# POPULAR BELIEFS AND SUPERSTITIONS FROM UTAH

Collected by

Anthon S. Cannon

# POPULAR BELIEFS AND SUPERSTITIONS FROM UTAH

Collected by

ANTHON S. CANNON

With the help of Jan Harold Brunvand, Austin E. Fife, Alta S. Fife,
Wayland D. Hand, Hector H. Lee, William A. Wilson,
and Others

Edited, With Introduction and Notes

by

WAYLAND D. HAND AND JEANNINE E. TALLEY

UNIVERSITY OF UTAH PRESS

SALT LAKE CITY

1984

**Library of Congress Cataloging in Publication Data**
Main entry under title:

Popular beliefs and superstitions from Utah.

   Bibliography: p.
   Includes index.
   1. Folklore—Utah. 2. Legends—Utah. 3. Folk medicine—Utah. 4.
Utah—Social life and customs. 5. Superstition—Utah. I. Cannon, Anthon
S. (Anthon Steffensen), 1906–1976. II. Hand, Wayland Debs, 1907–   .
III. Talley, Jeannine E.
GR110.U8P66   1984        398'.09792        84-5286
ISBN 0-87480-236-9

DEDICATED TO THE MEMORY

OF

ANTHON STEFFENSEN CANNON

1906–1976

# Contents

# Preface

The senior editor had been collecting Utah folklore intermittently since the late thirties, but did not concentrate on folk beliefs until the 1940s. The editing of the Frank C. Brown Collection of North Carolina Folklore, beginning in 1944, led to plans for a Dictionary of American Popular Beliefs and Superstitions. Both the California and the Utah collections carried on at the University of California, Los Angeles, are a part of this larger enterprise. When these facts became known to the late Anthon S. Cannon in the 1940s, he started to collect materials sporadically, and then ultimately enlisted the help of students in his sociology courses at the University of Utah. The bulk of the Cannon Collection, which constitutes over 80 percent of the total, fell in the period, 1954-66.

Austin E. Fife and Alta S. Fife, as part of their Moab, Utah, Folklore Project in 1953, contributed over 600 folk beliefs and superstitions from the multivolume Fife Mormon Collection which dates from the 1930s. With the introduction of systematic instruction in folklore at Utah State University in 1970 came almost 1650 additional entries from the classes of Austin E. Fife. Through the courtesy of Jan Harold Brunvand and William A. Wilson another 700 highly select items from the Folklore Archives of the University of Utah and Brigham Young University were placed at the disposal of the editors in 1975. This material, added to that of Cannon, the Fifes, Hand, Hector H. Lee, and a few other contributors, assured good coverage for all parts of the state.

To the collaborators named above, and to the University of Utah Press, the editors express their sincere thanks; likewise to Hugh Cannon, Anthon S. Cannon, Jr., and other members of the Cannon family whose timely financial assistance has made possible, after some vicissitudes, the publication of the Utah Collection. The editors are grateful to Norma Mikkelsen, who saw the manuscript through its early stages, and to Peggy Lee and Sharon Arnold who proved equal to the most diverse demands in copyediting the volume. In resisting the urge to normalize grammar and to eliminate other infelicities, these editors have preserved the hearty colloquial style of the scores of informants who made the Utah Collection a typical folk literary product of the Mountain West. Heartfelt appreciation also goes to the efficient Central Stenographic Bureau of the University of California at Los Angeles and to the late Director, Ellen Cole, for continuing help over many, many years in seeing thousands of individual entries move from a formidable bulk of slips and cards into a classified typescript so that the material could undergo further refinement. Help in compiling the Selected Bibliography came from Ernest W. Baughman, Jan Brunvand, Keith Cunningham, Austin E. Fife, and William A. Wilson. To them a hearty word of thanks. Without the work of collectors, typists, and classifiers over a period of many years the Utah Collection could not have turned into the important reference work that it is in the gradually developing scholarly investigation of American folk belief and superstition. Finally, for the inspiration and encouragement to carry on with the Utah Collection in the face of mounting professional obligations over almost forty years' time, the senior editor owes a deep debt of gratitude to Austin and Alta Fife. By unexampled hard and thorough work in the folklore of Utah and the Intermountain West since the late 1930s, the Fifes have set standards of excellence that have stood as beacons to seasoned scholars as well as to younger workers eager to husband the folk cultural resources of Utah and the West.

--W. D. H.
--J. E. T.

Whitsuntide, 1979

*Since this Preface was written Celeste Hand, with characteristic dedication, threw herself into the not inconsiderable task of reading proof on this bulky volume, including the checking of Index numbers.

# Introduction

The Utah Collection marks a new and important phase in the collection and study of American popular beliefs and superstitions. The scholarly interest in this basic and inveterate genre of American folklore, first manifest in New England and the eastern part of the United States in the 1890s and later seen in collections made in the southern states, beginning in the 1920s, was to reach its high point in 1935 with the publication of Harry Middleton Hyatt's epochal Folk-lore of Adams County, Illinois. The Hyatt volume, largest of its time, with a repertory of some 11,000 folk beliefs and superstitions, was expanded in a second edition (1965) by 5,588 items. Now as the country enters the final quarter of the century comes the first major collection from anywhere in the West. Sizable and representative enough to compare with the great collections made anywhere else in the United States and Canada, the Utah Collection is among the early systematic efforts to establish the spread and patterning of folk beliefs across the length and breadth of the land. It grew directly out of plans for a Dictionary of American Popular Beliefs and Superstitions made by Wayland D. Hand in 1944 as he began the editing of Popular Beliefs and Superstitions from North Carolina. The publication of this two-volume work in 1961-1964, with copious notes, provided a needed handbook for comparative study and set the stage for state and regional collections in all parts of the United States and Canada. Several of these tributary volumes have already appeared, and other collections are being readied for publication. Library deposit copies are also being compiled in different parts of the country so that archival holdings can be utilized.

Like most other collections of popular beliefs made in various parts of the country, the Utah Collection is of tolerably recent compilation. The earliest accessions came to hand in the late 1930s, but the bulk of the collection was brought together during the 1950s and 1960s. In spite of this outward circumstance a great part of the collection, as in all genres of folklore, is made up of age-old American folk beliefs and an even larger component of materials that derive from earlier European stocks. Representative items, old and new, including recent updates, are discussed later on in the Introduction. A few general observations on historical factors are in order here, even though the events of the founding and colonization of Utah are well known. Folk beliefs and superstitions prevalent in early nineteenth-century America, principally from the eastern and southern states, came to Utah with the pioneers of 1847 and for two decades thereafter. With the coming of the railroad in 1869 immigration into the Utah Territory widened in scope to include settlers from all parts of the country. To be noted in this period of growth, however, is the fact that converts to the Mormon church from Europe, beginning with the first influx of pioneers, have come to Utah in increasing numbers ever since. This has resulted in the constant engrafting of European folk beliefs on the earlier, if not entirely native stocks. With the era of modern transportation, and the free movement of people from state to state, particularly college students, one can now begin to speak of a general body of American folk beliefs and superstitions recoverable in any part of the country. This common leveling should, to be sure, not deter the serious worker from searching for deeper regional and ethnic connections, nor from trying to see the impress of earlier historical periods and events that unfold in the hundreds and thousands of popular beliefs that have been preserved over generations and centuries. The editors have been at pains to point out these connections in the Introduction, and to note them here and there in the body of the collection.

Since definitions and general discussions of folk beliefs and superstitions are now easily available in encyclopaedias, textbooks on folklore, and particularly in the long essay in the Brown Collection from North Carolina, we shall offer only brief theoretical conceptualizations here. We have chosen rather to approach the material inductively from actual texts adduced from the Utah Collection. These examples will give a practical demonstration of different categories of folk beliefs and superstitions and the attitudes of informants toward these beliefs as a part of their ways of thinking. Here and there the ideas expressed may throw light on earlier modes of thought and thus illumine certain facets of cultural history.

In terms of the origin of superstitions and their effect on people, scholars are increasingly coming to think of these materials as a body of beliefs and practices that derive from an earlier and less enlightened time. Ideas on these matters expressed by the senior editor over a decade ago still seem worth repeating today, even though America's growing egalitarianism has

given rise to many new distinctions and varying interpretations:

> As we search back in history for explanations of the proclivity to interpret phenomena and events in subjective terms, we are confronted with the fact that not all so-called superstitious pronouncements were made as a result of purely personal inference. There seems always to have been a body of thought inherited from an earlier time, a residual element, a superstes, or a superstites. This residuum often carried the connotation of a suspect or rejected element. The exact etymology of "superstition" has never been agreed upon, but the Germanic equivalents would seem to support the notion of a faith or false faith that has either lived on or has grown up outside the bounds of an accepted faith or belief. The German Aberglaube, the Dutch overgeloof, and the Danish overtro are terms that bear out both aspects, going somewhat beyond the Latin term in the matter of a noncanonical body of thought or a fabric of questionable ideas. Another Dutch term bijgeloof, clearly establishes the fact that such questionable notions lie outside accepted norms of thought and faith.[1]

For want of a more appropriate term "superstition" is used if notions expressed are harmful in terms of what people are impelled to do by virtue of an inbuilt logic or illogic. Similarly, if people refrain from doing needful things because of ancient taboos or modern constraints, the resulting harm is also referred to as superstition. As pointed out in earlier writings on the subject,

> small aberrations of the human mind involve primitive peoples

---

[1]Wayland D. Hand, "'Fear of the Gods': Superstition and Popular Belief," in Our Living Traditions: An Introduction to American Folklore, ed. Tristram P. Coffin, 215-16 (New York: Basic Books, 1968).

as well as members of civilized societies, and are encountered in the byways of religion no less than in the misapplications of learning and the perversions of science. Superstition is not the preserve of the unlettered only, but is a state of mind or a way of looking at things that may befall even the most sophisticated members of society. Professional people of all kinds, no less than tradesmen, are prone to many of the same conceits and mental errors, to which, for want of formal education, members of the humbler classes have fallen heir.[2]

If superstitions are encountered in all classes of society, and if educated people are subject to the same kinds of attitudes toward the objects and forces that surround them as are exhibited by those less favored in terms of formal schooling and experience, one need not be astonished at all to find the far less harmless folk beliefs and popular notions abounding and proliferating among people of all classes. People who might be hesitant to practice or advocate courses of action fraught with possible harm and danger, find no problem whatsoever in tolerating idle bits of fancy or whim, or even relishing these tidbits as a diversion from a more rigorous and disciplined way of thinking and doing things. These folk beliefs, by far more numerous, are naive and often misguided notions about the universe, the animal and plant kingdom, and the myriad activities of humankind. Humor and whimsy, quite as much as fancy and wistfulness, lie at the base of many of these notions. They are not harmful per se, but may contribute to benighted modes of thought that impair logical thought processes and an orderly pursuit of

human goals. Still other folk beliefs may rest in full or in part on fact, becoming folklore by the way they are received, utilized, and treasured. "From some points of view," to quote a previous formulation on this point, "one can apply Zola's famous dictum about literature to folklore, and paraphrase it somewhat as follows: folklore is fact refracted through human temperament, and enlarged upon by the wondrous and in exhaustible powers of the imagination."[3]

In the Utah material, unfortunately, collectors have rarely catechized informants about their real belief concerning the folk material they harbor. Wherever background information and interpretive remarks have been given, however, these communications have been made a part of the entry in question. Unusual explanations often appear in toto, and are given in the exact words of the informant. Most of the material for the Utah Collection had already been collected before the appearance of Alan Dundes' epochal essay on "Texture, Text, and Context."[4] Greater attention to contextual relationships would doubtless have revealed, as it has in all kinds of studies of folk belief, that materials are often transmitted in some meaningful pattern. Mothers or female relatives, for example, in recurring discussions of a family pregnancy, pass on to the expectant mother in a natural and understandable way, many things which they themselves heard decades earlier. The beliefs and customs of love and courtship are transmitted in the same way; likewise folk notions concerning other rites of passage, including death itself. Around the house, on the farm, in the school, on the playing field, and in the various social and recreational settings, folk beliefs are freely communicated. There need not always be an immediate raison d'etre for storytelling of this sort. Perhaps the best stories about hunting and fishing, and the myriad folk beliefs connected with these outdoor pastimes, to take a

[2]Wayland D. Hand, ed., Popular Beliefs and Superstitions from North Carolina, constituting Vols. VI and VII of the Frank C. Brown Collection of North Carolina Folklore, 7 vols., VI, xix-xx (Durham, North Carolina: Duke University Press, 1952-64).

[3]Hand, in Coffin anthology, p. 220.
[4]Alan Dundes, "Texture, Text, and Context," Southern Folklore Quarterly 28 (1964): 251-65.

conspicuous example, are recounted around the fire in the off-season, not in the wilds.

Oddly enough, folk beliefs have shown, perhaps better than folk narratives, songs and ballads, and other forms of folklore, that much material is retained without any clear memory of when and where an item was learned, and under what circumstances. This is another way of saying that there was something intrinsically interesting and vital about an item heard that made it survive in memory long after attendant circumstances had been forgotten. This cardinal fact, more than anything else that comes to mind, shows in what real esteem old folk traditions are held, and with what lasting and persistent force folklore lays hold on people's minds.

People have wondered to what extent education has helped to eradicate the outmoded beliefs and superstitions of an earlier day. No definitive answer can be given. While it is true that some older categories are slowly passing from view, one is continually astonished at the tenacity of the corpus by and large, and at the large number of young people who are still exposed to these popular traditions. Published and archival materials in the United States and Canada reveal that, along with folk speech, folk belief and superstition constitutes the single most viable and prolific genre of folklore in the country today. The relative neglect of this field of study is hard to understand; it is viewed, it would seem, as a limitless corpus, still largely uncharted in many parts of the country, and unstudied in relationship to the diverse cultural milieux from which it has sprung.

The physical hazard of earlier trades and occupations--navigation, lumbering, mining, the cattle trail, railroading, the building trades, and the like--has produced a colorful body of folklore, celebrated in song and story, in wit and saying, and in belief and custom. To these occupations, and to many other physical pursuits, including farming, have been added, or have come to greater prominence in recent decades, occupations and professions that involve mental and psychological hazard. Anything where uncertainty of any kind is to be reckoned with, is a fruitful field for the creation of odd or unusual ways of looking at things, and the observance of a whole congeries of favorable forces to deal with the exigencies of any matter at hand. Business, particularly the stock market, is a fertile field for the growth and nurturing of folk beliefs and customs; so are the gambling industry, commercialized sport, the entertainment world, the media, and even the classroom. The field of health care, with life often hanging in the balance, is perhaps the richest field of all for the investigator. These various matters will be pursued in somewhat greater detail below, with an effort being made to show by example what is meant and to indicate the almost limitless array of matters and situations upon which the imagination can lay hold. Definitions based on an actual corpus of field data are always more satisfactory than theoretical disquisitions, and this is particularly true if these theories are based only on models and constructs rather than on living folk traditions.

In considering the Utah Collection, and other modern American collections of folk beliefs and superstitions like it, one is struck, we believe, with the mixture of ancient and modern elements, with things that have a semblance of reason to them, as well as with things that have long since been outmoded, are patently without merit, outlandish or even wrong and harmful. This is not the place to chart the whole range of perception and reasoning that underlies the beliefs and superstitions themselves. In the space available we shall rest content to show enough variety in the kinds of logic and illogic that are pressed into service in given situations so that the discerning reader can at least develop some feeling for the principles of thought that are involved. In the ensuing discussions one will see for Utah in reasonably good array the whole gamut of irrational and magical ideas that are to be encountered in other major American collections of popular beliefs and superstitions. Involved are all nuances of sympathetic and contagious magic, associative thinking, strange reversals, symbolic transference, and other manifestations that stem from the vagaries of the human mind. Since many of these unusual modes of thought permeate beliefs and superstitions dealing with folk medicine, the human body, and the medical aspects of birth, infancy, and childhood, we can begin with this major area of folk belief where knowledge is generally more widely diffused among bearers of oral tradition than it is in other fields.

For those aspects of folk beliefs and superstitions that cannot be explained by causal relationships and logical thought processes, one must look to systems of thought and action that are based on forces in the universe, natural and supernatural, that can be brought to bear on human affairs. Supernatural powers may be made manifest in religious miracles or in various kinds of magic. Miracles are commonly understood as the workings of Providence to aid His children or otherwise to accomplish the Divine purpose with regard to all living things, even the inanimate creation. Magic, far less clearly understood, also represents a force in the universe, namely, a set of relationships and operating principles that can be manipulated by man to his own ends. In the same general way magic constitutes a set of precepts that itself brings results by mere juxtapositions or by meaningful conjunctures and a supposed indwelling dynamism. Sympathetic magic is a general description of these principles and forces, whether they be based on the law of similarity (homeopathic magic) or the law of contact (contagious magic). Magic based on these principles is not limited by the usual constraints of time and space, even though, as in the case of contagious magic, actual connection may have long since been disrupted. These two kinds of magic usually operate singly, though in many cases both homeopathic and contagious principles are effective at one and the same time. A few examples will suffice to acquaint the reader with these principles, and then he or she will be able to see the application of magical ideas throughout the Introduction as well as in the Utah Collection itself.

The notion that eating strawberries or carrots while pregnant will give the unborn child red hair (666, 668) is an act of imitative magic on the part of the mother. Ominal magic, based on similarities existing in the nature of things, rather than in any intervention by people in the course of events, is seen in the belief that if you live in a white house, your children will automatically be blond (753). Sympathetic attitudes on the part of a child toward objects placed before it on the floor are supposed to exercise prophetic force with regard to the child's future. With the choice of a Bible, a dollar, or a deck of cards, the child indicates by the first object it picks up whether it will turn out to be a preacher, a banker, or a gambler (1316). Even death is involved in these ominal relationships, for it is believed that a clock usually stops when a person has died (9318). The stopping of the clock being equated, in the popular mind, with the cessation of the beat of the heart itself. Distance, of course, is no impediment to the working out of homeopathic magic: If a pregnant woman sees a cross-eyed man, her baby will have crossed eyes (1063). Three excellent examples of homeopathic magic deal with phenomena that either cause harelip, or prevent it: If a child was born with a split lip, it is because the mother stepped across a threshold that had been split or hit with an axe (987); an earthquake tremor may cause the child to be born with a harelip (981). Preventive magic, involving a reversal, is seen in the belief that if a pregnant woman sees a rabbit she should quickly tear her petticoat so that the child will not get a harelip (983). In effect, by tearing her petticoat, the mother diverts the cleavage of the hare's lip from affecting her unborn child and turns it to a rent garment that can sustain the loss at far less cost. Reverse magic has imitative qualities that are expressed in other ways. If your child was a boy, and you want a girl next time, turn the bed around (552).

Homeopathic magic is no better seen anywhere than in folk medicine where diseases are combatted by remedies and curative measures that are in ways similar to the diseases for which they are employed. This principle of folk medicine is well expressed in the Latin precept, similia similibus curantur, 'similar things are cured by similiar means.' Cold, for example, is used to fight chills (3163), and heat to cure a fever (3461). Scarlet fever is cured by covering patients with scarlet blankets and giving them scarlet medicine (3948). Similarly, one should use red roses to cure anemia (3032). The classical example, of course, is to obtain the hair (or hide) of the animal that has bitten you (3367); for snakebite, kill the reptile and apply the fat to the wound (3969). This is in keeping with an ancient Indic prescription, 'let him who wounds also make whole,' and is seemingly, a rudimentary idea underlying some theories of immunology.

Like the principles of similarity, similia . . . , the Doctrine of Signatures, adumbrated in the writings of Paracelsus (1493-1541), and raised to a prominent theory of natural medicine by early herbalists in different parts of Europe, rests on homeopathic principles. Not only color is important, e.g., a person with yellow jaundice should be treated with yellow drugs, for yellow rids yellow (3717), but also shape: Kidney beans are good for the kidneys (3730). Harking back to the teachings of Crollius, a late sixteenth-century German scientist, is the notion that walnuts are good food for the brain, since meat of the nut looks like the brain and the shell resembles the skull (3081). It would indeed be interesting to know whether Ute Indian beliefs in the color, shape, and markings of plants, as indicating the human organs to which they should be applied (3766), is part of the Ute's ancient tribal lore, or whether this notion, like many another, has been borrowed from the white man. In any event, it is clear that the doctrines of Crollius did not reach Utah in the learned tradition of burgeoning European science; rather, these ideas were no doubt handed down from generation to generation in popular tradition, as is the case in folklore generally.

Contagious magic, like homeopathic magic, is subsumed under the general rubric of sympathetic magic, and therefore often operates according to the law of similarity, as mentioned earlier. The important difference is that the desired result is brought about by physical contact. For instance, if two people wash in the same water, their children will look alike (1213). If you cut your hair, don't throw it outside, or the birds will make a nest of it and you will have a headache (3560). If an expectant mother touches a toad, her baby will be born with warts (1118). A pregnant woman's hanging up clothes, or becoming entangled in any way in a rope, will cause the umbilical cord to wrap around the unborn child's neck and strangle it (1330). Contagious magic underlies much of conjury, and by the principle of contact the objects used to work harm on a person need not be presently connected with him; the magical bond is forever maintained, even beyond physical separation, e.g., an article of clothing once worn can be used to work a spell (10117), likewise hair clippings (10110, 10112), nail parings (10115) and the like. The extreme subtlety of sympathetic magic, both homeopathic and contagious, is seen in the following Utah example: If a woman divorces her husband and then remarries, the children born as issue of the second marriage will look like the first husband (1214). By this same magical transference the offspring of a mother are supposed to inherit the characteristics of a previous suitor of the mother (856).

Magical transference of disease, of course, involves contagious principles,[5] but goes well beyond the medical aspects of the transmission of infectious diseases. Diseases are communicated not only to fellow human beings, whether living or dead, but also to animals, and to plants, usually trees. In the classical examples, the disease, after leaving the sufferer, enters a new host, there to continue its ravages. Intermediate disposal agents, the so-called Zwischenträger, often are used to effect the translocation of the disease. If you have a fever, for example, cut your fingernails and put them on your neighbor's door with wax. The fever will then pass from you to the neighbor (3460). One may remove a

---

[5]Wayland D. Hand, "The Magical Transfer of Disease," in Magical Medicine: The Folkloric Component of Medicine in the Folk Belief, Custom, and Ritual of the Peoples of Europe and America, edited by Wayland D. Hand, 17-42 (Berkeley and Los Angeles: University of California Press, 1980). Cited: Hand, "Magical Medicine."

wart by borrowing a penny, rubbing it on the wart and throwing the penny away. The person who finds the penny will then get the wart (4398). Transference from person to person simply by another person's counting the number of a sufferer's warts is a rare case where the unit of measure, i.e., the counting of the warts, almost becomes a Zwischenträger, constituting, as it were, an intermediate agency in the transfer (4409). Communication of diseases to the dead is seen in the belief that toothache will cease if the gum above the tooth is rubbed with a newly cut off finger from a dead person (4148). Transference to animals is still commonly encountered, as witness the following examples: Three hairs taken from the cross of an ass will cure the whooping cough, but the ass will die (1129). Cats were taken to bed to absorb the patient's rheumatism (3382). The transfer of warts to a disposal agent and then to an animal was accomplished by getting a wart to bleed, rubbing the blood on a grain of corn, which was then fed to a bird (4284). Transference to animals by exhalation or kissing is seen in healing rituals where sufferers from a cold breathe deeply three times on a hog (3261), and those afflicted with toothache kiss a donkey (4150).

Transference to trees is either by Zwischenträger, namely, a string, a bandage, or something of the sort, and by various kinds of implantation, as treated below. If you rub warts with a piece of bacon, and then put the bacon on an aspen tree, the warts will disappear from you and grow on the tree; put the bacon in a slit on a tree, and the warts will grow on the tree as knobs (4229).

The classical form of transference to trees, of course, is by implantation. This is accomplished by plugging, wedging, nailing, and the like. To cure a toothache, take an eyelash, an eyebrow, trimmings of the fingernails and toenails of the patient. Bore a hole in a tree and put them in. The sufferer must not see the tree, and it must not be cut down or burned (4146). Cattle, bewitched and dying, can also be cured by an elaborate ritual of plugging (12767).

There is one further aspect of transference that must be considered, namely, the power of absorption that is thought to operate between persons and which seems to be a normal part of the biological process. An elderly person, for example, is thought to sap the strength of a young one if they sleep together (783), and among the Indians it is a custom when twins are born to let the weaker one die, lest it draw the vitality from its stronger sibling (578). These relationships between people of different station and physical makeup also apply to the sick: If two sick people are in the same house, and one dies, it means the other will get well very soon (2641). Even animals are involved in this strange symbiotic relationship with humans: If there is a sick pet and a sick person in the same family, the life of one is dependent on the other. If the animal dies, the person will live (2640).[6] Aspects of sacrifice are obviously involved in these notions, the living creature profiting, apparently, from the death of its counterpart. A simpler case, involving the transfer of headache from spouse to spouse by prayer, and by touching heads (contagious magic), must likewise be thought of in connection with these vicarious offices. In one such case it was reported that "grandpa, being in more robust health, was able to recover more rapidly" (2699). The most curious belief in the transfer of maladies among married couples to be encountered in the Utah Collection is an actual case in which a spouse reputed to have suffered from a white liver is supposed to have done in her mate in the marriage bed (9123). This strange notion, encountered in different parts of Europe, is not widely known in the United States. The absorption of arthritis and rheumatism by potatoes (3892), and of miasmas by garlic (3651), onions (3664), and the like, more properly represents divestment than it does

---

[6]These two items bear out George M. Foster's theory of the "limited good," that is, the notion that there is only so much of good or value, and that one can only profit at another's loss. See George M. Foster, "Peasant Society and the Image of Limited Good," American Anthropologist 67 (1965): 293-315; idem, "A Second Look at Limited Good," Anthropological Quarterly 45 (1972): 57-64.

transference, but these matters nevertheless belong in this general discussion on assimilation, absorption, and transference.

Passing through,[7] a ritual featuring movement through natural clefts in trees, split saplings, rerooted brambles, and the like, involves aspects of transference, but in many cases divestment seems the primary emphasis. If a person suffering from blackheads, for example, creeps on hands and knees under a bramble bush three times with the sun, he will be cured (2988). Crawl under your front porch to get rid of warts (4420). Passing through is also a promoter of health: Pass a child through a maple tree and it will live long (789), and this same ritual is an apotropaic measure to protect sheep and lambs from witches and fairies (12859). In this curative custom the animals are forced to jump through hoops at Halloween. Passing children underneath the bellies of donkeys and horses, still well known in the United States, is also encountered in Utah, namely, for the cure of a child's cough (1060).

Measurement as a means of diagnosing an ailment,[8] circumscribing it, or effecting a cure involves principles of both homeopathic and contagious magic. In some cases the unit of measure becomes the Zwischenträger itself, as the malady is physically communicated to the measuring device, whether a stick, beanstraw, or a string, etc. Even knots in a silk thread placed there by counting constitutes a prominent form of measurement and a means, apparently, of transference. To protect a child against croup, for example, a child is measured with a stick, and the stick is placed in a closet and kept until the child grows past the measure, and thus outgrows the croup (1069). Plugging, a form of divestment by contagious magic, also may involve measurement at the point where the hole is bored in a tree or doorjamb.[9] In the cure for undergrowth in children the hole is bored in a doorjamb at the exact height of the child (1117). Notching of a stick for warts, of course, is a form of counting, and throwing the unit of measure into a stream to float the warts away is homeopathic magic pure and simple (4346). The taboo against measuring a child with a tape measure (1152) somehow has to do with death, for adults also avoid measuring hands and feet with people in the fear that a death will occur (9072). Dogs are stopped from rolling in front of one's door on the theory that they are measuring ground for a grave (9393). Measuring a tablecloth between the elbow and one's hand in a ritualistic way is a means of determining whether a child is afflicted with the evil eye (1174).

We have seen counting as a means of riddance in the case of warts. Now we can see an example of counting as an act of imitative magic, namely, in the act of counting backwards. This is done where one seeks to diminish the pain, take away growths, and the like. To cure a headache, for example, say abracadabra, taking off the final syllable or letter each time this ancient magical formula is recited. Finally, in proceeding down page, as the inverted right-angled triangle is reduced to its lone syllable in the lower left-hand corner, namely, "ab" (or more normally, "a" where the triangle is diminished by only one letter at a time), one's headache will be gone (3584).

```
A B R A C A D A B R A
A B R A C A D A B R
A B R A C A D A B
A B R A C A D A
A B R A C A D
A B R A C A
A B R A C
A B R A
A B R
A B
A
```

---

[7]Wayland D. Hand, "'Passing Through': Folk Medical Magic and Symbolism," in Hand, Magical Medicine, pp. 133-85.

[8]Wayland D. Hand, "'Measuring' With String, Thread, and Fibre: A Practice in Folk Medical Magic," in Hand, Magical Medicine, pp. 107-18.

---

[9]Wayland D. Hand, "Measuring and Plugging: The Magical Containment and Transfer of Disease," in Hand, Magical Medicine, pp. 93-106.

This magical diminution is also often represented as an inverted isosceles triangle:

```
A B R A C A D A B R A
A B R A C A D A B R
A B R A C A D A B
A B R A C A D A
A B R A C A D
A B R A C A
A B R A C
A B R A
A B R
A B
A
```

A cure for hiccoughs involves the magical number 9 in three different connections, including the reverse "count-down":  To cure hiccoughs, take nine sips of water, count nine backwards, and then turn around nine times (3617).  Contagious magic is involved in a curative custom reported from Escalante, whereby amber beads worn around the neck on a leather thong are removed one at a time so that a goiter will gradually decrease in size as the numbers themselves decrease (3537).

In cases of contagious magic, where agents of disposal, or of measurement are involved, we have seen examples of a disease being "floated away."  More usual forms of divestment are burial, usually in wet places where the Zwischenträger will rapidly decay and thus cause the swelling or excrescence to dwindle by imitative magic.  Burial can take place anywhere, as for example, under the back stairs (4309), in a cemetery (4314), or in the side of a ditch bank (4379).  "Selling" a disease as a ritualistic act is seen in the selling of warts and moles outright (4390, 3785), or by placing the disposal agent, sometimes a coin as well as the more common items, in a conspicuous place where it can be picked up by an inquisitive passerby (4375).

One final example of contagious magic as it applies to folk medicine can be seen in the age-old custom of treating a nail, a splinter, or a fishhook that has inflicted a puncture wound, or any cutting tool for that matter.  Nails are cleaned and greased by the logic--and this is symbolic magic--that if the instrument can be kept from corroding in any way, the process of infection in the wound can likewise be stopped (4463, 4464).  Lockjaw and blood

poisoning are prevented in the same way (3764, 3048).  The student of medical history will see in these folk practices the application of "weapon salve," as promulgated by Sir Kenelm Digby of the Royal Society in the seventeenth century.

Beliefs connected with the human body, bodily functions, and bodily attributes are too numerous to survey adequately in these pages. Worth mentioning, however, are children born with a caul.  Since the child's face is enveloped by a veil as part of the amniotic sac, there is a natural association of such children with the sea and sailors.  A child born with a caul, for example, will never drown (1356), and by the same token will protect a ship on which he sails from sinking (7005). The unusual nature of the caul has also given rise to the notion that a child born with a caul is possessed of the devil (1188).  Such common bodily functions as spitting and urinating may be ritualized, thus assuming a folkloric importance not otherwise attained.  In medical and other magical rituals, for example, spitting on a rock will rid one of sideache (3951) and warts (4359). Likewise a sick horse may be cured by spitting in its mouth (12810).  Like saliva, urine is another bodily excretion considered efficacious for various ailments.  Urine rubbed on the top of a bald man's head, for example, is thought to cure baldness (2984), while young boys in swimming hole days were told to urinate on their legs to prevent cramps while swimming (3322).  A baby's wet diaper was rubbed on a person's face to cure freckles and tan (3519), and drinking the urine of a pregnant woman was believed to be a cure for snakebite (3983).  Conversely, urinating in the middle of the road, on the sidewalk, or in bed was believed to cause styes (4087, 4088).[10]  A reversal of this almost universally believed taboo is the belief that if you micturate in the middle of the road, your warts will go away (4427).  To rid a house of witches a child must urinate in the fireplace (10082).  Perhaps the most unique use of urine is a

[10]Wayland D. Hand, Padepissers and Wekschissers:  A Folk Medical Inquiry into the Causes of Styes," in Hand, Magical Medicine, pp. 261-72.

humorous ritual in which friends are prevailed upon to urinate on the wheel of a new automobile in order to initiate the vehicle (7793).

Prominent among modern superstitious actions are innocuous rituals performed to avert bad luck and to insure good fortune. Good examples of this are knocking on wood after bragging (10522), after making a prediction (10540), or voicing something one doesn't want to happen (10527). No doubt the original animistic meaning of these actions is expressed by one Utah informant who explained that knocking on wood calls the spirit from the wood (10530). Another ritual act involves spitting over the left shoulder three times when a black cat crosses your path (7759), and spitting on a cross made in the dust in front of a cabin when returning to it in order to ward off bad luck (7699). By the same rationale, if spitting can stop bad luck, it can also promote good fortune. It brings good luck to spit on dice before rolling them (8613). Spitting on a baseball bat will bring a home run (8719), and expectorating on a fish hook will cause fish to bite (8978). The simple gesture of crossing one's fingers when meeting a black cat is supposed to reverse the bad luck which is thought to result from such an encounter (7768). Ultimately, making the sign of a cross is operational on a dual level. As a Christian symbol, it opposes evil spirits (10307) and the devil (10231; 10232); on a magical level, however, the cross is a counteractant to something crossing one's path which usually signals danger or physical harm (7733).

Whistling is another bodily function that has gained an importance in folk beliefs and strange notions associated with such related functions as singing and even talking. It is uncertain why whistling has attracted so many superstitious notions which for the most part envision the consequences as dire. On a very basic level whistling bears a sympathetic relationship to wind and storms and it is therefore taboo on shipboard because it will call up a storm (7014). If a ship is becalmed, however, crusty old sailors can be depended upon "to whistle up a breeze of wind" (11303). The interdiction not to whistle when going past a cemetery as it will attract ghosts

may be explained by the widely held belief that the spirits of the dead inhabit the wind (10606; 10605). As so frequently happens in folk belief, the opposite view is also expressed that one should whistle when passing a cemetery (9856). The concept that evil forces lurk in the wind is extended to include the idea that whistling in the house invites the devil in (10221), or that whistling in the woods will call out a snake (12367), an animal commonly associated with the devil in the popular mind as well as in theology. It is apparent that this analogy of whistling with conjuring the devil deems that whistling in the chapel of a church will result in bad luck (8651). Many beliefs suggest that whistling is considered unfeminine. A whistling woman is bound to be an old maid (5001); if a girl whistles the angels in heaven weep (8652), or she will grow a beard (1624). Obviously in a community where marriage is regarded as the most rewarding goal and esteemed position for a woman, if whistling would guarantee her a life of spinsterhood, the cautionary advice against whistling might not be regarded lightly. Several variations on the verse whistling girls and cackling hens always come to a bad end (8655) perhaps afford an analogy of whistling and cackling to gossiping and noisiness. The negative connotation of whistling aboard ship has spread to other trades and professions where one may feel either physically or psychologically endangered. If a miner whistles in a mine, there will be an explosion (7101), and whistling in the editorial room or the dressing room of a theater will result in bad luck (7190). Even more threatening is the belief that a dancer whistling between performances indicates someone on the stage will be injured (7203). Contrariwise, when driving under a bridge everyone should whistle to bring good luck (7833).

In folk belief people have speculated not only about man's physical nature, but also about his spiritual and psychic nature and about the various projections of his personality, his soul, his shadow, and even his footprints and other manifestations of his presence. One of the more fascinating premises of the human mind is that the soul can dwell apart from the body, and that things in nature reflect the physical condition of an individual. This sympathetic relationship is most frequently felt to exist between trees and humans and underlies the custom of planting an evergreen when a child is born to insure the infant a long, healthy life (790). The tree is subsequently regarded as a life token and withering or unseasonal yellowing of the leaves is a sign that someone in the family is going to die (9563). An update of this concept resides in the belief that if a picture fades, that person is dead (9323). Just as one's hair or fingernails are bodily parts, which in the possession of an enemy can be used to harm, so too one's shadow is a projection of the self and thus vulnerable to evil forces (2281). Thus if a black cat touches or walks under one's shadow, bad luck will follow (11960). For some inexplicable reason if a person sees his shadow in the water in the month of May, it is believed he will die before the year is out (9127). Another belief, if a white man's shadow falls on the food of an Indian, the food is poisoned (3469), reflects the notion that the essence of personality is contained in the shadow. Behind this belief is the unhappy thought, borne in on us recently in concerns about the environment, that even the white man's shadow can bring about a desecration of nature. Conversely, evil beings such as vampires (10333) and the devil (10200), who have no soul, cast no shadow. This is also one of the telltale signs that a woman is a witch (10048). By means of contagious magic, the footprint is also representative of the whole person, and walking in another's footprints will give that person a headache (3557). One's name is likewise an extension of the self. If someone knows a person's real name, he is able to cast a spell on him (10094), and it is advised that the name of a very sick person be changed to fool the angel of death (2664).

We have seen representative kinds of folk beliefs and superstitions that deal with man in his physical relationships, particularly with regard to the human body and folk medicine. Since man's domestic and social relationships are more clearly understood than other aspects of his life, we are not attempting summaries here, but are referring the reader to appropriate chapters in the Utah Collection. Treatment can better be given to folk religion which strikes at the very heart of the whole system of folk belief. In this connection we have chosen to discuss certain aspects of death and the realm of the dead, because this universal human experience has captured man's imagination as have few other aspects of his many-sided and wondrous life. Death tokens are seen, as a glance at the Table of Contents will show, in a whole range of omens--the physical states of man himself and various parts of his body, the behavior of animals, birds, and even insects, the attitudes of trees, plants, and flowers, and the signs to be read in the moon, the stars, and other cosmic phenomena. Causal as well as ominal magic has given rise to various taboos. A central point of gravity in all of the beliefs about the dead is the notion that the dead are with us even beyond the grave. The treatise on ghostlore, while not as rich as in many other states, nevertheless gives a good conspectus of the subject. These items cannot be pursued in these introductory pages, so let us look in detail at just one aspect of the realm of the dead, namely, the corpse itself, the grave, and certain funereal paraphernalia such as the shroud, parts of the coffin, and even graveyard dirt. Finally we can consider the death of criminals by hanging, a subject that has yielded a rich folklore wherever the gallows is or has been, the executioner's deadly instrument.

As in shamanism and other primitive practices that link the living with their ancestors and the realm of the dead, things connected with death have a magical and even a numinous quality. Bodily parts of the dead, particularly a dead man's hand, are deemed to be efficacious in the treatment of cancer, where the afflicted part is touched with the hand (3140). Toothache is treated by rubbing the gum above the tooth with a finger newly severed from a dead person (4148). Sterility, more in keeping with the notion of death, is seen in a belief that if a corpse is taken across a field, that field will become barren, no matter how fruitful it may have been before (13004). Coffin nails, being of iron or steel, have a magic of their own by virtue of the metal itself. Additional supernatural power, of course, comes from the connection of the nails with coffins and with the dead.[11] Accordingly, merely removing a nail from a coffin is said to relieve rheumatism (3936). By contagious magic, and by the power and debilitating effect of death itself, a piece of wood from a coffin put in a tilled field will keep sparrows from vexing it (13155). Graveyard dirt, the American counterpart of England's churchyard mould, is used for a variety of things, including curing a child of eating ordinary dirt (1146). This is a practice so common that it has been held fast in the proverbial notion that a person must eat a peck of dirt before he dies. Simply going to the graveyard, for example, will help a person get rid of moles (3788). Walking over dirt fetched from a graveyard ten nights in succession is supposed to cure rheumatism (3937). Dirt taken from a freshly dug grave and sprinkled on the floor of an enemy will render him harmless (10123), and graveyard dirt put on top of a fence will keep away burglars (7553). At a less magical level, worms dug in a graveyard are reputed to be best for fishing (8981).

As one would expect, love rituals are rarely connected with the dead, but a Utah love charm exhibits at least three magical elements connected with death, hallowed earth, and funereal paraphernalia. To produce the charm a girl takes a needle which has been stuck into a dead body, covers it with dirt in which the body is buried, and then wraps the needle in a cloth cut from a winding sheet or shroud (4982). Implied in this bizarre ritual, obviously, is help for the love quest solicited from beyond the grave.

Death by execution or by hanging, a form of punishment not known in Utah except from early-day vigilante action, has given rise to additional notions connected with death and burial over and above folk beliefs connected with such executions per se. Grass, for

example, is not supposed to grow on a murderer's grave (7584), but lilies are said to grow from the grave of a person innocently executed (7597). A mole on the neck indicates that a person is in danger of death by hanging (7589); furthermore, should a woman work at a spinning wheel during pregnancy, it is believed that her child is destined to hang by a hempen rope (1323). Two widespread notions dealing with criminal aspects of death and punishment for murder are found in the Utah corpus: A corpse will bleed in the presence of its murderer (7578), and the man goes free if the rope breaks in a hanging (7593). The magic of the number thirteen has worked its way into the lore of the gallows: A hangman's noose must have thirteen turns in it (7592). It is instructive to note that here, as in so many other cases, Utahns have drawn on the age-old stock-in-trade of beliefs, even if the Utah connections are tenuous.

Punishment as a form of legal redress is one thing, punishment as the torture of conscience, suffered alone, and lasting a lifetime, is quite another. We are dealing here with one of the basic precepts of folk religion, and the whole matter must be considered in this broader matrix. Since taboos and interdictions of all kinds constitute a major category of folk belief, it will be instructive to see the kind of acts that bring penalties of different degrees of severity, as well as those that are serious enough to invoke divine retribution. The torture and killing of animals, a violation of nature, does not go unnoticed. A person killing a lizard, for example, brings down the death penalty upon himself (9515); anyone cruel enough to fracture an owl's wings himself must suffer broken limbs (3500), and disaster will follow anyone killing a mocking bird (12274). For reasons not explained, those who have made enemies of cats during their lifetime are destined to go to their graves by a storm of wind and rain (9381). Rarely are punishments meted out for violations of plant life, supposedly because plants are thought to be insensitive to pain. In this connection it has never been explained why one should suffer typhoid fever in Utah for burning locust wood in the fireplace (4178). The physical properties of the wood

---

[11]Wayland D. Hand, "Hangmen, the Gallows, and the Dead Man's Hand in American Folk Medicine," in Hand, _Magical Medicine_, pp. 69-80.

itself, and the gases produced, are a more likely explanation than anything having to do with punishment or taboo.

Somewhat different in spirit are transgressions of religious precepts or infractions of moral law, which itself is often rooted in religious teachings. Punishments for these offenses are taken more seriously, and may often be used to compel conformity to religious and moral teaching. Desecration of the sabbath by sewing, for example, is punished by the seamstress, having to rip the stitches out the following day (6566). This is a lesser penalty than the more common one, known in Utah as well as throughout Europe and America, by which the seamstress is forced to take the stitches out with her own teeth in hell. As far as we know, no one has ever catechized people professing these strange notions, yet one has a feeling that these warnings were not always taken literally. Even so, many a young seamstress has no doubt been kept from desecrating the sabbath because of these dire warnings voiced by older people.

More serious, of course, are deeds whose punishment involves physical and mental incapacity, sickness, and death.[12] Though rarely stated in so many words, it is generally implied the misfortune is visited upon the sinner by God himself, or that it results from infraction of moral law (2573; 2574). The most direct and striking example of direct intervention is the belief that if you take the name of God in vain He will strike you dead (9656). The fact that no one, so far as we know, has even been reported to have seen this sacrilege punished does not lessen in any way the threat in the minds of believers.

Punishments for lesser offenses range from blisters (3027) and cankers (3141) on the tongue for telling fibs and lying, or styes for the same offense (4086), to cold sores for kissing (3263). (The humorous "kissing the cook," known elsewhere, apparently has not been collected in Utah, though it

doubtless is well known.) In these cases the tone of voice and facial expressions of the person issuing the warning often indicate the half serious, and often cajoling nature of the threat. More often it is perhaps an indirect and clever way of indicating that people know what the offender has been up to, making the punishment nothing more than a telltale sign.

Sins and transgressions dealing with sexual matters, as one can imagine, have graver consequences. Sterility, for example, is thought to befall a person born out of wedlock (35), a hard fate involving the old religious notions of the transmissibility of sin and evil to children and their descendants over generations. There is seemingly more justice to sterility being visited on a woman for having borne a child without benefit of clergy (34). Masturbation is alleged to make one sterile (39), also practicing onanism (withdrawal during intercourse), with the affliction falling on the innocent female rather than her partner (36). Sterility and barrenness are also ascribed to men and women using contraceptives too long (37). Mental deficiency is said to result from excessive masturbation (1011), or it may befall a child born out of wedlock (1009), a notion that runs counter to the popular belief that bastards are brighter than most children and the widespread notion that they are often geniuses (824). The belief that insanity is caused by the devil getting into your soul or as a punishment of God (2879) harks back to primitive aetiologies of mental disease. Alcoholic mothers (1000), or fathers drunk at the moment of their child's conception, will produce feebleminded offspring (999). Similarly, if a pregnant woman drinks alcoholic beverages, the baby will be an alcoholic (217) or have defective germ plasm (219). Smoking is also strictly tabooed on the grounds of its evil effect on the unborn child (221-223). As a derived, though attenuated, form of punishment for seeing the bride nude before marriage, or seeing a nude woman at all, namely, blindness, there is a curious Utah belief that a groom who sees the bride in her wedding gown before marriage will go blind before they have been married ten years (3016). The strict pre-wedding taboos observed in many

---

[12]Wayland D. Hand, "Deformity, Disease, and Physical Ailment as Divine Retribution," in Hand, Magical Medicine, pp. 57-67.

countries, though dealing with seeming externals of the kind seen here, may really go back to the fundamental taboo of seeing a naked woman, a temptation to which blind Tiresias, the sage of antiquity, himself fell prey. Single items of interest connected with sexual matters, and not widely known in the tradition, are the notions that a child born out of wedlock will become criminal (7546), and that, quite arbitrarily, every sixth person in a house of prostitution will die (9198). It is not clear from the entry whether the operators of the establishment or the clients are intended. Neither is it known how widespread the belief is, nor how effective it has been as a deterrent to keep men from resorting at these establishments.

Legends are frequently the most effective means of reporting the punishments meted out to people for their misdeeds. A girl reported to have sunk into the earth for dancing in church (8621), would appear to be a variant of the legend of El Mal Hijo (Hija), a story encountered in Latin American tradition (9845).[13]

Sacrilege, particularly the profanation of sacred utensils and holy ordinances, is thought to bring swift retribution, and there is a whole cycle of stories about blasphemers, all the way from a Utah Valley sheepherder who was accustomed in thunderstorms to invoke the Deity with a violent oath and appellation to "send us another thunderbolt, you _____" to men reported to have mocked the holy church ordinances. Many of these are legends and memorats, really, of which item 2690 is a typical example. William A. Wilson has recently written on the subject.[14] Some of these stories are like the El Mal Hijo cycle of stories in the Latin tradition of the American Southwest as mentioned above. Other typical beliefs are: If you mock a preacher, you'll be cut down like a tree (9920); to damage a Bible in any fashion will cause very

_____

[13]T. M. Pearce, "The Bad Son (El Mal Hijo) in Southwestern Spanish Folklore," WF 9 (1950): 295-301.

[14]William A. Wilson, "The Paradox of Mormon Folklore," pp. 40-58, esp. 48-51.

bad luck (9950); if you don't believe in religion, but attend services anyway, and then laugh at the people and their practices, you will be punished with death or serious injury (9655).

The most severe punishments of all, of course, are meted out to apostates. The disfellowship itself is bad enough, even though such ostracism never has reached a point where backsliders are given the "silent treatment," as is reported to be the case among some of the primitive German churches in this country. Economic failure is part of the penalty paid for turning against the church, also sickness, melancholy, and heartbreak. Violent apostates from the church, and those who work actively against it, are thought to be possessed of evil spirits and of the devil himself. Furthermore, they are said to emit an extremely unpleasant odor (10202).

Among the different kinds of sins for which God metes out punishment are acts of supererrogation on the part of man, like Faust, seeking to know more about the universe than has been vouchsafed to humankind, and failing to acknowledge the providence of God in the bounties of nature and in the prudent use of that which God has provided. The Vanishing Hitchhiker stories, often confused with the cycle of the legendary Three Nephites, were found in Utah at the time of the Century of Progress Exposition in Chicago in 1933. These had to do with man's arrogance and failure to acknowledge the hand of God in the great technical advances of the twentieth century. It is believed by some, for example, that exploring outer space is condemned by God, and that such a presumption will lead to the experimenter's damnation (9979). Likewise, probing too far beneath the earth's surface will surely lead one to find hell (9980). This notion might hark back to the earlier resistance to exploring Utah's mineral resources on the ground that such quick wealth would undermine the religious fibre of people and invite exploiters into the state. The belief that the devil holds dominion over everything more than three feet beneath the earth's surface is apparently not the specific basis for the belief cited.

Devil lore is prominently represented in the Utah corpus, with descriptions of his Satanic majesty's person as well as his various activities and his dominion over man and beast (10207; 10208). In the wide array of devil lore one finds, for instance, the widespread notion that when the sun shines while it is raining, the devil is beating his wife (11006). Witchcraft is not so well represented, but one can trace the usual kinds of witchly depredations, the _maleficium_, whether the visitation is on man himself (10057), his animals (12766), or on other parts of his patrimony (10064). Witches' familiars, whether animals or birds (10040) are treated; likewise witch-riding (10034), and the means of combatting witches (10067), including the use of hot iron and silver (10083, 10084). The evil eye, of course, is related to witchcraft and the casting of spells. The Utah traditions are drawn largely from Mediterranean stocks (cf. 1167-1176) and involve animal as well as human victims (10143). Evil spirits are associated with devil lore, also, of course, with ghostlore and the realm of the dead. Evil spirits as the cause of physical ailments fall into demonic aetiologies of disease, causing such assorted ailments as headache (3556) and epilepsy (3395), also known as the "divine madness."

Fairy folk, elves, and other creatures of lower mythology are encountered in Utah popular tradition, but knowledge about them has been preserved in a learned, if not literary tradition, and is based on historical materials brought from the eastern part of the country, or directly from Europe. There is little or no living folklore concerning these creatures.

Religious folklore does not bulk large in the Utah Collection, but the items that have been collected give at least an adumbration of the kinds of religious folklore--Catholic, Jewish, Orthodox, Protestant, Mormon--that are encountered within the state. Following the leading writers on biblical and religious folklore--Saintyves, Hanauer, Rumpf, Weiss, Trachtenberg, Yoder, Fife, et al.--the editors have been at pains to utilize materials that represent folkloric extensions upon religious doctrines and miracles that are a part of conventional theological and confessional systems. By the same token the compilers have left out of

account theological and doctrinal matters that have strict denominational warrant, are either strange or otherwise contrast sharply with accepted views within churches and other ecclesiastical bodies. This divergence from normal standards of acceptance does not qualify the beliefs and exempla as folklore per se, unless the teller himself--and the hearer, too--let fancy reign to a degree, where extensions are created upon the perception of the normal workings of God and the Holy Spirit. Church authorities in all Christian and Jewish bodies are understandably not eager to see the scope of religious sacraments extended and the pastoral care of the church move from its time-tested conservative channels. Above all, these religious leaders do not wish the controls of religious life and action to get out of hand, take on a Pentecostal fervor, and deteriorate into a state of popular religious frenzy if not mass hysteria. They are concerned that speculations about the imminent second coming of Christ, the end of the world, glossalalia, dream fantasies, and other conjurings up of the human mind might, by their own tenuous character and transitory appeal give rise in time to disillusionment, apostasy, and the eventual scattering of the flock of Christ. Recent developments in American religious history, particularly in the primitive church and the gospel denominations, show these beliefs, fears, and apprehensions to be prevalent across the length and breath of the land. Religious ferment, as witnessed by Jesus freakism and other popular religious outpourings, has never been stronger since the revivalism that swept across the inhabited parts of America in the early nineteenth century.

Religious folklore is found throughout the Utah Collection, however. Much of this folklore is part of the general stock-in-trade of religious folklore found elsewhere in the country. Such lore is encountered particularly in the Life Cycle--birth, marriage, death--in devil lore, witchcraft and related fields, and to a lesser extent in the folklore of plants and animals. Baptism and christening as a means of improving the health of unthrifty or sick children, a belief which is well known in the religious folklore of xxx

Europe and many parts of the United States, is also reported from Utah (923, 901). Represented also in the Utah materials is a series of beliefs that belong to the well-known legend cycle of the devil as a builder, except that the devil pact for the first soul entering the church is not expressed. In these accounts the first child christened in a new church is claimed by the devil and is sure to die (1350). A variant of this notion is the belief that the first living thing to enter a new church becomes the property of the devil (10207). Likewise the devil claims the first corpse laid in a new church (10208). A group of folk beliefs dealing with Good Friday have general currency in religious folklore. Miners, for example, were afraid to enter mines on Good Friday, fearing a disaster (7089), and workmen and others were warned not to hammer on Good Friday, lest they hammer nails into the body of Christ (11845). In husbandry it was believed that removing bees on Good Friday would cause them to die (12700), and that eggs laid on this day would go stale (12677). On the positive side, a person washing his or her hair on Good Friday, and every Friday thereafter, was thought to be safe from headache (3580).

Mormon folklore having to do with the end of the world does not differ significantly from the general body of such lore in the United States. Common among these beliefs is the notion that the moon will be covered with blood (10001), that there will be violent extremes in weather--hot and cold--earthquakes, and the like (10003), and that if chickens lay more eggs than they're supposed to, the world will come to an end (9988).

Burial with feet toward the East, so that the dead can rise facing the sun on Resurrection morning is a belief and burial custom observed in religious denominations throughout America. This is also the case in Mormon tradition, with the explanation that the dead should be in the correct position when Gabriel blows his horn (9806). An exception is made, according to the same informant, who claims that the position is reversed for suicides as a punishment for their brash act (9806).

Religious legends of the Three Nephites, undying disciples of Christ's ministry in the Western Hemisphere, are found everywhere in the Mormon country.[15] Their ministrations to the sick and those in need are proverbial (2687); likewise, their instant appearances and leave-takings. Miraculous help in sickness are seen in cases involving a venerable, gray-bearded man who gave timely advice (2686), and two ministrants unknown to the mother with a sick child who cured the patient with a blessing (929). In the 1880s in Park City there was a cave-in in one of the mines and several men were trapped. As they were resting and pondering their sad fate, a form in a yellow slicker appeared and led them to safety. As the last miner crawled out and turned to thank the man, he had disappeared (9960). In the early days midwives were believed to be protected by an unseen power as they went about their work, and horses were reported to have taken the right road in blinding storms. By the same Providence the midwife was told by an unknown voice what to do when she was confronted with an unusual obstetrical problem (936). Miraculous and supernatural cures are reported in various parts of the chapter on Folk Medicine, e.g., the account of a man who cut his arm off with a saw in the mountains, and whose wounds were stanched by the power of prayer to save him from bleeding to death (2692).

Belief in the protective power of garments, ceremonial underclothing worn by worthy members of the Church of Jesus Christ of Latter-day Saints, is a part of the religious teaching of the church. Memorats and exempla about the protection afforded are

_____

[15]To the standard titles on the Three Nephites in the Bibliography under the names of Fife, Lee, and Wilson, should be added a series of modern updatings by Wilson in his article, "Folklore and History: Facts amid the Legends," Utah Historical Quarterly 41 (1973): 47-48. Wilson's unpublished corpus of Nephite stories numbers about one thousand entries, and will soon be published in monographic form. Many of these legends reflect the recent course of Mormon church history and policy, and are not to be found in the older works of Fife and Lee.

part of the faith-promoting religious legendry of the church. A typical story is told of a Mormon soldier in France who was saved from shrapnel that was stopped short of penetrating his body by the protective clothing (3542), and a person protected from burns in a hotel fire (3106). These stories can be multiplied by the hundreds.

Mormon missionaries are reputedly not allowed to swim while on their missions, because it is believed that the devil and evil powers will cause them to drown (9691). This is no doubt an extension of a curse placed on the waters by John the Baptist. In a lighter vein, and in keeping with the church teachings with regard to marriage, it is popularly believed that missionaries are married within six months after returning home from their missions (5727).

Thus far we have been concerned mainly with man and have had occasion to consider him in terms of his physical makeup and health, his mental and emotional qualities, and in his human and social relationships. Finally we have considered him in his affective life and in those parts of his makeup that respond to supernatural forces and concerns, whether they be spiritual and religious, or whether they tend to magic and the miraculous, or are concerned with folkloric matters by and large. We can now consider the concern of man with the physical universe and with the animate and inanimate creation.

Man has always been concerned with the things around him, mainly because he has been forced to use them for his own sustenance and welfare. It is a matter of record that the earliest scientific writing centers pretty much on the natural world, and that thinkers from the time of Empedocles and Aristotle, to Bacon, Galileo and Newton, and in our time, to Lord Kelvin and Einstein, have pondered the physical universe in an attempt to decipher man's role in the grand scheme of things. Many of the early ideas about the earth itself, the air and water which surround it, the flora which covers it, and the creatures that inhabit it contained a generous admixture of fanciful notions and downright folklore. Pliny's monumental Natural History compiled in the first century A.D. is a compendium of the writings of the ancients on these subjects, and still serves as a handbook for those who would understand man's notions of the surrounding world. The earth itself and the elements which it cradles have been of particular interest. The belief that metals of all kinds and in particular iron have efficacious qualities goes back to a pre-Christian concept that human and animal illness and natural disaster are the result of either divine punishment or malicious activities of one's supernatural enemies. That infants are especially regarded as being vulnerable to various malefic influences is illustrated in the practice of putting a key or steel of some kind in the baby's cradle for one of their own (1165, 1166, 1184). Apparently this same notion underlies the practice of putting an axe or knife under the bed of a woman in childbirth. Both in Europe and America the belief is widely held that sharp instruments placed beneath the bed during labor and delivery will prevent hemorrhage or drive away evil spirits. Nowhere in the Utah repertory is the belief expressed that the sharp instrument is placed in the crib to blind the fairy midwife as she comes to bring the changeling, a notion common in Europe. Three examples from Utah (244, 252, 306), however, have rationalized the use of the axe as being a means to "cut the pain." This wearing down or loss of the original meaning can be observed in the beliefs that picking up a rusty nail (6944), finding or carrying a horseshoe (12085; 10505) will bring good luck (12085; 10505), or that saying "pins and needles" will prevent bad luck (10590). Still a fair number of items in the collection retain an older notion that iron possesses magical properties. The apotropaic power of iron is thought to offset the bad luck associated with passing a priest on the street (7722), a preventive measure that in more recent times has deteriorated to clasping a button on one's clothing when one passes a person in the cloth, whether priest or nun (7720). Horseshoes are hung over the door to prevent a witch, the devil or evil spirits from crossing the threshold (10066, 10236, 10288). Another very old belief, commonly found in German-speaking countries, is that one may prevent a witch from riding a person by placing a knife or scissors under the bed (10067). One memorat from Utah (10084) reads as though it came from the annals of the early American witch craze:

There was an old woman who the neighbors were sure possessed supernatural powers. Even though she had never harmed anyone, she was still feared. It was also a known fact that she could not pass under steel. One day while it was raining she stopped at a neighbor's house. Someone slipped a steel knitting needle into the rafter above her head. Her clothes began to steam and she looked in agony, but she couldn't move until the steel knitting needle was removed.

Silver is likewise regarded as a means of warding off witches (10080) or bringing about the death of the witch by invultuation, namely, by piercing the heart of an effigy with a silver object (10083)

Both one's property and one's person can be protected from ghosts by laying cold iron across the front door steps (10673), by having steel in hand (10674), or by throwing a key at the spectre (10675). Silver bullets are supposed to kill a ghost or a werewolf (10676; 10326), while silver nails or screws used in a coffin are said to keep out the bad spirits that cause ghosts (10662).

As we have seen elsewhere in these pages, many of today's folk beliefs are an admixture of pagan and Christian concepts. A prime example of this juxtaposing of faiths is found in items in which the cross is employed to avert evil influences (10307). Here the cross functions as a Christian symbol, and, by virtue of its metallic composition, coincides with magical practices stemming from an archaic doctrine of disease and illness.

Another demon of disease which may be thwarted from its evil designs by metal is the nightmare, a creature believed to come during the night, transform a human into a horse and ride the person over hill and dale until dawn. By this time, of course, the victim is totally depleted, particularly when this attack follows night after night. To cure nightmare one must hang a horse's halter on the bed (10344).

Domestic animals, especially horses and cattle, are believed to be plagued by the same evil forces which beset humans, and therefore protective measures must be taken to prevent bewitchment of the animals which will impair their health or spoil their products. Such notions underlie the placing of a red-hot horseshoe into the cream when the butter won't come (5888), or under fowl eggs to insure they will hatch (12665). Further examples of practices intended to protect animals from havoc at the hands of malign beings are hanging a horseshoe over the barn door to ward off evil spirits (12598) and placing brasses on a horse's harness to keep the devil away (12827).

Folk notions are often based on archaic religious or mythological concepts of cosmology. Echoing throughout these tenets is the struggle for survival in the face of natural disasters such as storms, floods and drought, which since early times have been conceived as the punitive measures enacted by the Almighty against His children (11342). Lightning is God's spear (11347) with which he will strike down a person who takes His name in vain (11332). The idea that divine retribution is not only visited upon one's person, but also upon his means of sustenance is reflected in the beliefs that thunder and lightning cause milk to sour (5879; 5880; 5881), or make hens' eggs bloody (12674). A steel bar, however, laid across a barrel of beer during a thunderstorm will prevent the contents from souring (5931). Numerous beliefs show that metal and weapons in the mind of the folk are connected with lightning and thunder. There has long been a recognition that what is harmful may also be beneficial, an observation that has given rise to a number of inherently contradictory beliefs: To have iron or steel around you during a thunderstorm will bring safety (11384), but knives, needles and scissors should not be left in a conspicuous place such as on a table or on a window sill during an electrical storm (11369; 11372; 11373), because they will bring lightning into the house. By extension things struck by lightning are imbued with either demonic or sacred qualities. One is cautioned not to touch a person struck by lightning, as he is possessed with evil spirits (10266). These notions go back to classical antiquity. On the other hand wood which has been struck by lightning is efficacious in ridding one of warts (4353) and toothache (4157), or can be a powerful aid in getting someone out of jail (7570). The inherent sacredness of lightning-struck wood makes the burning of this wood a sin which brings about the death of the offender (9355).

The logic of some superstitions can only be recognized by excavating the mythological context in which they once functioned. For example, why does a feather bed or down-filled pillow (11377) protect one from lightning, and why is it believed that swans and chickens hatch during thunderstorms (12209; 12662)? In Germanic myth swans and ducks appear as zoomorphic forms of divinities who control weather and the change of seasons. Pillows and mattresses filled with down are thus considered to contain the essence of the divinity and for this reason have apotropaic power. It is unlikely that Europeans or Americans who know of this belief could state something approaching a "logical" reason for the belief, a circumstance which demonstrates the tenacity of tradition which often outlives the rationale and substitutes a new explanation.

Celestial phenomena and the weather figure importantly in man's doings, particularly in his husbanding of the animal and plant life on which he has come to depend for his living. The importance of the moon as a means of reckoning time is reflected in folk beliefs concerned with health, weather, plant and animal husbandry. Many of these beliefs and practices are continuations of an ancient astrological pseudo-science which attempted to provide a coherent view of the universe by uniting the microcosm with the macrocosm. Consistent with this view is the notion that celestial bodies influence human life from womb to tomb (11727). Early medical doctrine drew upon this same cosmological theory to establish the proper time during which treatments should be undertaken. In modern folk belief one still encounters the idea that curative rituals should take place only when the associated heavenly

bodies are in the proper position (2669). The moon's power is seen as capable of causing insanity (2898) or giving one nightmares (10343), as well as being able to wither one's warts (4367). As far as human health is concerned the malevolent effects of the moon far outweigh the beneficial ones. Widespread among Spanish speakers is the belief that if a pregnant woman views an eclipse, her child will be born with a cleft palate (1040), crossed eyes (1064) or a harelip (988). It is also believed that if she touches her body during an eclipse, the baby will be marked where she touched herself (383).

The doctrine that human ailments must be treated in accordance with the configuration of celestial bodies also pertains to the care of domestic animals and plants. One should butcher cattle during the proper phase of the moon so that the meat will not shrivel (12759), or to assure that the meat will increase in volume when cooked (12760). Likewise one must slaughter pigs during the appropriate phase of the moon or the bacon will turn out fat (12844). To prevent excessive bleeding animals should be castrated when the sign is in the foot (12594), or according to the moon (12822). Dehorning (12741), branding (12763), and weaning of cattle (12755) are regulated by the moon or the signs of the zodiac. The sympathetic bond thought to exist between cosmic entities and terrestrial life is expressed in numerous beliefs about planting by moon phases and signs of the zodiac. For example, cucumbers should be planted by the sign in the arms so they will be long and slim and not chubby (13071). It is even believed that lumber is affected adversely if the moon is in the wrong quarter. If a rail fence is laid at the wrong time of the year, the bottom rail will bury itself in the ground (13206). Wooden shingles must be put on at a certain time of year, or they will curl upwards and peel off (13205).

Similarly it is believed that weather changes occur with different phases of the moon (10869), that weather can be predicted by the position of the crescent moon (11124), or by the presence of a ring around the moon (11129). The very destiny of the world and its inhabitants can, by this logic, be interpreted by the movement and appearance of the astral spheres. Blood on the moon portends war or the end of the world (10001). A pale red setting sun foretells a plague (3846), and an eclipse of the sun on the 29th day of the month indicates there will be many deaths on the first day of the next month (9592).

Since weather has always been an element of vital concern to those engaged in agricultural pursuits, a number of beliefs concerning its prediction and control are still noted in rural farming communities. Some of these beliefs appear to date from the early period of cultivation and are based on common sense observation of animal behavior which coincides with the changes of season and weather. Because of their migratory patterns birds are by far the most popular omen of weather, whether good or bad. Bad weather is presaged when buzzards fly high (10935), or if the cuckoo sings in the direction of the south (10936). A dove singing at night foretells three days of good weather (10959), whereas noisy chickens about the farmyard are a sign of rain (11047). The behavior of other barnyard and domestic animals is also regarded as signaling various kinds of weather. Cows and horses refusing to drink in dry weather (11040) and horses frolicking in the fields (11037) are indicators of rain. A cat sneezing (11026) and a dog eating grass (11036) are signs of rain. Good weather is predicted when flies swarm (10962), warmer weather by a chirping cricket (10974), while ants retiring early is an omen of cold weather (10907). Humans too are granted some of the intuitive powers attributed to animals: Body aches, rheumatism, aching corns and bunions indicate rain is on its way (11007-11011). Even stones are considered to be in sympathy with the weather. The diamond is dull when the weather is bad, but sparkles during nice weather (10837).

Perhaps even more important than predicting the natural elements is controlling them. The killing of frogs, toads (11074), ants (11079), daddy-longlegs (11098), or owls (11068) is believed to bring rain. It is tempting to consider that the sacrifice of these creatures is a remnant of an earlier rain ritual. The widely encountered belief that killing a snake and hanging it on a fence will cause rain (11071) is no

doubt akin to the mythological theme of slaying the dragon to bring on rain. In the Middle Ages this ritual combat was dramatized in the Mummers Play and the Christianized St. George celebration of the old pagan dragon slaying which ushered in the spring. To some extent it would seem that geography has had a bearing on the types of beliefs which are retained. For example, in those climates where rain is more prevalent and thus often a threat to crops, rituals to stop or prevent rain are more prominent than in Utah where drought is more normal than flood. Only two items in this collection instruct how to stop rain: If you draw a circle on the ground, it will stop raining (11189); make a cross with ashes on the ground before it starts raining hard and the rain will stop (11190).

Time, numbers and systems of reckoning, directions, and the like are important parts of man's notions of the universe, cosmic phenomena and natural surroundings. To increase their effectiveness ritual acts of various kinds are carried out at favorable and magical times of day and night. Avoidances and taboos are also calculated to fit into these special times of the daily cycle. Midnight, for example, is regarded as an ominous and dangerous period when all sorts of supernaturals roam freely about the earth, and it is frequently referred to as the "witching hour." This is the time when werewolves (10322) and vampires (10329) strike or when a vampire can be killed (10341). Since the devil has control of things after midnight (10166), one is cautioned not to draw water from a well at 12:00 A.M. or court bad luck by strolling through a graveyard at this hour (9837), because the evil spirits will haunt one (10255). The hooting of an owl at midnight foretells calamity (12327), and the barking of a dog three times after midnight means death (9403). Miners believe this is the hour at which the earth rotates on its axis and therefore most cave-ins are thought to occur near midnight (7087). Dawn and sunrise, and the period before breakfast are likewise times of crisis and decision in the daily cycle. A snake will not die until sundown, even though its head has been severed (12397), nor will a turtle relax its bite until night comes (12430). Tides are also important in relation to the life cycle. Deaths are believed to occur at ebbtide (9882), and the dog days in the late summer are aggravated times for the healing of insect bites (3683), other wounds, and for one's state of health in general. The influence of Sirius, the Dog Star, on the canine species is especially bad at this time of the year.

Numbers figure prominently in folklore, and we have already cited sample folk beliefs in which numbers play a part. Three is a climax and a charmed number, not only in folk tales, but in folk beliefs as well. Things either happen in threes (11544), or the third time is either lucky or unlucky (11549), accidents come in threes (2806), and so do deaths (9634), as well as flat tires on a truck (9864). The common fancy concerning three people lighting cigarettes from one match, goes beyond the well-known belief that the last one will die, or the youngest of the three (9346), to include other human situations.

Seven and thirteen, as well as multiples of three (11546), are important numbers to be reckoned with in folk belief (11560). The seventh son, for example, is a born doctor (1315), and the seventh successive son has the power to cure boils (3075). If you sneeze seven times in a row, you will die (9109). In the European tradition thirteen is generally considered an unlucky number, although in some eastern Mediterranean and Middle East lands the reverse is true: Thirteen is lucky. If thirteen people sit down together to eat, there will be a death (9260), a notion derived from the betrayal at the Last Supper (9262). A clock striking thirteen, an unexpected mischance, prophesies the most dire consequence, namely, death (9316).

Directions are often associated with time and numbers. For instance, if you run around the house with a baby when it is nine days old, the baby will never have colds (1045). Another example of circumambulation involving three is the belief that if you spit under a cow chip and walk around it three times, you will cure the hiccoughs (3630). In playing poker, if you are having bad luck, get up and walk around the table three times to change your luck (8598). Doing things clockwise is a usual directional procedure, because the sun moves in this way (11505).

Stirring batter and mixing ingredients is usually done clockwise (5741). Magic rituals, as in folk tales, are often done counterclockwise, or "withershins." We have already noted counting backwards in connection with healing rituals to remove excrescences or to reduce swellings. In a directional orientation, walking backwards means you are showing your parents the road to Hell, or cursing them (1203). Standing a child on its head for a quarter of an hour to cure the croup is another example of a reversal of orientation and attitude (1059).

We have seen manifestations of folklore in the affairs of man, in the animal creation, and in the universe itself. It will be instructive in these broader connections to see how folkloric ideas are also applied to the hundred and one simple things that surround us in our daily activities inside and outside the home. We have already seen, for example, the odd uses of common kitchen utensils and household plunder--scissors, knives, thread, tape measures, keys, screws, nails, needles, feather beds, pillows, spinning wheels, etc.--and also such specialty items as beads, fishhooks, horse collars, horseshoes, baseball bats, coffins, grave clothing, etc., etc. As a study on variations let us look at the folklore of a household broom in a way that will bring out the manifold connections of this common implement of the domestic hearth.

If a broom falls across a doorstep, you'll have visitors (8197). If you want your guests to go home soon, put a broom behind the door and they will soon leave (8100). Buy a broom in May, sweep your friends away (9331). It is bad luck to take a broom with you when you move (6287). As a symbol of domesticity, the broom naturally figures in love matters: Your love will be true to you if you break a broom (4769). If a girl strides over a broom handle, she will be a mother before she is a wife (105); and to jump over a janitor's broom is a sign that you will soon marry (4768). By way of reversal: You are sure to be an old maid if you step over a broom (5039). As a sex determinant in keeping with the broom as a symbol of domestic life, it is believed that when a woman gets her feet in the way of a broom while sweeping, all her children will be girls (514). If you get hit with a broom, you will go to jail (7566). It is believed that if a new broom falls a death will occur (9332), and that it is a sign of death to put a broom on a bed (9330). This notion is associated perhaps with the bad luck supposed to follow putting a hat or shoes on a bed. As is well known, brooms are associated with witches, all the way from the well-known tradition that witches ride on broomsticks on Halloween (10034) to the belief that a broom across a doorway will keep witches out (10069), or the notion that if you pull a straw from a broom it will break the witch's back (10090). For reasons not explained, a broom hung in a chicken house will rid the chickens of lice (12685).

Sweeping brings additional variations on items connected with brooms that have already been mentioned, e.g., sweeping while company is in the home is a way of telling visitors to leave (8099). Sweeping under a girl's feet is a way of delaying her marriage (5206), or even causing her to become an old maid (5036). This applies to men also. If you sweep a baby every morning with a broom, it will grow faster (759), and if trash is swept over the feet of a crawling baby, it will begin to walk earlier than usual (749). In an updated version, one sees a reversal from the promotion of growth to stunting: When a person is vacuuming, a small child should never step in front of the moving equipment, for if it does, the child's growth will be stunted (770). Sickness and death are also involved in various beliefs about sweeping, e.g., if a spot is skipped while sweeping, the person's mother-in-law will lose the sight of one eye (3018). (Is this a punishment for the mother-in-law's overscrupulous surveillance of domestic activities?) Sweeping under the bed is a sickroom taboo, for the sweeper inadvertantly sweeps the sick person away with the dust (2645; 9138). If ashes are swept out of the house after dark, someone in the house will die before morning (9356), but sweeping out the house after a dead body has been removed is a way of preventing another death (9719). Sweeping dirt out of doors is tantamount to sweeping away your riches (7510). You should never sweep after sunset, for this supposedly stirs up the devil (10189); moreover, you should not sweep your house at night because a witch will come later during the night and take the broom (10030).

Like brooms, mirrors play an important role in folklore--all the way from the talking mirrors of the folk tale to the more common notions of mirrors as an extension of one's self or a projection of one's personality. Mirrors figure importantly in the nursery, and mothers and nursemaids are careful to keep a child from looking into a mirror before it is a year old (six months, and various other stated periods), lest it fail to develop normally (1158), become cross-eyed (1065), or even die (1373). A baby who looks at itself in a mirror will never marry (1319), and if an unmarried person breaks a mirror it is said that he or she will not marry for seven years (5204). By way of reversal, mirrors figure in love rituals, particularly those related in some way to the "dumb supper," whereby the girl sees the image of her true love looking over her shoulder (4792ff.). The bride, however, must not look into a mirror after she is fully dressed in her wedding gown (5374). The association of mirrors with one's personality, and even with one's essence or soul, readily explains the connection of mirrors with spirits and with death itself: Don't hold a child up to a mirror until it's a year old, as it will draw the attention of evil spirits (1178), a belief resting on the notion that spirits somehow live in mirrors or are reflected in them (9708). Burning a candle in front of a mirror, for example, is a way of summoning a spirit from another world (10631). Mirrors are covered at the time of death because a mirror is supposed to possess part of the deceased person's spirit (9708). In the Jewish tradition this is done in the belief that the first person to look in the mirror will be the next to die (9711). The association of mirrors with lightning strengthens the thesis that the common household looking glass is associated with superterrestrial forces (11374).

.     .     .

The importance of Utah as a depository for folk beliefs and

superstitions from elsewhere in the country was noted at the beginning of the Introduction. Throughout the collection are to be found items that stem from other parts of the country. Because of the lack of distribution studies, however, it is difficult to plot the provenience of these "imports," and it does not seem likely that there will ever be a kind of "union catalogue" of holdings against which state and regional collections can be measured for their local components.

Since the Utah Collection has been cross-referenced to the final two volumes of the Frank C. Brown Collection of North Carolina Folklore, comparisons may be drawn that will show the differences between these two major collections. The comparison will also throw light on general coverage of the field, category by category, in other parts of the country. First of all, the numerical superiority of the Utah Collection, 13207 items as against 8569 for the Brown Collection (64.8 percent) probably indicates a more intensive effort made in bringing the Utah corpus together. Of a total number of 21776 entries, only 2283 items were shared, or 10.4 percent. The greater coverage of the Utah Collection accounts, of course, for higher percentages of unique material. In Birth, Infancy, and Childhood, for example, the percentage runs to 68.5, and an even higher figure in Economic and Social Relationships (including Travel and Communication), namely, 69.9 percent. In Cosmic Phenomena and Weather, where the holdings in both states are more nearly equal (Utah, 925; North Carolina, 886), only 4.2 percent of the common totals are unique in Utah. In Hunting and Fishing, for example, Utah entries fall well below North Carolina levels, with only 93 unique items as over against 131 (70.9 percent). Since Utah is a sportsman's paradise for both hunting and fishing, one can only conclude that collectors did not talk with enough informants drawn from a growing host of devotees of field and stream. Even more difficult to understand is the deficiency in the Utah Collection of materials from the field of plants and plant husbandry, where the 259 unique Utah items still fall well behind the North Carolina totals of 478 by a 54.1 percent margin. Utah is still largely an agricultural state, but the bulk of the collecting was done in Salt Lake, Utah, and Davis counties, where an agricultural economy has gradually given way over the years to suburban living. People in these counties now largely find employment in Salt Lake and Provo, with lots of Davis County residents commuting to Ogden nearby for their daily work. The strength of the Utah Collection in Witchcraft, Magic, and Ghostlore, is completely unexpected, where the percentage of unique items runs to 57.2.

The enrichment of the American corpus of folk beliefs and superstitions by the influx of European materials is a general phenomenon encountered in all categories of folklore. As noted earlier, the influence of Mormonism and the church's proselyting efforts have played an important role in this process of acculturation. In this same general connection it should be noted that people from the Balkan Peninsula, either of orthodox or catholic faith, came to Utah's mine fields and to its smelter towns. This influx accounts for a whole series of beliefs not found in urban centers and in rural parts of the state. One unique popular belief and custom, not encountered except in the Pennsylvania German country, came to light after the Utah Collection had been completed. In the South Slavic folk traditions of Newtown, Tooele's ethnic enclave of smelter workers, a husband, wishing to sire a male child, approaches his wife in the marriage bed with boots on, and whistling. (This item, and many others like it, show that the folklore collector's work, really, is never done.) Jewish, Latin American, and Black ethnic elements, for understandable reasons, are not as pronounced in Utah as in other states of the area.

.    .    .

From this very cursory survey of the subject matter of folk beliefs and superstitions, and from the examples that have been given of the free array and manipulation of beliefs and ideas from field to field, and even from item to item, one will have been able to gain a presentiment, at least, of the appeal of this folk material to people, and the store they lay by it.  In tracing the geographical movement of these beliefs as well as the fluidity of the material itself, we have been able to show its dynamism as well as its general resilience and adaptability to changing conditions. Even so, in assessing the corpus of folk beliefs and superstitions in the development of culture in the lettered community, students of history and the behavioral sciences have generally relegated folk beliefs and superstitions to the realm of mental baggage handed down from an earlier day.  At best these folkloric notions are considered waifs and strays of a bygone time that can do little more than beguile us in an idle hour and provide amusement as we compare the ideas expressed with what has become a part of the logical systems of thought that govern our lives.  To the true scholar in the field of cultural history, however, folk beliefs and superstitions, along with the broader field of folklore itself, constitute an important part of a system of ideas and beliefs that have always been major components of human thought.  For in the old beliefs are embedded man's fears and hopes, his elation and his despair. Without this legacy, this residuum of man's earliest mental and spiritual yearnings and gropings, mythology, literature and art are empty indeed, and the key to much of associative thinking and symbolic representation that inform all thought, all art, and the creative process in general, are irretrievably lost.

What sense, one may ask, does it make to send anthropologists and ethnologists to the far corners of the earth to study the life of aboriginal peoples, if we are unwilling to examine the foundation of our own Anglo-Saxon heritage?  The Utah Collection of Folk Beliefs and Superstitions, fortunately, has preserved important parts of this ancient legacy, and the editors have tried to indicate here and there in the Introduction whence the material comes and how it coheres with other elements of our culture.  At the same time they have attempted to show, rather by example and induction than by theoretical discussion, the great resiliency and elasticity of folk belief in tying common, everyday things together into endless patterns.  Only a few of these ramifying musters of belief have been pursued to any length, but the Introduction taken as a whole will indicate to the thoughtful reader the ultimate riches and complexity of the material.  In assembling this motley array of old beliefs and folk notions the editors hope, along with the many hundreds of informants who have contributed material to the collection for over forty years, to have provided a useful tool for the study of Utah folk culture and folklife.  Many items in the collection, it is to be hoped, will contain useful clues for the reconstruction of the earliest cultural history of America, and the materials for piecing together the fabric of man's primal modes of thought, not only for this country, but also for Europe and the rest of the world.

## ABBREVIATIONS

The following abbreviations were used for locations, ethnic origins, and some occupations in the informant data that follows each entry:

| | |
|---|---|
| Alban | Albanian |
| Alta | Alberta |
| Amer Ind | American Indian |
| Anon | Anonymous |
| Arab | Arabian |
| Armen | Armenian |
| Aust | Austrian |
| Bas | Basque |
| Bav | Bavarian |
| BC | British Columbia |
| Belg | Belgian |
| Bulg | Bulgarian |
| Can | Canada, Canadian |
| Chin | Chinese |
| Czech | Czechoslovakian |
| Dan | Danish |
| DDS | Dentist |
| Du | Dutch |
| DVM | Veterinarian |
| Eng | English |
| Finn | Finnish |
| Fr | French |
| Fr Can | French Canadian |
| Ga | Georgia |
| Ger | German |
| Gr | Greek |
| Hosp | Hospital |
| Hung | Hungarian |
| Is | Israel, Israeli |
| Ind | Indian (see also Amer Ind) |
| Ir | Irish |
| It | Italian |
| Ja | Japanese |
| Je | Jewish |
| Lat | Latvian |
| Leban | Lebanese |
| Lith | Lithuanian |
| MD | Medical doctor |
| Mex | Mexico, Mexican |
| Norw | Norwegian |
| Obstet | Obstetrician, Obstetrics |
| Penn Du | Pennsylvania German |
| Pharm | Pharmacist |
| Pol | Polish |
| Pol Je | Polish Jew |
| PR | Puerto Rican |
| Que | Quebec |
| RN | Registered nurse |
| Rum | Rumanian |
| Russ | Russian |
| Scand | Scandinavian, Scandinavia |
| Scot | Scottish |
| S. Jordan | South Jordan |
| Secy | Secretary |
| Serb | Serbian |
| Slav | Slavic |
| SLC | Salt Lake City |
| SLCo | Salt Lake County |
| Span | Spanish |
| Swed | Swedish |
| US | United States |
| UT | Utah |
| W. Jordan | West Jordan |
| Yugo | Yugoslavia, Yugoslavian |

# I

# Birth, Infancy, Childhood

ORIGIN OF CHILDREN

Plant and Animal Agents

1  You find babies in cabbage heads (F,
   SLC, 1909); . . . under cabbage plants
   (F, Midvale, 1953).

2  Bad little boys aren't born--they're
   found under cabbage leaves (F, 79, SLC,
   1950).

3  Babies come from the pumpkin patch (F,
   SLC, 1958).

4  Where do children come from?  Children
   come out of an old hollow stump up
   beside the hill (M, Provo, 1972).  Cf.
   Brown 3.

5  Babies come from knots in the trees (F,
   SLC, 1958).

6  Babies are found in straw piles (F, SLC,
   ca. 1900).

7  Storks bring babies (M, Tooele, 1940).
   The belief in storks as bringers of
   babies is widespread, and the creatures
   are still made welcome to nest on
   rooftops and chimneys.  Even in America,
   where the bird is not native, the belief
   in this childlore persists, as notes in
   the Utah and other collections attest.
   Cf. Brown 1.

8  A stork dropped me from heaven into my
   parents' house (F, 19, Logan, 1970).

9  If you want a baby brother or baby
   sister, put a cube of sugar on the
   outside windowsill.  If a passing stork
   swoops down and picks it up, you'll have
   your wish (M, SLC, 1959).

10 The crow flew over and dropped you (F,
   Moab, 1953).

Medical Kits, Etc.

11 Children frequently believe that the
   doctor brings babies in his medical bag
   (F, Tooele, 1957).

12 We were told that babies were brought in
   the midwife's little black satchel (F,
   Woods Cross, 1953).

13 It is believed that babies are brought
   to the place of birth in saddlebags and
   then delivered (F, SLC, 1964).  Cf.
   Brown 6.

Miscellaneous

14 Babies are born by sprinkling dust on
   the windowsill (F, SLC, 1956).

15 When you put salt on the windowsill, it
   creates babies (F, 20, SLC, 1963).

16 Where do babies come from?  The angels
   grease the baby's bottom, and he slides
   down a rainbow (F, SLC).

17 Babies came from one's navel (F, SLC,
   1959).  Informant states that she
   believed this until after her third year
   of marriage and the birth of her first
   child.

18 I used to believe that God put His
   finger in babies' stomachs and said,
   "You're done," which caused the navel or
   "belly button."  The belly button was
   also where babies were born from (F, 21,
   Logan, 1970).

19 The mother plants a seed next to her
   heart and that is where the baby grows
   (F, 61, Bingham Canyon, 1911).

20 Spirits of our ancestors return in new
   born children (M, 43, Midvale, 1964).

FERTILITY

General

21 A man that has more than one wife
   usually has more than one child (M,
   Provo, 1961).

22 A bald-headed man is more fertile than
   one possessing hair on the head (M, SLC,
   1963).

23 If you get engaged on a full moon, it
   means the couple will be blessed with
   many children (F, SLC, 1962).

24 If you are having your period during
   your first date with your husband to be,
   you will be unusually productive during
   your marriage (F, SLC, 1959).

25 If a man marries a woman with red hair,
   he is assured a large family (M, 49,
   Midvale, 1925).

26 If you throw rice on the couple after
   they are married, it will make the
   marriage fertile and happy (F, 60,
   Odgen, 1930).  If the rice clings, you
   will have many children (M, SLC, 1960).

27  You will have more children if you decorate your house with green on Christmas (F, Ogden, 1960).

28  Grains of wheat grown in the house will make the family prolific (F, SLC, Obstet. ward, 1963).

29  To carry a New Zealand tiki charm will bring you luck if you are a man or fertility if you are a woman (F, 60, SLC, 1959).  Informant traded tiki charm for a rabbit foot.

30  Eat certain food on New Year's--as fish eggs--and have lots of children (F, 51, Ja, W. Jordan, 1938).

31  Eating of oysters will keep a woman fertile throughout her life (M, SLC, 1963; . . . makes a male fertile (F, 1964).

32  If you drink mandrake tea, it makes a woman fertile (F, SLC, 1920s).  Cf. Brown 8.

33  Because of its numerous seeds, pomegranates have become a symbol of fertility (F, 1908).

## STERILITY

### Causes

34  If a child is born out of wedlock, the mother will become sterile (F, SLC, 1964).

35  If a man and wife can have no children, one of them was born by means of illicit sexual relations (F, 19, SLC, 1960).

36  The act of withdrawal during intercourse will result in sterility in the female (M, SLC, 1880).

37  A man and woman can become barren if they use contraceptives too long (F, SLC, 1961).

38  Girls from a set of twins will be barren (F, Holladay, 1967).

39  Masturbation will make you sterile (M, SLC, 1969).

40  When you have the mumps you must not even so much as lift your head, let alone stand up.  To do so would cause sterility (F, Ogden, 1954).  Informant says: "When I was young and had the mumps, I was so afraid to even lift my head, that for the full duration of the illness I not only did not lift my head, but did not comb my hair."

41  If you eat white bread then you won't be able to have children (F, 17, SLC, 1963).

42  Celery causes sterility in women (F, Provo, 1971).

43  Black-eyed peas cause sterility (M, 65, farmer, SLC, 1964).

44  Too much lettuce in a garden is a sign of no more children (F, 85, SLC, 1964).

45  Paper flowers mean sterility in the owner (F, 54, 1972).

46  If the shadow of a pregnant woman falls upon a man she doesn't know, she'll never have more than one child (F, 38, Midvale, 1963).

47  When a man is involved with welding, it will cause him to become sterile (F, 80, SLC, 1974).

48  Flying above 20,000 feet will make a man sterile for 24 hours (F, Midvale, Obstet. ward, 1963).

49  Marlboro cigarettes make men sterile (F, SLC, 1962). . . . make you sterile (M, 20, SLC, 1963).

### Cures

50  Adopting a child will overcome sterility in a woman (Anon, Lehi, 1957).

51  A sterile woman should crawl on her knees up 150 stone stairs to a church with a Virgin Mary statue and pray and she will get a baby (F, 65, Du, SLC, 1965).

## BIRTH PORTENTS, INDICATORS

### General

52  All things happen in a series of three-- births, for instance (M, SLC, 1961).

53  Sadness in a dream means a birth (F, SLC, 1964).

54  Dreaming of milk means that the person is going to father or mother a baby (F, 18, SLC, 1965).

55  If a man develops a toothache, it means he will soon become a father (F, 78, SLC).

56  To see an image of husband with no clothes means pregnancy (M, Layton, 1934).

57  The first male who congratulates the new father will become the next father (F, SLCo, 1959).

### Domestic

58  If by mistake an extra spoon is put on the table before a meal is served, you will hear of a new baby (F, SLC, 1957).

59  If you drop a spoon while setting a table, a baby will be born in the family (F, 20, SLC, 1963).

60  Rocking an empty cradle is the sign of another child (F, 27, Charleston, 1972); . . . it will be filled with another baby within a year (F, Spanish Fork, 1959).  Cf. Brown 145.

61  The last person who puts a stitch on a quilt at a quilting will have the next baby (F, Moab, 1953).

62  If you break a needle while quilting, you will have the next baby (F, 57, SLC, 1963).

63  If a man and woman pour out tea at the same time or together, they will have a baby (M, SLC, 1963).

## Wedding, Showers

64  If you dream of a wedding, there will be a new baby in the family (F, 61, SLC, 1964).

65  If you break the bow on a wedding gift, you'll soon have a baby (F, SLC, 1961).

66  When opening up a shower gift, the bride must be careful not to break the ribbon, for a broken ribbon means that she will have a baby within the year (F, 19, SLC, 1958).

67  At a baby shower whoever gave the seventh gift that is opened will have the next baby (F, SLC, 1957); At a baby shower the giver of every seventh gift opened will have a baby (F, SLC, 1969).

68  The last person to have their gift opened at a baby shower will have the next baby (F, SLC, 1944).

## Baby, Baby Articles, Maternity Clothes

69  Never allow your visitor to lay her new baby on your bed or it brings a new baby to your house (F, 70, SLC, 1964); If a new baby lays on your bed and wets, you will have a baby (M, Park City, 1957).

70  If a baby wets on your lap while holding it, it means you will also have a baby (F, 42, Gr, SLC, 1964).

71  If a baby has early teething, there will be a new baby in the family soon (F, 1959).

72  If a woman leaves dirty diapers laying around, she will have another baby (F, 45, Price, 1961).

73  Never leave a wet diaper in someone's house because it brings a baby to the house you left it in (F, 68, SLC, 1964); Never change a diaper and forget to remove it from the bed . . . (M, SLC, 1957).

74  If you sell your baby carriage, etc., you are bound to need it yourself again (F, 44, SLC, 1961).

75  If you give all of your baby clothing away, you will be sure to get pregnant (F, 53, SLC, 1964).

76  The mother who gives away all her dead child's clothes will soon have another baby (F, SLC, 1962).

77  A woman should never give away her maternity dress, or pregnancy will occur again (F, SLC).

## Animals, Plants

78  Women that dream of fish will have a baby (F, 21, SLC, 1963).

79  Seeing fish in a clear stream means your wife is pregnant (F, SLC, 1958).

80  If you put salt on the windowsill and a bird comes, it means you're going to have a baby (F, 20, SLC, 1964).

81  Seeing four magpies means birth (F, Ir, SLC, 1960).

82  If a stork makes a nest on your chimney, a baby is due (M, SLC, 1953).

83  When a stork flies over a house, there is a birth about to take place (F, Ir, 1925, SLC); A stork hovering over a house means there will be an increase in the family (M, MD, SLC, 1959). Informant heard this belief throughout his medical career. Cf. Brown 1.

84  If a dog barks in the dark of the moon, there will be a birth (M, 49, Midvale, 1925).

85  If you are harvesting fruit and find a double, there will be an increase in the family (F, Dan, 1959).

86  A tree will fall each time a baby is born (M, SLC, 1964).

## Death, Cosmic Phenomena

87  Dreams go by opposites. If you dream of a death, there will be a birth (F, Tooele, 1957); Hear of death, hear of birth (F, 24, SLC, 1964). Cf. Brown 238.

88  If you dream of drowning, you will hear of a birth (M, 45, Sandy, 1945).

89  Falling stars are the souls of babies being born at the moment you see them fall (M, 17, SLC, 1961); Falling stars are souls coming down from heaven to animate newborn children (M, SLC, 1963).

## CONCEPTION

90  You're only supposed to be able to get pregnant two hours a month (F, Moab, 1953).

91  For the woman who cannot conceive, repeat the Nineteenth Psalm into her ear and say nothing thereafter. This helps with the will of God (M, 25, Je, SLC, 1965).

92  Pregnancy is possible long after the change of life has taken place (F, SLC, 1961). Informant says belief is a hangover from Sunday School tale of Abraham and Sarah.

93  If the bride dances with anyone except the groom at the wedding, she will have a baby in ten months (M, SLC, 1972).

94  A friend of mine thought you got pregnant from dancing close (F, 19, Logan, 1971).

95  It's bad luck to conceive a child in the dark of night (M, Ogden, 1961).

96  Conception is under the woman's will; by avoiding the last thrill of passion, she can prevent the ovules being displaced to meet the male sperm (M, 77, SLC, 1957).

## Human Body, Clothing, Domestic

97  If you fall up the stairs, you'll be pregnant (F, 25, SLC, 1953).

98  If you kiss a boy, you will become pregnant (F, SLC, 1959).

99  If you rub stomachs with a pregnant woman, you will become that way yourself (F, 21, SLC, 1963).

100 If a pair of men's trousers are hung on the foot of the bed, the woman will conceive and bear a child (F, SLC).

101 If you pick up a hanky, you will become pregnant (F, 68, SLC, 1964).

102 Only one person can pour tea at a tea party. If more than one does, someone will get pregnant (F, SLC, 1957).

103 Her mother always told her that the person who makes the tea must pour it. If one pours the tea that someone else has made, the person pouring it will become pregnant (F, 40, Midvale, 1972).

104 If two people make a bed, one gets pregnant (F, 35, SLC, 1964).

105 If a girl strides over a broom handle, she will be a mother before she is a wife (M, SLC).

106 If a visitor comes to your house, she should leave by the same door that she came in or she will become pregnant. The same is true if you go to someone else's house (F, Logan, 1935).

## Plants, Foods

107 A woman can become pregnant by eating watermelons (F, Clearfield).

108 If you swallow a watermelon seed, it will grow in your stomach and make you pregnant (F, Richfield, 1958).

109 Girls that eat green apples will become pregnant before marriage (M, SLC, 1964).

110 Put a potato under your bed if you want to get pregnant (F, SLC, 1964).

111 A woman will not accept the plant called "Wandering Jew" if she doesn't want to get pregnant. If she does want to get pregnant, she will accept the plant (F, 70, SLC, 1909).

112 A woman can become pregnant by drinking black coffee (F, Clearfield, 1962). Informant says it is a sure cure for infertile women.

## CONTRACEPTION

113 If a woman stands during sexual relations, she will not become pregnant (M, Eng, SLC, 1961).

114 You can't get pregnant during your period (M, SLC, 1959).

115 Many believe that a nursing mother cannot get pregnant (M, MD, Roosevelt, 1961). A woman will not become pregnant as long as she is breast feeding (F, Ute Indian, SLC, 1935). Informant learned it from Negro midwife.

116 You cannot have a baby if there is a double-bladed axe under the bed or wagon. It is bad luck (F, 70, SLC, 1964). Informant learned this belief from Indians in Kansas.

117 Put butter under the bed and you won't get pregnant (F, 38, SLC, 1935).

118 If you put perfume behind your knees, you won't get pregnant (M, SLC, 1965).

119 Aunt ---- used to insert a capsule of soda to keep from being pregnant (F, Moab, 1953).

120 Just use gunpowder in a gun to prevent conception (F, Moab, 1953).

121 To prevent future childbirths feed your husband dried placenta from the last child secretly in his food (F, 22, SLC, 1962). Heard during nursing training.

122 Eat chicken liver in order to stop from having babies (M, SLC, 1964).

123 Eating parsley prevents pregnancy (F, Eng, Logan, 1970).

124 A woman would not get pregnant for as many years as the number of cedar tree seeds she ate (F, 55, Logan, 1947). Learned from a black woman.

125 A yarn string saturated with turpentine worn around the waist for nine days is supposed to prevent childbirth (M, 20, Ogden, 1963). Advice given to male-- what he should do.

## MISCARRIAGE

126 If a pregnant woman steps over nails, she will lose her baby (M, 50, It, SLC, 1956).

127 If a pregnant woman develops a profound longing or craving for a particular food, her wish should be granted or she will have a miscarriage (F, Holladay, 1962).

128 Eating black jelly beans will make a woman lose a baby (F, 65, Farmington, 1937).

129 Eating red licorice will make a woman have a miscarriage (F, 65, Farmington, 1965).

130 A pregnant woman who works with tomatoes risks losing her child (F, 20, SLC, 1963).

131 If a pregnant woman works with warm meat--like if they've just killed a pig or something--if she touches the warm meat, she's supposed to lose her baby (F, Moab, 1953).

132 Exercise can cause miscarriages (F, 21, SLC, 1964).

133 Traveling distances in a car will always cause a miscarriage (F, 21, SLC, 1964).

134  Women who are pregnant should not bathe during their pregnancy or they will lose the baby (F, SLC, 1946).  Learned from Indian woman.

135  If you have a tooth pulled when you're pregnant, you will have a miscarriage (F, 21, SLC, 1963).

136  At a baby shower if the expectant mother breaks any ribbons, she will have a miscarriage before the baby is born (F, 25, Kearns, 1961).

137  When a pregnant woman smells nail polish, she will lose her baby to be (F, Eng, SLC, 1957).

138  Turpentine on the mother's umbilicus will cause a miscarriage (F, 50, Midvale, 1963).  Heard in hospital.

139  If a pregnant woman passes by a cemetery or meets a returning funeral party, she will swell or hemorrhage, which will result in a miscarriage (M, 58, MD, SLC, 1963).  Heard in Pittsburgh, 1930.

140  During pregnancy if a woman's hands are put above her head, this will cause a miscarriage (M, Eng, SLC, 1961).

141  If a pregnant woman paints, it will cause her to miscarry (F, Swed, SLC, 1959).

142  If a woman smells paint fumes when she's pregnant, she will have a miscarriage (M, 20, SLC, 1950).

## ABORTION

143  Take turpentine to cause an abortion (F, 1920).  Cf. Brown 23.

144  If a pregnant woman sits over a pan of hot turpentine water, she will have an abortion (F, Bear River City, 1957).

145  Soot from a chimney will cause an abortion (F, SLC, 1969).

146  Quinine and castor oil will cause an abortion (Anon, SLC, 1971).  Case reported from Holy Cross Hospital.  Cf. Brown 22.

147  If a woman paints at all when pregnant, the child will abort (F, 20, SLC, 1955).

148  Out on the desert there is a plant that has a little yellowish flower that grows up the stem.  I've heard if you make that into a tea it will cause an abortion (F, Moab, 1953).

149  A girl who sits over a pot of stewed onions will have a miscarriage (M, 19, SLC, 1963).  Cf. Brown 20.

150  Lay in the bathtub with mustard and flour in hot water for 15 minutes, covered from the waist to the knees, and you will abort (F, SLC).

151  It is bad luck to get a present for a baby that hasn't been born yet (F).  Mother-in-law of bride cited this as reason for an abortion.

152  For an abortion:  Jump off the fireplace stiff-legged (F, SLC).

## PREMATURE BIRTH

153  There is a worldwide superstition that a baby born prematurely will suffer injury to its head and be born with a permanently damaged brain (M, 39, MD, SLC, 1963).

154  A baby born at seven months will live (F, 50, Midvale, 1963).  Heard at Salt Lake General Hospital, Obstetrics Ward.

155  An eighth-month baby will live (F, SLC, 1950).

156  A premature infant born during the seventh month has a greater chance than one born during the eighth month (F, SLC, 1962).

157  If a pregnant woman passes by a cemetery or meets a returning funeral party, she will swell or hemorrhage which will result in premature birth (M, 58, MD, SLC, 1963).  Heard in Pittsburgh, 1930.

## PREGNANCY

### General Notions

158  A woman is more beautiful when carrying her unborn child (M, 55, SLC, 1964); . . . just before the birth of her first child (F, 77, SLC, ca. 1900).

159  Indians believed that a pregnant woman in a group indicated friendliness (M, 55, SLC, 1964).  A case from the Lewis and Clark Expedition.

160  Pregnant women have the devil in them (F, SLC, 1957).

161  Paint is harmful to a pregnant woman (M, SLC, 1961).

162  It is bad luck to take a picture of a pregnant woman (F, SLC, 1964).  Heard in Chicago about 1936.

163  It's good luck to have your ears pierced if you're going to have a baby (F, 35, SLC, 1965).

164  With every child a mother has, she loses a tooth (F, 88, SLC, 1964); . . . gives a tooth (F, 53, SLC, 1963).

165  Don't get your teeth filled while you're pregnant or they will fall out (F, 21, Logan, 1971).

166  For health purposes you shouldn't have any teeth filled while you are pregnant (F, 22, SLC, 1961); . . . or they will rot (F, 50, Orem, 1955); . . . or the fillings will fall out (F, SLC, 1960).

167  An expectant mother should not have her teeth pulled (F, SLC, 1935).  Cf. Brown 14.

168  A permanent won't take while you're pregnant (F, SLC, 1960).

169  Don't have a permanent when you are pregnant or your hair will fall out (F, 1962).

Indicators

170 When a woman has cravings for certain foods, it means she is pregnant (F, 18, SLC, 1963).

171 If a pregnant woman smells a certain food, she has to have it to eat (F, 29, Gr, Magna, 1964).

172 When you crave dill pickles, it means you'll soon be having a baby (F, SLC, 1959). Heard at a shower. Cf. Brown 85.

173 Eating strange foods like pickles and ice cream is a sign of pregnancy (F, 1962); Craving pickles and ice cream . . . (F, 19, SLC, 1963). Cf. Brown 85.

174 You're pregnant if you eat pickles and milk (F, 61, Richfield, 1929).

175 Eating pickles and strawberries is a sign of pregnancy (F, 18, SLC, 1963); Craving pickles and strawberries . . . (F, 20, SLC, 1958).

176 It was a legend handed down through the family that pregnant women crave watermelon and have strange desires to eat such things as dirt, or wood, or even to swallow small pebbles (M, 34, Ogden, 1950).

177 Pregnant women eat dirt because of a dietary deficiency (Anon).

178 A woman is pregnant if salad dressing tastes like rotten eggs (F, Brigham City, 1957).

179 Pregnant women have dark nipples (F, 19, SLC, 1963).

180 If the husband has a toothache or is taken sick, it means his wife is going to have a baby (F, Ger, SLC, 1961). . . . a man's sound teeth ache (F, 42, seamstress, SLC, 1964). Cf. Brown 13n.

181 When babies cut their teeth early, the mother will have another baby soon (F, 88, SLC, 1964).

182 A husband becoming ill is a sign that his wife is going to have a baby (M, 24, Brigham City, 1950).

Ailments of Pregnancy

183 Morning sickness is not to be avoided; the child will be more healthy and the delivery easier (F, SLC). A grandmother's notion.

184 If during the act the husband crawls over his wife and ends up on her side of the bed, he'll have morning sickness and his wife won't. This was how some women got out of having morning sickness (F, 43, Vernal, 1950).

185 If you eat a chocolate candy bar before getting out of bed, you will not have morning sickness (F, Moab, 1953).

186 If you are pregnant, eat raw eggs to stop from getting morning sickness (F, 25, SLC, 1964).

Conduct of Mother

187 Eat pickles when you are pregnant (F, 20, SLC, 1964). Cf. Brown 85.

188 Don't take a cold bath when pregnant (M, SLC, 1960).

189 The extreme of those who broke the "no cold water" taboo were the women who dowsed and swam the whole nine months, and fifteen minutes after the child was born took a cold water bath (F, SLC).

190 It is dangerous for a pregnant woman to look at a deformed person (F, 55, SLC, 1964). Cf. Brown 115ff.

191 A pregnant woman must not wash clothes lest she become deformed (M, 58, MD, SLC, 1963). Heard in Pittsburgh, 1930.

192 Among certain Indians a mother must withdraw into isolation for some time because she is condemned by her blood and dangerous forces of birth (F, 19, SLC, 1963). Hopi.

193 A pregnant woman should not watch or hear ghostly stories because she will dream of them (F, 79, Woods Cross, 1958).

194 Don't look at a dead baby while pregnant (F, Murray, 1964). Cf. Brown 114.

195 When you are pregnant you are not to go to a funeral because it is bad luck (F, 25, SLC, 1964).

196 It is bad luck for women to smoke when they are pregnant (F, 20, SLC, 1955).

197 Never drink water if you're pregnant because it could be dangerous (F, SLC, 1961).

198 A pregnant woman should never sit with a scissors on her lap or something terrible will happen (F, 55, Norw, SLC, 1959).

Conduct of Parents Affecting Unborn Child

199 Whatever happens to an expectant mother will affect the unborn child (F, SLC, 1961).

200 Everything a prospective mother sees, feels, and hears will influence her child's development. She should be protected against abnormal or dead things, sadness, fasting, thirst, or hearing about misfortune (F, SLC, 1962). Cf. Brown 97ff, 114ff.

201 A mother's state of mind will affect the unborn child (F, 72, SLC). Heard in North Dakota, 1922. Cf. Brown 195ff.

202 If a woman has bad thoughts while she is pregnant, her baby will be bad (F, 72, SLC, 1964).

203 Whatever a woman concentrates on during her pregnancy the child will become proficient in (F, 72, SLC, 1963).

204 When a woman is pregnant what she does continuously--such as a habit--her baby will more or less pick up the same thing (F, 20, SLC, 1963).

205 Never pick up someone else's baby when you are pregnant. Something will happen to yours (F, 21, SLC, 1949).

206 An expecting woman cannot have a permanent, for it will not take and it will be bad for the child (F, 43, SLC, 1964).

207 If you hold your nose at something that smells while pregnant, your child will always have bad breath (F, SLC, 1960).

208 Husbands of pregnant women are cautioned to avoid eating fish containing many bones lest injury befall the child (M, MD, 58, SLC, 1963). Heard in Pittsburgh, 1929.

209 If a baby is born and he shakes a lot, his mother has eaten a jellyfish (F, SLC, 1958). Indian belief.

210 A mother believed that her child's stuttering at the sight of peaches was caused by her bottling peaches just before the baby was born (F, SLC, 1959).

211 If a pregnant woman avoids food she dislikes, her baby will dislike the same food (M, SLC, 1957).

212 If a pregnant woman experiences various strong emotions, she can "mark" her unborn child in various ways. For example, my grandmother always insisted she had been made violently ill from smelling rancid butter during her pregnancy (F, Tooele Co, 1957).

213 If a woman abstains from meat during her pregnancy, her child will have a strong craving for meat (F, 38).

214 A woman must eat for two during pregnancy to make sure the baby will get enough (F, SLC, 1958).

215 A pregnant woman must eat sparingly of fat meat lest the child become too large and delivery too difficult (M, 58, MD, SLC, 1963). Learned in Pittsburgh, 1929.

216 If a pregnant woman doesn't eat the food she craves, her child will crave the same food (M, SLC, 1957). Cf. Brown 83f.

217 If a pregnant woman drinks alcoholic beverages, the baby will acquire a taste for alcohol (F, SLC, 1959); . . . the baby will be an alcoholic (F, 20, SLC, 1963). Cf. Brown 96.

218 If a mother becomes drunk while pregnant, the child will have a tendency toward alcoholism (M, SLC, 1958).

219 Parents who are alcoholics will produce children with defective germ plasm (F, SLC, 1959).

220 If the expectant mother drinks alcoholic beverages during pregnancy, it will affect the baby's nervous system (1957).

221 If you smoke and then quit while you are pregnant, your baby will grow up desiring to smoke (F, SLC, 1965). Learned in Nevada, 1930.

222 Smoking while pregnant will have bad effects on the baby (M, MD, Payson, 1913).

223 If a woman smokes while she is pregnant, her baby will have nicotine fits after it is born (F, 97, Syracuse, 1950).

224 If a pregnant woman is around fresh paint, the baby she is carrying will be adversely affected (F, Logan, 1960).

225 If a woman works while she is pregnant, her child will not be normal (M, SLC, 1961).

226 It is considered disturbing to the child being carried by a pregnant woman if she wears high heels (F, Granger, 1961).

227 Wearing high heels while pregnant puts hair on the back of the neck of the baby (F, 18, SLC, 1959).

228 If you dream that a baby will be deformed, it will be born perfect (F, 30, SLC, 1955).

229 If your feet get wet when you're pregnant, your baby will nearly drown sometime (F, 20, SLC, 1963).

230 If you are pregnant and see a fire, it is dangerous to the baby (F, 45, Bountiful, 1938).

231 If during pregnancy you dislike some person to a great extent, your child will also dislike that person (F, SLC, 1964). Heard in Texas, 1951; . . . you hate, the child will hate (M, Tooele, 1964).

## DELIVERY

232 There is a set of identical twin girls who have been very close all of their lives. One is married and the other is not. They live several miles apart. When the married twin gets pregnant, the unmarried one gets nausea (morning sickness) and suffers labor pains while the married twin has the baby (F, 33, Logan, 1970). Read in local newspaper.

## Prenatal Influences Affecting Delivery

233 If you look in the mirror while carrying your baby, you'll have a hard time at birth (F, SLC, 1964). Black belief.

234 If you sing while making your bed, you will have a hard or bad confinement (F, 53, Norw, SLC, 1961). Learned as young girl in Norway.

235 The expectant mother should be generous because if she isn't, she will have great labor in her delivery (F, 18, SLC, 1964).

236 Husbands with large genital organs will father babies so large that childbirth is difficult (F, 35, SLC, 1963).

237 A pregnant woman should never cross her legs or she may make her labor more difficult and painful (F, teacher, SLC, 1962).

238 During pregnancy, if a woman's hands are put above her head, this will cause a premature birth (M, Eng, SLC, 1961).

239 As soon as a woman begins to show signs of pregnancy, she should grease her hips and stomach with grease to have an easy delivery (M, 23, clothing salesman, SLC, 1960).

240 When a woman is going to have a baby, her friends give her a baby shower on the day of the dog. The reason is because dogs usually give birth without difficulty and it is thought that the expectant mother will do the same thing (Ja, SLC, 1963).

241 When pregnant, if you have a sudden desire to wash woodwork, it means that the baby will arrive on that day (F, SLC, 1958).

242 A woman about to become a mother wears her husband's shoes so that when her time comes she will suffer little pain (F, Ger, SLC).

243 Walking is good to bring on labor in a pregnant woman (F, 1933). Cf. Brown 25f.

244 Women about ready to deliver a child put an axe under the bed to cut the pain (F, 45, SLC, 1964). Learned in Arkansas. . . . put an axe under the mattress during delivery to prevent hemorrhage (M, MD, SLC, 1959). Heard from his patients. Cf. Brown 45.

245 Nails in front of the bed will ward off elves from women in childbirth (F, Swiss, SLC, 1959).

246 Tea made from raspberry leaves will bring on labor (F, 87, Providence, 1900).

247 A teaspoonful of turpentine will bring on labor (F, Lehi, 1957).

248 Castor oil may be used to induce labor in pregnant women (M, 18, Logan, 1971).

Easing Labor and Delivery

249 The presence of an owl near the home of a pregnant woman predicts an easy delivery (F, 70, SLC, 1915).

250 A Moab midwife said that all she needed to ease labor was a "bitch light" (F, Moab, 1953). (A "bitch lamp" or "bitch light" is an improvised light from a wick in a can of grease. --Eds.)

251 To make a delivery easier stay on your feet as long as you can (F, Moab, 1953). Informant claims that in biblical times they used to tie women to sticks and bounce them around to make it more painful.

252 Hold the edge of a sharp axe against the abdomen of a woman suffering from labor pains. This will take her mind off her trouble and ease the pain (F, SLC, 1964). An axe under the bed cuts the pain in half (F, 97, Syracuse, 1930). Cf. Brown 45f.

253 When you're pregnant and you're in pain, put a knife under the bed and it cuts the pain in half (F, 47, Sandy, 1965). A knife under a woman cuts the pain (F, Ir, SLC, 1957). A knife under a pillow . . . (F, 72, American Fork, 1963). Heard in Mississippi, 1908. A butcher knife under the mattress . . . (F, 36, SLC, 1957). Cf. Brown 49, 51.

254 For easy childbirth put a pair of shears under the bed to cut the pain (F, Bountiful, 1960).

255 If a red thread is tied to the index finger of an expectant mother during the labor period, it will assist the midwife in cutting the umbilical cord (F, 72, American Fork, 1963). Heard in Mississippi, 1908.

256 When a woman is in labor, if she drinks her husband's urine, her labor will be easier (F, 23, SLC, 1962). Heard in class for expectant mothers. Cf. Brown 19.

257 For labor pains boil a gold ring and drink the tea (F, 19, SLC).

258 The doors of a house should be left open when a child is about to be born. The mother will have an easy delivery (F, Richfield, farmw, 1910).

259 A window must be open at the time of birth so that the new soul can get in (F, SLC, 1961).

260 Fresh hog lard put in birth canal will ease birth (F, SLC, 1964). Black belief.

261 In the early days plural wives were hiding in the barn to keep out of prison. One of them started giving birth; the other, not knowing what to do, began praying. A lady appeared and stayed with them that night. A baby girl was born. The next morning the lady went out and wasn't seen again (F, 42, Manti, 1945). (This providential help is strongly reminiscent of aid often given by the Three Nephites. Typical features of the Nephite visitations, some of which are paralleled here, are the desperate need of the mother for help, and the mysterious appearance and disappearance of the unknown ministrant. For a survey of the Nephite legend, see Austin E. Fife, "The Legend of the Three Nephites Among the Mormons," *JAF* 53 (1940):1-49; Hector Lee, *The Three Nephites: The Substance and Significance of the Legend in Folklore*, University of New Mexico Publications in Language and Literature, No. 2, Albuquerque, 1949. The leading scholar in the tradition of the Nephites today, William A. Wilson, who has examined close to 1,000 versions of the Nephite stories, knows of only one other story in which the mysterious helper is a woman. --Eds.)

262 For a woman in delivery whose child will not emerge, say the following passage three times: "All these thy servants shall come down unto me, and bow unto me, saying 'Get thee out,' and all the people that follow thee, and after that I will go out" (Exodus 11:8; M, Je, SLC, 1965).

## Care of Mother After Delivery

263   A woman after childbirth is the most dangerous thing on earth. Demons are around her, and if she goes to a river to wash, the fish will go away (F, SLC, 1955).

264   The informant, pregnant one winter and very sick, had a miscarriage and remained ill because the afterbirth did not come. Since her family was living 100 miles from Logan and it was too risky to go to the hospital, they sent for her brother-in-law. He, with the rest of the family, made a circle around her bed and prayed. According to the informant, "I felt someone working on me, and when they were through I was just as well as I am now" (F, 68, Woods Cross, 1945).

265   After giving birth a woman should first be given bread soup. Brown some butter and put bread with it and water over it. Beat up an egg and put it in. It is easy to digest and filling and warm (F, 87, Providence, 1895).

266   After you have a baby you must stay in a dark room for ten days (F, 61, Richfield, 1928).

267   An axe placed under the bed of a woman who has just given birth to a child will stop her pain (F, SLC, 1964). Cf. Brown 45.

268   Stopping bleeding and pain: A midwife, to stop the newborn hemorrhage, said to stand an axe under the bed to cut the bleeding. The axe must be standing up (F). Cf. Brown 46.

## CARE OF NEWBORN

269   A dried malaga grape raisin boiled and opened and the fleshy part bound upon the navel of a newborn child was said to be a successful disinfectant (M, SLC, 1946). Cf. Brown 324.

270   A scorched cloth was laid on the navel of a newborn babe to prevent blood poisoning (M, SLC, 1946). Cf. Brown 322.

271   To bring good luck a baby should be rubbed with lard immediately after birth and before it is washed (F, 78, Midvale, 1920).

272   Rub a new baby with lard and spit on him and he will have a happy life (F, 48, SLC, 1964).

273   Spit upon a newborn baby and you will bring it luck (F, SLC, 1959); . . . ensure its happiness (F, SLC, 1955).

274   Spit on a newborn baby and you will have good luck (F, Richfield, 1958).

275   A newborn baby's face is swept with a pine bough to bring good luck (F, SLC, 1960).

276   It is good luck to kiss a newly born baby (F, Ogden, 1961).

277   Don't take a newborn child out in the night if the moon is full (M, SLC, 1961). Cf. Brown 219.

278   To protect a newborn baby from evil spirits, he is smoked, which is called "ukufutwa." Herbs are put in an earthenware vessel with some live coals which produce a dense smoke. The child is swayed to and fro in the fumes each morning at sunrise until it is six months of age (F, 53, SLC, 1964).

279   If a baby is brushed with a rabbit's foot at birth, this will avert the possibility of an accident (F, 59, SLC, 1963); . . . the baby will have good luck (M, 1963).

280   When a baby is born, one of the first things placed on its garments is a bit of gold. Sometimes an earring, a ring, or a gold piece. Superstition has it that on the first three days of a baby's life the fairies come to call on the baby. The fairies will be pleased and only predict good things (F, Gr, Tooele, 1961). (Apart from the obvious fairytale setting of this unusual folk belief ["Sleeping Beauty," Grimm No. 50], the reader should look beyond the modern fairytale manifestation to Classical and Germanic mythology where the Fates and Norns are thought to preside at birth and prophesy and ordain the newborn's future. The transition from the goddess-like figures of the Parcae to fairies, on the lips of the Greek woman from Tooele, is the kind of accommodation the folklorist is accustomed to seeing. Even so, adaptations of this sort in modern American folklore must be reckoned as utmost rarities. --Eds.)

281   It's bad luck to see a newborn baby without giving the child a piece of silver (F, 49, Can, SLC, 1964).

282   When a child is born, place a silver coin at his head and it will be lucky (F, Gr, Magna, 1926).

283   A silver spoon, as a present to a child, will act as protection to that child (M, Swed, SLC, 1961).

284   Giving a child a silver toy or a silver spoon is offering his life to Christianity (M, Swed, SLC, 1961).

285   Always put a silver dollar over a child's navel with tape to prevent it from sticking out too far (F, Ogden, 1971). Informant says she still has the silver dollar used on her because it is bad luck to throw it away.

286   For the first four months after a baby is born put a penny in its belly button and put a Band-Aid® over it and the baby won't ever have a hernia (F, Provo, 1972).

## BREECH BIRTH

287   If a baby is born backwards, it will always be backward (F, 36, SLC, 1956).

288   Breech births bring bad luck (F, 19, SLC, 1963).

289   If you eat pears when you are pregnant, your baby will be born upside down (F, 20, SLC, 1957).

## STILLBIRTH

290   A pregnant woman must not look at a dead body since this is likely to mark the baby and might cause it to be born dead (M, 48, SLC, 1936). Cf. Brown 102, 114.

291   If you take an airplane ride when you are pregnant, the baby will be born dead (F, SLC, 1959).

292   If a woman is going to have a baby, she should not lay down until just before it is to be born or it will be born dead (M, SLC, 1959). Heard in Pennsylvania, 1920.

293   If a man crosses his legs and his pregnant wife steps over them, the baby will be born dead (F, 25, SLC, 1945).

294   If a pregnant woman walked under a clothes line, her baby will be born dead (M, SLC, 1957).

295   If a woman is pregnant and already has one or more children and one child is a small child still, and she hangs out its tiny clothes in a position where a full moon shines on it, her baby will be born dead (F, 70, SLC, 1964).

296   If a woman washes windows with ammonia, her baby will be born dead (F, Ger, Ogden, 1960).

297   If you put a baby buggy in the house before the child is born, then the child will be born dead (F, 67, Bear River City, 1926). Informant claims she experienced this.

298   Don't look at a fire before a child is born or it will be born red, bloody, and dead (F, Ger, SLC, 1962).

299   If the mother is mournful, her tears may drown the child in her womb (F, 45, Provo, 1964).

300   If you stand in water when it's raining, your baby will drown if you're pregnant (F, 19, SLC, 1963).

301   To prevent stillbirth get all children in the neighborhood to beat tin pans in the sickroom to drive the devil away (F, 75, 1964).

## AFTERBIRTH AND AFTERPAINS

302   The placenta must be buried or hidden to protect the growth of the child (M, SLC, 1959).

303   The afterbirth must be buried or burned or the baby cannot go right to heaven when it dies (F, 50, Midvale, 1963). Informant heard this in Salt Lake General Hospital. Cf. Brown 57.

304   The father must step over the spot where the afterbirth is buried to assure that the child will listen to him and treat him with due respect (M, 58, MD, SLC, 1963). Heard in Pittsburgh, 1930.

305   The remains of birth should be buried in a dry place so that the mother and child will not become susceptible to strong pains in the stomach (M, 58, MD, SLC, 1963). Heard in Pittsburgh, 1930.

306   Place an axe under a newly delivered mother's bed, and it will cut away her "after pains" (F, SLC, 1961). Learned from black midwife in Pierce Co., Ga., 1935. Cf. Brown 66.

## LYING-IN PERIOD

### Well-Being of Mother; Conduct of Mother

307   Forty days after a woman has a baby she should be blessed. If she visits others within this period, it is bad. If in the presence of wine, it will curdle (F, Gr, SLC, 1964); After a baby is born, a woman cannot visit anyone for 40 days or bad luck will come upon the baby (F, Gr, SLC, 1959).

308   After childbirth the hair of the mother must not be combed for a month or all of it will drop out and never grow again. (F, SLC, 1960).

309   In Scotland it is considered unlucky for a mother and her baby to go outside until baby is baptized (F, Scot, Roosevelt, 1964).

310   When a mother is in bed with a newborn baby, visitors are not supposed to mention any sickness or disease during the conversation. It is no good luck (F, 62, Gr, SLC, 1963). Learned in Greece as a child in 1918.

311   If a new mother eats fish before her baby is a month old, she will get sick (F, SLC, 1964). Black belief. Cf. Brown 69.

312   Women shouldn't eat fish after having a baby. It brings bad luck to the mother and the baby (F, 40, Bountiful, 1926).

313   You must not sweep under the bed of a newborn for a month or the mother will catch a cold and never recover (M, 23, SLC, 1962).

## DEATH OF MOTHER

314   If you are born during a leap year, then you or your mother will die within a year (F, 84, SLC, 1965). Heard in Chester, Idaho, 1890.

315   If a new mother eats fish before her baby is a month old, she will die (F, SLC, 1964). Black belief. Cf. Brown 4899.

316   If a mother who had just given birth to a new baby ate fish and milk at the same meal, she would surely die (F, Eng, SLC, 1925).

317   If a pregnant woman bathed in cold water, she ran a great risk, and if her hands were put in cold water after confinement, she would surely die (F, SLC).

318 Don't have your teeth pulled when you are pregnant or you will bleed to death (F, 1962).

319 If you have childbed fever three times, you will die (F, Ger, SLC, 1936).

# BIRTHMARKS

## General Beliefs

320 Birthmarks are hereditary defects (F, SLC, 1957).

321 Some believe that birthmarks are caused by influences on the mother before the child is born (F, SLC, 1933). (For a discussion of birthmarks and related matters in this section, see Fife, "Birthmarks," pp. 273-83. --Eds.)

322 Different things that a pregnant woman sees will cause the child to be marked (F, Richfield, 1958).

323 If you have bad thoughts when you get married, your children will have birthmarks (F, 19, SLC, 1959); . . . bad thoughts during pregnancy . . . (M, professor of biology, SLC, 1961).

324 Don't think bad thoughts while you are pregnant or you will have a baby with a strawberry mark on it (M, SLC, 1962).

325 A birthmark is caused by a bad deed (F, SLC).

326 If you steal apples when a young child, when you become a mother your child will have a mark like an apple (M, 38, SLC, 1948).

327 If a woman has a tooth pulled while she is pregnant, the baby will have a birthmark (F, 84, Price, 1961).

328 Many an expectant mother lives in fear that she will mark her unborn child with a birthmark if she sleeps on her stomach (M, 42, MD, Murray). Heard in medical school, 1941.

329 A pregnant woman may never stretch to reach something. This will leave a scar on the baby (F, 71, It, SLC, 1963).

330 If you bump a lady while she is pregnant, birthmarks on the baby will result (M, SLC, 1961).

331 If you bruise a leg when you are pregnant, the baby will have a birthmark (M, MD, Roosevelt, 1961). Informant attributes this belief to Ute Indians. . . . bruise your body, baby will have a mark the same place on its body (M, 28, SLC, 1964).

332 If an expectant mother places her hand upon her body, the child will have a birthmark at that part of its body (F, 45, SLC, 1920); . . . places fingers on face or around the neck, child will have birthmark (F, 53, Orem, 1933). Informant has finger marks where his mother grabbed hold of somebody (M, Moab, 1953).

333 A pregnant woman should never wear real flowers, as it marks the child (F, 60, Port, SLC, 1959).

334 If a pregnant woman sees anything, she should take it--if not offered--or else the baby will have a birthmark (F, 37, It, Magna, 1932).

335 A birthmark in the middle of one's back will bring good luck and future wealth (F, 88, Yugo, SLC, 1905).

336 A birthmark in the shape of strawberries becomes red and itchy when strawberries are in season (F, 74, SLC, 1963).

## Fright

337 If a pregnant woman is badly frightened, her baby will be marked (F, 60, Tooele, 1970); . . . will be marked by whatever frightened her (F, Moab, 1953). See Fife, "Birthmarks," pp. 274ff.

338 If a child has a birthmark, the mother was scared by whatever the birthmark resembles (F, 55, SLC, 1965).

339 If an expectant mother gets frightened and touches herself, she will mark the unborn baby in the same spot (F, Crescent, 1915); . . . screams and touches her stomach, baby will have a birthmark (M, 53, SLC, 1930); . . . puts her hands to her face, baby will be marked (F, 25, SLC, 1943). Cf. Brown 98.

340 A frightened mother-to-be should never expose or grab her face or body as it causes birthmarks on the baby (F, Port, SLC, 1959).

341 A pregnant woman shouldn't look at anything frightening or it will give her child birthmarks (F, 60, SLC, 1963).

342 The result of some shocking sight or experience of the pregnant mother is a birthmark or defect in the child (F, Provo, 1959).

343 A mother's fear of the unknown or of a catastrophe will mark or deform an unborn child (F, SLC, 1959). Cf. Brown 97.

344 If a woman is frightened by an Indian when she is pregnant, the child will bear some kind of a mark when it is born (F, 95, Nephi, 1967).

345 If a pregnant woman has a bad dream, the baby can be injured or have a mark on it (M, Roosevelt, 1961).

346 If you see a monster in your dreams more than once, the baby you're carrying will have a birthmark like the monster (F, SLC, from informant born in Battle Mountain, Nev., 1945).

## Seeing Unpleasant Things, Violence, Etc.

347 If a pregnant woman looks upon anyone ugly or disfigured, it may mark the baby she is carrying (F, 60, SLC, 1964). Learned in Canada, 1927. Cf. Brown 111.

348   If a pregnant woman sees a horrible sight, it can cause her child to be marked (F, 90, SLC, 1964).

349   A pregnant woman must not look at a dead body since this is likely to mark the baby. In the early months of pregnancy women sometimes attend funerals but always take care not to look directly at the corpse, even if it is a near relative (F, 60, SLC, 1937). Cf. Brown 102f, 114.

350   "Lots of people believe that a baby can be marked by its mother's experience. Uncle George has a broken vein in his face, and his mother seen a neighbor hit his wife in the face with a hatchet just before the baby was born" (F, Moab, 1953).

351   "There is a spot on my forehead. Dad had been in town and had been hit on his head and it was all bloody, and he came in and Mama looked up and seen this, and when I was born, I had this red streak on my head. It shows up most when I am not well. When I was feeling bad, I would have this red streak on my forehead" (F, Moab, 1953).

352   If a pregnant woman sees a freak, her baby will have a birthmark (F, 1961).

353   Expectant mothers should stay close to home. If they see a limping man or deformed person their unborn child might have a birthmark (M, 56, Ir, 1920). A woman can mark her unborn child by close contact with a deformed person (F, Farmington, 1942).

354   If a pregnant woman sees a terrible accident, it will mark her baby (M, SLC, 1964).

## Burns, Fires

355   Any scar, injury, or burn will mark your unborn baby (F, 19, SLC, 1963).

356   If a pregnant lady gets burned, the child will have a scar where the mother was burned (F, 49, Milford, 1935).

357   If a mother is frightened or upset by a fire during the prenatal period, her child will be born with a large red mark on its face (F, SLC, 1959). A red birthmark was caused when the mother was frightened by a burning house (F, SLC, 1959). A pregnant woman can't look back at a fire or the child will get a birthmark (M, 25, Ja, SLC, 1965). See Fife, "Birthmarks," p. 275.

358   If during pregnancy a woman sees fire and touches her face, the baby will be born with a birthmark (F, 28, SLC, 1946). . . . sees fire and touches any part of her body the baby will have a scar where she touched, but if she rubs her rectum right away, this will prevent the baby from getting a scar (F, Ja, SLC, 1964).

## Animals

359   If a pregnant woman is scared by an animal, her child will look like the animal (M, SLC, 1958); . . . her child will favor that animal (F, SLC, 1960).

360   If an expectant mother is scared by an animal, the baby will be born with the image of the animal on it (F, 44, SLC, 1930). Cf. Brown 108f.

361   If you're carrying a child and you get frightened by an animal, wherever you touch your body you will mark the child the same way (F, Riverton, 1910).

362   A bat flew on her chest when she was pregnant and her child was born with a large brown mark on her chest (F, Emery, 1959).

363   A pregnant woman saw a shot beef cattle bleeding. When she gave birth to her child, it had a large, red birthmark (F, SLC, 1964).

364   If a pregnant woman steps over a black dog, her baby will have a black mark on him (F, Eng, SLC, 1962).

365   If a pregnant woman is frightened by a hawk, her baby will have a birthmark resembling a hawk (F, 48, SLC, 1963).

366   A hog chased a woman when she was pregnant and a birthmark in the shape of a hog appeared on the child (F, 74, SLC, 1963).

367   When a pregnant woman is frightened by a pig, her baby will have a patch of pig skin on his face (F, Eng, SLC, 1957).

368   If an expectant mother looks at a monkey, the child will be born with a birthmark (F, 72, American Fork, 1963). Learned as a child in Mississippi.

369   During pregnancy, if a woman is kicked by a mule, the baby will have a birthmark the shape of a mule (M, SLC, 1959).

370   If a pregnant woman is frightened by an insect, the child will have a birthmark which looks like the insect (F, 54, SLC, 1964).

371   If a pregnant woman gets scared by a mouse, her baby will have a red, furry birthmark (F, SLC, 1962). Heard in "preparation for childbirth class"; . . . scared by a mouse and touches herself, the baby will have birthmark on its body where the mother touched herself (F, 60, SLC, 1910).

372   If a pregnant woman sees a mouse, her baby will have a birthmark shaped like a mouse (M, SLC, 1957); . . . the child will have moles on its body (F, SLC).

373   A pregnant woman killed a mouse and when her baby was born it was on the baby's arm (F, SLC, 1963).

374   A brown birthmark is caused when the mother is frightened by a brown animal or rodent crossing her path when pregnant (F, SLC, 1959).

375   If a woman is frightened by a rat during her pregnancy, the child born will have a birthmark in the shape of a rat (M, SLC, 1959).

376 Margaret said she knew a woman who was
scared by a snake when she was pregnant,
and when the baby was born, the outline
of the snake went all the way around its
head and face, and the snake's head was
right between its eyes (F, Moab, 1953).
Cf. Brown 113.

377 If a pregnant woman is bit by a snake,
the baby will have snake marks on it (F,
Moab, 1953).

378 A woman and her husband were walking one
day when a snake crossed right before
them. The man killed it, but blood
splashed on the woman's cheek. The baby
was born with a birthmark on the cheek
(F, 26, SLC, 1963). (This entry
exhibits the contextual framework of
many folk beliefs, which is often
sluffed off in transmission.)

379 If a snake touches a pregnant woman, the
baby will have a birthmark in the same
place that the snake touched the mother
(M, Bountiful, 1959).

380 If a pregnant woman sees a reptile and
is frightened by it, the baby will come
with the picture of what she is
frightened by (F, 63, Monroe, 1964).

381 If you see a black widow spider when you
are pregnant, the next place you touch
on your body, your baby will have a mark
there (F, SLC, 1960).

## Moon

382 If a pregnant woman stares at a half
moon during a certain time of her
pregnancy, her baby will have a
birthmark shaped like a half moon (F,
39, Span, Grantsville, 1956).

383 If a pregnant woman touches her body
during an eclipse, the baby will be
marked where she has touched (F,
Bountiful, 1971).

## Craving Food, Fruit, Etc.

384 If a pregnant woman craves anything,
when the baby is born whatever she
craves will be marked on the baby (F,
Moab, 1953). The child of a woman who
is denied something will be marked for
life (M, SLC, 1961). Cf. Brown 86.

385 If a pregnant woman wants something to
eat, you're supposed to give it to her.
For if you don't, her baby will have the
imprint of the mother's craving on its
thigh (F, Gr, SLC, 1960); . . . gets a
craving for some food and doesn't get
it, the baby will be born with a mole
resembling the food (F, Ger, SLC, 1938).
See Fife, "Birthmarks," pp. 277ff.

386 If a pregnant woman puts her hand on her
back at the same time she has a craving
for something, the imprint of the
craving will be on the baby in the form
of a birthmark (F, SLC, 1961).

387 Her brother was marked with a chicken, a
roast chicken, and she said it was just
as plain a roast chicken as you ever
saw. Before he was born her mother went
into a neighbor's house. Just as she
went in the neighbor opened the oven and
pulled this chicken out to baste it, and
she said it just looked so good she just
went home and all day she wanted some of
that chicken so bad. She had it on her
mind so much that when my brother was
born, he had that chicken on him. She
said it was the leg. The leg stuck up
just like a chicken will (F, Moab,
1953).

388 "I've got a piece of bacon somewhere on
my neck because my mother wanted bacon"
(F, Moab, 1953).

389 "Mr. F was on the mountain, riding for
cattle, and I was in the valley, and he
came down, and he brought some fresh
beef. And I said, 'Well, I'd better go
and start supper.' And he said, 'I'll
cut some of that meat.' I made up my
mind just how I wanted it cooked, so I
put the skillet on the stove, and put
grease in it and got it just good and
smokey hot, and took that meat, the
slices on my hand, and laid it in that
grease, and it just all quivered, and
the blood came to the top and oh, it
smelled good. And I went on and put all
the meat in there, and the water was in
my mouth, the saliva, and I stood there
looking at it, and I turned around and
scratched my buttocks. And they say,
'Wherever you touch yourself, there's
where the mark will be.' And when that
child was born he had the prettiest bit
of raw meat on him you ever saw. It
lasted there all his life" (F, Moab,
1953).

390 "I have a fish this long (measuring on
her index finger and hand for about 4 or
5 inches) on my leg because my mother
didn't have much food to eat and had a
lot of fish while she was pregnant with
me" (F, 73, Moab, 1953).

391 If a pregnant woman craves a certain
fruit, her baby will be born bearing the
mark of the fruit (F, SLC, 1957); . . .
eats fruit during pregnancy, the child
will have a birthmark in the shape of
the fruit (F, 19, Ogden, 1963). Cf.
Brown 86.

392 If a woman craves strawberries while she
is carrying her child, when the child is
born it may bear a strawberry-shaped
birthmark (F, SLC, 1959); . . . eats a
lot of strawberries while she's
pregnant, her baby will have a
strawberry birthmark (F, 19, Sandy,
1960); . . . wants strawberries she
should be given some because if she
isn't and then touches herself with her
hands, it will leave a red mark on the
baby (F, 58, It, Murray, 1915). Cf.
Brown 93.

393 A pregnant woman fell down in a
strawberry patch, and the baby had a
birthmark resembling a strawberry (F,
SLC, 1910).

394 "Our little girl, before she was born--
of course, I was young and didn't know
much of anything, and I had a picture of
huckleberries hanging on the wall above
our bed. And I waked up one morning and
looked at that and I said, 'Oh, I would
like to have some of those. I wonder if
they have any of those in the West?'

Oh, during the day I think I talked to my mother about it. She says, 'Well, if there's any huckleberries in town we'll get them.' So they went downtown and got some canned huckleberries, but they didn't taste good. And it went on, and when she was born there was huckleberries right across the bottom of her lower jaw. They were blue, and kind of raised up a little, and they looked just like huckleberries that I imagined I seen. But we were afraid at the time that as she grew they'd grow out and bother her teeth. But they didn't. As she grew, the huckleberries grew down her mouth. They didn't hurt her teeth none, but they were always there" (F, Moab, 1953).

395  If a woman eats raspberries in the last three months of pregnancy, the baby will have a birthmark on it (F, SLC, 1960).

396  A red birthmark is caused from a desire for cherries (F, SLC, 1959). Brown 88.

397  "Before N was born Mama was standing on the ground and T was up in a tree and threw a cherry down and hit her on the leg. When he was born, he had a big cherry on his leg" (F, Moab, 1953).

398  If a pregnant woman sees a nut and doesn't eat it, but scratches herself, the baby will be marked at that spot (M, 50, It, SLC, 1956).

399  If a pregnant woman craves tomatoes, the baby will be born with a mark on its body unless she eats them (F, 23, SLC, 1964).

## Riddance of Birthmarks

400  When a baby is born with a mark, if the mother will lick the birthmark three times before sunrise for nine mornings the mark will disappear (F, 46, SLC, 1938).

401  Spit on a birthmark every day to cure it (M, SLC, 1964).

402  A birthmark can be removed by rubbing it with the thing it most resembles (F, 27, SLC, 1956).

## RESEMBLANCES, IMPRINTING, ETC.

403  An expectant mother should not see a dead person for if she does her baby's color will resemble the dead person (F, 60, Gr, SLC, 1961).

404  If a woman craves a certain food during her pregnancy, her child will like that food (F, SLC, 1941).

405  An expectant mother, at the first sensation of feeling life, the next person she sees her baby will resemble (F, 60, Gr, SLC, 1961).

406  If the mother is frightened during pregnancy, she will have a fearful baby (1957). Cf. Brown 197.

407  If a pregnant woman is frightened by a thunderstorm, her child will be born fearing storms (F, SLC, 1964).

408  Don't look at snakes while you are pregnant or your baby will always be afraid of them (M, 19, SLC, 1962).

409  "Her mother was one of those rare people who have a long tooth between her front teeth. Her brother had told her mother that this was because she had seen a dog when she was pregnant" (F, Provo, 1970).

## TIME OF BIRTH

### General

410  The leap year day brings good luck to the people who claim it as a birthday (F, 67, Pol, Provo, 1960).

411  A girl will be born two weeks earlier than a boy (F, SLC, 1962).

412  The time of day a baby is born is the same time of day that the mother conceived (F, 22, Milford, 1961).

### Day of Week

413      Monday's child is fair of face.
         Tuesday's child is full of God's
           grace.
         Wednesday's child is merry and glad.
         Thursday's child is sour and sad.
         Friday's child is Godly given.
         Saturday's child must work for a
           living.
         Sunday's child shall never want.
       (F, SLC, 1961). Brown 123f.

414  Wednesday's child is full of woe (F, SLC, 1920).

415  Wednesday's child is loving and giving (F, SLC, 1960).

416  Thursday's child has far to go (F, SLC, 1920).

417  Thursday's child works hard for a living (F, SLC, 1960).

418  It is always bad luck to be born on Friday (F, Ogden, 1960); . . . because Friday is a day of bad omens (M, 20, Midvale, 1949). Brown 125.

419  Friday's child is loving and giving (F, SLC, 1920).

420  If born on Friday, fair of face and never have to work for a living (F, Swed, SLC, 1957).

421  Friday's child is full of woe (F, SLC, 1960).

422  The child that is born on Saturday is bonny and blithe and gay always (F, SLC, 1959).

423  Saturday's child has far to go (F, SLC, 1959).

424  Saturday's child is full of woe (F, SLC, 1965).

425  The child born on the Sabbath Day is fair and good and wise and gay (F, SLC, 1920); . . . learned and wise (F, SLC, 1956).

426 It is good luck to be born on a Sunday (F, Ogden, 1959). Brown 128.

427 A child born on Sunday will be blithe and bonny, good and gay (F, SLC, 1944). Cf. Brown 129.

428 A child born on Sunday is loving and giving (Woods Cross, 1953).

429 Born on Sunday, full of God's grace (F, Woods Cross, 1953).

430 A child born on Sunday shall never lack for food (F, Lehi, 1957). Cf. Brown 127.

431 If a baby is born on Sunday he will have an easy time during his life (F, Murray, 1915); . . . is highly favored (F, SLC, 1959).

432 If born on Sunday, you are a person of leisure (F, 17, SLC, 1962).

433 The day of the week on which you are born should be your lucky day in every important matter (F, Ir, SLC, 1960). A child born on an unlucky day will have bad luck for the rest of its life (F, 45, SLC, 1939). Brown 121.

## Month, Day of Month

434 Anyone born in March is calm in facing their problems (F, 20, W. Jordan, 1959).

435 If you are born in May your life will be successful (F, 20, W. Jordan, 1962).

436 If one is born on the thirteenth day of the month, thirteen is his lucky number (M, Ogden, 1956). Brown 130.

437 Children born on Friday the thirteenth will always have bad luck (F, 1960); . . . but a part of this evil may be avoided by falsifying the record; if such a child ever does have any good fortune, it will be after the death of the last person who knows the true date (F, 69, SLC, 1930).

438 It's good luck to be born on Friday the thirteenth (F, 65, SLC, 1929).

439 Any person born on June twenty-first will not live to be twenty (F, 97, Syracuse, 1883).

440 It is unlucky to be born on either the sixteenth or seventeenth day of the month (F, SLC, 1961).

441 To be born on Christmas day is a sure sign of a carefree life (F, 40, SLC, 1938).

## Moon, Tide

442 The change in the moon has an effect on the births of children (M, Ogden, 1954). Brown 61.

443 More babies are born during full moon than any other time (F, SLC, 1959). Nurses say that when the moon is full there will be more babies. They call it a "full house" or "the blitz" (F).

444 A baby born during the night of the fullest moon will be blessed with success and happiness (F, SLC, 1957).

445 A pregnant woman can almost determine the day she will have her baby by the largest change in the face of the moon (F, Sandy, 1964).

446 A pregnant woman will have her baby at the time of the new moon (F, 67, SLC, 1963).

447 Babies are born with the incoming tide (F, 51, Ja, W. Jordan, 1963). Births occur at the flow of the tide (F, SLC, 1944).

## SEX OF BABY

### Conception

448 To produce a baby boy screw the girl six times in the morning (M, 22, Provo, 1972).

449 A baby conceived before midnight will be a boy; after midnight a girl (F, 50, SLC, 1963).

450 If you have intercourse with the lights on, the results will be a girl; if the lights are off, it will be a boy (F, SLC, 1960).

451 It is believed that a woman expecting a baby in the springtime is likely to have a girl, and that if the baby is born in daylight it will be a girl, whereas, if the baby is born at night, it will be a boy (F, Provo, 1971).

452 If you take garlic to bed with you, and a baby is conceived, it will be a boy (F, Provo, 1959).

453 If a boot is hung on the left side of the wall, a girl will be born, whereas the right is indicative of a boy (F, Provo, 1971).

454 If a couple puts salt in their bed, they will have a boy (F, Clearfield, 1964).

455 Dry weather during conception produces boys; rainy days are for girls (F, SLC, 1962).

456 When the moon is growing small and you get pregnant, you will have a girl. If you get pregnant when the moon is growing big, you will have a boy (F, Peoa, 1920). Cf. Brown 154.

457 If a woman gets pregnant on a full moon, the woman will have a boy, but if the moon is in process of changing, then the woman will have a girl (F, W. Jordan, 1929). Cf. Brown 146.

458 If a woman is tired before a sexual relation, she will have a girl. If refreshed and relaxed, a boy (M, SLC, 1961).

### The Mother's Body as a Determinant

459 Sprinkle salt on the head of an expectant mother to determine the sex of

the baby-to-be (when the mother is not looking ). Then sit back and observe the movements of the mother-to-be's hands. If she raises her hands towards her head immediately after this, the child will be a girl. If her hands go towards the lower part of the body, the baby will be a boy (F, Gr, Magna, 1961); . . . if mother scratches above the waist, it is a girl, below, a boy (F, 71, Gr, SLC, 1964).

460   If a girl who is pregnant has a happy and shining face, she will have a boy (F, SLC, 1971).

461   If a pregnant woman has color high on her cheeks, the baby will be a boy (F, 50, Midvale, 1963).

462   If a pregnant woman's face is swollen and bloated, the baby will be a girl (F, teacher of Obstet., SLC, 1962).

463   If you get freckles during your first pregnancy, it will be a girl (F, 48, SLC, 1964).

464   A mole on the right side of the chest means you'll have good health and most of your children will be boys (M, 1965).

465   If your nipples are dark during pregnancy, you'll have a girl (F, 37, SLC).

466   A pregnant woman can tell what sex her child will be by the stiffness of her shoulders--left, a boy, right, a girl (F, 74, SLC, 1964).

467   If a woman will kiss her elbow, she will have a boy (F, 68, SLC, 1924). Cf. Brown 152.

468   If a pregnant woman is told she has a spot on her arm, and if she looks at the outer side, she will have a boy. If she looks at the inner, she will have a girl (F, 19, SLC, 1964).

469   If a pregnant woman shakes hands with her left hand, she will have a baby girl (Sp, SLC, 1957).

470   If you place a baby boy on a bride's lap, she'll have a baby boy first (M, Gr, SLC, 1948).

471   If a pregnant woman is carrying a boy, she gets broader across the hips than if the child is a girl (F, SLC, 1959). A pregnant woman who grows big in the back will have a girl (F, 1960).

472   If a pregnant woman gets a charley horse in her left leg, it means she is carrying a boy; a charley horse in her right leg means a girl (F, SLC).

473   If a woman wants a boy she should ovulate from the left ovary; if a girl, from the right ovary (M, 58, MD, SLC, 1963).

474   Each ovary has charge of distributing one sex egg. If one of the ovaries has been removed, then that girl will have only girls or vice versa (F, Taylorsville, 1959).

475   Only males will be born to a woman after the removal of the left ovary (F, 1961).

476   If a woman is pregnant with a girl, she will tend to be fatter. If she is pregnant with a boy, she will be thinner (F, Grantsville, 1935). If you put on weight just on the front, it is a girl (F, Moab, 1953).

477   If you get high all over, it is a boy (F, Moab, 1953); . . . big all around, will have a girl, big in front, a boy (F, Logan, 1970). Brown 147.

478   Before birth a child's sex can be determined by the shape of the stomach. If it sticks out forward, it will be a girl; but if it lies more flatly and the ribs expand for it to lie from side to side, it will be a boy (F, SLC, 1964); . . . woman sticks out more in front, she will have a boy. Heavy all over, a girl (F, SLC, 1962); . . . larger in front, a boy (F, 27, Charleston, 1972).

479   A pregnant woman carrying a baby high will have a boy; carrying it low will mean a girl (SLC, 1960).

480   If during pregnancy the baby is carried high, it will be a girl; if it is carried low, it will be a boy (F, 19, SLC, 1952).

481   If a child is carried more to the right of the mother's body, it will be a boy; if to the left, a girl (M, 58, MD, SLC, 1963).

Bodily Functions

482   Sex in an unborn child may be determined by how the mother eats (F, 30, SLC, 1964).

483   The diet of the mother determines sex, meat for a boy and sweets for a girl (F, SLC, 1950).

484   When an expectant mother has a craving for sweets, she will have a girl baby. A desire for meats and vegetables indicates that a boy is coming (F, SLC, 1957).

485   If a pregnant woman eats lots of peas, she will have a girl (F, SLC, 1961).

486   If you're pregnant eat lots of broccoli, you'll have a boy (M, 19, SLC, 1964).

487   If a pregnant woman eats green beans, she will have a boy (F, SLC, 1961).

488   If a pregnant woman wants a boy, she will have one if she drinks goat's milk (F, 21, American Fork, 1960).

489   If an expectant mother drinks much lemon juice before the baby is born, it will be a boy (M, SLC, 1959).

490   If an expectant mother drinks much orange juice before she has the baby, it will be a girl (M, SLC, 1959).

491   If a pregnant woman gets out of her bed every morning from the right side, she will have a baby boy (F, 20, SLC, 1962).

492   A woman should put wood with a knot in it under her pillow to assure a male child (F, 45, SLC, 1964). Learned it in Arkansas as a child.

493 Whatever side a pregnant woman lies on will determine the sex of her child (M, SLC, 1959).

494 If a pregnant woman always lays on her right side, she'll have a girl, and if it is always on her left side, she'll have a boy (F, 18, SLC, 1955).

495 If a woman gives birth to a child while lying on the right side of the bed, the child will be a girl; if the mother is lying on the left side of the bed, it will be a boy (F, 43, American Fork, 1949).

496 If an expectant mother dreams about the baby, she will know the sex of the child before it is born (F, SLC, 1962).

497 When you dream that you are going to have a boy, you will get a girl instead (F, 52, W. Jordan, 1929).

498 If a woman who is pregnant starts up stairs with her right foot, she'll have a boy and left foot for a girl (F, 18, SLC, 1955).

499 If a pregnant woman starts walking with her right foot, she will have a boy, and if she starts with her left foot, she will have a girl (F, 20, Sunset, 1955).

## Illness as a Determinant

500 A great deal of morning sickness when you're pregnant indicates you will have a girl (SLC, 1960).

501 If the father gets morning sickness, the baby will be a boy (F, 50, Midvale, 1963). If a woman suffers much morning sickness, the baby will be a boy (F, 22, Ogden, 1963). (Sympathetic physical discomfort on the part of the husband during his wife's pregnancy is part of a psychological syndrome known as pseudocyesis and belongs to a larger complex of unusual male behavior before, during, and after the conception and birth of a child. Encountered in many parts of the world, including the Mediterranean parts of Europe and sporadically in the Americas, this aberration of the early life cycle is known as couvade, from the Fr. vb. couver, "to hatch." See Wayland D. Hand, "American Analogues of the Couvade," in Studies in Folklore in Honor of Distinguished Service Professor Stith Thompson, ed. W. Edson Richmond [Indiana University Folklore Studies, No. 9, Bloomington, Indiana, 1957], pp. 213-29. --Eds.)

502 When you are pregnant and have to take pills, take the blue end first if you want a boy and the pink end first if you want a girl (F, SLC, 1945).

503 If an expectant mother takes blue morning sickness pills during her pregnancy, she will have a boy; if she takes pink pills, she'll have a girl (F, 21, SLC, 1964).

## Activity of Fetus

504 The sex of an unborn infant can be determined by counting the rate of movement by the child in the womb. A high number of kicks indicates a boy, a low number, a girl. Count made at midterm (4 1/2 mos.) (M, Logan, 1970). (Informant received this information from a University of Kansas Education Department professor who claims to have validated this notion through scientific research.)

505 A very active fetus usually indicates you're going to have a girl (SLC, 1970).

506 Pour cold water on your navel and if it kicks, it's a boy; if it doesn't, it's a girl (F, 26, SLC, 1970).

507 If the kicking of the prenatal baby is hard and frequent, it will be a boy; if it is mild and infrequent, it will be a girl (F, SLC, 1959).

508 During pregnancy, if the baby kicks left, it will be a boy; if it kicks right, it will a girl (F, 19, SLC, 1950s).

509 A fast fetal heart beat indicates a girl, and a slow fetal heart beat indicates a boy (F, 50, Midvale, 1963).

## Domestic Pursuits

510 A pregnant woman who wishes to determine the sex of her child should get a cup of warm water, spit into it, and add one tablespoon of Drano. If the mixture becomes cloudy, the baby is a boy (F, Provo, 1974).

511 If you are expecting a child and you pick your napkin up in the center, you will have a boy. If you pick it up on the edge, you will have a girl (F, SLC, 1962).

512 Place a spoon under one chair and a fork under another. If a pregnant woman sits on the chair with the spoon, it will be a girl, if the fork, it will be a boy (M, PR, 32, SLC, 1965).

513 Spill wine on the table and a baby boy will be born in the family (M, 61, It, W. Jordan, 1936).

514 When a person (lady) gets her feet in the way of a broom while sweeping, this will mean she will have all girls (F, 58, SLC, 1925).

515 To have a boy, place a candle in the window for a week (F, SLC, 1961).

516 If you look at a picture of a boy baby long enough, your baby will be a boy (F, 18, Lynndyl, 1954). Concentrate on the picture of a baby boy for one hour every day and you'll have a baby boy (F, 18, Bountiful, 1961).

## Natural Domain

517 If you dream you are fishing and catch a catfish, it is a sign someone will have a baby boy (F, SLC, 1962). Learned in Georgia.

518 To know whether a baby shortly to be born will be a boy or a girl, hang a mutton bone (the shoulder) over the back

door.  If the person who first enters through the door is male, the baby will be male; if a female, the baby will be female (F, 83, Nephi, 1955).

519    When you kill a pig and you collect the lard, if you put the cut kidney into the cooling lard, you can tell if a woman is going to have a boy or a girl (F, 50, It, W. Jordan, 1920).

520    If you touch a fig leaf when you are pregnant, you will have a baby boy (F, SLC).

521    A forked stick pointed at a mother can be used as a device to detect the sex of an unborn child (F, 81, Nephi, 1964). (Diagnostic devices for predicting the sex of an unborn baby in Utah popular tradition are uncommonly rich, as entries between Nos. 527-42 show.  Most unusual, of course, is the use of a forked stick for the purpose.  The so-called "water witch," or forked stick used for locating underground water is most unusual as a divinatory ritual in predicting the sex of unborn children. For examples of various kinds of sticks and forked sticks in locating wells and underground watercourses, see Nos. 10444-57, below.  Divining rods and dowsing rods for the detection of precious metal are not well represented in the Utah Collection.  No. 10458, below, however, gives a presentiment, not of the use of the boughs of trees, but of the so-called "doodlebugs," metal and geophysical contraptions, used for their magnetic properties.  --Eds.)

522    If there is a full moon the night before the birth, it will be a girl (F, 20, SLC, 1950).  Cf. Brown 154.

523    When you are pregnant, if you look over your right shoulder at a full moon, you will have a boy; if over your left, you'll have a girl (F, 50, SLC, 1932).

## Wedding, Shower

524    Before the wedding march starts they let the bride hold a boy so her first offspring will be a boy (M, 66, Gr, SLC, 1963).

525    If your first wedding present is wrapped in pink, your firstborn will be a boy (M, 20, Idaho Falls, 1955). . . . wrapped in blue, your first baby will be a boy (M, 20, Idaho Falls, 1963).

526    At a baby shower if the gifts are dominantly blue, it means you will have a boy.  If they are pink, it will be a girl (F, 1960).

## Diagnostic Devices - Ring

527    An expectant mother may determine the sex of her child by attaching her wedding ring to a string and holding it directly over her stomach.  If it swings backward and forward, it will be a boy, and if it swings sideways, it will be a girl (F, SLC, 1959); . . . if it turns clockwise, the baby is a boy; counterclockwise a girl (F, 45, SLC, 1940).

528    To tell the sex of a child when pregnant take a hair from the expectant mother's head and tie it to a wedding band. Suspend the band over her stomach.  If it swings back and forth, it's a girl, if in a circle, it's a boy (F, 43, SLC); . . . swings in a circle your first child will be a girl, if it swings back and forth it will be a boy (F, 68, SLC, 1964).

529    Tie a gold ring on a string and hold it still over a pregnant woman's palm.  It will start moving on its own accord.  If it goes in a circle, the baby will be a girl; if it goes back and forth, the baby will be a boy (F, 40, SLC, 1943).

## Diagnostic Devices - Coins, Buttons, String, Etc.

530    If you hold a coin on a string dangling over the belly of a pregnant woman, you can tell that she'll have a boy if the coin spins.  You can tell she'll have a girl if the coin stays still (F, 22, Ogden, 1970).

531    Lay a pregnant woman down.  Twist a string, tie it on a coin.  Hang it over her.  If it goes back and forth, it'll be a boy.  If it goes around, it'll be a girl (F, SLC, 1960).

532    If you want to know if your baby is going to be a girl or boy, tie a long string around a dime (at one end).  Hold it out in front of you and spin the dime.  When it stops (facing you)--heads it's a girl, tails it's a boy (F, SLC, 1957).

533    Put a button on a string in front of a pregnant woman's stomach.  If the string swings sideways, it is a boy; and if it swings frontways, a girl (F, 18, Price, 1962).

534    If you hang a string over the abdomen of a pregnant woman and the end falls in a circle, the baby will be a boy; if the string slips sideways, it will be a girl (F, SLC, 1962).

535    Take an empty spool of thread, tie a string around the middle, hold it right in front of a pregnant woman.  If it swings from right to left the baby is a boy; if from front to back, the baby is a girl.  It works best if a married woman with several children holds the spool on the string (Logan, 1972).

## Diagnostic Devices - Needle, Pencil

536    A needle on a thread is held dangling above the palm of a pregnant woman.  If the needle swings around in a circle, the baby is a girl; if the needle swings back and forth, the baby is a boy (M, Provo, 1974).

537    Stick a needle and thread in the eraser of a pencil and hold it over your wrist. If it goes back and forth, it's a girl. If it goes up and down, it's a boy.  And if it goes around and around, you won't have any kids (F, Heber, 1965).

538 Dangling a pencil over a mother's wrist will tell the sex of her children and the order in which they will come (F, 21, SLC, 1964).

539 Hold a pencil on a string over your hand. If it moves crosswise, you'll have a baby girl. If it moves vertical, you'll have a baby boy. (Works only on married women.) (F, SLC, 1963).

540 In order to find out whether an expectant mother will have a girl or boy, tie a string around a pencil and hold it above the woman's left hand. If the pencil goes in a circle, she will have a girl (F, 21, SLC, 1964).

541 If a pin on the end of a string is swung over a reclining expectant mother and the string swings back and forth, the child will be a boy. If the string swings around, the child will be a girl (M, 72, SLC, 1930).

542 A pregnant mother should take a piece of thread and a needle and let the needle spin from the end of the thread. If the needle spins in a clockwise circle, the baby will be a boy. If it spins in a counterclockwise circle, the baby will be a girl (F, 18, Ger, 1961).

Miscellaneous

543 Parental temperament influences the sex of unborn babies. Phlegmatic husbands and vivacious, energetic wives produce mostly male children; nervous husbands and placid wives produce mostly females (F, teacher of Obstet., SLC, 1961).

544 When a mother has a new girl and comes home from the hospital, she should enter her home through the back door. For the girl is weaker and more girls will not be born to the family. With a new baby boy the mother must go through the front door. A boy is the stronger sex and therefore more boys will follow him into their home (F, Gr, SLC, 1909).

545 A baby's umbilical cord is saved and put in vinegar to become soft. The mother who is pregnant will tie this cord in a rag and wear it. If she wants a boy, she will wear the cord of a girl, vice versa for a girl (F, Gr, SLC, 1962).

546 If a woman has four boys in a row, she must wait until the seventh to have a girl (F, 52, SLC, 1964). Heard in Minnesota, 1940.

547 If a member of the family dies and a baby is due, it will be of the same sex as the person who passed away (F, 26, Bingham, 1959).

548 There is an old belief that in times of war there are more male children born than female. When the population gets overcrowded, a war comes on (F, Woods Cross, 1953).

549 On the holiday of the Cross in the Greek church they used to decorate the cross with basil. Women take three leaves of basil and they make a wish in order to have boys (F, 66, Gr, SLC, 1963).

Sex of Next Child

550 If the baby says "da da" first, the next child will be a boy; if it says "ma ma" first, the next child will be a girl (F, Riverton, 1900); . . . firstborn says "papa" first, next child will be a boy, if it says "mama" first, a girl (F, 60, SLC). Brown 151.

551 You can tell what the sex of the next child to be born in the family will be by the last child born. If the last child has a pointed hairline at the nape of the neck, the next child will be a boy. If there is a rounded hairline, the next child will be a girl (M, SLC, 1961). If a girl has a long hairline on her neck, the next baby will be a boy (F, Gr, SLC, 1962).

552 If your child was a boy and you want a girl the next time, turn the bed around (F, 27, Charleston, 1972). Brown 149.

553 When a birth takes place in the "growing of the moon," the next will be of the same sex (F, 51, SLC, 1964).

554 If a boy is born in the wane of the moon, the next birth will be a girl and vice versa (F, SLC, 1955).

NUMBER OF CHILDREN

Bodily Indicators

555 The number of wrinkles in the forehead shows the number of children you will have (1960); . . . wrinkles on face . . . (F, 50, SLC). Cf. Brown 139.

556 The number of crosses on your hand indicates how many children you will have (F, 19, Heber, 1972); . . . crease lines on the palm of your hand . . . (M, SLC). Brown 131.

557 Count creases in a doubled up fist on the little finger side and you'll have that many children (F, 19, SLC, 1964).

558 If you pull each finger on each hand, the number of fingers that pop at the joints will tell you how many children you are destined to have (M, Helper, 1958).

Wedding, Shower, Diamonds in Ring, Etc.

559 The number of ribbons the bride breaks at her bridal shower is the number of children she'll have (F, SLC, 1963). The bride will have a child for every ribbon that is cut . . . (F, SLC).

560 At bridal showers the ribbons from the packages are tied in the bride-to-be's hair. They must remain in her hair until her groom-to-be takes them out, and for each one he removes he gets a kiss. Each ribbon that he may break means a child (F, SLC, 1948); . . . tie the strings of gifts in the bride's hair (F, 19, SLC, 1961).

561 For every towel that is received for a wedding present you'll have a baby (F, SLC).

562    The number of safety pins you receive at a baby shower is the number of children you will have (F, 1960).

563    The number of diamonds in a girl's engagement ring is the number of children she'll have (F, Midvale).

564    If on your wedding night you drink wine from a glass and throw the glass on the floor, the number of pieces the glass breaks into predicts the number of children you will have (F, SLC, 1961).

Plants

565    The number of seeds in an apple indicates how many children you'll have (F, 27, Charleston, 1972). Cf. Brown 132.

566    We used to blow the fluff from a dandelion gone to seed and count the number of "blows" it took to clean it, saying that it indicated the number of children we would have (F, 52, SLC). Practiced as a child in South Carolina, 1920s. The amount of seeds left on the dandelion tell how many children (F, 55, SLC, 1964). Heard as a child in Brooklyn, N.Y., 1920s. Brown 136f.

567    To tell the number of children you will have, toss up the yellow centers of a daisy and catch them in one hand as they come down (F, SLC, 1964). Learned as a child. Cf. Brown 135.

568    If you pull off a leaf from a plantain weed and count the number of fibers hanging free from the broken end of the stem, this will tell you how many children you are destined to have (M, Helper, 1958).

Various Beliefs

569    The more sons, the more the happiness, if a woman (F, 39, Sp, Grantsville, 1948).

570    The more children a family raises, the bigger the rewards in life in heaven (M, 63, pastor, Tooele, 1958). Informant told this to his congregation to encourage them to have more children. "When my grandmother was sixteen she received a Patriarchal Blessing saying she would be the mother of a multitude. On last count in 1960 there were 15 children, 34 grandchildren, 59 great-grandchildren, and 5 great-great-grandchildren. However, it has increased in a sizable amount since then" (F, 52, Vernal, 1971).

571    When you wash dishes and you get your stomach wet, you are going to have a lot of children (F, 27, SLC, 1957).

572    If you rock an empty cradle, you'll have a lot of babies (F, 55, SLC, 1930). Cf. Brown 145.

573    A needle is stuck into the eraser of a lead pencil. A piece of thread is put through the eye of the needle and the pencil is held over the wrist of the person. The pencil will start to go into circles but when it goes in a north-south or east-west direction you count how many times it goes back and forth before it stops. That's the number of children you will have (F, 20, N. Logan, 1960).

574    If you dream of ants you will have a large family (M, Ogden, 1960).

575    Farmers who have a good harvest of grain during a period of three consecutive years will be given a good family of boys by his wife (M, 87, Ger, Corinne, 1963).

Twins

576    A woman who has twins is possessed with an evil spirit (M, 49, SLC, 1964).

577    The Ute Indians in Uintah County, Utah, used to kill the second child born if an Indian woman had twins because they thought God could create only one perfect child at a time (F, 42, Dragerton, 1958); . . . Indians kill the girl most of the time (M, Kanab, 1958).

578    Indians believe that when twins are born the weaker takes the strength from the stronger so they let the weaker one die (M, Roosevelt, 1961).

579    If when twins are born, the girl of a girl-boy set is born first, it is bad luck (F, SLC, 1960).

580    Twins of two sexes are more animal than human (F, Ja, 51, W. Jordan, 1963).

581    Boy twins brought bad luck, so mother gave one away (F, 51 Ja, W. Jordan, 1963).

582    If an expectant mother uses both hands equally during her pregnancy, then she will have twins, one a boy and one a girl (F, SLC, 1959).

583    If someone gives two of the same kind of gift at a wedding, it is an indication that the couple will have twins (F, 34, Sandy, 1939).

584    Hold an eraser or needle suspended on a string over the wrist of the pregnant woman. If it moves in circles, it will be twins (F, Provo, 1970).

585    If you open an egg on your wedding day and it has a double yolk, it is an indication you'll have twins (F, 34, Sandy, 1939).

586    When a couple make love and see a mocking bird, it means they will have children. If they see two mocking birds, they are going to have twins, and if they see three mocking birds, they will have many children (F, SLC, 1962).

587    If a coyote howls at the stroke of midnight, it means twins are being born (F, Bountiful, 1916).

588    If you find two violets with stems intertwined, it means you will have twins (F, SLC, 1958).

589 If two spoons are accidentally put by your cup, you will have twins before the year is up (F, 25, Bountiful, 1959).

590 Put two cubes of sugar on the outside of a windowsill and the stork will bring twins (F, 1960).

591 If the parents have intercourse twice in one night, the result will be twins (M, SLC, 1967).

592 Coitus during pregnancy will cause twins or triplets (F, teacher, SLC, 1962).

593 If you have twins, it means that you have been carrying on with another man and one of the twins must be put to death (F, 23, SLC, 1957).

594 A multiple birth signifies an unloyal wife (M, SLC, 1963).

595 If a man is unfaithful to his wife while she is in the hospital having a baby, she will have twins (M, 18, SLC).

596 An old explanation for why we have twins. They thought two children, two fathers, but since one child comes from conception of each father, one father must be a god. So one twin must be a child of god (F, SLC, 1964).

## FIRSTBORN, ORDER OF BIRTH, ETC.

597 The first one born in the family is the luckiest one (F, 18, SLC, 1955).

598 The third son has the brains of the family (M, Logan, 1950).

599 A seventh child is always lucky (F, 45, W. Jordan, 1935). Brown 221.

600 The seventh son of a seventh son can have nothing but good luck (F, 19, SLC, 1955). Brown 221n.

## NAMING, BAPTISM, CHRISTENING

601 It's bad luck to name a baby before it's born (M, 46, SLC, 1920s).

602 A child will become very wealthy if the initials of his full name spell a word (F, SLC, 1960).

603 You have to name baby after the first thing you see after it is born (M, Ute Indian, Roosevelt, 1961).

604 It is bad luck to change a baby's name on a wedding date (F, 46, Welsh, Marysvale, 1963).

605 A person with seven letters in his or her name is very lucky (F, 21, Richfield, 1949). A first name with seven letters is lucky (F, SLC, 1960).

606 If you want your children to be happy throughout life, give them happy names (F, SLC, 1957).

607 The name of Mary is lucky (Spanish Fork, 1959).

### Naming After Someone

608 It is very unlucky to name a newborn child after a dead child of that family (F, SLC, 1962).

609 If you name your baby after a living relative, the name will assure the child a long life too (F, Sandy, 1959).

610 The spirit of an ancestor returns to a newborn child and then the child should be named after that person (M, 20, SLC, 1956).

611 It is bad luck to name a child after someone you dislike (F, 21, SLC, 1963).

612 If one names a child after a mean person, the child will also be mean (F, SLC, 1940).

613 If you have suffered a lot and you name your baby after yourself, the baby will also suffer (M, SLC, 1957).

### Baptism, Christening

614 The parents of a newborn child should not accept sugar from its grandparents before it is christened. It is bad luck (F, SLC, 1918).

615 To call a child by name before it's christened is unlucky (F, 51, SLC, 1964).

616 It is believed that if a boy is very ill or is expected to die, this boy is to be baptized before he is dead. This is called baptizing in the air. Later, if the boy becomes well again, he is unable to become a priest (F, Gr, SLC, 1962).

617 It is considered unlucky to take a baby out of doors until the baby is baptized (F, 24, SLC, 1962).

618 A baby should cry when baptized to prove that the baptism is valid (evil spirits leaving the baby make him cry) (M, 27, SLC, 1949). A child's cry at baptism is the voice of an evil spirit being put out by holy water (F, 55, waitress, Swed, SLC, 1935). A child's cry means the devil is going out of it (F, SLC, 1964).

619 A child's crying at christening means that it won't like its name (M, SLC, 1921).

620 If a child cries while being baptized, he will be a saint (F, 19, St. George, 1964).

621 It is a bad omen if a child does not cry at its baptism (F, Holladay, 1959).

622 It is a sign of good luck if a child cries at baptism (F, 69, SLC, 1960). If a child cries at christening, he will have good luck all through his life (M, SLC, 1961).

623 Never kiss an unbaptized baby. It is thought to be a devil (F, SLC, 1910).

624 Butterflies are the souls of unblessed babies (F, SLC, 1959); . . . unbaptized babies (F, 54, SLC, 1964).

## NURSING, LACTATION

### Nursing

625    For sore nipples cut up a little mutton tallow and melt over hot or boiling water. Rub on nipples after each feeding (F, 67, SLC, 1915).

626    The milk is believed to be injurious to a nursing child when the mother is in her fourth or fifth month of pregnancy (F, 58, MD, SLC, 1963). Learned in Pittsburgh, 1930.

627    "Well, the first food that I recommend giving to them is just put them on the nipple. Let them nurse. There's a substance in the breast, if the baby gets that it seems to me it always gets along better. It will be a good-natured baby--better than if you give it something artificial" (F, Moab, 1953).

628    Put hands in cold water when nursing a baby and it will cause breasts to cake (M, MD, Roosevelt, 1961). Informant attributes this belief to Ute Indians.

629    Never give a new nursing mother much water as it will dilute her milk for the baby (F, SLC, 1961). Heard from a black midwife in Georgia, 1935.

630    If you iron while you are nursing, your milk will go bad (F, SLC, 1960).

631    After a woman has had a baby, if she dries up her breasts properly, they will not return to their original size but will remain as large as when the mother was nursing the baby (F, 22, Milford, 1961).

632    Make a very greasy hot cake, fry in lots of grease and put on breast. Bind tightly for breast fever (F, 67, Mt. Pleasant, 1915).

### Weaning

633    If you wean your baby in the dark of the moon, you will never get it weaned completely. It will always want to nurse (F, SLC, 1964).

634    You must wean babies when the sign is right. The day after a full moon (F, 73, Swiss, Midway). Cf. Brown 81.

635    Good Friday is the best day on which to wean children (F, 55, SLC, 1964).

636    Women should not have a second child until after the first one has been weaned, lest the first child be sick and weakly (M, 58, MD, SLC, 1963). Heard in Pittsburgh, 1930.

637    Sugar was placed in a small bag and worn around the neck of an infant. It was used in weaning and called a "sugar titty" (M, 46, SLC, 1918). Brown 80.

## DREAMS ABOUT BABIES, CHILDREN

638    Dreams about children mean bounteous favors to those to whom they appear (F, SLC, 1940).

639    If you dream about babies you will know happiness (F, 69, SLC, 1910).

640    If you dream of a baby laughing, then it's good luck (F, 69, SLC, 1904).

641    If you dream about a baby, bad luck will come your way (F, 55, Norw, SLC, 1961); . . . dream of baby crying, bad luck . . . (F, 69, SLC, 1904). Cf. Brown 165, 240.

642    A child in your dreams means danger in the near future (M, SLC, 1961). Cf. Brown 241.

643    If you dream about babies, be careful and avoid trouble (F, 59, Bear River, 1914).

644    If you dream of a baby, there will be a tragedy in the family (F, 20, SLC, 1964). Heard on T.V. Cf. Brown 241.

## WISHING ON BABY, ETC.

645    If you hold a baby in your arms for the first time and wish, you will get your wish within a year (F, SLC, 1962).

646    If you look at a baby before you look at the mother, and make a wish, it will come true (F, SLC, 1962).

647    First sight of a brand new baby, make a wish and it will come true for sure (F, 70, SLC, 1906).

648    A newborn baby laid on your bed brings you good luck for the year (F, Eng, Ogden, 1963).

649    If you are holding a baby and it wets on you, it's good luck (F, SLC, 1959).

650    Babies can see God (F, Clearfield, 1890).

## HUMAN BODY

### Hair

651    Children's hair is weaker and more delicate than that of adults (F, SLC, 1959).

652    To shave a child's head soon after birth will help bring prettier hair (F, 25, Ja, SLC, 1965).

653    It is said that if a baby is born with a double crown, it brings bad luck. The Indians used to sacrifice these babies because they were a bad omen (F, SLC, 1958).

654    A pregnant woman should not handle furry animals because the child will be hairy (F, 45, SLC, 1964).

655    A pregnant lady shouldn't look at a monkey or the baby will be born hairy (M, 21, SLC, 1956).

656    If you whip a horse, your baby will have hair (like horses' hair) on his back (F, 84, Price, 1961).

657    If there is a muskrat around the house when a baby is born, the baby will have a lot of hair (M, 55, Centerfield, 1964).

658    If you have a lot of heartburn during pregnancy, your baby will have a lot of hair (M, 22, SLC, 1964); . . . your children will be born with hair (F, SLC, 1959); . . . heartburn during the first pregnancy, the baby will be born with curly hair (F, 67, SLC, 1956); If the mother doesn't have heartburn, her baby will be bald (F, Ogden, 1961).

659    If you have a permanent during pregnancy, your child will have curly hair (F, Midvale, 1961).

660    If a pregnant woman eats toast that is burnt, her children's hair will be curly (F, 19, St. George, 1963).

661    If a pregnant woman drinks vinegar, her baby will have curly hair (F, 60, SLC, 1964).

662    Wet a baby's hair and curl it on the ninth day, and it will have curly hair (F, Kanab, 1956). Brown 190.

663    Lick a baby's hair and it will be curly (M, Ogden, 1950). Spitting on baby's hair will make it curly (F, 60, SLC).

664    The best way to insure that the child will have naturally curly hair is to wash her hair in toilet water. It never fails (F, Provo, 1971).

665    If a child loses his hair after scarlet fever, it will come in curly (F, 1917).

666    Eat strawberries while pregnant and your child will have red hair (F, 21, SLC, 1954).

667    If a pregnant woman craves strawberry ice cream, she will have a redheaded girl (F, teacher, SLC, 1960).

668    Eating carrots will give the unborn baby red hair (F, 50, Midvale, 1963).

669    When two people with shiny black hair marry, there is a probability that their children will have red hair (M, 18, SLC, 1962).

670    If a pregnant woman eats an orange, her baby's hair will fall out (F, teller, SLC, 1962).

671    If you cut a baby's hair before he is one year old, it is bad luck (M, Tooele, 1964); . . . it will bring him bad luck for many years to come (F); . . . bad luck the rest of his life (F, SLC, 1959).

672    Cutting a baby's hair before it was one year old would make its hair coarse (F, 53, SLC, 1964).

673    If you cut a baby's hair before he's one year old, it won't grow (F, SLC, 1930).

674    If a baby sees itself in a mirror before it is one year old, the baby's hair will not grow (F, 28, Murray, 1963).

Caul

675    If you are born in a veil (skin) you'll always be protected (F, 78, Dan, SLC, 1964). Learned in Denmark. Cf. Brown 245n.

676    If a baby is born with a veil over its face, the baby will have good luck (F, 52, W. Jordan, 1933); . . . good luck will follow it all its life (F, It, SLC, 1962). Thomas E. Cheney was recently shown his own caul, which had been preserved by a midwife because it would be lucky for him (SLC, 1960). Brown 244.

677    If a baby is born with a veil of skin over its face, whatever becomes of the veil will become of the child (F, 52, SLC, 1930).

Eyes, Ears, Mouth, Face

678    Food eaten during pregnancy will affect or influence the color of the hair and eyes of the baby (F, Murray, 1923).

679    If a pregnant woman looks at an animal with a blue and a green eye she will have a baby with two different colored eyes (F, 44, Ger, Orem, 1963).

680    If the baby is born on St. Patrick's Day, it will have green eyes (M, SLC, 1967).

681    A pregnant woman can stare at a brown-eyed doll to make her child so it would have brown eyes (F, 69, SLC, 1965).

682    If a child will eat his carrots, his eyes will always be healthy (F, 18, St. George, 1963).

683    If parents boast about their child or expose him unnecessarily, the child will develop big ears (M, 58, MD, SLC, 1963).

684    Dragonflies sew up the ears of children (F, 60, SLC, 1963).

685    Eating a small piece of bread and butter after a wedding by the bride will induce the children to have small mouths (M, 47, SLC, 1963). Small pieces of bread served to the bride by the best man will cause children to have small mouths (F, Swed, SLC, 1961).

686    If a child tells a lie, a dragonfly (or darning needle) will come along and sew up his mouth (M, Sunnyside, 1963).

687    When you see a dragonfly, you should stamp with your fingers stretched apart and your mouth open so he won't sew you up (F, 45, SLC, 1933).

688    If a baby has a dimple in its chin, it is a sign of good luck (F, SLC, 1962).

689    A dimple means that the baby was kissed by the angels before it came to earth (M, 64, SLC).

Teeth

690    It is bad luck if a child is born with teeth (F, Orangeville, 1959).

691   Put a coral on a chain around a child's neck to make sure that he will have good teeth (F, SLC, 1971).  Brown 380.

692   It brings bad luck to count a baby's teeth (F, Springville, 1961).  Cf. Brown 382.

693   If you let a baby look in a looking glass, its teeth will come in crooked (F, Magna, 1930).

694   If a baby sucks a pacifier, then he will have buck teeth (M, Logan, 1971).

695   If you have a loose tooth, don't pull it.  Let it fall out or the next one that comes in will be extra large (F, SLC, 1955).

696   The first teeth are supposed to bring you money from the good fairy (F, Moab, 1953).  Cf. Brown 387, 3388.

## Lost Tooth - Throwing Away, Burning

697   In order to have straight secondary teeth you must throw your baby teeth over the roof (M, 22, Ja, Midvale); . . . put your tooth in a crack or the next tooth will grow in crooked (F, SLC, 1964).  Cf. Brown 384.

698   If you pull a tooth, throw it to the sun and you will have another one (F, Span, SLC).  Cf. Brown 386n.

699   You must burn baby teeth so permanent teeth will develop (F, Sandy, 1957).

## Lost Tooth - In Glass, in Oven, under Pillow

700   When a child's tooth is pulled, place it in a glass of water and the fairies will take it and leave a gift (F, SLC, 1938); . . . the good fairy will turn it into money (M, 64, SLC, 1900).

701   Place a new pulled tooth in the oven. The fairies will exchange it for money (F, 47, Midvale, 1931).

702   When a tooth comes out, put it under your pillow and a fairy will come in the night (leaving a candy bar, if Dad has been to town, otherwise a penny, nickel, or dime).  If you listen carefully, you can hear her wings (F, Logan, 1919). Cf. Brown 387f.

703   Put your tooth under the pillow and a blue fairy will come and leave money or else take the tooth and build a castle (F, SLC, 1961).

704   Put an extracted tooth under your pillow and a fairy will bring you a gift (M, Layton, 1958); . . . fairy godmother will exchange money for it (M, 28, SLC, 1946); . . . fairy princess will bring you a dime (M, 23, SLC, 1947); If you don't put your tongue in the hole, the fairies will leave money under your pillow (F, Moab, 1953).  Brown 387f.

705   If you sleep with a tooth under your pillow, after losing it, it will bring good luck (M, SLC, 1959).

706   If you sleep on a tooth, your wish will come true (F, SLC, 1910).

707   To insure the proper growth of a new tooth, put the lost one under the pillow of the child who lost it (F, SLC).

## Lost Tooth - Gold, Black, and Dog's Tooth

708   When you lose a tooth, if you don't put your tongue in the hole, the tooth that comes in will be gold (F, SLC, 1959). Brown 383.

709   If your tongue goes in the hole where a baby tooth came out, the permanent tooth will come in black (F, 8, SLC, 1964).

710   If you lose one of your baby teeth and a dog swallows it, your tooth will grow in like a dog's tooth (F, 20, SLC, 1949); . . . burn it to prevent dog's tooth from coming in (F, Murray, 1959); . . . bury it to prevent dog's tooth from coming in (F, 42, Layton, 1970); . . . bury it under a rock, for if a dog runs over it, a dog tooth will come in its place (F, 19, Midvale, 1964); . . . throw it at the moon (F, 28, Midvale, 1939).  Cf. Brown 389ff.

## Teething

711   Don't let a baby look in a mirror before it's a year old; it will have painful teething (M, 53, SLC, 1944).  Brown 352.

712   In order to cut teeth without pain a baby must wear a red flannel vest (M, SLC, 1961).

713   If a spice bag consisting of a mixture of whole spice is tied around a baby's neck, it will aid the baby in cutting teeth (F, 69, Pleasant Grove, 1902).

714   To chew on the leaves and stems of onions will relieve the pain of swollen gums when a baby is teething (F, SLC, 1964).  Cf. Brown 373.

715   Ground eggshell for a baby cutting teeth (F, 60, Duchesne, 1930s).

716   The teething egg:  When children are teething, put an egg in a jar.  Seal it up and put it in a closet somewhere. There are gases in the egg that leak out into the air of the house.  They prevent the teeth from coming in crooked (F, SLC, 1971).

717   Rub a baby's gums with a silver thimble to bring teeth through (F, 1961).  Brown 375.

718   A piece of agate around a child's neck will assist him in cutting teeth (F, SLC).

## Teething - Animals, Animal Parts

719   A good bite of earthworm will cause a child to cut teeth without trouble (M, 50, Provo, 1925).  Brown 372.

720   Put a necklace of alligator teeth around the neck of a teething baby to make the teething easier (M, Midvale, 1961).

721   Tie a rabbit foot around the baby's neck so that cutting teeth will be easy (F, Tooele, 1961).  Brown 368.

722 The gums of a child cutting teeth are rubbed with the brains of a rabbit or another animal (SLC, 1946). Brown 365f.

## Bones, Heart

723 If a pregnant woman drinks a lot of milk, her baby will have strong teeth and bones (F, 19, Bountiful, 1953).

724 If a car splashes on you, your children will have weak bones (F, 19, SLC, 1964).

725 If a woman gets scared during pregnancy, her child will have a weak heart (M, SLC, 1961).

## Legs, Knees, Feet

726 If a woman eats rabbit while she is pregnant, the baby will have weak legs (M, 23, SLC, 1964).

727 If you drink coffee when you are a child, your knees will turn black (F, 82, SLC, 1955); . . . green tea . . . (F, 19, American Fork, 1949).

728 Never go barefoot. If you do, it will make your toes grow uneven (M, 58, Logan, 1925).

## Fingers, Fingernails

729 A new baby girl with short fingers was caused because the mother had been bitten by another child during pregnancy (F, SLC, 1964).

730 If a baby bites his nails, he will have stubby fingers (F, secy, SLC, 1948).

731 If a baby has fingernails, it was born at term (F, 28, SLC, 1964).

732 If you cut a baby's fingernails before he's one year old, he'll have bad luck the rest of his life (F, 19, SLC, 1959); . . . before three months old . . . (F, SLC, 1960). Cf. Brown 252, 8523.

733 Never cut the baby's fingernails during his first year, or the baby will be cursed. The mother should chew them off (F, 49, SLC, 1940). It is bad luck to cut baby's toenails; tear or bite them off (F, 42, SLC, 1937). To bring good luck to a new baby, bite its fingernails the first time they are to be trimmed (F, SLC, 1961).

734 A child's fingernails should not be cut until he is a year old, or you will not be able to raise him. Bite the nails off (F, 27, Kanab, 1940s). Brown 253f.

735 Do not cut the baby's nails until it is at about the age of one month (F, 46, SLC, 1932).

## BODILY FUNCTIONS

## Crying, Defecating, Sleeping

736 A sharp stare from a pregnant woman whose eyes are believed to be especially powerful may cause desperate and sustained crying from the baby (M, 58, MD, SLC, 1963).

737 If children mess in their pants, rub some of it under their noses and they will quit (F, Moab, 1953).

738 If you are not in bed asleep by nine o'clock, the sandman will come around and throw sand in your eyes (F, SLC, 1940); . . . sprinkle sand . . . (F, 28, SLC, 1945).

739 Catnip fed to babies to make them sleep (F, SLC, 1957).

740 If you want to get a baby to go to sleep, yawn and the baby will go to sleep (F, Moab, 1953).

741 To let a cat sleep in the same room as a baby will bring bad luck (M, SLC, 1957).

742 Cats sometimes suck the breath of sleeping babies (F, SLC, 1961). Brown 267.

743 When a baby smiles in its sleep, it is talking with the angels (F, 77, SLC, 1910); . . . dreaming of angels (F, 24, SLC, 1960). Brown 262.

## Talking, Walking

744 If a parent eats tongue during a woman's pregnancy, this will hinder development of the child's speech (M, 58, MD, SLC, 1963). Learned in Pittsburgh, 1930.

745 If you put a baby in front of a mirror, he will not be able to talk (F, 50, It, SLC, 1963).

746 Do not cut a baby's hair or nails or they will not talk (F, SLC). Cf. Brown 341.

747 Before babies learn to talk they are still in the spirit world and converse with the angels (F, Moab, 1953).

748 Children who lose their mothers in infancy always will be talkative (F, 44, Payson, 1936).

749 If a baby is crawling, sweep trash over its feet and it will begin walking (F, SLC, 1962). Cf. Brown 193.

## BODILY ATTRIBUTES

## Eyesight, Complexion

750 Eat carrots while pregnant and the child will have good eyesight (F, 53, Orem, 1933).

751 If a child is pale, he is said to have slept with the moon's rays on him (F, Scot, 1957).

752 When changing a baby's diaper, wipe the baby's face with the wet diaper to insure the baby of a good complexion (F, Mex, SLC, 1957).

753 If you live in a white house, your children will be blond (M, 1964).

754  If rain strikes a child's face before it is a year old, its complexion will become rusty and freckled (M, 22, Union, 1964). Cf. Brown 1519n.

755  If a pregnant woman eats strawberries, her baby will have freckles (F, SLC, 1956). Cf. Brown 1503.

756  Some Negro women believe that eating cornstarch during pregnancy will cause the baby to have lighter colored skin (F, SLC, 1967).

## Growth

757  When a child reaches two years of age, he is half the size he'll be when he is completely grown (F, 49, Charleston, 1972). Brown 174.

758  If a baby has hiccoughs, it means it is growing (F, 20, W. Jordan, 1950).

759  If you sweep a baby every morning with a broom, he will grow faster (M, 23, clothing salesman, SLC, 1962). Cf. Brown 178.

760  If you eat your dessert first, you'll grow upside down (F, Logan, 1972).

## Stunt Growth - Stepping Over, Measuring

761  If a person steps over a child crawling on the floor, the child will not grow any more (F, Spanish Fork, 1959). If an adult steps over a youth, it will stunt his growth (F, SLC, 1964). Don't jump over your little brother, it will stunt his growth (F, 68, SLC, 1939). Brown 181.

762  If you step across someone who's lying down, they won't grow. If you step back over, they will (F, Bingham, 1927). Brown 182.

763  Never step over a baby's head because it won't grow (M, 27, SLC, 1950). Brown 184.

764  When they play leapfrog, if they jump only once the youngster does not grow tall (M, 33, Gr, SLC, 1963). Cf. Brown 175ff.

765  Never measure a child's height with a measuring stick. It will stunt its growth (F, 19, St. George, 1964).

## Stunt Growth - Miscellaneous

766  If you smoke when young, it will stunt your growth (F, 47, SLC, 1957).

767  If a woman smokes, her babies are much smaller in stature than other babies (F, 30, SLC, 1960).

768  If someone remarks about how big a baby is getting, it will stunt its growth (F, It, Murray, 1958).

769  Until a baby is six months old his clothing must be put on over his feet rather than over his head to prevent stunting his growth (F, SLC, 1960).

770  When a person is vacuuming, a small child should never step in front of the moving equipment. If he does, his growth will be stunted (F, Gr, SLC, 1961).

771  Never pass a baby through a window. It will stunt its growth (F, 19, St. George, 1964).

772  Never set a bowl on top of your head because it will not let you grow any more (F, 40, Ja, SLC, 1964).

773  If children walk under ladders, it will stunt their growth (M, 45, SLC, 1963).

774  If you hit a person with bamboo or step over him while he is lying down, he will not grow any larger (M, SLC, 1957).

775  Peas placed in the shoes stop a child's growth (F, 58, Elsinore, 1963). Brown 187.

776  If a child is growing too tall, put a stone on his head (F, Swed, SLC, 1958).

777  Place a weight on a child's head to stop growth (F, SLC, 1957).

## Strength, Weakness

778  When a mother brings her new baby home, she must step on a piece of iron on going through the threshold. This will make her baby strong and give him long life (F, Gr, Magna, 1961). Learned from mother in Greece, 1920.

779  If a child eats spinach, he will grow to be a strong and healthy adult (F, 19, Provo, 1963).

780  You shouldn't cut a baby's hair until after one year of age, or they will lose their strength (F, SLC, 1959); . . . before two months old or you will weaken the body (M, SLC, 1965).

781  If a boy child is born under a full moon, he will never be a masculine-type man but a weakling and sissy (F, SLC, 1963).

782  The thirteenth child in a family will be a weakling (F, Lehi, 1949).

783  An elderly person will sap the strength of a young one if they sleep together (F, Bear River City, 1957); . . . will sap the vitality of the young person . . . (F, Lehi, 1957). Brown 274.

## Longevity, Age, Short Life

784  A child born on Monday will have a long life (M, SLC, 1961).

785  If a baby cuts its first tooth after it is a year old, it will live to be a hundred years old (F, SLC, 1957).

786  If a very old woman kisses a baby, it will have a long life (F, 19, SLC, 1964).

787  Never bring a new baby through the front door--always through the back door, then take it to all the corners in the house

for a long life (F, 52, SLC). Learned in Charleston, S.C., 1920s.

788 Cut a baby's lock of hair and put it in a hidden place and the person will live to an old age (F, SLC, 1951).

789 A child passed through a maple tree will live long (M, 23, SLC, 1959). (The passing of ailing children and other patients through holes in trees, split saplings, rerooted brambles, and the like, is a folk medical ritual known as "passing through" or "pulling through." The underlying notion of stripping and divestment also involves magical transference and implantation. In the present case, the child would appear to gain the strength and long life of the tree. For a discussion of this elaborate ritual, see Hand, "Passing Through." For the passing of the patient under the belly of a horse, see No. 1060, below. --Eds.)

790 If parents plant an evergreen at the birth of a child, the child will live a long healthy life (M, 79, Dan, SLC, 1898); . . . the tree will grow until the child's death, then the tree will also die (M, SLC). Another informant comments that Utah Mormons plant poplar trees as each child is born. One may see in eastern Nevada and Utah many farms surrounded by poplars.

791 If children are raised by wolves, they will live the same life span as the animal does (F, 19, SLC, 1964).

792 A mother must not take her baby after birth out of the hospital on Saturday, the end of the week, or the baby will have a very short life (F, SLC, 1967).

793 If a child learns rapidly and it is exceptionally bright it will not live very long (F, 26, Bountiful, 1940s).

794 If a child is born late in the mother's life, the child will have a short life (F, 44, Payson, 1945).

795 Cutting a baby's fingernails will shorten its life (M, SLC, 1957). You shouldn't cut a baby's fingernails for two months or it . . . (M, 84, Centerville).

796 Cutting a child's hair before he is two years old will shorten his life by two years (M, SLC, 1961).

Beauty, Ugliness

797 Expectant mothers that look at beautiful things have beautiful babies (M, MD, SLC, 1959). Heard from patients. Think of beautiful things, have a beautiful baby (F, 66, Tooele, 1925).

798 Your firstborn child will be good looking if you don't eat fish before his birth (M, SLC, 1961).

799 A beautiful baby makes an ugly adult and vice versa (F, 22, SLC, 1946). Pretty in the cradle, ugly at the table (M, Tooele, 1957). If a child is homely, it will be good looking when it gets older (F, 46, SLC, 1939). Brown 163.

800 If a pregnant woman looks at anything ugly, her baby will be ugly (F, 45, SLC, 1930). Cf. Brown 111.

801 Children under a year looking in a mirror will grow up to be ugly (F, SLC, 1958).

802 If a baby sucks its thumb, it will grow up to be hideous (M, 54, SLC, 1923); . . . grow up to be ugly (M, 56, SLC, 1934).

Miscellaneous Bodily Attributes

803 A baby born feet first will be very fast on foot. It was said Jim Thorpe was born feet first (M, Vernal, 1958).

804 If an expectant mother eats fish, she will have a lively baby (F, 44, SLC, 1926).

805 A green-eyed baby will grow up to be fat (F, 88, SLC, 1964).

806 Coitus during pregnancy will make the infant oversexed (F, teacher, SLC, 1961). Heard in her maternal child care class.

807 It is claimed that intelligence and physical virility were showered lavishly upon children of polygamous families, while the child of a monogamous union will only be mediocre (M, 80, SLC, 1964).

GIFTS, TALENTS, CHARACTER, ETC.

Mental Gifts

808 A child born on Sunday is wise and benevolent (F, SLC, 1965); . . . born on Sunday, very smart (F, 45, Price, 1961). Cf. Brown 123f.

809 A child will be smartest if he is born in the summer (F, 78, Yugo, SLC, 1900).

810 A gifted child will be born when it is a full moon (F, 85, Eng, SLC, 1900).

811 People born at sunrise will be clever (F, 21, Eng, SLC, 1963).

812 If a baby is born with a veil--the placenta--over his face, he will be a brilliant person (M, Magna, 1959); . . . with a membrane over his head, he will be smart (F, 45, Price, 1961). Cf. Brown 245n.

813 Babies born with a blue veil (caul?) over their faces will either die or be really smart (F, SLC, 1939).

814 A child will be an intellectual if it's born when the mother has a veil on (F, 70, SLC, 1964).

815 If a baby doesn't fall down the stairs its first year, it will be intelligent (F, 45, SLC, 1937).

816 If a pregnant woman eats fish, her child will be very intelligent (F, SLC, 1960).

817    When a woman is carrying her child, if she places a book on her stomach, her newborn will be intelligent (M, 55, Ja).

818    A birthmark on one's forehead means a high intelligence (F, 64, SLC, 1964).

819    Sprinkle salt on the head of an expectant mother so that the baby's brain will be salted and the baby will be born with good sense (F, Gr, Magna, 1920).

820    If a woman reads educational material during pregnancy, her child will be bright (M, 69, SLC, 1917). Cf. Brown 213.

821    If a hair from a wise man's head is wrapped around a baby's left little finger, the baby will have lots of wisdom during his life (F, Nephi, 1905).

822    If you are over thirty-five, your baby will be very brilliant (F, 48, SLC, 1964).

823    A third son is more intelligent than his brothers (F, Syracuse, 1951).

824    If a child is born out of wedlock, that child will become a genius (M, 43, teacher, American Fork, 1958). Cf. Brown 217.

## Supernatural Powers

825    If a baby is born with a blue veil over its face, this is considered better than the "gold spoon in the mouth"--he has the "call" (M, SLC, 1961); . . . born with veil, especially gifted or favored (F, SLC, 1964). ("Caul"?)

826    A child born with a caul or something over his head is supposed to be able to tell the future (M, Logan, 1970). Brown 245.

827    A child born with a caul will have the gift of second sight (F, SLC, 1957). Brown 245.

828    If you are born in a veil--hymen--you will always be psychic (F, 55, SLC, 1964); . . . born with black veil, you will have psychic powers (F, Moab, 1953). Brown 245.

829    The seventh son of the seventh son is blessed with great powers (M, 45, SLC, 1956). Brown 222.

830    The seventh son of a seventh son has second sight and can foretell the future (F, Ogden, 1963); . . . is a seer (M, SLC, 1961); . . . has mystic qualities (M, 20, Farmington, 1960).

831    A seventh son is able to see and hear spirits (M, SLC, 1961).

832    The seventh son or daughter of a seventh son or daughter has tendencies for healing people (F, SLC, 1961). Brown 223.

833    Persons born on Saturday can see ghosts (F, SLC, 1964).

834    As a rule the gift of foreseeing an approaching death is confined to persons born on Sunday (F, 72, SLC, 1964).

835    Children born during the hour of midnight have the power of the spirits (M, 1963); . . . the hour after midnight have the power through life of seeing departed spirits (F, SLC, 1955).

836    A child born at midnight on Christmas Eve can understand the speech of animals (M, Tooele, 1957).

837    A person born on Halloween has some evil spirits (F, 72, SLC, 1905).

838    It was believed that a boy with a caulic [sic] may have extra perceptary [sic] perception (F, 60, SLC, 1963). Cf. Brown 245.

839    A child born feet first has magical gifts (F, Brigham, 1930).

## Artistic and Musical Talents

840    If during pregnancy the mother will concentrate on any quality or talent which she wishes her child to have, the child will be blessed with this talent (F, SLC, 1960). Cf. Brown 213.

841    If an expectant mother studies certain subjects or attends certain cultural events, the child will be born with an appreciation for those subjects (M, SLC, 1959).

842    While pregnant, if a woman paints, the child will be a great painter (F, 20, SLC, 1957); . . . mother goes to an art gallery, the baby will be an artist (F, 19, SLC, 1950s); . . . mother goes to art exhibits, the child will be artistically inclined (M, 43, American Fork, 1958).

843    If while you are pregnant you stare at the moon incessantly, then your child will be the romantic type and will tend toward the arts (F, SLC, 1959).

844    If a child has long fingers, then he will be an excellent artist (F, Tabiona, 1955). Cf. Brown 214.

845    If a woman who is pregnant listens to music, her child will also be musically inclined (F, 18, St. George, 1955); . . . listens to classical music, her child will be a musician (F, 50, SLC, 1963). Brown 215.

846    If you want your child to be a musician, go to a concert before its birth (F, 49, Logan, 1964); . . . the mother should attend many concerts (F, SLC, 1958). If the mother goes to the opera, the child will be musically inclined (F, 22, SLC, 1962).

847    If you want your child to be interested in music, you should read musical books and play the piano during pregnancy (F, SLC, 1956). Cf. Brown 215.

848    If a woman sings while she is carrying her baby, the child will be musically inclined (F, Bountiful, 1960).

849  Musical ability is believed to be the result of diligent practice by the mother during pregnancy (F, Vernal, 1959).

850  If a woman plays the organ while she is expecting a baby, the child will be quite musical (F, Kearns, 1961); . . . plays the piano, the child will be a great pianist (F, 20, 1957).

851  If you bury the first parings of a child's fingernails under an ash tree, the child will be a fine singer (F, Logan, 1930).

852  If songs are sung as the afterbirth of a newborn infant is buried, the child will be a good singer (M, SLC).

853  If a baby cries while it is being blessed, it will be a good singer (F, 1935); . . . cries during baptism, it is a sign he will be a singer (F, 26, teacher).

854  If a child has a large mouth, it will be a good singer (F, SLC, 1914).

## Character, Other Traits

855  Your character and personality were determined by the position of the stars at the time of birth (M, SLC, 1957).

856  Offspring sometimes inherit characteristics from a previous suitor of the mother (F, Du, 1961).

857  If the cord on a baby boy is cut long, he will be a "Mama's Boy" (F, 50, SLC, 1963).

858  The baby must keep the dried cord stump because he would be tied to any woman who got it (F, 50, SLC, 1963).

859  People are born either good or bad according to the blood of their parents (Anon, SLC, 1961).

860  If you sing at the table, you will grow up to be bad (F, 74, 1904).

861  The actions and manners you hate so much in some people will usually show up in your children (F, Grantsville, 1960).

862  If the parents of newborn children are old, then the children will not have any ambition in life (F, SLC, 1959).

863  If you hang a picture crooked, the children will grow up getting into trouble (F, 74, SLC, 1964).

864  Never show a baby its face in the mirror, or it will grow up to be a vain person (F, 74, SLC, 1964). If baby looks at itself in a mirror before twelve months, it will be proud (F, Bountiful, 1964).

865  If you let a baby look in a mirror before it is one year old, it will grow up to be silly (F, 40, SLC, 1935).

866  A child under one year should not look at a mirror. If the little rascal does so he will surely grow up to be a deceiver and a liar (M, Chin, SLC, 1960). Brown 229.

867  If a baby is born on Tuesday, it will be certain to be ornery (M, SLC, 1967).

868  People born in the afternoon or at sunset will be lazy (F, 21, Eng, SLC, 1963).

869  If a baby is born with teeth, it is a sign of future greatness (F, SLC, 1961).

870  If a baby is born bald, it means that he is well-bred (F, SLC, 1959).

871  If a baby has red hair, it is evil (M, 38, Ogden, 1964). Cf. Brown 481n.

872  A blue-eyed baby will help her mother a lot when she grows up (F, 88, SLC, 1964). Cf. Brown 511n.

873  If a baby sleeps with its hands closed, it will grow up to be stingy (M, SLC, 1957); . . . keeps a tight fist . . . (F, SLC). Cf. Brown 579.

874  If a newborn baby has its fingernails cut, it will be a sissy and be characterized by bad luck (F, 49, Richfield, 1900s).

875  If a child or baby is not made to sleep in a dark room, he will grow up to be a coward (F, 19, SLC, 1950).

876  Brown-eyed babies will tell fibs (liars) (F, SLC, 1964).

877  If you bite a child's nails off rather than cut them, he will not steal (F, SLC, 1964).

878  If a child does not cry at his baptism, he will grow up to be a good citizen (M, SLC, 1963).

879  If a person is born under the planet Mars, he will be an evil doer in his lifetime (F, SLC, 1964).

## Disposition - Mother's Influence

880  The disposition of a pregnant woman will be the same in the child (F, 85, Charleston, 1972). Brown 195.

881  The amount of sleep a woman gets while she is pregnant determines what her baby will be like. If a lot of sleep, then baby will be congenial--if a little, then the baby will be cranky (F, 21, Logan, 1971).

882  If a woman cries when pregnant, she will have a sad child (F, 80, Eng, Midvale). Cf. Brown 196.

883  If an expectant mother cries, her baby will be cross (F, 44, SLC, 1930). Cf. Brown 196.

884  If the woman is grouchy while she is pregnant, so will the baby be grouchy (M, 1960).

885  If startled at night, when pregnant, the baby will be nervous (F, SLC, 1950).

886  Thinking bad thoughts will cause the unborn child to be born with a bad temperament (F, SLC, 1964).

887  If a woman worries during pregnancy, she'll have a high-strung child (F, 67, SLC, 1964).  Cf. Brown 8522.

888  If a woman is polite to people while pregnant, her child will also be polite (F, 22, St. George, 1963).

889  If the mother eats candy, the baby will have a sweet, sunny disposition (F, 50, SLC, 1963).

890  When you are pregnant think happy thoughts and look at pretty pictures, and you will have a happy baby (F, 67, SLC, 1908).

891  In order to have a happy child an expectant mother must be cheerful at all times (F, 53, Orem, 1933).

### Disposition - Weather, Cosmic Forces

892  The forces of nature which govern the weather also affect the formation of a newborn child's personality--permanently marking his life for good or ill (F, SLC, 1962).

893  If it is raining when a child is born, the child will be ill-tempered (F, 47, housewife, SLC).

894  If a child is born on a rainy day, it will be an unruly child (F, 82, SLC, 1900).

895  If a child is born on a sunny day, he will be a child of ease and grace (F, 82, SLC, 1900).

896  A person born under the planet Mars will have a violent disposition like that of Mars, the god of war (F, 45, SLC, 1928).

### Disposition - Various Influences

897  Children of the psychiatrist are the ones that develop abnormal personalities (F, 18, SLC, 1954).

898  Born on Friday--will have a bad temper (M, 61, W. Jordan, 1935).

899  Red hair on a child means it will grow to have a violent temper (F, Bountiful, 1950).  Brown 481.

900  If your baby wears clothes a dead baby has worn, your baby will be unhappy (M, SLC, 1957).

### HEALTH AND SICKNESS

901  Children will never thrive until they are baptized (F, 19, Ogden, 1953).  Cf. Brown 160.

902  Milk is not necessary for a healthy body (F, SLC, 1961).

### Indicators of Sickness and Health

903  If a child is conceived in the spring, it will be unhealthy (M, Payson, 1959).

904  A May baby is always sickly.  You may try but you'll never rear it (F, 29, SLC, 1949); . . . is always sickly and hard to raise (M, 21, Eng, S. Jordan, 1964).

905  If a baby does not cry when it is christened, it will become sick (F, 85, Eng, SLC, 1965).

906  An infant who cries during baptism will have good health (F, SLC, 1950).

907  Fat babies are always the healthiest (F, 21, SLC, 1964).

908  If a baby is born without the blue vein showing across the bridge of its nose, the child will live and be healthy.  If a blue vein does show, the child is a "terrier," and his chances of survival are not considered to be as good (M, SLC, 1961).

909  It's not normal for a baby to lie with its arms at its side.  Something is wrong with it.  The normal position is arms flexed across the chest (F, 1900).

910  A baby born in a moving car will be prone to becoming car sick (F, SLC).

### Promoters of Health

911  The more repulsive the health foods eaten by a pregnant woman, the more healthy the baby (F, 20, SLC, 1955).

912  If an expectant mother wears a hat decorated with feathers and ribbons during the delivery of her baby, the baby will live a long healthy life (F, 72, American Fork, 1963).  Learned from black midwife in Mississippi, 1908.

913  The baby will be healthy if rubbed with fat after birth (F, 67, Devils Slide, 1965).

914  To keep a child well, cut a lock of hair from his head (M, SLC, 1961).

### Causes of Disease, Illness

915  Engaged couples who try on each other's shoes means that their children will have ill health (F, 20, SLC, 1963).

916  A baby conceived from an elderly father will be weak and sickly (F, 50, SLC, 1963).

917  If an elderly couple have a baby, the child will be very slow and susceptible to diseases (F, 18, Sunset, 1963).

918  If a baby eats hot bread right out of the oven, it will stick to the top of the child's mouth and if swallowed will cause the child to become very sick, which illness will not be able to be stopped until medication is given (M, 23, Ogden, 1960).

919  It is unhealthy for a child to sleep with an adult (M, Tooele, 1957).  Cf. Brown 274.

920  If a baby is told that he is a pretty baby and not told at the same time "God bless you," he will get sick (F, 74, It, SLC, 1963).

921 Never let a baby eat watermelon before a year old, or it will get deathly sick (M, Hyde Park).

## General Cures

922 If a baby is sick, put a blue ribbon on the crib (F, SLC, 1962).

923 If a baby falls ill before it has been christened, give it a name and it will get well (F, 61, SLC, 1965). Brown 160.

924 Kissing a sore spot better is a commonplace in the nursery, comforting both child and adult (M, SLC, 1920).

925 If a child is ill, put two eggs in an ant bed and it will recover (F, SLC, 1925).

## Magical and Supernatural Illnesses and Cures

926 When a child has had the evil eye put on him, the grandmother has to say a prayer. If the child's sickness was from the evil eye, it will cause the grandmother to get tired after the prayer and during the drowsiness the sickness will pass from the child (F, 21, Gr, SLC, 1965).

927 If a person has an evil eye and speaks to a baby without saying "God bless you," then the baby will be cursed with illness (F, 43, Provo, 1935).

928 A severe illness of a baby may be cured if its breath could be supplemented by the breath of a man who is the seventh son of his father who is also a seventh son (F, 83, Nephi, 1919). Cf. Brown 418n.

929 There was a lady with a very sick child, and she prayed for help. Two men appeared at the door and they said they had been called to administer to her sick child. They came in, administered to the child, and the child was almost healed instantly. The lady didn't know who the men were, but she thought they might be the Nephites (F, 50, Manti, 1945). (For bibliographical references to the Three Nephites, see No. 261, above. --Eds.)

## Prevention of Disease, Medical Amulets, Etc.

930 Tie a red ribbon around the ankle of a child to preserve him from being harmed (F, 85, SLC, 1900).

931 Fresh bacon rind rubbed on a baby's head prevents disease (F, 45, SLC, 1957). Cf. Brown 2188.

932 Rubbing a piece of coral over a child's gums will protect that child from sickness (M, SLC, 1961). Cf. Brown 380.

933 Children should wear a bag of asafetida around their necks to ward off disease (F, SLC, 1958). Another informant comments that during the 1920s, when she was in elementary school, many of her classmates wore these bags and never took them off even to bathe (F, 56, Logan, 1970). Brown 735f.

934 Squeeze a new baby's tit until fluid appears to ward off infection (F, SLC, 1971).

## Medical Practitioners

935 One informant said when he first came to Utah (about 1919) there were a lot of midwives, but now all the babies are delivered in the hospital by doctors. He said the midwives did a pretty fair job, although their technique was poor, they did the best they could (M, MD, Moab, 1953).

936 In early times the midwives were often the only medical help to be had in a town. The stories suggested that the women doctors had been protected and guided by an unseen power. On stormy nights the horse was led to take the right road, or the midwife was told by an unknown voice where to go and what to do (F, 60, W. Weber, 1915).

# DEFORMITIES

## General

937 If you make love on a stormy night, you'll have abnormal children (F, SLC, 1964).

938 If you are in a car with your boyfriend and out making love while it's cloudy, you'll have abnormal children (M, SLC, 1957).

939 Dancing close when pregnant or any other sex with other than your husband will deform or kill the baby (F, SLC).

940 They say you're not supposed to marry close relatives or the baby will be crazy or deformed (F, Moab, 1953).

941 A pregnant woman who cradles a young child in her arms may cause his navel to become distended (M, 58, MD, 1963).

942 If you have a foreskin, you will have deformed children (F, 35, SLC, 1964).

943 If a person with an evil eye looks at a pregnant woman, the baby will be born defective (F, SLC, 1961).

944 A baby will be deformed if you cut its fingernails (F, SLC, 1962).

945 Deformed children are possessed of evil spirits (F, 47, SLC, 1964).

946 If a pregnant woman doesn't eat all the special and exotic foods she longs for, the unborn child will be damaged (F, Provo, 1959).

947 If a person has a mouth birth deformity, he won't eat in public because people think it will spoil the food (F, 21, SLC, 1962).

## Punishment

948 If a baby is born deformed, the mother is being punished for a sin (F, 50, SLC, 1963).

949  If a child is born without an ear, people think the mother has been unfaithful to her husband (F, 21, SLC, 1962).

950  Physical and mental defects are a result of some grave sin committed before or after the conception of a child (M, SLC, 1964).

951  If a child is born out of wedlock, it will have physical impairments (F, Provo, 1964).

952  If you laugh at a deformed person, God will punish you by giving you a child like that person (F, 39, Grantsville, 1950).  Brown 117ff.

## Conception, Pregnancy

953  Children conceived while the parents are under the influence of alcohol will be defective (F, teacher of Obstet., SLC, 1961).

954  If you have a nightmare the night the baby is conceived, it will be born deformed (F, SLC, 1962).

955  A pregnant woman must not lift heavy weights lest her child or she herself become deformed (M, 58, MD, SLC, 1963).

956  You shouldn't participate in any activities before a child is born because the child will be malformed (F, SLC, 1960).

957  If there is a tragedy in a pregnant woman's family, she will have a deformed baby (M, 20, Ogden, 1960).

958  If you go to a dentist while you're pregnant, your baby will be defective (F, 32, SLC, 1950).

959  If a pregnant woman sleeps on her back, the baby will be deformed (F, 19, SLC, 1963).

## Getting Excited, Seeing Things, Fright

960  It was a common belief then that if the pregnant mother saw something frightful, it would cause the child to be deformed (F, Logan, 1970).  (See Fife, "Birthmarks," pp. 274ff.  --Eds.)

961  If a pregnant woman should see a deformed object, her child will be deformed (F, 19, Kearns, 1950); . . . see something terrible, her child may be a monster (F, SLC, 1964).  Cf. Brown 115.

962  It is wrong for a pregnant woman to see a fire or her baby will be deformed (F, 31, Du, SLC, 1963).

963  During pregnancy if a woman sees an accident, like someone losing a finger, the baby will be born without the corresponding finger (M, Spring Glen, 1963).

964  If a child was born with no hands, the explanation is that the mother, during her pregnancy, saw a crushed hand and therefore gave birth to a child with a hand defect (F, Mt. Pleasant, 1959).

965  A child's uncle was the sheriff in Carbon County, Utah, and the sheriff had his arm shot off.  His sister was pregnant at the time and they called her and told her.  When the child was born, his arm looked just like his uncle's . . . it was gone, and he's got shot-marks in the arm (F, 69, 1957).

966  If a woman sees a man with only one leg while she is pregnant, her baby will be born with only one leg (F, 65, Farmington, 1931).  Cf. Brown 115.

967  If a pregnant woman sees something bad during her pregnancy, she will have a crippled child (F, teller, SLC, 1962).

968  If a pregnant woman saw a defect such as a cripple, her baby would be born with that defect (F, 75, SLC, 1926).  Brown 115.

969  It was believed that if a woman saw anything polka-dotted before becoming pregnant, she would have a polka-dot baby (M, 42, Kanesville, 1964).  Heard in Alaska, 1943.

## Making Fun of, Ridiculing Deformed Persons

970  It is bad luck to make game of old or deformed people, because evil will fall upon your children (M, 19, SLC, 1963); If a mother makes light of an afflicted person during her pregnancy, her child will be afflicted (M, 20, Union, 1964).  Brown 117, 120.

971  Don't make fun of a deformed child or you'll have one in your family (F, SLC, 1960).

972  If a pregnant woman criticizes someone else's baby, her baby will be deformed (M, SLC, 1957).  Brown 117ff.

## Animals

973  Birth deformities are due to seeing certain animals during pregnancy (F, 52, SLC, 1930).  Brown 102f, 109.

974  If a pregnant woman is frightened by a cat, her baby will have a cat's head when born (F, Farmington, 1959).

975  If a mouse runs across a pregnant woman's path, her child will have a tail (F, 40, SLC, 1930).

976  A neighbor said her sister-in-law was scared by a rat, and her child was half rat (F, SLC, 1958).

977  If an expectant mother eats frog legs, her child will have a defective limb (F, 44, SLC, 1964).  Heard in Nevada, 1926.

978  If a pregnant woman saw a snake, she believed that her child would be deformed (M, 38, SLC, 1965).  Cf. Brown 112f.

## Harelip

979  A sudden crash may cause the child to be born with a harelip (M, MD, SLC, 1963).

980 The sight of blood may cause the child to be born with a harelip (N, 58, MD, SLC, 1963).

981 An earthquake tremor may cause the child to be born with a harelip (M, 58, MD, SLC, 1963).

982 If the baby is born with a harelip, it is because the mother was scared by a rabbit (F, 53, Norw, SLC, 1961); If the mother was scared by a rabbit, the baby will look like a rabbit (F, 20, SLC, 1955); . . . mother sees a rabbit . . . (F, Salina, 1920).  Brown 110.

983 If you are pregnant and you see a rabbit, quickly tear your petticoat or your child will be a harelip (F, SLC, 1960).

984 If a woman gives birth to a harelip child, she is believed to have touched a rabbit in her pregnancy (F, 21, SLC, 1962).

985 When a pregnant woman helps her husband kill rabbits, the child will be born with a harelip (F, 72, tea leaf reader, Lark, 1960).

986 If the mother eats rabbit meat while pregnant, her baby will be born with a harelip (F, Ja, SLC, 1963).  Heard in Japan, 1930.

987 If a child is born with a split lip it is because the mother has stepped across a threshold that had been split or hit by an axe (M, Ogden, 1912).

988 If a pregnant woman goes outdoors on the eclipse of the moon, her baby will be marked at birth with a harelip (F, Mex, Magna, 1961).

989 If a child is born with a harelip, people believe that an evil curse was placed on the mother (F, 21, SLC, 1962).

990 If an expectant mother goes to the dentist, her child will be born with a harelip (F, Brigham, 1920).

991 If an expectant mother has strong impressions about harelips, the baby will be born with one (F, 49, SLC, 1964).

## Bowlegs

992 A pregnant woman who crosses her legs will cause her children to be bowlegged (F, SLC, 1961).

993 If you stand a baby up too soon, it will be bowlegged (F, 65, SLC, 1964).

994 If you drink tea, your legs will grow bowed (told to children). (M, SLC, 1960).

## MENTAL AND EMOTIONAL AILMENTS

## Mental Deficiency

995 If a baby can't talk by one year, he is an idiot (M, Dan, SLC, 1964).

996 If a couple is middle-aged and have a child, it will be an idiot (SLC, 1957).

997 If a pregnant woman sees a cross-eyed man, her baby will be an idiot (F, Brigham, 1930).

998 If a child is born late in the mother's life, it will be mentally retarded (F, 44, Payson, 1945).

999 If the father is drunk at the moment of conception, the child will be feebleminded (F, 58, Ogden, 1964).

1000 Alcoholic mothers produce babies with mental deficiency (F, Tooele, 1967).

1001 Feebleminded children are primarily a result of a first cousin marriage (M, 61, Ephraim, 1965).

1002 If a child doesn't fall down the stairs before he is a year old, he will be a fool when he grows up (F, 74, SLC, 1964).

1003 If a baby doesn't fall out of bed by the time it is eleven months old, he will be a fool when he grows up (F, 65, SLC, 1942).

1004 Don't look at anything frightening if you're pregnant or you will scare the child and make him a half-wit (M, 50, It, SLC, 1956).

1005 If a pregnant woman has her wisdom teeth pulled before her baby is born, the baby will be born without any wisdom and good judgment (F, SLC).

1006 Children born during the earliest part of parents' reproductive life will be inferior as compared to those born later (F, SLC, 1959).

1007 Children born in the month of July will not be very bright (F, SLC, 1962).

1008 Don't let baby play with a mirror.  If he sees his reflection before he is one year old, he will not be bright (F, SLC, 1960).

1009 If a child is born out of wedlock, the child will have mental impairments (F, 46, SLC, 1964).

1010 A child-bearing mother and father may not eat "fool hen," or the child will become a moron (F, 19, SLC, 1964). ("Fool hen" is a grouse that exhibits little alertness or fear of humans which permits it to be easily caught.  --Eds.)

1011 Mental deficiency is caused by excessive masturbation in childhood (F, 24, hosp. aide, Provo, 1960).

## Derangement, Insanity, Fear

1012 If a pregnant woman reads mystery books, her child will be affected, that is, it will have mental illnesses (F, 25, Kearns, 1961).

1013 If you marry your first cousin, your children will be insane (M, 25, SLC, 1945).

1014  If a baby is rocked too much, his brain will be addled (M, 28, SLC, 1961).

1015  If a pregnant woman sleeps in the light of a full moon, the baby will be crazy (F, 50, SLC, 1963).  Cf. Brown 219, 2759.

1016  If a new baby is born under a full moon, it will become a lunatic (M, SLC, 1962).  Brown 219n.

1017  A baby shouldn't be allowed to see itself until one year in a mirror as it will cause a baby to be crazy (M, 58, Centerville).

1018  If you tickle a baby's feet, it will make him go crazy (F, 44, SLC, 1970).

1019  Wolf teeth hung around a child's neck will prevent fear (M, 40, SLC, 1964).

## CHILDHOOD DISEASES

### Albinism

1020  Children born to parents who were married on Tuesday the thirteenth are expected to be albinos (F, SLC, 1964).

### Bedwetting

1021  A child should be through bedwetting at three years.  Lots get through younger, but they should be broke at three years (F, Moab, 1953).

1022  There is a flowering plant in St. George which the natives call "peebent flowers" and the kids were told if they played in them, they would wet the bed that night (M, Provo).  Informant didn't remember the plant's true name.

1023  If you pick dandelions, you will wet the bed (F, Provo, 1975); If the milk from the dandelions left a brown stain, one was jeered as a "pee-the-bed."  The flower was sometimes called by that name (F, Provo, 1971).  (It is also known as "pissabed."  --Eds.)

1024  A stye on your eye means that you wet the bed (F, SLC, 1964).

1025  If a child plays with matches, he will wet the bed (M, 52, Cedar City, 1964); If you play with fire, you . . . (F, 1925); . . . play at stirring a fire . . . (M, 19, SLC, 1959); . . . play with fire, you will wet your pants (F, 49, SLC, 1964).  Brown 278.

1026  If a child sings in bed, it will wet the bed (M, 20, SLC, 1955).

1027  Stick the finger of a sleeping person in ice cold water and it will make them wet the bed (F, 97, Syracuse, 1930).

1028  Feed children raisins to keep them from wetting the bed (F, Woods Cross, 1953).

1029  Feed a child mouse meat to cure him of enuresis (F, SLC, 1959).  Brown 279.

1030  If a child wets the bed late in life, feed him a fried mouse and he will stop (F, 48, SLC, 1964); . . . it can be cured by eating three roasted mice (F, 88, W. Jordan, 1890).  Brown 279.

1031  I've heard that if you set children in ice water it will cure them of bedwetting (F, Moab, 1953).

### Blindness

1032  A pregnant woman must refrain from eating eggs because the child will go blind (M, 58, MD, SLC, 1963).

1033  Babies with small hands usually will become blind and die (M, SLC, 1961).

1034  If you cut an infant's fingernails, the infant will become blind (M, SLC, 1957).

1035  If you hold a baby up to a mirror to see itself before a year old, the baby will be blind (F, 52, W. Jordan, 1964).  Heard in North Dakota, 1927.

### Blood Ailments

1036  They used sassafras for babies and they used lots of catnip tea.  Babies lots of time are awfully red and kind of pimply and sassafras brought the impurities of the blood out (F, Moab, 1953).  Cf. Brown 895f.

1037  Don't give a baby too hot a bath.  This causes blood poisoning (M, Granger, 1958).

### Cancer

1038  Don't lay babies in the hot sun.  This causes cancer (M, Granger, 1958).

### Chafing

1039  We used to brown flour and put it on a baby's bottom for chafing.  It was just as good as talcum powder.  Just brown the flour in a pan in the oven (F, Moab, 1953).

### Cleft Palate

1040  If a pregnant woman goes outdoors on the eclipse of the moon, her baby will be marked at birth with a cleft palate (F, Magna, 1949).

1041  A thick mixture of salt and water on a baby's soft spot will protect it from a cleft palate if it should fall (F, SLC, 1959).

### Colds

1042  If you stand in water when you're pregnant, the baby will have a cold (F, 20, SLC, 1964).

1043  If you eat ice cream when pregnant, your baby will catch cold (F, 19, SLC, 1963).

1044  No child ever catches cold from its own spit or its own pee (F, 70, Provo, 1900).

1045 If you run around the house with a baby when it is nine days old, the baby will never have colds (F, 58, SLC, 1963). Learned in Nebraska, 1923.

1046 Fenchel tea is the best thing to cure colds in small children (M, SLC, 1969). Fenchel is the German word for fennel.

1047 Put garlic and onions on a baby's feet to prevent it from getting a cold (F, MD, 1964).

1048 If you keep a black tie around your child's neck in the winter, he will not get a cold (F, Tooele, 1964).

1049 Tallow rubbed on a baby's foot will cure a cold (M, 48, Vernal, 1946). Cf. Brown 1131.

1050 For colds: Catch a skunk, take its fat, add camphor and quinine to it, and make a salve from it. Rub it at the "bole" of a child's head and on the bottom of his feet (F, black, SLC, 1964).

## Colic

1051 If a baby has hiccoughs, he won't have colic (F, 28, Logan, 1960).

1052 Put a jade stone around the baby's neck to prevent colic (F, SLC, 1963).

1053 Eating chocolate by the nursing mother will cause colic in the baby (M, MD, Roosevelt, 1961). Informant claims this item comes from the Ute Indians.

1054 For cure of baby's colic make catnip tea and add sugar to make it more palatable (F, 47, Monroe, 1928). Cf. Brown 290, 1156.

1055 A tea made from catnip and fennel will cure colic in a child (M, Tooele, 1957). Cf. Brown 290.

1056 As a cure for colic my ancestors fed a baby "clinker" tea. This is made by dropping a hot coal into a cup of water. They thought that it would bring the gas up from the stomach (F, 42, Sandy).

1057 Give babies a little whiskey for colic. But I have heard them preach that if you give them a taste when they are young, they will want it more when they are older. I never let any of mine have it for that reason (F, Moab, 1953).

1058 For baby colic put a thick coating of spice between two layers of cloth. Stitch them together and put on the baby. It may then be left on the baby for some time (F, 81, Sigurd, 1910).

1059 To cure the colic stand on one's head for a quarter of an hour (F, SLC, 1961). Cf. Brown 287, 1147.

## Cough

1060 A child's cough can be cured by passing him three times underneath the belly of a horse (F, 40, Logan, 1958). (For bibliographical references to "passing through," see No. 789 above. --Eds.)

## Cross-Eyes

1061 Never cross the legs when a woman is pregnant or the baby will be cross-eyed (F, 52, It, W. Jordan, 1928).

1062 Wearing high heels during pregnancy will make the baby cross-eyed (F, teacher of maternal child care, SLC, 1962).

1063 If a pregnant woman sees a cross-eyed man, her baby will have crossed eyes (F, Brigham City, 1930).

1064 If a woman, while pregnant, sees an eclipse, her baby will be born cross-eyed (F, SLC, 1963).

1065 If a baby looks into a mirror before it is six months old, it will go cross-eyed (M, 23, Ogden, 1960). Cf. Brown 307.

1066 If a baby crosses its eyes playfully, it will become permanently disfigured with crossed eyes (F, 40, Logan, 1938).

1067 To cure cross-eyes, pierce the child's ear and insert gold hoops (M, 55, SLC, 1926).

## Croup

1068 Keep an acidity [asafetida?] bag around your children's necks to keep away the croup (F, Morgan, 1961).

1069 To protect a child against croup, measure a child with a stick, put the stick in the closet and keep. When the child grows past the measure, he will never have any more croup (F, 58, Midvale, 1963). Brown 302. (For measuring rituals in folk medicine, see Wayland D. Hand, "Measuring with String, Thread, and Fibre: A Practice in Folk Medical Magic," in *Festschrift für Robert Wildhaber zum 70. Geburtstag am 3. August 1972*, ed. Walter Escher, Theo Gantner, Hans Trümpy, Schweizerisches Arhiv fur Volkskunde, 68-69 [1973], pp. 240-51. Cf. No. 1117, below. --Eds.)

1070 Chamber lye or urine was given to babies suffering from the croup (F, SLC, 1946).

1071 Charcoal is good to relieve children with croup (F, Tooele, 1957).

1072 Coal oil and sugar to cure the croup (M, 73, Laketown, 1965).

## Diarrhea

1073 Clean a chicken's gizzard and take the lining of the gizzard and dry it and pulverize it and give it to babies for diarrhea (F, 73, Moab, 1953).

## Diphtheria

1074 The child who wears a black silk cord around its neck will never have diphtheria (F, SLC, 1961).

## Dysentery

1075 Feed a baby the white of an egg to get rid of dysentery (F, 89, 1961).

## Earache

1076   Blow smoke into your child's ear to cure an earache (F, 50, Roosevelt, 1925). Cf. Brown 1338.

1077   Mothers used to breathe into the ears of children having earaches.  The warmth of the breath provided relief (F, 1925).

## Epilepsy

1078   If a pregnant woman touches a person having an epileptic seizure, her baby will be born an epileptic (F, Provo, 1971).

## Eye Ailments

1079   If you pierce the ear lobes of a child, it will improve its eyesight (F, 65, Fillmore, 1961).

1080   When a child has a cold in its eyes, the mother should squirt a little milk from her breast into the eyes in order to clear up the eye cold (F, SLC, 1971). Cf. Brown 306, 1363.

## Fits

1081   If a child has a spasm, the mother should pull his shirt off so it goes inside out.  The child will never have another one (F, Norw, SLC, 1960).

## Freckles

1082   Freckles will go away if the child wipes his face in a wet baby's diaper (M, 19, SLC, 1964).  Brown 1486.

## Growing Pains

1083   If your children run and they have a pain in their digits or in their sides, they are having growing pains (F, SLC, 1927).

## Headache

1084   If someone rocks a baby cradle without the baby in it, it will give the baby a headache (F, Centerfield, 1964).

## Heart Ailments

1085   The emotion of strong sorrow may cause the child to be born with a heart ailment (M, 58, MD, SLC, 1963).

## Hernia

1086   If a baby does not wear a bellyband for three to six months after birth, the baby will develop a hernia (F, SLC, 1960).

## Indigestion

1087   Bananas are indigestible for young children and should not be given to them (F, SLC, 1960).

1088   Milk is fattening and causes indigestion because of curd in the stomach, therefore only small children should have to have it (F, SLC, 1960).

## Lameness

1089   A child born feet first is certain to meet with an accident during its life and become lame, unless laurel leaves are rubbed on its legs within four hours of birth (F, SLC, 1955).

## Leukemia

1090   Don't give a baby too hot a bath.  This causes leukemia (M, Granger, 1958).

## Lisp

1091   If a child is dropped before it first speaks, it will have a lisp (F, 74, SLC).

## Moles, Mumps

1092   If a child is born with a large mole, its mother was a thief as a child (M, 21, Ogden, 1958).

1093   If a woman has a child with a hairy mole, it is thought that she touched a bird during pregnancy (F, 21, SLC, 1962); . . . bought two birds while pregnant (F, 63, SLC, 1950).

1094   If you see a goat when pregnant, your baby will have a mole with a hair growing out of it (F, 50, Price, 1935).

1095   Boil snake's eyes in water in the room of a child with the mumps to help stop the pain (M, Logan, 1950).

## Pinworms, Pneumonia

1096   Sulphur and molasses will cure pinworms in children (SLC, 1964).

1097   Never change a child from one bed to another in February because it's a pneumonia month (F, 43, SLC, 1942).

## Rash

1098   If a husband eats crackers in bed, the first child will be born with a rash (F, SLC, 1931).

1099   Baby rash was considered necessary for health (M, SLC, 1957).

1100   If there was no rash after three or four days, the baby was fed saffron tea.  In a few days the baby would be covered with baby rash (F, SLC, 1957).

1101   Newborn babies had to break out with a rash to cleanse the poisons in their bodies.  Catnip and saffron tea were used to cause the rash (F, 60, Duchesne, 1930).

1102   We gave newborn babies senna tea and they'd all break out in a rash, and it would clear up the skin--usually when

they were about three or four days old
we gave them that (F, Moab, 1953).

1103  Cornstarch for diaper rash (F, 57,
Logan, 1920).

1104  Flour browned in the oven would heal a
baby's sore bottom (F, Logan, 1954).

1105  For heat rash in babies bathe in soda
water several times daily and let it dry
on (F, 19, SLC, 1952).

## Rheumatic Fever, Rickets

1106  A child had rheumatic fever and the
informant gave her some of his tea and
the child was well by the next day.
(Informant sent a bunch of his tea to
Washington to have it analyzed and they
told him it was "Willy Romel." He
learned about the tea after Brigham
Young cured a woman with this tea.) (M,
Moab, 1953).

1107  If a baby sees itself in a mirror before
it is four months old, it will suffer
from rickets (M, SLC, 1963).

## Snakebite

1108  A child was bitten by a snake and wasn't
expected to live. An Indian doctored
the child with plug tobacco, wild
peppermint, and paint. The Indian also
came every morning as the sun was half
way up above the mountain and every
evening as it was half way down. The
child got better and her leg was saved
(F). Cf. Brown 2156ff.

## Sore Throat

1109  To cure sore throat in a child, spread
black pepper thickly on a strip of bacon
and wrap the bacon around his throat
with the pepper next to his skin (M,
Tooele, 1957). Cf. Brown 2199.

## Stomachache

1110  Washing baby's clothes in a washing
machine will give the baby a stomachache
(F, SLC, 1957).

1111  Tansy tea is good for children with
stomachache (F, St. George, 1967).

## Stuttering, Stammering

1112  If you tickle a baby, he will stutter
when he grows up (M, SLC, 1960); . . .
when he begins to talk (F, Moab, 1957).
Brown 343.

1113  Never tickle a baby under the chin as
this may make him stammer (M, 20,
Riverdale, 1962).

1114  If a baby's feet are tickled, it will
stammer in later years (F, 49, Payson,
1926). Brown 343n.

## Thrush

1115  If a mother will feed her young baby
nine live wood lice in some breast milk,

his thrush will be cured (F, Spanish
Fork, 1962).

1116  If you know a person who can cure a
baby's thrush, ask him to blow his
breath in the direction the baby lives
and his thrush will be cured (F, SLC,
1961). Brown 411ff.

## Undergrowth

1117  For a child which is undersize, measure
the child by the door jamb, a hole bored
by an auger at his exact height, a lock
of hair from the head of the child is
put in the hole, and a wedge driven in
and whittled off smoothly. The child
will grow rapidly (F, 22, Midvale,
1964). (For the interrelationships
between "measuring" and "plugging," see
Wayland D. Hand, "Measuring and
Plugging: The Magical Containment and
Transfer of Disease," Bulletin of the
History of Medicine, 48 [1974], pp. 221-
33. Cf. No. 1069, above, and 1174,
below. --Eds.)

## Warts

1118  If an expectant mother touches a toad,
her baby will be born with warts (F, 44,
SLC, 1964). Cf. Brown 2414.

1119  As a young child I had a wart wished
away by my grandfather. He said some
words out loud and in English. I don't
know whether he did anything else or not
(F, 28, Logan, 1950s). Cf. Brown
2689ff.

1120  Informant knows a lady who took a
chicken's liver, rubbed it on her
child's warts, and then buried it in the
corral. The warts disappeared (F,
1945). Cf. Brown 2452.

## Whooping Cough

1121  I've wore an asafetida bag lots of times
when we were children. It would keep us
from having the contagious disease,
whooping cough (F, Moab, 1953). Brown
2705.

1122  Tie a hairy caterpillar in a bag around
a child's neck. As the insect dies, the
whooping cough will vanish (F, 50, SLC,
1928).

1123  Use goose grease and molasses for
whooping cough (M, 44, Layton, 1970).
Cf. Brown 2726.

1124  To cure whooping cough, mix sugar in
kerosene oil and drink it (F, Logan,
1970).

1125  Cure for whooping cough. A flat turnip
sliced into a pan--put between each
slice muscavado [raw] sugar. Cover it
up, close with paste. When well baked
take the juice from it and give the
child to drink (entry from personal
diary dated 1836).

1126  The tooth of a dead horse rubbed over a
child's mouth will stop whooping cough
(F, SLC, 1910).

1127  When my grandfather was a boy, his parents believed that the cure for whooping cough was mare's milk (F, 67, SLC).  Brown 2716.

1128  A teaspoonful of mare's milk was administered three times a day for whooping cough (F, SLC, 1946).

1129  Three hairs taken from the cross of an ass will cure whooping cough, but the ass will die (F, 85, SLC, 1964).  (The cross of an ass is a natural cross formed by a different color of hair, usually black, found on the backs of donkeys near the loins.  --Eds.)

## Worms

1130  If a child picks its nose, he has worms (F, SLC, 1963).

1131  If a child has circles under its eyes, it has worms (M, 1960).

1132  Tooth grinding in a sleeping child indicates the presence of worms (F, SLC, 1961).

1133  For worms:  Give a child the size of a small bean of corvage molasses three times in the day.  The next day give a strong dose of castor oil or rubarb Indian Speufick Salree hard Sop Rosin brown sugar and flax seed oyle, eaqual quantitys (entry from personal diary dated 1836).

1134  Catch a mouse, kill it, scrape off the hair, mix it with lard, and give it to the child.  It will kill worms (F, Draper, 1955).

1135  To de-worm kids take some of the horse's tail, cut it into small pieces, mix it with honey, and feed it to the children (F, RN, Escalante).

## NURSERY ACTIVITY

### Preparations before Arrival

1136  It's bad luck to buy the baby's layette before you're pregnant (F, SLC, 1959).

1137  It's bad luck to buy a baby's bed before it is born (M, SLC, 1961); A child must have a bed before he is born or he will never own one (M, SLC, 1959); It is bad luck for the first child to sleep in a new cradle (F, SLC, 1960).

1138  Never buy a gift for an unborn child (F, 21, SLC, 1963).

1139  If you make a bonnet for an unborn baby, it is bad luck for the baby (F, 60, SLC, 1961); Never give a bonnet at a baby shower (F, Peoa, 1930).

### Dressing and Feeding the Baby

1140  It is bad luck to put a necklace on a male baby (M, Ogden, 1961).

1141  My grandmother has told me that her stepmother used to tell her when she was a child that she must never put her little sister's or brother's booties on the table or bad luck would follow the baby all through its life (F, 78, SLC, 1970).

1142  Never put a big pin on a baby's clothing or they will fall (F, Murray, 1957).

1143  Always dress a baby over its feet for several months after birth because its arms and shoulders are delicate (M, Tooele, 1957).

1144  Take some flour and brown it over the stove.  Then you mix enough water with it until it becomes a paste and feed it to babies.  It is especially good for them (F, SLC, 1967).

1145  Babies eat dirt because they lack something in their diets (Anon, SLC, 1959).

1146  If a child eats dirt, give him some off of a grave, and he will never eat any again (M, SLC, 1959).

## Thumb Sucking, Toilet Training, Nail Biting

1147  If a baby sucks his thumbs, then he is insecure (F, 21, Logan, 1971).

1148  Mother used to put red pepper on our thumbs to stop thumb sucking (F, 54, Logan, 1918).

1149  When a child cried loud and long without just cause, Grandma would say:  "Oh let him cry.  The more he cries the less he'll pee" (F, 83, Provo, 1920).

1150  Finely cut human hair was placed in the food of children afflicted with the habit of biting their nails (M, SLC, 1946).

## Other

1151  It is bad luck to let tears fall on a baby, especially a mother's tears (M, 19, Bountiful, 1963).

1152  It is bad luck to measure children with a tape measure (F, 56, SLC, 1954).  Cf. Brown 4880.

1153  When a newborn infant is first seen, the onlooker must give compliments and make "puffing" sounds into the child's face (F, Gr, SLC, 1964).

1154  When taking a newly born baby to visit members of your family, the relatives being visited should put something sweet in the baby's mouth so it will come to their home more often (F, Gr, SLC, 1961).

1155  When the father first comes to visit his offspring, it is good luck to put money in his hands (F, Dan, SLC).

1156  A baby's layette should contain something old (F, SLC, 1900).

1157  A newborn child must be carried upstairs to the top of the house for luck before being taken downstairs or out.  Even carried up a pair of steps is better than nothing (F, 78, SLC, 1964).  Cf.

Brown 210ff.  (For a discussion of the birth ritual of "rising in life," see Hand, "That the Child May Rise," pp. 77-80.  Cf. No. 1300, below.  --Eds.)

1158  Don't let baby look into a mirror or the baby will not develop normally (F, 18, Pol, Moab, 1964).  Cf. Brown 255.

1159  If you let a baby look in a mirror before it is six months old, it is bad luck (F, SLC, 1959); . . . before it is a year old . . . (F, 42, SLC, 1937).  Brown 255.

1160  If you look in a mirror a lot when you're little, you'll turn into a monkey (F, 23, Dan, SLC, 1959).

Religious and Magical Offices

1161  A baby born during a rainstorm is taken right out in the rain to be cleansed and blessed right from heaven, otherwise the priest is called in to baptize the infant (M, 34, Granger, 1964).

1162  A small baby must wear a coral bracelet to protect it from someone liking them too much (F, SLC, 1959).

1163  When a child is very young tie a scarlet thread around its neck to insure good luck (F, SLC, 1971).

1164  A squirrel's tail should be tied to a baby's cradle so that the child will be protected in case of a fall (F, 49, Logan, 1964).

Fairy Influences, Evil Spirits, Etc.

1165  If a piece of steel isn't kept in a baby cradle, an underground person could be exchanged for the baby (F, Norw, SLC, 1960); . . . evil spirits will switch a boy for a girl (F, Norw, SLC, 1964).  Steel is kept in cribs before baptism because a child is not safe until it's baptized (F, SLC, 1967).  (In Germanic Europe an "underground person"-- expressed in a plural substantive, "the undergrounds"--is a subterranean fairy creature.  --Eds.)

1166  Put a key in a baby cradle so that the baby will be locked in.  If not the fairies will steal it (F, Midvale, 1961).

Evil Eye, Evil Spirits

1167  When admiring a young child, it endangers them to bad illnesses because of the evil eye.  The evil eye comes especially from people with thick, dark eyebrows (F, Gr, 49, Midvale, 1934).  (Many of the folk beliefs and customs having to do with the evil eye as it applies to infants and children are taken up in Hand, "Evil Eye," pp. 183-89.  --Eds.)

1168  Avoid showing newborn infants for the first fifteen days in order to ward off the evil eye (F, SLC, 1971).  Informant comments that now this practice is usually dismissed as a protection against infection.

1169  When a newborn baby is first seen, the onlooker must follow compliments and comments with a "puffing" into the child's face.  The reason for this is that no one knows if they have the power to transmit the evil eye.  The "puffing" dispels the evil eye which the person may have cast upon the child (F, Gr, Magna, 1961).

1170  After the baby is born they apply a little soot on the back of the ear in order to avoid the evil eye (M, Gr, 73, SLC, 1963).  Learned in Greece in 1915.

1171  A coral band is given to a child as defense against "fascination" (F, SLC, 1957).

1172  Mothers who in their homes are neat usually arrange something untidy in the children such as socks inside out to keep the evil eye away from the children (M, MD, SLC).

1173  Get a glass of water and drop some oil in it.  If the oil sinks, it means that the child has the evil eye (M, Gr Orth priest, SLC, 1962).

1174  Measure a tablecloth the length from your elbow to your hand.  Put a pinch of salt in and tie it up.  If the tablecloth, when measured again, is shorter, the child still has the evil eye (F, Gr, SLC, 1957).  (For bibliographical references to "measuring" in its various aspects, see Nos. 1069, 1117, above.  --Eds.)

1175  To detect whether a child has the evil eye let a person with the evil eye touch a handkerchief, tie it in three knots and say a prayer.  If there are any knots in the hanky after she straightens it out, the child has the evil eye (F, Gr, SLC, 1962).  Learned in Greece in 1920s.

1176  If you suspect that your baby has been given the "eye," you can find out by breaking an egg in a bowl and putting the bowl over the baby.  If a little "eye" starts to form on the yolk, you can know that the child is under the curse or has been "given the eye."  So you must locate the one who cursed it quickly before the child gets any sicker (F, 55, Ogden, 1940).  (Egg rituals as diagnostic devices for the evil eye are found in Hand, "Evil Eye," p. 186. --Eds.)

1177  It is bad luck to praise the appearance of an Oriental baby, for this makes the spirits jealous (F, SLC, 1958).

1178  Don't hold a child up to a mirror until it's a year old as it will draw the attentions of evil spirits (F, 85, Pol, SLC, 1965).

1179  Before putting a baby in its cradle a mother turns around three times in front of the fire while singing her favorite song.  This wards off all evil spirits (F, SLC, 1958).

1180  If a person says something nice about a baby, they must add "for a fachina" so jealous spirits won't harm them (F, 50, It, SLC, 1963).

1181   A baby must wear a ring on its ring finger until the age of ten or evil spirits will enter his body (F, 43, It, SLC, 1964).

1182   A silver chain on a child's neck will keep it from evil spirits (F, Chin, SLC, 1920).  Cf. Brown 5702.

1183   Indians dry and grind the umbilical cord and attach it to the papoose board and it dispels evil spirits (M, MD, Roosevelt, 1961).  Informant attributes this practice to Ute Indians.

1184   A key under the pillow of a sleeping child will keep off evil (F, Midvale, 1961).

1185   When a child is born, a candle should be lighted so the evil spirits will stay away from the infant (M, 19, W. Jordan, 1955).

1186   Hold a child over the fire with a shovel.  If it is possessed with evil, it will fly up the chimney (M, 73, Russ, SLC, 1963).

1187   A child born on a Sunday is highly favored and is secure from malice of evil spirits (F, 78, SLC, 1964).

### Devil

1188   A baby born with a caul will be possessed of the devil (F, SLC, 1965).

1189   If you look at a baby covetously, the devil will enter into its body (M, 23, SLC, 1961).

1190   The father should never curse a child, or the devil will possess the child (F, 28, SLC, 1942).

1191   When a baby cries in its sleep, it has been talking with the devil (M, SLC, 1957).

1192   Singing a lullaby to children at night keeps the devil away (F, 60, Ogden, 1920).

1193   Praying for help and crying out will put Satan to flight when he comes to harm the baby (F).

### Pernicious Influences, Spells

1194   During the viewing of a corpse, if a child sneezed so his soul wouldn't be taken by the dead corpse (F, 49, Gr, Midvale, 1964).

1195   If you look at a newborn baby you have to touch it--if not a curse will come upon it.  To break the spell an egg has to be broken under its bed (M, 23, SLC, 1961).

1196   Tie red ribbons around the ankles of children so they won't be harmed when outside (F, Du, SLC, 1957).

1197   If a child is admired or praised in public, it will bring bad luck and the mother will have to beat or insult the child in order to counteract the bad spell (M, SLC, 1958).

### Snakes and Children

1198   One woman noticed that her child was not doing so well.  She watched him and he took his bread and milk and walked outside and sat on a little log in front of the house.  He'd take a spoonful of bread and milk and feed it to a (rattle)snake, pour it down its mouth, then he'd eat some out of the same spoon.  He got sick from it (M, 60, Manti, 1945).  (For a discussion of the friendly relationship between children and snakes, including the sharing of meals, as related in this section, see Wayland D. Hand, "Children and Snakes: A General Inquiry Based on Grimm No. 105, 'Märchen von der Unke,'" Literature Komparatystyka Folklore Ksiega Poswiecona Julianowi Krzyzanowskiemu [Warsaw, 1968], pp. 889-900. --Eds.)

1199   There was a little boy who herded cows who was very pale and sick looking.  They followed him one day and he started to feed a rattlesnake a spoonful of bread and milk.  They said he was absorbing small amounts of poison from eating from the same spoon as the snake.  They killed the snake, and the boy got all right (F, 42, Manti, 1945).

## PARENT-CHILD RELATIONSHIPS

1200   By stepping on cracks you can do some injury to your parents (M, 19, SLC, 1955).

1201   Children who kick up their heels and pout and run around the side of the house to hide will not be found again by their parents (F, Weber Co, 1936).

1202   A child who brings unhappiness to the parent will experience three times the unhappiness himself (F, 45, SLC, 1936).

1203   If you walk backwards, you are showing your parents the road to Hell (F, SLC, 1959); . . . cursing your parents (F, SLC, 1960).

1204   Never be mean to a baby or the baby, when it grows up, will be superior to you and will do you harm when it can and you will be inferior to its actions, wants, and wishes (F, 58, Richfield, 1930s).

1205   If you ever go against the word of your mother, it will always end in bad luck (M, 19, Kaysville, 1948).

1206   If the father is not with his wife when she is having their child, the child will never be close to his father (F, 50, SLC, 1964).

1207   The first baby must be born on its father's lap (F, 37, Syracuse, 1942).  Brown 33.

1208   When a woman clasps her hands together she should notice whether her left thumb is on the top.  If it is, this means she has a warm and sincere desire for children (F, SLC, 1961).

1209   If you cry in the movies, you will make a good mother (F, SLC, 1960).

1210 A woman who cuts bread thick on one side and thin on the other will make a good stepmother (M, SLC, 1920).

1211 If you spread butter on the little side of the bread (it is easy to tell the little from the big side with homemade bread), you will have a stepmother (F, Bear River City, 1957).

1212 It is good luck for a boy to resemble his mother and a girl to resemble her father (F, Provo, 1960). Brown 166.

1213 If two people wash in the same water, their children will look alike (F, SLC, 1959).

1214 If a woman divorces her husband and then remarries, the children born as issue of the second marriage will look like the first husband (F, 18, Sunset, 1963).

## CHASTISEMENTS

1215 It is believed that any parent who strikes their child is taking their own faults and failings out on the child (M, SLC, 1964).

1216 Do not hit a baby on the face. If it dies during its first year, your hand print will appear on its face (F, 20, SLC).

1217 Gypsies will kidnap any children who wander off when they are not supposed to (Bear River City, 1957).

1218 Alligators will get children who play near the ditch (Bear River City, 1957). (Since folklore often deals with unreal or idealized juxtapositions, one is accustomed to see unusual misplacements in the natural habitat. The present entry is an excellent example of anatopism, where creatures of tropical waters are made to inhabit ditches and other watercourses in northern Utah. Young minds, eager to believe anything told them in "good" faith, will ordinarily not bother to exercise a judgment in matters of the kind under discussion. --Eds.)

1219 If you're not good, the "boogy man" will get you (F, 19, SLC, 1950); The bugger man is waiting around to grab little children (F, Bear River City, 1957); . . . when going out at night (M, SLC, 1958). (This entry, and a few others in this section, deal with bogeymen and other frightening figures used by parents and older siblings to keep young children in line. John D. A. Widdowson, University of Sheffield, has devoted a whole dissertation to the subject, *If You Don't Be Good: Verbal Social Control in Newfoundland* (Social and Economic Studies, No. 21, Institute of Social and Economic Research, Memorial University of Newfoundland, St. John's, Newfoundland, 1977). --Eds.)

1220 If you get too close to the ditch, the Old Lady will get you (M, Orem); Children playing near canals on the outskirts of Salt Lake were told that the "boogie man" would get them (M, SLC, 1959).

1221 The boogie man is lurking in the cellar (F, 46, SLC, 1963).

1222 Children can't go out November's night or the "pookeys" will get them (F, Ir, SLC, 1960).

1223 Children were not to go to the school basement or the "Tommy Knockers" would get them (F, SLC, 1969). (For a discussion of "Tommy Knockers," phantom creatures of the mines, see Hand, "Utah's Silver Mining," pp. 142-44. See also this author's treatment of these fabled creatures in surveys of hardrock mining lore from California and Montana: "California Miners' Folklore: Above Ground," *CFQ* 1 [1942]: 128-31, passim; "The Folklore, Customs, and Traditions of the Butte Miners," *CFQ* [1946]: 3-8, passim. --Eds.)

1224 A child who sings in the early morning is tempting fate and might have to be whipped before the day is out (M, Holladay, 1959). Cf. Brown 468f.

1225 If your nose itches, you're going to get a whipping (F, 49, Midvale, 1929).

1226 If you dream of dirty water, it means you'll soon be punished (M, 19, Heber, 1972). Brown 470.

1227 If children lie to their parents, the devil will enter their bodies and take their souls (F, 49, Midvale, 1964).

1228 A dragonfly will sew up the mouth of a child who swears (M, Farmington, 1954).

1229 Cayenne pepper on the tongue will cure a child from swearing (M, 44, Layton, 1970).

## CHILDHOOD ACTIVITY

### Birthday

1230 If a child cries on its first birthday, it will have an unhappy life (F, SLC, 1960).

1231 If the date of your birth is divisible by seven, you will be lucky (F, 50, Bear River City, 1922).

1232 You will have extremely good luck in the year that you are as old as the number of the day of the month on which you were born. For example, if you were born on the sixteenth, when you are sixteen you will be very lucky. Good luck (though to a lesser extent) also follows you on multiples of this number (F, 20, Logan, 1972).

1233 Birthdays and age are very rarely mentioned in an Orthodox Jewish household because they believe this is an invitation to the Angel of Death who is always listening to call (F, SLC, 1956).

1234 If you wear red on your birthday, you will have bad luck (F, SLC, 1964).

1235 If it rains on your birthday, you will have good luck all that year (M, 47, SLC, 1922).

1236    Drinking red wine on your eleventh birthday brings good luck (F, It, SLC, 1963).

1237    On a child's birthday he should be spanked once for each year of his life, once for good luck, and once for growth (F, Nephi, 1961).

1238    What you do on your birthday, you'll do all year (F, 52, SLC, 1950).

1239    If you cry on your birthday, you will have bad luck all that year (M, 48, Midvale, 1922); . . . you will have an unhappy year (M, 16, SLC, 1958).

1240    Seven years bad luck if you cry on your birthday (M, 19, SLC, 1950).

1241    If you cry on your birthday, you will cry all year long (F, Ger, SLC, 1950); . . . you will cry every day of the year (F, 55, Logan, 1956); . . . you will cry every other day (F, 43, SLC, 1934). Brown 5976f.

1242    If you laugh on your birthday, you will laugh all year (M, 53, Logan, 1920s).

## Birthday Cakes, Gifts

1243    On a person's birthday if he eats the first piece of cake, it will bring him good luck (F, SLC, 1961).

1244    Baking a coin in a birthday cake will bring good luck to the person who finds the coin in his piece (F, SLC, 1957).

1245    A dime, a penny, a button, and a thimble, and a ring were put in our birthday cakes. The person who got the dime was the rich man; the penny, the poor man; the thimble, the old maid; the button, the bachelor; the ring, first one married (F, SLC, 1957).

1246    Make a wish before you blow out the candles on your birthday cake. However many candles are left burning that is how many years it will be before your wish comes true. If you blow them all out with the first breath, your wish will come true that year (F, 54, Logan, 1970). Cf. Brown 8505.

1247    Good luck if you blow out all the candles on a birthday cake (M, SLC, 1957); Candles on a birthday cake bring good luck (M, 9, SLC, 1964).

1248    Make a wish and blow out the candles on a birthday cake. Each breath it takes means a year before the wish is fulfilled. Pinch the wick on the last glowing candle and sleep on it (F, SLC, 1947). Cf. Brown 8505.

1249    If you tell your wish when wishing on a birthday cake, it won't come true (F, Bountiful, 1945).

1250    The last candle to be blown out on a birthday cake is a life-saver and should be kept until the next birthday (F, SLC, 1950).

1251    Place your ring around the birthday candle before blowing out the candles and then make a wish and the wish will come true (F, 14, 1961).

1252    It's unlucky to have a birthday party before your birthday (M, 52, SLC, 1925).

## Playing, Etc.

1253    If a child plays excessively with dolls, it is a sign she will be unable to give birth to a child of her own (F, SLC).

1254    Take a dandelion that has gone to seed and blow the down off. The number of seeds that are left indicates the number of hours before your mother wants you home (F, SLC, 1958). Brown 476.

1255    If two children washed in the same basin and wiped together on the towel, one of us would say: "Wash and wipe together, quarrel and fight forever" (F, SLC, 1954). Cf. Brown 3565ff.

1256    It is bad luck for a child to walk forwards when he is running an errand (F, 24, SLC, 1964).

## School

1257    The Indians believe that to send a child to school is bad luck. They always die (F).

1258    A boy that leaves school early will be subject to the pains of stupidity (F, SLC, 1961).

1259    To find a ladybug on the way to school is a good omen (F, 21, SLC, 1962).

1260    If a person will take the same path to school every day it will aid him in his school work (M, 21, Midvale, 1952).

1261    When you come home with a bad report card, you should take a bowl of oatmeal to stimulate the brain (F, Grantsville, 1964).

1262    To prevent bad luck after dropping a school book, kiss it (F, Midvale, 1964). Brown 432.

1263    Friday is an unlucky day unless you are going to school (M, SLC, 1960).

1264    If you get a red tray in the Ballif lunch line, you will have good luck all day (F, 18, SLC, 1962). (Ballif Hall is a dormitory at the University of Utah. --Eds.)

1265    Among the 300 or so dinner plates in the dining room, two or three are very slightly different from the others in having a thin green line around their circumference. If you are served one of the "green plates," you will have good luck for the next 24 hours, it is thought (M).

1266    If you get a yellow tray for dinner in Van Cott Hall, at the University of Utah, you'll have bad luck that day (F, SLC, 1964).

1267    A girl is not officially a co-ed at the University of Michigan until she has been kissed under the arch in the engineering building (F, SLC, 1964).

1268  To be initiated into a sorority one must give blood or else it is not a true sisterhood (F, SLC, 1966).

1269  If a pledge goes into a fraternity house unescorted by an active sorority sister, she may never go active in her sorority (F, SLC, 1966).

1270  If a student walks over the school seal, he will have bad luck (M, SLC, 1964).

Editors' note: No. 12573, below, referring to a metal slug in the sidewalk or road which is used by surveyors, belongs to a category of taboos having to do with stepping on cracks, seals, manhole covers, and the like. Even though the luck is reversed, the item apparently fits better here than where it was erroneously placed.

1271  In a college if a doctor is teaching a class he can legally be fifteen minutes late, a professor can be ten minutes late, and an instructor never later than five minutes late. If they are later than this the students have the right to leave without any jeopardy (F, 20, Ogden, 1960).

Exams

1272  Always think the other thing that you want to happen. If you want to get a good grade on a test in school, think that you will flunk it and then, if you study, you'll get a good grade on it (M, 25, SLC, 1963).

1273  On the day of an exam you must walk out the front door of your house and into the front door at night upon returning or it will be bad luck for you on the exam (F, 19, SLC, 1964).

1274  To write the middle initial on an exam which you're not quite sure of increases your chances of missing more questions. You should never write your initial on anything about which you have apprehension--it's bad luck (M, 27, SLC, 1964).

1275  If you do well on a test, the next time you take a test write your name exactly the same as you did on the previous test. It brings good luck (F, 19, SLC, 1963).

1276  Never turn in an exam before anybody else does even if you finish quite a while before anybody else. Wait until someone else has turned one in first (M, Helper, 1958).

1277  Put an X where it says seat number on the bluebooks at final time. It brings good luck (M, SLC, 1961).

1278  Always use the same pencil when taking exams, you'll do better (M, 24, SLC, 1958).

1279  You will do better on an examination if you cross your fingers first (M, 26, Logan, 1957).

1280  If a person will wear the same combination of clothes when they have a test, it will aid them while taking it (M, 21, Midvale, 1950). Cf. Brown 440.

1281  If you look up the answers immediately after an examination, your score will be lower than if you don't (F, 19, SLC, 1964).

1282  It is bad luck to get 100 percent on the test; thus, one should purposely make one error (M, 19, SLC, 1963).

1283  Fish is brain food. Eat it before exams (F, SLC, 1953); . . . eat fish, you will remember all the information (F, 19, SLC, 1964).

1284  Sleep with your books under your pillow and you may more easily pass an examination (F, 53, SLC, 1927); . . . to learn what is in a book (F, SLC, 1959). Brown 439.

1285  Rubbing the hand over a bald-headed man will help a student remember what is needed for an examination (M, 54, Magna, 1923).

1286  Shaving during finals is bad luck (M, SLC, 1960).

1287  If you step on a crack, you will fail your lessons (M, 14, SLC, 1964); . . . you will fail your next test (F, 19, SLC, 1964); . . . you will get an F in school (SLC, 1964).

1288  A hall in high school was tiled in black and yellow. If you stepped on a black square, you would fail a test (M, Vernal, 1959).

1289  To walk under a ladder means that you will miss your lessons (M, 9, SLC, 1962).

1290  If you study for a test on Sunday, you will fail the test (F, SLC, 1960).

1291  If you use a green tray in the cafeteria before a test, you will flunk (F, 20, SLC, 1960).

1292  When you are in school and are going to have a test, if you meet a priest on the way to the test you're going to fail (M, Gr, SLC, 1952).

CHILD'S STATUS AS ADULT

Fame, Prosperity, Success, Etc.

1293  The position of the stars and the time of birth influence a person's destiny (F, 45, Clearfield, 1964). Brown 242.

1294  The success or failure of your life depends upon what sign of the moon you were born under (F, 49, SLC, 1954).

1295  The seventh son of the seventh son will have choice blessings in life (M, SLC, 1949). Brown 222.

1296  If a baby doesn't fall off a bed before it is one year old, it is a sign of bad luck (F, 47, Provo, 1945). Cf. Brown 256.

1297  Unless a baby crawls before it walks, it will crawl in afterlife (M, 1960).

1298  If a child gathers all the eggs without dropping them, he will encounter good luck throughout his childhood (F, 42, Copperton).

1299   If you fall in a water well or in a pond of water when you are small, you will not succeed in this world (F, 25, Ja, SLC, 1952).

1300   A baby must go upstairs before it goes downstairs, or it will never rise in the world (F, 53, SLC, 1964); If you want your child to rise in the world, carry it up the stairs the day it is born (F, SLC, 1960). Brown 210ff. (For a bibliographical reference to the birth ritual of "rising in life," or "rising in the world," see No. 1157, above. --Eds.)

1301   While a baby is being baptized three drops of oil are dropped in the water. If the oil sets in the water with the sign of a cross, this means that the baby will become very important when he is older (F, Gr, SLC, 1962).

1302   When the mother comes with the baby from the hospital, have her step on a piece of iron in order for the baby to be prosperous (F, 62, Gr, SLC, 1963).

1303   Never walk on top of a kid's head when it is sleeping. Walk over their heads, otherwise they won't succeed in later life (F, 51, Ja, W. Jordan, 1963). Cf. Brown 3382.

1304   Keep a baby's first pair of shoes to bring him luck (F, Orem, 1941).

## Wealth, Poverty

1305   If one is born during an eclipse, he will suffer poverty and misfortune (F, 46, SLC, 1938); . . . will be poor (F, 58, Provo, 1947).

1306   If the palms of a baby's hands are washed before he is a year old, he will have no money (M, Gr, SLC, 1950).

1307   A child born on Wednesday will be blessed with money (M, SLC, 1961).

1308   A baby born with lots of hair will be rich (M, SLC, 1957).

1309   If a baby gets its first tooth on the bottom, it means wealth (F, 33, Bountiful, 1953).

1310   Put a silver piece in a newborn baby's hand and it will always be rich (F, 80, Midvale).

1311   As soon as a child is able to hold on to a half-dollar, they should be given it to keep. It will bring them money (F, SLC, 1971).

1312   If you put a five-dollar piece in a baby's hand, the baby will have money (F, SLC, 1959).

## Trades, Professions, Work

1313   If a child cries at birth and lifts one hand, it is born to command (F, SLC, 1960).

1314   A baby born on Sunday will grow up to be a preacher (F, Murray, 1957). Cf. Brown 205, 208.

1315   The seventh son is a born doctor (M, 16, SLC, 1964). Brown 224.

1316   If you place a child on the floor with a Bible, a dollar, and a deck of cards, the one that he picks up first indicates his future as a preacher, financier, or gambler (F, SLC); If you want to know what your child will be, set a tray of articles symbolic of various trades before him, and notice what he reaches for (F, 70, Provo, 1900). Cf. Brown 205.

1317   Give a baby girl spinning and cooking equipment so she will be a good housewife when she grows up (M, 50, SLC, 1964).

1318   Give a baby a bow and arrow so he will grow up to be a good hunter (M, 50, SLC, 1964).

## Marriage, Travel, Legal

1319   Never let a baby look at itself in a mirror or the baby will never marry (F, 33, Bountiful, 1964).

1320   When a baby boy is born, if it has two crowns, it means he will have two wives (F, 24, Murray, 1949).

1321   If a child is born with two crowns on her head, she'll live in two different countries (F, 80, Midvale). Brown 259.

1322   If a child's eyebrows are far apart, then he will move far away from where he was born (F, Pol, SLC).

1323   Should a woman during pregnancy spin at the spinning wheel, her child will be hanged with a hempen rope (M, Welsh, Midvale, 1961).

1324   If you steal something while you are pregnant, your baby will be a thief (F, 63, SLC, 1921).

1325   Never cut a baby's fingernails until they are a month old or they will become a thief (F, Weber Co, 1922); . . . before it is six months old . . . (F, SLC, 1928); . . . before it is a year . . . (M, 20, SLC, 1960). Brown 232ff.

1326   Don't cut a baby's fingernails with scissors or he will become a thief (F, SLC, 1959). Brown 233.

## DEATH OF CHILDREN

### Premature Babies

1327   A seven-month baby will die (F, SLC, 1950).

1328   A baby born at eight months of pregnancy will die (F, Midvale, 1963).

### Prenatal Influence on Child

1329   If you reach too high when pregnant, the cord will wrap around the baby's neck and choke it to death (F, 19, SLC, 1963); . . . raise your hands above your head . . . (F, 61, Ogden, 1935); . . . lift up high, the baby will be born with the cord around its neck (F, 63, SLC, 1921); . . . lift up arms too high ties the cord around the baby's neck (F, 21, SLC, 1964). Cf. Brown 4876.

1330 A pregnant woman's hanging up clothes, or becoming entangled in any way in a rope, will cause the umbilical cord to wrap around the unborn child's neck and strangle it. Don't walk under a washline or the cord will be around the baby's neck (F, Peoa, 1920). Brown 4876.

1331 If a woman hangs curtains while carrying a baby, it will strangle in the umbilical cord (M, 56, SLC, 1964).

1332 If a woman ties knots in her final month of pregnancy, her baby will be strangled by the umbilical cord (F, 21, Helper, 1963). Cf. Brown 4876.

1333 Pregnant women should never tie anything around their neck because it will choke the baby (F, 58, It, SLC, 1964). Heard in Italy in 1915.

1334 If a pregnant woman breaks a string or crosses ditches, she will tie a cord around the baby's neck (F, 51, It, W. Jordan, 1963). Cf. Brown 4878.

1335 Fathers mustn't tie knots securely during their wives' pregnancy for fear that the unborn child would become entangled in the umbilical cord (M, 58, MD, SLC, 1963).

1336 A pregnant woman must not sew or wind thread lest the fetus entangle itself in the umbilical and be strangled (M, 58, MD, SLC, 1963); Don't sew with a treadle sewing machine or it will wrap the baby's cord around his neck (F, SLC, 1971). Informant said the movement of the machine vibrates the baby until he is strangled.

1337 If a woman moves around too much while she is pregnant, the umbilical cord will wrap around the baby and cause its death (F, 20, SLC, 1955).

1338 A pregnant woman should never cross her legs or she may suffocate the unborn child (F, teacher of maternal child care, SLC, 1962).

1339 Crossing a fence while carrying an unborn child will make the cord wrap around the fetus (F, Salina, 1937).

1340 If a pregnant woman drinks too much (any liquid), the baby might drown in the "bag of water" (F, Tooele, 1967). Cf. Brown 4877.

1341 A pregnant woman must not look at a dead body or the expected baby will die (F, Ogden, 1961). Heard in Canada, 1940.

1342 If you step over a new grave while you're pregnant, your baby will die (F, SLC, 1960).

1343 If a pregnant woman breathes paint, the baby will die (F, 53, Mt. Pleasant, 1964).

1344 Pregnant women must not eat pork or their child will die (F, 21, Eng, SLC, 1963).

## Naming, Baptism

1345 A baby will die if you name it before it's a month old (F, Eng, SLC, 1965).

1346 A baby with the same name as a family member that has recently died will not grow very old (M, SLC, 1957); If a child is named for someone dead, it will die young (M, Tooele, 1957). Cf. Brown 4879.

1347 Don't name a child after someone that has died violently or they will die also (F, 1957).

1348 If you decide to name a child something and then for some reason change that name, it will die a violent death (F, SLC, 1963).

1349 Never call a baby angel. If you do, he will soon be one (F, 80, Midvale); . . . it will not live long (M, SLC, 1960).

1350 The first child christened in a new church is claimed by the devil and is sure to die (F, 69, Murray, 1915).

1351 A baby that does not cry at christening is too good to live long (M, 51, SLC, 1964); . . . that does not cry at baptism . . . (M, SLC, 1964).

1352 An unbaptized child cannot die (M, 1900); . . . unchristened child . . . (M, SLC, 1961).

## Parts of Body

1353 If a baby doesn't cut its teeth in order, it will die (M, SLC, 1957). Cf. Brown 4883.

1354 If a certain small blue vein shows on a baby's forehead, it is said it will die (M, 20, SLC, 1963); . . . die within a few days (M, 53, SLC, 1943).

1355 A child born with a veil over its face will soon die (F, SLC, 1965).

1356 It is lucky to be born with a caul or membrane over your face. It is believed to be a protection against drowning (F, SLC, 1959). Cf. Brown 245n.

1357 The sudden loss of hair means a loss of children (F, 81, 1965).

## Care of Child, Clothing

1358 Never wean a baby in May, you will wean the baby away (F, 60, Midvale, 1910).

1359 Never lay a baby on a table. To do so is significant of laying them out in death (F, SLC, 1960).

1360 If you cut your fingernails in the night time, then your children will die early (F, 25, Ja, SLC, 1954).

1361 If a child's nails are cut before it is a year old, it will bring it death (F, SLC, 1960); . . . before it is three months old . . . (F, 97, Syracuse, 1888).

1362    It brings bad luck and occasionally death to a baby if his hair is cut before it is a year old (F, 50, SLC, 1964). Cf. Brown 4881f.

1363    Shorten baby's clothes in May, you shorten its life away (F, SLC, 1961); . . . baby's dress . . . (F, Peoa, 1919).

1364    If you buy a bonnet for a baby before it is born, it won't live to wear it (F, 60, Dan, SLC, 1910).

1365    Never put a baby's shoes on the table or the baby will die (F, 43, Ogden, 1964).

## Animals as Portents and Causes of Death

1366    Do not leave a cat in the same room with a sleeping baby; the cat will suck the baby's breath and suffocate it (F, 23, SLC, 1950); Cats can smell milk on baby's breath and they try to get to it (F, SLC, 1969); Cats sit on babies' chests and breathe the air next to their faces (F, 62, SLC, 1963). Brown 4888.

1367    A cat should not be allowed around a small sleeping baby because he will suck out the life blood of the baby (F, Logan, 1970).

1368    Rats kill baby children (M, 19, SLC, 1950).

1369    It is very unlucky to hear a cow moo at night. If you are a parent, you will lose a child (F, SLC, 1959).

1370    To kill a white dove will cause you to lose your youngest child (M, SLC, 1961).

1371    Three months before my mother was due to have a baby my grandmother saw two birds trying to get in the kitchen window. When my mother had the baby--which turned out to be twin boys--we were staying with my grandmother to be near the hospital. Both of the babies died and my grandmother said she had felt this would happen after seeing the birds (F, 36, Payson, 1947).

1372    When two white doves follow a casket along the road, two children in the area will soon die (F, 59, Swed, Bear River, 1914).

## Miscellaneous

1373    If you let a baby look in a mirror before he is a year old, it will die (F, 62, Tooele, 1964); . . . it will not live long (F, Orangeville, 1959); . . . it will die before it is a year old (F, Santaquin); . . . die within a year (M, SLC, 1957); . . . before it is six months old (M, MD, Provo, 1959). Cf. Brown 4892ff.

1374    If you let a baby look in a mirror before it has one tooth, it will die before it is a year old (F, SLC, 1964).

1375    Before reaching his first birthday an infant must fall off the bed at least once or else he will die (F, 23, SLC, 1950). Brown 4884.

1376    To rock a cradle with the baby not in it is to bring about its early death (M, SLC, 1961). Cf. Brown 4890.

1377    If you think too much of a child, it will die (F, Sandy, 1957).

1378    Never leave or have clothes hanging out to dry when the New Year comes in because it will cause your child to die (F, 62, Garland, 1916).

1379    The child born in the interval between an old moon and the first appearance of the new moon will never reach the age of puberty (F, SLC, 1955).

1380    If you save your veil and corsage, your firstborn will die (F, 56, Grantsville, 1963).

1381    Children of people married in May will be likely to die (F, Scot, 1957). Cf. Brown 4767f.

1382    Wedding after sunset entitles a bride to a joyless life and the loss of children (M, SLC, 1961). Cf. Brown 4778.

1383    If you step over a child you have to back over it in the same way or it will die within a year (M, Magna, 1918). Brown 4886.

1384    If you're too smart as a child, you'll die young (M, W. Jordan, 1920); Bright or beautiful children will die soon after birth because they are near perfect (F, 80, Sandy, 1970). Cf. Brown 4887n.

1385    Small children should not get into empty boxes to play. This signifies death-- coffin (F, Gr, SLC, 1964).

1386    Young children never die, they turn into grass (M, SLC, 1964).

1387    When a baby dies, the mother is not supposed to go to the funeral. If she does, any other children she has will die (F, Gr, SLC, 1962).

1388    A week after a sick lady held a baby she died. Two weeks later the baby died because the dead woman loved the baby and wanted it for company (F, 21, Riverton, 1960).

## Burial of Children

1389    A woman buries her dead child with its favorite toy or with her own beautiful hair in the coffin. They believe this should be done or the child will be lonely in heaven (F, 19, Fr, Murray, 1956).

1390    It is lucky to have a stillborn child put into an open grave, as it is a sure passport to heaven for the next person buried therein (F, SLC, 1955).

# II
# Human Body

BLOOD, SKIN, ETC.

1391 One drop of blood from the left nostril signifies good luck (F, 83, SLC, 1940).

1392 Beets make your blood red (F, SLC, 1957).

1393 Tomato juice makes blood red or redder (M, SLC, 1945).

1394 Cinnamon will dry up your blood (M, SLC, 1971).

1395 If you eat too many lemons with salt, your blood will dry up (M, 43, SLC, 1938).

1396 Having your blood drawn for various medical tests can leave a scar on your left forearm (F, SLC, 1961).

1397 God will be angry if a young girl uses lipstick and nail polish, because to him they mean the same as blood (M, SLC, 1957).

1398 You know skaters on the water. If you go swimming when they are there, they will suck your blood (F, Moab, 1953).

1399 When you drink milk your arteries will harden (M, 18, SLC, 1964).

1400 If a person has a dimple in his chin, he will have good luck. If it shows only when he smiles, he will have good luck on the day he smiles (F, 25, SLC, 1960).

1401 Moles are lucky signs (F, SLC, 1961); . . . on the body are a sign of good fortune (F, 39, Draper, 1965); . . . on the right side of the face or body are lucky; on the left side they bring misfortune (F, 52, SLC, 1930).

1402 A round mole on your neck is good luck, but an oblong or misshapen one is bad luck (F, 18, SLC, 1959). Cf. Brown 631.

1403 If you lie, you'll get moles on your back (M, 57, SLC, 1964).

1404 If you have a mole on your arm, you will live on a farm (M, 42, Provo, 1938).

1405 A mole on the throat or back of the neck is a sign of good luck (F, 63, SLC, 1964).

1406 If you drink a glass of water with a teaspoon of molasses in it every week, your skin won't turn yellow and get scaly when you get old (F, Logan, 1920).

1407 Use buttermilk to keep your skin good (F, Moab, 1953).

1408 Rub your face with a baby's wet diaper to keep your skin white (F, Lehi, 1957).

1409 A poultice of cow manure will bleach your skin (F, Lehi, 1957).

1410 If you drink too much coffee, your skin will turn brown (F, Logan, 83, Can, 1970); . . . you'll turn dark-skinned, even black (M, SLC, 1960). (The temptation to think of this item in terms of the Word of Wisdom and the proscription of coffee as a beverage should be resisted, for this folk belief is encountered everywhere in the country. --Eds.)

1411 Carrots will make your skin turn brown (F, SLC, 1961); If you drink too much carrot juice, your skin will turn orange (F, Midvale, 1961).

1412 If you take a milk bath, you will have beautiful skin (F, 1962).

HEAD, TORSO

1413 Each part of the body is associated with certain heavenly bodies (M, 68, Midvale, 1960).

1414 Some of the chiropractors believe that the pull of gravity has a bearing on the body. In fact old Dr. So and So had all the beds in his nursing home running north and south. It has something to do with how the body functions, as related to the pull of gravity (F, nurse, SLC).

1415 The entire composition of the body changes every seven years (Anon, Lehi, 1957).

1416 Ironing underclothes prevents the body pores from functioning (M, SLC, 1957).

1417 The body goes into a trance while the soul is absent (F, 23, SLC, 1963).

1418 Salads are not necessary for a good body (F, SLC, 1961).

1419 All sound-minded people have the largest half of their head in front of their ears (F, 40, SLC, 1964).

1420 Knock on the head instead of on wood for continued good luck (F, SLC, 1965).

1421   If the crown of our heads itch, we will be advanced to a more honorable position in life (M, 32, bricklayer, SLC, 1958).

1422   If two people bump heads, they will be together when they grow old (M, Vernal, 1958).

1423   If a woman wears hats, her head will swell (F, 44, Payson, 1940).

1424   When April blows her horn (thunder), it's good for hair (M, 19, Logan, 1950).

1425   If you part your hair on the left side, you will have bad luck (M, 69, Sterling, 1920).

1426   One hair of a woman draws more than a team of horses (F, 19, SLC).

1427   If you pull out one hair, two will replace it (F, SLC).

1428   Pull a hair out of your head and lick it. If it goes straight, you will have a good day (F, 17, SLC, 1963).

1429   If a woman's hair grows in a low point in the center of her forehead, it presages womanhood (F, SLC, 1955).

1430   The scalp of a white man will bring good luck to the Indian (F, 20, SLC, 1964).

## Hair - Combing, Washing

1431   It is good for the hair to wash it in wild sage tea (F, Logan, 1968).

1432   An egg-yolk shampoo is good for the hair (F, Logan, 1968).

1433   Don't let hair get greasy. Use beer as a rinse for hair to make it soft and manageable (F, 19, Logan, 1971).

1434   For curly hair sagebrush was steeped in water and used as a wash (F, 53, SLC, 1964).

1435   If you are combing your hair and you drop the comb, the rats will come out (F, 68, Farmington, 1915). Cf. Brown 497ff.

1436   To comb your hair after dark will bring you bad luck (M, Santaquin, 1920s); If you comb your hair after dark you'll comb sorrows to your heart (F, 88, SLC, 1964); . . . with a black comb in the dark, it will bring bad luck (M, 21, SLC, 1955). Brown 487ff.

1437   If you dream that you are combing your hair and there are no snarls, something good will happen. If you dream that there are snarls in your hair while combing, something bad will happen (F, Gr, SLC, 1957).

1438   Some Greeks believe that it is unwise to say "Good Morning" without first combing your hair (F, 52, Provo, 1938).

1439   It is considered bad luck to wash your hair on Sunday (F, Gr, SLC, 1964); If you wash your hair on Sunday, it will fall out (M, 19, SLC, 1964); . . .you will never be successful (F, Gr, SLC, 1961).

1440   It is bad luck to wash your hair while menstruating (F, SLC, 1955).

1441   If a lady washes her hair in water from March snow, it will become pretty (F, 40, Logan, 1938).

1442   Twelve days after Christmas the girls did not wash their hair, for fear of bad luck (F, Gr, SLC, 1962).

1443   Wash your hair in the good time of moon (full) and it will be prettier (F, bank teller, SLC, 1962).

1444   Too frequent shampoos are harmful to the hair (F, SLC, 1959). Learned in beauty school.

1445   There was an old lady that used to tell us to wash our hair in buttermilk to make it glossy (F, Moab, 1953).

1446   The women used to wash their hair in water from the blacksmith's tub. The iron in the water was supposed to do something for it. We just couldn't keep water in the tub, the women were always taking it (M, Moab, 1953).

1447   Beat the whites of two eggs to a froth, rub well into the roots of the hair. Leave to dry. Then wash the head clean with equal parts of rum and rosewater. Rinse in clean, soft water (M, 1957). Taken from Woman's Favorite Cook Book.

1448   The fewer times you wash your hair, the more beautiful it will be (even to the extent of years) (F, 19, SLC).

## Hair - Tonics, Singeing

1449   Olive oil both softens and toughens the hair (F, 20, SLC, 1963).

1450   A preparation that has been in use many years and has been proved efficacious for strengthening the roots of the hair is made by taking a pint of bay rum, one-half pint of clear alcohol, one-half ounce of castor oil, one-quarter of an ounce of carbonate ammonia and one-half ounce of tincture of cantharides. They must be thoroughly mixed. Excellent to promote the growth of the hair (taken from Woman's Favorite Cook Book).

1451   Kerosene worked into the hair will give it thickness and lustre (F, 20, SLC, 1963).

1452   Singeing will correct a split-end condition (F, SLC, 1959). Learned in beauty school.

## Hair - Permanents

1453   If you have a permanent during your menstrual period, it won't take (F, 12, SLC, 1964).

1454   If you have a permanent during a full moon, it won't take (F, 20, SLC, 1963).

1455   Too many cocktails spoil the wave of hair (F, SLC, 1959). Learned in beauty school.

1456  Hair exposed to ether will never wave
(F, SLC, 1959).

1457  When I was in high school, one girl
reportedly used a setting lotion made
from flaxseed to curl her hair.  But
none of the rest of us knew how and she
never divulged her secret (F, 54, Logan,
1970).

Hair - Curly

1458  If you have natural curly hair and you
cut it off, the curl will never grow
back (F, 21, SLC, 1957).

1459  Curly-haired people have better luck (F,
20, SLC, 1964).

1460  When it rains, curly hair gets curlier
and straight hair gets straighter (F,
Logan, 1970).

1461  If you swim in the ocean, you will have
wavy hair (M, 25, SLC, 1950).

1462  Eat bread crusts and it will make your
hair curly (F, 20, SLC, 1964); . . .
bread crumbs . . . (M, SLC, 1964); . . .
black crusts . . . (F, Nephi, 1961);
. . . burnt toast . . . (M, 20, SLC,
1950).

1463  To make straight hair curl, eat charcoal
from burned food (F, 18, SLC, 1964).

1464  Eat a lot of carrots and your hair will
be very curly (F, SLC, 1920).

1465  Sweet apples are good for curly hair (M,
19, Ogden, 1964).

1466  Eating onions make your hair curly (F,
20, Taylorsville, 1964).

1467  If you eat spinach, your hair will
become curly (M, 19, SLC, 1964).

1468  If a cow licks straight hair, it will
make it curly (F, SLC, 1961).

Hair - Color

1469  Rub a redheaded girl's hair--good luck
(M, 19, 1963).

1470  Red hair is unlucky (M, Spanish Fork,
1959).

1471  Eat lots of carrots and your hair will
turn red (F, SLC, 1940).

1472  A man should beware of a girl with red
hair (F, 19, SLC, 1964).

1473      Redheaded sinner,
Come down to your dinner.
(M, 26, Bountiful, 1940).

1474  If you eat burnt crusts of bread, it
will make your hair black (F, Moab,
1953).

1475  Your hair will turn coal black if you
eat a lot of seaweed (M, Ja, SLC, 1963).

1476  Hair turns grey quite suddenly from fear
or fright (F, 1960); Shock will turn
hair grey overnight (F, SLC, 1959);
Worry . . . (F, 46, SLC, 1964).

1477  If you break a promise, your hair will
start to grow grey (M, 60, SLC, 1910).

1478  If you pull out one grey hair, two will
grow in to replace it (F, 40, Logan,
1972); . . . three will take its place
(F, SLC, 1949); . . . seven . . . (F,
51, SLC, 1918); . . . thirteen . . . (M,
61, SLC, 1964); . . . twenty . . . (F,
19, SLC, 1950).

1479  People's hair will sometimes turn white
after they die if they've had a scare
just before they died or they died a
violent death (F, SLC, 1967).

1480  They used to dip their combs in a brew
made from sage to keep their hair from
going grey (F, 87, Moab, 1953).

1481  Wash your hair in butter to stop it from
going grey (F, SLC, 1961).

1482  A person's hair can turn white overnight
by seeing something extremely
frightening or receiving news without
being prepared to have it arrive (F,
SLC, 1951); . . . from a great shock or
emotional experience (F, 20, Logan,
1956).

1483  If you pull out a white hair, two will
come in its place (M, 22, SLC, 1964);
. . . others will come in its place (F,
Ogden, 1963).

Hair - Growth

1484  If you stand out in a rain storm, your
hair will grow faster because of the
nitrogen in the rainwater (M, 18, W.
Jordan, 1971).

1485  Cut you hair on the first day of a full
moon and your hair will grow faster (F,
80, Vernal, 1913).

1486  If you cut your hair on a new moon, it
will grow faster (F, 18, SLC, 1953);
. . . cut your hair two inches when the
new moon is forming, your hair will grow
fast (M, SLC, 1957).

1487  Singe the ends of your hair on the night
of a full moon and it will grow longer
(F, 28, Midvale, 1936).

1488  Cut the ends of hair and put them near a
stream for a thicker growth of hair (F,
SLC, 1961); Trim edges of the hair every
six to eight weeks and bury them by a
stream to encourage long hair growth (F,
68, SLC, 1963).

1489  Cutting the hair will promote its growth
and improve it (F, SLC, 1959).  Learned
in beauty school.

1490  If you eat bullets, your hair will grow
out in bangs (F, 19, SLC, 1960).

1491  To make your hair grow cut some of it
off, wrap around a piece of grapevine
and plant.  If the vines take root and
grow, your hair will grow with them (F,
28, SLC, 1951).

1492  Wash your hair under a cactus and stay
there all night, and by morning your
hair will have grown to reach the ground
(F, Provo, 1971).

## Hair - Cutting

1493   Porter Rockwell never cut his hair because he had been promised if he didn't his enemies would never take him (F, Provo, 1946).

1494       It is better you were never born,
          Than on the Sabbath pare hair or
            horn.
       (F, 61, Du, SLC, 1964).  Learned in Holland 1933.  Cf. Brown 491.

1495   Hair should only be cut when the moon is on the increase (M, 22, SLC, 1963); Always trim hair by a new moon (F, 67, SLC, 1963); Trim your hair each new moon, it will make your hair more beautiful (F, 67, Du, SLC, 1964).

1496   You're not to cut your hair after dark. It is bad luck (F, Kanab, 1960).

1497   If your hair is cut on Sunday, you will later be embarrassed (M, SLC, 1964).

1498   A barber in ---- had to close his shop on Fridays because the people were so superstitious that they thought that if they had their hair cut on a Friday, it would never grow (F, 80, teacher, SLC, 1963).

## Hair - Disposal, Bats

1499   To throw hair combings out of a window is bad luck (M, 22, SLC, 1961).  Cf. Brown 492.

1500   Burning one's hair brings bad luck (M, 70, SLC, 1964).  Brown 494.

1501   Burying one's hair brings good luck (M, 70, SLC, 1964).

1502   Avoid bats.  They will get in your hair (M, Layton, 1934); As a child, one woman was not allowed to go out of the house at night without a scarf over her hair to keep the bats out (F, 58, Smithfield, 1959); If a bat gets in your hair, you'll never get it out (M, 30, SLC, 1964).

1503   Bats will eat your hair (M, SLC, 1952).

1504   There is a belief that if a woman had her hair done and didn't want to ruin it by washing it for a long time, a black widow spider would build a nest in it, bite her and kill her (F, SLC, 1971).

## Hair - Cowlick

1505   A cowlick is very lucky (M, SLC, 1964). Brown 484.

1506   A person with a double cowlick on his head has very good luck (F, 54, SLC, 1964).

## Hair - Legs, Chest, Body

1507   If you shave your legs, the hair will grow back double (F, SLC, 1950).

1508   If you shave your legs, the hair on them will turn black (F, 21, SLC, 1957).

1509   Liquor will make hair grow on your chest (F, 48, SLC, 1964).

1510   Don't drink beer because you will grow hair on your chest (F, 19, SLC, 1957).

1511   If you eat stew, you will grow hair on your chest (M, SLC, 1959).

1512   Eating spinach will cause hair to grow on your chest (M, SLC); Carrots will give one a hairy chest (F, 84, SLC, 1963).

1513   If you will eat the crust of your bread, you'll grow hair on your chest and a mustache (F, 84, SLC, 1939); If boys eat burnt toast, it will put hair on their chests (F, 40, Kearns, 1963).

1514   People with excessive body hair are descendants of Cain (F, 68, SLC, 1941).

## Face

1515   A full, plump, round face means that the person will have happiness in the future (M, 45, Ja, SLC, 1963).

1516   Keep your face clean or angels won't visit you (n.d.).

1517   If you hold your face in one position for a long enough time, it will freeze that way (F, 18, Price, 1963).

1518   If you pull a face and the wind changes, your face will stay that way (F, 39, SLC, 1964).

1519   If you go outside mad in the cold weather, your face will freeze (F, 20, SLC, 1943).

1520   Never let anyone look over your shoulder into a mirror or lines in your face will crack before you're old (F, 44, secy, SLC, 1961).

## Cheeks

1521   If you eat the dark brown crusts on burnt toast, you get rosy cheeks (F, 30, Ogden, 1945).

1522   Eating beets gives you rosy cheeks (M, 54, SLC, 1916).

1523   If you eat apples, you'll have rosy cheeks (F, SLC, 1957).

1524   The eating of carrots will make the cheeks rosy (M, 71, SLC, 1964).

## Ears

1525   Wear earrings and your ears are guarded (F, Sandy, 1960).

1526   The size of the bump behind the ear is indicative of the degree of the religious nature of a person (F, Lehi, 1915).

1527   It is good luck to have large ears (F, 87, Santaquin, 1914).

1528   Never put anything in your ear except your elbow (M, 83, Midvale, 1964).

1529 You can't go to heaven with holes (pierced ears) in your ears (F, 19, SLC, 1964).

1530 Pull your ears after sneezing for good luck (M, 1957).

1531 It is good luck for a bell to ring in your right ear (F, Dan, SLC, 1965).

1532 If you hear ringing in your right ear, it means good luck. But if it is in the left ear, it is bad luck (F, Gr, Magna, 1964).

1533 If your left ear rings, you will have good luck (M, 21, SLC, 1961).

1534 If your right ear rings, something bad is going to happen (M, 21, SLC, 1961). Brown 505.

1535 If your right ear burns, it's for spite (F, 18, SLC, 1964).

1536 A burning right ear signifies hate (F, 72, SLC, 1963).

1537 If your left ear burns, it is a very good sign (F, SLC, 1963). Cf. Brown 504.

1538 Dragonflies sew up people's ears (F, Mt. Pleasant, 1959).

1539 Earwigs will cement your ears closed (F, SLC, 1960).

## Eyes

1540 A cinder in the eye foretells unexpected pleasure (F, Axtell, 1958).

1541 To talk about eyes will bring bad luck (M, Gr, SLC, 1959).

1542 Rub the eyes with saliva every morning before breakfast (M, 20, SLC, 1964).

1543 A darning needle (fly) will sew up your eyes (M, 25, SLC, 1964).

1544 Hazel eyes are most expressive (M, 20, SLC, 1964).

1545 Brown eyes are supposedly bedroom eyes (M, 21, SLC, 1964). Cf. Brown 511.

1546 Blue-eyed beauty,
Do your mother's duty.
(F, 1920).

1547 Blue eyes are true eyes (M, 21, SLC, 1962). Brown 511.

1548 A person with blue eyes has good luck (F, 21, SLC, 1948).

1549 People with green eyes are bad luck (F, SLC, 1950). Cf. Brown 511.

1550 The color green is good for the eyes (F, Bear River City, 1957).

1551 If a woman's eyes are blue,
Watch the things she's apt to do.
If a woman's eyes are grey,
Heed the things you hear her say.
If a woman's eyes are brown,
Never let your own fall down.
If a woman's eyes are black,
Give her room and lots of track.
If a woman's eyes are green,
Whip her with a switch that's lean.
(F, Ogden, 1961). Cf. Brown 511.

## Eyes - Improve the Eyes

1552 If you eat a lot of carrots, you will have bright eyes and be able to see in the dark (M, 44, SLC, 1964); . . . it will make your eyes sharp (F, 20, SLC, 1964); . . . you will have good eyes (F, 19, SLC, 1947); . . . better eyes (M, 14, SLC, 1963); . . . your eyes will sparkle (F, 19, SLC, 1952); . . . your eyes will shine (F, 17, SLC, 1950).

1553 If an orange squirts in your eye, you will have shiny eyes (F, Eng, SLC, 1963).

1554 Strengthen the eyes by opening them in cold water every morning (F, SLC, 1961).

1555 Piercing the ears strengthens the eyes (F, 24, SLC, 1940).

1556 To have good eyes put an eagle's feather in your hat (M, SLC, 1961).

## Eyes - Itching

1557 If your right eye itches, it denotes good luck (F, 9, SLC, 1964); . . . is a sign of joy (F, Moab, 1953). Brown 513.

1558 When your right eye itches, it means sorrow (F, Bear River City, 1957); . . . one will shed tears (F, SLC); . . . something sad will happen (F, SLC, 1959). Cf. Brown 523, 526, 529.

1559 If your right eye itches, you will see bad (F, SLC, 1959); Your right eye is your cry eye. If it itches and you cry, it means that you shall have bad luck (F, 85, SLC, 1890).

1560 If your left eye itches, you will see good (F, SLC, 1959).

1561 If your left eye itches, you will be pleased (F, Murray, 1957); . . . something pleasant will happen (F, SLC, 1959); . . . it means happiness (F, SLC). Cf. Brown 515f.

1562 If the left eye itches, there will be sadness (F, Moab, 1953). Brown 532.

1563 If your left eye itches, it is bad luck (F, SLC, 1958); . . . means a disappointment (M, 29, SLC, 1950). Brown 520, 530.

## Eyes - Twitching, Watering

1564 Eye twitches, going to see someone you haven't seen for years (F, 28, SLC, 1942).

1565 You will have good luck if your right eye twitches (M, Layton, 1962). Cf. Brown 521.

1566 If your right eye twitches, something bad will happen (F, SLC, 1957).

1567 If your right eye twitches, something bad will happen (F, SLC, 1964).

1568  You will have bad luck if your left eye twitches (M, Manti, 1962).

1569  If your left eye twitches, something good will happen (F, SLC, 1957). Cf. Brown 519, 522.

1570  When the left eye waters, misfortune impends (F, 19, SLC); . . . watch out for bad luck (F, SLC, 1957).

### Eyes - Cross-Eyes

1571  Never look directly at a cross-eyed person. This will result in a series of events leading to disaster (F, SLC, 1959); . . . They bring bad luck (F, 30, Sandy, 1964).

1572  It is unlucky for a cross-eyed woman to look at you (F, 21, Provo, 1964).

1573  If you come eye to eye with a cross-eyed person, you should spit in your hat or you will have bad luck the rest of the day (F, 52, SLC, 1936). Cf. Brown 3634.

1574  If you see a cross-eyed person, cross your fingers or it will bring you bad luck (F, 50, SLC, 1964). Cf. Brown 3781.

### Eyebrows, Eyelashes, Eyelids

1575  Persons whose eyebrows meet will be lucky in all their undertakings (M, 49, SLC, 1964).

1576  If you find one of your own eyelashes which has fallen on your face or body, you may make a wish (F, 20, SLC, 1964).

1577  If you find an eyelash on you, you should blow it away and you'll have luck (F, 45, SLC, 1930).

1578  If you make a wish on an eyelash, it will come true (F, SLC, 1961).

1579  When an eyelash comes out, put it on your hand, close your eyes and make a wish and blow. If the eyelash is still there, it won't come true (F, 21, SLC, 1964). Cf. Brown 542ff.

1580  If an eyelash is placed on the tip of the little finger, and placed against someone else's little finger, both may make wishes and both will come true (M, Manti, 1970).

1581  When an eyelash falls out, put it on the end of your finger. Close your eyes, make a wish, blow the eyelash from your finger, and your wish will come true (F, 9, SLC, 1964); . . . blow the eyelash over your left shoulder . . . (F, 37, SLC, 1930); If you see an eyelash on your cheek, make a wish, blow it away . . . (F, 46, SLC, 1957). Cf. Brown 547ff.

1582  If an eyelash falls out, throw it over your shoulder for good luck (F, Murray, 1957). Cf. Brown 544.

1583  When you lose an eyelash, blow it away and good luck will follow (F, SLC, 1930).

1584  If an eyelash sticks to your finger and you can't get rid of it, you'll have bad luck (F, 45, SLC, 1930).

1585  If your eyelash twitches, you're full of jitters (M, Provo, 1960).

1586  If you eat an eyelash that has fallen out, it will grow back (F, 19, Sandy, 1969).

1587  Sleeping with vaseline on your eyelashes will make them grow (F, 21, SLC, 1964).

1588  Be careful when the dragonflies or darning needles are around, for they may sew your eyelids closed (M, 43, SLC).

### Nose

1589  It is bad luck to touch your nose before you take a bath (F, 19, SLC, 1950).

1590  Goldenrod causes yellow spots on the nose (F, SLC, 1961).

1591  People's noses never stop growing anytime during their lifetime (F, Ogden, 1958).

1592  If you would like your nose to be less wide, occasionally put a clothespin on it (F, 19, SLC, 1959).

1593  A nose which is too long may be shortened by rubbing it with wet grass on the night of a new moon (F, Orem, 1964).

1594  If your nose twitches, you're going to meet a fool (F, 28, SLC, 1942); . . . itches, you will soon be crossed or vexed by a fool (F, 22, Murray, 1954).

1595  If a person's nose itches, he will become very angry (F, 49, SLC, 1963).

1596  If your nose itches, you'll kick a fool (F, SLC, 1915).

1597  If your nose itches, it means you're about to get mad (M, 44, SLC, 1930).

1598  When your nose itches it means you are going to be coaxed (F, 67, SLC, 1908).

1599  If your nose itches, it's a sign of fright (F, 28, SLC, 1964).

1600  If your nose itches, you are going to fall (F, SLC, 1959).

1601  If one's nose itches, someone is waiting for that person (F, SLC, 1959).

1602  If your nose itches, you will walk with someone with holes in their britches (F, 77, SLC, 1964).

1603  If your nose itches, there are Indians waiting for you in the hills (M, 21, Holladay, 1958).

### Mouth, Lips, Tongue

1604  Devil's darning needles will sew your mouth shut (F, Moab, 1953); Swamp needles . . . (M, 18, SLC, 1950); Dragonflies, if you get near them, . . . (F, Monroe, 1964).

1605  If you stick your lower lip out, it may freeze (F, 19, SLC).

1606  It was believed that the dragonfly or darning needle had the capability of sewing one's lips together (M, 46, SLC, 1926).

1607  If you stick out your tongue, it will get cut off (F, 35, SLC, 1964).

## Teeth

1608  A fat man can eat more food than a thin man because his teeth are harder (M, 18, SLC, 1964).

1609  Spaced teeth mean good luck (F, 56, Orem, 1921).

1610  If your front teeth are spread far apart, it indicates a happy life (F, 45, SLC, 1930s).

1611  If you can get a sixpence between your front teeth, then it means you will be a very lucky person (SLC, 1967).

1612  A gold tooth will bring good luck (F, 44, SLC, 1964).

1613  When you dream about teeth, it is bad luck (F, Ja, SLC, 1964).

1614  If you dream of teeth, you're going to have good luck (F, It, SLC, 1963).

1615  If you get a tooth filled during your monthly period, the filling will fall out (F, 22, Ogden, 1970).

1616  It is bad luck when you dream about your tooth falling out (F, 45, Ja, SLC, 1963); Pulling a tooth is bad luck (M, 64, SLC, 1911).

1617  Old Greek and Italian people believe that if after the extraction of an upper cuspid tooth they were to remain in an airless, darkened room, their face would turn to that of a monkey (M, Price, 1959).

1618  If you touch any teeth that are coming in, they will become jagged (M, 63, SLC, 1951).

1619  If you put your tongue into the hole where you lost a tooth, it will grow in crooked (F, 16, Midvale, 1955).

1620  If you cast a tooth over your left shoulder, all your wishes will come true (M, SLC, 1959).

## Beard, Whiskers, Adam's Apple

1621  Put sour cream on your face and let the cat lick it; you'll grow whiskers on your face (M, 1910); . . . to keep from having whiskers (F, Moab, 1953).

1622  If you shave your beard, it will grow back faster (M, 17, SLC, 1958).

1623  If a woman shaves the hair on her face, it soon turns to whiskers and grows thicker (M, 44, Layton, 1970).

1624  If little girls whistle, they will grow a beard (F, 54, Richfield, 1935).

1625  If you wear beads, it will make your Adam's apple smaller (M, SLC, 1958).

## Shoulders, Breasts

1626  If you look over your left shoulder, it is bad luck (M, Spanish Fork, 1959).

1627  It is unlucky to hand anyone anything over your shoulder (M, 49, SLC, 1964).

1628  I thought if you run up and down stairs without a bra, you'll get big breasts (F, 19, Logan, 1971).

1629  My girl friend told me that if I slept on my stomach that I would develop flat-chested.  Because I got in the habit of sleeping on my back, I still do to this day (F, 17, SLC, 1971).

1630  Little girls who eat the ends of crusts of bread will develop well-rounded busts (M, 52, Du, SLC, 1964).

1631  My sisters and I were all quite flat-chested in our teens.  My grandmother used to tell us to not worry because, "What the Lord has forgotten, you can fill up with cotton" (F, 58, Logan, 1930).

## Ribs, Genitals

1632  Men have more ribs than women (F, SLC, 1964).

1633  If you swallow your gum instead of spitting it out, it will stick to your ribs (M, SLC, 1947).

1634  Colored men have larger sex organs than white men (M, SLC).

1635  A woman with a large mouth has a large vagina (M, SLC, 1925).

# EXTREMITIES

## Arms, Elbows, Muscles, Joints

1636  It's bad luck to fold your arms (F, Gr, SLC, 1942).

1637  A scratch on the left arm means a disappointment (F, Bear River City, 1957).

1638  If you knock your elbow, you will see someone you are very anxious to see (M, SLC, 1944).

1639  If you bump your right elbow, rub it and nothing bad will happen (F, SLC, 1960).

1640  If you bump your left elbow, something nice is going to happen (F, SLC, 1960).

1641  If you eat spinach, you will get big muscles (F, SLC, 1957).

1642  When your joints crack, it means you have not outlived your good days (M, 28, SLC, 1950).

Hands

1643   If your hands are warm, it means you
       have done an evil deed (F, 75, 1964).

1644   Spit in one hand and kiss the other and
       see which one gets fooled the fastest
       (F, 49, SLC, 1964).

1645   Never take anything from someone's hand;
       have them lay it down and then you pick
       it up (F, 17, SLC, 1962).

1646   It is considered bad luck to measure
       your hand against someone else's (M, 21,
       SLC, 1961); Never match hands with
       anyone (F, 24, SLC, 1964).

1647   If you get soot on your hands from the
       chimney sweeper, you'll have good luck
       (F, 19, Ger, SLC, 1963).

1648   If a person turns his hands over and
       over and keeps looking at them, he will
       have bad luck (F, It, Murray, 1958).

1649   Urinate on your hands to make them soft
       (F, 83, SLC, 1964).

1650   If your hand itches, rub it on your
       knee, and it will surely come to me (F,
       SLC, 1955).

1651   If your hand itches, good luck is coming
       (M, 55, SLC, 1964). Cf. Brown 572ff.

Hands - Right, Left

1652   The right hand is good; the left hand
       offsets the good with bad (F, 58, SLC,
       1930).

1653   Your right hand is the lucky hand (F,
       Roosevelt, 1961).

1654   Use of the right hand is normal.
       Substitution of the left hand is
       forbidden because it offsets the good
       (F, 38, SLC, 1930s).

1655   The left hand is evil (F, 76, Marysvale,
       1895); Using your left hand will bring
       bad luck (F, SLC, 1964). Cf. Brown 577.

1656   People who are left-handed are lucky (M,
       SLC, 1946).

1657   Left-handed people are exceptional (F,
       20, SLC, 1958).

1658   The use of the left hand of a right-
       handed person offsets the good (F, 50,
       Murray, 1928).

1659   It's bad luck to eat with a fork in
       one's left hand (M, 18, SLC, 1955).

Shaking Hands

1660   Shake hands with a chimney sweep for
       good luck (M, 1920).

1661   Always shake with the right hand for
       luck (M, 22, SLC, 1963).

1662   If the palm of your right hand itches,
       you will shake hands with a fool (F, 71,
       Woods Cross, 1953); . . . shake hands
       with a stranger (F, 1958); . . . left
       hand itches, shake hands with a fool (F,
       Scot, SLC, 1964).

1663   If your right hand itches, a person
       wants to shake it (M, 45, SLC, 1959).

1664   If your nose itches, you will shake
       hands with a fool (F, 62, SLC, 1964).

1665   Four people crossing arms to shake hands
       is bad luck (F, 45, Farmington, 1950).

1666   Come in the front door and go out the
       back or you will shake hands with a fool
       (F, SLC).

1667   It is bad luck to shake hands with a
       fool (F, 45, SLC, 1961).

1668   Shaking hands across a fence or through
       a window will bring bad luck to the
       other person (M, 23, Ger, W. Jordan);
       . . . will bring you bad luck (F, SLC,
       1960).

1669   It is bad luck to shake hands across the
       doorstep (M, SLC, 1964).

1670   It is unlucky to shake with the left
       hand (F, 21, SLC, 1963).

1671   Never shake hands left handed or the
       devil will shake it (F, 61, SLC, 1965).
       Cf. Brown 577.

1672   Shaking hands with the left hand means
       there is more sentiment in it. The left
       hand is closest to the heart (F,
       Springville, 1959).

Palms, Thumbs

1673   It is good luck to have the palm of your
       hand itch (F, 77, Santaquin, 1914).
       Brown 572.

1674   If your palm itches, you're going to get
       something (Anon, SLC). Brown 573.

1675   Inserting your thumb into your palm and
       wrapping the remaining four fingers
       around it will make your wish come true
       (F, 20, Bountiful, 1965).

1676   If you prick your thumb, something bad
       will turn up soon (F, 25, SLC, 1950).

1677   Making a circle with thumb and index
       finger means "OK" (M, 19, SLC, 1955).

1678   Stub your toe, kiss your thumb (M, 71,
       Santaquin, 1917).

Fingers

1679   If you get bumps on your fingers,
       something will linger; if you get them
       on your thumb, something will come to
       you (F, 50, SLC, 1935).

1680   When in need of good luck, tie a string
       around your finger (F, Tooele, 1964).

1681   To prick one's finger is a sign of bad
       luck (F, 28, Manti, 1942).

1682   It's bad luck to pop your fingers (M,
       19, Swed, SLC, 1964).

1683   Snapping the fingers or a tug brings you
       a lucky break (M, 54, Magna, 1923).

1684   Looking at the moon will make your
       fingers green (M, SLC, 1964).

1685 Open a book with your left hand only, or you'll lose a finger (M, 55, SLC, 1963).

1686 If you cut your finger on nails on Saturday, you will get joy tomorrow (M, 37, SLC, 1935).

## Crossing Fingers

1687 Cross your fingers for good luck (F, SLC, 1958); . . . and you will improve your chances for success (M, 52, SLC, 1950).

1688 Crossing your fingers acts as a safeguard against bad luck (M, 46, SLC, 1964).

1689 You should cross your fingers when you hope for something good (F, 25, SLC, 1950); When you want something good to happen, keep your fingers crossed (F, 74, SLC, 1920).

1690 Cross your fingers and your wish will come true (F, 23, SLC, 1964); . . . after making a wish or planning a new venture (M, Riverton, 1963).

1691 If you cross your fingers on both hands, it's bad luck (F, SLC, 1954); . . . it will bring a jinx (F, 20, SLC, 1958); . . . you'll double cross yourself (F, SLC, 1962).

1692 Crossed fingers behind your back while making a promise means you don't have to keep the promise (F, 20, SLC, 1952).

## Fingernails

1693 Never bite your fingernails. It is an ill omen and bad luck will result (F, 42, Gr, SLC, 1964).

1694 Black spots on fingernails presage misfortune (F, Parowan, 1959); White specks on the nails presage good fortune (M); White under your fingernails means good fortune (F, SLC).

1695 Bruises on fingernails indicate that you are mean to your mother (F, SLC, 1957).

1696 If a person has long fingernails, it is bad luck (M, 20, Cedar City, 1964).

1697 It is bad luck to file your nails on Sunday (F, 44, SLC, 1964). Brown 597.

1698 Large amounts of gelatin dissolved in water and eaten as a food supplement will strengthen fingernails (F, SLC, 1961); Jello will make your fingernails grow (F, SLC, 1961).

## Fingernails - Cutting

1699 It is very good luck to trim the nails of your right hand first (M, 20, SLC, 1964).

1700 It is considered bad luck to cut your nails in another person's house (F, 71, Gr, SLC, 1964).

1701 Never cut your nails on Wednesday or Friday--it stunts your progress (F, 49, Gr, Midvale, 1964).

1702 Never cut your nails on Tuesday or Friday. This will result in bad luck (F, 42, Gr, SLC, 1964).

1703 Cutting your nails on Friday brings bad luck (M, Ogden, 1963). Brown 595n.

1704 It is lucky to cut one's nails on a Friday (F, 27, SLC, 1961). Brown 594.

1705 Trim your nails any day but Friday (F, SLC, 1960).

1706 If you cut your fingernails on Sunday, you will get joy tomorrow (M, 37, SLC, 1949); Don't cut . . . on the Sabbath (F, 23, SLC, 1964).

1707 If you cut your fingernails on Sunday, bad luck will prevail (M, SLC). Brown 598.

1708 You will wish you had never been born if you cut your nails on a Sunday morn (F, Bountiful, 1930). Cf. Brown 604.

1709       Cut them on Monday, you cut them for news.
          Cut them on Tuesday, a pair of new shoes.
          Cut them on Wednesday, you cut them for health.
          Cut them on Thursday, you cut them for wealth.
          Cut them on Friday, a sweetheart you'll know.
          Cut them on Saturday, a journey you'll go.
          Cut them on Sunday, you cut them for evil.
          For all the next week you'll be ruled by the devil.
      (F, 61, Murray, 1963). Cf. Brown 490, 600, 602, 605.

## Legs, Knees, Shins

1710 If a woman makes a bodily gesture in crossing her legs, they should be turned sideways and make sure the dress covers. Don't spread the legs apart when sitting--it is mannish and totally unfeminine. It is also a gross, dirty gesture (F, 19, Logan, 1971).

1711 If you cross your legs in church, they will wither and dry up (F, 40, SLC, 1957). Cf. Brown 609.

1712 A person should never cross their legs at the knees. This denotes that they do not believe in Christ as their saviour (F, Gr, Magna, 1961).

1713 If you drink coffee before you are eighteen, it will make your knees turn black (F, SLC, 1959).

1714 You can't knock a Negro out by hitting him on the chin, you have to hit him on the shins (M, 44, Layton, 1970).

## Feet

1715 If you have a high arch, you will have a good smooth life (M, 42, Ind, SLC, 1964).

1716 If your feet ache, your arches will fall (F, SLC, 1957).

1717    When you go to bed at night, wash the bottom of your feet so when all the impurities drain to the feet during the day they will be washed from the body at night (F, SLC, 1960). (Riddance of disease in folk medicine is often accomplished at the extremities distal from the seat of infection or disease. Divestment takes place through gravity and drainage, as in the present item, or it is brought about by the violent shaking of the hands or the kicking of the feet once the disease has penetrated to the distal points. --Eds.)

1718    When your foot is asleep, two broomsticks placed across it in the shape of an "X" will surely cure it (F, 82, It, SLC, 1963).

1719    If your left foot itches, you will go to a dance (M, 49, Norw, SLC, 1963).

1720    Right foot itches, going to stand on pleasant ground (F, 58, SLC, 1915).

1721    Red pepper in your shoes will keep your feet warm (M, 1930).

1722    For beautiful feet walk in cow dung and chicken droppings (F, SLC, 1964).

## Toes

1723    If you stub your toe, you've done something wrong (M, 27, SLC, 1964).

1724    It is unlucky to stub one's toe (F, Clearfield, 1964); . . . bad luck to stump your toe (F, SLC, 1950); Stubbing left toe is bad luck (F, 46, SLC, 1938). Brown 621.

1725    If you stub your right toe, you will have good luck; if you stub your left toe, you will have bad luck (M, 36, SLC, 1935).

1726    If you stump your toe, you have to stop, step back and step over it or you'll have bad luck all day (F, SLC, 1954).

1727    If your second toe is longer than your big toe, it is a sign you are from a royal family (F, Ogden, 1958).

1728    If your second toe (the one next to the big toe) is the longest, you'll be the boss in your family (F, Bear River City, 1957).

1729    Webbed toes will give you luck all your life (M, 93, St. George, 1897).

1730    If someone has hammer toes, they will come to a bad end (F, SLC, 1966).

## Toenails

1731    It is very good luck to trim the nails on your right foot first (M, 20, SLC, 1964).

1732    Don't cut your toenails unless you ask one of your parents or else one of them will get seriously hurt (F, SLC, 1960).

1733    Never cut your toenails on Sunday or it will ruin the rest of the week (F, 39,

Swed, SLC, 1930); . . . it's bad luck (M, 52, Eng, SLC, 1963).

1734    When the moon grows cut your toenails; otherwise you will have ingrown toenails (F, Swiss, SLC, 1965).

## INTERNAL ORGANS

### Brain

1735    Brain breathing:  The brain needs oxygen to function.  Lean over as far as possible placing your head between the knees and inhale and exhale as fast as possible.  This will refresh the brain (M, 18, Sandy, 1953).

1736    Brains and beauty rarely go together (F, SLC, 1961).

1737    A man that goes bald young has lots of brains--hair and brains don't go together (F, Moab, 1953).

1738    When sewing on a garment while it is being worn, either mending it in any way or sewing on a button, if the person whose clothes are being mended does not chew on a piece of thread, his brains will be sewed up (M, 50, It, SLC, 1965).

1739    If you eat an animal's brain, your own brain will grow (F, Fillmore, 1960).

1740    Fish is a brain food.  Fish is said to contain phosphorus which the brain also contains.  Since both contain phosphorus, fish should be good for the brain (M, 61, SLC, 1930); Many people eat fish, believing it makes you smarter and causes you to learn faster (M, 48, MD, SLC, 1964); . . . makes the brain grow healthy (F, 75, Murray, 1964); . . . will enhance your mental powers (F, 21, SLC, 1950).

1741    Seafood is brain food (F, SLC, 1955).

1742    Celery is brain food (M, SLC, 1964).

1743    Lettuce is good to make the brain grow healthy (F, 75, Murray, 1964).

1744    Tomatoes clear the brain (F, Kanab, 1960).

### Heart, Stomach

1745    You should always sleep on the right side of your body or the heart may be crushed (F, Holladay, 1959).

1746    Every time you sneeze, your heart skips a beat (F, SLC, 1961; . . . your heart stops beating (F, SLC, 1960).

1747    If you bite your nails, they will lodge together in your stomach and poke holes in you (F, 19, Orem).

1748    Asparagus will pierce holes in your stomach, if you eat it on Friday (F, 54, SLC, 1915).

1749    If you swallow gum, it will stick your stomach together (F, 49, Bountiful, 1960).

1750  If you drink coffee, your stomach will turn black (F, 19, SLC).

## BODILY FUNCTIONS

### Arising

1751  Before getting out of bed wiggle your toes seven times to insure a lucky day (F, 49, SLC, 1942).

1752  Drink hot water before breakfast in order to get the system awake (M, 24, SLC, 1964).

1753  To arise early in May means a long troubled day (F, SLC, 1961).

1754  It is said if you get out of bed late, you will be angry with someone during the short part of the day that is left (M, 27, Logan, 1963).

1755  It is bad luck for a whole day if one doesn't arise before 9 A.M. on that day (F, 89, Dan, Crescent); . . . before 1 P.M. (F, 61, Swed, Midvale).

1756  Be pleasant until ten o'clock in the morning and the rest of the day will take care of itself (F, 10, SLC, 1964).

1757  When you get up in the morning and the first thing you see is a woman, you will have bad luck, and if you see a man, it will bring you good luck (F, Ger, SLC, 1959).

1758  Don't get out of bed on the wrong side. Sure as you do everything goes wrong (F, 23, SLC, 1964); . . . you'll have a bad day (F, Vernal, 1935); . . . you'll be cross and irritable (F, 1959); . . . you'll be grouchy all day (F, SLC, 1925); . . . you'll be hard to get along with (F, 51, Centerfield, 1964); . . . you'll have bad luck (M, 21, SLC, 1963); . . . you'll have an angry disposition (M, 27, SLC, 1964); . . . you'll be ornery for the rest of the day (F, 1960); . . . be out of sorts (F, 61, SLC, 1964); . . . be in a bad mood all day (F, 19, SLC, 1964); . . . be cranky (F, Farmington, 1958).  Cf. Brown 3103.

1759  If you get up on the wrong side of the bed you will hurt someone's feelings that day (F, SLC, 1964).

1760  If you are cross, it is a sign that you got up on the wrong side of the bed.  If you go back to bed and get up on the other side, the spell will be broken (F, SLC, 1958).  Cf. Brown 3103.

1761  If you don't get out of bed on the same side you got in, you'll have a rotten day (F, 46, SLC, 1930s); Don't get out of bed on the opposite side from where you sleep (F, Nephi).

1762  If you get out of bed on both feet, you can be sure not to start the day on the wrong foot (F, 20, SLC, 1963).

1763  If you get out of bed on the right side or on the right foot, you'll be happy all the day (M, 52, Du, SLC, 1964); . . . you must put out the right leg first; if the left leg is first then something unpleasant will happen or you

will be in a bad mood all day (M, 63, Russ, SLC, 1955).

1764  When you get out of bed in the morning, get out on the right side and put on your right shoe or you'll have bad luck (M, 28, SLC, 1963).

1765  It'll cause bad luck for anyone who gets up out of bed in the morning with his left foot first on the floor (M, SLC); . . . will be cross all day (M, SLC, 1960); . . . be grouchy during the day (F, SLC, 1958).

1766  Don't get out of bed on the left side or you will have bad luck all day (F, 65, SLC, 1945); . . . be cranky (F, SLC, 1952); . . . be in a bad mood (F, SLC, 1964); . . . be grouchy (F, 21, SLC, 1964).

1767  To take the first step of the day with the left foot is unlucky (F, SLC, 1953).

### Bathing

1768  If you throw water off your hands in the morning, you will lose your good luck all day (M, SLC, 1957).

1769  If you take a bath after you eat, you may have bad luck (F, SLC, 1961); It is not good to bathe immediately after eating (M, 1930).

1770  The first Monday after the second Friday you can't bathe (F, 63, Provo, 1915).

1771  It is bad luck to take a bath in the morning (F, SLC, 1961).

1772  If you take a shower before going on a hike, you won't get lost (M, 22, SLC, 1965).

1773  If two persons wash in the same water at the same time, it means bad luck unless one of them spits in the water (F, 25, Provo, 1963); It is bad luck to share the same wash basin (M, 52, Cedar City, 1964).

1774  Never have two people wipe on the same towel at the same time or they will both have bad luck (F, 53, SLC, 1964); . . . two people wipe hands on the same towel (F, 54, Ger, SLC, 1964).

1775  Wash and wipe together, you will live in peace together (F, 47, SLC).

### Breathing, Crawling

1776  Milk cuts your wind (M, SLC, 1964).

1777  Crawling under a fence means bad luck (M, 49, Lindon, 1920).

### Crying

1778  It is bad luck to cry before you have eaten in the morning.  If you do cry before eating, your whole day will be ruined and nothing will seem to go right (F, 29, Tooele, 1964).

1779  To sneeze twice before breakfast on Friday, you'll cry on Sunday (M, 27, SLC, 1964).

1780  If the hem of one's dress is turned up, one will cry during the day (F, 64, 1961).

1781  If you spill the salt, you will cry as many tears as there are grains of salt spilled before the day is over (F, SLC, 1958).

1782  If you spill salt, you will cry before the day is over (F, 25, Bountiful, 1964); . . . spill salt before dinner . . . (F, Ger).

1783  If you dream of grapes, you will have a bad cry during the next day (M, SLC, 1963).

1784  If you throw water out of the window, you will have cause to cry (M, 21, SLC).

1785  If you take laughing gas, you will cry (M, 19, Provo).

1786  He who talks too much will cry when others laugh (F, Bear River City, 1957).

## Crying - Eyes

1787  If your right eye itches, you will cry soon (F, Tooele, 1964).  Brown 536.

1788  The rubbing of your eye is a sign that you will soon cry (M, 27, SLC, 1964).

1789  If the nerve in your left eye twitches, it is a sign you will cry (M, SLC, 1957).  Cf. Brown 539.

## Crying - Singing, Whistling, Laughing

1790  Sing before breakfast, cry before dinner (F, Milford, 1959); . . . cry before supper (F, SLC, 1957); . . . cry before night (F, SLC, 1959); . . . cry before bed (M, SLC, 1910); . . . before the sun goes down (M, SLC, 1959); . . . cry before you sleep (M, 90, SLC, 1880); . . . cry before noon (M, Murray, 1959). Cf. Brown 2845ff.

1791  If you sing at the breakfast table, you will cry before night (M, SLC); If you sing at the dinner table, . . . cry before you go to bed (M, SLC).

1792  Sing before seven, you'll cry before eleven (F, SLC, 1957).

1793  If children wake up singing they will go to bed crying (F, Murray, 1915).

1794  Sing at supper, cry at night (F, 24, SLC, 1964).

1795  Singing after you go to bed means you'll cry before morning (F, SLC, 1961); Sing in bed and you'll cry the whole night through (F, Moab, 1953).  Brown 3088.

1796  Whistle before breakfast, cry before night (F, 52, SLC, 1964); . . . cry before dinner (F, SLC, 1962).

1797  Laugh before breakfast, you'll cry before night (F, 54, Logan, 1970); . . . cry before supper (F, Ogden); . . . cry before dinner (F, 63, Gr, SLC, 1963); . . . cry before lunch (F, 23, SLC, 1963); . . . cry before noon (F, 85, Ger, SLC, 1961).  Brown 2854.

1798  Laugh with the light, you'll cry before night (F, 1925); If you laugh in the early morning, you'll cry before night (M, Layton, 1946); If you laugh before seven, you'll cry before eleven (F, SLC, 1958).

1799  If you go to bed laughing, you will wake up crying (F, SLC, 1949).  Brown 3092.

1800  If you laugh before you eat, you cry before you sleep (M, Salem, 1958).

1801  If you laugh at the table, you'll be crying in half an hour (M, SLC, 1958); A person who laughs a lot early in the evening will cry before he goes to bed (F, Payson, 1959).

1802  Laugh today and you will cry tomorrow (F, Hyrum, 1950s).

1803  Laugh on Sunday, cry on Monday (F, Clearfield, 1959); Laugh on Friday, cry on Saturday (F, 52, W. Jordan, 1964).

## Dieting, Digestion, Dizziness

1804  A person can lose weight by drinking lemon juice or vinegar (F, 21, Richfield, 1958).

1805  Pine gum was chewed to aid in digestion (M, SLC, 1946).

1806  If you get dizzy whirling, whirl the other direction to unwind yourself (M, 41, SLC, 1964).

## Dreaming - General

1807  A dream is sometimes regarded as an experience in which the soul of the sleeper leaves the body. For this reason one should not waken a sleeper suddenly. His soul might not find its way back to the body (F, Clearfield, 1964).

1808  Dreams are the actual adventures of the spirit that has for a time left the body (F, Midvale, 1964).

1809  People dream real things before they happen (M, 23, SLC, 1964).

1810  Dreams last only a few seconds and occur right before you wake up (F, 20, SLC, 1955).

1811  When you dream about going to war, it is good luck (M, 45, Ja, SLC, 1963).

1812  Dreaming of blood means trouble ahead (F, 49, SLC, 1963).  Cf. Brown 8502.

## Dreaming - Special Persons, Animals

1813  Dream of a man, it is a fortunate omen-- to dream of a strange man, but not of a strange woman (F, SLC, 1957).

1814  When you dream about fish, the next day will be a bad one (F, SLC, 1960).

1815  If you lay a chip of wood under a sleeping dog's head, you will have the same dream he is having (M, Ogden). Brown 3115.

## Dreams Come True

1816    If you dream in color, it will come true
(F, 20, Logan, 1970).

1817    If you talk about a bad dream, it might
come true (F, 45, SLC, 1948).

1818    If you dream about something long
enough, that something is going to
happen to you or someone else.  It will
come true (M, 19, SLC, 1954).

1819    If you dream a dream more than six
times, it will come true (F, SLC, 1971).

1820    The first time you sleep in a new house,
if you count all the windows, the dream
you dream that night will come true (F,
24, SLC, 1964).  Cf. Brown 3116.

1821    To sleep in a strange bed for the first
time--your dreams will come true (M, 23,
SLC).

1822    Sleep under a new quilt and your dream
will come true (F, 41, SLC, 1940).
Brown 3121.

1823    Sneeze at the table and your dreams will
come true (F, 45, SLC, 1926).

1824    If you don't tell of a dream, then it
will come true (F, Brigham City, 1929).

1825    If one dreams just before breakfast, the
dream will come true (M, 34, SLC, 1940).

## Dreams Told Before Breakfast

1826    If you have a bad dream and tell it
before breakfast, it will come true (M,
SLC, 1962); Tell your dream before
breakfast if you want it to come true
(F, 1959).

1827    Don't tell dreams before breakfast on
Sunday, if you don't want them to come
true (F, SLC, 1957).

1828    Tell your dream before breakfast and it
will not come true (F, Bountiful, 1959).

1829    To tell a dream before breakfast is
unlucky (F, 45, SLC, 1933).

## Telling Dreams - Days, Time

1830    If you dream on a Friday night and tell
the dream the next day, the dream will
come true (M, 98).  Cf. Brown 3137.

1831        Friday night dreamed,
        Saturday told,
        Is sure to come true,
        Though ever so old.
(F).  Cf. Brown 3139f, 3142.

1832    Never tell your dream on Saturday that
you dreamed the night before (F,
Fillmore, 1960).

1833    If you tell your dream before sunup, it
will come true (M, 37, SLC, 1947).
Brown 3132.

## Dreams - Good and Bad Luck

1834    I've heard it said if you dream of
finding eggs, you are going to have good

luck (F, Moab, 1953); To dream of seeing
eggs is bad luck (F, Springville, 1924).

1835    If you dream of fire, the more flames,
the more lucky (F, 56, Ger, SLC, 1946);
. . . you will have bad luck (F, 24, Ja,
SLC).

1836    A dream of silver indicates good luck
(M, 50, It, SLC, 1965).

1837    If you dream of green, usually green
scenery, it signifies good luck because
green is the color of hope (F, 18, SLC,
1961).

1838    If you dream of clear water, it's good
luck (M, 39, SLC, 1964); . . . cloudy or
muddy water it means bad luck (F,
Midvale, 1962).  Cf. Brown 3109.

1839    If the person you are dreaming about
doesn't die, as in your dream, good luck
will come to them (F, It, SLC, 1963).

1840    If you dream of oil, then it is good
luck (M, Gr, SLC, 1962).

1841    It is bad luck if you dream of eating
(F, 80, Springville, 1924).

1842    If you dream of a hatchet, you will have
bad luck (M, SLC, 1961).  Cf. Brown
8512.

1843    Dream of rosary being given to you means
bad luck (F, 57, SLC, 1963).

1844    A dream of paper money foretells bad
luck (M, 50, It, SLC, 1965).

1845    If you dream of excrement, it is bad
luck (M, Gr, SLC, 1962).

## Dreams - Foretelling Trouble, Worry, Etc.

1846    If you dream of rain, you will
experience some unpleasant event the
next day (M, 73, Gr, SLC, 1963).

1847    To dream of fire means that there is
going to be trouble within the family
(SLC, 1962).

1848    If you dream of smelling smoke and can't
find the source, you will have a lot of
worry (M, SLC, 1961).

1849    If you dream about fruit out of season,
it brings trouble without reason (F,
Magna, 1918); . . . dream of things out
of season, you'll hear of things out of
reason (F, SLC, 1920s).

1850    If you dream of awful commotion, you'll
hear something bad (F, 74, Granite,
1964).

1851    If you dream of people eating, you will
have something terrible happen (F,
Joseph, 1964).

1852    If you dream of a rough wind, it means
treachery will be prevalent (F, 82, It,
SLC, 1963).

1853    If you dream of eggs, you are going to
have trouble (F, Bear River City, 1957).

1854    Dream of a fall:  To fall from a height
is a sign of misfortune, and the longer

the distance of the fall, the greater the coming trouble (F, SLC, 1957).

## Dreaming Three Nights in a Row

1855   Dreaming about the same thing three times in succession is a sure sign of the dream's fulfillment (M, SLC, 1964). Brown 3130f.

1856   Dream the same dream three times or more and it will come true (F, SLC, 1960); . . . the fourth day it will come true (F, 25, SLC, 1965).

## Dreams Go by Opposites

1857   Dreams forecast future just opposite (F, Copperton).  Cf. Brown 3123f, 8500.

1858   Dream of tears:  A contrary sign-- happiness awaits you (F, SLC, 1957).

1859   Dream of danger:  If you face it, you may expect success.  But if you avoid it, trouble will come (F, SLC, 1957).

1860   Dream of failure means success in real life (F, SLC, 1957).

1861   Dream of riches--unfortunately this is a dream of the contrary.  The more flourishing your affairs in your visionary world, the worse they will be in real life (F, SLC, 1957).

## Bad Dreams, Nightmares

1862   If you put your nightwear on wrong side out, you will have bad dreams (F, 75, Tooele, 1964).

1863   If you sleep on a feather mattress which has been turned on Sunday, you will have bad dreams for a week (F, SLC, 1952).

1864   If you have a bad dream, someone walked over your grave (F, 20, SLC, 1949).

1865   Reptiles bring troubled and fearful dreams (SLC, 1957).

1866   Bad dreams are caused by rich foods (F, SLC, 1959); If you eat before going to bed, you will have bad dreams (F, SLC, 1955); Bad dreams are caused by the food you eat before going to bed (F, 43, Logan, 1936).  Cf. Brown 2855.

1867   Eat a piece of pie before sleep and you will always have bad dreams (F, SLC, 1910).

1868   Don't eat raw hot dogs before going to bed or else you will have bad dreams (F, 46, Sandy, 1963).

1869   When a bad dream wakes you up at night, wipe your hand across your forehead, and you will forget it before morning (F, 40, SLC, 1926).

1870   If you have a bad dream, it won't come true if you don't tell anyone about it (F, 45, SLC, 1964).

1871   If you place your shoes neatly side by side at the edge of your bed when you retire, you will never have dreams that

you are being chased and cannot get away.  You can step quickly into your shoes and elude any pursuer (F, St. George, 1954).  Cf. Brown 3122.

1872   To cure yourself of bad dreams, hang a sock over your bed and you will no longer have them (F, 17, SLC, 1961). Cf. Brown 5663.

1873   To cut out bad dreams, sleep with a knife under your pillow (F, SLC, 1959). Cf. Brown 5706f, 5671f.

1874   It was believed that the topaz when placed under one's pillow or worn about one's neck would prevent bad dreams (F, 19, SLC, 1964).

1875   Sleeping with your head at the bottom of a bed will cause nightmares (M, 23, SLC).

1876   If you eat a large meal before going to bed, you will have nightmares (F, 18, SLC, 1955); Nightmares are caused by what you ate before you went to bed (M, 64, SLC).

1877   If you have meat for dinner, you'll have nightmares (F, SLC, 1960).

1878   If you eat a pickle before you go to bed, you'll have nightmares (F, 19, SLC, 1958).

1879   If you eat fresh strawberries, you will have nightmares that night (F, 20, SLC, 1964).

1880   If you don't eat your greens, you'll have nightmares (F, Logan, 1971).

1881   Never relate a nightmare before breakfast.  It will come true (F, SLC, 1957).

1882   If you go to sleep on your back, you will not have nightmares (SLC, 1947).

1883   Take one full teaspoon of honey before going to bed and you'll have no nightmares (F, 18, Huntington, 1968).

## Dreams - Miscellaneous

1884   Many people believe that smoking hashish before going to bed will make you have vivid in-color dreams called "hashish dreams."  I have smoked a lot of hash at bedtime and I didn't notice any significant alteration in my dream experience (F, SLC, 1971).

1885   If you dream of seeing soldiers, something good will happen quickly (F, Gr, SLC, 1962).

1886   If you dream of fire, you are too warm (M, 25, SLC, 1945).

1887   My wife believes and practices the superstition that her dreams are indicative of the children's behavior for the approaching day (M, Magna).

1888   Dream of hills:  These must be looked upon as obstacles.  If you succeed in climbing the hill, you will put things right with perseverance.  The easier the ascent, the better for your future (F, SLC, 1957).

1889   If you dream of hearing a cello, you will have a moving experience (M, SLC, 1956).

1890   If you dream of red, then something good will happen quickly (F, Gr, SLC, 1962).

1891   Dream of watching:  To dream of watching from a window or high place signifies you are being spied upon.  If you have secrets, guard them well (F, SLC, 1957).

1892   To dream that you go to school and cannot say your lessons right, shows that you are about to undertake something you do not understand (F, SLC, 1957).

1893   It is considered a fortunate omen to dream that you are at a party, but it is unfavorable if you yourself give the party, and the smarter the function, the worse the omen (F, SLC, 1957).

1894   If you have a dream that you can't understand, write it on the wall facing south.  When the sun shines on it, you'll be able to interpret it (F, 20, SLC, 1959).

1895   If you dream of a calm wind, it is a sign of a helping hand (F, 82, It, SLC, 1963).

## Drinking

1896   Don't drink water with your meals, it's bad for you (F, 20, SLC, 1964).

1897   You must drink at least eight glasses of water per day (M, Ogden, 1961).

1898   Drink coffee and you'll turn black (F, 80, Eng, Midvale, 1913).

1899   Drinking hot drinks on a hot day will make you cooler (F, Marysvale, 1961).

1900   If a fly is found in your drinking glass, it is good luck (M, 19, SLC, 1964).

1901   If your eyebrow itches, you are going to drink (F, 49, Salina, 1964).

1902   You should never drink water right at midnight.  It's "dead water" and will bring bad luck (F, 69, Swed, SLC, 1917).

1903   Water is fattening (F, SLC, 1961).

1904   If you can see the rocks in the bottom of a river, the water is safe enough to drink (M, SLC, 1957).

1905   Water drunk from the ground is somehow cleansed of all impurities (M, 22, SLC, 1959).

1906   If you're drinking out of a spring, don't move somewhere else and start drinking, it will bring bad luck (M, 48, SLC, 1964).

## Social Drinking, Heavy Drinking

1907   The last drink taken from a bottle on New Year's Eve will bring good luck to the drinker (M, 19, SLC, 1961).

1908   When drinking you should always go to higher alcoholic contents, never the reverse.  That is from beer to wine, to whiskey, never from whiskey to wine to beer (M, SLC, 1958).

1909        Wine and whiskey, mighty risky
             Whiskey and beer, never fear.
       (F, 49, SLC, 1954).

1910   To drink a beer with an egg in it is good luck (M, SLC, 1957).

1911   Before you drink champagne, if you rub a little bit behind your ear, you'll have good luck (F, SLC, 1955); It is good to put foam from the top of the champagne behind your ear (F, 1955).

1912   Never pour a glass of whiskey back into the bottle (M, SLC, 1930).

1913   It is bad luck to take the last drink from a whiskey bottle (M, 65, SLC, 1964).

1914   If a glass is used for beer, never use it for anything else (M, 37, Linden, 1964).

1915   You only stir martinis twenty-one times to the left or else the gin turns sour (M, 21, SLC, 1957).

1916   When drinking from a whiskey bottle, if one turns the bottle upside down before you drink it, you will have good luck (M, 19, Kaysville, 1959).

1917   Drinking champagne out of a slipper is good luck (F, 23, SLC, 1962).

1918   If you spill an alcoholic beverage, it means good luck will come your way (F, 41, Gr, SLC, 1964).

1919   If you get drunk on bootlegged liquor, you will have three years of bad luck (F, 19, Czech, S. Jordan, 1945).

1920   Alcohol affects brilliant people more than dull people (M, Ogden, 1956).

1921   If the weather is cold, drinking whiskey will warm you up (M, 24, SLC, 1964).

1922   A man should never drink alone as it means something bad will happen or has happened (M, 37, SLC, 1950).

1923   Drinking a lot of alcoholic beverages will give you a rosy nose (F, 46, SLC, 1938).

## Portents and Causes of Inebriation; Prevention

1924   If you splash water on a dress or apron, then your husband will come home drunk (F, 23, Murray, 1964).

1925   Aspirin in coke can make you drunk (F, 15, Bountiful, 1955).

1926   The amethyst is worn to prevent intoxication (M, 20, SLC, 1950s).

1927   Eat something before you drink any kind of liquor and the alcohol won't affect you so rapidly (F, Tooele, 1957).

### Hangover Cures

1928    The best way to get rid of a hangover is
        to have another drink (M, 22,
        Farmington, 1958).

1929    For a hangover eat honey.  It helps
        neutralize the acid of alcohol (M, 21,
        Logan, 1972).

### Drunks, Drunkards

1930    Tendencies toward alcoholism are
        inherited (F, SLC, 1961).

1931    If you pick marigolds, or even look at
        them long, you will take to drink (F,
        29, SLC, 1943).

1932    A person who has a red nose is an
        alcoholic (F, 21, SLC, 1962); People
        born with red noses . . . (F, 21, SLC,
        1960).

1933    Drunks see pink elephants (M, 19, SLC,
        1963).

1934    To cure a husband of drinking to excess,
        put a live eel in his drink (M, SLC,
        1953).

### Dropping Things, Eating

1935    If you drop something, it's because you
        subconsciously wanted to (M, 40, Logan,
        1960).

1936    It is unhealthy to eat the first snow
        that falls (M, 44, Layton, 1970).

1937    One should eat only those foods which
        are natural in his area (M, SLC, 1964).

1938    Never eat or drink anything that is not
        approximately body temperature because
        it is not good for the system.  It could
        even kill you (M, 57, Bountiful, 1964).

1939    If you eat before you go to the dentist,
        then your mouth will not take to
        novocaine (F, 21, SLC, 1956).

1940    You should never eat two starches or two
        fruits at the same meal (F, SLC, 1960).

### Falling, Jumping

1941    It is a good luck sign to fall out of
        bed.  It means you will live another
        year (M, 26, Tooele, 1962).

1942    To jump out of a window is considered
        bad luck (M, 20, SLC, 1964).

### Kissing

1943    If the number on your bus ticket adds up
        to forty-one, it means a kiss (M, SLC,
        1964).

1944    Come in the front door and go out the
        back or you will be kissed (M, 77, SLC,
        1963).

1945    The first girl that enters under a
        mistletoe all the members of the
        household all get to kiss (F, Moab, 1953);
        Kissing under the mistletoe insures good
        fortune (SLC, 1964).

1946    If you kiss the Blarney stone, you will
        have good luck (M, SLC, 1961).

1947    It is bad luck to be kissed by a fool
        (F, 45, SLC, 1961).

1948    It is bad luck to dream of kissing (M,
        56, SLC, 1960).

### Bodily Portents of Kissing

1949    If your left ear itches, you are going
        to be kissed (F, Woods Cross, 1957).

1950    When your eyes itch, that is the sign
        that you are going to kiss a fool (F,
        27, SLC, 1954).

1951    If your teeth itch, it means you want to
        be kissed (F, SLC, 1957).

1952    If your lips are chapped, you need to be
        kissed (F, 21, SLC, 1963).

1953    If your upper lip itches, a man with a
        mustache will kiss you (F, 28, SLC,
        1944); . . . lips itch, you're going to
        kiss a fool (F, Moab, 1953); . . . lips
        itch, it is a sign you want to be kissed
        (M, 23, Murray, 1964).

1954    If you get a hair in your mouth, you are
        going to kiss a fool (M, 39, SLC, 1964);
        . . . hair on your tongue . . . (M, 53,
        Logan, 1930).

1955    If your nose itches, you will kiss a
        fool (M, SLC, 1961); . . . blue-eyed
        fool (M, SLC, 1951); . . . it is a sign
        you will be kissed (F, 55, SLC, 1964);
        . . . kiss a stranger (F, 20, W. Jordan,
        1957); If you have a twitching nose, you
        will kiss a fool (M, SLC, 1920); . . .
        scratch your nose, you will kiss a fool
        (F, 55, SLC, 1964); If your nose itches,
        your mouth is in danger; you'll be vexed
        by a fool and kissed by a stranger (F,
        39, SLC, 1964); . . . nose tickles, kiss
        a fool (F, London, 1943).  Cf. Brown
        4161.

1956    Sneeze on Tuesday, kiss a stranger (F,
        Farmington, 1959).

1957    If the palm of your right hand itches,
        you will be kissed by a fool (F, Woods
        Cross, 1953); If your left hand itches
        . . . (F, 28, Scot, SLC, 1964).

### Domestic, Clothing Indicators of Kissing

1958    If you drop a knife, you will kiss a
        fool (F, 50, SLC, 1963).

1959    If a woman puts on a man's hat, she must
        kiss him (F, 47, SLC, 1927).

### Laughing

1960    Bad luck to laugh before breakfast (F,
        SLC, 1957).

1961    Cry before you eat, and you will laugh
        before you sleep (F, SLC, 1958).

1962    If you cry before eleven, you will laugh
        before seven (F, Roy City, 1964).

1963    If the nerve in your right eye twitches,
        it is a sign of laughter (M, SLC, 1957);

. . . left eye itches . . . (F, SLC, 1960).

1964 To dream you cry means that you will laugh when you are awake (M, 40, Orem, 1964).

## Masturbation

1965 Masturbation causes hair to grow on the palm of the hand (M, 21, Spanish Fork, 1961).

## Menstruation

1966 If a woman eats watermelon or tomato during menstruation, she will have severe cramps (M, SLC, 1957).

1967 A woman who has a great deal of discomfort during her menstrual period will have much less pain during childbirth than the woman who has little discomfort (F, MD, SLC, 1960). Told to her by many patients.

1968 If a woman doesn't menstruate, she will collect an accumulation of poison in her body (F, MD, SLC, 1960). Told to her by many patients.

1969 The moon controls the menstrual cycle of a woman (M, teacher, Wendover, 1964).

## Interdictions During the Menses

1970 Never get out of bed on the first day of your monthly period (F, 22, Ogden, 1955).

1971 During menstruation a girl must not exercise, take a bath, swim or go on a date (F, 21, Ogden, 1960).

1972 A girl shouldn't eat or drink anything cold during her menstrual period (F, MD, SLC, 1960). Told to her by many patients.

1973 A girl shouldn't eat anything sour during her menstrual period (F, MD, SLC, 1960). Told to her by patients; . . . should not eat pickles (F, Bear River City, 1957).

1974 A girl shouldn't wash her hair during her menstrual period (F, MD, SLC, 1960). Told to her by patients.

1975 A woman shouldn't take anything to relieve menstrual discomfort or she will not be prepared for the pain of childbirth and it will be worse (F, MD, SLC, 1960). Told to her by patients.

1976 You should not have a tooth pulled while menstruating (F, 1925).

1977 Don't have a tooth filled during menstruation. The filling won't last (F, SLC, 1933).

## Pointing, Reading

1978 It is bad luck to point at something (F, 22, Syracuse, 1949). Brown 580.

1979 Never read the last page of a book first; you will not only ruin the book but also the day (F, 22, SLC, 1960); Don't read the ending of a mystery first (F, 31, SLC, 1964).

## Sexual Intercourse

1980 You should never make love when there isn't a moon (M, 24, SLC, 1950).

1981 If you eat before sex, you will not satisfy your partner (M, Logan, 1970).

1982 Dreaming of snakes means you're thinking of sex (M, 29, SLC, 1964).

1983 Masturbation will alter the climax period in later sexual intercourse (Anon, Tooele, 1955).

1984 Sex on Thursday after midnight will bring those people bad luck. Refrain from doing so (M, 20, SLC, 1964).

1985 A theory is that every female child has a tiny cleft of depression in the end of her nose, and that this depression disappears after sexual intercourse (M, Bountiful, 1961).

1986 Girls are like buses. They come every fifteen minutes (M, 20, Bountiful, 1960).

1987 The sex urge increases in the springtime (M, 18, SLC, 1964).

## Shaving, Sitting

1988 Shave the right side of your face first to avoid cuts. The right side is less prone to cuts (M, 20, Provo, 1959).

1989 If you sit in your house in the same direction of the bathtub, you'll have good luck (F, 21, SLC, 1964).

1990 You mustn't sit on anything that does not have legs (M, 50, It, SLC, 1965).

## Sleeping

1991 If you accidentally bump heads with someone, you will sleep with them (M, SLC, 1958).

1992 Cats will suck a sleeping person's breath (M, 56, SLC, 1964).

1993 Never sleep in a household that doesn't have a Bible (F, 90, SLC, 1964).

1994 Don't sleep in room number thirteen (M, 20, SLC, 1950).

1995 Be sure to look under your bed at night to scare away any evil spirits (F, W. Jordan, 1961).

1996 Never sleep with your foot dangling over the side of the bed, else it'll get bitten off (F, 46, Midvale, 1927).

1997 If you get up with the sun, you should go to bed with it also to avoid misfortune (M, SLC).

1998 Sleep where night overtakes you. Otherwise misfortune will come (F, SLC, 1963).

1999   When you sleep at a strange house, check to see what side you are on when you wake up. If you are on your right side, you'll have good luck. If you are on your left side, you'll have bad luck (F, 41, SLC, 1964).

2000   It is important to be in bed before the sun comes up, or you will not sleep comfortably for the next week (M, 71, SLC, 1964).

2001   You get more out of sleep before twelve midnight than you get after that hour. You sleep deeper before (F, 20, SLC, 1958).

2002   An hour of sleep before midnight is worth two after midnight (M, SLC, 1959); The sleep you get before midnight is the best sleep that you get all night (M, Midvale, 1940). Brown 3083.

2003   Any sleep before midnight is "beauty sleep." Therefore, if you want to be handsome, go to bed early (F, 40, SLC, 1964).

2004   It is bad luck to lie on your face at night (M, 47, SLC, 1964). Heard in Kansas, 1935.

2005   Never step over a sleeping person's body (F, 49, SLC, 1964).

2006   An odd number of hours of sleep at night will make the person grouchy and irritable (M, SLC, 1961).

2007   Three in a bed is considered bad luck (F, SLC, 1960).

2008   It is unsafe and bad luck to wake a person out of a sound sleep (F, SLC, 1966).

## Peaceful Sleep; Inducing Sleep

2009   Spearmint and peppermint tea are good for putting you to sleep (F, 87, Providence, 1970).

2010   Parsley tea and dandelion greens are good for putting you to sleep (F, 87, Providence, 1970).

2011   A nightly honey and milk drink will lull any person to sleep (F, 55, SLC, 1964).

2012   Counting sheep will help one to sleep (F, 19, SLC, 1964).

2013   When you go to bed, make sure the toes of your shoes point in the same direction or else you will not have a good night's sleep (F, SLC, 1958).

2014   Put your shoes under the bed before you retire with the toes pointing under first, and you will sleep better (F, 42, Bountiful, 1964). Heard in Tennessee, 1944.

2015   If you want to sleep well, sleep on your right side (F, SLC, 1959).

## Position in Sleeping

2016   Never sleep with your head to the west. That is the way they bury the dead (F, SLC, 1958). Heard from Blacks in Oklahoma in 1938; When you sleep at night, your head should be facing the west (F, SLC, 1958).

2017   You should sleep with your head turned to the east or south never toward the north, because they bury the dead with their heads toward the north (F, 48, Ja, SLC, 1963).

2018   You aren't supposed to sleep with your head to the east for that is the way dead people are buried (M, 23, Ja, SLC). Cf. Brown 3079.

2019   You should sleep with your head pointing north and your feet pointing south (F, 46, Scot, SLC, 1964). Cf. Brown 3077.

2020   Lying on your left side when sleeping will let your left side be more relaxed (F, SLC, 1961).

2021   Don't sleep on your left side (F, Springdale, 1951).

## Troubled Sleep; Sleeping with Stranger

2022   If your shoes are above your head, you won't be able to sleep (F, 18, SLC, 1957). Brown 3082.

2023   If you leave your shoes pointing toward the bed at night, you will not sleep well (M, 46, SLC).

2024   If an elbow itches, you will be sleeping with a strange bedfellow (F, 19, SLC, 1960). Cf. Brown 3071.

## Talking, Walking in Sleep

2025   The soul of a person leaves him when dreaming, so you should not awaken sleepwalkers (F, 70, SLC, 1964); One must never awaken a sleeper lest his spirit be away on a journey (M, 69, Sterling, 1920).

2026   Hold a mirror over a sleeper's face and he will answer any questions you ask him (Bear River City, 1957).

2027   If you look at a full moon, you'll talk in your sleep (F, SLC, 1956).

2028   When a person talks in his sleep or sleepwalks during the night, never call his name because he may lose his voice (F, 51, Gr, SLC, 1957).

2029   Pull on the toe of a person asleep, if you want him to talk, or snip scissors by his ear (F, SLC, 1957).

2030   If someone is talking in his sleep, put his hand in cold water and he will tell you all about it (F, 89, SLC, 1964). Brown 3099f.

## Smelling

2031   Musk is a lucky odor (M, 47, SLC, 1946).

2032   Only bad or unpleasant smelling odors are dangerous (F, SLC, 1961).

## Smoking

2033  Cure a cowboy from smoking by cutting up ten strands of hair from his horse's tail and putting it into his Bull Durham (M, 44, Layton, 1970).

2034  When you smoke, burn the brand name or you'll have bad luck (M, 15, Orem, 1964).

2035  Only female marijuana plants will stone you (F, SLC, 1971).

## Sneezing

2036  Your spirit leaves the body when you sneeze (F, 42, SLC, 1963).

2037  A sneeze is a sign that a devil or evil spirit is trying to get out of your body (F, 21, Springville, 1964).

2038  If you sneeze in your house, the room is overheated (M, 31, SLC, 1959).

2039  Sneezing is good luck (M, 25, SLC, 1964).

2040  If one sneezes in a group of people, what is being said will come true (M, 48, Vernal, 1933).

2041  If you sneeze to the left, you'll have bad luck, but to the right you'll have good luck (M, 22, SLC, 1960).

2042  When you sneeze, you are very close to death (F, 48, Ogden, 1964).

## Sayings after Sneezing

2043  When you sneeze a spirit leaves the body.  To turn it into a good omen say, "God bless you"  (F, 45, SLC, 1923); Say "God bless my soul" every time you sneeze (F, Moab, 1953).

2044  When a person sneezes, a spirit is supposed to leave the boy.  That is where the phrase, "Gesundheit" originated (M, SLC, 1964).

2045  Saying "God bless you" after a person sneezes averts bad luck which could otherwise follow a sneeze (F, 21, SLC, 1964).

2046  If you sneeze, you must say "Febuta" or else you'll have bad luck (M, 23, It, SLC, 1964).

## Days of the Week

2047  Sneeze on Monday, sneeze for danger.
Sneeze on Tuesday, kiss a stranger.
Sneeze on Wednesday, receive a
  letter.
Sneeze on Thursday, something
  better.
Sneeze on Friday, sneeze for sorrow.
Sneeze on Saturday, see your lover
  tomorrow.
Sneeze on Sunday, your safety seek,
Or the devil will have you the rest
  of the week.
(F, SLC, 1958).  Cf. Brown 562.

2048  Sneeze on Monday, sneeze for news.
Sneeze on Tuesday, a new pair of

shoes.
Sneeze on Wednesday, you'll get a
  letter.
Sneeze on Thursday, something
  better.
Sneeze on Friday, sneeze for danger.
Sneeze on Saturday, kiss a stranger.
(F, Bear River City, 1957).  Cf. Brown 561.

2049  If you sneeze on a Sunday, you will have a very unsafe week (F, SLC, 1964).  Cf. Brown 559.

## Preventing, Stopping, Inducing Sneezing

2050  Look at the sun if you feel like you are going to sneeze (M, 48, SLC, 1964); . . . to prevent sneezing (F, 39, Coalville, 1933); If you have to sneeze but can't, look at the sun (F, Bear River City, 1957).

2051  If you have to sneeze but don't want to, press hard between your nose and your upper lip (F, Bear River City, 1957).  Cf. Brown 552f.

## Number of Sneezes

2052  A person who sneezes twice is a happy person (M, 29, SLC, 1964).

2053  To sneeze rapidly three times is a good omen (M, 20, SLC, 1964).  Cf. Brown 554.

2054  If you sneeze once, you'll sneeze three times (F, 19, SLC, 1964).

2055  Sneezing three times brings good luck, but sneezing a fourth time sneezes it all away (F, 85, SLC, 1964).

2056  Sneezing three times in a row will bring bad luck (F, 20, SLC, 1964).  Brown 554n.

2057  If you sneeze rapidly three times it is a good omen.  Sneeze once for a dill; twice for a letter; and three times for a wish, and four times for something better (F, Axtell, 1958).

2058  To sneeze four times in succession is good luck (F, 44, SLC, 1964).

2059  If you sneeze before a meal, however many times you sneeze, there will be that many more or that many less for the next meal (F, Moab, 1953).  Cf. Brown 558.

2060  If you sneeze five times, there is going to be a war (F, 18, SLC, 1954).

## Snoring, Spitting

2061  To make someone stop snoring, put his hand in water (F, 51, SLC, 1944).

2062  Spitting on the hands brings good luck (M, SLC, 1964).

2063  Spitting at a person means good luck (F, SLC); Spit after someone and you wish them good luck (F, 49, Norw, SLC, 1963).

2064  It causes bad luck to spit on anyone else (F, 19, SLC, 1955).

## Seeing, Looking

2065    If you stare at a person's back, you can make him turn around and look at you (F, SLC, 1958).

2066    If a person sees a beautiful girl the first thing in the morning, it will bring them good luck. If they see an elderly person first in the morning, it will be bad luck the rest of the day (F, 60, SLC, 1910).

2067    As a child my grandmother was told by her grandparents never to take a second look or look back at someone or she would turn into a pillar of salt (F, 70, SLC, 1964).

2068    It is good luck to see a person of whom you have just been speaking (M, Ger, SLC, 1965).

## Stepping

2069    When you step out of your house, you should go out with the right foot for good luck (F, 22, Ogden, 1964).

2070    Step in a hole and you break your mother's sugar bowl (F, Logan, 1970).

2071    If you step on a stake in the sidewalk which is really the boundary line between two properties, you may slug the next person that comes by (F, 20, SLC, 1954).

2072    If you see a pack of Lucky Strike cigarettes, step on it. If you don't step on it, bad luck will follow (M, Provo, 1959); . . . step on it and hit the closest person to you and say "lucky strike, no strike back" (F, 26, Magna, 1953).

2073    When you see a metal slug on the ground, step on it for good luck (F, 50, SLC, 1963). (See also Nos. 12573 and 12574.)

2074    Never purposely step on a crack in a sidewalk or you will cause your mother to have bad luck (F, Murray, 1940).

2075    Stepping on a crack in the sidewalk brings evil to someone you love (F, 11, SLC, 1964).

2076    Stepping on the sidewalk brings bad luck (M, 52, SLC, 1964).

2077    If you step on the cracks on a sidewalk, you will get bad luck for as many years as cracks that you step on (M, 61, Cedar City); . . . it will bring disaster to you (F, SLC, 1915).

2078    Skip the cracks in a sidewalk and don't step on corners of the curb (M, 45, SLC, 1963).

## Stepping Over

2079    It is bad luck to step over a person lying down (M, 46, SLC, 1929). Brown 615.

2080    If a person is sitting on the floor and someone steps over him, the person must step back over him the opposite way or

he will have bad luck (M, 24, Ogden, 1950s). Brown 616.

2081    One must not step over a fire, except during ceremonies (M, SLC, 1965).

## Stepping on Footprints, Blood, Shadow, Etc.

2082    If a person steps on the feet of anyone who is sitting, it is bad luck (F, 21, SLC, 1958).

2083    Don't follow in footprints or it will bring bad luck (F).

2084    It's bad luck to step in blood (M, Layton, 1934).

2085    One must not step on the shadow of another, for it brings bad luck to both persons (F, 45, Murray, 1925).

## Tripping, Stumbling

2086    If you stumble, you have to go back around the part of the sidewalk on which you stumbled before going on (F, 30, Ogden, 1950).

2087    It is bad luck to stumble or trip at the beginning of the day (M, SLC, 1959).

2088    After tripping one must step backwards seven steps or one will have bad luck (F, 22, Ogden, 1952); . . . three steps backwards . . . (M, SLC, 1938).

2089    If a person stumbles before leaving the house in the morning, it is a sign that the rest of the day will be a bad one (M, SLC, 1965).

2090    If you trip yourself, it's because you subconsciously wanted to (M, Logan, 1960).

## Urinating

2091    If you smell a dandelion, you'll wet your pants (F, 25, SLC, 1964).

## Walking

2092    Going upstairs backwards changes your luck (M, 42, SLC, 1964).

2093    It is bad manners to keep in step with the person you are walking with (M, 19, Ja, SLC, 1945).

2094    If you walk on the left side of the street, you'll have bad luck all day (M, 66, SLC, 1923).

2095    Never walk over a boarded hole (F, Murray, 1957).

2096    It is unlucky to walk under the grounding wire of a telephone pole (F, 16, SLC, 1958).

2097    It is bad luck to walk under a bucket filled with paint (F, Ger, SLC).

2098    It is bad luck to walk on the curb side of a telephone pole (M, 19, SLC, 1964).

2099    It is bad luck to walk between two poles (M, SLC, 1961).

2100    If you retrace your footsteps, it is bad luck (M, 19, SLC, 1961).

2101    Jay-walking brings bad luck (M, 19, SLC, 1961).

2102    If you walk along a picket fence, you must touch each picket or you'll have bad luck (F, 40, Ogden, 1935).

2103    Every time you walk under a telephone pole with a stabling wire extending to the ground, you must cross your fingers or it will mean bad luck (F, 19, SLC, 1964).

2104    Don't walk over an open manhole (F, SLC, 1964).

2105    To be able to walk the length of nine rails along the railroad track without stepping off will bring good luck that day (F, SLC, 1912); . . . seven rails without falling off . . . good luck (F, 18, Brigham City, 1960).

2106    Never walk between the ties on a railroad track (M, Orem).

2107    When crossing railroad tracks, never take more than one step in between tracks (M, Orem).

2108    If you walk on someone else's crutches, something will happen to you so that you'll have to use crutches too (M, 25, SLC, 1964).

## Divisive Objects While Walking

2109    If a man and woman walk on opposite sides of poles, they will have bad luck (M, 31, SLC, 1963).

2110    If a person is walking down the street and he lets his girl friend walk on the outside, this will bring him bad luck (M, 35, SLC, 1940).

2111    It's bad luck for two persons to separate and walk on opposite sides of a tree (M, 24, SLC, 1949); . . . they should walk around it together in the same direction (F, 50, SLC, 1964). Brown 3595.

2112    Never allow anyone to pass between you and your companion while walking together.  This brings bad luck (F, SLC, 1964); Two people should walk on the same side when passing a lamppost or fire hydrant (F, SLC).  Brown 3594.

2113    When you and another person are walking together and you approach a post or sign, if both of you walk on opposite sides of it and at the same time say "bread and butter," good luck follows (F, 41, SLC, 1963).  Learned in Canada, 1932; When two people walk on opposite sides of a telephone pole it is unlucky not to say "bread and butter" (F, 20, SLC, 1963); If two guys are going down the street and they split a post, the youngest should go back and go on the same side as the older or bad luck will come on him (F, 20, Price, 1950).

2114    If two people are separated by an obstacle, they cross their fingers so that they won't have bad luck (F, SLC, 1959).

## Wishing

2115    Hook little fingers with your friend to make a wish and say:
        I say chimney, you say smoke,
        Then our wish will never be broke
        (F, 19, Logan, 1963).

2116    If you wish bad luck on someone, you'll get it yourself (M, 21, Crescent, 1955).

2117    If the number on your bus ticket adds up to seven, it means a wish (M, 19, Ogden, 1964).

2118    If you take the middle stick of gum, you get to make a wish (F, 24, SLC, 1964).

2119    If you see an empty Lucky Strike cigarette package, step on it and very lightly hit the closest person next to you and make a wish, and the wish should come true (F, 21, American Fork, 1960).

2120    If you see a man with a patch over his left eye, you can make a wish (F, 18, SLC, 1961).

2121    Make a wish while untangling you hair (M, SLC, 1960).

2122    If while drinking soft drinks one's straw happens to be through a round piece of ice, this person gets one wish which will only come true if this person is not kissed before one week's time (F, 18, Midvale).

2123    Make a wish and throw something over your left shoulder (F, 70, SLC, 1964). Heard in Kansas City, 1901.

2124    If you turn around three times, it will help make a wish come true (F, 47, SLC, 1961).

2125    If you repeat a wish ten times, it will come true (F, 36, SLC, 1965).

2126    If once a person has made a wish and he tells the wish, the wish will not come true (F, 26, SLC, 1964).

2127    If you want something, you should wish on a wishing well (M, 12, SLC, 1960). Cf. Brown 8507.

## Yawning

2128    Always cover your mouth when yawning to stop bad spirits from getting in (F, 52, SLC).  Heard in South Carolina, 1920s.

2129    If you yawn in a crowd, pretty soon everyone will yawn (F, Moab, 1953).

## BODILY ATTRIBUTES

## Appetite

2130    Years ago children were given a tonic of sulphur and molasses every spring to make them healthier and give them a better appetite (F, 19, SLC).

2131    You should never eat when you have no appetite (F, Swed, SLC, 1960).

## Athletic Prowess

2132   Swallowing a fish's bladder will make you a swimmer (F, Midvale, 1964). Brown 647.

2133   Wearing red clothes makes you have more pep (F, 43, Bountiful, 1960).

## Beauty

2134   Smoke follows beauty (M, 44, Layton, 1970). Cf. Brown 675f.

2135   Yogurt is an aid in retaining beauty (M, Delta, 1961).

2136   To become beautiful wash your face in dew before sunrise on May Day (M, 37, SLC, 1948).

2137   On your face moles are supposed to be beauty marks (F, Moab, 1953).

2138   Eating carrots will make you beautiful (F, 44, SLC, 1963). First heard in Kansas City, Missouri, 1935.

2139   A widow's peak is a sign of beauty (F, 1958). Brown 674.

2140   If you have blue eyes, you'll be a beauty (F, SLC, 1959).

2141   If your nose doesn't have a bump on it, it's a sign of beauty (F, 47, SLC, 1964).

2142   If you eat raw chicken hearts, you will be good looking (F, Ogden, 1961). Cf. Brown 677ff.

## Complexion

2143   Natural things that I use for skin care are egg whites to tighten the skin and oatmeal for a masque (F, 19, Logan, 1971).

2144   One whipped egg white and a tablespoon of honey applied regularly to the face will result in a beautiful complexion (M, Logan, 1969).

2145   Honey is a fine cosmetic. There is no hand lotion as good for the face and hands as honey (F, Woods Cross, 1953).

2146   For an unblemished face, catch rainwater in a clean vessel during the last days of the month of April and the first four of May, and pour it into a glass vessel so that it will keep. The water will become as bitter as violet water or rose water (M, 50, It, SLC, 1965).

2147   Peaches and cream gives you a good complexion (F, 21, SLC, 1963).

2148   Buttermilk on the skin will bleach and soften it, and it is good against sunburn (F, Logan, 1968).

2149   They used buttermilk and cornmeal mixed together for your complexion (F, Moab, 1953).

2150   Washing your face in milk will improve complexion (M, SLC, 1957).

2151   Use vinegar in water (bath water) to cleanse your pores and allow your pores to breathe (M, SLC, 1964).

2152   Lemons are good for the skin (F, 20, Logan, 1971).

2153   Sagebrush tea will make you have a good complexion (M, Lehi, 1957).

2154   Use boiled quaken [sic] asp bark for a poor complexion (M, 55, 1971).

2155   If you eat raw carrots, you'll have a clear complexion (F, 55, Logan, 1926).

2156   Fresh cow dung facials are very good for the complexion (F, Bear River City, 1957).

2157   Baby urine is good for the complexion (F, Moab, 1953).

2158   For wrinkles eat ten to a dozen dry prunes every day (F, 56, Can, SLC, 1964).

2159   I used to think if you ate chocolate and too much of it, your face would be one big zit (blemish) (F, 19, Logan, 1971).

2160   Wearing red and blue helps hide the blemishes on your face (F, SLC, 1971). Learned in New York.

## Eyesight

2161   Rapid improvement in vision of old people is a good sign (F, 19, SLC, 1964).

2162   If you eat a lot of carrots, you will be able to see very well in the dark--like a cat (M, 27, SLC, 1964).

2163   If you eat a carrot without shaving the skin off, your eyesight will improve twice as much as it would if you peeled the skin off first (M, 58, Logan, 1970); . . . you never have to wear glasses (F, 43, SLC, 1937); You will go blind if you don't eat carrots (F, 55, SLC, 1964).

2164   Yellow fruits and vegetables are best for eyesight (M, 59, Dan, SLC, 1964).

2165   Pumpkins are excellent for eyesight (F, 28, SLC, 1964).

2166   Ground soybeans will give you good eyesight. It is said that you will be able to see clear to Tokyo (M, 45, Ja, SLC, 1963).

2167   Pierced ears help improve eyesight (F, 55, SLC, 1914).

## Fat

2168   One who drinks water with meals will get fat or temporarily bloated (M, Holladay, 1959).

## Growth

2169   Drinking liquor stunts the growth and impairs one's health (M, 20, SLC, 1964).

2170   Smoking will stunt a man's growth (M, SLC, 1960).

2171 If you drink coffee when you are young, it will stunt your growth (M, Ogden, 1961).

2172 If you cross over someone, the person will cease growing (F, SLC, 1960). Brown 638.

2173 If you step on a grave, you will never grow anymore (M, 28, SLC, 1964). Learned in South Carolina, 1952.

2174 If you let your hair grow too long, you will stunt your growth (M, 18, SLC, 1952).

2175 One should never carry a rake or a broom on his shoulders, or he will stop growing (F, SLC, 1920).

2176 To stop your growth, place a brick on your head (F, 19, SLC, 1950).

2177 Spinach will make you grow (F, SLC, 1961).

## Height

2178 Drinking milk will make you grow taller (M, 23, Provo, 1964).

2179 One will grow tall if he drinks well water (F, 43, Logan, 1935).

2180 If you put a broom on your shoulder, you'll only grow as tall as one (F, Ja, SLC, 1960).

2181 To grow tall, put a piece of grass in your shoes (F, SLC, 1961).

## Homosexuality

2182 You are queer if you wear green on Thursday (F, 14, SLC, 1963); You are weird . . . (F, 22, Logan). Heard in California, 1960.

2183 If you wear yellow on Thursday, it means you're queer (M, 33, 1960).

2184 Homosexuals are incapable of whistling and snapping their fingers (M, 21, SLC, 1965).

## Impotency

2185 The act of withdrawal during intercourse will result in impotence in the male (M, SLC).

2186 Eating vinegar will make a man impotent (F, 50, Midvale, 1963).

## Longevity

2187 The first one to wake up on the wedding night will live the longer of the two (M, SLC, 1961).

2188 Never have your bed facing the east if you want to live a long life (M, 30, Magna, 1930).

2189 Mummy powder is supposed to confer longevity (F, Midvale, 1964). (Is mumia meant here? --Eds.)

2190 If someone meets you and he does not recognize you, you will live long (M, 22, SLC, 1964).

2191 When you light a candle with your left hand, you are shortening your life by three days (M, SLC, 1963).

2192 If you gossip you can look for a short life (F, SLC, 1941).

2193 When you wind your watch backward and forward, you are shortening your life span (F, 27, SLC, 1956).

2194 The number of times you can walk the brick wall around Emo's grave in Salt Lake Cemetery determines how many more years you will live (M, Provo, 1972).

## Parts of Body as Signs of Longevity

2195 Heavy eyebrows are a sign of long life (M, 1961).

2196 If three moles form a triangle, the person will die at a very young and innocent age (M, 43, SLC, 1933).

2197 If the palms of your hands are always cold, it means your life will be very short (F, Dan, SLC).

2198 The length of the lifeline in the palm of the hand denotes the length of one's life (F, 49, SLC, 1963). Cf. Brown 666f.

2199 A long line around the thumb means a long life; a short line means a short life (F, 61, SLC, 1910).

2200 To cut your hand across the lifeline shortens your life (F, 80, Eng, Midvale).

2201 If a person is fat, he will die early (M, SLC, 1964).

2202 A person with a big earlobe will live for a long time; a small earlobe, a short life (M, 45, Ja, SLC, 1963). Cf. Brown 670.

2203 Tall people always die before short ones (M, SLC, 1964).

2204 A space between your teeth means that you will have a long life (F, 50, SLC, 1963).

2205 If the wisdom teeth cut through before the age of twenty, it means a short life (F, SLC, 1961).

## Eating, Drinking, Foods to Promote Longevity

2206 If you drink seawater every day from the time you are a child, you will live to a ripe old age (F, 23, SLC, 1950).

2207 To keep from getting old, drink buttermilk all your days (F, SLC, 1961).

2208 A shot of whiskey every day will insure long life (M, SLC, 1964).

2209 Drinking a glass of wine before dinner will prolong a person's life (F, 71, SLC, 1900).

2210   Eat yarrow whenever you can--at least once a week--raw, out of the garden. It will make you live until you're eighty (M, Hurricane, 1969).

2211   If a person eats black pepper, for each time he eats it his life will be shortened by one day (M, SLC).

2212   You must never pay back borrowed salt or it will shorten your life (F, 60, Weber).

2213   If your soup continues to boil after you take it off the heat, the cook will live to a good old age (F, 24, SLC).

2214   For every piece of food a person wastes, it will deduct a minute from a person's life (F, 46, Midvale, 1927).

Dreams as Prognostics of Longevity

2215   A dream of death will add years to your life (M, 50, It, SLC, 1965). Cf. Brown 649.

2216   If in a dream you see someone drowning, then you (the dreamer) will live a long life (F, 20, SLC, 1964).

Clothing, Jewels, Gold as Prognostics of Longevity

2217       Change your underwear in May,
           Wither your life away.
       (F, 53, SLC, 1918).

2218   Wearing a diamond will prolong a person's life (F, 61, Magna, 1922).

2219   If you wear a ruby, you will be assured of a long life (M, 20, St. George, 1964).

2220       If you fall for gold,
           You will become old.
       (M, SLC, 1957).

Plants, Animals as Portents of Longevity

2221   Ginseng is able to prolong life, and even restore it after death (M, Vernal, 1959).

2222   If one carries an acorn, he can be insured of a long life and general good luck (M, 29, Union, 1950).

2223   Eating the seeds of a grape will lengthen one's life span (F, SLC, 1963).

2224   On New Year's place bamboo and plum and fir tree in a wreath on the porch for courage, long living (F, 51, Ja, W. Jordan, 1963).

2225   If someone sends you lilies, it is an indication that you will have a long happy life (M, SLC, 1958).

2226   Count the number of buzzards that you see flying overhead. The number that you see will be the number of years you live (M, 67, SLC, 1936).

2227   When whippoorwills sing together at night making the sound "hohin, hohin" one should reply "no." If the birds stop singing at once, it is a sign that the hearer will die soon; but if the birds continue their singing, it means a long life instead (F, SLC, 1961).

2228   Never under any circumstances whip a dog, or it will bring bad luck to you. If the dog happens to die as a result of your whipping him, then you are destined to lead a short life (M, 21, Richfield, 1954).

2229   To find a snail in your yard will mean that your life will be long (M, SLC, 1961).

2230   It'll shorten your life to burn spiders (M, Ogden, 1961).

Sexual Change

2231   If you kiss your elbow, you will turn into a girl (F, 19, SLC, 1964).

Sexual Powers, Virility, Masculinity, Femininity

2232   Wheat germ is for sexual potency (F, Murray, 1964).

2233   Good teeth are a sign of sexual weakness (F, SLC, 1961); Bad teeth mean sexual prowess (F, SLC, 1961).

2234   A popular singer has the belief that Wheaties make him more virile (F, 49, SLC, 1964).

2235   Eggs and oysters incite to venery (F, Marysvale, 1900).

2236   Eating seafoods causes a man to be more virile (M, 20, SLC, 1954); . . . Rocky Mountain oysters . . . (F, 49, SLC, 1954).

2237   Wet dreams are signs of virility in the male (M, 29, SLC, 1964).

2238   The more virile men are bald (F, 23, SLC); Bald-headed men are the best lovers (M, SLC, 1952).

2239   "You're chewing ice"--means you're oversexed and horny (M, SLC, 1969).

2240   A man who can dance well is a man who will make a good lover (M, 43, It, SLC, 1930s).

2241   Latins are good lovers (F, 54, SLC, 1963).

2242   Men with a great deal of hair are more masculine (M, 21, SLC, 1960).

2243   One who looks at his hands with the fingers up is feminine (M, 19, SLC, 1963).

2244   Long eyelashes signify masculinity (M, 51, SLC, 1943).

Strength

2245   The weaker person with a superior wit wins the contest over a person with great strength (M, 21, SLC, 1962).

2246   Feathers of eagles bring strength (M, 21, SLC, 1950s).

2247 If you tie the white stones from the rooster to your right foot and say, "The Lord is a man of war," you will become strong (M, 25, Je, 1965).

2248 The Indians used to wrap the skin of a blacksnake around their bodies to make them strong (F, Moab, 1953).

2249 War paint makes a warrior stronger (F, 20, SLC, 1950).

## Eating, Drinking

2250 The eating of an animal's heart gives a man strength, courage and compassion (M, 18, SLC, 1964). Cf. Brown 646f.

2251 Drinking blood makes one strong (F, 45, SLC, 1963).

2252 Eating rare meat will make you strong (M, SLC, 1957).

2253 If you eat fish, it makes you stronger (F, SLC, 1964).

2254 To feel strong, take water from a rain barrel containing iron rust (M, 54, Magna, 1923).

2255 Eating spinach will make you strong (F, SLC); . . . twice as strong (F, 52, SLC).

2256 To eat garlic gives strength (M, SLC, 1960).

2257 If you eat raw eggs, it will give you extra energy (F, 30, Ja, SLC, 1964).

2258 If you leave your last bite of bread at the dinner table, then you leave your strength (F, 29, Gr, Magna, 1964).

2259 If you eat a certain kind of rice cake on New Year's, you will be nice and strong for the rest of the year (M, 45, Ja, SLC, 1963).

2260 An olive pit brings strength (M, Magna, 1963).

## Bodily Signs

2261 A man with lots of hair on his body is supposed to be strong (F, Moab, 1953).

2262 Long hair and whiskers are considered signs of strength (M, Beaver, 1964).

2263 Men with beards are usually physically stronger than those without beards (M, 33, 1964).

2264 Hairy chests are a sign of strength (F, 80, Spring City, 1930); Hair on the arms is a . . . ; Hairy arms are a sign of vigor (M, Tooele, 1957).

2265 Brown eyes denote strength (F, SLC, 1962).

## Thirst

2266 A pebble in your mouth will stop you from being thirsty (M, 49, Lindon, 1926). Brown 660.

2267 Spilling the first bit of a glass of water on the ground will make sure that you will never be thirsty (F, SLC, 1961).

2268 To alleviate suffering from lack of water, put a bullet in your mouth (F, 41, SLC, 1930).

## Virginity

2269 When I was in junior high school, my friends and I used to peel gum wrappers apart and if they tore, then that proved you weren't a virgin (F, 22, Logan, 1963).

2270 If a boy or girl can successfully peel off the label of a beer bottle, she or he is rightly claimed a virgin (F, SLC, 1971).

2271 If you have a widow's peak on your head, it means you're a virgin (M, 18, Magna, 1963).

2272 If a girl who is a virgin dreams she is pregnant, she should guard her virginity very closely, for she is soon to lose it (M, 63, Ogden, 1964). Learned in Wyoming, 1926.

## Weakness

2273 A heavy head of hair will sap the strength from a woman's body (F, Moab, 1953).

2274 No hair on a man's chest is a sign of weakness (F, 69, SLC, 1964). Heard in Ohio, 1910.

## Youth

2275 Yogurt is an aid in retaining youth (M, Delta, 1961).

2276 If a lady carries an acorn in her pocket or bag, she will be blessed with perpetual youth (F, Mt. Pleasant, 1960); . . . in her purse . . . (F, 1959).

2277 Young girls should wear an asafetida necklace to retain their youth (M, 52, SLC, 1960).

2278 If you want to regain your youthful appearance, eat snakes (M, 18, Sandy, 1959). Cf. Brown 10.

2279 Only young Indian maids are allowed to work on native woven blankets, so that the vitality of youth may be woven into the blanket to make it last a long time (F, 18, Provo, 1956).

2280 Some people still search for the fountain of youth (F, Roosevelt, 1964).

## PERSONALITY PROJECTION, SHADOW, IMAGE, PICTURE, PHOTOGRAPH, ETC.

2281 You must not let anyone step on your shadow, for if they step on it, it will injure your soul (F, 80, SLC, 1915).

2282 A picture or a reflection of a person is believed to possess part of his spirit, or to be his soul (F, SLC, 1964).

2283   Never look at your reflection through a double thickness of glass (F, 42, SLC, 1943).

2284   Some people believe that a picture captures their spirit (M, 49, Ogden, 1964); . . . if a photograph is taken of your body, you lose part of your spirit (M, SLC, 1961); . . . a picture of a person possesses part of his soul (M, 49, SLC, 1920).

2285   If a photograph in a frame is dropped and the glass breaks, a painful accident will befall the subject of the photograph (F, 21, Provo, 1964).  Cf. Brown 3052, 5064ff.

2286   You should not have your picture taken, because it can be defiled (M, 20, SLC, 1963).  Cf. Brown 634.

2287   It's bad luck to be photographed with a cat (F, 69, Payson, 1903).

2288   Never take a picture with three people because the middle person will have bad luck (M, 45, Ja, SLC, 1963).

2289   Never take a picture of a dead person or draw a picture of them.  If you do, they will bring bad luck to you and your family (M, 59, Richfield, 1924).

2290   If you stare at yourself in a mirror, your image will slap your face (F, SLC, 1958).

## Miscellaneous

2291   Everyone has a double somewhere in the world (M, SLC, 1957); . . . a twin (M, 34, SLC, 1954).

2292   It is bad luck to meet one's double (M, Bingham, 1957).

2293   If two men cut their arms and hold them together, they'll become blood brothers (M, 23, Magna, 1956).

2294   A coin or shell or pebble carried by a person becomes imbued with his personality (F, 85, Grantsville, 1964).

2295   Go to the cemetery, bury a dishrag, turn around three times, and you can change your name to one of your choosing (F, SLC, 1958).

## MENTAL ABILITIES, BRAIN POWER, MIND, KNOWLEDGE

2296   Baldness is a sign of unusual mental powers (F, SLC, 1959).

2297   People with high foreheads have many brains (M, 25, SLC, 1959).

2298   If a person has large feet, it's a sure sign of knowledge (F, SLC, 1957).

2299   Left-handed people are naturally bright (M, 18, SLC, 1955).

## Genius, Good Student, Intelligence

2300   A single white hair means genius.  It must not be pulled out (F, 60, SLC, 1964).  Learned in Idaho, 1920.

2301   Glasses are a sign of studiousness (M, 51, SLC, 1963).

2302   A person that is tall will be a good student (M, SLC, 1957).

2303   If you have a big head, you have more intelligence (M, SLC, 1957).

2304   To determine a person's intelligence one should study his countenance (F, SLC, 1961).

2305   Wide-set eyes indicate intelligence (M, 24, Ogden, 1950).

2306   Large ears are a sign of intelligence (F, 68, SLC, 1926).

2307   A long nose is a sign of intelligence (F, 57, SLC, 1964).

2308   A high forehead is a sign of intelligence (F, 71, Woods Cross, 1953); A wide forehead is a sign of high intelligence and leadership (F, 26, Bountiful, 1940s); A high brow . . . (F, SLC, 1957).

2309   If someone had a widow's peak, it's a sign of great intelligence (F, SLC, 1966).

2310   A receding hairline signifies intelligence (F, SLC, 1964).

2311   Men with fine light hair are intelligent and conceited (M, SLC, 1960).

2312   Big feet are a sign of intelligence (F, SLC, 1960).

2313   Small handwriting is a sign of intelligence (F, 1958).

2314   Messy writing is a sign of intelligence (M, 51, SLC, 1963).

2315   A left-handed person tends to be more intelligent and superior in the fields of study and practical work than the right-handed person (M, SLC, 1961).

2316   Eating fish makes you intelligent (F, SLC, 1950s).

## Quick-witted, Smartness, Wisdom

2317   Those who eat a lot of fish will be quick-witted (M, 58, Ger, SLC, 1963).

2318   A person with a high forehead is smart (F, 19, SLC, 1951).

2319   Left-handed people are naturally smart (M, 32, SLC, 1935); . . . smarter (M, Columbia, 1964).

2320   Eating calf brains makes a person smart (M, SLC, 1957).

2321   Fish will make you smart, if you eat it (F, 80, Eng, Midvale).

2322   If you eat carrots, you will become very smart (F, SLC, 1957).

2323   Itching skin foretells wisdom (M, 23, SLC, 1964).

2324   Lumps on your head are a sign of wisdom (M, SLC, 1957).

2325  If you eat crumbs, it will make you wise (F, 19, Granger, 1964).

2326  If you keep a key you have found, it will give you great knowledge (F, 19, SLC, 1964).

## ESP, Telepathy, Sixth Sense, Etc.

2327  A blind man is blessed with the power of revelation (M, SLC, 1960).

2328  If you have hooded eyes you are telepathic (F, SLC, 1963); . . . can see into the future (F, 20, Ogden, 1955).

2329  If you concentrate hard enough on an item, you can make it move (F, 18, W. Jordan, 1960).

2330  It is a common belief that the voices of the dead and the communication with the dead can be done by concentrating on some object of furniture belonging to them (M, 20, SLC, 1963).

## ARTISTIC ABILITY

2331  I've always heard if you have short, stubby fingers, you'll be an artist (F, Moab, 1953).

2332  Long, slender fingers mean the person is artistic by nature (M, SLC, 1950); . . . an artistic person (M, Provo, 1940s).

2333  A right thumb crossed over a left indicates artistic inclination (F, 21, SLC, 1963).

2334  People with black hair are very artistic (F, Bountiful, 1964).

## Dancing Ability, Musical Ability

2335  If your foot itches, you are going to be a dancer (F, SLC, 1959).

2336  I've always heard if you have long, tapering fingers, you'll be a great pianist (F, Moab, 1953); . . . a musician (F, Moab, 1953).

2337  When teeth are well separated, it signifies a fine voice (M, 38, dentist, SLC, 1963).

2338  Eat anything burned and it will make you a good singer (M, 71, Santaquin, 1920s).

## CHARACTER AND PERSONALITY

2339  A woman who stomps when she walks will be a work horse. If she trips lightly, she will be important (F, Eng, Hooper, 1963).

2340  Your character can be read by the bumps on your head (F, SLC).

2341  You can judge a person's character by looking at his face (F, SLC, 1958); . . . by looking at him (M, 30, Ogden, 1964).

2342  Looking people in the eye may be used as a criterion for judging people (F, SLC, 1958).

2343  The color of a girl's hair will give you a clue to her character (M, 58, Provo, 1963). Heard in Houston, 1910.

2344  A heavy growth of hair on a man denotes character (F, Moab, 1953).

2345  Find a nail and someone will attack your character (M, 1959).

2346  A person's handwriting shows and determines a person's personality. If he writes tall, it shows he is optimistic (M, SLC, 1964).

2347  People believe that if a person has a facial change, it changes their personality also (F, 21, SLC, 1962).

2348  If you are scared of the dark, you have a guilty conscience (F, 43, SLC, 1940).

## Adulterous

2349  If the veins on a woman's breast form the letter "A" she will become an adulteress (F, SLC, 1961).

2350  When the veins on the right hand form an "A," it means that if this is a female, she will become an adulteress (F, SLC, 1961).

2351  If a woman is unfaithful to her husband, she will take on a sulphur smell. This is the way you can detect unfaithfulness (M, 26, Ogden, 1963). (The sulphurous smell of the adulteress indicates that she likely fell victim to the enticements of the devil, with whom these acrid fumes are often associated. --Eds.)

## Affectionate

2352  A person with cold hands is considered to have a very warm heart and is very affectionate (F, SLC, 1961).

2353  Big eyes with little white means you're affectionate (M, 19, SLC, 1964).

2354  A woman with her slip showing will prove to be quite affectionate (M, 54, SLC, 1964).

## Aristocratic, Good Breeding

2355  Long noses are aristocratic (M, 24, Ogden, 1950).

2356  No hair on a man's chest is a sign of good breeding (F, 46, SLC, 1964). Heard in Ohio, 1938.

## Bad or Poor Character

2357  If you have close-set eyes, you are a bad person (M, SLC, 1964).

2358  Redhaired people are not good (M, Gr, SLC).

2359  If a dog does not like a man, it is a sign the man has a bad character (M, Nephi, 1961).

2360  A person with a receding chin has a weak character (M, SLC, 1959).

## Bad Tempered, Hot-Tempered, Etc.

2361  If the eyebrows meet, one is ill-tempered (M, 28, SLC, 1964).

2362  A mole on your left leg is the sign of a very bad temper (F, 21, SLC, 1958).

2363  A dimple indicates a bad temper (F, 21, SLC, 1958).

2364  Meat eating causes a bad temper (M, 54, Magna, 1923).

2365  Redheads always have a bad temper (F, SLC, 1958); . . . fiery temper (F, Spanish Fork, 1925); . . . are hot-tempered (F, SLC); . . . have violent tempers (F, SLC, 1960); . . . are quick tempered (F, 1957); . . . have a high temper (F, Moab, 1953); A redheaded woman has a bad temper (M, 20, SLC, 1962). Brown 481.

2366  A redhead is emotionally unstable, has a terrible temper and deserves to be burned as a witch (F, 17, Ogden, 1960).

2367  A redheaded person has got a temper like red pepper (F, Moab, 1953).

2368  A redheaded person sure has got an Irish temper (F, Moab, 1953).

2369  Red hair indicates a "spit fire" of a woman (M, 28, SLC, 1952).

## Bossy, Dominant

2370  If the second toe on your foot is longer than your great toe, you are a bossy type of person (F, W. Jordan, early 1900s); . . . you will be the boss in your family (F, Lehi, 1957); . . . you have a very dominant personality (F, 21, Logan, 1970).

2371  A bald-headed man will be master of his own house (M, 37, MD, SLC, 1963).

## Conscientious, Sincere

2372  A bump on the top of the head is a sign of conscientiousness (F, Lehi, 1915).

2373  Dark-haired girls are sincere (M, Kaysville, 1958); Brunettes . . . (F, 1961).

## Dishonest, Deceitful

2374  You can tell if a person is lying by looking at their eyes (M, 47, SLC, 1927).

2375  If a person can't look into your eyes, he or she is dishonest (F, SLC).

2376  A shifting eye denotes dishonesty (M, 50, SLC, 1935); Shifty eyes, shifty character (F, 33, SLC, 1963).

2377  Black eyes tell lies (F, 40, SLC, 1964).

2378      Brown eye pic-a-pie,
          Run around and tell a lie.
      (F, 17, Bountiful, 1960).

2379  Parted teeth are a sign of deceit (F, SLC, 1960); A broad space between the teeth indicates one is a liar (M, 22, SLC, 1959).

2380  Blondes are false (F, 1961).

2381  Light-haired girls are fickle and prove to be false friends (F, 47, Midvale, 1928).

2382  Short fingernails are a sign of a liar (F, 73, SLC, 1964).

2383  If you have spots on your fingernails, you are a liar (M, 33, It, SLC, 1939).

## Evil, Wicked

2384  A blond spot in your hair means you are evil (M, 22, Magna, 1963).

2385  There is a basic or innate evil in all redheads. Don't trust them (F, Ger, SLC, 1957).

2386  From bad company we draw in wickedness and faults (M, 64, SLC, 1920s).

## Generous, Unselfish, Etc.

2387  A person with big ears is generous (F, SLC, early 1900s); . . . unselfish (F, SLC, 1957); . . . broad front teeth . . . (F, Lehi, 1957); . . . thick lower lips . . . (M, Bountiful, 1962); . . . broad fingernails . . . (M, SLC, 1960). Brown 508.

2388  People who have crooked thumbs are spendthrifts (F, SLC, 1930s).

2389      If your shoe wears at the toe,
          You'll spend as you go.
          If your shoe wears at the ball,
          You'll spend it all.
      (M, 78, SLC, 1906).

2390  If you wear your heels out on the outside, it shows a generous nature (F, Axtell, 1958).

## Gentle, Kind

2391  If you have far-set eyes, you are a kind, gentle, good person (M, 20, SLC, 1964).

2392  A dimple in your cheek, you are gentle and meek (F, 79, Logan, 1970).

2393  Fine hair indicates a mild and gentle person (F, 54, Swed, SLC, 1963).

2394  If a person grows a flower garden, they will always be kind of heart (F, Eng, SLC, 1957).

## Good Dispositioned, Good-Natured

2395  Soft hands indicate that a person is friendly and easy to get along with (F, SLC, 1920s).

2396  Fat people are good-natured (F, 1959); . . . have a good disposition (F, Ogden, 1955).

2397  Grow a box of herbs on your kitchen window shelf and you will always be sweet and good-natured (F, Eng, SLC, 1960).

## Happy, Cheerful, Etc.

2398 Blue eyes mean contentment. A person is more apt to be contented (M, SLC).

2399 Blondes have more fun than girls with any other color of hair. They are more fun too (M, 22, SLC, 1963).

2400 Prominent dimples are a sign of a happy and congenial person (F, SLC, early 1900s).

2401 Fat people are always happy (M, 71, Pol, Provo, 1964). Heard in New York City, 1939; . . . cheerful (F, SLC, 1945); . . . jolly (Bear River City, 1957).

2402 A bachelor is said to be jolly (F, 46, SLC, 1938).

## Honest, Trustworthy

2403 I've always heard you can tell if a person is honest by looking him in the eye. If he can't look you in the eye, he may tend to be dishonest (F, SLC, 1958).

2404 An honest person can look the world in the face (F, 21, SLC, 1964).

2405 Big earlobes mean you'll be an honest person (M, 25, SLC, 1964).

2406 Brunettes are more trustworthy and less fickle and more intelligent than so-called dumb blondes (F, SLC, 1958).

## Ill-Natured, Cross, Etc.

2407 If you're always biting your fingernails, it shows that you're ill-natured (M, 49, Lindon, 1925).

2408 Pull out a hair, touch it with the flame of a match, and if it curls up quickly, it is a sign that you are cross in your disposition (F, 61, Du, SLC, 1964). First heard in Holland, 1920.

2409 If a person is in a good mood on Monday, he will be grouchy the rest of the week, and vice versa (F, SLC, 1940).

## Immoral

2410 Pimples and boils indicate that the person who has them has led an immoral life (F, 93, SLC, 1964).

2411 A hole in the toe of the right shoe is a definite sign of bad luck and immorality (M, 19, SLC, 1964).

## Innocent, Naive, Etc.

2412 Dimples signify naiveté (M, 51, SLC, 1963).

2413 A turned-up nose indicates that one is gullible (F, 50, SLC, 1963).

2414 A loud person is harmless (M, 70, SLC, 1964).

2415 On a bottle of beer if you can slit a label all the way down with your fingernail, you are innocent (F, 19, SLC, 1959).

## Jealous, Envious

2416 Green is the sign of jealousy (M, Orem, 1959).

2417 A person with green eyes is not to be trusted. He is considered to be violently jealous (M, SLC, 1964); . . . green eyes . . . envious (F, SLC, 1955).

2418 When your eyes water when you peel onions, you are jealous (M, SLC, 1957).

2419 If you have itches, you are jealous (F, 55, SLC, 1964).

2420 Those who wear a yellow flower are jealous (M, 19, SLC, 1962).

## Lazy, Nonpersistent

2421 If a person has a recessive chin, then he will lack persistence (F, Bountiful, 1964).

2422 Fat people are lazy (F, SLC, 1961).

2423 Fat and thick hands are lazy hands (F, Moab, 1953).

2424 If you hit a person with a broom, you will make him lazy (M, SLC).

## Loud Mouthed, Scolding

2425 If a woman has hair on her legs, that signifies she's a loud mouth (M, Gr, SLC).

2426 Don't break thread (when sewing) with the teeth, for it will cause you to become a scold (M, Welsh, SLC, 1960).

## Mean, Cruel, Etc.

2427 A person born under the planet Mars will have a violent disposition (F, 50, Murray, 1927).

2428 If you have a short stalky build, you have rash behavior (M, 20, SLC, 1964).

2429 People who have protruding eyes are dangerous (M, Farmington, 1932).

2430 Little lips mean you are mean (F, SLC, 1957).

2431 If a person is not able to make friends with a baby or an animal, he is considered mean (F, SLC, 1961).

2432 Eating a ferocious animal's heart makes a person cruel (M, Ger, SLC, 1963).

## Nontrustworthy

2433 Never trust a redhead (F, 20, SLC, 1964).

2434 A person with green eyes is not to be trusted (F, 48, SLC, 1939).

2435 Do not trust people with close-set eyes. They are sneaky (F, 47, SLC, 1930).

2436 A person whose eyebrows come together cannot be trusted (M, SLC, 1961).

2437 Never trust people with pointed teeth (F, 21, Brighton, 1952).

2438 No earlobes mean the person can't be trusted (M, 25, SLC, 1964).

2439 People born under certain zodiac signs cannot be trusted (F, 49, SLC, 1954).

2440 One should never stumble or trip over the threshold when entering anyone else's house. This is to mean that you cannot be trusted (F, 22, SLC, 1952).

## Stingy, Grasping, Etc.

2441     Green-eye greedy gut,
       Eat all the world up
(F, Moab, 1953); . . . gobble all the world up (F, Bountiful, 1960); Grey eyes are greedy (F, 23, Price, 1964).

2442 A person with eyes which are close together is a stingy person (M, 23, Ja, SLC).

2443 People with small ears close to the head are selfish (F, 19, Murray, 1964); . . . little ears are stingy (M, 19, SLC, 1962); . . . small ears are stingy (F, 56, SLC, 1964); . . . tiny ears are stingy (F, 22, SLC, 1963). Brown 509.

2444 A hooked nose (like an eagle's) indicates a noble but grasping manner (F, 54, Swed, SLC, 1963). Heard in Sweden, 1930s.

2445 A person having thin lips is a person of Scotch quality, namely, stingy (F, SLC).

2446 A person with short fingers is usually considered stingy (F, 61, SLC, 1930).

2447 A pigeon is supposed to be greedy, so a pigeon-toed person is supposed to be stingy (M, 28, Tooele, 1951).

2448 If you wear your heels out on the inside, it shows you have a stingy nature (F, Axtell, 1958).

2449 If your shoes squeak, you are stingy (F, 53, SLC, 1964).

## Strong Will, Strong Character

2450 A left thumb crossed over a right indicates strong moral character (F, 22, SLC, 1963).

2451 If you have a square jaw, you have strong character (F, 21, SLC); . . . strong will power (F, SLC, 1960).

2452 A person with a prominent chin or cheek bones is often considered to have a strong will (M, SLC).

## Stubborn, Obstinate, Etc.

2453 People born under Taurus, the sign of the bull, are likely to be stubborn and bull-headed, and always want their own way (F, SLC, 1958).

2454 People with narrow distance between their eyes have very stubborn dispositions (M, 22, SLC, 1945).

2455 Stiff hair indicates obstinacy (M, 22, SLC, 1950).

2456 Short thumbs mean a person is stubborn (F, 21, SLC, 1964).

2457 To like pepper is a sign you are spunky (M, 21, SLC).

## Timid

2458 A weak chin means a timid person (F, 14, SLC, 1964).

2459 When you shut your hand, if your thumb goes naturally inside your fingers, it is a sign of timidity of disposition (F, SLC, 1960).

## Good Traits

2460 If the front teeth are overlapping, one is close-mouthed (M, Richfield, 1961).

2461 Big lips mean that you are lovable (F, SLC, 1957).

2462 People who have prominent noses (Roman type) are inclined to be quick in doing work and making decisions (F, SLC, 1930).

2463 Anyone with lots of slick hair is a very patient person (M, 22, SLC, 1950).

2464 People with fine hair are more sensitive than people with coarse hair (F, 20, Granger, 1957).

2465 Long, flowing hair on a woman is a sign of fine character (F, SLC, 1957).

2466 Men whose hair turns grey prematurely are nearly always good fellows (M, SLC, 1960).

2467 If a person has a protruding chin, then he has persistence and the will to get things done (F, Bountiful).

2468 Thin people are energetic (F, SLC, 1961).

2469 A boy who reaches his ultimate height by his thirteenth birthday will also achieve his greatest popularity at the same time (M, SLC).

2470 Eating turtle hearts will cause a man to be brave (M, 22, Midvale, 1964). Brown 7325.

## Bad Traits

2471 Eyes situated fairly close together on the face indicate narrow-mindedness (M, SLC, 1963).

2472 Large ears are a sign of coarseness (F, 26, SLC, 1955).

2473 If the front teeth are wide apart, it means one can't keep a secret (M, Richfield, 1961).

2474 Women with turned up noses are frivolous and disdainful (F, SLC, 1920s).

2475 A man with a sharp tipped nose has a snarling character (F, SLC, 1963).

2476 A small chin is the mark of a coward (M, 75, SLC, 1929).

2477 If a man has facial paralysis, he is thought of as a tough guy (F, 21, SLC, 1962).

2478 If a woman has a red mole, she will be sullen and furious (M, 46, SLC, 1963).

2479 People who like the color and wear yellow to an excess are known to be cowards (F, SLC, 1960).

2480 People outside Utah are unsociable (F, 68, SLC, 1952).

Other Traits

2481 If a person's front teeth are far apart, he will be a wanderer (F, 47, SLC, 1964).

2482 A long nose pointing down indicates a person that is curious and prying (F, 54, SLC, 1963).

2483 Short men have inferiority complexes (F, SLC, 1962).

2484 A backward slant in one's penmanship is a sign of inferiority (F, 23, SLC, 1964).

2485 A markedly forward slant in one's penmanship is a sign of superiority (F, 23, SLC, 1964).

PROMOTERS OF HEALTH

Eating, Drinking

2486 On New Year's eat rye noodles before midnight for good health (F, 51, Ja, W. Jordan, 1963). Learned in Japan, 1938.

2487 If you eat chestnuts, you will be moving around all year and will be in the best of health (M, 45, SLC, 1963).

2488 If a person wants to be well, he shall eat the three first ants he sees in the spring, and throw three over his back with his left hand (F, SLC, 1940).

2489 If you eat beans, you will be healthy all year long (M, 45, Ja, SLC, 1963).

2490 Well water is purer than city water; its minerals will help you stay healthy (M, Moab, 1964). Learned in Kansas.

2491 Steep mountain graperoot tea and you'll be well the rest of the year (M, 84, Centerville).

2492 A man who avoids extremes in dress and eating will be healthier and better liked (M, 90, SLC, 1964).

2493 Italian foods are for Italian people, and they will be healthier if they eat Italian food (M, 43, It, SLC, 1930s).

2494 If you take sulphur and molasses in the spring, you will have good health (F, 40, Bountiful, 1963).

2495 An apple a day keeps the doctor away (F, 60, Ogden, 1970). Learned in Idaho, 1920.

Miscellaneous

2496 Marry on a Tuesday for health (F, SLC, 1964).

2497 If you go swimming on the first of June, you will not be sick the whole summer (M, 37, SLC, 1947).

2498 Smoking cigarettes is good for your health inasmuch as it prompts coughing, which clears your lungs of all foreign matter that may have settled in them. Perhaps this is an example of homeopathy (M, 45, Ogden, 1960).

2499 Keep a set pattern of sleep and diet without ever deviating (M, SLC, 1961).

2500 If a man will retire early in the night, he will be in good health (M, SLC).

2501 A cold winter is healthy. Snow takes the germs out of the air (F, 22, Syracuse, 1960). Brown 658.

HEALTH PORTENTS

2502 A mole on the bosom means your riches and your health will always be mediocre (M, 40, SLC, 1965).

2503 A mole on the right side of the chest means you'll have good health (M, 40, SLC, 1965). Cf. Brown 651.

2504 A cold nose means good health (M, SLC, 1961).

2505 Individuals with high color are always especially healthy (M, SLC, 1959).

2506 Sneeze on Tuesday for health (F, Weber Co).

2507 To sneeze means you will have good health (F, 68, SLC, 1964).

2508 To dream of a body of water that is clear and sparkling is a sign of good health (F, 69, SLC, 1964). Heard in Ohio, 1908.

2509 When we have a crop of cherries, we don't need doctors (F, 87, Providence, 1900).

PORTENTS OF DISEASE

Part of Body, Bodily Functions

2510 A bloody nose is a sign of sickness (M, Ogden, 1943); If only one drop of blood comes from the nose, it foretells severe sickness (F, 83, SLC, 1940).

2511  If you cut your finger, it means you will soon have a trip to the hospital (F, SLC, 1957).

2512  If you trim your fingernails on Sunday, you will be ill during the next week (F, SLC, 1957).

2513  If you break two fingernails on the same finger, within the same week, someone close will soon get sick (M, SLC, 1960).

2514  It is a sign of forthcoming illness if, while eating, one drops his food before putting it into his mouth (F, 53, SLC, 1929).

2515  If you laugh in bed or if you are very unhappy before going to bed, you will be ill when you awake (F, 55, SLC, 1923).

2516  If a nurse or doctor goes and sees a patient before noon on the first of January, the whole family will be sick (F, 46, SLC, 1960).

2517  A dream of teeth means there will be a sickness in the family (F, 69, SLC, 1920).

2518  To dream of a helpless baby is a bad sign.  It shows sickness (F, SLC, 1957).

2519  If you should dream of heaps of money, especially small change, someone in the immediate family is ill (F, 70, SLC, 1964).

2520  To dream that you are in a valley is a warning of ill health.  Do not overtax your powers (F, SLC, 1957).

2521  If a person dreams of a wedding, there will be an illness in the family (F, SLC, 1960).

2522  If one dreams about a disaster in the family, a relative or member of the family will actually become ill (M, SLC, 1955).

2523  A dream of lice means that someone in the family is about to get sick (F, 45, SLC, 1964).

2524  To dream of snakes is a sign of sickness which will soon follow (M, 84, Centerville).  Brown 717.

2525  If you dream about a black cat, you will have a great illness (F, 45, Midvale, 1964).

2526  If you dream of muddy water it means sickness (F, 69, SLC, 1964).  Heard in Ohio, 1910.  Brown 730.

2527  If you dream of being covered with water, you will have a long illness (F, Hooper, 1963).

2528  If you dream of mud, it's a sure sign of sickness (F, Magna, 1963).

## Animals

2529  If a bird flies in the house from the outside, someone will be sick (F, SLC, 1959).

2530  A crow in your yard indicates a sickness in your family (M, 65, SLC, 1910).

2531  A grey cat crossing your path is sickness (F, 57, SLC, 1963).

2532  If a cat meows loudly at midnight, someone close will be sick (M, SLC, 1958).

2533  If you dream about a horse, then someone is sick (F, 68, SLC, 1964).

2534  If a moth singed its wing on a candle flame, there will be sickness in that family (F, Ogden, 1960).

## Miscellaneous

2535  If a picture fades, the person in the picture is in pain (M, SLC, 1961).

2536  To break a pitcher indicates sickness (F, 28, SLC, 1956).

2537  If you see a broken cello, you will soon be ill (M, SLC, 1956).

2538  If a wind blows out a candle, sickness will come to the family (F, 60, SLC, 1915).

2539  To raise an umbrella in the house is a sign of bad luck, usually a forewarning of serious illness to some loved one (F, Copperton).

2540  If one sees a comet in the sky, it is a sign of sickness (F, SLC, 1940).

## CAUSES OF DISEASE

### Eating, Drinking

2541  Synthetic vitamins are harmful (F, SLC, 1959).

2542  Hot foods should be combined with cold foods.  If too much of either is taken alone, you will become very sick (F, SLC, 1964).

2543  People will get sick if they eat their dessert before their main course (M, 38, SLC, 1930).

2544  It is bad for the health to eat pork in the summer (M, Provo, 1950).

2545  Never eat an egg with a blood spot in it--it will make you sick (F, SLC, 1964).

2546  Fruits and vegetables eaten together explode in the stomach (M, SLC, 1960).

2547  Do not eat fruit at night, or it may make you ill (F, 65, SLC, 1940).

2548  Fruits, especially citrus and tomato, are too acidic to be handled by the body (F, SLC, 1961).

2549  You should not drink water after eating any type of seeded fruit.  If you do so, you will become severely ill (M, 23, SLC, 1965).

2550      If you want to be sick or want to be dead,
          Eat an apple and go to bed.
      (F, 32, SLC, 1964).

2551 One will get sick by drinking mixed drinks of any kind (F, 20, SLC, 1963).

2552 If you swallow green gum, it will form a big wad in your stomach and make you sick (F, 19, SLC).

## Bragging, Coveting, Fearing, Mocking, Etc.

2553 If bragging about not being sick for a long period, you will get sick unless you counteract the brag by knocking on wood (F, 60, SLC, 1911).

2554 "Don't paint the picture on the wall." This means if you act like you're sick, you probably will really get sick (F, 50, Ger, Logan, 1972); If you lie about illness you're painting a devil on your wall and illness will come to you (F, 52, Provo, 1920s).

2555 When a bacterial disease is prevalent in the community, you should never think about it, and especially you should not worry about it, because it only strikes those who think about it too much or have great fear of it (M, 23, SLC, 1964); If you are afraid of a particular communicable disease, you usually get it (M, SLC, 1957).

2556 Covet your neighbor's wife and yours will fall sick (M, 23, SLC, 1961).

2557 If someone sees your baby and comments on how beautiful he is, you must immediately pray for the person who made the comment or he will become ill (F, 37, It, Magna, 1963). Heard in Italy, 1934.

## Domestic, Clothing

2558 Sickness will come to you if you change the beds on Sunday, for you'll get sick on Monday (F, 1960).

2559 Rocking an empty chair brings illness (M, 23, Ger, W. Jordan).

2560 Don't sit thirteen people at a table on Friday or one will become ill (M, SLC, 1960); . . . on Friday 13th, one will become seriously ill (M, SLC, 1960).

2561 Never open an umbrella in a house or a close relative will get very ill (F, 19, Provo, 1963). Heard in Chicago, 1948.

2562 Laying one's hat on a bed is bad luck, for it causes an illness in the family (F, SLC, 1964).

2563 If you place your shoes on the bed, there'll be a sickness (M, SLC, 1959).

2564 Shoes can't be higher than the floor, because it could mean a sickness in the family (F, 60, SLC, 1963).

2565 Sleeping with stockings on will make you sick (M, SLC, 1957).

2566 If you find a bent safety pin on the sidewalk, do not pick it up, or you will suffer illness shortly (F, Murray, 1957).

## Animals, Plants

2567 Killing a spider will bring bad luck and sickness (F, 25, SLC).

2568 If a sweet potato plant winds around the house, it causes sickness (F, SLC, 1944).

2569 If a willow tree spreads its roots under a house, it brings sickness (F, 51, Ja, W. Jordan, 1963).

2570 If you leave a Christmas tree up over New Year's, you will have sickness (F, SLC, 1958).

2571 Cut flowers should never be kept in a bedroom at night; they will cause sickness (M, SLC, 1960). Cf. Brown 705.

2572 Leaving a cut onion in the house will bring sickness (M, It, SLC, 1965).

## Divine Punishment

2573 Sickness is God's way of punishing man (M, SLC).

2574 If you burn yourself in any way after taking the Lord's name in vain, it means you are being punished (M, 65, Mt. Pleasant, 1910).

2575 A person will get a scar upon his face if he touches a crossed "T" without thinking of Deity (F, SLC, 1964).

2576 If you laugh and have fun on Sunday, God will punish you because it is a day of reverence (M, Salem, 1951).

2577 Evil will follow one who tears the flag of his country (F, SLC, 1957).

## Miscellaneous

2578 If you go to bed with wet hair, you will wake up sick (F, SLC, 1960).

2579 Never shower after a meal or at noon, or you will become ill (F, SLC, 1961).

2580 Sickness will come if a non-family member walks all the way through the house without sitting down (F, SLC, 1960).

2581 Close and shutter all of the windows and doors at night, because the night air is very dangerous and will make the person who breathes it very sick (F, 19, Belg, SLC, 1964); From corrupted air we draw in diseases (M, 64, SLC, 1920s).

2582 A mild winter causes illness (F, Toole, 1957).

2583 A man that tries to seduce a woman before marriage will bring sadness and illness to all the members of his family (F, SLC, 1961).

2584 If you work on Sunday, you will be sick on Monday (M, SLC, 1945).

2585 If a person dies in a Negro family, the bees have to be told immediately or disease will result (F, SLC, 1957).

2586   When you smile at yourself in the morning, you will get sick (F, SLC, 1958).

2587   Never pay your doctor bill in full, or there will be sickness (M, 1955).

2588   Never walk on top of a relative's grave, or you can encounter illness (F, 58, Richfield, 1920).

2589   Evil spirits cause and spread disease (M, 58, SLC, 1930).


PREVENTION OF DISEASE

Food, Vegetables, Plants

2590   Bake bread on New Year's Day. Cut a piece of bread and keep it all year round. At the end of the year give it to the dog. This keeps the sickness out--both humans and dog remain well (M, Bas, SLC, 1967).

2591   To rid house of diseases, take onions and set them around the house. All diseases will go into the onions. Then throw the onions away (M, Springville, 1961); A piece of onion on a shelf will absorb all germs (M, Union, 1920).

2592   Plant sunflowers around the house to prevent all diseases (F, 65, SLC, 1940).


Domestic, Clothing

2593   Sulphur was burned in a little can in the house to kill germs and prevent disease, especially respiratory diseases or those that could lead to respiratory problems such as colds and bronchitis. The burning sulphur gives off a bluish smoke (F).

2594   Put a penny in your shoe to keep illness away from the family (F, 20, SLC, 1968).

2595   To ward off disease wear a gold earring in your ear. If it turns green though, it means that the wearer is going to become very sick (M, SLC, 1971).

2596   In the old days it was believed if you put sulphur into your shoes it would keep diseases away (M, SLC, 1964). Brown 772.

2597   The Italians in the community used to sew their children into greased jackets for the winter. They believed this would keep away diseases (F, Midway, 1900).


Miscellaneous

2598   When you see an ambulance go by, rub your head fifty times so you won't get the illness (F, 34, SLC, 1955).

2599   You can never catch a disease in church (F, SLC, 1957).

2600   When a person sneezes, which may be a sign of an approaching illness, the illness may be warded off by someone saying "Gesundheit!" (Good Health!), or "God bless you!" (F, 21, SLC, 1964).

2601   Saying the word abracadabra will ward off disease (M, 18, SLC, 1960).

2602   In the old days, if a communicable disease sign was displayed in the window of a home, a person walking by would walk across to the other side of the street and hold his nose with his fingers (M, 71, Ogden, 1924).

2603   A drop of turpentine on the tongue every day was thought to keep all diseases away (M, 71, SLC). Heard in Wyoming, 1915. Cf. Brown 770.

2604   The Japanese believe if you make a tea from the navel cord that has dropped off a baby and drink it, it will keep you from having anything. The Japanese woman here from whom we buy vegetables did that when her first baby was born (F, Moab, 1953).

2605   Magnets avoid (prevent?) and cure disease (M, 16, SLC, 1963).


MEDICAL AMULETS

2606   You must always carry a good luck charm into the operating room so you will have a successful operation (F, Provo, 1958).

2607   Punch a hole in a dime, put a string through it, and wear it around your ankle. You will never be sick (F, 21, SLC, 1964). Heard in Missouri, 1950.


Herbs, Plants

2608   Carrying a bag of bad-smelling plant substance will ward off disease (F, Midvale, 1964). Heard in Idaho, 1901.

2609   Bags of herbs worn on the body keep away germs (M, 53, SLC, 1922). Cf. Brown 752.

2610   A mustard bag around the neck wards away sickness (M).

2611   A bag of sassafras around one's neck prevents illness (F, 45, SLC, 1957). Cf. Brown 761.

2612   Hang a bag of antiphlogiston about your neck and it will keep all germs away (F, SLC, 1961).

2613   To ward off disease, wear an asafetida bag around the neck (M, 37, Logan, 1950). Brown 735f.

2614   Put a few drops of camphor on a handkerchief when you are going out in public to keep contagious diseases away (F, 65, SLC, 1940); Wear a bag of camphor around your neck to protect you against all ills (F, 19, Coalville, 1953). Cf. Brown 737.

2615   Garlic worn around the neck will keep away disease (M, 1950); . . . prevents illness (F, SLC, 1964); If you get around anyone who is very sick, put a piece of garlic around your neck on a piece of string so you won't get their sickness (F, 53, SLC, 1964).

2616   All sickness may be combatted or kept away by the wearing of a medicine sack filled with garlic, sulphur and cheese and tied with a red ribbon (M, 68, Bountiful, 1900).

2617 A spice bag tied around your neck keeps illness away (F, SLC, 1957). Cf. Brown 752.

2618 A water chestnut will prevent illness if worn in the left rear pocket (F, SLC, 1964); A horse chestnut in one's pocket . . . (M, 43, American Fork, 1938).

2619 Carry a buckeye to avoid sickness (F, 74, SLC, 1964). Heard in Idaho, 1904. Brown 755f.

## Animals, Animal Products

2620 By wearing a chameleon chained about the neck, it is supposed you will be protected from any disease (F, SLC, 1959).

2621 Whoever carries the right eye of a wolf fastened inside his right sleeve remains free from all injuries (F, 31, SLC, 1952).

2622 Wear a string of rattlesnake rattles around your neck to protect from all ills (M, 35, SLC, 1964).

2623 Carry a rabbit's foot around the neck to prevent contagion (M, 60, Morgan, 1915). Brown 746.

2624 The townspeople used to put suet (or pig fat) on a string and tie it around their necks to keep sickness away (M, 43, SLC, 1971). Learned in Arkansas, 1941.

## THE SICK

## General

2625 Sickness comes in threes (F, SLC, 1957).

2626 Put a red flag on the gate when someone in the family has a contagious disease (F, 76, Orangeville).

2627 A person who has been sick for a long time doesn't love his mother (M, SLC, 1964).

2628 Painful illnesses are less dangerous than painless ones (M, 18, Logan, 1971).

## Human Body, Bodily Functions

2629 When a girl with very long hair is sick, the hair saps much of her strength and she is more likely to die than someone with short hair (F, SLC, 1961).

2630 If you cut a sick person's nails, they will never get well (F, SLC, 1920). Cf. Brown 664, 696f.

2631 You should not look in a mirror when you are ill (M, 20, SLC, 1960).

2632 You should not eat when you are terribly sick, as you will feed the disease (F, SLC, 1960).

2633 It is very bad luck to push a patient feet first in the hospital (M, SLC, 1967).

2634 If your boyfriend is sick, you should take two baths every night and he will get better (F, 14, SLC, 1959).

2635 When you are sick, if you will take a bath in a cold river, and then go into a steam hut, you will get better (M, 53, Logan, 1927). Told to him by an American Indian.

2636 The kissing of the Blarney Stone is for good luck when an illness has occurred (M, 58, SLC, 1960).

2637 Walking every morning before breakfast will cure most minor and some major illnesses (F, 65, SLC, 1915).

2638 When a sick person sneezes, it is a sign that he will become well (M, 44, Manti, 1920s). Brown 662.

2639 Never talk about sick people when you are at a funeral, or they will die soon too (F, SLC, 1971).

## Death

2640 If there is a sick pet and a sick person in the same family, the life of one is dependent upon the other. If the animal dies, the person will live, and if the person dies, the animal will live (F, Lehi, 1922).

2641 If two sick people are in the same house and one dies, the other will immediately improve in health (M, 26, SLC, 1945).

## Domestic

2642 To avoid trouble, never lay an umbrella on the bed of a sick person, or a black garment or a pair of gloves. In the last case trouble may be prevented by instantly throwing the gloves into the fire (M, 23, SLC, 1963).

2643 A pillow filled with hops and slept on will help cure your ills (F, 34, Orem, 1964).

2644 If you burn sulphur in a room where there's sickness, it will kill the germs (M, 70, Copperton, 1964).

2645 Dust should not be swept from under a sick bed (F, SLC, 1964).

2646 You should never clean out the room of a sick person, or something serious will happen (F, Murray, 1940).

2647 A candle should always be lit when a person is sick to keep evil spirits away (M, SLC, 1957).

2648 Put a knife under the sick bed to cut the pain (F, Copperton); . . . and you will cut the pain in half (M, 28, Midvale, 1937).

## Plants, Vegetables

2649 The ginseng (clusters of scarlet berries) is a remedy for every illness (M, Vernal, 1959).

2650 Flowers must be removed from a sick person's room at night in order that they will not take up the oxygen needed by the sick person (F, SLC, 1957).

2651  To cure sickness, put a bag of small ripe onions in the person's room and the sickness will be gone by the next day (F, 15, SLC, 1961); . . . put a sliced onion at the side of a sickbed to collect the germs (F, SLC, 1958).

2652  Onions are good to have in a sick room because the odor will kill any germs that might linger in the stagnant air (F, 42, SLC, 1956).

### Animals, Animal Products

2653  A black cat on a fence facing a room that contains a sick person is a bad omen (F, Helper, 1959).

2654  Bird feathers placed in a sick room will help the patient recuperate (M, Pol, Je, Provo, 1964).

2655  A chicken bone put on a sick person's bed will bring health (M, SLC, 1964).

2656  When you are sick, rub a horse in the place where you are sick (arm, stomach, etc.) (F, 9, SLC, 1964). Attributed to Japanese.

### Cosmic Phenomena, Precious Stones, Coins

2657  Night air is deadly to someone sick (F, SLC, 1971).

2658  A person who sees a shooting star and is sick will recover within a month (F, SLC, 1958).

2659  The possession of certain stones will cure illness (M, 91, Eng, SLC, 1964).

2660  If you wear a pair of emerald earrings while you are sick, they will turn pale (F, 48, SLC, 1964).

2661  Amber is a health indicator; it changes color with the state of one's health (F, 25, Cedar City, 1961).

2662  It is good luck to throw pennies in the fountains for sick people (M, 56, SLC, 1964).

### Miscellaneous

2663  A person's warm hand placed upon a sick person's brow will make them well (M, SLC, 1964).

2664  Change the name of a very sick person to fool the angel of death (F, 84, Pol, Je, SLC, 1965).

2665  Put an ill person in the middle of paintings of sand to make them well (F, 19, SLC, 1955).

2666  When Gypsy leader, MM, was at St. Marks Hospital, April 1, 1964, critically ill, members of his tribe believed that if they got 1,000 members to visit him at the hospital, he would get well (M, 63, SLC, 1964).

2667  It will hinder a Gypsy's recovery when he is sick if a picture is taken of him in the hospital (M, 34, SLC, 1964).

2668  The more people around a sick person the better (F, 48, SLC, 1964).

## MEDICAL PROCEDURES

2669  Medical treatment should be given only when the associated heavenly bodies are in the proper position (M, 78, Murray, 1960).

2670  To draw water out of the body, wear or carry copper (F, 37, Bountiful, 1964).

2671  Bleeding a person who is sick will drain out the bad blood and the sickness (M, SLC, 1958); Bleeding is to rid the body of vapors and humors which are the roots of illness; If you're sick, cut your finger, and the sickness will run out with the blood (F, 31, Magna, 1953); When sick, put leeches on your skin, and they will suck out bad blood and disease (F, SLC, 1950).

## MAGICAL AND SUPERNATURAL CURES

2672  If the last child to contract a contagious disease in a family is dipped in seawater, that child will have the power to purify and disinfect the entire family (F, 69, Pleasant Grove, 1904). Informant's father witnessed this ritual aboard a ship from Liverpool to New York in 1848.

2673  An animal is buried alive to cure disease (F, SLC, 1963).

2674  Driving evil spirits out of a body causes the illness to disappear (F, Midvale, 1964).

2675  Bleeding a person during illness will relieve the body of evil spirits (M, 18, SLC, 1952).

2676  It was customary to shake the hands violently after rubbing someone's sore back to rid the hands of evil spirits (SLC, 1946).

2677  Diseases are caused by evil spirits residing in the body and these evil spirits can be expelled by sniffing the smoke of burning dung (M, 23, SLC, 1962).

2678  Burning incense in a room containing an ill person casts out all evil spirits (M, MD, SLC, 1959).

2679  Garlic is a most effective cure to ward off disease because the demons are afraid of the odor (M, MD, SLC, 1959).

2680  Sundance braves dance three days and three nights with nothing to eat or drink to cure themselves or a member of the family who is ill (M, 25, Roosevelt, 1964). Ute Indians.

2681  Water running north has a healing power; therefore, one should drink it as well as bathe in it (F, SLC, 1945).

2682  Unusual objects have powerful medical effects (F, 50, Murray, 1928).

2683   Burn a string the length of an ill person, and eat the ashes (F, 20, SLC, 1950s).

2684   If you touch a corpse, it will cure your hurt (M, 45, Ogden, 1957).

## MIRACULOUS AND RELIGIOUS CURES

2685   Holy water sprinkled on the sick during sleep secures the ill of a good night's sleep and cures the illness (F, Centerville).

2686   Consecrated olive oil which was blessed by the priesthood for healing is used for every illness (F, 68, Farmington, 1910).

2687   A woman was nursing the sick during an epidemic in Mexico when she heard someone beside her as she walked along. It was a grey-bearded man who told her what to do. It was a simple remedy, but it worked. She remembers looking down and when she looked up again, the man was gone (F, St. George, 1939).

2688   While on a mission, reading the Book of Mormon . . . "everything seemed to be black--wrong. . . . got to feeling so blue, so funny, so strange. All at once such a feeling of power and darkness came over me. . . . Finally there was such a struggle I thought I'd have to give up to the awful power of the Devil, but something told me, and I made one more effort to pray and everything was just as different as it could possibly be. I went back in the house and everything was all right . . . " (M, Washington, 1939).

2689   A woman in B was afflicted with evil spirits and confined to her bed. The Elders were called to administer to her and cast the devil out. At the moment that this occurred the woman's sister, who was in another part of town, was seized by the evil spirits which had departed from the body of her sister, and she began screaming and tearing around (F, St. George, 1946). (This is a rare case of the transference of a demonically induced condition. --Eds.)

2690   A man named C had been making light of the church ordinances and was struck dumb. He was a young fellow and very wild. But he lost his speech and did not regain it until he had been baptized. This happened in one of the southern Utah or Muddy Valley settlements (F, St. George, 1939).

2691   Spiritual disease can be cured by properly playing a flute (M, DDS, SLC, 1959). Heard from patients.

2692   There's an old man in southern Utah who cut off his arm up in the mountains. There was nobody there, and he knelt down and prayed that he could get to the doctor before he bled to death. He made it to the doctor's office; and the doctor said that all of his blood vessels were sealed over, and that there was nothing he could do. He was completely taken care of before he got to the doctor's (F, Kearns, 1967).

2693   Informant's younger brother got a very bad eye infection that the doctors said would not only make him go blind but would infect his brain and he would be an imbecile, if he lived. The family decided that the best thing for the boy would be to pray to God for the release of the boy's spirit. The entire community knelt around the bed, in relays, and prayed. After morning prayers, the next day, the boy could see. Examination proved that the infection was gone even though the sight of one eye was permanently gone. The infection to the brain, if any, was also cured (F, St. George, 1946).

2694   Informant's little brother was sick with pneumonia and wasn't expected to live. The Elders came in and when they finished he fell asleep. He hadn't slept since he had been sick and he slept all that night, and in the morning was well on the road to recovery (F, 24, Holladay, 1945).

2695   Informant had a problem with her voice in that she couldn't speak above a whisper. Her grandmother said she would pray for her until she had her voice. For three months, Grandma prayed night and day for the informant, until one day a man appeared at the door whom the informant knew was a Nephite. He put his hands on her head and neck, prayed for her and she suddenly had her voice. Informant has dutifully served the church since that time (F, 71, Bountiful, 1945).

2696   A woman with a kidney stone was told by the doctors that it would kill her if she didn't have the operation. She went to one of the patriarchs for a blessing and he told her she would have to work for the Lord with all her might and strength and that if she did, the stone would pass and she would be all right. She started to do the work and one morning she passed the stone with no problem (F, 71, Bountiful, 1945).

2697   A girl had appendicitis and wasn't expected to live. The family prayed, fasted and administered to her. One night, when she didn't look like she would live through the night, she said, "Mother, don't feel bad because I am getting better." The next day she was better and the following Sunday she walked over two miles to Sunday School, over snow three or four feet deep in places (F, 68, Woods Cross, 1945).

2698   The informant's son broke his leg and it mended wrong, with the broken leg shorter than the other leg. He underwent several operations but the bone matter was running out and was poisoning his blood. He wasn't expected to live. Apostle B, a distant relative of the family, came and administered to the boy and said that the boy would live and grow to the full stature of manhood. Sure enough, after two more operations, the leg healed and the broken leg is exactly the same length as the other leg (F, 68, Woods Cross, 1945).

2699   Informant's grandmother had been bedridden for a month with a severe headache and the doctors had given up hope.  Grandfather placed his head against hers and prayed that the pain would leave her body.  Shortly, the pain left Grandma and was transferred to Grandpa, who because of his robust health was able to recover rapidly.  Grandmother then arose from her bed, completely healed (F, 1945).

2700  A young man was stricken with an eye disease before he was to go on his mission to New Zealand.  The church officials told him to go to missionary school and a way would open up for him to serve his church.  His name was placed in the temple and all his friends and relatives prayed for him.  On the day he was supposed to leave on his mission, the doctor checked his eyes and found that he was completely cured and could see again (F, 1945).

2701  A neighbor was very near death and was unconscious and had a raging fever.  Elders of the Mormon Church came in to administer to her.  They stood in a circle around her bed, placed their hands on her head and prayed.  She fell asleep and the fever broke.  By the end of the week she was doing her daily chores (M, 1945).

2702  The informant's brother-in-law, R, was blown up in a black powder accident, and wasn't expected to live.  IOB, a recently returned missionary, came in to administer to him.  Brother B asked the Lord to give R a portion of the ministrant's strength to help him bear the pain.  The patient fell asleep and Brother B nearly fainted, for the Lord surely granted his request.  It was many hours before Brother B could go home (M).

2703  The informant was on her death bed when one of the Three Nephites came to her and said she would raise a large family and that she would live as long as she wanted to.  Informant lived to raise fifteen children of her own, and at this writing was 94 (F, Ferron, 1932).

2704  Mrs. G had been bedridden for years in Farmington or Bountiful.  She had a dream that a white-haired man came to her and told her to go to the Temple to the prayer circle and she would be healed.  She put it off until one morning she noticed the man she had dreamed about coming up the walk.  She let him in and he gave her twenty dollars to go to the Temple.  They went but for the next three weeks she was worse.  They went again and she left the Temple without her crutches and completely healed.  In testimony meeting two years later, as she sat down, Brother M, the man who had come to her, stood up and related the following.  He said he had a dream where the Lord came to him and told him to take the twenty dollars and go to this woman.  Brother M said he argued with the Lord because his own family needed the money.  He went on to say that the Lord told him that if he did this, his money would be returned four-fold.  A week or two after he had given the twenty dollars to Mrs. G, a man who had bought a heifer from him twenty years before sent him eighty dollars and told Brother M that he had owed him twenty dollars for so long that he would pay him the eighty (F, St. George, 1939).

2705  Informant's mother, as a young girl, was very ill with malaria.  The Elders were called in to administer to her.  They put their hands on her head to exorcize the spirit and she said she felt the evil spirit rise in her body and go out through the top of her head.  Those who were observing say her hair stood on end and those who had their hands on her head (including her father) felt a tingling in their hands as the spirit left.  Then she was cured.  This incident happened to the informant's mother when she was a child in Davis County around 1889 (F, 68, Logan, 1970).

2706  In crossing the plains in the early days, the informant's mother fell into a river, went down three times and wasn't expected to live.  The Elders in the wagon train rolled her on a barrel and administered to her every hour.  Towards morning she revived and lived (F, 42, Manti, 1945).

2707  Back in the  mid-1850s Mrs. B's grandmother was coming across the plains with one of the Mormon pioneer companies.  She was riding on the wagon box and as the wagon went over a bump, she was bumped off and the rear wheels of the wagon ran across her chest and crushed her.  Her family was afraid she would die and so they called the Elders in to administer to her.  As soon as the words of the blessing were pronounced she stood up and said, "What are we waiting for?  I'm going to Zion," and off she went (F, 46, Tremonton, 1971).

2708  Mrs. B's husband had left her and she was thinking of suicide.  One morning she had decided this was the time to do it when a man with a flowing white beard appeared at her door and told her to continue living and that within three months her husband would return to her and beg for forgiveness.  He told her that she should forgive him and that they would have three children and live happily.  This prediction came true and Mrs. B was very happy.  Mrs. B was convinced that the stranger was one of the Three Nephites (F, SLC, 1937).

MEDICAL PRACTITIONERS

2709  In R we had a Grandma C who had the gift of charming off warts and stopping bleeding.  She didn't rub the warts with anything, but did say some words and the wart would disappear in a few days.  The bleeding patients didn't need to see her.  Someone would call her and ask for aid, and in a very short time the bleeding would stop.  She also did this for injured animals.  This gift is passed from mother to son, and from son to daughter.  It always went from male members of the family to the female (F, 49, Richfield, 1958).

2710  If a woman marries a man with her own last name, she will be able to cure some diseases (M, 54, SLC, 1940).  (Onomastic magic is important in curative rituals, and healers often gain the curing virtue

merely by marrying a person of the same
surname, or with a name beginning with
the same initial letter.  The present
belief and related matters are taken up
in Wayland D. Hand, "The Folk Healer:
Calling and Endowment," Journal of the
History of Medicine and Allied Sciences
26 [1971]: 271-73.  --Eds.)

## MEDICINES

2711    For every evil under the sun,
        There is a remedy
        Or there is none.
        If there be one,
        Try to find it.
        And if there be none,
        Never mind it.
        (M, 1900).

2712 All medicines distributed by supposed-
to-be-traveling doctors would effect a
cure (M, 35, SLC, 1940).

2713 Magic words, when uttered, give power to
medicine (M, 38, SLC, 1964).

2714 There is more magic in disagreeable
drugs than in pleasant ones.  Pleasant
remedies are a sign of weakness in the
face of the enemy (M, MD, 74, SLC,
1964); The most repulsive medicine is
the most effective (M, MD, SLC, 1959).

2715 This gives you more energy, if you are
tired and worn out.  Rub body with olive
oil well into skin, then rub off with
alcohol to clean off (F, 87, Providence,
1950).

2716 Buy radium rocks, put them in water,
soak overnight and drink the water (F,
Sandy, 1969).  Informant said that
peddlers sold these radium rocks in
Uintah Basin around 1929.

2717 The rainwater of May has peculiar
beneficial qualities which that of no
other time possesses (M, MD, Provo,
1959).

2718 The mineral waters of hot springs in
Willard can cure most internal disorders
if one will bathe and drink the water
(M, 90, SLC, 1964).

2719 The Great Salt Lake can cure body sores
if one will swim in its waters three
days in a row (M, 90, SLC, 1964).

2720 A pinch of gunpowder washed down with a
cup of sour milk will cure anything (M,
21, Heber, 1961).

2721 Two older men in Helper are reputed to
use whiskey as a daily cure-all.  Both
men having their teeth extracted did not
want to have false teeth.  In order for
them to chew well they would gargle
daily with a stiff belt of whiskey or
bourbon.  They both seem to be able to
eat anything they want (M, Helper,
1966).

2722 Cranberry juice has some kind of magical
power and will cure anything (F, SLC,
1969).

2723 To cure all diseases take a massive dose
of Epsom salts (M, 38, Logan, 1937).

2724 Honey and vinegar is a panacea (F, 20,
SLC, 1960).

2725 Gasoline will cure anything (F, 70,
Provo, 1963).

2726 Use turpentine for a cure-all (F, 19,
SLC, 1953).

2727 Tobacco smoke is a disinfectant (F, 40,
SLC, 1961).

2728 Swallowing a capsule or a tablet whole
is quite correct (F, 40, SLC, 1961).

2729 Two colors of aspirin are made, but
people think that green ones are
stronger than white ones, just because
of their color (M, pharm, SLC, 1964).

## BOTANICALS

2730 If herbs are gathered at a certain time
of the year, it is more effective on
that person (M, 45, Ja, SLC, 1963).

2731 Golden seal, an herb, will heal
anything.  Taken dry or with water (F,
70, Provo, 1900).

2732 The roots of the ginseng are a remedy
for every illness (F, Pleasant Grove,
1906).

2733 It was believed that portions of
different plants cured different
ailments (M, 26, SLC, 1963).

2734 Rhubarb root is used for physic
(phthisic) (F, SLC).

2735 A piece of onion on a shelf will absorb
all germs (M, SLC, 1959).

2736 Nuts have certain curative properties
(F, SLC, 1960).

2737 Camphor kills germs at any time of day
(F, SLC, 1961).  Cf. Brown 737f.

2738 A very good hand lotion is made from
flaxseed (F, SLC, 1959).

2739 An asafetida bag is used for all
purposes in the winter (F, 67, SLC,
1964).  Brown 735f.

2740 The roots of the sego lily plant have
good nutritional and medical benefits
(M, SLC).

2741 For sickness we had catnip that we grew
in the garden (F, Moab, 1953).

2742 Many years ago it was believed that
parts of plants which looked like parts
of the body or the body itself, could
cure that part of or the whole body of
its ailments when taken (F, 23, SLC).

2743 The tops, middle portions and roots of
plants can cure diseases of head, chest
and legs, respectively (F, 80, Ja,
Midvale).

## TEAS AND TONICS

2744 A woman fell ill in Sanpete County and
was about to die.  President Young was
called for.  He sent her husband to the

bottom of a big canyon to gather a certain shrub which grew there and make tea for his wife. His wife was healed. To this day people still harvest this herb and use it for medicine (F, 84, SLC, 1950).

2745  The ladies all used to drink tea and rinse out the bit of sugar left in their cups and put it in the vinegar jar (F, Moab, 1953).

2746  There was a tall plant with little yellow blossoms that used to be used for a tonic. I can't think of the name of it (F, Moab, 1953).

2747  As a general medical regimen, the informant kept fast day by going off into the woods and having prayers. Made tea out of alder bark (M).

2748  Tonic was made from aspen bark (M, SLC, 1946).

2749  Brigham tea is made from leaves that look almost like alfalfa leaves (F, Woods Cross, 1953); Drink Brigham tea just to do you good (F, Moab, 1953); Mrs. I sent her boy up on the mountain to get some Brigham tea. She said, "Don't dry it. Just break it up and steep it like other tea." Lots of people still drink it as a laxative or for their general good (F, 50, Moab, 1953).

2750  In the early days if there was a need for medicine there was an Indian by the name of Arimo that we used to go to. We used to dry catnip, sage and yarrow and take them for sickness. President Young used to advise us to do that (F, 94, Logan, 1946).

2751  We used to use catnip tea and sage tea a great deal (F, 81, Logan, 1946).

2752  When you need iron, make a tonic of wild graperoot by pouring boiling water over the roots. Drink it all down while it is still hot (F, SLC, 1967).

2753  The mixture made from boiling linden tree bark in water is good for almost anything. "Linden" wood is lime wood or wood from the lime tree (M, Ger, SLC, 1969).

2754  Slippery elm tea was used as a tonic (M, SLC, 1946).

2755  Tea was made from wild mustard leaves (M, SLC, 1946).

2756  They give peppermint and catnip tea. That was to bring out skin eruptions--sometimes the skin was kind of pimply--and they claimed that it would bring out that (F, Moab, 1953).

2757  Herb tea to remain strong in old age is made from peppermint, comfrey, spearmint, alfalfa, dandelion greens. Dry them, steep, but do not boil. Honey may be added to improve the taste (M, 70, Logan, 1970).

2758  In pioneer times rhubarb, senna, and brown sugar were boiled together to form "syrup of rhubarb" which was used for a laxative (M, Tooele, 1957).

2759  We had wild sage tea for sickness (F, Moab, 1953). Brown 787.

2760  Sagebrush tea is a good spring tonic (M, Lehi, 1957); Sage and hop tea . . . (M, 44, Layton, 1970).

2761  Sage tea or mint tea are good for any ailment (F, 41, SLC, 1971).

2762  Peach leaf tea is made from boiling fresh peach leaves. Steep overnight and then drink (F, Hurricane, 1969). Brown 784.

2763  Sassafras tea is a good tonic (F, Bear River City, 1957). Brown 788.

2764  My husband's mother used to gather a wild plant, uva-ursi, every fall to make a tonic (F, Moab, 1953). (*Arctostaphylos uva-ursi* is known as kinnikinnick or bearberry. --Eds.)

2765  Use willow bark tea as a spring tonic (M, 44, Layton, 1970).

2766  Kerosene and sugar were mixed together and then taken internally by a teaspoon as a spring tonic (M, 46, SLC, 1964).

2767  For sickness drink a mixture of paregoric, water, flour and cinnamon (F, SLC, 1959).

2768  Use sulphur and molasses as a spring tonic (M, 44, Layton, 1970); . . . sulphur, vinegar and molasses . . . (M, SLC, 1900); . . . sulphur and treacle . . . (F, SLC, 1964); . . . honey and sulphur . . . (F, Moab, 1953). Brown 797.

2769  For a laxative which would flush out the body, mix sulphur and molasses together until quite thick. Use about a heaping teaspoonful, however, do not overdo (F, 81, Richfield, 1910).

2770  Beef tea kills germs (F, 1961).

SALVES, OINTMENTS, ETC.

2771  Bran is good for a poultice. Wet it with warm water and put it on as a poultice (F, Woods Cross, 1953).

2772  Bread and milk is a good poultice (F, Moab, 1953).

2773  Boil cactus roots to make juice. Mix juice with red clay and pack it on the affected parts (F, 30, SLC, 1964).

2774  Rub a mixture of camphor and lard on the neck and chest (F, 19, SLC, 1964).

2775  People used cow manure and sheep fertilizer as a poultice (F, Moab, 1953).

2776  Use willow bark tea as spring tonic (F, SLC, 1961).

2777  Poultices were made of pork (F, Moab, 1953).

2778  They used to use prickly pear for a poultice (F, Moab, 1953).

2779  A good salve for minor injuries is obtained by mixing powdered rhubarb and lard (F, 75, Layton, 1910).

2780  Sage leaves were boiled and used as a poultice (M, SLC, 1946).

2781  You take some snakeweed and it's a wonderful thing to make a poultice. Cook it up so it's kind of a mash and make a poultice out of it (F, Moab, 1953).

2782  People made sugar and soap poultices (F, Moab, 1953).

2783  In pioneer times a healing salve was made by mixing sulphur with lard (M, Tooele, 1957).

2784  Tobacco was used as a poultice (M, SLC, 1946).

2785  Make a poultice of tumblebugs. Mash the bugs up and put them on raw (F, SLC, 1964).

## ANIMALS, ANIMAL PRODUCTS

2786  Many animals possess the power of curing diseases (F, 85, Grantsville, 1964).

2787  Rub the body entirely with bacon grease and put bacon grinds about the throat and cover with long underwear. This is a winter remedy, and it will cure throughout the winter (F, 20, SLC, 1955).

2788  Relief from disease may be obtained by cutting off a cat's ear and using the blood (M, MD, SLC, 1959). Heard from patients.

2789  A cure for all ills is to boil earthworms in water and give the person the liquid to drink (M, 49, Ogden, 1962).

2790  Toads cure sickness (M, Clinton, 1959); The toad has a precious stone in its head that can cure sickness (M, MD, SLC, 1963).

2791  White or bright feathers are good medicine; dark feathers are bad medicine (M, 44, Roosevelt, 1964).

## ANIMALS IN BODY

2792  If you eat bread dough, it will cause worms to grow in your stomach (M, 35, SLC, 1940). (Among the early theories of disease, and a notion still widely encountered in primitive medicine, is the belief that animals insinuate themselves into the human body, and either gnaw at the vital organs, or exude substances that create infection. The early notion of worms as the principal culprit, particularly in the cause of toothache, has been expanded in folk medicine to include insects of all kinds, snakes, lizards, frogs, and other kinds of creatures. For a general statement see O. von Hovorka and A. Kronfeld, Vergleichende Volksmedizin: Eine Darstellung volksmedizinischer Sitten und Gebräuche, Anschauungen und Heilfaktoren, des Aberglaubens und der

Zaubermedizin [2 vols, Stuttgart: Verlag von Strecker & Schröder, 1908-1909], I: 452-53, and Wayland D. Hand, "Animal Intrusion into the Human Body: A Primitive Aetiology of Disease," in Hand, Magical Medicine, pp. 251-60. American examples can be found in Popular Beliefs and Superstitions from North Carolina, ed. Wayland D. Hand as vols., VI-VII of the Frank C. Brown Collection of North Carolina Folklore [7 vols., Durham, North Carolina: Duke University Press, 1953-1964], VI, 106-107, Nos. 718-22. The best deposit of such materials is to be found in Harry Middleton Hyatt's Hoodoo, Conjuration, Witchcraft, Rootwork [5 vols. (New York), Memoirs of the Alma Egan Hyatt Foundation, 1970-1978. Vol. VI, the Index, in preparation] will make it possible to locate this widely scattered information. --Eds.)

2793  If you swallow a hair, it will turn into a worm (F, 19, SLC, 1962).

## PLANTS IN BODY

2794  Never swallow a seed or it will grow (F, Murray, 1957).

2795  When you eat the core of an apple, you will have apple trees growing out of your ears (M, SLC, 1963); Watermelon grows out of your ears if you swallow the seeds (F, SLC, 1957).

2796  If you swallow apricot stones, an apricot tree will grow in your stomach (F, Lehi, 1957); . . . cherry stone . . . (F, 83, Logan, 1970); . . . grape seeds . . . (F, Bear River City, 1957); . . . watermelon seeds . . . (M, Bountiful, 1960).

2797  If soil is swallowed, growth of plant life will follow in the stomach (M, SLC, 1939).

2798  If you don't wash behind your ears, you will grow potatoes in your ears (F, 18, SLC, 1964). (A spoof, but it rests on a belief. --Eds.)

## DEFORMITIES

2799  If you dream of rough turbulent water, there will be a deformity in the family (M, 22, Magna, 1963).

2800  If a woman goes swimming during her menstrual period, her legs will shrivel up and she will become permanently crippled (F, 46, SLC, 1932).

2801  If a person makes fun of handicapped people, he is likely to suffer the same disability in the future (M, 27, Price, 1963); If you mock a crippled man, then God will make you crippled (F, 30, SLC, 1964); If you stare at a cripple, you might become one (M, SLC, 1957). Brown 116f.

2802  One must yield to another who is lame. Failure to do so results in your being lame (F, Brigham City, 1960).

2803  Too much idle thought will cripple a body (F, SLC, 1941).

2804 It was considered very good luck to bump into a hunchback (SLC, 1946); Touching the hump . . . (M, 19, Logan, 1970); Seeing a hunchback . . . (F, Axtell, 1958); . . . rub the hump (M, 19, SLC, 1963); . . . meet a hunchback (F, SLC, 1961); . . . rub your shoulder against a hunchback (M, 22, SLC, 1961). Cf. Brown 3661.

2805 It is bad luck to quarrel with a hunchback (F, 45, Midvale, 1964).

## ACCIDENTS

2806 Accidents come in threes (F, 21, Bountiful, 1952).

2807 Failing to drink tea before leaving home will bring an accident to that person (M, 18, Ja, SLC, 1965).

2808 When you cross the street in less than five steps, you will cause an accident at that place within twenty minutes (F, SLC, 1963).

2809 Stand on one foot and the next day you'll be in an accident (M, SLC, 1964).

2810 Fatal accidents should never happen at home. If they do, they're worse than ever (F, SLC, 1961).

2811 Dreams of pains in your head or about accidents are warnings of difficulties ahead of you (F, SLC, 1957).

2812 If you dream of muddy water, it means an accident will happen to you soon (F, Swed, SLC, 1957).

2813 If you dream of raw, bloody meat, it means an accident is near (F, 18, SLC, 1961). Cf. Brown 8502.

2814 When a dress or blouse is put on backwards, an accident will happen (F, Norw, SLC, 1960).

2815 Two knives should never be allowed to cross each other. It is very bad luck and may result in an accident or serious injury (F, Spanish Fork, 1974).

### Cosmic, Times

2816 If you go out on a stormy night, you will have an accident (M, 21, SLC, 1955).

2817 On Friday the 13th, if you step on a line, you will have an accident (F, 53, SLC, 1930s).

2818 If you look at a full moon over your left shoulder, an accident will befall you (F, 19, SLC, 1962).

### Travel

2819 If you step on a crack in the sidewalk, your mother will have an accident (F, SLC, 1959).

2820 Do not stop at the scene of an accident, because if you do you will have an accident shortly following (F, Provo, 1959).

2821 Do not follow a fire engine or ambulance, because it will cause you to have the same fate as the accident in which the fire engine and ambulance are going to (F, Provo, 1959).

2822 If you don't pick up your feet when you go over a railroad track, you'll get in a wreck within a year (M, 19, SLC, 1960).

2823 Black cars are very prone to get into accidents (M, 15, SLC, 1964).

2824 Carry a St. Christopher's medal while driving, and you will be protected from accidents (M, 40, SLC, 1939).

2825 To prevent accidents it is customary to make a churn handle of ash (F, SLC, 1959).

## AMPUTATIONS

2826 Amputated limbs will hurt until they are buried (F, Bear River City, 1957). Cf. Brown 807-809. (A definitive treatment of this subject is to be found in Douglas B. Price, "Miraculous Restoration of Lost Body Parts: Relationship to the Phantom Limb Phenomenon and to Limb-Burial Superstitions and Practices," in *American Folk Medicine: A Symposium*, ed. Wayland D. Hand [Publications of the UCLA Center for the Study of Comparative Folklore and Mythology, No. 4: Berkeley and Los Angeles, University of California Press, 1976], pp. 49-71. --Eds.)

2827 A person had an arm cut off. The pain increased continually until at last the person insisted the arm be dug up and straightened. It was done, the bones and fingers straightened and reburied. The person whose arm it was, said the pain lessened greatly (F, 54, Hoytsville, 1963).

2828 I recall that as a child after I lost my finger people told me that whenever my finger which had been cut off was hurt by anything I should feel a similar pain in the stub of that finger. Since my finger had been lost in a beet field and never properly disposed of I was at times concerned that my finger might be stepped on by animals, run into by cultivating tools, wagons, and so on, and that I should suffer from this circumstance (M, 36, Woods Cross, 1946). Cf. Brown 809.

2829 My brother had his leg cut off, and he just about went crazy. He swore up and down that there was something between his toes. A fellow up here had his finger cut off and they never thought of picking it up. He nearly went crazy, said the flies were crawling on it. He made them go back up in the mountains and find it and put coal oil on it to kill the maggots so the finger wouldn't itch. The finger was all swollen up and black and they poured kerosene on it and burned it and he was all right (F, Moab, 1953).

2830 An arm that has been lost by its original owner cannot be burned or the person who lost it will feel it burn (M, 20, Logan).

2831 Apply green leaves as a dressing for an amputation (F, 1900).

## MENTAL AND EMOTIONAL AILMENTS

### Forgetfulness

2832 To comb your hair at night makes you forgetful (F, Ogden, 1963). Cf. Brown 2767.

2833 Tie a string around your finger and you will not forget (M, 46, SLC); Wearing a piece of string on your thumb will help you to remember things (F, 40, SLC, 1961).

2834 If you momentarily forget something, you should go back to where you thought of it to remember it (F, 67, SLC, 1964).

2835 If you have forgotten something that you need to know, go sit on a bed and it will come to you (F, Provo, 1959).

2836 When you forget something you must sit down for ten minutes before you leave or you will have bad luck (M, 49, SLC, 1925).

2837 If you forget something that you have left behind, count to ten or you will be disappointed with something (F, 56, SLC, 1964). Heard in Pennsylvania, 1930.

### Loss of Memory; Weakened, Impaired Memory

2838 Eating cheese will improve the memory (F, Bountiful, 1960).

2839 You will lose your memory if you read gravestone epitaphs (M, 37, Blanding, 1939).

2840 Liquor permanently destroys memory cells in the brain, if taken in excessive amounts (M, 20, SLC, 1964).

2841 Inhaling a cigarette fogs the brain and destroys one's memory (M, 19, Orem, 1955).

### Absent-Mindedness, Weak Mind

2842 College professors are absent-minded (M, 19, SLC, 1959).

2843 Only the weak-minded can be hypnotized (M, 44, Manti, 1920s).

2844 A weak mind and strong back go together and a strong mind and weak back go together (M, SLC, 1958).

### Stupidity, Thick-Witted, Dumb

2845 An educated man is stupid in practical matters of life (M, 38, SLC, 1951).

2846 Blondes are dumb or stupid (M, 35, SLC, 1940).

2847 Beautiful women are always dumb (M, Salem, 1946).

2848 Big-footed men are dumb (M, SLC, 1962).

2849 Big earlobes indicate stupidity (M, 19, SLC, 1963).

2850 Coarse hair indicates a brutal or thick-witted person (F, SLC, 1963).

2851 People with big heads have little brains (M, SLC, 1964).

2852 A shallow brow means a shallow brain (M, 20, SLC, 1964).

2853 According to a Yiddish superstition, one should not do any sewing on a person's clothing when he is wearing them. There is danger that one will sew up his "wits," and he will become a dullard. If, however, he chews a piece of string during the sewing, or immediately afterwards, it will neutralize the "bad" effect that may ensue (F, SLC, 1969).

2854 You should not eat ginger, because it is too strong and it will make you dumb (F, SLC, 1964).

### Idiocy, Mental Deficiency, Low Mentality

2855 If moonlight shines on you through a window while sleeping, you will become an idiot (F, Weber Co, 1958).

2856 Girls who are attractive usually have poor capacity for learning, and girls who lack beauty have greater capacity for learning or higher intelligence (F, 1959).

2857 Short, stubby fingers on a man denote low mentality (M, SLC, 1957).

2858 A loud laugh indicates a vacant mind (F, 50, SLC, 1930).

### Emotional States

2859 If you spill salt, you will be angry (M, Hyrum, 1950). Cf. Brown 2884.

2860 It is bad luck to be vexed by a fool (F, SLC, 1961).

2861 If the day is clear upon which you start on an ocean voyage, you will not be homesick (F, 46, SLC, 1946).

2862 Freckles are a sign of insecurity (M, 51, SLC, 1963).

2863 Lean men are morose (F, SLC, 1945).

2864 Redheads are short tempered and emotionally unstable (M, 19, Kearns, 1963).

2865 A person should never pick a mandrake plant. It screams so loud that whoever hears it may go mad (M, Eng, SLC, 1964).

2866 Sneeze on Sunday, be mad all week (F, Weber Co).

### Nervousness, Etc.

2867 If you eat lettuce, it will help calm your nerves (F, Morgan, 1961).

2868   Sleep on a sage pillow for nerves (F, 60, RN, Duchesne, 1970).

2869   Steep tame sage leaves, then serve. This remedy is used for the nerves (F, 74, Delta, 1966).

2870   Celery is a nerve medicine (F, 75, SLC, 1964).

2871   A raw onion taken at bedtime will cure insomnia (F, Kanab, 1960).

2872   If you are nervous, or can't sleep, brew leaves and stems of catnip. Take two tablespoons (F, 70, Provo, 1900).

2873   To ward off nervousness, wear a bag of the bad smelling plant substance asafetida around your neck (F, SLC, 1959).

2874   Raw beef juice is a nerve food and medicine (F, 55, SLC, 1964).

2875   The white stones from the rooster will help you to sleep well (M, Je, 25, SLC, 1965).

2876   Nervous breakdown is (always) caused by financial trouble (F, SLC, 1961).

2877   If you wear your watch on your right hand, you will have a nervous breakdown (F, 39, SLC, 1945).

Mental Derangement, Insanity, Etc.

2878   Mental illness is inherited (M, SLC, 1964).

2879   Insanity is caused by the devil getting into your soul or by punishment by God (F, 20, SLC, 1961).

2880   Evil spirits spread mental illness (M, 24, SLC, 1964); Open a small cut in the skull so the evil spirits can escape when one is mentally ill (F, SLC, 1955).

2881   Insanity or mental disorders are caused by overstudy (F, SLC, 1960).

2882   Persons named Agnes always go mad (F, 1959).

2883   If your eyebrows grow together, it means that you will go crazy (M, 25, SLC, 1955).

2884   A streak of white hair indicates madness (M, SLC, 1946).

2885   Viewing oneself in a cracked mirror induces madness (M, 26, SLC, 1948).

2886   Staring at one spot for a long period of time will drive you insane (M, SLC, 1964).

2887   Whenever a person sits too long in one spot he becomes insane within himself to the extent that he thinks he is part of the furniture (M, SLC, 1961).

2888   If you say "Gesundheit" when someone sneezes, it will prevent insanity (M, SLC, 1959).

2889   A person that yawns all the time is mentally ill (M, SLC, 1964).

2890   If gaiety or liveliness increases with old age, it is then believed to be madness (F, 79, SLC, 1890).

2891   If you have "anything" to do with girls, you will go crazy (M, SLC, 1960).

2892   Copulating with a menstruating woman will cause men to become insane (F, SLC, 1961).

2893   A deranged man can be found out if he smells girls' bicycle seats in the summer (M, 35, SLC, 1940).

2894   Masturbation causes mental illness (M, 19, SLC, 1964); . . . insanity (M, SLC); . . . you to go crazy (M, 25, SLC, 1941); A young man may become insane if he "plays with himself" (M, 43, 1938).

2895   If a letter is written in red ink, it means the person who wrote it is insane (F, Moab, 1953).

2896   You must always burn and not throw away your hair, for the birds will take it and make nests of it, and you will become insane (F, SLC, 1961). Learned in Louisiana, 1949. Brown 2762.

2897   If you get bitten by a bat, you'll go crazy (M, SLC, 1961).

2898   If someone gazes at the moon, he will go insane (F, SLC, 1959); If you gaze at the moon for a long time, you will become "moonstruck" (F, 63, Roosevelt, 1964); . . . stare at the moon too long, you will go mad (F, 43, American Fork, 1951); People who watch the full moon for an extended period of time become lunatics (F, 23, SLC, 1952).

2899   Do not go out in the full of the moon after midnight alone or you will lose your sanity (F, SLC, 1961); Never go out at night without a hat, the moon will make you mentally ill (F, SLC, 1965).

2900   A person who tries to pick a four-leaf clover in the moonlight will become insane. The good luck of the four-leaf clover reverses itself (F, 23, SLC, 1964).

2901   If moonlight shines on a person's face while he is sleeping, he will go crazy (M, Ogden, 1964); A full moon shining on your face through a window will cause insanity (1960); Sleeping nine nights by the light of the moon causes mental distress, lunacy (F, 70, SLC, 1964); The moon shining on you during sleep will make you lose your mind (F, 49, Midvale, 1933); If the moon shines on you during sleep, you will be moonstruck (F, 75, SLC, 1964); . . . it affects one's mind (F, SLC, 1960). Brown 2759f.

2902   A lunatic is a person who has been viciously attacked by the moon (F, SLC, 1961).

2903   Jasper will cure madness (F, 61, Midvale). Cf. Brown 2765.

2904   The sapphire relieves insanity (M, 53, SLC, 1963).

# III

# Physical Ailments and Diseases

## ABSCESS

2905 They used to use plantain leaves for abscesses. Bruise it and put it on as a poultice (F, 71, Woods Cross, 1953).

2906 A bag of heated oats placed over an abscess will cause it to break and heal (M, 44, Layton).

2907 We used sliced pork on a finger abscess, or foot or hand, and bandaged it on (F, 71, Woods Cross, 1953).

## ACHES AND PAINS

2908 Epsom salts can be used for aches and pains (F, 20, SLC, 1963).

2909 To ease aches and pains, cover the area with lard (F, Swiss, 44, Midvale, 1964).

2910 Cow manure is a good cure for aches and pains (M, 44, Spring Glen, 1958).

2911 Any strong smelling, nasty tasting liquid will cure internal pains (F, 78, Ger, SLC, 1964). (This entry bears out the old folk medical notion that in order for medicine to be effective, it must be bitter, foul-smelling, or otherwise offensive. In external applications, the medicine had to be sharp and penetrating. In the words of one old Indian: "No smart-um--no cure-um." --Eds.)

2912 If you put a knife or scissors under your bed when you have pain, it will cut the pain (F, 18, Brigham, 1960).

2913 If you have a pain, turn a rock over and spit on it, and the pain will leave (M, 48, Price, 1961).

2914 Carrying a horse chestnut is supposed to relieve pains (F, SLC, 1958).

2915 A chestnut will relieve pain (M, SLC, 1959).

2916 For anything that causes pain (except an open sore) we use mud (M, Tooele, 1968).

## ACNE

2917 Acne is caused by masturbation (M, 44, Layton, 1970).

2918 Washing the face every night with rubbing alcohol is an excellent remedy for acne (F, 58, SLC, 1961).

2919 By eating onions regularly one can prevent acne (M, SLC, 1961).

2920 Rub a wet baby's diaper over your face to remove acne (F, 20, SLC, 1964).

## APPENDICITIS

2921 If you eat the seeds of fruits, you will get appendicitis (F, SLC, 1960); . . . apple seeds . . . (F, 49, SLC, 1964); . . . a cherry stone . . . (F, 49, SLC, 1964); . . . grape seeds . . . (M, 50, Bountiful, 1960); . . . a lemon seed . . . (F, 48, SLC, 1964); . . . strawberry seeds . . . (F, 1920); . . . orange seeds . . . (F, SLC, 1961); . . . watermelon seeds . . . (F, Bountiful, 1960).

2922 Never eat green apples. It causes appendicitis attacks (F, 48, Mapleton, 1963).

2923 Eat cherries and milk together, and you will have appendicitis (F, SLC, 1930s).

2924 Appendicitis can be cured by the process of freezing the appendix (F, SLC, 1961).

2925 Apply hot pans or hot towels over the region of the soreness for appendicitis (M, American Fork, 1958).

2926 To cure an attack of appendicitis, kill a chicken (leave the feathers on), cut the chicken in half lengthwise, and put it over the area where the appendix is. It must be put on while it is warm (F, 80, SLC, 1915).

2927 Cure for appendicitis: Kill and skin a cat and spread the skin over your stomach (M, 24, Ogden, 1950).

## ARTHRITIS

2928 Eat the wrong foods and you will get arthritis; eat properly and you won't get arthritis (F, 55, SLC, 1964).

2929 An excess of milk can cause arthritis (M, Ogden, 1958).

2930 If you pop your knuckles, you'll get arthritis (F, 31, Ogden, 1958).

2931 Alfalfa tea is good for arthritis. This is because alfalfa roots go way down and get all these minerals out of the earth (F, Orem, 1974).

2932    Make a tea out of the branches of the creosote bush and drink it to cure arthritis (M, 65, Moab).

2933    A teaspoon of honey a day, and you will not have arthritis (M, Logan, 1970).

2934    Apple cider vinegar mixed with honey is a remedy for arthritis (F, 54, Logan, 1955); Two teaspoonfuls of apple cider and two of honey in a glass of water each meal . . . (F, 54, Minersville, 1964); Vinegar and honey . . . (M, 1900); Vinegar and water . . . (F, 52, SLC, 1925). (This item is of particular interest since the vaunted benefits of cider vinegar and honey, as enunciated in C. D. Jarvis's best-selling work, Folk Medicine [New York: Holt, Rinehart and Winston, 1958], and in its sequel volume, Arthritis and Folk Medicine [New York: Holt, Rinehart and Winston, 1960], seem to have been known in Utah folk medical tradition much earlier. --Eds.)

2935    Sauerkraut juice applied to a joint suffering from arthritis will cure the arthritis (F, SLC, 1969).

2936    For arthritis in the hands rub vinegar into them (M, 70, SLC).

2937    To cure arthritis, hold a raw potato wherever you have the arthritis. After a few days the potato will become petrified from whatever was causing the arthritis. Just keep putting raw potatoes on it until it is gone (F, Tooele, 1968).

2938    You should carry a hickory nut in your pocket to ward off arthritis (M, 61, SLC, 1910).

2939    Puncturing a joint that has arthritis will cure it (F, SLC, 1969).

2940    Place the fur of a recently dead cat on your back to cure arthritis (M, 1960).

2941    Metal around the finger, arms or legs stops arthritis (M, Logan, 1970).

2942    If you wear a brass bracelet around your wrist, it will cure arthritis (F, Price, 1963).

2943    Wear a piece of copper wire around the wrist or the ankle to ward off arthritis (F, 63, Farmington, 1912); . . . copper bracelet . . . (Monticello, 1955); . . . copper bands . . . (F, 21, SLC, 1964); . . . copper band around your arm . . . (F, 55, SLC, 1964); . . . copper ring . . . (M, 61, SLC, 1910); Copper bracelets will suck out the pains of arthritis (F, Roosevelt, 1964).

2944    I've always been told that to get rid of arthritis you should tie a silver dollar and put it over the joint (F, SLC, 1967).

2945    If one suffers from arthritis, place some uranium under their bed at night to cure it (F, 19, SLC); Water that has had uranium ore soaked in it is very good for arthritis (F, Moab, 1953).

2946    If you sit in a uranium mine, you will be cured of arthritis (F, SLC, 1957). (There is a locally famous uranium mine near Boulder, Montana, where people spend time breathing the supposedly beneficial air for a variety of ailments. Richard Threlkeld did a CBS feature broadcast on this mine March 9, 1972. For the benefits of the air in mines, caves, and even earth gases liberated by the plow, see Wayland D. Hand, "Folk Medical Inhalants in Respiratory Disorders," Medical History, 12 [1968], pp. 153-63, esp. pp. 154-55. This essay is now conveniently available in Hand, Magical Medicine, pp. 273-86, esp. pp. 275-76. --Eds.)

## ASTHMA, ASTHMA BOIL

2947    Asthma is supposedly cured by a tea called comfrey. It was discovered by a man who picked some leaves off of a plant and chewed them. It seemed to help him sleep that night, but he couldn't decide how or what made him do this. He retraced his steps and remembered chewing this plant (F, 58, W. Jordan, 1971).

2948    Drink tea made from jimsonweed to cure asthma (M, Layton, 1922).

2949    To cure asthma, eat large quantities of carrots at every meal (F, 36, Murray, 1936); To cure asthma boil . . . (F, SLC, 1961).

2950    Asthma will be cured if you collect spiders' webs, roll them into a ball in your palms then swallow them (F, 48, SLC, 1961).

2951    To help cure asthma, try and eat chicken gizzards (F, 80, SLC).

2952    If you have asthma or any kind of breathing illness, you're supposed to sleep with a Mexican chihuahua. It will take away the illness, but it won't get it himself (F, Basque, SLC, 1969).

2953    Asthma can be cured by wearing a nutmeg (M, SLC, 1965).

2954    A rabbit's foot worn around the neck will prevent asthma (F, SLC, 1964). Brown 819.

2955    The topaz stone is worn for a cure of asthma (F, Vernal, 1959). Cf. Brown 826f.

## BACK AILMENTS

2956    Carrot and celery juice is good for back trouble (F, 65, Du, SLC, 1965).

2957    Tansy tea for backache (F, 60, Duchesne, 1970).

2958    Pepper vinegar is good for backache (F, 22, Farmington, 1963). Brown 837.

2959    For a backache crack an egg in the middle of your back and let it run down. When the egg yolk breaks in a particular spot, massage the yolk into the spot real good. Relax for awhile and the backache will be gone (F, Tooele, 1968).

2960    The person who has a backache lies down on the floor. Another person gets on his back and walks up and down until it goes away (F, Tooele, 1968). Attributed to Indians. (This manipulative cure, known as "trampling," is not widely encountered in the United States. It is known in other parts of the world, particularly in Japan and elsewhere in the Orient. --Eds.)

2961 A sexual relationship with a Negro will cure a back ailment (M, 45, SLC).

2962
    Step on a crack,
    Break your mother's back.
    Step on a line,
    Break your mother's spine
(F, 20, Logan, 1955); . . . break your back (F, 65, SLC, 1930).

2963 During World War II if you stepped on a crack in the sidewalk, you'd break a Jap's back (M, 24, Provo, 1964).

2964 If you step on a tack, you'll break your father's back (F, SLC, 1957); . . . step on a crack . . . (F, SLC, 1959).

2965 If you step on a crack, it will break your grandmother's back (F, SLC, 1962).

2966 Carry potatoes in your pockets to cure lumbago (F, SLC, 1925).

## BAD BREATH

2967 Dollar-leaf tea is an old folk remedy for bad breath (F, Midvale, 1961).

## BALDNESS

2968 If you wear your hat into the house, you'll go bald (F, 46, Sandy, 1953); . . . in a building . . . (M, 22, Magna, 1963). Brown 843.

2969 Baldness is due to frequent wearing of hats or hat bands that are too tight (M, SLC, 1959).

2970 If you get your hair cut on the first Friday following or on the 13th, you'll go bald (M, 24, SLC, 1962).

2971 Men are baldheaded because they burn up the roots of their hair thinking so hard (F, Moab, 1953).

2972 If a bat pisses on your head, you will go bald (F, SLC, 1958). Cf. Brown 844.

2973 It is believed that if a person shows his pride in an obvious way, he or she will begin to lose their hair (F, SLC, 1910).

2974 If one presses heavily when writing, it means he's bald (F, 23, SLC, 1964).

2975 Cutting one's hair keeps one from getting bald (F, 26, Morgan, 1959). Brown 838.

2976 It is possible to grow hair on a bald head (M, SLC, 1956).

2977 Wearing a stocking cap to bed at night will prevent loss of hair. My dad tried it, but his head became slick as a baby's (M, Magna, 1967).

2978 Baldness can be cured by rubbing your fingernails together (M, 19, SLC, 1961).

2979 Rubbing yarrow into a bald head will make hair grow (M, SLC, 1961).

2980 If a baldheaded man washes his head with sage tea, this will bring out a new crop of hair (F, 46, SLC, 1930).

2981 To insure against baldness and make one's hair curl at the same time, pour rum on the head (F, 28, Tooele, 1964).

2982 Salves made of animal grease will cure baldness (M, SLC, 1959); . . . prevent baldness (F, SLC, 1961).

2983 If you are bald put manure on your head and your hair will grow (M, SLC, 1971); . . . goose dung . . . (M, 70, W. Jordan).

2984 Urine rubbed on top of a bald man's head cures baldness (F, 19, SLC, 1950s).

## BED SORES

2985 To get rid of bed sores, place a bucket of spring water under the bed every night (M, SLC, 1963).

## BILIOUSNESS

2986 Reason for biliousness (headaches, tired feeling, aversion to food) was said to be due to an overflow of bile (F, SLC).

2987 The gall of rattlesnakes is thought to be excellent as a cure for biliousness (F, 86, SLC, 1964).

## BLACKHEADS

2988 If a person suffering from blackheads creeps on hands and knees under a bramble bush three times with the sun (clockwise?), he will be cured (F, SLC, 1959).

## BLACK PLAGUE

2989 Wild ducks carry the black plague (F, SLC, 1964).

## BLADDER AILMENTS

2990 Remedy for bladder trouble: Parsley tea. Gather shoots of parsley as well as leaves and stems, then steep and drink (F, 74, Delta, 1966).

2991 For bladder trouble, drink much tea from watermelon seeds (F, 53, Morgan, 1927).

## BLEEDING

2992 If anybody's bleeding externally or internally, cayenne pepper will stop the bleeding. Just pour it on; it clogs up the blood (F, SLC, 1975). Cf. Brown 866.

2993 A piece of chewing tobacco (already chewed) is a good thing with which to stop bleeding (F, SLC, 1961).

2994 Use milkweed lotion to stop bleeding (M, 57, SLC, 1961).

2995 Tapioca pudding will cure hemorrhages (F, SLC).

2996 To stop a wound from bleeding, apply the lining of an eggshell (F, SLC, 1960).

2997 Flour or cornstarch patted into a wound will stop bleeding (F, Bear River City, 1957).

2998 Soda placed on a cut will stop the bleeding (F, SLC, 1961).

2999 You can stop bleeding with cobwebs (F, Moab, 1953). Brown 858.

3000 To heal a wound that is bleeding, apply a poultice of soot and spider webs (F, SLC, 1958); A case was cited of a severed toe which was swathed in soot until the doctor sewed it back on (F, Moab, 1953). Brown 861, 2750, 2754.

3001 Pale blue stones worn around the neck will be an effective antidote to prevent and check bleeding (M, MD, SLC, 1959). Heard from patients. Cf. Brown 869.

3002 A blood red ruby applied to a bleeding surface stops the flow of blood immediately (M, MD, SLC, 1959). Heard from patients. Cf. Brown 869.

3003 Recite the Hippocratic oath to stop the flow of blood (M, SLC, 1966). Told by medical students, with some disbelief.

BLINDNESS

3004 Someone goes blind every time a pair of eyeglasses is broken beyond mending (F, 23, Cedar City, 1961).

3005 Never read when you have measles. To do so will risk blindness (F, 29, Ogden, 1953).

3006 If a person crosses his eyes five-hundred times in a row, he will go blind (F, 19, SLC, 1953).

3007 If you bump your head three times in one day, you will go blind within five years (F, SLC, 1957).

3008 Masturbation causes blindness (M, 23, Richmond, 1959).

3009 If you look at searchlights, you will become blind (F, 19, SLC, 1953).

3010 Never follow a lightning bug with your eyes. He may put them out (F, 87, W. Jordan); If fire from a lightning bug gets into your eye, it will put it out (M, 46, SLC, 1928).

3011 Grasshopper juice will blind you (M, SLC, 1964).

3012 Sleep in moonlight and you will go blind (F, 26, Morgan, 1960). Brown 884.

3013 Looking at an eclipse of the sun will make you blind (F, 19, Bountiful, 1962).

3014 Staring continuously for more than five seconds will cause a person to go blind (M, 22, SLC, 1953).

3015 When you smile at yourself in the morning, you will go blind that day (F, 18, SLC, 1958).

3016 If the groom sees his bride in her wedding dress before they are married, he will go blind before they are married ten years (M, 22, SLC, 1963).

3017 If you eat too many eggs, you'll go blind (M, SLC, 1954).

3018 If a spot is skipped while sweeping, the person's mother-in-law will lose the sight of one eye (M, 64, SLC, 1932).

3019 When I was a small child, my grandmother told me that if I looked at moon lilies, I would go blind (F, Hurricane, 1946). According to the informant, moon lilies, also known in Kanab as lunar-bloomers, are jimsonweed. If eaten, they are poisonous and cause temporary blindness or even death from the poison known as belladonna. (Unverified by the eds.)

3020 Never waste a kernel of rice either down the drain or on the floor, or you will go blind (F, Ja, SLC, 1964).

3021 If you leave your hat on in the house, it will lead to blindness (F, SLC, 1971).

3022 To keep from going blind, eat many carrots when you are young (F, 18, SLC, 1961).

3023 To prevent going blind, always wear earrings (F, 51, SLC, 1926).

3024 Gold earrings should be rubbed across the eyes of a blind person and he will see again (M, 89, Provo, 1946).

3025 A baby's first tear will cure a blind man's blindness (M, Layton, 1959). (For a discussion of the power of innocence in healing, and related matters dealing with the unblemished state, undiminished quality, etc., as they relate to healers and the means these practitioners employ, see Hand, "The Folk Healer," pp. 270-71. See Hand, Magical Medicine, pp. 48-49. --Eds.)

3026 If blind people are kind to ravens, they will learn how to gain back their sight (F, SLC, 1959).

BLISTER, SORE, LUMP, ETC., ON TONGUE

3027 If you tell a lie, you will get a blister on your tongue (F, 24, SLC, 1964); . . . you have told your husband a lie . . . (F, 39, SLC, 1933); . . . you have lied to your mother . . . (M, SLC, 1957). Brown 887.

3028 If you have a blister on your tongue, it means someone is talking about you (M, Norw, 22, SLC, 1965).

3029 If the tongue of an accused person blisters while drinking something hot, it means that that person has told a lie (M, 20, SLC, 1960).

3030 If you get sores on your tongue, it is because you have told a lie (F, 25, Centerville); . . . lumps on your tongue . . . (M, 20, SLC, 1964).

3031    A pimple on the tongue means you have told a lie (M, SLC, 1961).

BLOOD

3032    Red roses cure anemia (F, 19, SLC, 1964).

3033    The best thing for low blood is raw liver (F, 57, Logan, 1967).

3034    Vinegar and water improves circulation (F, 52, SLC, 1920).

3035    We used to drink Brigham tea--it was a good blood purifier (F, Moab, 1953).

3036    Choke cherries are a good blood tonic (M, 44, Layton, 1970).

3037    In order to build up the blood, drink plenty of clover blossom tea (F, 78, Provo, 1910).

3038    In the spring dig dandelions and wash them and brown the roots then make a drink from them. Make a tea from the tops of the plant. Dandelions prepared this way are very good in organizing the blood in the spring, clears the blood for the summer from the winter thickness (F, 86, Providence, 1900); To purify your blood, boil dandelion roots and hop roots into a kind of root beer. Add yeast and sweeten it (F, Logan, 1972).

3039    Onions purify the blood (F, 55, SLC, 1964).

3040    They used sagebrush as a blood purifier (M, 48, Moab, 1946); . . . sagebrush, stems and leaves, brewed, taken in the spring for blood purifier (F, 70, Provo, 1900); Steep white sage and take it in the spring and fall as a blood medicine (F, 49, Moab, 1953); Steep tender wild sage shoots, add milk and sugar . . . (F, 49, Delta, 1956). Cf. Brown 889.

3041    Sassafras tea in the spring will thin the blood (F, SLC, 1961). Cf. Brown 895.

3042    Sweet balsam, yarrow, saffron and mountain rush were used to purify the blood (M, SLC, 1946).

3043    Use tag alder bark to make a tea for a blood purifier (M).

3044    Sulphur and molasses will thin the blood in the spring to prepare for hot weather (M, SLC, 1920); . . . will purify the blood (F, SLC, 1960); . . . will clear your blood (F, 70, Provo, 1900); . . . are a good spring tonic for the blood (F, 74, SLC, 1964); Yellow sulphur and black strap molasses mixed together and taken internally will thicken the blood (M, 46, SLC, 1925).

3045    If you wear a penny in your shoe, it will change the direction of your blood and purify it (M, 36, Sandy, 1945).

3046    Electricity was thought to have been able to purify the blood. Machines were often invented to do just this (M, 46, SLC, 1932).

BLOOD POISONING

3047    Never pick a hair out of your nose. It means blood poisoning (M, SLC, 1958).

3048    If you step on a nail, you must find that nail and grease it, or you will get blood poisoning (M, 50, Midvale, 1920). (For a discussion of treating the wounding instrument rather than the wound itself, see the editorial note to No. 4463, below. Cf. also No. 3764, below. --Eds.)

3049    Mother had blood poisoning and her arm and hand were swelled up and as black as could be. Grandma B, as we called her, was considered to be a bit of a witch, but she was the first doctor in the country. She told us to go down to the river, dig three feet down into the swamp and get the roots of cattails. We then were to crush them and put new milk on them and make a poultice to put on Mom's arm. In sight (sic) of four hours there wasn't a thing wrong (M, 48, Moab, 1946).

3050    To cure blood poisoning, pack the wound with bread soaked in milk or raw tomatoes (F, 41, SLC, 1964).

3051    For blood poisoning, a person should put fresh cow manure in a cloth and put on the infected part (F, 63, Monroe, 1964).

3052    If you put leeches on you when you're sick, they'll suck out the poison from the blood (M, 24, Provo, 1964). Cf. Brown 888.

BLOOD PRESSURE

3053    Normal blood pressure is 100 plus the age of a person (F, SLC, 1961); . . . should be your age over 100 (F, 19, SLC, 1963).

3054    Normal blood pressure is 100 plus weight (F, SLC, 1961).

3055    To prevent high blood pressure, eat cooked cabbage (F, 75, Murray, 1964).

3056    Garlic cures high blood pressure (M, 52, Layton, 1964).

BOILS

3057    Boils are caused by impure blood (F, SLC, 1958); . . . bad blood (F, SLC, 1961). Cf. Brown 912.

3058    Having a boil means that the blood is purifying itself (F, SLC, 1961).

3059    The eating of too much pork causes boils (M, SLC, 1925).

3060    If you don't eat fruit, you get boils (F, Midvale, 1961).

3061    Apply bread and milk on boils to make them go away (M, SLC, 1925).

3062    Draw a boil out with fat bacon, honey and flour (F, 55, Syracuse, 1940). Brown 914.

3063    You may get rid of a boil by wrapping yeast with sugar in a towel around the boil, and it will burst (F, Gr, SLC, 1962).

3064    To cure a boil, eat carrots in abundance (F, Lehi, 1937).

3065    For a boil chop some onions and mix it together with sugar and salt. This is supposed to open the boil (F, Gr, SLC, 1962). Cf. Brown 934.

3066    Flaxseed poultices are good for boils (M, SLC, 1925).

3067    We used to use pounded peach leaves and cactus for anything you wanted to draw, a boil, or corpuscles (F, Moab, 1953).

3068    Indians say sage tea soaked in cold water for twenty-four hours will cure boils (F, 80, Ogden, 1918).

3069    For boils mix laundry soap and sugar together, adding as much sugar as possible. Put this bandage with the mixture on the boil overnight. Rake off the next morning. In most cases the core of the boil will come out also (F, 81, Sigurd, 1910); . . . make a paste of soap, sugar and spit (F, Magna, 1974). Cf. Brown 948.

3070    For treatment of a boil, keep castor oil on the area until it comes to a head (F, 49, SLC, 1963). Learned in Texas, 1930.

3071    Sulphur and molasses in springtime prevents boils (F, 54, SLC, 1964). Learned in Oklahoma, 1920.

3072    A chestnut pierced and hung on a string around the neck prevents boils (M, SLC, 1959).

3073    A necklace made out of nuts hung around the neck will cure boils (M, Monticello, 1963).

3074    A nutmeg pierced and hung on a string around the neck prevents boils (F, 23, SLC, 1963); Three nutmegs hung around one's neck will get rid of boils (M, 63, SLC, 1964). Cf. Brown 932f.

3075    The seventh successive son has the power to cure boils (F, Ir, SLC, 1960). (For the healing power ascribed to seventh sons of seventh sons, see Wayland D. Hand, "The Folk Healer: Calling and Endowment," Journal of the History of Medicine and Allied Sciences, 26 (1971), 265-67. See Hand, Magical Medicine, pp. 45-46. --Eds.)

3076    Put the top of a heated, narrow-necked bottle over a boil to draw it out (F, Bear River City, 1957).

3077    A person sick with boils and abscesses should walk three times around a grave of a person of the opposite sex at midnight or crawl three times over a grave three nights after burial and they will be removed (M, MD, SLC, 1959). Heard from patients.

BRAIN AILMENTS

3078    If you dye your hair, it will affect your brain (F, 76, SLC, 1956).

3079    Earwigs crawl in your ears at night and eat your brains out (M, 25, SLC, 1964).

3080    Sunshine will burn the brain cells (M, SLC, 1950).

3081    Walnuts are good food for diseases of the brain since the meat of the nut looks like the brain and the shell resembles the skull (M, Dan, SLC, 1958); Eat walnuts so you won't get brain disease (F, SLC, 1959). (The present entry is an excellent example of the Doctrine of Signatures, as propounded by Paracelsus of Hohenheim and later scholars. These included the sixteenth-century English botanist William Turner, the contemporary German alchemist Oswald Croll, and the later German botanist Johannes Franck. For a general discussion, see Fielding H. Garrison, An Introduction to the History of Medicine [4th ed., Philadelphia: W. B. Saunders Company, 1929], pp. 205-6, 237. --Eds.)

3082    A walnut is supposed to cure diseases of the brain if one sleeps with it under his pillow (M, 57, MD, SLC, 1950s).

3083    Nutmeg is considered a brain food and medicine (F, 55, SLC, 1964).

BRONCHITIS

3084    For bronchitis cut up onions in slices, cover with brown sugar and some water, and put over hot water until syrup forms and then give syrup to the patient (F, 63, SLC, 1915).

3085    To cure bronchitis, wear a stocking around the throat at night. The dirtier the stocking, the better (F, 65, Farmington, 1930). Brown 967.

BRUISES

3086    Put a raw piece of beefsteak on a bruise to draw out the inflammation (M, SLC, 1961).

3087    A bruise may be healed by applications of bacon (F, SLC, 1964).

3088    The skin of an egg white will cure black and blue marks (F, SLC, 1969).

3089    Wild sage made into a poultice is effective for getting rid of bruises and relieving soreness (F, SLC, 1967).

3090    Use Epsom salts and hot water for bruises (F, 71, Woods Cross, 1953).

BURNS

3091    If you burn your finger, stick it in your ear and the soreness will go away (M, 22, Brigham City, 1953).

3092    Spit on a burn to cure it (F, 21, SLC, 1964); Lick the spot with your tongue and apply salt . . . (F, SLC, 1925).

3093    When you burn yourself, put beaten egg whites on the spot that is burned (F, Gr, SLC, 1962).

3094    Mashed potatoes heal burns (F, 40, Logan, 1938). Cf. Brown 983.

3095 To cure a burn, put butter on it (F, 55, SLC, 1950); . . . preferably unsalted butter (F, 65, Farmington, 1955). Brown 975.

3096 Very strong tea (tannic acid) is good for burns, especially when used to soak a dressing (F, 20, SLC, 1963); Apply wet tea leaves to burns (M, SLC, 1961). Brown 984.

3097 The pine tree's inner bark, boiled in one gallon of water, is good for burns (F, 28, SLC, 1964).

3098 Put pepper on a burn to draw soreness out (F, 53, Morgan, 1930).

3099 I used to know an old lady--we called her a witch--and if she got a burn she would hold it over heat until it drew the heat out of the burn (F, Moab, 1953). Brown 991.

3100 Apply fresh tomatoes or cold catsup to burns (F, SLC, 1971).

3101 If you have a bad burn, cut off a chicken's head and let the blood run over the burn (F, 80, SLC). Cf. Brown 976.

3102 Cow manure will cure a burn and prevent scarring (F, Moab, 1953).

3103 Put a piddled diaper on a burn to cure it (F, 52, Provo, 1925).

3104 This little girl's dress caught afire and burned her clear to the top of her head. They smeared Frazier's axle grease all over her and her hair grew back (F, Moab, 1953).

3105 Church linen will heal a burn (F, SLC, 1949).

3106 A devoted Mormon was in a hotel fire and all the clothing was burned from his body except where his garments were. The only burns he suffered were on his hands and feet, which were not protected by the garments (F, SLC, 1946).

## CANCER

3107 Cancer is never preventable (F, SLC, 1961).

3108 Cancers are incurable and if cured, it is only by some chance. Actually you never really had cancer (F, SLC, 1961).

3109 All kinds of cancer are alike (F, SLC, 1961).

3110 The younger you are with cancer, the sooner you die (F, SLC, 1960).

3111 People with cancer are always sure they will get well (F, SLC, 1960).

3112 Cancers are produced by bruises (F, 65, Farmington, 1960). Brown 995.

3113 If you suck your hair, you will get cancer (F, 21, SLC, 1953). Heard as a child.

3114 If you light a cigarette filter, it's bad luck, and if you smoke into the writing, it will cause cancer (M, 19, SLC, 1965).

3115 Cancer is usually caused by a single injury (F, SLC, 1961).

3116 Cancer is directly inherited (F, SLC, 1961).

3117 Cancer is caused by a germ (F, SLC, 1961).

3118 Cancer is contagious (F, SLC, 1961); A face deformed by cancer is contagious (F, 21, SLC, 1962).

3119 Cancer is caused by badness coming out of you (F, SLC, 1961).

3120 If you don't sleep with an open window at night, you are more susceptible to cancer (F, 86, SLC, 1957).

3121 Don't eat bread red hot out of the oven, or you will get cancer (F, Provo, 1969).

3122 Foods cooked in aluminum will cause cancer (M, Delta, 1961).

3123 The skin of tomatoes clings to the lining of the intestines and tears the lining from both the stomach and intestines, causing cancer (F, SLC, 1961).

3124 Milk helps cause cancer (M, SLC, 1960).

3125 White sugar and white flour cause cancer (F, SLC, 1959). Heard from owner of health food store.

3126 Black jelly beans give you cancer (F, SLC, 1963).

3127 Cold drinks cause cancer (F, SLC, 1967).

3128 Touching a broken cattail pod will cause cancer (M, SLC, 1957).

3129 "Tobacco juice" excreted from the mouth of a grasshopper causes cancer (M, 46, SLC, 1925).

3130 If a person is born under the star sign of Cancer, he will die from the disease cancer (F, SLC, 1961).

3131 Cancer results from a curse (F, Woods Cross, 1946). (Case of first wife of a polygamous marriage, herself childless, cursing the second wife.)

3132 Kinnikinnick bark, wild cherry root and golden seal are made into a syrup for cancer sores (F, 60, RN, Duchesne, 1930s).

3133 Drinking carrot juice in great quantities can cure cancer (F, 57, SLC, 1935).

3134 By rubbing grapefruit over the skin in the area of a cancerous tumor, it will make it disappear (F, Sandy, 1967).

3135 Drinking lemon juice will cure cancer (F, Ogden, 1948).

3136 If you want to cure cancer, drink plenty of cucumber juice and then sleep on an ant hill (M, Logan, 1970). Read in "Dear Abby" column.

3137  Toads have the power of sucking the poison of cancer from the system (F, Brigham City, 1960). Cf. Brown 1001.

3138  To cure cancer of the breast, apply blood suckers (F, Lehi, 1960).

3139  An old-timer declared that cancer could be cured with an application of cobwebs (M, 19, SLC, 1957).

3140  A dead hand touched to a cancer will cure it (F, SLC, 1960). (For the power of the dead man's hand, see Wayland D. Hand, "Hangman, the Gallows, and the Dead Man's Hand in American Folk Medicine," in Medieval Literature and Folklore Studies, Essays in Honor of Francis Lee Utley, ed. Jerome Mandell and Bruce A. Rosenburg (New Brunswick, N.J.: Rutgers University Press, 1970), pp.323-29, 381-87. Reprinted in Hand, Magical Medicine, pp. 69-80. --Eds.)

## CANKER

3141  If you have a canker on your tongue, it is a sign that you have told a lie (F, 21, SLC, 1964); . . . in your mouth . . . (F, Eng, SLC, 1962).

3142  If you have a canker in your mouth, you have been eating bread that the mice have been near (F, It, SLC, 1963).

3143  A canker sore in the mouth (not on the tongue) means that you have been urinating in the road (F, Helper, 1958). Heard as a child. (For a discussion of relieving oneself in public places as an ascribed cause of styes, and for related scatological and erotic acts, see Wayland D. Hand, "Padepissers and Wekschissers: A Folk Medical Inquiry into the Cause of Styes," in Kenneth S. Goldstein and Neil V. Rosenberg, eds., Folklore Studies in Honour of Herbert Halpert: A Festschrift [Memorial University of Newfoundland, St. John's, Newfoundland, Canada, 1980], pp. 211-23. Reprinted in Hand, Magical Medicine, pp. 261-72. --Eds.)

3144  Walnuts cause canker sores and pain to the mouth (F, SLC, 1960).

3145  Canker medicine was made from honey, vinegar and golden seal (F, 87, Moab, 1953). Cf. Brown 1008.

3146  Make canker medicine out of golden seal, graperoot, peach leaves, barberry bark, honey and alum (F, 73, Moab, 1953). According to informant, an old Indian gave the recipe to Brigham Young, who gave it to the pioneers.

3147  Lemons are good for cankers in the mouth. Also salt and water are good for them. Wash mouth all through the day (F, Providence, 1950).

3148  To heal a canker, put cinnamon on it (F, Logan, 1970).

3149  Black gunpowder will cure canker (F, Bear River City, 1957). Brown 1007.

## CARBUNCLES

3150  Eat tar for carbuncles (M, 1900).

3151  To cure a carbuncle, fill a bottle full of hot water, dump out the bottle and place the open end over the carbuncle. The bottle will draw out the foreign matter (F, 36, Logan, 1970).

## CHAPPING OF LIPS, HANDS, FEET

3152  A girl can cure her chapped or rough lips by kissing the middle bar of a five-rail fence (F, Du, Ogden, 1961). Brown 1017.

3153  Urinate on your hands to keep them from chapping (F, Bear River City, 1957); Wash . . . in chamber lye . . . (M, SLC, 1946).

3154  Wash the hands in the first snow, and it will prevent them from becoming chapped (F, SLC, 1960).

3155  Rub buffalo tallow on chapped hands to heal them (M, SLC, 1922); . . . mutton tallow . . . (F, Logan, 1968).

## CHEST AILMENTS

3156  The middle of plants are for diseases of the chest (M, 16, SLC, 1963).

## CHILBLAINS

3157  If you rub your chilblains with snow, they will disappear (F, 22, Holladay, 1955). Cf. Brown 1040.

3158  For chilblains, take a pot, urinate in it and soak your feet for about fifteen minutes (F, 58, SLC, 1921).

3159  Fresh cow manure, while still warm, was used as a poultice for chilblains (Lund, 1900).

## CHILLS

3160  A chill is a warning of something bad that is going to happen to you or someone close (F, SLC, 1959).

3161  If you get cold chills, it means that someone is talking about you (F, 8, SLC, 1962).

3162  If you sit in the sun, it will give you chills (M, 60, Syracuse, 1950). Brown 1045.

3163  Cold is needed to fight chills (M, 31, SLC, 1964).

3164  To cure chills, wear nutmeg on a string around your neck (M, 20, SLC, 1964).

3165  Bark from the persimmon tree, when boiled with water, will cure chills and fever (F, 60, Ogden, 1915).

3166  To cure chills and fever, knot a string and tie it to a large pine tree, and the fever will disappear (M, 23, Midvale, 1964).

3167  If you feel a chill coming on, get a toad-frog, or have one got, put it in a paper bag, and hold in your lap fifteen minutes. The chill will go into the frog (M, 23, Midvale, 1964). Cf. Brown 1050, 1053.

## CHOKING

3168 You will choke on your food in heaven if you eat it before the blessing (F, Provo, 1974).

3169 When you choke, lift your left hand (F, Orem, 1972).

## CHOLERA

3170 When the pioneers were struck with cholera, it was a superstition that water should be kept from patients. I have a pioneer story where several were in a room with cholera (the water pail was guarded), but while a nurse was asleep one woman crawled to the pail and secured a drink. I think she was the only one to live (M, Lund, 1900).

3171 If you hang a bunch of onions in front of the threshold of the house, you will avert an epidemic of cholera (M, MD, SLC, 1959). Heard from patients, attributed to Japanese.

3172 If you eat cucumbers and ice cream together, you will get cholera (M, SLC, 1900).

## CHOLERA MORBUS

3173 It was believed that if one ate too much green fruit, one would die of cholera morbus (M, 46, SLC, 1926).

3174 One tablespoon of castor oil for "collery marbles" (cholera morbus) (M, Hurricane, 1969).

## COLDS

3175 If your throat itches, it is a sign you are going to have a bad cold (M, 63, Farmington, 1958). Brown 1097.

3176 Wear overshoes in the house, and you will catch a cold (F, Eng, SLC, 1962).

3177 If a cat sneezes or coughs, one person, at least, in the house will soon have a cold (F, 21, Vernal); . . . sneezes three times, a cold will run through the family (F, SLC, 1959).

3178 If you hit a skunk on the road and don't smell it, you will soon have a cold (M, Logan, 1972).

3179 "Rose Cold" is a dangerous kind of cold (F, SLC, 1961).

3180 If a person catches a cold on an even day of the month, he will get over it soon; but if he gets one on an odd day, he will have phenomena (pneumonia?) soon (M, SLC, 1957).

3181 If you take a bath while you have a cold in winter time, you'll surely not recover (M, 27, SLC, 1964).

## Internal Remedies

3182 Starve a cold and feed a fever (F, Bear River City, 1957).

3183 Feed a cold and starve a fever (F, 18, SLC, 1952); Eating a large amount of food is a good cure for a cold (F, SLC, 1963). Cf. Brown 1100f.

3184 Drown a cold, starve a fever (M, 44, Layton, 1970). Cf. Brown 1100.

3185 Camomile tea is good for colds (F, 87, Providence, 1900).

3186 Catnip and sage teas are used for colds (F). Brown 1106, 1120.

3187 Cayenne tea was used for colds and things (F, Woods Cross, 1953).

3188 Flaxseeds were boiled to form a thick substance, lemon juice was added to the strained liquid, and it was used for a cold remedy (F, 53, Provo, 1964).

3189 Drink hot ginger tea to cure a cold (F, 21, SLC, 1961). Brown 1107.

3190 Drink horehound tea for colds (F, 21, SLC, 1964). Cf. Brown 1108.

3191 A teaspoon of lemon juice and three teaspoons honey, heated. Take this when you feel a cold coming on and it will take it away (F, 21, SLC, 1963).

3192 For colds bake a lemon in the oven till it swells. Cut it up and put juice and rinds in some water. Steep on the stove for twenty minutes and drink (M, 64, SLC, 1950).

3193 Chew Oneida Love Medicine in the fall, and you will never have a cold during the coming year (M, 23, SLC, 1964). Learned in Wisconsin.

3194 Eat cooked onions for colds and to prevent colds (F, 67, SLC, 1964); . . . fried onions . . . (F, 19, Provo, 1964); Eat a whole onion and go straight to bed and keep covered up . . . (F, Gr, SLC, 1962). Cf. Brown 1112.

3195 Stewed, chopped onions were mixed with sugar and allowed to set until a thick, gooey syrup was formed. That was taken to eliminate colds (M, 71, SLC, 1963). Learned in Nebraska, 1912. Brown 1113.

3196 Make a tea out of Indian root to cure a cold. It is strong and nasty, but it works (M, 1945).

3197 Molasses and soybeans mixed together will cure a bad cold (F, SLC, 1962); Molasses and sulphur will prevent colds (F, 40, 1974).

3198 Infallible remedy for a cold: three parts mustard, two parts cornstarch, water. Mix and drink and cold will be cured (F, Ir, SLC, 1950).

3199 Sagebrush tea is good for colds (Anon, 1961).

3200 Sweet balsam, yarrow, saffron and mountain rush were used for colds (M, SLC, 1946). Brown 1123.

3201  Tabasco sauce taken when a cold is coming on will get rid of the cold (F, 19, SLC, 1963).

3202  Vinegar and honey can cure colds (M, 18, SLC, 1964); Make a syrup of vinegar, butter, molasses to . . . (M, 18, SLC, 1964). (For a discussion of the famous Dr. C. R. Jarvis vinegar and honey cures, see note to No. 2934, above. --Eds.)

3203  Whiskey and aspirin cures a cold (F, SLC, 1963).

3204  Drink whiskey with rock candy dissolved in it to cure a cold (F, 21, SLC, 1964). Cf. Brown 1109 (notes).

3205  To cure a cold, drink hot whiskey with honey and lemon juice (F, Helper, 1967).

3206  If you sprinkle yeast on your food, you'll get rid of any cold (F, 18, Hunter, 1964).

3207  Take a laxative for a cold. It will clean out the system (F, Woods Cross, 1964). Heard from a practical nurse.

3208  Put a drop of coal oil in sugar and eat it to cure a cold (F, 60, Midvale, 1972).

3209  Mix a few drops of kerosene and add one teaspoon sugar and swallow it down for your cold (M, 43, SLC, 1971). Brown 1121.

3210  Sweet spirits of nitre was used for a cold (F, 55, Monticello, 1946).

3211  Dried rats tails will cure a cold (F, 45, SLC, 1934).

## External Applications

3212  Rub a mixture of camphor and lard on the neck to cure a cold (F, 19, SLC, 1964). Cf. Brown 1133.

3213  Mustard plaster for congestion and heavy chest cold: four tablespoons flour, one tablespoon soda. Mix together dry, add enough water to spread. Place in a cloth sack and place on chest or back. Leave until skin begins to get red (a few minutes). Watch close or can burn and blister skin. Remove pack, dry skin with towel (F, 81, Logan, 1973); . . . hot mustard plaster applied to chest and left all night (F, 20, Salem, 1959). Cf. Brown 1132.

3214  Soak the feet in hot mustard water to break up a cold (F, 68, Farmington, 1917).

3215  Wear an onion plaster on your chest to cure a cold (F, 19, SLC, 1964); . . . on your neck . . . (F, 19, SLC, 1964).

3216  If you rub an onion on your feet before you go to bed, it will cure a cold (F, SLC, 1959).

3217  Fried onions on the chest and feet cure colds (F, 55, SLC, 1964).

3218  If you boil potatoes and leave them in their skins then put them around your feet, a cold will go away (F, SLC, 1967).

3219  Butterpflaster (butter plaster) on the chest will cure a cold (F, Ger, SLC, 1969).

3220  A live chicken was cut open and placed on the chest of one ill with a cold (M, SLC, 1946).

3221  To cure a chest cold apply warm cow dung (M, Midvale, 1964).

3222  Rub goat tallow on the neck and chest to cure a cold (F, 19, SLC, 1964).

3223  Grease rubbed on the soles of the feet heads off colds in the head (F, 65, SLC, 1965). Cf. Brown 1126.

3224  Rub yourself with goose grease to cure a cold (F, 78, SLC, 1964); Rub . . . on the chest, the palms, and the soles of the feet . . . (M, 67, SLC, 1940); . . . around the neck . . . (F, 19, SLC, 1964); . . . goose grease and turpentine . . . (F, SLC, 1964); A sock or rag rubbed in goose grease and camphor was worn about the neck in order to heal colds and keep away the "north wind" (M, 71, SLC, 1964). Heard in Wyoming, 1922. Brown 1126.

3225  To cure a chest cold, rub brown paper with lard and wear on the chest (F, Nephi, 1930).

3226  Hot lard rags are used for chest colds (F, 57, Logan, 1973). Learned in Idaho, 1920. Cf. Brown 1129.

3227  Grease the neck and chest with hot skunk oil to cure a cold (M, 19, Provo, 1964).

3228  Kerosene and butter plaster will cure a cold (M, SLC, 1969).

3229  A tablespoon of turpentine in a cup of warm, melted lard, rubbed on the chest was thought to be a good cure for colds (M, 46, SLC, 1925). Cf. Brown 1130.

3230  A worn stocking tied around the neck will cure a cold (M, SLC, 1961); . . . clean silk stocking . . . (F, 21, SLC, 1964); For a cold, tie a dirty sock around your neck, and it will ward off the evil spirits (F, SLC, 1964); . . . dirty woolen sock . . . (M, SLC, 1961).

3231  To cure a cold, dip underwear in cold water. Wear them to bed all night (F, Swiss, 44, SLC, 1964); To prevent a cold . . . (F, SLC, 1969).

3232  Cold remedy: Heat a brick, place it in a paper sack, and put it on your neck while reclining to obtain relief (F, 19, SLC, 1962).

3233  Cure for a cold: Put an ice pack on your head and a hot brick in a sock on your neck (F, SLC, 1963).

3234  Sweat a cold out by using hot rocks and blankets (F, SLC, 1964). Attributed to the Indians.

3235  The best cure for a cold is a hot steam bath for about two hours. Then plunge into an icy river to wash the cold away after it has been drawn out (M, 63, SLC, 1918).

3236 Paint the bottoms of your feet with iodine to prevent a cold (M, SLC, 1967).

3237 My dad used to make us put sulphur in our shoes and wear it all day long. We also used to burn it on the stove in the mornings. It was supposed to keep colds away (F, SLC, 1969).

3238 Wet your feet in salt water daily, and you will not get a cold (M, 49, SLC, 1964).

3239 Rub grease on the soles of your feet, and you won't get a cold (F, 82, SLC, 1964).

Miscellaneous

3240 Beads of amber around the neck keep off colds (F, SLC, 1967).

3241 Hang a bag of asafetida around your neck, and you won't catch cold (M, 56, Ogden, 1963); When you have a cold, putting asafetida around your neck will kill germs (M, 70, Copperton, 1964); A sack of asafetida around the neck will cure a cold (F, SLC, 1957); A piece of asafetida tied on a string around the neck will prevent colds (M, Bountiful, 1960). Brown 1099.

3242 Garlic in a sack around the neck will keep away colds (M, Vernal, 1961); Garlic in a dirty sock around the neck . . . (M, 54, Midvale, 1948); Garlic in an old sock . . . (M, Magna, 1963); Carry raw garlic around your neck, it will cure a cold (F, 44, SLC, 1965); A garlic necklace around the neck will cure a cold (F, 19, SLC, 1964).

3243 Hang a nutmeg around your neck, and it will clear up your cold (M, Bountiful, 1959).

3244 An onion hung around the neck will get rid of a cold (F, 20, Laketown, 1955); Hang an onion . . . and you won't get a cold (M, SLC, 1958).

3245 Hang a little bag of sassafras around your neck to keep from catching cold (F, SLC).

3246 To ward off a cold, wear a little sack of tobacco and garlic around your neck all winter (M, Ogden, 1957).

3247 If you put eucalyptus leaves under your pillow, it will cure a cold (F, Ger-Dan, RN, 1974).

3248 An onion under the pillow will ward off colds (F, 66, Bountiful, 1933).

3249 For a cold cut up onions and put them on the floor and walk around in them and you'll be cured (F, 19, SLC, 1962); Cure a cold by placing an onion on the floor and stomping on it (F, 19, SLC, 1955); Grind up onions to cure a cold and have them all around you for the night (F, 20, SLC, 1955); . . . put cut up onions all about the house and inhale the odor (F, 19, SLC, 1963); . . . quarter an onion and put each part in each window of the house (F, SLC, 1964).

3250 To dry up a cold, cut a potato in half. Place it cut side up under the bed and the cold will go away (F, SLC, 1960).

3251 Gargle a solution of salt and vinegar for a cold (F, 19, SLC, 1964).

3252 I once heard that people would have their heads cut open to release the pressure which built up from a cold (F, SLC, 1967).

3253 After a haircut, boys' heads were doused with cold water to prevent them from catching cold (F, 1957).

3254 If you tie a lock of your hair to a stick, it will cure a cold (F, 35, SLC, 1950). Cf. Brown 1145.

3255 Keep a black silk cord to protect against a cold (F, 42, Kearns, 1963).

3256 Any string around the neck keeps away a cold (F, SLC, 1961); . . . if a person has a summer cold, tie a string around their neck and the cold will go away (F, Hooper, 1963). Cf. Brown 1141.

3257 If you put on your shoes every morning after rising, you'll never get a cold (F, 20, SLC, 1954).

3258 If you accidentally fall into a creek, your cold will be cured (M, 48, Vernal, 1938).

3259 If you catch a falling autumn leaf, you will not have a cold all winter (F, 15, SLC, 1961).

3260 To cure a cold, you are supposed to plant a rusty nail six feet from the east side of your house, and in two or three days your cold will go away (M, 21, SLC, 1963).

3261 If you have a cold, breathe deeply three times on a hog, and the next day the cold will be gone (M, SLC, 1967).

3262 By dropping a spider in a thimble and plugging the thimble with a cork and wearing it on a string around the neck, a cold can be cured (M, SLC). Heard in Wyoming, 1910.

COLD SORE

3263 A cold sore on a girl means that she has been kissed. Sometimes they are called "kissing sores" (F, Tooele, 1957).

3264 Cold sores will not heal until they have been made to bleed freely (M, SLC, 1925).

3265 If you eat two servings of yogurt each day, it will cure cold sores; if you keep eating it each day, it will also keep them from coming back (F, Bountiful, 1969).

3266 To keep a cold sore from breaking out, rub it with a woolen cloth until it burns (M, Draper, 1920).

3267 Rub earwax on cold sores to cure them (M, 19, SLC, 1957).

3268    When you wet your finger, rub it behind
your ear, and then rub it on a cold
sore.  The sore will vanish (M, SLC,
1963); When you think you are getting a
cold sore, rub behind your ear and then
rub your lip (M, 22, SLC, 1960).

3269    Rub the head of a match over the head of
a cold sore to cure it (M, 19, SLC,
1964).

3270    Rub something pure silver on a cold
sore, and it will go away.  You can use
a spoon or a ring, or something like
that (F, Tooele, 1968).

3271    Take a needle and sterilize it.  Stick
it into one of the cold sores.  Then
without washing the needle or even
touching it, take the pus and put it
under your arm.  It is supposed to be a
method of self-inoculation.  I guess it
gives you immunity against the germs
which cause the blister (F, RN, Provo,
1969).

## COLIC

3272    To cure the colic, stand on your head
for a quarter of an hour (F, SLC, 1961).
Brown 1147.

3273    Catnip tea was used for colic (M, SLC,
1946).

## CONSTIPATION

3274    Milk and cheese will cause constipation
(M, 55, SLC, 1964).

3275    To cure chronic constipation, drink
three large glasses of warm water before
breakfast (M, 44, Layton, 1970).

3276    For constipation brew senna tea and give
to the patient with milk and sugar.
Give a whole cupful (F, 63, Welsh, SLC,
1907).

3277    Molasses and honey are good for
constipation (F, 87, Providence, 1900).

3278    When you have constipation, sew a piece
of sheep's intestine to your shirttail
(M, 22, SLC, 1964).

## CONSUMPTION

3279    If you gad about in the night air, you
will get consumption (F, Bountiful,
1915).

3280    Eating mustard on Fridays causes acute
consumption (M, SLC, 1962).

3281    Fresh blood from the slaughterhouse is
good for consumption (M, SLC, 1920);
Drink warm blood of a calf . . . (M,
SLC, 1920).

3282    The skin of a cat worn on the chest can
be used to cure consumption (M, SLC,
1957).  (As recently as the 1960s fine
Paris drugstores displayed in their
windows tanned cat furs for use in
various respiratory and arthritic
diseases.  --Eds.)

## CONVULSIONS AND FITS

3283    Don't go out on Friday night on the
thirteenth day, or you will have
convulsions that night (M, 12, SLC,
1964).

3284    A salt shaker under the pillow at night
was believed to cure fits caused by
worms (SLC, 1946).

3285    If you wear a string of nutmegs around
your neck, it will prevent fits (F, 80,
SLC).

3286    An emerald worn around the neck will
stop the person from having convulsions
(M, MD, SLC, 1959).  Heard from
patients.

## CORNS, BUNIONS, ETC.

3287    A pale sunset means there will be pain
in one's corns (F, SLC).

3288    Spit on corns every morning just after
you awaken, and they will disappear (M,
19, Clearfield, 1964).  Heard in
Arizona, 1955.  Brown 1198.

3289    Corns can be removed by making a cross
upon them with a saliva-moistened finger
immediately upon awakening in the
morning (M, SLC, 1946).

3290    Put onion skins on a corn to heal it (F,
18, SLC, 1964).

3291    To get rid of corns on the feet, soak
feet daily in sauerkraut (M, 22, SLC,
1963).

3292    Castor oil on corns will cure them (F,
SLC, 1969).

3293    To cure corns, steal a small piece of
beef and bury it in the ground.  As it
rots away, the corn will go away (F,
SLC, 1961).

3294    Put raw pork on a corn to cure it (F,
19, SLC, 1964).

3295    To cure corns and calluses, cover them
with chicken drippings (F, 41, SLC,
1964).

3296    To get rid of corns, apply cow's urine
to them (M, 78, SLC, 1964).  First heard
in Wyoming.

3297    To cure a bunion, make a plaster of
fresh cow dung and place it on the
bunion (F, 88, Union, 1925); . . . make
a solution of cow dung and whale oil,
the bunion will disappear (M, 47, SLC,
1963).

## COUGH

3298    Each time you cough you lose three
minutes of your life (F, 21, SLC, 1963).

### Teas, Syrups, Other Internal Remedies

3299    Horehound syrup for coughs (F, 60,
Duchesne, 1930s); horehound and molasses
(M, Tooele, 1957).  Brown 1208.

3300  For a cough eat boiling garlic as hot as you can stand it (M, 50, It, SLC, 1965).

3301  For coughs drink onion juice (F, 67, SLC, 1964).

3302  Make cough medicine out of honey and onions and brown sugar.  You stew the onions a little and crush the juice out and put it in with the honey and brown sugar and essence of peppermint or fresh peppermint (F, Moab, 1953); Put sugar on onions and squeeze it for cough syrup (F, SLC, 1964); Simmer onions, honey, and water together for hours to make cough syrup (M, Tooele, 1957).

3303  Mrs. F used to make a cough medicine.  It tasted like it had senna leaves and alum in it (F, Moab, 1953).

3304  We used powdered slippery elm for a cough.  Any mucilage drink is good for the lungs.  We also used flaxseed for a cough (F, 81, Logan, 1946).

3305  Milk and honey are good for a cough (M, SLC, 1959).

3306  Make a syrup of vinegar, butter and molasses for a cough (F, 72, SLC, 1964).  Cf. Brown 1219.

3307  Sugar and butter mixed together is used for cough medicine (F, 23, Spanish Fork, 1970).

3308  They used to make a cough syrup with honey, flaxseed, lemons and ipecac (F, Moab, 1953); . . . the juice of three lemons and honey (F, 70, Provo, 1900).

3309  Remedy for cough:  Wash an egg and put it, shell and all, in a quarter cup of vinegar.  Let it remain in the vinegar until the egg completely dissolves, then take a spoonful or two of the mixture every time you cough (F, 66, Woods Cross, 1948).

3310  Kerosene for a cough.  One teaspoon to a glass of water (F, 60, Duchesne, 1930s).

3311  For coughs:  One teaspoon sugar and two or three drops kerosene (F, 70, Provo, 1919).

3312  Make a syrup of kerosene, sugar and onion juice and take as often as needed to cure a cough (M, 28, Coalville, 1949).

3313  To cure colds and coughs, put an asafetida bag around the neck (F, Logan, 1970).

3314  When black velvet is put around the neck, a cough will be cured (F, 76, SLC, 1964).

CRAMPS, ETC.

3315  If you got the cramps, well then they used the camphor.  They would give you a few drops of it.  You know that's very stout.  They'd put it in hot water and give it to you (F, Moab, 1953).

3316  To cure a cramp, place a cork between the bed and the mattress, or between the sheets (F, 69, Eng, SLC, 1963).  First heard in England, 1910.

3317  If you lay raw potatoes on a person's stomach, it will stop cramps (M, SLC, 1961).

3318  A brass ring will stop cramps in the fingers (M, 23, Midvale, 1964).  Brown 1237f.

3319  If you tie a chicken wing above your knee, you will not get any charley horses (F, 63, Monroe, 1964).

3320  For cramps in the legs and feet at night, turn your shoes upside down under the bed when you retire, as a preventative (M, SLC, 1961).  Brown 1239ff.

3321  For cramps in the feet, put feet in hot ashes (M, Layton, 1959).

3322  To keep from getting the cramps while swimming, (in Richfield, Utah, boys used to) urinate on your legs (M, Richfield, 1920).

CROUP

3323  Night air helps the croup (F).

3324  Coal oil with honey was given for croup (F, Logan, 1968); Put five drops of coal oil on one-half teaspoon sugar and eat . . . (F, 52, Provo, 1925).

3325  Eat a teaspoon of kerosene to cure the croup (F, 22, SLC, 1964).

3326  Sugar and turpentine are good for the croup (M, SLC).

External Applications

3327  A plaster made out of milk and bread placed on the chest will cure the croup (F, 56, Logan).  First heard in Wyoming, 1941.

3328  To cure croup, rub coal oil over the throat (F, 92, SLC, 1883).

3329  Rub skunk oil or sweet cream upon the chest for croup (F, SLC, 1971).

3330  If you take an old wool sock and wrap it around the neck, it will take away your croup (F, Centerfield, 1930).

3331  Wear a black velvet ribbon (a croup string) around your neck to prevent getting the croup (F, Spanish Fork, 1917); Wear black thread . . . (M, 84, Centerville, ca. 1900); If you wear a string around your neck, you will keep the croup (a bad cold) away (F, 42, SLC, 1964).  Cf. Brown 1258.

3332  Wear a shammy skin jacket to keep the croup away (F, Spanish Fork, 1917).

3333  Wear a string with three knots tied in it around your neck to prevent croup (F, 65, SLC, 1963).

3334  To cure croup, one should tie a string of beads around their neck (F, 73, Eng, SLC, 1965).

3335  A chestnut pierced and hung on a string around the neck prevents croup (M, SLC, 1959).

CUTS

3336    Never give a present with a sharp edge
without enclosing a penny or the one who
receives the gift will get cut with it
(F, Murray, 1958).

3337    Treat the weapon that made the wound (M,
58, SLC, 1960).

3338    Chewed tobacco is used as an application
to cuts (M, 63, Farmington, 1930);
Spitting tobacco juice on cuts will
prevent infection (M, 44, Layton, 1970).
Brown 1266.

3339    Heat milk and bread, and put it on cuts
and scratches. This was supposed to
bring out the infection (F, 80, American
Fork, 1972).

3340    Put a salt pork poultice on a cut after
bathing it carefully (F, 54, Logan,
1970). First heard in Wisconsin, 1928.

3341    Raw turpentine was often used as a
disinfectant for cuts and scrapes (M,
46, SLC, 1931).

3342    The old Indian used to say when he cut
himself and put remedy on the cut:  "No
sting 'um, no cure 'um" (F, 60, SLC,
1911).

3343    For cuts on one's person, spit on wound
and hold it against the bark of a tree
and the poison will be drawn away from
the cut (M, SLC, 1959). Cf. Brown 1260.

3344    A dog was sometimes allowed to lick a
cut or scrape because it was thought
that a dog's saliva contained a
substance which would cause rapid
healing (F, 46, Ogden, 1925).

DANDRUFF

3345    Dandruff can be cured by a solution of
boiled hemlock (F, 65, SLC, 1964).

3346    For dandruff rub kerosene on your head
(F, SLC, 1960); To prevent dandruff,
. . . (M, 97, Bountiful, 1961).

DEAFNESS

3347    If earwigs crawl in your ears, you will
become deaf (F, 21, SLC, 1953); If you
sleep out at night then earwigs (bugs
with pinchers in the back) will crawl in
your ears backwards and snip your
eardrums off (F, SLC, 1971).

3348    Snake oil is good for deafness (M, SLC,
1957).

DIABETES

3349    Eating too many sweets will cause
diabetes (M, 24, SLC, 1964).

3350    Alfalfa tea or sauerkraut juice will
cure diabetes (F, SLC, 1961).

DIARRHEA AND SUMMER COMPLAINT

3351    A cup of ginger tea can cure anything
that you can come up with. It really

works well for diarrhea though (F, SLC,
1967).

3352    To check diarrhea, make a concoction
from the leaves of horehound (M, 23,
SLC, 1960).

3353    To prevent summer complaint, drink tea
made from horsetail leaves (F, 26, SLC,
1964).

3354    Licorice in wine juice cures diarrhea
(F, SLC, 1961).

3355    For diarrhea boil rice with water and
eat it. You may also squeeze the juice
from a pomegranate and drink it (F, Gr,
SLC, 1962); . . . drink water from
boiled rice (F, SLC, 1925).

3356    For the cure of diarrhea make a paste of
cream and flour. Take this in
tablespoon doses (M, 80, Monroe, 1905).

3357    Peppermint tea with zwieback will help
diarrhea (F, SLC, 1969).

3358    For summer complaint they used to just
get in the buggy and go up in the
mountains, and they'd be all right (F,
Moab, 1953).

3359    Boil rhinoceros tooth shavings in water
and drink the cool mixture to cure
diarrhea (M, Chin, MD, SLC, 1969).

DIPHTHERIA

3360    Diphtheria attacks only the throat (F,
SLC, 1961).

3361    Laws were passed to keep people from
entering a diphtheria area of town.  One
man was fined ten dollars for just
traveling down a street containing some
diphtheria cases (F, 28, Vernal, 1955).
Event took place ca. 1893.

3362    To disinfect a house from diphtheria,
take everything outside and put an open
container of formaldehyde in the center
of each room. Then shut the house up
tight. The fumes from the formaldehyde
will disinfect the house (F, 28, Vernal,
1945).

3363    Diphtheria was so dreaded that no one
was allowed to enter another person's
home to help. They even had to go out
at night and bury their dead (F, 28,
Vernal, 1955).

3364    They had diphtheria here so bad--it
practically cleaned out some families--
and they used to get a rabbit or bird or
a small animal and kill it and split it
down and bind it on the neck. In a
minute it would turn dark and draw out
the infection (F, Moab, 1953).

DOG BITE, BITES OF OTHER ANIMALS

3365    A plantain leaf poultice is a good
remedy for dog bite (F, Lehi, early
1900s).

3366    Rub axle grease on a dog bite to cure it
(F, 18, SLC, 1964). Brown 1291.

3367    To cure a dog bite, take the hair of the
dog that bit you, rub it on the place

where you were bitten, and it will be cured (M, 33, SLC, 1964); . . . apply hair of the dog . . . (M, Ger, SLC, 1963); . . . take hair from the dog to ward off sickness (M, 27, SLC, 1964); A hair from the animal which has bitten you will cure the bite (F, 56, Ogden, 1930). Brown 1293. (This suggested cure is a prime example of the medical doctrine of similia similibus curantur, 'similar things are cured by similar means.' Often this means that ailments are cured by the same agents that cause them. Cf. No. 3970, passim, below where various snake parts are employed to cure snakebite. --Eds.)

3368  To prevent rabies, kill the dog, and the person bitten will be safe (F, 14, Midvale, 1964); To prevent insanity caused by a mad dog bite, kill the dog immediately (Anon, Park City, 1930). Brown 1692.

3369  To kill a dog that bites you, put some of the blood from the bite on a piece of red flannel and burn (F, 28, SLC, 1948).

## DROPSY

3370  Milkweed made into a tea cures dropsy and purifies the blood in the brain (F, Orem, 1967).

3371  If you dig down below ground level and get the potato off a potato cactus, then cut it up and make a tea out of it, then have the person drink it, it will cure the dropsy right away (F, Provo).

3372  To rid oneself of dropsy, eat toasted toads (F, 19, SLC, 1962).

## DYSENTERY

3373  Raspberry tea is for dysentery (F, Logan, 1946).

3374  For dysentery drink water in which white writing paper has been soaked (F, 39, Layton, 1951).

## EARACHE

3375  If you eavesdrop on a telephone call, your ear will become diseased (F, 21, SLC, 1963).

3376  If you have a running ear, do not try to care for it, because it means the mischief is running out (F, SLC, 1958).

3377  Drink camomile tea to act as a sedative when you have an earache (F, 75, SLC, 1964).

3378  Have someone spit tobacco juice in your ear to cure your earache (F, 21, Price, 1955).

3379  Cure for an earache:  Pour a teaspoonful of warm water into the ear.  Let it remain a while, then let it run out slowly (F, 19, SLC, 1950).

3380  Drop one drop of very cold water into an aching ear.  This is a permanent cure for earache (F, SLC, 1952).

3381  Linseed oil boiled and put in a linen cloth should be applied to an earache to stop it (F, SLC, 1969).  Cf. Brown 1328.

3382  Put sweet oil or olive oil in ear to cure earache (F, 21, SLC, 1964).

3383  For an earache we used to heat molasses and drop a drop in the ear.  Also olive oil (F, 73, Moab, 1953).

3384  For a person who had an earache it was advisable to roast an onion and then put it in the ear.  Then place a cloth around the head to hold it in (F, 71, SLC, 1900).  Cf. Brown 1323f.

3385  A pepper pack (put pepper in a bag, dampen it with oil) is good for earache (F, Logan, 1968).  Cf. Brown 1326.

3386  To cure an earache, split a baked potato and pop it on the ear (F, 44, SLC, 1930).

3387  Put a raisin in the ear to drive away an earache (M, SLC).

3388  Put human milk in the ear to cure earache (F, 20, SLC, 1964).

3389  The wax in the ear of a person who does not have earache will cure the earache in another person's ear (F, 19, SLC, 1952).

3390  To cure an earache, pour warm urine into the ear (M, 21, SLC, 1964); . . . make a child piddle (urinate) in a saucer, then drop some in the ear (F, SLC, 1971). Brown 1318.

3391  The fat of a fox, when warmed and placed in the ear, will cure an earache (F, 43, Logan, 1935).

3392  An earache was cured by blowing into the ear (M, SLC, 1946).

3393  If one had an earache, it could be healed by having someone blow pipe smoke in the infected ear (M, 46, SLC, 1930); . . . cigarette smoke . . . (F, 52, Provo, 1925).  Cf. Brown 1327, 1338.

## EARS

3394  If your ears get clogged up, jump up and down on the opposite foot of the ear that's funny.  Then all of the stuff will just come right out (M, SLC, 1967).

## EPILEPSY

3395  Anyone with epilepsy is possessed by evil spirits (M, 53, Logan, 1925).

3396  For epilepsy pull the patient's shirt over his head, pull it out of the house through the chimney and bury it at the crossroads (F, Logan, 1958).

## ERYSIPELAS

3397  Fresh cow manure, while still warm, was used for erysipelas (M, Lund, 1900).

EYE AILMENTS

3398  You cannot cure nearsightedness by wearing glasses (F, 46, SLC, 1936).

3399  Wearing rubbers (overshoes) in a house will cause a person to develop weak eyes (M, Ogden, 1961); Wearing rubbers will give one sore eyes (M, SLC, 1920); . . . rubber-soled shoes causes bad eyes (M, SLC, 1960).

3400  If you wear glasses and drop them and break a lens, your sight will be worse thereafter (M, 21, SLC, 1959).

3401  Wear earrings for sore eyes (F, SLC, 1910).  Brown 1384, cf. 2108.

3402  If you have your ears pierced, you will not have sore eyes (M, 67, Ger, SLC, 1945); Gold earrings in pierced ears will cure weak eyes (M, 21, SLC, 1952). Heard from Gypsies.  Brown 1385.

Vegetable and Animal Products

3403  A slice of ripe cucumber placed over each eye served as a cure for sore eyes (M, SLC, 1946).

3404  Rub scraped potato on your eye (M, SLC, 1930).

3405  For inflamed eyes, make an eye wash from the roots of roses (F, 64, SLC, 1964).

3406  Tea is good for curing sore eyes (F, 72, Provo, 1921).

3407  A piece of toast, dunked in wine, is very good for a sore eye (F, Gr, SLC, 1962).

3408  Foreign particles in the eye:  Drop a drop of milk in your eye and the particle will come out (F, Provo, 1973). Brown 1361.

3409  A piece of linseed placed in the eye will attract to it and remove foreign objects and particles that have gotten into the eye (F, SLC, 1920).

3410  Crushed bedbugs mixed with salt and human bile serve as an ointment for sore eyes (F, 22, SLC, 1954).

3411  To remove a foreign object from the eyes, make a loop from a long horse hair.  Put it in the eye, close the lid. When the hair is pulled out, it will bring the foreign object with it (F, 30, SLC, 1964).

Rainwater, Snow, Etc.

3412  The first time you hear the swallow in the spring, if you go to a stream or fountain and wash your eyes, at the same time making a silent prayer, the swallow will carry away all your eye troubles (F, SLC, 1961).

3413  Pure rainwater is a sure cure for sore eyes (F, 44, Midvale, 1930); . . . collected on Easter . . . (M, 57, Midvale); . . . caught during the last days of April and the first four of May, is good for pain in the eye (M, 50, It, SLC, 1965).  Cf. Brown 1375.

3414  The first snow is good to rub sore eyes with (M, Ger, SLC, 1965).  Brown 1378.

3415  Catch the last snow of the season, melt and put into a bottle.  It will cure sore eyes (M, SLC, 1961).  Brown 1379.

3416  Whenever your eyes start really feeling tired or they get all bloodshot, just mix brine, salt and water and pour it on (M, SLC, 1967).  Cf. Brown 1381.

Miscellaneous

3417  Cigarettes are good for the eyes (M, SLC, 1949).

3418  Honey put in your eyes will remove cataracts without an operation (F, 86, Providence, 1950).

3419  If you have a foreign particle in your eye, put a flat, small pearl button in under your eyelid.  It will work itself down and when it comes out, the particle will be gone (F, Provo, 1973).

3420  If you rub cataracts with diamond particles, the cataracts will be absorbed (F).

3421  Place steel over your eyes to protect them from the sun (F, SLC, 1964).

Black Eye

3422  If you put a steak over your eye, it will draw out the swelling (M, 22, SLC, 1964); Set cold beefsteak on a blackened eye overnight (M, 46, SLC, 1924).  Brown 1391.

3423  Whenever you bump your eye and don't want it to go black, put a silver knife, fork or spoon handle on your eye (F, Provo, 1973).

Cross-Eyes

3424  If your eyes are crossed when the wind is blowing, and if the wind changes directions, you will stay cross-eyed (F, Tooele, 1964).

3425  If you cross your eyes at midnight with a full moon, they will stay that way (F, Provo, 1972).

3426  If you look cross-eyed, your eyes will stick (F, Spanish Fork, 1925); If you frequently cross your eyes, they may become crossed (M, Holladay, 1959).

3427  If you look cross-eyed at a rooster and it crows, you'll stay cross-eyed (F, SLC, 1949).

3428  If you go cross-eyed, you'll stay that way forever (M, 24, SLC, 1946).

3429  If you put your shoes on wrong it means cross-eyes (F, 20, Sandy, 1962).

Pink Eye, Snow Blindness

3430  For pink eye, wash the eyes with salt or sugar solution (M, 19, SLC, 1964).

3431 Lamp black, or any type of carbon, when placed on the eyelids and just under the lower lid, eases and helps to prevent snow blindness (F, 20, SLC, 1963).

## FAINTING

3432 If somebody fainted, they used the camphor (F, Moab, 1953).

## FALLEN PALATE

3433 A lock of hair tied very tightly at the top of the head will pull up a fallen palate (F, 21, SLC, 1946). Brown 1395.

## FALLING HAIR

3434 If you eat too much sugar, your hair will fall out (F, 47, SLC, 1957).

3435 If you wash your hair on Tuesday, it will fall out (F, Gr, W. Jordan, 1924).

3436 Never comb black hair with a black comb, or it will fall out (SLC, 1951).

3437 It is bad luck to comb the hair with a comb that has touched a corpse's head. The hair will all fall out (M, 20, SLC, 1958).

3438 If you have your hair cut during the sign of Cancer, it means you will lose your hair (M, 57, Heber City, 1910).

3439 Cutting hair makes it fall out (F, 80, SLC, 1954). Cf. Brown 839.

3440 Don't touch a rusty hair pin, or you will gradually lose your hair (F, Springfield, 1961).

3441 Falling hair can be cured by a solution of boiled hemlock (F, 65, SLC, 1964).

3442 Sage tea will restore fallen hair (F, 56, Centerville).

3443 To make hair grow, take garlic or onions and rub the place where the hair is falling or has fallen out. To make hair fall out, take the blood of a young sheep, and smear the hairy spot with it (M, 60, It, SLC, 1965).

3444 Singeing the hair prevents hair falling out by sealing the ends of the tubules (M, 53, SLC, 1925).

## FEVER

3445 Fevers are caused by swamp fogs and mists (M, 22, SLC, 1961).

3446 If you see a wooley-bear caterpillar, you must spit before it dies or you'll get a fever (F, Ogden, 1961). Cf. Brown 1413.

3447 Starve a fever and feed a cold (F, 45, SLC, 1928). Brown 1410f. (The historical development of this notion is treated by Stuart A. Gallacher in his article, "Stuff a Cold and Starve a Fever," Bulletin of the History of Medicine and Allied Sciences 11 (1942), 576-81. --Eds.)

3448 In treating someone for a high fever, take an apple and slice it in three parts. On the first day write on the first slice: "I shall not die, but live, and declare the work of the Lord" (Psalms 118:17). The next day write on the second slice: "The Lord hath chastened me sore; but He hath not given me over unto death" (Psalms 118:18). On the third day write on the third slice: "Open to me the gates of righteousness; I will enter into them, I will give thanks unto the Lord" (Psalms 118:10). Each morning give the patient a slice to eat before allowing him to eat anything else (M, 25, Je, SLC, 1965); an apple is eaten on Easter morning as a preventive of fever (F, Ger, 55, SLC, 1964).

3449 Ginger tea will cure fever (M, 44, Layton, 1970). Brown 1427.

3450 Soak the feet in hot mustard water to draw out fever (F, 68, Logan, 1970).

3451 Nannyberry tea will break a fever (M, 45, Midvale, 1964). (A tea made from sheep droppings. --Eds.)

3452 To get rid of a fever, rub onions on the soles of your feet (F, 88, St. George, 1963). Cf. Brown 1437ff.

3453 Raspberry leaf tea should be used to reduce a fever (F, 25, Logan, 1972).

3454 Sweet balsam, yarrow, saffron and mountain rush were used for fever (M, SLC, 1946).

3455 Eating watermelon will help reduce a fever (F, 72, Provo, 1938).

3456 Yarrow is used to break up a fever (F, SLC, 1957).

3457 My mother used to use a freshly killed small animal for fevers (F, Moab, 1953). Cf. Brown 1414f.

3458 Boiled bedbugs and beans cure fever (F, 71, Centerville, 1963).

3459 If someone you know has a fever, take a piece of their clothing and pray over it. They will then recover (F, 37, It, Magna, 1963).

3460 If you have a fever, cut your fingernails and put them on your neighbor's door with wax (M, MD, SLC, 1959).

3461 Heat is needed to fight fever (M, 31, SLC, 1964). Cf. Brown 1457.

3462 Put a hot stone on the head of a person having a fever, and it will go away (F, 79, Ogden, 1919).

3463 Cold water packs are used for fever (F). Cf. Brown 1459.

## FEVER BLISTERS AND SORES

3464 You get fever blisters from kissing (M, 25, SLC, 1950s); . . . when someone has been dreaming of kissing you (F, Axtell, 1958); . . . being kissed by your sweetheart (M, 71, Santaquin, 1910). Brown 4166.

3465   To cure a fever sore, let a dog lick it (F, Bear River City, 1957).

## FINGER, FINGERNAILS

3466   Don't point your finger at the moon, or it will rot off (M, Clearfield, 1935). Heard from Indians.

3467   For a mashed fingernail apply a baked potato to ease the pain (F, 72, Provo, 1910).

## FOOD POISONING

3468   Don't cook food in aluminum, or it will poison you (F, 75, Murray, 1957).

3469   If a white man's shadow falls on the food of an Indian, the food is poisoned (F, 18, Bountiful, 1963).  Indian belief.

3470   Eating a mixture of foods will result in food poisoning (F, SLC, 1961).

3471   If you drink milk while eating fresh cherries, you will get poisoned (F, 29, Ogden, 1952); . . . you'll die of a horrible disease (F, 18, SLC, 1962); Cherries and milk can only be eaten at bedtime, or you'll be sick (M, Box Elder Co, 1946); Choke cherries and milk . . . (F, 1957).

3472   The following combinations of foods are poisonous:  milk and orange juice or other citrus fruit; milk and fish (F, SLC, 1961).

3473   Never eat ice cream with berries, it is poison (F, Ger, SLC, 1961).

3474   Never use cold milk to make gravy, or it will poison you (F, 44, SLC, 1961).

3475   Never eat cucumbers and drink milk at the same meal.  The combination is poisonous (F, SLC, 1962).

3476   Raw cucumbers without salt are poisonous (F, SLC, 1942).

3477   Margarine is poisonous (F, SLC, 1959).

3478   Meat poisons the system (F, SLC, 1960).

3479   Pork is unclean as a food; likewise shellfish.  Meat from the waist down cannot be eaten.  Meat and dairy products cannot be consumed at the same time, a six-hour interval being prescribed between the consumption of foods of these two different categories (M, 60, It, SLC, 1965).

3480   One will get food poisoning from eating a mackerel which has been exposed to moonlight (M, SLC, 1959).

3481   Oysters are poisonous to those who were born in months with "R" in them, when they eat them during a month with "R" in it (F, 20, SLC, 1964); Oysters eaten in months without "R" give ptomaine poisoning (M, Holladay, 1959).  Brown 2820.

3482   Oysters and milk taken together cause poisonous effects (M, SLC, 1961).

3483   Oysters and beer eaten together can be poisonous (M, SLC, 1961).

3484   Never eat and drink pickles and milk together.  It will make you sick (F, 49, SLC, 1964); . . . pickles and ice cream . . . (F, SLC, 1958).

3485   Tomatoes are poison (F, 54, SLC, 1963); Fresh picked tomatoes . . . (M, 49, SLC, 1961).

3486   Tomatoes and milk don't go together. They will make you sick (F, 49, Eng, SLC, 1964).

3487   Watermelons turn poison if allowed to stand after being cut (F, SLC, 1925).

3488   Never have bread, honey and milk because honey and milk will form a poison which is bad for you (M, 56, Ogden, 1963).

3489   Never eat bread if it even has a speck of mold on it, or it will poison you (F, 61, Ogden, 1950).

## FRACTURE

3490   If you suck a lemon daily, you will never break a bone in your body (F, 45, Midvale, 1964).

3491   Dropping of a piece of chalk predicts the breaking of a friend's bones (F, 19, SLC, 1945).

3492   Never step on a cracker, or you'll soon have a broken bone (F, 74, SLC, 1964).

3493   Step on a stone and you'll break your mother's bone (F, Bountiful, 1947).

3494   A broken chair leg forewarns a broken leg (M, SLC, 1964).

3495   It is bad luck to carry the crutches of a person with a broken arm or leg, because you will be the next to break one (M, 19, SLC, 1963).

3496   Never put shoes on the shelf where hats are, or you are sure to break a leg while in a high place (F, 69, SLC, 1965).

3497   Never walk under a ladder, or you will break a limb (F, 80, SLC, 1964).

3498   If you step on a spider, you will break a leg (M, 26, Bountiful, 1945); . . . step on a granddaddy long-legs, . . . a bone (F, Vernal, 1958).

3499   If you kill a robin or destroy its nest, you will break a bone within a year (M, 18, SLC, 1957).  Cf. Brown 1481ff.

3500   If an owl is caught and its claws and wings are broken, the person who catches the owl will have his own limbs broken by some mysterious agency (M, 71, Midvale, 1911).

3501   If one kills a wren, he will break a bone before the year is out (F, Swed, SLC, 1964).  Brown 1483.

3502   After you break your arm, if you don't drink milk while it is healing, it won't grow straight (F, 54, Richfield, 1929).

## FRECKLES

3503  Freckles are marks where the sun kisses you (M, SLC, 1954).

3504  Freckles are a sign of good luck (F, 44, SLC, 1941).

3505  If a person touches a toad or frog, he will have freckles (M, SLC, 1960).

3506  If you wash your face in olive oil once a month, you'll never have freckles (M, SLC, 1957).

3507  To cure freckles, go to a stone and step over it three times backward and then three times forward (F, 65, SLC, 1944). Brown 1525.

3508  Before going to bed tie a string around the finger to keep freckles away (F, SLC, 1961).

### Rain, Dew

3509  Stand in the rain and don't wipe your face.  You will get freckles (F, 22, SLC, 1959).

3510  To get rid of freckles, go into the pasture early in the morning and put the dew from the middle of a cow pie on the freckles (F, 52, Provo, 1925).  Cf. Brown 1492.

3511  By rubbing dew on your face on the first day of spring, you will remove freckles (M, 22, SLC, 1964); . . . early morning dew . . . (F, 20, SLC, 1949). Cf. Brown 1509ff.

3512  Spread rainwater from a hollow log over your freckles to make them disappear (M, 9, SLC, 1963).  Cf. Brown 1519ff.

### Plant and Animal Products

3513  May flowers, gathered before sunrise, keep freckles away (M, Ogden, 1959).

3514  The juice of a dandelion will clear up freckles (M, SLC, 1945).

3515  To get rid of freckles, wash them in cucumber juice (F, Lehi, 1957); . . . rub with cucumber slices (M, Tooele, 1957).  Brown 1497.

3516  To get rid of freckles, wash your face in melon rind (F, SLC, 1961). Brown 1500, 1504.

3517  Rub lemons on freckles to make them disappear (F, 40, SLC, 1972). Brown 1499.

3518  To cure freckles and tan, wash your face in human urine every night (M, 44, Coalville, 1935).  Brown 1485.

3519  Rub a wet baby's diaper on your face to remove freckles (M, SLC, 1957). Cf. Brown 1486.

3520  Wash the skin in buttermilk every day to cure freckles (M, 24, SLC, 1950). Brown 1490.

3521  Wash your face in donkey's milk and it will get rid of your freckles (M, 78, SLC).

3522  To remove freckles, rub a live frog on them (F, 75, Moab, 1964); . . . wash your face in frog eggs (M, SLC, 1950).

## FROSTBITE

3523  For frostbite, bathe the feet in running water from a stream that runs west (F, 65, SLC, 1941).

3524  Frostbite was called chill pains back then, and it pains and itches, but all you have to do is take off your shoes and run in the snow, or set your feet in a tub of snow and your feet will stop hurting (F, Provo, 1973).  Cf. Brown 1532.

3525  For frostbite make a poultice out of rotten apples (F, Provo, 1973).

3526  Rub the gall out of the cow's bladder on frostbite, and that will heal it (F).

3527  Raw beefsteak will cure frostbite (F, Provo, 1973).

3528  Rub frostbite with coal oil (F, Provo, 1973).

## GALLBLADDER, GALLSTONES

3529  To cure any gallbladder trouble, drink apple juice for three days.  Take no other food during this time.  This will cure the trouble (M, 80, Monroe, 1905).

3530  One teaspoon vinegar and one teaspoon honey mixed in one cup water and drunk each morning will solve any gallbladder troubles (F, Sandy, 1969).

3531  If you eat red beets, you'll never have gallstones (F, 38, Logan, 1955).

3532  If you eat a cherry pit, you'll develop gallstones (F, 19, SLC, 1963).

3533  Eating a lot of grapefruit will help cure gallstones (F, SLC).

3534  Sheep dung boiled in milk and taken internally is a sure cure for gallstones (M, 91, Dan, Midvale, 1964).

## GOITER

3535  To rid oneself of goiter, eat a burned sponge (F, 19, SLC, 1962).

3536  In order to cure goiters, a person should wear beads (F, 60, SLC, 1963). Brown 1538.

3537  Amber beads around the neck will prevent goiter (M, SLC, 1910); In Escalante many of the women wore amber beads to reduce an enlarged goiter.  Remove a bead at a time and the goiter gets smaller (F, RN, SLC).  Brown 1539.

3538  If you cover pennies with olive oil and wear them around your neck, it will cure your goiters (M, Logan, 1970).

3539    If you rub a goiter with a toad, it will go away (F, 65, SLC, 1954).

## GOUT

3540    Wrapping snakes around your joints will cure the gout (F, SLC, 1967).

## GUNSHOT WOUNDS

3541    Informant's son had his hip joint shot away. She prayed to the Lord, and he told her to do the following: The ashes from the bark of the shagbark hickory were used to make a lye and this was put right into the wound. She made a poultice out of slippery elm to fill the wound, and poured a bottle of balsam into the wound to soothe the pain. After five weeks he was entirely recovered. A flexible gristle had grown in place of the missing joint and socket (F).

3542    HG of Woods Cross was fighting in France in 1944 when a piece of shrapnel hit him and penetrated his clothing as far as his garments. Mrs. A said that the boy's mother attributed his escape from injury to the protective power of the garments (F, 60, Woods Cross, 1945).

3543    A man was hit by a bullet during a fight with the Indians. One of his friends had a bottle of consecrated oil which he poured into the cleaned wound and administered to him. In two weeks the wound healed and never bothered him after that (F, 42, Manti, 1945).

3544    Porter Rockwell was promised by Joseph Smith that if he didn't cut his hair he would be immune from bullets and physical violence. Rockwell didn't cut his hair, and eventually he died a natural death (M, SLC, 1946). (This traditional account likely rests on the fabled strength of the Old Testament figure Samson, which was lost when he was shorn, as related in Judges, XVI. --Eds.)

## HANDS

3545    Rub the hands with the first wet snow that falls and you'll not have sore hands (M, SLC, 1961). Brown 1566.

3546    Use cream from the top of the milk bottle as a lotion for sore, rough hands (F, Moroni).

## HANGNAILS

3547    A mixture of sugar and soap will cure hangnails (M, SLC).

## HAY FEVER

3548    Hay fever is usually drawn to nervous adults (F, SLC, 1961).

3549    Hay fever is contagious (F, SLC, 1961).

3550    If camphor ice is taped in the navel, it will prevent hay fever (F, SLC, 1960).

3551    For hay fever eat the color out of violets each spring (F, SLC, 1969).

3552    To cure hay fever, smoke coffee grounds in a pipe (F, SLC, 1960).

3553    Chew a good wad of beeswax before the hay fever season, and it will substantially decrease your hay fever (M, SLC, 1969).

3554    Honey straight from the comb is a sure cure for hay fever (M, Box Elder Co, 1944).

3555    Hay fever is spontaneously cured after seven years (M, SLC, 1959).

## HEADACHE

3556    The entering of evil spirits into one's body can be detected by the coming of headaches and great pain (F, 42, SLC, 1956).

3557    Stepping continuously in another's footprints will cause severe headaches (M, 20, Butler, 1964); Walk in footprints in the snow, the person who made them will get a headache (M, SLC, 1957). Brown 1575f. (By the laws of contagious magic stepping in another person's footprints is a common way in which various ailments and magical harm and evil are transmitted. Contact with footprints is known in witchcraft as well as in conjury. Cf. No. 4147, below. --Eds.)

3558    I've known a lot of women that have had headaches constantly because they had a heavy head of hair, and they've had to go and have it thinned (F, Moab, 1953); Let your hair grow long to cure and prevent headache (F, 21, SLC, 1964).

3559    A woman's hair should never be cut in March--this makes it dull and lifeless and sometimes causes headaches which persist until midnight on March 31 (M, 44, SLC, 1950). Cf. Brown 1571.

3560    If you cut your hair, don't throw it outside; the birds will make a nest out of it and you will have a headache until the bird leaves its nest (M, SLC, 1961). Brown 1572, 1578ff.

3561    If you put on a hat without blowing off the dust, it means you will get a headache (M, 60, SLC, 1963).

3562    If you make up an excuse such as having a stomachache or a headache, it may come true (F, SLC, 1960).

3563    Drinking champagne gives worse headaches than the drinking of any other drink (F, 21, SLC, 1963).

3564    If eggshells are left in the sink, they will cause a headache (M, 50, It, SLC, 1965).

3565    Headaches are caused by exposure to the hot sun (M, SLC, 1930).

## Hot, Cold Packs, Etc.

3566    Soak the feet in hot water to cure a headache (M, 34, Layton, 1940).

3567 Hot cloths on the back of the neck for headaches (F, 57, Logan, 1920).

3568 Cold water packs are used for headaches (F, ca. 1860).

3569 Put plastic bags on your feet to ward off a migraine headache (F, SLC, 1963).

### Animal and Plant Products

3570 The rattles of a snake, if worn in the hat band, will cure the wearer of a headache (M, SLC, 1946); . . . will prevent headaches (M, Levan, 1957). Brown 1588.

3571 If you wear a snake skin around your head, you will never have a headache (F, 76, SLC). Cf. Brown 1589.

3572 Cobwebs across the bridge of the nose were supposedly good cures for headaches (M, 71, SLC).

3573 You can cure a headache by wearing a tooth around your neck (M, SLC, 1960.

3574 If you got a headache, then they used the camphor (F, Moab, 1953). Brown 1591.

3575 For a headache use a poultice of cornmeal (F, Ogden, 1959).

3576 A cucumber peel bound on a person's head will cure a headache (F, 48, SLC, 1964).

3577 Grasp tightly in the hand some scraped horseradish; your headache will go away (F, 29, SLC, 1964).

3578 Sliced potatoes on your forehead cures headaches (M, 19, SLC, 1950); A sliced cold potato on your head with a rag soaked in vinegar . . . (F, SLC, 1959).

3579 The last nine drops of tea poured from the teapot will cure a headache (F, 68, Grantsville, 1912).

### Miscellaneous

3580 If a person washes his hair on Good Friday and every Friday thereafter, he will never have a headache (F, It, Magna, 1961).

3581 Run bareheaded in a rainstorm on May Day, and you won't have a headache for a year (M, SLC, 1961). Cf. Brown 1610.

3582 Stick a match in your hair when you have a headache, and it will go away (M, 35, SLC, 1940).

3583 For a bad headache sleep with pennies under the pillow. It will go away (M, 19, SLC, 1964).

3584 Say abracadabra. Take syllables off. Take away pain as you take away syllables. When only ab is left, the headache should be gone (F, Roosevelt, 1964).

3585 Wear earrings to cure a headache (F, 20, SLC, 1964).

3586 Have someone spit tobacco juice in your ear to cure a headache (M, 60, Morgan, 1916).

3587 Blow smoke into the ear to prevent a headache (M, 67, SLC, 1951); . . . to cure it (F, 20, SLC, 1964).

3588 You can cure a headache by pressing the hand on the forehead so as to press each pulse-beating place (F, 65, SLC, 1931). Cf. Brown 1570.

3589 For a headache wrap your head with paper that has absorbed vinegar (F, 21, SLC, 1964). Cf. Brown 1599, 1603f.

3590 If you carry a horse chestnut when you have a headache, it will relieve the pain and cure the headache (M, 79, Pleasant Grove, 1908).

3591 Pale blue stones worn around the neck will be an effective antidote to alleviate headaches (M, MD, SLC, 1959). Cf. Brown 1608.

### HEART AILMENTS

3592 A pain in the left chest means a person is suffering from heart disease (F, SLC, 1961).

3593 Wearing a gold watch near the heart will cause heart disease (M, 50, Magna). Brown 1618.

3594 The way to cure any kind of heart trouble is to wear copper (F, SLC, 1969).

3595 Never eat garlic. It will ruin your heart (F, SLC, 1960).

3596 If you swallow gum, it will wind around your heart and kill you (F, Bountiful, 1960).

3597 If you sleep on your right side, your heart will be weak (M, SLC, 1964).

3598 For heart trouble, take two-thirds of the medicine given by the doctor and bury it in the ground (F, SLC, 1961).

3599 Put cayenne in a glass of cold water for a heart attack (Anon, SLC, 1975).

3600 Tea leaves mixed with clover is a good remedy to cure heart disease (F, SLC, 1965).

3601 To rid oneself of heart disease, eat a foxglove (F, 19, SLC, 1962).

3602 Step on a dart and you'll break your mother's heart (F, SLC, 1961).

### HICCOUGHS

3603 Hiccoughs are caused by someone talking about you. If you mention their name the hiccoughs will stop (F, 50, SLC, 1963); . . . . If you can guess who is talking about you, the hiccoughs will stop (F, SLC, 1920).

3604 If you have the hiccoughs, think of a member of the opposite sex. If that person loves you, the hiccoughs will go away (M, 21, Layton, 1964). Brown 1680.

3605  To cure hiccoughs, think of the one you love (M, 22, SLC, 1949).  Brown 1679.

3606  Think of someone who is thinking of you and your hiccoughs will stop (F, Bear River City, 1957); If you have the hiccoughs, someone is thinking of you (F, 49, Norw, SLC, 1963).

3607  To prevent hiccoughs, think of the last person you kissed (M, SLC, 1961).

3608  If you lie, you will get the hiccoughs (M, Ogden, 1959).

## Drinking Water, Swallowing

3609  To cure the hiccoughs, swallow nine times (M, 21, Holladay, 1964).

3610  To cure hiccoughs, swallow eight times and think of the one you love; if he or she loves you in return, they will go away (F, 52, Provo, 1925).

3611  To cure hiccoughs, swallow three times; hold your breath for the count of ten, and they'll be gone (M, 23, Magna, 1956).

3612  To cure the hiccoughs, drink a cup of warm water without taking a breath (F, Tooele, 1964); . . . drink a whole glass of water in one gulp (F, SLC, 1952). Cf. Brown 1643.

3613  To cure hiccoughs, drink nine swallows of water without breathing (F, Bear River City, 1957); . . . ten swallows . . . (M, 28, SLC, 1938). Cf. Brown 1647, 1650f.

3614  For hiccoughs you can drink across a cup (F, Moab, 1953); . . . drink from the wrong side of the glass (F, 25, Provo, 1948).

3615  Cure for hiccoughs:  Place a dishtowel over a glass of water and drink the water through the dishtowel.  Hold the breath for nine swallows while doing it (M, 15, Provo, 1964); . . . Drink through a handkerchief (F, SLC, 1967); . . . Drink through a napkin (F, SLC, 1961); . . . Drink through two paper towels (F, 48, Tooele).

3616  Drink nine swallows of water, holding your breath.  Then think of the person you love and take the tenth swallow.  If this person loves you in return, the hiccoughs will be gone (F, 23, SLC, 1942).

3617  To cure hiccoughs, take nine sips of water, count nine backwards, and then turn around nine times (M, SLC, 1947). Brown 1654.

3618  Place a pencil in the mouth and drink a liquid.  You will concentrate so heavily on retaining the pencil in your mouth, you will be cured of hiccoughs (M, SLC, 1971).

3619  Drink a glass of water and count to ten to cure hiccoughs (F, 54, SLC, 1963).

3620  Put about one-fourth teaspoon of cinchona bark that is powdered in a glass of water.  Give a teaspoonful every five minutes until the hiccoughs are relieved (F, Spanish Fork, 1974).

## Holding Breath

3621  You can cure hiccoughs by holding your breath and drinking water (M, 20, SLC, 1955).  Cf. Brown 1643.

3622  To cure hiccoughs, hold your breath for sixty seconds (F, SLC, 1952).  Brown 1660f.

3623  To cure hiccoughs, hold the breath and count to nine (F, SLC, 1961); . . . count to ten (F, 20, SLC, 1950); . . . count to twenty (M, 36, SLC).

3624  For curing hiccoughs hold your breath, count to one hundred, take a drink of water, swallow it all without breathing, take a tablespoon of vinegar (F, Logan, 1973).

## Breathing and Blowing into a Paper Bag

3625  When you have the hiccoughs, if you put a paper sack over your head, they will go away (F, 12, SLC, 1958).

3626  To cure the hiccoughs, place a paper bag over your head and hop around in a circle three times (F, 19, SLC, 1950).

3627  Blow as hard as you can into a paper bag to get rid of the hiccoughs (F, 40, Fillmore, 1930).

3628  Breathe into a sack to stop hiccoughs (M, 17, Kearns, 1963); . . . into a paper bag . . . (F, 47, Roosevelt, 1935); Blow up a paper sack and breathe in it . . . (M, 28, SLC, 1938); Breathe in a paper bag, hold the breath and pop the bag . . . (F, SLC, 1963).

## Miscellaneous

3629  Let someone scare the person who has hiccoughs and the fright will cure him (M, 44, Bishop, 1927); Give the person . . . a sudden shock . . . (F, 21, SLC, 1958).  Cf. Brown 1673.

3630  Spit under a cow chip and walk around it three times to cure hiccoughs (M, 44, Coalville, 1935).

3631  For hiccoughs put a cup of water over your head and say "peep" (F, 63, SLC, 1964).

3632  For hiccoughs kiss a widow in the dark (F, Moab, 1953).

3633  To cure the hiccoughs, wet the forefinger of the right hand with spit and cross the front of the left shoe three times (F, 58, Teasdale, 1927).

3634  Remedy for hiccoughs:  Put a penny in your navel and hold it there for a minute (M, 21, Logan).

3635  Lie flat on your back when you have hiccoughs.  This cures them (F, SLC, 1963).

## HOARSENESS

3636 Take turpentine or kerosene and sugar for hoarseness (F, Moab, 1953).

## HUMAN BITES, ETC.

3637 The bite of a Negro with bluish gums is poisonous (F, SLC, 1961). Brown 636.

3638 To get rid of "monkey" bites or "hickeys," rub them with a penny (F, 19, Bountiful, 1960s).

## HYDROPHOBIA

3639 Humans with hydrophobia bark like dogs and bite those around them (M, SLC, 1959).

## IMPETIGO

3640 To cure impetigo, boil dock in water then throw away the dock and drink the resulting liquid (F, 36, Logan, 1970).

## INDIGESTION, HEARTBURN, ACIDITY

3641 For indigestion eat the dried lining of a chicken gizzard (M, SLC, 1960). Brown 1697f.

3642 Sweet balsam, yarrow, saffron and mountain rush were used for indigestion (M, SLC, 1946).

3643 For heartburn drink water (F, Provo, 1973).

3644 Wearing a copper band around the wrist removes acid from the body (F, It, Spring Glen, 1959).

## INFECTION

3645 Some people wanted me to bring my children up to the temple to be baptized (for the dead) and I told them no because I had heard of cases of sinus infections being picked up there. These people were horrified at the thought that there would be any infection in the temple (F, 50, Logan, 1946).

3646 To clear infection out of the body, eat or make tea out of yarrow (M, SLC, 1900).

### Poultices and Various Applications

3647 An old pioneer notion was that hot griddle cakes cure a festering sore (M, 24, SLC, 1963).

3648 Bread and milk will draw out an infection (F, Bear River City, 1957). Brown 1743.

3649 Use a poultice of flaxseed soaked in water to draw out infection (F, 20, SLC, 1963).

3650 A poutice of red beets will draw out various infections (M, 44, Layton, 1970).

3651 Onion poultice for drawing out infection (F, 60, Duchesne, 1930s).

3652 Pitch from the pinon tree is good to draw any kind of infection (F, Moab, 1953).

3653 My father cured an infection in his hand by using blue clay, which he spread like butter on his hand (F, 81, Logan, 1946).

3654 Denver mud is used for drawing out infection (F, 60, Duchesne, 1930s).

3655 Bloodsuckers will draw out an infection (F, Bear River City, 1957).

3656 The inside of a freshly killed chicken will draw out infection (F, Dan, Bear River City, 1957).

3657 The skin just under the eggshell will draw out an infection (F, Bear River City, 1957).

3658 Egg yolk and salt mixed together are used to draw out an infection in any type of open cut (F, 18, Boulder, 1958).

3659 Infection may be cured by placing a piece of fat bacon over the infected part (M, Layton, 1961).

3660 Fresh cow droppings is a good cure for serious infections (M, SLC, 1948). Brown 1738.

3661 Sugar and soap will draw out infection (M, SLC, 1910); Sugar and water . . . (F, Lehi, 1915).

3662 Use Epsom salts and hot water for infections (F, Woods Cross, 1953).

### Miscellaneous

3663 Camphor carried on the person will ward off any infection (F, 54, SLC, 1964).

3664 A bag of garlic around your neck will keep away all infections (F, SLC, 1940).

3665 A string tied around an infected area prevents the spirit from going deeper into the body (M, MD, SLC, 1959).

3666 Smoke from burning raw wool will take away infection (F, Dan, Bear River City, 1957).

3667 To burn an old shoe prevents infection (M, 89, SLC, early 1900s).

3668 Set a piece of wood on fire to draw out infection. A person should hold the infected part over the fire (F, 63, Monroe, 1964).

3669 A magnet will draw infection out of the body. The magnet possesses magic powers (M, 89, Springville, 1964).

## INFLUENZA

3670 If you got the flu, it was always due to something you had done. It was your own fault because you were chilled or neglected yourself in cold or rainy weather. There was a reason behind every time you were taken down with the flu (F, SLC, 1913).

3671　If your nose itches, you'll shake hands with the flu (F, Midvale).

3672　We washed out hair in sage. When you have the flu, your hair comes out and you just take and wash your head two or three times a week with sage tea, and you'll have the prettiest hair you ever saw (F, Moab, 1953).

3673　Always drink hot tea and eat toast to get rid of the stomach flu (F, 75, Smithfield, 1970).

3674　Camomile tea is a good cure for intestinal flu. Use the flowers (F, 73, Logan, 1970).

3675　A good cure for intestinal flu is mint tea made from the mint leaves (F, 73, Logan, 1970); . . . spearmint and peppermint tea (F, 87, Providence, 1970).

3676　If you slice onions and put them around the window sills in a house, it will keep the flu out (F, 60, SLC, 1964).

3677　Put sulphur in your shoes to keep the flu away (F, 80, Ogden, 1918). Brown 1746.

3678　Burn orange peelings on top of a stove to cure or prevent influenza (F, 65, SLC, 1944).

3679　During the flu epidemic of 1918 some people wore a little bag containing asafetida around their neck, believing that this would keep them from catching the flu (F, Draper, 1918). Brown 1745.

## INJURY

3680　Kiss an injured spot to make it well (F, 1960).

3681　A string tied around an injured area prevents the spirit from going deeper into the body (M, MD, SLC, 1959).

3682　You should never give anything sharp for a gift because an injury with it will take longer to heal (F, 58, It, Murray, 1964).

## INSECT, SPIDER BITES, ETC.

3683　If insects bite you in "dog days," the bites are worse and will take longer to heal (M, 46, SLC, 1964).

3684　Sagebrush was used for making a poultice for insect bites. Use either dried sage or fresh. Roll it and put salt on it and then apply it. Dampen it with water or vinegar after it is on the affected part (F, 84, Price, 1946).

3685　The yolk of an egg and salt made into a paste are used for insect bites (F, ca. 1860). Brown 2266.

3686　For whenever you get an insect bite or a mosquito bite, you just rub a little salt on it and then it won't itch (F, St. George, 1967). Cf. Brown 2266.

3687　Use mud or bicarbonate of soda on insect stings (F, 20, SLC, 1963). Brown 2237f.

3688　If bitten by a poisonous insect, press an agate on the spot and the bite will come to no harm (F, 74, SLC, 1964).

## Bee Stings

3689　To prevent bee stings, rub your body with flowers (M, 52, Cedar City, 1964). Brown 2242.

3690　Don't try to remove a bee stinger by pulling it out; it only drives it in further. Take a knife and scrape it off (F, Roosevelt, 1920).

3691　Take a piece of garlic and rub it on a bee sting (F, Provo, 1969).

3692　Put a crushed plantain leaf on a bee sting to draw out the poison and make it stop hurting (F, Logan, 1972). Brown 2248.

3693　To cure the sting of a bee or a wasp, wrap the leaf of a tomato vine around it (F, SLC, 1957).

3694　Sagebrush and salt was used for making a poultice for bee stings. It can be mixed with water or vinegar (F, 84, Price, 1946).

3695　Fresh urine cures bee stings (F, 15, SLC, 1964). Cf. Brown 2230.

3696　Tape a slice of bacon over a bee sting to draw out the poison (F, 20, Logan, 1955).

3697　A liberal application of cow dung on a bee sting will alleviate the pain (M, 24, Morgan, 1964). Practiced by farmers in Morgan County.

3698　If you put mud on a bee sting, it will cause the sting to go away and swelling to go down (F, 20, Provo, 1960); . . . black mud . . . (F, Moab, 1953); . . . blackest mud from the ditch . . . (F, 41, Fayette, 1971); . . . mud and spit . . . (F, 57, Logan, 1963); . . . the mud sucks out the poison (F, 42, Sandy, 1971); . . . mud will take the stinger out (F, Bear River City, 1957). Brown 2241, 2262.

3699　For bee stings put soda on them (F, Moab, 1953). Brown 2237, 2257ff.

3700　For bee stings, put ammonia on it (F, Moab, 1953).

## Mosquito Bites

3701　If you take lots of vitamin C, the mosquitoes won't bite you (F, 60, Moab, 1970).

3702　Spitting on mosquito bites will cure them (F, 57, Logan, 1973).

3703　If you eat garlic, you will sweat out a powerful odor and that will keep the mosquitoes away. They can't stand the smell (F, Provo, 1973).

3704   Mosquito bites:  Apply water and salt on bite.  Leave it for a while.  It takes the itch away (F, 20, Salem, 1965).

3705   Rub a softened bar of wet soap over mosquito bites (F, 54, Logan, 1970).

3706   If you rub an Arizona mosquito plant on a mosquito bite, it won't swell or itch (F, 36).

## Stings of Hornets, Wasps

3707   Put tobacco juice on a hornet's sting to cure it (M, 77, Grantsville, 1900).  Cf. Brown 2232ff, 2250, 2252, 2254.

3708   Put mud on a wasp sting to draw out the poison (M, SLC, 1958).  Heard from a shepherder in Box Elder County in 1944.  Brown 2262.

## Stings of Ants, Spiders, Etc.

3709   Put mud on ant stings (F, Provo).

3710   Put coal oil on ant stings (F, Provo).

3711   If you have been bitten by a spider, catch a fly and press it over the wound; the fly will draw the poison into itself (M, 60, It, SLC, 1965).

3712   Pale blue stones worn around the neck will be an effective antidote to prevent spider bites (M, MD, SLC, 1959).

3713   The only cure for the bite of the tarantula is lively music which inspires the victim to dance until he falls exhausted, bathed in his own perspiration (F, 50, SLC, 1963); To cure a tarantula bite, you must dance until there is no more poison in you (M, Eng, 1957).

## INTERNAL INJURIES

3714   If you touch your navel while you are bathing, it will give you internal injuries (F, Swiss, SLC, 1959).

## ITCH

3715   To prevent the itch between the toes, tie a piece of red yarn around each toe (F, 64, SLC, 1964).  Cf. Brown 1754f.

## JAUNDICE

3716   Jaundice is cured by hanging a carrot in the basement.  When the carrot dries up, jaundice will disappear (F, 60, Ger, SLC, 1930s).

3717   A person with yellow jaundice should be treated with yellow drugs.  Yellow rids yellow (M, MD, SLC, 1959).  Heard from his patients.  (The color and shape of plants used as botanical cures were prominent features of the Doctrine of Signatures.  For a general discussion of these theories, see No. 3081, above.  For further examples of affinity of the color of the cure to the manifestations of the disease, see Nos. 3776 and 3948, below.  -- Eds.)

3718   To cure jaundice, eat nine lice on a piece of bread and butter (M, 93, St. George, 1910).  Cf. Brown 1756.

## JOINTS

3719   To relieve joint pains of the lower leg, place hot boiled onions in a sock, place upon the affected leg and it will take away the pain and it will not return (F, SLC, 1961).

3720   Wear a copper bracelet and you'll never get sore joints (F, 80, Eng, Midvale).  Brown 2052f (notes).

## KIDNEY AILMENTS

3721   A pain in the back means a kidney disease is present (F, SLC, 1961).

3722   Never eat anything with fins or feathers and you'll never get kidney stones (F, 49, SLC, 1964).

3723   Beekeepers do not have kidney trouble (M, 54, Ferron).

3724   Drink cranberry juice for a kidney infection (F, It, 1971).

3725   Egg white is injurious to the kidney (M, SLC, 1960).

3726   Parsley tea and dandelion greens are good for the kidneys (F, 87, Providence, 1970).

3727   Tansy tea for kidney (F, 60, Duchesne, 1930s).

3728   Raisins are very good relievers of kidney trouble (M, SLC, 1961).

3729   Burnt toast is good for your kidneys (M, Dan, SLC, 1969).

3730   Kidney beans are good for the kidneys (F, 65, SLC, 1964).

3731   Chewing a titty bag will clean out the kidneys.  You can use almost anything of nature to fill the titty bag (F, 41, SLC, 1964).

3732   Watermelon seed is good for kidneys (F, SLC, 1957).  Brown 1765.

3733   Eat radishes with rock candy to cure kidney trouble (M, 31, SLC, 1964).

3734   Every time you eat an apple, if you eat some of the seeds, you will never have kidney trouble (F, 65, SLC, 1964).

3735   Gather rabbit brush in the fall and it will cure a kidney illness (M, Morgan, 1961).

## LA GRIPPE

3736   La grippe can be cured by soaking your feet in a pail of water just as hot as you can stand it.  Also make a plaster of mustard and flour and put it on the chest, wrapping firmly with flannel (F, 76, Orangeville, 1920s).

3737   If you soak your feet in yarrow, it will cure la grippe (F, Morgan, 1961).

## LARYNGITIS

3738    Put a piece of onion on your foot when you go to bed to get rid of laryngitis (F, 18, Layton, 1971).

## LEPROSY

3739    Never go inside the gate where the dead are buried; you will get leprosy (F, SLC, 1965).

3740    Wear a gold ring on your left hand, and it will guard against leprosy (M, Midvale, 1961).

## LICE

3741    If a person drinks water instead of wine, they will develop lice (M, 23, SLC, 1960).

3742    Bathe the head in kerosene to kill lice (F, SLC, 1925).

## LIMBS

3743    Never strike a man with a creeping vine, or he will lose the use of one of his limbs (F, 62, W. Jordan).

3744    If you have a lump on the back of your hand or wrist, you can only get rid of it by slamming a Holy Bible on it (F, 21, Ogden, 1970).

## Ailments of the Legs and Feet

3745    If a person walks on the lines when walking on a sidewalk, he is wishing that his mother would break her leg (M, Midvale, 1957).

3746    A shovel brought indoors will cause leg problems (F, SLC, 1967).

3747    When your foot falls asleep at the dinner table, make a cross of water on it and hop around the table three times (M).  Cf. Brown 1399f.

3748    For cold feet take a pot, urinate in it and soak your feet for about fifteen minutes (F, 58, SLC, 1921).

3749    If you break a water pitcher, you will have foot trouble (M, SLC, 1961).

3750    Oranges are good for sore feet (M, SLC, 1964).

3751    For tired, sore feet, soak them in mustard water (F, 57, Logan, 1973). Heard in Idaho, 1920.

3752    Boil alfalfa and soak feet in the hot water to relieve swollen feet (F, 76, Logan, 1970).

3753    Alum and boric acid for galled feet (M, 70, Duchesne, 1970).

3754    Soak infected feet in fresh cow dung (F, Magna, 1974).

3755    Sagebrush tea is a good tonic to bathe frozen feet (F, Orem, 1967).

3756    A dead bee burned to ashes and sprinkled in the shoe will cure flat feet (F, SLC, 1961).

3757    You can cure athlete's foot by walking on the sand at the beach barefoot (F, Midvale, 1961).

## LIVER AILMENTS, LIVER SPOTS

3758    When the whites of the eyes have a bluish cast, liver trouble is indicated (F, SLC, 1925).

3759    Eggs are harmful to the liver.  Minor illnesses are ascribed to that organ's malfunction (M, 21, SLC, 1962).

3760    Tomatoes are a tonic for the liver (F, Kanab, 1960).

3761    To keep from getting liver spots, rub castor oil over your hands up to your elbows weekly (F, Provo).

## LOCKJAW

3762    Lockjaw is caused by a wound in the web between the thumb and forefinger (F, SLC, 1961).

3763    If children walk in horse manure, they will get lockjaw (F, SLC, 1960).

3764    To prevent lockjaw, remove the nail from the foot, grease the nail with tallow and drive it into a board or other wooden object where it will remain dry (F, 22, Midvale, 1964).  Cf. Brown 1781, 1782, 1783ff.  (For a discussion of "weapon-salve" see No. 4463, below.  Cf. also No. 3048, above.  --Eds.)

3765    If you have lockjaw, put a ball of yarn under your arm and unravel it and by the time it unravels the jaws will come unlocked (F, Moab, 1953).

## LUNG DISORDERS

3766    Cabbage leaves placed over the lungs, front and back, were thought to cure lung congestion or chest colds (M, 71, SLC, 1960).  Heard in Nebraska, 1910.

3767    Onions on the chest relieve lung infection (F, 40, Logan, 1938).

3868    Mullein is good for any kind of lung trouble.  Make a tea out of it, or dry it and smoke it (F, 81, Logan, 1946).

3769    Eat quantities of watercress as a salad to cure lung trouble (F, 22, SLC, 1964).

3770    For congestion in the lungs, take equal parts lard or olive oil, equal parts turpentine or coal oil.  Heat and wring the cloth out about every hour, placing it over the lungs and neck.  Breathe in the fumes (F, 70, Provo, 1900).

3771    For a cold in the lungs put heavy brown paper over the lungs (F, 78, SLC, 1964).

3772    A red flannel vest will cure lung disorders, if you wear it long enough (M, 70, Duchesne).

## MALARIA

3773 Malaria is carried on the night air, so keep the shutters closed while you sleep (F, Provo, 1900); Sleeping in the night air will cause malaria (M, SLC, 1963).

## MEASLES

3774 Measles is always a trivial disease (F, SLC, 1961).

3775 Bull frogs cause measles (F, SLC, 1963).

3776 Measles were cured by covering the patients with scarlet blankets and giving them scarlet medicine (M, MD, SLC, 1959). Heard from patients. (For a discussion of the Doctrine of Signatures and the symbolic association of the color of plants with the diseases that they are supposed to cure, see Nos. 3081, 3717, above, and No. 3948, below. --Eds.)

3777 Asafetida bags keep one from having the measles (F, Moab, 1953). Cf. Brown 1802.

3778 To bring out measles, drink ginger tea (M, SLC, 1929). Brown 1815.

3779 Tea made from sheep droppings will bring out the measles (F, Moab, 1953); . . . out of sheep fertilizer . . . (F, Moab, 1953); . . . sheep or nannyberry tea . . . (F, 67, Panguitch, early 1900s). Cf. Brown 1805f, 1809.

3780 To cure measles, eat a roasted mouse, well done (M, 26, Layton, 1953).

3781 If you carry a dead chicken around your neck, you won't have measles (F, 38, SLC, 1964).

## MENSTRUAL PAINS

3782 To avoid cramps during your menstrual cycle, eat an orange peel (F, 67, Bear River City, 1913).

3783 Hop tea for menstrual pains (F, 60, Duchesne, 1930s).

## MOLES

3784 If you step on a hole, you'll get a mole (F, SLC, 1941).

3785 If a person has a mole and can't get rid of it, he should get somebody to give him a penny for it, and it will soon disappear. Sometimes the person who bought the mole will get one in the same place (M, Midvale, 1957).

3786 If you have a mole, open a dried bean and rub it on the mole; bury it where no one can see you. The mole will fall off in a day or so (M, 45, Beaver 1964).

3787 Tie your own hair around a mole, and it will disappear (M, SLC, 1930s).

3788 Go to the graveyard to get rid of moles (F, 18, SLC, 1950).

## MOTION SICKNESS

3789 To overcome car sickness, put a piece of plain white paper between clothing and chest (F, SLC, 1963); . . . put a brown paper bag on your stomach, next to your skin (F, Grantsville, 1932).

3790 To cure airplane or boat sickness, place a brown paper over the stomach (F, 68, Farmington, 1917); . . . a folded piece of paper on your chest (F, SLC). Brown 2094.

## MOUTH SORES

3791 If a person tells lies, he will get mouth sores (F, SLC, 1952).

## MUMPS

3792 If it is suspected a person has mumps, have them eat a dill pickle. If it hurts them too much to even swallow it, they have the mumps (F, 19, SLC); . . . if the pickle locks their jaws, they have mumps (F, SLC, 1920).

3793 Put green tomatoes on the swellings when you have mumps. It will make the swelling disappear (F, SLC, 1969).

3794 Put a medicine bag around the neck to prevent mumps (M, 84, Centerville, early 1900s).

3795 For mumps make two little sacks with bran in them and get them warm and this will soothe them (F, Provo).

3796 When we were children we wore asafetida bags to keep from getting the mumps (F, Moab, 1953).

3797 When my brother had the mumps, my grandfather told my mother that tying a black cloth around the throat would keep the disease from falling to other parts of the body (M, Venice). Cf. Brown 1832.

3798 For the mumps you draw a five-star figure on the part that is swollen (F, Gr, SLC, 1962).

3799 Put a wool string around your neck and it keeps the mumps from going down (F, SLC, 1928); . . . sock around the neck . . . (F, 71, Hoytsville, 1909). Cf. Brown 1832.

3800 Wear lead around the neck, tied with buckskin string to prevent anything above this string from going down. It will keep diseases like the mumps above the string (F, Moab, 1953).

## MUSCULAR DISEASES

3801 Deer bring on muscular diseases (M, SLC, 1957). Belief attributed to American Indians.

## NECK AILMENTS

3802 Don't put a clothespin on the neck of shirts when hanging them out, or you will have a stiff neck (F, Vernal, 1958).

3803    A hot mush poultice was often used to help heal a stiff neck (M, 71, SLC).

## NEURALGIA

3804    A chestnut pierced and hung on a string around the neck prevents neuralgia (M, SLC, 1959); A nutmeg . . . (F, SLC, 1964).

## NIGHT SWEATS

3805    Sagebrush tea is good to cure night sweats.  Some people have them awful bad, and sagebrush tea will cure them (F, Moab, 1953).

## NOSE, NOSEBLEED

3806    To get rid of a stuffy nose, chew on a honeycomb (M, 81, Welsh, SLC, early 1900s).

3807    A person is love sick if his nose bleeds (M, 48, SLC, 1939).

### Water, Snow, Animal Products, Etc.

3808    A cold, wet cloth held on the back of the neck will cure a nosebleed (F, SLC, 1965).  Brown 1885.

3809    Pour water down your neck to stop a nosebleed (F, 19, Heber, 1972).  Cf. Brown 1885, 1888.

3810    If you put your feet in cold water, it will cure your nosebleed (F, 19, Heber, 1972).  Brown 1890.

3811    If in the winter you get a nosebleed, apply snow on the back of your neck, and it will stop (F, 22, SLC).

3812    A karate chop to a certain nerve on the back of the neck will stop a nosebleed (M, 1961).

3813    It is superstition that cobwebs will stop nosebleeds (F, 55, Ger, SLC, 1964).

3814    Local informants say that a bloody nose is effectively cured by eating the larvae of wasps (F, SLC, 1961).

### Paper

3815    If you have a nosebleed, put a piece of dark brown paper in the roof of your mouth (F, 50, SLC); . . . under the upper lip (M, 71, SLC).

3816    You can stop a nosebleed by putting a piece of paper under your tongue (F, SLC, 1964).

3817    If you put a piece of damp paper between your upper lip and your teeth, it will stop your nosebleed (F, SLC, 1945). Brown 1871.

### Yarn, String, Necklace, Etc.

3818    Wear a wool thread around your big toe to cure a nosebleed (M, 35, SLC, 1964).

3819    To cure a nosebleed, tie a string around your neck (F, 73, Eng, SLC, 1965).  Cf. Brown 1874.

3820    Carry a red string in your pocket to prevent a nosebleed (F, SLC, 1900); Put a red yarn around the neck to treat a nosebleed (pioneer remedies).

3821    A lead (metal) necklace will prevent nosebleeds (F, 68, Tooele, 1910); Lead on a silver chain . . . (F, Moab, 1953); Mash a lead bullet flat around a piece of string and wear it around your neck to . . . (M, 24, SLC, 1950). Cf. Brown 1894f.

3822    Wear a red necklace around your neck to cure a nosebleed (F, SLC, 1960).  Cf. Brown 1878ff.

### Knives, Keys, Coins, Stones, Etc.

3823    Hang a butcher knife down your back to cure a nosebleed (F, 21, SLC, 1950). Brown 1896.

3824    Cure a nosebleed by placing a knife on the forehead (F, SLC, 1925).

3825    Put a cold coin on the back of the neck to cure a nosebleed (F, 20, Provo, 1964).  Cf. Brown 1902.

3826    Put a nickel under the upper lip to cure a nosebleed (F, 21, Tooele, 1964); . . . a penny under the upper lip . . . (M, 71, SLC).  Cf. Brown 1905.

3827    Whenever you have a nosebleed, lie down and put a penny in the middle of your forehead and the bleeding will stop quicker (F, 19, Logan, 1972).

3828    Sit on a copper penny for five minutes and your nosebleed will stop (F).

3829    Place a key on the back of the neck to stop a nosebleed (F, Lehi, 1957); . . . cold key down the back . . . (M, SLC, 1961).  Cf. Brown 1899.

3830    To stop a nosebleed, pick up a stone and let a few drops of blood fall on it, then replace the stone and your nosebleed will stop (F, 21, SLC, 1964). Cf. Brown 1891.

3831    Nosebleeds are cured by a cold rock on the back of the neck (F, 74, Parawan, 1920s).

3832    Nosebleeds:  Put a matchstick about one-half inch long under your top lip and right underneath your nose and that will stop the bleeding (F, Provo, 1973).

## OBESITY

3833    Laughing just after you have eaten a large dinner will cause one to become fat (F, 21, Midvale, 1960).

3834    Eating bananas will make you fat (F, SLC, 1963).

## PARALYSIS

3835    Stepping on an ant while walking on a sidewalk will cause the foot that

performed the fatal step to become
paralyzed (M, SLC).

3836  If you let a chicken die in your hand,
it will give you paralysis (M, 23, SLC,
1962).  Cf. Brown 1913.

## PILES AND HEMORRHOIDS

3837  To cure piles, apply buffalo tallow
mixed with salt (F, 63, Coalville,
1964).

3838  Tea made from the leaves of wild currant
bushes cures hemorrhoids (F, Woods
Cross, 1946).

## PIMPLES

3839  Pimples are caused by "bad" blood (F,
SLC, 1961); . . . impure blood (M, SLC,
1925).

3840  If you get a pimple on one side of your
face, you'll get another one on the
other side in almost the same spot (F,
22, Clearfield, 1964).

3841  If you look in a mirror when you are
young, a pimple will grow on your nose
(F, SLC, 1917).

3842  Washing the face every night with
rubbing alcohol is an excellent remedy
for pimples (F, SLC, 1961).

## PLAGUE AND EPIDEMIC

3843  If you pay your fines, you won't be
stricken with plagues (M, Clinton,
1959).

3844  Dead bodies left unburied cause a plague
(F, SLC, 1961).

3845  If you dream about the dead, it means
someone in your town is going to catch a
plague (M, 54, Richfield, 1928).

3846  A pale red setting sun foretells a
plague (M, 20, SLC, 1964); A sun going
down in crimson . . . (F, 61, Midvale).

3847  Close the room and burn sulphur to ward
off illness in an epidemic (F, SLC,
1964).  Informant's mother practiced
this as late as 1910.

## PNEUMONIA

3848  Three-day pneumonia is the worst kind.
Put the patient's feet in hot vinegar
water overnight and a raw potato
poultice on his chest to cure him (F,
87, Providence, 1920).

3849  To cure pneumonia, dip your underwear in
cold water.  Wear them to bed all night
(F, 44, Swiss, Midvale, 1964).

### Plasters, Poultices, Etc.

3850  A poultice of onions, sliced onions and
fried just a little--be sure they are
good and hot--and make a poultice with
them and use it for pneumonia on the

chest.  That was very common (F, 71,
Woods Cross, 1953); . . . fried onions
on chest and feet . . . (F, 55, SLC,
1964).  Cf. Brown 1936.

3851  People were taught to use mustard
plasters on the chest and back for
pneumonia (F, 50, SLC, 1930).

### Animal Products

3852  For the cure of pneumonia put the skin
of a black cat on the sick person.  This
will draw out the poison.  The darker
the color of the cat, the more effective
it will be (F, 82, 1900, Monroe).

3853  For pneumonia rub the patient with skunk
oil and give him honey and whiskey, tea
and castor oil (F, 53, SLC, 1964).

3854  Hot cow dung spread over the chest cures
pneumonia (F, 20, SLC, 1964).

3855  Cut a live chicken in two and place it
over the lungs of a sick person to cure
pneumonia (F, SLC, 1960); . . . put the
entrails right over the chest . . . (F,
Moab, 1953).  Brown 1933.

3856  A dead dove placed on the chest of a
person suffering from pneumonia is
supposed to insure prompt recovery (F,
Magna, 1929).

## POISONING

3857  For lye:  Drink vinegar diluted with
water.  Wash out mouth with vinegar or
lemon juice, give milk (Logan, 1970).

3858  If you had poisoning in the body, put
twelve peppermint leaves in your shoe,
named after the twelve apostles, and
when the leaves have disintegrated, the
poison would be gone (F, SLC, 1910).

## POISON IVY, POISON OAK, ETC.

3859  Buckshot placed on poison ivy cures it
(M, 42, SLC, 1964).

3860  Rub pure apple vinegar on the poisoned
part infected with poisoned ivy to cure
it (F, SLC, 1957).

3861  Pack mud on a poison ivy sting to cure
it (M, Vernal, 1961).

3862  If you put mud on a stinging nettle, it
will cause the sting to go away and
swelling to go down (F, 20, Provo,
1972).

3863  Stinging nettle:  Rub the sore area with
regular old sage leaves, the ones you
cook with (F, Provo, 1973).

## POLIOMYELITIS

3864  If you drink too much soda pop, you'll
get polio (F, Bountiful, 1960).

3865  Swimming during August will cause polio
M, 26, SLC, 1950).

## PUNCTURE WOUND

3866    If you step on a rusty nail, grease the nail or you will have infection (M, Farmington, 1930). Brown 1781, 2756f.

3867    If you step on a nail, you must bring it in and put it in the oven for a month to stop infection and lockjaw (F, 63, SLC, 1914). Cf. Brown 1789.

3868    When my brother received a severe wound in his hand from a nail, a neighbor buried the nail in the ground in a place known only to her (M, SLC, 1940s).

3869    It is more dangerous to prick one's self with a pin than a needle (F, SLC, 1961).

## PYORRHEA

3870    For pyorrhea use a poultice of cow manure placed in cheesecloth in your mouth (F, 73, Moab, 1953). Informant received this treatment as a child.

## QUINSY

3871    A man with a beard will never have the quinsy (F, SLC, 1925).

3872    Wear a black silk cord around your neck to prevent quinsy or asthma attacks (F, Bountiful, 1967).

## RASH

3873    You get bather's rash from too many baths (F, SLC, 1900).

3874    Pickles and milk will give you a rash (M, 45, SLC, 1956).

3875    Catnip tea was used to bring out a rash (M, SLC, 1946).

3876    If you have a rash on your hands, put three copper pennies under your pillow and sleep on them and your rash will go away (F, 54, SLC, 1930).

## RHEUMATIC FEVER

3877    For rheumatic fever obtain fresh corn silk and soak it in water for a day. Strain the water through a clean cloth and drink the bitter liquid (M, MD, Bicknell, 1932).

## RHEUMATISM

3878    Soak your hands in water and you'll never have rheumatism (M, SLC, 1964).

3879    If a person sleeps with his stockings on, he will develop rheumatism in later life (M, 23, Vernal).

3880    If you hear a blaring radio, you will have rheumatism shortly (M, SLC, 1961).

### Animals, Animal Products

3881    Deer bring on rheumatism (M, SLC, 1957). Attributed to Indians.

3882    To cure rheumatism, take a cat to bed (F, 30, Ogden, 1964). Brown 1973.

3883    Fresh cow manure, while still warm, was used as a poultice for rheumatism (F, SLC, 1900).

3884    Carry a small round bone from a ham as a cure for rheumatism (F, 50, SLC).

3885    To get rid of rheumatism, rub the blood of a mole on it (F, 59, SLC, 1964). Cf. Brown 1984.

3886    Oil from the fat of snakes is supposed to be good for rheumatism (F, SLC, 1890).

3887    The rattles from a snake, if worn, will ward off rheumatism (F, SLC, 1960). Cf. Brown 1987.

3888    To cure rheumatism, get stung by a bee (F, 17, SLC, 1962). Brown 1969.

3889    If a person lets a horny toad crawl on their bare skin, it will take their rheumatism away when it gets off (F, 57, SLC, 1963). Cf. Brown 1993.

### Plants, Herbs

3890    You can cure rheumatism by putting mustard in your shoes (F, 26, SLC, 1964). Cf. Brown 2008.

3891    Dried potatoes in the pocket will protect you against rheumatism (M, St. George, 1963); A potato begged or stolen, carried in a pocket . . . (F, 18, SLC, 1958); A spoiled potato . . . (F, 23, SLC, 1952); A raw potato . . . (F, SLC); To protect against rheumatism, sew a potato into a slip and wear it around (F, Lehi, 1960). Brown 2017.

3892    If you place a raw potato in your hip pocket, it will draw the rheumatism from your body (F, 19, Sandy, 1946). Brown 2018.

3893    If an immatured potato is placed in the back pocket and it disintegrates, it means that there will be freedom from rheumatism. If it turns to a hard, petrified potato, it means rheumatism will return (M, MD, SLC, 1959).

3894    Some people wear a string ring made of a potato with a hole bored through it for rheumatism (F, 85, Grantsville, 1900).

3895    Cloths dipped in hot potato water are suggested for complete relief of rheumatism (F, 64, SLC, 1964).

3896    Carry a buckeye in your pocket and you will never have rheumatism (M, 54, Park City, 1920). Brown 1995.

3897    If you carry horse chestnuts in each pocket, it will help rheumatism (F, 74, SLC, 1964). Brown 2001.

3898    A chestnut carried in your pocket is a good cure for rheumatism (M, Eng, SLC, 1965).

3899    A nutmeg carried in the pocket will prevent rheumatism (F, SLC, 1955). Cf. Brown 2009f.

3900 A piece of cedar wood in the pocket will help cure rheumatism (F, 75, SLC, 1963).

3901 A cedar knot carried in the pocket will cure rheumatism (M, SLC, 1959); A cedar knot around your neck . . . (M, 19, SLC, 1964); A double cedar knot in the pocket . . . (F, 23, It, SLC, 1962).

3902 A man may carry a gall from the stems of the goldenrod for rheumatism (F, 85, Grantsville, 1900).

3903 Indian root is a cure for rheumatism (M, 48, Moab, 1946).

3904 Alfalfa tea is good for rheumatism (F, Moab, 1953).

3905 To relieve the pain of rheumatism, drink "Brigham's tea" which is made from the stock of the bush (F, 81, Sigurd, 1910). Cf. Brown 2007.

3906 A poultice of mashed burdock leaves was supposed to be an effective remedy for rheumatism (M, SLC, 1946).

3907 To cure rheumatism, drink tea made out of catnip weed (F, Lehi, 1960).

3908 For rheumatism drink fresh coconut milk (F, Du, SLC, 1960).

3909 To cure rheumatism, drink tea made out of dandelions (F, Lehi, 1960).

3910 Hot lemon juice is good for rheumatism (F, 80, Heber, 1972). Cf. Brown 2004f.

3911 To cure rheumatism, drink sage tea (M, Logan, 1950).

3912 For rheumatism make tea from soapweed leaves. The true name is oose-weed. It looks like the yucca plant (M, 48, Moab, 1946).

3913 Vinegar and water helps cure rheumatism (F, 52, SLC, 1920).

3914 For rheumatism use vinegar and pepper (F, 80, Heber, 1972). Cf. Brown 1997.

3915 A pillow filled with hops and placed under a sufferer's bed will cure rheumatism (M, 54, Magna, 1923).

## Flannel, Thread

3916 If a person wears red flannel, he will not get rheumatism (M, 20, SLC, 1963); Red flannel cures rheumatism (M, SLC, 1961); Red flannel underwear eases the pain of . . . (F, 70, Provo, 1900). Brown 2035f.

3917 Wrap a flannel around a knee for rheumatism (F, SLC, 1957).

3918 For rheumatism of the wrist, tie a black thread around the wrist in question and the pain will go away (F, 44, secy, SLC, 1961).

## Magnets, Copper, Brass, Etc.

3919 A magnet was believed to have the power of drawing rheumatism from a person's joints (M, 45, SLC, 1963).

3920 A strand of copper wire is often worn around the left wrist by older people in order to ward off rheumatism (M, 71, SLC). First heard in Nebraska, 1910.

3921 If you wear a copper bracelet or ring, it will stop you from getting rheumatism (M, 64, SLC, 1924); Copper bracelets worn around the wrists or ankles are a good remedy for . . . (F, Lehi, 1915); A copper wire around the neck like a necklace prevents . . . (F, Peoa, 1920); A copper band prevents . . . (F, 85, SLC, 1964). Brown 2052f.

3922 To get rid of rheumatism, wear a brass ring (M, Bountiful, 1959); . . . brass ring on the left thumb (F, Ogden, 1959); . . . on the middle finger (M, SLC, 1960); A brass bracelet around wrist prevents rheumatism (F, 21, Price, 1963).

3923 For rheumatism wear brass wires around the area (F, 19, SLC, 1964); . . . around the arms and ankles (F, 46, SLC, 1964). Cf. Brown 2056.

3924 Wear a brass belt to cure rheumatism (F, 63, SLC, 1920).

## Uranium, Sulphur, Buckshot, Gems, Etc.

3925 If you carry a piece of uranium in your pocket, it will keep away the rheumatism (F, SLC, 1957); Wear uranium in bags for rheumatism; it will cure anything that is the matter with you (F, Moab, 1953).

3926 If one suffers from rheumatism, place some uranium under the bed at night to cure it (F, 19, SLC).

3927 Water that has had uranium ore soaked in it is very good for rheumatism (F, Moab, 1953).

3928 Carry sulphur in your pocket to stop rheumatism (F, Ogden, 1959).

3929 Dust the inside of your shoes with sulphur as a remedy for rheumatism (F, Lehi, 1915).

3930 Buckshot carried in the hip pocket will prevent rheumatism (M, 21, SLC, 1964).

3931 Carrying and rubbing certain stones will make your rheumatism feel better (F, 73, Logan, 1900s).

3932 Wear amber beads about the neck for rheumatism (F, Ogden, 1959).

3933 If a woman wears a ruby, she will never have rheumatism (F, 48, SLC, 1964).

## Miscellaneous

3934 Drink cream of tartar for rheumatism (F, 57, Logan, 1973). First heard in Idaho, 1920.

3935 If a person suffers from rheumatism, he should carry a horseshoe nail in his pocket (M, 49, SLC, 1924). Brown 2050.

3936 To cure rheumatism, remove a nail from a coffin (F, 65, SLC, 1964).

3937　To get rid of rheumatism, get some dirt from the graveyard and walk over it for ten nights and then you will be cured (M, 80, SLC, 1930).

## RINGWORM

3938　Cats cause ringworm (F, 77, SLC, 1910).

3939　If you touch a red and white ringed cat, you will catch ringworm (M, SLC).

3940　For ringworm, burn paper on an axe, then rub the resulting material on the ringworm. This will cure it (F, 82, Monroe, 1910).

3941　Rub a cigar stub on ringworm and it will disappear (F, 18, SLC, 1964).

3942　If you have ringworm, keep staring at it. Wet your finger and touch it and it will die (F, SLC, 1960).

## RUNNING SORES

3943　If you eat red maize, you will have running sores about the mouth (F, SLC, 1961).

## ST. VITUS' DANCE

3944　If you can't learn to sit still, it will cause St. Vitus' dance (M, 24, SLC, 1964).

3945　Acorn tea was used as a sedative for St. Vitus' dance sufferers (M, SLC, 1946).

## SCABS

3946　If you don't eat ham on Easter morning, you will get scabs on your body (F, 89, SLC, 1930).

## SCARLET FEVER

3947　An asafetida bag around your neck will prevent scarlet fever (M, SLC, 1968). Informant wore this in Finland as a child.

3948　Scarlet fever was cured by covering the patients with scarlet blankets and giving them scarlet medicine (M, MD, SLC, 1959). Heard from patients. (For a discussion of the Doctrine of Signatures and the symbolic association of the color of plants with the diseases they are supposed to cure, see Nos. 3081, 3717, 3776, above. --Eds.)

## SEVEN-YEAR ITCH

3949　Sulphur baths will cure the seven-year itch (M, 44, Layton, 1970).

3950　Sulphur and lard will cure the seven-year itch (F, 70, Provo, 1900).

## SIDEACHE

3951　If you get a sideache from running, stop and spit on a rock and the pain will go away (M, SLC, 1961); . . . throw the spit side down . . . (F, 24, SLC); . . . put the rock back in the same place . . . (F, Ogden, 1940). Brown 2104.

3952　If you have a pain in your side, carefully stoop and spit under a clod and the pain will go (M, SLC, 1957).

## SINUS

3953　Sinus trouble is caused from cow's milk (F, SLC, 1959).

3954　Different parts of the feet control certain areas of the sinus cavity. A lady in Magna treats sinus conditions by massaging the feet (F, Murray).

## SKIN AILMENTS

3955　Taking too many baths can cause certain skin diseases (F, 18, SLC, 1958).

3956　If you have a skin sore, scrape mold off of old cheese and put it on the sore (F, 29, Garfield, 1943).

3957　Medical supplies in the early days consisted of catnip, tansy, yarrow, slippery elm, spearmint, hops, horehound and sage tea. Sulphur and molasses would cure many skin sores (F, 85, W. Jordan, 1900).

## SLIVERS, SPLINTERS

3958　If you don't remove a sliver, it will work its way to your heart and kill you (F, SLC, 1971).

3959　Never dig a sliver out with a pin; always use a needle (F, 52, SLC, 1930).

3960　Bandage a slice of bacon or other salted meat onto a sore spot to remove a sliver of metal (F, Logan, 1972).

3961　We used a bread and milk poultice to draw out a sliver--that's really good-- put it on warm (F, 71, Woods Cross, 1953).

3962　We used a soap and sugar poultice to draw out a sliver (F, 71, Woods Cross, 1953).

3963　To draw out a deeply imbedded sliver, use a small mouth bottle, fill it with hot water, pour out the water, then place the opening over the spot where the sliver is and let it cool (M, 44, Layton, 1970).

## SMALLPOX

3964　Cure smallpox by putting red hangings in the room (F, 60, SLC, 1930).

3965　Wear a lump of asafetida around the neck to ward off smallpox (M, 54, Park City, 1935). Brown 2115.

3966　Wear a string of rattlesnake rattlers around your neck to prevent smallpox (F, 18, SLC, 1955).

3967　Sheep manure was used in smallpox. It was made into a tea (F, 71, Woods Cross, 1953).

## SNAKEBITE

### Animals, Animal Products

3968 If a snake bites you, bite its head off and you won't die (Provo, 1900); . . . cure yourself by eating the snake (F, 20, SLC, 1955).

3969 For the bite of a snake, kill the reptile and apply the fat to the wound (M, 43, Vernal, 1936). Cf. Brown 2141f, 2144. (The medical precept, similia similibus curantur, 'similar things are cured by similar means,' applies here, where the agent causing the disease is also employed in its cure. See other examples in this section, and No. 3367, above, where the hair of a dog is recommended as a cure for a dog bite. --Eds.)

3970 If a rattlesnake bites you, kill it and cut the rattles off; put the rattles on a string and wear it around your wrist, then the bite will get better faster (F, 18, SLC, 1958).

3971 A rattlesnake bite can be cured by salt and fresh pork (M, SLC, 1957). Brown 2137.

3972 To cure a snakebite, drench the body with warm lard out of a bottle (F, 20, SLC, 1964).

3973 The yolk of an egg and salt made into a paste are used for snakebites (Utah pioneer, ca. 1860). Brown 2133.

3974 The hair of the dog is good for snakebites (F, Moab, 1953).

3975 If a dog which has been bitten by a rattlesnake and recovered will lick the wound of a person bitten by a rattlesnake, it will help cure the person (M, 50, Logan). Cf. Brown 2146.

3976 For a snakebite kill a bird, a chicken, a frog or a toad. As long as the blood is still warm, open it up and put it against the bite and it will suck the blood out (F, Moab, 1953). Brown 2130, 2134.

### Plants

3977 A rattlesnake will not bite you if you smell of tumbleweed (M, SLC, 1964).

3978 Snakebites were cut crosswise and treated with milkweed, tobacco, whiskey or black mud (M, SLC, 1946).

3979 Spit of tobacco on snakebite will help cure poisonous reaction (M, 70, Duchesne). Cf. Brown 2156f.

3980 A cut onion will draw the poison from a snakebite (F, 64, SLC, 1963). Cf. Brown 2152.

### Miscellaneous

3981 A drink of whiskey will cure or prevent the action of poisons from a snakebite (M, SLC, 1952); Whiskey will kill the poison in a snakebite if taken ten minutes after being bitten (F, SLC, 1961). Cf. Brown 2165.

3982 Never wear the clothes of anyone who has been bitten by a snake and died, or you may die too (M, 60, Richfield, 1921).

3983 If you get bitten by a snake, find a pregnant woman and drink her urine (F, Springville, 1960).

3984 If you get bitten by a snake, be very active and drive out the poison (F, 20, SLC, 1955).

## SORES

3985 Swimming in August causes a breaking out of sores on your feet (F, 74, SLC, 1964).

3986 Use vinegar for open sores (F, 44, Swiss, Midvale, 1964). Cf. Brown 2184.

3987 Use alum syrup for sore mouths. It has sugar and alum and I don't know what else (F, Moab, 1953).

3988 Any strong smelling substance will cure sores on the body (F, 78, Ger, SLC, 1964).

3989 Take a glass and light a piece of cotton in it and then place it on a sore spot. It will suck the evil spirits out (M, Price, 1963).

3990 If you have a sore that is slow to heal, rub skunk oil into it (F, SLC, 1920s).

3991 Cow manure will cure a sore (F, Moab, 1953).

3992 To cure all sores, rub on kerosene (F, 36, Logan, 1940).

3993 If you are pregnant, you can't heal a sore on another person (F, SLC, 1930).

3994 The ring finger stroked along any sore or wound will soon heal it (F, Spanish Fork, 1959). Cf. Brown 2174. (In folklore the ring finger is supposed to be more directly connected with the heart than any other digit of either hand; hence notions of vital force and efficacy. From early times the fourth finger has been regarded as the digitus medicus, and has been used for the application of salves and other medications, as well as for touching, stroking, and the like. In the early literature it was referred to as the lecheman, being connected with the early word for doctor, namely 'leech.' --Eds.)

## SORE THROAT

### Animals, Animal Products

3995 Wrap bacon fat around a sore throat and bind it securely (F, Orangeville, 1900s); . . . bacon soaked in turpentine . . . (M, 44, Layton, 1970); Use bacon rind hung around the neck for a sore throat (M, SLC, 1957).

3996  Wear a slice of fat pork under a flannel cloth around your neck to cure a sore throat (M, 20, SLC, 1964).

3997  A strip of salt pork bacon with drops of turpentine applied on the neck with a wool sock wrapped around it is good for a sore throat (F, 60, SLC, 1906).

3998  A strip of bacon, rubbed with pepper, and placed around the neck, will cure a sore throat (F, SLC, 1925); A slice of bacon sprinkled with pepper on a flannel cloth . . . (F, 53, SLC, 1964); Hold a peppered bacon strip in place with a dirty sock to . . . (F, Lehi, 1957); A strip of heavily peppered fat wrapped around the neck . . . (M, SLC, 1946). Cf. Brown 2188.

3999  Slices of salt pork are mixed with kerosene and taken internally to cure a sore throat (M, 71, SLC, 1964).

4000  For a sore throat tie a piece of unwashed lamb's hair dunked in brandy around your neck (F, Gr, SLC, 1962).

4001  To cure a sore throat, go to the chicken coop and gather the chicken's droppings, put them in a cloth and tie around your neck (F, 80, SLC, 1915).

4002  Hot cow dung and honey will cure a sore throat (F, SLC, 1964).

### Plants, Herbs, Vegetables, Etc.

4003  Cayenne mixed with fruit juices is a good tonic for sore throat (F, SLC, 1975).

4004  Hang a bag containing asafetida around your neck and it will keep sore throats away (M, SLC, 1961). Learned in Georgia, 1920; Asafetida on a rag around the throat will cure a sore throat (F, Bear River City, 1957).

4005  The petals from Canterbury bells will cure sore throats (M, Clinton, 1959); The Canterbury bell's petals are arranged to suggest a throat, hence the plant was and is supposed to cure a sore throat (F, SLC, 1964).

4006  Put carrots in cloth around your neck to relieve a sore throat (M, 35, SLC, 1940).

4007  In order to get rid of a sore throat, hang an onion around your neck on a wet string (F, SLC, 1963).

4008  Nutmeg worn around the neck is good for a sore throat (F, Ogden, 1959). Brown 2196.

4009  Boil the inner bark from an oak tree until you obtain a dark brown fluid. Cool and gargle three times a day to cure a sore throat (M, Vernal, 1961). Cf. Brown 2200.

4010  Eat raisins to cure a sore throat (F, SLC, 1964).

4011  Remedy for a sore throat: ginger tea. Put about one teaspoon of ginger in two cups of water and let boil a few minutes. Drink it down (F, 18, Draper, 1971).

4012  Mullein is good for any kind of throat trouble. Make a tea of it, or dry it and smoke it (F, 81, Logan, 1946).

### Pharmaceuticals, Minerals, Etc.

4013  Merthiolate will cure a sore throat (M, 52, Cedar City, 1964).

4014  To cure a sore throat, gargle gunpowder and glycerin mixed (M, 20, SLC, 1964).

4015  To cure a sore throat, take powdered sulphur and put in a tube made of paper; then blow onto sore throat (M, SLC, 1900); Use flowers of sulphur blown on a sore throat to treat it (F, SLC, 1969).

4016  A sore throat can be cured by gargling coal oil (M, 46, SLC, 1924).

4017  For a sore throat use an ointment throat rub of raw sliced onions in kerosene (F, 20, SLC, 1963).

4018  For a bad sore throat heat turpentine and lard together and dip in a piece of flannel and wrap around the chest and neck, and cut it off in small pieces. Don't take it off all at once (F, 63, SLC, 1912).

4019  Kerosene on a feather heals a sore throat (F, 65, SLC, 1964).

4020  For a sore throat, get some cinnamon and sugar. After they are mixed well, swab them down around your tonsils (F, Gr, SLC, 1962).

4021  Gargle with salt water every two hours, as hot as water as you can take it to cure a sore throat (M, SLC, 1961).

4022  A small bag of salt heated and placed on the neck before you go to bed will cure a sore throat (M, 18).

4023  A vinegar pack on the throat cures a sore throat (F, 52, Provo, 1920-25).

### Applications

4024  A red flannel cloth wrapped around the neck will cure a sore throat (M, SLC, 1957). Brown 2208.

4025  A silk stitched chain worn around the neck will prevent a sore throat (M, SLC, 1957).

4026  When you wrap a wet rag around your neck when you have a sore throat, the evil spirits are chased away (F, 50, SLC, 1928).

4027  Soak a rag in alcohol and wrap it around your neck. This is a sure cure for a sore throat (F, 29, Ogden, 1956).

4028  Prevent a sore throat by wearing glass beads (M, 36, Sandy, 1945); Wear a necklace of amber beads to cure or ward off . . . (F, 20, SLC, 1964). Brown 2218.

4029  Wear a rubber band around your arm to cure a sore throat (M, 20, SLC, 1964).

4030  If you wear a dirty sock around your neck, you won't get a sore throat (M,

43, Delta, 1930); . . . sock of the left foot . . . (M, SLC, 1958). Cf. Brown 2209f.

4031 To cure a sore throat, wear a woolen sock around the neck (F, SLC, 1957); . . . soiled wool sock . . . (F, Bear River City, 1957); . . . red wool sock . . . (F, 80, Heber, 1972).

4032 A string with sixteen knots in it will ward off sore throats in the winter if the string is worn around the neck (F, 60, Scot, SLC, 1966).

## AILMENTS OF THE SPINE

4033 Don't sleep on the right side of the bed or your spine will become curved (F, SLC, 1910).

4034 If you step on a line, you break your spine (F, SLC, 1963); . . . your father's spine (F, 32, SLC, 1941); . . . your mother's spine (F, SLC, 1964).

## AILMENTS OF THE SPLEEN

4035 If the palm of your right hand itches, it means your spleen is out of order (F, 40, SLC, 1920s).

## SPRAINS

4036 Arnica, or "arnicky" was always applied to sprains instead of soaking in cold and then warm water (M, 46, SLC, 1928).

4037 Use Epsom salts and hot water for sprains (F, Woods Cross, 1953).

4038 A sprain may be healed by applications of bacon (F, 20, SLC, 1964).

4039 Beat an egg white until dry, spread over the sprained area, and within a short time it will take the swelling and soreness out of the sprain (F, 64, SLC, 1962).

4040 Use wild sage for sprained ankles. Just make a tea out of it and soak the ankle (F, Woods Cross, 1953).

4041 Dandelion juice and alcohol is good for sprains and problems with the joints (F, SLC, 1969).

4042 To cure a sprain, place the injured member in a hat and turn it three times to the left at sunset (M, SLC, 1960).

4043 Cure sprains by twirling a half-bushel measure over the afflicted part of the victim (F, Ephraim, 1920). (The editors have been unable to find parallels of this ritual to explain the underlying notions of a regimen involving both "twirling" and "measuring."  --Eds.)

## SPRING FEVER

4044 Drink sassafras tea to prevent spring fever (F, 65, SLC, 1940).

4045 Drink molasses and sulphur to purify the blood and prevent spring fever (F, 57, SLC, 1964); . . . to cure spring fever (F, 41, SLC, 1964).

4046 Eat poke salad to get rid of spring fever each spring. You must parboil it several times, pouring off the water each time, and finally frying it in a large skillet with bacon (F, Logan, 1973).

## STOMACHACHE, BELLYACHE

4047 A person who eats green apples will get a stomachache (M, SLC, 1947); . . . a stolen apple . . . (M, 61, Ephraim, 1915).

4048 Citrus fruit causes an acid stomach (F, SLC, 1960).

4049 If you eat cherries and milk together, they will explode in your stomach (F, SLC, 1953).

4050 Eating pickles with milk will make a person sick to their stomach (F, 19, SLC, 1964).

4051 If you eat sweet milk and fish together, you will have a stomachache (F, SLC, 1958).

4052 In some cuts of round steak there is a piece of fat or gristle referred to as "bellyacher." If you eat it, it will give you one (F, 49, SLC, 1948).

4053 Stirring a drink with a knife will cause stomach pains (F, 60, Ogden, 1920).

4054 To prevent a stomach ailment, drink thick pea soup which puts a lining on the stomach (F, SLC, 1969).

## Cures

4055 Catnip tea for bellyaches (F, 73, SLC, 1910).

4056 A fern found growing on a tree will relieve a stomachache (F, 19, SLC, 1957).

4057 A warm lettuce leaf placed over the right side will cure stomach disorders (F, 49, SLC, 1961).

4058 For stomach disorders take the dried root of calomel, a swamp plant, and hold it in your mouth, swallowing the juices from it (M, 49, SLC). Heard in Missouri, 1925.

4059 Peach leaf or peach twig tea was a pioneer remedy for stomach upset (M, Tooele, 1957).

4060 Hop tea and cream of tartar for stomach disorder (F, 60, Duchesne, 1930s).

4061 Peppermint tea will cure stomachaches (M, 44, Layton, 1970); For stomachaches gather peppermint, wash when fresh and hang up to dry, steep (F, 70, Provo, 1900). Cf. Brown 1713.

4062 Use spearmint tea which is made from the weed of spearmint and water to cure a stomachache (F, 75, Smithfield, 1970).

4063 For stomach trouble take wormwood tea. It's also good for ulcers of the stomach and stomach flu (F, 85, Providence, 1890).

4064    Warm milk and egg whites are good cures for stomachaches (M, 37, SLC, 1961).

4065    For a sick stomach, take one-half teaspoon of black pepper in a glass of milk (M, Tooele, 1957).

4066    The lining of a chicken gizzard was thought to be especially good for stomach trouble (M, 71, SLC). Brown 1697.

4067    The skin of a hawk is good to wear on the stomach for the pain and coldness of it (M, 19, SLC, 1959).

4068    To cure a stomachache, kill and skin a cat and spread the skin over your stomach (M, 24, Ogden, 1950).

4069    Tea made of chimney soot from a wood-burning fire was supposedly used for troubled stomachs (M, 71, SLC).

4070    To settle an upset stomach, you have to drink water which has had three flies boiled in it (F, SLC, 1964).

4071    The best thing you can take for an upset stomach is a glass of pure rainwater. If it's clean it will help your stomach (M, 21, SLC, 1955).

4072    Always put the garbage out when you have a sour stomach. This will cure your sore stomach (M, 24, SLC, 1950).

4073    When your stomach first starts to hurt, you just take a piece of cardboard and paper and put it over your stomach (F, SLC, 1967).

## STRANGULATION, THROAT OBSTRUCTIONS

4074    It was believed that if chokecherries and milk were taken internally at the same time, strangulation would follow (M, 71, SLC).

4075    If you swallow a fish bone, just eat a slice of bread and it will take care of the bone (F, 18, Bountiful, 1972).

4076    If a fish bone gets stuck in your throat, pull on your big toe and it will come out (F, 29, SLC).

4077    To dissolve a fish bone caught in the throat, drink vinegar (F, 20, SLC, 1963).

4078    To clear the throat of any sharp or irritating object or substance, eat a dry crust of bread (M, SLC, 1920).

## STROKES

4079    Salt carried in the pocket will ward off strokes (M, 52, Cedar City, 1964). Brown 2272.

## STUTTERING, STAMMERING

4080    Tickling a person will cause him to stutter (M, SLC, 1920).

4081    A common belief of stutterers is that an "it" or something is inside them such as a little man which makes them stutter (F, 21, Bountiful, 1964).

4082    Stammering may be cured by reading out loud with teeth closed for two hours a day in three or four months (F, 64, SLC, 1964).

## STYES

### Human and Animal Connections

4083    If you don't wash your hair for a week or two, you will get a sty (F, 26, SLC, 1964). First heard in Wisconsin, 1946.

4084    If you stare at a sty, you will soon have one (M, 52, Cedar City, 1964). Brown 2274.

4085    A sty is caused by seeing something you shouldn't have seen (Anon, Lehi, 1957).

4086    A sty comes to the eye from telling a lie (F, 43, SLC, 1927).

4087    A sty in your eye is caused from wetting in the middle of the road; if you see someone with a sty you say, "Get out of the middle of the road to pee next time" (F, Moab, 1953); . . . urinating in the street (F, 19, SLC, 1961); . . . urinating on the sidewalk (F, Bear River City, 1957); . . . peeing on the ground (M, SLC, 1959); . . . going to the bathroom outside (F, 16, SLC, 1958); . . . urinating in the road at night (M, Roosevelt, 1961). (See Wayland D. Hand, "Padepissers and Wekschissers: A Folk Medical Inquiry into the Cause of Styes," Hand, Magical Medicine, pp. 261-72. Cf. Nos. 4135, 4203, below. --Eds.)

4088    Defecating on the street causes a sty (F, SLC, 1925).

4089    If you have a sty, that means you have wet the bed (F, SLC, 1961).

4090    Spit on a sty to cure it by rubbing a moistened finger on it (M, 20, SLC, 1964).

4091    If you have a sty in the eye, go at night to the crossroads and spit. The infection will be gone in the morning (F, 59, SLC, 1963).

4092    Put urine on a sty and it will cure it (F, 45, SLC, 1964).

4093    Cats cause styes (F, SLC, 1950s).

4094    To cure a sty, rub it with a cat's tail (F, 20, SLC, 1964). Cf. Brown 2277ff.

4095    A sty can be cured by the lick of a dog (M, SLC, 1959).

### Miscellaneous

4096    Rub scraped potato on your eye to cure a sty (F, 19, SLC, 1964).

4097    If you drop a piece of pie on the ground, you will get a sty in your eye (M, Orem, 1959).

4098    Rub turpentine on a sty that has just started (M, 20, SLC, 1964).

4099 To get rid of a sty you should recite, "Sty, sty go off my eye. Go on the next one I pass by." Then the next person you pass will get the sty and you won't have it anymore (F, Richfield, 1916).

4100 Rub a sty on the eye with a wedding ring by crossing it twice each day. It will disappear (F, SLC, 1957); Rub the sty with your gold wedding ring . . . (F, 44, Bountiful, 1964); . . . with a silver ring . . . (M, SLC, 1961); Rub the wedding ring on your clothes and get it warm as possible . . . (F, 20, SLC, 1953).

4101 Rub a gold wedding ring three times on a sty and it will go away (F, SLC, 1961); Rub a sty nine times with a golden wedding ring or any other piece of gold . . . (F, 74, 1898, Mill Creek); . . . rub a gold ring over it seven times . . . (F, 18, SLC, 1961); . . . rub a gold ring or anything gold across the affected part nine times and wash in onion water . . . (F, 34, SLC, 1960). Cf. Brown 2283ff.

4102 Rub a gold thimble on a sty and it will go away (F, SLC, 1955).

4103 For a sty take a penny, rub it until it's very hot and put it on the sty (F, SLC, 1944).

SUNBURN

4104 If a girl doesn't want to get burned by the sun in March, she must wear a red and white string around her wrist (F, Gr, SLC, 1957); The first day of spring (March 21) they tie red and white string on children's forefingers so they won't sunburn (M, Gr, SLC, 1963).

4105 On the first day of May if you tie a red ribbon on your right wrist, it will keep you from getting sunburned the rest of the summer (F, 49, Midvale, 1927).

4106 When sunburned, sit in a tub of cold water for four hours (F, 19, Logan, 1971).

4107 Vinegar will cure a sunburn (M, Cedar City, 1964).

4108 The best thing for sunburn: Take a bath in pickle juice. It makes it so it doesn't hurt so bad (F, Provo, 1969).

SUNSTROKE

4109 Light-skinned people get sunstrokes before dark-skinned people (F, 78, Provo, 1942).

SWELLING

4110 Epsom salts are excellent for reducing swelling (F, 20, SLC, 1963).

4111 To reduce swellings of bumps and bruises, place a cold table knife against the swelling (F, SLC, 1925).

4112 We used to use cow manure poultices on swellings (F, 81, Logan, 1946).

SYPHILIS

4113 Copulating with a menstruating woman will infect men with all sorts of diseases such as syphilis (F, SLC, 1961).

4114 If a man has a saddle, people think he has syphilis (F, 21, SLC, 1962).

TAPEWORMS

4115 An intestinal tapeworm always causes one to overeat, especially meat (F, SLC, 1961).

4116 If you put a piece of cheese on the tip of your tongue, a tapeworm will come up to get it and you can catch it (F, SLC, 1960). Cf. Brown 2329f.

4117 If you have a tapeworm, the thing to do is sit in front of a bowl of milk and this will make it come out (F, Ir, SLC, 1969).

4118 Eat honey and chopped up hair to kill tapeworms (M, 92, Ogden, 1961).

TEETH

Cleaning, Etc.

4119 Eating the crust on toast makes your teeth white (M, 21, Gr, SLC, 1963).

4120 To whiten dark teeth, take barley meal, honey and salt; mix them together and rub the dark teeth with it. Do this in the morning and at night (M, 50, It, SLC, 1965).

4121 Drink cold water for white teeth (M, SLC, 1964).

4122 Cleaning teeth with toothpaste prevents decay (F, SLC, 1961); A clean tooth never decays (F, 69, St. George, 1964).

4123 Some people believe that the plaque that forms on dentures is hair (F, SLC, 1971).

4124 Take a nail and pound the head into the gums of your teeth just enough to make them bleed, and you will never have any more decay (F, 23, SLC, 1964).

4125 If you pick your teeth in company, they will decay (M, 24, Ogden, 1963).

4126 Raw potatoes will rot a person's teeth (F, 75, Emery Co).

4127 You should not go to bed with wet hair. If you do, your teeth will fall out (F, Gr, SLC, 1964). Heard in Greece.

4128 Chew tobacco to cure a bad tooth (F, 34, SLC, 1964).

TEMPERATURE

4129 Rub pepper on a patient when his temperature is below normal (F, SLC, 1960).

## THROAT AILMENTS

4130  Turpentine can be used as a throat rub (F, 20, SLC, 1963).

4131  For phlegm in the throat make a paste from sugar and lemon juice and take as often as necessary (F, 20, SLC, 1963).

## TOES, TOENAILS

4132  Walk in a hole, break your mother's toe (F, 61, Dan, SLC, 1959). Heard in Denmark, 1903.

4133  Always cut your toenails straight across, or you'll get ingrown toenails (F, 29, Ogden, 1970).

4134  Bread and milk poultices draw the inflammation from an ingrowing toe. Warm milk, mix in bread to a mush. Wrap the toe in it with cloth and a wool sock for warmth. It draws out the pus (F, 69, SLC, 1925).

## TONGUE AILMENTS

4135  If you have a sore on your tongue, it means that you have peed in the middle of the road (F, 48, Mapleton, 1920s). (For relieving oneself in the road, and physical punishments deriving from this public desecration, see No. 4087, above, and 4203, below. --Eds.)

4136  A sore on the tip of the tongue means you have told a lie (F, 19, SLC); You get lumps on your tongue if you lie (F, Tooele, 1964). Brown 3670.

## TONSILLITIS

4137  Tie velvet around the throat to keep from getting tonsillitis (M, SLC).

4138  To cure tonsillitis, roast a potato and put half on each side of the throat (F, 81, Sigurd, 1910).

4139  For tonsillitis paint the tonsils with iodine either using a Q-tip or a pipe cleaner (F, SLC, 1972).

4140  Swab turpentine on the throat for tonsillitis (F, Moab, 1953).

4141  Cut open bullets and remove powder, grind to fine powder. Make a funnel out of paper and blow a small amount onto the tonsils (M, SLC, 1974).

## TOOTHACHE

### Human and Animal Connections

4142  A toothache is always a sign that you have not brushed your teeth regularly (F, 49, Holladay, 1945-47).

4143  Stop a toothache on the left side of the jaw by tying a string around the big toe of the right foot (F, 75, SLC, 1963).

4144  Cut your fingernails on Friday and you will never have a toothache (F, 67, Panguitch, 1920). Brown 2338.

4145  To cure a toothache, place a soiled diaper directly upon it (F, SLC, 1969).

4146  To cure a toothache, take an eyelash, an eyebrow, trimmings of the fingernails and toenails of the patient, bore a hole in a tree and put them in. The sufferer must not see the tree, and it must not be cut down or burned (F, 21, Butler City, 1964). Brown 2341.

4147  If you walk in someone else's footsteps, you'll get a toothache (F, Bountiful, 1960). (As in No. 3557, above, q.v., there is an underlying notion of contagious magic and perhaps conjury, even though no such idea is openly expressed. Headaches, fever, nausea, and stomach upsets are more common manifestations of harmful magic brought into play by contact with footprints than is a toothache. --Eds.)

4148  A toothache will stop if you rub the gum above the tooth with a newly cut off finger from a dead person (M, MD, SLC, 1959). Heard from patients. (See Hand, *Magical Medicine*, pp. 73-74, note 62. --Eds.)

4149  Carry a hen's tooth in your pocket for a toothache (M, 78, SLC). Cf. Brown 2343.

4150  If you want to get rid of a toothache, kiss a donkey (M, SLC, 1963).

4151  A safeguard against toothaches is to wear a spider enclosed in a nutshell around the neck; a mole's paw will do as well (F, SLC, 1961).

### Plant Remedies

4152  For a toothache scrape some carrots and put some in the tooth, inside and out. If this does not relieve the toothache, put a hot pancake on the face, holding it with a cloth (M, 59, Monroe, 1920).

4153  To cure a toothache, put clove syrup on a cotton swab and hold on the aching tooth (F, 61, Draper, 1965).

4154  For a toothache, smear the aching tooth with onion juice and the tooth will stop aching (M, 50, It, SLC, 1965).

4155  A toothache can be cured by wrapping boiled tea leaves or ground cloves in a cloth and lodging the cloth in the gums (M, 46, SLC, 1926).

4156  Chew tobacco to stop a toothache (M, 35, Ogden, 1940). Brown 2365.

4157  To cure a toothache, one can eat shavings from a tree that was struck by lightning (F, 73, Eng, SLC, 1965). Cf. Brown 2363f.

4158  Wear a walnut around your neck and it will help soothe a toothache until you can get to a dentist (M, Kamas, 1940).

4159  A double nut carried in the pocket will prevent toothaches (F, 36, SLC, 1949).

### Miscellaneous

4160  Hold whiskey in the mouth to deaden a toothache (M, SLC, 1961).

4161 For a toothache: Pack the tooth with salt in the hollow (F, SLC, 1964). Brown 2368.

4162 For a toothache, put some vinegar and salt on your tooth (F, Gr, SLC, 1962). Cf. Brown 2372.

4163 To cure a toothache, place a very cold stone against your face (F, 47, SLC).

4164 To cure a toothache, steal a dishrag and bury it (F, 73, SLC, 1964).

4165 Powdered jet (a mineral) is believed to have the power of curing toothaches (M, SLC, 1963).

4166 Put gunpowder on an aching tooth to ease it (M, 18, Peoa, 1964).

4167 An old horseshoe put under your bed will cure the toothache of the person sleeping in the bed (F, 85, SLC, 1964).

4168 To prevent a toothache, make a wish by the full moon (M, Provo, 1954).

4169 A nail driven into an oak tree will cure a toothache (M, 51, Murray, 1923).

4170 It is believed that a toothache can be prevented by driving horseshoe nails into the upper lintels of kitchen doors. If the nails come loose, they have to be driven securely home again in the lintel (M, 47, SLC, 1964).

## TUBERCULOSIS

4171 Tuberculosis is inherited directly (F, SLC, 1961).

4172 Tuberculosis is infectious and very easily contracted by adults (F, SLC, 1961).

4173 If you have tuberculosis, March will search you, April will try you, and May will tell you whether you will live the year out (F, SLC, 1961).

4174 If you have ever had smallpox, you will never have tuberculosis (F, SLC, 1961).

4175 If you have tuberculosis, stay in the sun (F, 48, SLC, 1964).

4176 The skin of a cat worn on the chest will cure tuberculosis (F, Pol, Wanship).

4177 Cure tuberculosis by eating raw meat to build up the lungs (F, 28, Vernal, 1955).

## TYPHOID FEVER

4178 Typhoid fever will develop in the person who burns locust wood in the fireplace (F, Bountiful, 1916).

4179 A pine knot placed in drinking water will prevent typhoid (M, 67, Ger, SLC, 1964). Brown 2396.

4180 Sponge cold water over the body several times each day to cure typhoid fever (F, 28, Vernal, 1945). This was prescribed by MD to her father in 1909.

4181 To cure typhoid fever, there's nothing better than to bathe in ice cold water (F, 87, Providence, 1970).

4182 To cure typhoid fever, soak in lukewarm water with salt so strong that you can float an egg. Then rub the body with olive oil (F, 87, Providence, 1915).

## ULCERS

4183 If a person drinks cold water, he will develop ulcers (M, 23, SLC, 1962).

4184 Raw cabbage juice cures ulcers (F, 20, SLC, 1962).

4185 The best thing for ulcers is cayenne pepper. It stops the bleeding and also heals the stomach (F, SLC, 1975).

4186 Mexicans have a lower percentage of ulcers because they eat hot peppers. In order to prevent ulcers or cure ulcers, eat hot peppers once a week (M, SLC, 1969).

4187 For ulcers boil some linen seed with water and drink it (F, Gr, SLC, 1962).

## VARICOSE VEINS

4188 If you cross your legs, you will get varicose veins (F, 21, Ogden, 1965).

4189 For varicose veins take cayenne and vitamin E. You can take cayenne in a capsule (F, SLC, 1975).

## VENEREAL DISEASES

4190 You will get venereal disease if you sit on a public restroom toilet (F, 21, Ogden, 1965).

4191 Venereal disease is caused by having the semen of two or more different men inside you. It is the semen that generates into venereal disease. This way two conclusions are reached: One, men can have as many wives as they want, but two, women can only have one husband each. This is also a handy way of explaining why prostitutes get venereal disease (F, Bountiful, 1971).

4192 If you can't touch the point of your nose while your eyes are closed, you have a venereal disease (M, 63, SLC, 1935).

## VOMITING

4193 For a good sedative and to control vomiting, simmer peach tree leaves in water and then drink (F, 75, Heber, 1895).

4194 To control nausea and vomiting, have the person lie flat on his or her back and place an egg (raw) on the neck (M, SLC, 1936). Cf. Brown 2401.

## WARTS

### Causes - Animal and Human Agents

4195 If you handle frogs, you'll get warts where the frog touched you (F, 46,

Granger, 1920s); . . . play with frogs
. . . (M, 52, Cedar City, 1964); . . .
handle toads . . . (F, 26, Bountiful,
1940s). Brown 2410.

4196  If frogs or toads wet on you, it makes
warts (F, Moab, 1953). Brown 2414.

4197  When handling a toad, the bumps on his
back will come off onto one's hands as
warts (F, 22, SLC, 1955).

4198  If a toad spits on your hand, it will
make a wart (M, 18, SLC, 1958).

4199  Cats cause warts (F, 21, SLC, 1950s).

4200  Don't count the warts on another person
or you will get the same number of warts
on you (M, SLC, 1957); If you touch
another's warts, they will appear on you
(M, 23, Heber, 1972). Brown 2417.

4201  If you have warts, it means you have
been kissing over the back fence (F, 23,
SLC, 1957).

4202  If you tell a lie, you'll get a wart (F,
20, SLC, 1965).

4203  If you urinate in the street, you will
get warts (F, 68, Farmington, 1906).
(Warts as a punishment for urinating in
the street is unusual. Far more common
is the notion that one will get a stye
for this act, or for defecating in a
public place. See No. 4087, above, for
literature on the subject, and No. 4135,
above, for another somewhat unusual
punishment for this same antisocial act.
--Eds.)

4204  If you point at a star, you will get a
wart (M, 15, W. Jordan, 1958).

4205  If you count stars at night, you'll get
warts on your hands (F, SLC, 1959).
Brown 2418.

4206  If you play with toadstools, you will
get warts (F, 23, Murray, 1946). Brown
2416.

4207  To wash your hands in water in which
eggs have been boiled is a certain way
to get warts (F, 74, SLC, 1964). Cf.
Brown 2405f.

## Cures - Animals, Animal Products

4208  Holding a dead cat in the light of the
moon gets rid of warts (F, 18, Ogden,
1960).

4209  If you swing a black cat overhead in a
graveyard at midnight, the wart will
leave (M, SLC, 1957); Whirl a black cat
around your head three times and put it
down on the warts and they will go away
(F, SLC, 1960). Cf. Brown 2451.

4210  To cure warts, you should take a dead
cat, at a full moon, and go to the
cemetery. You then say a little chant
and your warts are cured (F, 38, Nephi,
1935).

4211  Bury a dead cat by the light of the moon
and you'll get rid of your warts (F, 45,
SLC, 1930s); Kill a cat and bury it in a
black stocking . . . (M, 30, SLC, 1941);

Kill a black cat at midnight . . . (M,
13, Provo, 1964).

4212  To get rid of warts, kill a cat and bury
it at the crossroads (M, 19, Magna,
1964); . . . kill a black cat, drain the
blood and put it on the wart, bury the
cat (F, 34, SLC, 1965).

4213  To get rid of a wart, rub a cat's tail
on it; then bury the cat alive where no
one will bother it (M, 19, SLC, 1950).

4214  Tie a black cat to a tombstone, under a
full moon at midnight, and it will cure
your warts (F, 18, Price, 1962).

4215  Take a black cat to a graveyard and lay
it on a freshly dug grave to get rid of
warts (F, SLC, 1960); . . . at full moon
. . . (F, 19, SLC, 1961).

4216  To get rid of a wart, get a cat that was
killed by a Negro in a graveyard in the
full of the moon, and rub the blood of
the dead cat on your wart (F, 19, SLC,
1964).

4217  The first squirt of cow's milk will cure
warts (F, SLC, 1931).

4218  To get rid of warts, apply cow's urine
to them (F, 78, SLC, 1964).

4219  If you go into the pasture and get a bag
of warm cow manure and put it on your
warts, they will go away (F, 70,
Bountiful, 1900s).

4220  To cure warts, impale a frog on a stick
and rub the warts on the frog. They
will disappear as the frog dies (Anon,
SLC, 1953).

4221  To get rid of a wart, go out all alone
on a night without a moon and touch a
frog on the wart (F, SLC, 1959); . . .
toad . . . (F, 18, Aust, SLC, 1951).
Cf. Brown 2453.

4222  Bury a frog under a full moon to get rid
of warts (M, 19, SLC, 1964); Kill a frog
and bury it under the porch on the night
of a full moon . . . (M, 23, SLC, 1964).

4223  Rub a toad on a wart in the moonlight
and it will disappear (M, 40, SLC,
1963).

4224  To get rid of warts you must kill a toad
and then on the night of the full moon
must cut off one of its legs and let the
blood run onto the wart. If any of the
blood falls to the ground, you'll have
more warts grow around the original one
(M, 19, Logan, 1970). Learned in
Alabama. Cf. Brown 2478.

4225  Let a bird or a chicken peck at a wart
for three days in a row, and your wart
will disappear (F, SLC, late 1950s).

4226  To get rid of warts, tie a lizard by the
tail to a piece of string. Next rub a
slab of bacon on the wart and then on
the piece of string. Now drive a nail
into a tree and tie the string to the
nail. Then you wait. When the string
rots and the lizard falls to the ground,
the wart will fall off (F, Provo, 1971).
Learned in New Orleans, 1959.

4227 If you bury a fish in your backyard under a tree, you can get rid of your wart (F, SLC, 1964).

### Bacon, Meat, Bones

4228 If you soak bacon rind in vinegar overnight and then put it over a wart, the wart will be gone the next day (F, 35, Vernal, 1930s).

4229 If you rub warts with a piece of bacon and attach the bacon to an aspen tree, the warts will disappear from you and grow on the tree (F, 37, SLC, 1964); . . . put the bacon in a slit on a tree; the warts will grow on the tree as knobs (M, SLC, 1959).

4230 If you rub a piece of bacon rind on a wart and then secretly bury it, the wart will go away (F, 71, Midway, 1900); . . . rub a wart with salt bacon . . . (F, Bountiful, 1960).

4231 If a person has warts, one should steal a piece of bacon, smear it over the warts, put it under a stone and the warts will disappear (F, SLC, 1937). Cf. Brown 2467ff, 2471.

4232 To cure a wart, break it off, rub the place with a piece of salt bacon, and then bury the bacon (M, Tooele, 1957).

4233 To remove warts: In a full moon bury a piece of bacon in the back yard (F, 18, SLC, 1950).

4234 To cure a wart: Take a piece of bacon and on a dark night take it out and bury it--as the bacon rots away so will the wart. It is stipulated that you must not ever tell where you hid the bacon or the cure won't work (M, 28, SLC).

4235 Take a rind off of a slice of bacon and rub it on a wart. Say "Hocasty, pocasty, rotten tomato," and throw it over your shoulder and the warts will go away (F, SLC, 1964); Rub a wart with a piece of bacon and throw the bacon over your left shoulder . . . (F, Mt. Pleasant, 1920).

4236 If you bury salted ham in the ground, your warts will go away (F, 82, SLC, 1921).

4237 Rub salt pork on a wart to get rid of it, then bury the meat in an ant hill (F, SLC, 1959).

4238 If you have a wart: Rub fat on it, bury the fat, and when the fat rots, the wart will be gone. The person with the wart shouldn't know where the fat is hidden (M, 18, Norw, SLC, 1965). Cf. Brown 2472.

4239 Rub a piece of meat over a wart and then bury it. As the meat decays the wart will disappear (F, 45, Bennion, 1913); Put a steak on them and bury the steak and . . . (M, SLC, 1958); . . . dried up steak . . . (F, SLC, 1956); . . . raw meat . . . (M, 46, SLC, 1928). Cf. Brown 2458, 2461.

4240 To remove a wart, take the skin off the meat and rub the wart (F, 40, SLC, 1963); . . . rub it with a piece of stolen meat (F, 32, 1940s). Brown 2459.

4241 To get rid of warts: Take a freshly cut steak, hold it on the warts, turn around three times, tell the warts to leave and they'll disappear (F, 18, SLC, 1950).

4242 To get rid of a wart, throw a piece of beefsteak over your left shoulder (F, 18, SLC, 1961).

4243 Go out and find a bone, rub the wart and lay the bone down just as you found it. Don't look back or warts will return doublefold (F, 20, Du, SLC, 1963). Brown 2443.

### Fruits and Vegetables

4244 The apple is a good preventive medicine against warts (F, 55, Ger, SLC, 1920).

4245 Take an apple and break it in two. Eat one-half and have someone rub the other half on the warts and give to them to dispose of, and the warts will disappear (M, W. Jordan); Rub warts with half an apple, bury the apple (F, Roosevelt, 1961).

4246 To get rid of warts, rub them with a peeled apple and then feed it to a pig (F, 65, SLC, 1964).

4247 Warts can be removed by lemon juice (M, SLC, 1960).

4248 To get rid of a wart, you rub a fig on it, letting the juice contact the wart (F, 20, SLC, 1955). Brown 2524.

4249 Warts can be removed by rubbing the red juice from freshly picked beet leaves on the warts daily (M, 71, SLC).

4250 Rub a slice of onion over warts to cure them (M, Farmington, 1954).

4251 To get rid of a wart, rub one-half of a tiny onion on the wart. Put the onion back together and bury it where it will rot. Don't tell where it is buried (F, SLC, 1960). Cf. Brown 2531.

4252 To get rid of a wart, cut an onion in half, rub the onion on the wart, then tie the onion back together with a string and put it somewhere where it will dry out. When the onion is dried out, your warts will be gone (F, 46, SLC, 1963).

4253 To make a wart go away, rub a carrot on it. Cut the end of the carrot off and every time the carrot is rubbed on the wart, bite off the end (F, SLC, 1968).

4254 To remove a wart, rub it with a bean, and then bury it in the earth. As it decays, the wart should dry up (F, SLC); . . . a stolen lima bean (M, 23, SLC, 1962).

4255 If you have a wart, open a dried bean and rub it on the wart. Bury it where no one can see you. The wart will fall off in a day or so (M, 45, Beaver, 1964); . . . bury the bean under a rock . . . (F, Ogden, 1961).

4256   To cure warts, take a bean, burn half of it, put blood on the other half, and bury it (M, SLC, 1957); . . . a cooked navy bean . . . (M, 56, Ogden, 1963).

4257   To get rid of warts, cut a red bean in half. Rub the wart with one-half of the bean. Then bury one half on one side of the street and the other half on the other side of the street (F, SLC, 1964). Cf. Brown 2483.

4258   If you rub warts with beans and tie them in a bag and throw them away, your warts will disappear (M, SLC, 1961).

4259   To cure warts, rub a brown bean on each wart, wrap the beans in a present and take a walk. Drop the present and don't look back. The warts will disappear (F, 41, SLC, 1964).

4260   If you have a wart, take a green bean and rub it over the wart and then place the bean in a sack and throw it over your shoulder. When a person picks the sack up, they will get your wart from you (M, 26, SLC, 1946). Cf. Brown 2484.

4261   To get rid of warts: Take blood from a wart, dip a bean in the blood and plant the bean. The wart theoretically disappears when the bean sprouts (M).

4262   Cross a wart with a bean and feed the bean to the rooster. The wart will soon leave (F, 34, Echo, 1942).

4263   Remedy for curing warts: Rub the warts with stones, peas or beans and throw the latter in the roadway (M, Vernal, 1959). Cf. Brown 2534.

4264   If you throw a handful of peas into a well and run into the house before they hit the bottom, your warts will go away (M, SLC, 1957). Cf. Brown 2482.

### Potatoes

4265   To cure warts, rub them with a potato cut in two (M, 44, Layton, 1970).

4266   Warts can be cured by rubbing them with a raw potato, and as the potato rots the wart will disappear (F, 60, SLC, 1964). Learned in Idaho, 1920.

4267   Put a dried potato on a wart and it will go away (F, 77, Dan, SLC, 1964).

4268   Use a rotten potato on a wart, then throw the potato over your left shoulder. The wart should go (M, SLC, 1964).

4269   If you want to get rid of warts, rub a potato on them and throw the potato over your left shoulder, and don't tell anyone where it lands (F, Provo, 1959). Cf. Brown 2543, 2545.

4270   Take a potato and split it in two and rub it on the wart, and throw it off over your head (F, Moab, 1953). Cf. Brown 2544.

4271   Plant potatoes in the moonlight, and your warts will go away (F, 55, SLC, 1965).

4272   Plant potato peelings to get rid of warts (F, 55, SLC, 1920s).

4273   If a potato peeling is rubbed on a wart every night for a week, it will disappear (F, 46, SLC, 1928).

4274   Rub a raw potato peeling on a wart, bury it seven inches in the ground on the north slope of a hill. When the peeling rots, the wart will disappear (F, 45, SLC); . . . sliced potato . . . (M, 32, SLC, 1940); . . . as the potato decays in the ground the wart will disappear (F, 18, SLC, 1958); . . . when the potato is buried and sprouts, your warts will go away (M, Farmington, 1931); Bury a cooked potato . . . (F, 19, SLC, 1956).

4275   Rub a rotten potato on a wart and bury the potato afterward (M, 17, SLC, 1955).

4276   A potato is cut in half and rubbed on a wart, then buried in the back yard. In a few days the wart is supposed to dry up and fall off (F, 45, Magna, 1970); Cut a potato in half and rub it on the wart; bury it under the eaves of your house (Logan, 1959); . . . bury the potato in the ground under a full moon (F, 26, SLC, 1964); . . . bury the potato at midnight (F, 21, Brigham City, 1950). Cf. Brown 2547.

4277   To get rid of warts, rub them with a potato cut in half, put the halves together and bury (F, 19, Holladay, 1953).

4278   To cure a wart, steal a potato, cut it in half, rub it on the wart and bury it. As the potato perishes the wart goes away (F, 32, Logan, 1954).

4279   If you have a wart, cut a potato in half and bury it with a dishtowel. When the potato rots, the wart will go away (F, 20, SLC, 1954).

4280   To remove a wart, cut out the eyes of a potato and rub the wart with a piece of the potato eye. Then bury the potato where the person will never go (F, 50, SLC, 1959); . . . bury the potato in good soil . . . (M, 19, SLC, 1963).

4281   If a person has warts, bury an eye of a potato for every wart in the ground. This will make the warts go away (M, 59, Monroe, 1913).

### Cereals

4282   Bury a small bag of corn. When the corn decays, the wart will leave (F, 34, Ogden, 1942).

4283   To get rid of a wart, prick it with a needle, run the needle through a grain of corn, and bury the corn (F, SLC, 1900). Cf. Brown 2495f.

4284   To get rid of a wart, take a drop of blood from the wart and put it on a grain of corn and feed it to a bird (M, SLC, 1957). Cf. Brown 2502.

4285   Rub your wart with a grain of wheat and then plant the grain. When it sprouts, the wart will go away (F, 52, Logan, 1963).

4286 To get rid of warts, you take a stock of wheat, break it off at the first joint, rub it on the wart, and bury it when no one is around (F, Spanish Fork, 1932).

4287 You can remove a wart by rubbing a grain of barley on it and then feeding it to a chicken (F, 42, Kearns, 1930s). Cf. Brown 2497ff.

## Tobacco, Milkweed, Etc.

4288 If you wave a bag of tobacco over a wart, it will go away (M, 18, Magna, 1959).

4289 Milk from a milkweed plant rubbed on a wart will make it disappear within a week (M, 46, SLC, 1927); Sap from milkweed . . . (M, SLC, 1925). Brown 2527.

4290 If you put milkweed on a wart and turn around twice to the left, the wart will go away (M, 57, Heber, 1912).

4291 To remove a wart, one must rub the wart with the milk from a milkweed and bury the milkweed. When the milkweed decays, the wart will fall off (F, 65, Midvale, 1906).

4292 To get rid of warts rub dandelion juice on the wart, and it will disappear (F, 25, SLC, 1964); . . . milk of dandelion . . . (F, SLC, 1967). Brown 2522.

## Dishcloths, Rags, Fibre, Etc.

4293 Rub a dishcloth on a wart and it will disappear in three hours (M, SLC, 1955).

4294 Use a dirty dishrag wrapped around a wart to remove it (F, 54, SLC, 1964).

4295 To remove a wart, steal somebody's dishrag (F, 41, Murray, 1931); . . . wrap your hand in a stolen dishcloth (F, 38, SLC, 1964); . . . steal the dirtiest dishtowel in the house (M, MD, SLC, 1959); . . . steal a dishcloth from a neighbor (M, 55, Centerfield, 1964). Brown 2587.

4296 If you have warts on your hand, steal your mother's dishcloth, touch each wart with it, tie it in a knot and bury it. When the dishcloth has rotted, the warts will disappear (F, Eng, SLC). Cf. Brown 2593.

4297 Tie a knot in a dishrag for each wart that you have, bury the dishrag, and when the dishrag rots, the warts will disappear (M, 55, Roosevelt, 1919).

4298 To get rid of warts, throw away your mother's old dishrag (F, 53, SLC, 1964). Cf. Brown 2588.

4299 Steal a dishcloth, rub your wart and then throw the cloth away without looking where it landed. Your wart will disappear (F, 56, Grantsville, 1953). Cf. Brown 2592.

4300 To get rid of a wart, throw a dirty dishrag over your left shoulder in the light of a full moon (F, Bountiful, 1960).

4301 Take a dirty dishrag and rub it three times on your wart and throw it over your left shoulder. Bury it and your wart will disappear (M, Murray, 1957).

4302 To get rid of warts, boil your mother's best dishcloth, then wash the warts, and finally, bury the rag (F, 19, SLC, 1961).

4303 Bury a towel underground, and by the time it has rotted, your wart should be gone (M, SLC).

4304 Rub your warts with a dishcloth and then bury the cloth, not letting anyone know where you bury it. When the cloth rots, the wart will go away (F, 54, Nephi, 1920s); . . . bury the dishrag when no one is watching (F, 48, Ogden, 1920s); . . . spit on the dishrag and bury it, but don't let anyone know where you buried it (F, SLC, 1964).

4305 Place a dishrag on warts, then say a prayer; bury the dishrag soon afterwards (F, 24, Orderville, 1960).

4306 To get rid of a wart, prick it and rub an old dirty dishtowel in it, then go bury it in the back yard (F, Bountiful, 1959).

4307 If you have a wart and you want to get rid of it, you take an old dishrag and bury it in the back yard where no one can step on it. Forget it and your wart will go away (F, 20, SLC, 1949).

4308 If you rub a wart with an old dishrag and make a wish, then bury the rag under the porch, as the rag rots, the wart will rot away (F, 52, Provo, 1920); . . . under a step . . . (F, SLC, 1958); . . . under the front porch for three days . . . (M, 19, SLC, 1952); . . . under the back porch . . . (SLC, 1958).

4309 Steal a dishrag, rub it on a wart; bury it under the back stairs and the wart will go away (F, 21, SLC, 1961).

4310 Bury a dirty dishrag in the garden to get rid of your warts (F, SLC).

4311 To get rid of warts, bury a stolen dishrag in a chicken yard (F, Park City, 1957).

4312 Rub the wart with a rock, wrap the rock in a dirty dishrag and bury it. The warts disappear (F, SLC, 1957).

4313 Rub a dishrag on the wart and bury the rag under a rock to make the wart go away (F, 22, SLC, 1964).

4314 To remove a wart, rub it with a dirty dishrag and then bury the dishrag at midnight in the cemetery (M, SLC); . . . your mother's dishrag and bury it in a cemetery (F, 1958).

4315 Cure for warts: Rub with a greasy dishcloth, then bury the cloth under a tree, and never tell anyone where the cloth is buried (F, 70, Provo, 1900); Hide a dishrag in the stump of a tree (M, Vernal, 1959).

4316 Wipe your warts with a dishrag and bury it in manure, and your warts will disappear (M, Layton, 1934).

4317    To get rid of a wart, take an old dishcloth that has been dipped in creek water and rub the wart with the rag and then bury the rag at midnight on a night when there isn't a moon in the sky (M, 56, Ir, SLC, 1964); . . . bury it in the full of the moon (F, 45, Midvale, 1928); . . . bury it at midnight under a full moon (F, 51, Gr, Midvale, 1926).

4318    If you have a wart, take a rag soaked in vinegar and bury it and the wart is supposed to disappear (F, 31, American Fork, 1960).

4319    If you steal an old dirty handkerchief and rub it on the warts, then bury it, the warts will go away. The handkerchief should be stolen (F, 69, SLC, 1900s). Cf. Brown 2581.

### Thread, String, Hair, Knots, Etc.

4320    If you tie a string around a wart, it will go away (F, 22, SLC, 1944). Cf. Brown 2434.

4321    If you want to get rid of a wart, it can be done by pulling a string over the wart and then burying the string. As soon as the string is rotten, the wart will leave (F, 53, SLC, 1959).

4322    If you have a wart on you, put a string in your mouth and get it wet. Then wrap it around your wart for a few minutes. Then take it off and bury it, and your wart will go away (M, SLC, 1959). Cf. Brown 2427.

4323    To cure a wart, tie a silk thread for as many warts as you have and throw it away, and your wart will go away (F, 24, W. Jordan, 1953); . . . silk string . . . (M, Morgan, 1961).

4324    Tie a silk thread around a wart. Burn up the rest of the thread and the wart will go away (M, 50, Coalville, 1924).

4325    People claimed warts disappear from hands if you tie a red silk thread around them, mumble some words that no one can hear, then after a certain length of time, cut the thread from off the warts and bury it where no one can see and never tell (F, 71, Centerville, 1963).

4326    During grade school days a neighborhood tradition was that to get rid of warts, one need only to bury a spoon with a string tied around it someplace where no one else knew. By the time the string had rotted, the warts would be gone (M, 35, Milford, 1962).

4327    If you have warts, tie a string around them and rub them with a potato peel. Bury the string and the potato peel. When they decay, the warts will go away (F, Provo, 1955).

4328    Take a hair out of your own head and tie it around the wart, and it will go away (F, SLC, 1967). Cf. Brown 2429.

4329    Tie a horsehair around a wart and it will cut the wart off (M, 62, St. George, 1912); . . . a strand of horse's mane . . . (M, 19, Heber, 1972). Brown 2431f.

4330    To cure warts, wrap a horsehair around the wart and put vinegar on the wart and wrap it up (M, 45, Midvale, 1964).

4331    If you tie knots in silk thread, you will charm away warts (F, 68, SLC, 1920).

4332    One can tie seven knots in a piece of string and bury it. In about a week, the warts go away (M, 53, Richfield, 1930s).

4333    Tie a knot in a string and rub it on your wart; then bury the string and don't think about it anymore. The wart will go away (F, 43, Roosevelt, 1935).

4334    To get rid of warts, tie as many knots in a piece of string as there are warts. Bury the string and tell no one where it is. When the string rots, the warts disappear (M, Ogden, 1961); . . . bury the string under a stone . . . (M, Vernal, 1959). Cf. Brown 2438.

4335    To get rid of warts, rub a string over the wart, tie it in knots and bury the string in a damp place. When the string rots, the warts will disappear (F, 53, SLC, 1917); . . . place it where the rain drops off the house, and place some dirt on it. In three days the warts will be removed (M, 22, Midvale, 1964). Cf. Brown 2440.

4336    Tying knots in a string and burying it in the road at midnight will rid one of warts (M, SLC, 1959); Tie knots in a string and bury it at the crossroads. The first passerby will get the warts (F, Swed, SLC, 1963); . . . bury it under an oak tree (F, Swed, SLC, 1963).

4337    Take a red silk thread and place it around a wart; then tie three knots in it. Remove the thread and bury it under a tree stump; wait three days and the warts will vanish (F, Eng, SLC, 1964).

4338    If you count your warts, make a knot in a thread for every wart, and throw the thread away. The warts will be cured (F, 30, SLC, 1964); . . . throw the string over your head . . . (F, Panguitch, 1900); . . . whoever picks up the string will get the warts instead of you (F, 16, SLC, 1954).

4339    If you take a piece of silk thread and tie as many knots in it as you have warts and throw it into the wind, your warts will go away (F, 24, W. Jordan, 1950).

4340    To cure warts, take a cord or string and tie a knot in it for every wart. Rub the cord over the warts, without anyone knowing. Flush it down the toilet and the warts will disappear (M, 61, Grantsville, 1931).

4341    Tie knots in a piece of black silk thread--as many as you have warts. Give this to a charmer who will bury the thread. The warts will disappear when the silk thread has rotted (F, SLC, 1912).

4342    A Norwegian woman from Minnesota cured a wart on me. "I want you to give me that wart." I said, "Okay." "I will give you something for it," she said. She wrapped thread around it and tied a single knot. Then she removed the thread and hit it. She went home, and pretty soon I noticed the wart was gone (F, Moab, 1953).

4343 Warts: Take a needle with black thread. It has to be black thread. Put the needle and thread through the wart. Burn the thread and watch the smoke go up and disappear. The warts will disappear also (M, Provo, 1971).

Wood, Branches, Sticks, Etc.

4344 To remove warts, one must make as many notches on a piece of wood as he has warts, bury it, and when it rots, the warts will fall off (F, Midvale, 1955). Cf. Brown 2621.

4345 Notch a stick for each wart, and have somebody else bury the stick and by the time it decays, the warts will disappear (F, Moab, 1953).

4346 To do away with warts, go to a running stream, get a twig and cut as many notches in the stick as you have warts. Throw the twig into the stream, and never look back, and they will go away (M, 22, SLC, 1964). Brown 2628.

4347 Cure warts by cutting a notch in a stick for each wart, and throwing it in a field. The first person to cross the field gets the warts (F, 34, Swed, SLC, 1963). Cf. Brown 2625.

4348 To remove warts, cut a small willow branch with a sharp knife. Peel the bark away and rub the sap on the wart (F, SLC, 1958). Cf. Brown 2561.

4349 Break a green stick, rub it on your warts, put it back together, bury it; as it grows back together, it will take away your warts (M, Orem, 1959).

4350 To cure a wart, rub it with a green elder stick and bury the stick in the muck to rot (F, 44, Midvale, 1931).

4351 To make warts disappear, cut a pine needle the size of each wart and bury them. In a few days the warts will be gone (F, American Fork, 1924).

Rainwater, Stump Water, Teardrops, Etc.

4352 Wash your hands in the fresh rainwater in a hollow stump, and you'll lose your warts (M, SLC, 1959); . . . rainwater found in the stump of a white oak tree . . . (F, 46, SLC, 1928). Cf. Brown 2575f.

4353 To get rid of a wart, gather rainwater from a tree stump that has been struck by lightning and put it on the wart (F, SLC, 1960).

4354 Stump water is a cure for warts (M, 24, Provo, 1964); Punk water . . . (F, 49, SLC, 1961); Put stump water on the wart in the moonlight to cure it (F, 64, SLC, 1964). Cf. Brown 2578.

4355 If you want to remove a wart, go to the woods at midnight and splash stump water on it while turning around three times saying a chant. I've forgotten the chant (F, 13, Orem, 1964).

4356 Cure for warts: Collect stump water at midnight. Then collect a number of cobwebs, ants, spiders and bird feathers and place them in a bag; bury the contents in the ground, and when it rots, the warts will go away (F, 19, SLC, 1950s).

4357 Teardrops cure warts (F, 17, SLC, 1963). Cf. Brown 2530.

4358 Washing your hands in water that eggs have been boiled in will get rid of warts (F, 67, Devils Slide, 1965).

Rocks, Stones, Pebbles

4359 Pick up a stone and spit on it to get rid of warts (F, SLC, 1957). Cf. Brown 2426.

4360 To get rid of warts get a small stone and rub it on the wart. Carry the stone until you come to a large stream, throw it in, and if you don't hear a splash, the wart will go away (F, 75, Heber, 1898).

4361 If you want to get rid of a wart, rub pretty rocks on it every day at noon and it will go away (F, 15, Orem, 1964).

4362 Rub a black rock on a wart and throw it over your left shoulder and do not look back at it. It will cure warts (M, SLC, 1956). Cf. Brown 2633.

4363 If you spit on a flat rock, rub your warts, then throw the stone hard over your shoulder and don't look where it lands, your warts will go away (F, 74, SLC, 1964). Cf. Brown 2637, 2643.

4364 If you have a wart, rub a rock on it, put the rock in a sack, bury the sack in the absence of witnesses, and the wart will disappear (M, SLC, 1958).

4365 If you have warts, put one rock in a candy bag for each wart and whoever picks up the bag will get your warts (M, Midvale, 1948). Cf. Brown 2636.

4366 One can get rid of warts if he puts two dozen small pebbles in a can and sets the can in the middle of the road. When the first car hits the can, it takes five days from that time onward for the warts to go away. There will be no scar and no pain (M, 53, Richfield, 1936).

Moon

4367 By holding one's hands, palms up, to the moon, warts can be withered away (F, 46, SLC, 1932); Sit out at night when the moon is full; at twelve o'clock, hold out your hand and the wart will go away (F, 45, SLC, 1940).

4368 To get rid of a wart, one looks at a new moon, picks up dust from below his right foot and when the moon goes away so does the wart (F, 22, SLC, 1948); . . . pick up a pinch of dust from beneath your left foot, rub the wart with it . . .

(F, 85, Grantsville, 1900). Cf. Brown 2697.

4369    If you have a wart, watch the new moon and say, "What I see grows and what I touch goes away (F, Provo, 1959); . . . say, "What I see proves and what I touch goes away." Then touch your wart and it will go away (F, SLC, 1959).

4370    To get rid of a wart, spit on it in a full moon (F, 20, SLC, 1964).

4371    Cure for warts: At the full of the moon, toasted bread is rubbed upon the warts and then the bread is buried in secret in the light of the full moon (F, SLC, 1910).

4372    If you need to have a wart removed, go to the cemetery during the period in time when the moon is dark (M, It, Helper, 1959).

## Pins, Needles, Rings

4373    It is a superstition that if a pin is stuck in a wart, it will kill it (M, 21, SLC, 1964).

4374    If a wart is pricked with a pin and thrown away afterwards, the wart will disappear (M, 20, SLC, 1964). Cf. Brown 2656.

4375    In order to get rid of a wart, stick a pin in the wart and then pin it on a curtain when no one is looking. When someone discovers the pin and removes it from the curtain, your wart will be gone (F, Richfield, 1915).

4376    Warts can be removed by placing crossed pins on the wart and then throwing the pins away (F, 83, SLC, 1963). Cf. Brown 2666.

4377    If you stick a pin in a wart, hide the pin and wish the wart on someone else, and it'll go to that person (F, 24, SLC, 1946).

4378    Take a straight pin and rub it over and around the wart. Put the pin in a place where you will forget about it. As soon as the pin becomes rusty, the wart will be healed (F, 1970).

4379    To get rid of warts, bury a needle three inches deep in the side of a ditch bank (F, Springville, 1947); . . . rub a needle on the wart and then bury the needle in your back yard (F, 40, SLC, 1974).

4380    Heat a needle and burn out the middle of the wart, and it will go away (M, 21, SLC).

4381    If you stick a needle through a wart and then hide it, gradually the wart will go away (F, Midvale, 1961).

4382    Rub a wart with a gold ring, and it will disappear (F, 80, Eng, Midvale).

4383    Rub a gold wedding band until warm and put it on the wart. It will disappear (F, 53, SLC, 1918).

4384    To cure warts, prick them with a gooseberry thorn through a golden wedding ring (M, SLC, 1953).

## Burning Off and Cutting Off Warts

4385    It is bad luck to burn off warts (M, Pleasant Grove, 1961).

4386    To get rid of warts, cut off the head of a match and put the head on the wart. Light the head with another match and let it burn (F, 70, SLC, 1964).

4387    Warts were cured by burning them off by placing brimstone on them and lighting a match (M, SLC, 1946).

4388    To get rid of a wart, cut it off first with a razor blade and then pour salt over it (F, Bountiful, 1953).

4389    A wart will be removed if it is cut by the razor that was used to shave a dead person (M, DDS, SLC, 1959).

## Selling Warts, Coins

4390    If you have warts on your hands, you can get rid of them by selling them to someone else. It doesn't matter how much they give you just so they do give you some amount of money for them. They will not get the warts, but the warts will go away in a few days (M, 53, Richfield, 1927). Brown 2675.

4391    Grandma N used to give pennies for warts to people (F, Moab, 1953).

4392    Someone with a wart goes to an older person who gives him five cents for the wart and then rubs it. This is supposed to make the wart disappear faster, especially since the wart was sold, and really no longer belongs to the child. My father is in the wart buying business (F, 18, SLC, 1963); Warts can be sold for a dime (M, 1960). Cf. Brown 2683.

4393    A gifted person can charm warts and buy them for a pin each (M, 68, SLC, 1964).

4394    Spit on a penny, rub on wrist, and your warts will go away (M, SLC, 1950).

4395    To get rid of a wart, rub it three times a day with vinegar water that a copper penny has been sitting in (F, 34, Springville, 1963).

4396    To get rid of warts, rub a penny on them and then throw it away (F, SLC, 1923). Brown 2684.

4397    Rub the wart with a penny and give the penny away. The wart will go away (F, 20, SLC, 1964).

4398    One may remove a wart by borrowing a penny, rubbing it on the wart, and throwing the penny away. The person who finds the penny will then get the wart (F, SLC, 1957). Cf. Brown 2680.

4399    You can get rid of warts by rubbing a penny on them and burying the penny in the ground. The warts disappear in a few days (F, 46, Richfield, 1932); If someone finds the penny, the wart will come back (F, Salina, 1920). Brown 2686.

4400 Rub a new penny on the wart. Put the penny away for a while and the wart will go away and never come back (F, SLC).

4401 Place a coin on top of a wart and it will disappear (M, 52, Cedar City, 1964).

## Charming Off Warts

4402 A wart charmer can remove warts (M, 27, Spanish Fork, 1943); Warts can be charmed off by certain magic words (F, 67, Panguitch, 1900). Cf. Brown 2701.

4403 Mr. F would say something, and the warts would go off. He'd go around a wart, and he'd say something and they'd go off (M, Woods Cross, 1953).

4404 My aunt placed her finger over the wart and charmed it away (F, Orderville, 1913). Cf. Brown 2695.

4405 To get rid of warts, go out on a new moon and say in Greek, "Good-looking, beautiful, wonderful moon, new moon, since you're so good and can eat goats and lambs, eat this mud-soaked wart off my hand" (F, 19, Gr, SLC, 1965).

4406 My father's aunt could take warts off by rubbing broom straws on the warts and chanting something. She would then place the straws in his hand, and told him when he unconsciously dropped them, the warts would go away (M, Cleveland, 1971). Cf. Brown 2614.

4407 It was thought that if a person of opposite flesh pigmentation rubs her fingers over the warts of another, they will disappear (M, 71, SLC).

## Miscellaneous

4408 Never count warts if you want them to go away (M, 24, SLC, 1957); . . . ; the more you count, the more you will get (M, 21, SLC).

4409 I had warts on both my hands for ten years. Then one day I went to visit my grandma's friend, and she told me to count them up. Three months later they all went away (F, 18, Heber City, 1968). Cf. Brown 2674.

4410 Wish a wart on someone else and yours will go away (M, 78, SLC).

4411 To get rid of warts, rub salt on them (M, Richfield, 1920). Cf. Brown 2565f.

4412 Put ink on warts (M, SLC, 1925); Take the cork of an ink bottle and place it on a wart (F, 44, Morgan, 1926). Cf. Brown 2572.

4413 If you have a wart on your hand, arm, etc., and rub it on a screen door, the wart will go away (M, Layton, 1956).

4414 Put your toe in vinegar and it will take a wart away (F, 20, SLC, 1964).

4415 Rub your warts with butter to cure them (F, 21, SLC, 1964).

4416 Put a drop of castor oil on warts, at least twice a day, and they will drop off (F, Woods Cross, 1953). Cf. Brown 2487.

4417 If you want to do away with warts, rub molasses over the warts every night and within a week the warts will go away (M, 22, Midvale, 1964).

4418 Put mud packs on your hands once a week for thirty minutes and it will absolutely cure you from ever getting warts (F, 83, Can, Logan, 1900).

4419 If you have a wart and cover it with fingernail polish, it will suffocate it, and it will go away (M, 21, Provo, 1969).

4420 Crawl under your front porch to get rid of warts (M, 21, SLC, 1959).

4421 Rub the wart with the sole of your shoe, and as the sole wears away, so will the wart (M, 28, SLC, 1958). Brown 2480.

4422 A wart can be cured by plucking the seeds from it (M, 52, Cedar City, 1964). Brown 2422.

4423 If you carry a whole nutmeg with you in your pocket, it will keep warts away (F, 80, Midway, 1900).

4424 To cure or get rid of warts, suck on them first thing in the morning (M, 24, SLC, 1964). Brown 2425.

4425 When you first wake up in the morning you should take some saliva from your mouth and put it on the wart (F, SLC, 1967).

4426 If you have a wart, spit on it several times a day, and it will go away (F, Grantsville, 1964).

4427 If you piss in the middle of the road, your warts will go away (F, SLC, 1957). (This item represents a curious reversal of No. 4203, above, namely a reversal from cause to cure, but it is unique in the whole literature having to do with maladies resulting from relieving oneself in public places. See also No. 4087, above. --Eds.)

4428 Go through the motions of washing a dishpan (without water) and your warts will go away (M, SLC, 1957).

4429 Warts will disappear if one forgets about them (F, 23, Cedar City, 1964). Cf. Brown 2687.

## WEIGHT LOSS

4430 Potatoes are fattening and should not be eaten while trying to lose weight (M, SLC, 1960).

4431 Lemon juice in great amounts will cause one to lose weight (F, SLC, 1961).

4432 Unequal portions of natural vinegar and honey causes loss of weight (F, SLC, 1963).

4433 Rubbing your body with medicine will prevent weight increase. If you add bath powder, your weight will go down (F, SLC, 1961).

4434    Thyroid extract will cause a reduction in weight (F, SLC, 1961).

## WHOOPING COUGH

4435    Wear a bag of asafetida around your neck to keep you free from whooping cough (F, Logan, 1970). Cf. Brown 2705.

4436    If a person has whooping cough, they should hang onions in the room. When the onions turn black, they will soak up the whooping cough out of the person (F, 20, SLC, 1959).

4437    Chestnut leaves made into syrup will cure whooping cough (M, SLC, 1964). Brown 2723.

4438    Make a drug from the buttercup to cure whooping cough (M, SLC, 1964).

4439    A cure given by a man riding a white horse will cure whooping cough (M, Ir, SLC, 1960). (For further references to riders on white horses as healers, see Wayland D. Hand, "The Folk Healer: Calling and Endowment," Journal of the History of Medicine and Allied Sciences, 26 (1971), 274. [Hand, Magical Medicine, pp. 51-52.] For magical qualities attaching to white horses in a more general way, see the Brown Collection, VI, xxiv-xv. --Eds.)

4440    A sure cure for whooping cough can be obtained by asking and following the advice of a man riding a piebald horse (F, 46, Swed, SLC, 1964). Brown 2715.

4441    Drink warm mare's milk to cure whooping cough (F, 21, SLC, 1964). Brown 2716.

4442    Three hairs taken from the "cross" of an ass, that is, the mark running up the back and out at right angles over the shoulders, will cure whooping cough, but the ass will die (F, 46, Swed, SLC, 1964).

4443    To cure whooping cough, every night for four nights walk the patient around the block a different way (F, 43, SLC, 1945).

## WINTER DIABETES

4444    If you eat brown sugar and no white sugar, you will never get winter diabetes (M, 80, SLC, 1969).

4445    Mix equal parts of molasses and sulphur and drink each morning to cure winter diabetes (M, Hurricane, 1969).

## WORMS

4446    When a person's hair becomes dry and brittle and won't grow in the back, it is a sign they have worms (F, 89, Eureka, 1880).

4447    People who pick their nose have worms (M, 22, SLC, 1960).

4448    If you eat raw bread dough, you'll get worms in your stomach (F, 20, SLC, 1944).

4449    If you eat cookie batter before it's cooked, you will get worms (M, SLC, 1956).

4450    Pumpkins will give a person worms in the stomach, if eaten (M, 53, SLC, 1936).

4451    If you grit your teeth, it means you have worms. To get rid of worms, eat garlic (F, 20, SLC, 1949).

4452    Castor oil and turpentine will cure worms (F, 70, Provo, 1900).

4453    For cure of pinworms, apply a turpentine and water solution with a swab (F, Lehi, 1915).

4454    If you have worms, chop up the hair of a horse's tail and mix it with your food. When you eat this, the worm will die (M, 20, SLC, 1962).

## WOUNDS

4455    If you kiss a wound, it will heal more quickly (M, SLC, 1958). Cf. Brown 2746.

4456    Fresh, raw meat, changed frequently, should be placed over a wound (or a bruise, tho' it is not so effective), to draw out infection, promote healing and cure the pain (F, 20, SLC, 1963). Brown 2748.

4457    Raw egg whites are good for drawing a wound. They should be applied directly to the skin and allowed to dry, thus puckering the skin (F, 20, SLC, 1963); Beaten egg white with salt . . . (F, Moab, 1953).

4458    A boy's badly cut hand was bound up with a poultice of flour and not removed for three weeks. When unwrapped, the wound had healed well, though leaving a scar (F, St. George, 1946).

4459    For wounds take pitch from pinon trees and boil it and strain it through a piece of cheesecloth; then mix mutton tallow with it and carbolic acid, and make it so you can just spread it on (F, Moab, 1945).

4460    Wounds were cauterized by burning them with a hot iron (M, SLC, 1946).

4461    Empty the gunpowder of a bullet into a deep wound, and it will draw the bullet out (F, SLC, 1967).

4462    The ring finger stroked along any wound will soon heal it (F, SLC, 1959).

4463    Sometimes the weapon which inflicts a wound is treated. The wound is healed by applying salve to the weapon (M, 22, SLC, 1964). Cf. Brown 2756. (The treatment of the wounding instrument, rather than the wound itself, rests on sympathetic magic and on the principles of analogy. Vulnerary surgeons and other medical scientists of the seventeenth and eighteenth centuries were the proponents of this theory and regimen. To disinfect the cutting blade and the puncturing instrument they mixed so-called weapon-salve and compounded sympathetic powders, arguing that if the metal could be kept from rusting and corroding, the wound, _ex post facto_, could be kept from festering. Sir Kenelm Digby of the Royal Society was one of the principal adherents of these doctrines. See Emile H. van Heurck, _L'Onguent armaire et la Poudre de sympathie_ [Anvers, Imprimerie J. E. Buschmann, 1915]; Fielding H. Garrison, _An Introduction to the History of Medicine_ [4th ed., Philadelphia and London; W. B. Saunders Company, 1929], pp. 276-77, 286-88. Cf. Nos. 3048, 3764, above. --Eds.)

4464 When an individual is wounded, place a clean bandage over the wound, place medicated salve on a silver knife and tie the knife against the wound on top of the clean bandage. Each day remove the knife and replace the salve, tie the knife with the salve on it back in place. Do not at any time disturb the bandage. The wound will heal very well. This was once called the "sabre salve" treatment (F, SLC, 1961).

# IV
# Love, Courtship, Marriage

## BODY INDICATORS

4465 A mole on the left breast of a girl will enable her to choose any man she likes; she is irresistible (M, SLC, 1961).

### Head and Face

4466 If your eye twitches, it is a sign that someone loves you (F, SLC, 1950); If you have itching eyes . . . (F, 54, SLC, 1965); . . . itching of the right eye, you are in love (F, 84, Sevier Co, 1925).

4467 When your eyebrow itches, your sweetheart is talking about you (M, 50, It, SLC, 1965).

4468 When a girl's eyelash falls out, she may determine if a boy loves her. She places the eyelash on the tip of her index finger, then blows the eyelash. He loves her if the eyelash blows away. He does not love her if it clings to her finger (F, Provo, 1974).

4469 A burning left ear denotes love (F, 72, SLC, 1963).

4470 If your ear itches, your lover's thinking of you (F, 54, Logan, 1923).

4471 It is a sign that a person is lovesick if his nose bleeds (M, 35, SLC, 1960).

4472 If your nose itches, someone loves you (F, SLC, 1957); . . . your lover is thinking of you (F, SLC, 1962); . . . the man you'll marry is thinking of you (F, 19, SLC, 1963); . . . you'll see your true love before dinner time (F, 44, SLC, 1964).

4473 If your nose itches, you're in love with a fool (M, 21, SLC, 1959).

4474 If only one side of your nose itches, you are going to have a boyfriend (F, SLC, 1959).

4475 An itchy nose is a sign that the true lover will be seen before nightfall (M, SLC, 1964).

4476 If you show a blue vein on the bridge of your nose, you'll survive to wear wedding clothes (F, Santaquin, 1900s).

4477 If you have lipstick on your teeth, you are in love (F, SLC, 1959).

4478 If a girl's teeth are wide apart, she will find it hard to marry until she has them straightened out (F, Norw, SLC).

4479 If you see a man with a dimple on his chin, you will soon have a new love (M, SLC, 1964).

4480 The number of lines (wrinkles) in your forehead will tell the number of times you will marry (M, SLC, 1957).

4481 If a hair hangs over your nose, you'll get a love letter (F, SLC, 1960).

4482 If you pull a hair from a girl's head, she will love you (F, SLC, 1959).

4483    A dimple in your cheek
       Many hearts you will seek;
       A dimple in your chin
       Many hearts you will win.
    (F, SLC, 1951).

4484 If a girl combs her hair under a holly tree at the stroke of midnight, she will marry the next man she sees (F, 19, SLC).

4485 It is a sign that you are forsaken if your hair comes down (F, 52, SLC, 1963).

4486 If your hair parts straight and even, you will have a good marriage (F, 42, East Ind, SLC, 1922).

### Upper Extremities

4487 A person who has warm hands has a cold heart, and vice versa (F, 63, SLC).

4488 If your hands are cold and sweaty, you are in love (M, 23, SLC, 1956); A moist hand means thoughts of love (F, Midvale); A moist hand is a sign of an amorous disposition (F, Copperton). Cf. Brown 4176.

4489 When the side of the hand itches when a person is single, it means he will soon get married (F, 63, Monroe, 1964).

4490 If the creases in the palm of your hand form an "M," it is a sign that you will marry (F, 19, Logan, 1972); . . . you will have a happy marriage (M, Ferron, 1961).

4491 When you wrinkle your hand the lines will form the first initial of your future husband's last name (F, 52, Fielding, 1925).

4492    If the lines on the palm of your hand form an "N," that means you will get divorced (F, 43, SLC, 1963).

4493    When people cross hands when shaking hands, it means a secret engagement (F, Norw, SLC, 1960).

4494    When four people are together, if they cross over each other's arms while shaking hands, making a cross with their arms, it means that one of them will become engaged (F, 24, Norw, SLC, 1964); Four people crossing hands means there will be a wedding (F, 23, SLC, 1950); . . . one or both of the couples will get married (F, SLC, 1962); . . . there will be a marriage in the family (F, 20, SLC, 1949).  Brown 4179.

4495    When four persons meet and shake hands crosswise, it is a sign that one of the group will be married within a year.  If they are all married, it then means that any one of them making a wish will have it come true without fail (F, SLC, 1961).  Brown 4180.

4496    If you should cross hands with another girl while you're shaking the hand of another person, you will marry that girl (M, SLC, 1953).

4497    If two people cross arms while reaching at the table, it means marriage in the family (F, SLC, 1962).

4498    Hold somebody's pulse and call out names of possible boyfriends.  The boy named when the pulse beats faster is the boyfriend (F, SLC, 1969).

4499    By cracking one's fingers, one can tell by the number of cracks how many girl friends or boyfriends he or she has (M, Tooele, 1953).

4500    It is possible to determine if a person loves you by pulling the fingers hard.  If the knuckle cracks or pops, the person loves you (F, Lehi, 1957).

4501    If you finger cracks, you are having an unhappy love affair (F, Hung, SLC, 1963).

4502    If a girl has thick nails, she will marry young (F, 20, SLC).

4503    Every white spot on your ring fingernail represents a beau (F, SLC, 1958); White spots on fingernails . . . (F, SLC, 1957).  Cf. Brown 4193.

4504    If you cut your fingernails on Friday and go outside, the first man you see will be your husband (F, Ogden, 1961).

4505    If you cut your fingernails on Saturday, you will see your sweetheart on Sunday (F, 61, SLC, 1965).  Brown 4199.

### Lower Extremities

4506    If you are ticklish behind the knee, it means you are boy crazy (F, SLC, 1950).

4507    If you sit with your feet too high to reach the floor, you'll marry young (F, 53, Magna, 1921).

4508    Stub your toe and meet your beau (F, 60, SLC, 1963).  Heard in New York, 1930s.

4509    Stump your toe, kiss your thumb, you'll see your beau before bedtime comes (F, 70, SLC, 1905).  Cf. Brown 4203.

4510    Cold feet are a sign of a warm heart (F, 70, Provo, 1900).

### BODILY FUNCTIONS, ATTRIBUTES, ETC.

4511    Absence makes the heart grow fonder (M, 21, SLC, 1964); . . . for someone else (M, 57, SLC, 1964); Distance makes the heart grow fonder (M, 26, SLC, 1951).

4512    Dream of birth and there'll be a wedding (F, 61, SLC, 1964).

4513    Dream of home:  Indicates continued prosperity, especially to one in love (F, SLC, 1957).

4514    To dream of money is a sign of marriage (M, 1960).

4515    If you dream of seeing a young man drink, it is a sign that you are very much loved by your gentleman friend or lady friend (M, 61, SLC, 1962).

4516    Sadness in a dream means a wedding (F, 54, SLC, 1964).

4517    Dream of death, someone gets married (F, 20, SLC, 1963).

4518    It is bad luck to dream of a wedding (M, SLC, 1959).

4519    Never look back at a person passing by, or you will never marry that person (F, Eng, SLC, 1958).

4520    Persons fall in love when a cherub named Cupid shoots them in the heart with a dart of special make (M, 22, SLC, 1954).

4521    You fall in love three times before you fall in love with the person you're going to marry (M, 17, SLC, 1963).

4522    To find your true love, first spit in your hand, then hit the spit.  The way it falls is the direction where your true love is (F, 68, Midvale, 1910).  (Divination by flying saliva is usually employed in the finding of lost objects and straying animals.  Its use in love divinations is somewhat exceptional. --Eds.)

4523    If you accidentally stick yourself, you will have a new boyfriend (F, 66, Bear River, 1910).

4524    If you trip over a crack in the sidewalk, it means you are in love with someone (F, Logan, 1972).

4525    If you fall upstairs, you are in love (F, 45, SLC, 1964); . . . it's a sign of an approaching wedding (M, 48, SLC, 1934).

4526    If you trip while walking upstairs, you want to get married (F, 67, SLC, 1915).  Cf. Brown 4330.

4527    When entering a home, if you exit through the same door, it breaks up a possible matrimony in the home (F, 49, Midvale, 1930).

4528 Go for a walk and turn around; the first man you meet will be your husband (F, SLC, 1962).

4529 If you turn around four times with your eyes closed, after you open them the first boy you see you'll fall in love with him (F, 20, SLC, 1960).

4530 If a couple out walking together stumble, it is a sign that they will be married (F, SLC, 1961).

4531 If you get up early in the morning and walk nine steps backward before breakfast, you will find some of your lover's hair (F, 45, SLC, 1952).  Cf. Brown 4142f.

4532 If you walk eighteen rails on a railroad track without stepping off, you can get any man you want (F, 46, SLC, 1939). Cf. Brown 4214ff.

4533 Catholic maidens pray thusly to get a man, "St. Anthony send me a man as fast as you can" (F, 54, SLC, 1920s).

4534 Call anyone darling, and love will come your way (M, 1963).

4535 Make a rhyme, make a rhyme, see your beau before bedtime (F, 19, SLC, 1963).

4536 On accidentally making two lines rhyme, kiss your hand, and you will be so fortunate as to see your lover before nine that night (M, 54, SLC).  Heard in Mississippi, 1939.  Cf. Brown 4171.

4537 If you sing before breakfast, or at the table, you will be disappointed in love (F, 30, SLC, 1940).

4538 If you start to shiver without any apparent reason, you are in love (F, 46, SLC, 1945); If you shiver in the heat . . . (F, 20, SLC, 1964).  Brown 4133.

4539 If you hear bells and get cold chills, you're in love (F, 20, SLC, 1949).

4540 The first person you think of after you have had the hiccoughs loves you (F, 19, SLC, 1958).

4541 If you sneeze on a Saturday, the girl you are with will be your sweetheart (F, 88, SLC, 1964).

4542 Sneeze on Saturday, you'll see your sweetheart tomorrow (F, SLC, 1957). Brown 4162.

4543 Sneezing early in the morning means you will see your lover that day (M, 19, SLC, 1963).

4544 If you sneeze before breakfast, you will see your true love before Saturday night (F, 19, SLC).

4545 It is a sure sign of an approaching wedding if one sneezes before getting up on Sunday morning (F, SLC, 1964).

4546 Three sneezes in a row means a boyfriend (M, 28, SLC, 1955); Four sneezes in a row:  You are in love (M, SLC, 1962).

4547 A legal kiss is never as good as a stolen one (F, Logan, 1960).

4548 It brings bad luck to kiss a girl on the nose (M, 19, SLC, 1962); It will cause trouble . . . (M, 48, Vernal, 1935).

4549 If a person kisses you on the left cheek, kiss them back on the left cheek or it's bad luck (F, 19, SLC, 1963).

4550 A kiss on the forehead is a mark of special esteem and reverence (F, SLC, 1964).

4551 Never kiss a girl behind the ear, because it will bring bad luck (M, Hawaiian, SLC).

4552 If you kiss with your eyes open, it means you're thinking of someone else (M, SLC, 1958).

4553 If you don't close your eyes when kissed by your sweetheart, you will have bad luck with him (F, 23, Crescent, 1952).

4554 If a girl laughs or giggles before she is to be kissed, she is said to be cold (M, 56, SLC).

4555 If you kiss a boy on Sunday, you won't ever marry him (F, 65, Nephi, 1898).

4556 A kiss on the first date means an affair; a first kiss on the second date means thanks for taking me out; a first kiss on the third date means marriage (M, SLC).

4557 If your boyfriend or girl friend kisses you during the day, it is a sign that he or she really loves you.  At night it may be just a romantic action (M, SLC, 1959).

4558 If you make circles instead of dots when you dot your i's, you like to French kiss (F, SLC, 1957).

4559 The girl you kiss on New Year's Eve at twelve o'clock is the girl you will marry (M, SLC, 1958).

4560 The first person you kiss after the New Year begins will love you throughout the year (F, 20, SLC, 1965).  Cf. Brown 4167.

4561 Kiss a baby on the hand when it is about nine days old.  The first man to kiss your hand after this will be your future husband (F, SLC, 1962).

## NAMES, INITIALS

4562 To find out if you are suited for another person, you cross out the letters in your names that are the same. On each of the remaining letters you say, love, hate, friendship, marriage (F, 22, SLC, 1955).

4563 To find your future husband, put seven names in a hat and draw out one each day.  The one you draw out last is your true lover (F, Bountiful, 1960).

4564 It is bad luck if a bride doesn't change her last initial when she marries (F, 21, SLC, 1964); Change the name and not the letter; marry for the worse and not the better (M, 1963); . . . have an unhappy marriage (F, 45, SLC, 1964); . . . the marriage won't last (M, Ogden, 1958).

4565 If the initials of the person who you marry and your initials form a word, then you should never have married because your personalities will not mix well (F, SLC, 1959).

4566 To marry a lady whose last name begins with the next letter of the alphabet of her husband's name is a sign of great luck and happiness (F, SLC, 1900).

4567 If people of the same name marry, their marriage will be an unhappy one, such as Brown and Brown (M, SLC, 1959).

## JEWELRY, INTIMATE POSSESSIONS

4568 If a boy gives a girl a strand of pearls, it's bad luck to their courtship (F, Peoa, 1920); A pearl ring will mean bad luck for the couple (F, 20, SLC, 1964).

4569 If one lover gives another lover an emerald, it will fade if their love fades (F, SLC).

4570 If a boy makes a wish as he is putting a ring on a girl's finger, that wish will come true until the girl takes the ring off, which will break the wish (M, 19, SLC, 1964).

4571 A cameo is a jewelry gift on the basis of love, and if the love of a boyfriend or friend who gave you that cameo is ever broken, you must never wear that cameo again or it's bad luck for your friends (F, 19, SLC, 1963).

4572 When a girl wears a necklace and a charm touches the clasp, it means her boyfriend is talking about her (F, SLC, 1963); . . . thinking about her (F, Ger, SLC, 1950).

4573 When a young girl wears a locket around her neck, if the fastener is in front, it symbolizes love (F, SLC).

4574 If you are wearing an ankle bracelet on your left ankle, you will find a boyfriend within a week (F, 17, SLC, 1960).

4575 A hairpin suddenly dropping out of your hair lets you know that your lover is thinking of you (M, 44, SLC, 1937).

4576 If you find a hairpin, keep it, and you will have a new date (F, Provo, 1930). Cf. Brown 4153.

4577 If you find a hairpin on the ground, you will see your sweetheart before night (F, SLC, 1925).

4578 Keeping a hairpin in one's shoe all day will cause one to dream of one's sweetheart (F, 66, Provo, 1925). Brown 4155.

4579 A bobby pin in your shoe means you will talk to your boyfriend the next day (F, 22, Price, 1962).

4580 If a hairpin is put inside a girl's shoe, the first man she speaks to is the man she will marry (F, Nephi, 1961).

4581 If you find a hairpin with the open end facing you, pick it up and place it in your shoe. It will bring you good luck in finding a lover (F, 67, Farmington, 1936).

4582 If you find a hairpin and stick it in your shoe, the next boy you walk with will marry you (F, 51, Ogden, 1964).

4583 If you throw bobby pins or hairpins into a wishing well, you will get married (M, Layton, 1934).

## CLOTHING

4584 If a white thread hangs on your clothes, you'll get a love letter (F, SLC, 1960).

4585 If a girl sticks a pin in the lapel of her fiancé's coat, he will always return to her safely (F, 29, Logan, 1959).

4586 If your slip shows, you're looking for a boyfriend (M, 1959); . . . your boyfriend is thinking of you (F, 70, Bountiful, 1900s).

4587 When a girl's apron is unfastened accidentally, her lover is thinking about her (F, Ogden, 1964).

4588 If your boyfriend gives you a pair of gloves the day before Easter and you wear them on Easter, you'll get married and your love will last forever (F, Ger).

4589 If you walk nine ties on the railroad tracks, the first man you meet wearing a red tie will be your husband (F, SLC, 1957).

4590 Never kiss a date under a full moon if he's wearing a red tie, or the next man you meet wearing a red tie, you'll marry (F, 19, SLC, 1955).

4591 The fifth man you see after you see someone wearing a red necktie will be the man you will marry (F, Ogden, 1961).

4592 If you see three redheads walking down the street, all dressed alike, you will marry the next person you see (M, SLC); . . . dressed head to toe in lavender . . . (F, SLC, 1960); . . . dressed in blue . . . (M, 1960).

4593 A group of girls will determine a time span that they will run the contest and usually this would be a week. They were to pick a boy, usually in their class. The girl who gets the most of his fairy loops (hanging loops on the backs of men's shirts) would be the one to marry him (Provo).

## Dresses, Skirts, Blouses

4594 If the hem of your dress is folded up, a widower follows you (M, SLC, 1959).

4595 If a girl's hem is turned up by being caught, kiss it and she will see her boyfriend that day (F, 18, American Fork, 1960). Cf. Brown 4223f.

4596 If your dress is turned up at the bottom showing your slip, you'll catch a fellow (F, Panguitch, 1906); . . . you will have a new sweetheart (F, SLC, 1960).

4597 If when putting on a dress the hem flies up and stays up, you will be kissed before bedtime (F, 53, SLC, 1964).

4598 If the hem of your skirt is turned up, your boyfriend loves you (F, 12, SLC, 1964).

4599 If a girl's skirt is turned up, her lover is thinking of her (F, 19, Ogden, 1964).

4600 Tearing your dress under the arm means a wedding (F, SLC).

4601 Count the buttons on your dress: "He loves me, loves me not, etc." (F, 22, SLC, 1964).

## Shoes, Stockings

4602 If your shoestring comes untied, your sweetheart loves you (M, SLC, 1961).

4603 If your shoelace comes untied, then your true love is thinking of you (F, SLC, 1961); . . . is talking about you (F, SLC, 1962). Brown 4206.

4604 If your shoe comes untied, your girl friend is mad at you (F, 19, SLC, 1963).

4605 If you put a penny in your shoe, you will meet a girl soon (M, St. George, 1959).

4606 If you dream of a new pair of shoes, you will find a new lover (M, 51, SLC, 1964).

4607 If you place the toe of one shoe to the heel of the other at twelve midnight, you will see the person that you will marry (F, 75, E. Jordan, 1895).

4608 If a girl's shoe comes off, her lover is thinking about her (F, 19, Ogden, 1964).

4609 If a girl's stocking falls down, her lover is thinking about her (F, 19, Ogden, 1964).

## Hats, Handkerchiefs

4610 To sit on your hat is a sign that you are in love (M, 19, SLC, 1964).

4611 If you put on a boy's hat, you owe him a kiss (M, 26, SLC, 1959); . . . you'll get a kiss (F, 70, SLC, 1964). Cf. Brown 4218.

4612 When a girl puts her hat on backwards, it is a sign of a new lover (F, Axtell, 1958).

4613 The hundredth man who tips his hat to you will be your future husband (F, SLC, 1962).

4614 If you drop your handkerchief, it means that you want someone to follow you (M, Ogden, 1961).

4615 If you hang out a wet handkerchief on a full moon, when the handkerchief dries,

it will have the initials of your future husband on it (F, SLC, 1962). Cf. Brown 4227.

4616 On the last night of April hang a wet handkerchief out the window. When it dries, it will form the initial of the boy you will marry (F, 51, Ogden, 1964).

4617 A person will never marry his lover if he gives her a gift of a handkerchief (M, 20, Sandy, 1957).

## ANIMALS

## Cats, Rats

4618 If the cat of the house is black, the lovers of lassies will have no luck (M, 69, miner, Park City, 1918).

4619 If a cat is washing its face, your true love will come from the direction that the cat's tail is pointing (F, SLC, 1959).

4620 If you see a white cat on a moonlit night, it means marriage (F, SLC, 1959).

4621 Bury a rat, and the boy you love will have to marry you (F, 12, Orem, 1964). Heard on TV.

## Horses, Bulls

4622 If you spit in your hand when you see a white horse, you will have a good marriage (F, 54, Midvale, 1920).

4623 Make a stamp in the palm of the left hand for each white horse you see, and when you have reached the tenth horse, the next man you shake hands with will be the one you will marry (M, Manti, 1920).

4624 Count a hundred white horses, and after you have counted the hundredth, the first person who touches your hand will be the one you'll marry (F, 70, Provo, 1905); . . . will be your spouse (F, 18, SLC, 1965). Cf. Brown 4473, 4475.

4625 Count the white horses you pass on the road, and the rider on horse number one hundred will be your future husband (F, 67, Panguitch, 1900).

4626 If you dream of a black horse, a wedding is about to take place (F, SLC, 1962).

4627 If you dream of a bull, you will get a beau (M, 24, SLC, 1964).

## Chickens, Wishbones

4628 To hear hens cackle in a dream signifies joy and love (F, 43, SLC, 1964).

4629 If a hen lays two eggs in a day, it is a sign of relatives marrying (F, 24, Huntsville, 1951).

4630 If you see a hen flying with a red tail, you will marry the next person that sees her (F, SLC, 1961).

4631 If you put a wishbone over a doorway, the first name of the first man to enter will be the name of your intended (F, SLC, 1958); . . . you will see your beau (F, Orangeville, 1959).   Brown 4494.

4632   Put a wishbone of a fowl over the door, and the man that comes under it is the one you are going to marry (F, 71, Woods Cross, 1953); . . . will be your lover (F, Moab, 1953); . . . your true love (F, Murray, 1937).   Brown 4492.

4633   If you put the small part of the wishbone over the door, the next boy/girl who comes in the door is the one you'll marry (F, 16, Midvale, 1955). Brown 4495.

4634   When you wish on a wishbone, the person who gets the short piece will get his wish.  The one who gets the long piece has to hang it up over a doorway, and the first person to come through the door is the one this person will marry (F, 12, SLC, 1960).   Brown 4497, 4499.

4635   The long piece of the wishing bone denotes a coming marriage (SLC).

## Birds

4636   If you see a bluebird, you will see your sweetheart the same day (M, SLC, 1961). Cf. Brown 4516, 4519.

4637   A woman wishing marriage must first find and feed a dove (possibly the famous turtledove) (F, SLC, 1957).

4638   While walking on a bridge, if you see a dove sitting on it, it means the first man you see you will marry (F, SLC).

4639   If you find a nest with a bird's eggs in it, you will have a happy home (M, SLC, 1961).

4640   If a redbird flies across a girl's path, she is sure to be kissed twice before nightfall (F, Ogden, 1960).

4641   Unmarried women believe that if the whippoorwill's first call in the spring is not followed immediately by a second call, it means that they will have to wait another year for a husband (F, SLC, 1961).

4642   Seeing three magpies means a marriage (F, Ir, SLC, 1960); . . . a wedding (F, Ir, SLC, 1960).

## Reptiles

4643   If you dream of snakes, there will be a wedding in the family (M, SLC, 1961).

4644   When one sees two snakes in a house at once, it means that there will be a marriage soon (F, SLC, 1961).

## Insects, Butterflies, Spiders, Etc.

4645   To see a white cricket denotes that an absent love will return (F, 20, Murray, 1951).

4646   When a ladybug is on you, take it and throw it into the air and say, "Fly away east, and fly away west, show me where

lives the one I love best" (M, SLC, 1959).   Cf. Brown 4533.

4647   One method of finding where your sweetheart is residing:  Place a ladybug on the back of your hand and say:  "Fly north, fly south, fly east, fly west. Fly where my sweetheart likes it best." And whichever direction the ladybug flies you will find your sweetheart (F, SLC, 1959).   Brown 4533.

4648   When a butterfly lands on the head of a young woman, she will find a new sweetheart (F, SLC, 1960).

4649   If a butterfly gets in the house, it is a sign of an impending marriage (M, 63, SLC, 1964); If a dark butterfly . . . (F, SLC, 1959).

4650   If the first butterfly of the season is a white one, you will go to a wedding before the season is over (F, SLC, 1961).

4651   A spider on a wedding dress means a happy marriage (F, 1958).

## PLANTS

## Seeds, Leaves, Plants, Herbs, Etc.

4652       Yarrow, yarrow I pluck thee,
          In my bosom I put thee;
          The first young man who speaks to
              me,
          My true lover he shall be
       (Anon, a game played in Utah, 1870-1890); Yarrow, yarrow I do pick,/In my bosom I do stick, etc. (F, Fairview, 1930).   Yarrow pronounced "yerno" as kids.

4653   Lovers should pluck a twig from a laurel tree.  If they break it in two and each preserves a piece of it, it will keep them lovers (M, 15, Ogden, 1963).

4654   If you tie a knot in a cedar limb and name it and it grows, the person it is named for loves you (F, SLC, 1961). Brown 4601.

4655   A girl picks a cocklebur, names it after her lover, and throws it against her skirt; if it sticks, she knows that her lover is true to her; if it doesn't stick, she thinks he is false (F, 68, American Fork, 1920).

4656   If when shelling peas you find ten peas in a pod, you'll meet the man you'll marry (F, SLC, 1925).

4657   If you find ten peas in a pod, put it over your door and the first man or woman to enter will be your mate (F, SLC, 1925); . . . nine peas . . . the first to enter will be your own sweet one (F, 47, Midvale, 1931).   Brown 4545.

4658   If a girl is worried that her boyfriend may not love her, she should put some love vine on the shrubs back of the house.  If it grows this means that he does love her (F, Bountiful, 1961).

4659   No one will get married within a household if a wandering Jew plant is kept in the house (F, 25, Centerville).

## Flowers

4660 You can tell whether or not he loves you by plucking the petals from a daisy and saying, alternately, "He loves me, he loves me not" (F, Moab, 1962); . . . odd number of petals, he loves you; even, he doesn't (F, 20, SLC, 1963); . . . petals of a sunflower or use a drugstore straw . . . (F, Moab, 1953). Brown 4576.

4661 The first wild flowers you gather in the spring will give you the initials of your future husband (F, Axtell, 1958).

4662 When a boy wears a flower to school, he is hunting a girl (F, 46, SLC, 1943); . . . a red flower in his lapel, it signifies he is eligible for courtship (M, 27, SLC, 1964).

4663 If a bachelor's button grows in his pocket, he will end up marrying his sweetheart (M, 26, Riverdale, 1955).

4664 If the flower Bell of Ireland grows in your garden, someone will be married (M, Scot, SLC, 1961).

4665 Upon holding a buttercup under one's chin, if it reflects yellow on the chin, he is in love (F, SLC).

4666 If you rub a daisy under your chin and it leaves a yellow mark, someone loves you (F, 28, SLC, 1946).

4667 Twirl a yellow dandelion under your chin, and if your chin turns yellow, it means you are in love (F, 38, Ogden, 1964).

4668 If you can blow all the fluff off a dandelion with one puff, you will get the boy (or girl) of your dreams (F, Bear River City, 1957).

4669 Let a young woman pin a four-leaf clover over the door, and the first unmarried man who comes in the door will be the one she is to marry (F, 61, Du, SLC, 1964). First heard in the Netherlands, 1920. Brown 4553.

4670 If you put a four-leaf clover next to the address of a girl in your address book, she will fall in love with you (M, 21, SLC, 1958).

4671 Put a four-leaf clover into your shoe, go to sleep, and you will see the one you are to marry (F, SLC, 1961); . . . you will marry the first man you meet (F, SLC, 1961); Eat a four-leaf clover . . . (F, SLC, 1964). Cf. Brown 4550.

4672 If you find a lilac flower with three or five petals, instead of the regular four, take this flower and insert it in your shoe. The next boy that you meet will have a great influence on your life (F, Nephi, 1947).

4673 A passion flower is good luck when given by your love (F, 19, SLC, 1963).

4674 The red rose is the flower of love (M, SLC, 1959); A gift of red roses means undying love (F, SLC, 1958).

4675 Dew on a rose means your love is crying over you (M, SLC, 1961).

4676 Fold a rose petal so that a small air pocket is formed, then, the children with you will name it (boy or girl's name). The rose petal is then hit against the back of the hand. If it pops, the person named loves you (F, Lehi, 1957).

4677 When courting, send thirteen roses instead of twelve for good luck (F, 65, Du, SLC, 1965).

## Mistletoe

4678 If you stand under mistletoe, you can kiss a girl (M, 53, SLC, 1955); Kissing under mistletoe means good fortune (F, SLC, 1961). Brown 4564.

4679 If a girl stands under the mistletoe, this is an invitation to be kissed by any man. If she refuses, it is bad luck (M, SLC, 1964).

4680 If a girl is not kissed under the mistletoe during the Christmas holidays, she won't marry during the next year (M, SLC, 1957).

4681 Kissing under mistletoe assures lovers that no possible harm will befall them (M, 25, SLC, 1941).

## Fruit

4682 When you can eat a crab apple without frowning, you can get the person you desire (M, SLC, 1960).

4683 An apple, divided and eaten, produces love (F, 20, SLC, 1963).

4684 If you eat an apple in front of a mirror, your lover is bound to appear soon (F, SLC, 1962); A girl eating an apple while looking in a mirror on Halloween may see her future husband dancing over her shoulder (M, SLC, 1965). Brown 4417.

4685 Single girls bobbing apples on Halloween are supposed to get married in a certain length of time (F, 60, SLC, 1915).

4686 A common project in my childhood was to place an apple seed on each of the four fingers of the right hand. A friend named them, and the seed that stayed on the longest indicated the name of your husband (F, SLC, 1961).

4687 Name apple seeds, place them on the lids of the closed eyes, wink, and the first to fall off means your future husband (F, SLC, 1905).

4688 To see who you'll marry, name four apple seeds after four boys you know. Pick up the seeds and say: "This one I love, this one I like, this one I'll marry, this one I'll fight" (F, 51, Ogden, 1964).

4689 Say while counting seeds in an apple: Four I love with all my heart, five he runs away, six she loves, seven he loves, eight they both love, nine he comes, ten he tarries, eleven he courts, twelve he marries (F, 70, Provo, 1900); . . . eleven they kiss, twelve they marry (F, Woods Cross, 1953).  Cf. Brown 4578, 4591.

4690 Twist the stem of an apple while reciting the alphabet.  The stem will break when you reach the first initial of the person you will marry (F, Tooele, 1957).

4691 You can show if your boyfriend loves you by twisting the stem of an apple and with each turn saying, "He loves me, he loves me not, etc."  When the stem comes out, that's the answer (F, Ogden, 1953).

4692 While twisting the stem of an apple, say the names of fellows you know.  You will fall in love with the fellow whose name you are saying when the stem breaks (F, 70, Provo, 1900).

4693 Twist the stem of an apple to the number where it breaks, and it will tell how long it will be before you marry (M, SLC, 1959).

4694 Peel an apple so the peeling will form one long string, drop it; the initial it forms is the initial of the one you will marry (F, SLC, 1925).

4695 Let a girl pare an apple on Halloween and fling the skin over her left shoulder.  She will read in the twists the initials of her future husband's name (F, 78, SLC, 1964); Pare . . . your left shoulder.  If it doesn't break, the initial of your lover's name will be made of the apple peel.  If it breaks then both initials of your lover will appear (F, 67, Farmington, 1933).  Brown 4594.

4696 Look at the moon and throw an apple peeling over your left shoulder; if the peeling forms a letter, it is the letter of your lover (F, Sandy, 1957).

4697 You should peel an orange so it remains in one piece and then throw the peeling over your left shoulder.  If it lands on the sidewalk, it will form the initials of the girl or man you will marry (M, 52, SLC, 1964).


THE DOMESTIC SCENE


Food, Meals, Salt, Etc.

4698 A gain of appetite is a sign of true love (F, SLC, 1954); A loss of appetite is a sign of infatuation (F, SLC, 1955).

4699 The way to a man's heart is through his stomach (F, 46, SLC, 1964).

4700 If you always scrape your dish clean of food, it will rain on your wedding (F, Gr, SLC, 1957).

4701 If a particle of food drops from your plate, your lover is hungry (M, 50, It, SLC, 1965).

4702 If a girl wants to marry a well-mannered man, she should feed him spaghetti.  If he can eat it, he is well mannered (M, 43, It, SLC, 1930s).

4703 If one has a craving for pickles, he is in love.  This is usually more prevalent in girls, but is sometimes characteristic of boys, too (F, 49, Richfield, 1928); In order to settle your love, eat a pickle (M, 23, Holladay, 1960).

4704 If you eat onions on Saturday, you will not see your love on Sunday (M, SLC, 1961).

4705 If a girl likes lemons, it's a sure sign she is in love (F, SLC, 1925).

4706 Try to peel a potato without breaking the peeling.  Throw the peeling over your left shoulder, and whatever alphabetical letter it forms will be the initial of your future husband's last name (M, SLC, 1959).

4707 Prick an egg with a pin, and let the white drop into a wine glass three parts full of water.  Take some of this in your mouth and go for a walk.  The first name you hear mentioned aloud will be the name of your future spouse (F, Brigham City, 1960).

4708 If you drop an egg and it splashes on the floor, there will be a marriage in the family; and if you drop more than one, there will be more than one marriage (F, Kearns).

4709 While kneading bread dough, smack it a good one and give it a boyfriend's name.  If he is a good boyfriend, the bread will be delicious (F, SLC, 1957).

4710 If bread burns, your fellow is mad at you (F, 60, SLC, 1964).  Brown 4297.

4711 To take the last piece of bread and butter on the table, a bachelor may gain for himself a wife and money (M, SLC, 1964).

4712 If you take the last hors d'oeuvre on the plate, you will get a handsome husband (F, SLC, 1971).

4713 If two girls bake a cake on the same day without telling each other, stick the cake into the oven and bake it.  When the cakes are baked and out of the oven, the initials of their future husbands will be on the cake (F, SLC, 1962).

4714 Two people make a cake in silence.  Put a piece under your pillow and you will dream of your future husband (F, 51, Ogden, 1964).

4715 If a girl cannot carry a custard pie to the oven without spilling it, she is not ready for marriage (M, 53, Logan, 1925).

4716 A woman must eat herring or else she will not marry (F, Brigham City, 1960).

4717 Oysters, as a gift, foretell that lovers will obtain their wishes for each other (M, SLC, 1960).

4718 Bubbles on tea are a sign that you are going to be kissed (M, Ogden, 1960).

4719 Two tea leaves in a cup means there are two men in your life (F, Clearfield, 1962).

4720 If you are in love, you will not be able to drink tea (F, SLC, 1962).

4721   It is an old wives' tale that if you have a glass of water (it cannot be any other beverage) with two ice cubes in it, it is a sign of good luck in finding a husband if the two ice cubes fuse before they melt (F, 23, Logan, 1970).

4722   Sweetheart toast:  Drinking wine while arms are interlocked brings good luck (F, 20, SLC, 1964).

4723   If you put too much salt in the cooking, it means you're in love (F, SLC, 1960).

"The Dumb Supper"

4724   Have a midnight supper, do everything backwards (sit, serve), and each time you put some food on the table, say, "I bring this in the name of the devil." If you do this, your future husband will be present or walk into the room (F, 84, SLC, 1890).  Cf. Brown 4322f.

Table, Chairs, Cutlery

4725   If you sit on a table, you want to get married (F, SLC, 1962); . . . you'll get married before you're able (F, 38, Magna, 1934).  Brown 4284.

4726   Sing at the table, get married before you are able (F, Provo, 1971).

4727   If you sit on the table, it's a sign of a wedding (F, SLC, 1958).

4728   If a man sits on the corner of a table and crosses both legs, he is going to marry the girl of the house (M, 33, It, SLC, 1963).

4729   If you sit at a table with a person of the opposite sex, you will someday marry that person (M, 54, SLC, 1939).

4730   A girl should never sit on a table while talking to her boyfriend, for it's a sign she will never marry him (F, 15, SLC, 1961).

4731   If you break the back of a chair, you will hear of a wedding (F, 24, SLC).

4732   Having two forks at the dinner table means you will be married (M, SLC, 1958); . . . is a sign of a wedding (F, Orangeville, 1900); . . . a marriage in the family (F, American Fork, 1962). Brown 4287.

4733   If a young unmarried girl drops a fork, a gentleman who was going to visit her decided not to come (F, SLC).

4734   If you drop a fork, you'll acquire a spark (husband) (F, 65, SLC, 1914).

4735   If you drop a knife, you'll acquire a wife (F, 65, SLC, 1914).

4736   If you drop a knife, your boyfriend is coming to see you.  The blade points to the direction from which he will come (F, SLC, 1957); . . . a gentleman will call on you (F, SLC).

4737   Two spoons in a saucer foretell a wedding (F, Brigham City, 1960).  Cf. Brown 4293.

4738   If two spoons are accidentally put into a cup, it denotes a wedding (F, Midvale, 1963).  Cf. Brown 4294.

Bedroom, Bed, Bedclothing

4739   On Valentine's Eve the person you dream of will be the person you marry (M, 28, SLC, 1961).  (Helpful to the reader for many entries in the present section will be Frances M. Tally's article, "American Folk Customs of Courtship and Marriage: The Bedroom," in Forms Upon the Frontier, ed. Austin and Alta Fife and Henry H. Glassie, Monograph Ser., XVI, No. 2, Utah State University Press, 1969, pp. 138-58.  --Eds.)

4740   The first man a girl sees out of her bedroom window on Valentine's Day she will marry within a year (F, 19, Logan, 1972).

4741   It is believed that if a girl will get the same candied almonds that were carried on a tray at the wedding, sleep on three or four of them, and dream of the man she would like to marry, her dream will come true (F, Gr, SLC, 1962); . . . if a single girl or boy puts a Jordan almond from a wedding tray under the pillow, she or he will see their future spouse (F, 29, Magna, 1964).

4742   If you dream of the same person three nights in a row, you are sure to marry that person (F, SLC, 1962).  Brown 4378.

4743   If a girl sleeps with her legs crossed, it means that she is dreaming of her sweetheart (F, SLC, 1953).

4744   If a girl places her shoe beside her bed with the heel against the middle of the other, she will have happy dreams and good luck in love (F, 47, Granger, 1963).

4745   Put your shoes in the shape of a "T" at night before you go to bed and the first man you see the next day you are going to marry (F, 18, Price, 1962); Put your shoes in the shape of a "T"/Your own true love in dreams you'll see (F, 51, Ogden, 1964).

4746   Put your shoes to form a "T" three nights in a row and say these words, "I put my shoes in a "T" for my future husband to see, not as a groom and not as a suitor, but in his daily asure." The first stranger you meet will be your husband (F, 49, Norw, SLC, 1963).  (The meaning of "asure" is not known. --Eds.)  Cf. Brown 4374.

4747   If you sleep with a petticoat under your head, you'll dream of the man you'll marry (F, 19, SLC, 1963).  Cf. Brown 4384.

4748   After the wedding unmarried persons put wedding candy under their pillows overnight to dream of the one they will marry (M, 57, Gr, SLC, 1963).

4749   Before retiring, write the names of your possible mates on three slips of paper and place them under your pillow.  Throw one away before sleep and another the next morning.  The remaining name will

be that of your mate (F, SLC, 1960).
Brown 4363.

4750   Put a looking glass under your pillow,
and you will dream of your lover (F, 62,
SLC, 1946).

4751   If you place a raw egg under your pillow
at night, you will dream of the man you
will marry (F, 20, SLC).

4752   If you place a wooden chip into a glass
of water and place it under your bed,
during the night you will dream of
crossing a stream and the one that
assists you will be your future husband
(M, 23, SLC, 1960).

4753   Name the bedposts for four different
men.  The one you dream about you will
marry (M, Richfield, 1961).  Cf. Brown
4357, 4369.

4754   Name each of the corners in your room
for a boy that you like, and the one you
wake up facing in the morning is the one
you will marry.  For young girls (F, 70,
Provo, 1900).  Brown 4353f.

4755   Rub four bedposts with a lemon, and
carry the lemon in your pocket the next
day.  The first man you speak to you
will marry (F, 53, SLC, 1964).

4756   When sleeping in a room you have never
slept in before, if you will count the
windows, you will dream of the man you
will marry (F, 26, Finn, Morgan, 1965).

4757   The pop-tops from aluminum cans are used
to signify whether your boyfriend really
loves you.  All the pop-tops are hooked
together until they are as long as your
boyfriend is tall and then they are
strung over the curtain rod in your
bedroom, and if they stay up for as many
days as the boy is old, then you can be
sure that he really loves you (F, SLC,
1971).

4758   A girl should swallow a whole chicken
heart, and that night she will dream of
her future husband (F, Bountiful, 1960).
Cf. Brown 4484.

4759   If you eat a thimble of salt, don't
speak, go to bed backwards (walk
backwards, wear your clothes backwards,
etc.), and you will dream of your future
husband (F, 84, Provo, 1892).  Cf. Brown
4305, 4309f.

4760   If you put a level teaspoon of salt on a
hard-boiled egg, eat it, go to bed
backwards, and do not talk after going
to bed, the person you're going to marry
will bring you a glass of water in the
night (F, 52, SLC, 1935).  Cf. Brown
4306f, 4311, 4314.

4761   The night before Valentine's Day, if you
go to bed thirsty, you will dream of
someone of the opposite sex giving you
water to drink.  In later life you will
marry that person (M, SLC, 1963).  Cf.
Brown 4306.

4762   The night before Valentine's pick five
bay leaves, pin four to the corners (of
the bed) and one in the middle.  That
night you will dream of your sweetheart
(F, Bountiful, 1925).

4763   On Valentine's Day, take two bay leaves,
sprinkle them with rose water and lay
them under your pillow.  When you go to
bed, put on a clean nightgown turned
inside out.  When you go to sleep you
will see in a dream your future husband
(F, 57, Springville, 1904).

## Cleaning, Washing, Ironing, Sweeping

4764   If you leave the breadboard clean,
Prince Charming will come on a white
horse and carry you away (F, SLC, 1890).

4765   Drop a dishrag, pick it up and kiss it,
and your boyfriend will come see you (F,
SLC, 1958).

4766   To boil a dishcloth is to boil all your
lovers (M, SLC, 1961).

4767   If someone irons your back with a warm
iron, you'll dream of the man you'll
marry (F, SLC, 1958); . . . dream of the
girl you'll marry (M, SLC, 1960).

4768   To jump over a janitor's broom is a sign
that you will soon marry (F, 62, W.
Jordan).

4769   Your love will be true to you if you
break a broom (M, SLC, 1961).

## Sewing, Knitting, Etc.

4770   If three things go wrong with a dress
you are sewing, you will wear it at a
wedding (F, Axtell, 1958).

4771   If you find a pin, note which direction
the point is heading.  That's the
direction an admirer lives (F, 17, SLC,
1958).

4772   If you find a red piece of yarn, put it
down your neck, and the next man you
meet will be your new boyfriend (F, Fr,
SLC, 1960).

4773   If you find a piece of red yarn, put it
down your neck and make a wish to marry
the guy you want; your wish will come
true (F, Kanab, SLC, 1960).

4774   If you see five ladies knitting
together, it is the sign of a wedding
(F, 18, SLC, 1962).

4775   If a girl knits you a sweater, she is in
love with you (M, 21, SLC, 1963).

## Fire, Hearth, Firebrands, Matches, Candles, Etc.

4776   If a girl builds a good fire, her
sweetheart loves her (M, 48, Vernal,
1940).  Cf. Brown 4393.

4777   To see if a boy loves you, put a net on
the fire.  If it burns quietly, he is
sincere; if it jumps, he is not (F, 51,
SLC, 1964).

4778   To see a familiar face in the blaze of a
Yule log at Christmas is the sign of an
early marriage with the person seen (F,
SLC, 1960).

4779   When a lot of sparks are seen flying
from a chimney late at night, it means

that young kids are courting (F, SLC, 1950).

4780 Three candles burning in a room is a sign of a wedding (F, Murray, 1925).

4781 To blow out a candle accidentally is a sign of marriage (F, SLC); If you accidentally snuff out a candle . . . (M, 21, Bountiful, 1955).

4782 Name each of the candles of the birthday cake for a boy, and as you light the candles, make your wish. You say:
    Candles bright, upon my cake,
    Which of you will be my mate?
Blow the candles out. The last one smoking will be the future mate (F, Provo, 1972).

4783 If a candle goes around once, you will be pinned; if it goes around twice, you will be engaged; if it goes around three times, you will be married (F, SLC, 1962).

4784 If you stick pins through the end of a tallow candle and at the same time repeat a rhyme, your sweetheart will come to you (F, SLC, 1955).

4785 Light a candle and leave it, and your intended mate will blow it out (M, SLC, 1960).

4786 If you take a candle and walk downstairs backwards at night, you'll see the face of the person you're going to marry (F, Eng, SLC, 1964).

4787 Light candles in front of a mirror on New Year's Eve, and the man you see in the mirror will be the man you will marry (F, 26, Morgan, 1965).

4788 If you are smoking a cigarette and it keeps going out, it is a sure sign that your lover is two-timing you (M, Roy, 1962).

4789 Stamp out three cigarette butts in one day with the same foot, and look for your husband in the next male you meet (F, 60, SLC, 1930s).

4790 If a lighted match burns to the end without breaking, a girl is assured that a boy loves her (F, SLC, 1945). Cf. Brown 4409.

REFLECTIONS: MIRROR, WELLS, SPRINGS, ETC.

4791 Fill water in the sink. Go in the room and make sure that everything is completely dark. Look into the water and on the surface will appear the face of the man you are going to marry (F, Holladay, 1971).

4792 Hold a mirror and walk down the stairs backwards. The face that appears in the mirror will be your future husband (F, SLC, 1960). Cf. Brown 4428.

4793 If a boy looks over a girl's shoulder while she is looking in a mirror, the girl will marry that boy (F, 67, SLC, 1963).

4794 If you look in a mirror in a lonely place at midnight, you will see your

sweetheart looking over your shoulder (F, Scot, SLC, 1958).

4795 If you look at a mirror over your left shoulder on Halloween, you will see the image of the person you are going to marry (F, 55, SLC, 1964). Cf. Brown 4427.

4796 If you look in the mirror on New Year's Eve, you'll see the reflection of your future husband, but if you turn around and try to find him, something will happen to your love affair (F, 28, Brigham, 1939).

4797 If you look into a well, you will see the reflection of your true love (F, Bountiful, 1960); If you look into a well in May . . . (F, SLC, 1962); If you look into a well through a mirror on the first day of May . . . (M, 22, SLC, 1960). Brown 4430ff.

4798 If a girl gets up early on May 1, goes to the spring, and breaks a guinea's egg into a cup, she will see the face or initials of her husband-to-be (F, Du, Ogden, 1961).

4799 At twelve noon only the single girls and boys go to a well with a mirror. They cover their heads with a white cloth, then turn the mirror upside down. As they look in the well, they can see an image of the man or the woman they will marry (F, Gr, SLC, 1962). Cf. Brown 4438.

4800 If a girl looks into a stream before breakfast, she will see her future husband (F, SLC, 1945).

4801 If you look into a pool of still water, you will see your true love, if you are pure in heart (M, SLC).

4802 Roll the lovers' names up in a bit of clay or a piece of paper and put into water. The first that unrolls will be the spouse (F, Bountiful, 1961). Cf. Brown 4304.

4803 When you throw a pebble in a lake and the ripples disappear, you will see the face of the person in the water that you're going to marry (F, SLC, 1963).

DEATH AND FUNEREAL EVENTS AS INDICATORS

4804 A dream of death is the sign of a wedding (M, SLC, 1951); A dream of a funeral . . . (F, 21, SLC, 1963); . . . means a marriage in the family (F, 26, SLC, 1964). Cf. Brown 4389ff.

4805 If you dream someone is dying, someone is getting married (F, 37, It, SLC, 1964).

4806 Dream of death, you hear wedding bells (M, 41, SLC, 1964).

4807 To dream you read someone's obituary means news of their marriage (F, SLC, 1957).

4808 If someone dies in a family and you don't see the person after they're dead, then you'll be married in a short time (F, 20, SLC, 1964).

### Cards and Games as Indicators of Love

4809   If a person is unlucky in sports or games, this same person will be extra lucky at the game of love (M, SLC, 1961).

4810   Lucky in cards, unlucky in love (F, SLC); Unlucky at cards, lucky at love (M, 18, SLC, 1963).

4811   The ten of hearts means that a new lover is soon in store (M, 20, SLC, 1964).

4812   The queen of hearts means lucky in love (M, Ogden, 1961); . . . you will find your true love in three days (M, SLC, 1961).

4813   Take a deck of cards and lay out all the aces. Then take out any card from the deck but don't look at it. Name each of the aces for a boy. Now ask, "Who's going to kiss me?" Lay down the cards one at a time in a row on the aces until you match a suit with the ace. That will be the boy who will kiss you. Continue with the same procedure asking who will hug me, buy me a mink, take me on a honeymoon, etc., as long as the cards last. When the whole deck is gone you turn over the secret card and match it to the ace by suit. It determines who you will marry (F, Springville, 1972).

### CARS AND VEHICLES AS INDICATORS

4814   If you see a car with one light, it means that somebody loves you (F); . . . love in the near future (F, 67, SLC, 1963).

4815   If you see three cars with only one headlight, you'll see your lover (F, Midvale, 1955).

4816   If you see a car with only one light while you are with your girl friend or fiancée, you should kiss her (M, Tooele, 1958).

4817   If a girl counts the cars with only one headlight burning, the boy she's with on the hundredth one she'll marry (M, Magna, 1960).

4818   Count fifty red convertibles, the next boy you see will be the one you will marry (F, SLC, 1967); . . . one hundred red convertibles, the first man you speak to you will marry (F, SLC, 1959).

4819   If you see one hundred chartreuse convertibles in one day, the next boy you see will be your future husband (F, SLC, 1959).

4820   After you have counted one hundred yellow convertibles, the next girl you talk to will be your wife someday (M, 22, SLC, 1949).

4821   Count one hundred red convertibles and then a black tie, and the next man you see you will marry (F, 25, SLC, 1964).

4822   To find your future husband, follow this: Count one hundred red convertibles, then find a boy with a red sucker, then find a man with a green tie. The next unattached man is your true love (F, Bountiful, 1960); . . . the first unmarried fellow of appropriate age that wore a green tie that spoke to you would be considered your future husband (F, SLC, 1961).

4823   A girl is supposed to count one hundred red convertibles, then look for a fat woman with a purple dress, and a tall man with a green bow tie. The next man she speaks to will be her future husband (F, 22, SLC, 1955).

4824   After you see one hundred red cars, one black tie, a purple dress, and an out-of-state license plate, the next man you see is the man you will marry (M, 46, SLC, 1964).

4825   If a person has a car ticket where the figures add up to twenty-one and she gives it to a person of the opposite sex, it means that she loves whoever she gave it to, and she will be married at twenty-one (F, Provo, 1964).

### MOON AND STARS

### Moon, Full Moon, New Moon

4826   Lovers should never swear by the moon, because it is considered fickle (F, Sandy, 1958).

4827   A maiden who drinks white wine and rose water and then looks through a silk scarf at the moon will see her husband-to-be (M, SLC, 1964).

4828   If you will go to a vacant house on a moonlit night and throw a ball of string through the window, holding on one end of the string, then slowly wind it up, you will see the face of your husband at the other end (F, SLC, 1957).

4829   A full moon brings romance (F, SLC, 1964); If the moon is full, there will be lovers out that night (M, 48, SLC, 1939).

4830   A full moon means you'll fall in love with the boy or girl you are with (F, 19, SLC, 1964).

4831   If you see a full moon over your left shoulder, you'll marry soon (M, Eng, SLC, 1957).

4832   If you put a pail of water out in the moonlight when the moon is full, you'll dream of the person you're going to marry (F, Ogden, 1959).

4833   If a young couple are together on the night of the full moon, they will marry (F, 17, W. Jordan, 1963).

4834   Always bow to the new moon and turn the money in your pockets. In your life you will have prosperity in love (F, SLC, 1960).

4835       New moon, new moon, call down to me,
           And tell me who my true love will
             be.
       (F, 20, SLC, 1964). Cf. Brown 4451.

4836   When a new moon shines, say:
           New moon, true moon, true and
             bright,

If I have a true love, let me dream
of him tonight.
(F, 51, SLC, 1964).

4837 On the first new moon you see if you
happen to be the first to say this
little saying, you will find out what
you ask in the poem:
Blue moon, true moon,
Tell unto me
Who my true love is to be.
The color of his hair,
The clothing he doth wear,
And the day he is to be wed unto me.
(M, W. Jordan). Cf. Brown 4138, 4454.

4838 If you take a new shirt or dress and
shake it at the new moon, looking
closely at the moon and walking
backwards, you will see your future mate
there (M, 22, SLC, 1954).

## Eclipse, Stars

4839 If you and your boyfriend or girl friend
look at an eclipse together, you will be
together forever (M, SLC, 1959).

4840 If you look at a bright star intently
before retiring, you will dream of your
sweetheart (M, 54).

4841 Stare at the brightest star in the sky
and wink three times, and you will dream
of your true love (F, 51, SLC, 1964).

4842 Four stars in a row means a new love (M,
Eng, SLC, 1961).

4843 Look at a star nine times in a row
(consecutive nights). Then you will
dream of the man you are going to marry
on the ninth night (F, 46, Garland,
1964).

4844 If you see the morning star over your
right shoulder for seven nights in a
row, you will dream of the one you are
going to marry (M, 54, SLC, 1941).

4845 Count the big dipper for seven nights in
a row, and on the seventh night you'll
dream of the person you will marry (F,
18, SLC, 1955).

4846 Count seven stars for seven nights, and
on the seventh night you will dream of
the one you are going to marry (F, 65,
SLC, 1915); . . . nine stars on nine
consecutive nights . . . (F, 51, Ogden,
1964); . . . ten stars for ten
consecutive nights . . . (F, SLC, 1966).
Cf. Brown 4308, 4463, 4465.

4847 If you see a falling star, you'll fall
in love (F, 14, SLC, 1964).

4848 See a falling star while you are with
your lover and you will always be happy
(M, Vernal, 1959).

4849 If lovers see a shooting star and wish
for health, wealth, and happiness, their
wish will come true (M, SLC, 1959).

4850 If an engaged couple kiss when a star is
falling, they will have good luck in
marriage (F, Magna, 1960).

4851 When you see a falling star, you will
marry the next person you see (F, 19,
SLC, 1964).

## Miscellaneous

4852 Never put elastics around doorknobs.
They serve to keep love out (F, SLC,
1960).

4853 If an unmarried girl rubs herself with
olive oil, she will become beautiful and
will marry (M, Eng, Magna, 1960).

4854 If you find a 1936 nickel, it means that
you will soon meet someone new and
interesting of the opposite sex (F, 18,
Brigham City, 1960).

4855 After finishing a drink take a straw
and, starting at the bottom, crimp the
straw alternately at right angles and
alternately with the right and left
hand, all the while with each crimp
saying "She loves me, she loves me not.
. . . ." The statement upon reaching the
end of the straw will tell you how your
girl friend feels about you (M, Helper,
1958).

4856 Take a straw and pinch it in half, then
in fourths, etc. You will get the
initials of your husband (F, SLC, 1962).

4857 If one desires to know who he is going
to marry, he must fast the day before
St. John's Day (June 24) and sit in the
parlor at midnight. The person whom he
or she will marry will enter and look
upon him. If he is not to marry, a
casket will slide into the room (F, SLC,
1959).

4858 On St. John's Day, which falls once a
year, the single girls are supposed to
get a handful of ashes at night, and put
them on the inside of the door. The
next morning, a name is written on the
ashes of the man you are going to marry
(F, Gr, SLC, 1962).

4859 If you stand at a crossroad on New
Year's Eve, you will see the image of
the one you will marry (F, 75, E.
Jordan, 1897). The informant remarked
that one girl was said to have seen the
image of a headless horseman. Later her
husband had his head shot off at war.

4860 If the Angel Moroni waves to a
missionary when he leaves on his
mission, it means his girl will wait for
him (M, 20, SLC, 1960).

4861 It is bad luck to write love letters on
a typewriter (F, SLC, 1961).

4862 Sending perfumed letters means love and
affection (F, 24, SLC, 1964).

# DATING, GOING STEADY

## General

4863 Date only those who are of your caliber
(F, 64, Heber, 1910).

4864 You are supposed to have knowledge of
"your other half" if you feel a distinct
shock of love at first meeting (F, 21,
Sandy, 1957).

4865 Don't date a boy shorter than yourself
(F, SLC, 1961).

4866  Dating more than twelve girls brings bad luck in courtship (M, 23, SLC, 1961).

4867  Never give your correct age to a man, if you are a girl (M, SLC, 1961).

4868  No girl should start dating before the age of eighteen or nineteen (F, 64, Heber, 1910).

4869  It is not good taste for a young courting lady to let the fellow see her in her dress before the dance (F, 24, SLC, 1960).

4870  It is always bad luck to go courting on Friday (F, Ogden, 1960).

4871  Don't go out on a date Friday night with a blonde, or you will be tied to a date with her for Saturday (M, Wellington, 1916).

4872  Never go with a boy or girl whose birthday will come before yours or Christmas (F, SLC, 1959).

4873  If your foot itches, you'll want a date with someone (M, 33, SLC, 1949).

4874  If you wear a pearl necklace on your first date, you'll cry (F, 35, SLC, 1964).

4875  A couple going together should never act as best man or maid of honor at a wedding.  It is bad luck (F, 60, SLC, 1964).

4876  It is bad luck for a man to have a lady friend pay her own guest check (M, SLC, 1964).

4877  A hairpin found and kept signals a date (F, 20, SLC, 1965).  Brown 4152.

4878  Boys won't make passes at girls who wear glasses (F, SLC, 1935).

4879  Never pick a girl up on the first date driving a dirty car.  You will always have better luck with the girl, and have more of a chance for another date if you pick her up driving a clean car (M, 23, W. Jordan, 1963).

4880  The luck routine in dating:  Get ready for a date two hours early, and then wait around until it is time to go (M, SLC, 1971).

4881  You can tell how a boy feels about you by the time of day that he calls to ask you for a date.  If he calls before 7:00 P.M., he wants to get to know you better.  If he calls you after 7:00 P.M., he's only interested in sex (F, SLC, 1967).

## Clothing, Jewelry

4882  When I was in junior high school, if you were going steady (boys only), you would be sure to button the back of your neck button on your shirt.  If you were available, you would leave it unbuttoned (F, SLC, 1971).

4883  If you go with a girl wearing a red coat, you're in for trouble (M, 1960).

4884  If a girl wears red and yellow, she wants to be kissed (F, SLC, 1957).

4885      Red and yellow,
          Catch a fellow.
      (F, Moab, 1953).

4886  Always wear a favorite necklace on your first date with a boy.  It gives you confidence (F, 19, Midvale, 1959).

## Kissing, Etc.

4887      If you kiss on the first date,
          You'll never be a mate.
      (M, 86, Payson, 1894).

4888  Do not kiss a girl on the first date, or you will have bad luck (M, SLC, 1958).

4889  It's unlucky to kiss a boy before the third date (F, 19, SLC, 1962).

4890      A kiss in the night will bring
            lovers delight,
          But a kiss in the day will drive
            true love away.
      (F, 21, SLC, 1964).

4891  Count the dots on the Olympia Beer label:  One dot, you can hold hands; two dots, you can kiss; three dots, you can pet; four dots, there are greener fields (F, SLC, 1962).

## "Perdiddle," "One Eye," Etc.

4892  If you see three cars with only one light, you'll see your lover (F, Midvale, 1955).

4893  If you see a car with only one headlight, it means your boyfriend wants to kiss you (F, SLC, 1964); . . . you will soon be getting a kiss (M, SLC, 1959); . . . you can kiss the girl next to you (M, 21, SLC, 1954); . . . you can either kiss or slap your date (F, SLC, 1963).

4894  The custom of collecting a kiss for every car that you see with only one headlight is called a "padittle" (M, 19, SLC, 1956).

4895  If you see a car with one headlight, the boy owes a girl a kiss; if you see a car with only one taillight, the girl owes the boy a kiss (F, SLC).

4896  If you see a car with only one headlight or one taillight, you are going to be kissed (F, SLC).

4897  If a girl sees a car with one headlight out, she gets to slap the boy; if the boy sees one, he gets to kiss the girl.  This is known as the "pedittle" (F, Moab, 1962).

4898  If you see a car driving along at night with only one headlight, you call it "perdiddle."  For each perdiddle you call out before someone else in the same car can say it, a girl will automatically give you a kiss when you want one.  But if you try to take more kisses than you have perdiddles saved up, she will slap your face (M, 22, SLC, 1960).

4899  When a boy sees a car with one headlight out, he says "Perdiddle" and kisses the girl with him.  If the girl sees it first and says "Perdiddle," she kisses the boy (F, 23, SLC, 1964).

4900  When you see three one-eyed cars in one night, "stamp" them and you will get a date for the weekend (F, Logan, 1970).

4901  A car that has no working headlights is called a "wammy" by Salt Lake teenagers. This, like the "Perdiddle," enables a fellow to kiss the girl he is with at that particular time twice (F, SLC, 1961).

4902  "Perdiddle" is the word said when you see a car with one headlight.  Count up the ones you see and then when you meet your boyfriend, you get to kiss him that many times (F, SLC, 1969).

## Going Steady

4903  The early settlers of Grantsville, Utah, had a custom among their young people which must have been the forerunner of our present-day "going steady."  When a young man wanted a date, he did not ask for just a date for the dance.  He asked for a date for the season.  This assured a certain amount of certainty for all concerned as to the attendance at the year's affairs (M, Tooele, 1957).

4904  Putting a dime in the strap of loafer shoes means a boy is going steady (M, 24, Provo, 1964).

4905  If you walk around Temple Square three times with a girl, and the Angel Moroni blows his trumpet, you know you have the right girl.  This applies only to singles (M, Provo, 1972).

4906  This is a way for LDS missionaries to tell if their girl will wait for them. While in the mission home the missionary walks his girl around the Temple three times.  If Angel Moroni blows his horn, the girl will wait, if he doesn't, she won't wait (F, 19, Springville, 1963).

## PROPOSAL AND ENGAGEMENT

### General

4907  The engagement should last well over a year (F, 64, Heber, 1910).

4908  Girls who are not engaged for the minimum of a year are considered "hussies" (F, 64, Heber, 1910).

4909  A long engagement is an insurance policy against the failure of marriage (F, 64, Heber, 1910).

4910  When they are engaged, girls wear their flowers on their right shoulder, and after they are married, they wear them on their left (M, 53, SLC, 1964).

4911  During their engagement, a couple should break a piece of gold for luck (M, SLC, 1961).

4912  Every time the groom-to-be visits the bride-to-be's home, he must carry fresh fish to her home (F, Gr, SLC, 1962).

## Proposal

4913  It is lucky to receive a proposal at a dance and refuse it (M, SLC, 1925).

4914  A man proposing with his hat on is bad luck (F, SLC, 1967).

4915  On leap year day the girls can ask boys to marry them (M, 52, SLC, 1964); Every four years the girls can ask the boys to marry them (M, 51, SLC, 1963); . . . and the man must accept, if it is leap year (F, Tooele, 1964); Leap year is always when the girl catches her man (F, 45, Clearfield, 1940).

4916  When a boy marries a girl who has asked him to marry her on leap year day, he has to buy her a mink coat (M, SLC, 1964).

4917  If a man refuses a proposal of marriage from a girl in leap year, he must buy her a cow (F, SLC, 1925).

## Engagement Ring

4918  There will be bad luck if the groom shows the engagement ring to anyone else before the future bride (M, SLC, 1961).

4919  If your engagement ring gets turned with the stone on the inside of the finger before the wedding ceremony, then the wedding will never take place (F, SLC, 1959).

4920  It is bad luck to let someone try on your engagement ring before you are married (F, Ogden, 1960).

4921  If you try on an engagement ring of another person, the person's engagement will be broken, and it will bring bad luck to you (F, SLC, 1952); If a bride tries her wedding band on before the wedding, it will break the engagement (M, Sandy, 1945); If a friend tries on your engagement ring, you will have a bad marriage (F, 20, SLC, 1962).

4922  It is unlucky for a girl who is not married or about to be engaged to wear a glass or diamond ring on either her right or left hand (F, Oakley, 1960).

4923  The diamond symbolizes everlasting love and devotion (F, 19, SLC, 1963).

4924  It's bad luck to give the same diamond to two different girls (M, SLC, 1958).

4925  Emeralds should never be given as engagement rings, or bad luck will occur (F, 19, SLC, 1963); Opals . . . (F, 19, SLC, 1963).

4926  An engagement ring containing pearls will bring tears to the marriage (F, SLC, 1961).  Cf. Brown 4745.

4927  It's bad luck to take off your engagement ring during the engagement period (F, Springville, 1961); If you don't take off your ring until the day of the wedding, love will last forever (F, Ogden, 1961).

4928    After your engagement ring has been wished on, it is bad luck if you ever take it off (F, 33, SLC, 1945); . . . if removed, the wish is broken (F, 18, SLC, 1962).

### Engagement Time

4929    To become engaged on Christmas Eve is a sure sign of good luck in the marriage (F, SLC, 1964).

4930    Never get engaged during the dark of the moon, or you will have a dark, dismal marriage (F, 35, Richfield, 1949).

4931    If you become engaged on the night of a full moon, you will have a successful marriage (M, Magna, 1963).

### Breaking the Engagement

4932    If a maid drops a fork when laying a table, it means that her engagement will be broken (F, 20, Midvale, 1950).

4933    If a visitor comes in one door and goes out another, an engagement in the home will be broken (F, Gr, SLC, 1920).

4934    To pull the petals from a rose means a broken engagement (F, SLC, 1951).

4935    If an engaged couple are dreaming about each other, they will never get married to each other (F, SLC, 1959).

4936    When you cut your initials in something solid with your diamond ring, if the diamond falls out, it is bad luck, and the engagement will fall apart (F, 33, SLC, 1950).

4937    An engaged couple should never give each other a pin for a present, for it will kill their love (F, 53, Norw, SLC, 1961)

4938    To give your sweetheart a knife means that you want to break the engagement (F, Brigham City, 1960).

4939    If a courting couple are photographed together, the engagement will be broken (M, 19, SLC, 1961); . . . they will never marry (F, 23, SLC, 1965); . . . they will break up (F, 87, S. Jordan, 1949).

4940    Never give your girl friend your picture until engaged, or the engagement will break up (M, 56, SLC, 1940).

4941    After an engagement is broken, the ring should be broken so that another engagement can occur (F, Midvale, 1961).

### WEDDING SHOWERS, GIFTS

4942    If a bride-to-be wears a ribbon in her hair at a surprise shower, she will have good luck (F, SLC, 1959).

4943    Brides at showers should never cut strings on presents, for it means bad luck (F, SLC, 1959); . . . it will be an unhappy marriage (F, Woodland, 1959).

4944    When unwrapping gifts at a bridal shower, don't break any of the ribbons, or the bride will have bad luck (F, SLC, 1957).

4945    It's bad luck to untie shower ribbons yourself. You must let the future husband do so, and it must be just before bedtime (F, SLC).

4946    At a wedding shower the bride should have all of the ribbons from the presents placed and tied in her hair. This will bring good luck (F, 35, SLC, 1939).

4947    The bride-to-be should save all the bows from her shower gifts and use them as a makeshift bouquet for the wedding rehearsal. This will bring good luck (F, 45, SLC, 1964).

4948    It is bad luck if wedding gifts are wrapped in green or black paper. It will bring a life of misery to the couple being married (F, 48, SLC, 1928).

4949    If you wrap wedding presents in red and white, the bride and groom will have good luck (F, 24, Ja, SLC).

4950    You must never tear the wrapping paper on any shower gifts, or you will have bad luck (F, 21, SLC, 1950).

4951    It is good luck to receive salt and pepper shakers as a wedding gift (F, 65, Midvale, 1909).

4952    It is believed that a person should never give a pair of shoes as a wedding present, or any kind of a present, because it indicates or symbolizes the walking away or parting of a friendship forever (M, 29, Ger, SLC, 1964).

4953    Don't give any sharp instrument at a wedding. It is bad luck (F, Woods Cross, 1953).

4954    You are not supposed to give anything sharp for a wedding gift, or else you will bring bad luck to the marriage. To counteract this you are supposed to put a nickel in with the gift (F, 20, SLC, 1963).

4955    Don't give scissors as a gift at a wedding. It is bad luck (F, Woods Cross, 1953).

4956    The number of pins you have in your wedding gifts tells you the number of quarrels that you will have (F, 1962).

4957    A knife for a wedding present breaks good relations between man and wife (F, 52, SLC, 1965); . . . will bring bad luck to the couple (M, 12, SLC, 1960); . . . means the marriage bonds will be cut in half (M, SLC, 1961).

4958    If a person gives a gift of cutlery to the bride-to-be at a shower, then the bride must give a penny for each piece so the friendship will not be cut (F, 45, SLC, 1964).

4959    Giving your prospective mate a Bible before marriage is lucky (F, 24, 1964).

4960    It is believed to be unlucky for young lovers to give Bibles to each other before they are married (F, 27, SLC, 1950).

## APHRODISIACS

### Bodily Tokens

4961 If a member of the opposite sex crosses your shadow, that person will be your mate (F, Eng, Magna, 1960).

4962 If it's raining and the sun is shining and you find a rock that is half buried in the ground, dig it out and find under the rock a hair the color of your mate, or wife will have (M, Richfield, 1920). Brown 4135.

4963 If you pull a hair out of a girl's head, she will love you (M, 23, Holladay, 1958).

4964 If you will steal a piece of a boy's or girl's hair and sew it in your coat or dress, he or she will get crazy about you (M, 20, Midvale, 1964). Brown 4233.

4965 Hair from your lover's head placed under the band of your hat will make that person love you (F, 45, SLC, 1936). Cf. Brown 4237.

### Animal Products and Tokens

4966 If someone hates you, white stones from a rooster will cause him to love you (M, 25, Je, SLC, 1965).

4967 If you swallow a raw chicken heart in one gulp, you will be sexually attractive (F, Du, Ogden, 1961).

### Food and Drink

4968 Eat yeast and it will improve your sexual potency (M, SLC, 1959).

4969 Drinking gin makes you passionate (Anon, Lehi, 1957).

4970 If a mother and daughter have a child at the same time, and you take a little milk from mother and daughter and give it to your boyfriend, he will fall in love with you (M, Gr, SLC, 1953).

4971 Eggs will increase passion (F, Moab, 1953); Drink an egg in beer for sexual potency (M, 45, SLC, 1964).

4972 Hot liver is thought to be a passion food and the seed of a passion (F, 19, SLC, 1960).

4973 It is unwise to eat green olives, anything with sesame seeds on it or to eat bananas, for they are passion pills (F, 19, Logan, 1970).

4974 If you eat oysters, you will be sexually excited (M, 21, SLC, 1963); . . . sexually potent (M, 45, SLC, 1964); . . . increase passion (F, Moab, 1953).

4975 Eating radishes will increase the sex drive (F, 19, SLC, 1949).

4976 Too much pepper makes you passionate (F, 40, SLC, 1940).

4977 If you eat a lot of spices, you will become sexually excited faster and more often (F, SLC, 1959).

### Love Powders, Charms, Etc.

4978 If you go to a bruja (witch), she can give you a love potion that will make whoever you give it to fall in love with you (M, SLC, 1957).

4979 Goofer dust comes from the goofer tree. Sprinkle it in the shoes of the woman you love, and she can never get away from you (F, 19, SLC).

4980 For love, divide an ounce of quicksilver into three parts and cast one part into the fire every day for three days, while saying, "As I burn this quicksilver, so should the heart of so-and-so, the daughter of such-and-such, burn until she does my will and desire." When this has been said, recite the passage, "Fire shall be kept burning upon the altar continually; it shall not go out" (M, 25, Je, SLC, 1965).

4981 Churchyard dirt in a hat produces love (F, Ger, SLC, 1963).

4982 A girl can take a needle which has been stuck into a dead body, cover it with dirt in which the body is buried, and wrap the whole thing in a cloth cut from a winding sheet; this is supposed to be a very powerful love charm (F, Ger, Clearfield, 1961).

4983 If a girl puts salt on the fire for seven mornings, it will bring her absent lover home, if he wants to come or not (F, Ogden, 1961). Cf. Brown 4259.

4984 Dogstone, which is found in salt marshes, is used to make love potions (F, 29, SLC, 1964).

4985 If a mother has a child and her daughter has a child, they may mix their milk into a bottle of ink. Any single person may wish to write a letter with that ink to their boyfriend. This means that the boy will marry the girl (F, Gr, SLC, 1962).

4986 If a boy can contrive to have his eyes meet those of his girl and rub bluestone in his hands at the same time, she is his forever (F, 45, RN, SLC, 1948).

4987 To make a person love you, think of that person (F, 52, SLC, 1964).

4988 By saying some magic words while you clean your nails on Sunday, you can force your lover to visit you on Monday (F, SLC, 1961).

4989 For love, take a thorn, place it in a kerchief, and say: "Tartie, Partie, Gurtie." She must then run after you without her undergarments (M, 25, Je, SLC, 1965).

4990 If you like red, you are generally passionate (F, 21, SLC, 1960); Red governs affection (F, SLC, 1964); Red governs lust (F, SLC, 1964); Red governs love (F, SLC, 1964).

4991 Don't paint your bedroom red. Red brings out the sex attribute of men (M, 48, SLC, 1930); . . . red brings out the bad in the male sex (F, 56, Ogden, 1920).

4992 Wearing black beads will enhance your love life (F, SLC, 1971).

## Anaphrodisiacs

4993 Ants' eggs are an antidote to love (M, 19, SLC, 1961).

4994 An amber bead necklace will stop desire (F, SLC, 1959).

## SPINSTERHOOD, BACHELORHOOD

## Bodily Indicators

4995 If your eyebrows meet across your nose, you will never wear your wedding clothes (F, 51, SLC, 1931).

4996 A girl with excess hair on her earlobes is destined to be an old maid (F, SLC, 1967).

4997 If the creases in the palm of your hand don't form an "M," you will become a bachelor or an old maid (F, 19, Logan, 1972).

4998 If a girl has thin nails, she will never marry (F, 20, SLC, 1964).

4999 If a person falls up the stairs, it's a sign he will never marry (M, 17, SLC, 1958).

5000 To spit on yourself is a sign that you will not marry (M, 54, SLC, 1943).

5001 A whistling woman is bound to be an old maid (F, SLC, 1967).

5002 To sneeze three times in a row means that you will never marry (M, Provo, 1952); . . . be an old maid (F, 18, SLC, 1962).

5003 Stepping over a person's legs denotes they will be an old maid or a bachelor (F, Gr, SLC, 1961). Cf. Brown 4691. (The well-known beliefs about stunting the growth of children by stepping over them while recumbent or playing on the floor is carried over here, apparently, to thwarting the natural development of the love relationship. Cf. Nos. 761ff, above. --Eds.)

5004 If you stub your left toe, you will not marry (F, Hyrum, 1930).

5005 When riding in a car, if you don't lift your feet off the floor of the car when you go over railroad tracks or under a bridge, you will be an old maid (F, 19, Panguitch, 1960).

5006 If a young lady folds her arms while sitting, she will live to be an old maid (F, 26, Centerfield, 1964).

5007 If you dream of getting married, you will never be married (F, 23, SLC, 1961).

5008 If a girl dreams of wearing or seeing a white dress, it means she will not marry (M, 51, Midvale, 1935).

5009 To kiss a man with a moustache and get a hair in your mouth from it means you will die an old maid (M, Eng, SLC).

5010 If you sing while sitting on the toilet, you will never marry (F, Lehi, 1957).

5011 If you sing at the table, you will never marry (F, Lehi, 1957).

5012 To look into a tumbler when you are drinking is a sign that you will be an old maid (F, SLC, 1961).

## Food, Salt, Pepper

5013 If you look into a coffee pot, you will be an old maid (F, SLC, 1945); . . . you will never be married (M, SLC).

5014 They used to tell a girl that was making bread if she left dough in the pan she would never get married (F, Moab, 1953).

5015 If a girl is baking bread and it burns, the girl will never marry (F, SLC, 1920).

5016 If when serving cake at a birthday party, when putting it on a plate if it tips over on its side, the person being served will end up a bachelor or an old maid (M, SLC, 1959).

5017 If a girl eats the tip of a pie first, she'll be an old maid (M, SLC, 1960).

5018 If you eat a frozen egg, you can never marry (F, 38, SLC, 1940).

5019 The girl who eats the unpopped popcorn kernels will be an old maid (F, Ogden, 1961).

5020 If you spill a beverage on a saucer while pouring, the person who gets it will be an old maid (F, SLC, 1960).

5021 Always pass the salt and pepper together, or it means you will be an old maid (F, 22, Helper, 1956).

## The Last Piece of Food, Etc.

5022 Whoever takes the last drop of milk out of a bottle will be an old maid (F, SLC, 1950s).

5023 The one who takes the last piece of food off a plate will be an old maid or a bachelor (F, 60, Ogden, 1970); . . . the last serving at dinner . . . (F, 52, American Fork). Brown 4665.

5024 Do not take the last thing on the plate or buy the last item, or you will be an old maid (F, 37, Heber, 1963).

5025 Don't take the last biscuit, or you'll be an old maid (F, 25, SLC, 1945); . . . the last slice of bread . . . (M, 46, SLC, 1964). Brown 4668.

5026 If a girl eats the last piece of cake left on the cake plate, she will never marry (F, 19, SLC). Learned in Wyoming.

5027   A girl who eats the last piece of candy, etc., from a plate will be an old maid (M, SLC, 1957); . . . the last chocolate from a box . . . (M, SLC, 1930s); . . . the last cookie on a plate . . . (F, Ogden, 1940).

## Tables, Chairs

5028   If you sit on a table, you will be an old maid (F, SLC, 1910); . . . on the corner of a table . . . (F, 24, SLC, 1964).  Brown 4661.

5029   If a girl sits on a table while talking to her lover, she will never get married (M, SLC, 1963).

5030   If you tip a chair over while getting up, you will never marry (M, 44, SLC, 1962).  Brown 4685.

## Domestic Chores, Sewing, Sweeping, Etc.

5031   If a girl splashes dishwater on her stomach, she'll be an old maid (F, 29, Garfield, 1945).

5032   If you wash dishes on a stove, you'll never get married (F, Eng, SLC, 1965).

5033   Shake the tablecloth outdoors after sunset, and you'll never marry (F, 45, Centerville).

5034   If you sew buttons backward on a shirt, you will never have to worry about losing your heart (F, SLC, 1963).

5035   Sewing on Sunday means you will be an old maid (F, SLC, 1957).

5036   If you let someone sweep under your feet, you will not marry (F, 21, Moab, 1957); If you sweep under anyone, you will never marry (M, 67, Ger, SLC, 1929).  Brown 4687f.

5037   If an unmarried girl sweeps dirt across her feet, or if someone else sweeps some dirt across her feet, she will never marry (F, 23, SLC, 1953).  Cf. Brown 4689.

5038   If you are sweeping in a doorway when someone comes to the door, you will be an old maid or old bachelor (F, 54, Midvale, 1920).

5039   You are sure to be an old maid if you step over a broom (F, SLC, 1962).  Brown 4690.

## Animal Indicators

5040   A maiden who is particularly fond of cats will be an old maid (F, Provo, 1959); If a woman likes cats better than dogs . . . (M, 18, Dan, SLC, 1964).

5041   If black cat is kept in the family, the girls in that family will never marry (M, Ogden, 1951).  Cf. Brown 4695f.

5042   At a party throw a cat into the middle of a quilt; the girl toward whom it goes will be an old maid (F, SLC, 1961).

5043   If a young girl raises cats, she will be an old maid (F, SLC, 1957).

5044   Where cobwebs grow, love never goes (F, SLC, 1960); Where cobwebs grow, boys don't go (M, Clearfield, 1959).  Cf. Brown 4699.

5045   Where the cobwebs hang low, beaux never go (F, SLC, 1925).

## Participation in Nuptial Events

5046   When your favor at a shower is a thimble, you'll be an old maid (F, Ogden, 1970).

5047   Twice a bridesmaid, never a bride (F, 21, Bountiful, 1945).

5048   Three times a bridesmaid, never a bride (F, SLC, 1958); Three times in one season . . . (F, 22, Milford, 1961); The jinx will be broken if she is a bridesmaid seven times (F, Brigham City, 1960).  Brown 4754.

5049   Always a bridesmaid, never a bride (F, 18, SLC, 1952).

5050   If a girl tries on another girl's engagement ring, she won't get married (F, Copperton); . . . wedding ring . . . (F, SLC).

5051   If you try on someone else's wedding dress before you are married, you will never get married (F, 24, Norw, SLC, 1964).

5052   If a bride is robbed of all the pins about her dress by a single woman, all who pass one of the pins will be married within a year.  If the pin is bent, however, she will be an old maid (F, SLC, 1960).

5053   If you're the first one to sign the bridal book, you'll never get married (F, Copperton).

5054   If a girl reads the marriage in its entirety, she will never be asked to wed (F, Brigham, 1960).

5055   If the bridesmaid stumbles in the wedding march, she will be an old maid (F, 28, SLC, 1961).

## Miscellaneous

5056   Don't count the number of cars on a train.  If you do, you'll never get married (F, Ger, SLC, 1959).

5057   In the Greek Church they used to prepare boiled wheat for memorial services. After the service they distributed the boiled wheat to the people.  If you give this boiled wheat to a family in a house where there are unmarried girls, they believe that the girls will not get married (M, 73, Gr, SLC, 1963).

5058   A dime, a penny, a button, and a thimble, and ring were put in our birthday cakes.  The person who got the dime was the rich man; the penny, the poor man; the thimble, the old maid; the button, the bachelor; the ring, first one married (F, SLC, 1957).

5059   The one at the end of something is referred to as having a more likely chance of becoming an old maid (M, 55, Bountiful, 1954).

5060  If you raise an umbrella in the house, you will not marry (F, SLC, 1945). Brown 4678.

5061  If you walk under a ladder, you'll stay single (F, SLC, 1963).

5062  If you are cross when you are young, you will be an old maid (M, SLC, 1960); . . . grouchy . . . (F, SLC, 1962).

5063  Good guessers never marry (F, SLC, 1962).

5064  If there is an old maid in the family, there will be one in the next generation (M, SLC).

5065  A girl who is pricked by a rose will not marry (F, Eng, Magna, 1960).

5066  If a young man passes the age of nineteen before he marries, chances are that he will never marry (F, 35, SLC, 1964); If a girl doesn't marry before she is twenty-five, she will never marry (F, 35, SLC, 1964).

5067  If you visit a home, you must leave the place through the same door you entered, because a girl leaving another way is not going to get married (F, 62, Gr, SLC, 1963).

5068  A girl is old enough to get married when she can take the hair from the back of her head, put it over her head and down her face and wind it around her nose three times. She must stay single until this can be done (F, 68, Midvale, 1909).

5069  A girl who fails to look to the north before breakfast will remain a spinster (F, Brigham City, 1960); . . . when she leaves her house in the morning . . . (M, SLC, 1961).

5070  Eating dates with an old maid is considered unlucky (F, 57, SLC, 1963).

## FLIRTATION, JEALOUSY, DISCORD

5071  If flowers wilt quickly on a girl, it's a sign that she's a flirt (F, 18, Heber, 1972). Brown 4574.

5072  If a girl is sent flowers which number seven, then she will probably break up with the man who sent them (F, 27, SLC, 1964).

5073  If you look over the side when drinking from a glass, you are a flirt (F, SLC, 1961).

5074  If you wink at a girl with your left eye, in a storm, the next girl you see will be similar to your wife (M, SLC, 1960).

5075  If you kiss a girl on the nose, you will have a fight (M, SLC, 1961).

5076  If you want to lose a man, kiss him on the first date, if you can (F, 49, Ogden, 1930).

5077  When two lovers are walking and meet an obstacle, they should go on either side of it, or they will have a quarrel (F, 45, SLC, 1964).

5078  Never apologize to a girl, because it will cause bad feelings in the future (M, SLC, 1958).

5079  If a person goes to bed thinking about a loved one with whom they have a romantic interest, this relationship will change for the worse (F, SLC, 1961).

5080  Eat a pickle to solve your arguments with your best girl (M, SLC, 1959).

5081  If you sing before breakfast, you'll be disappointed in love (F, 24, SLC, 1964).

5082  The color yellow means jealousy (F, SLC, 1964). Cf. Brown 4644.

5083  If you are going with a boy or girl and break up with them, you shouldn't go with a boy whose first initial is the same as the last one's was (F, 20, SLC, 1959).

5084  If a young man is courting a girl, and one night she presents him with a bowl of nuts, the courtship is over, and the young man may no longer call (F, 59, SLC, 1963).

5085  Split hairs indicate an unhappy love affair (F, SLC, 1920s).

5086  If given a box of chocolates by your boyfriend, never eat the last piece or allow it to be eaten, because as soon as it is gone your relationship with the guy will end (F, 73, W. Jordan, 1960).

5087  If someone calls you by a wrong name in a dream, it is an unfortunate omen for your progress in love (F, SLC, 1957).

## LOSS OF SWEETHEART, SPOUSE

### Clothing, Gifts

5088  If a woman loses her garter, she'll lose her lover (M, 23, Heber, 1972). Brown 4649.

5089  If you break a shoestring, your sweetheart will turn to another (F, Axtell, 1958).

5090  If you buy your sweetheart a pair of shoes, your love will walk away from you (F, 62, Vernal).

5091  Girls should never give gloves as a present to the boys, or they'll be nothing but friends (F, Norw, SLC).

5092  Never give your lover a gift of a handkerchief. It will cause you to part (F, 67, Bingham, 1925).

5093  Never give your sweetheart anything with a sharp point, for it will cut your love (F, Orangeville, 1959); . . . cut your love in half (M, SLC, 1959). Cf. Brown 4337, 4652.

5094  If you give a person a knife for a present, it will cut the love off (M, SLC); To break off a courtship, a girl should present her lover with a knife (F, 19, SLC, 1964). Brown 4650.

5095 If a boy and girl are going together and the boy gives the girl, for her first present, a pin or something sharp, then it's bad luck (F, Peoa, 1930). Cf. Brown 4337, 4651.

5096 If you give something pointed to the one you love, your love will turn to hate (F, 49, SLC, 1964).

Domestic Portents

5097 To drop a fork while setting a table will end your love affair (F, 69, Riverside, 1920); . . . means you will get a divorce (F, 44, Swiss, Midvale, 1964).

5098 If you have two forks at your plate, someone will take your girl away from you (M, 21, SLC, 1949).

5099 If you don't get enough salt in your food, you'll lose your beau (F, SLC, 1925).

5100 If a girl forgets to salt the food while it's cooking, it means that she has lost her beau (F, SLC, 1925).

5101 You must peel an apple without breaking the skin; if you break the skin, you'll lose your boyfriend (F, 50, American Fork, 1925).

5102 If you eat the peel of a banana absent-mindedly, it means you have lost your true love (F, 28, SLC, 1960).

5103 If you put cream or milk in your tea before sugar, you may lose your sweetheart (F, 21, Eng, SLC, 1963).

5104 If you sit on a table with your sweetheart, you will break up real soon (F, 19, SLC, 1960).

5105 Don't sew on an article while it is still on you, or you will drive your suitors away (F, SLC, 1957).

5106 If while sewing the thread keeps tying up in knots, a husband or boyfriend is going to step out on you (M, SLC).

5107 Walk out the same door of a house you walked in, or you'll lose your boyfriend (F, 41, SLC, 1964).

Walking, Riding, Travel, Etc.

5108 If you don't raise your feet while crossing a cattleguard, you'll lose your boyfriend (F, 20, Smithfield, 1972).

5109 If you step on the rails of a railroad track when you are crossing, you will lose your boyfriend (F, SLC, 1949).

5110 When you go across the railroad tracks, you must lift your feet up until you cross them, or you'll lose your boyfriend (F, Murray, 1959); . . . don't lift up your feet, or you will lose your boyfriend (F, 20, SLC, 1964).

5111 As you go over railroad tracks in a car, if you raise your hands and feet and cross them, you will never lose your boyfriend (F, 19, Kamas, 1949).

5112 Lift your feet when going over railroad tracks or bridges when riding in a car. Also put your hands on the inside roof of the car when passing through a tunnel or archway. This is to insure that you don't lose your sweetheart (F).

5113 If you step on a manhole, you will lose your boyfriend or girl friend (F, 23, SLC); . . . a manhole cover . . . (F, SLC, 1964).

5114 If you let someone walk between you and your lover, you will have bad luck (F, SLC, 1960).

5115 When out for a walk with your girl friend and a tree is in your way, never let her walk on one side of the tree and you on the other because you will break up (M, 23, SLC, 1958); . . . a lamppost . . . (F, 44, American Fork, 1930). Cf. Brown 4658.

5116 If a couple are separated by an object when walking, they must cross their fingers immediately or they will be separated (F, SLC, 1958).

5117 When walking with your lover or friend, never let a barrier come between you. If it does, one of you must walk back around it, or it will cause a split with your lover or your friend (F, SLC, 1961).

5118 If a couple is walking together and come to an object such as a tree and one goes on one side of it, and one on the other, they should say "Bread-and-butter" when they get to the other side, or their romance will end (F, 71, Midway, 1910).

Miscellaneous

5119 Never leave hair in your comb. If you leave it in and another girl uses it and takes it out, she will take your sweetheart away (F, 19, Heber, 1972). Brown 4645.

5120 A full moon brings romance, but a new moon brings breaking up (F, 20, SLC, 1964).

5121 Rain on a summer day means that someone is crying over a lost loved one (M, SLC, 1961).

5122 To upset ink signifies a separation (M, 30, SLC, 1946).

5123 If a girl says "goodbye" to her lover, she is liable not to see him again. She should say "good night" (M, SLC, 1959).

5124 If you say "good night" to your girl while standing on the middle step of her porch, you will break up (M, 19, SLC, 1964).

5125 When you step on someone's heel, if you don't shake hands with him, he will take your sweetheart away from you (M, 26, SLC, 1959).

5126 To crush a rose is to crush your love's heart (M, SLC, 1961).

5127 To break a pane of glass is to break your love's heart (M, SLC, 1961).

5128 A boy should never give a girl a letter in her left hand, as it will break their friendship (M, SLC, 1960).

5129 If someone marries your lover, if you get two sticks and tie them together, then the couple will become as brother and sister instead of man and wife (M, Gr, SLC, 1945).

5130 If you mix dog hair with cat hair, and put it in front of a home in which a happily married couple live, they will start fighting and it will eventually result in their breakup (F, Gr, SLC, 1957).

MARITAL STATUS

5131 If you marry your cousin, you will have bad luck (F, Fairfield, 1905).

5132 All girls have met the boy they'll marry by the age of eighteen (M, 16, SLC, 1961).

5133 Two people born in the same month should never marry. It will not be a successful marriage (F, 80, Midvale).

5134 A man should marry only a girl whom he has had sexual experience with (M, Perry, 1964).

Bodily Attributes

5135 The desired wife is one who is plump, because she must know how to work, and if times are hard, she will have plenty stored (M, 26, SLC, 1963).

5136 When a man chooses his wife, he should pick a girl who is not too fat, not too skinny, not too tall and not too short. This means that she will be the ideal woman (M, Ja, SLC, 1963).

5137 If a blue-eyed man and a brown-eyed girl marry, the marriage will be all right, but if two people of the same color eyes marry, they will be incompatible (M, SLC, 1960); Grey eyes aren't to marry other grey eyes (F, 1963); Brunettes are not compatible married to the same (M, 23, SLC, 1962).

5138 Many girls marry men like fathers; and many boys project a marriage image of the mother (F, SLC, 1962).

5139 If your father has hair on his chest, it means you will marry a man with hair on his chest (F, SLC, 1962).

5140 A lot of hair on a man's chest, and especially high up to his neck, means he is very masculine and that he will make a wonderful husband (F, SLC, 1960).

5141 Men with fine brown hair, light or dark, make the best husbands (M, SLC, 1960).

5142 Don't sweep the floor and sing at the same time, or you will marry a stammering husband; and while you are sweeping, be sure to pick up everything--otherwise you will marry a bald-headed man (M, 50, It, SLC, 1965).

5143 People with long toes are less desirable as marriage mates (F, SLC, 1961).

5144 Two persons with false teeth should not marry, as it will be an unlucky union (F, SLC, 1961).

Age, Beauty

5145 If you marry a beautiful woman, you marry trouble (M, Providence, 1957).

5146 Whoever gets the last piece of pie on a plate will get a handsome husband or wife (F, 80, SLC).

5147 If you make a bed well, you'll get a handsome husband (F, SLC, 1890).

5148 To sweep the floors or walks after nightfall means that a young woman will marry an old man (F, Magna, 1933).

5149 It is a superstition that May and December weddings are not successful (F, 48, SLC, 1940).

5150 A marriage between a young man and an old woman is made by the devil, and both will abide with him (F, Brigham City, 1960).

5151 If you do not sweep the floor well, it means that you will marry an ugly husband (F, 71, Gr, SLC, 1964).

Character, Virtue

5152 Marriage usually takes place between persons with opposite personality characteristics (blonde-brunette, etc.), and such marriages are more likely to be successful (M, SLC, 1957); Opposites attract (F, SLC, 1962).

5153 Brownettes make the best wives; blondes are fickle, brunettes are suspicious (M, SLC, 1960).

5154 Never marry a man with red whiskers. This is worse than red hair, and it means that your husband will be cruel to you (F, 1963).

5155 If a wife's eyes are blue, she'll be a true mate (M, Layton, 1960). Heard in Colorado, 1924.

5156 Eyebrows that meet show a person with much passion and a disregard of marital fidelity (F, 51, SLC, 1931).

5157 For a young woman to dream of bananas foretells that she will be mated to an uninteresting and an unloved companion (M, 68, SLC, 1938).

5158 If you cannot start a fire and make it burn readily, you will have a lazy husband (F, Murray, 1952).

5159 If you can cut an even piece of pie, you will have an honest husband (F, SLC, 1962).

5160 For a single woman to dream of giving birth to a child, she will lose her virtue and be abandoned by her lover (F, 68, SLC, 1915).

5161 A girl will lose her virtue if she cuts her hair (F, 19, SLC, 1963).

5162 When an owl hoots among houses, a girl will lose her chastity (F, SLC, 1961).

## Mental Gifts, Talents, Domestic Ability

5163 A woman who can build a bright fire will marry an intelligent man (F, Dan, SLC, 1903).

5164 She who pricks bread with a fork or knife will never be a happy wife (F, Brigham City, 1960).

5165 If you're washing dishes before you are married, and you get your apron wet, you will be a slouchy housewife (F, 41, SLC, 1940).

5166 If you can't light the fireplace, you won't have a happy marriage (M, 20, SLC, 1963).

## Mental and Emotional Ailments

5167 If you sing at the table, you'll marry a crazy person (F, 16, SLC, 1964).

5168 If a woman, while washing clothes, wets the front of her dress, she'll marry a drunkard (M, SLC, 1920). Brown 4721.

5169 If you sit on a table, you'll marry a drunkard (F, Ogden, 1961).

5170 When a girl (in Mexico) is making tortillas, she is careful not to spill flour. If she does, they believe that she will marry a drunkard (F, 20, SLC, 1964).

## Trade or Occupation, Financial Status

5171 Count the buttons on your clothing saying: "Rich man, poor man, beggarman, thief; doctor, lawyer, merchant, chief." On the last button whichever is named will be your future husband's profession (F, SLC, 1957). Brown 4727.

5172 On reeds you find, count the separations as "Rich man, poor man, beggarman, thief, doctor, lawyer, merchant, chief--" The last one is the one you marry (F, 54, SLC, 1963); Pull petals out of a flower saying "Rich man," etc. . . . (F, 64, SLC, 1964). Cf. Brown 4728.

5173 Breaking a heel off your shoe while walking means you'll marry a lawyer (F, 60, Midvale).

5174 If your shoe wears at the side, you'll be a poor man's bride (M, 78, SLC, 1906).

5175 She who takes the last piece of bread on the plate will get a ten thousand-dollar man (M, SLC, 1961). Cf. Brown 4735.

5176 A marriage will never succeed if the wife is rich and the husband poor (F, SLC, 1964).

5177 If you put a penny in your shoe when you marry, it means your marriage will financially prosper (F, SLC, 1962).

5178 When other people see a single girl's hope chest, they throw a silver piece, rice and Jordan almonds into the lace. This denotes that when married she will never lack money, she will multiply as the rice, and be sweet and have a sweet marriage as the Jordan almonds (F, Gr, SLC, 1961).

## Miscellaneous

5179 If two people in the same family marry the same year, it means the marriages will fail (F, Gr, Magna, 1930).

5180 A woman who tries on a widow's cap before she is married is sure to be a widow within the first few years of her marriage (F, SLC, 1950); . . . tries on a widow's hat soon after she's married . . . (F, 52, W. Jordan, 1960).

5181 A woman born with a "V"-shaped hairline will be a young widow (F, 40, Payson, 1940); . . . whose hair grows in a low point in the center of her forehead . . . (F, 17, Ogden, 1958).

5182 A woman with a "widow's peak" will lose her first husband but will quickly remarry (F, 34, Willow Creek, 1939).

5183 A woman with black hair will outlive her husband (F, SLC, 1964).

5184 If they bury the dead person with the wedding ring on, the spouse never gets married (F, 38, Gr, SLC, 1963).

5185 He who married a widow will often have a dead man's head in his dish (F, SLC, 1961).

## ORDER AND TIME OF MARRIAGE, DELAYED MARRIAGE

## Body and Clothing Indicators

5186 If you fall up stairs, you won't get married for seven years (F, SLC, 1957); . . . you will not marry within the year (F, Axtell, 1958). Cf. Brown 4629.

5187 If you fall up stairs, you will get married soon (F, SLC, 1915); Stumble on the stairs, be married within the year (F, 80, Midvale); . . . get married very shortly (F, 19, SLC, 1964).

5188 If you fall down the stairs, you will be a bride within a year (F, SLC, 1962).

5189 If a couple stumble on the sidewalk, they will be married soon (F, SLC, 1962).

5190 If you are trying on a dress and a pin sticks you, you will not marry that year (M, SLC, 1961).

5191 When you go to bed, point your shoes to the west and you will be married within a year (F, 21, Logan, 1960).

## Animal Indicators

5192 The first person that a cat looks toward after washing its face will be the next to marry (SLC, 1959). Brown 4469.

5193    If you tie a knot in a horse's tail, you will marry within a year (F, 54, SLC, 1964).

5194    If two people pull on a wishbone, the one who gets the short end will marry first (F, 20, SLC, 1964).

## Food and Drink

5195    When bread is passed at a dinner, the one taking the last slice of bread from the plate will be married next (F, Murray, 1915); If an old maid takes the last piece of bread, she won't get married this year (F, SLC, 1959).

5196    If you "eat" the dime out of the plum pudding, you'll be the next to marry (F, 60, Ogden, 1970).

5197    If you get an almond in your porridge (cereal), you'll be married within the year (M, 27, Croydon, 1965).

5198    The person who gets the last drink out of a bottle is going to be the next person to get married (M, 29, SLC, 1964).

## The Domestic Scene

5199    A person who sits on a table will soon marry (F, Logan, 1957); If you sit on the table, you'll be married before you're able (F, 53, Ogden, 1963). Brown 4608.

5200    If you sit on the dining room table, you will not be married for at least a year (M, 56, Mt. Pleasant, 1965); . . . marry within a year (F, 20, Du, SLC, 1963). Brown 4609.

5201    If you sit on a corner of the table to eat, you'll not marry for seven years (M, 52, Du, SLC, 1964).

5202    If at a meal, an unmarried person is placed between a man and wife, the individual so seated will be married within the year (M, 23, SLC, 1962).

5203    When you spill the toothpicks, as many as remain will be the years before you marry (F, Weber Co).

5204    If you break a mirror, you won't marry for seven years (F, 26, Morgan, 1965).

5205    A person whose chair falls backward as he or she rises will be married during the year (M, SLC, 1957). Cf. Brown 4613.

5206    If you sweep under someone's feet, they'll be the last one married in the house (F, 46, Bingham, 1925). Cf. Brown 4619.

5207    If you are single and you enter a home where a woman is sweeping the floor, you will not get married that year (F, 53, Monroe, 1964).

5208    If you meet someone sweeping dirt out the door, you won't get married during the year (F, Bear River City, 1957).

5209    If one walks over a pile of sweepings he won't get married for seven years (F, Midvale, 1932).

5210    If a girl's dishwater boils, she will not get married that year (F, Norw, SLC, 1959).

## Nuptial Events

5211    At a bridal shower the one who brought the first gift that is opened will be the next to marry (F, Ogden, 1969).

5212    Sleep on wedding cake and you will be married or engaged within the year (F, Moab, 1953).

5213    The person who gets the first piece of wedding cake will be the next person to marry (F, 22, SLC, 1955).

5214    If a single girl puts a piece of her best friend's cake under her pillow, she will be the next bride (F, 23, Murray, 1959); . . . she will marry soon (F, 22, SLC, 1964).

5215    Bake a ring in the wedding cake, and the one who gets the slice containing the ring will be married next (F, SLC, 1959). Brown 4847.

5216    The girl who receives from the bride a piece of cheese cut before leaving the table, will be the next bride among the company (M, SLC, 1960).

5217    The bride throws an old shoe into the crowd at her wedding; the one who catches it will be the next to marry (F, SLC, 1961); . . . the right foot bridal shoe . . . (F, Bingham, 1960).

5218    All the girls that are ready to get married must write their names in pencil on a piece of paper. This is put in the bride's shoe, and the first name that is rubbed off is the first girl that will get married (F, Gr, SLC, 1962).

5219    A bride writes the names of her bridesmaids on the sole of the shoe she is to wear the day of her marriage ceremony. The first name to wear off will be the next bride (F, Gr, Magna, 1961).

5220    If the bride's flowers are worn by a person, then that person will marry in a year (M, SLC, 1961).

5221    Just before a bride is ready to leave with the groom on their honeymoon, the bride tosses her bouquet. The girl to catch it will be the next one married. The bride and groom ride away in a car with old tin cans tied on behind and lettering of "Just Married" all over the car. Rice is tossed as they leave showering them with it, in the belief their marriage will be blessed with children (F, 54, Logan, 1970). Brown 4854.

5222    The bridesmaid that catches the bride's bouquet will be the next one married (F, SLC, 1948); The girl in attendance who catches . . . (M, SLC, 1957). Brown 4855.

5223 The usher who snatches the garter will be next in line as a bridegroom (M, SLC, 1932).

5224 The boy who catches the bride's garter thrown by the groom is the next to be married (F, SLC, 1958); The attendant to the groom . . . (F, 1960).

5225 The bride should wear a blue garter, and after the wedding throw it to the male members, and whoever catches it, the next one he dates, he will marry (F, SLC, 1961).

5226 If you catch the jeweled hairpin which the bride throws (instead of the bouquet), you will be married next (F, Provo, 1959).

5227 If a bride is robbed of all the pins about her dress by a single woman, all who pass one of the pins will be married within a year (M, SLC, 1960).

5228 If you lend something to a bride or groom before the wedding, you will be married within one year (M, SLC, 1961).

5229 The first young couple to leave the wedding will be the next to marry (F, Bountiful, 1960).

5230 If you sign the bridal book first, you'll be the last one married (F, Midvale, 1958).

5231 The unmarried man who touches the groom last on the wedding night will be the next to marry (M, SLC, 1961).

## Miscellaneous

5232 He who marries late marries bad (M, 19, Brigham, 1951).

5233 If a couple elopes to get married, they will have bad luck in marriage (M, SLC, 1959).

5234 If a girl is kissed seven times in one day, she will marry within the year (M, 54, Magna, 1923); . . . kissed seven times under the mistletoe on the same day . . . (F, 70, Bountiful, 1900s); . . . kissed more than seven times in one day (F, SLC, 1960).

5235 A dime, a penny, a button, a thimble, and a ring are put in our birthday cakes. The person who gets the thimble is the old maid; the button, the bachelor; the ring, the first one married; the dime, the rich man; the penny, the poor man (F, SLC, 1957).

5236 When going over a railroad track while riding in a car, all of the unmarried women in the car should lift up their feet from the floor. This means they will get married soon (F, Logan, 1970).

5237 If you see three one-lighted cars in one night, you will be married within six months (F, 27, Copperton, 1948).

5238 If the first person a single woman sees outside her doorway on Valentine's Day is a woman, she won't be married that year. If it's a man, she'll be married within three months (M, SLC, 1959).

5239 If an unmarried woman sees a cornerstone being laid, she will not marry for at least a year (M, SLC, 1964).

## Postponed Wedding

5240 If a wedding is postponed, bad luck will follow (M, SLC, 1959); . . . it's a bad omen (F, 30, SLC, 1963); . . . your marriage will be unhappy (F, SLC, 1964); . . . the marriage will never take place (F, SLC, 1959). Brown 4751.

5241 If you postpone a marriage three times, you will never be married (F, SLC, 1961). Brown 4752.

## Weather

5242 The weather on the wedding day determines the future happiness of the bride and groom (F, Ogden, 1961). Brown 4777.

5243 If a bride's wedding day is bright and beautiful, her wedded life will be happy (F, SLC, 1942).

## Sunshiny Weather

5244 If a bride is married on a sunny day, she'll have a life full of sunshine (F, 22, SLC, 1964); . . . good luck and happiness will follow (M, SLC, 1956); . . . the future will be bright (F, SLC, 1961). Brown 4782f.

5245 A bright beautiful, sunny day--no clouds in the sky--means the couple will be happy forever (F, 19, Logan, 1972).

5246 If on the day you get married the sun is shining, the marriage will be long and happy (F, 72, SLC, 1900).

5247 The sun always shines on a happy bride (F, Roosevelt, 1961).

5248 Happy is the bride the sun shines on; sunshine on her wedding day means many children and a happy marriage (F, Farmington, 1959).

5249 The bride the sun shines on will travel far (F, 67, Panguitch).

## Rainy Weather

5250 Happy is the bride the rain falls on (F, 50, SLC, 1963).

5251 If a young couple gets married on a rainy day, they will have good luck through their marriage (F, 51, Centerfield, 1964); When there is rain on the wedding night, it means good luck for a long and prosperous marriage (M, 26, Bountiful, 1958).

5252 If it rains on your wedding day, your love will stay forever (F, 47, Swiss, SLC, 1965).

5253 If a bride gets rain in her veil, it means happiness (M, 18, Norw, SLC, 1965).

5254   It's bad luck to have rain on a wedding day (F, 65, SLC, 1965).  Cf. Brown 4784, 8550.

5255   Happy is the bride the sun shines on and sad is the bride it rains on (F, 45, SLC, 1964).  Brown 4785.

5256   If it rains on your wedding day, it means tears will be shed (F, Ogden, 1961); . . . you will shed as many tears as it rained that day (F, 50, SLC, 1958); . . . the couple will have sorrows (F, SLC, 1961).  Brown 4791.

5257   It is not supposed to rain on a wedding day, or the bride will cry for one month (M, 52, SLC, 1964).  Cf. Brown 4790.

5258   The bride who marries on a rainy day will have a stormy married life (F, 65, SLC, 1945).

5259   If it rains on the wedding day, gloom throughout the marriage is inevitable (F, SLC, 1962).  Cf. Brown 4788.

5260   If it rains on your wedding day, you will have an unhappy marriage (F, 75, Pleasant Grove, 1906); . . . your marriage will not be successful (F, 26, SLC, 1964); . . . you will have an unhappy life (M, 53, SLC, 1964).  Cf. Brown 4789.

5261   It is said that when the bride is married on a rainy night, she will be a cranky wife (F, Gr, SLC, 1962).

5262   A rainy wedding day makes the skies of marriage grey (F, Eng, SLC, 1965).

5263   If you get married on a rainy day, your marriage won't last (F, 52, SLC, 1964).

Weather, Phases of the Moon, Etc.

5264   If the wind blows toward a couple getting married, it means bad luck (F, 63, Monroe, 1964).

5265   If a couple marries on a stormy day, they will have an unhappy marriage (M, 30, SLC, 1956).

5266   To marry in a storm betokens an unhappy life (F, SLC, 1961).

5267   Snow falling on the wedding day means great happiness (M, SLC, 1917); . . . on the wedding night means a happy marriage (F, SLC, 1944).  Cf. Brown 4730.

5268   A snow storm brings luck on your wedding day (M, 44, SLC, 1964).

5269   If it snows on your wedding day, you will have lots of money (F, 18, SLC, 1964).

5270   A marriage under a new moon will be a successful one, but under a full moon, love diminishes with its size (F, 19, SLC, 1964).  Cf. Brown 4779.

5271   When a couple is married when there is a full moon, the marriage will be very happy (F, SLC, 1959).

5272   It's bad luck to get married when there is only part of a moon.  There should be a full moon (F, Brigham, 1959).

5273   Don't get married on the last quarter of the moon because you can't have children (F, 38, Gr, SLC, 1963).

TIME OF WEDDING

Seasons, Months

5274   If you marry when the year is new, your mate will always be constant, kind and true (F, Brigham, 1929).

5275   If you marry in January, you will be widowed before your prime (M, SLC, 1960); . . . wounded before your prime (F, 1960).  Cf. Brown 4764.

5276   If you are widowed and marry in January, you'll tread in time together (F, 75, SLC, 1964).

5277   Marry in February and you'll tread in time together (F, 84, SLC, 1905).

5278   If you marry in February, you will be together for life (M, Ir, SLC, 1960).

5279   A St. Valentine's Day for weddings is charming (F, SLC, 1961).

5280   It's bad luck to marry during Lent (M, Ogden, 1961); If you marry in Lent,/You will live to repent (M, 23, Midvale, 1964).  Brown 4765.

5281   Marry in March and you will be on a distant shore (F, 75, SLC, 1964); . . . your home will be in a foreign land (M, Ir, SLC, 1960).

5282   A wedding in either April or June is likely to succeed, but a marriage in March is unlucky (F, 41, SLC, 1964).

5283   If you marry in April, your life will be like a checkered path (F, Ir, SLC, 1960).

5284   Marriage in April means a happy life (F, 84, SLC, 1910); . . . you will have a happy path ahead of you (F, SLC, 1961).

5285   It is unlucky to be married in May (F, SLC, 1961); If you marry in May,/You'll rue the day (F, Ir, SLC, 1960); . . . repent always (F, 19, Orem).  Brown 4767.

5286   Marriage in May will soon decay (F, Logan, 1960).

5287   May is the month to marry bad wives (F, 1957).

5288   If you're married in May, you'll be surrounded with strangers (F, 75, Gunnison, 1920s).

5289   It is unlucky for a couple to marry in the month with a letter "A" in it, such as May (F, 27, Scot, SLC, 1963).

5290   A bridal dress is never cut out in the month of May, and no one is supposed to get married in the month of May. Everything is done before the month of May, or it is bad luck (F, Gr, SLC, 1962).

5291 Do not wed in May, because animals mate during this month (jackasses) (M, 32, Gr, SLC, 1963).

5292 It is unlucky to marry on May 3rd (M, SLC, 1961).

5293 June is the month of love and marriage (F, SLC, 1961); If you marry in June, you will have a happy, romantic marriage (F, SLC, 1958); A June bride is a lucky bride (F, 63, Fremont, 1920); For best success, marry in June (F, Provo, 1960). Brown 4769f.

5294 If a girl marries in June, her husband will be good to her (F, 65, SLC, 1932).

5295 It is lucky for a bride to be married on a sunny June day, because Juno is the goddess of women, and happy is the bride the sun shines on (F, Brigham City, 1960).

5296 Marriage in June is very lucky because it means happiness for the bride and prosperity for the groom (F, SLC, 1941); Marriage during the month with the longest day of the year is a happy symbol of a long successful married life (F, 48, SLC, 1964).

5297 Marry in June and life will be one long honeymoon (F, SLC, 1961).

5298 If you marry in July, your life will be full of bitterness (F, Ir, SLC, 1960).

5299 Sweet memories come with a July marriage (F, 63, Fremont, 1920).

5300 Marriage in August will be with a girl who has been your good friend (F, SLC, 1961).

5301 If you marry in August, you are guaranteed the love of your spouse (F, Ir, SLC, 1960).

5302 Marriage in September will bring a smooth and serene life (M, 86, SLC, 1910).

5303 If you marry in September, your life will be sour (F, Ir, SLC, 1960).

5304 Marriage in October will find you hardships (F, SLC, 1961).

5305 If you marry in November, you will have great fortune (F, Ir, SLC, 1960).

5306 If you marry in December, there will be growing love in marriage (F, Ir, SLC, 1960); . . . you will make a happier marriage year by year (F, SLC, 1961).

5307 Marriage on the last day of the year means good luck (M, 86, SLC, 1910); . . . brings bad luck (F, SLC, 1961).

5308 If married on Christmas, you'll have a happy life (F, SLC, 1961).

5309 Never get married on your birthday (F, 26, SLC, 1964).

5310 Marriage on the third of the month is always unlucky (M, 21, SLC, 1963).

5311 Tuesday the thirteenth is an unlucky day, and few marry on that day (F, SLC, 1964).

5312 The thirteenth day of the month is a bad day to be married on (F, SLC, 1961).

## Days of the Week, Time of Day

5313 A Sunday marriage is a happy omen (M, 44, SLC, 1964).

5314 It's bad luck to get married on a Monday (F, 20, SLC, 1964).

5315 Marry on a Monday for wealth (F, 75, SLC, 1964). Brown 4771.

5316 Health accompanies a Tuesday wedding (F, 49, SLC, 1964). Brown 4771.

5317 To be married on a Tuesday is lucky for the marriage (F, 52, SLC, 1930).

5318 Don't marry on Tuesday, for it is bad luck (M, Ogden, 1960); It is a bad omen to start a marriage on Tuesday (M).

5319 You should get married on a Wednesday (F, Richfield, 1940); . . . for the best of all (F, 75, Gunnison, 1964). Brown 4771.

5320 Marry on Thursday for crosses (F, 75, Gunnison, 1964). Brown 4771.

5321 Don't get married on Friday, or it won't last (F, Ogden, 1935).

5322 Marry on a Friday for losses (F, 75, SLC, 1964). Brown 4771.

5323 It is unlucky to get married on Friday the thirteenth (M, 65, Pleasant Grove, 1910); . . . the couple will always have bad luck (M, SLC, 1961).

5324 It is never wise to marry on a Friday because of what happened on Good Friday (F, It, SLC, 1961). Brown 4773.

5325 If the marriage occurs on Saturday, it is bad luck and means hard work for life (F, SLC, 1961); A Saturday flit makes a short sit. Get married on Saturday, and it won't last (F, 45, SLC, 1933). Brown 4774.

5326 Marry on Monday, you have far to go; marry on Tuesday, a tale of woe; marry on Wednesday, fair and sunny; marry on Thursday, pinch every penny; marry on Friday, sure to bode well; marry on Saturday, ne'er do well; marry on Sunday, stay close to heaven (F, It, SLC, 1960).

5327 Wedding day: Monday for wealth; Tuesday for health; Wednesday's the best day of all; Thursday for crosses; Friday for losses; and Saturday for no luck at all (F, Porterville, 1964); If you are going to marry pick your choice. If you marry on Monday, etc. . . . . Thursday is crossed; Friday is lost; Saturday is not lucky (F, SLC, 1962). Learned in Georgia, 1919. Brown 4771.

5328 Getting married before breakfast is unlucky (F, SLC, 1959).

5329 An early morning wedding will bring luck day after day (M, 44, SLC, 1920).

5330 Wedding after sunset entails a bride to a joyless life, the loss of children, or an early death (F, Swiss, St. George, 1961).  Brown 4778.

5331  Marry when the hands of the clock start upward, and your marriage will always be happy.  Marry when the hands start downward, and it will be filled with sadness (M, Park City, 1957).

## WEDDING CEREMONY

### Before the Wedding

5332  It is bad luck for a girl to buy silver for her trousseau (F, SLC, 1957).

5333  You will have lots of happiness if you break dishes for the bride and groom the night before their wedding (F, SLC, 1960).

5334  It is bad luck to break a lot of old china on the wedding eve (M, Ger, SLC, 1938).

5335  To burn an old shoe before marriage brings good luck (F, SLC, 1961).

5336  Saturday night, the night before you get married, you go to the bride's house and get all of her dowry.  This is transported to the groom's house, and a big party goes on.  They scatter everything, and even decorate the bed with pins underneath and with candy-covered almonds which have their names written on them (F, Gr, SLC, 1962).

5337  On the eve of your wedding, smear your feet with soot as you stretch out on the floor and you will always have a good and successful marriage (F, Ogden, 1961).

5338  If a cat sneezes on the day before a wedding, the bride will be lucky in her marriage (F, Ogden, 1961).

5339  The evening before the ceremony the groom should spend with men friends at a bachelor dinner.  He should not see the bride until the ceremony (F, SLC, 1960).  (The observance of this time-honored separation ritual in Utah is likely to be much more circumspect than similar rituals in the Latin countries such as the despido del novio of Spain and Spanish America, and the enterrement de garçon of France.  --Eds.)

5340  If the groom kisses the bride the day before wedding, the marriage will be a bad one (F, SLC, 1930); . . . the marriage will be rocky and stormy (F, 45, SLC, 1932).

5341  The bride and groom should not look at the moon over their left shoulder the evening before the day of marriage (F, SLC, 1960).

5342  It is bad luck for a groom to see his bride on the day of the wedding before the ceremony takes place (F, 54, Logan, 1970); The bride cannot see the groom . . . (F, SLC, 1946); . . . or bad luck will occur at the wedding ceremony (F, 19, SLC, 1955); . . . or it will spoil the marriage (F, 65, SLC, 1925); . . . or the marriage will be unsuccessful (F,

SLC, 1925); . . . or the marriage will not be a happy one (F, 22, SLC, 1965); . . . or the family will have bad luck (F, Brigham City, 1960).

### Wedding Rehearsal, Wedding Attendants

5343  It is bad luck to rehearse a wedding (F, SLC, 1961); . . . bad luck for a bride to rehearse her own wedding (F, SLC, 1930); It will bring an unhappy marriage . . . (F, SLC, 1959).

5344  It is lucky to have seven bridesmaids (M, SLC, 1959).

5345  It is bad luck to be a bridesmaid more than three times (F, SLC, 1959).

5346  The best man's duties are defending the bridegroom from a rival who might carry off the bride, as well as leading the bride to church (M, SLC, 1964).

5347  Legend has it that the best man was expected to bring the groom to the altar, by force in event of a change of mind.  Families in early days took no chances on brides being abandoned at the altar (F, 1960).

### Wedding Day

5348  A bride is supposed to be sure to jump out of bed on both feet on the morning of her wedding.  This is to prevent her from starting off her marriage "on the wrong foot" (F, 22, SLC, 1960).

5349  If on a girl's wedding morning the song of birds awakens her, or swallows fly past her window at dawn, this is an omen of good fortune (M, SLC, 1920).

5350  If the bride breaks a dish at her wedding breakfast, she will have an unlucky marriage (M, Honeyville, 1905).

5351  It is bad luck for a bride to go out the back door (M, Eng, SLC, 1958).

5352  Be sure that on your marriage day you do not go in one door and out another or you will always be unlucky (F, Norw, Provo, 1961).

5353  The bride-to-be was supposed to carry a bucket of water to her mother-in-law's house.  She would leave the water on the porch.  After she was married, she was able to enter the house (F, Gr, SLC, 1962).

5354  It will bring bad luck if the bride and bridegroom part the day they are married (F, SLC, 1961).

5355  Have a happily married man comb the bride's hair to insure happiness (M, 20, SLC, 1963).

5356  Pearls mean tears; do not wear them on your wedding day (F, 35, Magna, 1964).

5357  If drunk is the groom, then bad is the marriage (M, 44, SLC, 1964).

5358  If either bride or groom spills salt on their wedding day, it means bad luck will follow unless they take a pinch of it and throw it over their left shoulder to break the spell (F, Ir, SLC, 1960).

5359 When bride and groom speak together and say the same words at the same time, they should stop and exchange a kiss before going on or they will quarrel (F, Ger, SLC, 1960).

5360 Nothing but happy thoughts the day you are wed will bring you a lifetime of happiness (F, SLC, 1941).

5361 They do not permit an orphan to help the bride before the wedding, because this will bring bad luck to the bride (F, 62, Gr, SLC, 1963).

5362 If you dance in the sunshine on your wedding day, your marriage won't last (M, 38, professor, Norw, SLC, 1963).

5363 If a bride or a groom sneezes on the wedding day, they will have a marriage full of bad luck and unhappiness (F, SLC, 1960).

5364 To laugh on your wedding day will cause you to have unhappiness (F, SLC, 1961). Cf. Brown 4848.

5365 Should a dog pass between a couple on their wedding day, it means bad luck for the wedding (F, SLC, 1955).

5366 It makes for good luck for the family cat to be at the wedding (M, SLC, 1961).

5367 It is lucky for the bride if a cat sneezes in her house on the day of her wedding (F, 21, SLC, 1958); If a cat . . . it means a long, happy married life for the bride (F, SLC, 1959).

5368 If a cat sneezes on the day of a marriage, the bride will be unlucky in her marriage (F, SLC, 1961).

5369 It is unlucky if the bride does not weep bitterly on her wedding day (F, 86, SLC, 1949).

5370 If you cry on your wedding day, it will mean you will have a long marriage (F, SLC, 1961).

5371 If you cry on your wedding day, you will have unhappy wedding anniversaries (F, SLC, 1959); . . . a sorrowful married life (F, SLC, 1957); . . . you will cry all your marriage through (F, 1960).

5372 If the wedding is taking place in the house, no one is supposed to open any trunk on the day of the wedding (F, 38, Gr, SLC, 1963).

5373 Once you have left your home on your wedding day, do not return, for bad luck awaits you (F, 27, SLC, 1959).

## Looking in the Mirror

5374 A bride will have bad luck if she looks in a mirror after she is fully dressed in her wedding dress (F, 48, Midvale, 1938); . . . will make an unlucky marriage . . . (F, SLC, 1961).

5375 If a bride looks into a mirror as the last act before she takes her marriage

vows, she will have bad luck in the marriage (F, SLC, 1953).

5376 It is unlucky for the bride to look in the mirror before she leaves for the church (F, Brigham City, 1960).

5377 It is unlucky for the groom to see himself fully dressed in a mirror before the wedding ceremony (F, SLC, 1961).

## Wedding Clothes and Accessories

5378 It is unlucky to try on any wedding garments in a trousseau until the wedding day (F, SLC, 1959).

5379 The groom buys the bride's wedding clothes. This makes him the complete boss (F, 55, Magna, 1964).

5380 The bride should wear something at her wedding belonging to a happily married friend (F, 40, SLC, 1943).

5381 The bride should not put on all her wedding articles at the same time (F, 52, Eng, SLC, 1963).

## "Something Old, Something New," Etc.

5382 A girl should wear something old at her wedding for good luck (M, Murray, 1958).

5383 Something old transfers happiness from an older woman to the bride (M, 20, SLC, 1963).

5384 Something new at a wedding denotes an unspoiled beginning (M, 20, SLC, 1963).

5385 A girl should wear something new at her wedding for good luck in her marriage (M, Murray, 1958).

5386 A girl should carry something borrowed at her wedding for good luck (M, Murray, 1958). Cf. Brown 4818.

5387 A girl should wear something blue at her wedding for good luck (M, Murray, 1958).

5388 Brides wear a blue garter for "something blue" (F, SLC, 1964).

5389 The bride should never wear a borrowed yellow garter on her wedding day (F, SLC, 1962).

5390 For a successful wedding wear something old, something new, something borrowed, and something blue (F, 60, Ogden, 1970); For good luck and a happy marriage . . . (F, 65, SLC, 1965); Something old . . . at a wedding will bring good fortune (F, 51, SLC, 1964). Brown 4819.

5391 A bride wears something old, something new, something borrowed, something blue and a penny in her shoe (F, 22, SLC); . . . a sixpence in her shoe (F, Brigham City, 1960); . . . penny in the right shoe (M, Sandy, 1964). Cf. Brown 4820f.

5392 If you wear something old, something new, something blue and something borrowed on your wedding night, then you will have a successful marriage (F, 46, SLC, 1964).

5393  For a lucky married life, the bride
should wear:  something pink, something
blue, something old, something new,
something borrowed, something bought (F,
23, SLC, 1963).

5394  The bride is supposed to wear something
old, something new, something borrowed
and something blue to her reception (F,
Springville, 1960).

## The Wedding Gown

5395  It is bad luck for a bride to sew her
own wedding gown (F, 24, SLC, 1958).

5396  If a thimble is lost while making a
wedding dress for a bride, the bride
will have good luck (F, Joseph, 1964).

5397  When a bride-to-be went to a seamstress
to prepare for the making of the wedding
gown, members of both sides of the
families (the bride and groom) met at
the seamstress's home.  The bride cut
into the fabric first, and members of
the families showered the seamstress
with money (F, 49, Gr, Midvale, 1964).

5398  A stitch added to the bride's dress just
before she leaves for the church will
bring her good luck (F, SLC, 1959).

5399  If you try on your wedding dress just
before the ceremony, you will not be
happy (F, 49, SLC, 1964); . . . will
bring bad luck to the marriage (F, 22,
SLC, 1962); . . . will cause unhappiness
and disappointment (F, Provo, 1960);
. . . be an unlucky bride (F, Brigham
City, 1960).  Cf. Brown 4798.

5400  A groom should never see the bride's
wedding dress before the wedding or else
they will have bad luck in their
marriage (F, 19, SLC, 1961); . . . it
will bring unhappiness (F, 21, SLC,
1964); . . . the wedding won't come to
pass (M, SLC, 1959).

5401  It is bad luck for a bride to show her
bridegroom her wedding dress even in
pictures before they are being married
(M, 53, SLC, 1935).

5402  If a woman tears or splits any part of
her wedding ensemble, she will be
illtreated by her husband (F, Brigham
City, 1960).

5403  If the hem on the bride's wedding dress
gets turned up, and the bride sees this,
she can have a wish and it will be
granted on that night of her wedding.
She must make her wish before the hem
falls back down or it will not come true
(F, 21, SLC, 1957).

5404  If a bride tears her bridal dress, it is
a sign of much worry (F, 46, SLC, 1940).
Cf. Brown 4824.

5405  When she changes her wedding dress, the
bride must throw away every pin used or
she will have bad luck (F, 22, SLC).

5406  In a large family of girls, it is good
luck for them all to wear the same
wedding dress.  The best situation is
for the dress to be one that has been in
the family for several generations (M,
49, SLC).

5407  If a bride puts on another wedding dress
other than her own, on her wedding day,
then she will have bad luck on her
wedding day (F, Gr, SLC, 1960).

5408  A bride must never wear her wedding gown
after the wedding (F, Provo).

## Color of the Wedding Gown

5409  The bride wears white when she first
gets married.  Red or black and other
colors are not worn when she first gets
married (M, SLC, 1962).

5410  It is bad luck for her life, if a bride
chooses to be married in any dress other
than a white one (F, 21, SLC, 1964).

5411  White is the color of innocence, thus a
bride's dress is white (F, Porterville,
1964); . . . a white gown for purity (F,
SLC, 1962); A white wedding dress means
a bride is a virgin (F, 40, SLC, 1943);
. . . signifies chastity (M, 24, SLC,
1964).

5412  Wearing white on your wedding day will
bring you bad luck (F, 22, SLC).

5413  If a woman has had marital relations
prior to being married, she should not
be married in white, or she will have a
marriage full of sorrow (F, SLC, 1961).

5414  Never wear white at your second wedding
(F, 61, Ogden, 1940).

5415  It's bad luck for a bride to wear black
(F); If a bride wears black it's bad
luck for the rest of her life (F, 19,
SLC, 1961).  Cf. Brown 4804.

5416  Never wear black at a wedding, or it
will bring bad luck to the couple being
married.  If the couple wears black, it
means that they will live a short life,
or will have a short marriage (F,
Sevier, 1964); . . . the couple will
have a troubled marriage for one year
(F, 20, SLC, 1963).

5417  A bride's wedding dress used to be red,
as that was a sign of youth.  White used
to be considered a sign of mourning (F,
Ogden, 1958).

5418  If you get married in red, your married
life will be sad (M, SLC, 1957).

5419  Never wear red as a wedding dress.  It
signifies adultery or a "scarlet past"
(F, 20, SLC, 1963).

5420  Getting married for the first time in a
red dress will bring bad luck to the
marriage (F, 18, SLC, 1964).

5421  Unlucky will be the bride who marries in
green (F, SLC, 1961).

5422  If the bride has anything green in her
trousseau, she will have bad luck (M,
20, SLC, 1958).

5423  It is bad luck to be married in yellow
(F, Tooele, 1957).

5424  Wearing blue for your second marriage is
supposed to insure happiness and success
with your second husband (F, Logan,
1958).

5425 Yellow's forsaken, and green's foresworn, but blue and red ought to be worn (F, Brigham City, 1960).

5426 Marry in yellow, you'll get the wrong fellow; marry in blue, he'll always be true; marry in green, ashamed to be seen; marry in black, you're on the wrong track; marry in white, you'll always be right (F, Bear River City, 1957).

5427 Marry in yellow, you'll lose your fellow; marry in blue, he'll always be true; marry in pink, his feet will stink; marry in green, you're not fit to be seen; marry in white, everything's right (M, Tooele, 1957).

5428 Marry in white, everything right; marry in blue, lover be true; marry in pink, spirits will sink; marry in grey, live far away; marry in brown, live out of town; marry in black, wish you were back; marry in red, wish you were dead (F, Clearfield, 1959). Cf. Brown 4801ff.

5429 Marry in white, choose the right; marry in blue, always be true; marry in green, you'll never be seen; marry in brown, you'll live downtown; marry in black, you'll live in a shack; marry in pink, you'll smother in mink; marry in tan, he'll be a good man; marry in red, you'll wish you were dead; marry in pearl, you'll be in a whirl; marry in grey, you'll live far away (F, SLC, 1961).

5430 Married in black, you'll ride in a hack; married in pearl, you'll live in a whirl; married in pink, your spirits will sink; married in brown, you'll live out of town (F, Brigham City, 1960).

5431 Marry in white, you will live in delight (F, Scot-Ir, SLC, 1960).

5432 It is unlucky for a wedding guest to be dressed in black (M, Roosevelt, 1964); . . . , for it will bring sorrow to the bride (F, 19, SLC); . . . unlucky for guests to be in green or black (F, 85, SLC, 1964).

## The Bridal Veil

5433 The bridal veil is a symbol of virginity, and if the bride wears it falsely, her marriage will be unsuccessful (F, 22, SLC, 1963); . . . veil signifies chastity (F, 25, SLC, 1964).

5434 It is bad luck for a bride to put on the veil herself (M, Ger, SLC, 1938).

5435 It is bad luck for anyone to see a bride's dress, or for the groom to see her veil, before the wedding (F, 19, SLC, 1964).

5436 A bride wears a veil to protect her from evil spirits (M, 20, SLC, 1963); . . . to guard against the evil eye (F, SLC, 1962); . . . to keep the devil away (F, SLC, 1962).

5437 If the bride's veil is accidentally burned during the wedding ceremony, it means misfortune awaits her (F, Magna, 1929).

5438 If the candles at the marriage ceremony set the bride's veil on fire while she is at the altar, the marriage will be a failure (F, Gr, SLC, 1959).

5439 The ladies who prepare the wedding veil offer money for the bride in order to have good luck (M, 66, Gr, SLC, 1963).

5440 A newly married bride should never take off her wedding veil and comb her hair after the marriage ceremony, for a person near her can take the hair left on the comb and bewitch evil on the bride (F, Gr, SLC, 1961).

5441 After the wedding is over everyone helps tear up the veil for good luck (M, Ger, SLC, 1962).

## Shoes, Footgear

5442 A bride will have good luck in her married life if she wears old shoes when she gets married (F, 19, SLC, 1961).

5443 Old shoes will bring a bride and groom prosperity (F, 64, SLC, 1964).

5444 A bride who marries in old shoes is unlucky (F, Ogden, 1961).

5445 You should not wear your wedding shoes before your wedding. If you wear them before the ceremony, bad luck will follow you as you march down the aisle (F, 18, SLC, 1959).

5446 If a bride puts honey in the inner sole of the shoe she is to wear, she will have a sweet and happy marriage (F, Gr, Tooele, 1961).

5447 The bride wears a shiny new penny in her right slipper (F, 20, SLC, 1963); . . . sixpence . . . (F, 48, SLC, 1960).

5448 A penny is put in the bride's shoe for luck. If she can find a penny with her birth year on it, she'll have twice as much luck (F, 21, SLC, 1957).

5449 A bridegroom should give his bride a new penny to wear in her shoe at the wedding for good luck (M, 46, SLC).

5450 If the bride puts a penny in her shoe during the wedding and then gives it to the groom, and he wears it in his shoe, they will have good luck and fortune (F, 19, SLC, 1961).

5451 If a bride will place a penny in her shoe and keep it there during the wedding ceremony, she and her husband will never be poor (F, 21, Duchesne, 1970).

5452 If a bride will put a dime in her shoe when she is married, the marriage will be happy (F, 25, SLC, 1963).

5453 A penny in the shoe on the wedding day insures wealth (F, 20, SLC, 1963).

5454 If a bride places a silver coin in her shoe before the ceremony, she will have a happy and prosperous life (F, Brigham City, 1960). Cf. Brown 4827.

5455   If a father puts a penny in his daughter's shoe on her wedding day, it passes the love through the family (M, Ogden, 1961).

5456   If the groom's shoes are not shined, he will have bad luck in the wedding (M, SLC, 1961).

## Intimate Possessions, Jewelry

5457   The Mormon's undergarments (that look like Long Johns) are never taken off, not even while bathing, from the day of marriage until death (F, SLC, 1955).

5458   It brings good luck for a bride to carry another bride's handkerchief (F, SLC, 1961).

5459   Salt in a bride's left glove is a sign of loyalty (M, 20, SLC, 1963).

5460   It is bad luck for a bride to keep any of the pins that she used when she was married (M, SLC, 1961).

5461   The pearls a bride wears on her wedding day are the tears that she will shed (F, SLC, 1964).

## Bridal Bouquet, Flowers

5462   Knots in a bride's bouquet hold the wishes of her friends (F, 21, SLC, 1964).

5463   As many knots in the ribbons of a bride's bouquet, so many joys will be had in her married life (F, 20, SLC, 1963).

5464   A bride carries a bouquet for a fruitful marriage (F, 19, SLC, 1962).

5465   A bride who wears orange blossoms will have good luck (F, 43, SLC, 1937); . . . because the orange tree is believed to stand for a couple's everlasting love (F, 22, Sandy, 1957).

5466   Good luck is bestowed upon the girl that catches the bride's wedding bouquet (M, 22, SLC, 1954).

5467   The bride will throw one pomegranate in back of her. The fruit is thrown in place of the bridal bouquet (F, Gr, SLC, 1962).

## Wedding Gifts

5468   If a bride doesn't get something old for a wedding present, bad luck will follow (F, SLC, 1959).

5469   If newlyweds don't get a broom as a wedding gift, the bride will be a poor housekeeper (M, SLC, 1961).

5470   If someone gives you silver for a wedding present, you must send them a dime in return or have bad luck (F, SLC, 1966).

5471   If you give scissors or knives to a bride, it will cut your friendship (F, 48, SLC, 1963).

## Leaving for Church

5472   It is an old superstition that the bride must be led to the church between boys with bride laces tied with rosemary about their sleeves (F, Ger, Ogden, 1961).

5473   If you see a woman dressed completely in black on your way to your wedding, you will be a widow (F, SLC, 1961).

5474   If a white horse with a black rider passes the bridegroom going east or west, the bride and the marriage are cursed (F, 20, Springville, 1964); . . . the matrimony is forsaken (F, 16, SLC, 1964).

5475   On her wedding day the bride puts money in a round piece of white bread. As the bridal party walks to the church, if she is greeted by a young boy along the road, she gives him the bread, and she will have good luck throughout her marriage (F, SLC, 1969).

5476   It's a bad omen for two bridal processions to meet (F, SLC, 1963).

5477   It is unlucky for either the bride or groom to see a funeral on their wedding day. It promises a short life for whoever sees it first (F, Brigham City, 1960).

5478   It is unlucky for a pig to cross the path of a wedding party (F, Brigham, 1960).

5479   A marriage will be happy if the couple on the way to the church see a lizard (F, 66, Lawrence, 1920s).

5480   A marriage can never be happy if the bridal party on its way to the church sees a lizard cross its path (F, SLC, 1959).

## The Wedding Ceremony

5481   The bridegroom cannot see the bride before the wedding because they will never marry (M, 19, SLC, 1960). Cf. Brown 4760.

5482   During the marriage ceremony, the bride should have on her a small scissors, because if any curses are said during the ceremony, the scissors will cut them, and the curses will have no effect (F, Gr. SLC, 1957).

5483   It is lucky to carry a sprig of rosemary at a wedding (F, 19, SLC, 1963).

5484   A groom carries a lock of his bride's hair in his pocket during the ceremony to keep evil away (F, Gr, SLC, 1964).

5485   A candle should be lighted at the marriage ceremony to keep the evil spirits away from the bridal couple (M, SLC).

5486   In a Greek wedding ceremony the bride steps upon the foot of her husband. This is to keep him underfoot during their married life (F, Gr, SLC, 1964).

5487  If the officiating clergyman makes a mistake, someone is present who is opposed to the match (F, 45, SLC, 1950).

5488  During the wedding ceremony the bride should avoid looking at her reflection (F, 43, SLC, 1963).

5489  The bride walks on the left side of her father so that his right hand is free for combat (F, Eng, SLC, 1961).

5490  In a wedding, start down the aisle with the right foot (F, 51, SLC, 1965).

5491  A pinch of salt over the shoulder will make the groom happy in marriage (M, SLC, 1961).

5492  If you cry at your wedding, you will never be happy (F, 45, SLC, 1964); It is bad luck to cry when someone in your family marries (F, 45, SLC, 1964).

5493  If a bride doesn't shed tears at her wedding, she will be unhappy for the rest of her married years (F, 23, Bohem, SLC, 1964).

5494  If a marriage takes place while there is an open grave in the churchyard, it is a bad omen for the couple (F, SLC, 1949).

5495  The groom is supposed to kiss the bride for a happy and successful marriage (M, Tooele, 1944).

5496  A groom should be the first to kiss the bride (F, 44, Provo, 1956); The kiss symbolizes sealing of the marriage vows (F, Tooele, 1964).

5497  Good luck will come to the bride only if she is kissed in a church (F, SLC, 1961).

5498  Everyone attending a wedding must kiss the bride; then she will be a lucky bride bubbling with vigor and happiness her entire lifetime (F, 58, SLC, 1964).

5499  At a Jewish wedding, there is a small glass placed near the groom's left foot. Just before the Rabbi pronounces the couple man and wife, he is to stamp on the glass.  Their marriage will have as many years good luck and happiness as there are pieces of broken glass (M, SLC, 1957).

5500  It is an old wedding custom in the Czech ethnic group, that after the bride is proclaimed a wife, her husband puts a blue apron on her in order to symbolize that now she is a housewife (F, 21, Logan, 1973).

5501  At the conclusion of a Greek wedding ceremony the guests are given a favor of Jordan almonds.  They are good luck tokens (F, Gr, SLC, 1964).

## Wedding Ring

5502  If you wear a wedding ring, your marriage will succeed (F, Kearns, 1963).

5503  Marriage is not legal unless the ring is of gold (F, Ogden, 1961).

5504  It's bad luck for a girl to see her wedding ring before she marries (F, SLC, 1965).

5505  Never show anyone your wedding ring before your marriage, or it won't last (F, 19, SLC, 1960).

5506  In using a mother's wedding ring to be married some of their parent's good luck will rub off to the newly married couple (F, SLC, 1960).

5507  Never try on a wedding band before the wedding, or the marriage will be doomed (M); . . . this will bring the couple bad luck (F, Sandy, 1958).

5508  If you wear a ring on your left hand before you are married, your wedding ring will tarnish (M, SLC, 1964).

5509  Never wear another ring on your wedding ring finger, or you will never wear a wedding ring on it (F, SLC, 1961).

5510  If you let someone try on your wedding ring, you will have bad luck in your marriage (F, 41, SLC, 1964).

5511  It brings bad luck to a marriage if someone else wears your wedding band (M, Richfield, 1955).

5512  Never put on another person's wedding band, or your marriage will have bad luck (F, Morgan, 1961).

5513  Never try on another girl's wedding ring, or she will have more than one wedding (F, Murray, 1948).

5514  A wedding ring should be made specially for the bride, for if it is bought from a store it might have absorbed some bad luck from someone else's finger (F, Ogden, 1961).

5515  A diamond ring is the sign of loyal and everlasting love (M, SLC, 1960); . . . a long and faithful marriage (M, 19, Kearns, 1963).

5516  The diamond ring is worn on the left hand on the fourth finger, because it is thought to have a vein running directly to the heart.  The heart is the center of emotion, especially love (F, 22, Midvale, 1960); The wedding ring is worn inside the engagement ring because this puts the wedding ring closer to the heart (F, SLC, 1961); The wedding ring is placed on the left hand, because it is the shortest route to the heart (F, 19, SLC, 1949).

5517  The sparkling from the diamond protects the forthcoming bride from evil spirits (M, SLC, 1964).

5518  Never wear an opal for a wedding ring, for it brings bad luck (F, SLC, 1962).

5519  The exchanging of wedding rings is an outward bond of fidelity between the man and woman (F, SLC, 1964).

5520  A gold wedding ring signifies noble affection (F, 84, SLC, 1965).

5521  A round wedding ring means love will roundly flow from one to the other (F, SLC, 1964).

5522   The wedding ring is a symbol of a lasting marriage. It must be worn to keep love from escaping from the heart (F, Union, 1944).

5523   A wedding ring is customary because it symbolizes the circle of eternity (F, Brigham City, 1960).

5524   The ring is used to show that love has no ending. The ring depicts the moon which symbolizes endurance of the engagement or the wedding (F, SLC, 1962).

5525   The wedding band goes on first because it brings the couple close together (F, 19, SLC, 1955).

5526   After a wedding ring is placed on the finger at the altar, it should not be removed, because it will bring bad luck (F, 19, SLC, 1950); . . . should not be removed for seven years or bad luck will follow (M, 21, SLC, 1958). Cf. Brown 4851.

5527   You shouldn't ever take your wedding band off for any length of time after it has once been placed on your finger, except for death or divorce, or it will be bad luck (F, 18, SLC, 1964); . . . except in an emergency . . . (F, 40, Logan, 1938).

5528   If you ever remove your wedding ring, your husband or wife must be the one to put it back on (F, Dragerton, 1964).

5529   A bride should have her ring wished on, and if she never removes it, the wish will be fulfilled (F, 78, Ger, SLC, 1964).

5530   It is bad luck to drop the wedding ring during the ceremony (F, SLC, 1962). Cf. Brown 4850.

5531   To lose a wedding ring is an omen of unhappiness (F, Provo, 1960); . . . it is bad luck until you find it (F, SLC, 1961).

5532   If a married woman loses her wedding ring, she will lose her husband (M, S. Jordan, 1960).

5533   When a wedding ring is worn thin, it brings luck to the wearer's children (F, SLC, 1964).

5534   If a wedding ring is turned around three times, it will make a dream come true (F, 40, Logan, 1938).

## Leaving the Church

5535   If hot water is poured over the doorstep of a hall door as the bride and groom drive away after their wedding, another wedding is sure to be acted upon before it dries up (F, 24, Murray, 1961). Brown 4862.

5536   Rice is thrown as a token of good luck (M, SLC, 1962).

5537   Throwing rice at a wedding means that the marriage will have roots to grow on, and will be a happy one (M, priest, SLC, 1962); . . . signifies a good marriage (F, 19, SLC, 1952).

5538   Throwing rice at a newly married couple wishes them future prosperity (F, SLC, 1961); . . . so they will always have food aplenty (F, SLC, 1960); . . . a life of plenty (F, SLC, 1960).

5539   If rice is thrown at the bride and groom just before they leave on their honeymoon, they will have a happier marriage (F, 19, American Fork, 1960).

5540   Rice throwing at a wedding stems from the Oriental belief that rice is a symbol of health and prosperity. Rice also appeases the evil spirits around the couple (F, Brigham City, 1960); . . . keeps away bad spirits (M, SLC, 1962).

5541   During a Greek wedding ceremony the couple is showered with rice and Jordan almonds; they wish sweetness upon the future of the couple (F, 42, Gr, SLC, 1964).

5542   Rice and old shoes thrown at newlyweds will bring them good luck (M, SLC, 1954). Brown 4858f.

5543   Old shoes, tin cans, and rice bring luck to newlyweds (F, SLC, 1957).

5544   Always throw old shoes around a newly married couple to insure they will always have plenty of clothing (F, SLC, 1960); . . . tie tin cans on the back of the wedding couple's car to scare away bad luck (F, Clearfield, SLC, 1959).

## Tokens of Fertility and Sterility at Marriage

5545   If the sun shines on a bride, she is said to be very happy and will have many children which relate to a happy marriage (F, 26, Midvale, 1962).

5546   Throwing rice at a wedding expresses a wish for a fruitful marriage (F, 20, SLC, 1963).

5547   Rice, the symbol of health and prosperity, thrown at newlyweds is the charm to bless the marriage with many children (F, SLC, 1964).

5548   Sprinkle rice on the bride for fertility (F, SLC, 1959); . . . to increase the fertility of the bride (M, SLC, 1961).

5549   If rice thrown on the newly married couple stays in the hair of the bride, she will be a mother within a year (M, SLC, 1959).

5550   Old shoes and rice at the wedding symbolize a happy, loving marriage with many children (F, SLC, 1958).

5551   Rice and flowers were symbolic of the fertility wished for in the marriage (F, SLC, 1960).

5552   At a wedding, throwing flowers and grain has to do with wishing the couple productiveness (M, SLC, 1961).

5553   Upon marriage, the bride receives a pomegranate from her in-laws. This symbolizes a long and fruitful life (F, Gr, SLC, 1964).

5554 It is believed that a new bride is supposed to step on a pomegranate when first entering her home. This is to enable her to have children (F, 29, Gr, Magna, 1964).

5555 Bless eggs for a fruitful marriage (M, 20, SLC, 1964).

5556 The bride feeds the groom cake so they will have a fruitful marriage (F, SLC, 1962).

5557 During the wedding reception a young boy is placed on the bride's lap. This means that the bride will have a boy for her first child (F, Gr, SLC, 1962).

5558 To assure a large family, the bridesmaids must lay the bride's stockings in cross form on her bed (F, Brigham City, 1960).

5559 A bride who does not sit in the bride's chair will not have children (F, 44, Midvale, 1930).

5560 A bride must cut the wedding cake herself, or she will go through her married life childless (F, Brigham City, 1960).

# WEDDING RECEPTION

## The Wedding Feast

5561 At Greek weddings you get little favors with candied almonds inside. You're supposed to take this home and place it under your pillow and dream on it. This will assure that soon you will have a new boyfriend (F, 19, Gr, SLC, 1953).

5562 The bride's parents pay for the wedding and reception, or the bride will not meet her obligations (F, SLC, 1960).

5563 Upon being married the bride and groom at their reception break a plate to symbolize their break with the past (M, 53, SLC, 1962).

5564 In a Greek wedding, it is customary to break a dish over the best man's head for good luck (F, 42, Gr, SLC, 1964).

5565 After the wedding toast is drunk, the glasses are flung back over the shoulder or are smashed underfoot (F, 20, Gr, SLC, 1963).

5566 Throwing champagne glasses over the shoulder seals the bond of marriage (F, SLC, 1962).

5567 At your wedding throw your champagne glasses into the fireplace for good luck (F, 19, SLC, 1964).

5568 A common superstition is that of breaking champagne glasses at the stem at a wedding feast or the groom's farewell party. In the Greek Orthodox Church, the glass is completely broken (F, SLC, 1962).

5569 Drinking a toast to the bride and groom from the bride's shoe insures that they will always be lucky and wealthy (F, SLC, 1960).

5570 If a couple both drink out of a cup with both initials on it, it brings good luck (F, SLC, 1961).

5571 When both drink from the same cup on the wedding day or during the honeymoon, there will be good luck (F, 51, SLC, 1964).

5572 It is very bad luck for a bride to help cook her own wedding dinner (F, Norw, Logan, 1961).

5573 When a bride is first married, she's supposed to go to the groom's house where her mother-in-law will give her a teaspoon of honey. This is supposed to make her sweet the rest of her life (F, 19, Gr, SLC, 1953); . . . so the bride and groom's future will be congenial (F, 38, Gr, SLC, 1963).

5574 When newlyweds for the first time go to their new home, the groom's mother goes out and gives the bride honey to be sweet and then ties a scarf around both the groom and bride so as to be united and happy, and leads them into their new home (F, Gr, SLC, 1957).

5575 If you eat these long transparent noodles, you will have a long, happy life. These noodles are eaten at the wedding banquet (M, Ja, SLC, 1963).

5576 After the bride is married, she will go directly to the groom's home with a group of people. While on her way to the home, she must keep her eyes shut all the way until she is there. They say that if she opens her eyes, they will soon be divorced (F, Gr, SLC, 1962).

5577 A new bride should never eat too much on the first day at her mother-in-law's home, because she will eat her mother-in-law (F, Gr, SLC, 1957).

5578 If a bride carries a bouquet of wheat during her wedding and reception, etc., good luck and happiness will come to the couple (F, SLC, 1959).

5579 At an older sister's wedding the younger sister should dance without shoes; then she will find fortune and good luck (M, SLC, 1961).

5580 If the youngest daughter marries before the elder ones, they must dance barefooted at her wedding (F, Brigham City, 1960); In Mayfield, Utah, Mrs. M witnessed a wedding in the T family there in which an older unmarried sister of the bride danced in a pig trough because her younger sister married first (F, Duchesne).

5581 The sisters must all dance at the wedding of another sister without any shoes, or they will not find mates (F, Ger, Ogden, 1961).

5582 At wedding receptions they always used to have a dance, and the wedding couple would have the first dance. Well, if there was a bug on the floor around their feet while they were dancing, it was a sign for good luck (F, 61, Ogden, 1950).

The Wedding Cake

5583  A piece of the wedding cake will insure a happy marriage (F, SLC).

5584  The wedding cake signifies good luck and a good start for a couple (M, SLC, 1961).

5585  Today, the groom and bride's cake is usually a white cake. However, the wedding cake used to be a fruit cake, and the bride and groom each had their own cake (F, SLC, 1962).

5586  For a successful and happy marriage the bride should place a piece of the wedding cake under her pillow on her wedding night (M, SLC, 1961); If the bride places . . . , it will bring the couple a prosperous life (F, SLC, 1959).

5587  After the ceremony, it is good luck for a plate of the bride's cake crumbs to be thrown on the heads of the people below (F, Brigham City, 1960).

5588  If a plate covered with wedding cake is dropped from the window of the bride's father's home, and it doesn't break, there will be bad luck. If the plate breaks in many pieces, there will be much good luck (F, Swed, SLC, 1961).

5589  Silver coins are put on the wedding cake to bring good luck to the bride (F, 62, Gr, SLC, 1963).

5590  It is bad luck for anyone but the bride and groom to cut the first piece of cake, and they must do this together (F, SLC, 1964); . . . so they will be harmonious (F, 19, SLC, 1964); . . . to insure a compatible marriage (F, Brigham City, 1960).

5591  A newly married couple should always take hold of the same knife together to cut the wedding cake and the man should cut his piece for the woman and the woman should give her piece to the man. This will bring unity and happiness to the marriage (F, 40, SLC, 1963).

5592  The modern bride cuts the first piece of her cake to insure a happy marriage (M, SLC, 1959); . . . . If she doesn't, they will have bad luck (F, 28, SLC, 1950).

5593  It is good luck for the bride and groom to eat the first piece of a wedding cake (M, 20, SLC, 1964).

5594  For good luck, save the top layer of your wedding cake for the christening of your first child (F, 42, Brighton, 1963).

5595  Individual pieces of wrapped wedding cake were taken home and placed under the pillow. The person sleeping on it would dream about the one they were going to marry (F, SLC, 1960); Place . . . in a box under your pillow and you will dream of your future husband (F, SLC, 1962).

5596  A slice of bride cake thrice drawn through the wedding ring and laid under the head of an unmarried man or woman will make them dream of their future wife or husband (F, Ger, Ogden, 1961).

5597  If a bridesmaid takes home a piece of the wedding cake and sleeps on it, she will dream of her future husband (F, SLC, 1950). Cf. Brown 4830ff.

5598  Fruit cake is given to each single girl at a wedding, and they are supposed to put it under their pillows, and they will dream of the man they will marry (F, SLC, 1960).

5599  If you sleep with the groom's cake under your pillow, you will dream of your future husband or wife (F, SLC, 1962).

5600  If you go to sleep on a piece of wedding cake, the first boy you see when you wake up the following morning will be the man you marry (F, 24, SLC, 1953).

5601  You will have good luck if you sleep with a piece of wedding cake under your pillow for three nights in a row. This is supposed to make your romantic dreams come true (F, SLC, 1952). Cf. Brown 4834f.

5602  If you sleep on a small piece of wedding cake called "dream cake," obtained at a wedding, you will dream who your future love will be (F, 43, Tooele, 1918). Cf. Brown 4829.

5603  If you put a piece of wedding cake under your pillow, you won't be an old maid (M, SLC, 1961).

5604  If you put a piece of wedding cake under your pillow, it will bring you a wife (M, SLC, 1961).

5605  If you take a piece of wedding cake home and sleep with it under your pillow, you will have good luck (M, 20, SLC, 1964).

5606  Put a piece of wedding cake under your pillow, and you will always have joy and happiness (M, 37, SLC, 1932).

5607  Put a piece of wedding cake under your pillow and wish on it, and your wish will come true (F, Spanish Fork, 1930).

DOUBLE WEDDINGS

5608  Never have a double wedding ceremony. Bad luck will come to one of the couples (M, 25, Price, 1956). Brown 4749.

5609  If a double wedding ceremony is performed, one of the couples' marriages will end in bitter sorrow--by divorce, death or love for someone else (F, 19, SLC, 1957).

MARRIED LIFE

Activities After the Wedding

5610  It is bad luck for a couple to sleep in separate beds on their wedding night (M, SLC, 1961).

5611  It is considered bad luck for a couple to retire on their wedding night until the bed has been blessed (F, 80, Ger, Ogden, 1961).

5612  If the groom swears on his wedding night, he will have bad luck (M, 1961).

5613 If a couple argue on their wedding night, their marriage will be unhappy (F, SLC, 1961).

5614 Be sure that on your wedding night you do not go in one door and out the other, or you will always be unlucky (M, SLC, 1960).

5615 The day the bride gets married, the mother-in-law throws a hanky on her daughter-in-law's head. It is supposed to bring her good luck (F, Gr, SLC, 1962).

5616 If a person or a bride leaves for far away, you must not sweep the house for twenty-four hours, because they will go with the garbage (F, Gr, SLC, 1957).

5617 When a girl steps over a broom, it is a sign that she will be a poor housekeeper (F, 21, SLC, 1958).

5618 In a certain type of marriage in the South where after the service the bride and groom had to jump over a horizontal broom, it was considered bad luck for the marriage if either or both of the couple tripped on the broom (M, 20, SLC, 1964).

5619 It is unlucky for a stone to roll across the pathway of a newly married pair (F, Brigham City, 1960).

5620 After the wedding the bride enters the house, putting the right foot first for good luck (M, 66, Gr, SLC, 1963).

5621 If a bride walks across the threshold instead of letting her husband carry her, she'll have bad luck (F, 20, SLC, 1950); To carry your bride across the threshold will bring good luck (F, Sandy, 1957); The groom should carry the bride across the threshold to denote he takes full care and responsibility for her thereafter (F, Pol, SLC, 1960).

5622 It is bad luck for a bride to stumble over the threshold of her new home. Therefore, to assure that such a tragedy cannot happen, the groom must carry her (F, Eng, SLC, 1965); . . . if the bride walks and trips, the marriage will fail (F, 44, SLC, 1964).

5623 If the wife leads the groom across the threshold, you'll have a short unhappy marriage (F, 56, Centerville).

5624 Carrying the bride over the threshold provides the couple with a start to a successful future (M, 19, SLC, 1964).

5625 Carrying the bride over the threshold wards off trouble and assures good luck (M, 22, SLC, 1961); . . . so the family will get along (F, 18, Eng, SLC, 1950).

5626 Carry the bride over the threshold so that evil spirits in the doorway will not get her (F, 18, SLC, 1963); . . . for a spirit might be settling there (M, 47, Murray, 1964); . . . for fear a genie might be sitting there (F, 20, Scot, SLC, 1952).

5627 It is considered ill luck for a newly married couple to return home to an empty house. Therefore, some member of

the family must remain to keep the house open (F, 71, Gr, SLC, 1964).

5628 Newlyweds do not go to funerals for fear of bad luck (F, Gr, SLC, 1962).

5629 After the wedding ceremony the married couple is not supposed to witness any unhappy event (such as a funeral), because this will bring bad luck (M, 33, Gr, SLC, 1963).

5630 If the mothers of the couple do not weep on the wedding night, it means bad luck for the couple (M, SLC, 1961).

5631 It is unlucky if the bride does not weep on her wedding night (M, SLC, 1959).

5632 A new bride must put both feet on the floor at the same time when she gets up after her first-wed night. This is done to start her marriage off properly (M, 42, Provo).

5633 If a hen is taken into the couple's new home and made to cackle after the wedding, it will bring good luck (F, SLC, 1961).

5634 The bride should never bring peacock feathers in the house. Peacock feathers denote much sorrow (F, Pol, SLC, 1960).

5635 It was the custom to shivaree the bride and groom on their wedding night. Usually the couple was separated from one another (F, 28, Logan, 1970). Informant commented that the practice was quite extensive until about 1962.

5636 A bride is not supposed to go to church for a forty-day period after her marriage. If she does, this is bad luck (F, 19, Gr, SLC, 1960).

The Wedding Night, Honeymoon

5637 A full moon on your wedding night means good luck (M, 20, SLC, 1963).

5638 If on your wedding night, you drink wine from a glass and throw the glass on the floor, the number of pieces the glass breaks into predicts how many years your marriage will last. If it does not break, then your marriage will not last even a year (F, SLC, 1961).

5639 It is considered bad luck for a newly wed couple to sleep on a cotton mattress the first night of their honeymoon (M, SLC, 1925).

5640 A long honeymoon accompanies a June wedding (F, 63, Tremonton, 1920).

5641 A bride must take something borrowed with her on her wedding trip for good luck (F, SLC, 1900s).

5642 The honeymoon car is painted with good wishes and often gaily decorated (M, SLC, 1962).

5643 It is good luck to tie shoes on the back of a bridal couple's car as they are going away or making a journey (M, SLC, 1964).

## Householding

5644   A bride should cook the first meal eaten by her husband after their wedding, if the marriage is to last and be happy (M, 82, Perry, 1910).

5645   If the first meal that the bride prepares for her husband is burned, misfortune and sickness will befall the family (M, 18, SLC, 1959).

5646   The bride should serve the first meal to her new husband with bread she bakes herself.  This will ensure a long and happy marriage (F, SLC, 1960).

5647   The mother of the bride should buy the first set of dishes for everyday use. This is done for good luck (F, SLC, 1960).

5648   Pictures of married people or lovers should be placed in such a manner so it will appear they are facing each other (F, 40, Bountiful, 1943).

5649   If a husband can make a good fire, it shows he has an ambitious wife (F, Riverton).

5650   A woman with short fingers will be a good manager (M, SLC, 1954).

## THE MARITAL RELATIONSHIP

5651   Paintings placed on the outside of the house will insure a happy marriage (F, 20, SLC, 1964).

5652   If an Italian deserts his family, in the next life he will be all alone (M, 43, It, SLC, 1930).

5653   A woman who is skinny after marriage will be very hard to get along with (M, 43, It, SLC, 1935).

5654   Keep pictures hung straight if you would keep marriage straight (F, SLC, 1960).

5655   If a married woman's slip shows, the husband still loves her (F, Bountiful, 1915).

## Fighting, Quarreling, Etc.

5656   Spilling salt on the table will lead to a quarrel between a married couple (F, SLC).

5657   If the cook burns bread, her husband is angry (M, SLC, 1959).

5658   When drying dishes one should never cross the knives; they should be laid side by side in the utensil drawer.  If the knives get crossed, it means you will have a fight with your husband or wife (F, 48, SLC, 1925).

5659   The husband must lock the front door before the family retires for the night. Should the wife perform the task, there will be a quarrel during the night (M, SLC, 1953).

5660   If a dog runs between a woman's legs, her husband is going to beat her (F, Axtell, 1958).

5661   If you play with your wedding ring unthinkingly, you and your husband will have a fight (F, 20, SLC, 1963).

## Infidelity

5662   The husband should be the leader of the family, and is responsible for any infidelity on his wife's part (F, 18, Ger, SLC, 1964).

5663   If either husband or wife is untrue to each other, bad luck will befall the one who is untrue (F, SLC, 1961).

5664   If a ring suddenly breaks on a person's finger without any cause, this means his or her loved one has been unfaithful (F, Clearfield, 1961).

5665   If the sun shines on washday, your husband is true to you.  If it rains on washday, watch him, he's stepping out (F, Ogden, 1960).

5666   If the thread, while sewing, keeps tying up in knots, a husband or boyfriend is going to step out on you (F, SLC).

5667   The seventh year of marriage is the crucial one.  If a couple survives that year, they will never separate (M, SLC, 1957).

## Marital Difficulties, Unhappy Marriage

5668   Ill luck will pursue the married couple who had their banns published at the end of one quarter and were married at the beginning of another quarter of the same year (M, SLC, 1960).

5669   If the groom forgets to bring the wedding ring to the ceremony, the marriage will be a failure (M, SLC, 1961).

5670   If the wedding ring is accidentally slipped on the wrong finger, the marriage will be a failure (M, SLC, 1957).

5671   A broken wedding ring is a sign of marital difficulties (F, SLC, 1964).

5672   A lost wedding ring means an unhappy married life (M, 40, Price, 1965).

5673   If a bride takes off her wedding band, the marriage will fail (F, Magna, 1960); . . . marriage will fall apart (F, SLC, 1953); . . . marriage will be ruined (F, SLC); . . . marriage will be destroyed (F, 60, SLC, 1964).

5674   Once your husband has put on your wedding ring at the wedding, if you ever take it off after that, you will have an unhappy marriage (F, SLC, 1959).

5675   If someone closes a pocketknife at a wedding, the couple will not have happy marital relations (M, 22, SLC, 1960). (This is a symbolic locking of the "virgin zone."  --Eds.)

5676   The first person to congratulate the groom will have marital problems (M, SLC, 1959).

5677 If a couple do not take a honeymoon, they will be unhappy in their marriage (F, SLC, 1961).

5678 An unhappy honeymoon will bring an unhappy marriage (M, SLC, 1961).

5679 If the groom gets drunk on his honeymoon, the couple will have an unhappy marriage (F, SLC, 1961); . . . the groom will have bad luck (F, 44, SLC, 1964).

5680 Throw a hat on your bed, and you will be sure to have marital unhappiness (F, 67, Bear River City, 1963).

5681 A funeral following a wedding means that the marriage will not be successful (F, 52, Midvale, 1950).

## Loss of Spouse by Death, Divorce, Etc.

5682 If a girl has a very short lock of hair on either side of her forehead, it is a sign she will be a widow (F, SLC, 1960).

5683 If a woman parts her hair in a different place, she will be a widow before long (F, SLC, 1962).

5684 If you have an even number of children, your marriage is likely to break up (F, Brigham).

5685 If you drop a hammer in the kitchen, it means a divorce (F, 23, Murray, 1964).

5686 If you ever take off your wedding ring, it will break the bonds of matrimony (F, Scot, SLC, 1958).

5687 If your wedding ring is dropped during the ceremony, it means your marriage will not last long (F, SLC, 1961).

5688 If a wedding ring has worn so thin as to come to pieces, the woman will lose her husband (F, Brigham City, 1960).

5689 You should never remove your wedding ring unless in an emergency, or your marriage will not last (F, Murray, 1949). Brown 4872.

5690 If a married woman loves her wedding ring, she will lose her husband (M, Ogden, 1960).

5691 If the bride and groom do not cut their wedding cake for the first time together, their marriage will become separated (F, Ir, SLC, 1960).

5692 If the bride and groom on top of a wedding cake tip over, it means the marriage will meet disaster (F, SLC, 1950).

5693 If a bird in a cage dies on the morning of a wedding, the pair will separate (F, 1959).

## The Dominant Spouse

5694 When folding your hands, if your left thumb is on top, it means that when you marry your mate will be boss; if the right thumb is folded on top, it means you will be boss (F, SLC, 1955). Brown 4867.

5695 When a woman has the habit of resting her thumb inside her clenched hand, everybody knows that she will be ruled absolutely by her husband while if the thumb is held extended, the man who marries her will probably be henpecked (F, Ogden, 1961).

5696 If a girl's second toe is longer than her big toe, she will boss her husband (F, Tooele, 1957). Brown 4868.

5697 If a wedding happens on April Fool's Day, the wife will be the boss of the family (F, 70, Bountiful, 1900s).

5698 During a wedding ceremony when the priest is saying women should respect their husbands and husbands should respect their wives, if the man steps on the woman's foot, he will be boss; if not, the wife will be the boss (M, Gr, SLC).

5699 If the bride steps on the groom's foot during the wedding ceremony, she will domineer his life (F, 49, Gr, Midvale, 1964).

5700 If the newly married couple dance together on their wedding day, the wife will henceforth rule the roost (M, 18, Logan, 1971).

5701 Whichever of the new couple steps out of the church first will be the head of the new home (F, SLC, 1961).

## THE IN-LAWS

5702 If you don't drink all that is in your cup, you will have a bad mother-in-law (F, 65, SLC, 1940).

5703 Don't pour a drink into a cup that isn't empty, because if you do you will get a mean mother-in-law (F, SLC, 1964).

5704 If the couple, on their honeymoon, see any of their in-laws, the couple will have trouble with them in the future (F, SLC, 1961).

5705 Don't sit on the corner of a table while eating, for you will have a bad mother-in-law (F, SLC, 1958).

## WEALTH, PROSPERITY

5706 Giving a gold piece to the groom on the wedding day means he will acquire much wealth (F, Swed, SLC, 1960).

5707 If it snows on your wedding day, you will be rich (F, 74, SLC, 1900s).

5708 If it rains on the day of your wedding, it means that you will be rich (F, 42, Gr, SLC, 1964).

5709 If the bride has an engagement ring containing pearls, her husband will be assured of financial success (F, Ogden, 1957).

## WIFE SELLING

5710 It is a remarkable superstition that a man may lawfully sell his wife to another, provided he delivers her over with a halter about her neck (M, SLC, 1964).

5711    If a man walks on the inside and allows his wife or girl friend to walk on the outside, he wants to give her away (F, 67, Panguitch, 1920); . . . she's up for sale (F, SLC, 1930).

## NUMBER OF MARRIAGES

5712    If a boy has two cowlicks on his head, he is going to get married two times (F, 38, Gr, SLC, 1963).

5713    The number of creases on the wrist shows the number of times one will be married (M, Ferron, 1961).

5714    Two forks at your place when eating is an indication you will be married twice (M, SLC, 1953).

5715    If you have two spoons set on a table, a man will have two wives (M, SLC); Two knives mean you will have two wives (F, 47, SLC).

5716    If you spill salt, you will marry three times (F, SLC, 1900).

5717    If you sit on a table, it means you will be married more than once (M, 44, SLC, 1928).

5718    If two birds perch on your windowsill in one day, you will be married twice (F, Axtell, 1958).

## Miscellaneous

5719    A bride is never supposed to change her wedding day, or she will have bad luck (F, 46, SLC, 1964).

5720    Children of farmers always get married before those whose parents work in the city (F, 64, Heber, 1910).

5721    If a young man marries after age nineteen, chances are that he will not have any trouble with his marriage (F, SLC, 1964).

5722    Few girls married before twenty-four; these girls were considered "hussies" (F, 64, Heber, 1910).

5723    Girls who married men a great deal older than themselves were considered "hussies"(F, 64, Heber, 1910).

5724    In order to get along in marriage, it is best to marry a sign of the zodiac that is compatible with your own sign (F, SLC, 1958).

5725    The "lover's knot" is supposed to stand for love and duty. It is a symbol of oneness or unity. Today a marriage has taken place when "the knot is tied" (F, 22, Sandy, 1960).

5726    Blessing the bride and groom is essential to their happiness. In the Spanish wedding, the band plays the Intrega (giving away the bride) while the immediate family gives the couple the blessing (F, 100, Grantsville, 1963).

5727    When an LDS missionary returns home, he will be married in six months (M, 82, Perry, 1950).

5728    If married outside your own religion, the marriage is usually a flop (M, SLC, 1961); . . . the couple will have trouble throughout married life (F, 50, SLC, 1964).

5729    It is bad luck to dream of a wedding (M, Provo, 1959).

5730    If you dream of a wedding, it means there is trouble in the family (F, 26, Helper, 1955).

5731    If a bride dreams of a wedding, other than her own, on her wedding night, she will have bad luck the first three months of marriage (M, SLC, 1960).

5732    Don't buy a bridal book before your marriage, or it won't occur (F, Midvale).

5733    When a person is in love it makes them graceful (F, 18, SLC, 1968).

5734    If a bit of handwork--even one stitch-- is placed by the bride on each hope chest item, happiness and good fortune will be hers (F, Provo, 1960).

# V

# Domestic Pursuits

## COOKING, CULINARY PRACTICE

### General

5735 Keep a jar of pennies in the kitchen for good luck (F, 72, Fillmore, 1915).

5736 If you bang on a black kettle, you will get rid of evil spirits (F, 53, SLC, 1919).

5737 Never turn on stove burners before you're ready to cook, or your food will burn (F, Murray, 1957).

5738 Cooks will not give away food or any other things which they use in the kitchen. They will lend them, but giving them away brings bad luck (F, Ogden, 1960).

5739 Never whistle in the kitchen of a real good chef, for it results in disaster with the food all day long (F, 70, SLC, 1947).

5740 Never cook food in a soot-covered pan; it will ruin the food (F, 81, Helper, 1964).

5741 In preparing food, stirring must be clockwise, or it will fail when it is finished (F, 23, SLC,); When you stir clockwise and then reverse the direction, it brings bad luck (F, 26, SLC, 1949); It brings good luck to stir mixtures clockwise (F, 19, St. George, 1964). Cf. Brown 2776.

5742 To forget to put coffee in your coffeepot is a sign you're to get a prize (F, 52, SLC).

5743 To prevent food from sticking to a hot griddle, place salt in a small piece of cloth and fasten with a rubber band or string, and then rub the griddle briskly with a salt bag (F, 55, 1961).

5744 If a metal spoon is placed in a glass, it will prevent the glass from cracking when hot liquid is poured into it (F, 52, Nephi, 1964).

5745 Never watch a pot boil, or it will bring bad luck (F, SLC, 1962).

5746 A marble placed in the teakettle will keep deposits from forming on the sides of the kettle (M, SLC, 1925).

5747 Cold water will heat faster than hot water (M, 28, 1961).

5748 Never let water come to a boil, for every bubble brings bad luck (F, 78, SLC, 1964).

5749 If your pot boils over, rub your stomach, and it will stop (F, 28, SLC, 1952).

5750 To keep a pot from boiling over, place a green twig across its rim (M, 55, Weber, 1970).

5751 If you have a rocking pan on a coal stove, put salt under it, and it will stop rocking (F, Riverton, 1910).

5752 Never scrape the bottom of the pan when cooking or the contents will turn out poorly (F, Clearfield, 1964).

5753 If while a person is cooking he runs out of salt, it means bad luck (F, 26, SLC, 1964).

5754 Before opening a can of anything that can fizz all over you, tap the top of the can with a can opener, and it won't fizz (M, SLC, 1965).

5755 Having open cans in the refrigerator is a bad sign (F, 45, SLC, 1938).

5756 Use prickly pears or wood ashes to clear the water. The prickly pears cause the dirt to congeal at the bottom and the water will be nice and clear (F, 73, Moab, 1953).

### Vegetables, Fruit

5757 Boil a biscuit when cooking cabbage and the odor will disappear (M, SLC, 1961). Brown 2794.

5758 When slicing a cucumber, rub the end to draw out the bitterness, or to draw out the poison (F, SLC, 1957); . . . both ends should be removed and rubbed together (F, 45, SLC, 1933); If you cut a cucumber from the wrong end when you are slicing it, it will be bitter. The correct end to cut first is the end that the blossom was on (F, SLC, 1961).

5759 Cucumbers are poisonous unless soaked in vinegar (M, SLC, 1969).

5760 To see if mushrooms are poisonous, boil them for one hour in a pot with a silver coin on the bottom. If the coin turns black, the mushrooms are poisonous (F, SLC, 1971); . . . a dime . . . (F, 80, Lewiston, 1970); . . . a fifty-cent piece . . . (F, 19, SLC).

5761   To tell if mushrooms are poison or not, put a silver spoon in the pan they are cooking in, and if the spoon becomes tarnished, the mushrooms are poison (F, 47, Midvale).

5762   When boiling mushrooms grown on tree stumps, put a silver coin or a clove of garlic in the water. If either turns very dark, the mushrooms are poisonous. You do the same thing with clams and other seafoods (F, 1971).

5763   If when shelling peas you find a pod with nine peas in it, you should throw it over your left shoulder, and your wish will come true (F, SLC, 1961).

5764   Take nine peas in one pod, put them all in your mouth at once, and your wish will come true (F, Moab, 1953).

5765   Try to peel a potato without breaking the skin, throw the skin over your left shoulder and happiness is sure to occur as a result (F, 1960).

5766   On Sunday never cut the eyes out of potatoes; it's bad luck (M, 20, SLC, 1954).

5767   If you keep an onion under water or put a bread crumb at the end of the knife when you are cutting it, it will absorb the moisture (F, Moab, 1953); Holding an onion under running cold water will keep your eyes from watering while peeling it (F, Lehi, 1957). Brown 2802.

5768   When you are peeling onions, it won't bother you if you stuff bread in your upper lip (F, Moab, 1953); . . . hold a large piece of bread in your mouth (F, Ogden, 1947). Brown 2799.

5769   If you hold a pencil between your teeth while you're cutting an onion, your eyes won't water (F, 19, Logan, 1969); . . . a pin . . . (M, 1960); . . . a match between the teeth . . . (F, 22, SLC, 1955); . . . hold the sulphur end of a match in your mouth . . . (F, Ogden, 1948). Brown 2803.

5770   Burn your onion peelings for good luck (F, 39, SLC, 1940).

5771   If you can peel an apple without breaking the peeling, it means good luck (F, SLC, 1960).

5772   If you want your wish to come true, peel an apple. Start in one place and go around and around. Throw the peeling over your left shoulder, and if the peel doesn't break, you'll have good luck (F, 54, SLC, 1940).

5773   When peeling an apple, don't break the circle, or you'll have bad luck (F, 19, SLC, 1963).

5774   Peel an orange all the way around without breaking the peeling, and you'll have good luck (F, SLC, 1957).

5775   Never cut a melon with the point of a knife (F, 49, Logan, 1964).

## Meat

5776   When a pregnant woman touches meat, the meat will spoil (F, 60, SLC, 1958).

5777   If meat shrinks in the pot when cooking, it is unlucky (M, 20, SLC, 1961).

5778   When cooking a large order of steaks, touch the first steak's side to a dry grill on both sides, then salt it and put it on the moist side and the whole order will be good (M, SLC, 1959).

5779   When cooking large quantities of bacon, place them horizontally on a short pan and lay five pieces vertically between the rows, and the order will be good (M, SLC, 1965).

5780   If you get fresh venison, soak it overnight in milk and it tenderizes it and takes away the strong flavor (F, Moab, 1953).

## Baking

5781   Twelve for the baker and one for the devil makes up a baker's dozen (M, SLC, 1956).

5782   If you always stir the batter in the same direction, you will have good luck (F, 1955); It's bad luck if you don't . . . (F, SLC, 1950); Stir the batter in the same direction or you will make guests sick that eat your food (F, 43, Norw, SLC, 1964). Brown 2776.

5783   Whenever stirring a batter, be certain to stir it clockwise or you will have bad luck (F, Ogden, 1961); If you are stirring batter in a clockwise direction and you reverse the stirring, the batter will spoil (F, 18, Brigham City, 1960).

5784   Always stir batter in one direction only--from east to west (like the direction of the sun's path). Failure to do this results in bad batter (F, SLC).

5785   If the cook doesn't dip her thumb in flour before making pastry, it will not turn out (F, 71, SLC, 1964).

5786   If a person counts the tortillas as he makes them, the devil will write a message on them (F, Mex, SLC, 1920).

5787   When baking or cooking, before the food is put in the oven, the cook makes the sign of the cross. This insures that the food will turn out to perfection (F, Gr, Magna, 1920).

## Baking Bread

5788   If you wash the jar that the yeast rises in, the bread won't be as nice as otherwise. Never put yeast in a clean jar. When I was a little girl and we'd go to the neighbor's to get a start of yeast, they'd say, "Tell your mother to leave it in this jar" (F, Moab, 1953).

5789   Never double a recipe when making bread, as the bread will not rise (F, 22, SLC, 1955).

5790 A special bread made without yeast can be smelled all over the neighborhood. The only way it can turn out is if you don't tell anyone you are baking it. If you tell someone, it won't turn out (F, Gr, SLC, 1962).

5791 When making bread, after kneading it, the sign of the cross is done over it with the side of the hand. This insures that the bread will be blessed, and the bread will turn out good (F, Gr, SLC, 1961). Brown 2772.

5792 After the dough sets, making three crosses on it before baking will bring good luck (F, Columbia, 1963).

5793 If a girl for the first time bakes bread, the moon the night before must have been clear and full, because she then will always bake good and tender bread (F, Gr, SLC, 1957).

5794 Never make bread when the moon is scheduled to be full. It is a bad omen (F, 24, SLC, 1945).

5795 When you are baking bread, and one loaf cracks, you will have bad luck (F, Du, Ogden, 1959).

Baking Cakes, Pies, Cookies

5796 When beating a cake, keep the spoon going in the same direction, or you will unbeat the cake causing it to fail (M, SLC, 1950).

5797 Always stir a batter in the same direction or the cake will fall (F, Roosevelt, 1961); . . . if not, you will spoil the cake (M, Layton, 1952).

5798 To stir in the same direction all the time is bad luck, e.g., to stir cake batter in one direction will make it spoil (F, 19, SLC, 1952).

5799 Cake batter should be stirred clockwise to keep the cake from falling (F, Bear River City, 1957); . . . you must stir to the right . . . (F, 55, SLC, 1965). Brown 2777.

5800 When stirring a cake, stir quickly from left to right so the little imps sitting on the edge of the bowl will not fall in and spoil the cake (F, Logan, 1957).

5801 It is bad luck to have a cake fall in the oven if you are alone in the house at the time (F, 46, SLC). Cf. Brown 2790.

5802 Loud noises will cause a cake to fall (F, Bountiful, 1961); Slamming the kitchen door . . . (F, Spanish Fork, 1896). Cf. Brown 2786.

5803 Don't jump on the floor in the kitchen with a cake in the oven, or the cake will fall (F, Roosevelt, 1961); It is bad luck to walk across the floor when a cake is baking (F, 52, SLC). Brown 2787.

5804 Do not make a cake on a rainy day. It will not rise (F, 24, SLC, 1952).

5805 A menstruating woman will cause a cake to fall (F, 57, SLC, 1964). Brown 2789.

5806 An upside down cake is the result of a frustrated cook (F, 20, SLC, 1961).

5807 Never bake a white cake on Friday; it's bad luck. Never bake a brown cake on Sunday (F, 39, Sandy, 1940).

5808 If a housewife cuts the first cake from the oven, all the rest will be heavy (F, SLC, 1961).

5809 It is bad luck to throw away eggshells till after the cake is baked (F, 70, Bountiful, 1900s). Brown 2785.

5810 Place eggshells on top of the oven to make the cake rise (F, 25, SLC, 1948). Brown 2783.

5811 Stop the clock while baking a cake (M, 46, SLC, 1930). Brown 2788.

5812 In order to keep the layers of a double cake from sliding, a housewife will often put toothpicks in the layers to keep them together. When the cake is cut, those who have toothpicks in their piece of cake have good luck. They also get to make wishes and then break the toothpick (F, 21, SLC, 1950).

5813 If you swing on a gate, your pies will fail (F, SLC, 1961).

5814 If you are baking cookies and they don't turn out, it is because someone came in (F, Gr, SLC, 1962).

5815 If you burn the last batch while baking cookies, your next batch will be super-duper (F, SLC, 1957).

Candy, Meringue, Etc.

5816 Never make jelly or meringue icing on a stormy, cloudy day. The jelly won't jell, and the meringue won't congeal (F, Centerville, 1963).

5817 If you make candy on a cloudy day, it won't get hard (F, 25, Logan, 1948); Divinity candy won't turn out on a cloudy day (F, 50, SLC, 1963).

Various Foods

5818 If you stir gravy both ways, it will get lumpy (M, SLC, 1925).

5819 In making popovers, stir counter-clockwise or they will flop (M, SLC, 1959).

5820 When cracking eggs for commercial large-scale cooking, crack two eggs independently and put them in an omelet and the rest will crack evenly and the yolks won't break (M, 19, SLC, 1965).

5821 When an egg cracks while being boiled, add a pinch of salt to the water, and the egg white will not run out (F, SLC, 1925).

5822 While making soup, never allow your breath to blow on it, or the soup will have a bitter taste (F, 73, Eng, SLC, 1965).

Canning, Preserving, Pickling

5823   If you put up fruit during your menstruation period, the fruit will all spoil (F, SLC, 1964).

5824   If a woman cans food during her menstrual flow, the food will ferment (F, SLC, 1961).

5825   Don't put up fruit while you're pregnant, or it will spoil (F, SLC, 1959).  Cf. Brown 2797.

5826   If you bottle fruit when you are not feeling well and you feel sick, then all the fruit or some of it may turn out to be bad or not seal correctly and spoil in the bottle (F, 43, SLC).

5827   If fruit or jams boil over on the stove, throw salt on it quickly, or something bad will happen to the family (F, Paragonah, 1959).

5828   When canning mushrooms, if a fifty-cent piece is put in the pan when they are cooking, and turns black, the mushrooms are poisonous; if nothing happens to the fifty-cents, they are okay to eat (F, 19, SLC).

5829   Never can food unless there is a full moon.  It will spoil (M, 53, SLC, 1963).

5830   Menstruating women should not make pickles (F, Lehi, 1957).

5831   Old women should make the sauerkraut. If young women do, the kraut will spoil (F, SLC, 1925).  Brown 2795.

BELIEFS ABOUT FOOD

General

5832   Our landlady believed that it was bad luck to take back any food that was borrowed from her (M, SLC, 1959).

5833   The nutritive value of foods raised on depleted soil is poor (F, SLC, 1961).

5834   Aluminum cooking utensils taint the food (M, SLC, 1957); Food in contact with aluminum turns to poison (F, 46, SLC, 1938).

5835   Never accept food from a stranger; it may be poisoned (M, SLC, 1957).

5836   Dirt on the sink means the food is clean (M, SLC, 1964).

5837   It is bad luck to have anything edible broken in your hand (F, 78, Dan, SLC, 1965).

Bread

5838   Bread is the symbol of hospitality (F, Midvale, 1961).

5839   If you take the last piece of bread from the plate, you will kiss the cook (M, SLC, 1930s); . . . have to kiss the cook (F, SLC, 1900).  Brown 2862.

5840   Taking the last piece of bread off the plate or throwing it away is bad luck (M, 63, SLC).  Brown 2858.

5841   Throwing bread into the fire will bring you bad luck (M, Tooele, 1957).

5842   If you drop a piece of bread on the floor butter side down, it is bad luck (F, Orem, 1959).

5843   To step upon a piece of bread or to leave it lying upon the ground is an unpardonable sin (F, SLC, 1964).

5844   If one finds a piece of bread lying upon the ground, one must pick it up, kiss it and carry it until he finds a hole to place it in (F, SLC, 1964).

5845   It causes bad luck to break bread in anyone else's hand (F, 24, SLC, 1957).

5846   Two people should not butter their bread with the same knife (F, 54, SLC, 1964).

5847   It is bad luck to cut a hot loaf of bread (M, SLC, 1961).

5848   Always cut bread for seven people.  This means you will go to heaven (F, 52, W. Jordan, 1964).

5849   Stone-ground bread is better for you than regular bread (F, 15, Bountiful, 1961).

5850   A person is not supposed to put a loaf of bread on the counter or drain board or table upside down, or it will bring the person bad luck (F, 51, Centerfield, 1964).  Brown 2773.

5851   If you put the bread upside down, you insult Jesus (F, 27, SLC, 1963).

5852   A loaf baked on Good Friday will never go mouldy (M, 1900).

5853   Burning toast is a sign of a bad day to come (F, SLC, 1963).

5854   Toast has fewer calories than bread (F, SLC, 1961).

Pies, Cookies

5855   It is lucky to see two pies, but unlucky to see only one (M, 19, SLC, 1963).

5856   If you eat too much pie before bedtime, the Pie Lady will sit on your stomach (F, Bountiful, 1947).  (The Pie Lady is a locally known frightening figure, or bogey, used as a means of keeping children from eating too much pie before going to bed.  For a standard treatise on this subject see John D. A. Widdowson, *If You Don't Be Good:  Verbal Social Control in Newfoundland* [Social and Economic Studies, No. 21, Institute of Social and Economic Research, Memorial University of Newfoundland, St. John's, Newfoundland, 1977].)

5857   If the cookie jar is empty, bad luck is in store (F, 16, SLC, 1963).

## Meat, Fowl, Seafood

5858 It is bad luck to eat meat on Friday (M, SLC, 1957).

5859 It is very harmful to eat large quantities of meat (M, 90, SLC, 1890s).

5860 Never let the moon shine on fresh meat (M, 22, SLC, 1963).

5861 Meat should be chewed much more than bread or vegetables (F, SLC, 1961).

5862 Eating steak causes B.O. (F, 46, SLC, 1940).

5863 Don't eat beef liver on Wednesday (M, 40, SLC, 1963).

5864 If you eat cow's brain, you'll have bad luck (F, SLC, 1957).

5865 If a chicken with its head off runs into you or touches you, you should not eat it, or you'll have bad luck (M, 65, SLC, 1916).

5866 You can only eat wild rabbits during months that have "R" in them (F, SLC, 1962).

5867 Never eat of an eel because they are snakes in disguise (F, Scot, SLC, 1957).

5868 Don't eat oysters in any month that has an "R" in its spelling (M, SLC, 1963); Only eat oysters in months ending in "R" (F, Bountiful, 1915). Brown 2820.

5869 The quality of an oyster is determined by his size (F, SLC, 1961).

5870 The Navajo Indian believes that if they eat fish under any circumstances, the use of that food will be followed by a dreadful punishment (M, Brigham City, 1957).

5871 Navajo Indians wouldn't eat fish of the San Juan River, because they believed that the cliff dwellers' spirit went into the fish (F, SLC, 1920).

## Milk, Cream; Souring

5872 Don't stir milk with a knife because it cuts it (F, 23, Clearfield, 1964).

5873 A woman should never milk a cow while having her period. The milk will spoil (F, 49, Eng, SLC, 1964).

5874 One should never spin on the spinning wheel late Saturday evening, for the cream on the milk will be very thin (F, SLC, 1927).

5875 There are no living or dead germs in pasteurized milk (F, SLC, 1961).

5876 Sweet milk isn't good for grown-up humans to drink (M, Riverton, 1942).

5877 Skim milk has little nutritive value (F, SLC, 1961).

5878 Gnomes and goblins are full of mischief. They can cause milk to sour (F, 46, SLC, 1940); Elves turn milk sour (M, Swed, SLC, 1959); If the milk in a pail turns sour, it is a sign that the "Nisse" or elf has perched on the rim of the pail during the night (F, 74, Norw, Salem, 1900).

5879 Thunder and lightning cause milk to sour in a few hours, even in the coldest weather (M, 45, SLC); Thunder curdles cream (F, Eng, SLC, 1965). Brown 7568.

5880 Milk will turn sour on a rainy day (M, Bountiful, 1964).

5881 Milk sours quicker in cloudy weather (F, Lehi, 1957). Informant remarked that sour milk is called "blinky."

## Churning Butter

5882 Get the ugliest person you know to look in the cream jar, and it will turn so you can't churn it (M, 46, SLC, 1930); The look of an extremely ugly person will turn sour cream to butter (M, 44, Duchesne, 1970). Cf. Brown 7534.

5883 "I wish the Old Woman the butter would come, I wish the Old Woman the butter would come" (M, SLC, 1900).

5884 While churning the butter, it was common to say "Bum, bum, butter's come" (F, SLCo, 1900s). Cf. Brown 7553ff.

5885 Churning butter must be done in a clockwise direction, or you will have bad luck (F, Murray, 1920s).

5886 If you want butter to come more quickly, put salt in it (F, Moab, 1953). Brown 7540.

5887 If you do not throw salt into the fire before you begin to churn, butter will not come (F, 54, SLC, 1964). Brown 7540.

5888 Put a red-hot horseshoe into the cream when the butter won't come (F, Lehi, 1915). Cf. Brown 7552.

5889 The Cs lived across the creek from an old woman who was believed to bewitch children. The family was churning butter for dinner, but the butter would not come. They knew the old woman had bewitched it. Brother C heated a stove lid red hot and plunged it into the churn. The "Witch" flew out of her house all ablaze and dashed down to the creek to put out the flames. After that no one saw her anymore (M). Cf. Brown 7537.

## Eggs

5890 Eggs with two yolks are lucky, especially if found three or four in a nest (F, Eng, SLC, 1957).

5891 Breaking your egg yolk in the morning brings bad luck (M, SLC, 1961).

5892 If one dreams of counting eggs, it means trouble (F, Midvale, 1925); Dreaming of eggs . . . (F, Vernal, 1964).

5893 If you throw an egg over the house, it will bring good luck (F, Morgan, 1961).

5894    It is bad luck to burn eggshells (M, Farmington, 1961).

5895    To drop an egg on the floor and thereby break it is a sign of a serious disappointment (F, 23, Cedar City, 1961).

5896    Brown eggs are not as nutritious as white eggs (F, 47, SLC, 1937).

5897    If you want to borrow eggs, the person giving them to you must place them on the table, and you pick them up yourself (F, Gr, SLC, 1962).

5898    You will have good luck if your egg doesn't crack when you crack it with another egg (M, Gr, priest, SLC, 1962).

5899    To bring eggs in the house after dark is considered bad luck (F, 83, 1905).

5900    Never borrow eggs after dark. If you do, you will have bad luck (M, 73, Gr, SLC, 1963).

5901    Make a wish on the fruit of the season and it will come true (F, SLC, 1965); Wish on the first bite of the first fruit of the season for good luck (F, SLC, 1961). Brown 8426.

5902    Don't eat the first fruit because it always has too much pectin taste (M, 76, Kamas, 1910).

5903    How to tell if a watermelon is ripe: Place a straw from a broom on the melon, and if it turns or spins, the melon will be ripe and delicious (M, 6, Magna, 1970).

5904    You can tell if a watermelon is sweet by the number of times the bees have stung it (F, 20, Laketown, 1969).

5905    Whenever you eat a cherry make a wish on it and it will come true (F, 19, Jensen, 1961); You can make a wish if you eat the cherry on something last (F, SLC, 1967).

5906    The inside strips of the banana peel are poisonous (F, 54, Logan, 1970). Heard in Wisconsin, 1922.

5907    If you eat figs out of season you will have many sorrows (F, 42, SLC, 1930).

5908    The juice from a vegetable possesses more vitamins, etc., than the original vegetable (F, Eng, SLC, 1941).

5909    Never eat the parsley that is left on your plate in a salad or by the side of a steak or any other food, for it is bad for you to eat it (F, 59, SLC, 1961).

5910    Celery has to be banked up with dirt and frozen over before it really gets crisp and ready to eat (M, SLC, 1920).

5911    Tomatoes are thought to be poisonous when they are green on the vine (M, 46, SLC, 1926); Tomatoes were called "love apples" and were used only for decoration over the fireplace, because they were thought to be poisonous (F, SLC, 1969).

5912    If you eat a head of lettuce, you will be able to stay awake for three days (M, SLC, 1950).

## Food Fallacies

5913    Never eat cherries and milk together. The acid of the cherries will have a bad effect (F, Logan, 1970); . . . are bad for you (F, Moab, 1953).

5914    Eating oranges while drinking milk will curdle the milk (M, 49, saddle maker, SLC, 1961).

5915    Never eat dried fruits and milk at the same time (F, 45, SLC, 1953).

5916    Never eat tomatoes and milk in the same meal, or you will have bad luck (F, Murray, 1957).

5917    Milk and seafood should not be eaten at the same meal (F, Provo, 1959); Fish and milk . . . is bad luck (M, 21, SLC, 1963). Cf. Brown 2819.

## Oil, Vinegar

5918    Never borrow vinegar; you only borrow someone else's troubles (F, Eng, SLC, 1960).

5919    If you spill or drop a drop of oil, it means bad luck will befall you (F, Gr, Magna, 1926).

5920    If you spill olive oil, and you don't sprinkle salt in the form of a cross on it, bad luck will follow (F, 52, It, Bingham, 1929).

## Beverages, Liquids

5921    One must never drink cold liquids: warm milk only, hot tea, etc. (M, Provo, 1965).

5922    One must never drink any kind of liquid with food while eating, because it will sour the meal. Always follow the meal with hot tea (M, Provo, 1965).

5923    Never put cold water into anything before putting hot water in. It is for dead people only (M, Ja, SLC, 1960).

5924    If you put hot water in the icebox, it will freeze faster than cold water (M, 28, SLC, 1961).

5925    Never throw water out the door after dark, or you will have bad luck (F, Ger, SLC, 1960).

5926    Drinking black coffee will make you turn black (F, 18, SLC, 1962).

5927    It's bad luck to burn coffee grounds (M, Murray, 1957).

5928    Fruit juices do not contribute calories to the diet (M, SLC, 1961).

## Beer, Wine

5929    An upside-down Oly (Olympia Beer) can is good luck (M, SLC, 1964).

5930 The horseshoe on an inverted Olympia beer can brings good luck, preferably after being emptied (M, 18, SLC, 1964).

5931 Unless a steel bar is laid across a barrel of beer during a thunderstorm the beer will sour (M, 80, Ogden, 1961).

5932 After a woman has had a baby she should not enter anyone's home until forty days pass. If she does, the wine in the person's home will sour (F, Gr, SLC, 1920).

5933 When you want to empty wine in gallon bottles for storing, the moon the preceding night must have been full, because if it wasn't, the wine will be cloudy, not clear and sparkling like it should be (F, Gr, SLC, 1957).

5934 When a person pours the Japanese rice wine called sake into a container, he mustn't repour it back into the bottle for it would be ridiculing his ancestors (M, Ja, Midvale).

5935 Christ never drank wine, only grape juice (F, Murray, 1951).

Salt

5936 Salt is widely regarded as possessing magic qualities. It is believed to ward off evil (SLC, 1964).

5937 If you run out of salt, you will want for things (F, Norw, SLC, 1960).

5938 Never eat salt on the first day of the month, or all your food will taste too salty all month (F, SLC, 1941).

5939 It will bring luck and protection to you to give new neighbors a box of salt (F, 50, Helper, 1964).

5940 Finding salt on your doorstep is lucky (M, 10, SLC, 1962).

5941 If salt is thrown away, it brings bad luck (M, 23, SLC, 1963).

5942 Offering salt to a guest indicates a spirit of friendly hospitality (M, 35, SLC, 1964).

5943 Never help anyone salt his food, or you will be helping him to sorrow unless you make the sign of the cross over it (F, SLC, 1967).

5944 When you spill anything on the table throw salt over the left shoulder (M, SLC, 1961).

Magical Qualities of Salt

5945 Throw salt over your shoulder for good luck (F, 1962).

5946 Throw salt over your shoulder to avoid bad luck (F, Farmington, 1959); If something bad happens, throw salt over your shoulder to break the curse (M, 14, SLC, 1964); Salt over your left shoulder will counteract any bad omen (M, SLC, 1959).

5947 If you throw salt over your left shoulder, you will have good luck (M, Ogden, 1961); Throw a pinch of salt over your left shoulder with your right hand for . . . (F, SLC, 1963); A pinch of salt over the left shoulder brings bad luck (F, 46, SLC, 1964); . . . salt over your left shoulder to make a wish come true (M, 26, Bountiful, 1950).

5948 If you don't throw salt over your left shoulder when you swear, bad luck will follow soon (F, 46, SLC, 1952).

5949 When you go out to dinner make a wish and throw salt over your left shoulder (F, 15, SLC, 1965).

5950 Throw salt over your left shoulder with your back to a full moon and you receive good luck (M, Layton, 1959).

5951 Throwing salt over the right shoulder will bring good luck (F, SLC, 1959).

5952 It is good luck to throw salt over your right shoulder when you see a bluebird (F, SLC).

Borrowing and Lending Salt

5953 Never borrow or lend salt, as it will bring very bad luck (F, Bountiful, SLC, 1930). Brown 2886.

5954 If you have to borrow a cup of salt, throw a pinch over your right shoulder for good luck (F, 78, SLC, 1964).

5955 It is bad luck to borrow salt. It should be traded (e.g., a cup of salt for a cup of sugar) (F, 44, SLC).

5956 It is bad luck to return salt. Replace it with something else (F, SLC, 1964); To return salt will cause bad feelings (F, 50, Richfield, 1934); . . . signifies trouble (F, Lehi, 1957).

5957 If you borrow salt, never return it because it will bring bad luck to the lender if you return it (F, 76, SLC, 1940). Cf. Brown 2888.

5958 If you borrow salt, never forget to pay it back (F, Farmington, 1959).

5959 Never borrow salt--always pay for it. If you don't, you will have many days of sadness (F, 44, SLC, 1961); You can't lend or borrow salt; you must give or sell it (M, Hyde Park).

5960 Borrowed salt must be repaid in coins (F, 54, SLC, 1964).

Spilling Salt

5961 If you spill salt, you're out of luck (F, SLC, 1964); . . . it's bad luck (F, 30, Ger, Ogden, 1970); . . . you will meet trouble (F, 78, SLC, 1964). Brown 2879.

5962 Spilling salt will bring bad luck if not cleaned up right away (M, SLC, 1919).

5963 If you spill salt to your right, trouble will follow (M, SLC, 1964).

5964 If you spill salt carelessly, when you die you'll pick it up with your eyelashes (M, 75, Grantsville, 1959).

5965   If you spill salt, you will have bad
luck for one year (F, 19, SLC, 1954).

5966   Don't spill salt before dinner, or it
won't taste good (F, Ger, SLC, 1950).

5967   Because salt was spilled at the Last
Supper the spilling of salt is a bad
omen (F, Orangeville, 1959). (This
notion is believed to have originated at
the Last Supper of Christ, because when
Judas went to leave the table, he tipped
over the salt. --Eds.) Brown 2880.

5968   As many tears will be shed as are needed
to dissolve the salt that has been
spilled (M, 65, Kearns, 1963); If you
spill salt, your family will shed as
many tears as needed to dissolve it (M,
27, Sunnyside, 1964).

5969   If you spill salt, spell it: s-a-l-t
(F, 49, SLC, 1964).

5970   If you spill salt, throw it on the fire
to prevent bad luck (M, Eng, Ogden,
1958).

## Throwing Salt Over the Shoulder

5971   It is bad luck to spill salt unless you
throw some over your shoulder (F, SLC);
Throw a grain of salt over your shoulder
after you spill it; it erases any bad
luck (F, 24, Lindon, 1963).

5972   If you drop a glass salt shaker, whether
it breaks or not, you must quickly throw
a few grains of salt over your shoulder
to protect you against seven years of
bad luck (M, 51, SLC, 1963). Learned in
Florida, 1935.

5973   If salt is spilled on the table when the
salt shaker falls, the salt must be
thrown over the right shoulder.
Otherwise, there will be bad luck come
to the household (F, 43, Tooele, 1905);
. . . one should shake the salt shaker
over the left shoulder to avoid bad luck
(F, SLC, 1955).

5974   If one spills salt on the table or
floor, one must throw a few grains of it
over his right or left shoulder to avoid
disaster (M, SLC, 1961).

5975   Throw salt over your left shoulder if
you spill it; then good luck will follow
(M, SLC). Brown 2881.

## Passing Salt, Pepper, Etc.

5976   Never pass the salt at the table without
smiling, because it will bring bad luck
(F, 26, SLC, 1963).

5977   When you are at a dinner and you ask to
have the salt or pepper shakers passed,
it is bad luck to take them from your
neighbor's hand. You must pick them up
from the table (F, 51, SLC, 1920).
Brown 2885.

5978   It is bad luck to have either the salt
or pepper passed to you alone. They
should be together (F, 19, Kearns,
1950).

5979   If you spill salt or pepper, pick up
some of it and throw it over your left

shoulder to avoid bad luck (M, 50,
Bountiful, 1965).

5980   A bit of pepper sprinkled over the hot
stove will put bad luck out (F, Ger,
SLC, 1960).

5981   It is bad luck to pay back borrowed
pepper (M, 19, SLC, 1964).

## Sugar

5982   Spilling sugar on the table brings
happiness or bad luck (F, 45, SLC,
1964). Cf. Brown 2889.

5983   Spilling sugar brings worse bad luck
than spilling salt (M, 54, Magna, 1923).

5984   If you spill sugar, gather it up and
throw it over your left shoulder and
don't look back to change your luck for
the better (F, 25, SLC).

5985   When sugar is spilled accidentally it is
a lucky omen (F, 50, SLC, 1964).

5986   If you borrow sugar from a person, you
can't pay back sugar, or it will be bad
luck. You are supposed to pay back salt
(F, 60, Randolph, 1910).

5987   When you return borrowed sugar it is
unlucky to return it in the cup they
lent you. Return them separately (F,
SLC, 1914).

# HOLIDAY FOODS

## New Year's

5988   At twelve o'clock on New Year's Eve the
family should go out the back door,
circle the house and come in the front
to a meal of sauerkraut. This brings a
year of luck and happiness (F, 45, SLC,
1930s).

5989   Serve cabbage on New Year's Day to bring
good luck for the rest of the year (F,
Ger, SLC). Brown 2832f.

5990   Duck for New Year's dinner is good luck
(F, 75, Eng, Holden, 1899).

5991   If you eat kippered herring on the last
day of the year, it will bring good luck
for the following year (F, SLC, 1962).

5992   Eat twelve kinds of fruitcake on New
Year's Day and it will bring you a
year's good luck (F, SLC, 1961).

5993   The Japanese people believe that if on
New Year's Day they eat as many rice
cakes as they are years old, they will
have good luck during the coming year
(F, 21, Ja, Riverton, 1958).

5994   At New Year's a special kind of bread is
made and a coin is placed inside it.
The finder of the coin is to have a full
and prosperous year (F, 42, Gr, SLC);
. . . whoever finds a gold coin in the
bread will have good luck for the coming
year (F, Gr, SLC, 1957).

5995   You should eat rice and popcorn on New
Year's, because, like rice and popcorn,

your good fortune will increase (M, 20, Layton, 1972).

5996 Eat peas on New Year's (M, 54, Beaver, 1964).

5997 Eating black-eyed peas on New Year's Day will bring good luck all year (F, Ogden, 1961); . . . a year of good fortune (F, SLC, 1958); Eat black-eyed peas to avoid evil during the year (F, 19, SLC, 1963). Brown 2827.

5998 If you eat black-eyed peas on New Year's Day, you will have a prosperous year (F, 19, SLC, 1964). Learned in Missouri, 1952; . . . you'll get one dollar for every pea eaten (F, SLC, 1964).

5999 Serve black-eyed peas and hog jowl on New Year's Day and you will have prosperity for the coming year (M, SLC, 1961); . . . you'll have plenty to eat all year (F, SLC, 1963). Cf. Brown 2826, 2828.

6000 If you eat black-eyed peas, ham, and cornbread, you will have good luck and happiness in the coming year (F, 54, SLC, 1963). Learned in Tennessee, 1911. Cf. Brown 2830.

## Good Friday, Easter

6001 Eat hot cross buns on Good Friday to bring good luck (F, Ger, SLC, 1914).

6002 Easter loaves are baked and decorated with red eggs, and are considered as good luck in the home (F, 42, Gr, SLC, 1964).

6003 If a person finds a gold piece in a slice of Easter bread, this means that the person is to have luck the rest of the year (F, Gr, SLC, 1962).

## Christmas

6004 It is lucky to give food away on Christmas Day (F, Ir, SLC, 1960).

6005 It is unlucky to cut a Yule cake before Christmas Eve (F, 69, Garland, 1963).

6006 At Christmas time a coin is placed in each of a number of small loaves of bread. Whoever gets the coin in his piece of bread will never be poor (F, Gr, SLC, 1957).

6007 If someone puts a sixpence in a Christmas pudding, and you find it, it will bring you good luck (F, Eng, SLC, 1962).

6008 At Christmas the pudding contains one almond, and the person who gets the almond is promised good luck and happiness for the coming year (F, 11, Ir, SLC, 1950).

6009 It is good luck to have fish on Christmas (F, 44, Swed, Midvale, 1928).

## Miscellaneous

6010 It is bad luck to eat haws (hawthorn berry?) after November first (F, Ir, SLC, 1960).

6011 On a day in February you cook soybeans and throw candy out of the house to throw out bad spirits and leave in and invite in good spirits and happiness (M, Ja, SLC, 1963).

6012 It was the custom to serve baby pigs on Thanksgiving (M, 70).

## ABUNDANCE AND SCARCITY OF FOOD

6013 If you are eating when the New Year comes in, you will have plenty to eat throughout the coming year (F, 66, Eng, SLC, 1964).

6014 If your salt shakers are not full on New Year's Day, then your family will suffer want during the New Year (F, 25, SLC, 1945).

6015 If you let your salt supply run low, that means that you will need and want other food (F, SLC, 1960).

6016 If there is rice in your kitchen, you will always have plenty to eat (F, SLC, 1964).

6017 If you don't put out grain for the birds, you won't have enough food for the year (F, 67, Panguitch, 1900s).

6018 Taking food when you already have some means that someone is becoming hungry (M, SLC, 1957). Cf. Brown 2861.

6019 Never throw leftover food away; if you do, some time you will go hungry (F, Murray, 1925); If you waste food willfully, you'll live to regret it (M, 72, Mex, Grantsville, 1963).

6020 To throw food away is feeding the devil (F, 80, Eng, Midvale).

6021 If one is to throw a piece of bread away, one will someday want for that piece of bread (F, It, SLC, 1963). Cf. Brown 2835.

6022 To throw bread away is bad luck (F, SLC, 1960).

6023 If you burn bread, you will have bad luck. I think there is a saying, "Burn bread, want bread" (SLC, 1925); . . . you'll be hungry (Bear River City, 1957); It's bad luck to throw bread in a fire. You'll always be hungry (F, 70, SLC, 1964). Cf. Brown 2836ff.

6024 If you take a second piece of bread while you already have one buttered, someday you will starve (F, 41, SLC, 1943); . . . someone will go hungry (F, Kearns, 1963); . . . it is a sign that someone will come who will be hungrier than you (F, SLC, 1961); . . . you will go hungry (M, SLC, 1900). Cf. Brown 2860.

6025 When the cut end of a homemade bread faces the edge of the table, there will be hunger in your family (F, Ger, SLC, 1950).

6026 When finishing a meal, bread should be left on the table so it may be cleared from the table. This means that there will be food, and the family will never go hungry (M, Gr, SLC, 1961).

6027  Pastries must not be eaten on New Year's Eve, or the New Year will be marked by a shortage of food (F, Cedar City).

6028  When eating a bread roll or slice of bread always finish it. If you don't, you leave part of your strength behind (F, Gr, SLC, 1961).

## THE TABLE:  FOOD AND EATING, ETC.

### Eggs, Milk, Ice Cream

6029  If after eating a boiled egg you do not knock your spoon through the bottom of the shell, no luck will attend you (M, SLC, 1953).

6030  Eggs that are pointed on both ends will bring bad luck to he who eats them (M, SLC, 1961).

6031  Spilled milk is a sign of bad luck (F, SLC, 1961).

6032  If you eat the cherry last on a sundae, you can wish on it; but if you eat it first, you'll have bad luck (F, 30, Provo, 1964); While eating the cherry on a sundae close your eyes and wish; if it tastes sour, your wish will come true (F, SLC, 1958).

6033  If your ice melts before you finish a drink, you will have bad luck (F, Ogden, 1957).

6034  If a black and white cat crosses your path, you will have ice cream for dinner (SLC, 1925).

### Vegetables, Fruits, Nuts

6035  When greens are placed on a table, a person should twirl around three times to ward off evil spirits by the blessing (M, SLC, 1957).

6036  If you eat red cabbage on Monday, you'll have bad luck (F, Ogden, 1961).

6037  Fruit eaten in the morning is golden, silver at noon, and lead by night (F, SLC).

6038  To eat an apple without first rubbing it will bring bad luck (F, 1959).

6039  An almond in rice pudding drawn by a guest's spoon will bring good luck (F, SLC, 1959).

6040  Eating salted almonds is a lucky sign if they are wholesome and of good flavor (F, 45, SLC, 1930).

### Cake, Pastries, Etc.

6041  When a piece of cake is taken and set on one's plate and it tips over on its side, this is a sign of bad luck (F, 28, SLC, 1964).

6042  When you eat a piece of pie for dessert, cut off the point and put it aside and eat it last. Make a wish at that time, and the wish will come true (F, 34, SLC, 1964). Brown 2863.

6043  When eating pie, if the point of the pie is pointing to your left, make a wish and the wish will come true (M, 49, Price, 1964).

6044  It is good luck to have the piece of pie pointed to you (M, SLC, 1959).

6045  If you wait to eat the rim of a piece of pie last, you will have good luck (F, 20, SLC, 1963).

6046  For every mince pie you eat in a different house you will have a month's happiness (F, 21, Eng, SLC, 1963).

6047  If you have a piece of cherry pie and you happen to find a seed in you piece, make a wish, keep it a secret, and it will come true (F, SLC, 1964).

6048  If you offer to some person a dish with candies or pastries, it is not good luck if the person to whom the pastries are offered washes or clears the dish (M, 57, Gr, SLC, 1963).

### Coffee, Tea

6049  It is an old Finnish superstition that it is bad luck to sit at a table, unless your coffee cup is turned upside down (M, SLC, 1957).

6050  If a person eats the bubbles in a cup of coffee before they dissolve, this will bring him good luck (M, 35, SLC, 1945).

6051  If bubbles form on the top of a cup of tea, make a wish on them (F, 17, SLC, 1953).

6052  Bubbles in coffee bring bad luck (F, 49, SLC, 1964).

6053  You'll have bad luck if you have coffee grounds left in your coffee cup (F, 25, SLC, 1964).

6054  To stir the contents of a teapot is to stir up trouble (F, 34, Manti, 1939); . . . stir up strife (F, SLC, 1961).

6055  In serving tea, as you pour it, if the tea leaf stands up it is good luck (F, SLC, 1964).

6056  Don't drink milk in tea (F, 19, SLC, 1963).

6057  For two people to pour out tea from the same pot will bring bad luck (F, 21, Eng, SLC, 1963).

6058  It is bad luck to pour tea in someone else's house, also to have someone else pour tea in your house (F, SLC, 1957).

### Water, Etc.

6059  If a person should refuse you a drink of water, it would be the worse luck to him (F, 26, SLC, 1950).

6060  Don't drink water at night while standing up. Sit down (M, SLC, 1963).

6061  Don't drink out of a glass with your left hand, or bad luck will follow (F, 53, SLC, 1962).

6062 If you spill water and it runs toward you, it means you are going to have bad luck (M, 64, SLC, 1964).

6063 If you spill water on the right side of your water glass at dinner, bad luck follows (M, 21, SLC, 1964).

6064 It is unlucky to have an even number of ice cubes in a glass (F, 21, SLC, 1963).

6065 If you fill a glass to the brim, it is bad luck; you are supposed to leave the liquid a space from the top (F, 27, SLC, 1945).

## Wine, Toasting

6066 Don't step on a line, or your father will drink wine (F, 28, Copperton, 1942).

6067 If you drop or spill wine, you will have good luck (F, Gr, Magna, 1927).

6068 It is bad luck to spill wine (M, SLC, 1963).

6069 The host should always have the first taste of wine before serving the guests (F, 75, Eng, SLC, 1964).

6070 Passing wine at the table with the right hand gives good luck (F, 43, Logan, 1935).

6071 Don't pass the wine the wrong way at the table; it should follow the course of the sun (M, 46, Draper, 1963).

6072 Cork particles floating upon the surface of a newly opened bottle of wine announce a period of misfortune (M, 22, SLC, 1961).

6073 It is bad luck and bad taste to empty a wine glass completely (M, SLC, 1961); You must leave a small amount of wine in the bottom of the glass for good luck (F, It, SLC, 1963).

6074 Throwing a champagne glass in the fire is good luck (M, SLC); After a toast one should break the glass against the fireplace to bring luck and fulfillment of the toast (M, 66, SLC, 1964); Throw a wine glass into a burning fire for good luck in the future (F, 20, SLC, 1960).

6075 A toast to a person implies good luck and happiness (M, SLC, 1950).

6076 Toasting to anything with a glass of water will be unlucky to the person or the thing toasted (F, 20, SLC, 1959).

## Napkin, Tablecloth, Etc.

6077 Always leave the napkin the way you found it and you will be invited back (M, SLC, 1961).

6078 Never fold your napkin neatly. Always crumple it up or you'll not be asked back to your host's home again (F, SLC, 1967); A guest who folds his napkin after the first meal in a house will never return again (F, 79, SLC, 1964).

6079 It's bad luck to drop your napkin on the floor (M, Provo, 1949); . . . if you drop your napkin off your lap (F, 21, SLC, 1964).

6080 Shaking a tablecloth after dark means bad luck (F, 47, SLC, 1931).

6081 One should never shake a tablecloth outside, or it will bring bad luck (F, 69, Eng, SLC, 1964); . . . you shake away your good fortune (F, SLC, 1964); Never shake bread crumbs outdoors after sunset. It's bad luck (F, Gr, SLC, 1964).

## Seating at the Table

6082 Never seat thirteen at a table, or there will be a calamity (F, 44, SLC, 1964); . . . it is unlucky (F, 75, Smithfield, 1970); . . . bad luck will befall the people at the table (F, 66, Welsh, SLC, 1964); . . . brings bad luck to the hostess (F, 19, SLC, 1956); In the 1930s a lady in a suburb of Salt Lake had thirteen people at a dinner. When she discovered this, she went to a neighbor, prevailed upon the parents to get their little girl (the informant herself) out of bed, so she could come and make the fourteenth at the table (F, 1964). (In France, freeloaders advertise in newspapers to make a fourteenth at dinner, if needed. --Eds.)

6083 Don't seat thirteen persons at a table on Friday, or you'll have bad luck (M, SLC, 1958).

6084 On Friday the thirteenth never sit down to a table with thirteen or bad luck will soon come (F, SLC, 1960).

6085 If thirteen people are seated at a table, it is bad luck, and they must all join hands and rise as one person (F, 47, SLC, 1931).

6086 It's bad luck to have a seat vacant at a formal dinner (F, 43, Logan, 1935); . . . ; it should be removed (M, 33, SLC, 1964).

6087 If you invite an odd number of people to dinner, you will have bad luck (F, 67, SLCo, 1925); Never set a table for an odd number (F, 43, SLC, 1964).

6088 You should always sit at the same place at the table. It is unlucky to change (M, 22, SLC, 1950).

## Table Manners

6089 It is unlucky to cross hands while passing food at the table. One should set down what he is holding until the other person has passed the dish he is holding (F, SLC, 1957).

6090 Do not rest elbows on the table with your head between your hands. This will bring you misfortune, if you do (F, Gr, SLC, 1961).

6091 Don't cross your legs while at the dinner table (F, SLC, 1964).

## Miscellaneous

6092   Break your popsicle stick before you throw it away (M, SLC, 1963).

6093   Never serve anything in threes, because it is bad luck (M, 45, Ja, SLC, 1963).

6094   Leave something on the plate for good luck (M, SLC).

6095   Make a wish the first time you eat in someone else's house (F, Ogden, 1918).

6096   It's bad luck to eat in bed unless you're sick (M, 21, SLC, 1964).

6097   It's a sign of bad luck if when eating one misses the mouth with the food and it falls to the ground (F, 43, Logan, 1935).

6098   It is polite to belch after a meal to show satisfaction and appreciation for the food and the evening (M, E. Indian, SLC, 1963).

6099   If you brush your hands after a meal, it means it was fit for a devil (M, 19, Gr, SLC, 1964); . . . benefits none but the devil (F, Gr, SLC, 1964).

6100   If a small strand of hair is found in the food, a curse will be placed upon you (F, 23, SLC, 1960).

6101   Don't use tin on your table if you want to keep well (F, Eng, SLC, 1960).

6102   It's bad luck to put ashes on a dinner plate (F, Murray, 1957).

6103   Never take the last piece or portion of anything.  It brings bad luck (F, SLC, 1948).

6104   If a person takes the last bit of food from a dish, he should kiss the cook for good luck (M, 23, SLC, 1958).

6105   You will be lazy throughout the day if you have any second helpings at breakfast (M, SLC, 1954).

6106   No one can dine comfortably under the crossbeam of a house (M, 90, W. Jordan, 1920).

## EATING UTENSILS

6107   If you drop anything that sticks straight up, you'll have good luck (M, 47, SLC, 1925).  Brown 2867.

6108   Don't drop the silver or you'll have bad luck (F, 49, Brigham City, 1964).

6109   Don't cross silverware when setting a table.  It's bad luck (F, 62, SLC, 1910).

## Knives

6110   Stir with a knife, you'll have trouble all your life (F, 36, Draper, 1965); . . . stir up strife (F, Eng, Hooper, 1963).

6111   If you have to borrow a knife to cut fruit, return it laughing (F, 62, SLC).

6112   If you hand something sharp, such as a knife to someone, it will bring bad luck (F, 46, SLC, 1928).

6113   It's bad luck to hand a person a knife with the blade forward (F, 21, SLC, 1964).

6114   It's bad luck to give someone a knife open and have him give it back closed (F, SLC).

6115   Never pick up a knife if it is pointing toward you; it brings bad luck (F, 70, Bountiful, 1900s).  Cf. Brown 2870.

6116   Holding the blade of a knife toward the neck is a sign of bad luck (M, 19, SLC, 1964).

6117   If while setting the table you should place two knives together, it is very bad luck (F, 67, SLC, 1920).

6118   Don't turn the knife out on the table. This means you have something against the person next to you (M, 24, SLC, 1960).

6119   It is bad luck for knives to lie on their backs (F, 53, Monroe, 1964). Brown 2876.

6120   It is bad luck to use the back edge of a knife (F, 23, Cedar City, 1964).

6121   To drop a knife accidentally so that the point penetrates the floor and it stands upright, is a sign of success (F, Axtell, 1958).  Cf. Brown 2868.

6122   If you drop a knife, you will have bad luck (F, Nephi, 1961); . . . will experience disappointment (F, 18, SLC, 1961); . . . trouble is coming in the house (F, 82, It, SLC, 1963).  Cf. Brown 2877.

6123   Drop a knife, and you'll get a surprise (M, SLC, 1959).

6124   If you drop a knife, step on the handle with the left foot or you will burn yourself when you are cooking or you may cut yourself (M, Ogden, 1968).

6125   Never let two knives cross on the table (M, 52, Eng, SLC, 1963); . . . you'll have bad luck for ten years (F, 45, SLC, 1965).

6126   It is unlucky for two people to cross knives at the dinner table (F, Ogden, 1960).

## Knives as Gifts

6127   The placing of a penny with a new silver knife means the new owner will have good luck (M, 22, SLC, 1964).

6128   If you give anything sharp, give a silver coin with it, or you give bad luck (F, Park City, 1900).

## Knives and Forks

6129   If you cross your knife and fork at the dinner table, you're inviting bad luck (M, SLC, 1959).

6130  Never cross your knife and fork on your plate after your have finished eating, or you shall soon meet with trouble (F, 85, Eng, SLC, 1965).

6131  It's bad luck to hit your fork and knife together while you're cutting your food (F, Ogden, 1961).

## Forks

6132  If a fork is dropped, bad luck to a woman (F, Centerville, 1963).

6133  To drop a fork when setting the table will bring bad luck (F, 19, Ogden, 1956); . . . at the dinner table . . . (M, SLC, 1961).

6134  While you are washing dishes, you must not drop a fork, or it will mean bad luck (F, 61, Richfield, 1920).

6135  Putting two forks on the table at one plate means someone is starving (F, Ger, Sandy, 1933).

6136  If you drop a fork on the floor, throw salt over the right shoulder to prevent bad luck (M, 40, Provo, 1958).

6137  It is bad luck to eat with a fork in the left hand (M, 32, SLC, 1935).

## Spoons

6138  If you drop a spoon, you get a kiss (M, SLC, 1945).

6139  If you drop a spoon, trouble is coming your way (F, 63, Mex, Grantsville, 1963); . . . a disappointment will come into your life (F, 20, SLC, 1948); . . . a difficulty will arise in the near future (M, 62, Heber, 1963). Brown 2878.

6140  If a spoon is dropped, bad luck to a child (F, 72, Centerville, 1963).

6141  If you drop a spoon, a spoon or small amount of luck will come your way (M, 1960).

6142  Never pick up a spoon lying in the road, or you'll receive bad luck (M, Layton, 1960).

## Chopsticks

6143  When you use chopsticks, you mustn't cross them at the end, for it will bring you bad luck (M, 24, Ja, Sandy).

6144  Do not fight over food with chopsticks; this is bad luck (F, 25, Ja, SLC, 1958).

## China, Dishes

6145  Step in a hole and you'll break your mother's bowl (F, Bountiful, 1947); . . . mother's sugar bowl (F, SLC, 1918).

6146  If you break one dish, you'll break three (F, 60, Midvale, 1910); . . . two more the same day (F, 47, SLC, 1930); . . . you should hurry and break two

worthless objects so that the omen is fulfilled and you won't break anything of value (F, 20, Bountiful, 1969); . . . you will break seven more before you quit (F, 69, SLC, 1964). Cf. Brown 2891.

6147  If you drop a dish and it doesn't break, three good things happen. If it breaks, three bad things occur (M, SLC, 1930s).

6148  When you break a dish, turn around three times before cleaning it up to prevent bad luck (F, 25, SLC). Heard in Wyoming, 1950s.

6149  If you rub a snake skin in your hand, you will not drop and break any dishes (F, 28, teacher, SLC, 1958). Brown 2895f.

6150  If you break dishes, etc., you will avert other accidents (F, 25, SLC).

6151  If one breaks a dish, bad luck will follow (M, 64, Milford, 1964); It's a sign of bad luck to break a dish at a party (F, Sandy, 1957).

6152  It brings bad luck to break one dish; to reverse this bad luck, break another (F, 52, Provo, 1920).

6153  Breaking dishes will bring good luck (M, Swiss, SLC, 1957).

6154  Never return an empty plate to someone, or you will have bad luck (F, SLC, 1958).

6155  If you break a teapot, it is a sign of trouble (F, 31, Murray, 1963). First heard in Washington, 1939.

## Glassware

6156  If a goblet is broken at a dinner table, this means bad luck for those at the dinner (F, 60, SLC, 1964). First heard in Washington, 1940.

6157  If you break something that's glass, you will have to break three more things before your bad luck will stop (F, 82, SLC, 1961).

6158  If two glasses are broken during the course of a day, a third one must voluntarily be shattered; in this way an evil spell is broken (M, 50, It, SLC, 1965).

## DISHCLOTHS, TOWELS, WASHING DISHES

6159  Two people using a dishtowel at the same time is bad luck (F, 21, Vernal).

6160  Throwing a dishrag over the left shoulder will bring good luck (F, 41, SLC, 1952).

6161  It is unlucky to place a dishcloth over the left shoulder (SLC, 1946).

6162  It is bad luck to drop a dishrag (M, Layton, 1954).

6163  Dropping a dishrag means something special will happen (F, 43, Logan, 1936); . . . a wet dishrag . . . (F, 48, SLC, 1932).

6164    If you drop a dishrag on the floor, it is a sign that someone is going hungry (F, SLC).  Brown 2898.

6165    Never put a dishrag on the doorknob, or you will have bad luck (F, 50, SLC, 1964).  Brown 2899.

6166    Flour on the floor means a clogged drain (F, 21, Logan, 1970).

6167    At a shower, wedding, baby, etc., if you break a ribbon on a package, it means you have to do the dishes (Murray, 1969); If you break the string on a birthday present, you'll do dishes for the rest of the year (F, 22, SLC, 1955).

6168    If you are washing dishes and water drips down your arms to your elbows, it is very bad luck (F, Ogden, 1960).

6169    Don't pour dirty water down your sink on New Year's Day, or you'll have bad luck (F, 50, Eng, SLC, 1964).

6170    Every bubble in the dishpan means bad luck to that family (F, SLC, 1962).

### SOAP, SOAP MAKING

6171    If you want to borrow soap, the person giving it to you must place it on the table, and you pick them up yourself (F, Gr, SLC, 1962).

6172    It is unlucky if soap slips out of your hand and strikes the floor (M, 25, SLC, 1964).

6173    In making soap, throw in a handful of salt and it will come quicker (F, Moab, 1953).

6174    Make soap in the dark of the moon (F, SLC, 1964).  Cf. Brown 2806, 2811.

### TAKING UP ASHES

6175    On the day before New Year's, take the ashes out of the stove and sweep the floor so the devil won't come in (F, 83, SLC, 1964).

6176    Never carry ashes out on New Year's Day, or you carry your good luck out (M, SLC, 1957).  Cf. Brown 2908.

6177    Bad luck will come into the house if you fail to clean the dead embers out of the stove before retiring (F, SLC, 1960).

### SWEEPING, BROOMS, MOPS, ETC.

6178    Never sweep the floor with the light on (F, 36, Brigham City).

6179    Don't sweep dirt out the front door, or you'll sweep out the fortune of the house (F, 53, Roosevelt, 1964); Sweep all your luck away unless you sweep the dust to the middle of the room, and then carry it out the door in a dustpan (F, 45, SLC, 1930s).

6180    If you sweep dirt out of doors, you will sweep away riches (F, SLC, 1955); . . . you'll sweep out happiness (F, 57, Ger, SLC, 1963); . . . sweep dirt into the fire (M, 46, Swed, SLC, 1963).

6181    Sweeping the floor from the door in sweeps poverty into the house (F, 53, Norw, SLC, 1961).

6182    Never sweep dirt out the back door (M, 21, SLC).

6183    If you sweep scattered rice together with a broom rather than pick it up grain by grain, you'll have bad luck (F, 19, SLC, 1964).

6184    It is bad luck for two people to sweep the floor at the same time (M, 64, Milford, 1964).  Brown 2929.

6185    When you have swept your floor, don't empty the garbage outside.  It is bad luck (F, Gr, SLC, 1962).

### Sweeping under Someone

6186    It's bad luck to let a swamper (sweeper) sweep or mop under the bar stool when you're on it (M, 35, Hooper, 1970).

6187    Don't step over or sweep under a person's feet.  It is bad luck for the person if you do (F, Gr, SLC, 1964).  Cf. Brown 2925.

6188    If you sweep over someone's feet, you are sure to have bad luck (F, 28, Bingham, 1940).

6189    It's bad luck to sweep under a table while people are sitting there (F, 24, SLC, 1952).

### Sweeping the Bedroom of a Guest

6190    If you sweep out your guest room before a guest has been gone an hour, bad luck will befall the departed guest (F, SLC, 1962); . . . it's bad luck to a friend of the family (F, SLC, 1960); . . . it's bad luck to a member of the family (F, SLC, 1961).

### The Time of Day for Sweeping

6191    Sweeping the floor at night is bad luck (F, 19, SLC, 1964); . . . after sunset may bring misfortune to the home (F, 48, SLC, 1963); . . . after midnight is bad luck (F, SLC, 1945).  Cf. Brown 2913.

6192    If you sweep with a broom across the doorstep after dark, you will sweep your luck away (F, Nephi, 1961).  Cf. Brown 2914.

6193    Sweeping the floor at night will disturb the spirits who walk about at night (F, SLC, 1957).

6194    Sweep after dark, you'll sweep sorrow to your heart (F, SLC, 1960).

6195    Don't sweep the floor at night, or it will undo everything you have done that night (F, 45, SLC, 1963).

6196    Sweep dirt out of doors after dark and you'll sweep yourself out of a home (F, 65, SLC).  Cf. Brown 8480.

6197    Sweeping dirt out the back door after night means bad luck (F, SLC, 1959).  Cf. Brown 2917.

6198 Sweeping the sidewalk after dark is bad luck (F, 21, SLC, 1954).

6199 It is bad luck to sweep the porch after sundown (F, SLC, 1940). Cf. Brown 2916.

## Sweeping on New Year's Day

6200 Don't sweep or clean the house on New Year's Day, or you'll sweep out the good fortune of the year (F, Ja, SLC, 1963); . . . it will bring bad luck (F, 69, Eng, Midvale, 1964); . . . it is unlucky (F, SLC, 1959).

6201 If you throw or sweep anything out on New Year's, then everything will be going out and nothing will be coming in all year (F, SLC, 1958).

## Brooms

6202 It is bad luck to hold a broom after sundown (F, 54, SLC, 1963).

6203 A new broom should sweep something into the house before it sweeps something out of the house (F, 87, Dan, SLC, 1964).

6204 Have a new broom in your home on New Year's Day to bring good luck (F, Fillmore, 1960).

6205 A new broom sweeps cleaner than an old one (F, SLC, 1959).

6206 An old broom sweeps cleaner, because it knows where to find the dirt (F, Ogden, 1953).

6207 Never use a new broom until you have swept the ground with it first (F, SLC, 1961).

6208 Never buy a new broom except in the month of May (F, SLC, 1961).

6209 It is bad luck to jump or step over a broom (F, SLC, 1961); . . . a fallen broom (M, 24, SLC, 1964); . . . you'll be disappointed (F, 51, SLC, 1925). Brown 2931.

6210 To step over a broom going forwards is bad luck; you must step over it backwards (M, 22, SLC, 1961).

6211 If you walk over a broom, you are a lazy, slouchy housekeeper (F, 87, Providence, 1890); . . . trip over a broom . . . (F, SLC, 1957).

## CLEANING, HOUSEKEEPING

6212 A dirty house on New Year's will be dirty all the year (F, 50, SLC, 1921); If your housework is behind on the arrival of the New Year, you will be doing the thing you are behind in all year long (F, Scot, SLC, 1958); Work carried over into the New Year means bad luck (F, Scot, SLC, 1961).

6213 Don't throw out any dirt on New Year's Day. It's bad luck (F, 80, Eng, Midvale). Cf. Brown 2936.

6214 The house must be thoroughly cleaned before midnight on New Year's Eve in order to insure cleanliness as well as good luck for the New Year (F, 45, SLC).

6215 It is bad luck to do any work about the house on the Sabbath (F, SLC). You will have bad luck with your housework all week long if you . . . (F, 82, It, SLC, 1963).

6216 If a person sweeps the house on Good Friday, the house will have bugs in it the rest of the year (F, SLC, 1952).

6217 It is unlucky to spring clean a house after the month of May (F, 18, SLC, 1957).

6218 You're not supposed to empty the garbage outside at night. This is bad luck (F, 19, Gr, SLC, 1953).

6219 It is bad luck to shake a dust cloth out the front door (M, SLC, 1961).

6220 It is good luck to bring home a little dust from a church house and mix it with your own before dusting (F, Ger, SLC, 1933).

6221 People who have too clean a house have something to hide (F, 77, SLC, 1963).

6222 Don't clean house on Wednesday (F, 78, Provo).

6223 It's bad luck to hang things on a doorknob (M, Ogden, 1961).

6224 Never shake a rug in the house (F, Murray, 1957).

6225 Never shake rugs on the front porch, for it's bad luck (F, 40, Cedar City, 1936).

6226 It's bad luck to defrost your refrigerator on Sunday (F, Murray, 1957).

6227 You should never dust off a stove after dark, because there are spirits in the dust, and you should not disturb them at night (F, 84, Price, 1961).

6228 The way you keep your purse is the way you keep your house (F, 21, SLC, 1959).

## LAUNDRY

6229 Fruit stains cannot be removed from an item until the season of the fruit is over (M, 36, atty, SLC, 1955).

6230 To prevent shrinking and yellowing of Irish linen soak in urine (F, 41, SLC, 1964).

6231 It is bad luck to wash blankets in a month that doesn't have an "R" in its name (F, 19, SLC, 1964).

6232 Bubbles in a detergent mean that it has a lot of cleaning power (F, 52, SLC).

6233 Never wash the clothes after sundown; it is not good luck (F, 66, Gr, SLC, 1963).

6234 Wash your clothes on Monday and you'll have the whole week to dry (M, 45, SLC, 1940). Brown 2941.

6235   Don't wash on Wednesday because it brings bad luck to your husband (F, 49, Gr, Midvale, 1927).

6236   It is bad luck to wash on Friday (F, SLC, 1957); . . . Saturday (F, 25, SLC, 1964); . . . Sunday (M, 52, SLC, 1964).

6237   Don't ever leave the laundry out overnight; the dark air is unclean (F, SLC, 1963).

6238   If you step on a line in the sidewalk, it will break your mother's clothesline (F, 17, Sandy, 1956).

6239   If a Chinaman crosses in front of you, you'll have seven years of bad laundry (F, Provo, 1971).

## Laundering on New Year's Day

6240   Washing clothes between Christmas and New Year's is bad luck (F, 55, Ger, SLC, 1965). Brown 2937, cf. 2939, 8481.

6241   Clothes left hanging on the line overnight on New Year's Eve will bring the family bad luck during the year (F, SLC, 1930).

6242   It is a common belief that if you wash your hair, clothes, house or anything on New Year's Day, then you will "wash someone out of the family" (M, 19, Eng, Logan, 1970). Cf. Brown 2940.

6243   If you hang your clothes on a clothesline between Christmas and New Year's, someone in your family will hang themselves within a year (M, 48, Venice, 1930).

6244   If a woman washes clothes on New Year's Day, she will work hard all year (F, Brigham City, 1925).

6245   If you wash on New Year's, you'll slave all year washing (F, 56, Ger, SLC, 1964).

## IRONING

6246   Anything folded in a diamond fold brings bad luck (F, Layton, 1960).

6247   For every hour you iron on Sunday you will burn a day in hell (F, Nephi, 1961).

6248   An iron which lies flat after being dropped will bring bad luck (F, 46, Draper, 1965).

6249   Never lend a hot iron. No good luck (F, 57, Gr, SLC, 1963).

## NEW HOUSES, BUILDINGS--BUYING, SELLING

6250   A round wreath of green leaves is put on the house when the roof is put on. This is good luck (F, 25, Dan, SLC, 1964).

6251   A Christmas tree is put on top of almost finished houses and the next day is taken off (M, Logan, 1960).

6252   Rice cake is thrown from the top of the frame of a new house to bless it (M, Ja, SLC, 1963).

6253   When a new roof is to be put on a house, a party is given to the neighbors. It is good luck charm (F, 48, SLC, 1963).

6254   Never build a house at a diagonal. Always build it north-south or east-west. If you don't, odd things will happen to you (F, 58, Richfield, 1935).

6255   In building a house always construct an attic to catch the evil spirits before they enter the other parts of the house (M, SLC, 1964).

6256   Always let the foundation on a house set for about two weeks before building upon it, or the house could turn out to be crooked or lopsided (M, 45, SLC, 1954).

6257   A house built of all new lumber is sure to bring bad luck (M, 19, Richfield, 1957).

6258   It's bad luck to cut a doorway between two rooms after the house is built (F, Layton, 1956).

6259   If a building sways, this means it will never topple (M, 52, SLC, 1964).

6260   If when building something you bend a nail, never straighten it out and use it again, or it will cause a weak spot in your building (M, Kearns, 1958).

6261   Don't drive a nail after dark, because every nail is one in your coffin (M, 39, SLC, 1941).

6262   It is good luck to pick up an old nail (M, Hyrum, 1937).

6263   When hammering nails, if one falls over, throw it over your shoulder or you will have bad luck (M, 36, Murray, 1950).

6264   If you find your initials in spider webs near the door of a new home, you will be lucky as long as you live there (M, 22, SLC, 1955).

6265   You should place silver dollars on new things such as homes, etc. This is a token of good luck (F, Gr, SLC, 1964).

6266   Never live in a house that does not face the east (M, 49, saddle maker, SLC, 1961).

6267   When a house burns and another is built on the same spot, that too will burn soon (F, 61, Du, SLC, 1964). Cf. Brown 3035f.

6268   My father put a cross of tar over our storage house for the hotel with the belief that it would keep it safe and bring prosperity (M, SLC, 1967).

## MOVING

6269   A custom we brought with us from the old country was to give a friend a green plant when they move into a new house. The wish given with it is that as the plant grows and thrives so may happiness, love and life grow and thrive in the new home. The greatest gift and wishes that one can give to another are those of life (F, Ger, Provo, 1971).

6270 When moving into a new house or an apartment, count all the window panes, and whatever you dream that night will come true (F, 49, Norw, SLC, 1963).

6271 Never move downstairs in the same building (M, SLC, 1958).

6272 It's bad luck to move back into a house you have lived in before (M, 45, Murray, 1945).

6273 It is bad luck to leave the room clean when one moves (M, 64, Milford, 1964). Cf. Brown 2945f.

6274 One brings sweets to a new home so that life there will be happy (M, 50, It, SLC, 1965).

6275 If you break a glass or dish while entertaining your first guests in a brand new home, it means good luck (F, Gr, Magna, 1961).

## Portents of Moving

6276 If you open an umbrella in the house, you will move (F, 52, Eng, SLC, 1963).

6277 Two spoons given to one person denotes that that person will have two homes before the year is out (F, SLC, 1961).

6278 If you dream of ants you will move to a big city (F, Ogden, 1960).

## Time and Circumstances of Moving

6279 If you move on a rainy day, it means bad luck (M, Kaysville, 1958); . . . great unhappiness in the new home (M, SLC, 1959); . . . your new home will have many tears (F, 72, SLC, 1920).

6280 You should have good luck if you move on a Tuesday or a Thursday (F, SLC, 1967).

6281 It's bad luck to move on Friday (M, SLC, 1958). Brown 2951.

6282 Never change residence on a Saturday, because you won't stay very long at the new address (F, SLC, 1930); A Saturday flit is a short sit (F, SLC, 1960); . . . you will move in the next month (F, SLC, 1955). Brown 2952.

6283 You will have bad luck if you move on Sunday (M, SLC, 1961).

6284 Avoid the eleventh of any month for moving, as it is a most unlucky day (F, Ir, SLC, 1960).

6285 Never move into a house or sign a lease in the month of July (F, Ir, SLC, 1960).

6286 Misfortune will come if you move from one house to another in the dark of the moon (M, 19, Richfield, 1956). Cf. Brown 2948.

## Brooms

6287 When you move, if you take your broom with you, it will bring bad luck (F, SLC, 1959). Brown 2957.

6288 It's bad luck to take a new broom into a new house. You should always take your old wornout broom with you when you move (F, 49, SLC, 1964).

6289 When you move into a new home always burn your old broom, or your home will never be swept clean (M, SLC, 1958).

6290 It brings good luck when you move into a new house to take a broom in first (M, SLC, 1944).

## Broom and Bread, Bread and Salt

6291 The first articles taken into a new home should be a new broom and a loaf of bread. This is to insure a clean home and a full cupboard (F, 50, SLC, 1925); . . . ; it will bring good luck to the household (F, 26, Finn, Morgan, 1925).

6292 To bring luck to your new house you should go into every room bearing in your hands a loaf and plate of salt (F, 51, SLC, 1964).

6293 The first thing that you move into a new home is a little box with some salt in it for the spice of life, a dime so you won't ever want, and a piece of bread so you won't ever be hungry (F, 42, SLC, 1927). Cf. Brown 2949.

6294 The first things to be put into a new house should be: salt, a fresh loaf of bread, and a new broom. If this is followed, the family will never go hungry (F, 25, SLC, 1965).

6295 Before moving into a new house, always place a container with salt in it in the house (F, Ogden); Bring an old box of salt into a new residence; it should be kept until a new box is used (M, SLC, 1959); Take a bag of salt . . . to bring happiness (F, 50, Midvale, 1930).

6296 As soon as you move into a new house, sprinkle salt on the kitchen floor to keep away the devil (F, SLC, 1971).

6297 You should always take a box of salt to a friend in his new home (F, 46, Scot, SLC, 1964).

## Cats

6298 Never move a cat from one home to another, because it will bring bad luck to your new house (F, 78, SLC, 1964); . . . you will have three years of bad luck (M, SLC, 1952). Brown 2955.

6299 Never bring a cat from one house to another on Friday; it is a sign of bad luck (F, SLC, 1959).

## ENTERING AND LEAVING A HOUSE, ROOM, ETC.

6300 If two people open the door at the same time, the one who is on the side where the door swings will have bad luck (F, 49, Norw, SLC, 1963).

6301 When two people grasp opposite doorknobs at the same time, one will have an accident (M, 25, Wellington, 1964).

6302   If you open a door by accident and someone is standing there, bad luck may befall you (M, SLC, 1960).

6303   On entering a house some people will not leave without sitting down at least once (F, 19, SLC, 1960).

6304   When you come into the house, you should go sit on the bed before going out of the house again (F, SLC, 1964).

6305   It means ill luck to depart from a house leaving doors open throughout the house. The back door must be closed before the front door is opened (F, Swed, Sandy, 1963).

6306   When visiting a person, always leave by the same door that you entered; if not, bad luck will follow (M, 23, SLC, 1964); . . . ; it is unlucky to go out by a different door on the first visit (F, SLC, 1957); . . . you should leave by the same door in order not to break ties (F, Gr, SLC, 1964); If you go in one door and out another, bad luck will follow the next day (F, Ger, SLC); . . . it will bring bad luck to the person living there (F, 32, SLC, 1935). Brown 2969f.

6307   If you go into a room through one door, you must leave the room through that same door (F, 44, Eng, SLC, 1964).

6308   If there are more than two doors to a building, go in and out the same door (F, 60, SLC, 1964).

6309   The old Fillmore Post Office had two doors. It was considered bad luck to go in one door and out the other (F, Fillmore, 1960).

6310   Go out a different door than you came in for good luck (F, 18, SLC, 1963); . . . ; if you don't, it brings bad luck (F, SLC, 1947); Come in the front door and go out the back for good luck (F, 50, SLC, 1930).

6311   It is bad luck to enter a strange house by the back door (F, 19, Magna, 1954).

6312   It is bad luck to enter the house you are going to occupy by the back door. If you must do so, throw away the key with which you entered, and have a new one made (F, 22, SLC, 1960).

6313   If you enter a house with the left foot, bad luck will fall on the inhabitants (M, W. Jordan, 1959); . . . it is a bad omen (F, SLC, 1963); . . . you will bring evil to the inhabitants (F, SLC, 1960).

6314   If you step out of a building with your left foot, bad luck will come your way (M, 19, SLC, 1963).

6315   When coming into a house, put the right foot first, for this brings good luck (F, Gr, SLC,); . . . so you will have continued friendship (F, Gr, SLC, 1961).

6316   Don't walk backwards out of a door (F, Murray, 1957).

6317   Walk into a house backwards and you will have bad luck (F, 20, SLC, 1963).

6318   If a person walks into a room other than frontwards, it will bring him bad luck for the day (M, 21, Midvale, 1950).

6319   All people who go in and out of revolving doors one day will have bad luck the following day (F, SLC).

6320   Never leave a house by means of a window, or you will encounter very bad luck (F, SLC, 1962); Crawling out a window is bad luck to the house (F, 37, Midvale, 1964).

## WINDOWS

6321   Break a window and there will be seven years of bad luck (M, 15, Provo, 1964).

6322   Throw salt over the shoulder to break the bad luck incurred when breaking a window (M, 24, American Fork, 1963).

6323   It is bad luck if the windows rattle (F, 77, Santaquin, 1914).

6324   Smoking will cause windows to tarnish faster (M, SLC, 1963).

## DOORS

6325   Don't knock on your own door, or it will bring bad luck (F, 51, Park City, 1924).

6326   If a door closes without apparent reason, you'll have bad luck the next day (F, 20, Logan, 1972).

6327   If the wind blows the door open, bad luck enters (M, Pleasant Grove, 1959).

6328   Always shut the door of a room after you leave, or you'll never own a house (F, 19, SLC, 1955).

6329   Never leave the cupboard doors open when leaving your house, or it will bring bad luck (F, SLC, 1962).

6330   If you leave a stick behind the door, it will cause an accident (F, 20, Du, SLC, 1963).

6331   If you walk across a cellar door, it will bring you bad luck (F, SLC, 1945).

6332   Flint placed over a door prevents ill luck (M, SLC, 1959).

6333   If you hang garlic over your door, it will protect you (F, 58, Union, 1930).

## Horseshoes over the Door

6334   If you find a horseshoe, put it over your door, and you will have good luck (F, 80, SLC, 1940); . . . you will have a happy family life and a happy home (F, SLC, 1960); . . . it will bring good luck to all who enter (F, 50, Meadow, 1920). Brown 2961f.

6335   Anyone who finds a horseshoe must return it at once to his house, without speaking to anyone, and hang it over the door, prongs up. If prongs are hung downward, the luck will fall out (F, 23, Clearfield, 1964).

6336  A horseshoe above your door will keep away evil visitors (M, Bountiful, 1950); . . . evil spirits (F, 45, Monroe, 1928).

6337  Horseshoes over the door ward off bad luck (F, SLC, 1963). Brown 2963.

6338  A horseshoe barely tipped brings good luck (M, 1960).

6339  If you hang your horseshoe up, the good luck will stay in. If you hang it down, the good luck falls out (F, 20, SLC, 1949); . . . The open end of the horseshoe must point upward to keep the magical powers from running out (F, Bountiful, 1961).

6340  Placing a horseshoe upside down over a door brings good luck to the people in the house (F, Helper, 1959); . . . over the kitchen door . . . (F, Norw, SLC, 1963); . . . If the ends point downward, the good luck will run out into the household (M, SLC, 1958); . . . over the back door turned upside down . . . (M, 64, SLC).

6341  The horseshoe must be fastened with three nails, each driven by three blows (F, 54, SLC, 1945).

### Wishbones, Silver Dollars

6342  Hang a wishbone over the door for good luck (F, Moab, 1953).

6343  If you put a silver dollar over your front door, you'll have good luck (F, 19, SLC, 1950).

## DOORWAY, THRESHOLD, DOORSTEP

6344  Don't stand in a doorway and lean both hands on either side of it (F, Gr, SLC, 1964).

6345  The threshold is a favorite spot of the spirits (M, 40, SLC, 1940s).

6346  One must cross the threshold with his right foot, or it's bad luck (M, SLC, 1960).

6347  It is bad luck if a woman is the first to walk over the threshold of a house (F, SLC, 1961).

6348  A crack in the doorwalk means tragedy will strike the household (F, 74, SLC, 1964).

6349  To prevent bad luck, drive a rusty nail in the front doorstep (M, 22, SLC, 1963).

### Stairs

6350  An odd number of steps upstairs brings bad luck; an even number brings good luck (F, 20, SLC, 1960).

6351  It is unlucky to meet on the stairs (M, SLC, 1960). Brown 2998.

6352  Passing another person on the stairs going the opposite direction is bad luck (F, 20, SLC); . . . bad luck to cross on the stairs (M, SLC, 1960). Cf. Brown 2999.

6353  When walking upstairs, it is bad luck if you step on every step; you must skip some (M, SLC, 1930).

6354  Go upstairs two at a time, or you'll fall back three (F, 21, SLC, 1963).

6355  It's bad luck to hop down the stairs on one foot (F, 19, SLC, 1952).

6356  It is bad luck to fall downstairs and good luck to fall upstairs (M, Minersville, 1964); If you trip going downstairs, you will have bad luck the rest of the day (F, 19, SLC, 1961). Brown 3000f.

6357  If you stumble up the stairs, you're sure to be disappointed (F, 55, Brigham City, 1915).

## BRINGING TOOLS, GUNS, ETC., INDOORS

6358  If you bring an axe or any sharp tool in the house, it is bad luck. To break the spell you can take it back out the same door it was brought in (F, 59, SLC, 1964); . . . garden tools . . . (F, 66, Cedar City, 1964); . . . hoe . . . (F, SLC, 1959). Cf. Brown 2976f, 2981.

6359  If one carries a shovel or pitchfork through the house, doom will follow (F, 67, SLC, 1963). Cf. Brown 2978.

6360  A shovel in the house means bad luck. It has a connection with death in the digging of a grave (M, 1955).

6361  Don't hammer anything on Good Friday. If you do, it means you are hammering nails into Christ (F, 42, Gr, SLC, 1964).

6362  If you drop a hammer in the house, you will have mechanical trouble (F, 23, Murray, 1964).

6363  To bring old pieces of iron into the house will bring bad luck (F, SLC, 1915).

6364  If you pick up a rusty nail, it will bring you good luck (F, 76, Glenwood, 1893).

6365  All guns are bad, and to have one in the home is likely to bring bad luck to the owner (F, 50, SLC, 1964).

## HOUSEHOLD PESTS

6366  Use kerosene and sugar to kill ants (F, 14, SLC, 1964).

6367  A half and half mixture of borax and sugar was used to drive roaches away (F, SLC, 1920).

6368  Fleas may be driven away by scattering walnut leaves on the floor (M, 48, SLC, 1939).

6369  Put cotton dabs on the screen door to keep flies away. They think it is snow (F, 63, Monroe, 1964); Attach . . . to the front and back doors . . . (M, SLC, 1957).

6370 To get rid of flies, place white flowers on the table (F, 63, Monroe, 1964).

6371 If you catch a mouse in the house and burn it, your house will be free of mice (M, SLC, 1957).

6372 To rid a farm of rats, all that is necessary is to catch one and tie a bell to him, then let him go and the sound of the bell will frighten him into running away, and the rest of the rats, being scared, will follow (M, 57, SLC, 1964).

6373 When ashes gather and are not removed from the hearth, the salamanders will soon take over (M, 76, Provo, 1963).

## LAMPS, LIGHTS, CANDLES

6374 Never retire at night without leaving a light on somewhere in the house, or disaster will occur (F, 50, SLC, 1963).

6375 If a lamp goes out when full of oil, it is a usual sign of bad luck (M, 44, SLC, 1936).

6376 If water is applied to a lighted light globe, the globe will burn out much faster (F, SLC).

6377 Do not have three lighted lamps in the same room.  It is bad luck (M, SLC, 1961).  Brown 3022.

6378 It is bad luck for a lamp to be burning at sunrise (F, 59, Grantsville, 1920). Cf. Brown 3020.

6379 To give a person a light on Christmas Day will bring bad luck (M, Brigham City, 1960).  Brown 3017.

6380 A moving light will offset the influence of bad luck (M, SLC, 1960).

6381 When the candle wax forms a loop resembling a handle, this "coffin handle" portends bad luck (F, 19, SLC, 1953).

6382 Don't sit at a table with three lit candles, for bad luck will occur (M, 19, SLC, 1960).

6383 It is bad luck to put a lighted candle on a desk at night (F, SLC, 1960).

6384 A person who is making candles must absolutely be in a good mood; if not, the candles will not burn properly (F, SLC, 1945).

6385 It is bad luck to get a candle as a gift and not light it immediately (F, SLC, 1970).

## MATCHES, CIGARETTES, PIPES

6386 If you find a book of matches unused, you will have good luck (M, 19, SLC, 1964).

6387 When you blow out a match, be sure to wish, or else it will bring you bad luck (F, Ogden, 1950).

6388 It's bad luck to pay back borrowed matches (F, 64, SLC, 1964).

6389 If you strike a match, and it is the last in the box, you will have bad luck (F, Ogden, 1960).

6390 Three strikes of a match bring bad luck (M, 64, SLC, 1910).

6391 Never light more than two fires with one match (F, 19, SLC, 1964); It is unlucky to light three of anything with the same match (F, Santaquin, 1930s). Cf. Brown 3024.

6392 It's bad luck to light more than one cigarette with one match (M, SLC, 1962).

6393 It's bad luck to light three cigarettes on one match (M, Ogden, 1961); It is dangerous . . . (M, 73, Tooele, 1937); . . . ; the third man will have bad luck (F, SLC, 1958); To light more than three cigarettes on one match is bad luck (M, 23, SLC, 1964); The superstition originated in the First World War when three American soldiers were lighting their cigarettes on the battlefield. The first soldier lit the match and his cigarette; the Germans saw the light. The second soldier lit his cigarette; the Germans took aim.  The third soldier lit his cigarette and the Germans fired, killing him (M, 31, Murray, 1963). Brown 3025.

6394 When three people light an object from the same match, the youngest will have bad luck (M, 19, SLC, 1963).

6395 Lighting three cigarettes on one match will bring bad luck to all three persons (F, SLC, 1961).

6396 If you light more than two cigarettes on one match, it is bad luck.  If you do, break the match in half and throw it away (M, 46, SLC, 1965).

6397 It is considered good luck to light three cigarettes on the same match (M, 75, SLC, 1964).

6398 It is bad luck to light three pipes on one match (M, SLC, 1920).

6399 Don't light an unfiltered cigarette backwards or you'll have bad luck (M, 19, SLC, 1965).

6400 If a person opens a pack of cigarettes, he is supposed to give the first one away to take the curse off the pack (M, Tooele, 1964).

## FIREPLACE, FIRES

6401 A horseshoe hanging above the fireplace brings good luck (M, SLC, 1964).  Brown 3006.

6402 In the fireplace, if the sparks all gather in the soot, you are in for good fortune (M, 30, Scot, SLC, 1961).

6403 A fire in a fireplace indicates a happy home (F, 21, Bountiful, 1945).

6404 To throw a horseshoe into a fire is good luck (M, 20, SLC, 1964). Brown 3012.

6405 Licorice will put out a fire (M, Midvale, 1961).

6406 To let the fire on the hearth go out is a sure sign of ill luck (F, 29, SLC, 1964).

6407 Never look directly into a fire that is being kindled; if you do, it will not burn properly, and may bring bad luck to the whole household besides (M, 45, SLC).

## HOUSES AFIRE

6408 If one fire starts in an area, it's likely that another will start in the same area (M, 48, SLC, 1939).

6409 Fires always happen in a series of three (F, Park City, 1957).

6410 If a person sees a simulated flame over a house, it will soon burn down (F, SLC, 1959).

6411 There's a fire if a dog howls at night (F, Midvale). Cf. Brown 3026.

6412 If a rabbit runs along a road or a main thoroughfare, a house will catch fire during the day (F, 40, Midvale, 1961).

6413 It is a superstition that if a bird abandons his nest on a house, the house will burn down (F, 52, Ger, SLC, 1964); . . . if a swallow builds its nest on your roof and then leaves . . . (F, 67, SLC, 1963).

6414 A swarm of bees settling on a house means a fire (M, 71, Midvale, 1915).

6415 Hang an adder skin over the rafters of your house and it will never catch fire (M, SLC, 1961); . . . a snake skin . . . (F, SLC, 1945).

6416 A fire will never come where the stork has its brood (F, Ger, SLC, 1947).

6417 "Ladybug, ladybug, fly away home, your house is on fire, your children will burn." Never kill a ladybug, pick it up and place it on a plant or flower so your house won't burn (F, 71, Centerville, 1963).

6418 Rain on a hot tin roof will cause a fire (M, SLC, 1964).

6419 Firebugs can set your house on fire (F, SLC, 1960).

## FURNITURE, FURNISHINGS

### Tables

6420 Sit on the table if you love your dad the best (M, SLC, 1961).

6421 Knock under the table and say "Nine, seven, thirteen" to bring good luck (M, Dan, SLC, 1961).

6422 It is unlucky to sit on a table (F, 76, Glenwood, 1892); . . . a sign of coming disappointment . . . (F, 1961); . . . to sit on the kitchen table (M, 22, SLC, 1964). Brown 3049f.

### Chairs

6423 It is bad luck to put three chairs in a row (M, 75, SLC, 1964).

6424 It is bad luck for two persons to sit in one chair at the same time (F, SLC, 1949).

6425 Always go around your chair once before sitting down in a strange home (F, Murray, 1957).

6426 It brings bad luck to tip over a chair (F, Eng, SLC). Cf. Brown 3048.

6427 Straightening chairs around at night before going to bed is a good idea; in case the angels visit they will not stub their toes (F, SLC, 1925).

6428 It is bad luck to twirl an empty chair on one leg (F, Murray, 1957); Twirling an . . . brings seven years of bad luck (M, 23, Midvale, 1964). Cf. Brown 3040ff, 3046.

6429 It is bad luck to rock a rocking chair when one is in it (F, 19, Magna, 1952).

6430 It is bad to get out of a rocking chair when it is still rocking (F, 80, SLC, 1964). Brown 3038.

6431 Don't rock in a rocking chair in the light of a full moon. It is bad luck (F, 53, SLC, 1965). Cf. Brown 3037.

6432 Rocking an empty chair means there is a spirit in the chair (F, 44, Sandy, 1928); . . . is bad luck (F, Bountiful, 1960).

6433 Don't rock a chair with your foot and cause it to fall over, because it will bring you bad luck (F, 83, SLC, 1961).

6434 If you rock in a rocking chair at another person's house, it brings bad luck (F, 49, Gr, Midvale, 1932).

### Beds, Bedroom

6435 The bed should be in the same direction as the bathtub to have happiness in the home (F, 42, SLC, 1964).

6436 Beds should be placed parallel with the boards on the floor, or you'll have bad luck (F, 83, SLC, 1965).

6437 Your bed should not face the same way coffins are placed in the ground (east or west); this is bad luck (F, SLC).

6438 Always face the head of a bed north to insure a happy future (F, Grantsville, 1954).

6439 When you unfold a clean bed sheet and there is the shape of a diamond in the folds, it's good luck (F, 50, Eng, SLC, 1964).

6440 It is bad luck to sit on a made-up bed (F, 21, SLC, 1964).

6441 It is bad luck to place a weapon (gun) on a bed (M, 22, SLC, 1958).

6442 Don't put eggs on beds; it is bad luck (F, SLC, 1962).

6443   A housewife seeing a new moon for the first time should run quickly into her bedroom and turn a bed (F, SLC, 1955).

6444   It is unlucky to turn a feather bed on a Sunday (M, 29, Provo, 1960).

6445   Boiled water should never be left in a bedroom (F, Ger, SLC, 1959).

## Mirrors

6446   It brings bad luck for two people to look in a mirror at the same time (M, SLC, 1949); Looking into a mirror over someone else's shoulder brings bad luck (F, SLC, 1952).

6447   If you leave a mirror turned up, you will have bad luck (M, 23, Midvale, 1964). Brown 3057.

6448   If you look in a mirror at night, it's bad luck (F, Midvale). Brown 3058.

6449   To see one's face in a mirror by candlelight is bad luck (M, Honeyville, 1917).

6450   To see one's face in a mirror by candlelight is lucky (F, 72, SLC, 1964).

6451   Cracking a mirror means good luck for five years (F, Roosevelt, 1961).

6452   If you drop a mirror seven times, you will have one year of bad luck (M, 21, SLC, 1948).

6453   If you drop a mirror and it breaks, you will have bad luck (F, SLC, 1960); . . . it foretells a tragedy soon to occur (F, SLC, 1958). Brown 3059.

6454   If you break a mirror, the number of pieces will indicate the years of bad luck you will have (M, SLC, 1937); . . . the number of years of bad luck you will have depends upon the size of the mirror; up to seven years bad luck (F, 80, teacher, SLC, 1963). Brown 3060.

6455   The soul of an individual also lives in his image; therefore it is very bad luck to break a mirror (F, SLC, 1948); If you break a mirror, it will break your spirit (F, SLC, 1959).

6456   Don't break a mirror because it will cause seven days of bad luck (M, 13, Provo, 1964).

6457   If you break a mirror on your birthday, you'll have seven years of bad luck (M, 42, Du, SLC, 1964); . . . on Friday the thirteenth . . . (F, 10, Provo, 1964).

6458   If you break a mirror, it means seven years bad luck; the larger the mirror, the greater the bad luck (F, 51, Park City, 1920s); . . . nine years of bad luck . . . (M, Goshen, 1964).

6459   If you break a mirror and put it back together, you will only have four years bad luck (F, 51, Centerfield, 1964).

6460   If you put a broken mirror back together, you will change the seven bad luck years to good years (M, 19, SLC, 1964).

6461   If you break a mirror, it means seven years of bad luck, but if you throw a part of it over your left shoulder, it will break the spell (F, Orangeville, 1959).

6462   If you break a mirror, leave it in running water to wash away bad luck (F, 38, SLC, 1964). Cf. Brown 3061.

6463   If you break a mirror, it will bring you seven years of bad luck; however, there is a way to break this curse. If you throw a pinch of salt over your shoulder, it will counteract the bad luck produced by the mirror (F, 49, Richfield, 1924); . . . over your right shoulder . . . (M, 24, SLC, 1950).

6464   If you break a mirror into thirteen pieces, cut yourself with the largest and let it bleed for thirteen seconds (F, 13, Provo, 1964).

## Clocks

6465   Hearing the chiming of a clock at midnight is bad luck (F, SLC, 1958).

6466   Never turn a clock counter-clockwise (F, SLC, 1957). Cf. Brown 3055.

6467   To allow a wind-up clock to run down before winding it up brings bad luck (M, 23, SLC, 1960).

6468   It causes bad luck to have two clocks running in one house (M, SLC); . . . two clocks ticking in the same room . . . (F, 20, Logan, 1953). Brown 3056.

6469   It is bad luck to keep a clock in your house if it is not running (F, SLC, 1960).

## Photos, Pictures

6470   If a picture falls off the wall, disaster is near (M, 19, SLC, 1964); If a photograph falls, it is bad luck (M, Ogden, 1961); If a picture drops out of its frame, it is bad luck (M, 26, SLC). Brown 3052.

6471   If a picture of someone falls from the wall, they will bring bad luck to your household (F, Ogden, 1961).

6472   If when hanging a picture of Christ, you drop it, do not hang it up again, as He does not want His picture hung there (F, SLC, 1961).

6473   To have a picture drop out of a frame is a bad omen (F, 67, Riverton, 1963).

6474   It is bad luck for a picture to hang on the wall crooked (M, SLC, 1940).

6475   It is bad luck to turn a picture upside down (F, 78, SLC).

## Miscellaneous

6476   The performers on TV can see into the homes of the people watching (F, SLC, 1967).

6477   If you sit on an empty trunk, it is bad luck (F, 66, Provo, 1955).

6478 To sell furniture that has been in the family for years is unlucky (F, 26, SLC).

6479 If you break or shatter a vase, the scent of the flowers inside will remain forever (F, 22, Eng, SLC, 1963).

6480 To break pottery on Good Friday will bring good luck (M, 37, Blanding, 1939).

6481 All white rugs are good luck (M, Provo, 1950).

## PLANTS IN THE HOUSE

6482 If an acorn is hung on a window shade cord, it will bring that household good luck (F, 74, Salem, 1900).

6483 Never bring artificial flowers into the house; they bring bad luck (F, SLC, 1950).

6484 It is harmful to have flowers in one's bedroom at night (F, Cedar City, 1961).

6485 Bring flowers into the house on Saturday and you will have bad luck (F, 17, SLC, 1962).

6486 It is unlucky to bring flowers into the house that are out of season (F, SLC, 1960).

6487 It is bad luck to bring a dandelion in the house (F, 50, Eng, SLC, 1964).

6488 It's bad luck to bring a hawthorn blossom into the house (M, Eng, Ogden, 1958).

6489 Never let ivy grow in the house. It's bad luck (F, 19, SLC, 1963); If a person has ivy in the house, he will live a poor life (M, Gr, SLC, 1961).

6490 It is unlucky to take lilac into the house (M, 53, Cedar City, 1925).

6491 Mint in the house after dark is bad luck (F, 61, SLC, 1964).

6492 It's bad luck to bring mistletoe into the house except for the Christmas season (F, Farmington, 1936).

6493 The oleander, a large tree or plant, can be kept outside the home, but it is considered a curse or bad luck to bring it inside (F, 49, Gr, Midvale, 1964).

6494 A bag of scallions hung on a rafter in the attic of a new home will keep away bad luck (F, Ger, SLC, 1960).

6495 Don't have a wandering Jew plant in your house, because it means bad luck (F, 51, Park City, 1922); . . . you will be sure to lose something of value (F, 67, Bear River City, 1930); . . . it will keep the owners poor all life long (F, SLC).

## ANIMALS IN THE HOUSE

6496 Piutes believe that if they put a dead squirrel in their teepee, they will be protected from snakes (M, 20, SLC, 1963).

6497 Canaries are good luck to have in the home (F, 49, Eng, SLC, 1964).

6498 It is bad luck to find a bird in your house, especially in the attic (M, 57, Swiss, Heber City, 1913).

6499 A feather of a wren kept in your house brings good luck for as long as it is there (F, 50, Midvale).

6500 If you keep a peacock feather in the house, you will have bad luck (F, 36, SLC, 1959); . . . a picture of peacock feathers . . . (F, 53, SLC, 1918). Brown 3069.

6501 You should have peacock feathers in your home. They will bring you good luck (F, 58, SLC, 1964).

6502 Birds' eggs hung up in a house will bring bad luck (M, 79, SLC, 1964).

6503 It is bad luck to find a bat in your house, especially in the attic (M, Swiss, Heber City, 1913).

6504 If you keep the bone of a bat at home, it will bring good luck (F, 62, Gr, SLC, 1963).

6505 Don't keep goldfish bowls in the house; misfortune is yours (SLC); Don't take home a goldfish used in a magic act; it is bad luck (M, SLC, 1959).

6506 A cat and a rat will leave the home prior to a disaster (M, 22, Ja, SLC, 1965).

## LADDERS

6507 Always walk under a ladder before climbing it, if you are the one who placed the ladder on whatever you wish to climb (M, 42, SLC).

6508 If you walk backwards under a ladder, it will bring you good luck (F, Ogden, 1958).

6509 You should never put your hand through the steps of a ladder, it will bring bad luck (M, 20, SLC, 1964); Don't hand anything through a ladder (F, SLC, 1957).

6510 If one looks through a ladder, he should spit three times to prevent evil consequences (F, 19, SLC). Cf. Brown 3066.

6511 Walking under a ladder is bad luck (M, 15, SLC, 1964); . . . means bad luck the rest of the day (F, 14, Provo, 1964); . . . you will meet grave trouble (F, 67, SLC, 1963); . . . you will become part of a terrible disaster (M, SLC); . . . portends disappointment (F, 67, Riverton, 1963).

6512 If you walk under a ladder, an accident will follow (F, SLC, 1958). Brown 3064.

6513 Never walk under a ladder especially if someone is on top of the ladder (M, SLC, 1961); . . . because something will fall on your head (F, SLC, 1960).

6514    Don't walk under a ladder on Friday the thirteenth, or you will have bad luck (F, 10, SLC, 1964).  Brown 3065.

6515    Never walk under a step ladder (M, 47, Murray, 1963).

6516    If you walk under a ladder, you will have seven years of bad luck (M, 26, SLC, 1945); . . . thirteen years . . . (F, 72, SLC, 1919).

6517    If you are on a ladder and a black cat goes under the ladder, you will have bad luck unless you throw salt over your shoulder (F, 14, SLC, 1964).

6518    If you walk under a ladder, it means bad luck.  Cross your fingers or stop long enough to make a wish (F, 47, Midvale, 1929).  Cf. Brown 3067.

6519    If you walk under a ladder, you will have bad luck.  If you go backward through it again, you break the bad charm (F, SLC).

6520    It is bad luck to walk under a ladder.  The spell can be undone by turning around and walking back (F, SLC, 1961).

### UMBRELLAS

6521    It is unlucky to pick up an umbrella yourself.  Someone else should be called to perform the service (M, Midvale, 1958); . . . bad luck to pick up an umbrella by the handle after you have dropped it (F, Eng, SLC, 1958).  Brown 3063.

6522    Putting an umbrella on the table is bad luck.  Always put it on the floor (F, SLC).

6523    Putting an umbrella on the bed is worse luck than putting a shoe on the bed (F, 82, It, SLC, 1963); Never put an open umbrella on the bed, etc. (F, SLC, 1959).

6524    Close an umbrella before entering a house or building (F, 14, Orem, 1964).

6525    If you open an umbrella in the house, it will bring bad luck (F, 23, SLC, 1961); . . . a week of bad luck (F, SLC, 1959); . . . terrible trouble will follow you (F, 42, SLC, 1964); . . . terrible calamity will befall you (F, 80, SLC, 1894); It is especially bad luck to open a black umbrella in the house (F, SLC, 1964).  Brown 3062.

6526    To open a black umbrella in a house will bring one year of bad luck (F, Holladay, 1957); . . . seven years bad luck (M, 49, Brigham City, 1964).

6527    If you raise an umbrella in the house, it will bring bad luck to the people living in that house (F, Murray, 1957).

6528    Don't open an umbrella in the house, or the house will fall down (F, 20, SLC, 1964); . . . your roof will start leaking (F, 43, SLC, 1963); . . . it will cause disaster (F, Copperton); . . . will cause a tragedy (F, 46, Bingham, 1925).

6529    If you wear an umbrella inside a house, it's for dead persons, so do not open an umbrella in a house (F, 25, Ja, SLC, 1964).

6530    If you open an umbrella in a house, something will hit you from above (M, 59, SLC, 1915).

6531    The opening of an umbrella in a house, while it is raining outside, will bring misfortune (M, 1960).

### KEYS

6532    Never throw keys; always hand them or lay them down and let those who want them pick them up (M, 21, SLC, 1963).

6533    Keys on the table bring bad luck (M, 21, SLC, 1959).

### COLORS

6534    White is a sign of purity (M, 51, SLC, 1963).

6535    A lover of truth idealizes the color blue (M, Pleasant Grove, 1959).

6536    Green is an unlucky color (F, SLC, 1962); . . . on Thursday (F, Tooele, 1959).

6537    Yellow is unlucky (F, 58, Provo, 1945); . . . means silliness (F, SLC, 1964).

6538    Red is a lucky color (M, SLC, 1930); . . . means bravery (F, Moab, 1953).

6539    A person's spirits will sink if he believes in pink as a dominant color (M, Pleasant Grove, 1959).

6540    People who idealize the color grey live far away from everything (M, Pleasant Grove, 1959).

6541    The color black is considered bad luck (M, 20, SLC, 1964).

6542    People who idealize black think in the past and wish everything was back again (M, Pleasant Grove, 1959).

6543    Our lives are determined by color.  Each week we aspire to higher things and color helps us achieve this.

| Monday | Blue | Aspiration Day |
| Tuesday | Pink | Divine Love Day |
| Wednesday | Yellow | Wisdom Day |
| Thursday | Orange | Intuition Day |
| Friday | Green | Universal Day |
| Saturday | Black and | |
| | White | Organization Day |
| Sunday | Orchid | Spirituality |

(F, SLC, 1961).

6544    Red:  love, affection, or lust
Scarlet:  emotion, anger
Deep crimson:  animality
Bright red:  courage, confidence
Dull orange:  less understanding
Brownish orange:  worldly wisdom
Light yellow:  common sense
(M, SLC, 1957).

MISCELLANEOUS

6545  It's bad luck to break an ink pen (M, 45, SLC, 1964).

6546  Never pop a sack in the house (F, Murray, 1957).

6547  The greener the grass is in your front yard, the greyer the atmosphere will be inside of your house (M, SLC, 1961).

6548  It brings good luck to have placards placed about the home (F, Holladay, 1957).

6549  A singing teakettle means a happy home (F, Ogden, 1958).

6550  A cricket in a house signifies happiness in the home (M, Box Elder, 1958).

6551  Cutting a ribbon on a new building or highway means success and prosperity for that particular building or highway (F, 50, SLC, 1934).

6552  Skunk odor: Sprinkle soda and salt over the area where the skunk has been. Another remedy: Pour drain and crankcase oil all around where the skunk has been (F, Nephi, 1915).

6553  To eradicate skunk odor, dig down through the top layer of soil to where the ground is moist and humid, and shovel it all around the tainted area (F, Nephi, 1915).

SEWING

General

6554  If you bite the thread when sewing a garment, it will never stay sewn (F, 19, SLC, 1964).

6555  If you prick your finger while sewing on an article, throw the article away. It will bring you bad luck (F, 78, SLC).

6556  If you prick your finger while you are sewing, make a wish and suck the blood and it will come true (F, 52, SLC).

6557  When sewing, if you scratch yourself horizontally you will have good luck, but a vertical scratch is bad luck (F, 48, Murray, 1964).

6558  It is bad luck for you if you make a baby blanket for yourself before you are married (F, 18, Logan, 1970).

6559  When making a dress, it's unlucky to cut out anything that you can't finish that day (F, 53, Murray, 1964). Cf. Brown 3278.

6560  In making a dress, don't cut the cloth after sunset, because there will be no good luck (F, 38, Gr, SLC, 1963).

Sewing on Various Days

6561  Never sew on the thirteenth day, or it will not turn out right (M, 83, Ephraim, 1889).

6562  Choose a good day to cut out a dress, because the dress will bring you good luck (F, 45, Ja, SLC, 1963).

6563  It is bad luck to sew on Sunday (F, 49, Charleston, 1972); . . . the stitches will fall out (F, 22, Parowan, 1955); . . . all the stitches will have to be taken out on Monday (F, SLC, 1930s); . . . you'll have to take out twice as many stitches as you sewed (M, SLC, 1959). Cf. Brown 3261.

6564  If you sew on Sunday, you will surely prick your finger many times (F, 29, SLC, 1964).

6565  One stitch on Sunday means nine something in hell (F, Moab, 1953).

6566  If you sew on Sunday, your punishment will be to take out each stitch with your nose (F, 48, Mapleton, 1920s); . . . pick it out with your nose on Monday (M, SLC, 1958); . . . take out all the stitches with your nose when you die (M, SLC, 1963); . . . in the life hereafter (F, 40, Murray, 1961); . . . in the life hereafter (F, 40, Murray, 1961); . . . in the next world (F, 76, Lehi, 1900); . . . in heaven (F, 61, Bingham, 1916); For every stitch taken on Sunday, two stitches will have to be picked out by your nose in heaven (F, SLC, 1957); . . . in hell (F, Morgan, 1961); . . . on Judgment Day (F, Park City, 1957).

6567  Never sew on the Sabbath Day, or you will have to pull the stitches out with your teeth when you get to heaven (F, 80, Eng, Richfield, 1964).

6568  There is no harm in sewing on Sunday, if you don't use a thimble (F, 47, SLC, 1964). Brown 3262f.

6569  A dress cut out on Tuesday will be a "lemon." One way to avoid this is to cut out part of the dress on Monday night. This breaks the spell (F, Gr, SLC, 1961).

6570  If you make a dress on Tuesday it will never fit right (F, 42, SLC, 1948).

6571  Bad luck is connected with any sewing that is started on a Friday (F, Orangeville, 1959); Never cut out a garment on Friday that cannot be completed the same day, or you will never finish it (F, Lehi, 1957); A garment cut out on Friday will be endless to finish; you'll have to rip it out with your nose (F, 70, SLC, 1964); Never start a dress on Friday. It will never fit (F, SLC, 1960). Brown 3266, 3268ff.

6572  Never cut cloth for a dress on Saturday; it is no good luck (F, 38, Gr, SLC, 1963).

Sewing Clothes while They Are Being Worn

6573  It is very bad luck to mend clothing, or sew a button on when the person is wearing the article of apparel (M, SLC, 1957). Brown 3287, cf. 3296.

6574  Never sew something on your clothing while still wearing it. You will be sewn into something soon enough (F, 52, Helper, 1930s); . . . you'll have sorrow stitched to your heart (F, Eng, SLC, 1964).

6575    If you mend or sew on any apparel while wearing it, you will do something that you will be ashamed of (F, SLC, 1957).

6576        To mend your clothes on your back
        You will live much money to lack
(F, 30, Murray, 1963).  First heard in Boston, Mass, 1931.

### Mending, Darning

6577    It's bad luck to mend clothes on Sunday (M, Ogden, 1961); It's harmful to darn on Sunday unless you cross your feet (F, 51, SLC, 1964).

6578    If you have clothes mended while on you, you will come to want (F, 40, Garland, 1933).

6579    You should always mend the holes in your clothes of even the old ones of work so that when the night spirits come, they will harm your clothes not (M, Amer Ind, 53, Logan, 1929).

6580    It is bad luck to patch a man's garment with crosswise grains of the material. Always use it lengthwise (F, 45, Ja, SLC, 1963).

6581    It is bad luck to mend clothing with black thread even if it doesn't show, unless the cloth is that color (F, SLC, 1960).

6582    Never mend anything that a mouse has chewed up (F, 27, SLC, 1965).  Cf. Brown 3291.

### PINS

#### Rhymes

6583    See a pin and pick it up, and all the day you'll have good luck (F, SLC, 1958).  Cf. Brown 3338.

6584    See a pin and let it lay, bad luck will follow you all the day (M, 31, SLC, 1958).

6585    Drop a pin and let it lay, you will have bad luck all through the day (F, 24, SLC, 1964); . . . that will take your luck away (F, SLC, 1963).  Brown 3328.

6586    If you see a pin and let it lay, you'll need it by the end of the day (F, SLC).

6587    See a pin and let it lie, and you'll have need of a pin before you die (F, Draper, 1915).  Cf. Brown 3340.

6588    See a pin and let it lie, good luck that day will pass you by (F, 20, SLC).  Cf. Brown 3342.

6589        See a pin and pick it up,
        All day long you'll have good luck.
        See a pin, let it lay,
        Bad luck you'll have all day.
(F, Moab, 1953).  Cf. Brown 3344, 8534.

### General Notions

6590    If you take a pin for nothing, it is bad luck (F, 80, Springville, 1944).

6591    Pick up a pin, pick up sorrow (M, SLC, 1959).

6592    It is bad luck if you don't pick up a pin that is lying on the ground (F, SLC, 1955).  Cf. Brown 3332.

6593    Picking up a pin is bad luck (F, SLC, 1961).

6594    If you find a straight pin and it is pointing toward you, it means you will have bad luck (F, Murray, 1958).  Brown 3310.

6595    It is good luck to find a pin with the point, instead of the head, pointing toward you (F, SLC, 1957).  Brown 3309, cf. 8529.

6596    If you find a pin with the side toward you, it means that you will be going for a ride (F, 80, Springville, 1914).

6597    Finding pins and picking them up induces further finds (F, 45, Murray, 1925).  Cf. Brown 8527.

6598    One who finds a straight pin will receive bounteous luck if he pins it on his collar (F, 51, Bingham, 1931).  Cf. Brown 3322.

6599    If you are walking along and there is a pin in front of you, it's bad luck, but if you throw the pin over your left shoulder, it's good luck (M, 13, SLC, 1960).

6600    Sticking a pin in the lapel of a friend's coat will bring luck (M, 54, SLC, 1964).

### Safety Pin

6601    Don't pick up a safety pin; it is not good luck (M, 32, Gr, SLC, 1963).

6602    You will have good luck if you find a safety pin (F, 19, SLC, 1960).

6603    Don't let a safety pin lie on the floor, or it will bring bad luck (F, Bountiful, 1950).

6604    If you find a pin on the floor that is closed, you will have good luck; if it is open, you will have bad luck (F, SLC, 1964).

6605    Never walk past an open safety pin, or it will be bad luck; stop and pick it up (F, Moab, 1953).

6606    If you place a safety pin on a steel railroad track and let a train run over it, the safety pin will turn into a pair of brand new scissors (F, 94, SLC, 1900).

### Borrowing, Lending Pins

6607    Never lend a safety pin.  It brings bad luck (M, Union).

6608  It is bad luck to borrow pins (F, 23, Murray, 1964).

6609  If someone wants to borrow a pin, give them a penny (or coin) also to be returned when they bring back the pin. This will bring good luck (F, 27, SLC, 1964).  Cf. Brown 3337.

6610  Never take a pin from a person or it will bring you bad luck.  You must have the person put the pin on you, then you won't have bad luck (F, 80, SLC, 1920).

6611  Never lend a pin.  If anybody asks you for a pin say, "Take one.  I won't give it to you."  The borrower must not thank you (F, 47, Midvale, 1927).

NEEDLES

6612  If you find a needle pointing towards you, you will have good luck.  If the eye is towards you, it means bad luck (M, SLC, 1958).  Brown 3346f.

6613  If a person sees a needle on the road, he should not pick it up; it brings misfortune (F, SLC, 1959).

6614  It is bad luck to lend a needle (F, 27, Hyrum, 1948).  Cf. Brown 3293.

6615  You must not give a needle or pin directly to someone; rather, put it down, and let him or her pick it up (F, 27, SLC, 1965).

6616  When handing someone a needle, have the point toward yourself (F, 74, SLC, 1964).

6617  Dropping a needle on the floor brings bad luck to someone in the family (F, 19, SLC, 1951).

6618  You are a very poor sewer if you use a long piece of thread on your needle (F, 45, Ja, SLC, 1963).

6619  If you break a needle while sewing a dress, the person who wears the dress will be hugged in it (F, 53, SLC, 1925); . . . kissed . . . (M).

6620  It is bad luck if someone threads a needle for you and then ties a knot in the end (F, Ja, SLC, 1963).

6621  If you lose a needle, hang a pair of scissors on the doorknob and you will find the needle faster (F, 24, Korean, SLC, 1963).

SCISSORS, TAPE MEASURE

6622  If you drop a pair of scissors on the ground, it is bad luck, if the scissors poke in the ground (F, 28, Ger, Ogden, 1970); . . . it means a separation (M, Ir, SLC, 1960).  Cf. Brown 3304.

6623  If you drop a pair of scissors and they stick in the floor, standing straight up, dire things will happen (F, Park City, 1957).  Cf. Brown 3305.

6624  Leaving a pair of scissors opened on the floor means a mishap may occur in the house (F, 48, SLC, 1963).

6625  It is unlucky to pick up yourself a pair of scissors which you have dropped. Someone else should be called to perform the service (M, Midvale, 1958).  Cf. Brown 3308.

6626  Handing scissors to another person with the blade towards that person is bad luck (F, 41, SLC, 1963).

6627  Never hand anyone a pair of scissors, as it is very unlucky.  Put them down, and let the other person pick them up (M, SLC, 1957).

6628  It is unlucky to use scissors on Sunday (F, SLC, 1964).

6629  A knot in the tape measure is a sign of good luck for the sewer (F, 48, Murray, 1964).

BUTTONS

6630  A button received as a gift is always lucky, no matter what the color (F, SLC, 1945).

6631  It is good luck to find a button with two eyes (F, 19, Heber, 1972).  Cf. Brown 3297f, 3301.

6632  To drop a button means bad luck (F, SLC, 1961).

6633  When a button pops off the front of your clothing, it is a sign that trouble is near for you (M, 23, W. Jordan).

6634  If a person loses a button, he will have bad luck for every button remaining on his clothing (F, Murray, 1957).

6635  It is good luck to pull the middle button off your sports coat or suit jacket (M, SLC, 1964).

KNITTING, QUILTING, SPINNING, WEAVING

6636  Never knit on Sunday, or you will have to take every stitch out with your nose in heaven (M, 21, Hyde Park).

6637  While knitting if you stop in the middle of a row, your boyfriend will change his mind and go back home before he gets to see you (F, 49, Norw, SLC, 1963).

6638  It is bad luck to start a quilt on Friday (F, 49, Charleston, 1972).  Brown 3277.

6639  When you are quilting and end your stint, always leave the needle threaded and in the fabric ready for the next stitch, whether you will go on with it or someone else will.  This will prevent a needle from getting lost in the quilt, but simply putting an empty needle in a safe place will not do.  You must thread it and leave it in the quilt (F, 60, SLC, 1925).

6640  Any spinning started in the winter months has to be finished by the first of the twelve holy nights.  That is the time when Freya, wife of Wotan, inspects all the spinning wheels (M, Ger, SLC, 1938).  (This ancient allusion to Germanic mythology has as its counterpart the Christian spinning and weaving traditions that begin soon after the harvest has been taken up, and continue to Candlemas [February 2]. The Virgin Mary oversees this domestic activity and punishes those who work beyond the appointed time.   --Eds.)

## CLOTHING

### Getting New Clothes

6641   If your skirt is tucked up at the bottom, you'll have a new dress (M, Tooele, 1957).

6642   If your hem is turned up on a dress or skirt, spit on it and you will get a new one (F, 51, Park City, 1920s); . . . kiss the hem and you will get a new dress (F, 52, SLC, 1964).  Brown 3159ff.

6643   If a butterfly lands on you, you will get a new dress (M, 48, SLC, 1964); Bite off a butterfly's head and you will get a new dress or suit just like the butterfly (F, SLC, 1960).  Cf. Brown 3155f, 3164ff.

6644   If a ladybug crawls on you, you will get a new dress or new shirt (F, 60, Ogden, 1970); . . . a bug . . . (F, SLC, 1958).

6645   If you find a measuring worm on you, you are going to get some new clothes (F, Clearfield, 1959); . . . a new dress (F, SLC, 1900s); . . . a new pair of pants (F, SLC, 1959).  Brown 3146, 3157, 3170.

6646   If a caterpillar falls on you and starts crawling on an arm, he is measuring you for a new suit of clothes (M, 45, Price, 1930).

### ORDER OF DRESSING, UNDRESSING

6647   Those who make merry before dressing will have grief before underdressing (F, SLC, 1928).

6648   When a person gets out of bed:  First dress the right side (right shoe and sock, put in right leg and arm first, etc.).  If you always remember to do this, the day will bring good luck (F, SLC, 1964).

6649   If you want good luck to go with you all day, take your first step on the foot opposite to the one you put your first shoe on (F, Ir, SLC, 1960).

6650   Bad luck will attend you if, in donning a garment, you put the left arm in first (F, SLC, 1961).

6651   Always put the right glove on first, or it is bad luck (F, Orangeville, 1959).

6652   A person wearing only one glove will have bad luck until either that is removed or he puts the other glove on (M, 21, SLC).

6653   It's bad luck for men not to step into their trousers with their left foot first (F, SLC).

6654   Never take your nightgown off inside out, or you will have bad luck for the day (F, Logan, 1970).

6655   When taking off a dress, never turn the sleeves inside out, or you will have bad luck when you wear the dress again (F, 48, SLC, 1964).

6656   You should take off your left shoe first when undressing (M, SLC, 1959); Taking off the right shoe before the left means bad luck (F, 1959).

### Shoes, Stockings, Socks

6657   It is considered bad luck to put your left stocking on first while dressing (M, SLC, 1957).  Brown 3202.

6658   Put the left stocking on first and good luck will be with you for the day (F, 23, SLC, 1962).

6659   It is considered good luck to put your right stocking on first (M, SLC, 1964); It is bad luck all day . . . (F, SLC, 1961); When getting dressed put on your right stocking first, but your left shoe first (F, Axtell, 1958).

6660   Always put your left shoe on first, or you'll have a bad day (F, SLC, 1959).

6661   Never put the left shoe on first; bad luck will follow (F, SLC, 1957); . . . your affairs will suffer all day (M, SLC, 1957).  Brown 3214.

6662   If you are right handed and put your left shoe on first, you will have a bad disposition all day (F, SLC).

6663   Put your right shoe on first and the day will go well; put the left on first and you will have bad luck (F, Ir, SLC, 1962).

6664   It is bad luck to put on the right shoe first (F, 49, SLC, 1964).

6665   For luck always put the shoe and stocking on one foot before putting the stocking on the other foot (F, 1959).

6666   If one of your feet is dressed with both a stocking and a shoe before the other foot has a stocking on it, it will bring bad luck (F, 53, SLC, 1925); . . . you will have a disappointment (F, SLC, 1964).

6667   If you put your left shoe and stocking on first when you do your dressing in the morning, you will have good luck all day (F, 77, Pleasant Grove, 1912). Brown 3212.

6668   If you put your left shoe and stocking on first, it will bring you bad luck (F, SLC, 1900).

6669   When you get up in the morning be sure to dress your right foot first.  If you don't, you will meet with disappointment that day (F, 61, Du, SLC, 1964).  Cf. Brown 3211.

6670   When a person gets up in the morning, he must always remember to dress the right leg first; if he does not, the devil will be in his way the rest of the day (F, SLC, 1932).

## WEARING CLOTHES

6671  Wearing old clothes brings good luck (M, SLC, 1964).

6672  It is bad luck, when going some place, to change one set of clothes for another once they have been put on (F, 44, Sandy, 1928).

6673  If you wear your Sunday clothes on Monday, you will live in a rage (F, Eng, SLC, 1958).

### Changing of Clothes Worn Inside Out

6674  If you put your clothes on inside out, you had better get behind the door to change them or you will have bad luck (M, Layton, 1947).

6675  If you find clothing wrong side out, you should change it or it will be bad luck (M, SLC); If you put your sock on wrong side out, you must put the sock on seven times correctly or else you will have bad luck (F, 21, Bountiful, 1956); If you put a dress on wrong side out and change it, you'll change your luck (F, Moab, 1953); If you put a piece of wearing apparel on wrong side out, take it off and make a wish before putting it on again or it will bring you bad luck (F, Santaquin); If you put a shirt on backwards, . . . (M, SLC).

6676  If you put your pants on wrong side out and leave them that way, you will have bad luck. If you change them to the right way, you will have good luck (F, 1957).

6677  Don't change a garment immediately after putting it on inside out (F, Ir, SLC, 1960).

6678  To put an article of clothing on inside out is a sign of good luck (M, 91, S. Jordan, 1938).

6679  If, when dressing, you should by accident put any piece of clothing on inside out, do not take it off and change it. Leave it on throughout the day. To change it would bring bad luck. You may, however, take it off during the day if you should have to change clothes to go somewhere (F, 48, Murray, 1963); If you change them, something terrible will happen to you (F, 80, SLC, 1960).

6680  To put an article of clothing on inside out will bring bad luck (F, SLC, 1960).

6681  If you wear a garment inside out until twelve o'clock midnight, you will have good luck for thirteen years (M, 44, SLC, 1941). Cf. Brown 3183.

6682  If you put your sleeping clothes on wrong side out, you mustn't change them (F, SLC, 1958); . . . it's bad luck to change them (F, 19, SLC, 1963). Cf. Brown 3201.

6683  If you put your shirt on wrong side out, do not change it back that day, because

it will drive your luck away (M, SLC, 1961).

6684  If a person inadvertently puts a stocking on wrong side out, he should leave it, for it will bring him good luck for the rest of the day (F, SLC, 1957).

6685  If you happen to put your slip on wrong side out, don't take it off again or you will have bad luck all the day (F, Woodland, 1959); You can neutralize the bad luck by taking it off and putting it on again right side out, but front to back (F, SLC, 1969); If your underwear is put on wrong side out, don't change it, or you will have bad luck (F, SLC, 1957).

6686  If you put a blouse on the wrong side out, leave it until you go to bed, or you'll have bad luck (F, 68, SLC, 1964).

6687  If you put a dress on wrong side out, wear if for the rest of the day, or you will have bad luck (F, 80, Eng, Richfield, 1964); . . . it's bad luck if you change it (F, 69, SLC, 1964).

6688  If you accidentally put your apron on wrong side out, you must wear it that way. It brings very bad luck to change it (M, Tooele, 1957). Brown 3198.

6689  To put a garment on inside out is lucky, provided that you discover it and change it (F, Ogden).

6690  If you accidentally put an article of clothing on wrong side out, sit down for a minute before changing it, or you will have bad luck (F, 42, SLC, 1937).

### Wearing Clothes Inside Out

6691  If you put some article of clothing on inside out, it is a sign of bad luck (M, 14, SLC, 1961); If you change it to the right side, you will have bad luck (F, Spanish Fork, 1934).

6692  You will have bad luck if you wear your underwear wrong side out (M, SLC, 1964); . . . you'll get a bawling out that day (F, 52, Provo, 1920).

6693  If you wear your underwear inside out and don't realize it till the end of the day, it means good luck (F, SLC, 1971). Cf. Brown 3179, 3181.

6694  If you leave one sleeve wrong side out, it is bad luck (M, Layton, 1934).

6695  Socks worn wrong side out bring bad luck (M, SLC, 1965); . . . means a disappointment (F, 18, SLC, 1950); . . . matters will go crooked that day (F, 61, SLC, 1964).

### Wearing Clothes Backwards

6696  It is bad luck to put on clothing backwards (F, SLC, 1957).

6697  When getting dressed in the morning, if you put any article of clothing on backwards, it is bad luck to change it around (F, SLC, 1928).

6698 If you put something on backwards and leave it that way, or spit on it, you'll have bad luck (F, 46, SLC, 1933)

6699 If you put something on backwards as you dress, you must undress again and start all over, or bad luck will plague you the whole day (F, SLC, 1961).

6700 If you turn your cap and wear it backwards, you will ward off bad luck (F, Farmington, 1959); To put on one's hat the wrong way round is to invite all the bad luck there is going (M, 53, Crescent).

6701 If you put your undershirt on backwards, don't change it, or you will have bad luck (F, SLC, 1960).

6702 If you put your slip on backwards and leave it that way for the remaining day, it will be bad luck (F, SLC, 1960); . . . you should leave it that way or you will have bad luck (F, SLC, 1958); . . . it is good luck to leave it on backwards (F, SLC, 1959).

6703 Put a petticoat on inside out and backwards and your wish will come true (F, 79, Centerville).

6704 If you put your sweater on backwards, leave it that way or you will have bad luck (F, SLC, 1960).

6705 To put a shirt on backwards will bring you good luck (M, Ogden, 1960).

6706 A woman who puts on an apron backwards will have bad luck if she changes it (F, SLC, 1918).

### Clothes Buttoned Wrong

6707 Put a button or a hook into the wrong hole when dressing, and some unfortunate thing will happen to you during the day (M, Provo, 1960); . . . you will have bad luck all day (F, 14, SLC, 1961).

6708 To hook an eye into the wrong eyelet, or place a button in the wrong hole will bring you an unlucky day. This may be evaded however, if the garment is at once taken off, and then put on again (F, 74, Millcreek, 1898).

6709 To button a coat or waistcoat unevenly is a good sign (M, SLC).

6710 To button your coat wrong means matters will go crooked that day (F, 61, Du, SLC, 1964).

### Wearing New Clothes

6711 It is unlucky to put perfume on your clothes the first time you wear them (F, 55, SLC, 1960).

6712 Anyone appearing for the first time in a new dress should be pinched by a friend for good luck (F, SLC, 1960).

6713 If you put on a new dress, spit into it three times for good luck (F, 63, Monroe, 1964).

6714 Always try new shoes on the right foot first (M, 48, Midvale, 1945).

6715 Spit on a pair of new shoes for good luck (F, SLC, 1958).

6716 If new shoes squeak, it means you haven't paid for them yet (M, SLC, 1957); . . . you have stolen them (F, 45, SLC, 1957).

6717 If you tear your dress before it is washed, you will have bad luck (F, SLC, 1950).

6718 If you wear three new things on Easter, you will have good luck all year around (F, 53, SLC, 1957).

6719 Wear something new on Easter or the birds will skeet on you (M, 46, SLC, 1948).

6720 Before wearing a new hat, spit in it, and you will be lucky as long as you wear it (F, 55, Farmington, 1919).

6721 To dream you have a new hat portends success (F, SLC, 1964).

### Color of Clothing Worn

6722 To dress in a completely white outfit is bad luck (F, SLC, 1959).

6723 It is bad luck to ever put anything black on something that is white (F, SLC, 1958).

6724 Wearing black is bad luck (M, SLC, 1960); . . . on Monday is bad luck (F, SLC, 1960).

6725 If a woman wears a dress entirely black, unless she is in mourning, she will have bad luck (F, It, Murray, 1958).

6726 If black is worn on Friday the thirteenth, swallow one teaspoonful of salt; if white is worn, swallow one teaspoonful of pepper (F, SLC, 1964).

6727 When you wear blue not planning to, it means that you are in a bad mood or sad (F, 54, SLC, 1963).

6728 Owning a green dress is bad luck (M, Ir, SLC).

6729 If you buy anything green to wear, within a year you will mourn in black (F, Eng, SLC, 1958).

6730 It is bad luck to wear green on Thursday (F, Tooele, 1950).

6731 On St. Patrick's Day if you do not wear green, others may pinch you. If they pinch you and you are wearing green, you may pinch them back three times (F, SLC, 1945).

6732 If you wear red, white and blue together, others may pinch you saying, "Pinches for red, white and blue" (F, SLC, 1946).

6733 If you combine the colors of red and orange and wear them, it means that you will know a gay and pleasant time (F, 50, SLC, 1945).

6734 If a man wears two different colored stockings, he will have bad luck for the rest of the day (F, 20, SLC, 1964).

6735  If you put odd socks on in the morning, you must retrace all your steps or you'll have bad luck (F, SLC, 1957).

6736  Never wear black shoes with anything brown.  It's bad luck (F, 19, SLC, 1963).

## OTHER BELIEFS ABOUT CLOTHING

6737  Wear a new gift on New Year's Day to bring good luck (M, Fillmore, 1960).

6738  If there are still basting threads in a garment, it is a sign it still isn't paid for (F, 40, SLC, 1964).  Brown 3224.

6739  Never pull loose strings on clothes (M, 12, Provo, 1964).

6740  If you find a string on you, someone else has one on him (M, Orem, 1959).

6741  Carry a piece of clothing that has brought good fortune, and it will continue to do so (F, 1957).

6742  If a person is wearing certain clothes and something good happens, the clothes are considered good luck (M, 20, SLC, 1959).

6743  It is considered unlucky to wear your clothes outside your pants, etc. (M, 30, SLC, 1964).

6744  It is bad luck to go out of doors in stocking feet (M, 22, SLC, 1958).

6745  Carrying sharp things in your pocket is bad luck (M, 54, Eng, SLC, 1964).

6746  It is unlucky to wear a large feather on your person (F, 20, SLC, 1950).

6747  When a person possesses a peacock feather and wears it, he will have bad luck because of the eyes in the bird's feathers (F, 23, SLC, 1964).

6748  Wearing peacock feathers is good luck (F, 89, Midvale, 1964).

6749  Leather rots when pissed upon (F, 19, SLC, 1963).

6750  To help remove the odor of skunk from skin, animals or clothing, use tomato juice and tomato meat (F, 20, SLC, 1963).

6751  Do not discard any clothing until the last of spring (F, SLC, 1920).

6752  If you keep your old clothes seven years, they will come back in style and can be worn again (F, Bear River City, 1957).

6753  It is a sign of good luck to find a small spider on one's clothes (M, 29, Ogden, 1964).

6754  Hanging clothes on a doorknob brings bad luck, because it pulls your luck down (M, SLC, 1960).  Brown 3225f.

6755  If you brush your clothes at night, it will bring surprises (F, Axtell, 1958).

6756  To throw an article of clothing on a bed will bring bad luck (F, Sandy, 1957); . . . a coat . . . (F, SLC, 1940s).

6757  If any part of your clothing catches and is not torn, somebody is anxious to see you (F, SLC).

6758  If your hem is turned up and you discover it before it falls, you can make a wish (F, Ogden, 1961).

6759  When you notice a fold in your hem, close your eyes, make a wish, then pick up the first rock you see.  The number of rings you can count on it will be the number of years before your wish comes true (F, 19, SLC, 1953).

6760  If your hem is up, spit on it, make a wish and your wish will come true (F, SLC, 1964); . . . make a wish while turning it down . . . (F, SLC, 1960); . . . if you can lower the turned-up hem with one swat (F, 19, SLC, 1955); . . . if you kiss it before you turn it down (F, SLC, 1957).  Brown 3233.

6761  If you see a person's hem turned up, make a wish before it falls and then tell the girl about it (F, SLC, 1961).

6762  If a skirt or dress gets caught up, make a wish and twirl around three times (F, American Fork, 1959).

6763  If your skirt is found turned part way up in the morning, you'll be cranky and cross that day (F, 70, SLC, 1964); . . . you will be angry (F, 63, Monroe, 1964).

6764  You will have good luck if the hem of your dress turns up (F, Axtell, 1958); . . . If you kiss the hem, good luck is insured (F, 1960).  Cf. Brown 3231f.

6765  If the hem of your dress turns up, you will be invited to a party (F, 49, Norw, SLC, 1963).

6766  If a girl's petticoat hangs below her skirt, this means that her mother didn't love her as much as her father (F, 18, SLC, 1957); If your skirt is turned up at the bottom, you love your father better than your mother (F, Lehi, 1957).

6767  A crooked pin on a dress indicates that an old maid owns the garment (F, SLC, 1962).

6768  It is bad luck to have an odd number of buttons on your dress (F, 18, Heber, 1972); An even number . . . down the front of a shirt is unlucky (M, 29, SLC, 1960).

6769  If one wears a green flannel nightgown, one will have good experiences the following day (F, 18, SLC, 1960).

6770  A test to see if a girl can go without the support of a bra is to place a pencil under the breast.  If it stays, a bra should be worn. If the pencil falls, the girl could safely leave her bra off (F, 21, Logan, 1971).

6771  Don't leave a raincoat on the table (F, SLC, 1964).

## Hats

6772    If you wear your hat too tight on your head, you are apt to blow your top (F, SLC, 1963).

6773    Never rest your hat upside down, or your luck will run out (F, 18, Logan, 1972).

6774    It is bad luck to put a hat on a bed (F, Midvale); Bad luck will come to a visitor if his hat is laid on a bed (M, SLC, 1959).  Brown 3238.

6775    Don't throw your hat on the bed, or you'll have seven years bad luck (F, 49, Brigham City, 1964).  Cf. Brown 3239.

6776    A salesman never lays his hat on the bed.  It's bad luck (F, Grantsville, 1920).

6777    If you throw a hat on the bed before undertaking a big task, it will bring you good luck (M, 19, SLC, 1955).

6778    If you put a hat under the bed, it will bring bad luck (F, SLC, 1964).  Cf. Brown 3240.

6779    It is bad luck to put your hat on while in bed (F, Tooele, 1964).

6780    It's bad luck to sleep with a hat on your bed (F, 48, SLC, 1930).

6781    To throw a hat out of bed means you are in for bad luck (M, 21, 1970).

6782    If you hang your hat on a doorknob, it will bring you misfortune (M, 56, Mt. Pleasant, 1919).

6783    If a man comes into your home and leaves his hat, never give it back to him, or bad luck will follow (F, 61, Midvale, 1930).

6784    A gentleman's hat left behind means he will return (F, 46, SLC, 1943).

6785    If you put more than one hat on your head, you will get whipped (F, SLC, 1962).  Cf. Brown 3176.

6786    Never wear your hat into the home of a friend, or trouble will on him descend (F, 67, SLC, 1963).

6787    It's bad luck to put a hat on the table (M, SLC, 1960).

6788    To eat with your hat on will bring bad luck (F, Sandy, 1957).

## Shoes

6789    Squeaky shoes are good luck (F, SLC, 1960).

6790    Shoes that squeak means they won't last long (M, 44, Manti, 1920s).

6791    If your shoes squeak, it means they are not paid for (F, Bear River City, 1957); . . . not honestly paid for (F, Ogden, 1958.  Brown 3242.

6792    Never borrow a person's shoes without paying for them.  It is bad luck (M, Murray, 1961).

6793    To buy a pair of shoes for someone is bad luck (F, 54, Midvale, 1920); It is bad luck to give a person shoes or slippers; it means you wish them to walk away from you (F, SLC, 1959).

6794    If you put your shoes on the wrong feet, you will have bad luck (F, SLC, 1960).

6795    If you put the left shoe on the right foot, then something unlucky will happen to you (M, Midvale, 1961); . . . it is a bad sign and a forerunner of evil (F, 46, Sandy, 1963); . . . it will bring a day of frustration (M, 57, Heber City, 1914).

6796    If you put your shoes on the wrong feet, it means you will be putting your foot in your mouth the rest of the day (F, 56, SLC, 1915).

6797    If you switch shoes, a bear will come to your door (F, Ogden, 1958).  Heard on an Indian reservation at Washaki, Utah, 1947.

6798    It will bring bad luck to walk around with one shoe off and one on (M, SLC, 1957).  Brown 3206ff.

6799    It is bad luck to sleep with one's shoes on (M, Bountiful, 1961).

6800    If you wear boots inside, it's bad luck (F, Ogden, 1918).

6801    To kick off your shoes and have them alight on their soles and remain standing right side up is good luck; but if they fall over, bad luck is expected (F, 18, SLC, 1964).

6802    It is considered good luck to keep a pair of old shoes in your closet (M, SLC, 1961).

6803    Don't place shoes on the floor side by side in reverse position (M, 45, SLC, 1963); If your hose are crossed when they are off, it is bad luck (M, Layton, 1934).

6804    You aren't supposed to turn your shoes upside down when you take them off (F, Gr, SLC, 1962).

6805    Never put shoes over the head; it will bring you bad luck if you do (F, SLC, 1927); . . . above your head in a closet . . . (F, SLC, 1920s).

6806    If you set your shoes on anything but the floor, it will bring you bad luck (F, 33, SLC, 1940s).  Cf. Brown 3243.

6807    It is bad luck to put shoes on a bench (F, 44, SLC, 1944).

6808    Never put your shoes on the table, or it will bring you bad luck (M, 30, SLC, 1960); . . . new shoes that haven't been worn . . . (F, Norw, SLC); . . . bad luck through the day (F, 25, SLC, 1965); . . . bad luck will befall the family (F, 45, SLC, 1963).  Brown 3153.

6809    Putting shoes on the bed brings good luck (M, 18, SLC, 1963).

6810    Shoes on the bed are bad luck (F, Midvale); If you put . . . , misfortune

will befall you (F, 53, SLC, 1965);
. . . it brings bad luck to the family
(M, 60, It, Latuda, 1963); . . . evil
will enter (F, 19, SLC, 1963).

6811    If shoes are put under the bed, they
will hurt the feet (M, 35, SLC, 1963).

6812    It's bad luck to put your shoes under
the bed while sleeping (M, 25, SLC,
1953); . . . you'll have bad dreams (M,
19, SLC, 1952).

6813    If a person who is going to bed at night
places his shoes side by side, he will
have a good night's rest and a good day
(M, 19, SLC, 1963).

6814    You must always put one shoe a little
ahead of the other shoe at night.  It
will bring bad luck if you don't (M,
1959).

6815    Leave your shoes under the left side of
the bed, then get up on the right side
in the morning, and your day will be a
successful one (F, 1957).

6816    It is bad luck if your shoestrings come
untied (M, Snowville, 1936).

6817    When tying a shoelace, give the bow a
good twist for good luck (M, SLC, 1961).

6818    It is unlucky to burn a shoelace (M, 43,
SLC, 1963).  Cf. Brown 3221.

6819    Wear out your shoes at the toes, spend
as you go (F, SLC, 1935).

6820    If you wear your shoes at the heel, you
will spend a good deal (F, SLC, 1935).

6821    Good or bad luck is determined by which
shoe wears out first.  The left shoe
brings bad luck, the right shoe brings
good luck (M, Can, Magna).

6822    Don't throw both shoes away at the same
time.  It brings bad luck (F, Ogden,
1961).

6823    Don't ever burn old shoes, for it will
bring bad luck (M, SLC, 1930).

6824    Throw a shoe over your left shoulder for
good luck (F, SLC, 1961).

## Slippers, Stockings

6825    If a person crosses some slippers in the
house, it is a bad omen (M).

6826    If girls do not wear socks or nylons all
the time, they will have bad luck (F,
18, SLC, 1959).

6827    A hole in your stocking brings good luck
the first day, but bad luck on the
second (F, Axtell, 1958).

6828    If a stocking is put on crooked, it must
not be taken off and straightened or bad
luck will follow (M, SLC, 1930).

## Gloves

6829    It is bad luck to drop a glove (F, 60,
SLC, 1961); . . . ; you will meet with a
disappointment (F, 52, SLC, 1930).  Cf.
Brown 3237.

6830    If you drop one glove, you must drop the
matching glove, and pick up both of them
together, because if you don't you will
have bad luck (F, Gr, SLC, 1961).

6831    If a lady drops her gloves and picks
them up, she will have bad luck.  If
someone else picks them up for her, they
will both have good luck (M, 19, SLC,
1963); Someone who picks up another
person's glove will have a surprise (F,
SLC, 1960).

6832    Don't pick up another person's glove if
she drops it, for it means
disappointment (F, SLC, 1960).

6833    To drop one's glove means an
introduction (F, Ir, SLC, 1960).

6834    It is unlucky for a person to lose a
glove (F, 25, SLC, 1955).

6835    Finding a lost glove is bad luck (F,
SLC).

# INTIMATE POSSESSIONS

## Handkerchiefs

6836    Give a person a handkerchief and you
give him bad luck (M, 70, Duchesne).

6837    Put your handkerchief on top of your
head to change your luck (F, Kaysville,
1958).

6838    To find a handkerchief is a sign of good
luck (F, Axtell 1958).

6839    If you see a handkerchief on the street,
don't touch it.  Handkerchiefs are for
tears of sorrow, and if you touch it you
will be unhappy (F, 78, SLC, 1964); If
you find and pick up a handkerchief, you
will need it soon for tears (M, Midvale,
1961).

6840    If you find a handkerchief and cannot
turn it, you have a curse on you (F,
Murray, 1957).

## Combs

6841    Dropping a comb will bring bad luck (F,
American Fork, 1962).

6842    If you drop a comb, step on it before
you pick it up, or you will have bad
luck (F, 54, Midvale, 1920); . . . put
your foot on it and make a wish (F,
Ogden, 1960).

6843    If one steps on a comb when dropped, a
disappointment will be knocked out; if
not stepped on, a disappointment will
come (F, 82, It, SLC, 1963).

6844    If you drop a comb, you have someone
else pick it up, because you are not
supposed to pick up your own comb (F,
30, Sandy, 1964).

6845    A girl who drops the comb while combing
her hair is doomed to some sort of
disappointment (F, 21, SLC, 1958).

6846    If a comb breaks, it is a sign of bad
luck (F, 45, Ja, SLC, 1963).

## Wigs, Glasses, Etc.

6847  To have your wig blown off means that you will have to answer an embarrassing question (F, SLC, 1961).

6848  Breaking your glasses is bad luck (F, SLC, 1957).

6849  If you break the left lens of a pair of sunglasses, you will have bad luck (M, 29, SLC, 1963).

## Watches, Purses

6850  A watch will never keep good time while worn to bed (F, SLC, 1957).

6851  If the band on your watch breaks while you are wearing it, then time will go by all too soon (M, SLC, 1930).

6852  Do not wear a watch with a broken face, or you will have bad luck (M, 27, SLC, 1963).

6853  Don't look at the back of a pocket watch, or you will have bad luck (M, 31, SLC, 1960).

6854  When you buy a new purse, always put a penny in its first thing, and you'll never run out of money (F, 33, SLC, 1945).

6855  Never hand someone an empty purse, it's bad luck (M, 32, SLC, 1943).

6856  Never lay a purse on a bed, or that person will have bad luck (F, SLC, 1961).

6857  If you empty a purse, you'll never get it filled up again (M, 21, Midvale, 1950).

## JEWELRY

## Rings

6858  When you get your high school ring, you wear it with the symbol facing you; when you graduate, you wear it away from you. This is supposed to insure a successful future (F, SLC, 1956).

6859  An iron ring made from a horseshoe nail is the luckiest of all rings (M, Midvale, 1961).

6860  It is unlucky to wear a different ring on each finger (F, 21, Oakley, 1960).

6861  A ring worn on the forefinger indicates a haughty, bold, and overbearing spirit; on the long finger, prudence dignity and discretion (F, Ger, Ogden, 1961).

6862  Never wear a ring on your middle finger, or you will have bad luck (F, 16, SLC, 1964).

6863  Spitting through a ring will bring good luck (F, 1961).

6864  When a friend or sweetheart wishes a ring on your finger, it's bad luck to take it off (F, 36, SLC, 1963); . . . you will have good luck until you take it off (F, 19, SLC, 1964).  Cf. Brown 3247.

6865  when a friend makes a wish on the ring you are wearing, you can't take it off until your boyfriend kisses it off, or the wish will not come true (F, Logan, 1957).

6866  If a wedding ring, or any ring, is wished onto the finger of a woman by a man, then the wish will be broken if it is taken off (F, 21, SLC, 1951).

6867  Twist a gold ring on your finger three times, and it will bring good luck (F, SLC, 1959); When you put on a ring for the first time, make a wish and then turn it around three times.  The wish will come true if you don't take the ring off (F, SLC, 1958). Cf. Brown 3246.

6868  If you put a ring on a girl's finger and turn it around three times, and if it isn't removed before the special time, she will receive a wish (M, SLC, 1959).

6869  If you turn another person's ring around eighteen times and make a wish, it will come true (M, SLC, 1943).  Cf. Brown 3251.

6870  Take off your ring, drop it over a candle, make a wish and blow the candle out (M, 19, SLC, 1964).

6871  It will bring bad luck if a fellow removes the ring from the finger of a girl (F, 61, Draper, 1965).

6872  Moving rings from one finger to another brings bad luck (F, SLC, 1957).

## Birthstones, Diamonds and other Precious Stones

6873  Wear your birthstone for good luck (F, SLC, 1957).

6874  Diamonds are considered good luck (M, SLC, 1959).

6875  A solitaire stone is the luckiest of all (M, SLC).

6876  The Hope Diamond is unlucky (F, SLC, 1948).

6877  A diamond will lose its sparkle if touched by a traitor's hand (F, SLC, 1956).

6878  An emerald worn in spring will bring happiness (F, 54, SLC, 1965).  Cf. Brown 3254.

6879  The opal is an unlucky stone and will bring misfortune and ill luck to its owner (M, Vernal, 1959).  Cf. Brown 3256.

6880  The opal, a sinister stone, is the birthstone for those born in October. Anyone not born in October who wears this stone will meet with misfortune and tragedy (F, SLC, 1962).  Cf. Brown 3259.

6881  It is a sign of good luck to find a pearl in an oyster (F, 47, SLC, 1961).

6882  A necklace of pearls is said to attract loving associates (F, 19, SLC, 1963).

6883 Pearls are supposed to bring bad luck to the wearer. Only people born in June will have luck when they wear pearls (F, 19, SLC, 1959); Pearls bring tears to the wearer (F, 48, SLC, 1953); . . . sadness . . . (F, SLC, 1961).

6884 A ring set with a pearl is unlucky (F, SLC, 1964); A string of pearls means sadness (F, Farmington, 1959). Cf. Brown 3260.

6885 Pearls have been said to be formed from teardrops and would bring tears to the possessor (F, 53, Ogden, 1919); A pearl is a tear from the sea. Never wear it when there is trouble or sorrow in your house (F, 19, SLC, 1962).

6886 If you cut out the eye of a fish and bury it, it will turn into a pearl (F, 53, SLC, 1964).

6887 If you wear a ruby, it will prevent all evil and impure thoughts (M).

6888 A person wearing a ruby ring, unless it is their birthstone, will have bad luck (M, 60, SLC, 1958).

6889 A turquoise small charm stone will bring you good luck (M, 18, SLC, 1964).

6890 If a person wears jade, it becomes a part of him (M, 23, SLC, 1964).

## Miscellaneous

6891 If one wears a horseshoe pin, always wear it with the ends up so that one's luck won't run out (F, 43, SLC, 1956).

6892 Good luck bracelets are good luck (F, 44, SLC, 1930).

6893 It is bad luck to wear stick pins in your tie, because someone who doesn't like you can come up and stick it through your heart (F, 53, SLC, 1935).

6894 When you see a friend with the hook of her necklace in front with a jewel, make a wish, turn the hook around to the back, and your wish will come true (F, 20, SLC, 1964).

6895 When wearing a necklace on a chain with a clasp, you get a wish if the clasp touches the hanging pendant portion of the necklace. You must close your eyes and hold the clasp and touching pendant between your thumb and index finger. After the wish has been made, you must immediately return the clasp to the back again (F, 17, Bountiful, 1972).

6896 If the clasp of a necklace is in the front, turn it around three times and get a wish (F, 19, SLC).

6897 If you wear a particular item of jewelry when doing something (such as taking an exam), and you are lucky while doing this, then you must wear that same item of jewelry the next time you do this thing (F, 19, SLC).

6898 If you break a strand of beads and don't gather them all up, you will have bad luck (F, Kaysville, 1949).

6899 To wear a chain around your ankle will bring good luck (F, Holladay, 1957).

6900 People wear jewelry so that they will have magic powers (F, Midvale, 1960).

## GIFTS

## Portents and Inducements

6901 If your right hand itches, you will soon get a present (F, 49, SLC, 1964).

6902 If a person has a white spot on one of his nails, he will soon receive something new (F, SLC, 1948).

6903 If you sneeze in the morning, you will receive a present soon (F, 27, Riverside, 1950); Sneeze three times before breakfast and you'll receive a present during the day (F, 48, SLC, 1965); . . . sneeze before breakfast, you'll receive a present before the week is out (M, Sandy, 1963).

6904 If a person finds a hole in a garment, it is a sign you will receive something (F, 66, Provo, 1955).

6905 If an apron is put on wrong side out by mistake, you will receive a present (F, Lehi, 1957); If you wear your slip backwards all day, you will receive a gift (F, Ogden, 1961).

6906 If you lose a stocking, you will receive a present (F, SLC, 1959).

6907 If you drop a tablespoon, you will receive a package (F, Bountiful, 1953).

6908 Tie a string around your little finger when you go to town, and you will receive a gift you are not expecting (F, 28, SLC, 1948).

## Various Gifts

6909 If you want to receive a gift, you must spit over the little finger (M, 15, Midvale, 1960).

6910 To hear a goose cackling means you will get a gift (M, 20, SLC, 1949).

6911 Dream of a nest and you will receive a gift (F, SLC, 1960).

6912 If you walk through a field of daisies, you will get a gift soon (F, SLC, 1961).

6913 If you find a piece of silk or velvet, you will receive a present (F, 25, Monroe, 1964).

6914 If you are building or making something for someone and drop it, it is a sign that it will suit the person for whom it is being made (M, SLC, 1964).

6915 It is bad luck to give a woman an umbrella (M, 19, SLC, 1963).

6916 Don't give away gifts that someone else gave to you. It will mean bad luck for the person you gave it to (F, 42, SLC, 1964).

6917 Put a paper with 100 "Xs" on it under a rock, and in five days the paper will be gone and a gift will be there. Usually money or candy (F, 69, SLC, 1902).

## Unwrapping of Gifts

6918 When opening a present, don't break the ribbon, or it's bad luck (M, 56, Ir, SLC, 1964).

6919 Never cut the ribbon on a gift package when opening or it will bring bad luck (F, 61, SLC, 1964).

6920 To rip the wrappings of a gift will bring one bad luck (F, 21, Bountiful, 1950); If you tear the paper on the package you're wrapping, bad luck follows (F, 19, SLC, 1963).

## Sharp Objects as Gifts

6921 Giving a sharp instrument for a gift means bad luck for the person that receives the gift (M, It, Helper, 1959); . . . bad luck to the giver and receiver (F, 50, SLC, 1964). Brown 3579.

6922 Don't give something sharp to anyone without your letting them pay for it, or you will have bad luck (F, 80, SLC, 1961).

6923 Never give sharp gifts such as knives, scissors, ice picks, or nut picks to your friends unless you wish them some trouble (F, 49, Ogden, 1949).

6924 Never accept a pair of scissors as a present without giving a coin in exchange; they will bring you bad luck (F, 44, Sandy, 1963); . . . you should give a penny (F, Farmington, 1959); . . . a nickel (F, 97, Fairfield, 1964).

6925 Whenever you give a pointed gift, put a penny in the package for good luck (F, 88, SLC, 1963).

## Gifts of Purses and Wallets

6926 Never give an empty wallet or purse as a gift, or bad luck comes to the receiver (F, Murray, 1958). Brown 3451.

6927 Never give an empty purse or wallet, or it will always be empty (F, SLC); . . . they will be poor forever (F, Ger, Magna, 1964).

6928 Never give a purse without a penny, because you'll lose what you have (F, Midvale).

6929 A new penny in a new purse is good luck (F, SLC, 1963); . . . It will bring prosperity (M, 52, Du, SLC, 1964); . . . The receiver will never be broke (M, SLC, 1959).

## BORROWING AND LENDING

6930 It is considered bad luck to borrow from your neighbors after sunset (F, 71, Gr, SLC, 1964).

6931 It's bad luck to not pay back what you borrow (M, 19, Midvale, 1948).

6932 He who comes twice to borrow comes thrice (F, SLC, 1925).

6933 The best days for borrowing are the last three days in March, or the first three in February (M, SLC).

6934 Do not lend or give on the first day of any month, or it brings bad luck to the home (F, 49, Gr, Midvale, 1930).

6935 Never loan a pocketknife with the blade open, because it is bad luck (M, 38, SLC, 1963).

## FINDING AND LOSING

6936 It is bad luck to give away or spend anything that you find (M, 21, Holladay, 1964).

6937 It is good luck to find a postage stamp (F, 25, Monroe, 1964).

6938 If you find something gold, you will have good luck (M, 48, SLC, 1964).

6939 If you find an arrow, you will be unlucky afterwards (M, SLC, 1959).

6940 It is good luck to find a round stone with a hole in it (M, 24, SLC, 1953).

6941 It's good luck to find a key (F, SLC, 1964).

6942 To find a knife or razor will bring disappointment (M, SLC, 1959).

6943 It is unlucky to find a rusty knife (M, SLC, 1957).

6944 You will have good luck if you find a rusty nail (M, SLC, 1961).

6945 If you should lose an object, go to the general area where it was lost and then read any selection from the Bible, and it will tell you where to locate the lost article (M, 71, SLC, 1964).

6946 The resting place for all lost objects is the moon (M, 24, SLC, 1956).

6947 Fish Lake is a bottomless lake. Anything lost there will be lost forever (M, 65, SLC, 1933).

6948 If you place a straw in your chimney, you will find a lost article (F, Ir, SLC, 1960).

6949 If you lose something, count to ten, and you will find it sooner (F, 26, SLC, 1964).

6950 If you lose something, throw something like it over your shoulder, and it will lead you to the lost one (F, Dan, SLC, 1967).

6951 Spit, spat, spy,
If you don't tell me
Where my ball (or whatever) is,
I'll hit you in the eye.
Spit in the palm is flipped (M, SLC, 1926).

6952 If you lose something, say "Spit, spit, spy, tell me where my shoe (or whatever you are looking for) is, or I'll hit you in the eye."   Then spit in your hand, and you will walk right to it (F, 84, SLC, 1910).

6953   If you have lost something, spit in the palm of your hand, hit it with your fist, and hunt where the spit flies. You will find what you lost (M, Park City, 1957).

6954   When searching for something (whiskey) spit excessively in your palm, slap it with your two fingers, and say, "Spit, spat, spy, tell me where the whiskey lies."   Wherever the spit goes, the whiskey is (M, 40, Magna, 1964).

6955   When a little boy loses his top and he spits in the palm of his left hand and says:
    "Spit, spit spider,
    Tell me where my top lies,
    Or I'll kill you today and hang you
        tomorrow."
Then he would hit the spit with the index finger of his right hand and the spit was supposed to fly in the direction of the lost object (F, St. George, 1954).

# VI

# Economic and Business Affairs

## General

6956 Pull the petals off a sunflower, saying "Rich man, poor man, beggarman, thief, doctor, lawyer, Indian chief," and the one on which you end is what you will turn out to be (F, 47, Moab, 1925).

6957 We used to count the buttons on our dress. Everybody wore lots of buttons, and this is the way we'd count them: "A rich man, a poor man, a beggarman, a thief; a doctor, a lawyer, a merchant, a chief." Then start all over again if you had more buttons (F, 71, Woods Cross, 1953).

6958 It is bad luck for a male child not to specialize in the same profession as his father (M, 45, SLC, 1964).

6959 Stumpy fingers are a sign that one must work for a living (F, 40, SLC, 1964).

6960 It is bad luck to meet a woman on the road to work (F, 63, Monroe, 1964).

6961 To finish a job is to invite bad luck (M, 54, Magna, 1923).

6962 To dream of a hawk signifies the start of a new enterprise (F, 43, SLC, 1964).

6963 To have soup boil over signifies a change of employment (M, 26, SLC, 1963).

6964 Some people believe that if you do any work on rest or taboo days you will have bad luck (F, Kaysville, 1958).

6965 It is bad luck to do work on the Sabbath (F, 19, Payson, 1964); Work on Sunday, you'll have it to do over during the week (M, 84, Centerville, 1958); Those who on the Sabbath labor will never live their money to savour (F, SLC, 1925); . . . the amount you earn will be paid out double during the week (M, Ogden, 1958). Brown 3458.

6966 It is good luck to start your work on a Monday if it is a hard job (F, Ogden, 1959).

6967 Do not start any new work on Monday, or you will have bad luck (M, 63, Russ, SLC, 1964).

6968 It is bad luck to start a new job on Friday (F, 66, Provo, 1925); Never begin a job on a Friday that can't be finished on the same day (F, 1957); . . . you will never finish (F, Ir, SLC, 1962); . . . you will lose money and it won't be successful (M, 45, SLC, 1964). Brown 3455, 5999ff.

6969 It is bad luck to accept a job on Friday (F, 88, SLC, 1964).

6970 If you walk under a ladder, you will lose your job (F, 80, SLC, 1964).

6971 If one blows up a paper sack in the house and bursts it, a member of the household will lose his job (F, 44, SLC, 1964).

## SAILORS

### General Beliefs

6972 If you touch a sailor's collar, it will bring you good luck (M, SLC, 1963).

6973 If you point at a ship, you will bring bad luck to it (M, 14, SLC, 1962).

6974 An anchor is a sign of success and honor (M, SLC, 1958).

6975 A barnacle broken off from a ship turns into a solan goose (M, SLC, 1961).

6976 Some sailors say blue is the most lucky color to paint a boat; others, that blue is bad luck, unless you put on white, as in stripes which avert the evil (F, 21, SLC, 1963).

6977 If a ship creaks, it can never be destroyed (M, 52, DU, SLC, 1964).

6978 If you see the shadow of a ship in the fog, it is a sign of a shipwreck (M, 49, SLC, 1964).

6979 If the moon is red, something awful and bad is going to happen. Sailors think that the red signifies blood (F, SLC, 1959).

6980 A boat will sink when floating in pure spring water (M, SLC, 1964).

6981 To lose a mop or a bucket overboard a ship is bad luck (M, 47, Wendover, 1943).

6982 Sailors think it is a good omen to cross the bow of a foreign vessel (F, Grantsville, 1964).

6983 Throw oil on a stormy sea to hold the waves from breaking (F, SLC, 1958).

6984 If the wind is blowing, hoist a blue pennant, and if the day is clear, raise a red one, and you will have good and safe sailing (M, Du, SLC, 1965).

6985    Always throw the garbage over the starboard side for good luck (M, SLC, 1965).

6986    Aboard ship, when one apple is left in the barrel, the ship is near its destination (M, SLC, 1959).

6987    It is bad luck for a sailor or marine to have a two-dollar bill, so they tear one corner off (M, 61, SLC, 1934).

6988    Sailors believe that a pierced ear with a ring through it means stronger eyesight (M, 21, SLC, 1953).

6989    A sailor shouldn't lay his hat on a bed (M, 27, SLC, 1964).

6990    Never watch your sailor sail away, or he will never return (F, SLC, 1961).

6991    It is unlucky for a sailor to wear the clothes of a fellow sailor who died at sea (M, SLC, 1957).

6992    The petrel bird is supposed to be under the protection of Virgin Mary, and each bird is believed to represent the soul of a sailor lost at sea (M, Vernal, 1959).

## Christening the Ship

6993    All ships must be christened before going to sea.  Then the ship is free from all evil (M, 36, Milford, 1964).

6994    Christening a boat or ship will bring good luck and safety (F, 17, SLC, 1958).

6995    It is good luck to break a bottle of champagne on the bow of a ship (M, SLC, 1957); . . . ; it removes evil spirits from the ship (F, Ogden, 1959); If a ship has been christened by a bottle of wine, it will have fine sailing (M, SLC, 1959); . . . will prevent the ship from sinking (M, 40, SLC, 1940); . . . will insure many a successful voyage (F, SLC, 1958).

6996    If at the christening of a ship the bottle of champagne does not break, it is very unlucky, and the ship will have a rough journey, or something will go wrong on its maiden voyage (M, 39, lawyer, SLC).  Learned in San Francisco, 1955.

6997    It brings bad luck for a boat to be christened with anything but champagne (F, 73, SLC, 1964).

6998    He who owns the boat must give the name, or else it will sink (F, Brigham City, 1960).

6999    Disaster will overtake a ship that has changed its name (F, 18, SLC, 1957).

## Launching, Boarding Ships, Setting Sail

7000    When entering a vessel, never put the left foot down first; to do so will bring disaster (F, 50, SLC, 1964).

7001    Don't go to sea on Tuesday.  This is bad luck (M, Ogden, 1960).

7002    Seamen fear to sail from port on a Friday (M, SLC, 1959); The ship will have bad luck if you . . . (F, 36, Scofield, 1944); Sailors will not sail on a ship that leaves port at midnight on Friday.  The sailing time is 12:05 on Saturday (M, 56, Ir, SLC, 1964).  Cf. Brown 3462.

7003    If you heave a penny over the ship's bow when going out to sea, you will have a successful voyage (F, 21, Eng, SLC, 1963).

7004    Sailors must not mention the port for which they are bound, or bad luck will result (M, Swed, SLC).

## Amulets, Charms

7005    A child born with a veil (skin loosely hanging down over the face) will bring good luck to a ship's captain.  If he keeps this veil, his ship will never go down (F, 74, SLC).

7006    A sailor with "Mother" tattooed on his chest will not drown (M, Woods Cross, 1958).

7007    Sailors carry as good luck a small bone from the head of a fish (F, Grantsville, 1964).

7008    Sailors carry as good luck a bone from a living turtle (F, Grantsville, 1964).

7009    If a sailor is given a farthing by a Scotchman and if he loses it, his ship will sink (M, 21, SLC, 1956).

7010    A sailor will carry a small potato to prevent disease (M, SLC, 1959).

7011    The seamen carry on the boat an ikon of St. Nicholas, patron saint of all seamen; they burn a holy light before it throughout the entire trip.  Should it go out, it brings ill luck (M, 66, Gr, SLC, 1963).

7012    Putting a pin-up on the rear of a ship will bring good luck in a sea battle (M, SLC, 1958).

## Taboos - Whistling, Women and Others Aboard

7013    Whistling aboard ship brings bad luck (F, 43, Logan, 1935).  Brown 3467. (Whistling aboard ship, as seen in this entry and the two items following, likewise on fishing vessels [7058], is a taboo that has spread to other occupations such as mining [7099ff], the stage [7190ff], dance [7203], and to newspapering [7147].  In the days of sail, mariners were often requisitioned as stagehands because of their skill at handling rope.  In an increasingly mobile society, many a sailor also found work in the mines.  The passing on of maritime traditions, on a limited scale at least, resulted from this social interaction.  One other notable transmission from sea to shore was the taboo of women on a working ship.  Cf. Nos. 7016ff and 7056, below.  The taboo against women in a mine is seen in Nos. 7111ff, below.  --Eds.)

7014 If you whistle aboard ship at sea, you will call up a storm. If you whistle aboard while tied up, you will cause disaster to the ship on the next voyage (M, SLC, 1960).

7015 In shipyards no whistling is allowed on deck while a diver is down below (F, Gr, SLC, 1964).

7016 To have a woman on board a ship means bad luck (M, SLC, 1961). Brown 3465. Cf. No. 7013, above.

7017 Women on a sailer or navy ship is bad luck for the crew and the safety of the ship (M, 19, SLC, 1964).

7018 Women on old sailing ships brought bad luck (M, 30, SLC, 1964); If there's a woman on a sailing vessel, there's always disaster (F, Brigham City, 1960).

7019 If one woman is on board a ship with all men, the ship will sink (M, 26, SLC, 1963).

7020 In 1809, there was an old lady known as the "Woman in Black," who was supposed to have the power of casting evil spells. If she was seen on the docks as a boat prepared to depart, they would cancel the trip and depart the next day (F, Gr, Magna, 1961).

7021 Red-haired women on deck are a sign of bad luck and ships won't sail (F, 71, Gr, SLC, 1964).

7022 Never let a woman on a naval base (M, SLC).

7023 Chinamen on ships bring bad luck (M, 30, SCL, 1964).

7024 Preachers on a ship are bad luck (F, 48, SLC, 1964). (For a discussion of preachers aboard a ship, also horses, see California Folklore Quarterly, 5 [1946], 109-10. --Eds.)

7025 Disaster will overtake a ship on which a dead person is carried (M, 49, SLC, 1964); If . . . the ship cannot make her way along the route (F, 20, SLC, 1963).

## Cats, Rats, Animals on Board

7026 Sailors like a cat aboard for good luck (F, Farmington, 1959); . . . assures favorable winds and prevents shipwreck (F, SLC).

7027 Cats on a ship are bad luck (M, SLC, 1958); . . . an invitation to disaster (M, SLC, 1960); . . . mean the ship is doomed to sink (M, 29, SLC, 1964); . . . will bring storms (M, 21, Midvale, 1964).

7028 The mewing of a cat on board a ship foretokens a serious voyage (F, Brigham City, 1960).

7029 To throw a cat overboard is considered to bring you bad luck (F, SLC, 1959).

7030 A ship without rats is bad luck (F, 80, Midvale).

7031 If mice leave a ship, it's an omen of shipwreck (M, SLC, 1961); . . . it's a

sign that the ship will sink (F, SLC, 1958). Cf. Brown 3464.

7032 When rats are seen deserting a ship ready for sea, it is regarded as an evil omen (F, SLC); . . . the ship will sink on her next voyage (M, SLC, 1964); . . . the ship is doomed (M, Farmington, 1944).

7033 Don't speak of a four-footed animal while on the ocean. It will bring bad luck (M, lawyer, SLC, 1957).

7034 It is bad luck if a pet jumps overboard (M, 40, SLC, 1963).

## Albatross, Other Birds

7035 The albatross holds a strange spell over the sailor. He believes this bird, following a ship for days at a time with seemingly motionless wings, possesses an unnatural power, and no sailor is so bold as to harm one of them (F, Heber, 1959). (This item and the following seven entries probably derive from literary tradition rather than from folklore transmitted locally. --Eds.)

7036 The albatross is a bird of good omen (M, 45, SLC, 1961); . . . when it follows a ship, it's a sign of good luck (M, 20, SLC, 1963).

7037 As long as a ship is accompanied by an albatross, no misfortune will befall it (M, SLC, 1960).

7038 It is good luck when an albatross lands on a ship's mast while at open sea (F, 41, SLC, 1963).

7039 When an albatross follows a ship at sea, it is a foreboding sign of evil (M, SLC, 1964).

7040 If an albatross lands on a ship, the ship is doomed (M, 40, SLC, 1963).

7041 The albatross is a sign of good luck to seamen. To kill the bird will bring doom to any ship (F, 19, SLC).

7042 If an albatross was following a ship and was killed by a sailor, the sailor who killed it would have to put it around his neck and wear it for good luck (M, 19, SLC, 1964).

7043 It's bad luck if a bird alights on a boat before it sails (M, SLC, 1963). Brown 3463.

7044 Sailors believe a bird on the rigging is good luck (M, 27, SLC, 1963).

## Porpoises, Dolphins, Sharks

7045 If you see a porpoise at the start of a voyage, it will be a good trip (M, 12, SLC, 1960).

7046 As long as porpoises accompany and play about a ship, nothing bad will befall it (M, SLC, 1960).

7047 It is bad luck to kill a porpoise (M, 23, Ogden, 1964). Brown 7331.

7048    A sailor should never harm a porpoise, because the porpoise will push a man ashore who falls from a ship (M, SLC); . . . porpoises will push the body of a drowned sailor to shore (M, SLC, 1960).

7049    Never kill a porpoise, because they are believed to be reincarnated sailors (M, SLC, 1957).

7050    Dolphins and porpoises, when seen playing about, are said to foretell storms; so they are considered unlucky omens by sailors (M, 18, Moab, 1953).

7051    It is bad luck to kill a dolphin if you are sailing (M, 16, SLC, 1961).

7052    When a shark follows a ship persistently for a few days, it means that someone on board is going to die (M, 27, SLC, 1962).

## FISHERMEN

7053    Fish, such as sharks, are guardians over fishermen; these fish will not harm them but protect them (F, SLC, 1959).

7054    If a fisherman comes across a school of porpoises when fishing, it will bring him good fishing (M, 19, SLC, 1964).

7055    If a white whale is sighted at sea, it means that someone will die soon; maybe a whole fishing boat will be lost (F, 19, SLC, 1963).

7056    If a woman is on a fishing boat, they will have bad luck and not even see any fish (F, 19, SLC). (See note to No. 7016ff, above. --Eds.)

7057    For a fisherman to meet a woman wearing a white apron as he is going to his ship to go to sea, means he will have bad luck during the voyage (F, Ogden, 1960). First heard in Boston, 1920.

7058    Whistling while in a fishing boat is bad luck (F, 19, SLC, 1964). Cf. No. 7013, above.

7059    If a pelican lands on your boat, you will not catch fish. If a seagull lands on the bow of the boat, you will catch fish (F, Eng, Vernal, 1958).

7060    Tuna fishermen can't eat meat, or it'll jinx fishing (M, 29, SLC, 1963).

7061    It is unlucky to pass a barefooted woman before going on a ship. You will scare all the fish away (F, Scot, SLC, 1957).

7062    Fishermen refuse to ship out on Friday, unless it's one minute after midnight (M, 48, SLC, 1939).

7063    Horseshoes are nailed to the masts of fishing vessels for luck (M, SLC, 1959).

7064    A wife won't let a son or husband spin yarn because if they go out to sea with a fish net and a storm comes up, they will be caught in the fish net (F, 24, Norw, SLC, 1964).

7065    When a fishing boat is lost, it is good luck to the lost sailors to light a lamp in the window of their homes (M, 22, Norw, SLC, 1963).

## MINERS

### General

7066    A man came in here with a girl who was a medium, and he would hypnotize her, and she would tell him where to dig. They would hold these meetings night after night and the spirits would tell her where the mine was (F, 55, Monticello, 1946).

7067    Tom McNelly was a spiritualistic medium who came with John Barbee to help him locate his mines. He was a strange man but a real wizard. Barbee's claims were laid out just as the spiritualist told him to (F, St. George, 1939).

7068    "Old Man Peay" dreamed that descendants of Nephites brought their records north, and made trail signs leading to Alpine, Utah. Mr. Hutchings had seen one of the signs, shown him by Mr. Peay. For thirty-five years Mr. Peay dug at a site near Alpine, but when he got to a certain point, his hole would fill with gravel. Every year it would be filled right up, and they would have to start digging from the same spot again. He said once or twice persons had appeared to him and prevented him from digging. He said the site had signs of having been dug before--chisel marks on the rock, etc. Original dream of his was before 1900. He died in 1938 (M, Lehi, 1946).

7069    There's a vein of gold at every place in a rock where the quartz veins cross (M, 22, SLC, 1964).

7070    A black rock has gold inside of it (M, SLC, 1964).

7071    Brigham Young made a prophecy that there is a gold mine in southern Utah. Someday God will open the mine, and it will feed all the people in the world that are left (M, SLC, 1900).

7072    Zeke Johnson tells of being out prospecting in southeastern Utah. His pack mule became frightened and began backing, getting over the edge of the dugway so that its hind feet slid over. Zeke knelt down and prayed, and saw a giant hand reach up under the feet of the mule and lift it right back onto the trail (M, 52, Clearfield, 1946).

7073    If a miner hears a falling rock, he believes that he can't sneeze or it is bad luck (M, 43, SLC, 1948).

7074    If a miner washes his back, he will suffer from weakness in the back (F, 29, SLC, 1964).

7075    If you don't put your left boot on first, you'll die with your boots on (M, 49, Park City, 1920). Superstition among miners in Park City.

7076    After scarring the land from mining activities, return the land as much as possible to its original condition, or the earth will reclaim the wealth (M, 63, Hennifer, 1913).

7077    Never go into a coal mine alone (M, SLC, 1964).

7078    Miners in the Bingham area would not take new gloves into the mine (M, 50, Milford).

7079    Bad luck will come to a miner who turns back to his house after leaving for the pit (M, SLC, 1957).

7080    A summary of our interview with Bishop Koyle (he would not allow us to make notes while we were talking) reveals his intense belief in the theology of Mormonism with respect to dreams, visions, visitations, and his justification of his own supernatural experiences in the field of mining, such as an angelic messenger taking him inside the mountain and showing him exactly where the veins of precious ore lay, and how to get to them.  At a certain point in drilling the tunnel, he would know that he was directly over the "nine rooms" (M, over 70, Salem, 1946).

## Dowsing

7081    The forked hazel twig is a magic divining rod that points to the place where precious minerals lay hidden (M, 53, SLC, 1963). (For a treatment of divining rods, see California Folklore Quarterly, 1 [1942], 34-6.  --Eds.)

7082    Bend a piece of wire with a sample of what you want to locate (such as oil) attached to the far end.  When you hold it over an area which has some of the same material in the ground, the far end of the wire will pull down (M, 57, 1968).

7083    If you put some precious metal such as gold in a nonmetallic container like a little bottle and suspend the bottle from a string, it will (being energized with human brain waves) swing in the direction of other gold.  This will help locate where to prospect for gold.  If you are directly over the gold, it will swing in a clockwise circle (M, 57, Ogden, 1970).

7084    One old fellow said he could find gold with a forked stick like they use to find water (M, 77, Ogden, 1946).

7085    A divining or lightning rod is used to find gold.  When the rod quivers, there is gold underneath (F, 19, SLC).

## Mine Accidents, Etc.

7086    Canaries at the porthole are a sign of bad luck.  Some men take it that you should never enter a mine when you see canaries anywhere near a portal or inside the mine, for canaries are used to test bad air or gases in the mines (M, Lark).

7087    Miners believe that the earth turns on its axis at midnight, and that there is ground movement at this time.  It seems that all the cave-ins occur near midnight (M, 58, Lark).  DR, a geologist at the Lark Mining Company, stated that there actually is a rock tide, just as there is a tide in the ocean.

7088    Accidents in a mine always occur in sets of three (F, 50, Midvale, 1949).

7089    Miners who are superstitious object to entering mines on Good Friday or Christmas Day, fearful that some catastrophe will attend the breaking of a prescribed custom (F, 25, Bingham, 1955).

7090    If there is a Christmas tree in the first load of ore going to the hill or smelter, it is a good omen that the mine is going to be prosperous (M, Lark).

7091    If all is quiet in a mine, an accident is soon to occur (M, Moab, 1962).

7092    After the mine explosion in the Daly West Mine which killed thirty-eight men, miners who saw a white mule in the mine (where none were used) were always killed in mine accidents (M, Park City, 1957).  (The entry is not too clear, but phantom white horses and white mules in the mines have long been looked upon as harbingers of mine disasters and death. See Wayland D. Hand, "Folklore from Utah's Silver Mining Camps," Journal of American Folklore, 54 [1941], 145. --Eds.)

7093    If a Mexican miner were killed in a mine, his partner would make a cross on the wall with a carbide lamp, and no other miner would work in the place. The cross was indelible (M, SLC, 1958).

7094    Miners believe it is bad luck to speak of the shift that will be their last one (M, SLC, 1960).

7095    Miners believe you should never go down the mine shaft on your last shift or when planning a vacation, because many people have been killed in doing this (F, Park City, 1959).

7096    The ghost of a miner killed underground will stay in that spot (F, 50, Lark, 1949).

7097    When Park City was in its boom, one of the mines had an explosion in it. Several men were reportedly killed.  It was not reopened until several years later.  When the passage where the men were killed was opened, they found one of the old miner's hair growing on a tunnel post (M, 49, Park City, 1923).

7098    A miner who falls down a shaft will never hit bottom with his boots on (M, 21, Park City, 1960).

## Whistling, Music, Noises

7099    It is bad luck to whistle in a mine (M, SLC).  Cf. the note to No. 7013, above.

7100    Whistling in mines causes a high pitch which, in turn, causes vibrations for cave-ins (M, 37, Lark).

7101    If a miner whistles in a mine, there will be an explosion (M, Moab, 1962).

7102    The sound of music or the feeling of the miners that one is playing music is expressed by some miners.  One man said it was string music like a violin.  Some believe it is gases escaping from the rocks making the sound or water dripping (M, 53, miner, Lark).

7103   Tommy Knockers:  If one hears strange noises in the mine, it's those old stope cats who have come back to work in the mine.  They are drilling by hand (M, miner, Lark).

7104   Groaning timbers in the mine are bad luck (F, SLC, 1967).

## Rats, Mice

7105   Never kill mice in a mine, or it will bring bad luck (M, 47, Price, 1961).

7106   If rats are in the underground mine, the area won't cave in (F, 50, Lark, 1949).

7107   Miners won't enter a mine if there aren't any rats in it (F, 46, Bingham, 1925).

7108   If a miner sees mice leaving the mine, it is a sure sign of a forthcoming accident (F, 19, Bohem, Helper, 1964); . . . it's a sign of a cave-in or bad gas (M, miner, Lark).

7109   If you see mice or rats going back into the tunnels of a mine, it means there is going to be a catastrophe outside (landslide, etc.) (M, 49, Bingham, 1925).

## Women in the Mines, Etc.

7110   To meet or see a woman on the way to the pits in the middle of the night will bring about bad luck (F, 79, Eng, SLC, 1964).

7111   The presence of a woman in a mine was an evil omen.  It was a sign of ill luck merely to meet a woman on the way to work in the mines (M, miner, Heber, 1959).  Brown 3481.  (See note to No. 7013, above.  --Eds.)

7112   A woman was not allowed to enter a mine when the miner had found a vein of gold, silver, copper, etc., because she would stop his luck (M, 70, Bingham Canyon, 1913).  Cf. Brown 3482.

7113   When a woman enters a newly discovered mine, the mine won't produce, because of its jealousy of a woman (M, miner, SLC, 1963).

7114   Miners believe that if a woman comes to look at their work, and the miners see her, they stop working for the day because they say an accident will occur (M, 60, Bingham, 1930); . . . she will bring a disaster in the mine (F, SLC, 1960).

7115   If a woman enters a mine, there will be a death among the miners within six months (M, 22, SLC, 1954).

7116   Sandhogs driving tunnels from Bingham Canyon to Copperfield, Utah, would leave the moment women entered a tunnel (M, 50, 1930s).

## Construction and Other Fields

7117   Architects avoid building buildings of thirteen stories (M, SLC, 1958).

7118   If you step on a contractor's marking, it will bring you good luck (F, 22, Clearfield, 1964).

7119   A brick mason, when laying the first brick for a structure, always holds the trowel in both hands to insure a sturdy foundation (M, 42, SLC, 1963).

7120   You shouldn't start a construction job on Friday, or you'll never finish it (M, 84, Centerville).

7121   When the steel construction has been finished on a new building, the workers hang a Christmas tree on the top beam for good luck (M, 53, SLC, 1964).

7122   To finish a job is to invite bad luck. Don't place the last brick in a house, etc. (M, 43, American Fork, 1935).

7123   It's good luck to grow a beard for St. Patrick's Day if you're an engineer (M, 64, SLC, 1963).

7124   If you see a chimney sweep, it is good luck (F, 30, Ger, Ogden, 1970).

7125   When you can feel the ground shake under you around a drilling rig for oil, then the oil is not far off.  Every time the hammer falls, the earth shakes (M, 45, SLC).

7126   If when a cross arm is being set up a line pole, a ground man ties a granny knot when it should be a slip knot, the linesman comes down to allow the bad luck to dissipate (M, Magna, 1967).

7127   It is bad luck for a logger to kill a weasel (M, Midvale, 1958).

7128   It is bad luck if a logger brings an axe in the bunkhouse (M, Midvale, 1958).

7129   It is bad luck for loggers to have a female cook (M, Midvale, 1958).

7130   No harm or accident will befall a blacksmith (F, 53, Plain City, 1924).

7131   A cattleman should always wear his pants inside his boots (M, 45, Ogden, 1964).

7132   Cowboys want to die with their boots on (M, Layton, 1934).

7133   Cowboys should put the left boot and right spur on first for good luck (M, 35, Hooper, 1970).

7134   If cowboys eat raw meat, they will be eaten by wild animals (M, 1900s).

7135   It is unlucky for herdsman to carry a stick not made of ash (M, 1961).

7136   It is unlucky for a ranch to have anything but Basque or Spanish sheepherders (M, Grantsville, 1959).

7137   A sheepman must always wear his pants outside his boots (M, Ogden, 1964).

7138   The guards at Utah State Prison believe that riots usually occur in the spring. Men are restive after being cooped up all winter, and feel the urge to be free in the spring more than at other times (M, prison guard).

7139 During the Second World War in the South Pacific it was supposed to be good luck to be in the first assault (M, 55, Bountiful, 1964).

7140 A belief during World War I was that if you didn't wash your mess kit after using it, you would never use it again (F, 63, Monroe, 1964).

7141 It's bad luck to take off your helmet while in combat (M, Bountiful, 1964).

7142 If you wear your "blood wings" when you jump from a plane, it is bad luck, because you may cover them with blood (M, SLC, 1966).

7143 A hobo who has received food at your house will mark the gate in a way that only hobos understand so that the next one through will know to come in (F, Tooele, 1957).

7144 Never turn a beggar away from your door. If you do, it's bad luck (F, 80, Eng, Midvale, 1964); . . . his occupation will be yours (M, Midvale).

## VARIOUS PROFESSIONS

7145 If a dressmaker drops a pair of scissors accidentally, she will shortly have a mourning order (F, dressmaker, 1959).

7146 Long tapering fingers represent a stenographer; they are supposed to denote character (F, Moab, 1953).

7147 It is bad luck for a reporter to whistle in the editorial room (M, Payson, 1959). Cf. note to No. 7013, above.

7148 It is bad luck for a woman to enter the press box (F, SLC, 1957).

7149 If the first customer of a barber shop asks for a shave, the shop will have a good day (M, barber, SLC, 1957).

7150 Barber chairs must be red and every barber shop should have a red and white barber pole (M, barber, SLC, 1957).

7151 Long fingers mean that a person will be a doctor (F, Moab, 1953).

7152 If a nurse knocks over a chair, a new patient will soon be arriving (F, 44, nurse, SLC, 1956).

7153 If while dressing, a nurse twists her apron strings, she will be taking over new work soon (F, nurse, SLC, 1959).

## ACTORS

### General Beliefs

7154 A cat backstage is good luck (F, 15, SLC, 1962).

7155 In a theater black cats mean good luck (M, 22, SLC, 1957).

7156 It is bad luck to step on a spider backstage. Never do it (F, SLC, 1967).

7157 Actors will stay off a stage if there is a picture of an ostrich present, because of the bad luck that follows (F, Heber, 1961).

7158 Peacock feathers are never used on stage, as they bring bad luck (F, 53, SLC, 1965); . . . they curtail finances (M, 64, SLC, 1964).

7159 If you open an umbrella in the showhouse, bad luck will come to the actors (F, 49, SLC, 1925).

7160 Actors believe that it's bad luck to have someone backstage that is cross-eyed (F, 19, Granger, 1964).

7161 In the theater tragedy comes in threes (M, 18, SLC, 1964).

7162 Movie stars always die in groups of three (F, 24, SLC, 1964).

7163 Never really kiss your leading man (F, SLC, 1962).

7164 Stage people keep lucky objects, especially if something has gone right for them with these objects (F, 60, SLC, 1964).

7165 Actors will never take a two-dollar bill, because bad luck will follow (F, 74, SLC, 1964).

7166 Don't smoke in the greenroom before going on stage. It brings bad luck (F, SLC, 1962).

7167 If you should walk on a stage before the curtain rises, you'll be lucky (M, 22, SLC, 1964).

7168 In a theater it's bad luck to count the house (M, 22, SLC, 1957).

### Clothing and Accessories

7169 If an actor throws his hat on the bed opening night, the play will be a flop (F, SLC, 1961).

7170 If you go backstage in a theater, never lay your hat on a bed, for it is bad luck (M, 46, SLC, 1956); If an actor sees a hat on a bed before a performance, it is bad luck (M, Ogden, 1958).

7171 Any green worn out on the stage will be unlucky for the play and the actors (F, 72, SLC, 1964).

7172 Actors consider yellow an unlucky color (M, 22, SLC, 1964).

7173 Actors believe it's bad luck to change out of a costume after it has once brought you good luck (F, Heber, 1930).

7174 If an actor's costume catches a piece of scenery, he will have bad luck (F, 19, SLC, 1964).

7175 If an actor's shoes squeak, he will be well received by the audience (F, 19, SLC, 1964).

7176 Never wear jewelry on stage. It's bad luck. If you're really mad at someone, give them a piece of jewelry just before they go on stage (F, SLC, 1967).

## Wishing Good Luck

7177  Don't wish a person good luck on opening night of a play, or it will bring bad luck.  Wish misfortune upon them for good luck (M, SLC, 1953).

7178  Never wish a person good luck just before going on stage; rather say, "Break a leg" (F, SLC, 1955).

7179  If you pinch an actor's shoulder just before he goes on stage, he will have good luck (F, SLC, 1960).

7180  It brings good luck to kick someone gently in the seat before they go on stage (F, SLC, 1956).

7181  Never congratulate theater people on opening night, because it is bad luck (F, SLC, 1948).

## The Rehearsal, the Performance

7182  If you clap at a dress rehearsal, the performance will be a failure (M, Nephi, 1961).

7183  While rehearsing a play, speaking the last line will bring bad luck (M, SLC, 1958); . . . means the play will be a flop (M, SLC, 1959).

7184  A lousy dress rehearsal always means a good first performance (F, 60, Ogden, 1950).

7185  If you drop a hairpin on stage during dress rehearsal, you must pick it up and throw it backwards over your left shoulder into the orchestra pit.  This is to prevent bad luck during the performance (F, SLC, 1967).

7186  Never open telegrams or letters before a performance (F, 15, SLC, 1962).

7187  The second night of a performance is always the best (F, SLC, 1955).

7188  The first night of a performance the actors should never look out from the curtains before show time; the show will be a flop and it's bad luck if you do (M, 20, SLC, 1964).

7189  Never be seen by an audience before a performance (F, 15, SLC, 1962).

## Whistling in the Dressing Room, Etc.

7190  If you whistle in a dressing room, while off stage, someone will get hurt (F, SLC, 1960); . . . go out the door and turn around three times (F, 18, SLC, 1962); . . . it will bring bad luck and a bad performance (F, SLC, 1958). Cf. Brown 3477.  (See note to No. 7013, above.  --Eds.)

7191  If you whistle in a dressing room, then you have to go outside, say the dirtiest swear word you know, and spit over your left shoulder, or you'll have bad luck on stage (F, SLC, 1958).

7192  Don't whistle backstage.  It's bad luck (F, SLC, 1961).

7193  Never whistle in the theater before putting on a show, or the audience will be whistling at you during the performance (F, SLC, 1965).

7194  Actors never sing in their dressing room, for it is considered to be unlucky, and they will have trouble in their movie (M, Murray, 1959).

7195  Never whistle or sing "Home, Sweet Home" in a theater dressing room (F, SLC, 1920).

## DANCERS

7196  A dancer should never practice in black toe shoes, because she will be more susceptible to accidents (F, 19, SLC, 1953).

7197  Never rehearse your dance number the same day as the performance.  The routine will not look fresh and new for the audience (F, 21, SLC, 1963).

7198  Never throw away toe-shoe ribbons; sew them on new toe shoes or wear ribbons in your hair (F, SLC, 1967).

7199  Never throw away old toe shoes; give them to a younger dancer to bring them luck (F, SLC, 1967).

7200  Never throw away ballet shoes even if they are old.  You should keep them because they have character (F, SLC, 1967).

7201  It is bad luck to wear any part of your ballet costume without wearing it all (F, SLC, 1967).

7202  If you tip the rosin box over, you must step in what you have spilled and walk around it three times (F, SLC, 1967).

7203  If a dancer whistles in a dressing room, someone on the stage will be injured (F, SLC, 1958).  Cf. note to No. 7013, above.

7204  In the dressing room of a *corps de ballet*, if someone whistles in the room, the dancer closest to the door will have an accident (F, 21, SLC, 1958).

7205  Chorus girls are never supposed to have the number thirteen; if they have this number, they don't do well (F, SLC, 1964).

## MUSICIANS AND ARTISTS

7206  Musicians consider yellow an unlucky color (M, 22, SLC, 1964).

7207  Singers will not sing the "Witches Song" from *Macbeth*, because of the bad luck spell that goes with the song (F, Heber, 1930).

7208  A paint brush is guided by the gods (M, Provo, 1936).

7209  If the first two or three strokes on a canvas are not interesting or exciting, then the picture will not be a success when finished (F, 22, Clearfield, 1964).

PROSTITUTES

7210 Girls are supposed to walk with one foot in front of the other. Walking with the feet turned out is the sign of a common whore (F, 22, Price, 1963).

7211 If a frequenter of a house of ill fame can make a whore come, her services come free to him (M, 66, SLC, 1920s).

7212 Whores are "altered" so as not to become physically depleted as a result of their work (M, 66, SLC, 1920s).

7213 Light one of the matches, then turn the matches around so that two head in one direction and the remaining one in the opposite direction. If the two matches separate, it means you're a whore (F, SLC, 1971).

BUSINESS, TRADE, FINANCIAL MATTERS

General Beliefs

7214 Dreaming of children means success in business (F, SLC, 1957).

7215 It is the cigar-store Indian that makes the cigar store successful (M, 1957).

7216 The pig is a sign of good luck in business ventures (F, SLC, 1958).

7217 Cheaters never prosper (F, SLC, 1964).

7218 If you hear someone playing a flute, it means that you will meet an old friend, and in due time you will have a financial gain (F, Dan, SLC, 1964).

7219 If a man puts his hat on backwards, he will have good luck in business (F, Axtell, 1958).

7220 A business is never started on a day that bad luck occurred on before (F, 45, Ja, SLC, 1963).

7221 It is bad luck for businessmen to use red ink (F, 22, SLC, 1963).

7222 If you sing before breakfast, you will be unlucky in your business of the day (M, 41, SLC, 1946); . . . you will be disappointed in business (F, SLC, 1940).

7223 Put a pile of salt in the door of the establishment and it will draw many customers (M, Magna).

7224 The eighth day of the month is a good day to transact business (M, SLC, 1961).

7225 Don't make any business transactions on Monday, or the rest of the week will go bad (F, Pol, 22, Moab, 1964).

7226 If you drink whiskey on Sunday, you will gain nothing financially during the week (M, SLC, 1961).

7227 If you go where you don't have business, you will find business (M, 1959).

7228 Rain in the morning means you'll make money that day (M, SLC, 1964).

7229 If your business building is facing east, it is good luck because the sun rises in the east, and your business will also rise (M, 55, Ja, Elberta, 1963).

7230 It is believed if a man has a crooked smile, he will be unfair with you in his dealing or business transactions (M, 23, SLC, 1964).

7231 If you see more than ten sunspots on the moon at one time, the market will drop (F, 19, SLC, 1959).

First Customer; First Transaction

7232 You must make a sale to the first person in on a Monday morning, or business will be bad all week (M, 57, Ogden, 1970).

7233 If the first customer who comes into your shop in the morning doesn't buy something, no matter the size, business is said to be poor the rest of the day (M, 21, SLC, 1960); . . . the entire week (M, SLC, 1969); If a merchant makes a sale to his first customer of the day, he will have a good day (F, 67, SLC, 1963).

7234 Keep the first dollar you make in business for good luck (M, 19, SLC, 1963).

7235 Storekeepers often save the money they receive from their first customer. They hang it on the wall of their store to bring them good luck (M, 48, Midvale, 1964); . . . frame the first dollar (M, SLC, 1957).

Financial Trouble, Reversals

7236 A dull penny brings financial troubles (F, 54, SLC, 1964).

7237 To find an arrow is a bad omen, and it denotes failure in business matters (M, 68, SLC, 1936).

7238 To see an old, decrepit beggar is a sign of bad management (M, Dan, SLC, 1964).

7239 A pharmacy with a soda fountain leaves old gum that is stuck under the counter edge there, because business leaves when it is removed (M, Murray, 1930s).

7240 People who throw onion peel on the ground are likely to suffer financial reverses (M, 19, Richfield, 1958).

7241 If a person happens to be financially successful, he should prefer not to have anyone mention his success, or praise him for it, since this open admission may bring on a reversal of fortune (M, 50, It, SLC, 1965).

Making Business Deals

7242 No matter how you cheat or pull "fast deals" on people, it always gets done to you sooner or later (F, 23, Murray, 1964).

7243 Always shake hands to close a deal (F, 46, SLC, 1964).

7244    Spit in your hands when you are trading, and you will always get the best of the bargain (F, 28, SLC, 1948).

7245    Never start a business deal on Friday (F, 88, SLC, 1964).

7246    It is never wise to make a business deal on a Friday, because of what happened on Good Friday (F, 18, SLC, 1961).

7247    If someone sneezes during the interim of an agreement, or some other incident regarded as a bad omen occurs, the deal is off (M, SLC).

7248    If a hen crows like a rooster, its owner will get an office (M, 47, Clover, 1940).

## MONEY

### General

7249    If a baby has croup, you will have to raise money very soon (F, SLC, 1945).

7250    If the first one to enter your house on the New Year brings a piece of money with them, your money matters will be good during the entire year (M, SLC, 1957).

7251    Spitting on money brings good luck (M, SLC, 1950s).  Cf. Brown 3441.

7252    While smoking, blow smoke rings, stick your hand through them and you should receive money (F, Murray, 1932).

7253    It is unlucky to receive money in round numbers (F, SLC, 1958).

7254    Don't count your money on a sunny day (F, SLC, 1961).

7255    If you break the dial on your watch, the bank where you keep your money may not be safe (M, SLC, 1960).

7256    Saving stamps up to a certain amount will bring an inheritance in the same amount of dollars (F, SLC, 1940).

7257    The ten of diamonds means there is a larger sum of money in store for you (F, 21, SLC, 1964).

7258    If you talk to yourself, you have money in the bank (M, 20, SLC, 1952).

7259    If you are walking down the street and unconsciously happen to turn money over in your pocket, you will have a good day (F, SLC, 1961).

7260    Fold money toward you and more will come; fold it away from you and it will go fast (M, 29, SLC, 1964).

7261    Never take all of the money out of your purse.  Always leave a coin, as money attracts money (F, 60, SLC, 1906).

7262    Once you find money, more money will continue to come to you (F, 19, SLC, 1963).  Brown 3444.

7263    Finding a purse with a penny inside means it will never be without money (M, SLC, 1959).

7264    When a person finds some money, they should make a cross on the spot.  If they do so, they will find some more money (F, 20, SLC, 1964).

7265    Money found is lucky money (F, 52, SLC, 1964).

7266    To find a gold piece is lucky, and it should be kept in a safe place (M, 37, Richfield, 1938).

7267    If you find silver money on New Year's day, you will have good luck all year (M, Ogden, 1958).

7268    Pull someone's ears and say "brickle brits," and gold will flow from the ears (F, SLC, 1961).  (This belief apparently is based on Grimm 36, "The Wishing-Table, the Gold Ass, the Cudgel in the Sack."  --Eds.)

7269    If you dream of silver, you'll have a hard life (M, SLC, 1961).

7270    If you dream of gold, your life will be easy (M, SLC, 1961).

7271    It is bad luck to refuse to give money to a beggar (M, SLC, 1959).

7272    Do not knock icicles off a house; if you do, you will lose money (F, Sandy, 1957).

7273    If you see a woman die, you will lose property (M, 54, Swed, SLC, 1963).

## BODY PARTS AS INDICATORS

### Head and Chest

7274    If your teeth are far apart, you'll have money (F, Woods Cross, 1953).

7275    If your teeth don't hurt when pulled, you will pay money (F, 68, SLC, 1964).

7276    If your nose itches you're coming into money (F, 17, SLC, 1958).

7277    If the ears are not close to the head, the person is loose with his money (F, SLC, 1957).

7278    If the ears are close to the head, this indicates a person is tight with his money (F, SLC, 1957).

7279    If one's right eye itches, it is a sign of impending good fortune (M, SLC, 1959).

7280    If a bald-headed man has hair on his chest, he will have money (F, 67, SLC, 1963).

### Hand and Palm

7281    If the palm of your hand itches, you will get some money (F, 27, Bountiful, 1941); . . . you'll receive money from an unexpected source (M, doctor, SLC, 1964); . . . you will inherit some money (F, SLC, 1935); . . . you will soon receive a large sum of money (M, SLC, 1958).  Brown 3392ff.

7282   If the palm of your hand itches, knock on wood and you will receive some money (F, 52, SLC, 1963); . . . scratch your hand with wood, and you will receive some money (M, SLC, 1964).  Brown 3396.

7283   If the palm of your hand itches, there's money in your britches (M, 78, Laketown, 1894); . . . money in your husband's britches (F, 80, SLC, 1893).

7284   When the palm of the hand itches, it means you will be receiving money soon. Don't scratch the area with the nails, but rub it with the thumb or you will scratch your money away (M, 56, Ir, SLC, 1964).  Brown 3395.

✗ 7285   When the left palm itches, money will cross your palm (F, 19, 20, SLC, 1958); . . . you'll receive money unexpectedly (M, 1959); . . . receive some money that day (F, 21, SLC, 1963).  Brown 8536f.

7286   If your left hand itches, you will count money (F, 42, SLC, 1963).  Cf. Brown 3398.

7287   If your left palm itches, you will give money away (F, SLC); . . . it is a sign you will spend money soon (M, SLC, 1957); . . . you are going to lose some money (F, Ogden, 1960).  Brown 3401f.

7288   If your left palm itches, rub it on wood and say, "Money, money, money" and you will get money.  If your right hand itches, you will lose money (F, Ger, SLC, 1952).

✗ 7289   When the palm of your left hand itches, scratch it three times on wood and wish for money (F, Provo, 1959).

7290   The itching of the palm of the right hand means that it will shortly receive money (F, 83, SLC, 1965); . . . you will count money (F, 49, Norw, SLC, 1963); . . . scratch it with wood, and you will receive money (M, Layton, 1934).  Cf. Brown 3399, 8535.

7291   If the right palm of your hand itches and you scratch it on wood, you will give money to someone (M, SLC, 1957).

7292   If the palm of your right hand itches, someone wants money (M, 1959).

7293   An "M" in the lines in your hand means money (F, Moab, 1953).

7294   A thumb that turns back shows you can't save money (M, 1959).

7295   If your thumb bends back extremely far, you have money (M, 51, Bountiful, 1920s).

Fingers, Fingernails

7296   If your finger itches, you'll come into money very soon (SLC, 1960); If your fingers tingle, you can expect money before the day's end (F, SLC, 1964).

7297   If you have rounded fingernails during childhood instead of square, when you grow up you will acquire much money (M, 57, Swiss, Heber City, 1916).

7298   Put the cut-off pieces of your fingernails in the door hinge and you will receive money (Bountiful, 1971).

BODILY FUNCTIONS, ATTRIBUTES

✗ 7299   When you sneeze three times in succession, it means you are going to get some money (F, 19, SLC, 1962); . . . someone will give you money (F, 54, SLC, 1935).

7300   If one trips up the stairs, one is going to fall into money soon (M, SLC, 1964).

7301   If you dream of death, it means that one day you will have great amounts of money (F, SLC, 1962).

7302   Dreaming of money is an omen of bad luck (F, SLC, 1960); . . . means you are going to have trouble (F, 50, Magna, 1959); . . . brings bad luck (F, Logan, 1943); Dreaming of a small amount of money is bad, but of large bills is good luck (F, SLC, 1915).

7303   You should beware of theft if you dream of money (F, SLC, 1957).

7304   If you dream about money, you will shortly lose some (F, Murray, 1957).

7305   If you dream of an airplane, it is a sign of making money, but watch your speculations, or you will be caught and lose instead of gain (F, SLC, 1957).

7306   If you dream of a strange place, it is a sign of inherited money soon to come to you (F, SLC, 1957).

7307   If you have a mole on your neck, you will have money by the peck (F, 22, SLC, 1964); A mole on your nose means money when it snows; a mole on your back means money by the sack; a mole on your arm means money by the swarm; a mole on your leg means money by the keg (F, Richfield, 1936).  Brown 3390f.

CLOTHING INDICATORS

7308   If you mend your clothes on your back, you will receive much money (M, SLC, 1960).

7309   If you wear a garment with a hole on Christmas, you'll lose money (F, Midvale).

7310   If your shoe squeaks, you will receive money (F, 19, SLC, 1964).

7311   If your skirt is turned up at the bottom, you'll get some money (M, SLC, 1957).

7312   You can't bum money off someone wearing a red tie (M, 18, SLC, 1965).

DOMESTIC

7313   If you want good luck and money, take a piece of bread and sugar and put a piece of silver in it, wrap up the silver in the bread and sugar, and have some friend hide it in your house.  And then you forget about it (F, Moab, 1953).

7314    If you don't want to be without money, buy lots of salt always, and you'll always have lots of money in the house (F, Moab, 1953).

7315    On New Year's Day one must eat "Hopping John." The amount of peas eaten determines how much money you will have for the year (F, 47, SLC, 1965). Heard in Georgia, 1924. Cf. Brown 3406f.

7316    If you open a parasol in the house, you will soon have money to save (F, SLC, 1960).

7317    Bubbles in your coffee mean you're going to come into money (F, 20, Sandy, 1961). Cf. Brown 3428.

7318    If you catch the air bubbles that form on the top of your coffee when you pour it in your cup, it means you'll get some money (F, 40, SLC, 1940).

7319    If any bubbles should stay on the top of tea you are drinking, it means money (F, 67, SLC, 1920); . . . you'll inherit money (F, 19, SLC, 1952).

7320    If you drink the bubbles on top of tea, you'll receive some money (F, Fillmore, 1960). Brown 3430.

7321    When you drink tea, the leaves which are left in your cup after drinking the tea are supposed to represent the money which you will have (F, 22, SLC, 1964).

7322    Always spoon the foam off of a cup of tea or coffee and say "Money, money," and you will receive some money (F, 61, Bingham Canyon, 1910).

7323    Bubbles in a hot beverage mean money (F, 45, SLC, 1930); Foam on your Postum . . . (M, SLC, 1958); Bubbles on cocoa . . . (F, Ogden, 1935).

7324    If you have bubbles on a liquid, scoop them out with a spoon and it will bring money (F, 60, SLC, 1964).

## ANIMAL INDICATORS

### Various Animals

7325    A white cat crossing your path means money (F, 57, SLC, 1963).

7326    Start counting white horses. After you have reached 100, the next person you meet will give you some money (F, 42, SLC, 1957). Cf. Brown 3415.

7327    Upon seeing a white horse spit in your hand, then slap it and make a wish. This means money (F, 67, SLC, 1912). Cf. Brown 3416.

7328    To dream of a horseshoe is a good sign that you will receive some unexpected money (M, 35, Ibapah, 1947).

7329    If you dream of finding or gathering eggs, you will receive money (F, 44, SLC, 1964). Cf. Brown 3425.

7330    Dreams of mice mean money coming (F, 53, SLC, 1965).

7331    Count the spots on a leopard and you will find a dollar for every spot you count (M, SLC, 1960).

7332    If the cuckoo bird calls on New Year's Day and you have money in your pocket, you will have money for the rest of the year (F, 55, Aust, SLC, 1965); . . . turn over the money in your pocket and you will have money the year around (M, 19, Provo, 1964).

7333    If you hear a cuckoo by the forest, you should shake your money bag (M, 45, Ger, SLC, 1963).

7334    Bad luck will follow if you have no money in your pockets when you hear a cuckoo (M, SLC, 1956).

### Insects, Spiders, Etc.

7335    If you dream about bees, you are going to get money (F, Magna).

7336    Bees around a door mean money (F, SLC, 1960).

7337    If you kill a bee on the first day of May and keep it in your purse, you will always have money (F, 68, Murray, 1963).

7338    Keep a bumblebee in your wallet so you won't have it empty (F, SLC, 1960).

7339    It is unlucky to kill a ladybug, as it brings money (M, 44, Hyrum, 1964).

7340    Crickets on the hearth mean you will have money (F, 20, SLC, 1964).

7341    If you dream of lice, it means you will come into some money (M, Swiss, Heber City, 1916).

7342    If you dream about a spider, you will come into money (F, Ger, SLC, 1959).

7343    A spider in the house is an omen that the occupants will receive some money (F, 1946); . . . money spider . . . (F, Eng, SLC, 1943).

7344    Small black house spiders mean money; money means spiders (F, Ogden, 1935).

7345    A white spider found on the person means that the person will soon come by some money (F, Jordan, 1900s).

7346    When a spider crosses your path there is money in store for you (F, 84, SLC, 1963); . . . you will inherit some money (F, 46, SLC, 1964).

7347    Spider webs in a house bring prosperity to the members of the household (F, SLC, 1964).

7348    Killing a spider means you'll receive money (F, 75, SLC, 1904).

7349    Never kill a spider; you'll lose money (F, 80, Eng, Midvale, 1964).

7350    The gift of a yellow flower foretells a gift of money (M, 19, SLC, 1964).

7351    If you find the first daffodil of the spring in someone else's garden, you will have more gold than silver that year (F, Brigham City, 1960).

7352   If you will carry a four-leaf clover in your wallet, you will never be broke (M, 22, SLC, 1959).

7353   Dream of flowers and you will receive money (F, 54, SLC, 1965).


COSMIC PHENOMENA

7354   If you see a shooting star, you will get some money soon (F, 12, SLC, 1960).

7355   Say, "Money, money before the week's up" while a star is falling, and you will get money before the week's up (F, Bear River City, 1957).

7356   When you see a star fall, say, "Money, money, money." If you are able to make the third repetition before it fades, you will get some (M, 44, Layton, 1970).

7357   If you see a falling star, clap your hands and say, "Money, money, money," and you'll receive money (F, 13, American Fork, 1951).

7358   If you see a falling star and count to ten before it disappears, you will come into some money or good fortune (F, Murray, 1958).

7359   If you see a star fall, you are going to find some money (F, 55, Logan, 1970).

7360   If the first time you see the moon at night it's over your right shoulder, you'll get some money (F, 59, American Fork, 1920).

7361   If you show your money to a new moon, it will cause it to grow in value (F, 19, SLC, 1954). Cf. Brown 3432.

7362   When you see the new moon, turn your money over and it will accumulate (F, 50, Eng, SLC, 1964); . . . turn your money in your purse and you'll always have money (F, SLC). Cf. Brown 3434, 3436.

7363   During a full moon turn your money over in your pocket and you will save money in the future (F, 21, SLC, 1950).

7364   If a person buries money in the full of the moon, it will grow as the moon grows brighter (M, SLC, 1955).


DENOMINATIONS OF MONEY

Bills

7365   A two-dollar bill is good luck (M, 19, SLC, 1963); Carrying a two-dollar bill in your wallet . . . (F, 43, SLC, 1964); If someone gives you a two-dollar bill . . . (F, 24, SLC, 1940); If the corner is torn off . . . (M, SLC, 1958).

7366   Keep a two-dollar bill for over a year, and you will be lucky the rest of your life (F, 45, American Fork, 1960).

7367   It's good luck to keep a two-dollar bill in circulation (F, SLC, 1959).

7368   It is unlucky for a person to have possession of a two-dollar bill (M, 44, SLC, 1940s).

7369   Never cash a two-dollar bill (F, 35, SLC, 1956).

7370   It is unlucky to possess a two-dollar bill that does not have one of the corners torn off (M, SLC, 1959).

7371   A two-dollar bill is bad luck and should be handed on as soon as possible; but always tear one or more corners off (M, 22, SLC, 1960). Cf. Brown 3447, 3449.

7372   Save two-dollar bills, turn the corners down, and they bring good luck (F, 25, SLC, 1949). Cf. Brown 3448.

7373   A dollar bill with all four corners torn off will bring bad luck to the receiver (M, 67, SLC).


Coins

7374   If you find some money, pick it up with your left hand; if you pick it up with your right, it will bring bad luck (M, Puerto Rican, 32, SLC, 1965).

7375   See a coin and pick it up, and all the day you'll have good luck (F, Spanish Fork, 1929).

7376   It's good luck to find a coin before breakfast (M, 69, SLC, 1964).

7377   If you find a coin and you keep it, it will bring good luck. However, if you spend it, you will have bad luck (F, 63, Monroe, 1964).

7378   If you find a coin that is made with a statue on one side and an institution of God on the other, it is good luck (M, 53, Logan, 1929).

7379   Always put the head end of a coin on the counter or in a slot (M, 20, SLC, 1963).

7380   A two-faced coin means good luck (M, 19, SLC, 1963).

7381   It is lucky to receive a coin with a hole in it as change (M, 19, Midvale, 1960).

7382   If a coin is dropped, step on it for good luck (M, 1957).

7383   If a man walks up to you and gives you a coin, you will have bad luck until you give the coin to someone else (F, Murray, 1957).

7384   If you flip a coin, it will tell you the right way to go (M, SLC, 1957).

7385   On the flip of the coin, always choose heads (M, Richfield, 1961).

7386   If a coin is extra thin (worn), it is supposed to bring an extra amount of good luck (F, Moab, 1953).

7387   The gift of two coins to a cripple will bring good luck (F, 19, Granger, 1964).

7388   Don't spend a lucky coin, or you will have bad luck for the next year (M, Eng, SLC, 1964).

7389   If coins are put in the left-hand pocket, you will never have a penny as long as the garment lasts (M, 19, SLC, 1965).

7390    One should turn silver over in their pocket to bring good luck (F, Provo, 1960).

7391    Never under any circumstance throw any kind of money away; it will bring bad luck for at least five years (F, 20, SLC, 1962).

7392    Buffalo nickels bring good luck (M, SLC, 1957).

7393    You will have good luck if you drop a nickel and it sticks up on the floor (F, 46, SLC, 1949).

7394    If you swallow a pickle, you'll get a nickel (F, 25, SLC).

7395    An Indian-head nickel is the sign of good luck (M, 56, Logan, 1970).

7396    If you find a dime, throw it over your shoulder and make a wish (F, 42, SLC, 1963).

7397    If you step on a line, you will find a dime (F, Fillmore, 1960).

7398    If you find fifty cents, something will happen for the better (F, 13, SLC, 1963).

7399    If you find a silver dollar, it means you will have good luck (M, SLC, 1961).

7400    Pieces of aluminum or tinfoil rolled in a ball and kept over a period of ten years will eventually turn into silver dollars (M, 46, SLC, 1925).

7401    A silver dollar will bring good luck to its owner (F, 71, SLC, 1930).

### Pennies

7402    Wishes made on a penny, the date you were born, will come true (F, 9, SLC, 1964); A penny made the year of your birth is good luck (F, Bountiful, 1959).

7403    To dream of a penny is bad luck (F, Santaquin, 1914).

7404    Always have a penny in your purse for good luck (F, Provo, 1959); Keep your last penny for good luck (M, SLC, 1961).

7405    You should carry or keep a gift penny for good luck (F, Sandy, 1957).

7406    It brings good luck to carry three cents (M, Provo, 1953).

7407    Anyone who carries a penny bearing the date of a leap year will have good luck (F, SLC, 1958).

7408    If you have a jar of pennies in the house, you will have good luck (F, SLC, 1963).

7409    As long as you keep a penny you have found, you will have good luck (M, 18, SLC, 1963).

7410    See a penny, leave it lay, have bad luck the rest of the day.  See a penny, pick

it up, all the day have good luck (M, 34, SLC, 1964).

7411    A penny found with the face up means good luck (M, 20, SLC, 1955).  Cf. Brown 3443.

7412    By finding a new penny, it will bring you new and good fortune (F, SLC, 1961).  Cf. Brown 3445.

7413    If you find an old penny, it will bring you good luck (F, 19, Midvale, 1957).

7414    If you find a penny with your birth date on it, you will have good luck (F, 18, SLC, 1960).

7415    If you find a penny with your birth date on it, you must kiss the penny and then throw it over your shoulder (M, SLC, 1961).

7416    If you find a penny, you'll find a greater sum (F, SLC).

7417    If you find a penny under your bed, you will have good luck all day (F, Ogden, 1958).

7418    If you find a penny, throw it over your shoulder and you will have good luck (M, Logan, 1972).

7419    If you drop a penny, it's bad luck to pick it up again (F, Logan, 1972).

7420    An Indian-head penny is bad luck (M, Helper, 1958).

7421    To get rid of bad luck, throw a penny over your shoulder, and the one who picks it up will get all the bad luck (M, SLC, 1964).

### Wishing Wells, Fountains, Etc.

7422    It is good luck to throw coins, especially pennies, into a fountain (M, 53, SLC, 1964); . . . If you throw it down a well, the well will repay you by always being full (F, 20, SLC, 1964).

7423    Throw a penny in a fountain and make a wish come true (M, 12, SLC, 1961).

7424    Three coins in a fountain mean good luck for one of the persons throwing the coins (F, 51, Centerfield, 1964).

7425    If you make a wish, then drop a penny in a well, your wish will come true (F, 21, SLC, 1964).

7426    If you throw a penny over your shoulder into a wishing well, the wish will come true (F, SLC, 1964).

7427    If you cast coins into a waterfall, the good spirits will be pleased and reward you with good luck (F, 74, Norw, Salem, 1899).

7428    Throw a coin over your shoulder into a pond, make a wish, and your wish will come true (F, 39, SLC, 1963).

7429    Never take money from a wishing well. If you do, two times the luck given by the money to the contributor will fall upon you, but in reverse (bad luck) (F, Logan, 1972).

## PROSPERITY

7430 Prosperity and happiness in life are the results of being born under a lucky star (M, SLC, 1957).

7431 If more girls than boys are born in a year, that year will be prosperous (F, Gr, SLC, 1964).

7432 Dream of gold and you'll see prosperity (F, SLC, 1960); . . . have money (F, 22, Bountiful, 1964).

7433 To dream of seeing trees and shrubs in blossom denotes a time of pleasing prosperity is nearing you (M, SLC, 1934).

7434 A prosperous person has big earlobes (F, SLC, 1960). Cf. Brown 3350.

7435 Teeth wide apart indicate prosperity and happiness (F, Monroe, 1960).

7436 If you have an accidental fire in the morning, you'll be prosperous (F, SLC, 1960).

7437 To ride backwards in a wagon indicates prosperity (M, 42, Ioka, 1930).

7438 If the first bird you see at the turn of spring is a robin, the next year will be prosperous (F, 40, SLC, 1964).

7439 A stork in the chimney means prosperity (F, SLC, 1957).

7440 Spider webs in a house are a sign of prosperity (F, SLC, 1960).

## RICHES, WEALTH

### Body and Clothing as Indicators

7441 If your eyebrows meet, you will be rich (F, Richfield, 1961).

7442 If a person's teeth are spaced wide apart, it is a sign that that person will be rich (F, 66, Woods Cross, 1948); . . . will be wealthy (F, 58, Provo, 1949).

7443 To dream of having a tooth pulled means future riches (F, 67, Park City, 1946).

7444 Two cowlicks are a sign of riches (M, 24, SLC, 1964).

7445 People with hairy arms always become rich (F, 83, SLC, 1960); . . . much hair on their arms and hands will at some future time gain wealth (F, 21, SLC, 1964).

7446 Long hair on the back of one's hand is a sign of him becoming rich (M, 53, SLC, 1936).

7447 Itching of the palm insures forthcoming wealth (M, 50, It, SLC, 1965); . . . in the palm of your left hand means great wealth (F, 12, SLC, 1960).

7448 When the palm of your hand has the letter "M" in it, you will be rich at some time (M, 19, Magna, 1957).

7449 If your palms are hollow, someday you will be wealthy (F, Copperton).

7450 Persons with a line across their palms will be rich (F, Ja, SLC, 1960).

7451 Always keep your nails clean and you will be rich (M, 22, SLC, 1964).

7452 Toenails filed on Thursday will bring riches on Friday (M, 21, SLC, 1965). Cf. Brown 3355.

7453 Large moons on your fingers means you'll be rich (F, 80, Eng, Midvale).

7454 If you have a freckle on your neck, you'll be rich (M, Murray, 1960).

7455 Anyone with a lot of moles will be wealthy (F, 50, SLC, 1935); Moles on your neck are a sign that you'll become rich (F, 18, Heber, 1972); Moles in the middle of your back . . . (F, Moab, 1953). Brown 3351ff.

7456 A mole on the throat means you'll gain riches through marriage (M, SLC).

7457 If a person has many warts, he will become rich (F, SLC, 1959).

7458 If you sneeze three times in a row, you're going to be rich (M, SLC, 1949); Sneeze on Monday for wealth (F, Weber Co).

7459 An ugly person is much more likely to acquire riches in later life than a good-looking person (M, 57, Swiss, Heber City, 1917).

7460 The boy that wears his trousers out at the knee will be rich (F, Axtell, 1958).

7461 Wear a coin in your shoe, and you will always be wealthy (M, 23, Ger, W. Jordan).

### Domestic Portents

7462 If you eat goose on New Year's Day, you will be rich (M, 45, Midvale, 1964).

7463 If tea leaves stay close together in a cup, you will be rich (F, 22, SLC, 1963).

7464 If bubbles rise to the top of a cup of coffee, you will be rich (M, 43, SLC, 1964); . . . you will catch the bubbles in a spoon . . . (F, 35, SLC, 1938); Pour coffee in a cup and watch the bubbles that form. If they move over to the side of the cup, your ship is coming in; if they stay in the center, your ship will remain at sea (M, SLC, 1966); . . . see an increase in your wealth (M, 22, SLC, 1964). Brown 3360.

7465 Bubbles in your tea means you will have great wealth (M, Dan, SLC, 1964).

7466 If you have a slight film on the top of your hot chocolate, it's a sign that you will be rich some day (F, 70, SLC, 1964).

7467 If a film is on top of your hot milk, you will be rich (F, 19, Kaysville, 1964).

7468   Never waste food intentionally, or you will never become wealthy (F, 20, SLC, 1963).

7469   To dream of nuts means you will become wealthy through an inheritance (M, 68, SLC, 1936).

7470   If someone sweeps under your chair while you are sitting on it, it is a sign you'll never get rich (F, Moab, 1953).

7471   The amount of dirt you sweep up shows how rich you will be (F, 44, SLC).

## Various Beliefs

7472   Marry on a Monday for wealth (M, SLC, 1964).

7473   If the initials of your name spell a word, you're sure to be rich (F, Ogden, 1960); . . . you will accumulate great wealth (F, 67, SLC, 1963).  Brown 3349.

7474   A dime, a penny, a button, and a thimble, and ring are put in birthday cakes.  The person getting the dime will be a rich man; the penny, a poor man; the thimble, an old maid; the button, a bachelor; the ring, first one married (F, SLC, 1957).

7475   If you find a penny, it is good luck and you'll get rich (F, 60, Ogden, 1970); . . . pick up a penny and put it in your pocket . . . (F, 19, Ogden, 1950); . . . put it in your left pocket . . . (F, 19, Ogden, 1950); Pick up a lost penny, come into great wealth (F, 67, Norw, SLC, 1964).

7476   If the sun shines on the day of graduation, a future of riches awaits you (M, 70).

7477   Turn money in your pocket over when you see a new moon, and you'll get rich (F, 83, SLC, 1964).  Cf. Brown 3368.

7478   When you see a falling star, if you pull a handkerchief from your pocket, put a knot in it, and return it to your pocket before the star has disappeared, you will be rich for the rest of your life (M, 19, SLC, 1958).

7479   If you see a shooting star and say, "Money" three times before it goes out of sight, you will become rich (F, Brigham City, 1960); . . . wealth will await you (F, SLC, 1961); . . . say money ten times . . . (F, 20, SLC, 1964).

7480   If you never try to loosen and untie knots, you will not become rich.  Do not cut the string (M, 25, SLC, 1964).

7481   If you fold your money, it's a sign you're going to be rich, or double your money (F, SLC, 1969).

## Animal Portents

7482   The possession of a cat's eye will bring riches (M, SLC, 1959).

7483   If a mouse pokes his head out of a hole and says cheese, it means wealth (F, 1962).

7484   If you dream of a white horse, you will be rich (F, 48, SLC, 1921).

7485   If you dream of gathering or finding eggs, it means you're going to have riches (F, Moab, 1953).  Cf. Brown 3363.

7486   If one finds two yolks in an Easter egg, he will get rich (F, 56, SLC, 1913).

## FORTUNE

7487   If you mark a coin and spend it, and it returns to you, you'll inherit a fortune (F, Midvale).

7488   Specks on the fingers, fortune lingers; specks on the thumbs, fortune surely comes (F, SLC, 1961).

7489   If the soap slips out of your hands while you're washing, fortune will slip through them the same way (F, 78, SLC, 1964).

7490   To see three butterflies together means you will soon acquire a fortune (M, 23, SLC, 1951).

7491   Dreaming of broken eggs means you will lose a fortune.  Dreaming of unbroken eggs means you will come into a fortune (M, Ger, 23, SLC).

7492   Dreaming of burning houses means improved fortunes (F, SLC, 1957).

## POVERTY

### Body and Clothing Indicators

7493   If you have large holes between your fingers when you hold them together, you will be poor all you life.  The space between the fingers is where the money will fall out (F, SLC, 1971).

7494   If your second toe is longer than your first toe, you will be poor (F, 22, SLC).

7495   You should never have your hair cut on Thursday, Friday, or Saturday.  If you do, you will risk becoming or remaining poor (M, 20, SLC, 1964).

7496   If you have an empty pocket on New Year's Eve, then you will be poor all year (M, SLC, 1964).

7497   If you sew up your clothes while on your back, you will not have much money in your life (F, Richfield, 1910); . . . mend your clothes upon your back, poverty you'll never lack (F, Payson, 1920); . . . you will come to want (F, 74, Millcreek, 1900).

7498   You'll never have any money, until your wedding clothes are worn out (F, Ogden, 1959).

7499   Whenever skirts get longer in length, we are going to have a depression (M, 57, Ogden, 1935).

7500   If you empty a purse, you'll never get it filled up again (M, 21, Midvale, 1950).

7501 If you put shoes on the table, you'll have financial trouble (F, Roosevelt, 1900s).

## Domestic Portents, Etc.

7502 If you cut a loaf of bread from both ends, it will bring bad luck and poverty (F, 26, Finn, Morgan, 1965).

7503 Brushing crumbs from a table with a broom will cause poverty (M, 50, It, SLC, 1965).

7504 You should never run out of salt, or you will become poor (F, 24, Norw, SLC, 1964); . . . have a whole year's poverty (F, 63, Gr, SLC, 1963).

7505 If you spill salt, you will live in poverty (F, SLC, 1915).

7506 Sing at the table, and you'll die in the poor house (M, SLC, 1930s).

7507 People should never take food or furniture from one's home at night to give to someone else. This will make the giver poor (F, Gr, Tooele, 1961).

7508 Empty cupboards on New Year's Eve brings a year of poverty (F, SLC, 1961).

7509 If you keep changing your furniture to different places, it means you'll be poor (F, 42, SLC, 1956).

7510 If you sweep your trash out the door, your money will sweep away (F, SLC, 1962). Cf. Brown 3374.

7511 If you see a straight pin and don't pick it up, you'll be poor (F, 50, SLC, 1925).

7512 If there is an accidental fire in the afternoon, you'll become poor (F, Ja, SLC, 1960).

7513 A bouquet of peacock feathers in the home means you will always be poor (F, 70, SLC, 1964).

7514 When you go to visit a home for the first time on New Year's Day, you must carry something. If you go empty-handed, the people you visit will live in poverty (F, SLC, 1957).

## Various Beliefs

7515 Carry a good-luck penny, and you'll never go broke (F, SLC).

7516 Carry a special coin on your person at all times, and you will never be in want of money (M, 52, Du, SLC, 1964).

7517 Rubbing two coins together will keep poverty away from your family (M, SLC, 1961).

7518 If you drop your money on the floor, you will reap poverty (F, 53, Norw, SLC, 1961).

7519 A person retrieving a penny from a cake will be poor (F, SLC, 1957).

7520 If you have a child born during an eclipse, you will be stricken with poverty and misfortune (F, 55, Helper, 1925).

7521 If one sees a comet in the sky, it is a sign of depression (F, SLC, 1940).

7522 To dream you are an heir to property signifies you will be left penniless by those of your relatives who are wealthy (M, SLC, 1957).

7523 If a man owns seven dogs, he will be on poverty row (M, 84, Centerville).

7524 Killing a spider will bring either ruin or poverty (M, 54, Nephi, 1964).

7525 Never throw away string and you will never want (F, SLC, 1960).

## DEBTS

7526 Debts are not to be paid on Monday for fear of bringing bad luck (F, 40, Sandy, 1937).

7527 It is good luck to return borrowed money (M, 24, SLC, 1961).

7528 All debts must be paid within a year's time or else bad luck will come (F, SLC, 1960).

7529 All bills should be paid before New Year's, or you will have bad luck (F, 44, Sandy, 1928).

7530 If one does not throw bad, wilting flowers out, one will be surrounded by bad debts (F, It, SLC, 1963).

## LEGAL AND QUASI-LEGAL BELIEFS

7531 If the rooster crows three times, someone has been betrayed (M, 18, SLC, 1958).

7532 A glove hung up in a church is considered a public challenge (F, 84, SLC, 1950).

7533 The white stones from the rooster are good for lawsuits (M, 25, Je, SLC, 1965).

7534 Break the heel of a high-heeled shoe, and you'll soon need a lawyer (F, 58, SLC, 1915).

7535 If you are called before a judge on Friday, it will always bring bad luck (F, Ogden, 1960).

7536 An eye for an eye, and a tooth for a tooth (M, SLC).

7537 It is unlucky to get back anything that has been stolen (M, SLC, 1964).

## CRIME, CRIMINALS

7538 A ship refuses to move with a guilty man aboard (F, SLC, 1963).

7539 A mill will not grind stolen wheat (F, SLC, 1963).

7540 A ring around the moon means it's a good night for crime (F, SLC, 1959).

7541  More people are kidnapped on a full moon (F, 10, SLC, 1962).

## Body Portents, Etc.

7542  If a man has facial scars, people think he is an ex-convict (F, 21, SLC, 1962).

7543  Persons with small beady eyes are supposed to be criminal in nature (M, SLC, 1964).

7544  Anyone with their ears attached on their lower lobes has a tendency to be a lawbreaker (M, 57, Swiss, Heber City, 1916).

7545  Redheaded people are never put in jail (M, 22, SLC, 1964).

7546  If a child is born out of wedlock, that child will become a criminal (F, 43, American Fork, 1958).

7547  If a pregnant woman reads mystery books, her child will be affected, that is, it will become a delinquent (F, 25, Kearns, 1961).

7548  If you stub your toe in the dark, it means that your house will be robbed (M, 41, SLC, 1964).

## THIEVES, THIEVERY

7549  If a person has eyes which are close together, he is likely to be a thief (F, Midvale, 1955).

7550  A sign of a thief is unattached earlobes (M, 24, SLC, 1963).

7551  If one's shoes are turned at the heels, he is a thief (M, 52, Cedar City, 1964).

7552  If you steal salt, throw some over your left shoulder, or it will bring bad luck (F, 61, SLC, 1964).

7553  Graveyard dirt put on the top of a fence will keep away burglars (F, 51, SLC, 1963).

7554  A guardian rattlesnake will bite a burglar who has come to steal a miner's gold dust (F, 19, SLC).

7555  If a watermelon thief has left the stem of the melon behind him, throw it into the creek and the thief will die (F, 28, SLC, 1950).

7556  When stealing fruit, it is good luck to eat the fruit there, for you will be caught trying to get away (M, 23, SLC).

7557  If you wear a toad's heart concealed about your person, you can steal without being caught (M, 93, Price, 1900).

7558  If you purposely kill ants, you will become a thief (M, 25, SLC, 1963).

7559  If you find a dead cat on your premises, look out for robbers (F, SLC, 1959).

7560  If you dream of a parrot, a thief will try to rob you (M, 26, SLC, 1964).

7561  No one should whistle at night, because it is a signal for the burglars to come in (F, 40, Ja, SLC, 1964).

7562  Stealing from white people or from other tribes was bravery, but stealing from one's own tribe was severely punished. An elder of the tribe would heat a piece of iron; this would be held close to the eye of the thief until the eye burst (F, 50, SLC, 1964).

## CONVICTS, LAWBREAKERS

7563  It is very unlucky for a child to know about the facts of life before he or she is at least fifteen, because they will turn out to be wild and bad teenagers (F, 68, SLC).

7564  If you fall from a rail, you will put your father in jail (F, 20, SLC, 1946).

7565  Step on a nail and put your father in jail (M, Roosevelt, 1961); . . . you'll put your mother in jail (F, SLC, 1957).

7566  If someone should hit you with a broom, it is a sign that you will soon go to jail (M, SLC, 1957).

7567  If someone sweeps your foot with a broom, you will go to jail (M, 25, SLC, 1963).

7568  Peanut hulls scattered about a door mean that you will go to jail (F, 18, SLC, 1964).

7569  If you wish to free a man from prison, walk outside the city at night, when the open sky is above you, and recite Psalm 30, which begins: "A song at the dedication of the House of David" (M, 25, Je, SLC, 1965).

7570  Splinters taken from the north side of a tree that has been hit by lightning will have power to get someone out of jail (M, 20, SLC, 1963).

## MURDER

7571  A person with a dimple in his cheek will never commit murder (F, 82, Parowan, 1964); . . . dimple in the chin . . . (F, 49, SLC, 1964).

7572  If you're tall and thin, you're a homicidal and have premeditated murder (M, 20, SLC, 1964).

7573  Every twentieth president is assassinated, or dies for some reason (M, 54, Bountiful, 1964).

7574  When the moon is full and there is a ring around it, there will be a murder on that night (F, 71, SLC, 1900); . . . a white ring . . . (F, 56, SLC, 1964).

7575  If a high wind blows continually for three days, it means a murder has been committed (M, 64, SLC, 1911).  Cf. Brown 3689.

7576  If your canary sings after dark, it is a sign that you will shed blood that day (F, 1961).

7577 To see a dead canary is a sign you will shed blood that day (F, SLC, 1959).

7578 A corpse will bleed in the presence of its murderer (M, 24, Tooele, 1949). Brown 3695.

7579 Blood springs from a murderer's finger when he touches the victim (F, SLC, 1963).

7580 If a person has been murdered, bury the murdered man face downward, and the murderer will not be able to leave the locality until the body is turned over (F, SLC, 1960). Cf. Brown 3701f.

7581 The retina of a murdered person's eye records the image of the murderer (F, 1961).

7582 When a murder is committed with a knife or a club, and it cannot be proven, sometimes the ghost of the murdered person will return and show a ghostly knife to the murderer and frighten him into confessing (F, SLC, 1967).

7583 The spirit of a murdered person is reincarnated as a musical instrument such as a harp or flute (F, SLC, 1964). (This belief is reflected in Grimm 28 "The Singing Bones," and in the ballad of "The Twa Sisters" [Child 10]. --Eds.)

7584 Grass does not grow on a murderer's grave (F, SLC, 1963).

7585 When avenging the death of your brother, you should remove the head of the murderer (M, SLC, 1963).

7586 The informant's grandfather knew Porter Rockwell and related the story that Brigham Young had told Rockwell that if he never cut his hair, his enemies would never get him. Once two men plotted to kill Rockwell and they were discussing the plans for the murder in the rear of a store sitting on a barrel. Rockwell was hiding in this barrel, overheard the plans and he got them first (M, 50, Bountiful, 1944).

## HANGING, EXECUTION

7587 A person born on Christmas Day will never be hanged (M, 19, SLC, 1964).

7588 No man with the Christian name George has ever been hanged (M, SLC, 1961).

7589 A mole on the back of the neck means the possessor is in danger of hanging (M, SLC, 1961). Cf. Brown 3705.

7590 If you place a person's boots or shoes on a chair or table, that person will die of hanging (F, 88, W. Jordan, 1910).

7591 If you wash between Christmas and New Year's and hang it on a line, someone will hang themself [sic] (F, Ger, SLC, 1950); . . . someone in the family will be hanged during the year (F, 60, Ger, SLC, 1965).

7592 A hangman's noose must have thirteen turns in it (M, 32, SLC, 1964).

7593 If the rope breaks in a hanging, the man goes free (F, SLC, 1957).

7594 A man condemned to be hanged could escape this if some woman would come forward and say she would like to marry him (F, SLC, 1964).

7595 It is thirteen steps from the cell of the condemned prisoner to the gallows or to the electric chair (M, 56, SLC, 1964).

7596 Executed criminals never find rest in the grave (M, 16, SLC, 1964).

7597 If an innocent person is executed, three yellow lilies will grow on his grave (F, 48, SLC, 1963).

7598 A piece of the rope by which someone hanged himself brings good luck (F, 19, SLC, 1964).

## WILLS, HEIRS, LEGACIES

7599 Have a Gypsy bless a will, bury it, and good fortune will follow (F, SLC, 1964).

7600 If you give a relative a knife as a gift, you have to also give him a penny so he will not cut you out of his will (F, Ogden, 1961).

7601 It is unlucky to make a will. None of it will come true (M, SLC, 1957).

7602 To change a will is unlucky (M, SLC, 1961).

7603 If you carry plenty of insurance, nothing will happen (F, Ogden, 1960).

7604 Seeing six magpies means a legacy (M, Ir, SLC, 1960).

7605 If you find a lost book, you will receive a heritage (M, 48, Junction, 1964).

# VII
# Travel and Communication

## TRAVEL

### BODY PORTENTS

#### Various

7606 Eyebrows set far apart mean that a person lives far away from his home territory (M, 18, SLC, 1964).

7607 A cinder in the eye is a sign of an unexpected trip (M, 42, SLC, 1963).

7608 If your teeth are wide apart, you will be lucky and travel (F, 21, SLC, 1963); . . . you will be a wanderer (M, 60, SLC, 1964).

7609 If you have two crowns in your head, you will cross the ocean twice (F, 55, SLC, 1965).

7610 It is a superstition that if you have two bumps on the back of your head, you will travel across the ocean sometime in your life (F, 19, SLC, 1964).

7611 A scratch on the right arm means a ride (F, Bear River City, 1957).

7612 If your hand itches, you will take a long ride (F, 44, Provo, 1949).

7613 A man walking down the street with his hands in his pockets is going on a trip (M, SLC, 1966).

7614 If you can bend your thumb far back, you will travel (M, 18, SLC, 1950).

7615 Every white spot on your little fingernail represents a journey to go (F, Richfield, 1916). Cf. Brown 3710.

#### Feet

7616 If your toes are webbed, it means you are going to travel (F, SLC, 1959).

7617 If your feet itch, you want to travel (F, Ogden, 1952); . . . you will soon be going to new places (M, 90, SLC, 1964).

7618 If your foot itches, you are going to take a trip (F, 41, SLC, 1965); . . . you will travel far (F, Green River, 1936). Brown 3711.

7619 If your foot itches, it means you will travel in a foreign land (F, SLC, 1961).

7620 If the bottom of your foot itches, it is a sign that you are going to set down on strange ground. It did not mean strange ground of any great distance, just someplace you had not been before (F, 48, Murray, 1963); . . . you'll walk on new ground (F, SLC, 1961); . . . you'll walk in a strange land (M, 53, SLC, 1936). Brown 3712.

7621 If your feet itch, it means you are going someplace you were told not to go (M, SLC, 1959).

7622 If the bottom of your foot itches, it means you are going to take a trip (M, 41, SLC, 1964); If the sole of either foot itches, you will walk on a strange ground (F, 55, SLC, 1964).

7623 If your right foot itches, you will soon start on a journey (F, 46, SLC); . . . you are going on a pleasant journey (F, SLC, 1959); . . . you are going to step on a strange soil (M, Ogden, 1961). Brown 3714f.

7624 If your left foot itches, you will go where you're not wanted (M, 45, Centerville); . . . you are going on an unpleasant journey (F, SLC, 1959). Brown 3897.

#### Miscellaneous Portents

7625 If the leaves left in a teacup are formed into a line, it means that the person who drank the tea will be going on a long trip (F, 72, Eng, Lark, 1963).

7626 If you drop a dishtowel on the floor, it means a trip in the near future (F, 24, SLC, 1964).

7627 If a cigarette burns down on only one side, the person smoking it will travel (M, Gr, SLC).

7628 If you find a button, you'll go on a trip (F, SLC).

7629 Always pick up a pin with its head toward you, for that will insure your having a ride soon (M, 60, Du, SLC, 1964).

7630 If a sparrow builds a nest above one's window, one may expect taking a trip (F, SLC, 1964).

7631 To see a bird flying south means that you will travel soon (M, SLC, 1961).

7632    If a bird flies into your house, it means you are going on a journey (F, SLC, 1961).

## AUSPICES, PREPARATIONS, HAPPENINGS

7633    If you postpone a trip, you will never take it (M, SLC, 1962); . . . postpone a trip twice . . . (M, SLC, 1959).

7634    If you are in a car with a group of people that are planning to take a trip and someone sneezes once, it would be bad luck to go on the trip (M, 28, SLC, 1963); . . . someone sneezes twice, the trip will bring good luck (M, 28, SLC, 1963).

7635    When starting on a journey, it is unlucky to meet an old woman (F, SLC).

7636    One woman traveling in the company of five or more men will bring good luck to the journey (M, SLC, 1960).

7637    Sit down before you leave, and you won't forget anything (M, SLC, 1925).

7638    Direction in travel is important; if you go the wrong way, backtrack first before going on (F, 51, Ja, W. Jordan, 1963).

7639    Don't leave home with the left foot first (F, SLC, 1964).

7640    It is bad luck to hear someone weeping when you are starting to take a trip or journey (F, SLC).

7641    It's bad luck to wish a person good luck on a trip (F, SLC, 1936).

7642    When leaving the house for a trip or vacation, get the house in "dying" order. This applies to cleaning the oven, making the beds, straightening the bathroom, cleaning the dishes, etc. (F, Ogden).

7643    If the blind on your window flips up with a bang, something terrible will happen on the trip (F, Provo).

7644    If a person looks back at his house after leaving it for a journey, or returns after starting out, this will bring misfortune (F, 17, Murray, 1958).

7645    Leaving home in a hurry and leaving the back door open means the person will come into some rain before he reaches his destination (M, 21, SLC, 1955).

7646    Don't carry rough dry clothes on a trip. It is bad luck (M, 50, SLC, 1963).

7647    It is bad luck to pack anything wet when traveling (M, 68, SLC, 1928). Brown 3738.

7648    It is bad luck to carry a black suitcase on a train trip (F, 66, Provo, 1940). Cf. Brown 3737.

7649    It's good luck to slide your car keys in and out of the ignition once before you start your car, and this may prevent an accident (M, 31, SLC, 1955).

7650    Kiss the Blarney Stone for good luck when going on a trip (M, 58, SLC, 1960).

7651    Before people leave for travel, they should drink green tea for good luck (F, 51, Ja, W. Jordan, 1957).

7652    Place a St. Christopher statue in the car in front by the windshield. He will protect you from accidents on the highway (M, 52, Du, SLC, 1948).

7653    You should carry peacock feathers with you when you travel. They will bring you safety and good luck (F, 58, Eng, SLC, 1964).

7654    Save and throw old shoes after the carriage when a member of the family goes on a trip. This will bring them safely home (F, 78, SLC, 1964).

7655    It is lucky to burn old boots before starting out on a journey (F, 44, Midvale, 1930).

7656    When starting on a journey, it is unlucky to break a shoestring (M, 24, SLC, 1961).

7657    When on a car trip, one should never talk of flat tires, or he may get one (M, SLC, 1953).

7658    If you see someone with car trouble on a road, cross your fingers so that it won't happen to you (F, 21, SLC, 1964).

7659    If you see a white ball of fur on a stick, there will be safe passage (M, SLC, 1963).

7660    If you are traveling and you see a wayside inn, you will have good luck (M, 53, Logan, 1929).

7661    Seeing a load of empty barrels on a truck will bring the viewer good luck (M, SLC, 1957).

7662    If you ever look at the rear of a load of hay, you will not get home safe (F, Eng, SLC, 1958).

7663    After a farewell party on board ship you should toast and throw glasses overboard. This means a safe journey (F, SLC, 1957).

## TIME OF DEPARTURE, ARRIVAL

7664    Never leave on a trip on a Monday; it will cause great danger (F, 45, SLC, 1930s); . . . it's bad luck (F, Roosevelt, 1961).

7665    It is bad luck to travel on a Monday (F, 20, SLC).

7666    It's good to travel on Tuesday (F, 78, Provo, 1954). Cf. Brown 3720.

7667    Never start a trip or arrive on a Tuesday (M, Provo, 1960); Don't travel on Tuesday the thirteenth (F, SLC, 1964).

7668    You should never start a trip on Thursday, for bad luck will follow (M, Scot-Ir, SLC, 1960).

7669    Never start a trip or arrive on a Friday (M, Provo, 1960); . . . you will never finish it (F, SLC, 1962); . . . the trip will be a bad one (M, 54, Croydon, 1965); . . . you will have an accident (M, Vernal, 1958); . . . this is tied in with the fact that the Savior died on Friday and the trip will end in some disaster for the persons involved (M, SLC, 1958). Brown 3721ff.

7670 Never take a trip on Friday the thirteenth, or you will have bad luck on your journey (M, 21, SLC, 1964); . . . the journey will end in disaster (M, SLC, 1960).

7671 Never start a journey on the thirteenth of a month (F, 88, SLC, 1964). Brown 3727.

7672 Never start a trip on the weekend (F, 49, Richfield, 1964).

7673 Never start a trip on Sunday (F, SLC, 1958). Cf. Brown 3726.

7674 Sunday is a lucky day to go on a voyage (F, 82, Parowan, 1964).

7675 Only begin a trip at the time of the new moon (F, 46, SLC, 1964).

7676 A storm is a bad sign for vacationing. Delay your trip or vacation if it starts to storm (F, 61, SLC, 1964).

## SAYING "GOOD-BYE"

7677 Never tarry after once saying "good-bye" (F, Murray, 1957).

7678 Never say "good-bye" to someone you want to see again. It is bad luck to do this; say "so long," or "I'll be seeing you," or anything else rather than "good-bye" (F, SLC, 1962).

7679 To say "good-bye" gives bad luck (F, 21, SLC, 1964).

7680 Never say "good-bye" more than once (M, 69, Scot, SLC, 1964); . . . If you say "good-bye" twice, you will never meet again (M, 9, SLC, 1962). Brown 3730.

7681 When saying "good-bye," never look back more than twice (M, 42, SLC, 1963).

7682 Never shake hands in the moonlight when parting from a friend. It brings bad luck (M, 50, SLC, 1934).

7683 When friends are leaving, throw a glass of wine into the fire and friendship will be restored (M, 21, SLC, 1964).

7684 If you say "good-bye" to a friend on a bridge, you will part forever (M, 90, Jordan, 1930); . . . beside a bridge . . . (F, Brigham City, 1960).

## WATCHING SOMEONE OUT OF SIGHT

7685 It is bad luck to watch a loved one go out of sight (M, SLC, 1964); . . . if you do, they may not return (F, 42, Sandy, 1964). Cf. Brown 3732.

7686 Turn your back after saying "good-bye" to a friend, or you may never see him again (F, 86, Heber, 1902).

7687 Waving to friends in farewell until they are out of sight is to write a permanent farewell. It is better to turn one's back after saying "good-bye" (F, 40, Logan, 1938).

7688 A bad omen is watching a soldier leave for battle (F, Dan, SLC, 1965).

## TURNING BACK, LOOKING BACK

7689 To turn back after starting a journey will mean bad luck for the rest of the day (M, 49, SLC, 1964); . . . for the rest of the trip (F, SLC, 1959). Cf. Brown 3756.

7690 If a person is leaving on a trip and has forgotten something in the house, and he returns to the house to pick up the article, his trip will not be a success (F, SLC, 1959). Cf. Brown 3760.

7691 If you're going on a business trip and leave the house and then for some reason return, the venture will not turn out (M, Gr, SLC).

7692 One who finds a horse and a shoe must return to his house (M, 80, SLC, 1963).

7693 To look back at your house after leaving it for a journey is surely a sign of bad luck (F, 73, Payson, 1943); . . . will bring misfortune (F, SLC, 1960); . . . brings bad luck to the inhabitants (M, 46, SLC).

7694 If you look back at where you have been, you will never return (F, 26, SLC, 1964).

7695 When traveling north, never look back, or bad luck will ensue (M, 23, SLC, 1964).

## Counteractants to Turning Back

7696 It's bad luck to leave the home and then turn back without sitting down (M, 52, Eng, SLC, 1963); . . . always sit down a second (F, 19, SLC, 1961). Cf. Brown 3766f.

7697 If you've forgotten something, when going back for it count to seven (F, 23, SLC); . . . count to ten to break bad luck (F, Eng, SLC, 1964); . . . sit down and count to twenty (F, SLC, 1914). Cf. Brown 3768f.

7698 If you forget something in the house and go back in for it, you must turn around three times and sit down for one minute before you go back out (F, Ogden, 1961).

7699 When you return to a cabin, you should make a cross in the dust in front of it and then spit on it. If you don't, it will bring bad luck (M, 21, SLC, 1956). Cf. Brown 3764, 3770ff.

7700 If you should strike your left elbow while leaving the room on an undertaking of any kind, go back (M, 32, SLC, 1952).

7701 If you leave the house and have to return for something you forgot, it will bring you bad luck unless you go in and out three times (F, Hooper, 1963).

7702    If you leave and then enter once again, leave the second time by the same door. It is bad luck if you don't (F, 43, SLC, 1963).

7703    If you start a trip and forget something which you must return to get, wait a day and make a new start (F, 49, Richfield, 1925).

## MEETING AND PASSING PERSONS

7704    It is lucky if you meet a young person in the morning, and it is unlucky if you meet an old person in the morning (F, Yugo, SLC, 1960). Cf. Brown 3794. (The meeting and passing of persons and animals is a prominent folklore motif, but unfortunately there are no general discussions of the subject for the English reader. These encounters belong to the earliest auguries of classical and Germanic antiquity, and have in time come to apply to almost any kind of chance meeting or sighting of people, animals, birds, and the like. An excellent treatise on the subject is to be found in the Handwörterbuch des Deutschen Aberglaubens, I, 409-35, s.v. Angang. --Eds.)

7705    It is unlucky to meet a man with flat feet on Monday morning (F, SLC, 1961).

7706    If a stranger walks up to you on the right, it's a sign of good fortune (F, 40, Cedar City, 1941).

7707    It is bad luck when you meet a cross-eyed man (F, 80, Midvale). Cf. Brown 3781f.

7708    It is unlucky to meet a cross-eyed woman, but lucky to meet a cross-eyed man (M, SLC, 1961).

7709    You will have good luck if you see a red-haired girl coming up the street (F, 46, SLC, 1943). Cf. Brown 3797.

7710    Meeting a redheaded woman the first thing in the morning is bad luck (M, Ir, SLC, 1960). Cf. Brown 3795.

7711    If you happen to meet any Gypsies on the road, you are supposed to greet them cordially saying, "Good Day" to them, or if you don't it will bring you bad luck. The Gypsies will supposedly cast a bad spell on you if you aren't friendly (F, 80, Eng, Richfield, 1964).

7712    To see a Chinaman wearing a queue is a sign of good luck (F, SLC, 1961).

7713    It is a sign of bad luck to meet a beggar soon after leaving one's house in the morning. One must return and begin again (F, 28, SLC, 1964).

7714    If you see a beggar on a walk, it is a sign of danger (F, 85, SLC, 1964).

7715    It is unfortunate to meet a left-handed person on a Tuesday morning or Friday morning, but fortunate to meet one on other mornings of the week (F, SLC, 1955).

7716    If the right palm itches, you will meet a stranger (F, Lehi, 1964).

7717    If the palm of the right hand itches, you will meet a fool (some say a friend) (F, SLC, 1957).

## Special Persons

7718    It is lucky to see a blind man in the street, and especially lucky to help him (F, 59, Ibapah, 1964).

7719    It is a Greek saying that if a priest crosses your path, it is bad luck. Therefore, if a priest ever crosses your path, you must tie a knot in your handkerchief, and that means that the priest is with you and no harm will come to you (F, 56, Gr, SLC, 1957).

7720    It is bad luck to meet a nun or priest first thing in the morning (F, 53, Ir, SLC, 1963); To meet a . . . means a day of bad luck (M, 1963).

7721    If you meet or shake hands with a priest, hold onto your button till passed (F, 20, SLC, 1962).

7722    It's unlucky to pass a priest unless you touch a piece of iron (M, Fr, SLC, 1957).

7723    If you see a chimney sweeper, you must hold on to a button until you see a man with glasses go by, and then you can make a wish and it will come true (F, 24, Swiss, SLC, 1964).

7724    To meet a hunchback is lucky (M, 16, SLC, 1964).

7725    Meeting a hunchback on a dark street will bring you very bad luck (F, 58, Dan, SLC, 1964).

## MEETING AND PASSING ANIMALS

## Various Animals

7726    When you see a white horse, a redheaded woman, and a black cat all at the same time, it is very good luck (F, SLC, 1967). (See the note to No. 7704, above. The discussion found there refers to items 7704-7725, as well as to Nos. 7726-7789. --Eds.)

7727    It is unlucky to meet a flock of sheep on the road when making a journey (M, SLC, 1959).

7728    Dream of a wolf before a trip and you will have an accident (M, SLC, 1960).

7729    If a fox crosses your path, it's good luck (M, Arab, SLC, 1963). Cf. Brown 3802.

7730    If a person crosses the trail of a coyote, then the person will have bad luck (F, 20, Mex, SLC, 1964); If a coyote crosses your path, serious trouble lies ahead (F, 35, Amer Ind, SLC).

7731    If a squirrel passes in front of you, it will bring good luck (F, Monroe, 1960). Brown 3876, cf. 8546.

7732    It is bad luck for a crow to cross one's path (F, 63, Monroe, 1964).

7733 If a magpie crosses the path of a traveler, the journey will not be successful unless the traveler crosses himself (F, SLC, 1957).

7734 If one hears an owl at night, he won't lose his way in the dark (M, 31, SLC, 1942).

7735 If a toad crosses your path, you will have one year of bad fortune (F, SLC, 1959).

## Cats

7736 It is bad luck if a cat crosses your path (F, Woods Cross, 1953).

7737 If a cat crosses your path from right to left, good luck will be yours all the way; from left to right, look out for bad luck (M, SLC, 1959). Brown 3808.

7738 Don't cross a cat's path, or you will have bad luck (M, Layton, 1954).

7739 Don't let a black cat cross your path (F, 44, Magna, 1920); . . . it is an evil omen (M, SLC, 1964); . . . a sign of future bad luck or disaster (M, Ogden, 1961).

7740 If a black cat crosses the road in front of your car, beware (F, 67, SLC, 1964).

7741 If a black cat crosses your path, it means bad luck except if you're born on the thirteenth (F, 67, SLC, 1964).

7742     When in dark rooms,
        Don't put on your hats;
        Crossing dark streets,
        Beware of black cats.
    (F, SLC). Brown 3809.

7743 To see a black cat cross the road is lucky (M, 53, Cedar City, 1925).

7744 If a black cat follows you, you will have good luck (F, 31, SLC, 1964).

7745 It is considered good luck if one meets a black cat and strokes it three times from head to tail (F, 21, Springville, 1964). Cf. Brown 3810.

7746 A black cat crossing your path will result in seven years of bad luck (F, 37, SLC, 1964); Don't walk in the path of a black cat, or you'll have nine years bad luck (F, 20, Ogden, 1963). Cf. Brown 3814.

7747 If you see a black cat at midnight, you will have a serious accident (M, SLC, 1964).

7748 If a cat crosses your path from right to left, good luck is yours all the way (F, SLC, 1960). Brown 3808.

7749 A black cat crossing your path from right to left will mean bad luck in the near future (F, SLC); . . . from left to right is bad luck (M, SLC, 1938). Brown 3819f.

7750 It is bad luck to have a black cat walk in front of your path when there is a bright moon out (M, 18, SLC, 1963).

## Counteractants

7751 If a black cat crosses your path, turn and go the other way. You will meet with calamity if you don't (F, 67, SLC, 1963); . . . bad luck will strike before you return or reach your destination (M, Murray, 1958). Brown 3821.

7752 If a black cat crosses your path, turn about face and head in the opposite direction, else you will have bad luck (M, SLC, 1962). Brown 3822.

7753 Change your course when you see a black cat, or he will cast a spell on you (M, SLC, 1960).

7754 If a cat crosses in front of you, turn around three times and stomp your foot, or you will have bad luck (F, SLC, 1962). Cf. Brown 3825.

7755 If a black cat goes across your way, turn and go through another street (F, SLC, 1963). Cf. Brown 3824.

7756 If a black cat crosses one's path, stand right where you are and turn around in your tracks seven times to ward off the evil spirits (M, 36, SLC, 1960).

7757 A black cat crossing in front of you means bad luck, but if you take seven steps backward and then go forwards, you will kill the bad luck. It might be twelve steps backward instead of seven (F, Moab, 1953).

7758 To reverse the bad luck caused by a black cat crossing your path, you must back up fourteen steps and turn around seven times (F, 40, Ogden, 1970); . . . walk backward thirty paces (M, 22, SLC, 1948).

7759 If a black cat crosses the road in front of you, spit over your left shoulder three times so you won't have bad luck (F, 25, Bountiful, 1964).

7760 If a black cat crosses the street in front of you while you are driving your car, stop the car, then drive around in a circle three times before proceeding on down the street. Otherwise you will have bad luck (F, SLC, 1930); . . . make a circle on the ground and spit in it (F, SLC, 1908). Cf. Brown 3828.

7761 When a black cat goes in front of you, turn around and spit in your tracks to scare away bad luck (F, Roosevelt, 1961).

7762 You will have bad luck if a black cat walks in front of you. If you spit while the cat is in front of you, you will have good luck (M, SLC, 1957).

7763 If a black cat crosses your path, spit in the left palm and hit it with the right fist (F, 53, SLC, 1927).

7764 If a black cat crosses your path, you must walk around it backwards to receive good luck (F, 21, SLC, 1956).

7765 If a black cat crosses your path, draw an "X" on the ground and spit in it to break the curse (F, Logan). Brown 3828.

7766 If a black cat crosses your path, you will have bad luck; but if a white cat then crosses your path, it will cancel the spell the black cat caused (M, SLC, 1955).

7767 If a black cat crosses your path, you should wait until someone else goes first, or bad luck will come (F, 50, Eng, SLC, 1964).

7768 Cross your fingers when a black cat crosses your path so that the bad luck won't harm you (M, 52, SLC, 1964). Brown 3829.

7769 Turn your hat around on your head; it breaks the spell of a black cat crossing your path (F, SLC, 1965). Brown 3835.

7770 If a black cat crosses your path, you must catch it to avoid bad luck (M, Nephi, 1961).

7771 You can break the spell of a black cat crossing your path by rolling up your pant leg and saying "Bread and butter" (F, 61, SLC, 1920). Cf. Brown 3842.

7772 If a black cat runs across your path while you're driving the car, you must get out and run around your car seven times to break the bad luck spell (M, Venice, 1966).

7773 If a white cat crosses your path, you are in for some very good luck (M, Murray, 1958).

7774 If a white cat crosses your path, serious trouble impends (F, 35, Amer Ind, White Rock).

7775 A white cat crossing your path from right to left means much misfortune (F, SLC).

Dogs

7776 When starting on a journey, it is unlucky to meet a shaggy dog (M, 24, SLC, 1961).

7777 Hear a dog bark in the night before a planned trip, and you'll have an accident (M, SLC, 1960).

7778 When you go by a big dog, clench your fist (with the thumb tucked inside), and he won't bite you (F, Logan, 1970).

7779 It is unlucky to meet a barking dog early in the morning (F, SLC, 1961).

7780 Never cross the street after a dog, because you will have bad luck or a dog's life (M, 46, Logan, 1943).

Horses

7781 Passing a white horse, or seeing one always brings good luck (F, 49, SLC, 1963).

7782 It is unlucky to meet a white horse on leaving home unless you spit on the ground (F, 17, SLC, 1957).

7783 If you can count one white horse for every mile you travel, your trip will be successful (F, 67, SLC, 1963).

7784 While traveling and you see a white horse, lick your two fingers and slap them in your hand without looking back. No harm or danger will befall you (M, Provo, 1933).

7785 Do not pass a white horse without saying, "Lucky, lucky white horse, bring us good luck!" If you pass without saying this, you will never return from your trip (F, 30, Sandy, 1939).

7786 While traveling after seeing eleven white horses and repeating this after each one, "Lucky, lucky white horse, bring me a dime," you should find a dime at your destination (F, 22, SLC, 1964).

Rabbits and Hares

7787 If you see a hare running across the road, you'll have bad luck (F, Sevier Co, 1930). Brown 3849.

7788 If a rabbit crosses your path in front of you, it is lucky; but if he crosses in back, it is unlucky (M, 18, Wendover, 1964); It is good luck to see a rabbit run across the road (F, SLC, 1965). Brown 3846.

7789 If you see a white hare, you are unlucky, but if you see a black hare, you will have luck (M, SLC, 1964).

VEHICLES

Cars

7790 A pair of baby shoes hung on the inside of the car is held to protect the driver against accident (F, SLC, 1950).

7791 You should place silver dollars on new things such as cars as a token of good luck (F, 42, Gr, SLC, 1964).

7792 When you buy a new car, throw a piece of silver money into it so that its occupants will always travel in safety (F, 42, SLC, 1963).

7793 When a person purchases a new automobile, all of his friends initiate it by urinating on the wheel (M, 31, SLC, 1963).

7794 If you open an umbrella inside a car, bad luck will follow (F, 26, SLC, 1954).

7795 If you drive a car with a cracked windshield, the car will bring you good luck (M, 29, SLC, 1962).

7796 There is a town called Scipio in central Utah just off Highway 91 which is a bad luck town for some. No matter which way you are going--either north or south--if you can make it past Scipio, your car will not break down during the trip (SLC).

7797 The first person to see "Beetle eyes" gets to slug the person of his choice. "Beetle eyes" are taillights of a '59 Chevrolet (M, 22, Bountiful, 1964).

7798 It is bad luck to have five people in a car (M, 51, SLC, 1963).

7799  If a person sees fifty red convertible cars, it will bring the person good luck (F, Provo, 1959).

7800  If you see seven yellow cabs without seeing any other kind, you get your wish (M, SLC, 1959).

7801  It is bad luck to ride in a vehicle painted green (M, 24, Provo, 1969).

7802  When they saw a "lucky" cab with phone number 7-11, they would lick the first two fingers of their right hand and press them to their left forearm for good luck (M, SLC, 1965).

7803  Children slap the palm of the left hand with the index and middle finger of the right hand, then double the fist and strike it into the palm. The same applies every time they see an out-of-state license (F, SLC, 1928).

7804  If you see a car license plate on which the numbers add up perfectly to thirteen, then you get to make a wish (F, 25, Logan, 1972).

7805  Being in a driveway when a car goes by is bad luck (F, SLC, 1959).

7806  If you see a car going slow, you can be sure it's an old man with a hat (F, 19, SLC, 1963).

## Cars with One Headlight

7807  Seeing a car with one headlight at night means good luck (F, 20, Midvale, 1958); Seeing a car with a pop eye . . . (F, 22, Ger, SLC, 1942).

7808  If a person sees a car that only has one headlight, it means the person is going to have some bad luck (F, 20, SLC, 1964).

7809  If you see a car with one headlight out, you are supposed to duck or bad luck will follow (F, 24, SLC, 1964).

7810  The more one-lighted cars you see, the better luck you'll have (F, SLC, 1957).

7811  If you see a one-eyed car, you are supposed to clap your hands and count to ten for good luck (F, 23, Murray, 1963).

7812  Always cross your fingers when you see a car with one light (F, Murray, 1957).

7813  If you see an automobile with one light, blow your horn or blink your lights, or it's bad luck (M, SLC, 1960).

7814  A one-lighted car is bad luck if you fail to lick your right thumb, place it in your left palm, then hit it with your right hand before the one-lighted car passes you (M, 25, SLC, 1940s).

7815  Make a wish on a car with only one headlight, and it will come true (F, SLC, 1959); After you see three cars with just one headlight you can make a wish (F, SLC).

7816  Every car you see with one light say "Pididle." After three "Pididles" you get a wish (M, SLC, 1959).

7817  When you see a car with one headlight, you're supposed to say "Perdidle," then lick your pointer finger, press the finger to your palm and then stamp your fist to the place you've pressed (F, SLC, 1969).

## Cars Crossing Railroad Tracks

7818  It is good luck to lift your feet as you go over a railroad track when riding in a car (F, 20, SLC, 1955); Pick up your feet . . . to assure a safe journey (F, Moab, 1958).

7819  In a car, if you go over railroad tracks, you are supposed to lift your feet, or bad luck will befall you (F, 24, SLC, 1964).

7820  If you lift your feet while crossing a railroad track, you will fall flat on your face (M, Ogden, 1961).

7821  When you cross railroad tracks, if you lift your feet and cross your fingers, you will have good luck (F, SLC, 1964).

7822  Crossing your fingers when you cross the railroad tracks brings good luck (F, 19, SLC, 1963).

7823  When crossing railroad tracks in a car or wagon, lift up your feet and make a wish. The wish will come true (F, 21, SLC, 1960).

7824  When going over railroad tracks, lift your feet and put your hands on the ceiling and make a wish, and the wish will come true (F, 46, SLC, 1964).

7825  Cross your fingers and legs when you cross a railroad track, and make a wish. Your wish will come true (M, 18, SLC, 1958).

7826  When you drive your car across railroad tracks say, "Jinks, Jacks, on the railroad tracks" and it's good luck. If you don't, you get stalled on the tracks sometime (M, SLC, 1962).

## Cars Passing over or under Bridges, Etc.

7827  If you duck your head when going under a bridge or an overpass, you will have good luck (M, SLC, 1961).

7828  When I was young, my father used to tell us to duck our heads when we went under a bridge in a car, or we would bump it on the bridge (F, 19, Cedar City, 1958); When going under a bridge in a car, if you don't duck, an Indian will hit you on the head (F, 24, SLC, 1964); . . . your head will be cut off, or a bear in the tunnel will bite your head off (F, SLC, 1954).

7829  When one rides under a bridge in a car, it is good luck to knock the top of the car (F, 21, SLC, 1964).

7830  Whenever we would go out riding in the car my grandmother would lick her index and middle fingers, and touch the roof of the car every time we went under a bridge. She actually believed that this would bring you good luck (F, SLC, 1950s).

7831 If you don't hold your head while going under an overpass, it will cave in on you (F, SLC, 1954).

7832 If you hold your ears when you go under a bridge, the mouse won't get you (F, 20, SLC, 1963).

7833 When driving under a bridge everyone should whistle to bring good luck (F, 25, SLC).

7834 Talking while passing under a railway bridge will bring good luck (F, 44, Midvale, 1930).

7835 If, while passing in an automobile under a bridge, you lift up both feet at the same time, no harm will come to you that night (F, 19, SLC, 1964); When you go under an overpass if you lift your feet and cross your fingers, you will have good luck (F, 21, SLC, 1964).

7836 If you are walking under a bridge and a car passes over you, you'll have bad luck (F, 21, SLC, 1964).

7837 If you stop on a bridge, you will have bad luck (M, 48, Midvale, 1926).

## Wishing on Bridges, Trestles, Etc., and in Underpasses

7838 Make a wish going over a new bridge, and it will come true (F, 1964). Cf. Brown 3739.

7839 Put your finger on your tongue and make a wish under a viaduct or in an underpass (M, 21, SLC, 1945); Lick your pointer finger, touch the top of your car and make a wish . . . (F, SLC, 1969).

7840 Hold your breath when you go through a tunnel and make a wish. If you can hold your breath all the time till you come out of the tunnel, your wish will come true (F, SLC, 1962); Hold your breath while crossing a bridge . . . (M, Ogden, 1961).

7841 When going through an underpass, lift your feet and make a wish and it will come true (F, 20, SLC, 1958).

7842 When you drive through an underpass, wet your index finger and press it to the top of the car, raise your legs, make a wish, and it will come true (F, SLC, 1960).

7843 Suck on the forefinger of your right hand before going through an underpass, touch the ceiling of the car with it as you are going through and make a wish, and it will come true. If there is another vehicle moving above you on the pass, make two wishes, and they'll both come true (F, 12, Orem, 1964).

7844 When you go under a viaduct, lift your feet, wet your finger and put it on the ceiling and make a wish (F, 17, Sandy, 1958).

7845 When crossing a bridge, cross your fingers, hold your breath, and make a wish. It will come true (F, 32, SLC, 1963).

7846 When you're going under a bridge, if you cross your fingers, touch the roof of the car, lift your feet, and close your eyes, your wish will come true (F, 20, SLC, 1964).

7847 When you go under a bridge, close your eyes and hold your breath and make a wish. If you do this, the wish you make will come true (F, Logan, 1970).

7848 When you go through an underpass, you must cross your fingers, close your eyes, hold your breath, and make a wish, and it will come true (F, 28, Bingham, 1940).

## Honking Horns, Etc.

7849 Honk your horn before going under a bridge. Make a wish, and you will get it (F, SLC, 1959).

7850 Always toot your horn twice and hold the top of your car with one hand as you enter an underpass. If you don't, it is bad luck (M, SLC).

7851 When driving through an underpass, blow your horn three times and make a wish (M, SLC, 1960).

7852 Whenever crossing under a bridge, put the left hand on the ceiling of the car, and honk the horn with the right (M, 17, SLC, 1961).

7853 When you go through an underpass, put your index finger on top of the car, inside, and honk the horn. Then make a wish, and it is believed to come true (F, 20, American Fork, 1960).

7854 When going under a bridge or through a tunnel, honk the car horn and cross your fingers. This enables you to make a wish come true (M, 23, Provo, 1948).

7855 When you drive under a bridge, through a tunnel or underpass, passengers put their hands on the ceiling of the car and take their feet off the floor while the driver honks the horn. Close your eyes, and wish, and the wish will come true (F, SLC, 1962).

7856 When you go under a viaduct, always honk your horn, and you'll never have a wreck (M, SLC, 1957).

7857 When going through an underpass, raise your feet, whistle, blow the horn, put your hand on the ceiling, make a wish, or you will have bad luck (F, 21, SLC, 1963).

7858 When going under a bridge, honk your horn, or the bridge will collapse (F, 19, SLC, 1950).

7859 It is bad luck not to honk when driving through an underpass (F, 20, SLC, 1963).

## TRUCKS, MOTORCYCLES

7860 A pair of miniature baby shoes hung on the inside of the cab of a truck will protect the driver against accident (F, SLC, 1964).

7861 When you see a mail truck, you should cross your fingers. When you see a dog, you can make a wish and uncross your fingers (F, Murray, 1960); . . . a Wycoff mail truck . . . (F, Provo, 1974).

7862 If you see a hay truck on the road, make a wish (F, SLC, 1962).

7863 If you count red trucks, it's a sign of good luck (M, 60, SLC, 1964).

7864 Flat tires on a truck always come in series of three (M, 48, SLC, 1940).

7865 If a motorcycle isn't working, take it home, wash it and let it rest for two days, and it will get better (M, Ger, SLC, 1962).

## BUSSES, OTHER PUBLIC VEHICLES

7866 If you don't sit in a certain place on a bus or train, you will never get to your destination (F, 24, Bountiful, 1956); Sit in a certain seat . . . to get to your destination in safety (F, 38, SLC, 1964).

7867 If a number on your bus ticket adds up to twenty-one, you will be lucky all month (M, bus driver, SLC, 1964).

7868 If you miss the bus, it will give you bad luck (F, 12, SLC, 1960).

7869 It causes bad luck for a passenger who wishes to stop a streetcar to ring the bell three times (M, 22, SLC, 1959).

7870 To meet an ambulance three times in one day is a sign of ill luck (M, 24, SLC, 1962).

7871 It is bad luck to see an ambulance, but the bad luck can be averted by saying this rhyme:
> Touch your knee,
> Touch your toe,
> Hold your collar,
> And never let go
> Until you see a four-legged animal.
(F, Provo, 1970).

## TRAINS, AIRPLANES

7872 It is unlucky to walk under a bridge when a train is going over (M, 18, Wendover, 1964).

7873 If you count the cars of a train, you will have good luck the rest of the day (F, 22, SLC, 1964); . . . bad luck . . . (M, 20, SLC, 1964).

7874 Midshipmen from the United States Naval Academy on their way to Philadelphia, when passing through Baltimore, should pull the train shades to avoid bad luck (M, 22, SLC, 1958).

7875 If a child spits on the last coach roof of a train, good luck will be his (F, 69, SLC, 1964).

7876 When we were children, if a freight car painted yellow came along, we "stamped" it for good luck. "Stamping" consists of licking the index finger of the right hand, wiping it once in the palm of the left hand, and then hitting the palm of the left hand with the fist of the right. We considered it bad luck to omit this procedure on the sight of a yellow freight car (F, 34, Woods Cross, 1946).

7877 Pilots, during the war, would not fly without their good luck charms. When they forgot it, they were killed in action (SLC, 1964).

7878 It is good luck to have a silk scarf of your girl friend, or wife, on your person when you are flying a plane (M, SLC, 1950).

7879 A pilot will take a baby shoe and rub it along the leading edge of the wing. This will bring good luck (M, 22, SLC, 1963).

7880 It is unlucky to fly in an airplane unless you tap each of the gauges on the instrument panel before you start the airplane. Just tap lightly the face of the glass dial with your finger. This could one time jar enough a sticky instrument and give you a correct reading (M, 29, SLC).

7881 A pilot of an airplane never has his picture taken before take-off (SLC).

7882 When someone you like takes off in a plane, it is bad luck for you to look at the plane take off (M, SLC, 1964).

7883 Airplane crashes come in threes (F, 18, SLC, 1964).

7884 A falling star means that a plane will crash the next day (M, SLC, 1961).

7885 The safest seat in an airplane in case of crash is in the back (M, SLC, 1951).

## RETURNING TO A PLACE

7886 Throw a coin over your shoulder into the Fountain of Trevi, and you'll go back to Rome (M, 58, SLC, 1964); If you throw a coin into the fountain and wish to return, and see a shooting star the same night, it means you will return to that very spot one day (M, 19, Provo, 1964).

7887 The English translation of an Arabic inscription at a Mosque in Cairo reads, "He who comes to Africa and drinks from the waters of the Nile will surely return to drink again" (M, 53, SLC, 1964).

7888 When leaving the Hawaiian Islands on a ship, throw your lei overboard. If it floats to shore, you will return; if it sinks, you will never return (F, SLC, 1959); . . . you will return if the lei reaches shore before your ship is out of sight (F, SLC, 1965).

7889 If you leave a lighted lamp in the window, it will bring the wayfarer home safely (M, Dan, SLC, 1959).

## MISCELLANEOUS

7890 It is bad luck to have a crutch fall across your path (F, 45, Midvale, 1964).

7891  While walking in a forest, make a small
      mark on trees every so often to keep the
      trail friendly (M, 45, Box Elder, 1925).

7892  When you're going over a state border,
      you're supposed to touch the roof of the
      car and make a wish (F, SLC, 1971).

7893  Go home from the University a different
      way each night and vary the daily
      routine so that no one will kidnap you
      (F, 19, SLC).

7894  Never cross a stream without a paddle in
      hand or disaster will occur (M, 22, SLC,
      1963).


COMMUNICATION


NEWS


Various

7895  If the teakettle should start singing
      very suddenly, it means you will soon
      receive some news (F, SLC, 1900).

7896  Dream about someone, and you will hear
      from/of them very soon (F, SLC, 1920).

7897  If you dream of a wedding, you will hear
      from an old friend (M, SLC, 1957).

7898  If you dream of anybody that's died,
      you'll hear from the living (F, 87,
      Providence, 1895).  Brown 4079.

7899  If you see a fire, you will have sudden
      news (M, SLC, 1961); Dreaming of fire
      means hasty news (F, 51, Park City,
      1927).


Human and Animal Portents

7900  If your right eye twitches, you will
      receive news (M, SLC, 1964).

7901  When your ear itches, news is coming (F,
      SLC, 1960).  Brown 4080.

7902  Persistent ringing in your ear means you
      will soon hear important news (F, Norw,
      SLC).

7903  If your nose itches, it means you will
      hear some very important news (M, 35,
      SLC, 1963).

7904  If a stray cat comes to live with you,
      and you keep it, you will hear from
      someone you haven't seen in years (F,
      57, SLC, 1963).

7905  A cock crowing means you'll receive news
      (F, 80, Eng, Midvale).  Cf. Brown 4082.

7906  If a bird flies in your house, it means
      you're going to get a message (F, Moab,
      1953).

7907  If a butterfly lands on your shoulder,
      you will receive news (F, SLC, 1960).

7908  If a spider comes down on a string right
      in front of you, it means you are going
      to get a message from a long distance
      (F, Moab, 1953); If you see a spider, be
      prepared for news (M, 66, Gr, SLC,
      1963).


Good News

7909  Itching of the right eye betokens good
      news (M, 50, It, SLC, 1965).  Brown
      4089.

7910  A buzzing sound in the ear is a sign of
      good news (F, 20, SLC, 1965).  Brown
      4086.

7911  If you get a ringing in your right ear,
      you'll receive good news (M, 52, Du,
      SLC, 1964); . . . pleasant news (F, SLC,
      1959).

7912  Drink cream in the morning, and you'll
      have good news in the afternoon (F, 43,
      SLC, 1930); . . . good news will come
      with the afternoon mail (F, 55, Brigham
      City, 1917).

7913  When a woman is opening a jar of fruit,
      and some of the juice spatters into her
      face, it means that she will hear some
      welcome news very soon (F, 20, SLC,
      1964).

7914  If you spill sugar, you will hear good
      news (F, 68, Ogden, 1910).

7915  If coffee grounds cling to the sides of
      the cup, high up, it is a sign that
      company is coming with good news (F, 19,
      SLC, 1964).

7916  A singing teapot foretells pleasant news
      before long (F, 31, Murray, 1963).

7917  If you dream of clear water, good news
      will come (F, 82, It, SLC, 1963).

7918  When bees fly in the window, expect good
      news (F, SLC); . . . a bumblebee . . .
      (F, 48, SLC, 1930).

7919  If you see a spider at noon, it is
      bringing you good news (F, SLC, 1961).


Bad News

7920  Itching of the left eye betokens bad
      news (M, 50, It, SLC, 1965).  Brown
      4097.

7921  If you get a ringing in your left ear,
      you'll hear bad news (M, 52, Du, SLC,
      1964); . . . unpleasant news (F, SLC,
      1959).  Cf. Brown 4095.

7922  If your right ear rings, then you will
      receive bad news (F, 68, SLC, 1964).
      Cf. Brown 4094.

7923  If you think you hear a knock on the
      door, there will be bad news (F, 65,
      SLC, 1962).

7924  If you drop a dish of food, it means you
      will hear bad news (M, 41, SLC, 1964).

7925  If a person drops a dishrag, then they
      should throw it away, or a person will
      come to the house and bring them bad
      news (F, SLC, 1964).

7926  To say "Farewell" or to overhear it
      means bad news is coming your way (F,
      45, Woods Cross, 1964).

7927  If you dream of a witch, you'll get bad
      news (M, SLC, 1930).

7928 Dreaming of a bell or bells means coming news, but it may not be favorable (F, SLC, 1957).

7929 If you dream of a rifle, you will hear bad news (M, Iran, SLC, 1963).

7930 Walk in muddy water and you'll get bad news (M, Hyrum, 1948).

7931 Dreaming of mud and water will bring bad news the next day (F, SLC, 1958).

7932 When a dog howls it is a sign of bad news (F, 45, Ja, SLC, 1963).

7933 If the hen crows, you will hear bad news (M, 33, Gr, SLC, 1963).

7934 A rooster's crowing at night brings bad news the next day (M, 18, SLC, 1961). Brown 4100.

7935 The cooing of a strange dove by the window is a sign of bad news (M, 54, SLC, 1963).

7936 If any bird or any other animal should try to get into your house (other than one's pets), it means they have come to prepare you for bad news (M, Beaver, 1936).

7937 If a bat flies in your path, you will receive bad news (F, 67, SLC, 1963).

## MAIL

### Various Beliefs

7938 If you burn a letter, it will cause good luck (F, SLC, 1945).

7939 To dream of receiving a letter is a sign of unexpected news; but to dream of sending one portends some unexpected difficulty that will upset your plans (F, SLC, 1957).

7940 If you write a letter in red ink, it means you love the person (M, SLC, 1961).

7941 Get a letter on Monday, and you'll get six more during the week (F, 63, SLC, 1964).

7942 If the number of your bus ticket adds up to twenty-one, you will get a letter (M, 19, Ogden, 1964).

7943 If you dream of someone dead, you will get a letter (F, 70, SLC).

7944 If a girl signs letters with anything but "love," then luck will follow (M, Provo, 1964).

7945 When you receive a red tray for one of your meals at Ballif Hall (University of Utah), you will receive a letter that day (F, SLC, 1960).

7946 If you receive a chain letter, it is bad luck to break the chain (M, 64, SLC, 1964).

7947 A friendship letter is a chain letter that is received and must be passed on according to direction. It is bad luck if you break it (F, SLC, 1971).

### Body Indicators

7948 If your right ear itches, you will get a letter soon (M, SLC, 1961).

7949 If a hair hangs over your nose, you'll get a love letter (M, SLC, 1959).

7950 If your nose itches, you will receive a letter (F, 21, SLC, 1959). Brown 4106.

7951 Every white spot on your middle fingernail represents a letter you will soon receive (F, SLC, 1916).

7952 If your left hand itches, you'll receive a letter (F, SLC, 1950); If the palm of your left hand . . . (F, 49, Norw, SLC, 1963). Brown 4111.

7953 If your right hand itches, you will get a letter soon (F, 32, SLC, 1948).

7954 If a person sneezes three times in a row, this means they are about to receive a letter (M, 60, SLC, 1920).

7955 If you sneeze on a Wednesday, you are going to receive a letter (F, SLC, 1964). Brown 4109f.

### Domestic Portents

7956 If your bread accidentally falls into your soup, you will receive mail soon (F, Swiss, SLC, 1957); . . . in a cup of coffee . . . (F, 80, SLC).

7957 If you are drinking tea, and a small amount of the tea leaf drops over the side of the cup, a letter will come (F, 82, It, SLC, 1963).

7958 If you drop something of liquid (water, coffee, etc.), you will get a package the next day (F, Swiss, SLC).

7959 If you drop a piece of silverware, you are going to get a letter (F, Salina, 1921); . . . a fork . . . (F, 46, Provo, 1929); . . . a knife . . . (F, 51, Centerfield, 1964); . . . a spoon, it means you will receive an important letter that day (F, Swed, SLC, 1957).

7960 A candle showing a bright spark will bring a letter to the person sitting opposite of the spark (F, 54, SLC, 1942).

7961 When a spark forms on the end of the wick in the candle flame, moisten the tip of your finger with your tongue, touch the spark lightly with it, and if it adheres to your finger, you can confidently look for a letter within a day or two (F, Du, SLC, 1964).

### Clothing, Intimate Possessions

7962 If the hem on your skirt turns up, you will receive a letter (F, 63, Monroe, 1964). Cf. Brown 4113.

7963 If a woman finds a large hole in her stocking, there is a letter waiting for her (M, Layton, 1946). Cf. Brown 4112, 4115.

7964 If you have a piece of cotton on your dress and you pick it off, it means you will soon receive a letter (F, 54, Eng, SLC, 1964); To pluck a thread off someone's apparel is to receive a letter (F, 50, Eng, SLC, 1964); If a white thread hangs to your clothes, you'll also get a love letter (M, SLC, 1959).

7965   If you have a thread on your clothing, take it off, wind it around your index finger saying the alphabet; you will get a letter or see or hear from someone whose name starts with the letter at which the thread ends (F, 35, Murray, 1964).

7966   If you find a button, you will get a letter within two days (F, Ogden, 1959). Cf. Brown 4121.

7967   To find a handkerchief is a sign of a letter (M, 21, SLC, 1964).

7968   Find a hairpin, get a letter (F, 37, SLC, 1950). Cf. Brown 4122.

## Animal and Plant Indicators

7969   If a bird flies to your window, you will receive a letter (F, 1959).

7970   Seeing one magpie means you will receive a letter (F, Ir, SLC, 1960).

7971   If you kill a cricket, you will receive a letter from a friend (F, Nephi, 1961).

7972   If there is a big fly around the house, a letter will arrive soon (SLC, 1963). Cf. Brown 4127.

7973   If a honeybee circles around you, you will receive a letter in the mail (F, SLC, 1960).

7974   If a moth is flying around a light, you will receive a letter or a message (F, 82, It, SLC, 1963); A moth flying around in a room means . . . (F, 45, SLC, 1963); If a moth flies toward you . . . (F, 56, SLC, 1936).

7975   If you see a spider and do not step on it, you will receive a letter that day (F, 37, SLC, 1964).

7976   If a person sees a spider coming down a wall (or anything), it means that they are going to get a letter. If it is a white spider, it means that it will be a letter from a boy (F, 20, SLC, 1964). Cf. Brown 4128.

7977   If you find a one-leaf clover, you will get a letter from your sweetheart (F, 46, SLC, 1938).

7978   Touch wood if two people speak at the same time and say, "Knock on wood." The first one to get to wood will receive a letter (F, 57, Eng, SLC, 1964).

## Position of the Stamp

7979   Putting a stamp upside down on a letter means that you love the person to whom you are sending the letter (Lehi, 1957).

7980   If the stamp is on the envelope sideways, it's usually a lover expressing deep love (M, SLC, 1963).

7981   Postage stamps upside down means "I don't love you" (F, 67, SLC, 1957).

7982   If you put the stamp upside down on a letter, it means you don't want an answer (F, Bear River City, 1957); If you accidentally put a stamp on bottom side up, you will not receive an answer (F, Lehi, 1957); . . . you don't want the person to write ever again (F, Riverton, 1910). Cf. Brown 4130.

7983   If you desire an immediate reply to a letter, simply place your stamp on the letter upside down (F, SLC, 1960).

7984   A stamp on a letter upside down means a lie inside (F, Orangeville, 1959).

7985   Putting a stamp upside down on an envelope is good luck (F, 19, SLC, 1950).

## TELEPHONE CALLS

7986   When a telephone rings only once and when you pick it up and no one is there, it means that trouble will be coming your way before the next twenty-four hours are up (M, SLC, 1957).

7987   The first person to call you on the New Year will have good luck (M, 24, SLC, 1963).

7988   Never hang up the phone first, for it's bad luck (F, 14, SLC, 1964).

7989   Never answer the phone with your hair put up, or you'll have bad luck (F, 18, SLC, 1963).

## SPEECH

## Various Beliefs

7990   Mormons must never say "Joe Smith" when they are speaking of Joseph Smith, or something bad will happen (F, 67, SLC, 1900s).

7991   Don't marvel at things. Especially don't say "ohhh" or "oooo" (F, 42, Gr, SLC, 1964).

7992   Never make an affirmative statement about the future, or the opposite will come to pass (F, 19, SLC, 1963).

7993   Never boast about your good luck, or bad luck will follow (F, SLC, 1960); . . . brag about good fortune, or you will have bad luck (M, 21, SLC, 1964).

7994   There is a belief that the mention of misfortune or evil will bring misfortune on one (F, 50, Murray, 1928).

7995   If you compliment a person, it will bring bad luck (M, SLC, 1959).

## SPEAKING ABILITY, VOICE

7996   Eat sugar and it will make your voice sweet (F, Murray, 1957).

7997   Kissing the Blarney Stone loosens your tongue (F, Ir, SLC); . . . gives you the

gift of gab (F, Ir, SLC, 1960); . . .
the gift of blarney (F, 53, SLC, 1964);
. . . will give you the power of sweet
talk (F, 46, SLC, 1936).

7998    If girls eat too many eggplants, they
will lose their voice (F, 45, Ja, SLC,
1963).

7999 ✗ Whenever you are in a wind storm never
shout, because you will lose your voice
(F, Gr, SLC, 1957).

8000    An old settler in our town took the
Lord's name in vain a lot. The Bishop
told him if he didn't stop, he would
lose his voice. This happened. He
never spoke again (F, Logan, 1958).

## SPEAKING IN UNISON

8001    Saying the same thing at the same time
as someone else brings bad luck (M,
Kaysville, 1958).

8002    If two people say the same thing at the
same time, they will have good luck (F,
SLC, 1947).

8003    If two people start to say the same
thing at the same time, it means that
these two people will be together next
year at this same time (M, 52, Du, SLC,
1964).

8004    If you say something the same time
someone else does, whoever counts to ten
first yells "You owe me a Coke" (M, 21,
Spanish Fork, 1950).

8005    Whenever you speak and say the same word
as another person at the same moment,
you must say, "Jinks, winks" or it is
bad luck (F, 18, SLC).

8006    When two friends say something at the
same time one says, "Jinks, you owe me a
drink" (F, SLC, 1957); . . . the first
to say "jinks" gets a Coke (F, SLC,
1962).

8007    If two people say the same thing
simultaneously, they should shake hands
and turn around (F, 55, Murray, 1920).

8008    If two people say the same thing at the
same time, they should knock on wood (F,
18, Logan, 1950).

8009    If two people say something at the same
time and touch unpainted wood, you can
make a wish and it will come true (F,
26, Finn, Morgan, 1965).

8010    If two people say the same thing at the
same time, they should make wishes,
touch wood, touch blue, and their wishes
will come true (F, SLC, 1960).

8011    Say "Needles and pins" when you say the
same thing at the same time. This
prevents a quarrel (F, 47, SLC, 1928).

## Hooking Fingers, Wishing

8012    When two people say the same thing at
the same time, they should clasp little
fingers to avoid bad luck (M, SLC,
1961).

8013    When two people start to speak
simultaneously, or say the same thing
simultaneously, hook the little fingers
of the right hands together for a
moment. Then neither one can speak
until someone asks one a question. If
the person speaks before the spell is
broken, he will have bad luck (SLC,
1925).

8014    If two people say the same thing at the
same time and cross their fingers, they
will have good luck (F, Weber Co, 1958);
. . . they will have a chance to wish
(F, 53, SLC, 1921).

8015    If two people happen to start talking to
each other simultaneously, they should
stop, lock little fingers and make a
wish (M, 57, Swiss, Heber City, 1914).

8016    If two people are talking and say the
same word at the same time, they should
hook little fingers, make a wish and
pull. The one who can hold out longest
wins and gets his or her wish (F, 74,
SLC, 1964).

8017    If two people say the same word at the
same time, they should lock their little
fingers with each other and make a wish,
then pull to break the lock. After
that, the first one of them to say
another word loses his wish, but the
other person's wish comes true (F, SLC,
1945).

8018    If two people talk together and say the
same thing at the same time, they help
the tailor get to heaven, and they can
make three wishes (F, 24, Swiss, SLC,
1964).

## Reciting Verses and Formulae

8019    When two people start to say something
at the same time, they join little
fingers and say, "Needles and pins,
triplets or twins; when a girl marries,
triplets or twins" (M, SLC, 1965); . . .
they hook little fingers saying
"Needles, pins, triplets, twins, now our
wish begins" (F, SLC, 1926).

8020    To speak the same words simultaneously
with another, hook right little fingers
together and repeat together, "Needles
and pins, when a man marries the trouble
begins." Release the little fingers and
press the right thumbs together in a
hand clasp as you repeat the verse (F,
70, SLC, 1964).

8021    If two people say the same word at the
same time, they must hook their little
fingers together, make a wish and say
alternately, "Needles, pins, kings,
queens," and their wish will come true
(F, SLC, 1957).

8022    When two people say the same thing at
the same time, they must lock little
fingers and say the following verse, one
person saying lines 1, 3, 5, and 7, and
the other saying lines 2, 4, 6, and 8:
       "Needles,"
       "Pins,"
       "Buffalo
       "Skins."
       "What goes up the chimney?"
       "Smoke."

"What comes down the chimney?"
"Santa Claus."
Then they press their thumbs together
and make a wish (F, Bear River City,
1957).

8023    If two people say the same word or
phrase at the same time, if they will
immediately after saying it together say
"Jinx." Then one says, "What goes up
the chimney?" and he says, "Santa
Claus." Then he says, "May this wish
never be broken." Then the baby fingers
of both people are interlocked and they
make a wish privately and try to pull
the fingers apart. The person who first
releases his finger loses his wish and
the person who didn't let go gets his
wish (F, 21, Bountiful, 1950).

8024    If you say the same word as someone else
and at the same time, you say, "What
comes out of a chimney?" He says,
"Smoke." You say, "What do you put on
bread?" He says, "Butter." Then you
both get good luck (M, 36, SLC, 1964).

8025    If two people say the same thing at the
same time, they must lock their little
fingers and say alternately, "Red, blue,
needles, pins, shakes, pears,
Longfellow." They each may make a wish
(F, SLC).

8026    If you happen to say something at the
same time as someone else says it, you
will have good luck if you say "Bread
and butter" right after (F, 56, SLC,
1964).

## SILENCE

8027    At a party there will be complete
silence every twenty minutes (F, Lehi,
1957). Brown 8515.

8028    Silences in conversations come on the
hour or the half hour (F, Bear River
City, 1957).

8029    When a general silence occurs in a group
conversation, it will be either twenty
minutes after or twenty minutes before
the hour (F, Tooele, 1957).

## SECRETS

8030    Don't tell any secrets in a cornfield,
because it will bring bad luck (F,
1959).

8031    If a white person dreams they are dark-
skinned, a dark secret from the past is
about to be known by others (F, SLC,
1964); . . . if you dream of a Negro,
you have some desire or secret you wish
to withhold (F, 78, It, SLC, 1963).

8032    If you can handle hot pans without
burning yourself, you will be able to
keep a secret (F, 60, Bingham Canyon,
1910).

8033    If you wish to be successful in finding
out a secret, carry an old key in your
pocket (F, 45, Woods Cross, 1964).

## CURSING, CUSSING, SWEARING, ETC.

8034    If your nose itches, you'll be cursed by
a fool (F, 55, Midvale, 1963).

8035    If your hand itches, you are going to be
cursed (F, 64, SLC, 1964); If the palm
of your right hand itches, you will be
cussed (F, Woods Cross, 1953).

8036    It is bad luck to be cussed by a fool
(F, 45, SLC, 1961).

8037    It is bad luck if somebody curses at
someone else, even if only a jest. One
must cross oneself three times (M, Ger,
SLC, 1938).

8038    Come in the front door and go out the
back, or you will be cursed (F, 83, SLC,
1963).

8039    There was a great deal of conflict
between Brigham Young and the "Gentile
City" at Corinne. Many felt that
Corinne would become the "Chicago of the
West" and should be the capital of Utah.
Once Brigham Young visited Corinne,
astride a mule. The people heckled him
so much about his mode of transportation
that he put an eternal curse on the
city. It was not long before the town
went from a wild place of over 2,000
people to a virtual ghost town (F,
Ogden, 1971).

8040    If you swear on New Year's Eve, you will
swear every day for a year (F, SLC,
1959).

8041    Anyone who swears a lot will have snakes
and toads come from his mouth (F, Moab,
1953). (This curse appears to derive
from Grimm 24, "Dame Holle." --Eds.)

8042    A dragonfly will sew up your lips if you
swear in its presence (Cedar Valley,
1957); If you swear and a darning needle
bug hears you, it will sew your mouth up
(M, 36, Murray, 1950).

## ASSEVERATIONS OF TRUTH

8043    If you begin to tell something and
forget what you were saying, that is a
sign that it was true (F, 61, Du, SLC,
1964). Brown 3674.

8044    If you sneeze after you have made a
statement, it is a sign that the
statement is true (M). Brown 3662.

8045    "Cross my heart and hope to die, and I
won't tell a single lie" (F, 23, SLC,
1964); Making a cross over your heart
makes you tell the truth (F, Farmington,
1959). Brown 3663f.

## LYING

### Various

8046    If you tell a lie, it may come true (F,
1962).

8047    To tell if a person is lying ask him to
repeat what he said. If he doesn't tell
it the same way as before, it is a story
(F, 26, Bountiful, 1940s).

8048    If you drop a dishrag, you're going to
have a dirty lie told on you (F, 58,
SLC, 1915).

8049   If an apple falls on you while you are talking, what you are saying is a lie (F, 61, Richfield, 1930).

8050   If you pluck a plantain weed, the number of veins hanging out of the stem tells the number of lies told during the day (F, 49, SLC, 1964).

8051   The white strings in the stem of a dandelion leaf will tell how many lies you have told in your life (F, Ogden, 1961).

8052   You will always be punished for your lies, even though no one knew you lied (F, 39, SLC).

8053   If you tell a lie, lightning will strike (M, SLC, 1958).

## Body Signs

8054   Green eye, pick a pie.  Run around and tell a lie (F, SLC, 1925); Brown-eyed pickle pie, never known to tell a lie (F, SLC, 1910).

8055   If your ear twitches while you are talking, you are telling a lie (M, SLC, 1963).  Cf. Brown 3666.

8056   If you tell a lie, your nose will turn red (F, 20, SLC, 1958).

8057   If you rub the side of your nose while talking, it means you're lying (F, 18, SLC, 1959).

8058   Telling lies makes the nose grow longer (F, SLC, 1961).

8059   Blushing is a sign of lying (F, 55, SLC, 1964).

8060   If you bite your tongue, it is because you have lied (M, Riverside, 1920).

8061   If you bite your tongue while talking, you are telling a lie (F, Murray, 1957); . . . while eating . . . (F, 1900). Brown 3673.

8062   Any reference to the left shoulder is thought to be a falsehood (F, 55, SLC, 1963).

8063   If you tell a lie, your soles will curl (M, SLC, 1950).

8064   Darning needles can sew up your eyes if you tell a fib (M, SLC); . . . your ears . . . (M, SLC).

8065   Dragonflies sew up your mouth if you tell a lie (F, 17, SLC, 1949); If a darning nettle flies by and you have ever told a lie, it will sew your mouth shut (F, SLC, 1964).  (Darning needle? --Eds.)

8066   Darning needles can sew up your fingers if you tell a fib (M, 64, SLC).

8067   If you tell a lie, mosquitoes will sew your mouth shut (F, Provo, 1974).

8068   If you tell a lie, your tongue will grow as long as a dog's (F, 80, Panguitch, 1900).

8069   If you can't remember what someone said, it must have been a lie (M, SLC, 1935); If you forget what you started to say, it was a lie (F, Murray, 1957).

8070   If you are about to tell a story and forget it, it means that it was untrue (M, Murray, 1963).

8071   Short fingernails reveal a person that lies (F, 29, SLC, 1964).

8072   If you tell a lie, you will get white spots on your fingernails (F, 20, SLC, 1959); Specks of white in your fingernails indicate you have been telling fibs (F, 52, SLC); A white speck in your nail means you have told a falsehood (F, 43, SLC, 1947).  Brown 3677f.

8073   White spots on the fingernails indicate the number of lies you have told (F, SLC, 1920).

8074   You have told a lie if your joints crack when you pull your finger (F, Vernal, 1964).  Cf. Brown 3675.

## Clothing

8075   As many stitches as you take on you, you'll have that number of lies told about you (M, 60, Du, SLC, 1964).

8076   If you mend your apron or dress while on you, someone will lie about you (F, 55, SLC, 1964).

## Counteractants

8077   Cross your fingers when you say something untrue (F, 1960); It's okay to lie if you cross your fingers (F, Ir, SLC, 1960).  Brown 5843.

8078   If you tell a lie and you have your fingers crossed, it isn't really a lie (F, 27, SLC, 1963); . . . it means you are just kidding (F, Ogden, 1947); . . . you are only fooling (F, 23, SLC, 1963); . . . it won't matter (F, SLC, 1964).

8079   Crossing the fingers on both hands is bad luck, while crossing fingers on one hand is good luck, or allows you to fib and not be called dishonest (M, SLC, 1961).

8080   If you cross your fingers while telling a lie, it will not be discovered (M, SLC, 1957).

8081   In order to cancel a spoken untruth, cross your fingers (F, 76, Glenwood, 1894).

8082   Crossing the fingers while telling a lie is supposed to prevent harm (F, 65, Fillmore, 1961).

8083   If you cross your fingers, you can tell a lie with a clear conscience (F, SLC, 1961); . . . it will take away the guilt (F, SLC, 1959); . . . it nullifies you from the sin of lying (M, Woods Cross, 1958); . . . save yourself from being punished later on (F, 54, SLC, 1964); . . . it excuses you from that lie (F, 16, SLC, 1963).

8084    Crossing the fingers while telling a lie will make it so that it doesn't count against you in heaven (M, 64, SLC).

8085    If you tell a lie, cross yourself with the sign of the cross in order to be forgiven (F, 100, Mex, Grantsville, 1963).

8086    Crossing your fingers behind your back will allow you to tell a lie without any bad effects.  But if the person you're telling it to suspects that you are lying, he merely has to cross the fingers of both his hands behind his back and you are double-crossed (1963).

8087    A reference to the left shoulder is supposed to reverse the meaning of a falsehood (M, 48, SLC, 1964).

8088    If you tell a lie and want to undo it, walk backwards through your steps and it will take the lie away (F, Logan, 1970).

# VIII
# Social Relationships, Recreation

VISITORS AND COMPANY; MEETING AND GREETING

8089 If a person doesn't feel welcome at a friend's house, he or she should throw his hat in the door. If the host doesn't pick up the hat, the guest is welcome (F, 80, SLC, 1964).

8090 If you want your company to come to your house again, throw water into the air after they leave (M, 28, Iran, SLC, 1963).

8091 Never let a stranger into your home before eleven in the morning, lest the day be filled with grief (F, SLC).

8092 If you drop a dishrag, you'll have an unwelcome dinner guest (F, Delta, 1930); . . . a bigger slob than you is coming to dinner (F, SLC, 1968); If you drop a dishtowel, you will have an unwelcome female guest (M, SLC, 1968). Cf. Brown 4045.

8093 If a blind flips up, bad company is coming (F, SLC).

8094 A person who stumbles at the steps in going to someone's home will know that he is not wanted there (M, 44, salesman, SLC, 1944); If you stub your foot on walking to a house, you know that you are . . . (F, Provo, 1960). Brown 3898.

8095 If a person visits his neighbor and enters through the front door, then goes out the back, he must re-enter the back door and go out the front door before he goes home, or he is fated never to be welcome again (M, SLC, 1957).

8096 Do not come in one door and go out the other. It will bring unwelcome company (F, 71, Ger, Magna, 1964). Cf. Brown 4054.

8097 A horseshoe put up over the door is an infallible armor against unwanted visitors (M, 46, radio repairman, SLC, 1942).

8098 If company comes that you don't like, put salt in their tracks and sweep it out the door, and they will never come back (M, 30, Dugway, 1963); . . . put some salt behind the person . . . (M, priest, SLC, 1962). Cf. Brown 3903f.

8099 Never sweep the floor when company is around, or you are telling them to go home (M, 61, W. Jordan, 1932).

8100 If you want someone to leave and not sit and sit, put a broom behind the door where it cannot be seen (F, 55, Magna, 1964); . . . stand a broom upside down behind the door (F, 16, SLC, 1963); . . . stand a broom upside down with salt on it . . . (M, SLC, 1961). Brown 3901.

8101 Never put the broom behind the door, or you'll have bad visitors (F, 27, SLC, 1963).

8102 If you do not like the visitors in your home, throw away or break a black dish after they leave, and they will not return (M, 28, Iran, SLC, 1963). First heard in Iran in 1950.

8103 If you handle a key when you're talking to company, you are telling people to go home (M, 61, W. Jordan, 1942).

## Body Signs

8104 If a tress of hair hangs down in the forehead, you will have guests (F, 62, Gr, SLC, 1963).

8105 If your skin itches, you're about to have a visitor (F, 19, SLC, 1950).

8106 If your eye twitches, you will see someone you haven't seen for some time (F, 42, Gr, SLC, 1964). Cf. Brown 3906.

8107 When your ears ring, someone is coming to visit you (F, 45, American Fork, 1960).

8108 If your right ear itches, it means someone is going to come and see you (F, 19, Woods Cross, 1958).

8109 If your nose itches, you're going to have company (F, 75, Holden, 1899). Brown 3912.

8110 If your nose itches, it means you will have to sleep with company (F, Granger, 1961).

8111 If your nose itches, you're going to have a cheeky visitor (F, W. Jordan, 1935); . . . nosey visitors (F, 19, SLC, 1964); . . . snoopy company is coming (M, Panguitch, 1912).

8112 If your nose itches, someone is coming with a hole in his britches (F, 80, Springville, 1890); . . . a stranger is coming with patches on his britches (F, SLC, 1959). Brown 3921f.

8113   When the nose itches, it means a stranger will visit you (F, 84, SLC, 1955); . . . you will meet a stranger (F, 52, Provo, 1924).

8114   If the palm of your hand itches, you will shake hands with a stranger (F, 31, Murray, 1964).  Brown 3928f.

8115   When your left hand itches, you will have a male visitor (F, 36, Mex, SLC, 1963).

8116   When the palm of your right hand itches, you are going to shake hands with someone (M, Ogden, 1961).

8117   If your hand itches, you're going to shake hands with someone important that day (F, 19, SLC, 1964).

8118   If your left hand itches, you are going to shake hands with a fool (F, 60, SLC, 1910).

8119   If your fingers seem slippery, and everything seems to drop, it is a sure sign of a visitor (F, Axtell, 1958).

8120   An itching thumb means visitors (M, SLC, 1959).

8121   If you knock your elbow, you will see someone you are very anxious to see (F, Axtell, 1958).

8122   If the bottoms of your feet itch, you are going to have visitors before the sun sets (F, SLC, 1959).  Cf. Brown 3933.

8123   If your feet ache, it means that company is coming (F, Ogden, 1961).

## Sneezing

8124   If you sneeze before seven, you will have company before eleven (F, Murray, 1912).

8125   Sneezing before breakfast is a sign that company is coming (F, 47, SLC, 1961); If a woman sneezes before breakfast, company will arrive before noon (F, 64, Ogden, 1930).

8126   If you sneeze before you eat, you will have company before you go to sleep (F, 82, SLC, 1964).  Brown 4002, cf. 4033.

8127   If a person sneezes on Saturday, it means he'll have company on Sunday (F, SLC, 1934).

8128   If you sneeze consecutively three times, it means you are going to have company (F, 20, Logan, 1970); . . . five times . . . (F, 18, SLC, 1962).

8129   If you sneeze, this means there is someone coming with a hole in his socks (M, 22, SLC, 1963).

## CLOTHING, INTIMATE POSSESSIONS

8130   An apron slipping to the floor means you are about to meet a man (F, 65, SLC, 1962).

8131   If you ever see a hat on a bed, it means that company will be coming (F, SLC, 1962).

8132   A thread on a coat means that company is coming (F, 60, SLC, 1963).

8133   Don't put your slip on inside out, or you will have guests (F, 51, SLC, 1955).

8134   If you drop a handkerchief, you will meet a stranger (F, 58, SLC, 1955).

8135   If the comb is dropped while you are combing your hair, a visitor is coming (M, 44, SLC, 1962).  Brown 4051.

## ANIMALS

## Various

8136   If a cat washes behind his ears, you can expect company (F, Du, SLC, 1964); . . . its face . . . (F, SLC, 1920).  Brown 3935.

8137   A cat washing its face on a doorstep means that visitors are coming from the direction in which the cat's tail is pointing (F, 53, Monroe, 1964).  Cf. Brown 3934.

8138   If a cat licks his paws, expect company to come (F, Murray, 1940).

8139   If the cat licks its face before breakfast, you'll have company before dinner (F, Scot, SLC, 1959).

8140   When a dog is lying upside down on his back, it means that the person who sees him will have company.  Unless the person who sees the dog puts a glass of water on the dog's stomach, bad luck will come to the company, but nothing will happen to the company if water is placed on the dog (F, 20, Mex, SLC, 1964).

8141   When a mouse comes into the house, it means you will have company (F, 59, SLC, 1962).

## Fowls and Birds

8142   If a rooster crows, company is on the way (SLC, 1946); . . . three times . . . (F, SLC, 1964).  Brown 3939.

8143   If a rooster crows near the front door, it is a sure sign of company (F, Moab, 1953); If a chicken crows in the doorway . . . (F, 20, SLC, 1965); . . . crows on the front porch . . . (F, SLC, 1918); . . . on the doorstep . . . (F, Moab, 1953); . . . one person for every crow (F, Scipio, 1961); If the rooster comes in front of the door . . . (M, SLC, 1957).  Brown 3947, 3941, 3956f.

8144   If a rooster crows in your yard, it means company is coming to dinner (F, Murray, 1959).  Cf. Brown 3946, 3953.

8145   When roosters fight at the door of your house, it is time to start watering the soup.  That long lost relative is about to appear for a free meal (F, SLC, 1959).  Cf. Brown 3962ff.

8146 When a rooster crows in front of a window, it means you are going to have company (M, 67, SLC, 1962).

8147 Hearing a rooster crow at noon is a sign that a stranger will soon arrive (M, SLC, 1957); . . . in the afternoon . . . (F, 55, SLC, 1965).

8148 If the rooster crows in the evening, company is coming (M, 23, SLC, 1958).

8149 If the rooster crows on the back fence, it is a sure sign of company coming (M, 35, SLC, 1943). Cf. Brown 3944.

8150 If a bird flies to your house, it means someone is coming to see you (F, SLC, 1958). Cf. Brown 8547.

## Insects, Spiders, Etc.

8151 If a bee enters your house, you will have a visitor (F, SLC, 1961); . . . bee flies in through a window . . . (F, 1961).

8152 If a bumblebee enters your house, you will have a visitor (F, SLC, 1959); . . . a distinguished caller (F, SLC, 1958).

8153 If there is a big fly around the house, visitors are coming (F, SLC, 1962).

8154 If a butterfly enters the house through an open door, people will soon have a lady visitor with a dress the same color as the butterfly (F, SLC, 1960). Cf. Brown 3986.

8155 If a spider spins a web in your house and falls down in front of you, it means that company is coming (M, 20, Ogden, 1963). Cf. Brown 3987ff.

8156 The crawling of a spider on your bed foretells the coming of a stranger (M, 22, SLC, 1951).

## DOMESTIC PORTENTS

## Food, Meals, Etc.

8157 If you take more of a food when you already have some on your plate, then someone is coming who really likes that food (M, Farmington, 1936); . . . someone is coming to the house hungry (M, 17, SLC, 1952). Brown 4035.

8158 If you accidentally take two helpings of the same food at once, it means that someone hungry is coming to visit you (M, Tooele, 1957). Brown 4036.

8159 Long stems in tea indicate you will have gentlemen visitors (F, Bountiful, 1936); Tea leaves floating in a cup mean company (F, 19, Dragerton, 1964).

8160 A tea leaf floating on the tea in a cup foretells that a stranger will be paying a visit. If the leaf has a little stem on it, the stranger will be tall (F, 74, Farmington, 1899).

8161 A soft tea leaf in a cup of tea means you will have a lady visitor while a hard leaf means a man visitor (F, 68, SLC, 1914).

8162 When you pour tea, and a tea leaf sticks right up or stands up in the tea cup (upright), that means that you are going to have a visitor (F, 62, Ja, SLC, 1964).

8163 Tea leaves in the bottom of a tea cup mean that a visitor will come. Put the leaves on the back of your hand and slap the other hand over them, repeating a day of the week with each slap. When the leaves fall off, that is the day to expect a visitor (F, 20, SLC, 1955).

8164 Bubbles in a tea cup are supposed to foretell visitors (SLC, 1964).

8165 If you leave the lid off the teakettle, you will have company (F, Bountiful, 1950).

8166 If you pour coffee and see some grounds, company is coming (F, 23, Murray, 1964).

8167 If there are bubbles in your coffee, you're going to have visitors (F, 39, SLC, 1946).

8168 If bread falls butter-side down, you'll have company (F, Midvale); . . . unexpected visitors (M, 12, SLC, 1964).

8169 If you take a piece of bread and already have one, it means someone is coming hungry (F, 19, Holladay, 1964). Cf. Brown 4037f.

8170 If there is any bread left over on the table, be prepared for company (M, 73, Gr, SLC, 1964).

8171 Burned cake means unexpected company (F, SLC, 1961).

8172 If you spill sugar on the table, a visitor will come (F, 20, Du, SLC, 1963).

8173 If you spill salt, it will bring company, unless you throw some over your shoulder (F, SLC, 1959).

8174 If you spill salt, the next visitor will be a female; if you spill pepper, the next visitor will be a male (M, 21, SLC, 1964).

## Silverware

8175 Dropping a fork while company is visiting is bad luck (M, SLC).

8176 If you drop a spoon at the dinner table or while setting the table, an unexpected guest will come. A spoon dropped will be a child, a fork a woman, a knife a man (F, 47, SLC, 1964). Brown 4009, 4012.

8177 If you drop a knife, a woman is going to call (M, Ogden, 1960). Cf. Brown 4004, 4007.

8178 Drop a knife and a child will come and see you (M, SLC, 1960).

8179 If you drop a knife while washing dishes, some children will visit you (F, Murray, 1958). Cf. Brown 4005.

8180 If you drop a fork on the floor accidentally, a man will visit you (M, 50, It, SLC, 1965). Brown 4006.

8181 Dropping a salad fork means a boy visitor (F, 21, SLC, 1946).

8182 If you drop a fork while washing dishes, a man will come to visit (F, Murray, 1958); . . . a single man . . . (F, Moab, 1953); . . . a hungry man . . . (F, Norw, SLC, 1960).

8183 If you drop a fork, a child is coming to visit (F, 23, Murray, 1964).

8184 If you drop a spoon, it means a woman will come to your house (F, 68, SLC, 1964). Brown 4010.

## Dishes

8185 If you set an extra plate at your table, guests will drop in (M, SLC, 1959).

8186 If you accidentally set an extra plate at the dinner table, someone hungry is coming (F, Bountiful, 1935).

8187 Dropping a dish means that company is coming (F, Ogden, 1964); . . . a stranger is coming to call (F, 20, Vernal, 1964).

8188 If you get water on your stomach while you're doing the dishes, it means a visitor is going to come (F, SLC, 1961).

## Dishcloths, Towels

8189 Dropping a dishtowel while company is visiting is bad luck (M, PR, 32, SLC, 1965).

8190 If you drop a dishcloth, it means company is coming (F, Orangeville, 1959); . . . dishrag . . . (F, Provo, 1959). Brown 4016.

8191 When you drop a dishrag, if it falls wadded up, a man is coming; open, a woman is coming (F, Ogden, 1935); . . . if it falls in a ball, a woman; falls flat, a man (F, SLC, 1961). Brown 4018f.

8192 If you drop a dishrag, some big drip will come to dinner (M, Midvale).

8193 If you drop a dishrag, someone dirtier than you is coming (F, Moab, 1953); . . . the company will be as dirty as the dishcloth (F, 60, SLC, 1964).

8194 If you drop the dishrag while washing the dishes, you will have sloppy company (F, 67, Panguitch); . . . a bigger slob than you is coming to dinner (F, 55, Brigham City, 1915). Cf. Brown 4021, 4028ff.

8195 Drop a dishrag, and a poorer housekeeper than you will come to see you (F, Woods Cross, 1953); . . . a dirtier housekeeper . . . (F, 60, Ogden).

## Brooms, Sweeping, Cleaning, Etc.

8196 If a very young child without being told picks up the broom and sweeps the house, it is a sure sign of a visitor (M, 44, salesman, SLC, 1964). Brown 4049f.

8197 If a broom falls across a doorstep, you'll have visitors (M, 25, Huntsville, 1948); . . . across the door . . . (M, SLC, 1950).

8198 If a straw falls out of the broom, a stranger is coming (F, Nephi, 1961).

8199 If the broom falls over, company is coming. If the mop falls over, dirty company is coming (F, Ogden, 1935).

8200 If you sweep the floor at night, you will have company (F, 23, SLC, 1964).

8201 If you are sweeping the floor and you make a black mark on the floor, happening to hit a coal or something, that is a sign that a tall person is coming, or a short person (F, Moab, 1953).

8202 It is said that when the house is most dirty, you will be sure to have visitors (F, 48, SLC, 1926).

8203 Have the house clean from top to bottom, or company will come (F, SLC, 1960).

## Fire, Fireplace

8204 A hot cinder popping out of the fire is a token of a coming guest (F, 47, SLC, 1964). Cf. Brown 4063.

8205 When a fire burns without blowing, you'll have company without knowing (M, 50, American Fork, 1947).

8206 If there is coal soot on the bars of your fireplace, a visitor is coming (F, 50, Eng, SLC, 1964).

8207 Soot hanging from the front grate bars of a fireplace while the fire is burning is a sign that a stranger is coming to the house (M, Ogden, 1958).

## Miscellaneous

8208 If you go visiting, and go in one door and out the other, you will return (F, Farmington, 1959).

8209 Visitors come in threes (F, 18, SLC, 1950).

8210 If you dream of the dead, the living will visit (F, SLC, 1959); . . . it means a visit from a good friend of the deceased (F, 45, SLC, 1964).

8211 Two bells ringing in a house at the same time foretell a parting (M, 20, SLC).

8212 If you talk about someone, they'll soon appear (F, 20, SLC, 1958).

8213 Misplacing words while you are talking is the sign of a coming stranger (F, SLC).

8214 Invite the first person who comes to your door in for a visit, or you may be turning away luck (F, SLC, 1960).

8215 If the floor creaks, company is coming (M, 17, SLC, 1958).

8216  Entertain a guest three days before asking him a question.  Failure to do so will bring sorrow to your home (F, Eng, Brigham City, 1960).

8217  If a child crawls in the house, you are going to have visitors (M, 33, Gr, SLC, 1963).

8218  If a woman comes visiting first thing in the morning, you'll have company all day long (F, 54, Midvale, 1920).

8219  Keep a free seat for an unexpected guest (M, SLC, 1961).

8220  If you accidentally find two chairs with their backs together, you will have company (F, 18, SLC, 1950); . . . put chairs back to back, a stranger is coming to call (F, Ogden, 1960).

8221  As a woman rocks in her rocking chair, if it moves across the floor, this means she should be expecting company (F, 89, SLC, 1964).  Heard in South Dakota, 1927.

8222  If you don't sit down when you go to someone's house, you will bring them bad luck (M, 54, Benjamin, 1923).

8223  If you raise a flag pole, a distant friend will visit you (F, 85, SLC, 1964).

8224  If you watch for a person to come, that person will not come (F, 12, SLC, 1964).

8225  If you leave something behind you when you leave a place, it shows that you enjoyed your visit (F, 31, Logan, 1950).

8226  If you drop a pin and pick it up, someone will visit you that day (F, SLC, 1947).

## DAYS OF THE WEEK, TIME OF DAY

8227  If on Monday morning a woman comes to your house before a man, you will have bad luck that week (M, 37, SLC, 1955).

8228  If you have company on Monday, so goes the rest of the week (F, 67, Devils Slide, 1965).  Brown 3894.

8229  If you have company at your house on Sunday, it means you'll have company every night during the coming week (F, 49, SLC, 1924).

8230  It is a bad omen to accept company on a Saturday night, which is bath night (F, Norw, SLC, 1910).

## HOLIDAYS

### Christmas and New Year's

8231  On holidays a woman must never walk in a door of a house before a man.  If you don't have a man with you, get one off the street or have the woman wait outside until one shows up (F, 20, SLC, 1961).

8232  A dark-haired man should be the first to enter your house on Christmas day (F, 20, SLC, 1961).

8233  When Mrs. A was a small girl, they used to go out singing Christmas carols Christmas Eve, and then when they got home Christmas morning, her mother wouldn't let them back in the house until a dark-haired man came and wished them Merry Christmas (F, 80, Eng, Richfield, 1964).

8234  It is good luck to see a member of the opposite sex who is not one of your own family on New Year's Day morning (F, SLC, 1964).

8235  If you visit someone on New Year's Eve, you must eat something or you will take the happiness of the house away with you (F, SLC, 1959).

8236  If a person comes to your house on New Year's Day and says "Good Evening" when it's still afternoon, you will have bad luck the rest of the year (F, Gr, SLC, 1951).

8237  If there is a dark man and a blonde woman present at a New Year's party, the following year will be a lucky year (M, 55, Centerfield, 1964).

## FIRST-FOOTING AT NEW YEAR'S

### Gift Bearers

8238  The first person entering your home on New Year's will determine your luck for the coming year, according to the luck of the person entering the home (F, 42, Gr, SLC, 1964).

8239  At twelve o'clock midnight on New Year's Eve the patriarch of the family was to be the first person to go out the back door of the house and come in the front door.  This action was to bring good luck to the family (F, Eng, SLC, 1966).

8240  When visiting on New Year's Day, be sure to carry a present for the first person you visit; otherwise, the first person will have bad luck (M, 69, Scot, SLC, 1964).

8241  It is good luck to have a dark man be first to enter the house at the first of the year bearing a gift for the house (F, 49, Gr, Midvale, 1935).

8242  A family will have good luck for the next year if the first person to come into their home after midnight New Year's Eve has dark hair and is carrying something black in his hands (M, 23, SLC, 1964).

8243  On New Year's Day a man has to walk from the front door to the back with a piece of coal before anyone can enter (F, SLC, 1961).

8244  The first caller on the first day of a new year should bear gifts of coal, matches and wood so the new year will be one of plenty (F, 55, Eng, SLC, 1963).

8245  For good luck give one piece of coal to the first male to visit your home after New Year's arrival (F, SLC, 1964).

8246  A custom of the Irish on New Year's Day is that the first person to enter your home that day will bring with him a piece of coal, a piece of shortbread, and a bottle of ginger beer. This signifies that you will enjoy food, drink, and heat throughout the year. The greeting is "Lang may your lum reek" which means "Long may your chimney smoke" (F, SLC, 1963).

8247   The first foot through the door after midnight on New Year's Eve should be a man carrying matches and coal. It will bring you good luck for one year (F, SLC, 1969).

8248   On New Year's Eve the first man through the door must pay the owner of the house a dime, or they will have bad luck the rest of the year (F, 23, Dan, SLC, 1963).

8249   The first person to enter a house on New Year's Day will carry a rock in with him. It is said that the house will have as much gold in it as the weight of the rock (F, Gr, SLC, 1964).

8250   If the first person that comes to your home after the New Year does not bring you any food, you will have bad luck all year (F, SLC, 1958).

8251   A dark-complexioned man should open the door first on New Year's and bring fresh fruit into the house (F, Eng, Hooper, 1963).

## Dark-Complexioned First-Footers

8252   The first person to enter your home after the old year ebbs is your "first foot." For a prosperous year he must be a "dark man" (F, 55, Ir, SLC, 1963); . . . He brings good luck all through the coming year (F, SLC, 1957); . . . a brunette (M, SLC, 1957). Cf. Brown 3887.

8253   It is always good luck for the entire year if a black-haired person enters the door first after New Year's strikes (M, SLC, 1961).

8254   On New Year's Eve, the first tall, dark stranger that comes to your home will bring you good luck (M, 23, SLC, 1963).

8255   The first foot over your doorstep on New Year's Day determines your fate for the year. If it is a dark man, you will have extremely good luck. The Irish always arrange to have the father of the house or some neighbor man to be the first one over their doorstep (M, 64, SLC, 1963).

8256   If the first person to enter your house on New Year's Day is dark-complected, you will have a bad year (F, 78, SLC).

## Fair-Complexioned Visitors

8257   If a light-headed person enters the door first after New Year's strikes, it means the household will have seven years of bad luck (M, SLC, 1961).

8258   On New Year's Day, if the first stranger to enter your house is blue eyed, it means good luck for the coming new year (F, 63, SLC, 1912).

8259   If on New Year's a light-complexioned person comes to your door, it means good luck (F, Farmington, 1959).

8260   It is bad luck for a light-complexioned person to bring you home on New Year's Eve (M, 61, Eng, SLC, 1964).

8261   Don't let a blond man in your house on New Year's Day. It's bad luck (F, 80, Eng, Midvale).

8262   On New Year's morning if a fair person, especially a woman, comes to your door, it will bring bad luck for the year (F, Woods Cross, 1953).

## Male Visitors, Female Visitors

8263   If the first person to come in your home after the New Year is a man, it will bring good luck (F, 52, Provo, 1920); . . . it will bring a prosperous and happy year (M, 52, Du, SLC, 1964). Cf. Brown 3886, 3888.

8264   On the first day of the New Year if the first person to enter your home is a boy, your home will be strong as a rock (F, Gr, SLC, 1920).

8265   After New Year's if the man comes through the door before the woman, it is bad luck (F, 61, SLC, 1964).

8266   The first person in your house on New Year's Day will be a man with a black hat (F, Provo, 1937).

8267   On the first day of the New Year, if the first person to enter your home is a girl, this will bring good luck (F, Gr, SLC, 1920).

8268   On New Year's Day the first one to enter your house should be a dark woman. She should come in the back door and walk straight through the house without speaking to anyone. She should go out the front door, and doing this, she will take away all the bad luck for that year (F, 58, SLC, 1964).

8269   If the first person to enter your home in the New Year is a woman, you will have a year of troubles and bad luck (M, 52, Du, SLC, 1964). Cf. Brown 3890.

8270   If a woman comes on the first day of the year, someone will come every day in the year (M, 37, SLC, 1947). Cf. Brown 3884.

8271   On New Year's Eve, if a chimney sweeper comes to your door, the rest of the year will be lucky (F, 37, Eng, SLC, 1964).

## FRIENDS AND ENEMIES

### Various

8272   When something is wrong between two people, you can feel it in your bones (M, 21, SLC, 1964).

8273   If there is someone who does not like you, they will throw soap and water outside while you are walking by. This means that you will have bad luck (F, Gr, SLC, 1962).

8274 Never shake a stick at a close friend or an enemy, or the bad luck will fall on you (F, SLC, 22, SLC, 1962).

8275 If you enter into another's quarrels, and try to set them right, you will lose both friends (M, 60, SLC, 1925).

8276 When you lend money to anyone, he becomes your enemy (F, 51, W. Jordan, 1942).

8277 Hum a tune you heard from an old actor, and you will lose a friend (F, Heber, 1930).

8278 People born in the same month do not get along (M, 21, SLC, 1959).

## BODY INDICATORS

8279 If you dream of being in public not fully clothed, be cautious of word and act, or gossip will distress you (F, SLC, 1957).

8280 If a woman's hair is parted crooked, there will be a quarrel at her home (F, 52, SLC, 1935).

### Facial Parts

8281 If your face burns, someone is thinking about you (F, Murray, 1950); . . . someone is talking about you (F, 24, SLC). Brown 3529f.

8282 If your eye itches, someone wants to see you and can't (F, 61, SLC, 1927).

8283 If your cheeks burn, it is the sign of someone talking about you (F, 63, Riverside, 1920).

8284 If your chin itches, it is a sign you may lose a friend (F, 53, Monroe, 1964).

8285 A mole on the chin means your friends hold you in high esteem (M, SLC).

8286 If your left ear feels warm, someone is talking bad about you; if your right ear feels warm, someone is talking good about you (F, SLC, 1958).

8287 If your ears sting or itch someone is talking about you somewhere (M, 44, SLC).

8288 If your ears are cold, people are not talking well of you (F, SLC, 1961).

8289 If your ear aches now and again for only a minute, someone is talking about you (F, 1960).

8290 Pinching your ear will cause ill-talkers of you to bite their tongues (M, 40, SLC).

8291 Someone is thinking about you if your ear burns (F, 65, Eureka, 1965).

8292 If your ears burn, someone is talking about you (F, Farmington, 1959); . . . if it's the right ear, someone is saying nice things . . . (M, 32, SLC, 1965). Brown 3509f.

8293 If your ears burn, someone is saying unkind things about you (F, SLC, 1961);

. . . you are being gossiped about (F, SLC, 1960); . . . someone is speaking ill of you (F, 67, SLC, 1936); . . . if it's the right ear, it is bad (F, Farmington, 1959). Cf. Brown 3517.

8294 If your ears burn, someone is talking about you. If it is the right ear, it's for spite; if the left, it is for love (F, 56, Centerville). Brown 3506, cf. 3514.

8295 If your left ear burns, someone is talking ill of you (M, SLC). Cf. Brown 3507, 3513, 3515, 3519.

8296 If your ear itches, it means that somebody is talking about you (M, Helper, 1958). Cf. Brown 3505.

8297 If your ears itch, someone is saying bad things about you (F, SLC).

8298 When your ear itches, someone is talking about you; the right one, it's favorable; the left one, it is unfavorable (M, SLC, 1958); . . . left ear for spite, right ear, things are all right (F, 52, SLC, 1925). Cf. Brown 3512.

8299 If your left ear itches, someone is talking about you who loves you (F, 82, It, Bingham, 1916).

8300 When your ears ring, someone is talking about you (F, 19, SLC, 1953); Bells ringing in your ears means . . . (M, 19, SLC, 1964); . . . someone is gossiping about you (F, 49, Gr, Midvale, 1930).

8301 When you hear ringing in your ears, someone is praising you (F, 52, SLC).

8302 If your ear rings, it is a sign that someone is talking about you. If it is the right ear, they are saying good things about you; if it is the left ear, they are saying bad things (F, SLC, 1959).

8303 If your right ear rings, someone is saying something bad about you (F, 45, Ger, SLC, 1963); . . . someone is speaking evil of you (F, 47, Midvale, 1928).

8304 If your left ear rings, someone is saying something nice about you (F, Ger, SLC, 1963).

8305 If your ear rings, someone is thinking of you (M, SLC, 1959). Brown 3508.

8306 If there is ringing in your ears, have someone say a number quickly while the ear is still ringing. Count the number off in the alphabet, and someone whose name starts with that letter is thinking of you (F, Holladay, 1960).

8307 When you hear a ringing noise in your ear, someone is talking about you. To find out who it is, you say several names. When the ringing noise stops, the last name you said is the one who was talking about you (M, 49, SLC, 1963).

8308 When one's ears tingle, lies are being told about him (F, 19, SLC).

8309  If your right ear tingles, somebody is speaking well of you; if your left ear tingles, someone is speaking ill of you (F, 28, Riverside, 1949).

8310  If your nose itches, someone is watching you (F, 19, SLC, 1964).

8311  If your nose twitches, someone is saying something nice about you (F, SLC, 1963). Cf. Brown 3525.

8312  If your nose itches, you'll shake hands with a friend (F, 43, Delta, 1930).

8313  If your nose itches, you will shortly be crossed, or vexed by a fool (F, 29, SLC, 1964).

8314  If your nose itches, you are going to have a quarrel (F, 20, Vernal, 1950); . . . you are going to have a fight (M, Midvale, 1950); . . . you will get into an argument (M, 33, Gr, SLC, 1963). Brown 3527.

8315  When your nose itches, it is a sign that someone is talking about you, or thinking about you (M, 22, SLC, 1963); . . . someone is gossiping about you (Scofield, 1938).  Brown 3526.

8316  If your nose itches, someone is talking about you.  If it itches on the right side, the person is saying good things about you, but if it itches on the left side, the person is saying bad things about you (F, 21, Bountiful, 1960).

8317  If you have an itchy nose, your girl friend is talking about you (M, 42, SLC, 1963).

8318  A pimple on your tongue means someone is talking about you (F, Midvale).

8319  If you bite your tongue accidentally, you will be quarreling with someone (M, 30, Ethiopian, SLC, 1964).

8320  Itchy lips means someone is talking about you (F, 30, SLC, 1945).

8321  When a person gossips, the darning needle or dragonfly will sew up his lips (F, 88, SLC, 1963).

8322  If you dream about your teeth, you have enemies (F, 35, Bountiful, 1955).

8323  If you dream that you lose a tooth, you will lose a friend (M, Provo, 1953). Cf. Brown 3531.

## Arms, Hands, Feet

8324  If you break arms when you pass anyone, it is the sign of a quarrel (F, 21, Morgan, 1960).

8325  If your arm itches, someone is talking about you (M, SLC, 1960).

8326  Don't look at other people's hands; it is likely to start a fight (M, SLC, 1960).

8327  Itching of the palm is a sign of a fight (F, 55, SLC, 1964).

8328  If hands are crossed by two persons while reaching for food, they will quarrel (M, 53, SLC, 1936).

8329  Your hand will itch when somebody near or far away is thinking about you (M, SLC, 1959).

8330  If your right palm itches, it means you will meet a friend (M, 42, SLC, 1964).

8331  If your right hand itches, you will shake hands with a friend (F, Moab, 1953); . . . an old acquaintance (F, 49, Gr, Midvale, 1929).

8332  If your palm itches, that means that someone is talking about you (M, 20, Cedar City, 1964).

8333  Don't use your left hand to shake hands in a greeting, or the greeting will not be a friendly one and you'll depart as foes (F, 43, SLC, 1964).

8334  Every white spot on your pointer fingernail represents a foe (F, SLC, 1958); . . . on your thumbnail represents a friend (F, SLC, 1958). Brown 3532f.

8335  Biting of the thumb is considered a sign of picking a quarrel (F, 83, SLC, 1950).

8336  If your left foot goes to sleep, an enemy is thinking of you (F, Axtell, 1958).

8337  If you put your feet up on a table, you'll get in a fight (F, 19, SLC, 1962).

8338  If your big toe itches, your honey is thinking of you (F, 74, SLC, 1907).

## BODILY FUNCTIONS

### Various

8339  If you are walking down the street or sidewalk, don't step on the cracks, or you'll have a fight with someone (F, 20, SLC, 1953).

      Editors' note:  Entry No. 12574, below, dealing with stepping on a metal slug in the pavement, might more appropriately have appeared here.  It could not be moved, however, because of considerations in numbering and indexing.

8340  When you have the hiccoughs, someone is talking about you (F, 68, SLC, 1964); . . . someone is thinking of you (F, SLC, 1930).

8341  When you sneeze, someone is talking about you (F, 45, Ja, SLC, 1963).

8342  When you have a cold shiver, it means that someone is talking about you (F, 20, SLC, 1955).

8343  To change from one side to another while walking with a friend will bring bad luck (M, 20, SLC, 1964).

## Dreaming

8344  To dream you hate a person denotes you will always have a friend in time of need (F, 43, SLC, 1964).

8345  To dream of burns is a sign of a valuable friendship in your life (F, SLC, 1957).

8346  To dream you are dying means empty promises will be fulfilled (F, 80, Pleasant Grove).

8347  To dream of an angel is a fortunate dream, and applies especially to affairs of the heart and friendships (F, SLC, 1957).

8348  If you dream of a calm wind, you'll have a helping friend; a rough wind, you'll have a spiteful friend (F, 82, It, Bingham, 1916).

8349  Dream of dirty water and you will have an enemy (F, 60, Weber).

8350  To dream of washing dirty diapers means that someone is going to be underhanded, or pull a dirty deal in the near future (F, 22, SLC, 1952).

8351  Seeing one in a dream means an argument with that person soon (F, Ir, SLC, 1960).

## Talking, Thinking, Calling by Name

8352  If you call someone by the wrong name, the person whose name you used is thinking about you (F, 68, SLC, 1964); . . . is talking about you (F, SLC, 1957). Brown 3494f.

8353  If you say a person's name when you mean someone else, it means you are thinking about them (F, Ogden, 1961).

8354  The first person you think of after you wake up in the morning is the first person you'll see (F, 40, SLC, 1937).

8355  To find a red stone is a sign that someone is thinking of your brother (M, SLC, 1959).

8356  If you gossip about a certain person, that person is bound to show up (F, 45, Ja, SLC, 1963).

8357  It is bad luck to talk about a preacher behind his back (F, 21, SLC, 1964).

## CLOTHING

### Various

8358  To find some buttons means new friends (F, Axtell, 1958).

8359  If you put your clothes on backwards, leave them that way, or you will lose a friend temporarily (F, 52, SLC, 1916).

8360  If you have your dress or any clothes mended on your back, you will be ill spoken of (F, SLC, 1960).

8361  If you lose your belt, you will also lose a friend (F, Ephraim, 1960).

8362  Losing your apron means losing your best friend (M, 44, SLC, 1963).

8363  Give a tie to bind your friendship together (M, 20, SLC, 1964).

8364  A person should not pass handkerchiefs from one to another, for this may cause the breaking of friendship (F, 48, SLC, 1963).

### Footgear

8365  If you put your shoes on the table, there'll be a quarrel (M, SLC, 1959); . . . new shoes on the table, you will have a fight (F, 52, SLC, 1920).

8366  Take someone else's shoes off the table and there is bound to be a fight (F, 19, SLC, 1963).

8367  Shoes placed upside down will cause an argument (F, 27, SLC, 1965).

8368  Never let a good friend give you a pair of shoes. You will have a quarrel (F, 66, Bear River City, 1910).

8369  If your shoelace is untied, someone is thinking of you (F, 52, SLC); . . . someone is talking about you (F, SLC, 1962); If the right shoe is unlaced, somebody is talking about you (M, 54, Roy, 1925). Brown 3534ff.

8370  It is bad luck to give a friend a pair of slippers unless you put a penny in the toe, because they will walk away (F, SLC, 1935).

## JEWELRY AND INTIMATE POSSESSIONS

### Jewelry, Rings, Gems

8371  If the clasp on your necklace turns forward and is facing others, someone is thinking about you (F, Tooele, 1964).

8372  If you let someone wear your ring, it will cut your friendship (M, SLC, 1957).

8373  To draw a ring from a person's finger severs friendship (F, SLC, 1961).

8374  Do not remove a ring from the finger of a friend, or you will have an argument (F, Ir, SLC, 1960).

8375  If you want friends, wear a topaz (F, Moab, 1964).

8376  If a strand of pearls breaks and scatters, gather them all up, or your family will be split up (F, 22, Hurricane, 1952).

### Hairpins, Purses, Combs, Etc.

8377  If you find a hairpin, you will find a friend (F, Nephi, 1961). Cf. Brown 3498.

8378  If you lose a hairpin, you will lose a friend (F, Nephi, 1961). Cf. Brown 3501f.

8379    If you drop a hairpin, you must not pick it up, or you will lose a fight (F, 27, SLC, 1965).

8380    If someone dislikes you, never take anything such as candy, or a comb that they might offer (F, 20, Amer Ind, SLC, 1963).

8381    Whenever giving gloves or a purse to anyone, you must have your palm crossed with silver, or you will have bad luck and your friendship will be broken (F, 59, SLC, 1964); Don't give someone a purse without putting a penny in it, or it will break up a friendship (F, 44, Ogden, 1935).

8382    If you forget your gloves at a friend's house, then go back for them, you will never visit that friend again (M, Draper, 1961).

## DOMESTIC

### Food, Eating, Etc.

8383    To dream of eating is a sign of family quarrels.  But if you see other people eating in your dream, it shows a valuable friendship (F, SLC, 1957).

8384    A person should not pass vinegar from one to another, for this may cause the breaking of friendship (F, 48, SLC, 1963).

8385    When a woman burns light bread, so that the crust is black, it is a sign she will fly into a rage before the day is over (M, 24, Ogden, 1961).

8386    While cutting bread if you cut your finger, you will lose a friend (F, 80, SLC).

8387    If you take a piece of bread, if you butter it and take a bite out of it, then set it down and forget about it and take another piece, without thinking, and butter it and take a bite, it means that you have a hungry friend (F, 61, Ogden, 1960).

8388    If the biscuits you just baked burn, it means that somebody is mad at you (F, 85, Charleston, 1972).  Brown 3549.

8389    When the teakettle sings on the stove and makes strange noises, someone is talking about you (F, SLC, 1960).

### Salt, Pepper, Paprika, Etc.

8390    Take a box of salt as a present to a friend in his new home.  Salt is believed close to friendship (F, 54, SLC, 1924).

8391    Throw some salt over your left shoulder, and you will have new friends (M, Provo, 1960).

8392    Never pass a salt shaker and give it to another in the hand; set it down, or else you will have a quarrel with that person (F, SLC, 1960).

8393    If you take a salt shaker directly from another hand, you will have a fight with that person unless you throw salt over the left shoulder (M, SLC, 1930s).

8394    A person should not pass salt from one to another, for this may cause the breaking of friendship (F, 48, SLC, 1963).

8395    Never accept salt and pepper shaker when passed to you directly into your hand. Have them placed on the table near you. If accepted into your hand from someone else's hand, you will have trouble with the other person (F, 74, SLC, 1907).

8396    To spill pepper is a sign of a fight (M, Bountiful, 1960).

8397    If you borrow sugar and then return it, your friendship will be broken (F, Dan, SLC).

8398    If you use paprika to season food, you will have an argument with someone of the Latin race (F, SLC, 1961).

### Borrowing, Lending, Spilling Salt

8399    Never lend salt; always give it away, as it breaks friendships (F, SLC, 1958).

8400    To loan salt to a neighbor means that you will be disgraced by that neighbor (F, 63, SLC, 1920).

8401    Never borrow salt from a neighbor; you may make an enemy (F, 70, SLC, 1964); . . . you'll fight (M, Hyrum, 1948).

8402    When you borrow salt, it's a sign of a quarrel (F, SLC, 1959).

8403    If you borrow salt, it will break your friendship with the person you borrowed it from (M, Sandy, 1900).

8404    Never return borrowed salt; if you do, your friendship will be severed (F, Moab, 1953); . . . you'll quarrel (F, 64, Granite, 1918); . . . pay back sugar instead (F, SLC, 1928); . . . it will break your friendship (F, Axtell, 1958).

8405    Spill salt, and there'll be a quarrel (F, SLC, 1960); . . . to avoid a quarrel, throw salt over your left shoulder (F, SLC, 1958).  Brown 3551f.

8406    Don't tip over the salt, or you'll quarrel with someone.  If you do tip it over, throw some salt over your right shoulder (F, 51, Park City, 1922).

8407    If salt is spilled at the dinner table, it means that there will be a fight among the members of the family (M, 20, SLC, 1950); . . . you will get in an argument that day (F, SLC, 1938).

8408    If salt is spread out over any surface, it's a poor sign and will mean a feud with someone (M, 63, Russ, SLC, 1964).

8409    Throw some of the spilled salt over your left shoulder, and you will have new friends (M, SLC, 1959).

8410    If you spill salt, sprinkle it with sugar, so that it won't spoil your friendship (F, 67, Devils Slide, 1965).

Sharp Objects, Knives, Etc.

8411 If you give your friend something sharp like a razor, it will cut your friendship off (F, 62, Vernal); . . . break the friendship (F, Fillmore, 1960); . . . sever your friendship (M, 19, SLC, 1957); . . . sour the friendship (F, SLC, 1961).  Brown 3578.

8412 A sharp gift given at a wedding shower will break up your friendship (F, Eng, Weber, 1964); If you send knives to a wedding, it cuts your friendship.  To redeem the friendship, send a penny in return (F, 21, SLC, 1961).

8413 Never hand any person a sharp object, or it means that you cut friendship. Instead lay the sharp object down and let the other person pick it up (F, 51, Park City, 1920).

8414 If someone gives a sharp instrument to a person, it requires a penny in return or their friendship will be forfeited (F, 22, SLC, 1964); . . . gives you a sharp instrument, pay them for it . . . (F, Moab, 1953); . . . if the friend doesn't give you a coin, you'll quarrel within a year (F, SLC, 1964); . . . a silver coin . . . (F, SLC, 1956).  Brown 3577.

8415 You will break a friendship if you give something sharp, unless you put a penny in it (F, SLC, 1960); You will quarrel . . . (F, 61, SLC, 1964).

8416 If you borrow something sharp from a friend either give them a penny for it, or have them lend a penny too, or it will sever the friendship (F, 1957).

8417 It will bring bad luck to a friendship to give someone a knife as a present (F, 20, SLC, 1954); Giving someone . . . cuts the friendship (F, 50, SLC, 1963); . . . a pocket knife . . . (M, Tooele, 1964).

8418 Never give anything sharp like knives, or you'll quarrel (F, 74, Granite).

8419 If you give a person a new carving set, you should include a penny in it.  If you do not, you are cutting your bonds of friendship (F, 21, SLC, 1955); . . . give a penny for each knife in a set of knives . . . (F, 19, SLC, 1958).

8420 If someone gives you a pocketknife, you must give something personal in return so it will not cut friendship (F, SLC, 1962).

Silverware

8421 Never hand the blade of a knife to a friend, because the friendship will end if you do (F, 54, SLC, 1948).

8422 If one person drops a knife, then someone else should pick it up.  If the same person who drops the knife picks it up, then they will have bad words with a friend (F, 28, Scot, SLC, 1964).

8423 While you are eating, if you drop your knife, you will have a quarrel with a lady friend that day (M, 42, Du, SLC, 1964).

8424 If you drop a knife, it means that you have an enemy (M, 26, SLC, 1963).

8425 To lay a knife and fork crosswise is to bring about troubles and crosses (F, 74, SLC, 1965).

8426 If two knives cross on the table, it means an argument (F, 35, Murray, 1964); . . . you will have a fight (M, 44, Roy, 1938); . . . it is a sign of a serious quarrel (M, Odgen, 1958); . . . you have made an enemy (M, Park City, 1957); . . . sharp words with someone (F, 25, SLC, 1964); . . . will cut a friendship (F, 43, SLC, 1964).

8427 Don't cross a knife while eating; it means you will fight with your dinner partner (M, SLC, 1960).

8428 If accidentally two knives lie with crossed blades on a table or somewhere, it means a fight among family members or friends will soon start (F, 47, Swiss, SLC, 1965); Don't cross knives while cooking . . . (F, 80, Eng, Centerville, 1963).

8429 Two knives at one place on the table mean there will be a fight (F, SLC, 1959).

8430 If you stir anything with a knife, you'll surely stir up some strife (F, 25, SLC, 1964).

8431 Turn sharp knives away from you in the drawer if you would avoid sharp tongues and gossip (F, SLC, 1960).

8432 If a knife's sharp edge is not pointing down, it will cut a friendship (F, 20, SLC, 1964).

8433 Never borrow a knife, for it will cut your friendship (F, 70, Croydon, 1965).

8434 If you drop a fork, you're going to have a fight (M, 23, Du, SLC, 1963).

8435 If you drop a fork while eating, you'll have a quarrel with a male friend that day (52, Du, SLC, 1964).

Scissors, Pins, Needles

8436 If you pick up a pair of open scissors, you'll cut off a friendship (M, 56, SLC, 1965).

8437 One should not hand scissors to another person.  If this happens, their friendship will be cut (F, Gr, Magna, 1961).

8438 Never give anybody a present with a sharp edge, such as scissors, unless you put some money in with it, or it will cut your friendship (F, SLC, 1946); . . . without a penny in return . . . (F, 40, SLC, 1950).

8439 You should never leave a pair of scissors lying open, because it means you are being talked about (F, 41, Gr, SLC, 1964).

8440 Pick up a pin or lose a friend (F, SLC, 1920); Pass up a pin, pass up a friend (M, SLC, 1959).

8441    Pick up a pin, and you'll win a friend (F, SLC, 1957).

8442    If you find a straight pin, pick it up, and you will find a new friend. If it is bent, he will be crooked (M, Clearfield, 1933).

8443    A person should not pass pins from one to another, for this may cause the breaking of friendship (F, 48, SLC, 1963).

8444    When sweeping, never sweep a pin out of your door, or you will lose a friend (F, Santaquin, 1925).

8445    If you pick up a pin or another sharp object with the point towards you, you will receive some sharp remarks from someone (F, SLC, 1958).

8446    Give pins to a friend and the friendship ends (F, Bear River City, 1957); . . . it will pierce your friendship (F, 63, SLC, 1915); . . . it will puncture a friendship (F, Logan, 1957). Cf. Brown 3582.

8447    If a friend gives you a decorative pin or a writing pen or anything sharp, your friendship will end, unless you give one penny in return (F, Ogden, 1961).

8448    If you give a person a pin or needle, you must prick both your hand and the other person's, or you will have a continuing feud with this person (M, 63, Russ, SLC, 1964).

8449    If you drop a box of pins and they go all over the floor, it's a sign of a quarrel. If someone helps pick them up, it breaks the quarrel (F, 52, Eng, SLC, 1963).

8450    When sewing and you drop your pins, the next person you meet you will quarrel with (F, 48, Murray, 1964).

8451    If you do not return a borrowed safety pin, you are going to lose the friendship of the person loaning it to you (F, 24, SLC, 1960). Cf. Brown 3582.

8452    If you borrow a needle and do not return it, you will become an enemy of the person loaning it to you (F, 24, SLC, 1956).

8453    Never return a borrowed needle, for it will break a friendship (F, SLC, 1960).

8454    If someone gives you a needle, you must pay for it, or you will have bad luck (F, 19, SLC, 1958).

8455    If you take a needle from someone, there will be a fight (F, 27, SLC, 1940s).

8456    A person should not pass needles from one to another, for this may cause the breaking of friendship (F, 48, SLC, 1963).

### Washing, Wiping, Etc.

8457    If you wash together, you will be friends forever (M, 18, SLC, 1964). Brown 3560.

8458    When two people wash their hands together in the same bowl, they will quarrel before nightfall (M, 21, Provo, 1959). Cf. Brown 3555f, 3559.

8459    Do not empty the water that someone else has washed in, as a quarrel will follow (F, Manti, 1956).

8460    Don't wash the cup of a friend, or else you will lose one (M, Provo, 1960).

8461    Two people who wipe on a towel together will be friends forever (F, Moab, 1953). Brown 3568.

8462    If two people wipe on the same towel at the same time, they will have a quarrel (F, Axtell, 1958). Brown 3561, 3570.

8463    If two people use the same towel, they will soon quarrel unless the towel is twisted (F, SLC, 1962). Brown 3571.

8464    If you dry hands on a towel with someone else, it's a sign you will have a fight with each other (F, Uintah Co, 1927). Brown 3572.

8465    Don't dry your hands on a towel; it will break up friendships (M, SLC, 1964). Cf. Brown 3566.

8466    Never take soap from a person's hand, because if you do, a terrible argument will follow (M, 64, 1963).

8467    Never take soap from a person's hand, or you will lose their friendship (F, 32, Gr, SLC, 1964); When passing soap to someone, put the soap down and let the person pick it up, or you will have a quarrel (F, 56, SLC, 1964); . . . you will have a fight (F, Gr, Magna, 1961).

8468    Do not leave drawers or cupboard drawers open, for other people will gossip bad things about you (F, Gr, Magna, 1961).

### Dishcloths, Brooms

8469    If you drop a dishcloth, you'll have an argument with a family member (F, 52, Honeyville, 1922).

8470    Buy a broom in May, sweep your friends away (M, 24, SLC, 1965).

8471    To borrow a broom, you will sweep your friends away (F, SLC, 1915).

### Chairs, Mirrors

8472    Put a slice of lemon under the chair of a visitor to insure his friendship (F, 48, SLC, 1964).

8473    To turn a chair around on one leg is always bad luck and leads to family quarrels (F, 19, Magna, 1960).

8474    To turn a chair around means you are going to have a fight (M, 26, SLC,). Cf. Brown 3586.

8475    If you stand looking at your reflection in a mirror, side by side with a friend, you will have an argument shortly (F, Ir, SLC, 1960); . . . you will have a fight (F, Gr, Tooele, 1961).

8476 If you break a looking glass, you'll lose your best friend (F, 74, Venice, 1915).

## Fire, Matches

8477 To dream about fire is the sign of a quarrel (F, 39, SLC, 1964). Cf. Brown 3542.

8478 If you dream of fire, enemies are trying to harm you (F, Park City, 1957); . . . you will have an enemy waiting for you when you wake up (M, SLC, 1958).

8479 When a fire pops, someone is mad at you (M, 45, Murray, 1940). Brown 3545.

8480 If the fire pops, there will be a quarrel in the family (M, 44, SLC, 1962).

8481 To put the poker and tongs on the same side of the fireplace will mean a quarrel in the house (F, 29, SLC, 1964).

8482 If you spill a box of matches, you'll have a fight with somebody, or else you'll have trouble (F, Ger, SLC, 1950).

## Various Domestic Portents

8483 If an umbrella is opened inside a house, there will be a quarrel (F, Norw, SLC, 1960).

8484 To put an umbrella on the bed causes disputes (M, 22, Midvale, 1964). Brown 3587.

8485 You should leave a friend's house by the same door you entered, because failure to do so will result in a serious quarrel (F, 1960); . . . you will break your friendship (F, Eng, Hooper, 1963).

## ANIMAL AND PLANT PORTENTS

## Various Animals, Birds

8486 Dreaming of rats means the making of enemies (F, 53, SLC, 1963). Cf. Brown 3609.

8487 If you dream of a cat, you have a gossip for a friend (F, 82, It, SLC, 1963).

8488 To dream of a cat means sudden deceit from someone in whom you trust (F, 80, Pleasant Grove, 1961).

8489 If you dream of cats, it is the sign you are going to get into a fight (F, 54, Ger, SLC, 1963).

8490 If you get a cat from somebody, give him some money to avoid future fights (M, 57, Gr, SLC, 1963).

8491 If you dream of a dog, you have a good friend (F, 83, It, SLC, 1963).

8492 If you dream of being bitten by a vicious dog, it means one of your friends is going to turn on you (F, 60, SLC, 1964).

8493 If you dream of a horse, you have a strong reliable friend (F, 83, It, SLC, 1963); . . . a good friend (F, 48, SLC, 1960).

8494 If a rooster crows three times, someone has been betrayed (M, SLC, 1958).

8495 If you dream of a bird, you have a weak friend (F, 82, It, SLC, 1963).

8496 If you dream of eggs, you will quarrel with a friend (F, SLC, 1960). Cf. Brown 3611.

8497 If you dream of eggs, the number of eggs you dream of tells you the number of enemies you have (F, 61, Hanksville, 1961).

## Snakes, Lizards

8498 A dream of snakes results in the making of an enemy (F, 65, Eureka, 1965).

8499 If you dream of a snake, you have a deceitful friend (F, 82, It, SLC, 1963).

8500 If you dream of snakes, it is a sign that a friend is betraying you (F, Nephi, 1961).

8501 If one dreams of snakes, he will lose a friend (F, 61, Midvale, 1921).

8502 If you dream of killing a snake, you've killed your enemy (F, Moab, 1953).

8503 If you see a snake in a dream, you have enemies. If you kill the snake, you have made a friend of an enemy (F, SLC, 1940). Cf. Brown 3617.

8504 If you dream of snakes, you have enemies; if they bite you, they will do you harm (F, SLC, 1959).

8505 If you dream you are bitten by a snake, it means you have an enemy that will get the upper hand over you (F, 60, SLC, 1964); . . . your enemy will strike soon (F, SLC, 1959). Cf. Brown 3614, 3616.

8506 When you dream about snakes but they don't bite you, you have deceitful friends. If you dream about snakes and one bites you, you will have a fight with one of your friends (F, Peoa, 1920). Cf. Brown 3616.

8507 Kill the first adder you see in the spring, and you will triumph over your enemies (M, 19, SLC, 1964). Cf. Brown 3619, 3622.

8508 To dream of lizards is a sure sign of treachery. It means that you have a secret enemy (F, 22, SLC, 1956). Cf. Brown 3613.

## Insects, Spiders

8509 If a fly flies around you, someone is worried about you and wants to see you (F, 43, SLC, 1957).

8510 A bee sting means you are being betrayed (F, 70, Bountiful, 1900s).

8511 To dream of spiders means that you have an enemy who is trying to destroy your happiness (M, 52, Du, SLC, 1964).

## Plants

8512    You can find out how many friends you have by winding the stem out of an apple (F, 23, Murray, 1963).

8513    To make a friend for life, plant a pine tree (M).

## DIVISIVE OBJECTS

### Various

8514    When walking together side by side, don't let anything higher than your head come between (M, SLC, 1958).

8515    Two people walking on either side of an obstacle means an argument (F, 41, SLC, 1963); . . . a fight (M, SLC, 1938); . . . a quarrel will part your friendship (F, 58, SLC, 1963); . . . you'll split your friendship (M, Magna).

8516    If you let someone or something come between friends while walking, the friendship will break (F, 22, SLC, 1962); . . . the friendship will end (F, 73, Scot, Ogden, 1964); . . . it will split your friendship (M, Hyde Park); . . . it will terminate the friendship (F, 20, SLC, 1964). Cf. Brown 3592.

8517    If two people are walking together and they come upon an object, and one goes on one side and the other goes on the other side, they should go back and both go on the same side, or it will cause a quarrel (F, 63, Monroe, 1964). Cf. Brown 3593, 3603.

### Posts, Poles

8518    When a couple is walking together, it is bad luck to let a post or a dog come between them (F, SLC, 1962).

8519    To walk on the opposite side of a post from a companion will bring on a quarrel (F, 46, SLC, 1939); . . . an argument (M, SLC, 1957); . . . disagreements (F, Sandy, 1957); . . . a fight (F, 42, SLC, 1964). Brown 3596f, 3599.

8520    It's bad luck to let something, such as a post or tree, come between yourself and someone else when walking together, unless you say "Bread and butter" (M, Orem, 1958); . . . they will have a fight (F, 52, Logan, 1970).

8521    When walking don't let a post separate you and your partner, or it could mean permanent separation (M, 45, SLC, 1943).

### Trees

8522    Never separate to go around a tree, or it will bring bad luck (M, 61, SLC, 1964).

8523    If two people walk around a tree on opposite sides, they will have a quarrel (F, 58, SLC, 1964); . . . fight before night (F, SLC, 1961).

8524    When two people are walking together and they come to a tree, both go on the same side, because if they go on different sides, their friendship is cut in two (F, Roosevelt, 1911); . . . the friendship will break up (F, 70, Provo, 1905); . . . it will split up the friendship (M, 28, SLC, 1963).

8525    If you're walking with a friend and come to a tree, both of you should walk on the same side of it. If one goes on one side and the other goes on the other side, they will be enemies (F, 41, SLC, 1964).

### Counteractants

8526    When an object comes between two people, they have to say "Horseler" (F, 19, SLC, 1964).

8527    If you are walking with someone and something comes between you, say "Bread and butter" so you won't quarrel (M, SLC, 1959). Brown 3605.

8528    If two people walking together down a street or walk should pass between a pole or similar object, one to either side, each should clasp his fingers together and say "Bread and butter," so they will not fight later on (F, 70, SLC, 1964).

8529    If something goes between a couple that is holding hands, the couple must say "Bread and butter," or the couple will have a fight (F, Bountiful); . . . they will be separated in the near future for a long time (M, Midvale, 1959).

8530    If you and your friend go opposite ways around an object, you will lose that friend. This can be averted if you say: "What goes up a chimney?" Then you both answer in unison and if you say the same thing, you will remain friends (M, 55, Roosevelt, 1919).

8531    If you walk hand and hand with a friend and an obstacle, such as a tree, comes between you, unless you retrace your steps, you'll lose your friendship (F, 69, SLC, 1964). First heard in Ohio, 1903.

8532    If a girl and boy are walking down a street, and a pole comes between them, they must snap fingers and say "Lucky" and make a wish, and the wish will come true (F, 18, Farmington, 1963).

## MISCELLANEOUS

8533    You should never cut or break a ribbon on a gift, or it will break the friendship with the person who gave the gift (M, 1960).

8534    Five small pebbles from a bottom of a brook will protect you from enemies (M, 42, SLC, 1964).

8535    A poorly kept fence will cause trouble between neighbors (M, 71, Pol, Provo, 1964).

8536    A broken fence between two neighbors means a broken relationship is imminent (M, 40, SLC, 1964).

INDOOR RECREATION

GAMES AND DIVERSIONS

CARDS

Various Beliefs

8537  Face cards are evil (F, 61, Richfield, 1923).

8538  It brings bad luck to play cards any place near where a murder has been committed (SLC, 1959).

8539  When a person plays cards, he is under the spell of the devil (M, SLC, 1957).

8540  Never play against a left-handed dealer (M, SLC).

8541  It is bad luck to play cards with a cross-eyed man (M, 21, SLC, 1964).

8542  It is lucky to play with cards from which you have drawn a high card (F, 34, SLC, 1964).

8543  If you get into a passion while playing cards, you will have bad luck (M, 21, SLC, 1964).

8544  Put a handkerchief on your head to change your luck when you are having bad luck at cards (F, SLC, 1957).

8545  To carry a badger's tooth in your pocket will bring you good luck at cards (F, SLC, 1964).

8546  If you wish a person to win at cards, stick a pin in his coat (M, 21, SLC, 1964).

8547  If you have bad luck at cards, you can stroke the head of a bald man, and you will have good luck (M, 47, Kearns, 1943).

8548  In cards, if you have bad luck, have someone else touch your cards (F, 20, SLC, 1960).

8549  In cards, your luck will change with a new dealer (F, 20, SLC, 1960).

8550  To change luck at cards, change decks (M, 1960).  Brown 3652.

8551  If you win the first hand at cards, you will lose in the end (M, 50, SLC, 1963).

8552  In cards it's bad luck to win the first hand (M, 22, SLC, 1957).

8553  If you sing while playing cards, you will lose the game (M, Farmington, 1959).

8554  Don't play cards on Sunday (F, 19, SLC, 1964).

8555  Unlucky in love, lucky in cards (F, 55, SLC, 1967).

Handling Cards

8556  It's bad luck to cut a deck of cards more than once (Lehi, 1957).

8557  If you cut a deck of cards thin, you'll win; and if you cut a deck of cards deep, you'll weep (M, 44, 1965).

8558  When playing cards, and the person to the right of the dealer cuts the cards, a sloppy cut is good for the person who is dealing (M, 63, SLC, 1940).

8559  When playing cards, a sloppy shuffle means a good hand for the dealer (Anon, Bear River City, 1957).

8560  If you shuffle a deck of cards three times, the person who shuffles is likely to get a good hand (F, 20, SLC, 1964).

8561  Never receive the ace of spades coming the wrong way (upside down).  If you do, turn it right side up before putting in your card hand (F, 55, SLC, 1967).

8562  It brings good luck to pick up the cards with your left hand (SLC, 1959).

8563  Bad luck when playing cards can be caused by lifting up the cards before your complete hand is dealt (F, SLC, 1959).  Brown 3650.

8564  Never look at your cards before all the cards are dealt.  It is bad luck (M, 20, SLC, 1956).

8565  Put the top card on the bottom, and the bottom card on the top before picking up a dealt hand (M, 18, SLC, 1965).

8566  To drop a card on the floor during a game is bad luck (M, SLC, 1961); . . . means you will be unlucky the rest of the game (M, 21, Sandy, 1963); . . . you will lose the game (SLC, 1959).  Cf. Brown 3651.

Special Cards

8567  There is never a good hand at cards with the four of clubs in it (M, SLC, 1959).

8568  A hand of high diamond cards means success (M, SLC, 1961).

8569  If ace, two, three, four of hearts are played consecutively, it is lucky for the dealer (M, 22, SLC, 1963).

8570  A lone ace of spades in a card player's hand is bad luck (M, Park City, 1957).

8571  A queen of hearts is the last card of life (M, Ir, SLC, 1963).

8572  In cards the queen of spades is bad luck (F, 24, SLC, 1958).

8573  The jack of spades is the devil and will bring you bad luck (F, 19, SLC, 1964).

8574  A one-eyed jack means that evil will follow you for one year (M, SLC, 1961).

CHAIRS, TABLES, SEATING

8575  You will have good luck at cards if you sit in the same direction as the bathtub (F, 54, Logan, 1952).

8576  One who is unlucky when playing cards can change his luck by changing chairs with his partner (F, Sandy, 1957).

8577    To change your luck when playing cards, walk around the chair (F, Sandy, 1957); . . . get up and walk around your chair three times (F, Park City, 1957). Brown 3648.

8578    When you are unlucky at cards, you can change your luck by standing up and walking clockwise around the chair and picking it up (M, 22, SLC, 1963).

8579    Walk once around the table to change your luck in a card game (F, Bear River City, 1957); Walk around the table three times . . . (F, Sandy, 1957). Brown 3645, 3649.

8580    To play cards on a table without a tablecloth is unlucky (M, SLC, 1964); . . . on a bare table . . . (F, 52, Joseph, 1964).

## BRIDGE

8581        Cut 'em thin,
        You're sure to win;
        Cut 'em thick,
        Lose every trick.
    (M, SLC, 1967).

8582    When playing bridge and the cards are spread out to cut to see who deals first, you have to deal the first hand with the deck that was cut, not the one that wasn't cut, or you won't have good cards (F, Monticello, 1961).

8583    A black ace fallen on the floor during a game of bridge is the sign to stop playing (M, 40, SLC, 1949).

8584    In playing bridge, if the ace, two, three, and four of a red suit fall on a trick, the trick is lucky.  Place your hand on the cards and wish.  Your wish will come true (M, SLC, 1956).

8585    If ace, two, three, four of spades are played consecutively at bridge, it is unlucky for the dealer (M, 21, SLC, 1963).

8586    When playing bridge, face in the same direction as the bathtub in the house, and you will have good luck (F, SLC, 1959); Good hands always go with the bathtub (F, SLC, 1967; . . . you will always win (F, 44, SLC, 1964).

## GAMBLING

8587    It used to be an old southern superstition that all gamblers have black legs (M, SLC, 1957).

8588    Never gamble after you have taken a bath, or you will have bad luck all the way (M, 19, Ogden, 1956).

8589    When making a wager, never touch the other man's money until you have won (M, SLC, 1957).

8590    If you lend money while playing cards, you will lose (M, 21, SLC, 1964).

8591    Gamblers turn the chair around to change their luck (F, 45, American Fork, 1960).

8592    To change bad luck at gambling, get up and walk around your chair three times (M, SLC, 1955).

8593    It is good luck when playing the slot machines to leave a few nickels, dimes, or whatever the machine pays off, in the pay-off tray.  Apparently the money in the machine is attracted to the money in the tray (M, SLC, 1967).

8594    You must, after hitting a jackpot, wipe the smile off the slot machine or you will not hit any more jackpots in the future (M, SLC, 1959).

## Poker

8595    When playing poker, never smile when you deal, or you will lose money on the hand (M, Logan, 1970).

8596    When playing poker, the player on the north side will win most of the time (M, Logan, 1970).

8597    It's bad luck to sit in the same seat in poker for any long length of time (M, SLC).

8598    In playing poker, if you are having bad luck, get up and walk around the table three times, and you will have good luck (F, 18, SLC, 1964).

8599    In poker the early winner will be the biggest loser (M, SLC).

8600    When playing poker, never count your money, or you will start losing it (M, SLC, 1959).

8601    In poker, it's bad luck for a man with a good hand to raise the bet (M, SLC, 1959).

8602    In poker, don't stack chips when winning, or it will bring bad luck (M, Magna, 1959).

8603    If a fellow goes broke in a poker game, don't lend him money, or he will end up by winning (M, SLC, 1958).

8604    A hat, a home type, should be worn while playing poker to bring the wearer luck. If a hat (usually a unique hat) isn't used at home, some other sort of strange wearing apparel is (M, SLC).

8605    Put a single dice on a stack of poker chips during a poker game, turn the dice until a win comes, and leave it on that number.  You will continue to win (M, 45, SLC, 1963).

8606    In playing poker, the number of seven and eleven are supposed to bring good luck to the person that gets them (M, 55, Centerfield, 1964).

8607    The ace of spades is bad luck in a hand of poker (M, 32, SLC, 1939); . . . means death . . . (M, 24, Provo, 1964).

8608    It is unlucky not to bet the ace of spades in poker (F, 20, SLC, 1963).

8609    If you get a pair of aces and eights in poker, you will lose.  This is what Bill Hickok had when he was killed (M, 21, SLC, 1964); . . . aces and eights in a poker hand is the death hand (M, Layton, 1958).

## Dice, Craps

8610  It is bad luck to drop the dice in a crap game (M, SLC, 1957).

8611  If in picking up dice you drop one, you will lose, for you have lost your leader (M, 23, SLC, 1958).

8612  If a person in a dice game will talk to the dice, they will bring him good luck (M, SLC, 1952).

8613  If you spit on your dice before you roll them, it will bring you luck (M, 40, SLC, 1964).

8614  A kiss or a blow on the dice before throwing will bring it up to the numbers desired (M, 24, Provo, 1964).

8615  If one throws dice seven times and wins, he should quit, or he will lose all his previous gains (M, 19, SLC, 1956).

8616  In playing with dice if a person rolls "snake eyes" (a two), that person is supposed to have bad luck (M, 55, Centerfield, 1964).

## Roulette

8617  Never stand on the right of someone who is playing roulette (M, 47, SLC, 1960).

8618  It is unlucky to bet a number on the roulette wheel right after you have won on that number (M, SLC, 1959).

8619  If a person speaks while winning at the roulette wheel, he will cease to win (M, 20, SLC, 1958).

## DANCING AND PARTIES

8620  Bad luck will follow if you cross your feet while you are dancing (F, 19, SLC, 1964). Brown 3625.

8621  A girl sinks into the earth for dancing in the church (F, Norw, SLC, 1963).

8622  Swedes always drink beer before they folk dance. It guarantees good luck (SLC, 1967).

8623  The Basque folk dancers always drink the wine out of wine glasses even after dancing around it during a performance. This is good luck (SLC, 1967).

8624  Russian folk dancers always eat caviar before they dance (SLC, 1967).

8625  If your right hand itches, you will be invited to a party (F, SLC, 1950).

8626  If you find a hairpin, you will be invited to a party (F, 1958).

## MUSIC, SINGING, WHISTLING

## Music, Singing

8627  Never play a piano piece right before a recital, or it will be a failure (F, 21, Clearfield, 1964).

8628  If you drop a song book, you will never learn a song from it (F, 53, SLC, 1921).

8629  Do not sing Christmas songs during the year (F, 73, Ger, SLC, 1964).

8630  If a person has a long narrow tongue, then he will be a good singer. He's supposed to be able to touch his nose (F, Tabiona, 1955).

8631  A man who can sing well is an honest man (M, 43, It, SLC, 1930s).

8632  Singing in the house is bad luck (M, Farmington, 1958).

8633  If you sing before getting out of bed, it will bring very bad luck (F, SLC, 1959). Cf. Brown 3086.

8634  If you sing in the morning, you'll have trouble at night (F, Ger, SLC, 1950).

8635  Never sing in the morning unless you have accomplished something worthwhile, or it's bad luck (F, 40, Cedar City, 1964).

8636  Sing before breakfast, and you will be happy the whole day through (M, 24, SLC, 1946).

8637  If you sing before breakfast, it brings bad luck before supper (F, 47, SLC, 1935).

8638  Sing before breakfast, and you'll be sad before dinner (M, 63, Salina, 1930); . . . trouble during the day (M, 22, Norw, SLC, 1965); . . . you will have sorrow before dinner (F, SLC, 1962); . . . causes anger before night (M, SLC, 1963).

8639  It is bad luck to sing at the breakfast table (F, 39, SLC, 1963). Heard in Kansas, 1931. Cf. Brown 2842, 2844.

8640  Don't sing at the dinner table, or you'll be disappointed in something (F, 52, SLC, 1935).

8641  Singing at the table means that you were born in a stable (F, 71, SLC, 1964).

8642  If you sing before you bathe, you will have good luck all your life (M, SLC, 1960).

8643  If you sing unconsciously in the bathtub, it brings good luck (F, Farmington, 1959); . . . in the shower . . . (F, 76, Glenwood, 1897).

8644  To sing in bed brings bad luck (M, SLC, 1961). Cf. Brown 3085.

## Whistling

8645  Eat the crusts of bread, and you'll be able to whistle (M, SLC, 1944).

8646  It's rude to whistle if guests are present (F, 46, SLC, 1964).

8647  It's bad luck to whistle at the table (M, Layton, 1934).

8648  Whistling in a house is to invite bad luck (F, 43, Logan, 1935); It is bad luck to whistle in a house at night (F, 29, Gr, Magna, 1964); A whistle in the house invites the devil in (M, SLC, 1959).   Brown 8488.

8649   Never whistle in the dark (F, 47, SLC). Cf. Brown 3093.

8650   If you whistle before breakfast, you will have bad luck (M, SLC, 1959).

8651   Whistling in a chapel of a church will bring bad luck (M, 17, SLC, 1961).

### Girls, Women, Hens Whistling; Roosters, Etc.

8652   If a girl whistles, the angels in heaven weep (F, SLC, 1960).  Cf. Brown 8491.

8653   A whistling woman comes to no good end (F, 70, Bountiful, 1964).

8654   A whistling woman is whistling in her own bad luck (F, 45, SLC, 1938).  Cf. Brown 8490.

8655   A whistling girl and a crowing hen always come to no good end (F, 30, Midvale, 1942).  Cf. Brown 8492f.

8656   A whistling maid and a crowing hen are sure to come to some bad end (F, Peoa). Brown 8494f.

8657   A crowing hen and a whistling woman ain't good for nothin' (F, SLC, 1962).

8658   A whistling woman and a crowing hen are the unluckiest things under the sun (M, 55, Provo, 1920).

8659   Whistling maids and crowing hens are neither fit for God nor men (F, SLC, 1961).

8660   A whistling wife and a crowing hen will bring bad luck to all men (M, SLC, 1957).

8661   A whistling girl and a crowing hen are neither fit for cock nor men (F, Lehi, 1940).

8662   Girls that whistle and roosters that crow will surely have trouble wherever they go (F, 31, Beaver, 1950).

## OUTDOOR SPORTS AND PASTIMES

### GENERAL BELIEFS ABOUT SPORTS AND ATHLETES

8663   In sports the number eleven is usually lucky when worn (M, 27, SLC, 1950).

8664   Many participants don't wear the number thirteen (M, SLC, 1961).

8665   Eat the same food before every game (M, SLC, 1961).

8666   It's bad luck to shave on the day of an athletic contest (M, SLC, 1960).

8667   In almost all types of sports the favored person or team will fail to win (M, SLC).

8668   Athletes never date before a game, if the game is to be won (M, 21, SLC, 1963).

8669   In a contest keep your fingers crossed to win (F, SLC, 1957).

8670   If you spit in your hand before a game, you'll win (M, 26, Charleston, 1972). Brown 3628, cf. 3632.

8671   In high school, if you want to win a game, wear the other school's colors on Thursday and your own on Friday.  Friday is usually the day the game is played (F, 21, SLC, 1957).

8672   If you wear two different colored socks while you are participating in an athletic event, it will bring you good luck (M, 20, SLC, 1964).

8673   Never wash your sweat socks when on a winning team (M, SLC, 1961).  (This proscription holds for baseball [No. 8743], football [No. 8770], and basketball [No. 8790].  The taboo against playing in a clean uniform [No. 8676] is not so widespread.  Even on the job, a workman appearing in a new set of overalls is likely to encounter some gentle reproof, if indeed the new outfit or shoes are not dirtied or scuffed up. --Eds.)

8674   It's bad luck to wash your socks before the season is over (F, 22, SLC, 1965).

8675   Superstitious athletes will wear the same piece of clothing worn in a lucky game (F, 1959).

8676   It is unlucky to play a game in a clean uniform (M, 21, Holladay, 1961).

8677   Playing in a dirty uniform in any athletic contest is bad luck for the wearer of the uniform (M, SLC, 1958).

8678   In a winning streak wear the same pair of socks on the outside in any sport (M, 20, SLC, 1965).

8679   Athletes have good luck with a specific sweatshirt or sweater (M, 18, SLC, 1962).

8680   To cause his good luck to continue an athlete must wear the same suit (F, Holladay, 1957).

8681   If a coach is winning, he dresses the same way for every game (M, 44, SLC, 1965).

8682   If a coach is winning, he should put the right sock on first before each game to keep up the winning streak (M, 44, SLC, 1965).

8683   When a team is traveling by bus and they go under an overpass, it is good luck to honk the horn (M, SLC, 1950).

8684   If an athletic team jokes or laughs while going to an athletic contest, it is an indication that they will lose (M).

8685   In high school athletics, if the members of the team talk about the game on the day of the game, it is an indication of being beaten (M, SLC).

8686   Some sporting teams have an animal for good luck; this animal is called a mascot (F, 49, SLC, 1964).

8687 Coins placed in certain statues at institutions bring luck to players before competitive games (F, 53, Murray, 1964).

8688 If you whistle in the dressing room before an athletic event, it will bring you bad luck (M, 19, SLC, 1964).

8689 It is bad luck to wish a person good luck in the dressing room before a game (M, SLC, 1961).

8690 A black cat is a sign of good luck when it is associated with an athletic event (M, SLC, 1957).

8691 If a butterfly should light on a person's hand, you can win at play (F, SLC, 1959).

8692 If a pregnant woman happens to touch sporting equipment, bad luck will befall her husband or the person who is using the equipment (M, SLC, 1962).

8693 Tie the heart of a bat with a red silk string to your right arm, and you will win every game at which you play (F, 1957).

## BASEBALL

8694 A ball team should not have its picture taken before a game (M, SLC, 1955). Cf. Brown 3626.

8695 When baseball players are going to the game, if they pass a truck load of hay or barrels, it means good luck (F, SLC, 1958).

8696 Baseball teams who carry a mascot with them believe that they will have good luck and win the game (M, 52, Midvale, 1964). Heard in Idaho, 1922.

8697 A skunk means bad luck to a baseball team (M, SLC, 1958).

8698 A softball will never sink in the ocean (M, SLC, 1964).

8699 A baseball player tears the corner off a two-dollar bill to bring good luck (F, 23, Riverton, 1955).

8700 In baseball, when the teams change sides, an outfielder will touch one of the bases to bring good luck (M, SLC, 1959); . . . should always touch first and/or third base for good luck (M, 30, SLC, 1961); . . . step on second base . . . (M, coach, SLC, 1958).

8701 Baseball players never step on the foul line; they always step over it, believing it would be bad luck to step on the line (M, SLC, 1958).

8702 To change lockers during a baseball season is bad luck (M, 21, Holladay, 1960).

8703 The day of a big ball game should not be cluttered with other thoughts, or bad luck will ensue (M, 18, SLC, 1957).

8704 In baseball, you shouldn't get a haircut if you have a winning streak going (M, 27, Murray, 1964).

8705 Teams which lead the National and American leagues on the Fourth of July will be the ones to play each other during the World Series (M, SLC, 1967). Heard on TV.

## Pitcher, Catcher, Umpire, Etc.

8706 A left-handed pitcher is peculiar and may be a wild man (M, 58, Ger, SLC, 1963).

8707 A left-handed pitcher is a good luck charm (M, 18, SLC, 1961).

8708 If a baseball pitcher finds a penny on the pitcher's mound, he will win his game (M, SLC, 1958).

8709 It is considered bad luck for a baseball pitcher to step on the base line when going from the dugout to the pitcher's box (M, SLC, 1957).

8710 In baseball, a relief pitcher will be ineffective if he strikes out the first man he pitches to. He will be effective if he walks him (M, SLC).

8711 If the pitcher strikes out the first batter, the pitcher's team will lose (M, SLC, 1956).

8712 If the first pitch of the ball game is a strike, then that team will win the game (SLC, 1964).

8713 If a pitcher walks the pitcher of the opposing team, it will start a rally (M, SLC, 1944); . . . it's bad luck and he will lose the game (M, 53, Heber, 1972).

8714 If someone mentions a pitcher's winning streak to the pitcher, the winning streak will be broken (M, 19, SLC).

8715 If a pitcher has a no-hitter up to the fourth inning, no one thereafter will mention a no-hitter until after the game (M, SLC, 1957); . . . if someone mentions it, the other team will get a hit (M, SLC, 1958); . . . the string will break (M, SLC, 1954); . . . the pitcher will blow it (M, 19, Layton, 1964); . . . the chances of a no-hit game are spoiled (M, 18, SLC, 1961); If someone on TV mentions a no-hit game, the pitcher will allow a base hit (F, SLC, 1960).

## The Bat

8716 In baseball, if a new bat is used in a game before it has been used in batting practice, it will put a jinx on the bat (M, SLC).

8717 Never let anyone use your baseball bat, for it only has so many hits in it (M, SLC, 1959).

8718 Rubbing your baseball bat with a bone will make you a better hitter (M, 16, SLC, 1961).

8719 In baseball, spitting on the bat will bring a home run (M, SLC, 1960).

8720 Spit in a mitt and kiss a bat, and you will play good baseball (M, 19, SLC, 1965).

8721  Baseball players sometimes put a piece of gum on their bat believing that it will help their hitting (M, 47, SLC, 1945).

8722  If one drops a baseball bat between the home base and the catcher, bad luck will follow (M, 22, SLC, 1958).

8723  Never cross your bats while playing baseball, or you will have terrible luck throughout the game (M, SLC, 1959); . . . the player's batting average will come down (M, Sandy, 1957); . . . you won't get a hit (M, SLC, 1960); . . . all the hits escape from the bats (M, 20, SLC, 1959); . . . you will break your leg or something terrible like that (M, Provo, 1971). Cf. Brown 3637.

8724  It causes bad luck to change bats after you have taken one in your hand (M, SLC, 1953); To change bats after the second strike is unwise (M, SLC, 1954). Cf. Brown 3636.

8725  Strike the ball with the side opposite the label, or your bat will break (F, Tooele, 1957).

8726  If a batter breaks a bat, he's bound to lose the next two games (M, SLC, 1967).

8727  If a player breaks a bat, it means a playing or batting slump (F, 44, SLC, 1940).

8728  It is an old baseball superstition that you will lose the game if you put the bats in the bag before the game is over (M, SLC, 1950).

## The Batter

8729  For every carrot you eat, you will get a hit (M, SLC, 1954).

8730  If a player hits well in batting practice the day before a game, it is better to cut him short and save the hits until the game (M, 20, SLC, 1963).

8731  It is bad luck to run off the base lines in a ball game, for your next time at bat you won't get a hit (M, 16, SLC, 1961).

8732  If baseball players walking along the street see a hairpin, and pick it up, they will get a hit (M, SLC, 1958).

8733  If a batter finds a bobby pin on first base, he will get a sure hit (M, SLC, 1967).

8734  It brings especially bad luck to be put out on third base (M, SLC, 1956).

8735  When going to bat, always walk between the umpire and the catcher (M, SLC, 1944); Baseball players walk around the umpire, not in front, to keep their batting average up (M, SLC, 1960); Jackie Robinson always walked behind the catcher before he went to bat (M, Vernal, 1958).

8736  It's unlucky for a batter to spit on home plate (M, 1960).

8737  In baseball, if when you're up at bat you don't touch the left corner of home plate, you won't be able to hit the ball (M, 22, Magna, 1963).

8738  Tap the plate seven times with your baseball bat before confronting the pitcher (M, SLC).

8739  When they come to bat many baseball players make a cross on home plate for luck (M, 21, SLC, 1950).

## Uniforms, Gloves, Etc.

8740  Baseball players always wear the same suit and never have it cleaned if they are on a winning streak, because they feel if they wash their suit, it might break their winning streak (M, SLC, 1957).

8741  If a ball player wears a particular sweatshirt in winning a crucial game, he should continue to wear the sweatshirt for good luck (M, 18, SLC, 1960).

8742  Baseball players must wear the same sweatshirt, or they will have a bad day with many errors and no hits (M, Helper, 1959).

8743  Ball players believe that if they are winning in a series of games and they wash or change their socks, they will lose their good luck (F, 24, Murray, 1952). Cf. No. 8673, above.

8744  Don't change baseball athletic socks until the team loses a game (M, 23, Helper, 1946).

8745  Baseball players put the same sock on a certain foot each time (M, SLC, 1957).

8746  A baseball player will always put his right shoe on first for good luck (F, 18, SLC, 1964); . . . tie the right shoe before the left . . . (M, 49, SLC, 1963).

8747  A baseball player will get good luck if he hits his shoes with the bat before hitting (M, SLC, 1958).

8748  In baseball, a manager will not change his underwear during a winning streak, but will wait until the streak is broken (M, SLC, 1959).

8749  In baseball, when a player is having a hot hitting streak, he does not change or wash his underwear (M, SLC, 1957).

8750  Baseball players who play the outfield put grass in their hat for good luck (M, SLC, 1950).

8751  Baseball players put bubble gum in their hats for good luck (M, SLC, 1965).

8752  Don't let anyone use your baseball glove, for it only has so many good catches in it (M, SLC, 1959).

8753  When playing baseball, never leave your baseball glove face-up in the field when you come in to bat. It is bad luck (M, SLC, 1950).

8754  Always lay the ball glove with the palm up. It is bad luck if you don't (M, SLC, 1944).

8755 Among baseball players, if they change their mitt, they will commit an error (M, Helper, 1959).

8756 Ball players always throw gloves in the same spot at the end of an inning (M, SLC, 1965).

FOOTBALL

8757 A football player has Roman blood (M, SLC, 1957).

8758 Football teams who carry a mascot with them believe that they will have good luck and win the game (M, 52, Midvale, 1964).

8759 If players on a football team sing before a game, they will lose the game (M, 23, SLC, 1950).

8760 Rub football cleats on tar and draw a dragon on the grass, and you will make better runs and will fear falling so much you won't fall (M, 19, SLC, 1965).

8761 Some football coaches will not allow pictures taken of their players on a Friday (M, 41, SLC, 1950). Cf. Brown 3626, 3639.

8762 It is bad luck to shave before a football game (M, 26, Charleston, 1972). Cf. Brown 3627, 3638.

8763 To win a football game things must always be done the same as on the day the last game was won (M, SLC, 1961).

8764 Football players should never date on the night before a football game (M, 21, SLC, 1963).

8765 Some high school football teams believe that if they win their first game, they have to wear the same jerseys, pants, shoes and socks they had on for every remaining game (M, Fillmore, 1960).

8766 A winning football coach has one article of apparel he will wear at every game, during a winning streak, to bring him and the team good luck (M, SLC, 1957).

8767 To wash your practice clothes while using them during football season is bad luck (M, SLC, 1953).

8768 For any member of a football team to wear dirty socks will bring bad luck and loss of the game (M, SLC, 1954).

8769 One must wear dirty socks while playing football in order to play his best (M, 51, Bingham, 1931).

8770 If a football team has a winning streak, the players should wear the same socks each game for good luck (M, 23, SLC, 1958). Cf. No. 8673, above.

8771 Before a football game put your socks on first (M, SLC, 1960).

8772 Always put the left football shoe on before the right, or you will get hurt in the game (M, 25, SLC, 1956).

8773 Put the same shoe on first every time, or you will lose the game that will be played that day (M, 30, SLC, 1961).

8774 It is bad luck for a team to call a time-out in the process of a drive (M, SLC, 1954).

8775 Get the same number locker, T-shirt, shoulder pads, etc., as your jersey number (M, SLC, 1965).

8776 The trainer should not touch a player's clothes before a football game (M, 19, SLC, 1963).

8777 Football players that go into pro ball think they must have their same numbers that they had before, or they will have bad luck in playing (M, 30, SLC, 1961).

8778 If a football team had been winning, the team used to get in the huddle and in the same order each time and holler the same chant in order to continue their luck (M, 23, SLC, 1969).

BASKETBALL

8779 Basketball teams who carry a mascot with them believe that they will have good luck and win the game (M, 52, Midvale, 1964).

8780 If you go to a basketball game and your team is losing, sit on your hands and your team will win (M, 18, SLC, 1959).

8781 You should never change the sheets on your bed on the day of a basketball game, or the team is sure to lose (M, Bountiful, 1960).

8782 The pep club always sings the school song before the basketball game and the half-time performance so that they will do a good job with their march (F, Midvale, 1963).

8783 Always make the first two shots in practice by shooting easy lay-ups (M, 18, SLC, 1963).

8784 When playing basketball, you should try to make the last basket when warming up before the game; if you don't you won't make any points in the game that day (M, 25, SLC, 1954); It is bad luck if you leave practice missing the last shot (M, 57, basketball coach, SLC, 1964).

8785 Before the start of each game or each half, some players jump up and touch the ring of the basket for good luck (M, 30, SLC, 1961).

8786 Wilt Chamberlain wears a rubber band on his wrist while playing in every game (M, 21, SLC, 1963).

8787 Wear a high school letter jacket on the days you play basketball (M, 22, Orem, 1963).

8788 In order to win a game, you must always wear the same suit of clothing as you did in previous games (M, SLC, 1961).

8789 Do the same things on the day of a basketball game every week in order to have a set pattern which will make you a little luckier (M, 20, Midvale, 1962).

8790 One must wear dirty socks while playing a game, such as basketball, in order to

play his best (M, 51, Bingham, 1931).
Cf. No. 8673, above.

8791  Don't wash your gym shoes during the
state basketball tournament if you want
to have good luck (M, 19, Midvale,
1962).

8792  If a team loses its first game in new
uniforms, the basketball suits may cause
bad luck.  In one case on record, the
new uniforms were discarded (F, Midvale,
1967).

8793  The team that scores first in a
basketball game will win the game (F,
SLC, 1957).

8794  It is bad luck for a basketball player
to make more than two baskets in a row
(M, SLC, 1959).

8795  If a basketball player makes his first
field goal attempt, he will not get
another for the rest of the game (M,
SLC).

8796  Before you shoot a basketball, always
bounce the ball twice (M, SLC, 1960).

8797  In basketball bounce the ball three
times before taking a free-throw shot
(M, 22, SLC, 1963); . . . twice . . .
(M, 1960); . . . bounce the ball with
both hands four times before making a
foul pitch (M, 23, SLC, 1969).

8798  If a player is about to set a record in
basketball, don't talk about it, or he
won't make it (M, SLC, 1963).

## TRACK

8799  Hold your breath while running, and you
will run faster (M, 19, Provo, 1964).

8800  If a track man wears his hat during the
track meet, it will bring him good luck
(M, SLC, 1956).

8801  Never go onto the track before you run
in a track meet (M, 20, SLC, 1963).

## TENNIS

8802  White is always worn in tennis to show
the pureness of the game and good
sportsmanship (Provo, 1970).

8803  If you touch a basketball before a
tennis match, you will lose your match
(F, 55, Moab, 1933).

8804  Many tennis players will not step on a
line between points (M, 41, SLC, 1950).

8805  You will have bad luck if you drop your
tennis racket during a match (F, 55,
Moab, 1940).

8806  In tennis, the small tag that tells the
size of the racket handle is left on (M,
SLC).

8807  To hold more than two balls in one hand
while playing tennis will bring bad luck
to the player (M, 19, SLC, 1961); If you
hold three balls while serving, you will
default or miss a serve for sure (M, 19,
SLC, 1962).

## GOLF

8808  A golfer, when nervous, is said to have
"The Yips."  The yips are like little
gremlins who cause the otherwise
accomplished golfer to miss short putts,
use the wrong clubs, or make stupid
mistakes in general (M, 24, Logan,
1960).

8809  In playing a golf match it is bad luck
to watch another player swing (M, SLC,
1961).

8810  If you change golf clubs after selecting
one, you will muff the shot (M, SLC,
1960); . . . blow your next shot (F,
Provo, 1960); . . . you will flub the
stroke (M, SLC, 1962).

8811  A golf ball will never come down if hit
higher than 500 feet (M, SLC, 1964).

8812  Using a golf ball with the number of
three on the ball makes people
subconscious of three-putting the green
(M, 21, SLC, 1963).

8813  Never go out with a golf ball without
unwrapping the paper covering; if you
don't, you will have a bad round of golf
(F, 19, Midvale, 1963).

8814  By placing the name title of a golf ball
toward the hole, the life of the ball
will be lengthened (M, SLC).

8815  It's bad luck to leave two golf balls in
a golf cup at the same time (M, 51,
Magna, 1965).

8816  When the person putting ahead of you
sinks his putt, take the ball out of the
hole, or you will miss your putt (M, 50,
Magna, 1963).

8817  Grass is the best cleaner for ball
stains on a golf club (M, SLC, 1961).

8818  It is bad luck to use more than one golf
tee for eighteen holes of golf (M, 20,
Beaver, 1964).

8819  A tee in a golfer's hat will bring the
golfer good luck (M, 20, Beaver, 1964).

8820  Gary Player, a one-time winner of the
Professional Golf Association, is
superstitious in that he wears all black
in all of his tournaments, because he
says it makes him feel strong (M, SLC,
1963).

8821  When I have a good game of golf, I use
the same socks in the next game and
continue to use them until my luck runs
out (M, SLC, 1961).

## HORSE RACING, DOG RACING

8822  To have a green ticket at the race track
is bad luck (M, 24, Provo, 1964).

8823  A jockey wearing green will never win a
race (M, SLC, 1955).

8824  Never bet on a horse with four white
stockings (M, 31, SLC, 1963).

8825  It is good luck to pat a hunchback on
the back at the racetrack (M, SLC,
1958).  Brown 3661.

8826   A greyhound dog with a pure white spot and a round one on its head will bring good luck to its owner in a race (M, 35, Provo, 1951).

## CAR RACING

8827   No race car will ever start with the number thirteen, will ever have a green paint job, and its driver will never wear a green colored helmet in a race (M, SLC).

8828   Never wish a race driver good luck; wish him just the opposite, and he will have good luck (M, 37, Bountiful, 1964).

8829   Never wear green when you're race driving a car, or misfortune will follow (M, 18, SLC, 1963).

8830   It's unlucky to drive a green car in a race (M, SLC, 1959); . . . on the Indianapolis Speedway (M, SLC, 1959); . . . they cause wrecks (M, SLC, 1956); . . . they are a sign of death (M, SLC, 1957). (For a carry-over of this taboo to horse racing, see No. 8823, above. Since horse racing was an established sport long before the advent of car racing, historical research might show that borrowing took place in logical historical order. --Eds.)

8831   Seven is an unlucky number in automobile racing (M, 20, SLC, 1963).

8832   Car racers think it is bad luck to have a woman down by the cars before or during a race (F, 18, SLC, 1961); . . . will not let the wife in their pit (F, 22, Granger, 1964).

8833   Never see a girl before a race (M, 20, SLC, 1963).

8834   It is bad luck to eat peanuts at a sports car race. A fellow in the USSA was killed when his car skidded on some peanut shells and so no one eats peanuts (M, SLC, 1961).

## RODEO

8835   It's bad luck to wear yellow when performing or riding in a rodeo (M, 27, Logan, 1970); . . . bad luck to wear a yellow shirt the day before you are going to ride (M, Provo, 1971).

8836   The wearing of clothes in a rodeo that you've been hurt in once before is bad luck (M, 27, Logan, 1970).

8837   A rodeo rider won't ride with a new hat because it is bad luck (M, 38, SLC, 1963). Heard in Nebraska, 1940; . . . bad luck to ride with more than one hat in a season (M, Provo, 1971).

8838   Rodeo cowboys think a clean hat will cause them to lose (F, Copperton).

8839   Rodeo cowboys think cleaning a hat will make them lose (M, Midvale, 1942).

8840   A cowboy never puts his hat on any bed. It will bring bad luck (M, SLC).

8841   Rodeo equipment or gear on or under the bed is bad luck (M, 27, Logan, 1970).

8842   If you borrow someone else's spurs to compete, you'll never win. You have to wear your own (M, Paragonah, 1962); It is bad luck to wear a different pair of spurs in the same season (M, Provo, 1971).

8843   It is good luck to walk under a ladder just before riding in a rodeo as a contestant (M, 35, Hooper, 1970).

8844   It is bad luck to use saddle soap with rosin when you rosin your bull rope (M, Provo, 1971).

8845   When riding a Brahma bull in a rodeo, it will bring good luck to stroke the "pig tail" on the rigging before coming out of the shoots (sic) (M, 30, SLC, 1955).

8846   It is bad luck to spit on the bull's head before you mount (M, Provo, 1971).

8847   Peanuts in or around the rodeo arena are bad luck (M, 27, Logan, 1970). (This belief may represent a borrowing from the well established taboo in car racing against the eating of peanuts in the pits or near racing cars. Note also that the taboo has been extended to include popcorn and Cracker Jack as well [No. 8848]. --Eds.)

8848   It is bad luck to eat Cracker Jack or popcorn before you ride in a rodeo (M, Provo, 1971); Popcorn in or around the rodeo arena is bad luck (M, 27, Logan, 1970).

## BULLFIGHTING

8849   It is unlucky for a bullfighter to have any feminine company on the day of a fight (M, SLC, 1957).

8850   A matador always dedicates his bull, usually to a beautiful lady. He also carries an article of hers during the fight (F, 20, SLC, 1957).

8851   It's good luck for a strange woman on invitation to watch a bullfighter dress (F, 20, SLC, 1965).

8852   A matador will always visit a chapel before a bullfight (F, 20, SLC, 1961).

8853   When praying for success, a bullfighter must be alone, dressed in costume and unarmed (F, 20, SLC, 1965).

## DIVING, SWIMMING, SURFING

8854   Divers stand on the edge of the board and count to ten before diving (M, SLC, 1963).

8855   A person should not go in bathing while he is warm (F, SLC, 1961).

8856   Do not swim in water where the bottom has not been found. It will bring bad luck (M, 21, Richfield, 1957).

8857   It is bad luck to dream of swimming or being in water, especially totally submerged (F, 42, SLC, 1963).

8858   Eating a lot of fish will make you a better swimmer (F, SLC, 1962).

8859   A family that swims together stays together (M, SLC, 1955).

8860   If you swim in the rain, you will never swim again (M, 45, SLC, 1963).

8861   It is bad luck to surf where there are no seagulls (M, 19, SLC, 1963).

SKATING

8862   It is bad luck to hang skates on a hook. Always place them on top of something solid (F, SLC, 1940).

8863   Many skaters won't skate in any competition without using a certain pair of skates (F, 19, SLC, 1957).

SKIING

8864   A snow snake is a mysterious animal that causes people to fall while skiing (F, Brighton, 1967).

8865   The worst weather offers the best skiing days. It is either a stormy or a cold day (F, 60, Logan, 1970).

8866   If you go skiing on Sunday, it is bad luck (M, 19, SLC, 1958).

8867   If a skier decides to quit skiing for the day, and then after that he goes skiing some more, he is supposed to meet with a serious accident (M, SLC, 1957).

8868   A Saint Bernard dog is a luck charm for skiers (F, 19, SLC, 1960); A St. Bernard medal protects skiers (F, SLC, 1960).

8869   Good luck charms are worn for luck in ski races. One wears such things as St. Christopher medals, pins, or necklaces (F, 20, SLC, 1961).

8870   Always wear a certain ring in a ski race for good luck (F, 19, SLC, 1963).

8871   Never go skiing without a good luck coin. It's bad luck (M, 20, SLC, 1960).

8872   Wear a double racing number, 9933, to have better luck when ski racing (F, 19, Midvale, 1963).

8873   When skiing it is good luck to wear yellow (M, 18, SLC, 1963).

8874   There is an old German guy who is on ski patrol up at Brighton who goes around telling everyone if they "piss on their boots," the boots will mold and fit to their feet better (F, Brighton, 1967).

8875   Wear red stretch pants when in a ski race. It brings good luck (F, 20, SLC, 1963); . . . white stretch pants . . . (F, 17, SLC, 1963); . . . green pants . . . (F, 19, SLC, 1961); . . . a white shirt . . . (F, 19, SLC, 1960).

8876   A Ullr medal will protect one while skiing (F, 19, SLC, 1959); . . . Ullr is the god of skiing (M, 20, Midvale, 1963).

8877   Skiers always have a favorite pair of stockings to wear when skiing. If they don't wear them, they believe that bad luck will come to them (M, 45, SLC, 1936).

8878   Kiss the sleeve of a ski sweater for good luck during a ski contest (F, 22, SLC, 1963).

BOXING, WRESTLING

8879   It is bad luck for boxers to put on the right boxing glove first (M, SLC, 1958).

8880   When a boxer hangs up his gloves, it is bad luck for them to ever come off the wall (M, SLC, 1961).

8881   It is bad luck to enter the ring first in a boxing bout (Salt Lake Tribune, August 6, 1967).

8882   Wrestling in the dark brings bad luck (F, 20, SLC, 1965).

8883   A woman with a saddle nose is believed to be a woman wrestler (F, 21, SLC, 1962).

BOWLING

8884   If you use someone else's bowling ball, you will not raise your score, but you will lower the ball owner's score by quite a bit. You never use anyone else's ball, even if you are offered the ball. If you do, there's hell to pay (M, Provo, 1971).

8885   Being the first one on the bowling line will bring good luck (F, 27, SLC, 1959).

8886   Having your name spelled a certain way on the bowling line-up brings you good luck (F, 27, SLC, 1959).

8887   Bowlers bowl with special balls to suit their needs. One bowler, for example, uses only a number 52 to have good luck (F, 19, SLC, 1963).

8888   Never roll your ball if the alley next to you has a split pin spare you do not wish to have, or your pins will copy it. Have them roll first and wait for the lane to clear (F, 49, SLC, 1963).

8889   Don't make the score until it is necessary on the bowling sheet (F, 27, SLC, 1959); If you have three or more strikes in a row, your luck will be broken if the score is written in while the bowler is still getting strikes (F, 30, SLC, 1964).

8890   A red and black checkered shirt is necessary to bowl about 150 (M, Dan, SLC, 1961).

POOL

8891   If you go in to play pool and do good, keep your ring on; if doing bad, take it off (M, 19, SLC, 1965).

8892   It is bad luck to break the cue sticks in pool (M, SLC, 1964).

8893   It is bad luck to see a woman in a pool room (M, 50, SLC, 1961).

## VARIOUS SPORTS AND GAMES

8894 I never shave the day of a soccer match (M, Provo, 1970).

8895 One soccer player I know always imagines in his mind before the game begins a goal being scored in a particular place. He says invariably that if he scores in the game, it will be in the place imagined (M, Provo, 1970).

8896 In the game of marbles, spit on the marble (taw) for good luck before taking a shot (F, Fountain Green, 1950s).

8897 A criss-cross is made to keep one's opponent from "spotting dead" in marbles (M, SLC, 1915).

8898 Cat-eye marbles bring good luck (M, SLC, 1943).

8899 It is unlucky to let anyone "scope" you while shooting in a rifle match (M, SLC).

8900 When starting to play jacks, if you throw the ball up, slap the ground and catch the ball before it bounces. It is good luck (M, SLC, 1967).

## FISHING AND HUNTING

## FISHING

### Various Beliefs

8901 He who wishes well-being will never burn fish bones (M, SLC, 1957).

8902 By measuring the depth of the lake with a very long string and a weight and by calculations as to its temperatures, one can figure out what depth the fish will be swimming at (M, SLC, 1967).

8903 Test the temperature of the water with a thermometer, and you will know how deep to fish. The warmer it is at the surface the deeper you must fish (M, SLC, 1967).

8904 To catch a trout unexpectedly signifies hope (F, 50, SLC, 1940).

8905 The first two fish caught are mates (M, Provo, 1957).

8906 If a fisherman loses the first fish that he has on his line, the fishing trip will be unsuccessful (M, SLC, 1964); . . . he will not get any more bites (M, Sandy, 1956). Cf. Brown 7816f.

8907 If you catch a fish on the first cast, there will be no other bites the remaining part of the day (M, 54, 1964).

8908 If a fish gets off the line, you won't catch any more fish in the hole all day (M, 53, Heber, 1960).

8909 When you are fishing, always throw back the first fish caught, because it will bring luck to the fishing party, and will satisfy the rest of the fish that it is all right to take the bait (M, 54, Richfield, 1944).

8910 If you waste the fish you catch, you won't catch any more (M, 53, Heber, 1955).

8911 If you curse while you are fishing, the fish will not bite (M, 22, SLC, 1957). Brown 7814.

8912 If you boast of a fish on the line before it is caught, you will fail to catch it (M, 53, SLC, 1961).

8913 People couldn't talk of the fish they were going to catch while fishing at night; if they did, they wouldn't be able to catch any fish. In fact, if anyone mentioned fishing before they reached the boats, they would all just turn around and go home, as the fish wouldn't bite (M, 48, SLC, 1965).

8914 If you count the number of fish you have caught, you will catch no more that day (M, 43, Sandy, 1963).

8915 Don't cut a twig to string your fish on until you catch your first fish. If you do, you won't catch any (M, 58, Mt. Pleasant, 1965).

8916 If you are right-handed, you should never cast a line with the left hand, or you will have no fish to creel (M, Sandy, 1956).

8917 If you walk heavy, fish won't bite (M, Moab, 1953).

8918 If your shadow gets on the water, the fish will not bite (M, Moab, 1953).

8919 You can't carry fishing gear in the side of a car, or fish know something's wrong and will be cautious of you (M, 53, Heber, 1920s).

8920 If anything sour is eaten on a fishing trip, you'll have a bad day fishing (M, SLC, 1960).

8921 You can't have a gun, bow and arrow, or slingshot with you, or you won't catch fish (M, 53, Heber, 1965).

8922 Don't touch a fishing stream with fish entrails (M, 53, Heber, 1960).

8923 Beer, fruit, or vegetable cans in the water scare the fish (M, 53, Heber, 1920).

8924 Many fishermen have to wear a special type of hat to have the greatest fishing success (M, SLC, 1961).

8925 Don't wear light or flashy dark clothes when fishing. Always blend with the surroundings (M, 53, Heber, 1920).

8926 It is bad luck to wear white in a fishing boat (M, 67, SLC, 1964).

8927 If you smell like smoke, you won't catch fish (M, 53, Heber, 1920).

8928 It is bad luck to take a woman along on a fishing trip (F, 19, SLC, 1964). Cf. Brown 7806ff.

8929 If you don't pay your tithing, you can't catch fish (M, 53, Heber, 1920).

8930 If the fishing is bad, contribute money to a charity, or help a little kid who is fishing (M, 53, Heber, 1925).

8931 Slap your hand on the water for luck when fishing (M, SLC, 1964).

8932 A long stick placed across a river will draw the fish to the surface (M, SLC, 1964).

8933 When fishing, start small fires on the bank the night before to trail the fish (M, 25, Daggett Co, 1950).

8934 Holding your mouth a certain way will enable you to catch more fish (M, Logan, 1970).

8935 When you're fishing and someone is drowning, never put them in the boat directly, just pull them into shore. Bad luck in fishing will follow if you put them in the boat (M, 20, SLC, 1964).

## Animal Influences

8936 It brings bad luck to take a dog on a fishing trip, for you will catch no fish (M, 22, SLC, 1949).

8937 If a dog's shadow hits the water, fish won't bite (M, 53, Heber, 1920).

8938 If you see three white horses while on your way on a fishing trip, you'll be the first to catch your limit (M, Eng, SLC, 1957).

8939 A loon on a lake means that the fishing will be poor (M, 65, SLC, 1910).

8940 It is a sign of bad luck if a dragonfly lights on your fishing pole (M, 44, Layton, 1970). Cf. Brown 7783.

## Fishing Time

8941 Sunday is the best day to go fishing (M, SLC, 1964).

8942 Never catch fish on Sunday (M, 53, Heber, 1920).

8943 You will catch more fish on the incoming tide (M, SLC).

8944 I used to have a fishing partner that had a good time for fishing figured out by barometric pressure. He would say, "We will fish up to ten-thirty, then wait until about one. They won't bite between then." By golly, it would work out about like that (M, Moab, 1953).

8945 Fish bite best just after sunrise and at dusk (F, Logan, 1970). Cf. Brown 7796.

8946 A trout always sleeps from one to two o'clock in the afternoon (M, Provo, 1951).

8947 When the moon's red, there will be good fishing (M, 44, SLC, 1965).

8948 Fish bite best when the moon is full (M, 50, Goshen, 1964). Cf. Brown 7745f.

8949 When you go fishing, you should go after a full moon, because if you go during a full moon, your luck will be bad (M, 22, Sunnyside, 1963); If the moon shines bright, the fish will feed at night. Hence fishing will be no good (F, Lehi, 1957).

8950 For good fishing you should go when there has not been a full moon the night before (M, SLC, 1958).

8951 When it is the light of the moon, fish won't bite during the next day (M, SLC, 1957).

8952 If there is a full moon, the fishing will be poor, and if there is no moon, the fishing will be good (M, 40, Bountiful, 1926).

8953 When a Friday falls on the seventh of the month, and the moon happens to be full that night, the fishing will be poor (M, 22, Ja, SLC).

8954 It is best to go fishing when there has been a dark of the moon. The fish will bite better, because they didn't eat in the night when there was no light (M, 71, Centerville, 1926).

8955 Fish for lake trout in the dark of the moon (M, Logan, 1970).

8956 Oh, that picture in the front of the almanacs. That's what she used to go by. If you want to go fishing, you want to get good fish, you go by the signs in the feet. The fish are at the bottom of you (F, Moab, 1953). Cf. Brown 7744.

## Fishing Weather

8957 If fish jump out of the water, it is poor fishing weather (M, 50, Goshen, 1930s).

8958 When the sun goes behind a cloud, fish always bite the best (M, 44, Woods Cross, 1964).

8959 Fish bite best just before a rain. They bite very poorly just after (F, Logan, 1970). Brown 7772.

8960 Fishing is best when it rains (M, 39, SLC, 1964). Heard in the Virgin Islands, 1958. Brown 7773.

8961 Fish near the surface, quick to bite. Catch your fish when rain's in sight (M, SLC, 1930s).

8962 The fish won't bite when it rains (M, 19, SLC, 1964).

8963 It's good fishing during a summer storm (M, 27, SLC, 1948).

8964 Fish will not bite a hook when it is thundering, but if it is only raining, that is the best time to fish. This pertains to fishing in lakes (M, 54, Richfield, 1944). Cf. Brown 7779ff.

8965 A rainbow is a sign of good fishing (M, 20, SLC, 1950s).

8966 Fish only by the barometer (M, 74, Sanpete, 1903).

8967 Fishing is no good if the wind is blowing (F, Lehi, 1957). Brown 7751.

8968 When the wind is in the west, the fish will bite best (M, 50, Goshen, 1930s).

8969 When the wind blows north, fishing is usually good (M, 23, Draper, 1964).

8970 When the wind is in the east, then the fishes bite the least;/when the wind is in the west, then the fishes bite the best;/when the wind is in the north, then the fishes do come forth;/when the wind is in the south, it blows the bait in the fish's mouth (M, SLC, 1957); . . . when the wind's from the north, smart fishermen goeth not forth . . . (M, 44, Ogden, 1972). Cf. Brown 7752, 7755ff, 7765.

8971 If the Northern Lights are bright and abundant, people say: "That's good for the fisherman, it's a sign that there will be a good expedition of herrings" (F, SLC, 1927).

## Fishing Pole and Line

8972 Fish with a colored line, and the big fish will attack (M, SLC, 1964).

8973 To carry a pole into the house will prevent your catching any fish (M, 22, SLC, 1958).

8974 If someone steps over your fishing line, you will have bad luck (M, 22, SLC, 1956). Brown 7822, 7824.

8975 If someone steps across your fishing pole, you won't catch any fish that day (F, SLC, 1959). Brown 7823.

8976 If a fisherman consistently steps over his fishing pole or line on the ground, he'll catch no more fish that day (F, Farmington, 1946).

## Fishing Bait, Hook

8977 If you bait your hooks with leather gloves, you will have much better luck fishing (M, SLC, 1963).

8978 If a fisherman spits on the hook before the cast into the water, good luck will come (M, SLC, 1955); . . . the fish will bite (M, Moab, 1953); It's good luck to spit on the worm . . . (M, Layton, 1934); . . . you will catch more fish (M, Ogden, 1958). Cf. Brown 7833ff.

8979 If you spit tobacco on fishing bait, the fisherman will have good luck and catch many fish (M, 55, American Fork, 1963). Brown 7840f.

8980 Chew sweet anise and spit on your hook for luck at fishing (M, 22, SLC, 1964).

8981 Worms dug in a graveyard are best for fishing (F, SLC, 1957). Brown 7832.

8982 When looking for worms for fishing, if you hang a string on a rail fence overnight, it will turn into a worm, (M, 23, SLC, 1963).

8983 The best worms come from where the weeds grow that you threw dishwater on (M, 53, Heber, 1920).

8984 You won't catch fish with worms you catch near where you threw coffee grounds (M, 53, Heber, 1920).

8985 To have good luck in fishing, bite an angle worm in half in front of a witness (M, SLC, 1964).

8986 If you cut a fishing worm into pieces, each piece will become a complete worm (M, 14, SLC, 1958).

8987 When fishing with your back against the sun, your bait will work best if you break it in half (M, Logan, 1962).

8988 Kiss your fishing bait for luck (M, 20, SLC, 1950).

8989 If you change hooks while you are fishing, the fish will stop striking (M, 22, SLC, 1940).

8990 It is good luck to throw away your hook after you are through fishing (M, SLC, 1960).

8991 If you catch a fish on one type of lure one day, the lure won't catch fish until after the next day of fishing (M, 20, SLC, 1963).

8992 Fish will bite at any awkwardly moving thing in the water because he will think it is crippled and that it will not be able to get away so fast (M, SLC, 1967).

8993 If you are fishing for catfish, they will bite any stinging bait (M, Moab, 1953).

# HUNTING

## Various Beliefs

8994 Always carry water when hunting, or when you kill an animal you will soon be lost (M, Provo, 1964).

8995 It is bad luck to sharpen a hunting knife before going on a hunt (F, Orangeville, 1959).

8996 Never go hunting with your wife; it's bad luck (M, SLC, 1964); When you get up to go hunting if the first person you see outside your home is a woman, you will have bad luck on the hunting trip (M, Gr, SLC, 1949).

8997 Put gunpowder around your neck while hunting, and you will never be shot (M, SLC, 1963).

8998 If you go hunting and you mention or talk about fish, you will have bad luck (M, 32, Gr, SLC, 1963).

8999 In the southwestern United States when a larger animal was killed by a hunter, the hunter had to clean it, and then wash his entire body with its blood. This was to have rid him of the sin he had just committed (F, 18, SLC, 1963).

9000 A boastful person never fares well on a hunt (M, 29, Sandy, 1964).

9001 When hunting, if you find a dead animal, you won't find the game you are looking for (M, Logan, 1972).

9002    When the moon is new, if the point turns up so an Indian can hang his powder horn on it, the season will be rainy, and he will not be able to hunt. If the point does not turn up, the season will be dry and good for hunting (F, SLC, 1957).

9003    Leave dressed animals outside till the evil spirits have left before you eat it (M, SLC, 1957).

## Wild Game

9004    While hunting, if you wound an animal and have to chase the animal, do not speak of it. Because this will give the animal the extra strength, and he will get away (M, 18, Moab, 1971).

9005    When hunting game, if you spit into the wind, you won't get any game (F, 48, SLC, 1964).

9006    If a huntsman while going out in the morning sees a fox cross his path, or an old woman, he should return home. If he sees a fox, he will find no game; and an old woman, he will shoot a man in the bushes (F, 83, SLC, 1964).

9007    To see a fox while hunting is a good omen bringing good hunting without accident, provided you don't harm the fox (M, 30, SLC, 1958).

9008    The killing of albino game brings bad luck (M, 22, SLC, 1954).

9009    Jays call out to warn other animals when you are hunting (M, Logan, 1970).

9010    It is always said that the bird "Camp-robber" always flies ahead of hunters chirping loudly to warn the deer, and that if you can avoid the bird, you will get a deer (M, SLC, 1957). (Gray jay. --Eds.)

9011    To meet a man with red hair while deer hunting is bad luck (M, 46, Midvale).

9012    When you shoot your first deer, never wash your hands until after sundown. If you do, you will have bad deer hunting luck the rest of your life. If you do not wash your hands, this will bring you much luck hunting for as long as you hunt (M, 34, Richfield, 1948).

9013    Night time is the best time to hunt deer (M, SLC, 1964).

9014    If you like to hunt and eat rabbits, you should only hunt and eat them during the months without the letter "R" in them. This prevents disease (M, 27, SLC, 1943).

9015    Saturday mornings are the best time to rabbit hunt (M, SLC, 1950).

9016    By closing one eye while hunting rabbits, you can spot the leading rabbits more easily (M, SLC, 1964).

9017    A rabbit when chased by dogs will return to its starting point, lick its four paws, make a jump, and the dogs can no longer trace it (M, 26, SLC, 1945).

9018    To shoot a squirrel will bring bad luck on the person doing the shooting (F, 61, Midvale).

9019    Never shoot a bear, and never venture near a bear cub (M, Willard, 1900s).

## Guns

9020    It is considered very bad luck to look directly into the muzzle of a gun (F, Cedar City, 1964).

9021    A loaded pistol should never be put in the hot sun (M, SLC, 1964).

9022    When hunting, bite the lead of a bullet so your teeth marks are on it. This will make the bullet fly true (M, Jensen, 1958).

9023    It's bad luck to step over a gun in camp while hunting (M, SLC, 1965). Brown 7905.

9024    If you kiss the end of your gun before you shoot, you can't miss (M, SLC, 1964).

9025    It's bad luck for a hunter to return home with an empty gun (F, Ogden, 1960).

9026    Never sell a dead man's guns; they must be given away or bad luck will follow (F, Draper, 1960).

# IX

# Death and Funereal Customs

## GENERAL BELIEFS ABOUT DEATH

9027 All short people die miserable deaths (M, SLC, 1964).

9028 Never start anything on Friday that can't be finished before sundown of the same day, or else you'll be dead before you finish it (F, SLC, 1958).

9029 It's bad luck for anything to die in your hands (M, 39, SLC, 1934).

9030 Just before a sudden death the life of the victim passes in review before his eyes (M, SLC, 1959). (This is commonly said to be the case in death by drowning. --Eds.)

9031 If you are talking about a person and he surprisingly enters the room, it means that he won't die that year (M, Norw, SLC).

9032 Black means death (M, SLC, 1959).

9033 If a white cloth is placed over your face, it means there is going to be a death (F, SLC, 1962).

9034 Rocking a cradle without a baby in it prognosticates an early death (F, 90, American Fork, 1945).

9035 For every birth there is a death in the family (F, 45, SLC, 1964).

## AUDITORY MANIFESTATIONS

### Singing, Ringing, Etc.

9036 If you hear music when you are in bed, someone is going to die (F, 18, SLC, 1963). Cf. Brown 4915.

9037 If your ears ring, you will soon hear of death (M, 44, Layton, 1970); . . . there will be a death in the family (F, SLC,); . . . it is the death toll (M, 67, SLC, 1962). Cf. Brown 4910ff.

9038 If there is a ringing in your right ear, a man will die (F, 71, Park City, 1964).

9039 The continuous hearing of bells means the death of one's grandmother (M, Ger, SLC, 1938).

9040 Crying is frequently heard before a death (M, 58, SLC, 1930).

9041 A banshee's wailing announces the approach of death (F, 63, Roosevelt, 1964); . . . that someone in the family will die (F, 18, Aust, SLC, 1964); A howling banshee . . . (M, Ir, SLC, 1960); The screaming of the banshee . . . (F, 41, SLC, 1937).

9042 If you sing Christmas songs out of season, a member of your immediate family will die (M, 24, Ger, SLC, 1964).

### Knocks, Rattles, Etc.

9043 When there's a knocking at your window or door with no one doing the knocking, it means that there will be a death of one of your relatives far away, not from your own town (F, Gr, SLC, 1964).

9044 Three knocks on your door foretell of death to someone close to you (F, 52, SLC, 1920); . . . one of the family (F, 74, SLC, 1964).

9045 If a church door rattles without any reason, it is a sign that it will soon open and admit a coffin (M, Ger, SLC, 1961).

### Shivering, Shuddering, Etc.

9046 Cold shivers indicate that someone is walking over the spot that will be your grave (F, SLC, 1964). Brown 4921.

9047 If you shiver without apparent cause, death is touching you (M, SLC, 1959).

9048 If you shudder, this means there's a rabbit running across your grave (M, 22, SLC, 1963). Cf. Brown 4923, 5238f.

### Chills, Goose Pimples

9049 If you have chills down your spine, someone is walking across the spot where your grave will be (M, SLC, 1964).

9050 When you get a quick chill and shiver all at once for no apparent reason, it means a goose has just crossed over your grave, and it means bad luck is coming (F, Logan, 1970); Goose pimples mean a goose has just run over your grave (F, SLC).

9051 If you have a chill, a snake is crawling over your grave (M, 68, SLC, 1963).

9052 When you get a chill up your spine, it means a rabbit has run over your grave (F, SLC). Brown 5239ff.

PARTS OF BODY

## Various

9053    If your cheeks itch, someone very close to you will die (F, Gr, SLC, 1957).

9054    If your chin itches, you will hear of death (F, SLC, 1960).

9055    An itching left ear means that someone soon will die (F, SLC, 1960).

9056    If you show a blue vein on the bridge of your nose, you will never survive to wear wedding clothes (F, 87, S. Jordan, 1910).

9057    If you bleed from the nose, and only one drop of blood comes out, it foretells death (F, 83, SLC, 1940).

9058    An uneasy feeling in the stomach means that someone is walking across your grave (F, SLC, 1971).

9059    A signal of death is when legs are placed on something which is above the height of the knees (F, Logan, 1964).

9060    When your feet itch, it means you'll walk on graveyard dirt (F, SLC, 1959). Brown 4922.

## Teeth

9061    A dream of teeth means that a person will die (F, 18, SLC, 1965). Cf. Brown 4945.

9062    If you dream that your teeth are loose, and if in the dream it hurts, it is a sign of death (F, Bear River City, 1957).

9063    If you have a dream about pulling teeth, then a death will occur in the family or to one of your close friends (F, 45, SLC, 1930); Dreaming of pulling decayed teeth means a death will occur (F, 77, Dan, SLC, 1964). Brown 4946, 4950.

9064    If you have a dream that you lose a tooth, there will be a death (F, 24, Norw, SLC, 1964); . . . it means the death of a friend or relative (F, SLC, 1964).

9065    If your teeth hurt when pulled, there will be a death (F, 68, SLC, 1964).

9066    If you pass a Catholic sister or mother dressed in black, and you smile and allow her to see your teeth, you will surely die (F, SLC, 1900).

## Hair, Eyebrows

9067    Black hair on a chair means don't sit down, or death will follow (F, Ogden, 1959).

9068    If two people work on your hair at the same time, you'll die (F, 50, Ogden, 1963). Cf. Brown 485, 4942.

9069    If you cut your hair in the month of March, you will die before the year is over (F, SLC, 1961). Brown 4943f.

9070    After cutting your hair be sure to burn it. If a bird should get the hair and make a nest with it, you'll die of pains in your head (F, 28, Murray, 1963).

9071    If your eyebrows meet across your nose, you'll never live to wear wedding clothes (F, 1900).

## Hands, Fingers, Fingernails, Etc.

9072    If you compare hand measurements, someone will die (F, SLC, 1963); Measuring of arms or hands with someone else portends a death in the family (F, SLC, 1925).

9073    If you shake hands across someone else's handshake, it means someone will die soon (F, 22, Norw, SLC, 1965); . . . one of the three will die (F, SLC, 1960).

9074    A break in the lifeline in the palm of the hand means death (F, SLC, 1958).

9075    Don't sit with your face cupped in your hands. It is a sign of grieving for the loss of a loved one (F, 42, Gr, SLC, 1964).

9076    Measuring fingers with another is asking for a death to either party (F, 63, SLC, 1964).

9077    It is unlucky to die with long finger- and toenails (M, 54, SLC, 1963).

9078    Never throw fingernails in a fire; it attracts calamity, and you will soon die (F, Scot, SLC, 1957).

9079    If you cut your fingernails when they are soft, for instance after taking a bath, you will not be able to see your parents at their deathbed (F, Ja, SLC, 1964); . . . cut your fingernails at night . . . (M, 25, Ja, Clearfield).

## Sleeping

9080    Sleeping with your head at the bottom of a bed will cause death (M, 23, Ger, SLC). Cf. Brown 4964.

9081    Sleeping with your feet to the east is a sure sign of death soon (F, Milford, 1964).

9082    Never sleep with your head to the west, or you'll die early (M, 38, Sandy, 1950); . . . you will die before morning (M, 57, Gunnison, 1925).

9083    If you sleep in a room that a person has recently died in, that person will come back and take you with him (M, SLC, 1957).

9084    The first to go to sleep at night will be the first to die (M, 20, Ogden, 1964).

9085    A sleepwalker must never be awakened, or he may die (M, 46, SLC).

## Dreaming

9086    If you dream that you die, then you will die at that same moment (F, 15, Hurricane, 1955).

9087  Dream three times of dying, and you will die (F, Logan, 1958).

9088  When you dream of a birth, there will be a death in your family (F, 23, SLC); . . . you will hear of a death (F, 20, Round Valley, 1970). Brown 5138.

9089  To dream of a helpless baby is a bad sign. It shows death (F, SLC, 1957); . . . you will have a death in your family (F, Eng, SLC).

9090  If you dream of nakedness, someone will die (F, 64, SLC, 1964). Cf. Brown 4952.

9091  If you dream that someone has killed you, you will never wake up (M, SLC, 1957).

9092  To dream of a person who has died is a bad omen, but to speak to that person means a death in the immediate family (F, 49, Richfield, 1925); . . . don't tell about the dream for twenty-four hours, otherwise a member of the family will die (F, 19, SLC, 1964).

9093  If you dream about the dead, it means someone in your town is going to die (M, 54, Richfield, 1928); . . . someone in your family . . . (M, 21, SLC, 1963).

9094  If you dream you are being left, the person leaving will die (F, SLC, 1960).

9095  If you dream that some dead person takes something from your home, someone in your family will die (F, Gr, SLC, 1957).

9096  When you have a dream and see a coffin with the lid open, it means that someone you know is going to die (a close friend or relative); if the lid is closed, it indicates that someone the dreamer knows is going to die (F, 21, SLC, 1956).

9097  If you dream of a large crowd, a death will follow of someone you know (F, 80, Centerville).

9098  If the oldest member of a family dreams of a person in the family, another person in that family will die (F, SLC, 1961).

9099  Usually when you have a dream that you are falling, you wake up before you hit, but if you don't wake up before you hit, the shock of hitting will kill you (F, Roosevelt, 1964); . . . if you hit bottom, you will never live to tell about it (F, 1961); Dreaming that you fall from a great height means . . . (M, 23, Magna, 1951); . . . if you fall off a mountain and hit bottom . . . (F, 1960); . . . a cliff . . . (F, 61, Hanksville, 1961); . . . a ledge . . . (F, SLC, 1957).

9100  If a person pictures everything in a dream as being white, death will follow in the morning (F, SLC, 1957). Cf. Brown 4954.

9101  If you dream of a dead person, it means that they wanted to talk to you before they died (M, SLC, 1957).

9102  Do not tell your dreams before you eat breakfast, or you will have a death in the family (F, 23, W. Jordan, 1954).

Sneezing

9103  If you sneeze at the table, it will cause a death to occur (F, 84, Springville, 1964).

9104  If you are at the table eating and someone should sneeze with food in his mouth, it is a sign of death (M, SLC, 1957). Brown 4925f, 4935.

9105  When someone sneezes at the altar of our church, it means that someone in the congregation is going to die (F, Gr, SLC, 1962).

9106  If you sneeze by a dead body, somebody else is going to die (M, 57, Gr, SLC, 1963).

9107  If you sneeze twice before breakfast, someone will die before supper (F, 79, Centerville). Cf. Brown 4928f.

9108  If you sneeze four times in a row without stopping, you will die (F, Logan, 1960).

9109  If you sneeze seven times in a row, you will die (F, 21, SLC, 1964).

Stepping, Walking, Tripping, Etc.

9110  Don't step on a crack in the sidewalk, or someone in the family will die (M, 64, Can, SLC, 1964); . . . your mother will die (F, SLC, 1915); . . . your uncle . . . (F, 1959); . . . you will die (F, 27, Logan, 1957).

9111  Walking around the house in bare feet invites death for a member of your family (M, 50, It, SLC, 1965).

9112  Walking around with only one foot slippered will cause the death of your mother or father (M, 50, It, SLC, 1965).

9113  If six men walk slow with you, you are on your way to your funeral (M, 65, Provo).

9114  If you trip over nothing, you are losing your best friend by death (M, Murray, 1957).

9115  If you meet someone when going up or down stairs, one of you must turn back or someone might die (F, 80, SLC, 1899).

9116  If a girl jumps in cold water during her period, it will kill her (F, SLC, 1959).

Other Beliefs

9117  When a person is playing baseball on Sunday, he will probably die before he is twenty (M, SLC, 1961).

9118  If one falls down on his birthday, he will never live to have another (M, Murray, 1957).

9119  If a person falls from a great height (150 feet or more), he loses consciousness, or is dead before he strikes the ground (M, SLC, 1957).

9120  Sing before breakfast, and you will die before night (F, SLC, 1961).

9121  If a chorus hums the song "Oh My Father," it means the death of one of the chorus members (F, Bountiful, 1960).

9122  Never sing the song "No Place Like Home," on the front lines of a battlefield, because to do so will bring death (M, SLC, 1957).

9123  A person with a white liver will soon kill off his or her mate in the marriage bed (M, Du, SLC, 1930s). (This belief, of tolerable rarity in the United States, is found in different parts of Europe.  --Eds.).

## PERSONALITY PROJECTION

9124  If you see a vision of a member of your family or some relative, the person seen in the vision will pass away (F, 24, SLC).

9125  People shouldn't give a child the name of a living relative, for fear the relative will die (F, 89, Midvale, 1964).

9126  One twin follows the other in death (F, Sandy, 1957).

9127  If a person sees his shadow in the water in the month of May, he or she will die before the year is out (F, SLC, 1959).

## DISEASES

9128  If you have a row of shingles (the disease) on each side of the body, and it grows from the spine to the center of your abdomen and meets, you will die (F, 18, SLC, 1963).  Brown 4987f.

9129  If a rash or eruption encircles the patient, death will ensue (F, SLC, 1961).

9130  To scratch oneself with a rusty nail always causes death (F, SLC, 1961).

## THE SICK

9131  On New Year's Day you must not visit the sick, or they will die before the day is out (F, 97, Syracuse, 1882).

9132  You will die if you visit your mother when she is sick (M, 43, SLC, 1964).

9133  When a person is deathly sick and wants to be lifted, if he is lifted, he will die (F, SLC, 1960).

9134  The rattling sound in the sick person's throat is the death rattle and a sure sign that he will die (F, Murray).

9135  If you cut a person's fingernails while they are sick, they won't live long enough for them to grow again (F, Murray, 1957).

9136  Change a sick person from one room to another, and he will surely die (F, 74, SLC, 1927).

9137  Don't turn the bed of a sick person, or they won't get well (F, 1959).  Cf. Brown 4991.

9138  Don't sweep under the bed when someone is sick, or they will die (M, SLC, 1965).  Cf. Brown 4992ff.

9139  Three knocks at the head or foot of a sick person's bed is an omen of his death (M, SLC, 1957).

9140  If you have a sick person in the house and you hear three knocks, the person will die before the next morning (F, SLC, 1964).

9141  If a person is sick, never feed them fish, or they will die and become like the fish, having cold blood (M, 38, SLC, 1935).

9142  If a black cat is sitting on the bed of a sick person, this means sure death (F, Ogden, 1960).

9143  If a dog howls around the house of a sick person, the sick person will die (M, SLC, 1900); When a dog howls at the bedside of a sick person . . . (F, SLC, 1961); When a dog looks up to the moon and howls . . . (F, 69, SLC, 1964). Brown 5001.

9144  If a bird taps on the window of a sick room, it is a sign the sick person will die (M, 28, SLC, 1943).

9145  When a person is seriously ill and a crow is seen nearby, the person will die (F, SLC, 1960).

9146  A hoot owl hooting over a house of a sick person means they will die before morning (F, SLC).  Cf. Brown 5008.

9147  For a robin to tap the window of a room of a sick person, he will die (F, 1959).

9148  A person cannot die if his bed is stuffed with game feathers (F, 78, Midvale, 1964).

9149  No one can die on pigeon feathers (M, SLC, 1961).

9150  Bird feathers in a sick person's room will delay his death (M, 44, SLC, 1964).

9151  Never accept white flowers while ill. It is a sign of death (F, 62, W. Jordan, 1924).

9152  If you send a yellow bloom to a sick person, they will die (F, 60, SLC, 1961).

9153  A sick man cannot die until the ebb tide begins to run (F, 85, SLC, 1964).

## THE DEAD, THE DYING

### Various Beliefs

9154  Dream of the dead and you will have trouble with the living (F, SLC, 1958); If you dream about the living, you will hear from the dead (F, Ogden).

9155  If you dream of a person in a casket but you can't see them, you'll have bad luck (F, W. Jordan, 1920).

9156 If you dream of a dead person giving you something, it signifies that something bad will happen soon (F, 57, SLC, 1963).

9157 If you dream of a loved one who has passed on, try to listen and understand them. They are telling you something of importance (F, 37, Price, 1963).

9158 When a deceased family member appears at the end of the bed, someone in the family will die (M, 57, Gunnison, 1925).

9159 A dead person visits the earth periodically (F, SLC, 1963).

9160 The dead walk the streets looking for their body (M, SLC, 1960).

9161 If a person dies at sea, it is believed that a lot of times this dead person will come to call other persons to come to join him in death, at the same place where the person died at sea (F, Ja, SLC, 1964).

9162 It is bad luck to occupy a room and be the first to do so after a death has occurred (M, 34, SLC, 1965); . . . it will bring you death (M, 22, SLC, 1959).

9163 A plate of salt placed in the room of a dead person is a purger of that person's sins (F, 80, Pleasant Grove, 1961). Cf. Brown 5423. (One should read the note in Brown with some care, for at play here are reflections of the obsolescent notions of the sin-eater, who consumed salt from the body of the dead, to remove, symbolically, at least, their sins. --Eds.)

9164 If the eyes of a person who has just died do not close, he is looking after his followers (M, 64, SLC, 1960).

9165 If someone dies with his eyes open, the person he is looking at will also die soon (F, 18, It, SLC, 1961). Cf. Brown 5014.

9166 The last name that a dying person calls is that of the next to follow (F, 74, SLC, 1964). Brown 4908.

9167 If a person who has been real close dies, you will soon follow (M, SLC, 1957).

9168 If a dying person hits or bats another person, that person will die soon (F, 23, SLC, 1963). Brown 5016.

9169 If the body of a dead person remains limp for some time after death, it is a sign that some member of the family will soon follow (F, 31, SLC, 1948); If a corpse gets stiff then becomes limber, there will be another death in the family (M, SLC, 1958). Brown 5422.

9170 If one twin dies, and the limbs do not stiffen rapidly, the dead one is waiting for the other (F, SLC, 1955).

9171 When a Gypsy leader dies or is dying, the more people and the more noise they can make, the better the chances for the Gypsy to live (M, 21, SLC, 1964).

9172 A person cannot die so long as any lock is locked and bolts are shut in the house (F, SLC, 1959); . . . the soul will have a hard time leaving the body (M, SLC, 1938); When a person is on a deathbed, all locks in the house should be opened and kept open until after death (F, 74, SLC, 1964).

9173 The bed of a dying person should always be placed facing east and west with the head toward the west (M, 21, SLC, 1963).

9174 Navajo Indians believe if a person dies in their hogan, they would have to move; so if a person is ill, they put him outside to die (F, 53, SLC, 1918).

9175 Promises given to dying people must be kept to insure their resting peacefully (F, 47, SLC, 1964).

9176 After people who are just about to die are administered the last rites, but are not dead yet, they are said to have the power to make their curses come true for sure (F, SLC, 1971).

9177 If a man confesses anything on his deathbed, it is the truth, for no man could stare death in the face and lie (F, 19, SLC, 1960).

## Hard Death, Easy Death

9178 If a person dies hard, it is a bad sign; he will haunt the survivors (F, 31, SLC, 1945).

9179 If a person is found dead with their eyes shut, they have had an easy death (F, 67, SLC, 1959).

9180 If you find a dead person with their eyes open, it means they had a painful death (F, 67, SLC, 1959).

9181 The dying are held back from their repose by the love that will not give them up (F, SLC, 1961).

9182 If a person is dying, never sit on the bottom of his bed, or he will agonize for days (F, SLC, 1962).

9183 Anyone who has owned a dog during their life will die without pain (F, SLC, 1959).

9184 A person will die easier if his head is toward the east (F, 56, SLC, 1931). Brown 5011.

## Talk about, Kiss, Touch the Dead

9185 Never mention the name of a dead person (F, 46, SLC, 1964).

9186 To speak bad of the dead will bring bad luck or ill fortune (M, SLC, 1965).

9187 If you talk about a dead person, they will turn over in their grave (F, SLC, 1959).

9188 When you talk about a dead person, you are not letting them rest (M, SLC, 1957).

9189 When an old person asks about people who died long ago, they too will soon die (F, SLC, 1960).

9190    Think too much of the dead, and you'll be next (M, 84, Centerville).

9191    You are not supposed to kiss the dead, or you will be the next to die (F, 97, Syracuse, 1896).

9192    If a child doesn't kiss a dead person (this is usually at a viewing), the dead person's spirit will not follow the child during the child's life. That is to bring the child good luck and keep the child out of trouble (F, SLC, 1971).

9193    Kiss the dead and you won't dream about them (F, SLC, 1958).

9194    To touch the dead body of a loved one who has died will help to remove the sorrow and sadness of death (F, 21, Logan); If you touch the hand of a dead person, you will never be afraid of the dead (F, SLC, 1930). Brown 5421.

9195    Never touch a dead person, as it will bring death to a loved one (F, SLC, 1960).

## DEATH OF SPECIAL PERSONS

9196    A president elected in a year ending in zero runs the risk of being shot in office (F, SLC, 1963); Ever since 1840 every president of the United States elected to office in intervals of twenty years has died in that office (SLC, 1961); The United States government broke a treaty with an Indian tribe about 1830. The witch doctor of that tribe cursed the government that every president elected every twenty years would die in office. This curse has been realized in the deaths of Harrison (1840), Lincoln (1860), Garfield (1880), McKinley (1900), Harding (1920), Roosevelt (1940), and Kennedy (1960) (F, 19, SLC, 1964); Every twenty years a president dies in office (M, SLC, 1964).

9197    To dream of a white-haired man, especially a Negro, means the death of a friend (M, 61, SLC, 1962).

9198    Every sixth person in a house of prostitution will die (M, 20, Ogden, 1959).

9199    Before fighting, the Cheyenne warrior was not to eat with an iron utensil or he would be killed with a bullet or metal point (M, Ja, SLC).

## LOVE AND MARRIAGE AS INDICATORS OF DEATH

9200    A person who has been disappointed in love is said to die of a broken heart (F, 21, Sandy, 1958).

9201    To dream of a wedding is a sign of a death (F, SLC, 1957); . . . means you are going to hear of a death (F, Moab, 1953); . . . means the death of a loved one (F, 41, SLC, 1963); If you dream of marrying it means . . . (F, SLC, 1959). Brown 4979ff.

9202    If you dream of a wedding, there will be a funeral (M, 75, SLC, 1964).

9203    Whoever goes to sleep first on the wedding night will be first to die (F,

69, Riverside, 1920); If a bride goes to sleep first on the wedding night, she . . . (F, Ger, Ogden, 1961).

9204    If a doctor visits a wedding, someone will die that year (M, SLC, 1961).

9205    On the way to the church the bride or groom must not turn their heads. If either does, it means that he or she is looking for another companion and the present one will die soon (F, 47, SLC, 1964).

9206    If you postpone a wedding date, it is a certain sign that one of the contracting parties will die within a year (F, SLC, 1940).

9207    When a wedding pair join hands before the altar, the one whose hands are coldest will die first (F, 46, SLC, 1940).

9208    After the wedding ceremony, the first one to leave the altar dies first (F, SLC, 1957). Brown 4973.

9209    A bridal couple returning from church after the ceremony must pass the threshold at the same time, else the one passing it first will die first (F, 47, SLC, 1964). Cf. Brown 4977.

9210    If you sneeze during a wedding ceremony or a sermon, you will die (M, 21, SLC, 1955).

9211    If you dream that you help a bride prepare for her wedding, it means you are going to see a dead person (F, 24, SLC, 1964).

9212    If either the bride or groom loses their wedding band, this means that the partner will die first. Example: if the bride loses her band, her husband will die sooner than she (F, Gr, SLC, 1964).

9213    If a wedding ring has worn so thin as to come to pieces, or if it breaks, either the wife or the husband will die (F, SLC, 1955).

## CLOTHING

### Various

9214    Wearing black is a sign of death (F, SLC, 1957).

9215    Don't wear black on Friday the thirteenth, or you will soon wear it again in mourning (F, 14, SLC, 1964).

9216    If you wear green, someone in the family will die (M, 52, Eng, SLC, 1963); . . . you will go into mourning before the year is out (F, Ir, SLC, 1960). Brown 4958.

9217    Hanging clothes on a doorknob means death to someone (F, 51, Centerfield, 1964).

9218    Do not lay a coat on a bed, or someone will die (M, 30, SLC, 1960).

9219 If a man wears a hat in the house, it is a sign of death in that house (F, 15, It, W. Jordan, 1957).

9220 Don't throw a hat on the bed, or it brings death to the family (M, 23, Price, 1950); . . . someone will soon die (F, 53, SLC, 1918).

9221 If a man leaves a hat on the desk, it is a sign of death in the family (F, SLC, 1964).

9222 Never change underwear "till May's out," or you will die within the year (F, Eng, SLC, 1958); Change winter underwear in May, you'll waste your life away (F, 56, Centerville).

9223 Never put your underclothes on backwards, or you'll hear of a death (F, 57, SLC, 1963).

9224 Dreaming of a clothesline of white clothes means a death in the family (F, 50, Richfield, 1925). Cf. Brown 4954.

9225 Aprons are tied with bows horizontal; dead people's clothes are tied with the bows vertical (F, 48, Ja, SLC, 1963).

9226 When you wear a kimono and you put the left side over to your right hand, this is symbolic of the dead person (F, 25, Ja, SLC, 1964).

9227 If you find a black handkerchief, there will be a death (F, 48, Joseph, 1964).

9228 A young girl was dressing for a party and because she felt that the garments did not conform to the style of her rich attire, she left them off. She was killed in a motor accident (M, SLC, 1946).

9229 The Indians killed these people, and when they unbuttoned their shirts and saw the garments they had on, they didn't even scalp them. But the others were just riddled. There were five of them, I believe, in Southern Utah (F, 40, Woods Cross, 1944).

## Shoes

9230 Putting your shoes or feet on the table is a sign of death (F, Tooele, 1958); . . . means there will be a death in the family (F, Granger); A new pair of shoes on the table means you will not live to wear them out (F, 47, Midvale, 1928).

9231 To put baby shoes on the table will cause a death in the family (F, 46, Marysvale, 1963).

9232 A loose heel on a shoe means that you will die by tripping downstairs (F, SLC, 1915).

9233 Don't keep shoes tied or buckled when not worn. It is a sign of death (F, 42, Gr, SLC, 1964).

9234 If you wear a hole in the middle of your sole, you will die rich (F, Eng, Hooper, 1963).

9235 One shoe on and one shoe off is a sign of death (F, 75, SLC, 1935). Cf. Brown 4960.

9236 If you die with your shoes on, you will not be able to rest in death (M, SLC, 1959).

## JEWELRY, GEMS

9237 The person giving away the rings of a dead relative will die soon (F, 44, SLC, 1939).

9238 Pearls represent death (F, 21, SLC).

9239 Large opals are lethal, because the person who wears them will die a tragic death (M, SLC, 1961).

## DOMESTIC INDICATORS OF DEATH

### House

9240 If a house is added to other than at the gable end, a death will occur in that house (Anon, 30, Beaver, 1960s). Cf. Brown 5038.

9241 It is bad luck to live in a house where anyone has died. It is a sign of another death (F, Springville, 1924).

9242 To build a new house where the old one stood will cause a death in the family (M, Provo, 1938).

9243 If plaster falls off the wall, it is a sign of death (M, 26, SLC, 1962). Brown 5039f.

### Doors, Doorknobs

9244 Never go out the same door you came in; it means certain death (F, 59, SLC).

9245 If you walk in through the front of a house and out the back, there will be a funeral (M, 50, It, SLC, 1965).

9246 If you board up a door, someone will die (F).

9247 If you are going to open a door to go out and someone opens it from the outside at the same time, it means there will be a death soon (F, 22, Norw, SLC, 1965).

9248 When two people on opposite sides of a door turn or touch the doorknob at the same time, it means a death in the house (F, SLC, 1930).

9249 Never hang anything on a doorknob, or there will be a death in your family (F, Axtell, 1958). (The bad luck associated with hanging things on doorknobs, and even death, as here, has never been satisfactorily explained. William E. Koch's recent collection from Kansas, however, contains a useful clue: "People never used to hang a bonnet or anything on the door knob, because that was a sign there would be a death in the family within a year and that crepe would be hanging on the door," p. 162, No 1975. The mortuary practice of hanging a grey or black satin crepe over the doorknob, or fastening it to the door to announce a bereavement, is a custom long since fallen into desuetude. --Eds.)

9250   A dishcloth hung on a doorknob is a sign of death in the family (F, 74, SLC, 1964).

## Windows, Shades, Etc.

9251   If a person jumps through an open window, this person's mother will die (F, 20, SLC, 1964).

9252   If a blind runs up quickly, someone in your family will die (F, Park City, 1957); If a window shade flies up in the night, a death will soon follow (F, 43, SLC, 1930s).

9253   A falling blind is supposed to signify that a death will take place in the family that lives in that house (F, 19, Sandy, 1963).  Brown 5095.

9254   If the wind blows the shutters into an arched position, it is a sign of approaching death in the family (M, 23, Ogden, 1959).

## Chairs

9255   If you whirl a chair around on one leg, someone will die (F, Fillmore, 1960). Cf. Brown 5089.

9256   Never set chairs with backs together; it is a sign that death is imminent (F, 1957).

9257   To place three chairs accidentally in a row means a death in the family (F, 1960).

9258   If you rock an empty rocking chair, an older person or a baby in the family will die (F, 76, SLC, 1964); . . . it is an invitation for death to visit you, and to sit in the chair (M, 25, It, Helper, 1946).  Cf. Brown 5092.

9259   If a rocking chair starts rocking alone, there will be a death in the family (F, 45, SLC, 1930); . . . rocks all night, there will be a death in the family (F, SLC, 1959); . . . for every rock, someone will die (F, 20, Ogden); . . . the next person who sits in the rocker will die (M, Murray, 1958).  Cf. Brown 5093.

## Tables

9260   There will be a death if thirteen people sit down together to eat (F, 60, SLC, 1964); If thirteen . . . , one of them will die within a week (F, Copperton, 1967); . . . there will be a death in the family within a year (F, 58, Logan, 1970); . . . the thirteenth person to sit down will die (F, 87, Providence, 1895).  Cf. Brown 5073.

9261   If thirteen sit up to a table, one must never get up and leave without all getting up at once, or the one who gets up is the one who'll die (F, 87, Providence, 1900); . . . the one who rises will not live through the year (F, 55, SLC, 1964).  Cf. Brown 4905, 5074.

9262   Don't ever seat thirteen people at the supper table.  It denotes the Last Supper (F, 42, SLC, 1964).

9263   Never put lilies on the dinner table. They're the flower of death (M, 21, SLC, 1963).

## Silverware, Glassware, Dishes

9264   Never spin a knife, for death will come to the one it points to (M, Ogden, 1958).

9265   Don't cross two knives, for a death will occur in the family if this is done (M, 22, SLC, 1957).

9266   If by mistake an extra knife is put on the table before a meal is served, you will hear of a death (F, SLC, 1957).

9267   If you cross a knife and a fork, there will be a death in the family (F, 80, Midvale).

9268   Two spoons on a plate mean death (F, Cedar City).

9269   You should not cross your chopsticks, because it is bad luck.  Dead people's bones are picked that way (F, 40, Ja, SLC, 1964).

9270   If chopsticks are not paired, the person being served will die (F, SLC).

9271   If your drinking glass breaks, the person nearest you will die (M, 44, SLC, 1935).

9272   It's an old shipboard saying that if you run your finger around a glass and make it ring, a person on ship will die that night (M, SLC, 1960).

9273   Setting an extra place at dinner, i.e., counting wrong and setting an extra place, is inviting death to dinner (F, 44, Sandy, 1928).

## Food, Meals

9274   When you cremate a family member, the oldest son or next to the oldest son has to go in the cremation pit to pick out the bones and such with a pair of chopsticks and pass it down the line of the other people also using chopsticks. So one must not pass food by chopsticks, for it's ridiculing the dead and cremation ceremonies (M, 22, Ja, Midvale).

9275   Dreaming about food in any form is a sign of death in the family (F, SLC, 1961).

9276   If you eat seafood on the beach, someone fishing with you will die (F, 26, SLC, 1964).

9277   To eat taboo food brings misfortune or even death (F, 75, Pleasant Grove, 1906).

9278   Eat an egg every day for a year, and you will die (M, 44, Layton, 1970).

9279   Don't ever drink milk in the same meal you drink buttermilk, or it will kill you (M, SLC, 1959).

9280   If you drink milk after eating cherries, you will die (M, 38, SLC, 1935).

9281 If you eat choke cherries and milk together, you will die immediately (F, 18, Brigham City, 1960); . . . you will choke to death (F, 66, Tooele, 1906).

9282 Don't eat sour cherries and milk or rhubarb and milk, or you will die (F, Moab, 1953).

9283 Eat chili and drink milk together, and you will die (M, SLC, 1958).

9284 If you eat pickles and ice cream together, you will die (F, SLC, 1958).

9285 Never eat the first pickle in a jar; it will bring certain death to someone you love (F, 71, It, SLC, 1963).

9286 If you eat a pickle late at night, you will die (F, SLC, 1961).

9287 Dreaming of eating strawberries means a death in the family (F, 77, Dan, SLC, 1964).

9288 When you dream about black cherry or blackberry and then eat some, you will have something unpleasant happen, or even a death in the family (F, Peoa, 1920).

9289 Eat lobster and ice cream together, and you will die (M, SLC, 1958).

9290 If you dream of raw meat, there will be a death in your family (F, 88, SLC, 1964).

9291 If you put rice in the rice bowl above the rim, it means that this is for a dead person (F, Ja, SLC, 1964).

9292 When you eat rice, if you eat with one chopstick, it means you will die soon (F, 25, Ja, SLC, 1964).

9293 If you stick your chopsticks straight up in your bowl of rice, someone will die (F, 25, Ja, SLC).

9294 Always fill the rice bowl with more than one motion, because one motion only is for dead people (F, 41, Ja, SLC, 1963).

9295 If you dream of ripe fruit, being eaten, picked, or in any other way present, it means there will be a death of someone close to you (F, 45, Venice, 1935). Cf. Brown 5369.

9296 The whiter the bread, the sooner you're dead (F, SLC, 1961). A slogan of Clinton's Bread Company.

9297 If there is a hole in a loaf of bread, there will be a death in the family (F, 58, Logan, 1970); . . . a grave has been dug for someone in the family (F, 59, SLC). Brown 5085.

9298 If the bread burns, it means there will be a death (F, 70, Provo, 1900).

9299 A loaf of bread upside down on the table means a death in the family (F, 51, Tooele, 1923). Brown 5086.

9300 One should never give bread from their home after sunset, for the bread symbolizes the staff of life and will bring death to the giver (F, Gr, Tooele, 1961).

9301 If the cake you are baking falls, someone will die (F, 60, SLC, 1917); . . . someone is digging your grave (F, 70, Bountiful, 1900s).

9302 If you spill olive oil on the floor and you do not put salt on it in the form of a cross, a death will occur (F, 51, W. Jordan, 1963).

9303 Don't return salt to the person who lent it to you, for it means death (F, SLC, 1960).

9304 Never pour anything backhand--they wash dead people that way (F, 48, Ja, SLC, 1963).

9305 Do not warm over the food of your lover, for he will surely die (F, Eng, Brigham City, 1960).

9306 If the leaves left in a teacup form the shape of a tree and a person standing near the tree, it will mean that there will be a death in the family (F, 72, Eng, Lark, 1963).

9307 If a person enters the room at the same time a family has finished eating, he will die soon (F, SLC, 1940).

## Beds, Bedding

9308 If three people help make a bed, a death will occur in that house in one year (F, 40, W. Jordan); . . . someone in the family will die . . . (F, Murray, 1969). Cf. Brown 4967.

9309 If your bed faces east, you will die (F, 45, SLC, 1920s).

9310 If the headboard on your bed is on the west side of the room, you will die young (F, SLC, 1964).

9311 Three knocks on a person's bed means he is close to death (F, SLC, 1947).

9312 If a fresh sheet when spread on the bed has a diamond in the center from folding, there will be a death in the family (F, SLC, 1957).

9313 When someone dies in a bed at home, nobody is allowed to sleep in that bed for three nights. It is believed that the soul will not leave the house for three days (F, It, Helper, 1967).

9314 If you keep the pillow that a person has died upon, you will find the feathers have formed a crown (M, SLC).

9315 A rose shaped by your pillow means death (F, 53, SLC, 1964).

## Clocks, Mirrors

9316 A clock that strikes thirteen prophesies death (F, Ogden, 1959); . . . a death in the family (M, 29, SLC, 1949). Cf. Brown 5051.

9317 If a clock strikes or chimes more than it should, there is going to be a death (F, 78, Provo, 1900).

9318 It is a superstition that a clock usually stops when a person has died (M,

21, SLC, 1964); A clock stopping means the death of a near relative (F, 72, SLC, 1964).  Brown 5052.

9319   If you break a mirror, it means that there will be a death in the family before the year ends (F, 78, SLC, 1964); . . . someone close is going to die (F, SLC, 1964).  Cf. Brown 5059f.

9320   If you look in a mirror after you eat, you may have bad luck, or possibly die (F, SLC, 1961).

9321   If you see a dead person's face in a mirror, you will be the next to die (F, SLC, 1952).

## Pictures, Photos

9322   A photograph in which every member of the family appears is considered an omen of bad luck.  One of the group will surely meet an early death (SLC, 1946).

9323   If a picture fades, the person in the picture is dead (M, SLC, 1961).

9324   If a picture hangs crooked, someone is going to die (F, 19, SLC, 1950).

9325   If a portrait of someone falls, the person will die (F, 50, SLC, 1963); . . . someone in the house will die within a month (F, SLC, 1961).  Cf. Brown 5064.

9326   If a picture falls from the wall and breaks, a death will follow (F, Sandy, 1957).  Cf. Brown 5066f.

## Sweeping, Brooms

9327   If you sweep the floor after dark, you are sweeping the dead (F, 58, It, SLC, 1963); . . . you are disturbing the dead (F, 24, It, SLC, 1964); . . . someone in the immediate family will die (M, 53, SLC, 1964); . . . you'll have a death before morning (F, 55, SLC, 1963).  Cf. Brown 5110.

9328   You must sweep under your bed, for if you don't, the dust will accumulate and the image of a person who has died will appear beneath your bed (F, 28, Bingham, 1940).

9329   When someone is sweeping and accidentally hits their spouse with a broom, this means they will die shortly (F, 39, SLC, 1932).

9330   It's a sign of death if you put a broom on the bed (F, 20, SLC, 1964).  Cf. Brown 4968.

9331   Don't buy a broom in May, or you'll sweep all your friends away (F, 45, SLC, 1963); . . . sweep away a member of the family (F, 51, Centerfield, 1964).

9332   If a new broom falls on the floor from a place of rest, a death will occur (F, It, Helper, 1964).

## Washing, Wiping

9333   Don't wash on New Year's Day, or there will be a death in the family (F, Eng, SLC).  Cf. Brown 5118ff.

9334   If you leave your clothes out on the line over New Year's Eve, there will be a death in the family that year (F, Logan, 1958); If the wet clothes are hanging in the house . . . (M, SLC, 1957).

9335   Any laundering during the twelve holy days of the Yule Festival will cause the death of a relative (M, Ger, SLC, 1938). Cf. Brown 5115f.

9336   Leaving the clothes on the line outside overnight means death (F, SLC, 1961).

9337   Dreaming of a clothesline of white clothes means a death in the family (F, 49, Richfield, 1925).

9338   Wash blankets in May, wash one of your family away (M, Eng, Park City, 1957).

9339   Two persons should never wipe themselves at the same time on the same towel, or one of the persons will die (F, Ger, SLC, 1938).  Brown 5122.

## Candles, Lamps, Matches, Etc.

9340   If you see a ghost carrying a candle, it means you are going to die (F, 60, SLC, 1963).

9341   If you let a candle burn until it goes out, a close relative will soon meet a tragic death (F, 24, SLC, 1964).

9342   If a candle burns out by itself, someone in the family will die (M, 22, Hurricane, 1952).

9343   If a lamp goes out for no reason at all, a person will die within a month (F, Moab, 1953).

9344   If a lamp blows over, there will be a death (F, Orem, 1959).

9345   A third person on a match dies a terrible death (M, SLC, 1957).

9346   Three on a match means the youngest of the three will die (M, Syrian, SLC, 1963).

9347   During the war, men in foxholes were never to light three cigarettes on the same match, as the third one will die (M, 37, SLC, 1965); Three on a match means that the enemy is spotting the light on the first soldier, sights in on the second soldier, and on the third, he pulls the trigger (M, 23, SLC, 1963); . . . the third person will die before the others (F, 52, Nephi, 1965).

9348   Never light more than two cigarettes with one match, or one of the people will die.  "You know, there was a girl here in town that was to a card party, some kind of bridge, and somebody lit a cigarette and then lit somebody else's and she said, 'Light mine too.'  But he said, 'No, I won't,' and she said, 'Oh, light my cigarette with it.'  So he did, and that night their airplane caught fire, and she was killed" (F, Moab, 1953).  Brown 5173.

9349   The third man to light his cigarette on one match will die in a house of

prostitution (M, 21, Bingham, 1961);
. . . on a whore's doorstep (M, SLC,
1960); . . . in a French whorehouse (F,
SLC, 1960).

9350 If the kitchen fire burns out on
Christmas Eve, it is a sign that some
member of the household will die before
another Christmas season (F, SLC, 1957).

9351 If you dream that your home is burning,
someone will die in your family, or one
of your friends (F, SLC, 1957).

9352 To see a fire in the distance is a sign
of death (M, 39, SLC).

9353 When there is a hollow in the fire a
grave will be dug for a member of the
family (M, 91, Dan, Midvale, 1964).

9354 If you see a green ball of fire coming
from nowhere, a member in your family
will die (F, 24, Ja, SLC).

9355 Never burn wood that has been struck by
lightning, as it will bring death (M,
SLC, 1957).

9356 If you sweep ashes out of your house
after dark, someone in your family will
die before morning (M, Provo, 1975).
Cf. Brown 5107.

9357 If you carry the ashes from the stove or
furnace out on New Year's Day, it means
that you will carry somebody dead out
before the year is out (F, Eng, SLC,
1968). Cf. Brown 5099f.

## Umbrellas

9358 Put up an umbrella in the house, and
someone will die right away (F, 66,
Woods Cross, 1920); . . . a member of
the family will die suddenly (F,
Santaquin, 1925). Brown 5096.

9359 Never open a black umbrella in the
house. It means death (F, Bear River
City, 1957).

9360 Never ever put an open umbrella in front
of your hearth to dry, or death will
strike your home (F, 47, Swiss, SLC,
1965).

9361 Don't put an umbrella on the bed; it
will bring a death into the family (F,
82, SLC, 1961).

## Implements Brought into the House

9362 If you carry a sharp tool through the
house, it is the sign that someone in
the family will die within a year (F,
84, Provo, 1892). Brown 5390.

9363 Carrying a shovel through the house
means a death in the family (F, Moab,
1953); . . . a spade . . . (M, SLC,
1966); . . . means that person will dig
his own grave (M, Murray, 1958).

9364 Bring a hoe into the house and there
will be a death in that house (F,
Marysvale, 1963); . . . a casket will
follow (F, SLC, 1959); . . . someone in
the family will die within a year (F,
Tooele, 1958). Cf. Brown 5393f.

9365 If you bring a hoe or shovel into the
house and carry it from one door to the
other, someone in the family will die
(F, Moab, 1953).

9366 Bringing an ax into the house means
death to someone (F, 80, Eng, Midvale).
Cf. Brown 5391.

9367 If you bring an ax, shovel, or hoe into
the house, don't take it out the same
door, or someone will die (F, 19, SLC,
1964).

## Sewing

9368 If you start sewing an article on
Tuesday, you will never live to see it
completed (F, 67, Farmington, 1936).

9369 If you ever begin to make a dress on a
Friday, you'll never live to wear it (F,
Swed, SLC, 1957); Always complete a
dress cut out on Friday before the day
is ended, or you will not live to finish
it (F, Spanish Fork, 1962); . . . the
one wearing it will die before the dress
is worn out (SLC, 1946). Brown 5126f.

9370 If a person starts to make an article of
clothing on Saturday and does not finish
it before midnight, the wearer may never
live to wear it out (M, SLC, 1957).
Brown 5128.

9371 Leaving some stitches unfinished in a
gown means it will soon finish the life
of the wearer (F, 45, Murray, 1930).

9372 If in sewing a garment three needles are
broken, the person who wears the garment
will not outlive it (M, SLC, 1964).

9373 If you mend clothes while you are still
wearing them, you will never live to
wear them out (M, SLC, 1959).

## Miscellaneous

9374 If a teakettle sings, that is a sign of
death (F, 66, SLC, 1962).

9375 Dropping a dishtowel means a death in
the family (F, 55, SLC).

9376 To drop soap is a sign of death (F, 29,
SLC, 1952).

9377 On New Year's Eve, Germans take down
everything that is hanging such as
curtains, because they believe that
there will be a death if they don't do
so (F, 19, SLC, 1950).

9378 If an iron drops, it means that someone
in the house will die (F, 26, SLC,
1964).

9379 Don't sharpen a pencil at both ends, or
your father will die (M, SLC, 1969).

## ANIMALS

9380 A death in a family is always preceded
by an animal howling or screaming (M,
50, Roy, 1920s).

Cats

9381   If anyone during his life has made
       enemies of cats, he will go to his grave
       by a storm of wind and rain (F, 85,
       Grantsville).

9382   Kill cats, and die in rags (M, 65, SLC).

9383   If a black cat crosses your path in
       front of you, you will be killed (F,
       Paragonah, 1959); Cross a black cat's
       path and it is a sign of death (F, Moab,
       1953); If you let a black cat cross in
       front of you, some member in your family
       will die (F, 80, SLC, 1923). Brown
       5185.

9384   When a white cat crosses in front of
       you, it means a death in the family (F,
       SLC, 1957).

9385   If a strange cat enters the house, death
       will call soon (F, Holladay, 1957).

9386   If a cat rolls on its back in front of
       your door, someone will soon die (M, 19,
       SLC, 1963).

9387   If a cat jumps over a dead body, another
       person will die (M, 73, Gr, SLC, 1963).

9388   If you are rocking in a chair and rock
       on a cat's tail, it means you are next
       one to die (M, SLC, 1958).

9389   If a cat purrs around a man, even if it
       is repeatedly driven off, it is a sign
       he is about to die (F, SLC, 1959).

Dogs

9390   Dogs can sense death (M, 18, SLC, 1950).
       Cf. Brown 5186.

9391   Kill dogs, and die in rags (M, 65, SLC).

9392   If a dog rolls over on your front lawn,
       someone will die in your house that day
       (M, 64, SLC).

9393   If a dog rolls on its back in front of
       your door, someone will die (M, 19, SLC,
       1963).

9394   If a dog digs a hole in your garden,
       there will be a death in the family (F,
       49, Logan, 1935).

Dogs Howling

9395   Every time a dog howls someone will die
       (F, 71, Ger, Magna, 1964); . . . it
       means the death of a loved one (M, 52,
       Du, SLC, 1964); . . . a death in the
       family within three days (F, SLC, 1961);
       . . . death in the neighborhood (F, 63,
       Monroe, 1964).

9396   The howling of a dog announces a death,
       because he can smell death (F, Woods
       Cross, 1953).

9397   When a person is dying, dogs will howl
       (M, 44, Layton, 1970); When a dog gives
       a mournful wail with a howl rising in
       crescendo, and a very eerie pitch, it is
       an indication that someone near and dear
       to you is dying (F, 54, Logan, 1922).

9398   When a dog cries, it means his master is
       going to die (M, Gr, SLC).

9399   If a dog howls and gets down on the
       ground and rolls, he is rolling in the
       lint of someone's grave (M, Garfield,
       1905). Brown 5219.

9400   A dog barking at night while facing you
       means that you're next to die (F, 13,
       Orem, 1964).

9401   Never look over your left shoulder when
       you hear a dog howl, or what you see
       will frighten you to death (F, Weber
       Co).

Time and Place of Howling

9402   A dog howling at night means death (M,
       SLC, 1959); . . . a death in the
       household (M, 18, SLC, 1964); . . . a
       death in the family (F, 50, SLC, 1964);
       . . . a death soon (M, 1960); . . .
       someone in the neighborhood has just
       died (M, SLC, 1957); . . . a death
       before morning (M, SLC). Brown 5209.

9403   If a black dog barks three times after
       midnight, you will die (F, 20,
       Springville, 1963); . . . there will be
       a death in the town the next day (F,
       Alton, 1957).

9404   A dog howling in the middle of the
       night, right next to your window, is
       predicting a death in the night (F, 22,
       SLC, 1963). Cf. Brown 5207.

9405   If a dog howls after twelve midnight and
       howls for an hour, then someone will die
       (M, 75, SLC, 1964); . . . someone in the
       family . . . (F, 19, Salina, 1954);
       . . . someone in the house . . . (M,
       SLC, 1958). Cf. Brown 5213.

9406   If you hear a dog howl on a stormy
       night, there will be a death in the
       family (M, 21, SLC, 1958).

9407   A howling dog during the day means there
       soon will be a death (M, SLC, 1958).

9408   A dog howling in the house is bad luck
       and could cause death (F, 19, SLC,
       1965).

9409   If a dog howls under a window, it is a
       sign of death of a person in that home
       (F, Moab, 1953).

9410   A hound howling in front of a house is a
       sign of death (F, 50, SLC, 1935); . . .
       means a sudden death in the house (F,
       SLC, 1958).

Howling at the Moon

9411   If a dog sits and howls at the moon, it
       is a sign of death (F, Nephi, 1961); If
       someone dies, a dog will bay at the moon
       (F, Moab, 1953); If a dog is howling
       with his nose pointed toward the moon,
       it means someone will die in the
       neighborhood (M, Swiss, Heber City,
       1915).

9412   When you hear a dog howling at a full
       moon, someone will be dead by morning
       (F, 44, SLC, 1961); . . . a member of
       your family . . . (M, 63, SLC, 1920).

9413   A dog howls by the light of the moon if the master is going to die (F, 74, SLC, 1964).

## Cows, Cattle

9414   If a cow puts her head over the fence and bellows, it means there will be a death in the family (F, Midway, 1900). Cf. Brown 5189f.

9415   If a cow lows three times in your face, it is a sign of death (F, SLC, 1961). Cf. Brown 5193.

9416   The lowing of cattle at night foretells the death of some person in the neighborhood (F, 21, Vernal); . . . after midnight is a warning of an approaching death in the family (F, 24, SLC, 1963).  Brown 5194ff.

9417   An ox or cow breaking into your garden means a death will come in your house (F, Eng, Brigham City, 1960).

## Horses

9418   If you dream of a white horse, someone in your family will die soon (F, 85, Eng, SLC, 1965).  Cf. Brown 5232.

9419   When you lead a horse to water do not wrap the rope around your hand, or you can be drug [sic] to death (M, Box Elder Co, 1925).

9420   Seeing a black horse with a white rider means death (M, SLC, 1964).

## Sheep, Pigs

9421   If a family butchers a lamb, they examine the shoulder bone, and if they find two black spots, somebody is going to die in the house (M, 66, Gr, SLC, 1963).

9422   If you dream of a pig being slaughtered, there will be a death in the family (F, 19, Murray, 1963).

## Fowls

9423   When a rooster crows before light, someone will die in a three-mile radius (M, Hyde Park).

9424   A rooster crowing at night is a sign of death (M, 44, Layton, 1970); If it crows in the evening, it will be a sad death (F, SLC, 1962); If a rooster crows before midnight, someone is going to die (F, Morgan, 1961).  Cf. Brown 5252.

9425   The crowing of a rooster is the sign of some event affecting the family.  If the head of the house feels the rooster's feet and they are cold, it means death; if not, it means good luck (F, 52, W. Jordan, 1962).

9426   If a chicken crows before sundown, it means a death in the family.  If it crows nine times by nine days, there will be a death in the family (F, Moab, 1953).

9427   If you hear a chicken making a sound like a rooster, you are supposed to cut its head off right away.  If you don't kill the chicken, there will be a death (F, Gr, SLC, 1962).  Cf. Brown 5248, 5250, 5257.

9428   A rooster that crows at a doorway is a symbol of death within the family (F, 40, Grantsville, 1955).  Brown 5256.

9429   If a rooster crows three times in the morning and you are first to hear it, you will be the next to die (F, Swiss, SLC, 1957).

9430   A chicken or turkey backbone can tell the future like death, etc., by its clearness, sharpness on the top, and any odd piece on the end (F, Gr, SLC, 1957).

9431   A wisp of straw hanging on a hen's tail means death in the immediate family (F, Ir, SLC, 1960).

## Wild Animals

9432   If a monkey dies in the circus, it means that another member of the troupe will also die (F, 47, SLC, 1964).

9433   The scream of a mountain lion means that someone in the family will become sick and die (M, 90, SLC, 1964).

9434   Wolves howl and circle near a starving man or corpse (F, 71, Centerville, 1963).

9435   If you hear a wolf cry or howl, someone has died (F).

9436   Jackals howl and circle near a starving man or corpse (F, 71, Centerville, 1963).

9437   If a person sees a coyote running east, it means that he will die (M, 23, SLC, 1961).

9438   A coyote howling in the moonlight means someone has just died (F, SLC, 1957).

9439   If a mouse runs over a person, it is a sign that the person is approaching death (M, 31, Ogden, 1964).

9440   If you hold a guinea pig by the tail, its eyes will fall out, and you will die (M, 50, SLC, 1948).

9441   The cry of bats means the death of someone in the house where you live (F, 19, SLC, 1964).

9442   If you kill a bat, there will be a death in the family (F, SLC, 1961).

## BIRDS

## General Notions

9443   To dream of a bird means death (F, 49, SLC, 1963).

9444   If a bird flies down a chimney, a dreadful death will follow (F, 67, SLC, 1963); If a bird roosts on your chimney, it means a death in the family (M, 43, Hinckley, 1927).

9445  If a bird hits you, it is a sign of death (F, 58, SLC).

9446  If you find a dead bird, someone is going to die (F, SLC, 1960).

9447  A broken feather found on the doorstep means death is coming (F, Murray, 1957).

9448  Death will enter a house in the form of a bird (F, SLC, 1962).

9449  If a bird pecks on the house, count the number of times, for they signify the number of days before a death will occur in that house (M, 54, Midvale, 1964). Brown 5278.

Birds Inside the House

9450  If a bird flies into the house, someone will die (F, Roosevelt, 1900s); Letting a bird loose in the house means . . . (M, 24, SLC, 1963); . . . someone you know is dying (F, 42, Magna, 1932). Cf. Brown 5285.

9451  A bird flying through an open door means that a death will occur (F, 60, Duchesne, 1930s).

9452  A bird flying around inside a house means there will be a death in the family (F, SLC, 1948). Cf. Brown 5280.

9453  If a bird should come into the house, it is a messenger of death. If it lights on a person, it is sure to be the death of a near and loved one (F, 49, Richfield, 1925). Cf. Brown 5283, 5287.

9454  If a bird flies into your home, it is the death omen that a death will occur in three days (M, SLC, 1961).

9455  If a bird flies in a house before midnight, it means someone will die (F, Morgan, 1961).

9456  If a bird comes into your bedroom and sits on the head of your bed, you will die within twenty-four hours (F, 80, SLC, 1918). Cf. Brown 5284.

Birds at or near Windows

9457  If a bird lights on your window sill, it means death (M, 28, SLC, 1963).

9458  A bird in the east window means death (F, SLC, 1915).

9459  If a bird looks through the window at a sick person, he will die (F, Bountiful, 1915).

9460  If a bird hovers at the window, it is a sign of death in the immediate family (F, SLC, 1928). Cf. Brown 5279.

9461  If a bird flies into your closed window, it is a sign of death in your family (F, 40, SLC, 1920s); . . . it means death to a dear friend (F, SLC, 1964).

9462  If a bird pecks on the window, someone in the family is going to die (F, 34, W. Jordan, 1963); If a bird knocks on a window . . . (F, 24, Norw, SLC, 1964); A bird tapping on your window means . . . (F, 67, SLC, 1963). Brown 8558.

9463  If a bird flies into the windshield of a moving automobile, someone close to the driver is surely on his deathbed (F, 43, Tooele, 1924).

9464  If a bird flies in the window, it will bring news of a death (F, SLC); . . . someone will die (F, 24, Midvale, 1959); . . . there will soon be a death in the family (F, Bountiful, 1959); . . . a member of the family will die within a year (F, 80, SLC, 1918). Brown 5281.

9465  If a bird flies in a window of a house and circles the entire four corners of the room, there will be a death in the family (F, SLC, 1957). Brown 5282.

9466  For a bird to fly in and out of a room by an open window predicts the death of the inmate of the house (F, 74, SLC, 1903).

Blackbirds

9467  If a blackbird comes into a house, it is a sign of death (M, 20, SLC, 1964).

9468  If a blackbird lands on your window sill, it means there will soon be a death in the family (F, 21, Logan, 1970).

9469  Two blackbirds sitting together on a window sill or a doorstep are an omen of death in the family (M, SLC, 1933).

9470  If a blackbird is perched on your door or comes inside, it is a sign that someone in the house is going to die (F, SLC, 1966).

9471  A blackbird sitting on a fence means that death is near (M, SLC, 1961).

Doves and Pigeons

9472  A dove in the window means death (F, SLC, 1957). Cf. Brown 5296.

9473  When a dove mourns in the spring, it means death (F, Bear River City, 1957).

9474  A mourning dove cooing in the morning is a sign of death (F, Moab, 1953); A mourning dove cooing within hearing of the house .. . (F, SLC, 1940). Brown 5297.

9475  If it's raining and you hear a mourning dove, it means someone in the neighborhood has died (F, SLC, 1928).

9476  If a dove tries to get into the house or flies at the window, it is a sign of death in the family (F, Magna).

9477  If a dove released at a funeral lands on you, it means death (F, 33, Bountiful, 1964).

9478  A white pigeon fluttering round a house is an omen of death (M).

9479  If a pigeon flies against the window, there will be a death in the household (M, 22, SLC, 1961). Cf. Brown 5318f.

9480  If a white pigeon lands on a chimney, it is a sign of death in the house (F, SLC, 1945). Cf. Brown 5317.

9481   There will be a death in the house on whose chimney a white pigeon makes his nest (F, 12, Sandy, 1963).

## Robins and Sparrows

9482   A robin flying into a church and singing means a death in the parish (F, Midvale).

9483   If a robin taps your window, someone in your family will die (F, Park City, 1957).

9484   If a robin stays around in the yard for a period of time and chirps, it is a sign of death (M, 64, SLC, 1964).

9485   The singing of a sparrow is a sign of someone mourning a death (F, 17, SLC, 1961).

9486   If a sparrow pecks on a window, it means impending death (F, 67, SLC, 1964).

9487   If a sparrow flies into your house, it means a death in the family (F, 52, SLC, 1920).

9488   If a sparrow flies down the chimney, there will be a death in the family (M, 24, Ogden, 1950).  Cf. Brown 5325.

9489   If a sparrow kills itself in flying against a window, there will be a death in the family (F, Spanish Fork, 1962).

## Crows, Ravens, Magpies, Etc.

9490   If a crow circles around the house and then lands on it, it means someone in the house will die (F, 24, Norw, SLC, 1964).

9491   If a crow flies over a house and croaks three times, someone in the family will die (M, 90, Price, 1900).

9492   When crows caw in the evening, it is a sign someone is going to die (F, 51, Ja, SLC, 1963); . . . at night . . . (F, 17, SLC, 1961).  Cf. Brown 5292.

9493   When a raven appears, there is going to be a death (F, Norw, SLC, 1960).

9494   If black ravens perch on the top of a house and crow, it means someone is dying in the neighborhood (F, Swiss, SLC, 1957).  Cf. Brown 5320.

9495   If a raven feather drops in your yard, a death will soon follow (M, SLC, 1943).

9496   If a single magpie croaks around a house, someone will die (M, 53, Ogden, 1964).

9497   To see a magpie means death (M, 60, Plain City, 1917); . . . five magpies . . . (F, Ir, SLC, 1960).

9498   If you shoot a magpie, someone in your family will die (M, 57, Swiss, Heber City, 1918).

9499   If you see a buzzard on the housetop, it is a sign of death (F, SLC, 1959).

9500   Vultures howl and circle near a starving man or corpse (F, 71, Centerville, 1963).

## Owls

9501   If you ever hear an owl cry, there will be a death (F, Norw, SLC, 1964); . . . somebody is dying in town (M, Ger, SLC, 1938).  Brown 5303.

9502   If you hear the hoot of an owl, you will hear of the death of someone you know (F, Provo, 1959).

9503   If you hear an owl hoot at night, a close one will die (F, 29, Gr, Magna, 1964); . . . hoot in the light of the moon . . . (M, 49, Midvale); . . . hoot at your door, someone in the family is going to die (F, 84, Price, 1961).

9504   If you have an owl in your back yard, death will follow (M, 21, SLC, 1964).  Cf. Brown 5308.

9505   It is bad luck for an owl to screech outside of a bedroom window.  It means there will be a death (M, 25, Dugway, 1963).  Cf. Brown 5310.

9506   An owl sitting on a window sill of your house brings death (F, Morgan, 1961).

9507   If an owl passes over your head at night, you will die within a week (M, 18, SLC, 1963).

## Various Birds

9508   The appearance of a white-breasted bird means sure death (F, 63, Eng, SLC, 1964).  Cf. Brown 5288.

9509   A hummingbird is a symbol of death, if it lands on you (F, 31, Grantsville, 1956).

9510   If a road runner runs across the porch and drops a feather as it runs, a death in the family is foretold (F, SLC, 1957).

9511   If you see a single swan, it means that a death will occur (F, SLC, 1957).

9512   When whippoorwills sing together at night making the sound "hohin, hohin" one should reply "no!"  If the birds stop singing at once, it is a sign that the hearer will die soon (F, SLC, 1961).  Cf. Brown 5331.

9513   A woodpecker pecking on a house is a sign of death (M, SLC, 1958).

9514   Three seagulls flying together are a sign of death (F, Riverton, 1941).

## OTHER ANIMALS

## Lizards, Snakes, Frogs

9515   If you kill a lizard, you'll die within a year (M, 73, SLC, 1910).

9516   Two snakes moving down a road mean that sickness and death will follow (M, SLC, 1961).

9517   Dreaming about snakes means there is a death in the family (F, 21, SLC, 1963); If a snake bites during a dream, it means death (F, 49, Richfield, 1925).

9518   Kill frogs and die in rags (M, 65, SLC).

## Fish

9519   If you have some goldfish and someone in your family dies, get rid of the goldfish, or someone else will die (F, 61, Midvale, 1921).

## Insects, Etc.

9520   If a person dies in a Negro family, the bees have to be told immediately, or another death will result (F, SLC, 1957).

9521   Bees seen in a swarm foretell death (M, 44, Manti, 1920s); If bees swarm on dead wood, the owner will die (M, 91, Dan, Midvale, 1964); . . . on the dead branch of a live tree . . . (F, SLC, 1959).

9522   A swarm of bees settling on a house means a fire, and if one leaves the swarm for no reason, it is a sign of death in the family within a year (M, 71, Midvale, 1915).

9523   A beetle heard tapping in the wall of a house means sure death (F, 22, SLC, 1950).

9524   A black beetle crawling on your shoe means that one of your friends is going to die (M, Ogden, 1964).

9525   You'll die an unnatural death if you kill a butterfly by sticking pins in it (F, SLC, 1959).

9526   If a black butterfly flies into the church when someone is getting married, one or the other person getting married will die (F, 49, Green River, 1918).

9527   If a black butterfly comes into the house, it means a death in the family (M, PR, 32, SLC, 1965).

9528   A white moth in the house foretells a death (F, SLC, 1900).

9529   If you find a cricket in your house, it means death (F, 61, Riverton, 1962). Cf. Brown 5337.

9530   If a cricket leaves the house, it is a sign of death (F, SLC, 1959).

9531   When a person dreams of lice, it is a sign that there is going to be a death in his family (F, Provo, 1959). Cf. Brown 5344.

9532   A peculiar noise somewhat resembling the ticking of a watch is made by various species of insects, which bore into the walls and furniture of old houses. People believed this ticking sound predicted a sudden death in the family (M, Vernal, 1959). (These insects are called the "death watch." --Eds.) Brown 5049.

9533   If you destroy a red ant, you will die within a year (M, 64, SLC, 1945).

9534   If a firefly is in the house, it means that there will be one less person in the house the next day (M, 54, SLC, 1964). Brown 5342.

9535   If a lightning bug comes in the house, someone is going to die (M, Roy, 1956). Brown 5343.

## Spiders, Etc.

9536   If you try to kill a black spider and it escapes, it is an omen of death (M, 24, SLC).

9537   A white spider is a sign of death (F, Eng, SLC).

9538   To be bitten by a tarantula is sure death (F, Magna, 1960).

# PLANTS

## Various Plants

9539   If you touch hemlock, your mother will die (M, Ogden, 1938).

9540   Never have a Wandering Jew plant in your home, or there will be a death in the family (M, SLC, 1957).

9541   Never thank a person for giving you a plant, for you will die (M, SLC, 1967).

## Vegetables

9542   If you string garlic across the doorways, death will not come (F, SLC).

9543   If in a row of beans one should come up white instead of green, there will be a death in the family within a year (F, Spanish Fork, 1959).

9544   Maize was created by the Great Spirit during a famine, and whoever wastes it will be doomed to wander hungry and alone, and eventually die (F, Amer Ind, SLC, 1961).

9545   If a farmer fails to plant a row of corn in the cornfield by oversight, some member of his family will die before the harvest time (M, 54, Midvale, 1964). Cf. Brown 5348ff.

9546   If sweet potato plants wind around the house, it causes death (F, 28, SLC, 1944).

## Flowers, Bushes

9547   A lady called yoond (the crier) walks through the streets at night. She carries a tray of flowers and anyone who sees her meets sure death (F, 20, Amer Ind, SLC, 1963).

9548   If you dream of flowers, especially purple ones, it's a sure sign of death (F, 52, Provo, 1920).

9549   If you dream about flowers, you'll hear from the dead (F, 87, Providence, 1895).

9550   If a flower fades, someone is dying (F, SLC, 1963).

9551 To have flowers bloom out of season it means a death in the family (F, SLC, 1958). Brown 5353, 5360.

9552 If a Christmas rose blooms at any other time of the year than at Christmas time, there will be a death in the family that year (F, Axtell, 1958).

9553 Cut flowers should never be kept in a bedroom at night; they will cause sickness and death (M, SLC, 1960).

9554 Never mix red and white flowers in an arrangement for a person in the hospital. It will bring sudden death (F, SLC, 1967).

9555 Never send yellow flowers to a funeral. To do so means you will be next to die (F, Magna, 1960).

9556 If you pick a flower from a grave, you will die the next day (F, 47, SLC, 1964).

9557 When a dandelion goes to seed, blow as many seeds away as you can. Count the remaining seeds and that is the number of years you have left (F, 67, Farmington, 1934).

9558 To bring a flowering hawthorn into a house will bring death into the family (M, Ogden, 1929).

9559 If one brings home white water lilies, someone in the family will die (F, 47, SLC, 1964).

9560 Use lilies only for funerals, for they tempt death (F, SLC, 1950).

9561 It is unlucky to plant a bed of lilies of the valley, as the person who does so will die in the course of twelve months (F, 75, SLC, 1964).

9562 If one has a wild pansy given him, there will be a death within a year (F, 47, SLC, 1964).

## Trees

9563 If the leaves on a tree in your yard turn yellow, other than in the fall, somebody in your family is going to die (F, 52, Midway, 1972).

9564 If a dead tree falls when the wind is not blowing, it is a sign of death (F, 31, SLC, 1950). Cf. Brown 5372.

9565 For a fruit tree to bloom the second time in one season is a sign of a death in the family (M, 1957). Cf. Brown 5370.

9566 If an apple stays in the tree until spring, there will be a death in the family that owns the tree (F, 87, S. Jordan, 1964).

9567 If all the blossoms on the pear tree blow off, except one or two on the top of the tree, there is going to be a death in the family (F, 33, SLC, 1963).

9568 When a plum tree blossoms in December, it means death to the owner (M, SLC, 1963).

9569 If bay leaves wither on a tree, it is an omen of death in the family (M, SLC, 1961).

9570 Sitting under a pine tree on Christmas Eve brings death near (F, 87, W. Jordan); . . . means you will hear the angels sing and you will die shortly afterwards (F, 20, SLC, 1961).

9571 If one transplants a cedar tree, he will sure die as soon as the tree has grown enough to cover a grave (F, 46, Cedar City, 1964). Cf. Brown 5377ff.

9572 If you plant a weeping willow, someone in the family will die (F, Bear River City, 1957). Brown 5384.

9573 If a willow tree spreads its root under a house, it brings sickness and death (F, 51, Ja, W. Jordan, 1963).

## WEATHER

9574 If it rains when the sun's shining, a death will soon occur (M, 32, Magna, 1947).

9575 If it rains while a man is dying, or if the lightning strikes near his house, the devil has come for his soul (F, SLC, 1960).

9576 If it rains within an open grave, a relative of the deceased dies (F, Midvale).

9577 The barometer affects old people. There are a lot of old people that die after the first storm of the year (F, SLC, 1971).

9578 A black Christmas (no snow) means a full graveyard (M, Ogden, 1957).

9579 A green Christmas means a full cemetery in the spring (M, SLC, 1961); . . . a full graveyard (F, Eng, Hooper, 1963); . . . a fat graveyard (F, Lehi, 1957); . . . a rich graveyard (F, Bear River City, 1957). Cf. Brown 5151f.

9580 Three thunderbolts in a series means death (M, SLC, 1964).

9581 If you are touching metal when lightning strikes, you will be struck dead (M, 21, Holladay, 1964).

## PHYSICAL WORLD

## Stars, Meteors

9582 If you count the stars, you will die (M, SLC, 1960). Cf. Brown 5142.

9583 When someone dies, a new star is lit in the heavens (F, Garland, 1963).

9584 A falling star means someone has died (F, SLC, 1959); A shooting star . . . (M, 51, SLC, 1942); . . . is a sign some friend will die (F, Lehi); . . . a death of some of your close relatives (F, Moab, 1953); . . . a sign of a great person dying (F, SLC, 1961); . . . signifies that someone has gone to heaven (F, Lehi, 1957). Cf. Brown 5143, 5148, 8555f.

9585  A shooting star is the soul of someone who just died (F, 60, Ogden, 1919).  Cf. Brown 5147.

9586  A falling star means a witch has died (M, 21, SLC, 1962).

## Moon, Eclipse

9587  When the moon is red, someone close to you has died (F, 18, SLC, 1954).

9588  A full moon indicates that a death has occurred (M, 22, SLC, 1963).

9589  A certain sign of death is looking at the moon over your left shoulder (M, 26, SLC, 1963).

9590  Never look at a full moon through a window.  It means sure death (F, 80, Eng, Midvale).

9591  If the moon shines on your face while you are sleeping, you will die very soon (F, Bear River City, 1957).

9592  If an eclipse of the sun occurs on the twenty-ninth day of the month, there will be many deaths on the first day of the next month (M, It, Helper, 1959).

## Earth, Dirt, Water, Etc.

9593  All rivers flow over graveyards somewhere along their path (M, SLC, 1964).

9594  If you dream of mud or muddy water, it is a sign of death (M, SLC, 1957); . . . someone close will die (M, Midvale); . . . it means a death in the family (F, 20, Murray, 1957); . . . the person whose face appears in the water will die (F, 37, SLC, 1964).  Brown 5175.

9595  If you dream of yourself swimming in muddy water, someone in your family will die (F, 66, Bear River City, 1910).

9596  You have to eat a ton of dirt before you die (F, Bountiful, 1960).

9597  If you dream of beautiful mountains, someone in your family will die (F, 30, 1970).

## MONEY, WILLS

9598  He who earns his coin on Sunday never lives to enjoy his earnings on Monday (F, SLC, 1958).

9599  If you spend a two-dollar bill you have had for sometime, it means bad luck or death (F, SLC).

9600  A man who makes a will will soon die (M, SLC, 1961); The day you make a will, you'll sign your death warrant (F, 18, SLC, 1961).

9601  If you change your will, you will die three years sooner (M, SLC, 1959).

## TRADES AND PROFESSIONS

9602  Women in a mine will cause a miner's death (F, 46, Bingham, 1925).

9603  Wearing earrings will guarantee a sailor against drowning (F, 1900).

9604  If a dancer whistles between performances, someone will die that night (M, SLC, 1960).

## VEHICLES, CARRIERS

9605  Never count the cars on a train as it goes by, or someone will die (F, 80, Eng, Midvale); . . . you will die (F, 48, Ogden, 1920s); . . . it will cause a death in the family (M, 38, Logan, 1970).

9606  If you dream about a train, it is a sign of death (F, SLC, 1962).

9607  When three buggies, or carriages got in a line accidentally, someone in one of the buggies would die (M, Park City, 1900).

9608  The right hand seat of a car is the death seat (M, 20, SLC, 1963).

9609  If someone has died in a car, don't ride in it, for death will occur again (M, SLC, 1959).

9610  If you see an ambulance, hold your collar and don't swallow until you see a dog.  If you don't do this, the person in the ambulance will die (F, Ogden, 1964).

9611  The safest place in a plane is the back seat.  If a crash occurs, the person in this seat will be the last to die (F, SLC, 1960).

## TRAVEL, GIFTS

9612  When a person sees a friend coming along the road and he does not recognize him, the friend will soon die (F, SLC, 1920).

9613  Never begin a journey on Friday, or a death will occur in your family (M, 21, SLC, 1963).

9614      Watched out of sight,
          Dead before night.
      (F, Nephi).

9615  If you visit someone on New Year's and you don't take a gift, you mustn't go in, or the person you are visiting will die (F, 67, Farmington, 1942).

9616  Never give sharp objects, such as scissors, as a gift, for bad luck or death from stabbing will result (F, 28, SLC, 1964).

9617  Never give anyone a present that is black in color, because it is a sign of death in the family (F, 40, SLC, 1943).

9618  Packages wrapped in black and white mean death (F, Ja, 25, SLC, 1965).

9619  If you dream that you are giving a dead person a gift, someone will die (F, Gr, SLC, 1962).

## MAIL, COMMUNICATION

9620  If you dream about the living, you will hear from the dead (F, Bountiful, 1958).

9621   When opening a newspaper, if the first page you turn to is the obituary, this is a sign of a death in the family (F, SLC, 1959).

9622   The back of a letter edged in black means a death in the family (F, Magna).

9623   If you put a stamp on a letter upside down, it means death (M, SLC, 1963).

9624   If you address a letter and never send it, the person on the address will die (F, 44, SLC, 1964).

9625   When the phone rings and no one speaks at the other end, death is calling (F, 54, SLC, 1920s).

9626   Some people will not say "good-bye" at the end of a telephone call, because they feel they will die if they do (F, 19, SLC, 1958).

9627   "I dreamed that someone was dead. I could just see the telegram, and the next morning when I went to get the mail there was the telegram. But I saw that telegram that night just as plain as day" (M, Moab, 1953). (This is a "death token" story. --Eds.)

PLAYING CARDS

9628   If one gets all black spades in a hand of cards, it means there's going to be a death (M, Holladay, 1959).

9629   The ten of spades is a death card in fortune telling (F, SLC, 1957).

9630   If the ace of spades turns up in the cards, it means death (F, SLC, 1959); Draw an ace of spades from a deck of cards, and you will soon die (M, 13, Orem, 1964).

9631   If someone cuts the ace of spades out of a deck of cards, it's a sign of death (M, Tooele, 1957).

9632   If you turn up or drop the ace of spades while playing cards, it means a death (F, 40, SLC, 1947).

9633   When you draw a black queen card out of a deck, it means there will be a death (F, SLC); . . . the queen of spades . . . (F, Roosevelt, 1964).

COUNTING, NUMBERS, CALENDAR

9634   If someone you know dies, then there will be two more deaths very soon after. Death always comes in threes (F, 49, Ir, Tooele, 1972); One death in the family means there will be three in a row (F, Bountiful, 1960). Brown 4903.

9635   If after a long period the death is a male, three deaths will follow. If it starts with a he, it will always take three (F, 65, SLC, 1918).

9636   If a female dies in the family, three other females in the family will follow (F, Tooele, 1958).

9637   Famous people die in groups of three, never singly (F, 22, Logan, 1970).

9638   Three funerals always follow one another in quick succession (F, 19, SLC, 1964).

9639   Each Japanese individual has certain unlucky days during the year. For example, if May 2 is your unlucky day, you will die on that day. Soon after a close friend will die, for you will come to get him (M, Ja, SLC, 1962).

9640   One's unlucky, two's lucky, three's health, four's wealth, five's sickness, six is death (F, 38, Ger, SLC, 1940).

9641   Never hang a calendar of the New Year before January 1st, or death will occur in the family (F, Wattis, 1950).

MISCELLANEOUS

9642   If you wish someone were dead, you will die instead (F, Bear River City, 1957).

9643   You have to treat an older person really nice before they die, because they have closer contact with the spirits, and when they die, they decide what will happen to you (F, 18, American Fork, 1960).

9644   Anything that lands crosswise indicates a coming death (F, Norw, SLC, 1960).

9645   If you get lost in a building, you will die soon (F, 45, Midvale, 1964).

9646   If you throw a nail into a whirlpool, you will see your mother's coffin (M, 25, Dugway, 1963).

9647   Every cigarette you smoke is one more nail for your coffin (F, 22, SLC).

PREMONITIONS, DEATH TOKENS, BANSHEES, ETC.

9648   One night when the informant's mother was asleep, she awoke to see someone sitting on the foot of her bed. The personage or being spoke to her saying, "Which will it be, B or O?" She said, "O is higher in the priesthood," whereupon the personage disappeared. The next day the informant's mother received word that her son O had been killed in a mining accident at Bingham Copper Mine in Utah. He was only twenty-one and the eighth child. Six years later B was killed in a coal mine in Consumers, Utah (F, 52, Price, 1927).

9649   It brings death to answer a mysterious voice (M, SLC, 1961).

9650   If a stranger in black speaks to you on a foggy night, you will die within the year (F, Butlerville, 1957).

9651   If you hear a banshee wail at your door, it means a death in the immediate family (M, 30, SLC, 1961).

RELIGIOUS ELEMENTS, CURSES, ETC.

9652   When the N family came to Alpine, they used to let out wheat--a peck to plant for a bushel back in the fall. People were so hard up, they couldn't get seed, and had to give them anything they asked for to get it. Someone prophesied that

WN would die in a ditch like a dog, and that the Ns would lose all their property. Darned if they didn't. Look at that house now. W had a fit, and died out on the sidewalk (F, 63, Woods Cross, 1945).

9653    If a man swears on a skull and lies, he will be struck dead (M, 50, Manti, 1930).

9654    If you die at night, your spirit won't find its way to heaven (M, 22, Amer Ind, SLC).

9655    If you don't believe in a religion but attend the services anyway, and then laugh at the people and their practices, you will be punished with death or a serious injury (F, 56, Grantsville, 1963).

9656    If you use the name of God in vain, God will strike you dead (F, SLC, 1945).

9657    If you see God in a dream, it means someone will die (M, SLC, 1961).

9658    A Mr. C warned a dissenter from the LDS Church (who claimed to have walked and talked with Christ) that if he didn't stop his anti-LDS activities he would die soon. Two years later the dissenter arranged meetings in Provo, and dropped dead after the second meeting. Mr. C believed this to be fulfillment of his warning (M, 89, Provo, 1946).

9659    My aunt, ET, always believed that she was responsible for the death of my father. She said that when the angels came for her she was too stubborn to go; so they took my father instead (F, 38, Logan, 1961).

9660    Roman Catholics have this ritual every Palm Sunday; they give out palms to the people in church. If you put these palms over the head of your bed, you will not pass away at night in your sleep (M, 21, Logan, 1972).

9661    When the informant's father was a young man, he was in a saloon and there was a fellow making fun of the religion (LDS), and he held up his glass of whiskey and said, "Be there a God, may he strike me dead if I put my finger in this whiskey." He put his finger in his whiskey and died right then and there (F, 69, 1957).

## TIME OF DEATH

9662    Deaths mostly occur at the falling of the tide (F, 19, SLC, 1964); Death is delayed until the ebb of the tide (F, SLC, 1959). Brown 5180.

9663    Most deaths occur between two and six in the morning (F, 30, SLC, 1955).

9664    When it comes a person's time to die, fate arranges it so that it happens at a certain place (i.e., when several people are killed in a plane crash, fate intended for all of them to go that day and arranged the crash) (F, SLC).

9665    If you were born on Monday, you will die on Monday (M, SLC, 1964); Born on Friday, die on Friday (M, SLC, 1961).

9666    If a death occurs during the twelve days before Christmas, twelve more deaths will follow in due course (F, 19, SLC).

9667    Lent means a double funeral (F, 23, Midvale, 1954).

9668    When an Indian dies at night, he won't go to the happy hunting grounds (F, Bountiful, 1915).

## PREMATURE DEATH, EARLY DEATH

9669    People who kill animals for any reason other than to eat their meat will die horrible and premature deaths (M, 72, Willard, 1964). Heard in Wyoming, 1900s.

9670    If you're born on an odd numbered day in October, you're fated for ill luck and early death (F, 79, SLC, 1935).

9671    The good die young (M, SLC, 1960); Only the good die young (M, 25, SLC, 1964).

9672    A straight line in the palm of the hand is an omen of early death (F, SLC, 1961).

9673    If you measure hands with a friend, one of you will die at an early age (F, 41, SLC, 1964).

9674    If the palms of your hands are usually cold, it means you will die very young (F).

9675    Don't put a hat on the bed, or you will die young (M, Bountiful, 1962).

9676    Never sleep in a bed with the head facing east, because if you do, you won't live long (M, Du, SLC, 1964).

9677    A wedding after sunset entails an early death for the bride (M, SLC, 1961).

9678    The old English proverb says, "Early wed, early dead" (M, Providence, 1958).

9679    If you laugh during a marriage ceremony, you will die young (M, Ogden, 1961).

9680    You will die before your time if you lay a loaf of bread upside down on the table (F, Ogden, 1961).

9681    If you prick your finger while sewing and the blood gets on the garment, and you wear it, you will have an early death (M, 54, SLC, 1964).

## Accidental Death, Suicide

9682    A dream of raw meat means death by accident (F, 57, SLC, 1963).

9683    There is an old adobe church in town where a man hanged himself. If anyone enters this church, they will have bad luck (F, Fillmore, 1960).

9684    Those who threaten to commit suicide seldom do (M, 24, Cedar City, 1964).

9685    Suicides are not given a funeral service in the church (M, Gr, SLC, 1962).

9686 People that meet with an untimely death (suicide) come back to spend the rest of their time on earth (F, 58, SLC).

## Drowning

9687 If you possess a caul, you will never drown (F, Tooele, 1957).

9688 If one relaxes, he can't drown (M, 55, SLC, 1915).

9689 A drowning person cannot drown until he has gone down for the third time (F, SLC, 1959).

9690 It is unlucky to hold a chair on one leg. It is a sign of impending drowning (SLC, 1946).

9691 Mormon missionaries are not allowed to swim while on their missions because the devil or evil powers may cause them to drown (M, 21, Logan, 1970).

9692 Never attempt to save a drowning person, because it invites misfortunes to the rescuer (M, SLC, 1960).

9693 As you go over a bridge lift your feet, or you'll drown (F, 19, SLC, 1963).

9694 If you spill tea into the saucer, someone in the family will drown (F, 44, SLC, 1964).

9695 To fall into a dike means that you will meet death by drowning (F, Du, SLC, 1961).

9696 If a person sleeps with his eyes open, he will die in water (F, SLC, 1959).

9697 A drowned woman floats face upwards, and a drowned man floats face downwards (F, Wendover, 1964).

9698 If a person dreams of floating or drowning in a river or muddy water, it is a sign of death (F, 31, Bountiful, 1963).

9699 If one dreams of drowning, there is a death in the family (F, Price, 1959); If you see someone drowning in a dream, you will live a long life. But if the water is clear, it means that a woman is going to die (F, 20, SLC, 1964).

9700 A drowned person cannot rest in peace (F, 60, Norw, SLC, 1963).

## Finding a Drowned Body

9701 A boy drowned. They dragged the river for days and days, then got the peepstone woman (from Logan) up here and she told them right where he could be found in the river, but later he appeared. He hadn't been drowned at all (F, 60, 1946).

9702 The position of the drowned body may be discovered by floating a loaf of bread. Reason: The loaf of bread is apt to be carried by a current of water just as a body is (F, 51, SLC, 1963).

9703 A loaf of bread with a little quicksilver in it will float to and

stand over the place where a body is (M, 20, Midvale, 1960).

9704 Shoot a cannon over the water, and a dead body will rise (M, SLC, 1963).

9705 When search is made for the body of a drowned person, a live sheep is thrown into the water and is supposed to indicate the position of the body by sinking near it (F, Provo). (In contrast to the three preceding entries, which are well known, this ritual has not, to our knowledge, been reported from elsewhere in the United States. --Eds.)

9706 Drowned bodies float on the ninth day (F, SLC, 1961).

## CARE FOR THE DEAD

### Clocks, Mirrors, Pictures, Etc.

9707 The owner's clock should be stopped at the moment of his death, or it will bring bad luck to the family (F, 54, Nephi, 1918); All the clocks in the house should be stopped . . . (F, 33, SLC, 1955). Brown 5405ff.

9708 Mirrors are covered at the time of death in a home, because a mirror is supposed to possess part of the deceased person's spirit (M, 46, SLC, 1925); . . . so the spirit won't see its reflection in the mirror when it leaves (F, 49, Gr, Midvale, 1927); Cover all mirrors with a dark cloth at the time . . . so that no reflection of death appears (F, 29, Gr, Magna, 1964). Cf. Brown 5408.

9709 In time of death, turn all mirrors to the wall to prevent further disaster (F, SLC, 1960). Cf. Brown 5416.

9710 It means death or bad luck if another person sees the corpse of a dead person in the wall mirror (F, 46, SLC, 1963).

9711 It is a Jewish belief that if someone dies in the family, all of the mirrors must be covered, for the first to look in the mirror after the death will be the next to die (F, SLC, 1961). Cf. Brown 5412ff.

9712 Unless mirrors and pictures of a person who has died at home are turned to the wall, the spirit will catch the reflection and haunt you (M, SLC, 1961).

9713 When death occurs, the mirrors and picture in the room should be turned to the walls so the glass will not fog (M, 45, SLC, 1963).

9714 In the olden days if a loved one's pictures were facing out when the corpse was brought home, they turned the picture over or removed them, because it was believed the corpse would take the person's soul (F, 49, Gr, Midvale, 1934).

9715 When people die, it is customary to cover up the piano. It is not to be played for at least a week after the death (F).

## Preliminary Ministrations

9716   After death all the windows and doors in the house must be opened in order that the soul of the dead may be released and fly away (F, SLC, 1959); . . . to let the spirits out (F, 70, Bountiful, 1900s).   Cf. Brown 5430ff.

9717   Indians burn the tepee after the person dies so that the person's soul will go up in flames and reach the afterlife (F, 19, SLC, 1956).   Cf. Brown 5433.

9718   Burn incense to purify yourself and wish happiness to the persons passed away (M, 20, Ja, SLC, 1963).

9719   When someone dies in your house and the body is taken away, you're supposed to sweep your house out real good.  This will assure that no one else will die (F, 19, Gr, SLC, 1953).

9720   If somebody dies in a house, break a glass or dish in order to have good luck (F, 38, Gr, SLC, 1963).

9721   When a dead person leaves a home, break a piece of glassware to frighten away the spirits, or else someone in the family will die (F, Gr, SLC, 1957).

## Care of the Corpse

9722   One must not speak ill of the dead until they are buried, because the soul remains near the body until burial (F, 72, SLC, 1964).

9723   A candle is lit at the head of a corpse to keep the evil spirits away (F, 65, Fillmore, 1961).

9724   If a dead person has a smile on his face in the casket, he will take someone from his family to the grave (F, Gr, SLC, 1961).

9725   When a person dies, one is supposed to leave a small cup or bowl of water in the presence of the body for the first twenty-four hours so that the spirit of the body may partake of the water when it wants to (F, 1959).

9726   Tears of mourners should not be allowed to fall on the dead, or it will hinder his rest (M, SLC, 1929).

9727   A corpse must be carried from a room feet first (M, 44, Layton, 1970); . . . from the house . . . (M, SLC, 1963).  Brown 5429.

9728   Never carry a corpse to church by a new road (F, 49, SLC, 1962).

9729   Cats will enter funeral parlors at night and proceed to eat the noses and ears of any corpses which may be at hand (M, 17, SLC, 1958).  Brown 5427.

9730   A dog and a cat are not allowed to go near a dead body, for fear that the spirit will bother the living people (F, Gr, SLC, 1962).

9731   It is an unlucky omen to have a cat jump over a corpse (F, SLC, 1959).

9732   It is a pleasant omen for a butterfly to hover over a corpse (F, SLC, 1959).

9733   The mouth of the dead body must not touch any of the clothing else it will bring all the relatives after him (M, 51, SLC, 1964).

9734   If you hold a body over Sunday, somebody else will die in the family (F, 50, SLC, 1918).

9735   If some close relative dies, and you don't touch the body before it is buried, you will always dream of the dead person (F, 22, Helper, 1948).

## Laying out the Corpse

9736   Always put coins on the eyelids of a dead person as soon as he dies, and he will rest in peace (F, 49, Ogden, 1916); . . . a silver coin on each eye . . . (F, 20, SLC); . . . to keep the eyes closed (F, Bear River City, 1957).  Brown 5424.

9737   If you do not close the eyes of the dead, he or she will come and take another victim with him or her (M, 33, It, SLC, 1963).

9738   When my grandmother died, my mother saved a lock of hair, and she says it has always been the custom (M, 19, SLC, 1963).

9739   If a person dies away from home and he wished to have a tomb built in his honor in his home town, he should have someone send the remains of his fingernails and hair to put into the coffin in his home town (F, 62, Ja, SLC, 1964).

9740   Position of the arms (folded) in life is right over left; in death, left over right, or opposite (F, 28, Ja, SLC, 1964).

9741   As soon as a person is dead and arrayed in his grave clothes, a dish of salt is put on his breast to prevent the body from swelling (F, 31, SLC, 1948).  Cf. Brown 5423.

9742   The toes of a dead person may be pinned together to keep him from becoming a ghost (M, 20, SLC, 1963).

9743   When a person dies, his or her mouth, nose, and eyes are "stuffed" to prevent the spirit from leaving the body (F, SLC).

9744   Break a plate on the spot where a body has lain in state; it breaks the chains of death (F, 49, Gr, Midvale, 1964).

## Wake

9745   When someone dies, the body is never left alone until it is buried.  Someone remains with it all night (M, 77, Spring City, 1905).

9746   Never knit or crochet at a wake, because you will catch the dead souls in the yarn (F, SLC, 1971).

9747   After a person dies, they take the body to the home of the parents where friends will mourn over the body. After this, as the people are leaving, they will receive a candied almond if the person dead was young, and koliva, a mixture of wheat, sugar, and spices, if the person dead was old (F, Gr, SLC, 1962).

9748 One brings sweets to a house of mourning to offset sadness (M, 50, It, SLC, 1965).

## The Shroud, the Coffin, Items Put in the Coffin

9749 It used to be that a casket was put on two chairs in a home where the body was mourned over. After the casket was removed, the chairs were immediately turned downward. If they were not, it meant that someone else was to die (F, Gr, SLC, 1962).

9750 If you use scissors to cut a garment for a dead person, you must put the scissors in the casket (F, 38, Gr, SLC, 1963).

9751 If you dream of a closed coffin, it will mean a death of someone dear to you (F, SLC, 1961).

9752 It is unlucky to pass in front of a casket (M, SLC, 1957).

9753 A lighted candle is to be placed at the head of a dead person's coffin. Its purpose is to light the soul's way through the darkness of the afterlife (F, SLC, 1959). Cf. Brown 5518.

9754 If at a funeral a member of the dead person's family sneezes, they should remove an article they are wearing and put it in the casket. If this is not done, the person who sneezed will be the next to die (F, Gr, SLC, 1961).

9755 If an unmarried person dies, you are supposed to put a ring on his finger designating marriage, and you then bury the body. After six years you again dig up the body and take the ring for a good luck piece (F, Gr, SLC, 1957).

9756 If a married person dies, you must not put his wedding rings with him, because if the live partner ever decides to marry again, it will be bad luck to her or him (F, Gr, SLC, 1957).

9757 If a spouse dies, he should not be buried wearing his wedding ring. For if the living spouse remarries, the person they marry will die soon afterwards (F, Gr, Magna, 1961).

9758 A dead person should never be buried without money in his hand, for you never know when he will need it (F, Gr, SLC, 1961).

9759 Indians bury articles with their dead so that they will be prepared in the afterlife (F, 19, SLC, 1955).

9760 Indians put food, implements, and weapons in the graves of their dead to help them when they get to the "happy hunting ground" (M, 58, Gunnison, 1920).

9761 Indians bury their horse, bow and arrows, and possessions with their dead to make the journey to the happy hunting grounds easier (M, 46, Magna, 1928).

9762 Ute Indian: Concerning burial of an Indian, the relatives or friends must bury favorite possessions with the corpse. They used to bury the horse and blanket, now they just bury the blanket. Visitors to the casket place jewelry and bright scarves in on the corpse, and give a message for the corpse to take to God (M, reverend, 41, Whiterocks, 1958).

## FUNERAL SERVICES

### Funerals

9763 If you offer boiled wheat used for memorial services in a family, then return the plate or dish, don't wash it as it brings bad luck (M, 73, Gr, SLC, 1963).

9764 If you have a funeral on a certain day, you will draw friends to death with you (F, 51, Ja, SLC, 1963).

9765 It is bad luck to twiddle your thumbs at any time other than during a funeral (M, 21, SLC, 1963).

9766 If when going to a funeral the wind should turn your umbrella out, that means you are next to die (F, Swiss, SLC, 1957).

### Funeral Processions

9767 Children singing while going along the street are forerunners of a funeral procession (F, 72, SLC, 1964).

9768 A funeral procession should never cross a river twice. It is bad luck (M, 30, Dugway, 1963). Cf. Brown 5457.

9769 Do not take the horses across a bridge going to a funeral (F, Midvale, 1963). Brown 5458.

9770 The first to drive a hearse is the next to die (M, 65, Provo, 1964).

9771 If you ride in a funeral procession without lights on, you'll go to hell instead of heaven (F, 52, SLC, 1920).

9772 The lights are turned on in the funeral cortege to light the way for the departed soul (F, SLC, 1961).

9773 When taking a person who had passed away to the cemetery, if there is a large space between the vehicles, it means that there will be another death in the family (F, Murray, 1959).

9774 While a dead body is being carried by your house on the way to the cemetery, you are supposed to throw a bucket of water on the road (F, Gr, SLC, 1962).

9775 White horses were not allowed in a funeral procession for fear of bad luck (F, SLC, 1910).

9776 In former days when a warrior was killed, his favorite horse was killed also and put by his grave. The horse was to serve his master in the new world. Today the horse isn't killed, instead the horse is used in the funeral procession.  The horse bears the empty saddle with the riding boots facing backwards.  This signifies the fact that his master will never remount his favorite horse again (M, 23, Ja, SLC).

## Seeing or Meeting a Funeral Procession

9777   If a hearse stops in front of your house, there will be a death in the family (F, 62, SLC, 1963); If a casket stops in front of your house while going to the graveyard, someone in the family will die (F, 76, SLC, 1964).

9778   If a hearse stops alongside a person, it is bad luck for that person (M, SLC, 1920).  Cf. Brown 3800.

9779   Take five steps back if a hearse crosses your path to prevent death in the family (F, 55, SLC, 1967).

9780   It is good luck to have a hearse go by your home (F, SLC, 1959).

9781   Touch a button when a hearse goes by so you won't die (F, 21, Payson, 1958); . . . so someone close to you won't die (F, 21, SLC, 1964).

9782   When a hearse goes by you are to grab a button on your clothing and say, "Wiggle, waggle, spiggle, spaggle, I hope I'm not the next to die."  If you don't, you might be the next to die (F, 20, Payson, 1950).

9783   If you laugh when the hearse goes by, you will be the next to die (F, 21, 1952).

9784   It is unlucky to look at a funeral procession through a window (F, SLC, 1957).

9785   To meet a funeral procession is bad luck (M, 20, SLC, 1957); . . . ; if driving, you will have an accident before your drive is over, unless you turn back (M, Fillmore, 1960).  Brown 5442.

9786   Don't pass in front of a funeral procession, or it means bad luck of some kind (M, 64, SLC, 1950).  Cf. Brown 5443.

9787   Never cut across a funeral procession, because someone will die, either the person who cut the line, or the person who was in the funeral line (F, Gr, SLC, 1957).  Cf. Brown 5444ff.

9788   You must walk three steps with a passing funeral procession, or else you will die (M, Ir, SLC, 1960).

9789   If you are walking and meet a funeral procession, it is a cause of death in your immediate family (F, Moab, 1953).  Cf. Brown 5441.

9790   When two different funeral processions meet, it is bad luck (F, 49, Midvale, 1964).

9791   If a funeral procession passes you on Friday the thirteenth, you are condemned to death (M, SLC, 1964).

9792   It is not lucky to follow a funeral procession; let another car go by first (F, 80, SLC, 1964).

## Counting Vehicles in a Procession

9793   Never count the cars in a funeral procession, because it's bad luck (F, 41, SLC, 1964).  Brown 5452.

9794   When you go to a funeral, do not count the cars, because half of them will come to your home (F, SLC, 1963).

9795   Don't count the cars, wagons, or horses in a funeral procession, or someone in your family will die (F, 20, SLC, 1949); . . . a loved one will die (F, 51, Park City, 1920s).  Brown 5453.

9796   Never count cars in a funeral procession, or you will be next to die (F, SLC, 1946).

9797   If you count an odd number of cars at a funeral procession, you're next (F, SLC, 1925).

9798   If you count the carriages in a funeral procession, you will have that many days to live (F, SLC).

9799   One who counts cars at a funeral will die within a year (M, SLC, 1960).

## Funereal Dress, Burial Clothing

9800   Wearing black at a funeral is an old custom.  It shows respect and mourning (M, SLC, 1960).  Cf. Brown 5473.

9801   It is bad luck to wear new clothing to a funeral (F, Ogden, 1960).  Cf. Brown 5465ff.

9802   A Mr. F of Salt Lake dreams that his mother dies, and is buried "improperly dressed," meaning not in regulation LDS burial clothing.  Six months later his mother did die, and he reminded his father of the dream.  His father assured him that everything would be done properly.  The evening after the burial, his sister found some of the mother's clothing which should have been put on her.  They dug the woman up and put the clothes on her (F, 68, Woods Cross, 1950).

## BURIAL

9803   Getting buried on Friday is bad luck (F, SLC, 1963).

9804   Suicides must not be buried in hallowed ground (F, Lehi, 1957).

9805   When a person dies, they always bury him facing east, so when he is resurrected, he will be facing the rising sun (F, 19, SLC, 1963); . . . bury the head toward the west . . . (F, SLC, 1910).

9806   In Mormon society, the dead are buried with their feet pointing towards the east.  This is so that they can always "see" the sunrise and will be in the "correct" position to sit up when Gabriel blows his horn.  An exception is made for suicides, who are punished in burial by having their position reversed (F, 55, Logan, 1956).

9807 People should be buried on the sunny side of the hill, so as to always be warm (F, Chin, SLC).

9808 Indians are sometimes buried in the ground feet first, so the spirit may leave easily (F, SLC, 1957).

9809 Indians always bury their dead above the ground, because they believe they will be closer to heaven (M, 64, SLC, 1910).

9810 Indians bury their dead up on a pedestal to keep the wild animals away (F, SLC, 1965).

9811 If an Indian wasn't buried in one piece, he wouldn't live again (M, SLC).

9812 To leave a grave before it is filled, or to be the first one to leave the cemetery is a pointed invitation for death (F, Scipio, 1961); . . . means you will be the next to die (M, 45, SLC, 1963).  Brown 5523f.

9813 If a man dies and all his possessions and worldly goods are burned before he is buried, then they will go with him to the other world (F, 19, SLC, 1949).

9814 Never bury a person with his mouth open, for the spirit may return (F, Richfield, 1947).  Brown 5529.

9815 Indians considered it bad luck to sleep in a bed that someone had died in, so they buried the dead in their bed (M, 23, SLC, 1950).

9816 It is good luck to throw the ashes of the dead in the river, as it transports the spirit to heaven (M, SLC, 1945).

9817 After death your soul can't rest as long as any part of your body is above ground (F, SLC, 1957).

9818 Bury with the corpse the left-over medicine (M, SLC, 1963).  Brown 5501.

9819 Trees are sometimes planted in cemeteries in memory of the dead.  A birch tree, for example, was planted in a Provo cemetery for a son killed at Guadalcanal (M, 57, Provo, 1945).

## THE GRAVE

9820 A grave should be dug east and west so that the dear dead will be facing Gabriel when he blows his horn (M, 35, SLC, 1959).  Brown 5482.

9821 Graves on the south side of a church are the holiest (M, 21, SLC, 1962).

9822 The tools used in digging a grave should be left by the grave for several days (F, 44, Beaver, 1933).  Brown 5484.

9823 Never stand on someone's gravestone (F, 49, Ir, SLC, 1930).

9824 Leave a lamp on the grave, and it will lead the deceased to glory (F, Midvale, 1963).  Brown 5518.

9825 Broken dishes are occasionally seen on graves in Utah (F, SLC, 1910).

9826 A cup, knife, and a fork are often placed on the grave (F, Kanab, 1930s).

9827 If you take a flower from a new grave, there will be a death in your family (F, Murray, 1958).  Cf. Brown 5496.

9828 Never pull weeds or pick flowers from a grave, or you will kill the soul of the person in the grave (F, 44, SLC, 1964).

9829 The Japanese believe if they put fruit on graves, the bodies will come up and eat that food (M, SLC, 1958).

9830 It is unlucky to dig up or plow any land where a body has been buried (M, Garland, 1940).

9831 Don't dig up graves out of the graveyard (M, Clearfield, 1964); Digging up old Indian graves will cause bad luck (M, Tooele, 1958).

9832 If you lie on a grave at midnight, the spirit will overcome you (F, 48, SLC, 1964).

9833 Salt Lake teen-agers go to the city cemetery to a particular grave called "Emo."  Tradition has it that if at night a person strikes a match and walks around the large headstone three times, he will see "Emo" looking at him.  Actually he sees his own reflection in a small window inside which contains "Emo's" ashes in an urn (F, 21, SLC, 1958).

9834 Curses fall on people who enter tombs (M, SLC, 1958).

9835 It's bad luck to pick up white rocks in a cemetery (M, 20, Ja, SLC, 1954).

9836 An open grave over New Year's means another death in the family (F, Dan, SLC, 1908).

9837 It is bad luck to visit a graveyard after dark (F, Sandy, 1957); . . . you will never leave it (M, SLC, 1959); Walking through a graveyard at midnight brings bad luck (M, SLC, 1957).  Brown 5477.

9838 Never go to the cemetery at night, or evil spirits will surround you and bad luck will follow (F, 23, SLC, 1964); . . . death will follow (F, 20, SLC, 1964).

9839 Indians never walk in the graveyard at night because the dead are walking around (F, 19, Heber, 1950).

9840 If you walk through a cemetery at midnight, you must carry a rabbit's foot for protection from spirits (M, 14, Orem).

9841 When the moon is full, if you go to the cemetery and walk around the grave three times and then lie down on it and ask "Who is there?" the dead will answer, "Me, just me" (M, SLC, 1959).

9842 If you walk past a cemetery on Halloween night, you'll have bad luck all the next year (F, 20, Logan, 1972).

9843  At midnight all the graves open up, and the dead walk the earth (M, 36, Bingham, 1935).

9844  Dreaming of a freshly made grave is a sign you are suffering for the wrongdoing of others (M, Ger, 23, W. Jordan).

9845  Never slap your mother, or your hand will stick out of the grave (F, 19, SLC, 1964).

## Stepping on, Pointing at Graves

9846  If you walk across a new grave, you will have bad luck or a death in the family (M, Murray, 1958).  Cf. Brown 5491.

9847  Never walk on graves; you won't sleep that night (M, 45, SLC, 1963).

9848  Walking on a grave disturbs the dead. They then will rise and haunt the life of whoever wakened them (M, 37, SLC, 1964).

9849  Don't walk over anyone's grave, or they will come to get you (F, Murray, 1964); Never walk on top of a relative's grave, or you will surely join them soon (F, 58, Richfield, 1920); . . . it will hasten your own death (F, 52, SLC); . . . or your family will die that night (F, 39, SLC, 1964).  Brown 5492, 5495.

9850  Don't point your finger at a grave; you might be the next person to die (F, 71, Bountiful, 1912).  Brown 5479, 5487f.

9851  If you point at a grave, your finger will rot off (F, 31, SLC, 1941).  Brown 5489.

## GRAVEYARD, CEMETERY

9852  A beautiful, well kept cemetery means much happiness (F, SLC, 1961).

9853  It's bad luck to pass a cemetery without holding you breath (F, Ogden, 1961).

9854  Make a wish and hold your breath while you go past a cemetery (F, 21, Bountiful, 1946).

9855  Hold your breath, cross your fingers when you pass a cemetery, and you'll have good luck (M, SLC, 1960); Hold a button . . . (F, SLC, 1971).

9856  You should whistle while going past a cemetery (M, 12, SLC, 1960).

9857  If you stumble or fall in a cemetery, you will be the next one to die (F, Ir, SLC, 1960).

## BURYING WEATHER

9858  It always rains during a funeral (M, Layton, 1959).

9859  Happy is the corpse that rain rains on (F, 52, SLC, 1925).

9860  Blessed is the dead that the rain falls on (F, Woods Cross, 1953).  Brown 5504f.

9861  Rain in an open grave is bad luck (F, 1961).  Brown 5507.

9862  If it rains in an open grave, there will be another death soon (F, 54, Midway, 1972); . . . a death in a week (M, SLC, 1960).  Brown 5510, 5512.

9863  If it rains or snows on an open grave, there will be another death in the family within a month (M, 57, Swiss, Heber City, 1917).

9864  If it rains on the day of a funeral, there will be another death in the family within a year (M, 55, SLC, 1964); If it storms into an open grave . . . (F, 43, Swiss, SLC, 1963).

9865  If it rains in an open grave, the person to be buried there was wicked (F, 67, Panguitch); . . . will go to hell (M, 50, SLC, 1963).  Brown 5520.

9866  If it rains on a coffin, the soul of the departed has arrived safely (F, SLC, 1964).  Cf. Brown 5516f.

9867  If it rains the day of a funeral, the person buried was well loved and even the heavens weep at their passing (M, 52, Du, SLC, 1964).

## AFTER THE FUNERAL

9868  You should break a glass at the front doorway after returning home from a funeral.  It is supposed to break the trend of deaths (F, 41, Gr, SLC, 1964).

## MOURNING

9869  When a family is mourning, the other members of the family should not dance. For if they do, the dead person will take the member dancing with him to the grave (F, Gr, Tooele, 1961).

9870  Members of a family where there has been a recent death should not attend church for forty days, because the dead person's spirit may be roaming about (F, Gr, Magna, 1961).

9871  At the death of a close relative, one must not listen to music for forty days (F, 32, Gr, SLC, 1963).

9872  Forty days after someone close dies you should not have any form of entertainment (M, Murray, 1950).

9873  If you go dancing the same night a family member has died, you will be the next member to die (M, SLC, 1957).

9874  A dead person's immediate family is not supposed to eat any kind of meat for a period of forty-nine days (F, Ja, SLC, 1964).

9875  The dead man's widow should stay in mourning for forty-nine days (F, Ja, SLC, 1964).

9876  After a loved one dies, you must wear black and restrain yourself from all activities and entertainments for a year, so that you can show your respect for the dead (F, 100, Tooele, 1963).

9877  If a close relative dies, you should wear black for one year, or your own life will be shortened and marred with bad luck (F, Bountiful, 1964); . . . you will soon die (F, Dan, SLC, 1964).

9878  Wear black during mourning so the Angel of Death won't find you (F, 85, Pol, SLC, 1965).

9879  Sometimes lavender is worn for mourning, especially by a widow (F, Moab, 1953).

9880  Don't wear red or lipstick if someone in your family dies (F, 56, Grantsville, 1963).

AFTER DEATH

9881  The fingernails of dead people continue to grow after they die (M, 24, SLC, 1964).

9882  The hair and beard grow after death (M, Santaquin, 1964).

9883  All of the dead people's spirits live right here on earth with us and dogs can see them (F, SLC, 1967).

9884  Dead relatives always return to look at you through a window (F, SLC, 1966).

9885  The dead can reappear on earth, especially on Christmas and New Year's Eve (F, 19, SLC, 1964).

9886  On Christmas Eve the dinner table must be set with nine items of food. After the meal is finished everything is left on the table, including the dirty dishes. These items remain on the table overnight for the dead who will come home to eat (F, It, Helper, 1967).

9887  When you eat the favorite food of a deceased person, some people believe you should say to yourself, "For the soul of _____." If you do this and the person is hungry, he will receive some of his favorite food (F, It, Helper, 1967).

9888  It is a custom that you are to give food to the dead before you eat yourself (F, Ja, SLC, 1964); . . . at the Memorial Day Service (F, Ja, SLC, 1964).

9889  To celebrate a person's memorial service, you should eat no fish or meat, only vegetables for three or four days (F, 51, Ja, W. Jordan, 1963).

9890  If you are not kind to old men and women, they will pull your feet when they die (F, 42, Grantsville, 1963).

9891  The ghost of the last person buried keeps watch over the churchyard until another is buried, to whom he delivers his charge (F, SLC, 1959).

9892  When a person has been dead for one year, the body is dug up to be moved to another place. If the body has not disintegrated, it is believed that this person had many sins (F, Gr, SLC, 1962).

9893  As many grains of salt as one has wasted during one's life, so many hours or minutes the dead one must wait at the gate of heaven (F, 47, SLC, 1964).

REINCARNATION

9894  When you die, your soul is reincarnated in the body of an animal (M, 24, SLC, 1958).

9895  Some believe that when you die if you've been good you will return as a child again, but if you're bad, you will return as an animal (F, SLC).

9896  Anyone who mistreats an animal or insect in this life will in the next life take the form of the mistreated creature and be subject to the same abuse (M, SLC, 1961).

9897  When an evil person dies, his spirit enters into the body of an owl (F, 49, SLC, 1961).

RESURRECTION, RESUSCITATION, ETC.

9898  Always have your bed facing the east for Resurrection Day (F, 43, SLC, 1924).

9899  If you lose a limb and if it is not buried, you will be resurrected without it (F, SLC, 1958).

9900  People who have been resurrected will create spirits instead of bodies (F, 25, Logan, 1971).

9901  Lightning struck a man and killed him during a storm at North Platte. Informant's mother ran out and anointed him with olive oil, and he recovered. Informant's mother said her feet were blistered, and even today when a thunder storm comes up they swell and tingle (M, 74, Woods Cross, 1945).

9902  During the influenza epidemic of 1917-1918 the sister of WB got the flu and died. Her body was placed by an open window. The girl's fiancé and friend stepped through the open window, administered to the girl and prayed that life would be restored to her. She came back to life, was healed, and subsequently married the young man (F, St. George, 1946).

9903  Ginseng can restore life after death (F, 75, Pleasant Grove, 1906).

# X

# Religion, Lower Mythology, Witchcraft, Magic, Divination, Ghostlore

## RELIGION

### God, Gods, Holy Spirit

9904 If a person holds a live rattlesnake in his hands, it will prove to others that he has faith in the Lord (M, 55, American Fork, 1963). First heard in Mississippi, 1920.

9905 If you eat in an outside toilet, you're feeding the devil and starving the Lord (F, W. Jordan, 1925).

9906 Never curse God, or he will cause hard luck to follow you (M, Salem, 1950).

9907 One should not cut his nails or hair and leave them on the floor, because if he does, he is considered as cursed by God (F, 48, SLC, 1963).

9908 A man sitting alone in a cabin is likely to speak with God (M, SLC, 1964).

9909 If a person sits on hot coals, it will insure protection from the Lord (M, 55, American Fork, 1963). First heard in Mississippi, 1920.

9910 Certain Indian dances are done in secret, for the presence of strangers would offend the religious gods (F, Magna, 1964).

9911 When the first telegraphs were installed, the company invited a number of Indians to send messages to other Indians over the wires. The Indians believed the great spirit was talking to them through the wire, so they never caused much trouble for the telegraph company (M, 66, SLC, 1911).

### Christ, the Cross

9912 The Indians, when they string beads, always leave out one bead to make it imperfect. They believe that only one thing is perfect and that is Christ, and nothing else can be as perfect as he was (F, W. Jordan, 1971).

9913 If you wear a cross and are not Catholic, you will have bad luck (M, SLC, 1957).

9914 In Greek Orthodox churches at Easter time, a large flower-bedecked catafalque is used to denote the bier of Christ. It is considered good luck to crawl beneath this catafalque, first from the crosswise section, making the sign of the cross. This brings good luck throughout the year to the person (F, Gr, Tooele, 1961).

### Saints, Virgin Mary

9915 If it rains on the day you bury someone, they will become a saint (F, 29, Ir, SLC, 1964).

9916 If you lose an article, talk to St. Joseph, and he will direct you to it (F, 22, Ger, SLC, 1963).

9917 Petrels are supposed to be under the protection of the Virgin Mary (F, 75, Pleasant Grove, 1906).

### Angels

9918 If someone points his finger at the moon, he will blind an angel (F, 18, SLC, 1950).

9919 You should never point a finger at the stars, for you might blind an angel (F, Eng, SLC, 1958); Never point a stick at a star . . . (M, SLC, 1961).

### Clergymen, Prophets, Nephites

9920 If you mock a preacher, you will be cut down like a tree (M, SLC, 1957).

9921 If the words of wisdom from the would-be prophet are to be acceptable as guidance, you must be born between March 30 and April 22 (F, SLC, 1947).

9922 The three Nephite Apostles, who, like John, never die, come to the aid of the faithful when they're threatened by evil (M, 24, SLC, 1963).

### Sin

9923 Red is the color of sin (M, SLC, 1960).

9924 In Utah, some people confess and some don't. It is considered a sin or a crime if you don't confess. Here, as opposed to Greece, it is not such an obvious crime (F, Gr, SLC, 1962).

9925 If you have tragedies in this life, it means you are paying for your misbehaviors in the pre-existent life (F, 43, SLC, 1961).

9926    To bathe in brine water brings about remission of previous sins (M, 53, Midvale).

9927    If a white person dreams he is dark-skinned, a sin he has committed is soon to be exposed (F, 19, Provo). Heard from a Gypsy fortune teller in Orem.

9928    If a person swears while he kills a snake, he will be punished for nine sins (F, SLC, 1927).

9929    If a person kills a snake, he will receive forgiveness for nine sins (F, SLC, 1927).

## Church, Divine Service, Church Bells

9930    The east doors of the St. George Temple are properly hung, but they have never been opened, and will not be, until Christ walks through them at the Second Coming (F, 65, St. George, 1940s).

9931    The doors of the church should not be closed or locked during a ceremony, as no one should be shut out from a ceremony, for good luck (M, Ger, SLC, 1960).

9932    It is bad luck to break church windows (F, SLC, 1963).

9933    It is sacrilege for a dog to enter a church (M, 81, SLC, 1964).

9934    Greeks never cross their hands, legs, or arms while in church. It is believed that this is a disrespectful action towards the crucifixion of Christ (F, 18, Gr, SLC, 1963).

9935    You must not cross your legs in church, because you should make the sign of the cross only with your hands (F, 32, Gr, SLC, 1963).

9936    Always smile before going into a church (M, SLC, 1964).

9937    If your knee itches, you will very shortly be kneeling in a strange church (F, 78, Midvale, 1964).

9938    During Easter services, it is considered good luck to carry home a lighted candle from the services (F, 71, Gr, SLC, 1964).

9939    When at a protestant church and the dish is passed, it is bad luck if you put your offering in and it makes a clinking sound (F, 67, SLC).

9940    One should never look to see how much there is in the collection when the plate is passed. If they do, this is bad luck (informant data not available).

9941    Bats in the belfry means the church bells won't ring (F, SLC, 1957).

9942    If you hear a church bell ring three times and only three times, it is good luck (M, 54, SLC).

## Religious Ceremonies, Processions

9943    Circular religious processions follow the direction of the sun, from east to south, west, and never in a clockwise direction (F, 80, Ja, Midvale).

9944    Luminaries are burned on fiesta days and holy days (Christmas, etc.), so the saints can find their way to the place of celebration (F, 55, Magna, 1964).

9945    It is considered good luck to carry home a lighted candle from the Resurrection services of the Greek Orthodox Church held always at midnight Saturday. These candles are used to make the sign of the cross above the entrance of the house to ward off evil during the year (F, Gr, SLC, 1961).

## Prayers, Blessings, Benedictions

9946    Holding a prayer book during a ceremony assures all prayers will be answered (M, SLC, 1960).

9947    When you pray, face the Temple (F, 70, Provo, 1900).

9948    If you don't say your prayers at night, you will have bad luck (M, 19, Kaysville, 1948).

9949    Indians use cigarettes as prayer offerings (F, Midvale, 1961).

## Bible, Book of Mormon

9950    To damage a Bible in any fashion will cause very bad luck (F, Tooele, 1957).

9951    To throw away a Bible brings bad luck (F, Marysvale, 1900).

9952    If you read anything but the Bible on Sunday, you will come to a bad end (M, 49, SLC, 1964).

9953    A Bible upon the floor brings sorrow upon the owner (M, SLC, 1962).

9954    Dropping the Book of Mormon will cause bad luck (F, 23, Provo, 1958).

## Divine Providences, Miracles

9955    One of the companies of the handcart pioneers ran short of water. They came to a well, but the lady had padlocked it and turned them away. The pioneers went on and one of the ladies fell by the wayside with heat and thirst and said that the woman's well would dry up. A year or two afterwards, some of the brethren wrote and said that the well had dried up (M, Provo).

9956    Mr. EM and family were going to attend the April conference when the Indians ran off with all their horses except one lame one. The family tried to make the trip with this horse but had to stop after a while. The children were afraid but the mother reassured them by saying that she hoped that the Lord didn't let the Indians destroy them because their father had been working in the mission field. A white horse appeared, and they hitched their wagon to him. When they got into town and unhitched the horse, it just disappeared (F, 1945).

9957 When the Church at Kirtland was broken up in the spring of 1838, the Saints were advised to go into the woods to work to get the means to go to Missouri. They prayed to the Lord and one day they heard the puffing of a steamboat and the rattling of wagons in the air. It was seen by many people and it was filled with people. When the steamboat arrived over the Temple, part of it turned back and went north. The rest went to the west. The breaking off of the boat is doubtless a reference to the apostates who refused to follow the church to Missouri. The rest of the boat showed the Saints the way to go (M, SLC, 1948).

9958 Three black men entered the temple in Salt Lake and the attendant told them they couldn't come in unless they had a recommend. They kept going, and she said a prayer. Suddenly a policeman was at the entrance and escorted the black men outside. He told the attendant that he had been standing on a corner two blocks away one moment, and the next moment he found himself at the Temple, and he didn't know how he had gotten there (F, 20, SLC, 1969).

9959 One day our cow had strayed away and my father went to go look for her. It was a dark and stormy night, and I was worried that my father wouldn't be able to find her. I went behind a bush and prayed that he would find the cow and return safely. When he came back, he said he had started in one direction and a voice had told him to turn around and go back. He did just that, and found the cow not far away. I knew my prayer had been answered (F, 72, SLC, 1930).

9960 In the late 1880s in Park City, Utah, there was a mine cave-in and several men were trapped. They dug their way into another passageway but realized they were hopelessly lost. As they were resting, a form in a yellow slicker appeared and led them to safety. As the last miner crawled out and turned to thank the man, he had disappeared (F).

9961 Informant's great-grandmother who helped her family homestead in Benson tells the following story. When she was about eight, one winter, the only thing they had to eat was coarse wheat. Her mother had a dream in which she saw a mill in an abandoned nearby farm. The daughter was sent over to look for it, and sure enough, she found it (F, 96, Logan, 1973).

9962 Great-grandfather took his oldest son to go courting a sixteen-year-old neighbor. One night, great-grandfather had a vision in which the Lord had commanded him to marry this young girl, even though she was supposed to marry his son. The next day, he told of his vision to the girl's parents and they reluctantly agreed. He married her and went to Canada, leaving behind a wife and twelve children (F, Logan, 1973).

9963 Apostle M believed that the Temple was a sanctuary from which he could never be taken. He and GQC were in the Temple, and a constable walked in looking for them. M said, "We will walk in one of the sacred rooms . . . and he will never see us, will never bother us." The man walked right through without seeing them. The spirit of the Lord blinded him (M, Logan, 1946).

## Baptism

9964 Candles lighted at a baptism must be allowed to burn out, or misfortune will follow (F, SLC).

9965 The composition of blood changes when a Gentile is baptized and adopted into the House of Israel (M, 24, SLC, 1963).

## Souls: Heaven, Hell, Purgatory

9966 The soul leaves one body and enters another (F, SLC, 1963).

9967 Firing a bullet into a dead body will destroy its soul (M, 57, Midvale).

9968 Broad bean flowers contain the souls of the departed (M, SLC, 1963).

9969 If an Indian's final resting place is disturbed, his soul will have no rest (M, 30, SLC, 1964).

9970 The soul wanders until the corpse decays (F, 60, SLC, 1963).

9971 To dream of heaven means your life will be spiritually happy (F, SLC, 1964).

9972 We appear in heaven in whatever attire we're buried in, i.e., die in (M, 24, SLC, 1963).

9973 If you point your finger at a grave, the spirit of the corpse will try to keep you out of heaven (F, SLC, 1967).

9974 White people go to heaven, and if darker skinned races join the Mormon Church, they'll become white and go to heaven too (M, 24, SLC, 1963).

9975 When people die, they either go to heaven, which is in the sky, or they go to hell, which is under the ground (F, 44, SLC, 1964).

9976 No Basque can go to hell. At one time the Devil went to the country and tried to learn the language. It was too difficult for him, so he went away. He has not bothered with Basques since, because he can't get them without knowing the language (F, Basque, SLC, 1969).

9977 To dream of hell signifies bodily and mental agony (F, SLC, 1964).

9978 If a woman kills a snake, she will save seven souls from hell (F, SLC, 1916).

9979 Exploring outer space is condemned by God and will surely lead to the experimenter's damnation (F, SLC, 1964).

9980 Probing too far beneath the earth's surface will surely lead one to find hell (M, 19, SLC).

9981 Never spit in an open fire, or you will boil in hell (F, SLC, 1962).

9982   The shavings from whittling on Sunday will in hell be used to burn the back of your hand (F, SLC, 1940).

9983   Anybody that lies with real intent will burn forever in hell (F, Bountiful, 1961).

9984   All the souls in purgatory are freed one day on All Soul's Day, November 2 (F, Eureka, 1900).

Signs, Events of the Millennium, Etc.

9985   Two hundred years after World War II the world will end (M, Provo, 1950).

9986   Mrs. L said when the news came over the radio that President Herer J. Grant was dead she went next door and told her neighbors. The girl threw her hands in the air and said, "Why this is the end of everything. You know that in the Temple there is room enough for only seven pictures to hang, and President Grant's is the seventh. There will never be another president (F, 34, Bountiful, 1945).

9987   There are seven different colored horses. When each one has appeared, the end of the world is here. There is only one more horse to appear. When he does, the end is here (M, 20, Logan, 1969).

9988   If the chickens lay more eggs than they're supposed to, the world's supposed to come to an end (M, Moab, 1953).

9989   The world will end in fire (M, SLC, 1964).

9990   There will be a lack of food and water at the end of the world (F, 48, SLC, 1971).

9991   Fathers will turn against sons and mothers against daughters (F, 20, SLC, 1971).

9992   The devil will be bound by God and there will be one thousand years of peace (M, 25, Logan, 1971).

9993   There will be a long time of wars and then peace in which Satan will be bound at the time of the millennium (F, 20, Provo, 1971).

9994   Neighbor will turn against neighbor. There will be many wars. And there will be internal strife within families. Parents and children will hate each other (F, 48, SLC, 1971).

9995   Missionary work in Europe will end with the Second Coming of Christ (M, 25, Logan, 1971).

9996   The United States will unite with Russia, the Bear, and go against the Dragon, the Republic of China (F, 20, Provo, 1971).

9997   Women's hair will fall out from wearing wigs and bleaching their hair when the millennium comes (F, 20, Provo, 1971).

9998   You won't be able to tell the boys from girls. All girls will wear hooped earrings just before the Second Coming of Christ (F, 20, Logan, 1971).

9999   I've heard that the moon will turn to blood, seasons will be hard to tell from each other, and all righteous people will have to walk to Jackson County, Missouri. I think the purpose is to cleanse the earth and get resurrected. I don't know what order anything will happen in (F, 17, SLC, 1971).

10000   I've heard the usual stuff like the season will be strange and the moon will turn to blood, and that two missionaries will be killed in Jerusalem (F, 20, Provo, 1971).

10001   If there's blood on the moon, then the world's coming to an end (M, Brigham City, 1900).

10002   The belief was that some day a missile would be shot into the sky into the atmosphere. It would puncture the moon, and make it bleed (F, 44, Provo, 1910).

10003   In the last days there will be extreme weather and many earthquakes. There will be hot and cold temperatures in unusual places (F, 48, SLC, 1971). Cf. Brown 8520.

10004   When the world comes to an end Angel Moroni will blow his trumpet which is on the Temple (M, 74, SLC, 1900).

10005   If you eat the yarrow root, it will save you in the last day (F, 52, Ogden, 1970).

Mormons

10006   Mormons (the LDS church members) have an extra eye in the back of their heads (F, 25, SLC, 1950).

10007   Mormon mythology has it that the tragedies of the Donner party were their punishment for being murderers of the Prophet Joseph Smith or hirelings of the devilish Boggs, or just plain persecutors of the Saints (M, 26, SLC, 1963). Read in The Year of Decision, 1846, by Bernard DeVoto.

10008   The story of the sea gulls consuming all of the crickets at a pertinent time in the Mormon history, thus bringing salvation to these people, obviously is a manifestation of God (M, 23, SLC, 1963).

10009   One superstition is based on the old Mormon belief that Cain is a black man who wanders the earth begging people to kill him and take his curse upon themselves (M, 24, SLC, 1963).

10010   A Mormon traditional superstition connected with the afterlife states that those who lose babies on earth will raise them in the hereafter (M, 24, SLC, 1963).

10011   The Gadeanton Robbers of the Book of Mormon fame were seen by freighters hauling between St. George and southern Nevada (M, 21, SLC, 1962).

10012  According to an old Mormon belief the Sons of Perdition can be counted on the fingers of one hand (M, 24, SLC, 1964).

10013  Curses befall enemies of the Church (M, 24, SLC, 1963).

10014  The Mormons don't allow visitors in their Temple, because that's where they keep all their extra wives (F, 19, SLC, 1958); Women are held as prisoners in the Mormon Temple (F, 18, Bountiful, 1961); Mormons carry off young girls and imprison them in the top of the Temple (F, SLC, 1961).

## Miscellaneous

10015  Mrs. S said that when she was a girl a Mrs. S used to come to her mother's home in Alpine as a Relief Society teacher. Mrs. S used to tell them that they must never take their garments entirely off. She said when taking a bath to always leave one leg and one arm in the garments (F, 65, Woods Cross, 1946).

10016  Navajo Mountain, on the border between San Juan County, Utah, and Arizona, was and still is a sacred mountain to the Navajos. Formerly they made an annual pilgrimage there and held a ceremony. Today, even with a shortage of good land, sheep will only be grazed there sparingly. Also, they are very quiet there. We took a pack trip that crossed Navajo Mountain twice and saw only one herder. Where we had previously greeted all Indians and old buddies, the guide was silent here. He said you did not talk on Navajo Mountain (F, Navajo Mountain, 1962).

10017  When someone is kind to you, it means that you did something for them in the pre-existence (F, SLC, 1958).

10018  The funny feeling we occasionally experience that seems to have happened before is actually part of our pre-existence (M, 24, SLC, 1963).

10019  I understand that being a minister's son, I will mostly go wrong in life (M, 18, SLC, 1956).

10020  A dream about fire means that your conscience will be seared (F, 53, Du, SLC, 1961).

10021  The history of religious activity in the age will be lost following the Third World War (M, Ogden, 1950).

10022  A short man is always more religious than a big man (M, SLC, 1954).

10023  A person who carries a mustard seed will have faith (F, SLC, 1951).

10024  Years ago God put a curse on the people in Nauvoo for killing Joseph Smith. It was supposed to last for three generations. But to this day there is still an evil feeling in spirit in Nauvoo (F, Centerville, 1971).

## WITCHCRAFT

## WITCHES, WIZARDS, HEXES

## Various Notions

10025  People are superstitious about believing in any witchcraft or idols, because they fear wrongdoing will come to them if they don't worship these idols (F, SLC, 1960).

10026  Some people believe that witches will haunt you if you have bad luck (F, Kaysville, 1958).

10027  If you are out alone on the eve of the witches' sabbath and gaze on it, then you are doomed to damnation (F, SLC, 1961).

10028  The mandrake is a fleshy root and resembles the human body. It is believed the mandrake is stewed in the witches' caldron (M, Vernal, 1959).

10029  If you carry a four-leaf clover on Christmas Eve, you can see witches (F, Ger, SLC, 1960).

10030  Never sweep your house at night, because a witch will come later during the night and take the broom (F, 20, SLC, 1964). Heard in Mexico, 1953.

10031  A witch comes out when the moon is full (F, 19, SLC, 1945).

10032  Twelve midnight is the witches' hour. Goblins, witches and their ilk come out at this hour (F, 55, SLC, 1964).

10033  Witches come out on Halloween (M, SLC, 1959).

10034  On Halloween it is believed that witches ride around on broomsticks (F, 1959).

10035  Winter brings with it the witches that live in the lands of the north (M, Bountiful, 1961).

10036  People believe in witches and their power to curse and cast evil spells. There are only bad witches, not good ones (F, 19, SLC, 1964).

10037  Certain people are still witches and can cast an evil eye on their enemies (F, Helper, 1959).

10038  Always crush eggshells so that witches cannot use them as boats (F, Ogden, 1971). Brown 5621.

10039  If you see a falling star, a witch will die (F, 25, SLC, 1950); . . . a witch has died (M, SLC, 1963); . . . a shooting star . . . (F, 19, SLC, 1962).

## Appearance and Attributes of Witches

10040  Witches can appear in any object under the sun, animal or vegetable (F, 100, Mex, Grantsville, 1963).

10041  A witch frequently takes the form of a black cat (F, Sandy, 1957). Brown 5592.

10042    The owl is the animal that inhabits witches (F, 100, Mex, Grantsville, 1963).

10043    Rats without tails are witches (M, 21, SLC, 1964).

10044    Wizards can take the form of a wolf, hunt as an animal by night and then resume their human form at daybreak (M, 57, SLC, 1952).

10045    A redhead deserves to be burned as a witch (F, 46, Scot, SLC, 1964).

10046    If your eyebrows meet, you are a witch (M, SLC, 1959).

10047    A witch cannot weep, has a hidden birthmark, long slanted eyes, and she stops when she sees a broom and counts the straws (F, 58, Ogden, 1964).

10048    If a woman stands in the sun and doesn't cast a shadow, she's a witch (M, Magna, 1940).

10049    Witches always dress in black (M, 27, Hyrum, 1948).

10050    The witches' circle is a barren circular plot of land where nothing grows. The informant's friend's pet dog would not enter the circle, and growled when they tried to force it to enter by pulling on the leash. When one of the people was in the circle and the other was outside, the person within could not hear the voice of the person outside (M, 23, Logan, 1969).

10051    People that never look you in the face are witches (M, SLC, 1964).

10052    If a warm current of air is felt, witches are passing (F, Lehi, 1957). Brown 5601.

10053    Witches and other supernatural beings fear water and cannot cross it (F, 20, SLC, 1963).

10054    A lady is thrown in a river; if she comes to the top instead of staying on the bottom and floats, she is a witch (F, 47, Eng, SLC, 1964).

10055    Women thrown in a fire that don't burn are witches (F, 25, SLC, 1964).

10056    My brother used to scare me all the time. I was always afraid of the dark and going to bed was quite an ordeal. I had this superstition which my brother had instilled in me that there was a witch under my bed. Each night I would say my prayers with the lights on, take one leap and land in bed. It was a rule that only one leap could be taken. I could never have any part of my body hanging over the bed, for the witch was sure to grab it, and that would be the end of me (F, Brigham City, 1972).

## Bewitchment, Signs of Witches' Activities

10057    There are individuals who have the power to wish others misfortune and cause it to happen. This is called a hex (M, SLC, 1958).

10058    A woman was accused of resorting [sic] with the devil, and the townspeople took her into the mountains to burn her. She cursed Mendon and said it would never be prosperous, and she also proclaimed that the tree she was being burned on would never die, because her soul would remain to haunt it. She also said no bush or tree, bird or animal would go near the tree. To this day, Mendon has not been prosperous, and there is a tree in the forest which stands alone in a large clearing (M, 19, Logan, 1970).

10059    There was an old man and woman who had once been Mormons but had forsaken the faith. One night a boy recovering from a long illness suddenly began to cry and could not be quieted. Someone noticed the old man outside, and when he was driven away, the child quieted right down. It was evident to all present that he had bewitched the child (M, SLC, 1946).

10060    Place a salt shaker with some salt spilled in front of the house; it will bewitch the people inside the house (F, Helper, 1959).

10061    If you let a ball fall in a swift stream, you are in the witches' power (F, Eng, Holladay, 1963).

10062    If you have premonitions, you are bewitched (M, 21, SLC, 1955).

10063    If a person is left-handed, it means he is bewitched (F, 21, SLC, 1960). (This appears to mean that a left-handed person is a witch rather than being under temporary bewitchment. --Eds.)

## Prevention of Witchcraft

10064    Dutch people paint their barns all odd designs so the witches will be confused and not stop there and burn them (M, Du, Magna, 1940).

10065    I have seen witch signs on barns around Park City, probably a cross-cultural transplant from New England. The signs are supposed to keep the barn from burning down (M, 21, SLC, 1960).

10066    If you hang up horseshoes in your door, the wicked witch will pass you by on Halloween (M, 57, SLC, 1963). Cf. Brown 5627.

10067    To prevent a witch from riding a person, put a case-knife, a pair of scissors, or some mustard seed under the bed or pillow (M, 22, SLC, 1963). Cf. Brown 5671f, 5674.

10068    To avoid being bewitched, never lie on your back while asleep (M, 21, Midvale, 1964). Brown 5665.

10069    If you are afraid of witches, place a broom across the doorway (F, 77, Pleasant Grove, 1900). Cf. Brown 5634f.

10070    If you upset the salt, throw a little over your left shoulder to keep witches away (F, Scipio, 1961).

10071    One eagle's egg boiled and eaten by two persons will keep witches away (M, SLC, 1961).

10072 Witches flee from the odor of garlic (F, SLC, 1961).

10073 The hawthorn used to be hung up at the entrances of houses in May to guard the dwelling from witches (F, SLC, 1964).

10074 The white stones from the rooster are a charm. They will serve against witchcraft (M, 25, Je, SLC, 1965).

10075 If you put a dress on wrong side out, it will keep the witches away (M, 58, SLC, 1930s). Cf. Brown 5657, 5660).

10076 If you put your stockings on inside out, you'll catch witches (F, SLC, 1942). Cf. Brown 5662.

10077 Churchyard dirt in a hat prevents witchery (F, Ger, SLC, 1963).

10078 If a neighbor puts a hex on you, you must gather all his handkerchiefs and burn them before the hex can be broken (F, Murray, 1957).

10079 Tie the hair of a witch to control the witch (F, Provo, 1970).

10080 A silver pen will keep away witches (F, 19, SLC, 1958).

Laying Witches

10081 To drive the demons out of a witch dunk her in water (M, SLC, 1961).

10082 Mrs. B reported the belief she had heard in St. George that to get rid of witches in a house a child must urinate in the fireplace (F, St. George, 1946).

10083 If you want to kill a witch, pierce the heart in effigy with a silver object (F, 19, SLC, 1958). Cf. Brown 5694.

10084 There was an old woman who the neighbors were sure possessed supernatural powers. Even though she had never harmed anyone, she was still feared by everyone. It was also a known fact that she could not pass under steel. One day in the midst of a rain, she stopped into a neighbor's house to dry off. Someone slipped a steel knitting needle into the rafter above her head. Her clothes began to steam and she looked in agony, but she couldn't move until the steel knitting needle was removed (M, SLC, 1946).

10085 In the River Heights cemetery in River Heights, Utah, there is what is known as the "Bloody Stake." It is a stake, sticking up about three feet out of the ground, with red splashed down the edges. A long time ago M was considered to be a witch and was beheaded. She said she would return to haunt them and various people have seen her head on this stake laughing and jeering at them (M, 22, River Heights, 1969).

10086 If you kill a witch, bury the heart at the intersection of four roads to protect yourself from bad luck (M, 66, Ir, SLC, 1964).

10087 If you burn a witch, all your sins will be taken away (F).

10088 The only way you can kill a witch is to burn her to [sic] the stake (M, SLC, 1964).

10089 MC was a woman who lived in a shack in Provo Canyon. The children would tease her and chant "Burn witch, burn." She got herself a watchdog and one day the kids came and killed it. She chased them into the woods, but they circled around and set a torch to her shack. She came back and went inside and fell asleep. She woke up, but it was too late to leave the burning house. If you go up there now, you can hear her screaming (F, 19, Logan, 1970).

10090 If you pull a straw out of a broom, it will break a witch's back (M, Murray, 1952).

10091 The head of a beheaded witch mends if rubbed with salt (M, SLC, 1963).

CONJURY

10092 The ability to charm is passed from male to female and female back to male members of a family (M, SLC, 1925). Brown 5532.

10093 In casting magic spells you have to know how to throw and catch the spells (M, 66, SLC, 1940).

10094 One's actual name is sometimes kept secret since by means of it another person might bewitch the owner (F, 50, Murray, 1928).

10095 Sometimes you can make a person turn and look just by staring at his back (F, 63, Black, SLC, 1965).

10096 If a witch doctor points a stick at a person, the person will soon become very sick (M, SLC, 1960).

10097 A Gypsy will cast an evil spell on you if you don't feed them when they come to your door (M, Farmington). Heard in Missouri, 1948.

10098 An old Indian chief, when his land was taken away, placed a hex on the presidents of the United States that everyone would die in a fire (F, 40, Sunnyside, 1963).

Images, Pictures, Dolls, Etc.

10099 Make an image of someone and stick pins in it, and you will bring bad luck to that person (F, SLC, 1920).

10100 To cause someone to become sickly and die, take an image of the person and bury it, face down, three feet in the ground (M, 50, It, SLC, 1965).

10101 An evildoer makes an image of the victim in wax or clay; then he burns, buries, or pierces it with thorns or pins, thus injuring the victim and causing his death (F, 50, Murray, 1928).

10102 A sure way to kill a man is to place his picture under the eaves at the corner of your house during rainy weather and let the water pour upon it (F, Ogden, 1964).

10103   There is an objection to having a picture taken, lest the representation be used for witchcraft (M, 48, SLC, 1964).

10104   Turning someone's picture upside down will bring that person bad luck (F, 40, Logan, 1938); If you want someone punished, turn his picture upside down (F, SLC, 1958). Cf. Brown 5554.

10105   If you dislike someone, make a voodoo doll, ugly as possible with lots of pins in it. It's supposed to represent all the bad luck possible and shows dislike of a person after you give it to them (F, SLC, 1964).

10106   A voodoo doll made in the image of a person can be used to inflict harm on that person by sticking pins in it (F, SLC, 1963); Sticking pins in dolls will bring pain or death (M, 20, SLC, 1947); Sticking pins or knives in a doll, or burning it, can bring death or injury to the person who looks like the doll (M, 19).

10107   A doll is made and named for the person someone wants cursed. To have pains come to the person, they stick pins in the doll and finally stick it in the heart. It is supposed to make the person die (M, Provo, 1961).

10108   If you want to hurt someone, make two miniature effigies of him. Bury one and stick pins in the other. To overcome the harm caused by this you must dig up the buried miniature, take it to the mountain top and light a candle upside down. The wind blows the candle out (F, Provo, 1959).

10109   There are different types of voodoo baptism. One general way is to get a frog and put a name on a piece of paper and put it in the frog's mouth. Then they sew up the mouth of the frog in the name of the person they want to affect. The frog is turned loose but still has its mouth sewn up. Gradually the frog becomes weaker and weaker until it dies. This is the effect it has on the person for whom it was baptized (M, Provo, 1961).

## Use of Bodily Parts in Conjury

10110   Never let a person play with your hair; if they happen to get even one strand, they can bewitch you (F, 20, SLC, 1963). Heard on an Indian Reservation.

10111   Don't chew strands of your hair. If you do, it means you will destroy yourself (F, 42, Gr, SLC, 1964).

10112   If you carry a lock of hair of a person, you will have power or control over that person (M, 62, Midvale, 1964); Locks of hair can be used to cast a spell (F, 45, Murray, 1927); If people get a piece of your hair, nail clippings, etc., they can work magic against you (F, 19, SLC, 1964). Brown 5546.

10113   Never pick up a human hair which is lying in the road. It will "hoodoo" you (F, SLC, 1959).

10114   Never keep a lock of hair. If you do keep someone else's hair or your own, it is bad luck for you and the owner of the hair. The only way to break the curse it to burn the lock of hair (M, Eng, 19, Logan, 1970); Locks of hair are used to cast spells if not burned (M, 57, SLC, 1964).

10115   Never let nail parings, excrement, hair fall into the hands of another person, for he may do you harm. As a result of this, the Navajos were very careful and even went so far as to take the hair they combed loose, rolled it into a ball of some sort, and put it into the hair that was tied at the nape of the neck (Navajo Indian, 30, Brigham City, 1930s). Brown 5547.

10116   Wet a rag in your enemy's blood. Put it behind a rock in the chimney. When it rots, your enemy will die (F, 58, Midvale, 1964). Brown 5550.

## Personal Possessions Used in Conjury

10117   An article of clothing once worn can be used to work a spell (F, Midvale, 1964).

10118   A glove might be buried with appropriate incantations, with the notion that as the glove rots, so will the person who once wore it go to his end (M, 69, Sterling, 1905).

10119   If an article is dropped by a thief and thrown into the grave at the next funeral, the thief will soon die a slow and painful death (M, 26, SLC, 1964).

## WARDING OFF SPELLS

10120   Magic words when uttered protect against danger (F, 48, SLC, 1964).

10121   Some people believe they have the power to cast out evil spirits by uttering magic words (F, 46, SLC, 1930).

10122   A red cloth is often used to counteract or enhance magic (F, Ogden, 1964).

10123   If you take a handful of earth from a fresh made grave and sprinkle it on the floor of an enemy's house, he can do you no harm (M, 49, SLC, 1956).

## EVIL

10124   Painting something red on your property keeps away evil (F, 44, Sandy, 1928).

10125   Put hex signs on your barn to ward off evil and keep it safe (M, 19, SLC, 1964).

10126   Beware of no shadow, for evil follows (F, SLC, 1957).

10127   Wearing your clothes inside out invites all evil power and trouble (informant data not available).

10128   The mention of evil things may bring about evil unless safeguards are taken such as knocking on wood (M, 20, SLC, 1950).

10129 Salt wards off evil and spirits (F, 35, SLC, 1960).

10130 If someone wishes evil or says evil about you, their spell must be broken with bread by inviting them into your home and giving them bread. It must be bread (F, SLC, 1966).

10131 The image or design of an eye throws evil back to its source (F, SLC, 1948).

10132 Five fingers of the hand or any design associated with the number five will protect against evil (F, SLC, 1950).

10133 Wear an asafetida bag around the neck to keep away evils (M, Roosevelt, 1961). Attributed to the Ute Indians.

10134 Mistletoe is believed to ward off evil influences (M, 22, SLC, 1962).

10135 If you kill a rooster, put blood on the doorstep to keep evil away (F, 47, Midvale, 1931).

10136 The night is full of evil (M, 21, SLC, 1950s).

10137 The sword is a sign of an evil attack (M, SLC, 1956).

EVIL EYE

Various Beliefs

10138 There is a belief that some people have an evil eye (F, Roosevelt, 1964); . . . evil can be transmitted by the eyes of certain persons (F, SLC, 1948).

10139 Cross-eyed people have the evil eye, and you must not look them in the face without giving an evil eye sign as protection (F, SLC, 1971). Cf. Brown 5701.

10140 An evil eye brings bad luck (M, 19, SLC, 1964).

10141 One possessing the evil eye can lure you to your downfall (F, SLC, 1959).

10142 Be careful to never look at a person with the evil eye (F, Scot, SLC, 1957).

10143 There once lived in Magna a woman now dead named Mrs. F who possessed the evil eye. She made HM very sick with it and killed a horse with the evil eye (F, 19, Gr, SLC, 1958).

10144 If on any day something goes wrong, you would always say that the first man you met on the street that day was obviously the man who cast the evil eye (F, Gr, SLC, 1962).

10145 Anyone can possess the power of the evil eye, and it doesn't indicate whether one is bad or good. It is thought that the evil eye is passed on by a compliment such as: "Oh, how pretty she is. Isn't she beautiful. Doesn't she sew well." The result is that the person complimented may become sick unto death. Always, the one complimented is seriously ill. Not only people are affected with this, even plants, trees, etc. (F, Gr, SLC, 1962).

10146 There is a special prayer that qualified people are prepared to give a person who has a long or serious illness. If while the prayer is being given the individual yawns often, the ill person is known to have had the evil eye (F, Gr, Magna, 1961).

Preventing the Evil Eye

10147 Among certain people the purposes of prayer before meals was to counteract by the blessing of a higher power the evil eye which might be in the food (F, It, Spring Glen, 1959).

10148 If you are given an odd look, and you believe it to be of no good, quickly say a short prayer to throw off the evil eye (F, 18, SLC, 1961).

10149 The white stones from the rooster are a charm against the evil eye (M, 25, SLC, 1965).

10150 Garlic in a sack around the neck will keep away the evil eye (M, Vernal, SLC, 1961).

10151 A red cloth is often used to ward off the evil eye (F, 21, Grantsville, 1964).

10152 To avoid the evil eye, wear a part of your clothing inside out and no harm will come to you caused by the evil eye (F, Gr, SLC, 1957).

10153 To prevent evil eye, gather snakes' skin, or snakes' heads, tie them in a handkerchief, and wear them on any part of your clothing so they can't be seen (F, Gr, SLC, 1962).

10154 Get a fish net and tie forty knots in it. Then cut it into a triangular shape and wear it. This is to prevent the evil eye (F, Gr, SLC, 1962).

10155 To prevent the evil eye, you are supposed to wear a necklace which has a picture of a human eye on it (F, Gr, SLC, 1962); . . . wear an evil eye to ward it off (F, 23, SLC, 1964).

10156 Indian superstition: Some people have an evil eye and when they cast a look on someone else, he is cursed. To avoid having an evil eye cast on one, wear a red string tied on the finger (F, Provo, 1959).

10157 A charm that looks like an eye will throw the evil back to its source (M, 16, SLC, 1964); The design of an eye will throw back evil spirits (F, 49, SLC, 1964).

10158 Peeking through the fingers is a means to avoid the evil eye (M, SLC, 1959).

Abating the Evil Eye

10159 When another person sees one he believes is pretty or lovely and praises the other person, he must comment at the end with a puffing sound so he won't give the person he is admiring the evil eye (F, Gr, Tooele, 1961).

10160 The only way that someone can get rid of the power of the evil eye is this: Once a compliment has been uttered, the one given the compliment gets the evil eye, and one must immediately say a prayer over them; the plant or person will come to life again or the person will become well again. Not even the priest can pray over them (F, Gr, SLC, 1962).

10161    If someone has been given the evil eye, you are supposed to gather three sticks from a crossroad and burn them along with some incense. After this you are to wave the incense around the room. This will drive the evil eye away (F, Gr, Price, 1962).

10162    If a person has the evil eye, get a flower off of Christ's casket on Easter. Take it home and burn it. You then take the smoke from the flower and bless the person with the evil eye. This is supposed to drive the eye away (F, Gr, SLC, 1962).

## CREATURES OF LOWER MYTHOLOGY

## DEVIL

### Various Notions

10163    If a woman has hair on her legs, that signifies she's a loud mouth and a devil (M, Gr, SLC).

10164    The devil controls the waters (M, 20, Garden City, 1969).

10165    When children are playing out of doors at night, their parents tell them that unless they come in the house the devil will take their toys (F, 20, Mex, SLC, 1964).

10166    The devil has control of things after midnight (M, 22, SLC, 1953); The devil does his best work after midnight (F, 36, Brigham, 1946).

10167    A person is not supposed to get water from a well at twelve noon or twelve midnight for fear that the devil will be there (F, Gr, SLC, 1962).

10168    If you say your prayers after going to bed, you say them to the devil (F, 45, SLC, 1920).

10169    If you swear, the devil will take you away (M, SLC, 1957).

10170    People who curse will go to the devil (F, Tooele, 1958).

10171    The devil hears all bad things you say (F, 68, Tooele, 1910).

10172    If you make a wish when there is a ring around the moon, the devil will grant your wish (M, 18, SLC, 1963).

10173    If you keep thinking of something strong enough, you can bring the devil or one of his followers to do the act for you (F, SLC, 1961).

10174    Don't say aloud any favorite wish, because the devil will hear it and thwart you (F, 70, Provo, 1900); Never tell anyone what you are going to do, or

the devil will stop what you are doing (F, 77, SLC, 1963).

10175    Never let the devil know your plans. He will join you (F, 62, W. Jordan).

10176    God sends a bee to overhear the devil's secrets (F, SLC, 1963).

10177    If you walk on the cracks on the sidewalk, you will break the devil's dishes (F, SLC).

10178    Bishops' sons always go to the devil (M, SLC, 1946).

10179    If a person does not do everything his bishop, priest, rabbi, etc., tells him to do, he will be cast to the devil (F, SLC, 1959).

10180    If a person dreams of a person with a split hoof, it means he will be tempted by the devil in the near future (F, 72, tea-leaf reader, Lark).

10181    A cramp in your leg is a sign that the devil is near to tempt you (F,78, SLC).

10182    Talk to yourself and you talk to the devil (M, SLC, 1964).

10183    A typewriter speaks for the devil (M, SLC, 1940).

10184    Ouiji boards are dangerous and are directly influenced by the devil. If used, they may bring harm to the individual who is using them. They are very fascinating, which is a way of tempting one to play with the devil. Once the devil has tempted one enough, he may eventually render the individual completely helpless and cause him to do things under his influence which would not be done otherwise (M, 53, Richfield, 1930); If you have a ouiji board in your house, God will never enter your house, because the devil is within the ouiji board (F, 20, SLC, 1963).

10185    Don't burn trash on Sunday, or the devil will put you on the moon for everyone to see (F, Clearfield, 1959).

10186    Sew on Sunday, see the devil on Monday (F, W. Jordan).

10187    If you are vain and look in the mirror too much, one of those times the devil will be looking over your shoulder (F, 74, Ir, SLC, 1954).

10188    You should look in the mirror as soon as you get out of bed in the morning. Failure to do this brings bad luck for the day. The devil is behind the mirror, and you should confront him or scare him off, or he will remain to bring bad luck (M, Logan, 1970).

10189    You should never sweep after sunset. It supposedly stirs up the devil (F, 42, Gr, SLC, 1964).

10190    Do not turn a loaf of bread upside down, because the devil will dance on it (F, SLC, 1966).

10191    If you eat in the toilet, you are feeding the devil (F, Bear River City, 1957); . . . you're feeding the devil and starving the Lord (F, Magna, 1925).

10192 Never brush your hands at the end of a meal. It denotes the food just consumed benefits none but the devil (F, 42, SLC, 1963).

10193 The "baker's dozen" is twelve for the baker and one for the devil (F, 23, SLC, 1959).

## Physical Appearance and Characteristics of the Devil

10194 The devil appears before many men and women in different forms (F, 100, Grantsville, 1963).

10195 A rattlesnake is a form of the devil (M, 23, SLC, 1961).

10196 If a black cat follows you, it is a sign of the devil, and you should turn around three times and cross yourself (F, SLC, 1958).

10197 If you see a goat on a bridge at night, the devil has entered his body (F, SLC, 1964).

10198 Red is the color of the devil (M, SLC, 1960).

10199 Strange lights around a lonely dwelling mark a visit from the devil to that habitation (M, SLC, 1959).

10200 If a man stands in the sun and doesn't cast a shadow, he's a devil (M, Magna, 1940).

10201 Some young boys were teasing and chasing some pigs in a pen in a field when one of them looked up and saw a "character" dressed from head to toe in some sort of very tight suzy-long-leg type clothes. He had on a tight red cap with a black tassle on it. The boys started to run and fell down. When they looked up, the man was gone. They searched the field but found no trace of him. They figure it was the devil, and that he had gone into the pigs (M, 71, Bountiful, 1970). First heard in Idaho, 1913.

## Possession by the Devil

10202 Violent apostates from the Mormon church are sometimes possessed of evil spirits (the devil). Such persons emit an extremely unpleasant odor (M, 1970).

10203 If the lobes of your ears are hard, you're possessed by the devil (M, 1959).

10204 "May the devil take me, if . . . ." When a person says this, the devil does (F, 60, Norw, SLC, 1963).

10205 If you lay [sic] on a grave at midnight, the devil possesses you (M, 8, Magna, 1963).

10206 If it rains while a man is dying, or if the lightning strikes near his house, the devil has come for his soul (F, SLC, 1960).

10207 The first living thing to enter a new church becomes the property of the devil (F, 69, Murray, 1915). Underlying the belief in question is a well-known

legend involving a pact with the devil, wherein the devil contracts to build a church--or some other edifice--in exchange for the first thing to enter. Various subterfuges are resorted to, including sending in an animal, casting one's shadow into the church, and the like. This legend, and the stratagems employed to circumvent the results of the bargain, are treated in a learned monograph by August Wünsche, *Der Sagenkreis vom geprellten Teufel* [Leipzig und Wien, 1905]. --Eds.)

10208 The first corpse laid in a new churchyard is claimed by the devil (F, SLC, 1964).

10209 Yawning is caused by the devil so that he can enter through the mouth (M, SLC, 1959).

10210     Sing at the table,
    Dance at the bed,
    The devil will get
    You by the hair of the head.
(M, Parowan, 1959).

10211     Sing at the table,
    Dance to your bed,
    The devil will surely
    Get hold of your head.
(F, Fillmore, 1960).

10212     If you sing at the table,
    Sing in the bed,
    She devil will get you
    When you're dead.
(M, 19, SLC, 1964).

10213     Sing at the table,
    Read in bed,
    You'll go to the devil
    When you're dead.
(M, SLC, 1900); Sing at the table, / cry in bed, / the devil will get you / before you're dead (F, SLC, 1900).

10214 Sing in bed, see the devil before you're dead (F, W. Jordan).

10215 A sneeze is a sign that a devil or evil spirit is trying to get out of your body (F, 20, SLC, 1955).

10216 Sneeze on Sunday, your safety seek, or the devil will have you the rest of the week (F, Farmington, 1959). Cf. Brown 5773f.

10217 Dimple on the chin means the devil within (F, SLC, 1958).

10218 Trim your nails on Sunday, and the devil will be after you for a week (F, W. Jordan, 1957); . . . the devil will be with you the rest of the week (M, 84, Centerville). Cf. Brown 5775.

10219 The most binding way to get a signature is in blood. Then if this person should breach [the pact], the devil will come and take his life (M, 22, SLC, 1963).

10220 When walking along and your shadow is behind you, it means the devil is trying to steal it (M, Eng, SLC, 1957).

## Invoking the Devil

10221 To whistle in the house invites the devil in (F, Farmington, 1959); . . .

calls the devil (F, Norw, SLC, 1960); Never whistle in the dark, because the devil will know where you are, and he will seek you out (M, 23, Dragerton, 1963); Whistling in the dark is calling the devil (F, Gr, SLC, 1920); Whistling on Sunday invites the devil (F, SLC, 1958).

10222   If you whistle, you are playing for the devil who then is dancing (F, SLC, 1950).

10223   If you open a door to the wind, you're inviting the devil in (F, 19, SLC, 1963); If you say "come in" when a door blows open, you invite the devil (M, SLC, 1962).

10224   Rocking an empty chair invites the devil to sit (F, 92, SLC, 1890); . . . means you invite the devil (M, SLC, 1962).

10225   Speak of the devil, and he will appear (M, Bountiful, 1915).

10226   The Lord's Prayer said backwards calls up the devil (F, 54, SLC, 1963); Say the . . . backwards and you will see the devil (F, 40, Logan, 1938).

10227   If you eat an apple without rubbing it, you are calling the devil (M, 90, Draper, 1875).

10228   Don't count the stars, because if you count the right number, the devil will appear before you (F, 56, Grantsville, 1963).

10229   Take a pigeon and kill it. Sew it in the lining of a coat and the devil will visit you (F, SLC, 1969).

## Warding off the Devil

10230   The devil can't come into a room where there's a priesthood bearer (M, 24, SLC, 1963).

10231   It is believed that if a person comes to a crossroad, they must make a cross before this road in order to keep the devil away, because they believe the devil is at these crossroads (F, Gr, SLC, 1962).

10232   Whenever you yawn you should make the sign of the cross on your mouth, so the devil cannot enter (F, 17, SLC, 1963).

10233   Wearing a crucifix and keeping Holy Water in the room will keep devils away (F, 35, SLC, 1940).

10234   Wearing garlic will keep the devil away (F, 21, SLC, 1950); . . . garlic and a cross . . . (M, 22, SLC, 1958).

10235   When you sneeze the devil is coming out of you, but you'll be okay if someone says "God bless you" (F, 33, SLC, 1963).

10236   If a horseshoe is hung with the prongs up, it has the power to destroy the devil if he comes too near the threshold (M, 79, Pleasant Grove, 1901).

10237   Automatically when you hang clothes on a doorknob the devil comes into your house. You must then burn one inch of

string in the keyhole to chase the devil out (M, Logan, 1968).

10238   An "X" on the heel of the shoe will prevent the devil's bad influence (M, 19, SLC, 1958).

10239   If you put ashes on the forehead, you can keep the devils away (F, 27, SLC, 1963).

10240   If you boil pins, the devil will go away (F, Midvale, 1959).

10241   It is necessary to look under the bed before you retire in order to ward off the devil (F, SLC, 1959).

10242   Throw salt over the left shoulder to keep the devil at a distance (F, 19, SLC).

10243   When you spill salt, throw a few grains of it over your left shoulder to blind the devil (F, 44, SLC, 1961).

## DEMONS

10244   Souls may be extracted from their bodies or detained in their wandering, not only by ghosts and demons, but also by men, especially sorcerers (F, 80, Midvale).

10245   A full moon brings out demons (M, SLC, 1964).

10246   Wells and springs are the gathering place for demons. It is well to avoid these places (F, Helper, 1950s).

10247   Demons enter the bodies of pigs (F, Sandy, 1957).

10248   A demon may assume the image of an angel (M, 64, SLC, 1918).

10249   You shouldn't strike the dishes with utensils, because it releases bad demons (F, 19, SLC, 1958).

## EVIL SPIRITS

### Various Notions

10250   There are two kinds of spirits on the earth, those of the Lord and those of the devil. If you encounter one of these, ask it to shake hands. An evil spirit will disappear at this request (F, 18, SLC, 1967).

10251   Most spirits are evil (M, 40, SLC, 1930s).

10252   People believe that there are evil spirits all over trying to influence us (M, 32, Grantsville, 1960).

10253   When you sneeze, an evil spirit leaves your body (M, SLC, 1957); . . . you are getting the evil spirits out of your body (F, 39, Nephi, 1935).

10254   Evil spirits are out when there's no moon (M, 48, Ogden, 1964).

10255   After twelve midnight evil spirits come out, and if you are out of your house after midnight these evil spirits will haunt you (M, 19, SLC, 1964).

10256  If two people walk around a room at midnight and in the darkness, they will never meet; one of the two will be spirited away (F, 1959).

10257  Never face into the wind.  It carries evil spirits (F, 19, SLC, 1963).

10258  If one ventures into a cave, he'll catch an evil spirit (F, 18, SLC, 1960).

10259  Wells and springs are the gathering place for evil spirits.  It is well to avoid these places (F, Helper, SLC, 1950s).

10260  Singing in the house is an attraction to evil spirits (M, 36, Milford, 1948).

10261  A crack in the wall allows evil spirits to enter (F, SLC, 1964).

10262  If the front and rear doors of a house are in alignment, evil spirits will go in one door and out the other (M, SLC).

10263  If you shake a tablecloth outside at night, it lets the evil spirits into the house (F, Gr, SLC, 1961); Don't shake the crumbs off a tablecloth after dark, or it will invite the evil spirits (F, Gr, SLC, 1961).

10264  In a house where an evil spirit dwells or a person who possesses psychic powers, there will be the sound of nails or pebbles dropping on the roof.  Sometimes small pebbles will be found outside the house and appear to have fallen off the roof (F, Provo, 1975).

10265  Never step over a dead body, because the spirits will deprive you of your life (F, Gr, SLC, 1957).

10266  Never touch a person struck by lightning, as he is possessed with evil spirits (M, 50, SLC, 1963).

10267  The Arches National Monument is full of evil spirits who make sure that bad luck follows those who enter and especially those who destroy any part of the monument (M, Moab, 1962).

10268  The Gadianton robbers lived in ancient times near St. George, Utah, and their spirits still roam from time to time (M, SLC, 1958).

10269  The Gadianton robbers were evil spirits of Satan who tried to prevent the establishing of the Mormon church.  In an early community, tools would disappear, women would set their bread out to raise and it would be turned upside down.  If they turned their backs while they were ironing, their irons would disappear.  The sawmill would start running at night and would cease if the men came out.  These episodes went on for several months and then stopped as quickly as they had started.  They were all blamed on the Gadianton robbers (M, 1945).

10270  An Indian will not go near a house where death has occurred because he believes that evil spirits are there after the death (F, SLC, 1962).

10271  The Ute Indians were always afraid of the Great White Throne, a great mountain

in Zion Park.  They believed evil spirits lived there who wished to trouble them (M, 80, SLC, 1964).

Warding off Evil Spirits

10272  The drawing of Os and Vs on the cheek with the index finger will ward off the evil spirits (M, 19, SLC, 1964).

10273  Close all doors to your room at night so that the evil spirits can't get in (M, 17, SLC, 1950).

10274  If you sprinkle water across the back porch at night, the evil spirits will be kept away (F, SLC).

10275  Never look at the moon over your right shoulder; always over your left shoulder.  This wards off evil spirits (M, 54, SLC, 1945).

10276  When you talk about a dead person and you sneeze, pull up on your right ear to chase away the evil spirits (M, 50, It, SLC, 1965).

10277  Wearing a dead person's clothes will keep out evil spirits (F, 50, W. Jordan).

10278  Carrying a small bag of salt around your neck will ward off evil spirits (M, SLC, 1957).

10279  Salt sprinkled on something will get rid of evil spirits in it (M, 30, Ja, SLC, 1959).

10280  To throw a pinch of salt over your left shoulder will keep the evil spirits away (F, 54, SLC, 1920); In the olden days the bad spirits were believed to live on your left side, so by throwing salt you could ward off the bad spirits (M, Murray).

10281  If you throw salt on the fire, you will drive away the evil spirits (F, 67, SLC, 1963).

10282  Light a candle at night to keep evil spirits away (F, 87, W. Jordan).

10283  On Halloween you must always have a lighted pumpkin on your porch or window to scare away evil spirits and goblins (F, 18, Bountiful, 1972).

10284  A fire will ward off evil spirits (F, 19, SLC, 1954).

10285  All family members get together to untrim the Christmas tree to cut it up and burn it in the fireplace.  This must be done before New Year's Eve to drive evil spirits away (F, 71, Centerville, 1963).

10286  You can frighten evil spirits away by burning rubber (M, SLC, 1961).

10287  There is a knife that Scotchmen carry in their stockings named "Skeen Dhu" that keeps away evil spirits and brings good luck (M, 30, Scot, SLC, 1961).

10288  A horseshoe nailed over the door will catch the evil spirits and prevent them

from going inside (M, 22, Kamas, 1960);
. . . horseshoe nail . . . (M, SLC,
1959).

10289  Shoot a silver bullet over the house,
and it will scare away evil spirits (M,
55, SLC, 1965).  Learned in Tennessee,
1915.

10290  If you paint a barn red, the building
will bear a hex sign and frighten away
evil spirits (F, 41, Provo, 1942).

10291  Part the hairs of a horse's tail, rub
oil in it, and you'll never be followed
by evil spirits (F, 17, SLC, 1958).

10292  After eating fresh killed meat wipe the
grease on your arms to bring good luck
and ward off evil spirits (M, 61, Amer
Ind, Crescent).

10293  Wear an asafetida bag to ward off evil
spirits (M, 75, Honeyville, 1902); . . .
around your neck . . . (F, Grantsville,
1964).

10294  A bag of herbs worn around the neck
wards off evil spirits (F, Lynndyl,
1954); . . . a bag of spices . . . (F,
80, Spring City, 1920).

10295  To keep evil spirits away wear garlic
around your neck while sleeping (M, SLC,
1959); Garlic hung around the house on
Halloween Eve will prevent bad spirits
from entering (M, Midvale).

10296  A charm to keep away evil spirits is a
bag containing garlic, some soil, a
piece of wood, and the toenail of a dog
or rabbit, or a bird's beak, or the hair
of a dog (F, SLC, 1967).

10297  Mistletoe over a doorway keeps the evil
spirits out (M, SLC, 1959).

10298  If you burn pepper on the stove, all the
evil spirits will stay out of your home
(F, 69, Tooele, 1963).

10299  Red pepper put in the heel of a shoe
will keep away evil spirits (M, 47, SLC,
1963).

10300  Guard your home from evil spirits by
branches of certain trees (M, Roosevelt,
1964).  Heard from Ute Indians, 1930s.

10301  Knocking on wood will keep the evil
spirits away (M, 15, Du, SLC, 1961).

10302  Knock on wood so that the evil spirits
won't hear what you say (F, SLC, 1959).

10303  Beat on a kettle to drive away evil
spirits (F, 71, Richfield, 1911).  Heard
from the Indians.

10304  Bamboo wind chimes are supposed to keep
evil spirits away (F, Logan, 1972).

10305  Whistling in the dark keeps away evil
spirits (F, 65, Eureka, 1965).

10306  Confetti throwing, old shoes and
noisemakers have the function of scaring
spirits away (F, SLC, 1960).

10307  A Christian cross on a door will keep
away evil spirits (F, SLC, 1956).

10308  Santissima Maria (Holy Mary) is used by
many Spanish Catholics to rebuke evil
spirits (F, 100, Mex, Grantsville,
1963).

10309  Hot cross buns are made to ward off evil
spirits (F, 18, SLC, 1963).

10310  Many people keep in their possession
some charm such as a coin or rabbit's
foot to ward off evil spirits (M, SLC,
1959).

10311  Hang a glass eye in the window to keep
out evil spirits (F, SLC, 1961).

10312  Hang an evil eye in your window at night
to ward off the evil spirits (F, Gr,
SLC, 1961).

10313  If an Indian on the reservation steps
outside at night without a blanket, he
will be carried off by evil spirits, and
will never be heard of again (M, Roy,
1920s).

10314  The Indians thought if they danced and
feasted they would rout out evil spirits
(F, 47, SLC, 1964).

10315  Navajos always leave a break in the
border of a blanket for the evil spirits
to get out (M, 64, SLC, 1910).

10316  A group of Indians leave white thread
clear to the edge of the border of the
cloth they are weaving to let the evil
spirit escape (F, 40, SLC, 1963).

10317  Indians always make one mistake in
anything they weave to let the evil
spirits out (F, 20, Heber, 1952); When
weaving a rug you should purposely make
a mistake on the last stitch (F, SLC,
1971).

## WEREWOLVES

### Various Notions

10318  A werewolf is a person who has done
something very evil and as punishment
God has turned him into a wolf until
some other person draws blood from him
(M, 38, Norw, professor, SLC, 1963).

10319  People who owe debts when they die will
come back in the form of a werewolf (F,
80, Tooele, 1963).

10320  If a werewolf becomes wounded, he
becomes a human in form almost
immediately but retains the wound (M,
57, SLC, 1963).

10321  If your eyebrows meet, you are a
werewolf (M, SLC, 1959).

10322  During the first night of the full moon
some men turn into werewolves (F, 15,
SLC, 1965); . . . the wolfman is
supposed to come out (F, SLC, 1957);
Werewolves come out at midnight on a
full moon (M, 20, SLC, 1950s).

10323  At every full moon the werewolf claims a
victim (F, W. Jordan, 1956).

10324  When there is a ring around the moon,
the werewolves come out (F, 12, Orem,
1964).

## Warding off and Killing Werewolves

10325   To be protected from a werewolf a cross is good. You can't tell a werewolf from other wolves when hunting. The only way to kill them is to put a cross on a bullet or knife (F, 18, SLC, 1956).

10326   To kill a werewolf, shoot it with a silver bullet (M, 38, Norw, professor, SLC, 1963).

## VAMPIRES

### Various Notions

10327   If a cat enters the room where a person is dying, and it crosses their body, they will both become vampires (F, SLC, 1964).

10328   Vampires come out when there is a new moon (M, 31, SLC, 1942).

10329   Vampires strike at midnight when the moon is full (M, 23, Provo, 1949).

10330   When the cocks crow, the vampire, or living corpse, must return to its grave (M, 57, SLC, 1956); When the morning church bells ring . . . (M, 57, SLC, 1955).

10331   A vampire will die if daylight strikes him (F, 45, SLC, 1963).

10332   A vampire is invisible in a mirror (M, SLC, 1959).

10333   Vampires don't throw shadows (M, 65, SLC, 1940).

10334   Ghosts come out of their graves at night and suck the blood of human beings (F, SLC, 1962). (This item is a good example of the phenomenon of stable function and variable agent, for which reason it is listed under "Vampires" rather than under "Ghosts." --Eds.)

### Warding off and Killing Vampires

10335   Wear a cross around your neck to keep the vampire away (M, Layton, 1933).

10336   You can ward off a vampire by sticking a cross in front of its eyes (M, 58, SLC, 1915).

10337   Crosses outside your window will keep vampires away (F, SLC, 1964).

10338   If one believes in vampires, he should eat garlic before going out at night, as that will scare away any nearby vampires (M, 1961).

10339   If you carry a clove of garlic around your neck, it will protect you from vampires (M, 32, Murray, 1964).

10340   If you leave garlic outside of your house, the vampires won't be able to get you (F, 38, SLC, 1964); A garlic plant in a room will keep vampires away (M, 23, SLC, 1959); . . . outside the front door . . . (F, Eng, SLC, 1963).

10341   To kill a vampire drive a wooden stake through his heart (M, 18, SLC, 1963); . . . at midnight (M, 19, SLC, 1964).

## NIGHTMARE

10342   Nightmares are a form of the devil's work (M, 17, SLC, 1963).

10343   Reading by moonlight will give one nightmares (F, Provo, 1970).

10344   Hanging a horse's halter on your bed will cure nightmares (M, SLC, 1957). (Mention of the halter connects nightmares with the basic notion of a nightmare as a creature that enters the sleeper's room, either to crouch on his chest, or otherwise to oppress the victim by interfering with the breathing. In the compound, "mare" is not necessarily a horse, but any kind of frightful creature. The halter, of course, would restrain the creature. For an excellent typology of nightmares, their appearance, function, etc., see Carl-Herman Tillhagen, "The Conception of the Nightmare in Sweden," in Wayland D. Hand and Gustave O. Arlt, eds., Humaniora: Essays in Literature, Folklore, Bibliography Honoring Archer Taylor on his Seventieth Birthday [Locust Valley, New York, 1960], pp. 317-29. --Eds.)

10345   Hang little figures made of mistletoe twigs on the heads of beds to keep off nightmares (M, Midvale, 1961).

## JACK-O'-LANTERNS AND WILL-O'-THE-WISPS

10346   A jack-o'-lantern will bewitch men and lead them into pools and ditches (M, 63, Cedar City, 1964). Cf. Brown 5764f.

10347   The will-o'-the-wisp is a corpse candle carried by ghosts (F, 50, SLC, 1963).

10348   The will-o'-the-wisp is a bog sprite that lures lost travelers to their death in swamps (F, 50, SLC, 1963).

## ELVES, LITTLE PEOPLE

10349   At Christmas you put rice pudding outside, and if it is gone in the morning, the elves have blessed your house (F, 23, Dan, SLC, 1963).

10350   At Christmas time always put out mush for the elves in the stall; the elves will eat it, and it is supposed to bring luck to the family (F, SLC, 1930).

10351   About two weeks before Christmas little elves sit on your nose to keep track of your good deeds and bad acts; so you better be good (F, 26, Bountiful, 1940s).

10352   The elf can be blamed for any good or evil or mishap that one has (M, 21, Ger, SLC, 1964).

10353   If you put a cross above the keyhole in a door or on a window sill, it will keep out the "Nisse" (elf). The Nisse is responsible for all subnormal happenings (F, 74, Salem, 1900).

10354   Those who believe in the "little people" (elves, etc.) never come to any harm (F, 22, Eng, SLC, 1963).

10355   When your nose itches, an invisible elf is tickling it (M, Dan, SLC, 1959).

10356   All little people of Ireland have red hair (M, SLC, 1962).

10357   All little people of Ireland put dead leaves in people's pockets (M, 19, SLC, 1957).

10358   If you leave an untopped whiskey bottle out for the little people, you'll have good luck if they like it (F, 19, SLC, 1953).

10359   If little people are found, a pot of gold will also be found (F, 37, SLC, 1940).

FAIRIES

10360   Fairies, spirits, elves are helpful to human beings (M, 40, SLC, 1930s).

10361   If you get hurt, it is because of the bad fairy (M, SLC, 1960).

10362   Fairies are always dressed in white (M, 27, Hyrum, 1948).

10363   They say when there's a ring around the moon, the fairies and elves will come out and play (F, SLC, 1969).

10364   On stormy nights the family is to retire to rest at a very early hour, so that the good fairies may enter unobserved to find shelter and repose (M, SLC, 1959).

10365   Every time a person says that they don't believe in fairies, a fairy will die (F, SLC, 1962).

10366   The last bit of food on the plate should be left for the fairies (F, Lehi, 1957).

10367   A ring of mushrooms and toadstools means the fairies will be there at night for a dance (F, 19, Ja, SLC, 1956).

10368   Toadstools in a circle is where the fairies have been dancing (F, 40, SLC, 1930).

10369   Dust blowing along a road is from the movement of fairies; so always tip your hat (F, 39, Ir, SLC, 1963).

LEPRECHAUNS

10370   Leprechauns are small, evil people (F, 68, SLC, 1931).

10371   In Ireland the people believe in leprechauns, nice little people that do good deeds for people (F, 60, Ir, SLC, 1964).

10372   An Irishman believes that a leprechaun will guard and protect them (M, 59, Dan, SLC, 1964).

10373   As a child the informant was never allowed to wear the color green, as her Irish grandmother said that this was the leprechaun's color, and they would be displeased if people wore it (F, 35, Ir, SLC, 1963).

10374   It is a common belief by people of Irish descent that to say anything bad about fictitious characters such as leprechauns will bring much bad luck (M, 21, SLC, 1963).

10375   To bring happiness to your home leave your doors unlocked so that the leprechauns can enter at night (M, SLC, 1961).

10376   To catch a leprechaun, one must not take one's eyes off of it (M, Ir, SLC, 1960).

10377   Catch a leprechaun and you'll have good luck (F, 22, Syracuse, 1948); . . . you will inherit all his charms (F, 49, Gr, Midvale, 1927).

10378   If you catch a leprechaun, he must grant you three wishes (F, 23, SLC, 1964).

10379   If you catch a leprechaun, he will give you his pot of gold and bring you good luck (F, 24, SLC, 1964); . . . he has to show you where his gold is hidden (M, Ir, SLC, 1961).

10380   The leprechaun will leave a pot of gold at the end of a rainbow (F, SLC, 1964).

10381   "I was born and brought up on a farm in Ireland. My grandmother told me that if one didn't leave cheese and milk out for the 'little men,' the butter would not cream and the milk would be sour" (F, Ir, 46, SLC, 1964).

10382   If you leave a bowl of milk on your porch, a leprechaun will drink the milk and in return clean your house while you are sleeping (F, 61, SLC, 1900s).

10383   People put a saucer full of milk out; if the milk is gone, a leprechaun has been and wished good fortune on the house (F, Eng, SLC, 1964).

10384   It is impossible to take a picture of a leprechaun (F, 19, SLC, 1959).

GOBLINS

10385   The goblins will get you if you go out at night (M, 55, Roosevelt, 1919).

10386   On Halloween night goblins come out (M, 19, SLC, 1950).

10387   A full moon means the goblins will be out (F, 12, SLC, 1964).

10388   If you cover up your head to sleep, the goblins will carry you up the chimney (F, Box Elder Co, 1936).

10389   If you are bad, there will be goblins under your bed (F, SLC, 1960); If you don't mind your parents, the goblins will carry you away (F, 20, SLC, 1958).

10390   It is believed that a patch of mushrooms is the place where elves and goblins gather for their midnight revels (F, Heber, 1959).

## TROLLS

10391  Trolls live under small wooden bridges (F, 19, SLC, 1958).

10392  If a milkmaid snatches the hat of a troll and throws it to the cobblestone floor of the milking house, the hat will instantly be back on the troll's head (F, 74, Norw, Salem, 1900).

10393  If you aren't good to the trolls (supernatural beings), they will come and get you or eat you or have you as their baby if you aren't good (F, Swed, SLC, 1959).

## MISCELLANEOUS SUPERNATURAL CREATURES

10394  The Abominable Snowman is a type of human who has survived the ages. He is enormous and powerful, but yet needs no clothes for his warmth (F, 20, SLC, 1960).

10395  The Irish believe in a phantom called the banshee, whose wailing announces the approach of a misfortune (F, Ir, SLC, 1959).

10396  If you leave a bowl of milk out at night for the brownies to eat, they help do your work for you (F, 23, SLC, 1964).

10397  If you see a dwarf with a humpback, touch his back and you will get your greatest wish (F, 18, SLC, 1961).

10398  If something happens to an airplane, the gremlins have fixed it (F, Murray, 1960).

10399  Gnomes are the cause of mischief (M, 19, SLC, 1960).

10400  Geniis sometimes take the forms of cats, dogs or other creatures. Sometimes they have human form (M, 69, Sterling, 1901).

10401  In Kearns, Utah, young people were made to believe that if they slept out at night, there was a man who crept around on roof tops and jumped down on them and beat them with a lead pipe. They called him the "Lead Masher" (M, Taylorsville).

10402  The Grimees lived in your closet and in your drawers, and when you go to sleep at night, if some of your closet doors or drawers are not closed, the Grimees jump out and play in your room. "When I used to forget to close my closet, Mom always reminded me of the Grimees, and they seemed to have a negative connotation, so they must be bad people" (F, Orem, 1974).

10403  Wearing a crucifix and keeping Holy Water in the room will keep poltergeists away (F, 35, SLC, 1940).

10404  Looking up at the sky during a storm will anger the Wild Hunter who rides in the storm and will blind or kill anyone who sees him (M, Ger, SLC).

10405  The appearance of the Flying Dutchman means the skipper of a ship has to say a prayer for the restless souls, or his ship will be doomed (M, Ger, SLC).

10406  Frost patterns on the windows are painted there by Jack Frost (F, Helper, 1958).

## FORTUNE TELLING AND DIVINATION

## FORTUNE TELLING

### Various Notions

10407  Some people believe that a fortune teller is either a good or bad omen (M, Kaysville, 1968).

10408  Wizards, witches, medicine men, fortune tellers, can foretell the future and read the secrets of the past (M, Vernal, 1959).

10409  Anything a fortune teller says about a person, whether good or bad, is right (M, SLC, 1959).

10410  Gypsies can tell fortunes (F, 19, SLC, 1955).

10411  People with hooded eyelids (slant eyes) have insight into the future (F, 19, SLC, 1962).

10412  A ouija board works and is never wrong (F, 13, SLC, 1961). Cf. Brown 5847.

10413  The future is foretold by stars (M, 18, SLC, 1955); Reading the Star Gazer often determines the events of the rest of any day (M, 19, Price, 1960).

10414  Always follow what your horoscope tells you to do, and never go against it, or you'll never have good luck (M, 26, SLC, 1948).

10415  In order to find the future, melt solder and pour in cold water. The different shapes foretell different things in the future (F, 26, Finn, Morgan, 1965). (The custom of pouring molten lead into water as a means of divination was widely practiced in many parts of Europe until recently. Most often this ritual was carried out on St. Sylvester Day as a way of determining what would ensue during the new year. --Eds.)

10416  A person has his fortune told by dropping oil on water and seeing the way the oil goes (F, 21, SLC, 1959).

10417  Break an egg in some vinegar on Christmas Eve, and you can tell your fortune (M, SLC, 1960).

10418  The future may be foretold by jumping over a lighted candle (F, Vernal, 1959).

10419  When a family is going to move, they go to a fortune teller to see what direction they should move. If they move in the wrong direction, misfortune will befall them (F, 31, Ja, SLC, 1963).

10420  If you can't make your mind up about something, make an omen or a sign and do what it says (F, SLC, 1964).

10421  Any unusual sight or sound is a warning of danger (F, SLC, 1959).

10422 The future can be predicted by reading one's fortune from fortune cookies (F, 80, Ja, Midvale).

10423 The future can be told from the order in which a rooster eats grains of corn placed on markers on the ground (F, 50, Murray, 1928).

10424 Your future can be told by watching a fountain or the flight of birds (F, 80, Ja, Midvale).

10425 By looking through spectacles you can see magic (F, Midvale, 1961).

Palmistry, Phrenology

10426 A person's future may be revealed by the lines and markings in the palms of their hands (F, SLC, 1960); . . . by the palm of the right hand (M, SLC, 1928). Cf. Brown 5846.

10427 The lines in the palm of one's hand tell their entire life cycle (M, Milford, 1938); . . . indicate one's fate (M, 23, SLC, 1940s). Brown 5852.

10428 Fortune-telling rhyme to say when counting white spots on the fingernails:
   A friend, a foe,
   A present, a beau,
   A journey to go.
(M, Tooele, 1957).

10429 Physicians predict the future by the shape of a person's skull or in the lines of a man's palm (M, 69, Sterling, 1910).

10430 A person's destiny can be read by the lines in a person's face (M, SLC, 1964).

10431 Futures can be read from the bumps on a person's skull (M, 20, SLC, 1950s).

Fortune Telling by Crystal Ball, Seerstone, Etc.

10432 Some people forecast the future by looking into a crystal ball and going into a trance (F, SLC, 1900).

10433 There is a belief in seerstones and crystal balls (M, 24, SLC, 1963).

10434 Friday is the best day to tell fortunes with cards (F, 22, Moab, 1964).

10435 Reading cards predicts your future (F, 18, Heber, 1965). Brown 5848.

10436 Fortunes told with cards should involve the use of a new deck (M, 1960).

10437 The future can be predicted from the order in which cards are dealt (F, 40, Union, 1937).

10438 Three aces together mean change of places (F, SLC).

10439 The ace of spades in fortune telling tells of bad luck (M, 53, SLC, 1961).

Fortune Telling by Tea Leaves, Coffee

10440 The future of a person can be determined by tea leaves (F, 67, SLC, 1963); . . .

by the interpretation of tea leaves in the bottom of a cup of tea (M, SLC, 1959); By the way tea leaves fall a person can predict what kind of day he or she will have (M, SLC, 1964). Brown 5858.

10441 If leaves of tea in a teacup form the shape of a bird, it means good tidings for the one who drank that cup of tea (F, 72, Eng, Lark, 1963).

10442 Read coffee grounds in a cup to tell your fortune (F, Sandy, 1940); Turn a coffee cup upside down with Turkish beans in it . . . (M, Moab, 1953). Brown 5856.

10443 After drinking coffee turn cup upside down for good luck. If any grounds are left, someone can read fortunes in it (F, 15, SLC, 1963). Cf. Brown 5857.

WATER WITCHING

10444 To find the best place to dig a well, hold a forked stick in both hands out over the ground as you walk slowly. When this stick turns in your hand, you should dig the well there (M, Farmington, 1910); . . . "with the prong out he'd walk around, and when it tipped down, he claimed--I don't know whether there was anything to it or not--but he claimed when it was over water why that end would tip down, you know. I remember he switched for two or three different places, and he got water all right, you know. His son was here last summer, and he tried switching, but it didn't work so good" (M, Moab, 1953); "We asked her if she knew anything about water witching. O, her brother, said he had used one of those in his hand and it really worked. He said that it found water all right. He said the stick turned right over while he held it. It had a little twig on it. I don't know what kind of wood it was" (F, Woods Cross, 1953); You can find water with a "Y" stick. It will quiver when you are near water (F, 19, Ja, SLC, 1950).

10445 A divining rod will locate water (F, Bountiful, 1964); A divining rod, or forked stick, is supposed to be attracted by water as a magnet is to steel (F, 46, SLC, 1940).

10446 Get a forked branch for to find water (M, SLC, 1900).

10447 Water can be found with a water "witch stick" which will move violently by itself when over a spot where water is underground (F, 34, SLC, 1964).

10448 Ten people standing in a row on a dirt road can find a spring by holding hands (M, SLC, 1964).

Divining Rods and Dowsing Rods

10449 One can find water with a forked greenwood stick (M, 67, SLC, 1915). Brown 5871.

10450 Water can be found underground by use of a forked branch from a green birch tree. The two forked branches are held in either hand parallel to the ground. Wherever the extended end points downward, water will be found (M, 29, St. John, 1950s).

10451 To find a good place to dig a well, you use a forked hazel stick having a hold of the two branches. Then as you walk around, the trunk part will turn down to underground water (M, 44, Layton, 1970).

10452 If used properly, a forked hickory stick will bend down to underground water (F, Eng, SLC, 1952). Brown 5874.

10453 A divining rod or forked willow stick will seek out water (M, Vernal). Cf. Brown 5882.

10454 A forked, green willow stick will point to water under the ground (M, SLC).

10455 Take a peach branch, a limb from a peach tree, and if the water is close, the leaves will turn down (F, Moab, 1953); . . . peach or other fruit twigs . . . (F, 60, Ogden, 1950). Brown 5876ff.

10456 "The Mormon settlers usually chose their land near a stream for irrigation purposes. If the spring could not be found, a well had to be dug and this duty was left to a man said to have the gift of water witching. This was accomplished by a divining rod, most often a forked twig from a peach tree. The twig was held close to the ground as he walked. When a likely place was reached, it is said that the twig bent firmly toward the spot where water would be found" (F, 60, Weber, 1920); . . . this practice is called "well witching" (M, 57, Swiss, Heber, 1916).

10457 For water witching use a peach limb, a tamarack or black willow, or any willow or green branch that has a high water content, and bailing wire. You make a kind of spring out of the bailing wire by bending it. You fold it up a couple of times on one end, then you hold it in your hand with your finger on the wire, kind of on the edge of the wire to guide it, and then the wire, if there is water down there, will start to dip up and down (M, 50, Moab, 1953).

10458 Divinity [sic] rod: A brass rod in a V shape, total length, four feet. Hold it straight outward or bend it at the elbows so that it is in a horizontal plane with the earth but vertical to a man's body. When walking over an ore body, it begins to pull down so hard that one cannot hold it. There is supposed to be ore located at this point (M, SLC).

HIDDEN TREASURE

10459 Don't dig for buried treasure on a Friday. It's bad luck (F, 13, Orem, 1964, from Tom Sawyer).

10460 If you bury money and then die, your soul will not rest until someone digs the money up (M, 32, PR, SLC, 1965).

10461 Black goats on lonely paths are a sign of hidden treasure (F, Ogden, 1960).

10462 Serpents and demons are supposed to guard the mines from intrusion (M, 1961).

GOLD

10463 If you find a spider there is gold nearby. You must find them in multiple numbers (F, Scot, SLC, 1957); When you see spiders in abundance, there will be gold there (F, 85, SLC, 1964).

10464 If you hold down a daddy longlegs spider by one leg, the opposite leg will point to a pot of gold (M, SLC, 1961).

10465 If you dig at the end of a rainbow, where it touches the ground, you will find a bag of gold (F, Moab, 1962); . . . a box full of golden coins (F, SLC, 1963); . . . a pot of gold (M, 20, Vernal, 1964); . . . a bucket of gold (F, SLC, 1962). Brown 5901.

AMULETS AND CHARMS

Various Notions

10466 If you wear amulets or charms, you will avoid ill luck (M, SLC, 1959).

10467 A charm that looks like an eye will throw the evil back to its source (F, 18, SLC, 1950).

10468 It is unlucky to pay money for good luck charms as they will lose all of their luck (F, 20, SLC, 1964).

10469 Machine made lucky charms are extremely bad luck (M, 25, SLC, 1964).

Amulets of Human Parts

10470 Carry a fingernail for good luck (M, 19, SLC, 1963).

10471 During the war if you carried a lock of hair close to your heart, you would come home safely (F, SLC, 1964).

Animal Amulets

10472 Persons use the ear stones (white stonelike objects found in the small sac near the internal ear of a fish) as a lucky charm, like a rabbit's foot (M, Vernal, 1959). Cf. Brown 5810f.

10473 If you carry the small bone of a fish head, luck comes when you lose the charm. You have to lose the bone in order to have good luck (F, 35, SLC, 1945).

10474 If you save the swords off a swordfish, you'll have good luck (M, 21, Bountiful, 1965).

10475 Carry a fish scale in your purse and it will bring you good luck (F, 39, SLC, 1964).

10476 An elk's tooth brings good luck (M, SLC, 1960).

10477 The shark's tooth worn around the neck is good luck (F, SLC, 1963).

10478   Wearing a hound's tooth on a watch fob is good luck (M, SLC, 1963).

10479   If the eyes of a black cat are extracted and carried with you, it is a good luck charm (M, Ogden, 1960).

10480   White rats are good luck charms (M, 53, Logan, 1931).

10481   To find grace in everyone's eyes, take the stomach of a black rooster, and there you will find small white stones; carry these same stones about with you (M, 25, Je, SLC, 1965).

10482   If they wear an eagle's head around their necks, they will be protected from the buzzards (M, 20, SLC, 1963). Ute Indian belief.

10483   A rattle from a rattlesnake worn around the neck is good luck. This is an old sheepherder's superstition (F, Magna, 1960).

10484   To carry the knucklebone of a ham will bring good luck (M, 55, SLC, 1964). Brown 5805.

10485   A raccoon's penis bone is good luck to pick your teeth with (M, Hiawatha, 1955).

10486   To place a piece of paper from a wasp nest in your clothing will bring good luck (M, SLC, 1960).

## Rabbit's Foot, Etc.

10487   Carrying a rabbit's foot insures good luck (F, SLC, 1958); . . . on a key chain . . . (F, Moab, 1953); . . . will protect you from harm and bring you good luck (F, Bear River City, 1957). Brown 5789, 5792.

10488   Carrying a rabbit's foot will bring you good luck. My father adds, "The rabbit carried four of them, but it didn't help him keep them" (F, SLC, 1964).

10489   A rabbit's foot supposedly is a good luck charm, enabling the owner to lead a charmed magic life (F, 39, SLC, 1962); . . . you to have success in every undertaking (F, 67, SLC, 1964).

10490   Rub a rabbit's foot and you will get good luck (F, SLC, 1960).

10491   A rabbit's foot is good luck only if it is a white one (F, 20, SLC, 1963).

10492   To kill a rabbit and preserve his foot is excellent luck (M, 47, SLC, 1962).

10493   The possession of a rabbit's foot brings ten years of good luck (M, 22, SLC, 1962).

10494   A rabbit's foot brings bad luck (M, SLC, 1960).

10495   Carry the right front paw of a rabbit with you for good luck (M, SLC, 1961). Brown 5794.

10496   If you carry the hind foot of a rabbit, it will bring you good luck (M, 13, SLC, 1963); . . . the left hind foot . . .

(M, Ogden, 1958); . . . left hind foot of a graveyard rabbit . . . (M, Holladay, 1959). Cf. Brown 5796.

10497   A rabbit's left hind foot carried in your left pocket is considered good luck. One of the reasons a rabbit is considered lucky is because a northern rabbit changes colors for the different seasons (M, Murray, 1959).

10498   Carrying a rabbit's foot in the right pocket of your pants assures good health (M, SLC, 1961).

10499   Part of a rabbit bone hung around your neck will bring you good luck (M, SLC, 1950); A rabbit's foot around your neck . . . (M, SLC, 19 64).

10500   A rabbit's foot hung from the belt is good luck (M, SLC, 1964); . . . on a loop of your pants . . . (F, Peoa, 1959).

10501   Carry a rabbit's foot in your purse for good luck (F, SLC, 1963).

10502   If you carry a rabbit's tail with you, you will always have good luck (F, SLC, 1960).

10503   Dogs, wolves, coyotes howl at the dark of the moon, but if you wear a rabbit's foot, they will never hurt you (F, 69, SLC, 1900).

## Horseshoes as Amulets

10504   Horseshoes have power as talismans (M, SLC, 1945).

10505   Carry a horseshoe with you for good luck (M, SLC, 1949).

10506   If you have a horseshoe on your key chain, every place you go will be in safety (M, SLC, 1964).

10507   I usually carry a horseshoe shaped charm with a penny in it around my neck as a symbol of good luck (M, 39, SLC, 1965).

## Plants as Amulets

10508   Wear a bag of herbs around the neck to ward off bad omens (F, Eng, SLC, 1957).

10509   Carry an acorn for good luck (M, SLC, 1959); . . . and you will have good luck, especially a long life (F, Monroe, 1960).

10510   If a lady carries an acorn in her pocket or bag, she will be blessed with good luck (F, 44, SLC, 1963).

10511   A buckeye carried in the pocket will surely bring good luck (F, 31, SLC, 1952). Cf. Brown 5817f.

10512   It is good luck to carry a comb of corn stalks in the sweat band of your hat to ward off bad luck (M, 20, SLC, 1964).

10513   Carry a horse chestnut as a lucky charm (F, 58, Union, 1925). Brown 5819.

10514   Hickory nuts bring good luck (F, 85, SLC, 1900).

10515 It is good luck to carry a horse chestnut in your purse (F, 84, Provo, 1908).

10516 A four-leaf clover is a good luck charm (F, 1960).

10517 If you put a four-leaf clover in your shoe, it will bring you good luck (F, 24, SLC, 1964); A . . . pressed and put in the right shoe will bring permanent good luck (M, SLC, 1960).

10518 If you wear a mustard seed in a charm, you will have much good luck and fortune (F, 19, SLC, 1964).

10519 A nutmeg worn about the neck is said to be very lucky (F, 19, SLC, 1963).

10520 A potato carried in the pocket brings good luck (F, Eng, SLC, 1961).

10521 If you want good luck to pass real fast, carry a potato in your purse (F, 34, SLC, 1950).

## Knocking on Wood, Etc.

10522 If you brag, knock on wood (M, SLC, 1959); . . . knock on wood three times (F, SLC, 1957). Brown 5837.

10523 If bragging about something like you've never had a wreck, you'll soon have one unless you knock on wood (M, SLC, 1918). Cf. Brown 5839.

10524 Knock on wood if you want good luck to continue (F, SLC, 1959).

10525 Knock on wood three times and you'll have good luck (F, 18, SLC, 1950).

10526 You can ward off bad luck by knocking on wood (F, SLC, 1955).

10527 After you have made an unhappy statement you must knock on wood or it might come true (F, SLC, 1962); When you say something you don't want to happen . . . (F, SLC, 1959).

10528 Knock on wood after saying "never," or you'll have misfortune (F, SLC, 1960).

10529 Knock on wood to take away a bad omen from a wish (F, SLC, 1943).

10530 Knocking on wood brings luck from the spirit in the wood (F, SLC, 1957).

10531 Knock on wood if you say something and want it to be true (F, SLC, 1960); Knocking on wood after making a wish will make it come true (M, Ogden, 1964).

10532 If you knock on wood, then you won't have a flat tire (F, 19, SLC, 1957).

10533 Don't knock on wood if you want good luck to continue. Kick the ground (M, 54, SLC, 1965).

10534 When someone is going to do something, if they knock on wood first, it is good luck (F, 44, SLC, 1932); Knock on wood before undertaking a project (M, SLC, 1964).

10535 Knock on wood when you speak of the future to avoid disaster (F, 19, SLC, 1963).

10536 Don't knock on someone's head if they say "Knock on wood" (M, 45, SLC, 1963).

10537 If you knock on cedar wood, you will have good luck (M, 60, SLC, 1915).

10538 Never tempt fate without knocking on wood (M, 53, Provo, 1964).

10539 Knock on wood for success (M, American Fork, 1930).

10540 After making a prediction, knock on wood three times (F, SLC, 1945); To assure the happening of something you've just verbalized, knock on wood (F, 19, Sandy, 1958).

10541 When you say or see something good, knock on wood to ward off the evil spirits (M, 20, SLC, 1954). Brown 5836.

10542 When you see something bad or hear of something tragic, you should touch something of wood to ward off the bad luck (M, 20, SLC, 1953).

10543 If your hand itches, rub it on wood and it will come to some good (F, SLC, 1958).

10544 To prevent a coincidence, knock on wood (M, SLC, 1958).

10545 Knock on wood to keep things status quo (F, 44, SLC, 1965).

10546 Touch wood to ward off bad luck (M, SLC, 1959).

10547 When he was a child if you touched wood during a game, you were "safe" (M, 24, Ogden, 1946).

10548 Knock on ivory for luck (M, Woods Cross, 1958).

## Coins and Bills as Amulets

10549 Carry a coin for good luck (M, SLC, 1959).

10550 Carrying a bent coin means good luck (F, 40, Logan, 1938).

10551 A coin with a hole in it is good luck (M, SLC, 1959); . . . is an especially lucky piece (F, Farmington, 1959).

10552 Carrying a lucky penny will bring the carrier good luck (F, 51, Centerfield, 1964). Brown 5823.

10553 If you find a penny and always carry it with you, you will always have good luck (F, 38, SLC, 1964).

10554 If you carry a penny with a hole in it in your pocket, you'll have good luck (M, 19, Bountiful, 1964).

10555 Hang a 1944 penny around the neck for good luck (F, SLC, 1960).

10556 Wear a coin in your shoe for good luck (F, 40, Fillmore, 1933); Always put a penny in a new shoe . . . (F, Ogden,

1962); If you find a penny, pick it up and put it in your shoe and it will bring good luck. Wearing pennies in "penny loafer" shoes also brings good luck (F, 18, SLC, 1964).

10557 If you find a penny, put it in your left shoe and it will bring you good luck (F, 19, SLC, 1964); . . . put it in the shoe of the right foot . . . (F, 18, SLC).

10558 On the day of an election if the father gives you a penny and you put it in your shoe, it will bring you good luck (F, 19, SLC, 1964).

10559 If you carry a wooden nickel in your back pocket, it will bring you good luck (M, Dan, 59, SLC, 1964).

10560 A shined dime is a good luck charm (F, 54, SLC, 1964). Cf. Brown 5825.

10561 Three silver dollars carried in the left pocket of your pants is a good luck charm (M, SLC, 1961).

10562 A silver coin will bring good luck if worn in a necklace about the neck (F, SLC, 1960).

10563 Always carry a gold piece for a good luck charm (M, Ogden, 1961); "My mother always carried a two and a half dollar gold piece wherever she went as an amulet for good luck" (F, Logan, 1958); "My step-dad when he died had two twenty dollar gold pieces he carried for years and years" (F, Moab, 1953).

10564 Carrying a two-dollar bill in your pocket or purse will bring good luck (F, Ogden, 1959).

## Religious Amulets, Medals, Etc.

10565 To ward off bad luck, carry a Holy Book or charm (M, SLC, 1952).

10566 A cross around the neck will keep supernatural spirits away (M, SLC, 1960). Cf. Brown 5821.

10567 When you take a religious medal or a ring off to bathe, they should be placed on one another for mutual protection (F, 19, SLC, 1955).

## Intimate Possessions and Jewelry as Amulets

10568 If you find a hairpin, put it in your shoe and you will have good luck (F, Fillmore, 1960).

10569 As long as you carry a white, nylon comb in your left pocket your luck will be good (M, 19, SLC, 1964).

10570 If you wear a charm bracelet, you will have good luck for as long as you wear the bracelet (F, 21, American Fork, 1960).

10571 The Moslems keep a string of beads with a tassel on the end for good luck (F, 18, Price, 1962). Cf. Brown 5832.

10572 Some little thing such as a key chain or cuff links can be lucky for someone (M, 19, SLC).

## Miscellaneous Amulets

10573 The wearing of a bag which is supposed to have a magic power protects the wearer from harm (F, 46, SLC, 1934).

10574 To carry a miniature hunchback is a powerful bringer of luck (F, SLC, 1961).

10575 Troll dolls bring good luck (M, SLC, 1964).

10576 It is good luck to carry a crust of bread in one's pocket or pocketbook (M, 63, SLC, 1964).

10577 Having a safety pin on you somewhere will keep you safe (F, 26, Bountiful, 1940s).

10578 Some people keep a lucky thimble in their purse (F, 18, SLC, 1962).

10579 Salt possesses magic qualities (F, 23, SLC, 1960).

10580 If you carry a lucky bone in your pocket, you will have good luck (M, 78, SLC).

10581 Never use a cat's eye flint as a taw, because it is bad luck; only carry them for luck (M, 56, Ogden, 1963).

10582 To ward off bad luck, walk with small rocks in your shoe (F, 44, SLC, 1964).

10583 Coral has a special sympathy with nature (M, SLC, 1957).

10584 Carry a seashell with you, and you will never drown (M, 45, SLC).

10585 Magnets possess magical powers (F, 54, SLC, 1950).

10586 If you wear a mascot, it will bring good luck (F, 50, SLC, 1964).

## VERBAL CHARMS

10587 In order not to fear judges and elders and to avoid harm, pick up a handful of earth and repeat the following three times: "Terror and dread falleth upon them; by the greatness of thine arm, they are as still as a stone." Then say this backwards. Now take the earth, and throw it down on the ground in front of two houses (M, 25, Je, SLC, 1965).

10588 Whenever you say something like "I've never been sick," you say "Seven, Nine, Thirteen." It's like knocking on wood (F, 23, Dan, SLC, 1963).

10589 Say "One, two, three, good luck for me," if you know you have said or done something unlucky, and it will break the spell (F, 39, SLC, 1964).

10590 Say "Needles and pins" to prevent bad luck (F, Midvale, 1961).

## REALM OF THE DEAD

## Revenants, Resurrected Beings

10591 Among the first settlers to Mink Creek was a father who had committed a very bad crime in the town and who knew there was a curse on those who committed crimes. One night during a bad storm, the lights flickered out and the fire dimmed. When the fire became bright again, the oldest daughter lay dead with teeth marks on her neck. Each succeeding storm, one of the daughters died until all five were dead (F, 21, Preston, 1952).

10592  When the sun rises, the living corpse must return to its grave (M, 57, SLC, 1960).

10593  The informant's grandfather explained that you can tell if someone is resurrected by whether he offers to shake your hand or not. A resurrected being will; a spiritual being will not (M, 38, Ogden, 1970).

## GHOSTS AND SPIRITS

### Nature and Manifestation

10594  Some people have seen ghosts or shadows of ghosts (F, Logan, 1957).

10595  If a cat or a dog should jump over the bier of a newly dead person, the dead person will become a ghost and haunt the family (F, Gr, SLC, 1961).

10596  People believe in the return of the spirit or ghost of the dead to its former haunts (F, 37, Logan, 1964); Dead people come back to haunt others in the form of ghosts (M, SLC, 1960).

10597  If a person treats another person badly, when the person treated badly dies, his spirit will come back and haunt the other (M, 20, SLC, 1958).

10598  If a person dies hard, it is a bad sign; he will haunt his survivors (F, SLC, 1960).

10599  Never speak unkindly around the body of a dead person, or you will be cursed by his haunting (F, Bountiful, 1959).

10600  If you have been ignorant and mean to someone during their lifetime, chances are that he will come back to haunt you (F, 100, Mex, SLC, 1963).

10601  If you walk over a grave, that person will haunt you till you die (F, SLC, 1957).

10602  Never walk by a graveyard in the dark of the moon at midnight, or your closest relative that is buried near there will haunt you for a year, until you return to the same spot (F, 69, SLC, 1912).

10603  The dead sweetheart haunts the faithless lover (M, SLC, 1963).

10604  Falling stars are the souls of people coming back to earth to haunt their enemies (F, 50, SLC, 1963).

10605  A sudden warm breeze means the passing of a ghost (M, SLC, 1961). Cf. Brown 5714.

10606  The wind blowing down the fireplace means ghosts are coming (M, SLC, 1950).

10607  When the wind howls, it is a sign of spirits, and if you stay in it too long, you are sure to have bad luck (F, SLC, 1958).

10608  The mist at night on the streets are spirits that haven't gone to heaven or hell. They want to get your spirit too (F, Murray, 1954).

10609  If a door opens of itself, a ghost is the operator (F, Lehi, 1957). Brown 5717.

10610  If you have stairs in your house, you will be visited by spirits, and if you don't have stairs in your house, the spirits will stay away (F, 20, SLC, 1970).

10611  When a wagon refuses to move, it is because a ghost is sitting in it (F, SLC, 1963).

10612  Three knocks that seem to come from nowhere is a warning of danger from the spiritual world (F, 30, Bountiful, 1964).

10613  A long, lonely train whistle means the train is carrying a spirit (F, 44, Eng, Sandy, 1928).

10614  When the curfew sounds, it is the signal to ghosts for their walking (M, SLC, 1961).

10615  Midnight is the bewitching hour when spirits come out (M, SLC, 1945).

10616  On Halloween night ghosts come out (M, SLC, 1950).

10617  At Christmas Eve, spirits walk (M, SLC, 1960).

10618  When you have a cold shiver or a chill, it means that someone from the spirit world has touched you (F, 52, SLC, 1925).

10619  A person always meets his ghost just before he or she dies (M, 34, SLC, 1963).

10620  The ghost carries its own dead body (F, Ger, SLC, 1963).

10621  The ghost punishes the person who mocks him (F, Eng, Holladay, 1963).

10622  Spirits live in trees (F, 38, SLC, 1930s).

10623  You must never step on leaves, because they are little spirits (F, 80, SLC, 1923).

### The Detection of Ghosts and Spirits

10624  If you comb your hair in the dark, you will see ghosts (F, 52, SLC, 1918). Cf. Brown 5720.

10625  When speaking of a dead person you must say "May he rest in peace," or you will offend his ghost (M, 48, Midvale, 1923).

10626  Animals can see spirits (M, SLC, 1959). Cf. Brown 5721f.

10627 If a dog howls at night, you will be visited by the dead (F, 25, American Fork, 1945). Cf. Brown 5739.

10628 Spirits enter the bodies of pigs (F, Logan, 1957).

## Summoning Ghosts and Spirits

10629 Magic words, when uttered, summon spirits (F, 89, Midvale, 1964).

10630 Don't whistle at night. It attracts ghosts (M, SLC, 1963).

10631 Burning a candle in front of a mirror is supposedly a method of summoning spirits from another world. I placed a candle in front of a mirror in my bedroom. If it summoned spirits, they have not made their presence known to me (F, SLC, 1971).

## The Ghostly Return to Right Wrongs and Settle Accounts

10632 Spirits are watching all of us to see if we are good or bad (M, SLC, 1959).

10633 If a person is killed or dies a hard death, his spirit will be seen (M, SLC, 1961).

10634 If you haven't been good, and you walk alone at night, the dead will appear (M, SLC, 1957).

10635 A ghost exists to right a wrong or avenge a crime (F, 46, SLC, 1930).

10636 If a man is killed and sheds blood, he will keep coming back (F, 51, SLC, 1963).

10637 Before a woman's grandmother died she said she would be back to get her brother. Her mother was told by a neighbor that if she did not come in a year she wouldn't come. Her mother was very anxious until the year expired (F, Murray, 1959).

10638 After the death of my uncle D, his brother, F, constantly had dreams of him. D would go to F and beg him "to get it done for me." After several nights of this, F realized that D's temple work hadn't been done. He went ahead and did the work, and Uncle D never came to bother Uncle F again (F).

10639 Informant said that she had heard the father of Myra York Hancock tell that while he was working in his field, Daniel Webster appeared before him and told him to do his (Webster's) temple work. Mr. York did nothing about it for more than a year, then Webster appeared before him again and insisted that the work be done, so Mr. York went to the Manti temple and performed the ceremony (F, SLC, 1946).

10640 This story is related by Mrs. HP, Castle Dale, Utah. As a child, Mrs. P and her sister kept seeing a man clothed in white. They found he was their uncle who had died on the cattle range many years before. He had been buried on the range without any services. Mrs. P's parents finally had the remains of this uncle buried under the ritual of the LDS Church. After this burial neither Mrs. P nor her sister saw the personage again. It was believed that the spirit was trying to communicate with them that he wanted a proper burial (M, Orangeville, 1937).

10641 R and her brothers and sisters were told to stay off the hill behind their house, because of rattlesnakes. One day they went up there and R said she saw an uncle who had died two months earlier, standing in the bushes about a foot off the ground. They ran home and told their father, and he said that this uncle was looking out for their safety by warning them to stay off the mountain (F, 21, Logan, 1971).

10642 L, whose mother died when she was twelve, was in the habit of riding her horse too fast down a mountain. One night she saw the figure of an elderly woman clothed entirely in white with a hood of semitransparent material over her head. The figure floated along with L each night when she passed the hill. Her friends also saw the figure and the figure only appeared on those nights that L rode too fast. The explanation was that the figure was L's mother endeavoring to have her ride more cautiously (M, SLC, 1946).

10643 A family living in Logan was a large family--eight children--and very close, except for the father, who everyone hated. While he was on his deathbed, he cursed them by saying that one child would die every six months from the time he died. Sure enough, six months later, the oldest boy caught pneumonia and died. This continued until all the children and the mother died. In the Logan Cemetery there is a large statue of a lady sitting down, who seems to be weeping. Around the statue there are eight graves and all have died within six months of each other. If you go to the statue at midnight on the date of the day the last child died, you can hear her weeping and feel the tears on her cheek (M, 20, Logan, 1972).

## Haunted Places

10644 Old empty houses are haunted, and it pays to stay away from them (M, SLC, 1958); Ghosts live in empty houses and for that reason people would go blocks out of their way to avoid an empty house (F, Murray, 1894).

10645 There is a certain house east of Tooele that is haunted by a woman who disappeared just minutes after she was married in the house (F, 57, Tooele, 1925).

10646 A local superstition of the old Salt Lake City was that the Lee Mansion was haunted (M, 24, SLC, 1963).

10647 The Gadianton robbers haunt the area around Red Creek in Uintah Basin. A famous band of robbers in that area, they are supposed to ride their phantom horses down the old Red Creek road at night (F, 57, Vernal, 1910).

10648   To pass a haunted place, turn your pockets inside out; the haunt will not trouble you (M, 22, SLC, 1963).

10649   If you move into a house where someone has recently died, you will be haunted all the time you live there (M, 59, Dan, SLC, 1964).

10650   There is a house down by Spring City called X's house. The story goes that Mr. X killed his wife and buried her under the porch of the house. No one knew she was dead until her ghost came to haunt Mr. X and drive him out of the house. Since then no one has been able to live there because she haunts the house until they leave (M, 21, Logan, 1972).

10651   One night after the sawmill had been going all day, the men were awakened by the sound of the sawmill running at full blast. They got up and opened the door to see who was running it. When they opened the door, all sound stopped. No wheel turned, no lumber was disturbed and no sawing had been done. As soon as the men closed the door, the sawing started again. This continued all night with no explanation (F, 85, W. Jordan, 1893).

10652   There is a haunted house in Salt Lake in the Avenues on "I" Street. When this house was being built, the carpenter that was working on the house had to stop work because of bankruptcy. The carpenter was married and had a mistress on the side. He took his mistress to the unfinished house. While they were there this woman's boyfriend found them, and in his disgust he shot her and killed her. She haunts the house, and the family who has lived there fifteen years just accepts her presence in the house (M, SLC, 1966).

10653   One must never leave an empty rocking chair rocking. It may either cause a death or welcome some evil spirit to haunt the house (F, Springville, 1974).

Various Notions about Ghosts and Spirits

10654   It is said that people going past the old Branch Agriculture College auditorium at midnight have heard weird strains of "Deep Purple" coming from a piano somewhere in the darkness. The performer is said to be a young woman, an accomplished pianist, who had suddenly died of a heart attack after completing a rendition of "Deep Purple" at a recital in the auditorium (F, Cedar City).

10655   The railroad tracks used to go close by the slag dumps out of the Garfield Refinery and the story goes that hobos used to get off the trains looking for work, and when they couldn't get a job, they'd camp at the foot of the slag pile. They always found cans and stuff and ashes of campfires to show they'd been there. The guys around here claim some of them were burned alive while they slept when the hot slag was poured down over them. And a lot of guys claim right now they've seen the spirits of those hobos floating around the slag dumps (M, Magna, 1967).

10656   There was a hill in the neighborhood where many Indian relics had been found, and the children would never go up there alone for fear of the Indians' ghosts (M, Ogden, 1945).

10657   Spirits walk in a cemetery (F, SLC, 1957).

10658   Cemeteries are haunted during the night, especially between twelve and one, that time being the ghost hour (M, Ger, SLC, 1938); Ghosts lurk in graveyards after nightfall (F, 80, Pleasant Grove, 1961).

10659   A ghost named "Emo" talks to people in the Salt Lake City Cemetery every night at midnight (F, SLC, 1959).

10660   In Heber there is this cemetery. In this cemetery there's a light that looks like it is coming from one of the tombstones. One night a kid went into the cemetery to find out where the light came from. He never came back. They say some ghost got him. Now no one dares go in there at night (F, SLC, 1966).

10661   No person who touches a dead body will be haunted by its spirit (M, 22, SLC, 1961).

10662   Silver nails or screws in a coffin will prevent the dead from haunting the scenes of its existence in the flesh (M, 22, SLC, 1961).

10663   If a person dies by accident or suicide and he spills blood, you must throw sesame seeds on the body, and then his spirit won't haunt anybody during the night, because by the time the dead person's spirit has counted all the sesame seeds, it is dawn and the spirits then rest (F, Gr, SLC, 1957).

10664   If you play hide and seek, the ghost will come out and take you to hell (M, 23, Logan, 1970).

10665   Very bad boys would be taken by ghosts, all crawling on their hands and knees, high into the hills where the unruly youngsters would freeze to death and turn into stone (F, 47, Magna, 1964).

10666   There was a lady in Logan who claimed a crystal ball that was unearthed when the Logan Temple was being built. She became known as the "Peepstone Lady" and could do miracles with her crystal ball. Once, after a prominent man had disappeared, the Peepstone Lady, by looking into her crystal ball, told the searchers where to look. She first communicated with the spirit of the dead man and then found where his body was by looking into her crystal ball (F, 1945).

10667   There's a strange white light that you can see in Spring Canyon, a ghost town by Helper, Utah. This strange white light is supposed to be the White Lady of Spring Canyon looking for her baby, which died at birth (F, Coalville).

10668   A ghost appearing to a bride in the form of a white horse, was considered to be the very best omen (F, SLC, 1959).

10669   A person should not sit in "Nigger Heaven" (the balcony) at the movie because the "Nigger Spirit" is there, resulting in something black and terrible happening to anyone sitting in the balcony. Each time I went to the movie with my cousin I would hear the call "Now remember not to sit in single Nigger Heaven" (F, Centerville).

## Dispelling and Laying Ghosts and Spirits

10670   Upon seeing a spook or ghost a German should say: "Alle guten Geister loben Gott den Herrn!" (all good spirits praise the God our Lord) (M, Ger, SLC, 1940).

10671   On moonlight nights draw the window shade, because if the moonlight shines on you, a ghost or an angel will take you away (F, SLC, 1912).

10672   To keep ghosts away, place a feather duster in the doorway (M, SLC, 1961).

10673   Cold iron across the front door steps keeps ghosts out (M, Ogden, 1961).

10674   If you have steel in your hand, a ghost cannot harm you (F, SLC, 1959).

10675   Throw a key at a ghost, and you break its power to harm you (F, SLC, 1961).

10676   If one shoots at a ghost with silver bullets, he will kill him (M, SLC, 1961); . . . --it must be made with a silver quarter-- . . . (M, 22, SLC, 1963).

10677   A person may be kept from becoming a ghost if he is placed face down in his grave (F, 51, SLC, 1963).

# XI
# Weather, Cosmic Phenomena, Time, the Universe

SEASONS OF THE YEAR

SPRING

10678  An early Easter means an early spring
(F, SLC, 1955).

10679  Early thunder, early spring (M, 24, SLC,
1963).

10680  In winter if you see a bluebird, spring
is coming (F, SLC, 1923).

10681  If you see a robin in February, it is a
sign of an early spring (F, Swed, SLC,
1957).

10682  A robin is the first sign of spring (M,
44, Layton, 1970).  Brown 6050.

10683  If you see a robin towards the end of
winter in a snowstorm, it is an omen
that the coming spring will be cold and
changeable, and bad weather will plague
the area for the rest of the year (F,
19, SLC, 1964).

10684  If the first bird you see at the turn of
spring is a robin, the spring will be
warm and beautiful (F, 40, SLC, 1925).

10685      If Candlemas Day be fair and bright,
           Winter will have another flight.
           But if Candlemas Day bring clouds
              and rain,
           Winter is gone and won't come back
              again.
(F, SLC, 1961).

10686  If the ground hog sees his shadow when
he comes out for the first time, then
spring is here (M, 12, Orem, 1964).

10687  If the ground hog sees his shadow on
February 2, he will retire for another
six weeks, but if it is cloudy, he will
remain out, anticipating an early spring
(F, SLC, 1962); . . . spring will come
in three weeks (M, SLC, 1960); . . .
spring will be delayed by six weeks (M,
SLC, 1960); . . . spring will be late
(M, SLC, 1957).  Brown 6044f.

10688  When frogs start to croak, winter will
come to an end (M, 22, Midvale, 1964);
. . . it is a sign of spring (M, SLC).
Cf. Brown 6043.

10689  Spring arrives when you can set your
foot on twelve daisies at once (F, 49,
SLC, 1964).

10690  Wet May was never kind yet (M, 55, SLC,
1930).

SUMMER

10691  A cold winter is followed by a hot
summer and vice versa (M, Vernal, 1961).
Brown 6060f.

10692      If February gives much snow,
           A fine summer it doth foreshow.
(F, Bountiful, 1970).

10693  Snowy winter, dry summer (M, SLC, 1960).

10694  If you see a crow flying backwards,
there will be record temperatures
throughout the summer (M, SLC, 1957).

10695  Rain the first day of spring means a
happy summer (F, 65, Manti, 1964).

10696  When you see the morning ground torn up
by ants, you will know that summer has
begun (M, 37, SLC, 1941).

10697  There is not much summer left after the
24th of July (M, SLC, 1957).

AUTUMN

10698  It's a sign of an early fall if many
caterpillars are seen crawling on the
ground (M, SLC, 1964).

WINTER

Various Portents

10699  Older people say that you can expect to
have an extremely cold and stormy winter
every seven years (M, SLC, 1967).

10700  It is a good sign if the first three
days of winter are dark and cloudy (F,
SLC, 1957).

10701  An early frost means an early winter (M,
SLC, 1960).

10702  Hot summers bring a cold winter (F, SLC,
1941).

10703      If Christmas be fair and clear,
           Two winters will you have this year.
(F, SLC, 1965).

10704  Never put long underwear away till after
June 16th, or winter will still come (F,
Eng, SLC, 1960).

10705  Never do house cleaning for spring until
after June 16th, or else winter will
still come (F, Eng, SLC, 1960).

10706 When rheumatism begins acting up, winter is coming (F, 50, Weber, 1920).

10707 If thunder is heard in the spring before the leaves are on the trees, there will be six weeks more of winter (F, SLC).

Animal Portents and Indicators

10708 The type of coat grown by animals in the fall (heavy or light) predicts the kind of winter ahead (F, Nephi, 1963). Attributed to the Indians.

10709 Beavers know by instinct whether the coming winter will be mild or severe (M, 71, SLC, 1965).

10710 If the bear sees his shadow on February 2, there will be six more weeks of winter. If he does not see his shadow, it will be spring (F, Bear River City, 1957).

10711 If a gopher sees his shadow on February 2, you'll have more winter (M, 52, SLC, 1950).

10712 The weather for six weeks following Ground Hog Day (February 2) depends on whether the ground hog sees his shadow on that day (F, Sandy, 1957); . . . if he sees his shadow, there will be forty more days of winter (M, SLC, 1961); . . . six more weeks . . . (M, SLC, 1958); . . . seven more weeks . . . (M, 20, SLC, 1941); . . . sixty more days . . . (M, 22, SLC, 1952).

10713 If the ground hog sees his shadow on the first of March, there will be six more weeks of winter (M, SLC, 1960).

10714 If the ground hog sees his shadow, it will be a long winter, and if he doesn't, summer will be here soon (F, 19, SLC, 1960). Brown 6068.

10715 If February 2 is fine and clear, there'll be two winters in that year. The ground hog will have seen his shadow (F, SLC, 1957). Cf. Brown 6069.

10716 You can tell what kind of winter it will be by the shape of the pig's smelt [sic] (spleen) (M, 76, 1946).

10717 You can tell what kind of winter it is going to be by watching how the squirrels carry their tails (F, 58, SLC, 1958).

10718 The amount of nuts a squirrel stores up indicates the length of the coming winter (M, 46, SLC, 1926); If the squirrels store a lot of nuts, winter will come early and will last a long time (F, 54, Logan, 1970).

10719 When geese fly south early, it's a sign of an early winter (F, SLC, 1925). Cf. Brown 6065.

10720 The chirping of crickets early in the summer means an early winter (F, 60, Logan, 1915).

10721 The chirping of locusts in fall is a sure sign winter is near (F, SLC, 1960).

10722 Caterpillars forecast the amount of cold for the coming winter. Orange color predicts warm weather, while amounts of black predict cold weather (M, Logan, 1970).

10723 When a woolly bear caterpillar is seen hurrying across an open space, it is taken for granted that winter is close behind (M, SLC, 1960).

Plant Indicators

10724 The number of layers of an onion indicates the nature of the following winter (M, 54, SLC, 1930).

10725 When poplar trees shed their leaves early, it points to an early winter (F, SLC, 1925).

10726 Rain and lightning over a leafless tree means six more weeks of winter (M, 50, SLC, 1963).

Cold, Severe Winter

10727 An unusually severe winter will follow an Indian summer (F, 1957).

10728 If there is an extremely hot summer, there will be an extremely cold winter (M, 44, Woods Cross, 1964). Brown 6071.

10729 The nearer to a full moon on Christmas, the harder will be the rest of the winter (M, SLC, 1965).

10730 Heavy moisture on a clothesline means there will be a hard winter (F, SLC, 1961).

Animal Portents of a Severe Winter

10731 A heavy fur on the animals means that it will be very cold in the winter (F, 70, Provo, 1900). Brown 6076.

10732 You can expect a very hard and severe winter ahead when you see wild birds or beasts grow a heavier coat of feathers or fur for the winter (M, 35, SLC, 1964).

10733 When the animals get long fur, the winter will be a long hard one (F, Grantsville, 1964).

10734 Migration of animals indicates a strong winter (M, Provo, 1935).

10735 When fur-bearing animals get their winter coats early in the fall, a hard winter will follow (M, SLC, 1957).

10736 If small game is scarce during hunting season, a hard winter will follow (M, SLC, 1958).

Horses, Hogs, Pigs as Indicators of a Severe Winter

10737 If a horse has a heavy fur, there is going to be a long, hard winter (F, 65, SLC, 1962); If a horse gets a lot of hair on its stomach, there will be a heavy winter (F, SLC, 1957).

10738 Farmers tell how hard the winter is going to be by the growth of the hogs.

If they are fat, the winter will be hard (F, SLC, 1959).

10739 When you kill a hog and cut it open, if the melt is fat, then bad winter follows (M, SLC, 1958); . . . if there is more melt in the front of the pig, the beginning of the winter will be hardest (M, 70, Duchesne, 1970).

10740 When you kill a pig in the fall, look at the pancreas. If it is wide at the top and tapers off at the bottom, the first part of the winter will be severe, and the end will be more mild. If it is narrow at the top and widens at the bottom, the reverse will be true (M, 38, Ogden, 1970).

## Various Animals as Indicators of a Severe Winter

10741 If the deer come down from the hills in early September, it means a bad winter (M, Bountiful, 1964).

10742 If bears and squirrels hibernate early, there will be heavy snow that winter (F, SLC, 1957).

10743 The Indians believe that if the squirrels hold their tails high, the winter will be severe (M, 45, Beaver, 1937).

10744 Squirrels and chipmunks storing an unusually large supply of pine nuts is an omen of a hard winter (1946). Cf. Brown 6078, 6080.

10745 It is a hard winter when the squirrels store their nuts up high (F, SLC, 1960).

10746 It's a sign of a hard winter if pine squirrels leave the hills and come down into the valleys (M, 50, SLC, 1964).

10747 If rats have an extra large store of nuts, it is going to be a long cold winter (F, Moab, 1953).

10748 If beavers build their dams high, there is going to be a long winter (M, 38, SLC, 1963). Heard in Nebraska, 1932.

10749 If a rabbit has extra thick fur, there will be a hard winter (M, SLC, 1959).

## Birds and Fowl as Indicators of a Severe Winter

10750 You can tell winter weather by the breast bone of a chicken. A dark bone means a severe winter (M, SLC, 1957). Cf. Brown 6086.

10751 Lots of feathers on the chickens, and there's going to be a hard winter (F, Moab, 1953). Brown 6081.

10752 If a turkey has thick feathers by Thanksgiving, look for a hard winter (M, Spanish Fork, 1964).

10753 Five birds flying south means that the winter will be hard for all (M, SLC).

10754 When ducks go south in early fall, it's a sign of a hard winter (M, Woods Cross, 1964). Cf. Brown 6083f.

10755 When the wild geese fly south in early August, a severe winter is ahead (F, SLC, 1961). Cf. Brown 6085.

10756 Busy woodpeckers mean a severe winter (F, 46, SLC, 1935).

## Insects, Spiders and other Creatures as Indicators of a Severe Winter

10757 A cricket on the hearth of the fireplace means a hard winter (M, Vernal, 1958).

10758 When there are a great number of moths during the summer months, it is a sure sign that the following winter will be very hard (F, Nephi, 1963).

10759 A heavy winter will come when bees make their nests up high (M, SLC, 1961).

10760 If you see a lot of bees in the fall, it will be a hard cold winter (M, 57, Swiss, Heber City, 1918).

10761 Low hanging hornets nests are signs of a severe winter (F, 40, Sandy, 1937); If hornets' nests are in the trees, it should be a bad winter with plenty of snow (M, 21, Manti, 1971).

10762 If the wasp builds nests high in a tree, it means it will be a hard winter (F, 42, SLC, 1963).

10763 When the woolly bear caterpillar grows a heavy coat, it means the winter to follow will be a hard one (M, 65, Granger, 1915); . . . the length of the red hairs on his back indicate a long or short winter; if long, a long winter; if short, a short winter (M, 1968).

## Plants as Indicators of a Severe Winter

10764 Look for a heavy winter when buds have heavy coats (M, SLC, 1920s).

10765 If leaves are thick and heavy on the trees, it means a cold winter (F, SLC, 1957). Brown 6093.

10766 A lot of wild fruit and berries in the mountains is a sign of a hard winter (F, 67, Woodruff, 1965). Brown 6096f.

10767 If there is an abundant supply of seeds on plants, it will be a hard winter (F, SLC, 1961).

10768 When one observes many weeds which have exceeded their growth and are very tall, one can expect a hard and severe winter to follow (M, 35, SLC, 1964). Heard in Texas, 1940.

10769 If there is a large crop of chokecherries, there will be a hard winter (F, 60, SLC, 1963).

10770 Abundant blooms on dogwood in the spring indicates a severe winter to come (M, 39, SLC, 1964).

10771 If a geranium has more than three blooms on the same stem in one year, a bad winter is coming (M, 42, SLC, 1949).

10772 If there is an abundance of sunflowers in autumn, there will be a hard winter

(F, Bountiful, 1948); Indians believed that if the sunflowers were thick during the summer . . . (M, 47, W. Jordan, 1936); Tall weeds and sunflowers forecast severe winter so the birds can feed (M, 84, Centerville); . . . there will be a lot of deep snow that winter (F, Grantsville, 1964).

10773  If there are many acorns on the ground, it will be a hard winter (F); An oversupply of acorns is nature's way to tell of a hard winter (M, 39, SLC, 1964).  Brown 6100.

10774  If acorns are big, it is going to be a bad winter (M, American Fork, 1962). Learned from an Indian; A big acorn crop means a hard winter (M, Layton, 1936); A lot of acorns on the oak bush . . . (M, 57, Swiss, Heber City, 1917).

10775  If there is a heavy nut crop, it is the sign of a hard winter (F, Ogden).  Brown 6099.

10776  A large crop of pine nuts means a hard winter (M, 44, Layton, 1970); An extra heavy load of piñon nuts or pine cones . . . (F, Park City, 1957); If pine nuts fall easily, it . . . (M, SLC, 1957).

10777  If no pine nuts can be found in the trees in early fall, it's a sign of a hard winter (F, Payson, 1957); The chips and squirrels have gathered them in for a long winter's supply (F, 22, SLC, 1950).

10778  Heavy or thick corn husks mean bad winter (M, 44, Layton, 1970); A tight husk means . . . (F, SLC, 1961).  Brown 6088f.

10779  If the corn grows high in the summer, it means there is a hard winter on the way (M, 43, SLC, 1940).

10780  If the corn is red, there will be a hard winter (M, St. George).

10781  If the skin of an apple is tough, it will be a long cold winter (F, 38, Ogden, 1945).

10782      Onion's skin thick and tough,
           Coming winter cold and rough.
       (F, Murray, 1940); If the onion skin is hard . . . (F, SLC, 1961).

10783  If onions have more than one coat (covering), it will be a hard winter (F, SLC, 1961).

## Animal Indicators of a Mild Winter

10784  An Indian superstition is that the thickness of fur on various animals and the color and texture of the skin indicate a mild or heavy winter (F, SLC, 1957).

10785  If an animal's fur is thin, it will be a mild winter (M, Spanish Fork, 1961).

10786  When you kill a hog and cut it open, if the melt is long and thin, there will be a good winter (M, SLC, 1958).

10787  Farmers tell how hard the winter is going to be by the growth of the hogs.

If they are slim in the fall, the winter will be easy (F, SLC, 1959).

10788  One can tell winter weather by the breastbone of a chicken: a light bone means a mild winter (M, SLC, 1957).

10789  If bear tracks are seen after the first snowfall, expect a mild winter (M, Provo, 1970).

10790  If the coat of a hibernating fox is light, then the winter will be mild (M, 47, SLC, 1964).

10791  If rabbits are thick during hunting season, the winter will be mild (M, 23, SLC, 1958).

10792  If you see two birds flying south, it means that the winter will be mild (M, SLC, 1961).

10793  A mild winter will come when the bees make their nests low (M, SLC, 1961).

10794  It will be a mild winter if hornets build their nests in bushes and low (M, 21, Manti, 1971).

## Plants as Indicators of a Mild Winter

10795  If there are a lot of nuts on a tree, it means there will be a good winter (M, 48, SLC, 1963).

10796  If there are few pine nuts on the trees during summer, a mild winter will come (F, 48, Milford, 1955); An abundance of pine nuts means a light winter (F, 22, SLC, 1953).  Cf. Brown 6110.

10797  If corn kernels are large, there will be a mild winter (M, 68, Roosevelt, 1909).

10798  If corn kernels are small, it will be a mild winter (M, 68, Roosevelt, 1909).

10799  If corn has an open husk around the ear, it means there will be a mild winter (F, SLC, 1961).

10800  Short weeds that die off mean a mild winter (M, 84, Centerville).

10801  If sunflowers appear in April, there will be a short winter (M, 28, SLC, 1961).

10802      Onion's skin very thin,
           Mild winter coming in.
       (F, SLC, 1961).

## WEATHER INDICATORS; PILOT DAYS AND TIMES

10803  Rheumatic pain was the pioneers' most reliable weather forecaster in the 1800s (M, SLC, 1964).

10804  A bunion is a weather forecaster (M, 42, SLC, 1963).

10805  The chirping of crickets can be used to estimate temperature.  Count the number of chirps in fourteen seconds, add forty, and you will have the temperature in degrees Fahrenheit (F, SLC).

10806  The thickness of an onion skin can predict a season's weather (M, SLC, 1959).

10807 The first twelve days of January tell the weather of the twelve months respectively (M, SLC, 1957). Brown 6113.

10808 The first three days of any season determines the weather for that season (M, SLC, 1945).

10809 Weather on Easter Sunday will be the weather for the six following Sundays (F, Eng, Ogden, 1963).

10810 A green Christmas means there will be a white Easter (F, 57, SLC, 1964).

10811    As far as the sun shines on Ground
            Hog day,
        So far will snow blow in before May.
        As far as the snow blows on Ground
            Hog day,
        So far will the sun shine out before
            May.
    (M, SLC, 1965).

10812 If we don't get a good Indian summer during October, we will get it in the winter (M, SLC, 1965).

10813 The weather of the first Friday in the month governs the next month (M, SLC, 1961).

10814 As the weather is on Friday, it will also be the following Sunday (F, Norw, SLC, 1959).

10815 If it rains on Friday, the sun will shine on Sunday (F, SLC, 1961).

10816 Between twelve and two you will see what the day will do (M, Draper, 1920). Cf. Brown 6142.

10817 April showers bring May flowers (F, SLC, 1948). Cf. Brown 6119f.

10818 If March comes in like a lion, it goes out like a lamb. If March comes in like a lamb, it goes out like a lion (M, 20, Vernal, 1964). Brown 6117.

10819 The moon has effects on the weather (M, SLC, 1959). Cf. Brown 6121.

10820 By looking at the moon in the evening, you can tell the weather for tomorrow (F, 59, SLC, 1962).

10821 Stars at night, sailors delight (M, SLC, 1957).

10822    Red sky in the morning, fisherman's
            warning;
        Red sky at night, fisherman's
            delight.
    (F, 1960).

10823    A red sky in the morning,
        Is a sailor's warning (rain);
        A red sky at night,
        Is a sailor's delight (clear).
    (F, SLC, 1957); Red sunrise in the morning, sailor's warning; red sunset at night, sailor's delight (M, 29, SLC, 1950). Brown 6130.

10824    Red in the morning, sailor's
            forlorning,
        Red at night, sailor's delight.
    (M, 19, SLC, 1964).

10825    Red in the morning, a sailor's
            warning;
        Pink at night is a sailor's delight.
    (F, SLC, 1954).

10826 Evening red, the sailor's dread (F, Bear River City, 1957).

10827 Red clouds at night is sailor's delight (M, 78, Eng, Provo, 1963). Brown 6131.

10828 Red clouds in the morning is a sailor's warning (M, 78, Eng, Provo, 1963). Brown 6132.

10829    Red sails at morn,
        Sailor's take warn;
        Red sails at night
        Are a sailor's delight.
    (F, 26, SLC, 1963). Cf. Brown 6138.

10830    A sunset in the morning
        is a sailor's warning.
        A sunset at night,
        is a sailor's delight.
    (F, 39, SLC, 1962).

10831    Rainbow in the morning, sailors take
            warning;
        Rainbow at night, sailors' delight.
    (F, Centerville, 1930). Brown 6124f.

10832    Dark sky at night, sailors' delight;
        Red sky in the morning, sailors
            take warning.
    (F, Magna).

10833    Red sky at night is sheepherder's
            delight;
        Red sky in the morning is
            sheepherder's warning.
    (F, SLC, 1900s).

10834 Pink sky in the morning is a shepherd's warning (M, 20, SLC, 1950).

10835 Pink sky in the night was a shepherd's delight (M, 20, SLC, 1950).

10836    Rainbow at night, a shepherd's
            delight;
        Rainbow in morning, a shepherd's
            warning.
    (F, SLC).

10837 My mother has a diamond ring. We could tell what the weather would be like by how it sparkled or how dull it was. It might not happen for about one week, but it always seemed to work (F, 20, Logan).

## BAD (FOUL) WEATHER

10838 If we have bad weather, it always takes frost to clear up the weather (F, 20, SLC, 1962).

10839 When you go visiting, if you don't eat all the food on the table, the weather will be bad the next day (F, 23, Dan, SLC, 1963).

10840 Never do spring house cleaning till after June 16, or more bad weather will come (M, 1960).

10841 If soot falls down the chimney, the weather is going to be bad (F, 67, SLC, 1965). Cf. Brown 6167.

10842   Smoke staying near the ground means bad weather (M, 44, Layton, 1970). Brown 6165.

10843   A nightgown or slip worn inside out means bad weather will follow (F, SLC, 1971).

## The Human Body as an Indicator of Bad (Foul) Weather

10844   Aches in the back,
Bad weather's back.
(1946).

10845   When bones ache, it means bad weather (F, 65, SLC, 1962).

10846   People can tell when the weather is going to be bad by the aching of a healed broken bone (F, Peoa, 1924).

10847   If you have a corn or a bunion and it starts hurting, it is a sign that there is going to be bad weather (F, SLC, 1961); A corn or . . . or other pains in the feet forecast bad weather (F, 45, Monroe, 1928). (Belief in the connection between corns, bunions, and rheumatic joints and changes in the weather is so widely held in this country that "corn and bunion" predictions are deemed close to infallible by many a votary. See Nos. 11007ff, below, passim. --Eds.)

10848   Rheumatic people can tell when bad weather is on the way by their aching joints (M, SLC, 1920); Unusual twinges in a person with rheumatism means bad weather (F, Syracuse, 1943).

## Animals as Indicators of Bad (Foul) Weather

10849   When beasts eat greedily, foul weather will occur (F, 61, SLC, 1945).

10850   When a hog carries a piece of wood in its mouth, it means bad weather (F, 18, Kamas, 1961). Brown 6178.

10851   If a ground hog sees his shadow, it's a sign of a couple of months of bad weather (M, SLC, 1960); If the ground hog sees his shadow on February 2, there will be six weeks of bad weather (F, 54, Nephi, 1920). Brown 6176.

10852   Birds flying against the wind indicates a long siege of bad weather to come (M, 16, SLC, 1960).

10853   Whenever a flock of birds fly southward, bad weather follows (M, SLC, 1957).

10854   If swallows fly low, the weather will be bad (M, SLC).

10855   A sea gull inland means bad weather (M, SLC, 1960). Brown 6193.

10856   If the robin sings in the bush,
The weather will be coarse;
If the robin sings on the barn,
The weather will be warm.
(F, 1961).

10857   If crows make a sorrowful hoarse noise, it means that bad weather is coming (M, SLC, 1950).

10858   It is a sign of bad weather when ants are busier than usual (M, 56, SLC, 1960).

10859   When you kill a cricket, then there will be bad weather for twenty days (F, 45, SLC, 1925).

## Cosmic Phenomena as Indicators of Bad (Foul) Weather

10860   A red sky in the morning means bad weather that day (F, 19, SLC, 1964); . . . red sunrise . . . (M, SLC, 1960). Cf. Brown 6144.

10861   A ring around the moon means bad weather coming (M, Granger, 1915); . . . the bigger the ring around the moon, the worse the weather (M, SLC, 1960); When there's a circle around the moon on a clear night, it's going to be bad weather the next day (F, 22, SLC, 1972); A ring around the moon means ten days of foul weather (F, 49, Ogden, 1930). Cf. Brown 6151.

10862   If a quarter moon looks as though water would run out of it, there will be bad weather (F, 36, SLC, 1940). Brown 6154.

10863   If the moon's crescent is at the top, bad weather will come (F, 51, SLC, 1937).

10864   A rainbow on Saturday is sure to be followed by a week of bad weather (F, Price, 1930).

## CHANGING WEATHER

10865   If the day has been stormy and clears up during the night and the sun comes clear, it is going to storm that day. If the storm has cleared up before sunset and the sun goes down clear, it will be clear the next day (F, 66, SLC, 1964).

10866   The sudden shining of the sun on a cloudy day is a good sign (F, SLC, 1964).

10867   Wind from the north indicates a change in the weather, usually bad (M, 15, SLC, 1957).

10868   A rainbow seen during rain means that the rain is giving way to sunshine (F, 49, Murray, 1914).

10869   The weather changes with the different phases of the moon (F, 48, Fillmore, 1926). Cf. Brown 6199.

10870   A ring around the moon means a change in the weather (F, 21, Vernal, 1965); . . . it will change for the worse (M, Murray, 1958). Brown 6203.

10871   The number of stars within the ring around the moon denotes the number of days until the weather will change (F, 21, Vernal, 1965).

10872   If there is a sundog (colors like a rainbow) in the sky, there is going to be a change in the weather. For example, if it is cloudy and rainy and there is a sundog in the air, it will clear up (F, 87, W. Jordan, 1971). Cf. Brown 6198.

10873 Sundogs on either side of the sun during the winter indicate a change in the weather, usually colder (M, 43, 1970).

10874 Rheumatic pains indicate a change in the weather (F, Scipio, 1961).

10875 Animals at play are an indication of a change in the weather (F, 63, Monroe, 1964).

10876 The sneezing of a cat means there will be a change in the weather (F, Magna, 1960).

10877 If a cat sleeps on the back of her head, it means a change of weather (F, 66, SLC, 1962).

10878 When the rooster crows after eight o'clock in the evening, it is a sign that the weather is going to change (M, 66, Gr, SLC, 1963). Cf. Brown 6208.

10879 Excessive hooting of owls means a change in the weather (M, Logan, 1970).

10880 When the water boils away fast while boiling potatoes, there will be a change in the weather (F, Peoa, 1915).

10881 If furniture in the house cracks and creaks, it is a sign of a break in the weather (F, 55, SLC, 1950).

## CLEAR WEATHER

10882 A clear sky with a single puff of cloud is a bad omen (M, 29, SLC, 1963).

10883 The higher the clouds, the better the weather (M, SLC, 1910). Brown 6386.

10884 Sailor's belief: If there's a sunset in the evening, it'll be clear the next day (M, 23, SLC, 1959).

10885 If the sunset is bloody red, the next day will be clear (M, SLC, 1962); If the sunset is clear . . . (F, Springville, 1964). Brown 6223.

10886 A rainbow in the evening means clear weather (F, 52, Spanish Fork, 1940).

10887 If you see two rainbows or a double rainbow, it will clear up (F, 87, Providence, 1900).

10888 The hazy circle around the moon means a clear day will follow tomorrow (M, 57, SLC, 1964).

10889 When the point of the new moon points up, it will be a clear day (M, 62, Swiss, Heber City, 1912).

10890 Stars at night mean a clear day (M, SLC, 1960).

10891 If the chickens roost with the birds, you will enjoy clear weather in three days (M, 28, Logan, 1969).

10892 If ducks fly high, there will be clear weather (M, 1960).

10893 If ants come out early, the sun will shine (1946).

## COLD WEATHER

10894 When the days get longer, the cold gets stronger (M, 62, Swiss, Heber City, 1912).

10895 If the moon is far in the north, cold weather is approaching (F, Murray, 1951). Brown 6263.

10896     When the sunset is clear,
     A cool night draws near.
(F, Provo, 1970).

10897 A new moon will bring clear, cold weather (M, Logan, 1970).

10898 There will be colder weather in the full of the moon (F, 20, Logan, 1972).

10899 A sundog (colored clouds with rainbow colors) is a sure sign of cold (M, 1957); If you look at the sun and see sundog spots on the north side of the sun, it's a . . . (F, 60, Ogden, 1950); If sundogs are seen in the west, it's a . . . (M, 68, SLC, 1962).

10900 Clouds in the sky mean the night will be cold (M, SLC, 1964).

10901 The northern lights bring cold weather with them (M, 19, SLC, 1963); The brighter the northern lights, the colder the weather (F, 66, SLC, 1962). Brown 6267.

10902 Comets bring cold weather (M, Layton, 1958). Cf. Brown 6266.

10903 Thunder will almost always be followed by cooler weather (F, 34, SLC, 1950). Cf. Brown 6269f.

10904 If a cat's fur snaps with electricity, it is a sign of cold weather (M, SLC, 1959); If you see sparks when you rub a cat's back the wrong way, it is a sign of cold weather (F, 29, Ogden, 1964). Brown 6280.

10905 If the ground hog sees his shadow on February 2, another six weeks of cold weather will follow (M, 65, Granger, 1920). Brown 6282.

10906 When birds fly southward, it is a sign of cold weather (F, SLC, 1960). Cf. Brown 6292.

10907 Ants retiring early is an omen of cold weather (1946).

10908 Butterflies seen late in the autumn are signs that cold weather will arrive very soon (F, Ogden, 1960).

10909 If a fire burns well, it is a sign of coming cold weather (M, 28, SLC, 1948).

10910 Never put long underwear away till after June 16, or cold weather will come again (M, SLC, 1960).

## DRY WEATHER

10911 If the curve of the crescent moon is down low, it's holding water; if it's high, it's dry (M, 61, Hooper, 1910).

10912    When the new moon stands on end, the weather during the following month will be dry (M, SLC, 1919).  Cf. Brown 6316.

10913    If a new moon is on its back, there will be a dry season ahead (F, 59, SLC, 1962).  Brown 6313.

10914    If the new moon is cup-shaped with the cup opened upward, you will have a dry month (M, 37, SLC, 1964).  Cf. Brown 6314f.

10915    When the new moon has the points down, you cannot hang up your powder horn, so it will be dry enough to hunt (F, St. George, 1954); If you can hang a powder horn on the new moon, there will be a dry spell (F, 63, Monroe, 1964); If you can hang your powder horn on the tip of the crescent moon . . . (F, SLC, 1960).  Brown 6318.

10916    A quarter moon on its back means there will be a period of dry weather (M, American Fork, 1962).

10917    If the half moon is in a position where it can hold water, it will be dry (M, SLC, 1961).

10918    When points of the moon are turned up, the following month will be dry (F, 21, SLC, 1961); If the moon is turned so that it cannot hold water, it is a sign of a coming dry season (M, 35, SLC, 1943).  Brown 6315, 6317, cf. 6322.

10919    Lightning in the south means dry weather (M, Eng, SLC, 1957).  Brown 6333f.

10920    Red lightning foretells a dry spell (M, SLC, 1964).

10921    Lightning in November means dry weather (F, 47, SLC, 1964).

10922    A red sunset is supposed to promise at least twenty-four hours of dry weather (F, 19, Lehi, 1964).  Brown 6310.

10923    If a twig of green leaves falls to the ground, a drought is coming (F, 61, Loa, 1916).

10924    If you plant strawberries next to beets, there will be a drought (F, 47, SLC, 1926).

10925    When the swallow's nest is high, the summer is dry (F, SLC, 1961).

10926    Hair should not be cut, or a dry season will result (M, 22, SLC, 1965).

## FAIR WEATHER

10927    If the sun sets clear, there will be three days of fair weather (F, SLC, 1952).  Cf. Brown 6250, 6344.

10928    If the sunset is red, the weather will be fair in the morning (F, Sandy, 1957); A red sky at night means fair weather the next day (M, 54, SLC, 1950).  Brown 6346.

10929    If the clouds at sunrise fly to the west, the weather will be fair (F, 20, Ioka, 1949).

10930    If you see a rainbow in late evening, it will be a fair day the next morning (F, SLC, 1956).  Brown 6358.

10931    When the points of a half moon are pointing up, it means fair weather (F, SLC).

10932    If, on a rainy day, it clears in the west just before sunset, the next day will be fair (F, Tooele, 1957).

10933    If the ground hog sees his shadow on Ground Hog Day, fair weather is ahead (F, Orem, 1959).

10934    Bats coming out of their holes quickly after sunset, and sporting themselves in the open air, announce the coming of calm, fair weather (M, 45, W. Jordan, 1925).

10935    Buzzards flying high indicate fair weather (F, SLC, 1959).

10936    If a cuckoo sings in the direction of the south, the weather will be fine (F, Grantsville, 1964).

10937    When ants travel scattered, it will be fair weather (M, Spanish Fork, 1964).  Cf. Brown 6378.

10938    If you can hear frogs croaking, the next day will be fair weather (F, SLC, 1964).

10939         Welcome the sound of crackling hair,
              It tells of weather clear and fair.
         (F, Provo, 1970).

10940    Fair weather may be secured by sleeping with a flower under your pillow (F, 45, nurse, SLC, 1958).  Brown 6382.

10941    To predict weather for the evening, look at your coffee in the morning.  If the bubbles that rise after the sugar has been dropped in stay in the center of the cup, it will be fair (F, SLC).

10942    If everything is eaten off the table, it will be a fair day tomorrow (F, 64, Granite, 1964).  Cf. Brown 6368, 6383.

10943    If smoke rises, it's a sign of fair weather (M, 36, Milford, 1964).  Brown 6366f.

## GOOD WEATHER

10944    If the sun rises real red, it will be a nice day (M, 68, SLC, 1962).

10945    Red sky at night means good weather (F, 34, 1964).

10946    A red sunset promises a nice day tomorrow (F, 68, Du, SLC, 1964); A red sky in the morning means good weather (F, SLC, 1957).

10947    If the sun goes down shining after a big storm, it will be a good day tomorrow (M, SLC, 1962); If the sun goes down clear, it will be a nice day on the morrow (M, SLC, 1900).

10948    A cloudy morning brings forth a sunny day (M, SLC, 1961).

10949 A ring around the moon means that the weather is going to be good (F, SLC, 1954).

10950 A moon tipped upwards means good weather (F, 60, White City, 1963).

10951 If the new moon is tipped, good weather is coming (F, 74, SLC, 1964).

10952 If a quarter moon looks as if it will hold water, there will be good weather to come (F, 46, SLC, 1940).

10953 If the moon's crescent is at its bottom, good weather will come (F, SLC, 1964).

10954 If the big dipper is right side up, the weather will be good (F, SLC, 1964).

10955 Rain on Friday, fine on Sunday (M, 19, SLC, 1959).

10956 If cows are lying down in the fields, it's going to be a good day (F, SLC, 1931).

10957 Cows trail to the west when the weather is best. They travel to the east when the weather is least (F, 22, Ogden, 1949).

10958 If the ground hog sees its shadow, the weather will be good (M, 18, Logan, 1950); . . . sees his shadow on the first of March . . . (M, 21, SLC, 1963).

10959 If you hear a dove at night, the weather is going to be good for three days (M, 45, Ja, SLC, 1963).

10960 If a bug flies toward a light, then the next day should be a good day (F, SLC, 1964).

10961 Easygoing ants are an omen of fine weather (1946).

10962 Good weather will come if flies swarm together in sunbeams (F, 48, SLC, 1965).

10963 A grasshopper flying into the sun indicates good weather to come (M, 15, SLC, 1956).

10964 Cobwebs on the grass early in the morning prophesy good weather (F, 40, Logan, 1938).

10965 If smoke goes up a chimney straight, it is an indication of good weather the next day (M, SLC, 1959). Brown 6390.

10966 If a person sneezes three times in a row, good weather will come (F, Du, SLC, 1956).

10967 If you want good weather, you must eat everything put on your plate (F, 25, Bountiful, 1964); If there is no food left on the table, it will be a good day tomorrow (F, Murray, 1927).

10968 The passing of the calumet, or ceremonial pipe, is believed to be able to invoke good weather and banish evil spirits (F, Heber, 1959).

## WARM (HOT) WEATHER

10969 August is the hot month (M, 16, SLC, 1960). Brown 6393.

10970 A hazy morning or sun seen through mist is an omen of a warm day (1946).

10971 When the sun is in the far south, it is a sign of warm weather (F, 91, Logan, 1970).

10972 White clouds mean it will be hot and sultry (F, Moab, 1953).

10973 If the robin sings on the barn, the weather will be warm (F, SLC, 1961).

10974 A chirping cricket means warmer weather (F, 45, Monroe, 1925); If you want to find out how hot it is going to be the next day in the summertime, you sit out at night and count the number of cricks a cricket makes in a minute and that's the temperature number (F, Provo, 1972).

10975 When ladybugs swarm, expect it to be warm (F, SLC, 1965).

## WET (FALLING) WEATHER

10976 If the points of the new moon turn down, it is thought to indicate wet weather; the moon with points turned down resembles an inverted bowl, hence symbolizing the pouring out of water, which is called dry and wet moon (M, 23, SLC, 1964); If the moon is tipped enough to hang a powder horn on . . . (M, SLC, 1960). Brown 6404, 6407.

10977 If the points of the moon are turned down, the next month will be wet (F, 21, SLC, 1961). Cf. Brown 6403.

10978 If the new moon is cup shaped with the cup in a vertical position, you will have a wet month (M, SLC, 1964).

10979 If a half moon is in the position in which water can run out, it will be wet (M).

10980 If the moon is shaped to hold water, this foretells a wet season (M, 35, SLC, 1943).

## VARIOUS NOTIONS ABOUT RAIN

10981 One should never carry a rake on his shoulder; it will soon rain if he does (F, Norw, SLC, 1959).

10982 If you step on a crack, it will rain (M, SLC, 1960).

10983 Whistle to bring rain (M, 28, SLC, 1964).

10984 When you hear a train whistle close by, it means that it is going to rain (F, 25, Ja, SLC, 1964); . . . the next day (F, 30, Ja, SLC, 1964).

10985 There's a mountain near Grass Creek, Utah, called Pilot Mountain, and when the clouds or fog settle on Pilot Mountain, there will be rain or snow, depending on the season (M, SLC, 1967).

10986 April is the rainy month (M, 16, SLC, 1960).

10987 Wet May was never kind yet (M, Layton, 1938).

10988   It rains because the angels in heaven are sad and are crying (F, 19, Bountiful, 1960); Raindrops are tears from angry angels (F, 21, SLC, 1944); Rain is tears shed by the angels on our behalf (F, 46, Provo).

10989   When it rains, the heavens are crying (M, 24, SLC, 1948).

10990   The reason it rains is because God has a cinder in his eye (F, 44, SLC, 1964).

10991   When the Mormons meet, the angels weep (M, Midvale, 1950); You can expect rain when the LDS Church has its Mormon conferences (M, 21, SLC, 1956); The weather will always be rainy and stormy during spring and fall conference (M, SLC, 1957); When the saints meet, the heavens weep (F, 60, SLC, 1925). Cf. Brown 6438.

10992   It never rains on the Mormon pageant in Palmyra, New York (F, 33, Logan, 1970).

10993   The rainwater of May has peculiar qualities which are beneficial which no other time has (F, 85, SLC, 1964).

10994   If it rains right hard, people say it rains toads (F, Moab, 1953).

10995   Worms fall with the rain (F, Nephi, 1964).

10996   The "J" as seen from Utah County at Mt. Timpanogos, if still filled with snow by July 1, means there will be enough water for the summer (F, 37, Tremonton, 1937).

10997   You can smell rain (M, SLC, 1963).

10998   Rain on Wednesday is good luck (M, 31, SLC, 1942).

10999   Rain on the window brings good luck to the house (F, 19, SLC, 1963); . . . good fortune . . . (F, SLC, 1963).

11000   Don't stand under a tree when it's raining (M, SLC, 1960).

11001   When it is raining outside people inside begin to feel generous and happy (M, SLC, 1961).

11002   If the sun shines while it's raining, it's good luck (F, Eng, Holladay, 1963); To walk outdoors during a rain in which the sun is still shining is to bring good luck (M, 30, SLC, 1964).

11003   If it rains and the sun is shining, it is a monkey's birthday (M, 36, Murray, 1950). (In the Kuusi monograph cited at the end of No. 11006, below, there are cited whole categories of animal behavior and specific acts. These range from being born, to attending to eliminative functions, sexual encounters, grooming, frolicking, fighting, bathing, and other animal activities. The present item falls within these general limits. Also, to emphasize the unusual nature of concomitant rain and shine, animals are depicted in a variety of purely human functions that are as unusual and unexpected as rain and sunshine at the same time. --Eds.)

11004   When it rains and thunders, Satan is beating his wife (F, SLC, 1964).

11005   When the sun is shining and it's thundering, it means the devil is beating his wife (F, SLC, 1965); . . . the devil is breeding his wife (F, 49, Milford, 1938).

11006   If it rains and the sun is shining, the devil is beating his wife (M, Roosevelt, 1961); . . . whipping his wife (F, Moab, 1953); . . . quarreling with his wife (M, 59, W. Jordan, 1912); . . . beating his wife with a dishrag (F, Helper, 1940s); . . . the devil is beating your wife (F, SLC, 1957). Cf. Brown 6468, 6471ff. (In one of the most remarkable historical-geographical studies on record, Regen bei Sonnenschein: Zur Weltgeschichte einer Redensart [Folklore Fellows Communications, No. 171, Helsinki, 1957], Professor Matti Kuusi, eminent Finnish folklorist, has shown how people have sought to explain the unusual occurrence of rain and shine at the same time by a series of equally unusual occurrences involving divine personages, unusual human types, and the dead, as well as a variety of animals, usually wild. In all there are fourteen different categories of actors, and sixteen different kinds of activities. With free association and no limits to the imagination one is able to see many unusual and highly improbable acts, as well as many patent impossibilities. A sample of the latter: . . . cuckolds are going to heaven; . . . witches are buried at the end of the world; . . . mice are celebrating a wedding; . . . in the realm of the dead the child of a whore is being baptized; . . . the fairies are baking; . . . a liar is paying his debts; . . . the devil is baking pancakes, etc., etc. The devil beating his wife for a variety of different reasons, as in this entry and the previous one, is the favorite form of this humorous figure of folk speech in Anglo-American tradition. --Eds.)

HUMAN INDICATORS OF RAIN

11007       When teeth and bones and bunions ache,
            Expect the clouds to fill the lake. (F, Provo, 1970).

11008   It's a sign of rain if your arthritis bothers you (F, 28, Logan, 1970); . . . if your rheumatism hurts (M, 21, Magna, 1964); . . . when your rheumatism gives you fits (F, Bear River City, 1957); . . . when one's back aches like rheumatism (M, SLC, 1961). Brown 6647.

11009   Aching bones mean rain (F, 20, Logan, 1970); If your joints ache, it . . . (F, 20, Magna, 1952). Cf. Brown 6640.

11010   If your bursitis hurts, it will rain (F, 20, SLC, 1955).

11011   If your bunions hurt, it's going to rain (F, Moab, 1962). Brown 6641.

11012   If your corn hurts, it will rain (F, Woods Cross, 1953); If the corns on your feet hurt . . . (F, Moab, 1953); If your corns itch . . . (M, SLC, 1959); . . . a corn on the little toe . . . (M, SLC, 1959).  Brown 6641.

11013  If your nose itches, it's going to rain soon (F, SLC, 1964).  Brown 6643.

11014  If your ear itches, it is going to rain (F, 68, SLC, 1964).

11015  A crook in your back means it's going to rain (M, 38, SLC, 1940).

11016  If your knees itch, it is a sign that it is going to rain (F, Ogden, 1961).

11017      Pains in the knees,
          Rain through the trees.
       (1946).

11018  If your feet hurt, it will rain (M, SLC, 1960).

11019  If your big toe aches, it is a sign of rain (F, SLC, 1960).

11020  It is going to rain if your hands get sweaty (F, Provo, 1970).

11021  When straight hair limps, rain is near (F, 22, SLC, 1942).

11022      Sing afore you go to bed,
          You'll get up with a wet head.
       (F, SLC).

11023  If you dream of a dead person, it will rain the next day (M, 73, Gr, SLC, 1963).  Cf. Brown 6650.

11024  If anyone dies, it will rain (M, SLC, 1961).  Cf. Brown 6652.

## ANIMAL INDICATORS OF RAIN

### Mammals

11025  Many indicators of rain are found in the activities and behavior of animals (F, 18, Kamas, 1961).

11026  If a cat sneezes, it is a sign of rain (F, SLC, 1959).

11027  If you see a cat curled up in a ball sleeping with his nose in the air, it's a sure sign of rain (F, 52, Provo, 1920).

11028  If a cat licks his tail, it's going to rain (F, 77, SLC, 1964).

11029  When a cat washes his ear three times, it is a sign of rain (M, 23, SLC, 1964); A cat washing his face or ears . . . (F, 20, SLC, 1964); A cat scratching its ears all day . . . (1946).  Brown 6658f.

11030  If a cat is washed, it will rain the next day (M, 63, SLC, 1964).  Brown 6662.

11031  If a cat's fur looks bright, it is likely to be fine, but when they lick their feet, it means rainy weather (F, 83, Venice, 1910).

11032  If the cat sleeps on its back, it is going to rain (F, Bountiful, 1915).

11033  When cats eat grass, it means it's going to rain (F, 40, SLC, 1951).  Brown 6663.

11034  When cats are restless and rush about, they are "running up a storm," and rain will soon follow (F, 70, Logan, 1920).

11035  It will rain if a dog sleeps on his back with his feet up in the air (M, Bountiful, 1964).

11036  When a dog eats grass, it's a sure sign of rain (M, Box Elder Co, 1944).  Brown 6671.

11037  When horses frolic in the fields, it will rain in the next few days (F, 20, SLC, 1949).

11038  Horses sweating in a stable is a sign of rain (M, Bountiful, 1970).  Brown 6672.

11039  If you see horses standing together, it means rain (F, 65, SLC, 1962).  Cf. Brown 6654.

11040  If cattle and horses refuse to drink in very dry weather, it is a sign of a coming cloudburst (M, 22, SLC, 1963).

11041  When cattle lie down as they are put to pasture, rain is on its way (F, 78, Dan, SLC, 1965).  Cf. Brown 6665f.

11042  Sheep and cows will start down off the top of the mountain two or three days before a big rain comes (M, 60, Plain City, 1930).

11043      When the ground hog his shadow sees,
          Six more weeks of rain there'll be.
       (F, Provo, 1970).

11044  If prairie dogs hill up around their holes, it means rain (M, 70, Duchesne, 1970).

11045  If elephants are restless, there will be rain (M, SLC, 1963).

### Fowl, Birds

11046  If the chickens pick themselves, it is a sign of rain (F, Moab, 1953); If the hens in the barnyard are curling up and picking . . . (F, 40, Logan, 1938).  Cf. Brown 6676f.

11047  If chickens are unusually noisy, it is a sign of rain (F, 40, Logan, 1938).

11048  If the chickens eat grass, it will soon rain (F, SLC, 1920).

11049  If hens gather on rising ground and trim their feathers, it is a sure sign of rain (F, 29, SLC, 1964).  Cf. Brown 6680.

11050  When it starts to rain, chickens will stay out if the rain will fall the rest of the day or longer, but will run for cover if it's just going to be a shower (M, Logan, 1970).  Brown 6683,

11051  If chickens remain outside during a rain, it will only be a very brief shower (M, Murray, 1955).

11052  If a cock crows when he goes to bed, he will always wake up with a wet head (F, 18, SLC, 1950); . . . he wakens with a watery head (F, Eng, SLC, 1965); If a rooster crows a lot at nightfall, there will be rain before morning (F, Syracuse, 1945). Brown 6686f.

11053  Old hens are noisy before a rain (M, 39, SLC, 1964).

11054  If a bird makes a noise like "spirit," it is going to rain (F, 45, SLC, 1964).

11055  If birds sit close to the ground, it is a sign of rain to come (M, Vernal, 1961).

11056  Birds flying means rain (M, 19, SLC, 1964).

11057  If you see a group of black birds singing in a tree, it's a sign of rain (F, SLC, 1957). Cf. Brown 6702.

11058  It is going to rain all day if you hear a dove cry in the morning (M, 45, Ja, SLC, 1963). Cf. Brown 6703, 6716.

11059  If the cuckoo bird is hoarse when he crows, there will be a lot of rain (F, SLC, 1959).

11060  If a cuckoo sings in the direction of the north, it will rain (F, Grantsville, 1964). Cf. Brown 6714f.

11061  If you see a robin on the lawn, it is going to rain the next day (F, Dan, 1959). Cf. Brown 6729.

11062  A peacock or any bird's harsh clamor forecasts rain (F, 63, Eng, SLC, 1964). Cf. Brown 6724f.

11063  When a sea gull flies inland, you may expect rain (M, 21, Midvale, 1964). Brown 6730.

11064  Swallows flying close to the ground are an omen of rain (1946). Cf. Brown 6701, 6733.

11065  If you hear a woodpecker chirping and pecking, it is an omen of rain in twelve hours (1946). Cf. Brown 6736.

11066  The cry of the buzzard is a sign of rain (F, SLC, 1959).

11067  Crow on the fence,
Rain will go hence;
Crow on the ground,
Rain will come down.
(F, 68, SLC, 1964).

11068  If a person kills an owl (in any way), it will rain for twenty days (M, 59, SLC, 1964).

11069  If it is going to storm, a live hoot owl will sit on the chimney and call (F, 76, Orangeville, 1966). Cf. Brown 6719.

11070  If ravens caw in the day, it is a sign of rain (F, Moab, 1953).

## Reptiles, Amphibians, Fish

11071  If you kill a snake and hang it on a fence, it will rain in three days (M, 56, SLC, 1915); . . . belly up . . . (M, Moab, 1953). Cf. Brown 6755f.

11072  Take a dead snake and hang it over a fence, and it will rain before sundown (F, Moab, 1953). Cf. Brown 6745, 6749.

11073  If, when you kill a snake, if you leave it awhile, and when you go back and look at it, if it's turned over on its back, that means it's going to rain (F, Moab, 1953). Cf. Brown 6743.

11074  It will rain if you kill a frog or toad (F, 53, Ogden, 1931); It will rain for a week . . . (F, 67, SLC, 1964). Brown 6765.

11075  If a frog croaks in the daytime, it will rain (M, SLC, 1961); Frogs croaking loudly at night will mean rain tomorrow (F, 52, SLC). Brown 6762ff.

11076  If you see a dry-land terrapin crawling, he is hunting higher ground because it is going to rain (M, SLC, 1959). Brown 6758f.

11077  If fish are biting eagerly, it means rain is coming (F, 25, SLC).

11078  If a fish jumps above the water, you may expect rain (M, 1961). Brown 6774.

## Insects

11079  If you step on an insect, it is going to rain (M, 24, SLC, 1964).

11080  If you kill a bug, it will rain the next day (M, 13, Orem, 1964).

11081  Step on an ant, and it will rain (M, SLC, 1900s); If you kill a number of ants . . . (M, 24, SLC, 1964); If you kill an ant, it will rain the next day, one drop for every ant (Provo, 1964).

11082  When ants travel in straight lines, expect rain (M, 24, Spanish Fork, 1950); If the army ants are on the march, it will be heavy weather (M, SLC, 1963).

11083  When bees enter the hive, but do not leave it, rain is coming soon (M, 91, SLC, 1923). Brown 6779.

11084  If you step on a caterpillar, it will rain (F, Logan, 1972).

11085  If you kill a cricket, it will rain (F, 20, Oakley, 1959); . . . in the house . . . (F, W. Jordan, 1925); If you step on a cricket, it will rain tomorrow (M, 19, SLC, 1965).

11086  Loud singing of crickets indicates rain coming (F, Logan, 1970). Brown 6780.

11087  When flies bite, it is a sign that a rainstorm is soon coming (F, SLC, 1961); Flies bite more before a rain (M, SLC, 1900s). Cf. Brown 6784f.

11088  If flies stick to the screen door in the summer, it will rain (F, 65, SLC, 1962). Cf. Brown 6783.

11089  When flies gather under a shelter, there will be rain (M, 44, Layton, 1970).

11090  Mosquitoes bite more before it is going to rain (M, 45, Spanish Fork, 1936).

11091  If you step on a stink bug, it will bring rain (M, 21, SLC, 1964); . . . rain the next day (M, SLC, 1959).

Spiders, Daddy-Longlegs, Etc.

11092  Spider webs on a fence in the morning indicate rain (M, SLC, 1955).

11093  If spiders are numerous, rainy weather will come (1946).

11094  If spiders desert their webs, rain is coming (M, SLC, 1963). Brown 6799.

11095  Rain may be produced by sweeping the cobwebs in the house (F, SLC, 1958).

11096  A spider in the house is a sign of rain (F, SLC, 1971).

11097  It will rain if you kill a spider (M, Ibapah, 1942); If you step on a spider, it will rain tomorrow (F, SLC, 1961); If you step on a spider and kill it, it will rain (F, 62, Vernal, 1901); If you squash a grey spider it will rain (F, Bountiful, 1960). Brown 6797.

11098  If you step on a daddy-longlegs spider, it will rain (M, SLC, 1961); . . . it will rain the next day (F, 19, Roosevelt, 1944).

PLANT INDICATORS OF RAIN

11099  If you burn brush, it will rain soon (F, SLC, 1929).

11100  If you burn ferns, you will bring down rain soon (M, Ogden, 1911); . . . burn ferns at dusk . . . (M, 67, Crescent, 1921).

11101  When the morning grass is dry, it will rain (M, 38, SLC, 1964). Brown 6814, 6816.

11102  Take an onion and split it twelve ways. Then you salt each piece of numbered onion slice and leave it overnight. In the morning the piece of onion with the most moisture will be the month you will have the most rain (M, 21, SLC, 1955).

11103  On New Year's Eve a family takes twelve onions and labels each one for one of the coming months, then peels the onions, and the ones with the most water in them will be the rainiest months (F, SLC).

11104  When the wind blows the leaves so the backs of them are showing, then it means rain (F, 46, SLC).

11105  It is said that certain flowers, which ordinarily close at dusk, sometimes remain open all night. This is a positive indication that it will rain very shortly (F, SLC, 1955). Brown 6829.

11106  When flowers smell especially strong, it will probably rain (F, Provo, 1970). Brown 6829.

11107  Moss is dry and brittle in clear weather, but soft and limp before rain (M, Provo, 1970).

11108  A piece of seaweed hung up will become damp previous to rain (F, Provo, 1970).

11109  If the leaves on a tree turn up, it is a sign of rain (M, Bountiful, 1953); . . .

the underside of leaves . . . (M, Monroe, 1964). Cf. Brown 6809, 6823.

COSMIC PHENOMENA AND WEATHER AS INDICATORS OF RAIN

SKY, CLOUDS, SUN, ETC.

11110  When radio programs are peppered with static,
There'll be lightning and thunder and weather aquatic.
(F, Provo, 1970).

11111  If the sunset is gray, the next day will be rainy (F, SLC, 1964). Cf. Brown 6453.

11112  If there is a yellow sky at evening, or if the sun sets in a dense bank of clouds, it will rain the following day (1946). Cf. Brown 6480f.

11113  A red sunset means rain the following day (M, SLC, 1963).

11114  Morning red brings down rain upon your head (F, Moab, 1953); . . . red sky in the morning . . . (F, SLC, 1930). Cf. Brown 6449.

11115  A sheep sky never left the ground dry (SLC, 1969).

11116  Dark clouds indicate rain (F, Moab, 1953).

11117  If the sun sets beneath a cloud, it will rain in the third day thereafter (F, SLC, 1959). First heard in Norway. Cf. Brown 6457, 6484f.

11118  When the morning sun is red,
The ewe and lamb go wet to bed.
(F, American Fork, 1900).

11119  If there is a ring around the sun, it will rain (M, Cedar City, 1944). Cf. Brown 6460.

11120  If the sun shines while it is raining, there will be rain again tomorrow (F, SLC, 1961); . . . it will rain the same time the next day (F, Holladay, 1960). Brown 6448.

THE MOON AS AN INDICATOR OF RAIN

11121  If the moon goes over a cloud, it will rain the next day (M, SLC).

11122  Shadow on the moon means rain (F, SLC, 1965).

11123  If a new moon falls on Saturday, there will be twenty days of wind and rain (F, 20, Joseph, 1958).

11124  A tilting quarter moon means rain (F, SLC, 1964); . . . tipped too far up . . . (F, SLC, 1946); . . . a new moon tipped over . . . (F, SLC, 1957). Brown 6536.

11125  If the moon is in its quarter stage, with the convex side down, it is full of water and rain will soon fall (F, 19, SLC). Brown 6539.

11126    If the moon looks like a tipped bowl which water could run out of, it is called a wet moon and is a sign of rain (F, SLC, 1957); An Indian sign was that if the moon was tipped, it was going to rain (Moab, 1953).

11127    A crescent moon upside down means rain (F, Bear River City, 1957).

11128    When the point of the new moon is down, it will rain (M, 62, Heber City, 1963). Heard in 1912 from father who came from Switzerland; When the points of the half moon are down, it will rain (F, SLC, 1945). Cf. Brown 6538.

11129    If there is a yellow ring of light around the moon, it is going to rain (F, 46, SLC); . . . a circle around the moon . . . (M, SLC, 1959); . . . a halo around the moon . . . (M, Layton, 1958); If a full moon has a ring around it, expect rain (F, SLC, 1957); . . . rain in the near future (M, 19, SLC, 1963). Brown 6545.

11130    A ring around the moon means it will rain, and the number of stars in the ring are the number of days before it will rain (M, Price, ca. 1930). Cf. Brown 6547, 6549f.

11131    Count the rings around the moon to see how far away the rain is (M, SLC, 1956).

### STARS AS INDICATORS OF RAIN

11132    The number of stars inside the ring around the moon indicates the number of days until it will rain (M, Sandy, 1957); A circle around the moon with two stars in the circle is an omen of rain in two days (1946). Brown 6552.

11133    If the big dipper is upside down, it will rain because the water will spill (F, 41, SLC, 1964).

11134    Unusual clearness of the atmosphere or unusual brightness or twinkling of the stars indicates approaching rain (M, 30, Cedar Breaks National Monument, 1966).

11135    If there are a great number of stars, there will be rain within two days after (M, SLC, 1959). Cf. Brown 6554ff.

### Rain, Rainbows as Indicators of Rain

11136    If raindrops stick on a window after a rain, it is a sign of more rain (M, SLC, 1961).

11137    Large raindrops mean a brief shower; small drops mean a long shower (F, Layton, 1940). Brown 6860.

11138    When it rains, if the drops form big bubbles, it is a sure sign of continued rain (F, 80, Ogden, 1918). Cf. Brown 6568.

11139    When rain bounces, it will rain for three days (M, Eng, Hooper, 1963).

11140    If it rains the first Sunday of the month, it will rain every Sunday of the month (F, Willard, 1964). Cf. Brown 6440ff.

11141    If it rains or is a bad day Saturday, Sunday will be the same. If Friday is a good day, then so will the weekend be (M, 20, Layton, 1972).

11142    Rain on Friday, rain on Sunday; rain on Saturday, rain on Monday (F, 51, Ogden, 1964).

11143    If it rains on Easter Sunday, it will rain six more Sundays (M, SLC, 1964); . . . rain the next five Sundays (F, SLC, 1968); . . . rain for seven Sundays after (F, 71, Woods Cross, 1953); . . . rain for the next seven days (F, 22, Murray, 1950). Brown 6429.

11144    If it rains on St. Swithin's Day, it will continue to rain for forty days and forty nights (M, SLC, 1961); If it rains on July fifteenth . . . (F, 50, SLC, 1963). (July 15 is St. Swithin's Day. --Eds.) Brown 6434.

11145    If you see a rainbow, it is a sign of showers (F, SLC, 1960). Cf. Brown 6569.

11146    After a rainfall, if the rainbow appears, then all is well as God is at peace. If no rainbow appears, more rain is to come and God is mad (F, 21, Logan, 1970). Cf. Brown 6870.

11147    A rainbow on Saturday is sure to be followed by a week of rainy weather (F, 51, Levan, 1927).

11148    A rainbow in the morning means rain will follow (M, 65, Granger, 1915).

11149    To point out a rainbow is unlucky. It will bring back rain (M, 44, Ibapah, 1964).

11150    A rainbow on Saturday is sure to be followed by a week of rainy, rotten weather (M, 49, Midvale).

11151    If you see a rainbow over the mountain while it's raining, it'll rain the same time tomorrow (M, 59, SLC, 1964).

11152    A rainbow is a sign of heavy rain (M, 20, SLC, 1950s).

### VARIOUS KINDS OF WEATHER AS INDICATORS OF RAIN

11153    If you see steam rising from a field, it means more rain (F, SLC, 1910).

11154    When ditches and cellars smell moist, a long rain is near (F, 58, SLC, 1935).

11155        Fog goes up with a hop,
    Rain comes down with a drop.
(F, 29, SLC, 1946). Cf. Brown 6589.

11156    What goes up as fog, comes down as rain (M, 65). Cf. Brown 6590.

11157    Ninety days (approximately) after a fog there will be a rainstorm or some other form of storm that will provide moisture (M, 43, 1970).

11158    Eastern winds are a sign of rain (M, SLC, 1960). Cf. Brown 6566, 6598.

11159    When there is a north wind, it means it will be cold and wet (F, Moab, 1953).

11160 Lightning in the north means rain (M, Eng, 1957). Brown 6610.

## FIRE, SMOKE AS INDICATORS OF RAIN

11161 If smoke comes out of a chimney straight up, it means rain (F, Murray, 1959). Brown 6629.

11162 If smoke comes down to the ground from a chimney, it will rain that day (M, Bountiful, 1964). Brown 6630.

11163 All of the fireworks set off on the Fourth of July produce rain the following day (M, 21, Holladay, 1964).

## DOMESTIC INDICATORS OF RAIN

11164 When doors and windows swell, it's a sign of rain (M, 69, SLC, 1920). Cf. Brown 6839.

11165 When windows won't open and salt clogs the shaker, the weather favors the umbrella maker (F, Provo, 1970).

11166 When the taps in the bathroom are sweating, there will be rain before too long (F, Peoa, 1920).

11167 When a glass sweats, it is the sign of rainy weather (F, 42, SLC, 1964). Brown 6583, 6586.

11168 When the refrigerator sweats, it is going to rain (M, 21, Layton, 1972).

11169 To predict weather for the evening, look at your coffee in the morning. If the bubbles go to the side after the sugar has been dropped, it will rain soon (F, SLC).

11170 If there is hot food in a bowl, and it gets damp underneath, it will soon rain (F, SLC, 1945).

11171 At mealtime never leave leftovers, because if you do, it means it is going to rain (F, 69, Syracuse, 1890).

11172 If you drop a fork, it will rain (F, American Fork, 1946).

11173 If a lamp flickers continually, there will be rain (F, 51, SLC, 1930). Brown 6637.

11174 If you rock a rocking chair, and there's no one in it, it will rain (F, Midvale); . . . it causes rain (M, Midvale, 1948).

11175 If you open an umbrella in the house, it will bring rain for sure (F, SLC, 1962); . . . on the following day (M, 24, SLC, 1964). Brown 6842.

11176 If you sing on wash day, it will rain (F, 49, SLC, 1925).

11177 If you wash your clothes or your car on a cloudy day, it will surely rain (M, SLC, 1955); . . . it will rain the next day (F, 46, SLC, 1938).

11178 Washing your windows on a beautiful sunny day will make it cloud up and rain (F, 26, SLC, 1963); . . . the next day (M, 26, SLC, 1948).

11179 It will rain after you have watered the lawn (F, SLC, 1952).

11180 If you put the top down on a convertible, it will rain (F, SLC, 1959).

## CAUSING RAIN

11181 In order to insure a sufficient rainy season, a man in Springville would precede his spring planting by repeating the following wish in the form of a chant. It is supposed to be an Indian rain song: "Mee la beh lu lu unshenbel" (M, Springville, 1957).

11182 Dancing can bring about rain (M, 25, SLC, 1952); Dance for rain during times of drought (M, Vernal, 1961).

11183 Rain may be produced by crossing two matches and sprinkling salt on them (F, 28, SLC, 1958).

11184 If you place a cross under a tree, it will start raining (M, SLC, 1957).

11185 To bring rain, kill a black snake and hang him in a tree with his belly up (M, 21, Midvale, 1964); "When we first moved to Logan, in about 1915, I used to accompany my older brothers to Providence . . . to cut wood for my grandmother. On more than one occasion I remember her instructing us as we left for home to go by a trash dump where there were lots of water snakes so that we could kill some and turn them over, belly-up to the sun, in order to make it rain" (M, 37, Woods Cross, 1946). Brown 6750.

## STOPPING RAIN; NO RAIN

11186 If chickens come out and begin feeding, the rain will soon stop (F, Logan, 1970).

11187    Rain before seven,
       Clear before eleven
(M, Draper, 1915); Rain before seven, shine before eleven (M, 46, Beaver, 1933). Brown 6862ff.

11188    Sunshine and shower,
       Won't last half an hour.
(F, 36, Payson, 1946). Brown 6849f.

11189 If you draw a circle on the ground, it will stop raining (M, SLC, 1957).

11190 Make a cross with ashes on the ground before it starts raining hard and the rain will stop (M, 32, PR, SLC, 1965).

11191 If it is cloudy and about to rain, take an ax and chop at the clouds; then they'll separate and you won't get rained on (M, Magna, 1940).

11192 When the rain would come Grandma would sing this rhyme to us: "Rain, rain, go away; / Come again another day. / Little Ninna wants to play / Down the meadow on the hay" (F, SLC, 1967). Brown 6866ff.

11193 To make a big bonfire will bring on clouds and rain and thunder (F, SLC, 1967).

11194   When there is dew in the morning, it will not rain during the day (M, 38, SLC, 1964).  Cf. Brown 6872ff.

11195   If there is enough blue in the sky to make a pair of bloomers, it will be a good day, with no rain (F, 65, Midvale, 1908); . . . enough blue in the sky to make a pair of pants, the rain or storm will clear up (F, Provo, 1972).  Brown 6855.

11196   If the sky is grey and a patch of blue appears large enough to make a Dutchman a pair of breeches, it is a sure sign of a beautiful day (F, SLC, 1960); . . . it will not rain (F, 67, Bingham, 1900); If there is enough blue in the north to make a Dutchman a pair of pants, it will quit raining (M, 78, Eng, Provo, 1963).

11197   It will never rain when there is a full moon (F, SLC).

11198   The new moon lays on its back to hold the water (rain) (F, Woods Cross, 1953); . . . a quarter moon . . . (F, 77, SLC, 1964); If the new moon is like a cup, it will not rain cause the water won't fall out (M, SLC, 1930); If the new moon is tipped like a bowl . . . (M, SLC, 1957).

11199   If the new moon is tipped, it means no rain (M, SLC, 1958).

11200   When the crescent of the moon is curved so that it will hold water, it won't rain (M, Woods Cross, 1964).  Cf. Brown 6856.

11201   When the moon was straight up, then they figured no rain.  The Indians used to have that for their sign of wet weather (M, Moab, 1953).

11202       When apple blossoms bloom at night, For fifteen days, no rain in sight. (F, 78, SLC, 1965).

11203   Carrying an umbrella will ward off rainy weather (F, SLC, 1960).  Brown 6890.

## FLOODS; TIDAL WAVES

11204   When you see a dream about a flood, it's bad luck (F, Ja, 25, SLC, 1964).

11205   If the first days of April are foggy, there will be floods in June (M, 90, Union, 1910).

11206   Whenever you can see the ridges of the horseshoe, the flood danger or season is over (M, Fountain Green, 1920).

11207   The rainbow in the heavens shows that the world will never be destroyed by water (F, 42, SLC, 1964).  Brown 6894.

11208   When the smoke goes straight up, it's a sign that a tidal wave is coming (M, 57, Ogden, 1970).

## STORMS

11209   If a storm starts before seven, it will end before eleven (M, 68, SLC).

11210   Hide the looking glass during a storm to prevent breakage which would lead to bad luck (F, 67, SLC, 1964).

11211   There is always a calm before the storm (M, 22, Logan, 1954).

11212   It's always darkest before the storm (M, 22, SLC, 1954).

11213   It is bad luck to raise your eyes from the ground while a storm is raging (M, Ger, SLC, 1938).

11214   When the corn husks are tough and stand straight, there is a storm coming (M, 45, Payson, 1941).

## Human and Domestic Signs

11215   Some people always feel sleepy and drowsy before a storm (M, Logan, 1970).

11216   Arthritis and rheumatism make you ache the worst twenty-four hours before a storm (F, 52, Provo, 1920); The bones of rheumatics ache . . . (F, 40, SLC, 1964); You can tell a storm is coming by rheumatic feelings in your joints (F, 64, Spring Glen, 1963).

11217   When your back aches, it means that a bad storm is on the way (F, SLC, 1959).

11218   When your feet hurt, it means that a bad storm is on the way (F, SLC, 1959).

11219   If your corns hurt, it is going to storm (M, Bountiful, 1915).

11220   A hollow tooth will throb when it is going to storm (M, 45, Payson, 1942).

11221   A leaky water tap means a storm is coming (F, SLC, 1920).

11222   When water boils out of a pot, it means a storm is coming (F, 64, SLC, 1962).

11223   A singing kettle means a bad storm is coming (F, 25, SLC).

11224   When food cooking on the stove scorches too quickly, a storm is on the way (F, Ger, SLC, 1960).

11225   If a wife burns her bread while she is baking, it is a sign of a storm (F, Provo, 1959).

11226   When it's storming, open two doors so if the lightning comes in, it will have a way out (F, W. Jordan, 1925).

## Cosmic Phenomena, Weather as Indicators of a Storm

11227   During the first of the month the position of the moon determines the weather for that month.  If the moon is standing on end, it means that month will be stormy.  If it is a full or half moon, the weather will be pleasant (F).

11228   If there is a ring around the moon, it is the sign of a storm (F, Fillmore, 1960); . . . a large white ring . . . (F, 45, Logan); . . . a red ring . . . (M, SLC, 1961); . . . a circle of light . . . (F, 30, Bountiful, 1935).  Cf. Brown 6906.

11229   A ring around the moon signifies a storm.  The closer the storm the larger the ring (M, 35, SLC, 1941); . . . the number of rings determines how many days it will be, one ring for one day (M, SLC, 1959); . . . a storm within three days (M, 22, SLC, 1953); . . . there will be a storm before the moon changes (F, 1953).

11230 A circle around the moon means a storm is coming and the number of stars in the circle tells how many days before the storm (M, 55, SLC, 1964). Brown 6204.

11231 If there is a halo around the moon, a storm will follow (M, 56, SLC, 1918). Brown 6906.

11232 A ring around the moon, referred to as the "moondog" is a sign that a storm is coming (M, 23, Henefer, 1963).

11233 If you see a "sundog" (sun reflection) on each side of the sun, it is the sign of a storm (M, Jensen, 1958); . . . a storm within three days (M, 41, Ger, Bountiful, 1964).

11234 When there's a big ring around the sun, we'll have a storm soon (F, 29, Ogden, 1950).

11235 If a new moon lies on its back, it will storm for a period (F, 63, Monroe, 1964).

11236 A moon tipped downwards means a storm (F, 50, White City, 1963).

11237 When the new moon is cuplike it holds water and a storm comes (F, 72, Centerville, 1963).

11238 A quarter moon on end means it's going to storm (M, American Fork, 1962); When the new moon is with both points up, you can hang your powder horn on it, because there will be storm and you cannot hunt (F, St. George, 1954); As long as an Indian can hang his powder horn on the moon, there will be stormy weather (F, Ogden, 1958).

11239 The Indians say that if you cannot hang a powder horn on the moon, it will storm (Scofield, 1957).

11240 A full moon brings stormy weather (M, Logan, 1970).

11241 When a rainbow is around the moon, it is a sign of a storm (F, 72, Centerville, 1963); If you see only one rainbow, it will storm again (F, 87, Providence, 1900).

11242 A rainbow in the morning indicates a storm within twenty-four hours (F, 52, Spanish Fork, 1940); . . . stormy weather will continue (F, SLC, 1961). Cf. Brown 3476.

11243 If the sun comes up clear after a rain or a snowstorm, it means the storm is not over (F, 63, Monroe, 1964).

11244 If the sun sets clear on Friday, it will storm on Sunday (M, 58, SLC, 1920s). Brown 6900.

11245 The sun produces severe storms as it crosses the equator (M, SLC, 1957).

11246 If the sun goes down in the west and shines to the east and makes all the windows shine and glitter, you've seen how they can sparkle, then a storm's coming (F, 87, Providence, 1900).

11247 A red sky in the morning is supposed to mean that a storm is on its way (F, 46, SLC, 1930).

11248 Red clouds in the morning means a storm (M, 59, Swiss, Heber City, 1914).

11249 Mackerel sky means a storm is nigh (M, 29, SLC, 1964). Cf. Brown 3475.

11250 When the wind whistles when it blows, it means there is going to be a storm (F, 44, Sandy, 1928).

11251 When the winds are in the east, an approaching storm will be a lasting one (M, Logan, 1970).

11252 When it rains and the road steams, it means there is going to be more storm (F, 58, SLC, 1938).

11253 If the rain bounces when it hits the ground, it is going to be a long storm (F, 58, SLC, 1963).

11254 If it storms the first Sunday in the month, it will storm every Sunday in the month (F, 29, Ogden, 1964).

11255 If you whistle aboard a ship at sea, you will call up a storm. If you whistle aboard while tied up, you will cause disaster to the ship on the next voyage (M, SLC, 1960). Cf. Brown 3474.

## Animal Indicators

11256 Animals frolic and jump around the barnyard before a rain storm (M, Logan, 1970). Cf. Brown 6924.

11257 When a cat washes her face over her ears, there will be a storm (F, W. Jordan, 1959).

11258 A cat scratching on the bark of a tree points to the direction where the next storm will come from (M, SLC, 1964).

11259 A storm is approaching if horses run around, snort, and hold their heads high (F, SLC, 1964).

11260 When the cattle run through the fields, there is going to be a storm (M, Eng, Woodland, 1959); If cows kick up their heels when they run, it will storm the next day (M, SLC, 1959); If on a sunny day cattle run for no apparent reason with their tails on their back, a storm is sure to be brewing and will soon come (F, SLC, 1961); Cattle cutting capers is an omen of storm in twelve hours (1946).

11261 If you see a hog scratching its back, it's a sure sign of storm (M, Riverton, 1918).

11262 If you see the pigs in a pen eating and playing with the husks off of the ears of corn, it is a sign of storm (M, SLC, 1964).

11263   When chickens huddle together, it is a sign of a storm (F, Logan, 1970). Brown 6925.

11264   When baby ducks huddle it means a storm will come (M, 66, Gr, SLC, 1963).

11265   If the rooster crows before twelve, it is going to storm (F, SLC, 1960); . . . in the middle of a day, it foretells a storm (M, 54, Richfield, 1964).

11266   The crowing of a rooster during the daytime foretells a storm or bad weather (F, 49, Richfield, 1925).

11267   When coyotes howl close to town there is going to be a bad storm (F, 76, Orangeville, 1966).

11268   On a rainy day birds fly above the storm to protect their leaders (M, SLC, 1963).

11269   If you see birds perched on a tree, it indicates that a storm will soon come (M, SLC, 1964).

11270   When blackbirds gather in a group, a storm is coming (F, Eng, Hooper, 1963).

11271   The meadowlark sings when it is going to storm (F, 55, Logan, 1970).

11272   When petrels appear a storm will follow (F, 75, Pleasant Grove, 1906). Cf. Brown 6928.

11273   When sea gulls fly inland a storm is coming (F, Norw, SLC, 1960). Brown 6928, 6932.

11274   Swallows and bats fly close to the ground just before a storm (F, 24, SLC, 1954).

11275   If owls hoot at night, it is an indication of a storm (F, Moab, 1953).

11276   You must bury a dead snake immediately, or else it will storm that night (M, 52, SLC, 1964).

11277   When fish go in deep water it's a sign of a storm (M, SLC, 1960).

11278   When dolphins and porpoises play about, it foretells a storm (M, SLC, 1950).

11279   Ants milling around outside of an anthill predict that a storm is coming (M, 27, Sandy, 1963); Nervous, excited ants are an omen of a storm (1946).

11280   A swarm of bees very active around their hive indicates a coming storm (Anon).

11281   If crickets sing at night, it is an indication of an oncoming storm (F, Moab, 1953).

11282   When the crickets stop chirping, and all of the insects go into hiding, there is going to be a big storm (F, 65, Layton, 1962).

11283   A storm can be predicted when flies seem to crowd into a room (M, 38, SLC, 1940).

11284   Killdeers fluttering or flies clustering in a window are storm omens (1946).

11285   If angleworms come up and make little piles on the ground, there will be a storm (F, 87, Providence, 1900).

11286   If you see a spider in the room, it means a storm is coming (F, 40, SLC, 1940).

11287   If you kill a daddy longlegs, it will storm (M, SLC, 1967).

## Smoke, Fire

11288   If the chimney smoke doesn't rise but falls to the ground, there will soon be a storm (M, 57, Swiss, Heber City, 1918).

11289   Smoke drifting from the chimney to the ground is a sign of an approaching storm (Carbon Co, 1939); Smoke over your house real low is a sign of a storm (F, Moab, 1953); When the smoke from a chimney bends with the wind, there will be a storm (M, Price, 1959); If smoke comes out of a chimney and flattens out . . . (M, SLC, 1959).

11290   The crackling of the burning log means a coming storm (F, 50, Murray, 1928).

## NO STORMS, PROTECTING AGAINST AND PREVENTING STORM

11291   There are no heavy storms the first ten days or the last ten days of each month (M, 44, Woods Cross, 1934).

11292   When the moon's crescent is on end, the moisture has drained out and no storm is due (F, 72, Centerville, 1963).

11293   If the moon is in this position ⌣ , it won't storm. It is full (F, 87, Providence, 1900).

11294   A quarter moon in the form of a cup indicates that the moon will hold water back, and that there'll be no storm (1946).

11295   If the moon is tipped up, it won't storm (F, 83, Nephi, 1964).

11296   Storms usually don't last long when there is thunder (F, SLC, 1925).

11297   If you throw salt over a form of a cross, it's supposed to quit storming (F, SLC, 1925).

11298   Ringing church bells will keep a storm away (F, Orem, 1964).

## WIND, HURRICANES

11299   March is the windy month (M, SLC, 1960).

11300   Cold winds blow when the oak buds (F, SLC, 1961).

11301   If you stand on your head behind a door and look through the crack of the door, you'll see the wind blow (F, 59, SLC, 1921).

11302   If the wind blows the door open, bad luck enters (F, SLC, 1959).

11303 Whistling will cause a breeze (M, 24, SLC, 1964).

11304 A suicide is followed by a strong wind (F, 19, SLC, 1964).

11305 If the sun sets in red, then it will be windy tomorrow (M, 50, SLC, 1964). Cf. Brown 6940.

11306 If you see a ring around the sun, it is going to be windy (M, SLC, 1964); When the sun is red and colorful, it is an indication of wind the next day (M, 44, Woods Cross, 1964).

11307 If the sky is red in the west when the sun goes down in the evening, the wind will blow the next day (F, Grantsville, 1964). Brown 6940f.

11308 Clouds cling to the mountains along the east of the valley for awhile before one of those three-day east winds (M, 74, Ogden, 1945); When the clouds start rolling over the mountains to the east of Davis and Weber counties, there is going to be a big wind--90 mph (F, 38, Layton, 1962).

11309 Some people say that the angle at which a star falls somehow indicates the direction of the wind which will arise the next morning (F, 20, SLC, 1962). Brown 6957f.

11310 If a wood or coal fire sings, it is going to blow hard (F, American Fork, 1962).

11311 Cold winds are always from the north (M, 25, SLC, 1940); Wind from the west on two successive days plus a layer of clouds hovering over the mountains east of Centerville are sure signs of an east wind on the third day (M, 85, It, Centerville, 1964).

11312 Wind from the east is no good for man or beast (F). Cf. Brown 3096, 6965ff.

11313 If the wind is in the east, the weather won't be fit for man or beast (Logan, 1970).

11314 When the wind is in the east, it isn't safe for man or beast; when the wind is in the west, that is when the weather's best (F, 21, Vernal, 1965). Brown 6965f.

11315 In the area of Bountiful when the east wind blows, either it stops or blows hardest at six or twelve o'clock (M, 44, Woods Cross, 1964).

11316 A wind in the east calls to your priest (F, 51, SLC, 1965).

11317 An east wind will blow three days (M, SLC); An east wind in Salt Lake always blows three days (F, SLC, 1925).

11318 The east wind is evil. All windows and shutters are kept closed at night on the east side (F, 69, SLC, 1965).

11319 Wind from the north--time to go forth; wind from the south--stay quiet and shut your mouth (M, Norw, SLC, 1960).

11320 Wherever the wind lies on Ash Wednesday it continues throughout Lent (M, 1961). Brown 6963.

11321 If the wind blows a certain way on Easter Sunday, it will blow that way for six weeks (M, 22, SLC, 1960).

11322 If the wind doesn't stop blowing by six, it will blow all night (F, Lehi, 1957).

11323 If a cat tears at cushions and carpets or moves about uneasily, a wind is coming (F, 19, SLC, 1953). Cf. Brown 6977f.

11324 Birds on the clothesline mean a wind is coming (M, SLC, 1964).

11325 When the smoke goes straight up, that's a sign that a hurricane is coming soon (M, 57, Ogden, 1970).

11326 An ache in your toe means the wind's going to blow (M, Provo, 1970).

## LIGHTNING, THUNDER

11327 A clasp [sic] of lightning is an omen of things to come--usually bad (F, 63, Milford, 1964).

11328 Lightning never strikes twice in the same place (F, 62, SLC, 1964); . . . never strikes two in the same place (F, 1959). Brown 7024.

11329 If you carry a piece of a falling star, you can't be hit by lightning (F, 19, SLC, 1965); Meteoric fragments are protection against lightning (F, 61, SLC, 1920). Cf. Brown 7020.

11330 Ringing church bells will keep thunder and lightning away (F, 69, Murray, 1905).

11331 Holy water keeps away lightning (M, 48, SLC, 1957).

11332 If a person takes the Lord's name in vain, he may be struck by lightning (M, 17, SLC, 1948).

11333 Broken pieces of blue glass are thought to bring good luck, because they have been struck by lightning (M, 71, SLC, 1964).

11334 When it lightnings and thunders at the same time, it has struck somewhere (F, 87, Providence, 1895).

11335 After you hear thunder, count until you see the lightning flash. What number you get is how many miles away the lightning is (F, Logan, 1956).

11336 If it thunders and the sky is cloudless, it is a sign of good luck (F, SLC, 1960).

11337 Thunder in the morning, all the day storming; thunder at night is a traveler's delight (F, Ogden, 1961).

11338 If there is a lot of snow on the ground all winter, there will be a lot of thunder during the coming spring and summer (F, 60, SLC, 1964).

## Explanations of Lightning and Thunder

11339   The old Germanic peoples believed that thunder and lightning were caused in this way: Donnar [sic] or Donderdag (in Dutch) rides across the sky in a wagon. A goat with eight legs pulls the wagon so that it will go faster. When he is angry, he throws his ox (ax). This causes lightning. The goats' feet cause the thunder (F, 20, Du, SLC, 1963).

11340   When it thunders it means the man in the moon is beating his wife (F, SLC, 1958).

11341   Greeks and Romans used to believe that thunder and lightning were the signs of the gods. It represented their anger (F, 20, SLC, 1964).

11342   Thunder and lightning are God's way of showing displeasure towards his children (F, Ir, Ogden, 1962); When it thunders it means the Lord is angry (M, 55, SLC, 1915); The sound of thunder is God walking on clouds when angry (F, Ogden, 1961).

11343   To the Indians lightning and thunder mean that their great leader is angry (F, Provo, 1959).

11344   Thunder and lightning are said to be caused by a great black snake with rattles on its tail, on whose back a supernatural being rides (F, 44, Ogden, 1964).

11345   When it thunders it means the devil is beating his wife (M, SLC, 1964).

11346   Lightning is God winking (F, SLC, 1963). Brown 5970.

11347   Lightning is the spear God throws (F, Ogden, 1961).

11348   When there is lightning the heavens are on fire (M, 24, SLC, 1948).

11349   Thunder is God stepping or God speaking (F, SLC, 1930s). Brown 5971.

11350   Thunder is God pushing his table across the floor (F, Moab, 1953).

11351   Thunder is God rolling his chariot across the cobblestones (F, Moab, 1953).

11352   Thunder is Thor throwing his hammer at someone or some other god he's mad at. Noise is produced when the hammer hits the person or thing (F, 50, Norw, SLC, 1915).

11353   Thunder is a war in heaven (F, SLC, 1949).

11354   Thunder is the devil rolling rocks (M, 84, Centerville).

11355   When it's thundering, they're moving furniture upstairs (F, 80, Ogden, 1940).

11356   When it's thundering, potatoes are rolling down the hill (F, 61, Richfield, 1915); . . . it is God pulling his potato wagon across the sky (M, SLC).

11357   Thunder is made by clouds bumping into each other (F, SLC, 1900).

11358   When it thunders, it means that the mountain men are bowling (M, 47, SLC, 1965).

11359   Thunder is the sound of Captain Drake's crew knocking down a pin (F, 19, SLC, 1956).

## Domestic Precautions

11360   Stay away from the windows during a thunderstorm (F, SLC, 1920).

11361   Don't leave a window open during a storm, for lightning will follow the draft inside (M, Logan, 1970).

11362   Don't sit by an open window or an open door during an electric storm (F, Bear River City, 1957).

11363   Never stand in a draft in an electrical storm, or you will get hit by lightning (M, Sandy, 1950); Never sit in a draft . . . (M, 84, Centerville).

11364   Unplug the radio and all other electrical appliances during a lightning storm; if you don't, lightning will strike your home (F, 56, SLC, 1964).

11365   Never look at TV when there is a lightning storm, because lightning will strike from the sky and hit your house (M, 78, SLC).

11366   When it is lightning outside, it is necessary to cover up a sewing machine (electric or treadle), because a sewing machine is made of metal which particularly attracts lightning (F, Lehi, 1957).

11367   Don't talk on the phone while it is lightning, or you'll be struck by lightning (F, 42, SLC, 1963).

11368   When an electric storm comes up, throw out all the silverware and any article that might draw lightning (F, Moab, 1953).

11369   Never leave a knife on the table during an electrical storm, or it will bring the lightning into the house (F, SLC, 1961).

11370   Never eat during lightning, or you will be struck (F, 50, SLC, 1938).

11371   Do not eat while there is lightning in the sky, because God is scolding the people (F, Ger, SLC, 1963).

11372   Don't put knitting needles in the window during a storm because lightning will strike them (F, Norw, SLC, 1960).

11373   You should never leave scissors on a window sill, because lightning will strike them (F, 81, SLC, 1964).

11374   When it thunders and lightnings, hang a piece of cloth over a metal or a mirror, so that lightning won't strike (F, Ger, Granger, 1961); A looking glass should be turned to the wall during an electrical storm (M, SLC, 1925); . . . turn the mirrors down so the lightning won't strike (F, SLC, 1925); Lightning is attracted to mirrors (M, SLC, 1965). Brown 7025.

11375  Looking at lightning in a mirror is bad luck (M, 30, Ir, SLC, 1965).

11376  During a thunderstorm a handful of salt in a wooden container on the front stairs will pacify Thor's rams (M, Ger, SLC, 1938).

11377  Lightning will not strike during a thunderstorm, if one gets himself a feather bed (F, 46, SLC, 1938); . . . if you crawl under a feather mattress (F, 58, Layton); . . . are sitting on a down-filled pillow (F, 44, Sandy, 1928). Brown 7026.

11378  You should get under the bed during a thunderstorm (M, 70, Copperton, 1964).

11379  My dad tells about when he was a boy his mother used to gather all of her children and put them in a closet whenever it started to thunder and lightning.  She believed that if they were in a dark closet, they couldn't see or hear it and so it couldn't hurt them. Many other mothers used to do this (M, 45, American Fork, 1972).

11380  Always hide in a cellar during a storm if you don't want to be struck by lightning (M, SLC, 1959).

11381  The safest place during a lightning storm is in the car (F, 50, Goshen, 1929).

11382  Never take a bath during a lightning storm (F, 21, Ogden, 1958).

11383  Never wash dishes during a lightning storm (F, 50, Goshen, 1929).

11384  To have iron or steel around you during a thunderstorm will bring safety (M, SLC, 1961).

11385  Lightning cannot strike you if you are dressed in white (F, 45, SLC, 1930s).

11386  Lightning will not strike a person if he has his suspenders twisted (F, 39, SLC, 1963); . . . if suspenders are crossed in the back (F, Provo, 1972).

## Animal and Plant Life

11387  A cat draws lightning (M, 36, Bountiful, 1950).

11388  A dog coming into a house during a storm will draw lightning (M, 26, SLC, 1950). Cf. Brown 7007.

11389  Horses get jittery just before a lightning storm is coming (M, 60, Plain City, 1930).

11390  An elder tree is safe from lightning (F, SLC, 1961); During a thunderstorm stand under a tree to avoid being hurt (M, SLC, 1940).  Cf. Brown 7017.

11391  Lightning never strikes twice in the same place.  It is safe to stand under a tree that has once been struck by lightning (M, 19, Bountiful, 1964).

11392  Never stand under a tree during a lightning storm (F, 21, Ogden, 1960); . . . you will surely be killed if you do (M, 22, SLC, 1963); If you walk under a tree during a lightning storm, you will be struck by lightning in your life time (F, 16, SLC, 1953).

11393  A wreath fashioned of flowers picked during full moon at midnight under the sign of Taurus, will, if hung on the wall, protect the house from lightning (M, Ger, SLC, 1938).


## HAIL, SNOW

### Various Notions

11394  When it hails, you should burn palm leaves, and it will stop (M, 16, SLC, 1963).

11395  It is bad luck to eat the first snow of the year (M, SLC, 1966).

11396  Make a wish at the first snowstorm of the season, and you will have your wish (M, 22, SLC, 1964).

11397  Snow falling on Thursday will be bad luck for the day (M, 31, SLC, 1942).

11398  Deep snow means deep sorrow (F, SLC, 1941).

11399  An early snowfall means a long ski season (M, 23, SLC, 1964).

11400  The snow at the bottom of a drift is warm because of the pressure (M, 65, SLC, 1910).

11401  When it snows, it is mother nature combing out her dandruff (F, 15, SLC, 1959).

11402  When it's snowing, someone in heaven is getting married (M, 24, SLC, 1948).

11403  Snow is old Mother Goose picking her geese (F, Centerville).

11404  When it is snowing, children are told that the old woman is shaking her feather bed (F, SLC, 1963).  Brown 5969.

11405  If it snows when the sun is shining, it is a sign that the devil's wife is shaking her feather bed (F, SLC, 1957); Whenever it gets real dark and snows great big flakes of snow, it means the devil's wife is angry and beating her feather tick (F, 50, Nephi, 1967).

11406  If it snows when the sun's shining, it means the devil is beating his wife (F, 21, Richfield, 1955).

11407  Snow is the result of an angels' pillow fight (F, 19, Can, SLC, 1963).

11408  Snow is the poison from outer space (M, SLC, 1963).

11409  If the fire sparkles, it means snow (F, 56, SLC, 1964).

11410  If a stove makes a tromping noise in the evening, it will snow before morning (F, Park City, 1957).

### Human and Animal Indicators

11411   When grandpa gets pains in his legs, it is going to snow (F, 21, SLC, 1964).

11412   For a dog to go hunting at night in winter is a sign of snow (M, SLC, 1963).

11413   Sheep and cows will start down off the top of the mountain two or three days before a big snow comes (M, 60, Ogden, 1970).

11414   A flock of birds is a sign of snow (M, SLC, 1960).

11415   If birds build their nests high up in a tree, it means that the snow will be deep (M, Norw, SLC, 1965).

11416   When the wild geese fly to the southeast, expect a blizzard (M, 86, Payson, 1894).

11417   A robin entering a peasant's house is a sign of snow (F, 49, SLC, 1964); A robin that enters the home is a certain indication that snowstorms and severe frosts will follow (F, SLC).

### Plant Indicators

11418   The snow next winter will be as high as the thistles grow in the summer (F, SLC, 1930).

11419   Tall sunflowers, deep snow (M, 1945); The Ute Indians believe that the amount of snow for the following year can be predicted in advance by studying the growth of sunflowers. The collected snow would pile up to but never exceed the extended blossom (M, 45, Ogden, 1962); The taller the sunflowers grow, the deeper the snow will be. This is because the seed of the sunflower must be above the snow so the quail can get them (M, 51, SLC, 1971).

11420   When the pine trees on the mountains appear almost black, it will snow (F, Park City, 1957).

11421   Long grass means there was much snow that winter (M, SLC, 1964).

11422   The snow brings with it material to make green leaves grow (M, SLC, 1964).

### Cosmic Phenomena, Weather

11423   What date the first snowstorm come on, there will be that many snow storms during the winter (M, 84, Centerville). Cf. Brown 7028.

11424   It is believed that when snow falls late in the spring that the next snowfall for the following year will be exceptionally early and heavy (M, 23, SLC, 1940).

11425   If it snows the first day of March, there will be snow on the ground for a month (M, 22, SLC, 1949).

11426   When snowflakes are very large, it means that the storm won't last long, but if they are small, the storm will be a long one (F, 1960); Little flake, much snow; big flake, little snow (F, 20, SLC, 1964).

11427   If it snows and the sun is shining, it will snow tomorrow (M, 68, SLC, 1962).

11428   If the sky is pink, there is a bad blizzard coming (M, Ogden, 1961).

11429   Low clouds indicate snow (F, Moab, 1953).

11430   Thunder in winter means snow (M, 20, Ja, SLC, 1963). Cf. Brown 7043.

11431   If it thunders in February, there will be snow in May (M, SLC, 1956).

11432   If it thunders before the leaves are out, it will snow after they are out (F, 90, SLC, 1964).

11433   When the north winds blow, you can look for snow (F, Lehi, 1957).

11434   If rain comes between eight and nine o'clock in the morning, snow will follow that night (M, SLC, 1963).

11435   A rainbow during a snowstorm means snow at the same time tomorrow (F, 19, Santa Clara, 1959).

11436   John D. Lee always marked the first snow and the age of the moon when it fell. There would be as many tracing snows that season as days the moon was old (F, St. George, 1954).

11437   A halo around the moon means snow (M, Layton, 1936); . . . it will snow the next day (M, 20, SLC, 1964); A white ring around a full moon means snow (F, SLC, 1960); A circle of frost around the moon indicates a snowstorm and cold weather ahead (F, Logan, 1970).

### FROST, ICE

11438   Fog in February means frost in April (M, 38, SLC, 1933). Cf. Brown 7077.

11439   It usually freezes on June 14 and September 10 in Parowan Valley (M, SLC, 1967).

11440   The frost will come in the spring if no snow fell in the winter (M, Willard, 1910).

11441   A purple sunset means frost that night (F, Provo, 1972).

11442   When there is a clear moon, there will be frost soon (M, 21, Midvale, 1964). Cf. Brown 7070ff.

11443   As the moon grows bigger, it's a more likely time then to get frost than any other time (F, 87, Providence, 1900). Cf. Brown 7069.

11444   No frost on a clear night (M, SLC, 1960).

11445   A clear, bright night in winter indicates a hard freeze (also in the fall) (F, Logan, 1970).

11446   If it thunders in the winter, it means there will be a heavy frost (M, 1959).

11447   Large, bright stars in the winter promise a frost for the following day

(F, SLC, 1960); Many stars . . . (F, 32, SLC, 1949). Cf. Brown 7072.

11448   In the fall a frost will turn the leaves a brighter color than if there is no frost (F, 23, SLC, 1961).

11449   A robin entering a peasant's house is a sign of frost (F, 49, SLC, 1964).

11450   When the crickets start chirping from the trees, within thirty days the first killing frost will come (F, 26, Bennion, 1971).

11451   When you hear the first cricket of the fall, it is just six weeks till the first frost (M, SLC, 1930).

11452   There will be frost three months after the first katydid is heard (M, 65, Provo); The first frost is six weeks away . . . (M, SLC, 1960). Cf. Brown 7088ff.

11453   Grandpa D had a way of foretelling frost that was completely infallible. There was a little patch of maple in the foothills that you could see from the kitchen window, and after it turned red on the mountain there would be frost in the valley within ten days. It never did fail. I guess that's because turning red meant frost on the mountain, and it always got down into the valley, into the town within ten days (F, Summit, 1930s).

11454   If the ice on a river hardens early in the winter and cracks again, the ice will be bad all winter (F, American Fork, 1960).

11455   On a certain spring day the cold man is supposed to come and bring so many days of icy weather. The number of days varies with the informant, but the cold day is always the same (F, Provo, 1971).

## MISCELLANEOUS WEATHER BELIEFS

11456   The coldest part of the night is just before sunrise (F, SLC, 1920).

11457   Every winter I injure my leg. It is a bad season of the year (F, 19, SLC, 1960).

11458   When the sun is shining the heavens are happy (M, 24, SLC, 1948).

11459   It is bad luck to walk on the same side of the street that the sun is shining on (F, 47, SLC).

## PHYSICAL UNIVERSE

## WATER

### Clear, Muddy Water, Etc.

11460   Dreaming of clear water means good luck (M, 68, Bountiful, 1911).

11461   If you dream of clear water and fish, something good is going to happen (M, 41, Ger, SLC, 1964).

11462   To dream of deep water means trouble (F, Brigham City).

11463   If you dream of turbulent water, trouble will come about (F, 82, It, SLC, 1963).

11464   If you dream of clear water, it means a sad experience is near that will cause tears (F, 18, SLC, 1958); . . . something bad will happen to cause tears (F, 57, It, SLC, 1963).

11465   It is a sign of bad luck or sorrow if you dream of muddy water (F, Orangeville, 1959); Bad times will come in your life . . . (F, Park City, 1957); Troubles lie ahead . . . (F, 67, SLC, 1963); Something terrible will happen to you or your loved ones . . . (F, W. Jordan).

11466   If you dream about water and it is black, bad luck will come (F, 60, SLC, 1927).

11467   If you dream of muddy water, you will have good luck. If you dream of clear water you will have bad luck (F, Norw, SLC).

### Bodies of Water

11468   Always spit in a body of water three times before crossing (F, SLC, 1961).

11469   Every seventh wave is a bigger one (F, 39, SLC, 1964).

11470   If you drink from the river springs in Moab, you will always return to Moab (F, 22, Moab, 1964).

11471   Utah Lake is extremely deep and it covers a Nephite city (M, 18, Provo, 1949). (Nephites, according to the Book of Mormon, were part of an ancient Pre-Colombian civilization in the Western Hemisphere. Legends of sunken cities are found around the coastal perimeter of Europe, and are also frequently mentioned in connection with inland bodies of water. Such stories are fairly rare in America. Often cities are said to have been engulfed because of the wickedness of the inhabitants, their profligate ways, or their disdain of the poor and the afflicted. A good general treatise on the subject for Europe is Franz Schmarsel, Die Sage von der untergegangenen Stadt [Litterar-historische Forschungen, No. 53, Berlin, 1913]. --Eds.)

11472   Parowan got its name when an Indian maiden drowned in the Great Salt Lake when it used to cover the state. So the Indians named the site where she drowned Parowan which means 'evil waters' (M, 18, Parowan, 1967).

11473   The Great Salt Lake has an underground outlet to get rid of some of the water that flows in from the Bear and Jordan Rivers (F, SLC, 1895).

11474   It is bad luck to look into a well at noon (M, 19, SLC, 1963).

11475   Bridal Veil Falls in Provo Canyon was made when an Indian princess jumped off a cliff because she thought she had been forsaken by her lover, and her lover came and cried so hard that he started the waterfall (M, 56, Provo, 1964).

## MUD, DIRT, SAND, GROUND, ETC.

11476 The origin of sandstone buttes in southeast Utah: Paul Bunyan was hired to carve the Grand Canyon. While he was busy, the Blue Ox, his companion, roamed the flat countryside. Wherever he defecated one today finds the massive outcroppings of rock (M, 75, Price, 1920s).

11477 If you dig something out of the ground, you should put something in its place (F, 48, Ogden, 1964).

11478 If you dig a hole deep enough, you will dig away and arrive in China if you jump into it (F, 19, SLC, 1964).

11479 If a person dreams of dirt, then there will be a tragedy (F, SLC, 1964).

11480 If you dream of mud, there will be trouble (F, 56, Ger, SLC, 1964); . . . sorrow will come (F, Bear River City, 1957). Cf. Brown 3110.

## OIL, COAL

11481 Oil is really prehistoric mammal blood (F, 62, SLC, 1900).

11482 When grass grows naturally oil can usually be found (M, SLC, 1964).

11483 Wherever lightning strikes you'll find oil (M, 48, SLC, 1939).

11484 Lightning striking during a rainstorm changes small puddles of water into oil (F, 46, SLC, 1925).

11485 If you pick up a piece of coal, it's good luck (F, 50, Eng, SLC, 1964).

## STONES, ROCKS, PEBBLES, SEASHELLS

11486 As the earth rotates, the centrifugal force throws the rocks out from deep down in the earth up to the surface (F, SLC, 1967).

11487 A black rock with a solid white line that completely circles it is good luck (F, SLC, 1941).

11488 If you find a gray rock with a white circle around it, spit on the rock and make a wish then throw the rock in the stream over your shoulder so you can't see where it lands and your wish will come true (F, SLC); . . . over your right shoulder . . . (M, 19, SLC, 1964).

11489 There is a rock named Pleebamarnock (black with a white ring around the middle). If you find one, spit on it and throw it over your right shoulder and you will have good luck (M, 30, SLC, 1961).

11490 When one finds a flat stone with a white strip through it, one should spit on it and toss it without noticing its location (M).

11491 Finding a stone with a ring around it brings good luck if you throw it over your left shoulder (F, 82, SLC, 1961).

11492 A grey stone completely encircled by a thin band of white is a wishing rock. I throw it over my left shoulder and make a wish (F, SLC, 1961).

11493 Throw a striped rock over your shoulder to overcome any bad luck (F, 12, Provo, 1964).

11494 If you throw a rock in a river and it skips twice, your wish will come true (M, SLC, 1957).

11495 An open stone brings bad luck (M, 20, SLC, 1950s).

11496 To find a seashell full of sand is a good luck omen (F, SLC, 1959).

11497 Put your ear against a seashell and listen to the waves. You can tell whether it's calm or rough (F, 23, Eng, SLC, 1964).

## VOLCANOES, EARTHQUAKES

11498 Bamboo plants have large roots; in an earthquake run among them and the earth doesn't split because the roots hold the earth together (F, 51, Ja, SLC, 1963).

11499 Standing under a doorway during an earthquake keeps you safe (F, 43, SLC, 1925).

11500 Animals will not be caught in an earthquake. They seem to know when one is going to happen. They will leave an area before the earthquake occurs (F, 33, Logan, 1970).

## NIGHT AIR

11501 Night air is poison (F, Weber Co, 1958).

11502 Night air was believed to have been very harmful to one's physical being, because it often originated in swamps and polluted areas. The sun wasn't able to purify the air (M, 71, SLC).

## DIRECTIONS, GEOMETRIC FIGURES, PROGRESSION OF EVENTS, NUMBERS, ETC.

## DIRECTIONS, GEOMETRIC FIGURES

11503 If you look to the south, it will bring out good luck (F, SLC, 1961).

11504 Ceremonial movements must correspond to movements in nature (M, 20, SLC, 1958).

11505 Do things clockwise for good luck: Today and yesterday's people go clockwise whenever doing something in a circle because mainly, the sun goes in a clockwise motion (M, Murray, 1959).

11506 Maypole dancing must be done in a clockwise direction, or you will have bad luck (F, Murray).

11507 Draw a circle to enclose good luck (F, 40, Logan, 1938).

11508 When a lamp chimney broke, the whole family would try to see what it looked like. Some broke in the form of a coffin, meaning a death; some in the form of a gold nugget, meaning wealth; but if it broke in a circle it meant good luck (F, 48, SLC, 1964).

11509 When in a magic circle never circle to the left, but always circle to the right (M, 56, Ir, SLC, 1964).

11510 Make an X and spit on it for good luck (M, 60, SLC, 1914).

PROGRESSION OF EVENTS, REVERSALS, ETC.

11511 If you do anything wrong against nature, nature will get even with you (M, SLC, 1956).

11512 A common belief is that good luck happens in streaks and then one has streaks of bad luck. The two types don't seem to integrate but come all at once (F, 21, SLC, 1962).

11513 Reversing usual procedure brings bad luck (F, 27, SLC, 1963). Cf. Brown 5988.

11514 The first person to find a broken key on the piano will have bad luck until the key is removed (F, Murray, 1957).

11515 If you drop something, it's good luck to immediately look up instead of down (F, 99, Norw, SLC, 1963).

11516 If you drop something, let someone else pick it up and do not say thank you, and you will have a pleasant surprise (F, 35, Murray, 1964).

11517 If things go too smoothly, you are heading for a big letdown (F, 22, Clearfield, 1964).

11518 It is bad luck to go in a show in the middle (F, SLC, 1961).

11519 If you refuse to help someone, you will be refused yourself when someday you are in dire need of help (F, It, SLC, 1963); If one lends a helping hand, one will receive a helping hand when one needs it the most (F, It, SLC, 1963).

11520 If you have the wrong attitude towards something, then for a week bad luck is sure to befall you (F, 1959).

11521 A person must every so often throw something away of great value to them, or he will have bad luck (M, Salem, 1946).

11522 Never change your plans once you have made them, or something bad will happen (F, 62, W. Jordan, 1962); When you have a choice in anything, stick to the first choice; it's better (M, 18, SLC, 1963).

11523 If one speaks badly of another, he will have bad luck himself (F, 18, SLC, 1960).

11524 If you pull a mean joke on someone, the joke will come back to you many, many times (M, SLC, 1960).

11525 If a person keeps thinking about something and wanting it to happen, it won't. If you don't care one way or the other, it usually happens (F, SLC, 1960).

11526 A person who thinks evil will receive more evil than he thinks (F, 35, SLC, 1964).

11527 If one talks about his achievements too much or too often, he is letting himself in for a big disappointment (F, 22, SLC, 1964).

11528 A man invites bad fate, if he tries to take precautions against it (M, 43, It, SLC, 1930s).

11529 If one speaks of misfortune of another, it'll bring misfortune upon him (F, 22, SLC, 1960).

11530 When you do something, it will happen to you again (F, 16, SLC, 1958).

NUMBERS

11531 If a president is elected in a year ending in zero, it's bad luck (M, 19, SLC, 1964).

Odd Numbers

11532 Odd numbers are considered lucky (F, Garland, 1940).

11533 There is good luck in odd numbers except thirteen (M, Nephi, 1961).

11534 Odd numbers are lucky, especially in combinations of three (F, 19, SLC, 1964).

11535 There is luck in odd numbers: seven, three or nine (F, 18, SLC, 1954).

Numbers One and Two

11536 The number one is very lucky (M, 30, Ja, SLC, 1959).

11537 Misfortunes never come singly, they always come in twos (M, 22, SLC, 1952).

11538 Happiness comes in pairs (F, 23, Layton, 1958); Good things come in pairs (F, SLC, 1964).

11539 Blessings always come singly; misfortunes come in pairs (M, 68, SLC, 1964).

11540 If one does a thing once, then the chances of good and bad luck are equal (M, SLC, 1964).

11541 Never ring for an elevator twice (F, Murray, 1957).

11542 Two or more people in a telephone booth are bad luck (M, SLC, 1955).

11543 It is bad luck to do something twice (M, SLC, 1964).

Number Three

11544 Everything happens in threes (F, 1959).

11545    Number three and multiples of this number are mystic numbers (M, 22, SLC, 1963); Three is a magic number (M, SLC, 1959).

11546    Three is a lucky number (M, Ja, SLC, 1965); Good luck happens in threes (M, SLC, 1963); . . . it comes from the Holy Trinity (M, 20, SLC, 1964).  Brown 6027.

11547    Number three is unlucky (M, 21, SLC, 1953); Bad happens in threes (M, 19, SLC, 1963); Things in threes are unlucky (F, 50, SLC, 1964); Bad luck runs in cycles of three (F, 20, SLC, 1963); One disappointment is usually followed by two others (M, 22, SLC, 1965); All trouble comes in threes (M, SLC, 1958); Misfortunes always come in threes (F, SLC, 1958); Tragedies come in threes (F, 19, SLC, 1955).  Brown 6031.

11548    If you repeat something three times, you will never forget it (F, 52, SLC).

11549    The third time you try something it will work, because the third time is the charm (F, SLC, 1962); If some incident happens three times, it is a charm (F, 66, SLC, 1918); Things always work the third time.  Three's the charm (F, 21, SLC, 1964); The third try is a good charm (F, 47, SLC, 1940).

11550    A great many things happen in three's: If something happens twice, it will likely happen again (M, 19, SLC, 1963); Things or events always happen in three's, i.e., two airplane crashes followed by a third (M, SLC, 1958). Brown 6029f.

11551    The number three is unlucky; it has been said that two good events may occur, but the third event will be sad (M, Murray, 1959).

11552    Deaths and catastrophies always occur in threes (F, SLC, 1935).

11553    When something happens it happens in threefold; for instance, a man got divorced, broke his leg, and wrecked his car in one week (M, 34, SLC, 1963).

11554    You always break three things in succession (F, Moab, 1953); If you break one article, two other breakages are sure to follow (F, Lehi, 1957).

## Numbers Four, Five and Seven

11555    Number four is very unlucky (M, 30, Ja, SLC, 1959).

11556    Bad things happen in fours (M, 19, SLC, 1963).

11557    Five and multiples of five are lucky (F, 10, SLC, 1963).  Brown 6027.

11558    The five fingers of the hand, or any design or phrase associated with the number five will protect against bad luck (F, 50, Murray, 1928).

11559    Keep anything seven years and you can use it again (F, SLC, 1960).

11560    The number seven or any number with seven in it (17, 27) is a lucky number (M, SLC, 1958); Number seven and multiples of this number are mystic numbers (M, 22, SLC, 1955).  Brown 6027.

11561    It's lucky to have only seven letters in your first or last name (F, 46, SLC, 1964).

11562    The number seven is lucky (i.e., the seventh son of a seventh son has phenomenal luck) (M, 20, Salem, 1964).

11563    If seven is your lucky number, you can never lose (F, 38, SLC, 1964).

11564    Bad luck happens in sevens (M, SLC, 1963).

11565    Some people believe that the number seven is bad (F, Woods Cross, 1953); Seven is always unlucky (F, 21, SLC, 1964).

## Numbers Eight to Eleven

11566    It is superstition that the number eight is a sign of misfortune (F, 56, SLC, 1964).

11567    Eight is an unlucky number (M, 28, Provo, 1954).

11568    Nine is always lucky (F, SLC, 1964).

11569    Ten is the lucky number for the tenth child in a family (M, 65, SLC, 1963).

11570    Number eleven is lucky (M, 29, SLC, 1964).

## Number Thirteen

11571    Number thirteen is lucky (F, Bountiful, 1959).  Brown 6033.

11572    The number thirteen brings ill fortune at all times (M, SLC, 1960); Anything to do with the number thirteen is unlucky (F, 43, SLC, 1964); Anything that starts with the number thirteen is bad luck (F, 49, SLC, 1964); . . . is unlucky as hell (M, SLC, 1965).  Brown 6027.

11573    Number thirteen is unlucky.  This originated when Christ had thirteen apostles.  He was betrayed by the thirteenth (F, 49, SLC, 1964).  Brown 6033.

11574    A baker's dozen is bad luck (F, 74, SLC, 1900).

11575    Men with thirteen letters in their names should add one for good luck (F, SLC, 1958).

11576    It is bad luck to seat thirteen people at a dinner table or to invite thirteen people to a party (F, 21, SLC, 1964); "We went up the canyon when L was a baby (fifty years ago) and when we got up there, there were thirteen in the party and at the table, and you know there was members of that party wouldn't sit down at the table to make the thirteen" (F, Woods Cross, 1953).  Brown 6036f.

11577    The number thirteen on an apartment door is unlucky (M, SLC, 1961); If the number thirteen is on the door, the person who walks in will have bad luck (F, 43, SLC, 1964).

11578   The thirteenth floor is unlucky (F, 1957).

11579   Never stay on the thirteenth floor of a hotel. It will bring bad luck (M, 28, SLC, 1965); Hotels leave out the thirteenth floor. They go from twelve to fourteen (M, 30, SLC, 1964); Going to the thirteenth floor in a building is bad luck (F, 51, Centerfield, 1964).

11580   If the number of your hotel room is thirteen, this will result in bad luck (M, SLC, 1959). Brown 6038.

11581   Ships have no room numbered thirteen (M, 30, SLC, 1964).

11582   Riding chair number thirteen on the ski lift is unlucky (M, SLC, 1959).

11583   No airplane will have good luck if it has the number thirteen (M, 32, SLC, 1960).

## Numbers Twenty-One and Up

11584   If the number on your bus ticket adds up to twenty-one, you will be lucky all month (M, 25, Ogden, 1964).

11585   Twenty-three is an unlucky number (F, SLC, 1960). Brown 6027.

11586   When a lady is thirty-three years old she has to be very careful, because it is the age of bad luck (F, 45, Ja, SLC, 1963).

11587   When a man is forty-two years old he must be very careful, because it is the age of bad luck (F, 45, Ja, SLC, 1963).

## COUNTING

11588   It is bad luck to count to the number thirteen and stop (M, SLC, 1959).

11589   To count the numbers of persons in your dream foretells power, satisfied ambition, and dignity. Lucky numbers are three, seven, nine, eleven and seventeen (F, SLC, 1957).

11590   Take a dandelion and then blow the seeds. The seeds left tell what time it is (F, 21, SLC, 1963).

## COSMIC PHENOMENA

## MOON

## Various Notions

11591   The moon is made of cheese (M, SLC, 1964); . . . is full of cheese (F, 43, SLC, 1924); . . . is made of green cheese (Lehi, 1957). Brown 5911.

11592   In autumn when the moon is large and red-orange, it is said that there is blood on the moon (F, 20, Laketown, 1957); . . . it is an evil omen (F, 21, SLC, 1964).

11593   If you look at the new moon when it is in the following shape each month for a year, you will always be lucky (M, 28, Iran, SLC, 1963).

11594   If you can see the new moon very clearly, it means that you will have good luck throughout that lunar period (M, SLC, 1957).

11595   If you see a new moon straight in front of you, you will receive good luck the rest of the season (M, SLC, 1953); If you look at a full moon straight ahead . . . (F, 65, SLC, 1964).

11596   The time to break old habits is when there is a new moon (M, 72, cowboy, Willard, 1900s).

11597   It's good luck to look at the first new moon of the year from outdoors (F, 49, Norw, SLC, 1963).

11598   For good luck you should bow to the moon three times (M, SLC, 1960); . . . the new moon three times (M, 30, Farmington, 1950); . . . nine times (F, 70, Bountiful, 1900s).

11599   Don't go out at twelve on the night of a full moon (F, 15, Provo, 1964).

11600   If the old moon can be seen sitting in the lap of the new, harm will come (F, Vernal, 1959).

11601   When there is a full moon out, it predicts honor and happiness (M, SLC, 1958); Good luck comes with a full moon (F, 20, Ja, SLC, 1963); A full moon brings good luck to that person all of his life (M, 64, Bountiful, 1900).

11602   Never spit in the full moon (M, SLC, 1963).

11603   If a cow lies down all day, there will be a full moon at night (M, SLC, 1964).

11604   If the moon is full and at night the light shines across your bed, tomorrow will be a lucky day (F, 21, SLC, 1963).

11605   The waning moon is supposed to bring bad luck (M, 53, SLC, 1963).

11606   A crescent moon with prongs up brings good luck to the onlooker (F, 45, Murray, 1925).

11607   Pointing at the moon brings good luck (M, SLC, 1964). Cf. Brown 5947.

11608   Never let the moon shine in your eyes while in bed, or you will have bad luck (F, 1961).

11609   A ring around the moon is bad luck (F, SLC, 1962); . . . means a good night for evil (F, SLC, 1959); A moon with a cloudy ring around it means bad luck is coming (F, 44, SLC, 1964).

11610   A misty moon is a sign of ill luck (F, 27, SLC, 1963).

11611   Throw soup over your right shoulder in the light of a new moon, and you will have good luck (F, SLC, 1957).

11612    If you look at a new moon over your left shoulder, spill some salt (F, Vernal, 1960).

11613    You shouldn't let the full moon shine over your left shoulder, or you will have bad luck (F, 13, Orem, 1964).

11614    There is a man in the moon (F, SLC, 1957).

11615    A red moon is a sign of war (F, 49, SLC, 1929).

11616    No man will ever reach the moon (M, 82, Perry, 1950s).

11617    In the year 2000 the moon will fall to earth (M, SLC, 1964).

11618    All lost articles eventually end up on the moon (F, 21, SLC, 1964).

### Seeing the Moon over the Shoulder

11619    Seeing the moon over your right shoulder will bring you good luck for the following month (M, SLC, 1957). Cf. Brown 5920.

11620    When there's a quarter moon, if you look over your right shoulder, it's good luck (F, 10, Bountiful, 1964).

11621    If you first see the moon over the left shoulder, it means good luck (F, 27, SLC, 1940s).

11622    If the moon is seen over the left shoulder, this is a sign of a misfortune (M, 48, SLC, 1939).

11623    If you see the moon over your left shoulder on Halloween, it is bad luck (M, 46, Logan, 1927).

### Seeing the New and Full Moon over the Shoulder

11624    Never look over your shoulder at a full moon; it is a sign of bad luck (M, Ogden, 1961); . . . you will have bad luck for the rest of the month (F, 41, SLC, 1964).

11625    You should look at the new moon only over your right shoulder (F, 73, Ogden, 1964); . . . you will have good fortune (F, SLC, 1958).

11626    It is bad luck to see the new moon over your right shoulder (F, 78, SLC, 1964).

11627    Viewing the new moon over the left shoulder brings bad luck (F, Payson, 1925).

11628    If you see a new moon over the left shoulder, it brings good luck (F, 63, Monroe, 1964); . . . the full moon . . . (M, SLC).

11629    It is bad luck to see the new moon the first time over the left shoulder (F, 1959). Cf. Brown 5924.

11630    If a new moon's in the west, don't look at it over your left shoulder, or disaster will happen to the person who does (F, 83, Nephi, 1964).

11631    Many look at the new moon over their left shoulder with a mirror for good luck (F, 46, SLC, 1964).

11632    Never look at a full moon over your shoulder, or you will have bad luck (F, Eng, Hooper).

### Wishing on the Moon

11633    A wish made on a new moon will come true (M, SLC, 1961); . . . will come to pass (M, SLC). Cf. Brown 5914.

11634    If you make a wish on a new moon before speaking to someone, your wish will come true (F, SLC, 1958).

11635    On the night of a new moon, the boys bow three times to the moon, and the girls curtsy three times. They then make a wish (F, 42, SLC, 1935).

11636    When there is a full moon, you are supposed to be alone. You curtsy three times and your wish is supposed to come true (F, SLC, 1950).

11637    Look over your shoulder at a new moon, make a wish, and the wish will come true (F, SLC, 1900s); Look at the new moon over your right shoulder . . . (F, 54, Midway, 1925); . . . over your left shoulder . . . (F, SLC, 1961); Make a wish over your left shoulder on a full moon (F, Bountiful, 1960).

11638    When first viewing the new moon, it must be seen over the left shoulder, or you will lose your deepest wish. To regain the wish, spit over your left shoulder, look at the moon, and wish again (F, SLC, 1961). Cf. Brown 5923.

11639    If you see rings around the moon, you can wish on them and your wish will come true (F, 44, SLC, 1964).

### Wishing on the Moon with Money

11640    When wishing on the moon, jingle your coins and your wish will come true (F, SLC, 1961).

11641    Flip a coin at a full moon, make a wish, and it will come true (F, SLC, 1961).

11642    Turn a piece of silver over and make a wish when you see a full moon (M, 41, SLC); One must see the new moon for the first time over the left shoulder and turn the silver in one's pocket to have good luck (M, 53, SLC, 1963); Turn all the money in your pocket over on a new moon and wish . . . (M, Eng, Ogden, 1948).

11643    You'll have good luck if you sight the new moon over your left shoulder, having both hands full. You should also say: "Money, money, money!" (M, Draper, 1920).

### Seeing the Moon through Windows, Glass, Etc.

11644    To look at a new moon through a windowpane is believed to bring bad luck (F, 83, Venice, 1900); . . . through a new window . . . (M, SLC, 1959); . . . bad luck unless you throw a quarter over

your left shoulder (M, 24, SLC, 1964).
Cf. Brown 5942.

11645  It is bad luck to look at a full moon
through a window; you should be outside
(F, 18, SLC, 1964).

11646  Seeing the new moon through glass means
bad luck (F, Ir, SLC, 1960); . . . it
will bring much sorrow and distress to
you (F, SLC, 1961); . . . the first new
moon of the year . . . (F, 49, Norw,
SLC, 1963).

11647  Don't look at the new moon through
glasses (M, 52, Eng, SLC, 1963). Cf.
Brown 5944.

## Seeing the Moon through Trees and Clouds

11648  To see the new moon through the leafy
branches of a tree means bad luck
throughout the month (F, 21, SLC, 1958);
. . . sorrow (F, 26, SLC, 1964); Never
look at a full moon through the branches
of a tree (F, Fillmore, 1960).  Brown
5933ff.

11649  Never stand under a tree when the moon
is full.  A shadow of bad luck will
always follow you if you do (F, SLC,
1964).

11650  If a cloud crosses the moon at night, it
will cause bad luck (F, SLC, 1961).

## STARS

## Various Notions

11651  If you dig a well deep enough, then you
can see the stars in the daylight (M,
38, Logan, 1970).

11652  On dark, cloudy days, when the house dog
runs about the house whimpering and
crying, it means that the Great Mother
Dog is running in the sky (M, Ger, SLC,
1960).

11653  Stars rule life (F, SLC, 1957); Stars
influence a person's life (F, 43, SLC,
1964); There is a star in the sky that
looks out for you.  It's a lucky star
(M, 21, SLC, 1964).

11654  If the stars are not in your favor, you
will have a bad day.  If they are, you
will have a good day (M, SLC, 1959).

11655  Your future can be determined by the
stars (M, 30, Ogden, 1964).

11656  If you count seven stars for seven
consecutive nights, your wish on the
last night is sure to come true (F, SLC,
1960); If you count ten stars for ten
consecutive nights . . . (F, 22, SLC,
1964).  Brown 5960.

11657  If you can count all the stars in the
heavens, you will be blessed with
outstanding good fortune (F, 40, Cedar
City, 1940).

## Evening Star, the Big Dipper, Etc.

11658  Always wish on the evening star (F,
Murray, 1957); When the evening star is

the only star out, you can make a wish
and if you don't tell anyone your wish,
it will come true (M, Panguitch, 1950);
The evening star is lucky and brings
good fortune if wished upon in June (F,
20, SLC, 1964).

11659  The big dipper is full of happiness, and
as the world turns the happiness pours
out over the world (M, SLC, 1961); The
big dipper tips over and spills millions
of stars which spread the happiness over
the earth (F, SLC, 1961).  Heard on TV.

11660  Make a wish on the big dipper (F, Bear
River City, 1957).

11661  If you make a wish on the brightest star
in the sky, it will come true (F, 50,
1964).

11662  If you wish on a star, spit in the palm
of your hand and slap it, and it will
come true (M, SLC, 1957).

11663  If there is only one star in the sky,
you can wish on it (F, Tooele, 1964).

11664  If you wish on a star, and turn coins
over in your pocket, it will bring good
luck (F, 49, Gr, Midvale, 1964).

11665  If you wish the same wish for a week
under the stars, the wish will come true
(F, 84, Price, 1961).

11666  When you first look into the sky at
night, if you see one star alone, this
is bad luck.  But if you see two
together, it is good luck (M, 24, SLC,
1963).

11667  If you look at a star over your left
shoulder, your wish will come true (F,
20, SLC, 1963).

## Wishing on the First Star

11668  The first star seen in the sky at night
will bring you good luck (M, 74, SLC,
1900).

11669  The first star that appears in the sky
after dark has the power to make your
wish come true (F, SLC, 1920).

11670  The first star in the sky will make all
of your fondest dreams come true (F,
SLC, 1960).

11671  If you wish on the first star out at
night, you will get your wish (F, 67,
SLC, 1963); . . . if you tell anyone
what the wish is, it will not come true
(F, 25, SLC, 1948).  Brown 5953.

11672  If you're the first member of a group to
see the first star at night, your wish
will come true (M, 20, SLC, 1955).

11673  Make a wish on the first star you see in
the night, and then find another before
looking at that same one, and your wish
will come true (F, Brigham City, 1960).

11674  Throw three kisses on the first star you
see at night, don't look at it again,
and your wish will come true (F, 40,
SLC, 1920s).  Cf. Brown 5957.

11675  The first star you see in the evening
say:

Star light, star bright,
First star I see tonight;
I wish I may, I wish I might,
Have the wish I wish tonight.
(F, 70, SLC, 1964); . . . grant the wish
I wish tonight (F, 54, Midvale, 1964).
Brown 5956.

### Falling Stars, Meteors

11676   To see a falling star is good luck (F, Kaysville, 1958).

11677   A shooting star is a good omen (F, SLC, 1963).

11678   When you see a falling star, whatever you are thinking will come to pass (M, 25, SLC, 1942).

11679   Count to ten before the light of a falling star goes out and you will have good luck (F, 67, Farmington, 1927).

11680   If you see a falling star and you can say, "Money, money, my five cents," before the star fades, you'll have good luck (M, Magna); . . . the more times you can say "Money, money, money" while watching the falling star, the more good fortune you will get (F, 74, SLC, 1964).

11681   If you see a star fall and tell someone, you will have bad luck (F, SLC, 1960). Cf. Brown 5965.

11682   Point at or speak of a shooting star, and you'll lose your next wish (M, 45, Centerville). Cf. Brown 5966.

11683   A man can predict good fortune if he sees the paths of two falling stars cross (M, 72, Willard, 1920s).

11684   If you see a meteor flashing across the sky, you will have sudden short-lived success (M, SLC, 1961).

11685   Meteors are believed to foretell a great event (M, SLC, 1959).

11686   When people see a meteor in the sky, destruction of the world will follow in its path (F, Swiss, SLC, 1965). Cf. Brown 5904f.

### Wishing on Falling Stars

11687   Make a wish upon a falling star, and your wish will come true (F, 20, SLC, 1958); . . . it will come true within a month (F, 50, Murray, 1925).

11688   If you see a falling star, shut your eyes and make a wish. As long as you don't tell your wish, it will come true (F, SLC, 1958).

11689   If you wish on a falling star and tell the wish, it is bad luck (M, 19, SLC, 1963).

11690   If you see a falling star, make a wish before it fades, and your wish will come true (F, 50, W. Jordan, 1964); . . . before it hits the ground . . . (F, 39, SLC, 1964). Brown 5963f.

11691   You must make a wish when a star passes overhead, or you will soon be plagued by bad luck (F, 57, Crescent, 1930); . . . you will be unlucky all the year (F, 76, SLC).

11692   If you see a falling star, you get three wishes (F, Norw, SLC, 1960); . . . ask for three wishes and they will come true (F, SLC, 1963).

11693   When you see a falling star wish for money (F, 21, Bountiful, 1957).

11694   If you wish on a falling star while holding hands with the person you love, the wish will come true (F, SLC).

11695   When you see a shooting star, make a wish and kiss the person you're with, and your wish will come true (F, 50, Ogden, 1963).

11696   Lovers who see a shooting star and wish for health, wealth, and happiness will have their wish fulfilled (F, SLC, 1958).

11697   If you make a wish when you see a meteor and your wish is said before the meteor disappears, your wish will come true (F, SLC, 1945).

### COMETS

11698   Falling comets are a sign of the Lord's anger (M, 34, SLC, 1956).

11699   Comets are malevolent vagabonds who prowl about the heavens and bestow evil on anyone who sees them (F, Heber, 1959).

11700   A comet seen in the sky is a forewarning that bad things will follow (M, SLC); . . . is a sign of disaster (M, 19, SLC, 1964). Brown 5908.

11701   A comet is a sign of a coming war (M, SLC, 1959). Brown 5907.

### SUN, SUNSET

11702   It is real bad luck to look at the sun (M, 20, SLC, 1964).

11703   One can see the sun dance on Easter morning if one goes up on a hill just as the sun rises (F, Norw, SLC, 1959).

11704   If you look at the sun over your left shoulder, something terrible is going to happen (M, 18, Magna, 1963).

11705   The sun rises as a result of the animals' call (F, SLC, 1963).

11706   Some Indian tribes believe that the sun is a great god, the moon is his wife, and the stars are the children (F, SLC, 1957).

11707   The sun shines every Saturday but three during the year (M, SLC, 1935). Cf. Brown 6247f.

11708   A really blood red sunset indicates the approach of a coming war (blood will flow) (F, 47, Swiss, SLC, 1965); . . . there is a bloody fight up there (F, Ogden, 1958).

11709 The sun hides its face before any great sorrow or a national disaster (F, 19, SLC, 1963).

11710 When the sun doesn't shine, the end of the world is near (M, SLC, 1950).

CLOUDS, SKY, RAINBOW

11711 If you see a silver lining in the sky, it means good luck will follow (F, 45, SLC, 1963).

11712 A rainbow is a bridge between heaven and earth (F, 60, Ogden, 1910).

11713 Rainbows bring good luck (M, 20, SLC, 1950).

11714 Wishing on a rainbow brings good luck (F, 40, Sandy, 1937). Brown 5968.

11715 A rainbow means that your plan is approved and will be successful (F, 70, Provo, 1900).

11716 It is bad luck to point at a rainbow (F, 20, SLC, 1963).

11717 The rainbow is a sign foretelling war (F, 50, SLC, 1963).

11718 No rainbow seen in one year means the year will come to an end (M, 37, SLC, 1965).

ECLIPSE

11719 An eclipse is the pursuit of the sun and moon by two enormous wolves who now and then nearly succeed in devouring our chief sources of light (M, 53, SLC, 1963).

11720 An eclipse is caused by an enormous bear that is trying to devour the sun and now and then nearly succeeds in doing it (M, 20, SLC, 1950s).

11721 The solar eclipse is caused by a great dragon attempting to swallow the sun (M, Vernal, 1959).

11722 An eclipse of the sun means the destruction of the world (F, SLC, 1959).

11723 If there is an eclipse of the moon on Good Friday, the world will have a time of great disaster (SLC, 1968). Cf. Brown 5909.

11724 When there is an eclipse, there is going to be a war (F, Gr, SLC, 1964); The world is going to end in 1972 because of the eclipse of the sun at that time (M, 19, SLC, 1959).

AURORA BOREALIS

11725 The northern lights change color if you honk your car horn (M, 25, SLC, 1964).

11726 The northern lights will change colors the faster you drive into them (M, 25, SLC, 1964).

THE ZODIAC

11727 The positions of the sun, moon, stars, and planets influence human life (M, 20, SLC, 1959); . . . influence one's destiny (F, 62, Sandy, 1920); . . . govern one's life (F, 46, SLC, 1931).

11728 Astrologers can predict the future through the zodiac (M, Vernal, 1959).

11729 Reading of one's horoscope determines whether one's day is going to be good or not (F, 20, SLC, 1954).

11730 Rely on astrologers; after all, they predicted the crash in the stock market of 1929 (F, 94, SLC, 1964).

MISCELLANEOUS

11731 Electricity from lightning is sparks from outer space (M, SLC, 1964).

11732 The world will be destroyed because of a catastrophe caused by the planets (F, 1959).

11733 World War Two will be a product of outer space intrusion (M, SLC, 1941). (WWIII? --Eds.)

11734 If an atomic bomb explodes, there is no way to escape the radiation. It can penetrate anything (M, 20, SLC, 1940s).

TIMES, DAYS, HOLIDAYS

TIME

Various Notions

11735 Your lucky day is determined by the number of stars in the sky the day of your birth (M, SLC, 1961).

11736 "I believe that when I go to school that if there are songs on the radio that I like, it will be a good day. If the songs aren't good, the day will be lousy" (F, SLC, 1969).

11737 It's unlucky to show gaiety as the day begins when nothing has been done to merit it (M, SLC, 1959).

11738 Twelve o'clock midnight is a bad hour (F, 80, Eng, Midvale).

11739 If there is a sudden silence in a crowded room, it means it is either twenty minutes before or after the hour (M, Ogden, 1961); If there is a sudden silence in a group talking together, someone will probably say: "It must be twenty minutes after." This usually refers to the death of Abraham Lincoln. He was believed to have died at 8:20 (F, Midvale, 1963).

11740 If you can step on your shadow, it is noon (M, 41, SLC, 1964); . . . the head of your own shadow . . . (F, SLC, 1959).

11741 You can tell time by the size of a cat's pupils (F, SLC, 1959).

## DAYS OF THE WEEK

### Monday

11742    As goes Monday so will go the rest of the week (M, 84, Centerville). Cf. Brown 5974, 5990.

11743    If you are in a bad humor on Monday, you will be in bad humor all week long (M, SLC, 1961).

11744    Monday is a day of good omen (M, SLC, 1959); . . . is a lucky day for men (F, SLC).

11745    Monday is an unlucky day for all women who are born in April (M, 48, Vernal, 1933).

11746    Don't let a woman in your house on Monday, because it brings bad luck (F, 80, SLC, 1961).

### Tuesday

11747    Tuesday is one of the best days to take up a new post if you are a woman (F, Ir, SLC).

11748    No unordinary tasks should be begun on Tuesday. It is an unlucky day, and things will turn out bad (F, 71, Gr, SLC, 1964).

11749    Don't start anything on Tuesday. Any big job that you might start will be unsuccessful (F, Gr, SLC, 1962).

11750    If you begin something on Tuesday, you will never finish it (F, Gr, W. Jordan, 1920).

### Thursday

11751    You don't start anything on Thursday. Any big job that you might start will be unsuccessful (F, Gr, SLC, 1962).

11752    Thursday has one lucky hour, namely, the hour before the sun rises (M, 20, Ogden, 1957).

### Friday

11753    Friday is the unlucky day of the week (M, SLC, 1961); Friday is the most unlucky day of the week (F, Woods Cross, 1953). Brown 5994.

11754    The first Friday of each month tells you what the rest of the Fridays will be for that month (M, 47, SLC, 1965).

11755    Well begun is half done, but never begin on Friday (F, SLC); Don't ever start anything on Friday, because it brings bad luck (F, 50, SLC, 1909); Never start a new task on Friday (F, 1959). Brown 5996.

11756    Never start anything on Friday, because you will never finish it (F, SLC, 1959); A new task begun on Friday will never be finished successfully (F, 50, Lark, 1950). Brown 5997.

11757    Start things on Friday and it will take you six weeks to finish (M, Clearfield, 1959). Cf. Brown 5999.

11758    Fridays are the best days to take up a new post if you are a woman (F, Ir, SLC, 1960).

11759    Friday is an unlucky day for all women born in April (M, 48, Vernal, 1933).

11760    Friday is always the fairest or foulest (F, 56, Murray, 1919). Brown 5993.

### Saturday

11761    You should never start a project on a Saturday (M, 44, Provo, 1953).

11762    Anything started on Saturday will not be completed (F, SLC, 1960); . . . this means to sew a dress, start your vacation, etc. (F, Gr, SLC, 1962); If you begin anything Saturday, it must be finished that day, or it will never get finished (M, SLC, 1961). Cf. Brown 6005.

11763    On Saturday the sun always shines if only for a moment (F, 17, SLC, 1961).

### Sunday

11764    If you break anything Sunday, you will continue to do so every day of the week, or as you commence Sunday, so you will go through the week (F, 1961).

11765    Sundays are the luckiest days for men (F, Ir, SLC, 1960).

11766    If you go to a show on Sunday, the show house will burn down (F, Bountiful, 1960).

11767    Sunday is the day Noah's flood came (M, SLC, 1952).

11768    Don't do anything but rest on Sundays (F, SLC, 1959).

11769    "Since the Bible says to rest on the seventh day, my grandmother and other people felt that if they did work on Sunday, the work would be wrong or poorly done, and they would only have to do it over on Monday" (F, Spanish Fork, 1900).

## DAYS OF THE MONTH

11770    It is bad luck to trust women on the odd days of the month (M, SLC, 1961).

11771    If the first day of the month is a good day, the rest of the month will be good and vice versa (M, Gr, SLC).

11772    Say "White rabbit" as soon as you wake up on the first day of the month, and you'll have good luck for the rest of the month (F, Bear River City, 1957); The first day of the month is "Rabbit-rabbit" day. First thing in the morning you jump up and down on your bed yelling "Rabbit, rabbit," and then the rest of the day before speaking to anyone you must say "Rabbit, rabbit" (F, SLC, 1969); On March 1 when you wake up you say "White rabbit," three times, and you'll have good luck the rest of the year (M, 52, Eng, SLC, 1963).

11773  If something terrible happens on the eleventh of any day of the month, something terrible will happen the eleventh of the next month (F, 15, Orem).

11774  The thirteenth of each month brings bad luck (M, 80, SLC, 1964); Do not start any new work on the thirteenth day of each month no matter the day of the week, or you will have bad luck (M, 63, Russ, SLC, 1964).

11775  Astronomers believe January 1, 2, 4, 5, 10, 15, 17, 29 are unlucky days (M, SLC, 1961).

11776  If you want to borrow something, the last three days in March or the first three in February are the best (F, SLC, 1959).

11777  February 19, 1943 was a witches' day, and so all February 19th's are bad luck (M, SLC, 1953).

11778  Beware the Ides of March. This day is unlucky (M, 52, SLC, 1964); "The fifteenth day of March is a bad day for me. For two years I have had an automobile accident on that day" (F, 20, SLC, 1958).

11779  Circles are drawn around dates on a calendar for good luck (M, SLC, 1959).

11780  Don't tear off the calendar page of the month passing until the first of the next month, or you will have bad luck (F, SLC, 1960).

11781  It is bad luck to put up a new calendar before the sunup on New Year's Day (F, Farmington, 1945).

## Friday the Thirteenth

11782  One must be cautious on Friday the thirteenth (F, Ir, SLC, 1960).

11783  Black Friday or Friday the thirteenth is feared to bring bad luck (F, Eng, SLC); . . . is the unluckiest day of the year (M, SLC, 1964); . . . is a day of misfortune (F, SLC, 1964).

11784  Friday the thirteenth should be spent in bed, especially if it is your birthday (F, 45, SLC, 1930s); Get out of bed on the wrong side, then Friday the thirteenth won't bring so much bad luck (F, SLC, 1964); To prevent bad luck you should stay in your house on . . . (F, 48, American Fork, 1960).

11785  Anything undertaken on Friday the thirteenth is doomed to fail (F, 73, SLC, 1930); . . . is an unlucky day for all ventures (M, Tooele, 1964); . . . everything you do on that day will go wrong (F, Kanab, 1960); . . . everything you do will end in trouble (M, SLC, 1959); If you start a project on Friday the thirteenth, you will never live to finish it (F, 67, Eng, SLC, 1913). Brown 5995.

11786  Never do anything out of the ordinary on Friday the thirteenth, for that day is bad luck (M, Murray, 1958); . . . unfavorable for any important venture (M, SLC, 1945).

11787  Don't go swimming on Friday the thirteenth (F, SLC, 1959).

11788  It is bad luck to start a project on a Friday, or on the thirteenth day of the month (M, Eng, SLC).

11789  Friday the thirteenth is an unlucky day; so keep your fingers crossed (F, 20, SLC, 1963); . . . is a doubly unlucky day. If you do not have your fingers crossed, a person may say "Jinx on you," and you will then have to do any deed or favor they ask you to (F, SLC, 1958).

11790  On Friday the thirteenth knock on wood to prevent bad luck (F, SLC, 1959).

11791  If you try anything involving cheating on Friday the thirteenth, you will surely have bad luck (M, 23, SLC, 1964).

11792  Don't make a wish on Friday the thirteenth (M, 12, Provo, 1964).

## SPECIAL DAYS AND HOLIDAYS

### New Year's

11793  Bells are rung on New Year's Eve to signify the death of the old year (M, SLC, 1959).

11794  After the New Year whistle blows, go outside and bring something in and you will have a prosperous year (M, SLC, 1958).

11795  The last drink taken from a bottle on New Year's Eve will bring good luck to the person who gets it (M, 46, SLC, 1963).

11796  Sweeping out the old at the stroke of twelve on New Year's Eve and sweeping in the new will bring good luck (F, 21, SLC, 1950). Cf. Brown 6023.

11797  As the clock strikes twelve on New Year's Eve, you should open the door of your home so the old year may leave and the new year may come in (F, Ir, Richfield, 1908); . . . open all the windows and doors in the house . . . (F, 50, Eng, Hyrum); At the hour of midnight on December 31, you should open the front and then open the back door of your house to let in the new year and let the old one out (M, 20, Jordan, 1963).

11798  Putting a bowl outside on New Year's will mean that the New Year's baby will fill it (F, 36, SLC, 1964).

11799  On New Year's Eve at midnight always take the old year out the door and go completely around the house and bring the new year in (F, Weber Co).

11800  If you open your windows on New Year's Eve, the bad luck goes out and the good luck comes in (F, SLC, 1956). Heard on TV.

11801  On New Year's Eve the family was ushered out of the house and at the stroke of midnight, in order to insure good luck, the patriarch of the family entered through the front door and exited by the back door (F, 20, SLC, 1967); After twelve o'clock midnight on New Year's Eve the father must be the first person to enter the home from the outside, for he is believed to be lucky, and bring good luck to the home (F, Gr, SLC, 1961).

11802    Every New Year's Eve a girl's grandfather used to run around the house three times with a loaf of bread under each arm. This was supposed to protect his home during the coming year (F, 18, SLC, 1963); . . . to insure the family food for the next year (F, 48, SLC, 1964).

11803    Every New Year's everyone took a piece of coal out the back door and came around and through the front door. It was bad luck not to do so, and you would have a bad year (F, Provo).

11804    On New Year's Day a pomegranate is supposed to be rolled throughout the house in closets and rooms. This insures that the rooms and closets will be filled with riches just as full as the pomegranate. The pomegranate is rolled around by the feet of the father (F, Gr, Magna, 1961).

11805    Someone blonde must open the door to let in the New Year, or you will have bad luck (F, SLC, 1958).

11806    On New Year's morning if a woman calls on the telephone or comes to the door, you should either hang up or not let her in, because it means that you will have bad luck for the rest of the year. However, it is perfectly all right if a man calls on the phone or comes to the door (F, Bountiful, 1971).

11807    If a man is the first person to wish you a happy New Year, the entire year will be filled with good luck (F, SLC, 1969).

11808    If you bring in new things to your home on New Year's Eve, you will insure one year of good luck (M, 28, SLC, 1963); If anything comes into your house that's new on New Year's, it is good luck (F, 51, Ja, SLC, 1963).

11809    On New Year's Eve bring a rock in the house. This will bring a year of prosperity (M, 22, SLC, 1962).

11810    At New Year's the father would knock each of his children on the forehead lightly with a rock and say "Happy New Year." This meant that the rock was strong and his children would be also (F, Gr, SLC, 1962).

11811    The father of the house is supposed to carry in his pocket the largest rock he can find, and walk around his house on New Year's Day. And in and out of every room in his house. This is supposed to insure that the house will be rich in money, and through the year the pocket will be as heavy with money as the rock he carries (F, Gr, Magna, 1961).

11812    On New Year's take anything into a house, but don't take it out; wait until the next morning. You'll have a better year (F, 60, Midvale, 1910).

11813    What one does during New Year's Eve he will be doing for the rest of the year (F, SLC, 1938); Whatever you do on the first day of the year, you'll do all year (F, Copperton). Brown 5978.

11814    Everything must be in order on New Year's Eve, or it will not be in order for that following year (F, 73, Weber Co, 1964).

11815    If you're unhappy on New Year's Day, you'll be unhappy all year (F, SLC, 1957).

11816    If you work on New Year's, it means you will labor hard all the coming year (M, SLC, 1961). Cf. Brown 5979.

11817    Don't go outside on New Year's Day until you have something to go out for, or you'll go every day without something to go for (M, 84, Centerville).

11818    If you bathe on New Year's Day, you will be clean for the whole year (F, Spring Glen, 1959).

11819    Don't spend money on New Year's Day, and you will have money the year-round (F, 60, Midvale, 1910).

11820    Japanese people believe that if they pay all of their bills on New Year's Day, they will have good luck and fortune during the coming new year (M, 24, Logan, 1971).

11821    It's very good luck to receive money on the very first day of the year before you pay out any (F, 49, Norw, SLC, 1963).

11822    When it strikes twelve midnight and the change of the year, you must open the water from the faucet to have the year come clear, quick and good like water from the faucet (F, Gr, SLC, 1957); . . . every faucet in the house should be running. If this is done, everyone in the house will have good luck and evil will flow away from them and their home (F, Gr, Tooele, 1961).

11823    To let a fire die on New Year's Eve is very bad luck (F, Ogden, 1920); If you leave ashes in a stove or fireplace past twelve midnight on December 31, you will have bad luck in the new year (F, 75, SLC, 1898).

11824    If on New Year's Day you greet all your friends, your year will be good (M, 18, SLC, 1963).

11825    If you see a tall dark man on New Year's Day, you will have bad luck (F, 18, SLC, 1964).

11826    If the first people you see out on the street on New Year's Day are old, it means bad luck (F, Swiss, SLC, 1957).

11827    If a chimney sweep crosses your path on New Year's Day, it brings good luck (M, SLC, 1957); If you see a chimney sweep on New Year's Day, the whole year will be happy and gay (F, 47, Swiss, SLC, 1965).

11828    If you see a goat the first of the year, there will be no good year (M, 33, Gr, SLC, 1963).

11829 If you give anything away on New Year's Eve, you will have one year of bad luck (M, 28, Iran, SLC, 1963).

11830 At the stroke of twelve on New Year's Eve you stand on chairs, holding all your cash, the more the better, and then jump. This brings good luck (F, 49, Norw, SLC, 1963).

11831 For New Year's usually the father will give his children a silver dollar and a sweet candy. This means that you will be sweet and happy (F, Gr, SLC, 1962).

11832 On New Year's Day silver coins should be given to all who visit you that day. This is for good luck (F, Gr, 42, SLC, 1964).

11833 If someone places a bundle of hay in your arms on New Year's Day, you will have lots of good luck during the year (M, Ir, SLC, 1957).

11834 If you put a cabbage over your door on New Year's Day, it will bring you good luck (F, SLC, 1925).

11835 For New Year's the people put cotton in the toe of their shoes for good luck (F, Gr, SLC, 1962).

11836 Throw rabbits up the chimney on the New Year to bring good luck (M, Ir, SLC).

11837 Lobsters are used as a plate of decoration when celebrating an occasion such as New Year's. This is to wish for good luck. If, however, one of its antennae is broken off, bad luck will come (F, 23, Ja, SLC).

11838 On New Year's seeing a turtle and a crane brings good luck. People believe the turtle lives one million years and the crane one thousand years (F, 51, Ja, SLC, 1963).

11839 On New Year's dreaming of Mt. Fujiyama, a hawk and an eggplant brings good luck (F, 51, Ja, SLC, 1963).

11840 Six days after New Year's (Epiphany), a custom in Greece and many towns in America is to throw a cross into a river, and have all the boys dive for it. Whoever gets it is accorded great honor and will be the luckiest person for the year (F, Gr, SLC, 1962).

## ST. PATRICK'S DAY

11841 It is lucky and proper to wear something green or something with green in it on St. Patrick's Day (M, SLC, 1959); It is bad luck not to wear something green on St. Patrick's Day (F, Springville, 1964).

11842 If you don't wear green on St. Patrick's Day, everyone can pinch you (F, SLC, 1959); . . . one of your playfellows will say, "Greenie on you!" (M, SLC, 1920).

11843 On St. Patrick's Day, if you wear an item of red, this indicates that you will get a kiss from each boy (F, 21, SLC, 1963).

11844 Growing a beard for St. Patrick's Day means good luck (M, 45, SLC, 1901).

## GOOD FRIDAY, EASTER

11845 You should never hammer or pin anything on Good Friday, because it means you are piercing Christ (F, Gr, SLC, 1957).

11846 The sun does not shine brightly on Good Friday (M, 47, Lindon, 1947).

11847 If Easter falls in March, it will be a bad luck year (M, 62, SLC, 1964).

11848 Rabbits lay eggs on Easter (M, 22, SLC, 1964).

11849 On Easter a good bunny rabbit, commonly known as the Easter Bunny, hops about from house to house delivering gaily colored eggs (M, SLC, 1964); . . . hides eggs in the yard for the children to find (F, 24, SLC, 1964).

11850 On Easter morning all the children in the family have to hide in the bedroom while the Easter Bunny comes and leaves them lots of goodies. Then the parents hurry to hide the presents around the living room, and the kiddies all come out and hunt for their own things (F, 21, SLC, 1963); . . . bunny rabbits bring candy and eggs (F, SLC, 1958).

11851 Rolling eggs or finding eggs at Easter time is a sign of good luck (F, 43, Logan, 1935).

11852 For Easter the Greek people paint all of their Easter eggs red, to stand for happiness (F, Gr, SLC, 1962); . . . the eggs are dyed red, and are dyed only on Holy Thursday or Saturday. Any other day is considered bad luck (F, 42, Gr, SLC, 1964).

11853 Unless you wear something on Easter Sunday which is new, you will be unlucky the following year (F, SLC, 1958).

11854 Wear three new things on Easter and you will have good luck all year (F, 16, SLC, 1964).

11855 If you don't wear new clothes on Easter, then the birds will mess on you sometime during that day (F, 19, Murray, 1964).

11856 The bells fly to Rome for Lent, dispersing goodies on their return home in time for Easter (M, 22, SLC, 1963). (The informant had likely heard this interesting belief in folk tradition. The muffling of church bells from Maunday Thursday until Holy Saturday is explained by the notion that the bells have gone to Rome to be blessed and renewed. In this somewhat battered version, not only is the period widened to include the whole Lenten season, but festive elements are introduced more in keeping with Easter Monday than Easter proper. --Eds.)

11857 If you look at the sun through a piece of smoked glass on Easter Sunday morning, you will see the sun shouting in praise of the risen Lord (M, 30, SLC, 1950).

11858 In Easter services it is considered good luck to carry home a lighted candle from the Resurrection services, held always at midnight on Saturday (M, 66, Gr, SLC, 1963).

11859 At Easter time the custom is to light candles in church the night of the event when Christ rises.  If you can take your candles from church to home still lit, you will have good luck (F, Gr, SLC, 1962).

11860 The first Monday after Easter Sunday, if you bathe in a brook, you will begin a new life (M, 88, Ger, SLC, 1963).

11861 The first Monday after Easter Sunday, before the children wake up, the parents go break off a new willow switch and then go wake the children up.  They feel since they have given so much to their children, this is the one day of the year they have a right to get something from them (M, 88, Ger, SLC, 1963).

## CHRISTMAS

11862 When a fly comes into the house at Christmas time, it is called the "Christmas fly" and is considered to bring good luck (F, 92, SLC, 1963).

11863 To give a person a light on Christmas Day will bring bad luck (M, 31, Ogden, 1964).  Cf. Brown 3017.

11864 It's bad luck to sing Christmas carols before November (F, 20, SLC, 1964).

11865 Dress up between Christmas and New Year's, and if you can frighten someone, you will have a good year (F, Ger, SLC, 1965).

11866 Drawing water from a well on Christmas means happiness for oneself and family for the coming year (F, Ir, SLC, 1960).

11867 During Christmas and New Year's holidays, put a piece of lettuce over the front doorway for good luck (F, 18, SLC, 1961).

11868 If the wine ferments in the barrels on Christmas night, it means a good year will follow (F, SLC, 1960).

11869 Light a bayberry candle at midnight Christmas Day and allow it to burn until the midnight of New Year's Day, and you will have good luck the entire year (F, SLC, 1961).

11870 During the last week of this forty-day fast at Christmas, you must not eat oil. Neither may you use it on your food (F, Gr, SLC, 1962).

11871 Don't hang any curtains a week before Christmas; you'll have an unhappy Christmas (M, SLC, 1952).

11872 If the weather is bad on Christmas Day, it will be a lean year (F, Norw, SLC, 1959).

## Christmas Decorations and Greens, Christmas Tree and Yule Log

11873 To take holly into the house before Christmas Eve is bad luck (F, 20, SLC, 1961).

11874 It will bring bad luck to hang up mistletoe in the house before Christmas Eve (F, 81, SLC, 1964); . . . if you do, you will never catch anyone under it (M, 19, Butler, 1963).

11875 At Christmas time you have to kiss a person who stands under mistletoe, or you won't be around next year (F, 43, SLC, 1964).

11876 Burning logs at Christmas time brings peace to the home (M, SLC, 1961).

11877 The yule log must be kept lit during the night, or bad luck will follow for the coming year if it goes out (F, Eng, SLC, 1957).

11878 Save some of the embers of the Twelfth Night fire to use to start the fire next Christmas.  This will bring good luck (F, Eng, SLC, 1910).

11879 Blue lights on Christmas trees mean Christmas presents for everyone will be scarce (M, Provo, 1959).

11880 Once a Christmas tree is brought into a house, it shouldn't be taken out, it should be cut and burned inside.  It is bad luck if the tree is taken out (F, 34, Sandy, 1939).

11881 You are defying God if you burn your Christmas tree (F, 59, SLC, 1960); Christmas greens must not be burned but must be thrown away, or else bad luck will befall you (M, SLC, 1959).

11882 It's bad luck to sit under a Christmas tree (M, 95, SLC, 1964).

11883 Take the Christmas tree out before New Year's Day, and you will have good luck (F, SLC, 1964).

11884 Taking the Christmas tree out of the house before New Year's Day will mean bad luck for the house (F, Midvale, 1928); You must have the Christmas tree down before the New Year, or you'll have bad luck from the previous year (F, 51, Layton, 1963); If you leave your Christmas tree up after January, you'll not get another tree for five years (F, 19, Provo, 1959).  Brown 6020.

11885 Christmas trees should be taken down before the sixth of January, or bad luck will follow (M, SLC, 1956).

11886 It's bad luck to keep Christmas decorations up past New Year's Day (M, Ogden, 1961); Never keep Christmas decoration up after the twelfth day after Christmas (M, SLC, 1963); If your decorations are not down by January 6, your house will have bad luck all the year (F, SLC, 1967); It is unlucky to keep Christmas decorations hanging after Ground Hog Day (F, SLC, 1965).  Cf. Brown 6021.

Christmas Gifts, Santa Claus

11887   If you don't put out porridge for Santa
        Claus, he will leave no toys (F, 67,
        SLC, 1963); Refreshments should be left
        on the table for Santa Claus (F, Bear
        River City, 1957).

11888   Santa Claus watches all little girls and
        boys all year round and when Christmas
        comes, he gives them all presents (F,
        44, Eng, SLC, 1964).

11889   Putting a shoe in the window for twelve
        days before Christmas brings a gift from
        the Christmas spirit (F, Ger, 71, Magna,
        1964).

11890   If a child isn't good before Christmas,
        Santa Claus will leave sticks in his
        stocking (F, Bear River City, 1957);
        . . . coal and sticks . . . (F, SLC,
        1957); . . . a shovel of coal . . . (F,
        51, SLC, 1964).

11891   If you break the string on your
        Christmas presents, you have to do the
        day's dishes (M, 23, SLC, 1964).

11892   Trimming a Christmas tree under the
        light of the setting sun means Santa
        won't come to your house (M, 22, SLC,
        1958).

11893   Santa Claus and his reindeer fly through
        the sky with a sleigh (F, SLC, 1943).

11894   If a child throws his Christmas list
        into the fire and the back door opens,
        it means he will get all of the things
        on the list (F, SLC, 1948).

11895   It is luckier to receive money on
        Christmas than to give it (F, Ir, SLC,
        1960).

ANIMALS AT CHRISTMAS

11896   If there are many birds in the corn
        stalks on Christmas Eve, it indicates a
        prosperous year (F, SLC, 1935).

11897   At midnight on Christmas Eve all the
        animals can speak (F, 53, Ir, SLC,
        1965).  Cf. Brown 6015.

11898   Every Christmas Eve all the animals in
        the field will kneel down at midnight
        (M, Woods Cross, 1958); Cows in the
        stalls rise to their knees and bow on
        Christmas and Easter (F, 54, SLC, 1964);
        At midnight on Christmas Eve cattle will
        kneel and face the east (M, SLC, 1961).
        Cf. Brown 6012.

11899   At midnight on Christmas Eve the cattle
        bow down in honor of Christ (F, 44, SLC,
        1964); Oxen in their stalls go down on
        their knees in an attitude of devotion
        (F, Logan, 1935).

11900   Cows kneel at midnight on the Eve of Old
        Christmas (M, SLC, 1963).  Brown 6013.

VARIOUS HOLIDAYS

11901   If you try to April Fool someone on
        April 2nd, you're the biggest fool there
        ever was (F, 23, SLC).

11902   To lose one's temper at a practical joke
        on April Fool's Day will bring bad luck
        (F, 46, SLC, 1938).

11903   Every Wednesday after the first Tuesday
        of the seventh month never take a
        shower.  It will make the whole year bad
        (M, 20, SLC, 1948).

11904   Every July 24th the Mormons sharpen
        their horns on the mulberry bush (F, 19,
        SLC, 1965).

11905   July 29 is the luckiest day in the whole
        year (F, Springville, 1964).

11906   Orange and black should only be worn on
        Halloween (F, 19, SLC, 1964).

11907   You must always tell what you're
        thankful for on Thanksgiving (F, Murray,
        1957).

# XII
# Animals, Animal Husbandry

ANIMALS

## Various Notions

11908  Certain types of men and women can change themselves into animals (F, SLC, 1959).

11909  Always keep a part of wild animals that you kill such as teeth, foot, horn, etc., and you will take a part of the courage of that animal (M, 51, Bountiful, 1964).

11910  The intelligence of an animal is in proportion to its bodily heat (M, SLC, 1959).

11911  The wildlife animals have two lives to live (M, Provo, 1957).

11912  Animals that live in the ground usually have short fur (M, SLC, 1964).

11913  If an animal likes a certain person, that person is all right (F, 45, Ja, SLC, 1963).

11914  If you eat a thimble full of salt on Halloween night and go out to the barnyard at midnight, you can understand the language of the animals (F, SLC, 1926).

11915  If you see a dead animal, spit over your little finger so that you may avoid bad luck (SLC, 1959).

11916  A wild animal will never attack a person that lies down as if he is dead (M, SLC, 1950).

11917  If a man takes precautions against wild animals, they will come to test his precautions (M, 72, Willard, 1900s).

11918  A hair from certain animals brings bad luck (F, 26, Finn, Morgan, 1965).

CATS

## Various Notions

11919  A cat has nine lives (F, 12, Orem, 1964); Do not kill a cat for they have nine lives (M, 91, S. Jordan, 1964); . . . seven lives (M, SLC, 1959). Brown 7157.

11920  A cat that never purrs is as dangerous as a snake (F, SLC, 1959).

11921  If you pick up a cat and hold it by its tail, its eyes will fall out (M, 58, Logan, 1928).

11922  Look into the eyes of a cat. If the pupils are larger than usual, it is good luck (F, 23, SLC, 1964).

11923  Cats can see apparitions (M, SLC, 1964). Read in the Salt Lake Tribune.

11924  A cat draws lightning (F, 28, SLC, 1948).

11925  If a cat catches and eats a robin, it will die shortly (F, 88, W. Jordan, 1885).

11926  If you spit on a cat, it will avenge itself, and you will have bad luck (F, SLC, 1959).

11927  It's bad luck to stroke a cat backwards and then touch something made of metal (M, 54, SLC, 1965).

11928  One who stops a cat from singing will lose their next venture (F, SLC, 1959).

11929  It is unlucky to let anything touch a cat's ear (M, SLC, 1959).

11930  If a cat licks your face, expect much trouble in the near future (F, SLC, 1959).

11931  The Irish are extremely superstitious-- the beliefs about cats probably come from the Irish (F, Woods Cross, 1953).

11932  Never watch a cat fight another cat, or you will have bad luck (M, Logan, 1963).

11933  If two cats fight on the porch at night, they will bring good luck (M, SLC, 1957).

11934  It is bad luck to wake a sleeping cat (F, 62, SLC, 1964).

11935  Never carry a cat across running water if you want to have good luck. It will ruin your life (F, 1959).

11936  It is very bad luck to be photographed with a cat (M, 18, SLC, 1964).

11937  To kill a cat will bring some misfortune (F, Sandy, 1957); . . . seven years of bad luck (F, Sandy, 1957); . . . bad luck for the rest of your life (F, 49, SLC, 1964). Cf. Brown 7159f.

11938  Persian cats are bad luck (M, 22, SLC, 1960).

11939   If a strange cat kills your canary, bad luck will prevail for two years (F, 18, Tooele, 1955).

## Stray Cats and Cats of Various Colors

11940   Stray cats who come in the gate are good luck (F, 51, Ja, W. Jordan, 1963).

11941   A three-colored cat running across the street is bad luck, while one sitting still is good luck (M, 45, SLC, 1963).

11942   If you own a tortoise-shell cat, it will bring you good luck (F, 63, SLC, 1915).

11943   A cat with three colorings is always a female (F, SLC, 1925).

11944   A white cat is a sign of an angel (F, SLC, 1958).

11945   It is good luck to see a white cat (F, 17, Ogden, 1956).

11946   If you see a white cat, it's bad luck (M, 22, SLC, 1965).

11947   If you own a white cat, you will have bad luck all your days (F, SLC, 1964).

11948   A pure white cat is usually deaf (M, SLC, 1916).

11949   If you have six yellow cats, no harm can befall you (M, 29, SLC, 1963).

## Black Cats

11950   Cats bring bad luck, especially black ones.  Witches take the form of cats, and cats will suck a baby's breath (F, 58, Ibapah, 1964).

11951   A black cat is surely a sign of bad luck--one must avoid them (F, 47, It, SLC, 1963).  Brown 7150.

11952   If you see a black cat, you will have bad luck (F, 12, SLC, 1960).

11953   Seeing a black cat at night is a danger signal (F, 67, SLC, 1964).

11954   Don't let a black cat walk in front of you (F, 45, Ja, SLC, 1963).

11955   A black cat is good luck (F, Chin, SLC, 1964).

11956   To see a black cat without a single white hair is a lucky omen, especially if seen on a white fence (F, Axtell).

11957   To see a black cat cross the road is lucky (F, 1963).

11958   If a black cat walks into your room, you will have good luck (F, Richfield, 1905).

11959   It is good luck if a strange black cat visits your house (F, SLC, 1953).  Cf. Brown 7152.

11960   You will have luck if a black cat touches your shadow (F, 19, Provo, 1964); . . . walks under your shadow (F, SLC, 1960).

11961   A black cat with a white face is very suspicious (F, SLC, 1959).

## DOGS

11962   A stray dog following you is a sign of good luck (M, 40, Lost Creek); A strange dog . . . (M, 45, S. Jordan, 1964). Brown 7163.

11963   A dog with a white stripe down the middle of its forehead is bad luck (M, SLC, 1960).

11964   A black dog is a killer (F, SLC, 1959).

11965   If you spot three dogs in succession after a horse, you will have good luck (M, SLC, 1960).

11966   It's bad luck to kill a dog (M, 56, Union, 1918).  Cf. Brown 7174.

11967   A barking dog never bites (F, 60, Ogden, 1910).  Cf. Brown 7175.

11968   If you go where cross dogs are and you put your thumbs under your fingers, the dogs will not bite you (F, 21, SLC, 1963).  Cf. Brown 7176.

11969   A dog will bite you if you stare at him into his eyes (M, SLC, 1964).

11970   Never go out at night when you hear a dog cry (M, SLC, 1961).

11971   A howling dog is a sign of trouble (M, SLC); . . . bad luck (M, SLC, 1959); . . . disaster (F, 20, SLC, 1964).  Cf. Brown 7165ff.

11972   A dog that has a wolf howl is bad luck (M, SLC, 1960).

11973   A dog baying at the moon signifies bad luck (M, SLC, 1963); It is bad luck to have a dog howl at a full moon facing you (F, 20, SLC, 1955).

11974   A howling dog at dusk is bad luck for the Irish (F, 67, SLCo, 1910).

11975   A family will have bad luck if the dog howls on the front porch (F, Payson, 1959).

11976   Ringing bells will make a dog howl (F, Moab, 1953).

11977   A dog may be stopped from howling by turning a shoe upside down (M, SLC, 1950s).  Brown 7170f.

11978   If a dog is howling, put the master's hat in the window to quiet him (M, 78, Monroe, 1964).

11979   Never trust a laughing dog (M, SLC, 1961).

11980   A dog will cry tears if you beat him with a bone (F, SLC, 1957).

11981   A dog with a black mouth inside is smarter than one without (F, SLC, 1960).

11982   A dog turns around twice before lying down so as to have a peaceful sleep (F, 63, Milford, 1964).

11983  Dogs have the ability to tell if there are spirits present and can see them (F, 49, SLC, 1961).

11984  Dogs can sense the presence of invisible human beings (F, SLC, 1959).

11985  A dog was felt to have the power to see invisible demons (M, Logan, 1935).

11986  Don't let a dog look in a mirror. It is bad luck (F, 60, SLC, 1964).

COWS, BULLS

11987  If you kill a cow, you'll turn into a cow (M, 20, SLC, 1964).

11988  Cows are believed to forecast the future (M, SLC, 1959).

11989  If a cow moos after midnight, it brings bad luck to the owner (F, SLC, 1964). Cf. Brown 7095.

11990  Cattle have natural rhythm (pertaining to music) (M, 24, SLC, 1964).

11991  If a maverick winks his eye, there will be good luck (F, SLC, 1967).

11992  It is said that whenever a bull sees red he becomes enraged (M, SLC, 1946); . . . he will charge (M, SLC, 1961); If you are wearing red and go in a field where a bull is, the bull will attack you (F, Woodland, 1959); A red flag will enrage a bull (M, 79, Pleasant Grove, 1900).

11993  It is believed that bulls become enraged when they see red, but this is false because it has been proven that they are color blind and only see shades of grey (M, Murray, 1959).

11994  An encounter with a mad bull will bring safety if you look it squarely in the eye (M, 54, Magna, 1923).

11995  It is bad luck if you dream about being chased by a bull (F, SLC, 1959).

HORSES, MULES

11996  A horse draws lightning (M, 44, Layton, 1970); A horse is likely to get hit by lightning during a storm (M, Ogden). Brown 7009.

11997  The saliva of an angry horse is poisonous (F, 60, Ogden, 1918).

11998  It is considered bad luck to walk in back of a horse (M, 24, SLC, 1964).

11999  If you see a piebald horse you are lucky, but if you see a skewbald horse you are unlucky (M, Ogden, 1964).

12000  Grey horses are bad luck (F, 86, Provo, 1945).

12001  A grey horse is good luck (M).

12002  A black horse with a white spot on his forehead is good luck (F, SLC, 1957).

12003  If you see a black horse in a pasture, stop and throw salt over your left shoulder so as to break any bad spells one might incur (F, 59, SLC, 1962).

12004  It is good luck to see a white and grey horse (M, Payson, 1959).

12005  If a horse has a white streak from its forehead to its nose, the horse will bring bad luck to the home that owns the horse (F, Gr, SLC, 1957).

12006  A horse with four white feet is bad luck (F, Ja, SLC, 1960).

12007  A horse with four white feet is lucky (M, Park City, 1957).

12008  If you see a man on a horse with a dog following, you will have good luck for the rest of the day (F, 74, Salem, 1889).

12009  To dream of horses brings good luck (F, SLC, 1957).

12010  The Indians kill a horse by breaking its neck so as to spill no blood. The reason for this is so the Indian will have his horse in the "Happy Hunting Ground" (F, Peoa, 1909).

12011  If a horse rolls over three times, you will have good luck, i.e., if you see him while he is rubbing his back (M, 81, SLC, 1964).

12012  If a horse stumbles, it is a sign of bad luck (M, 70, Riverton, 1903).

12013  If your horse throws a shoe, stop and save the horseshoe, or you'll have bad luck (F, 90, SLC, 1964).

12014  A horse has a sixth sense that enables it to foretell danger, such as a rotten board on a bridge (M, 71, Bountiful, 1900).

12015  The people of St. George considered a pinto horse to be an unlucky horse (M, SLC, 1966).

12016  The people of St. George don't trust a "broomie" (a wild mustang from the Arizona strip), no matter how well he had been trained. It was said to be a killer horse (M, SLC, 1966).

12017  You can make a wish on a white mule (M, Bountiful, 1964). Cf. Brown 7143.

White Horses

12018  To see one white horse in a group of colored ones is lucky (F, 21, SLC, 1964).

12019  It is bad luck to see a white horse (M, 21, SLC, 1965); . . . especially lucky . . . after dark (F, 17, SLC, 1959); If you see a . . . , spit in your hand and you will have good luck (M, 53, SLC, 1964); . . . spit over your little finger (F, Murray, 1969).

12020  If you see a white horse, and repeat a certain verse, you will become lucky (M, SLC, 1948).

12021  It is bad luck to see a white horse after dark (M, SLC, 1959).

12022  If you see a white horse twice, it is unlucky (M, SLC, 1964).

12023 It is bad luck to dream of white horses (M, SLC, 1964).

12024 Whenever you dream of or see white horses you'll have a week's good luck (M, 22, SLC, 1950).

12025 When you see a white horse say, "White horse, white horse, give me good luck" three times (F, 49, Ogden, 1925). Cf. Brown 7100.

12026 When you see a white horse, spit so that you don't have bad luck (M, SLC, 1961). Cf. Brown 7104.

12027 See a white horse, spit on your shoe and make a wish (M, SLC, 1940s).

12028 If you see a white horse and you cross your fingers and spit, you will have good luck (M, Eng, SLC, 1964).

12029 When you see a white horse, if you can get out of sight before you think of the tail, it will bring you good luck (M, 22, Bountiful, 1960).

12030 See seven white horses in a row, and it will bring you bad luck (M, SLC, 1900).

12031 Count white horses and each one hundred will bring good luck (F, 50, SLC, 1960).

12032 Never borrow a white horse, for he will bring bad luck (F, Brigham, 1960).

12033 When you see a white horse you will soon see a redheaded woman (M, SLC, 1935). Brown 3804.

12034 A white horse and a redheaded girl seen one after another will bring you good luck (F, 47, SLC, 1964).

## Wishing on White Horses

12035 Snap seven white horses, two white billy goats, a man with a white beard, and your wish will come true (F, 21, SLC, 1963).

12036 Make a wish on all white horses. They are good luck (F, 52, Honeyville, 1922). Brown 7101.

12037 If a person sees a white horse and makes a wish on it, the wish will come true (M, SLC, 1958). Brown 7101.

12038 Always wish on a white horse without looking back (F, Murray, 1957). Brown 7102.

12039 If you see a white horse, you can make a wish, and if you don't tell anyone, it will come true (F, 45, Panguitch, 1935).

12040 When you spot a pure white horse, close your eyes and make a wish. Your wish will come true (F, 19, SLC).

12041 If you see a white horse say: "Lucky, lucky white horse, one, two, three," and wish, and it will come true (M, Park City, 1957).

12042 If you wish on a white horse, and ask for a dollar, your wish should come true (F, 46, SLC, 1928).

12043 If you should see a white horse, spit on the ground and make a wish, and the wish will come true (F, Santaquin, 1925).

12044 If you see a white horse in pasture, spit in your hand and make a wish and it will come true (M, SLC, 1964); . . . spit in your fist (F, 35, SLC, 1943).

12045 Make a wish on a white horse, and your wish will come true after you've seen a redheaded woman (F, 1963).

12046 Make a wish on a white horse. When you have seen one hundred white horses, the wish will come true (F, SLC).

12047 If you see a white horse, the moon, and the sun all at the same time, and you make a wish, it will come true (F, 26, Finn, Morgan, 1965).

12048 If two people see two white horses in a field, they should lock little fingers together and make a wish, and it will come true (M, 57, Swiss, Heber City, 1914).

12049 Making a wish while riding a white horse is good luck (F, 51, Centerfield, 1964).

12050 Wish on a load of hay drawn by a white horse, and your wish will come true (M, 20, SLC, 1964).

## Stamping White Horses

12051 If you see a white horse, lick your hand and stamp it on your knee (F, SLC).

12052 If you see one hundred white horses and stamp your hand each time, you will find a dollar (M, SLC, 1958).

12053 When you see a white horse, lick your fingers and touch it to the palm of your other hand and then "stamp" it. This will bring you good luck (F, 60, Ogden, 1970); . . . stamp the palm of the left hand with the fist of the right hand and make a wish (M, 58, SLC, 1910); . . . lick your right forefinger, wipe it on your left palm and then stamp your left palm with your right fist . . . (M, Helper, 1958); The first person who sees a white horse, licks his finger and stamps his feet gets his wish (F, 21, SLC, 1963). Brown 7105.

12054 When you see a white horse, if you spit on your hand and slap it and pull your fist away quick, you will have good luck (M, 56, Provo, 1964).

12055 Spit in your hand and hit it three times when you see a white horse, and your wish will come true (F, 52, SLC, 1964).

12056 If you see a white horse in a field, you spit in your hand and hit your other fist into it and you count to seven; you will have good luck (M, SLC, 1959).

12057 If you find a white horse after dark, you have to lick your thumb and press it into your hand if you do not want bad luck (M, 64, SLC, 1963); . . . spit in the palm of your left hand and make a wish (M, SLC, 1960). Cf. Brown 7106.

12058 To stamp three white horses means good luck (M, SLC, 1957).

12059  If you see and stamp seven white horses in a row, you will have good luck (F, Logan, 1970); . . . you should spit in your hand and clap seven times (F, 50, SLC, 1925).

12060  Stamp for a white horse. The first one to get ten will have good luck the rest of the day (M, 56, Ogden, 1963).

12061  Stamping fifty white horses is good luck (M, 55, Roosevelt, 1919); . . . one hundred . . . (F, Bear River City). Brown 7108.

12062  If you see a white horse in the country, lick your index finger, touch it to the palm of the other hand, and hit the same spot with your fist. This is called "spitting for luck," and after the hundredth time you will find something valuable (F, 70, Midway, 1910).

12063  If you wet your finger and rub the palm of your hand with that finger and then hit the palm every time you see a white horse, and then make a wish, upon the one thousandth time you do this (it will not work if you count), the wish will come true (F, 20, SLC, 1955).

## Verses While Stamping White Horses

12064  Stamp white horses in the usual way and say: "Lucky, lucky white horse, one, two, three," stamping once for each number. The person winning is treated with beer, or whatever, by the loser at the end of the trip (M, SLC, 1915).

12065  When you see a white horse say, "Lucky, lucky white horse, bring me a dime." After saying this you were supposed to find or be given a dime (M, SLC, 1960).

12066  If you see a white horse, lick your finger and press it to your hand, then say "Luck, luck, white horse, one, two, three," then clap your hands together and make a wish and it will come true (F, 35, Davis Co, 1944).

12067  When you see a white horse if you recite, "Good luck to you, good luck to me, good luck to every white horse I see," and then lick your finger, stamp it on the palm of your hand and stamp that spot with your fist--you will have good luck (F, SLC, 1944).

12068  When you see a white horse say: "Lucky, lucky white horse, one, two, three." Then spit in your palm and slap it with your other hand. This is supposed to bring you good luck (F, Nephi, 1919).

## HORSESHOES, MULESHOES

12069  The horseshoe is a sign of good luck (M, SLC, 1964). Brown 7114f.

12070  Hang a horseshoe on a nail on a rainy day, and you will have good luck (M, Fillmore, 1960).

12071  If a horseshoe is hanging inside your home, it means your home is always open to anyone in times of need. It is also a sign of good luck (M, SLC, 1957); . . . if you walk under it, you will have good luck (F, 16, Norw, SLC, 1964).

12072  Horseshoes, contrary to popular belief, are extremely bad luck (M, 25, SLC).

12073  For good luck always have a horseshoe in your possession (F, SLC, 1961).

12074  Finding a horseshoe brings good luck (M, 16, SLC, 1965); Picking up a horseshoe . . . (M, 55, Roosevelt, 1919). Brown 7116.

12075  If you find a horseshoe with nails on it, it will cause good luck (F, 42, SLC, 1963); . . . the more nails, the better the luck (F, 20, SLC, 1952). Brown 7117.

12076  If you find a horseshoe and make a wish before you pick it up, your wish will come true (M, Bountiful, 1925).

12077  If a person finds a horseshoe and doesn't return to his house, bad luck will follow (M, SLC, 1959); . . . he must run home without speaking to anyone or bad luck will ensue (F, SLC, 1960).

12078  If you find an old horseshoe, make a wish and try to throw it over the nearest fence or building. If it goes over, your wish will come true (M, SLC, 1959).

12079  Spit on a rusty horseshoe and throw it over your head. It will bring good luck (M, 55, SLC, 1920).

12080  If you find a horseshoe, spit over your left shoulder, and you will have good luck (M, SLC, 1951). Cf. Brown 7120.

12081  Make a wish on a horseshoe and throw it away. If you never find the horseshoe, your wish will come true; if you do find it, it won't (F, Eng, SLC, 1961). Cf. Brown 7121.

12082  When throwing a horseshoe, if it is turned upside down, you'll have bad luck (M, SLC, 1964).

12083  If you find a horseshoe, spit on it and throw it away without looking at where it lands, and it will bring you good luck (F, 83, Nephi, 1964). Cf. Brown 7124.

12084      See a horseshoe in your path,
       You'll have a happy aftermath.
    (M, SLC, 1957).

12085  If you find a horseshoe turned toward you, it is good luck; if turned away from you, it is bad luck (M, Fillmore, 1960). Cf. Brown 7118.

12086  If you walk toward an open horseshoe, it brings good luck. If you walk toward the back of a horseshoe, it brings bad luck (F, 71, Ger, Magna, 1964).

12087  If you see a horseshoe, you have to turn it over and you will have very good luck. If you don't turn it over, you will have bad luck (F, 85, Eng, SLC, 1965).

12088  If you keep a horseshoe, you will always have good luck (M, 18, SLC, 1963).

12089  If you hang a horseshoe upside down, the luck will run out (M, 25, Bountiful, 1972). Cf. Brown 7130.

12090   It is good luck to keep a horseshoe nail in your hat (M, Ogden, 1959).

12091   Horseshoe magnets are good luck (M, SLC, 1950s).

12092   Finding a mule's shoe brings bad luck (M, Eng, SLC, 1957); Picking up a muleshoe . . . (M, 55, Roosevelt, 1919).

## Horseshoes Thrown over the Shoulder

12093   For good luck, kiss a horseshoe and throw it over your shoulder (M, SLC, 1964).

12094   If you find a horseshoe, spit on it, wish and throw it over your shoulder and don't look back and you'll get good luck and your wish (M, 25, Roosevelt, 1964).

12095   Throw a horseshoe over your shoulder and it will bring you good luck if it lands before you turn around; it is bad luck if you turn around before it lands (F, 34, SLC, 1935).

12096   If you spit on a horseshoe and then throw it over your shoulder, it will bring you good luck (M, 49, SLC, 1964); . . . over your right shoulder . . . (M, Spanish Fork, 1924).

12097   If you kiss a horseshoe and throw it over your shoulder then turn around and can't see it by the time you count to six, you will have good luck (F, SLC, 1959).

12098   Throwing a horseshoe over your shoulder without looking back will bring you seven years of good luck (F, SLC, 1950).

12099   Find a horseshoe, throw it over your shoulder, and if it lands with the two ends away from you, it means bad luck. If the two ends are toward you, good luck is indicated (F, 12, Provo, 1964).

12100   Throw a horseshoe over the right shoulder and never see it again for good luck (M, 30, SLC, 1947).

12101   If you find an old horseshoe, spit on it, make a wish and throw it over your right shoulder and don't look where it went or your wish will not come true (F, 76, Glenwood, 1893); . . . toss it with your left hand over your right shoulder (M, 1960).

12102   If you find a horseshoe, and the open end is toward you, you must throw it over your right shoulder and not look back to prevent bad luck (M, SLC, 1957).

12103   If you find a horseshoe and throw it over your right shoulder and do not look to see where it lands, you will have good luck (M, 21, SLC, 1958).

12104   If you throw a horseshoe over your left shoulder, it will give you good luck (M, 30, Ogden, 1955); . . . a rusty horseshoe . . . (M, 57, Swiss, Heber City, 1914).

12105   If you find a horseshoe, spit on it, throw it over your left shoulder with your eyes shut (M, 50, Bountiful, 1965).

12106   Find a horseshoe and kiss it, throw it over your left shoulder not watching where it lands, and you will have good luck (M, SLC, 1964).

12107   If you find a horseshoe, throw it over your left shoulder and make a wish (F, SLC, 1957).

12108   When you find a horseshoe if you spit on it and throw it over your left shoulder and make a wish, the wish will come true if the horseshoe remains where it lands until it rusts (F, SLC, 1959).

## SHEEP, LAMBS, GOATS

12109   Sheep to your left will mean happiness and joy (M, 30, SLC, 1958).

12110   If you see a white sheep, clench your fist, and you will have good luck (F, 20, Swiss, SLC, 1965).

12111   In the springtime if you see the lamb's tail first, it's good luck (F, 50, Eng, SLC, 1964).  Cf. Brown 7180.

12112   The Polish people believe that the goat is the best sign of luck (F, 24, Midvale, 1959).

12113   It is very good luck to own a goat (M, Eng, SLC, 1957).

## DEER

12114   Deer travel in groups because it helps to protect them from disease (M, Provo, 1949).

12115   Deer have three lives to live (M, SLC, 1950).

12116   Wild deer always go to a stream at night-time (M, Provo, 1941).

12117   According to Indian legend every white deer has a madstone in his stomach, which was given to him by the Great Spirit.  This protects him from poison while eating grass (F, 35, SLC, 1940).

## BUFFALO

12118   Indians believe the white buffalo was a sign of good fortune.  Some tribes will not kill one (M, Vernal, 1958).

12119   Indians believe the imaginary white buffalo stands for peace (F, 20, SLC, 1965).

12120   White buffalo on the prairie means that the gods will send conditions for a good year (F, 57, SLC, 1965).

12121   Never kill a white buffalo, or it will bring bad luck (F, SLC, 1950).

12122   If you see a white buffalo, make a wish, and it will come true (F, 14, SLC, 1963).  Heard on TV.

12123   Only a person true of heart will see a white buffalo (F, 19, SLC, 1954).

## ELEPHANTS

12124 Elephants bring some people luck, especially pink ones (F, 8, SLC, 1964).

12125 The symbol of elephants with curved trunks up is good luck (F, SLC, 1958).

12126 Statues of elephants must always face east, or they will cause bad luck (F, 51, SLC, 1963).

12127 If you see an elephant with its trunk up, it is good luck; if the trunk is down, it is bad luck (F, SLC, 1959).

12128 If you throw a lot of white paper over your shoulder, no elephant will come around (M, 18, SLC, 1960).

12129 Elephants are afraid of mice (M, 20, SLC, 1951).

12130 Elephants all go to the same place to die (M, 20, SLC, 1963).

## LIONS, LEOPARDS

12131 An encounter with a lion will bring safety, if you look it squarely in the eye (M, 54, Magna, 1923).

12132 A mountain lion can see as good at night as he can during the day (M, SLC, 1964).

12133 If a mountain lion follows your tracks, next time he'll wait to kill you (M, 84, Centerville).

12134 Never capture a spotted leopard, or you will have bad luck (F, SLC, 1962).

## GUINEA PIGS, HAMSTERS

12135 If you hold a guinea pig by his tail, his eyes will fall out (M, 43, American Fork, 1949).

12136 Hold a hamster by its tail and its eyes will fall out (M, 51, SLC, 1964).

## RATS, MICE

12137 If you dream about a rat, it means bad luck (F, Bountiful, 1948). Cf. Brown 7179.

12138 It's bad luck to kill a rat (M, 23, SLC, 1964).

12139 Flutes will attract rats (M, 20, SLC, 1949).

12140 People used to believe that if you put dirty rags, paper, cheese in a dark place they would turn into rats (F, SLC, 1964).

12141 A mouse running over a person is an unlucky sign (M, 30, SLC, 1942).

12142 If you catch a mouse and shut it alive in a pollard ash, you will shut up your bad luck (M, 90, W. Jordan, 1920).

12143 If you dream of mice, it is lucky (F, Ger, 56, SLC, 1964).

12144 Mice are a sign of loss of valuables (F, SLC, 1958).

## RABBITS

12145 Rabbits have red eyes so they may see in the dark (M, 31, SLC, 1964).

12146 If a rabbit runs along a house top, a disaster will occur (F, 64, Salina, 1917).

12147 The way to catch rabbits is to put salt on their tails (F, 62, 1914).

12148 It is good luck to kill the first rabbit that you see in winter (M, Ogden, 1959).

12149 Rabbits only eat food they can get water from (M, SLC, 1953).

12150 Rabbits are very dangerous when in groups (M, Provo, 1964).

12151 Finding a rabbit's foot brings good luck (M, SLC, 1965).

## PORCUPINES

12152 If you come too close to a porcupine or agitate them, they will throw their quills at your face. The quills are filled with poison (M, 20, Price, 1945).

## FOXES, COYOTES

12153 It is a dangerous sign to see a fox lick a lamb (F, SLC).

12154 To see several foxes together is unlucky; but to see one alone is lucky (F, Brigham City, 1960).

12155 Coyotes won't bother a man who has eaten prepared green chilis (M, SLC, 1957).

12156 If the coyotes are howling, throw rusty nails in the open fire to make them stop (F, SLC).

12157 To prevent coyotes from entering a campsite, urinate in several places surrounding the camp (M, 21, Logan, 1970).

## WOLVES, BEARS

12158 The Polish people believe that the wolf is a sign of bad luck (F, 24, SLC, 1959).

12159 Baby bears are born without any shape and are licked into shape (F, 20, SLC, 1963).

12160 Shoes on the wrong feet bring a bear to your door (M, Layton, 1934).

12161 If you step on a crack in the sidewalk, a bear will jump out and grab you (M, SLC, 1961).

12162 Never go hiking in shorts or the bears will get you (M, SLC, 1964).

12163 If you eat bear's liver, it will come back and haunt you (F, Midvale, 1961).

12164 A bear kills not for hunger but for hate (M, Provo, 1960).

12165 To prevent wild animals from entering a campsite, urinate in several places

surrounding the camp.  This will keep
bears away (M, 21, Logan, 1970).

## VARIOUS ANIMALS

12166  Beavers don't climb trees (M, SLC,
1964).

12167  Step on a crack, break a camel's back
(M, SLC, 1959).

12168  If you feed nuts to a chipmunk, you will
have good luck (F, SLC, 1961).

12169  If a ground hog sees his shadow on
Ground Hog Day, six weeks of bad luck
will follow (M, SLC, 1957).

12170  The marks on a hog's front ankles, seven
of them, are marks where the seven
devils came out of them when they
drowned themselves at the time of Christ
(M, SLC, 1925).

12171  If you see a black hair floating down
the river, there is a hog up above (M,
SLC, 1963).

12172  Don't ever shoot a black monkey, or
something bad will happen to your mom or
dad (M, 30, SLC, 1963).

12173  A monkey's paw brings bad luck (F, SLC,
1965).

12174  If you step on the circle of the
sidewalk contractor which is usually
imprinted at the end of the sidewalk,
you will turn into a skunk (F, 21,
Logan, 1955).

## BATS, VAMPIRE BATS

12175  Bats bring bad luck (F, Sandy, 1957); A
bat in the house . . . (F, Woods Cross,
1953).  Brown 7183.

12176  Bats carry common lice or bedbugs (F,
50, SLC, 1963).

12177  Bats fly by radar (M, 22, SLC, 1954);
Bats are telepathic (M, SLC, 1963).

12178  Bats suck blood out of people while they
are asleep at night (F, 60, SLC, 1963).

12179     Bat, bat, come under my hat,
          And I'll give you a piece of bacon.
       (F, Moab, 1953).

12180  If a bat alights on your head, he will
stay there until it thunders (F, SLC,
1960).

12181  Vampire bats can change their form
during a full moon (M, 23, SLC, 1960).

12182  To keep vampire bats away, place garlic
leaves outside your windows (M, 23, SLC,
1963).

## HENS

12183  The son of a white hen brings luck (M,
65, SLC).

12184  If a chicken screeches for a period of
time, it means that you are going to
have bad luck.  You can prevent this by
cutting his head off and throwing it on
top of the roof (F, Gr, SLC, 1962).

12185  It's bad luck to hear a hen crow (F,
Murray, 1957); Evil is close at hand if
you . . . (M, 90, W. Jordan, 1915); If
you . . . , it is a warning that
something will happen (F, 46, SLC,
1934).  Brown 7192.

12186  If a hen crows, you must always cut its
head off (F, SLC, 1957).  Brown 7193.

12187  Whistling hens and cackling hens always
come to a bad end (F, Ogden, 1961).

12188  Giggling girls and crowing hens always
come to real bad ends (F, 67, SLC,
1963).

12189  Hens fighting means women arguing (F,
36, SLC, 1965).

12190  A chicken or turkey backbone can tell
the future, such as war, by its
clearness, sharpness on the top, and any
odd piece on the end (F, Gr, SLC, 1957).

12191  A chicken feather brings good luck (M,
SLC, 1964).

## ROOSTERS

12192  If a foot of a cock is warm, it is a
sign of good fortune (F, 85, SLC, 1964).

12193  If a man gets an egg laid by a rooster,
he will always be fortunate (F, 59,
Grantsville, 1936).

12194  If you are the first in your house to
hear the rooster crow, you'll have good
luck that day (F, SLC, 1964).

12195  If a rooster crows at night, it will be
bad luck for the family (M, SLC, 1959).
Cf. Brown 7189, 7191.

12196  It is bad luck for a rooster to crow in
the doorway of the house (M, 35, SLC,
1964).  Brown 7185.

## WISHBONES

12197  A wishbone is good luck (M, 67,
Farmington, 1937).

12198  You take a wishbone from a chicken and
let it dry.  Two people pull it apart
and the one who gets the bigger end,
will have his wish come true (M, SLC,
1961); . . . the one getting the part
with the bottom piece still intact gets
the wish (M, SLC, 1959); . . . the wish
of the person who has the top after it
is broken will come true (M, SLC, 1959);
. . . the one who gets the "knot" on his
end gets his favorite wish (F, 45, SLC,
1964).  Cf. Brown 7197f.

12199  If two people break a wishbone and the
middle part breaks off, the wish won't
be granted (F, 20, SLC, 1949).

12200  The short piece of the wishing bone
brings good luck (M, 19, Park City,
1964).

## DUCKS, GEESE, SWANS

12201    Three ducks fighting together is a sign of unhappiness (M, SLC, 1961).

12202    A blind duck is poisonous (M, 18, SLC, 1963).

12203    A duck flying south will never return (M, Provo, 1950).

12204    A redheaded duck is the greatest and most noble kind of duck (M, Provo, 1960).

12205    Ducks eat worms so they can walk better (M, Provo, 1955).

12206    Ducks always nest their eggs in cedar grass (M, SLC, 1947).

12207    Never let a goose get behind you (M, SLC, 1963).

12208    Wild geese passing south make the initials of each state over which they pass (M, 26, SLC, 1945).

12209    Swans are hatched during thunderstorms (F, 56, Orem, 1964).

12210    Just before a swan dies it will sing a beautiful song (M, SLC, 1959).

## BIRDS

### Various Birds

12211    If a bird pecks on a window, it means death for another bird (M, 42, SLC, 1964).

12212    Birds signifying spring are good omens (F, 43, SLC, 1964). Cf. Brown 7205.

12213    It is bad luck for a bird to be in the house (F, Fillmore, 1960).

12214    When a bird flutters at your window, some misfortune will soon come (F, Sandy, 1957); . . . against the window . . . (M, Murray, 1958); . . . on your window sill . . . (M, 34, SLC, 1954). Brown 7213.

12215    If a small bird flies in a house and lands on a mirror, it means bad luck for all in the house (F, SLC); . . . it means disaster (F, 59, Mt. Pleasant, 1964).

12216    If a bird flies down your chimney into your house, it will bring a year of bad luck into your home (F, Swed, SLC). Cf. Brown 7214.

12217    It is bad luck for a bird to get in the house and circle over your head (F, 19, SLC, 1952).

12218    If a bird flies in your window, it's good luck. If you don't keep it, it's bad luck (F, SLC, 1963). Cf. Brown 7209f.

12219    Birds are God's messengers; so you should always leave food for them (M, SLC, 1957); . . . messengers of the spirits . . . (M, SLC, 1959).

12220    If a bird flies into the church during the service, he will bring good luck to all those present at the service (F, SLC, 1967).

12221    A white bird brings good luck (M, SLC, 1964).

12222    Birds will peck out the eyes of the wicked (F, 20, SLC, 1971).

12223    Birds never feather the nest until they have a mate (F, 70, Provo, 1900).

12224    If you tear down a bird's nest, you'll have bad luck (M, 56, Union, 1916). Cf. Brown 7217.

12225    If you kill a bird, it will bring you bad luck (M, SLC, 1960).

12226    If a bird with beautiful plumage comes to you, it brings good health and good fortune (F, 52, SLC, 1962).

12227    If you want a bird to talk, just split its tongue with a knife (M, SLC, 1948).

12228    Birds who sing too early in the morning will be food for the cats at night (M, SLC, 1959). Cf. Brown 7219.

12229    If you see a bird over your left shoulder, you will have bad luck; if it's over your right shoulder, you will have good luck (M, Iran, 28, SLC, 1963).

12230    If a bird drops anything on you, it is good luck (F, 25, Norw, SLC, 1964).

12231    If a bird of prey flies over someone, and its shadow falls across that person, that person will have very bad luck (F, 54, SLC, 1964).

12232    It's bad luck to count the birds in a flock (F, Brigham City, 1926).

12233    When one sees birds flying in the sky, count them: One is for sorrow, two for joy, three for a letter, four for a boy, five for silver, six for gold, seven for a secret never to be told (F, 44, SLC, 1964).

12234    Counting the birds in a flock: One's unlucky, two's lucky, three's health, four's wealth, five's sickness, six is death (F, 19, SLC, 1964).

12235    Birds always whistle at four o'clock in the morning (M, SLC, 1964).

12236    You will have bad luck if you break a bird's egg (M, SLC, 1961). Cf. Brown 7218.

12237    Birds' eggs hung up in the house will keep good luck out (F, SLC, 1957); . . . will bring bad luck (M, SLC, 1947).

12238    Put salt on a bird's tail and it won't be able to fly (F, 68, SLC, 1934); . . . you'll be able to catch him (F, SLC, 1950). Brown 7220.

### Canaries, Parrots

12239    Whenever a canary remains silent for too long a period, there is evil in the air which prevents the bird from singing in its accustomed happy fashion (F, SLC, 1961).

12240  When canaries are in the same house with goldfish, harmony is there to stay (F, SLC, 1961).

12241  It is good luck to own a yellow canary (F, Springville, 1959).

12242  If you see a dead canary, it's a sign you will see blood that day (F, 20, SLC, 1960).

12243  Parrots love mice (M, SLC, 1963).

## Doves and Pigeons

12244  A mourning dove cooing in the evening is a sign of joy (F, Moab, 1953).

12245  A white dove brings you good luck (M, 19, SLC, 1964).

12246  A white dove flying into your yard or near you brings good luck (M, 68, Fairview, 1905).

12247  Pigeons can talk or communicate (M, SLC, 1941).

12248  If a pigeon settles on a table, it means bad luck (M, 90, Price, 1895).

12249  Feeding strange pigeons will bring good luck (F, 65, Provo, 1922).

12250  Don't kill pigeons; it's very bad luck (M, 24, SLC, 1963).

## Bluebirds, Blackbirds, Larks, Starlings

12251  If you see a bluebird, it is good luck (F, SLC, 1958).

12252  Bluebirds around the yard are good luck (F, 50, Bingham Canyon, 1942); . . . bring happiness (M, 22, SLC, 1964).

12253  If a bluebird builds his nest by your front door, good luck will come to you (F, 71, SLC, 1905); . . . on the porch . . . (M, SLC).

12254  If you see a bluebird and make a wish before it flies away, then the wish will come true (M, SLC, 1961). Brown 7234.

12255  Bluebirds on the head mean bad luck (M, SLC, 1942).

12256  Blackbirds bring bad luck (F, 50, Midvale, 1963).

12257  If a lot of blackbirds land in the back of your house, near your door, it's a sign of danger (M, 53, Heber, 1971).

12258  You'll have good luck if you hear a meadowlark sing (F, 70, Provo, 1900).

12259  When the sky falls, larks can be caught (F, SLC, 1958).

12260  When you hear a meadowlark sing, if you can count to seven before it stops, you will have good luck (M, Price, 1959).

12261  Starlings are generally lucky birds of passage (F, SLC, 1961).

## Redbirds, Cardinals, Sparrows

12262  If you see a redbird, make a wish and it will come true (F, Kaysville, 1958); . . . make three wishes . . . (F, 19, SLC, 1952). Brown 7223.

12263  Blow a kiss to a cardinal or redbird, and the wish will come true (F, SLC, 1965). Brown 7228.

12264  When you see a redbird fly over and turn right, you will have good luck (M, SLC, 1959). Cf. Brown 7230f.

12265  It is bad luck to kill sparrows (F, 51, Murray, 1927).

## Cuckoos

12266  The cuckoo bird is a bird of omen (M, SLC, 1961).

12267  A cuckoo is supposed to bring you good luck. She sucks birds' eggs to make her voice clear (F, Moab, 1953).

12268  Whatever you happen to be doing if you hear a cuckoo, that's what you will be doing most frequently the rest of the year (M, 76, Eng, SLC, 1963).

12269  Whatever you are doing when you hear the cuckoo clock for the first time, you will do that most often in your life (F, 23, SLC, 1954).

12270  It is unlucky if you have no money in your pockets when you hear the cuckoo for the first time in the season (M, SLC, 1935).

12271  When you hear a cuckoo in the spring, you are supposed to turn your money over, and it will bring you good luck (F, 80, Eng, Richfield, 1964).

12272  If a person can get under the tree where the cuckoo bird crows, his desires will be granted (F, SLC, 1937).

12273  To see a cuckoo implies the treachery of one woman to another (F, SLC, 1961).

## Mocking Birds, Robins

12274  Never kill a mocking bird, or disaster will follow (F, SLC, 1965).

12275  The robin got its red breast from being scorched by the flames of hell (F, Morgan, 1961); . . . from a drop of Christ's blood (F, Morgan, 1961).

12276  Catch a robin; for good luck rub his breast and let him go (F, 74, SLC, 1964).

12277  If the first robin you see in the spring flies up, you will have good luck (M, 20, SLC, 1964).

12278  Don't harm robins, for they bring good luck (M, 63, Orem, 1964).

12279  A robin on the property of a farmer means good luck (M, SLC, 1948).

12280  A robin's nest near one's house will bring him luck (M, 63, Fillmore, 1918).

12281 If you can put salt on a robin's tail, you can catch a bird (M, 23, SLC, 1963).

12282 For good luck salt a robin's tail (F, 25, SLC).

12283 When you see the first robin in the spring, you lick your thumb and moisten your palm and then hit your palm for good luck (F, SLC, 1959); If you lick your index finger and slap it into your palm and then hit your palm with a clenched fist, for every robin you see, it will bring good luck (F, 60, SLC, 1964). Cf. Brown 7236.

12284 Count, lick and stamp robins. The first twenty-five bring good luck (M).

12285 A male robin will always kill the young birds when they are touched by human hands (M, SLC, 1957).

12286 It is very unlucky to keep or to kill a robin (M, SLC, 1961). Brown 7238.

12287 Don't kill a bird when it is singing, or a bird's song will bother you from that day on. If a robin is singing in a tree and you shoot it, robins will bother you from that day on (M, 22, SLC).

## Swallows, Martins, Swifts

12288 Swallows bring good luck (M, Provo, 1937).

12289 Barn swallows bring good luck to cattlemen (M, Syracuse, 1947).

12290 It's good luck when the swallows make a nest under the roof next to the wall (F, Peoa, 1920); . . . in the eaves of your house (F, 19, SLC, 1960).

12291 It is unlucky if a swallow starts to build a nest on a house and then deserts it (M, 52, Ogden, 1928); It's a bad omen . . . (F, SLC, 1961).

12292 If you destroy a swallow's nest, you will have bad luck (F, 50, Richfield, 1932).

12293 To kill a swallow is unlucky (F, SLC, 1961). Brown 7241.

12294 It is unlucky to kill a martin (F, 19, SLC, 1964). Brown 7240.

12295 If you see a swift on the wing, it is not only lucky, but if you can make a wish before it is out of sight, the wish will soon come true (F, SLC, 1961).

12296 If a chimney swift builds his nest in your chimney, you will be warm all winter (M, Vernal, 1956).

## Whippoorwills

12297 In the spring when you see the whippoorwill's breast it means sorrow; if you see his tail first, it means joy (F, Norw, SLC, 1959).

12298 It is a sure sign of trouble if a whippoorwill sings near the house (F, 33, Bountiful, 1964). Cf. Brown 7242.

12299 Make three wishes when you hear the first whippoorwill (F, 25, SLC, 1946). Cf. Brown 7245f.

12300 What you are doing when you hear the first whippoorwill, that you will do most of the year (F, 1959); . . . the rest of the year (M, 58, Mt. Pleasant, 1914).

## Peacocks, Pheasants

12301 Peacock feathers are very bad luck (Anon, SLC, 1964).

12302 When a person possesses a peacock feather and wears it, he will have bad luck because of the eyes in the bird's feather (F, 19, SLC, 1964).

12303 It is good luck to find a peacock's feather (F, 22, SLC, 1963).

12304 If you see a white pheasant, it is good luck (M, 81, SLC).

## Sea Gulls

12305 Three sea gulls flying overhead together are a sign of bad luck (M, 25, W. Jordan).

12306 The sea gulls all were, and always will be, the fingers of God (M, SLC, 1903).

12307 It is unlucky to kill a sea gull (M, SLC, 1962); To kill a sea gull is bad luck, for the soul of a gull is someone's life (F, 17, SLC, 1961); . . . , for gulls are the souls of the dead (F, 61, Crescent, 1916).

## Storks

12308 The stork is a good luck bird (F, Mt. Pleasant, 1959).

12309 A stork nesting on a person's roof means good luck for the coming year (M); . . . the house will be prosperous (F, 45, Midvale).

13210 When a stork builds its nest in the chimney, it's good luck, but if the stork moves it, it will bring bad luck (M, SLC, 1958).

13211 It is unlucky to kill a stork (F, 85, Grantsville, 1964).

## Ravens, Crows, Magpies

12312 Crows and ravens are witches' messengers (M, SLC, 1957).

12313 If you see four ravens sitting on a fence, it is very bad luck (M, 81, Welsh, SLC, 1964).

12314 A croaking raven brings bad luck (F, 36, Helper, 1947).

12315 There are ravens living at the Tower of London. If ever they leave, the Tower will fall (F, 44, Eng, SLC, 1964).

12316 If a raven comes to your house, it means that some bad luck is about to come (M, SLC, 1958).

12317   To see a crow flying alone is a token of bad luck (M, 22, SLC, 1963).

12318   If you want to make a crow talk, split its tongue (F, SLC, 1961).

12319   A scarecrow will scare away crows (M, SLC, 1959).

12320   To see a single magpie is an omen of grave and serious incidents to follow (M, Eng, Ogden, 1958).

12321   If you see a magpie and do not cross yourself, you will be unlucky (M, 53, Ogden, 1964).

12322   If a magpie flies to the right of you, good luck will come; but if it flies to the left, you'll receive bad luck (F, 84, Sevier Co, 1930).

12323   Seeing two magpies means mirth (F, Ir, SLC, 1960).

Owls

12324   An owl is wise (F, Sandy, 1957).

12325   The owl is a bird of evil omens (F, 60, Ogden, 1920).

12326   The hooting of an owl is taken as a very bad sign (F, 85, Grantsville, 1900); To hear an owl hoot twice is a bad omen (M, SLC, 1964); An owl shrieking means coming misfortune (F, SLC, 1960). Cf. Brown 7259.

12327   Hearing the hooting of an owl at midnight brings bad luck (F, SLC, 1958); . . . foretells calamity to the house (M, SLC); . . . indicates evil is in the air (F, 19, SLC, 1963); If you hear two owls on the same night, you'll have bad luck (F, 12, SLC, 1964); If an owl hoots over your house, it's bad luck (F, SLC, 1960). Cf. Brown 7260ff.

12328   To see or hear an owl during the night means that something bad is going to happen (F, 48, SLC, 1963).

12329   If you hear an owl hoot, you should throw salt in the fire, or you'll have bad luck (M, Magna, 1956). Brown 7277.

12330   To chase away an owl from the bedroom window, you should turn a shoe upside down under the bed (M, 25, Dugway, 1963). Cf. Brown 7264ff.

12331   If you're troubled with owls at night, then tie a knot in the corner of your handkerchief, and they will be silenced (F, Midvale, 1961). Cf. Brown 7272, 7280.

12332   To see an owl during daylight hours will bring bad luck (M, 21, SLC, 1965); . . . in the sunlight . . . (M).

12333   It is bad luck if an owl flies over your path at night (M, 56, Ir, SLC, 1964).

12334   If you see an owl in a cemetery, it will bring bad luck (F, SLC, 1931).

12335   Whenever an owl enters a building, it's bad luck (F, 24, SLC, 1950).

12336   If an owl nests in your yard or field, it brings you good luck and good crops (F, 64, Moroni, 1910).

Eagles, Hawks, Buzzards

12337   If you rob an eagle's nest, you will have bad luck for a week (M, 45, SLC, 1960).

12338   A hawk flying overhead means a mountain lion just made a kill (M, SLC, 1964).

12339   It is good luck to see a hawk flying overhead (F, SLC, 1957).

12340   If you see a hawk flying, you will have a period of depression (M, SLC, 1961).

12341   If a buzzard lands on your house, you will have bad luck (F, 19, SLC, 1964).

Various Birds

12342   Kill a woodpecker and there will be a lack of lumber to build your home (M, SLC, 1961).

12343   An ostrich buries his head in the sand to hide from danger (M, 21, SLC, 1964).

12344   If you kill an albatross, you will have bad luck (F, 20, SLC, 1958).

SNAKES

Various Notions

12345   The snake is a sign that foretells misfortune (M, SLC, 1958).

12346   Snakes' legs can be seen if you throw them in the fire (M, SLC, 1962). Brown 7308.

12347   Because of the snakes in the Garden of Eden, men are now innately afraid of snakes (M, professor, SLC, 1964).

12348   Snakes live in snake grass (F, SLC, 1900); Snakes are always found around snakeweeds (M, SLC, 1958).

12349   Snakes always travel in pairs (M, Midvale, 1953).

12350   Snakes can outrun men (M, 20, SLC, 1963).

12351   Snakes are blind during Indian summer (F, 45, SLC, 1935).

12352   If you look at a snake in the eye, it will put a charm on you (F, 52, Nephi, 1964); If a snake looks at you in the eye, you become paralyzed (F, SLC, 1958).

12353   Never look a snake in the eyes, for it will bring you two years of bad luck (M, SLC, 1961).

12354   Music will charm snakes (M, 24, SLC, 1950s).

12355   Snakes devour their prey and then regurgitate them (M, 23, SLC, 1963).

12356  Snakes swallow their young to protect them (M, SLC, 1962).

12357  The whip snake is said to attack human beings whom it whips and lashes to death with its long tail (M, Vernal, 1959).

12358  Let an adder go alive, and bad luck will attend you (M, 1961).

12359  If you handle a snake, it's bad luck (M, 18, Magna, 1963).  Brown 7298.

12360  Step on a snake and some harm will soon come to you (F, Vernal, 1964).

12361  If you step over a double snake track, you will have good luck (F, Bear River City, 1957).

12362  A wavy snake track in the dust means that a poisonous snake has passed (M, 21, SLC, 1964).

12363  If you touch a snakeskin, it is bad luck forever (M, 1959).  Cf. Brown 7294, 7299.

12364  Hang an adder skin over the chimney and it will bring you good luck (M, SLC, 1961).

12365  A garter snake will shed its tail to escape from your hand (F, SLC, 1960).

12366  When you whistle at night a snake will come out (F, 30, Ja, SLC, 1964).

12367  Never whistle in the woods for fear of attracting snakes (M, 44, SLC, 1930).

12368  If you see a snake before sunrise, there will be danger during the day (M, 70, Devils Slide, 1965).

12369  Snakes used to suck eggs, get in a chicken coop and suck eggs (F, Moab, 1953).

12370  "I went down here to Grandma H's one day and there was a bull snake curled up in a pan of milk, and it had drank nearly every drop of that milk.  She said it was just bloated up till it was about as big as her arm, and just curled right up in the milk" (F, Moab, 1953).

12371  A king snake is commonly called a milksnake because it steals milk from cows (M, 30, Providence, 1970); Black snakes suck the milk from cows (M, SLC, 1959); Milksnakes will climb a cow's leg and suck her milk (F, 89, Eureka, 1878). Brown 7528.

12372  If the cows don't give enough milk, a blowsnake will come and milk the cows (F, 20, SLC, 1949).

12373  The number of rattles on a rattlesnake's tail tells its age (F, 19, SLC, 1963). Brown 7312.

12374  Rattlesnakes can charm birds so that they can eat them (M, SLC, 1962).

12375  If you catch a rattlesnake and rub the rattles on your eyes, you can always see a rattlesnake before he sees you (F, 45, SLC, 1936).

12376  Rattlesnake skin is bad luck (M, SLC, 1962); Handling a rattlesnake skin will bring bad luck (M, SLC, 1962).

12377  In 1849 settlers in Manti moved into caves on Temple Hill which became infested with rattlesnakes in November. After prayer circles and fasting by the settlers, the snakes disappeared.  No one was even killed on account of the snakes (M, 21, Manti, 1971).

12378  Blowsnakes will keep rattlesnakes away (M, 50, Logan).

## Warding off Snakes

12379  Snakes may be kept off by the carrying of a snakeroot (M, 22, SLC, 1941).

12380  Pouring oil around the house will keep rattlesnakes away (M, Logan, 1970).

12381  Wearing of the green on St. Patrick's Day is a way to ward off the snakes (F, 49, Gr, Midvale, 1926).

12382  Rattlers can be kept out of a camp by sprinkling pepper in a circle around the campsite (M, 21, Logan, 1970).

12383  To keep away rattlesnakes, sleep on a blanket made out of horsehair (M, Morgan, 1961).

12384  Always put a hair rope around your sleeping bags to keep out rattlesnakes, because the snake cannot and will not cross the rope (M, 25, Tooele, 1965); . . . a snake won't cross a horsehair rope (F, Copperton).

12385  If you put a rope in a circle around a snake, the snake won't go over it (M, 23, SLC, 1952).

12386  When camping in the desert, circle a rope around your camp to keep the rattlesnakes out of your camp.  The snakes won't crawl over the rope because they don't like the scratchy feeling (M, 60, Moab, 1971); . . . a rattlesnake won't cross a rope that surrounds sleeping men (M, 44, SLC, 1965).

## Killing Snakes

12387  Never kill a snake with your hands (M, SLC, 1961).

12388  If you once kill a snake, you cannot charm others (M, 32, SLC, 1962).

12389  To kill a snake is bad luck because they are full of evil spirits (F, Bountiful, 1971).  Cf. Brown 7297.

12390  If you spit on a snake's tail, the snake will die (M, 54, SLC, 1944).

12391  Kill a snake by spitting tobacco juice on its head (M, 70, Duchesne, 1970).

12392  A rattlesnake may be easily killed with a gun because the snake's head will follow the muzzle of the gun hypnotically (M, 20, SLC, 1964).

12393  After cutting a snake in two, if you put the pieces back in water, they will join together again (M, SLC, 1960).

12394   If you chop a snake up into little pieces, all of them will draw together again before sundown (M, 27, SLC, 1963). Cf. Brown 7314f.

12395   If you kill a snake in mating time, its mate will come to the body (M, 54, SLC, 1945).

12396   When you kill a snake leave him there and don't return; for his mate will go there and wait to bite you (F, 60, SLC, 1964); . . . its mate will come looking for you (M, SLC, 1964). Cf. Brown 7322.

## Dying Snakes

12397   Snakes won't die until sundown (M, Fillmore, 1960); If you cut a snake in half, it will wiggle until sundown (M, SLC, 1961); A snake shot in the morning wriggles till night (F, SLC, 1957); If you chop off a snake's head, its tail will wag until sundown (F, SLC, 1959); . . . this belief is attributed most likely to the fact that muscles will contract for some time after the snake has been killed (M, 20, SLC, 1963); A snake never dies until the sun sets. If it does, it is bad luck (M, Orem, 1959). Brown 7317ff.

12398   When a snake is killed, its tail does not die until the sun goes down (M, SLC, 1957); A snake's tail never dies till sunset (M, 63, Logan, 1952); . . . its tail will switch 'til sundown (M, Layton, 1958); A recently slaughtered rattlesnake is not completely dead and will strike until sundown (F, 46, Ogden, 1926).

12399   If you don't chop a snake's head off until after sunset, it will not die (M, SLC, 1958); If a snake is killed after the sun sets, it will not die (M, SLC, 1959).

12400   If you kill a snake, its body won't move until sundown (M, SLC, 1965).

## Snakes Striking and Biting

12401   Rattlesnakes were thought to have been able to "spit" their venom and poison an intruder (M, 46, SLC, 1925).

12402   A rattlesnake can only strike in a direct line from his sight, so therefore you can have two fellows, one in front attracting it, and the other to the side to kill it and it will work (M, 14, Calleo).

12403   A cottonmouth will not strike under water (F, 19, SLC, 1963).

12404   All rattlesnakes rattle before they strike (F, 19, SLC, 1960); A rattlesnake rattles three times before it bites (M, 63, Logan, 1952).

12405   If a rattlesnake strikes a piece of steel (such as a pickaxe), the piece which was directly struck will become discolored and fall off (M, 20, SLC, 1964).

12406   A rattlesnake never strikes the same person twice (M, 48, Farmington, 1964).

12407   Snakes sting with their tongues (M, SLC, 1962). Cf. Brown 7310.

12408   A dead snake can bite until the sun goes down (M, 24, SLC, 1964).

## Dreaming about Snakes

12409   When you dream about snakes, the next day will be lucky (M, SLC, 1960).

12410   If you dream about a rattlesnake, it's good luck (F, 25, Ja, SLC, 1964).

12411   Dreams of snakes mean bad luck for the following year (F, Eng, Hooper, 1963).

12412   If you dream of a snake biting you, you will be in serious trouble (M, SLC, 1957).

## Horsehair Turning into Snakes

12413   Put a hair from a horse's tail in water, and it will turn into a snake (F, 1959); Indians believed that if you place a piece of hair in water, it will turn into a snake (F, 24, Ja, SLC).

12414   Horsehairs turn into water snakes (M, 56, Ogden, 1963).

12415   A hair taken from the tail of a horse will turn into a snake if it is left in water for about six months (F, 20, SLC, 1963); Hairs from the mane or tail of a horse placed in stagnant water will turn into slender snakes (F, 50, SLC, 1963). Cf. Brown 7301, 7303.

12416   If a hair from a horse's tail is placed in a bucket of water, the hair will turn into a snake (M, 51, Farmington, 1919); . . . in a rain barrel . . . (F, Bountiful, 1915); . . . in a horse trough . . . (M, 12, SLC, 1964); . . . in a bathtub . . . (F, 98, SLC, 1964). Cf. Brown 7300, 7302.

12417   If you drop a piece of horsehair into a river, it will turn into a snake (M, 25, Dugway, 1963). Cf. Brown 7304.

12418   If you get a hair out of a horse's tail and put it in a bottle of water overnight, it will turn into a snake (F, SLC, 1958); Bury a horsehair in a bottle of water; one year later it will turn into a snake (F, 20, SLC, 1963); If you take horsehair and put it in a bottle of salt water for a period of one week, if the moon is right, the hair will turn into a horsehair snake. The moon is supposed to be a new one, or else the experiment will not work (M, 18, Richfield, 1951). Cf. Brown 7305ff.

12419   If you put a hair from a horse's tail in a glass of water and leave it, it will turn into a snake (M, SLC, 1958); Tie a knot in a horse's hair, place it in a glass of water, and it will turn into a water snake in seven days (F, 69, SLC, 1900s).

12420   Place a horsehair in a bottle of whiskey, and it will soon turn to a snake and wriggle (M, SLC, 1963).

12421   Pull out a horsehair, and it will turn into a snake (F, SLC, 1957).

12422  If you leave a rope in water, it will change into a snake (M, Provo, 1964).

12423  A hose will dig into the ground if it is left alone and turned on hard enough to turn into a snake (M, 13, Orem, 1964).

## Hoopsnakes, Etc.

12424  A hoopsnake takes his tail in his mouth and forms a hoop.  Then he rolls downhill (M, SLC).

12425  A hoopsnake has a sting on the end of his tail (M, SLC, 1962).

12426  If a hoopsnake stings a tree with his tail, the snake will die (M, SLC, 1962).

12427  Snakes make a hoop out of their bodies and chase people by rolling at great speed (M, 20, SLC, 1950); A certain type of snake will put its tail in its mouth and roll down a hill in the form of a hoop and strike you with its poisoned tail, if disturbed (M, 20, SLC, 1954); The hoopsnake is a very poisonous reptile.  It can put its tail in its mouth and roll with lightninglike speed after its prey.  The only way to avoid it was to quickly jump through its hoop as it passed (F, 44, Provo, 1912).  Cf. Brown 7311.

12428  Rattlesnakes have mystic powers and they will roll up into a ring and chase people (M, 32, SLC, 1950).

## TURTLES, LIZARDS

12429  The symbol of a turtle brings good luck (F, SLC, 1958).

12430  A snapping turtle won't quit biting until it thunders (M, SLC, 1962); . . . will hold on until night comes (M, SLC, 1959); . . . will never let go until sundown (M, 21, Magna, 1964).  Brown 7014f.

12431  If a turtle bites you, put straw in its nostril and it will let go (M, 48, SLC, 1930).

12432  To dream of lizards is a sure sign of treachery (M, SLC, 1961).

12433  When a lizard is killed, if the tail is cut off, it will wiggle until sundown (M, Tooele, 1957).

12434  A lizard will shed its tail to escape from your hand (F, SLC, 1960).

12435  Snakes turn into lizards at midnight (M, SLC, 1945).

## POLYWOGS, FROGS, TOADS, NEWTS

12436  "My great grandfather was taught in school that polywogs hatch out of horsehair and stagnant water" (F, 67, SLC, 1970).

12437  If you hit the ground right in front of a frog, it will stand right still and you can pick it up (M, SLC, 1967).

12438  If you hurt a frog, he will revenge himself (F, SLC, 1940).

12439  If you kill a frog at a spring, it will dry up (M, SLC, 1959).  Brown 7336, cf. 7341f.

12440  Frogs spit poison (F, Holladay, 1959).

12441  If you bring a frog into the house, it will bring you good luck (M, Garland, 1963).

12442  A toad brings good luck (F, SLC, 1961).

12443  It is good luck to have a toad in the garden (F, 49, Eng, SLC, 1964).

12444  If a toad crosses your path, ill fortune will be yours for one year (F, 21, SLC, 1950).

12445  Toads can cast magic spells (M, 20, SLC, 1950).

12446  A horned toad spits blood (M, SLC, 1959).

12447  A toad is poisonous and has a precious jewel in its head (F, Murray, 1957).

12448  Horny toads with a yellow belly are poisonous (M, 21, SLC, 1970).

12449  If you kill a toad, something will haunt you at night (M, 52, SLC, 1964).  Cf. Brown 7343.

12450  Newts are endowed with a deadly poison (M, 53, SLC, 1963).

## FISH, EELS, ETC.

12451  When a crawfish grabs you it will not let go until it thunders (F, 19, SLC, 1957).

12452  If you keep a horsehair in water long enough, it will turn into an eel (F, 49, Logan, 1935).

12453  It is bad luck to drown an eel (M, 61, Ger, SLC, 1964).

12454  An octopus kills on Friday the thirteenth (M, 27, SLC, 1963).

## INSECTS

### Ants

12455  An ant must follow the same path back to his hole, or he'll get lost (M, 25, SLC, 1964).

12456  If ants make a heap near your door, it is good fortune (F, Axtell, 1958).

12457  Stepping on ants is bad luck (M, Murray, 1963).

12458  Step on ants in the day, and they'll haunt you at night (F, Spanish Fork, 1961).

12459  It is always unlucky to destroy an ant hill (F, Ogden, 1931); . . . a colony of ants (M, Ogden, 1959).

12460  If you dream of ants, you will be happy (M, Ogden, 1960).

Beetles

12461    It will bring bad luck if a beetle enters your room where you are staying (F, 1959).

12462    Beetles who make clicking noises when calling their mates are called "death watchers" (M, SLC, 1957).

12463    To kill a beetle is to court bad luck (M, 1961).

Butterflies

12464    If a white butterfly comes to your window in the spring, it is a sign of good luck (F, 83, SLC, 1964).

12465    If the first butterfly you see all year is a white one, you will have bad luck (F, 1959).

12466    In the spring if a black butterfly comes to your window, it is bad luck (F, 83, SLC, 1964).

12467    To see a dead butterfly usually brings tears during the week (F, SLC, 1959).

12468    It is good luck to see three butterflies together (F, SLC, 1959).

12469    A butterfly perched on your shoulder is a sign of good luck (M, 21, SLC, 1954).

12470    If you catch the first butterfly you see in the spring, it will bring bad luck the remainder of the year (F, Ogden, 1960).

12471    Wish when you see the first butterfly of spring, and it will come true (M, 34, SLC, 1956).

12472    Kill the first butterfly you see each year, or you will have bad luck (F, 12, 1959).

Crickets

12473    A cricket in the house will bring good luck (F, SLC, 1960); . . . foretells mirth and plenty (F, Axtell, 1958). Brown 2992.

12474    A cricket on the hearth means good luck (F, 18, Price, 1962); . . . keeps insects out of the house (F, SLC, 1961); . . . brings happiness to the home (F, SLC, 1925). Brown 3010.

12475    If a cricket comes into your home and sings, he brings luck to your hearth (F, SLC, 1961); The song of a cricket inside your door / Means good fortune for you is soon in store (F, 62, SLC, 1964).

12476    A cricket in the house brings good luck. Its departure is a sign of coming misfortune (F, 64, SLC, 1915); If you are kind to a cricket that comes into your house, it is a sign of good fortune. If you kill it, you will meet with ill fortune (M, SLC, 1957).

12477    A cricket in the house means bad luck (F, 80, SLC, 1964); . . . signifies evil (F, 83, SLC, 1965); Crickets chirping in the house mean bad luck (F, Bountiful, 1960).

12478    Never kill a cricket found inside the home, for it represents a symbol of protection against disaster (F, Dan, SLC, 1900s); It is bad luck to kill a cricket, especially on Sunday (F, Wellington, 1937); . . . you will get seven years of bad luck (M, 14, Provo, 1964); Do not kill a cricket on the hearth; pick it up on a piece of paper and carry it outside (M, 64, SLC, 1963). Cf. Brown 2993, 3009, 7352.

12479    Killing a Mormon cricket will bring bad luck (M, SLC, 1958).

12480    It's bad luck to kill a black cricket (F, 22, Price, 1960).

12481    If you kill a cricket, it will eat holes in your socks (F, Ogden, 1961).

12482    When you see a cricket, kill it. They are bad luck (M, Layton, 1934).

12483    It brings bad luck if you step on a cricket (F, SLC, 1961); Misfortune will befall you . . . (F, SLC, 1963).

12484    If a house has crickets chirping at night, it will be a harmonious home. No chirping means trouble (M, 60, Layton).

12485    If when you're walking at night and the crickets stop singing and you don't whistle for a second, you won't be able to sleep well that night because of the singing of the insects. This applies only in the hot summer months (M, 89, Provo, 1900); When the crickets sing, it's a quiet night (M, SLC, 1960).

12486    If the cricket chirps on Christmas, it means good luck for the following year (F, Ir, SLC, 1960).

12487    If we could understand the cricket's talk, it would tell us the history of the world (F, SLC, 1961).

12488    Catch a cricket on the first night of the harvest moon, and good fortune will be yours through the next harvest moon (F, SLC, 1962).

12489    If you turn a cricket on its back, you will have good luck (M, 67, Farmington, 1929).

12490    It is good luck to keep a cricket in a cage (M, 20, SLC, 1964).

Flies, Bees, Etc.

12491    Release a fly that is buzzing along the windowpane, and it will bring good luck (F, Ogden, 1960).

12492    If you dream of flies, it means much trouble ahead (F, 59, Bear River City, 1914).

12493    Kill a fly in May and keep a hundred away (F, 19, SLC, 1953).

12494    If you kill a fly, two more will come to its funeral (F, 39, SLC, 1964); . . . ten flies . . . (F, 14, SLC, 1960). Cf. Brown 2987.

12495    It is unlucky for a stray swarm of bees to alight on your premises (M, SLC, 1961).

12496  If bees come and build a nest on your roof, or in your yard, it will bring good luck to your home (F, Gr, SLC, 1957).

12497  When a bee flies in the window, expect good luck (F, Axtell, 1958); A wild bumblebee in the house brings good luck (F, SLC, 1960).

12498  A yellow honeybee is a sign of good luck (61); A yellow honeybee flying around a person brings good luck (M, 43, Orem, 1937).

12499  Don't be afraid of bees.  A bee won't sting you unless you bruise him or if he is mad.  Don't be afraid.  They know it and will sting you (F, Moab, 1953); Stand still as a post and the bee will go away (M, 17, SLC, 1953); A bee which is ignored will not sting (F, 19, Can, SLC, 1964).

12500  A bee can't sting you when you hold your breath, for the reason that your pores close when you hold your breath; therefore the bee's stinger can't penetrate your skin (M, 38, Woods Cross, 1963).

12501  Bees sting redheaded people, but overlook idiots (M, Orem, 1937).

12502  A bee will never sting a man with one son (M, SLC, 1961).

12503  Little bees sting more than large ones (M, SLC, 1959).

12504  To kill a bumblebee is a sure omen of misfortune (F, SLC, 1959).

12505  Dragonflies ("snake feeders" in this area) feed snakes.  Whenever you see a dragonfly, you know there is a snake nearby (F, Bountiful, 1964).

## Grasshoppers, Cicadas

12506  Grasshoppers spit tobacco (M, Layton, 1934).

12507  Upon seeing grasshoppers, children would call out "Spit tobacco or I'll kill you."  The grasshopper often spat (F, 60, SLC, 1915).

12508  Grasshopper legs are good luck (F, 69, Ir, SLC, 1957).

12509  When cicadas swarm, it means war is approaching (F, 56, Orem, 1964).

## Ladybugs

12510  Ladybugs are all women (F, SLC, 1960).

12511  A ladybug is good luck (F, 22, SLC, 1948); If you catch a ladybug, it will bring you good luck (F, SLC, 1964).

12512  If a ladybug is found in the house, it means good luck (M, 30, SLC, 1964).

12513  To find a ladybug on the way to school is a good omen (F, 21, Ogden, 1949).

12514  If a ladybug lands on you, it is good luck (F, SLC, 1961); . . . you are charmed for life (F, SLC, 1961).

12515  If a little ladybug should land on you, make a wish before she flies away, and this wish will then come true (F, 21, SLC, 1963); Make a wish on a ladybug that lights on you by saying:  "Ladybug, ladybug, fly away home; your house is on fire, your children will burn" (F, SLC, 1958).

12516      Ladybug, ladybug, to your home you
              must turn,
       Your house is on fire and your
              children may burn.
       (F, SLC, 1961); . . . your house is on fire and your children are alone (M, SLC, 1958).

12517      Ladybug, ladybug,
       Fly away home,
       Your house is on fire,
       Your children are alone.
       They're all burned up,
       But little Mary Ann,
       And she hid under
       The frying pan.
       (M, SLC, 1925).  Cf. Brown 7370ff.

12518      Ladybug, ladybug, fly away home,
       Your house is on fire, your children
              alone.
       One is upstairs making the bed,
       The other is downstairs making the
              bread.
       (F, Moab, 1953).

12519  Ladybugs are good luck, so you should let them crawl all over you (F, 20, SLC, 1963).

12520  If you kill a ladybug, you'll have very bad luck (M, 20, SLC, 1957); Bad luck will come to anyone who kills a ladybird (F, SLC, 1959).  Brown 7374.

## Various Insects

12521  Bugs live in holes because light kills their sex drive (M, Provo, 1945).

12522  A centipede seen at night is good luck (F, SLC, 1960).

12523  If you break a centipede in two, it will grow into two bugs (M, 36, Murray, 1950).

12524  Draw a chalk ring around a cockroach and it will not leave (F, 19, SLC, 1963).

12525  If a firefly gets in the house, there will be either one more person or one less person in the house the following day (M, 48, SLC, 1939).

12526  It is unlucky to kill firebugs (M, 55, Roosevelt, 1964).

12527  At a sidewalk intersection, the middle square (the only one surrounded by four other squares) is a flea square, and if you step in this square, you will get fleas (F, SLC, 1956).

12528  If you hold your breath while a mosquito is biting you, he will be unable to withdraw his bill, and you can kill him (M, 19, SLC, 1963).

12529  If you kill a stink beetle, you will have an unlucky day (M, 89, SLC, 1920s).

12530   If you kill a stink bug, you will stink forever (F, SLC, 1962).

12531   Drive a nail in a hole made by termites, and it will stop them (F, 20, SLC, 1949).

SPIDERS, DADDY LONGLEGS, ETC.

12532   If one sees a spider in the morning, it means bad luck, but if one sees a spider in the evening, it means good luck (F, 44, SLC, 1965).

12533   A spider in the morning means heartache and sorrow (F, Gunnison, 1960).

12534   If you see a spider in the morning, it is a sign of a good day (F, 24, Korean, SLC, 1963).

12535   A spider at noon will bring good luck soon (F, 47, Swiss, SLC, 1965); . . . good luck for the morrow (F, Gunnison, 1960).

12536   If one sees a spider at noon or in the evening, he will find happiness and be lucky (F, SLC, 1958); A spider in the evening has only the best meaning (F, 47, Swiss, SLC, 1965); . . . means repose and comfort (F, Gunnison, 1960); . . . it will bring you joy and delight (F, SLC, 1961).

12537   If you see a spider at night, it's bad luck (F, 25, Ja, SLC, 1964); . . . you will have bad dreams (M, SLC, 1960).

12538   White spiders are signs of good luck (F, Cedar City, 1964).

12539   A black spider walking in front of you is a good omen (F, 55, SLC, 1963).

12540   To have a spider on you is a sign of good luck (F, SLC, 1956); If a spider falls on your face, it is . . . (F, 56, Orem, 1964). Brown 7375.

12541   It is a sign of good luck to find a small spider on one's clothes (F, 19, SLC, 1963).

12542   A spider in your house brings good fortune (F, 18, SLC, 1950).

12543   If you see a spider walking backwards, you will have very bad luck (F, 18, SLC, 1961).

12544   It is bad luck for a spider to drop from the ceiling and drop on your head (M, SLC, 1961).

12545   A spider crawling over your hearth stones is a bad omen (F, 47, Swiss, SLC, 1965).

12546   Stepping on a spider brings bad luck (M, 57, Swiss, Heber City, 1913); Stepping on a white spider brings bad luck (F, Murray, 1936).

12547   Stepping on a black spider brings good luck (F, Richfield, 1936).

12548   To kill a spider is a sign of bad luck (F, 50, SLC); Do not kill a spider in the evening, or bad luck will follow (F, SLC, 1960); Killing a black spider is bad luck (F, 55, SLC, 1963).

12549   If you find a spider in your house, don't kill it, or it will bring you bad luck (M, 18, SLC, 1950); . . . seven years of bad luck (M, 20, SLC, 1964); . . . but if you retain the spider's body, you will have good luck (F, 97, Syracuse, 1891).

12550          If you want to live and thrive,
            Let the spider run alive.
        (M, 54, Magna, 1923). Brown 7379.

12551   To undo the bad luck that is to befall you after killing a spider, take a whisk of a broom and break it in four pieces and burn them, then bury the remaining ashes (F, 42, SLC, 1964). Cf. Brown 7378.

12552   If you kill a spider, you will have good luck (M, 22, SLC, 1949). Cf. Brown 7377.

12553   Kill a spider in the morning, and good luck will follow all day (F, SLC, 1960).

12554   A daddy longlegs by your door will bring you good luck (F, 59, SLC, 1962).

12555   Daddy-longlegs are the most poisonous of all spiders, but their mouths are too small to bite (F, SLC, 1900). Brown 7383.

12556   Never kill a grand-daddy longlegs; it is bad luck (F, 74, SLC, 1964).

12557   If you see a black widow spider in the morning, you'll have bad luck (M, SLC, 1958).

12558   When you find a rock that has a black widow spider under it, you will be the first to be bitten by a spider (M, SLC, 1957).

12559   Black widows bite murderers (M, 19, SLC, 1963).

Cobwebs, Spider Webs, Etc.

12560   A cobweb in the house means bad luck (F, Vernal, 1963).

12561   It's unlucky to destroy a cobweb (M, 90, W. Jordan, 1880).

12562   If you find your initials in spider webs near the door of a new home, it is a sign that you will be lucky as long as you live there (F, 19, Ogden, 1960).

12563   A spider spinning a web in front of you will bring you good luck (M, 64, SLC, 1910); If a spider comes down on a web from the ceiling in front of you, it will bring you good luck (F, 67, Bear River City, 1913).

12564   It is good luck to have a spider spin his web downward toward you, but bad luck when he rises toward you (F, 85, SLC, 1964).

12565   If you are lying in bed and you see a spider, and it spins a web over your head, it means good luck (F, 25, SLC, 1964).

## CATERPILLARS, WORMS, ETC.

12566 If you find a hairy caterpillar, throw it over your shoulder for good luck (F, Kamas, 1945); . . . for good luck throw it over your left shoulder (F, SLC, 1959).

12567 Worms come from horses' hair (M, SLC, 1958); When a horsehair hits water, it turns into a worm (F, 76, St. George, 1894); A hair from a horse's mane or tail, when put in water, will turn into a worm (F, 57, Vernal, 1915); . . . put in rainwater . . . (F, SLC, 1957); Put a horse's hair in water and leave it for three weeks . . . (M, SLC, 1964). Cf. Brown 7385.

12568 Worms come out for air at night (M, SLC, 1964).

12569 If you make loud noises, earthworms will crawl out of their holes (M, 21, SLC, 1964).

12570 To get night crawlers to come out of the ground say, "Doodle-bug, doodle-bug, come and get sugar" (F, 21, Midvale, 1964). Cf. Brown 7358f.

12571 Glowworms will give off light if put in a bottle in a dark place (F, SLC, 1960).

## SNAILS

12572 If you throw a snail over your shoulder the first day of May, you will be lucky all year (F, SLC, 1960).

12573 If you step on a slug (landmark), it is good luck (F, 19, SLC, 1954).

12574 When you step on a slug, you can hit people (F, 19, SLC, 1964).

Editor's note: A misreading of the above two entries resulted in their having been placed here rather than with Nos. 1270, 2073, or 8339, where they might have appeared to better advantage. Difficulties of numbering and indexing made such a reordering impossible.

## LEGENDARY, MYTHICAL ANIMALS

12575 The Sidehill Wampus Cat has two short legs on the left side, resulting from its habitat, going around hills constantly. It lays a square egg that will not roll downhill (F, Panguitch, 1940).

12576 An animal enigma. Its hind legs have the hoofs of a moose and its forelegs the claws of a bear, making it very hard to track. When it tires of using one set of legs, it travels on the other set. It is fierce in appearance, but shy and harmless (M, 19, Provo, 1963).

12577 The Sidehill Dodger was an animal that lived on the sides of hills only. It had two short legs on the uphill side. It burrowed in hillsides, having a number of such burrows and was always dodging in and out of these (M, 79, Lehi, 1920).

12578 The Luferlang attacked its prey without provocation, and its bite was certain death (M, 77, Lehi, 1935). It is a curious animal with a bushy tail in the middle of the back. Its legs were triple-jointed, and it could run equally fast in any direction (informant data not available).

12579 The hoary beast that lived in the hollow trunks was the Argopelter. From this point of vantage it dropped chunks of splinters of wood on its victims. It seldom missed its aim, and a considerable number of people were often victims on its gunnery (M, Moab, 1920).

12580 The Goofang fish swims backward instead of forward. This was to keep the water out of its eyes (M, 76, Eureka, 1899).

12581 The Bear Lake Monster was first sighted about twenty-five years ago. Skin divers have found caves under the lake going into the mountain, which are possibly the habitat of the alleged monster (F, 21, SLC, 1963).

12582 People living around the area of Bear Lake are well acquainted with the many tales of the Bear Lake Monster. It was reported by hundreds of people that a monster would arise out of the lake to seek food on the land (F, 21, Laketown, 1950).

## ANIMAL HUSBANDRY

12583 Salt the tail of animals to tame them (F, SLC, 1957).

12584 Albino animals are bad luck because they are outcasts from the flock (M, 24, Ogden, 1950).

12585 If there is a sick pet and a sick person in the same family, the life of one is dependent upon the other. If the animal dies, the person will live, and if the person dies, the animal will live (F, Lehi, 1922).

12586 When an animal is right thin, the chance of conception is greater. They will pick up (M, Draper, 1925).

12587 If an animal is bleeding to death, apply mashed mushrooms, puff balls, snuff, cobwebs, or soot (M, 44, Price, 1930).

12588 For wire cuts on stock, throw lime or puff balls in the cut (F, 24, SLC, 1964).

12589 Apply blue vitriol directly to any animal wounds (M, Hurricane).

12590 Blow powdered calument [sic] into an animal's eye to cure a film over the eye (M, 22, SLC, 1964).

12591 Any butchering should be done by the light of the moon (M, Logan, 1970).

12592 Only kill animals for eating in the dark of the moon. It will be easier, and the meat will last longer (M, 73, Wellington, 1928).

12593 Never kill and eat an animal the same day, because the soul will enter your body (M, 38, SLC, 1935).

12594    Castrate when the sign is in the foot (M, SLC, 1963). Cf. Brown 7392.

12595    When animals are dying off rapidly from some disease, a healthy one sacrificed alive at the forks of a road will cure the rest (F, 28, SLC, 1948).

12596    Bury carcasses of all domesticated animals to keep other domesticated animals from becoming discontent (M, 37, Fountain Green, 1939).

12597    A horseshoe nailed above a barn entrance will bring good luck. Always be sure the ends are turned upwards, however, or the luck will run out. I have never seen horseshoes nailed up except in pairs. This must mean something (F, Logan, 1970); . . . to place the horseshoe in the position of the letter "U" (F, Dan, SLC, 1958).

12598    "We always kept a horseshoe over the door of the barn. You had to stop under and say 'Whoa' three times before you passed on into the barn. This not only gave you supernatural protection, but insured adequate warning to the horses, so they would not kick at you" (F, Logan, 1958). Cf. Brown 7661ff.

12599    It is good luck for farmers to hang a shiny horseshoe over the barn door. It keeps out evil spirits (F, 76, St. George, 1894).

12600    Never shut the barn door after the horse leaves, or your fortune will flee (F, SLC, 1962).

12601    The more cobwebs there are in a stable, the more fortunate it is (F, 24, SLC, 1954).

12602    The barn will burn down if the doors are closed for a week solid (M, SLC, 1964).

12603    To keep harmful birds away, nail a dead crow or hawk on the barn door (M, 40, SLC, 1930).

12604    In raising pigeons, if they are dipped in rainwater, they will have good luck (F, SLC, 1960).

CANARIES

12605    Unless you cover a canary's cage at night, it will sing all night and die (F, 47, Vernal, 1937).

12606    When a person has canaries and wishes them to have young, put a sage leaf with the eggs and they will hatch (F, SLC, 1959).

12607    If your canary bird sings after dark, it is a sign that it will not live much longer (F, SLC, 1959).

CATS

12608    If you have a cat with double paws, it will bring you good luck (F, 63, SLC, 1915).

12609    A cat in the house brings the family good luck (F, 1958).

12610    You will have good luck if a cat follows you home (M, SLC, 1959).

12611    If a cat comes to live with you, it will bring good luck (M, 84, Centerville); If a stray kitten comes to your home and you feed it, it will bring you good luck for many days (F, SLC, 1961).

12612    If you take a stray cat into your house, you'll have bad luck (M, 44, Ogden, 1935).

12613    A black cat that comes to stay brings bad luck (M, 84, Centerville). Cf. Brown 8562.

12614    Never leave the house with a cat inside; it is bad luck (F, Murray, 1957).

12615    A cat sneezing brings good luck (F, SLC, 1925); If a cat sneezes while you are looking at it, you will have a happy life (F, SLC, 1959).

12616    If you cut off a cat's whiskers, he can't smell mice (F, 58, SLC, 1963).

12617    A cat with mittens catches no mice (M, 18, SLC, 1950).

12618    It's good luck to own a black cat (F, 55, Eng, SLC, 1963).

12619    A black cat that is treated with kindliness will bring good fortune to its owner (F, SLC, 1951).

12620    Never give a black cat away, but lend it (M, 22, SLC, 1963).

12621    Paper sacks are to put cat food in for good luck (M, SLC, 1964).

12622    Carry cats in your arms when visiting with neighbors, so your cat will stay home (F, 70, SLC, 1930).

12623    If you castrate a cat, it will never stray from home (F, SLC, 1959).

12624    If you move and don't want your cat to return to your old house, put cream on its paws, and the cat will stay at your new house (F, SLC, 1958); Butter a kitten's feet, and it will forget its old home and be contented (F, SLC, 1959); Grease a cat's feet . . . (F, 71, Midway, 1900). Brown 7397.

12625    The common way to keep a cat at home is to cut the tip of its tail off and bury it under the doorstep (F, 21, SLC, 1963). Brown 7398.

12626    Always lock all the doors in the house before a cat is about to have baby kittens, or she will go outside and eat the young (M, SLC, 1947).

12627    A baby and a kitten can't get along in the same house, and if the cat has kittens the same time as a child is born, then the kittens must be destroyed (F, 83, Venice, 1910).

12628    If you let a dog lick a cat, the latter will recover from its illness (M, 67, Ger, SLC, 1939).

12629    It's bad luck for a cat to have more than three owners. A cat has the power to put an incantesimo on you (F, It, SLC, 1971).

12630 It is good luck to have a black kitten or kittens born on Halloween (F, SLC, 1967).

12631 It is unlucky to let a cat die inside the house (F, 87, Dan, SLC, 1900).

## DOGS

12632 Keep a yellow dog around for good luck (F, 90, SLC, 1964).

12633 Dogs always take on the characteristics of their masters (F, 20, SLC, 1963).

12634 It is bad luck to sell a dog that has a black spot (M, Ogden, 1959).

12635 To keep a dog at home, cut a piece from the end of its tail and bury it under the doorstep (F, 21, SLC, 1963). Brown 7411ff.

12636 If your dog is inclined to stray, wear a piece of cheese on the heel of your boot (F, SLC, 1959).

12637 If you lose your dog, whistle through a knot hole, and he will return (F, Axtell, 1958).

12638 If you form a dog's head out of a snowball tree's leaf, your dog will die, or else you will get a new one (F, 19, SLC, 1965).

12639 If you look at a dog or other animal covetously, its hair will fall out and it will die (M, 23, SLC, 1961).

12640 If you have a young puppy dog and he insists on howling at night, you can quiet him by providing him with an alarm clock and a hot water bottle. If one of these is not present, either will work. This makes him feel with their sound and warmth that his mother is near, and he will go to sleep (F, 58, Richfield, 1915).

12641 If you stir a dog's food with a knife, it will make him mean (F, 49, Roosevelt, 1964).

12642 Milk will starve a dog (F, Bountiful, 1964).

12643 A frothing dog is crazy or has rabies (M, 55, SLC, 1915).

12644 For a dog that has been poisoned with strychnine cut the end of his tail off so it will bleed and let the poison out of the dog's system. By doing this the dog will lose the poison as the blood drips from the cut tail (M, 44, Ephraim, 1939).

12645 To remove porcupine quills from a dog's mouth, cut them off close to the flesh and they will draw out easily. Do not pull them with pliers (F, 20, SLC, 1963).

12646 If a dog drinks fresh milk, he will have fits. This is so because the fresh milk coming from a cow has foam on it and a mad dog foams at the mouth (M, 38, Logan, 1970).

12647 If a dog has fits, feed him four doses of gunpowder (F, SLC, 1960); . . . running fits . . . (M, 42, Clearfield, 1948).

12648 Feed a dog four doses of chewing tobacco to cure its fits (M, SLC, 1920).

12649 Give a dog a clove of garlic, and it will cure worms (M, Holladay, 1967).

## CHICKENS

### Setting and Hatching

12650 Carry eggs over running water if you want them to set (F, Moab, 1953). (Streams and other bodies of running water are highly magical, demarcating boundaries as they often do, or offering asylum from pursuit. Creatures of lower mythology, including witches, are said not to be able to cross running streams, and thus haunt bridges and watercourses. Taboos extend to wedding parties and funeral corteges, yet here, as throughout folklore, reverse magic is often operable. See Wayland D. Hand, "Crossing Water: A Folkloristic Motif," in For Max Weinreich on His Seventieth Birthday: Studies in Jewish Languages, Literature and Society [The Hague, 1964], pp. 82-92. --Eds.)

12651 Sprinkle water on a hen's head, and she will go to setting (F, 29, SLC, 1963).

12652 Don't borrow eggs to set a hen from one family if you have a young one who has a birthday in the same month (M, 33, Gr, SLC, 1963).

12653 For the best result, set a hen on thirteen eggs. You go by the dozen, and the extra one is given. This is known as a "setting" (F, Tooele, 1920); There was almost a family ceremony when hens were set (F, Tooele, 1920). Brown 7433.

12654 Set a hen at night (F, Tooele, 1910).

12655 If you set a hen to hatch her eggs on a holiday or a Sunday, none of the chicks will turn out (M, Orem, 1975).

12656 Never let a hen sit on an uneven number of eggs (M, 20, Mt. Pleasant, 1964); . . . ., for none will hatch (M, 90, W. Jordan, 1901). Cf. Brown 7432f.

12657 In setting eggs, if you desire all the chicks to be hens, let a woman carry the eggs to the nest in her lap (F, 45, SLC, 1935).

12658 If water touches the eggs that are set, the chickens will drown (M, Grantsville, 1963).

12659 When eggs are set under a hen, they are usually marked to distinguish them from eggs which might be laid later in the nest. The marks up on the shell will be reproduced on the chicks (M, 26, SLC, 1945).

12660 To stop a hen from setting, dowse her in a tub of cold water (F, 45, SLC, 1935); . . . get a bucket or a barrel and put the hen in with the water and every time she sits down, she will stand up (F, Moab, 1953). Cf. Brown 7429.

12661 Chicken eggs won't hatch if it thunders and lightnings (F, Bear River City, 1957). Cf. Brown 7443f, 7504.

12662 A thunderstorm will make little chickens hatch (F, Centerfield, 1920).

12663 If a hen is setting on eggs and an awful electric storm occurs, the forming chicks in the eggs will die (F, 31, Centerville, 1963); . . . chicks will go crazy (M, Thistle, 1911).

12664 Never wash eggs which are to be put under a setting hen, or they will not hatch (M, SLC, 1957).

12665 Put a horseshoe under eggs, and they will hatch (F, 68, Ogden, 1958).

12666 To have a hen sitting on eggs and all the eggs turn out to be cocks is unlucky, and the hen should be eaten as soon as possible, or the rest of the hen's eggs will turn out to be roosters (F, 51, Provo, 1930).

12667 If you set your hen on big eggs, they'll all hatch into roosters (M, 93, Eng, SLC, 1965).

12668 If the first person that comes to your house on New Year's Day is a woman, nearly all your young chickens will be hens; but if your first visitor is a man, they will be largely roosters (M, 54, Midvale, 1964). Brown 7442.

12669 If you give away a chick, your luck goes with it (M, Kaysville, 1938).

Laying Eggs

12670 A setting hen lays no eggs (M, SLC, 1961).

12671 Baked eggshell will make the chickens lay (M, SLC, 1925). Cf. Brown 7453.

12672 Red pepper is put into the mash to make chickens lay (M, SLC, 1925).

12673 The lucky fellow gets eggs from his rooster and has hens whose eggs have two yolks (F, 46, SLC).

12674 Eggs laid during a thunderstorm will be bloody (F, Bear River City, 1957).

12675 If there is a thunderstorm while a hen is laying an egg, she'll never lay again (M, SLC, 1969).

12676 If you frighten chickens, they will lay bloody eggs (F, 20, Sandy, 1956).

12677 Eggs laid on Good Friday will go stale (F, 83, Pleasant Grove, 1908). Cf. Brown 7456.

12678 It is a bad omen to gather eggs and bring them into the house after dark (M, SLC, 1961).

12679 It brings bad luck to count eggs on Sunday (M, SLC, 1961).

12680 If you see a hen trying to crow like a rooster, you should cut off its head and

lay it on the porch. Otherwise the flock will turn homosexual and the egg production will decrease (M, 45, SLC, 1963).

12681 If you go in one door of the chicken coop or farmhouse, you must go out the same door when you leave, or you will ruin the chicken lot, namely, the number of eggs laid by the chickens (M, 52, SLC, 1964).

12682 If it rains on Valentine Day, your chickens will stop laying (M, 59, Beaver, 1920). Brown 7455.

Chickens' Diseases, Tonics, Etc.

12683 The informant's son, four years and one month old, wanted to bless one of the baby chicks that was sick. The parents let him, and by that afternoon the chicken was well and lively. Then the mother told the children that the chick was well. The boy said that he knew it would be (M, from his missionary journal, 1893-1896).

12684 Sprinkle ashes on animals and fowls on Ash Wednesday, and they will not be bothered with lice (M, SLC, 1963). Brown 7391, 7470.

12685 A broom hung in a chicken house will rid it of chicken lice (M, 52, Kenilworth, 1921).

12686 Grease little chickens' heads with lard and kerosene, mixed into an emulsion, to keep away lice (F, SLC, 1920). Brown 7471.

Chicken Hawks

12687 Put a bright object, cans or something, up high to keep hawks away from chickens (F, Moab, 1953).

12688 A hawk cannot catch a chicken if he sees a horseshoe (F, 80, SLC, 1963). Cf. Brown 7488.

Loss of Chickens, Death, Killing, Etc.

12689 To kick a cat will make it steal chickens (M, SLC, 1959).

12690 If a freshly killed chicken starts to jerk, place the chicken upon a cross drawn on the ground and it will stop (M, SLC, 1957). Brown 7497.

12691 To kill a chicken unexpectedly will bring bad luck (F, 56, SLC, 1963).

12692 If a chicken which has just had its head cut off should touch you, you should not eat it (F, SLC, 1925).

Miscellaneous Beliefs about Chickens

12693 Before the death of a farmer his poultry will go to roost at midday, instead of the usual time (F, 29, SLC, 1948).

12694 Feathers picked on the increase of the moon will be plentiful (M, SLC, 1963). Brown 7501.

TURKEYS, DUCKS, GEESE

12695  Little turkeys do better when mothered
by a hen than by a turkey (F, SLC,
1920).  Brown 7510.

12696  If a little duck gets wet on its back,
it will die because it doesn't have
waterproof feathers yet (F, Moab, 1953).

12697  Baby geese come from swamp plants (F,
Bountiful, 1960).

BEES

12698  A swarm of bees in May is worth a load
of hay; a swarm of bees in June is worth
a silver spoon; a swarm of bees in July
isn't worth a fly (M, 84, Centerville).
Brown 7515.

12699  It is unlucky at times to sell bees (F,
85, SLC, 1964).  Brown 7517.

12700  To remove bees on Good Friday will cause
them to die (M, Honeyville, 1915).

12701  If the owner of a beehive dies, the bees
must be told about it before sunup the
next morning, or they will weaken and
die (F, 68, Ogden, 1958).  Cf. Brown
7519, 7520.

12702  Before you put bees in a new hive, you
must knock three times and tell them you
are moving them.  If you don't, you'll
get stung by spiteful bees (M, SLC,
1961).

12703  Imitate a storm to settle the bees; have
the sun flashing off a pie tin to make
lightning, and bang tins to make thunder
(F, Moab, 1953).

12704  When the bees swarmed we used to take a
looking glass and throw a reflection of
the sun on them to settle them (F, Woods
Cross, 1953).

12705  To settle a swarm of bees, throw sand
among them, or make a big noise (F,
Moab, 1953).

12706  When the bees swarmed we used to go with
kettles and spoons and things and drum
them to settle the bees (F, Woods Cross,
1953); If you beat on a pan while bees
are swarming, they will light and you
can catch them--reason:  The bees think
the noise is thunder and lightning
nearby (M, 38, beekeeper, Woods Cross,
1941).

12707  If a man dies that raises bees, tell the
bees about the death before sunup or
there will be no honey (M, Grantsville,
1961).

12708  Bees will leave unless told of death (M,
SLC, 1963).  Brown 7519.

12709  Stolen bees will not thrive but will die
(F, SLC, 1963).

COWS

Various Beliefs and Practices

12710  The Irish believe when passing a
farmyard where there are cattle, it is

well to say "A blessing of God be on you
and your labors" (M, MD, SLC, 1959).

12711  A mean or crusty cow always has curved
horns; usually the horns are turned up
or out away from the head of the cow (M,
56, Parktown, farmer, 1940).

12712  When you want a cow to stand still you
say, "So, Bossy" (F, Moab, 1953).

12713  Dry cows off on Sunday morning, and they
will come in during the daytime (M, 78,
SLC).

12714  Feed your cow sugar, and it will come
home at night (M, 47, SLC, 1930).

12715  When there is any large wild grass in
your pasture the cattle will not eat (M,
SLC, 1964).

12716  If you drive cattle with an ash twig,
they will provide you with good butter
(M, Park City, 1957).

12717  Cows eat buttercups to help them make
better butter (F, 49, Logan, 1930).

12718  If cows and sheep run in the same field,
the sheep will ruin all the food.  The
cows won't eat it because it smells (M,
44, Kamas, 1935).

Milk, Milking

12719  Cows eat buttercups to make more milk
and cream (M, 7, SLC, 1962).

12720  If you sing to a cow, she will give more
milk (M, 48, SLC, 1963); People who used
to keep dairies said that singing when
milking had a gentling effect on the
cows (F, 71, Woods Cross, 1953).

12721  If a cow kicks a lot, rub her side with
milk (F, 45, nurse, SLC, 1937).

12722  Spilling the milk while milking a cow
will bring bad luck (M, 21, SLC, 1955).
Cf. Brown 7527.

12723  A bob-tailed cow gives sour milk at
night (M, Altonah, 1913).

12724  If a crow flies over the barn, there
will be blood in the milk (M, SLC,
1962).

12725  If one kills a frog, the cow will give
bloody milk (M, 53, SLC, 1936).  Brown
7524.

12726  If you smash or kill a toad, the cow's
milk will be bloody (F, 53, SLC, 1914).
Cf. Brown 7525f.

12727  If you kill a cricket, your cow will
give bloody milk (F, Clearfield, 1959).

12728  If you put a fork in the milk, the cow
will go dry (F, SLC, 1961).

12729  If a milkmaid does not wash her hands
after milking, her cows will go dry (F,
74, SLC, 1964).

12730  A cow dries up when trees begin to
flower (M, 24, SLC, 1946).

12731  Don't kill a cricket, or your cow will
go dry (M, SLC, 1959).

## Loss of Cud, Hollow Tail

12732  If a cow loses her cud, stuff chewing
       tobacco down her throat (M, 70,
       Duchesne, 1970).

12733  A dishrag can be used to restore a cow's
       cud (M, 70, Duchesne, 1970); A greasy
       dishrag . . . (M, 78, Monroe, 1964).
       Cf. Brown 7573.

12734  If a cow has a disease known as "holler
       tail," you must split the tail open and
       apply a mixture of salt and vinegar,
       then bind it up with woolen yarn (F,
       SLC, 1960).  Cf. Brown 7591f, 7594ff.

## Various Ailments, Preventions

12735      Let May come early or late,
           It will make an old cow quiver and
              quake.
       (M, 77, Pleasant Grove, 1900).

12736  If a goat grazes with a herd of cattle,
       they will remain free of disease (F, 39,
       SLC, 1963).

12737  A man can't raise both cattle and sheep,
       because disease will kill them if they
       are kept together (M, 72, Willard,
       1900s).

12738  When a cow's horns are cold she is sick
       (F, 63, Monroe, 1964).

12739  Failure to put the right glove on before
       the left when inside the barn will
       result in hoof and mouth disease of the
       stock (M, 36, Heber, 1954).

12740  Pump a cow's udder up with air for milk
       fever (M, 70, Duchesne, 1970).

12741  Farmers dehorn cattle according to the
       phases of the moon to stop the bleeding
       (M, SLC, 1936).

12742  Wild sage was used for a sprained ankle
       or a sprained wrist, and was used even
       on cattle (F, Woods Cross, 1953).

## Straying Cows, Ill Omens, Death

12743  Never turn cows into summer grazing
       pasture when the wind is in the east as
       they will continually break the fence to
       get out of the pasture (F, SLC, 1956).

12744  If you feed a cow a bunch of her own
       hairs, she will forget her old home (M,
       SLC, 1959).

12745  If a farmer has lost his cows and he
       finds a daddy longlegs spider, he will
       say, "Longlegs, longlegs, tell me where
       the cows are," and the spider will crawl
       in the direction of the lost cows (M,
       46, Beaver, 1930).  Cf. Brown 7393,
       7611.

12746  It is unlucky to put your hand on a
       calf's back.  The calf will fall ill, or
       meet with an accident (F, Brigham City,
       1960).

12747  When a cow becomes sick, if you keep her
       on her feet she will not die, but if she
       falls to the ground, she will surely die
       (M, 35, SLC, 1964).

## Calves, Calving

12748  Always dry up a cow that is going to
       have a calf at least two months in
       advance, or the calf will be small and
       scrawny when born (M, 61, farmer, Kamas,
       1940).

12749  When a cow that is going to have a calf
       lies down on her right side instead of
       rolling to the left, her calf will be
       born in the next twenty-four hours (F,
       62, Kamas).

12750  When a cow is to freshen, if the front
       teats are longer, the calf will be a
       heifer; if the back ones are longer, it
       will be a male (M, 68, SLC, 1964).

12751  If a cow's milk dries up on an odd-
       numbered day, her calf will be born
       hind-end first instead of the right way
       (M, 19, Centerville, 1954).

12752  To relieve a cow from afterbirth, feed
       her an old dishrag (M, 78, Monroe,
       1964).

12753  A mother cow will leave her young if
       milked (M, SLC, 1964).

12754  It is unlucky to put your hand on a new
       calf's back (M, 50, S. Jordan, 1950).

12755  If a calf is taken from its mother
       during the dark of the moon, the mother
       will not grieve the loss (F, SLC, 1952).

12756  A calf has to be weaned from its mother
       when the moon has gone down so that he
       is not in the light of the moon.  This
       will prevent the calf from bawling after
       the separation (F, 83, Ir, Nephi, 1964).

12757  If a cow watches another cow, steer, or
       bull get slaughtered, she will never
       calve again (M, 67, Layton, 1910).

## Butchering, Branding, Castrating

12758  To run an animal before you kill it will
       make the meat tender (SLC, 1959).

12759  You should butcher beef during the time
       of month when the moon is light so that
       the beef won't shrivel (F, 25, Kearns,
       1961).

12760  If the cattle are butchered during the
       increase of the moon, it is believed
       that the meat will increase in volume
       when cooked (F, 1959).

12761  You should never buy beef in September
       because the cows are changing pasture,
       and the meat will taste funny (F, SLC,
       1968).

12762  Mrs. B believed that when the equinox
       was at its point during late July or
       early August (when the sun was directly
       overhead instead of to the south or
       straight overhead), the fattest one of
       the cattle should be killed and eaten to
       bring good luck to the rest of the herd
       (F, 94, Richfield, 1900).

12763  Brand cattle in the waning moon so that
       the brand will not grow.  If you brand
       them in the growing moon, the brand
       spreads all over (F, St. George, 1954).

12764 Castrate cattle in the last quarter of the moon, because the blood is high in the animals, and they won't bleed freely (M, Spanish Fork, 1974).

## Bewitchment of Cattle

12765 If your cow will not give down her milk, it is a sign that you have an enemy, and that he has cursed you (F, Lehi, 1900s).

12766 There was an old woman in Farmington who was believed to be a witch and could make cows go dry and ruin crops. She was found dead in her hut one morning, and the extracted ball was found to have been made of a silver coin. This was evidence of the ancient belief that only silver bullets would kill a witch (M, SLC, 1946).

12767 Brother C's cattle were bewitched and were dying. A strange man appeared and told him to go to the timber in the mountains and bore an inch hole through as many trees as he had cattle. Take the cattle into the grove, cut off their tails, drive the tails into the holes, wedge them in solid, then drive the cattle away, and the spell would be broken. This was done, and he lost no more cattle (M). Cf. Brown 7625.

12768 If you put the ice pick into the ceiling, the neighbor's cow will go dry, and you will be able to milk the ice pick (F, Swed, SLC, 1966).

## OXEN

12769 During an exploration of Colorado for the church, Mr. B's oxen drank some poison water and were dying. He got down on his knees and laid a hand on each of his oxen and prayed to God to give life and heal the oxen. He did, and the oxen stood up with the poison water running out of them in streams. The oxen were weak, but were healed (M, from his journal, 1888).

12770 Coming from the east, President Young overtook a company of Norwegians who were traveling with ox teams that were heavily loaded. One of the wagons was stuck in the mud and the Norwegians were whipping and yelling to the oxen but the wagon was still stuck. President Young took the whip from the Norwegians, talked to the oxen in a tongue which was not understood by English or Norwegians, touched the oxen lightly with the whip and the oxen instantly pulled the wagon out of the mud (M, SLC, 1948).

## HORSES

### Habits, Training, Etc.

12771 Years ago, it was considered bad luck to load horses on a steamboat unless you first saw a white dog (M, SLC, 1957).

12772 Quakers load or handle hay using a three-pronged pitchfork over the right shoulder. Hay pitched in any other way is condemned, because it will poison horses (M, 34, Granger, 1964).

12773 If a horse has three white spots on his stomach, he will be a fast runner (M, 81, Welsh, SLC, 1964).

12774 If you wind a horse's tail, it will run faster (F, Kamas, 1957).

12775 Indians will never buy a horse with four white feet. They will buy one with one white foot or two, or three, but never with four (M, SLC, 1959). Cf. Brown 7633.

12776 If horse chestnuts are fed to horses, the horses will have long lives (M, SLC, 1959).

12777 Never feed a horse from your left hand. You'll get bitten (M, 1960).

12778 It is bad luck to uncover a horse before a horse show (M, SLC, 1957).

12779 It is bad luck to buy a horse and then change its name (M, 54, Magna, 1923). Cf. Brown 7390.

12780 If you buy or trade for a horse, never ask its name. Give it a name yourself and avoid bad luck (M, 24, SLC, 1963). Cf. Brown 7641.

12781 A horse with one white leg is weak, and should not be bought (F, Manti, 1930).

12782 When a horse gets down and rolls on the ground, every time he makes a complete roll from one side to the other, he's worth fifty dollars. If he rolled over three times, he'd be worth one hundred-fifty dollars (M, 28, 1967). Cf. Brown 7637.

12783 A horse will throw a woman who is menstruating (M, SLC, 1957).

12784 Never mount the right side of a horse (M, 21, SLC, 1964); If you get on a horse by its right side, it will not be nice to you (F, 21, SLC, 1964).

12785 To get on a horse on the left side rather than the right side will bring you bad luck (F, 21, SLC).

12786 If you ever hit or spook a horse in the night, it will throw you the next day (F, SLC, 1960).

12787 If a horse runs with its ears down, he is in top condition (M, jockey, SLC, 1964).

12788 If a horse is missing one shoe, it is immediate bad luck to ride the horse more than once a day (M, 73, Crescent).

12789 Never guide a horse by pulling his ears, or he'll think you don't like him (F, SLC, 1964).

12790 Never ride a horse near blood, and always shield a horse's eyes from fire (M, 72, Willard, 1900s).

12791 To ride a black horse is much more fortunate than riding a horse of some other color (M, 54, Magna, 1923).

12792 Keep a white horse for good luck (F, 74, SLC, 1964).

12793   A narrow distance between the eyes of a horse indicates he is mean (M, 19, SLC, 1963).

12794   If the white of a horse's eye shows all around the iris, it means that the animal is a killer (F, 1960).

12795   A brown horse will always have a brown offspring (M, SLC, 1964).

12796   If you wean a colt when the sign (of the zodiac) is in the heart, it will cry itself to death (M, 48, Vernal, 1931).

12797   A colt born in May will not cross water while young (F, 87, Midway).   Brown 7634.

12798   A colt born in May will always lie down while being driven through water (M, 26, SLC, 1945).

12799   "My mother once became infuriated with some men for mistreating a horse. Pointing to the horse she cried, 'I wish that horse would drop dead.'  Instantly the horse fell to the ground, and died on the spot.  One man thought that mother was a witch, but she was as surprised as they at the incident" (F, Logan, 1958).

## Stray or Lost Horses, Bewitchment

12800   There was a man that lost two horses and he couldn't find them and he went to the Peepstone Woman [Logan] and she told him right where they were, but it was too late for him to go after them.  He went up the next spring.  They had starved to death on the range--he went right up to where she had told him they were (F, 60, 1946).

12801   Mrs. CP of Logan used a peepstone.  Mrs. C's parents lost a valuable horse, and Mrs. P looked in her stone and told them where to find it (F, 81, Logan, 1946).

12802   "My husband's brother's daughter bought a ouija board.  We lost a team of horses and asked ouija where they were.  It said, 'Down by the depot behind a pile of lumber,' and there they were.  We asked ouija where it got its information, and it said, 'From the devil'" (F, 81, Logan, 1946).

12803   When a horse's mane is tangled, goblins have been riding it during the night (M, 23, Holladay, 1953).  Cf. Brown 7663f.

## Divers Equine Ailments, Castration

12804   Goats kept in stables with horses will keep disease away from the horses (M, Park City, 1957).

12805   Sheep in a field will make a horse get swaybacked (M, 44, Kamas, 1963).

12806   If one of your animals gets sick, round up all your horses, and with a sharp knife split the end of each animal's tail, just so it can bleed a few drops (F, 1960).

12807   If a horse acts sick and tired, take sandpaper and rub the inside of his upper lip until it just bleeds, and he will pick up (M, Ogden, 1960).

12808   "One time one of the neighbors had gone away and just left a little girl, and I was over helping her to do the chores. We were mowing alfalfa for the pigs with a scythe.  I was swinging the scythe and the horse stepped back just as I swung the scythe, and it cut her hind leg and the blood just spurted out.  I was scared, and she was too, and I said, 'Good land, we'll get some pig manure and put on that and maybe it will stop bleeding.'  So we did and bound it up, and in a week you couldn't tell the horse had ever been hit.  I don't know that I ever used cow manure" (F, Moab, 1953).

12809   If a man wants to raise particularly good horses, or if he wants to protect his herd, he should keep one well-groomed, healthy white one with his horses (F, 21, SLC, 1964).

12810   If the horse is sick and you spit in his mouth, the horse will get well (M, 73, Gr, SLC, 1963).

12811   Jump a horse off a high place to make him stop choking (M, 21, SLC, 1964).

12812   For stiff joints in a horse, let the animal stand in a cold creek for twenty-four hours (F, 30, SLC, 1964).

12813   "If a horse is cut by a sharp instrument such as an ax, the rider should immediately face the sharp instrument toward the earth and very very slowly push the instrument into the ground up to the handle.  This will stop the bleeding of the animal.  I saw this happen when I was seven or eight years old" (F, 42, Bicknell, 1934).

12814   "Once a man came to BC's grandfather in Richfield, Utah, to have him stop the bleeding in a horse.  All his grandfather did was to ask the name of the horse.  After about twenty minutes the man asked when he was going to stop the bleeding.  His grandfather replied that it had stopped bleeding twenty minutes ago.  On checking up later, the man found that it had stopped at the time stated" (M, 1952).

12815   Pat gopseed into the wounds of a horse to coagulate the blood (F, Bear River City, 1957).  (Although gopseed is unknown among botanists, it is a locally recognized remedy for treating horse wounds.  --Eds.)

12816   Use sage tea to bathe horses' sore backs or sore noses.  It is very good for that (F, Moab, 1953).

12817   Spread strong bacon grease over a horse's saddle sore (M, 19, SLC, 1964); Apply axle grease . . . (M, 22, SLC, 1964).

12818   Put a teaspoonful of coal oil in each ear and then ride or drive the horse to cure distemper (M, 21, SLC, 1964).

12819   Use salt water for horse galls (M, 70, Duchesne, 1970).

12820   Feed horses tobacco to cure worms (M, 70, Duchesne, 1970); Take about three cigarettes and shred them up and put them in some grain. Have the horse eat them, and it is supposed to rid the horse of worms (F, Provo, 1972).

12821   An alum solution will prevent abortion in horses (M, 44, Layton, 1970).

12822   Horses should be castrated according to the phases of the moon (M, Bear River City, 1957).

12823   Old ranchers wait until the moon is right before castrating horses. Apparently the moon should be full in order that all will be well with the surgical operation (M, 44, DVM, Box Elder Co, 1970).

12824   Don't throw castrated testicles in front of the horse. Throw them behind him and he will be a runner (M, 44, DVM, Tremonton, 1970).

12825   If a horse is branded during the full moon, a good brand will result. If on a quarter moon, the brand will shrink or blot out (F, SLC, 1967).

12826   If you own a horse that gets killed by lightning, you'll have a year of bad luck (F, Cedar City, 1967).

12827   You must always have brasses on a horse's harness to keep away the devil (M, SLC, 1963). Cf. Brown 7668.

## HOGS

## Health, Appetite, Habits, Etc.

12828   Men with extra hairy legs are always good at hog raising (F, Syracuse, 1960).

12829   A little pig will not be healthy unless its tail is curled at the end (M, SLC, 1925).

12830   If a pig's tail curls to the right, he's a better animal than one whose tail curls to the left. If his tail is straight, he is no good (M, SLC, 1958).

12831   If chickens are fed to hogs, the feathers will work right through into the hams (M, Draper, 1925).

12832   Milk will feed a hog (F, 70, Bountiful, 1964).

12833   Sweet milk can kill hogs (M, Syracuse, 1960).

12834   You can't poison a pig except with salt (M, Draper, 1925).

12835   Care for ill hog when poisoned by eating poison grain: Cut his tail and ear, and then rub salt into the cuts (F, 60, SLC, 1930).

12836   A pig with two owners will die of hunger (F, 88, SLC, 1964).

12837   Hogs should not be too heavy when bred (M, Draper, 1925).

## Fattening and Slaughtering Hogs

12838   You should kill pigs by the proper phase of the moon, or the bacon will turn out fat (M, 71, SLC, 1964); . . . the meat won't be good (F, SLC, 1957).

12839   If pork is killed in the "shrink of the moon," it will shrink and fry up into "frizzliness" (M, Draper, 1920); . . . when the moon is waning, it means bad luck with the bacon, as it is certain to shrink in the pan (F, SLC, 1961); A pig should not be killed in the waste of the moon . . . (M, 20, SLC, 1952). Cf. Brown 7710ff.

12840   Don't kill a hog on the wane of the moon, or the meat will spoil (M, SLC, 1963). Brown 7715.

12841   If a hog is killed in the old of the moon, it will have a lot of lard on it (M, 48, Vernal, 1940). Cf. Brown 7716, 7719f.

12842   If a pig is killed by the dark of the moon, the bacon from it will shrivel up when frying more than if the pig were killed by the light of the moon (M, 68, Payson, 1906).

12843   If you want good salt pork, you are to kill the pig in the dark of the moon. If killed in the light of the moon, the ends of the bacon curl up, but by the dark of the moon the ends will lay flat (F, 87, W. Jordan, 1950). Cf. Brown 7721.

12844   You can't render any lard from a hog killed in the new moon, and the whole hog will render fat if killed in the full moon. For equal rendering and meat, kill it during a quarter moon (F, SLC, 1957).

12845   Never kill a hog in a new moon, or the bacon will fry away (M, 48, Salem, 1963). Cf. Brown 7700, 7702.

12846   If you kill pork when the moon is getting larger--from crescent to full-- it will have a lot of good meat with lots of fat (M, Kearns, 1958). Cf. Brown 7693.

12847   A hog butchered in the light of the moon yields more lard than when killed in the dark of the moon (M, SLC, 1964). Cf. Brown 7725.

12848   You have to kill a pig under a full moon (M, 70, Copperton, 1964). Brown 7703ff.

12849   If you butcher hogs on a Sunday, the meat will be tough (M, St. George, 1959).

12850   You can't kill a hog when the tide is out, or the meat will go bad (M, 38, Norw, professor, SLC, 1963). Cf. Brown 7733ff.

12851   Only kill pigs when they are so fat that they can't stand up (they sit on their haunches). The pig will have more meat on it (M, Wellington, 1928).

SHEEP

12852  A leap year is a bad year for sheep (F, SLC, 1958).

12853  A black lamb foretells of good fortune to the flock (M, SLC, 1963); . . . is lucky for a shepherd (M, 32, Ogden, 1950). Brown 7741.

12854  A black lamb that is born into a flock will bring bad luck (F, Ogden, 1960); Bad luck will attend a flock into which a black lamb is born (M, SLC, 1961); . . . indicates trouble ahead (M, 42, SLC, 1964).

12855  Viewing the first lamb of the season from the front is good luck (M, Ir, SLC, 1960).

12856  Viewing the first lamb of the season from the rear is bad luck (M, Ir, SLC, 1960).

12857  If you clip the eyelashes on the lower lid of your sheep, it will keep them from jumping the fence (F, 87, W. Jordan).

12858  If the lambing season starts with twins, the flock will prosper in the coming year (M, 70, sheepherder, Devils Slide, 1965).

Passing Through

12859  On Halloween force all the sheep and lambs through the hoop to ward off all witches and fairies (M, 47, SLC, 1942). (For a general treatment of this ancient apotropaic and curative ritual, see Wayland D. Hand, "'Passing Through': Folk Medical Magic and Symbolism," in Magical Medicine, pp. 133-85. --Eds.)

GOATS

12860  Keep a billy goat in the yard always as a preventive or cure-all (F, 65, SLC, 1944).

# XIII
# Plants, Plant Husbandry

## PLANTS

### CLOVER

12861 A shamrock, or four-leafed clover is extremely lucky (M, SLC, 1959); . . . will bring good luck to the bearer (M, SLC, 1962). Brown 7909.

12862 If you find a four-leaf clover, pick it and keep it, for good luck will come your way (F, 19, Fairview, 1960); . . . as long as you have it in your possession you will have good luck (F, Tooele, 1964); When you find a five-leaf clover it is more good luck, and when you find a six-leaf clover, it is all the more good luck (F, 23, SLC); . . . you will have a fortnight of good fortune (F, SLC, 1964). Brown 7910.

12863 If a person finds a four-leaf clover on his property, it will bring him good luck. If it is found on someone else's property, it will have no effect (F, Murray, 1964).

12864 A four-leaf clover is good luck if you place it in your hat (F, 48, Farmington, 1935).

12865 Find a four-leaf clover, press it in a book, and it will bring good luck (F, SLC); . . . put them in a box and preserve them (F, Moab, 1953).

12866 It is bad luck to find a four-leafed clover and leave it unpicked (F, 21, SLC, 1964).

12867 A four-leaf clover will bring good luck if you throw it over your left shoulder and make a wish (F, Moab, 1953).

12868 If you find a four-leaf clover, you will have good luck, but if you find two on the same day, you will have bad luck (F, SLC, 1959).

12869 If you find a four-leaf clover and make a wish on it, your wish will come true (F, SLC, 1945).

12870 It is good luck to sleep with a four-leaf clover under your pillow (M, Pleasant Grove, 1961).

12871 If you find a clover with more than four leaves, it is bad luck (M, Layton, 1934). Cf. Brown 7920.

12872 If you find a five-leaf clover, bad luck will follow (F, 20, SLC, 1955); . . . it will bring you bad luck unless you throw it away as soon as possible (M, 56, Murray, 1919). Brown 7921f.

12873 If you find a four, six or eight-leaf clover, you will have good luck (F, SLC, 1961).

12874 A six-leaf clover is bad luck (F, 12, SLC, 1960).

12875 To hold a shamrock is good luck (F, 50, SLC, 1950).

12876 Picking a four-leaf clover will induce further finds (F, 40, Sandy, 1937).

### GRASS

12877 Grass will not grow under a "gallus" where a man is going to be hung (M, 41, SLC, 1964). Cf. Brown 7925.

12878 Grass will never grow from a forest that has been burned (M, SLC, 1964).

### PLANTS

12879 Never give your mother a plant on Saturday, because it is a bad omen (F, 48, SLC, 1945).

12880 Ginseng roots save themselves by moving from place to place underground (F, 75, Pleasant Grove, 1906).

12881 To stamp on a holly berry will bring good luck (F, 20, SLC, 1962).

12882 If you catch a ball of milkweed, make a wish and then blow it away again for good luck (F, 17, SLC, 1950). Cf. Brown 7929.

12883 The mistletoe is said to bring happiness, safety and good fortune so long as it does not touch the ground (F, Vernal, 1959).

12884 Mistletoe is hung up for good luck (F, Moab, 1953); No mistletoe, no luck (F, 19, SLC, 1964).

12885 Mushrooms and toadstools come down in the rain (F, 68, SLC, 1926); . . . are numerous before rain (M, Provo, 1970).

12886 Leaflets three, let it be, in reference to poison ivy (F, Logan, 1971).

12887 Poison ivy will not harm a truly good person (M, 17, SLC, 1958).

12888   Ivy or Jewish climber plants are bad luck (F, 40, SLC, 1936).

12889   The sage plant must never bloom, for the flower brings misfortune (F, 51, Park City, 1920).

12890   You should always be careful around snakeweed (horsetails), for they grow only where snakes have been (M, Helper, 1958).

## FLOWERS

12891   Don't bring flowers home from a cemetery, for this will bring you bad luck (F, 33, SLC, 1963).

12892   All flowers are dead people's brains (M, SLC, 1950).

12893   Black flowers are the food of snakes (M, SLC, 1964).

12894   If a girl wears a flower during her menstrual period, it will wilt (F, 19, SLC, 1955).

12895   Pick edelweiss in the spring for good luck and love (F, 19, SLC, 1963).

12896   Find a daisy; ask it a question you please that can be answered by "yes" or "no," and then, one at a time, pull off the petals.  For the first say "yes," for the second, "no" and so on.  The word that falls to the last one is your answer (F, 51, Du, SLC, 1964).

12897   If you find five petals on a lilac, it is good luck for you (M, 36, Sandy, 1950); Children hunt a five-petaled lilac and place it in their shoe for good luck (F, SLC, 1954).

12898   Beware of tall sunflowers because after dark they will trip you (F, 20, SLC, 1958).

12899   If you rub a sunflower by your nose and your nose turns yellow, it means you like butter (F, SLC, 1946).

12900   The roots and flowers of violets are supposed to moderate anger and will comfort the heart (M, 24, SLC, 1959).

## BUTTERCUP

12901   If you hold a buttercup under your chin and your chin turns yellow, it means that you love butter (F, 25, Ger, SLC, 1964); . . . this works only on a sunny day when you are facing the sun (F, SLC, 1971).

## DANDELION

12902   If a dandelion held under the chin reflects yellow onto the skin, it means you like butter (F, Bear River City, 1957).

12903   Blow dandelion fluff three times, and the number of seeds left tells you what time of day it is (F, Bear River City, 1957).  Brown 6006f.

12904   If you can blow the fluff off the dandelion in one puff, your mother needs you at home (M, Tooele, 1957).

12905   If you can blow all the fuzz off a dandelion that has gone to seed and make a wish in one breath, your wish will come true (F, SLC, 1959).

## ROSE

12906   Misfortune hovers around when someone sees a rose leaf fall to the ground (F, 85, SLC, 1964).

12907   White roses mean I am worthy of you (M, 54, SLC, 1964).

12908   Red roses mean I love you (M, 54, SLC, 1964).

12909   If you pick the first rose in the springtime, it will bring you bad luck all summer long (F, 65, Manti, 1964).

12910   Scattering the petals of a red rose on the ground is bad luck (F, 69, Murray, 1910).

12911   If the petals of a red rose are allowed to fall to the floor, it means bad luck will come to the sender of the flowers (F, 16, SLC, 1961).

## SHRUBS

12912   Growing an oleander shrub is unlucky (F, Fillmore, 1960).

12913   To dream of green hedges is a sign of agreeable circumstances (F, SLC, 1964).

## TREES

### Various Notions

12914   It is bad luck to kick a tree (M, 75, SLC, 1964).

12915   You can drive a green pole (sapling) into the dry ground (M, 33, Logan, 1970).

12916   To catch a leaf as it falls from a tree gives a wish or a day's luck (F, 49, Ogden, 1964).

12917   If you see the last leaf on a tree fall in the autumn, you will have good luck (M, Vernal, 1958).

12918   When it rains in the summer, go out and pull a leaf off the highest tree, and it will bring luck and a long summer (F, 19, Gr, SLC, 1950).

12919   It is a man, Mr. Jack Frost, who paints the leaves of the trees in winter time (M, 27, SLC, 1964).

12920   People who go around chopping trees are insensitive and won't succeed (F, 51, Ja, SLC, 1963).

12921   Lightning-struck trees must be avoided (F, 49, Logan, 1964).

12922   Never burn wood that has been struck by lightning, as it will bring bad luck (M, SLC, 1957).  Brown 8454ff.

12923   If a hoop snake rolls down a hill and the tail smacks out, if it hits the tree it will kill the tree (F, 20, SLC, 1949). Cf. Brown 7949f.

## Aspen and Bay Trees

12924 The cross upon which Christ was crucified was made from aspen wood. At the time the boughs were filled with horror and have trembled ceaselessly (F, Morgan, 1961).

12925 Quakin' asps always quake even when there is no wind. Some people claim this is because Christ's cross was made from quakin' asps (M, 19, Logan, 1971).

12926 Bay leaves placed under the pillow will bring pleasant dreams (F, 55, Plain City, 1921).

12927 Bay leaves placed under the pillow will bring good luck (M, SLC).

## Various Trees

12928 To find an even ash means good luck (F, SLC, 1952); . . . an even ash leaf . . . (M, SLC, 1961); . . . an even ash limb . . . (F, Lehi, 1964).

12929 To have an even ash blown on your porch will bring good luck (F, 50, Eng, SLC, 1958).

12930 The Irish people believe the black hawthorn tree is enchanted, and they call it Fairy Tree (M, 30, Ir, SLC, 1965).

12931 If you gnaw on cedar wood, you'll have good luck (M, 47, SLC, 1929).

12932 Oak trees are mysteriously protected and bring good luck (F, 63, Roosevelt, 1964).

12933 Plant a weeping willow, you will have cause to weep (F, Weber Co). Cf. Brown 7960.

## MOSS, HAY, HAY WAGON

12934 If you are lost in a forest, look at a tree trunk. The side that has moss on it is facing north (M, 57, Swiss, Heber City, 1915).

12935 "There's supposed to be this tree up in Mill Creek Canyon that, if you drive up there at night, turn on your bright lights, and wait, the moss on the tree will start to bleed--real blood. I don't know if it's true or not; I've never been up there, but it's supposed to bleed" (F, SLC, 1969).

12936 To dream you cut hay indicates you will have a great influence in society (F, SLC, 1964).

12937 Always pull some hay from a passing hay cart. This will bring good luck (F, 60, SLC, 1964).

12938 It is unlucky and harmful to burn hay (M, 23, Smithville, 1961).

12939 If you see a wagonload of hay drawn by a white horse, make a wish and it will come true (F, 1959).

12940 If you can count to ten before a load of hay passes, you can make a wish and the wish will come true (M, 55, Centerfield, 1964). Cf. Brown 8565.

12941 If you see a load of hay coming your way, make a wish. It will come true if you do not look at the hay again (F, SLC, 1957); . . . see a truckload of hay, make a wish and look away (F, SLC, 1963). Cf. Brown 7931ff.

12942 If the hay wagon passes you on the right side, it is good luck; if it passes you on the left side, it is bad luck (F, SLC, 1940).

12943 Wish on a haystack and it will bring you good luck (F, 19, Clearfield, 1964).

12944 If you see a bale of hay, make a wish and look away, and it will come true (M, SLC, 1959).

## SEEDS, NUTS

12945 A mustard seed brings good luck (M, SLC, 1964).

12946 An acorn found in the spring will mean good luck all summer (M, 52, Holladay, 1940).

12947 The Jordan almond should be passed at all festive occasions to bring out the good luck for all (F, 48, Magna, 1928).

12948 Hickory nuts bring good luck (M, SLC, 1959).

12949 Horse chestnuts bring good luck (M, SLC, 1959).

12950 If you accidentally step on a peanut and it does not crack, you will have good fortune (F, SLC, 1963).

12951 If you open a walnut without breaking the nut, you will have good luck for the rest of the year (F, 17, SLC, 1959).

## PLANT HUSBANDRY

12952 You have to talk to your plants. Plants like it (M, Provo, 1972); You can encourage plants to grow by talking lovingly to them (F, 33, Logan, 1967).

12953 Greasewood on uncleared land is a sign that the land has little agricultural value (M, SLC, 1920).

12954 Sagebrush on uncleared land vouches for its fertility and usefulness (M, SLC, 1915).

12955 Never dig holes after sundown. Bad luck will surely result (F, 42, Gr, SLC, 1964).

## PLOWING

12956 It's unlucky to start plowing a new field on Friday (M, 78, SLC, 1895). Cf. Brown 7966.

12957 When plowing a field, if sea gulls come and look to eat worms and bugs in the freshly turned earth, your crop the coming growing season will be bothered by birds, if it is that kind of crop where birds can destroy or harm it, e.g., such crops as strawberries, raspberries, grapes, etc. (M, 89, Provo, 1897).

12958 When plowing, mowing, or planting, never run over or step on a pheasant's nest and eggs, or you'll bring bad luck to the neighborhood (F, 90, SLC, 1964).

12959 Never leave stones unturned in a newly plowed field, or it will bring bad luck (F, SLC, 1962).

12960 Quakers never plow a field with a red horse on the right side of the harness; it will poison any crop they put in the ground (M, 34, Draper, 1964).

FERTILIZING

12961 The best fertilizer for soil is all left-over food (M, SLC, 1967).

12962 When there's a full moon, it fertilizes your crops (F, 10, Bountiful, 1964).

PLANTING

Phases of the Moon

12963 The moon has effects on the crops (M, SLC, 1959); The moon influences the growth of plants (F, 39, SLC, 1945).

12964 Farmers should plant their crops according to the moon for a healthy crop (M, SLC, 1960). Brown 7969.

12965 If you plant your crops under the wrong phase of the moon, they will bring you bad luck (M, 26, SLC, 1956). Cf. Brown 7970.

12966 The change in the moon influences the growth of plants (F, SLC, 1958); Always plant crops by the change of the moon (M, Murray, 1959).

12967 If there is a haze around the moon, farmers should plant crops for a good harvest (F, 19, Roosevelt, 1964).

New Moon, Waxing Moon, Etc.

12968 A new moon when plants are planted means that there will be a good harvest (M, 22, SLC, 1964).

12969 If a person wants to have a large harvest, he must plant his crops the first day after a new moon (M, 50, Roy, 1924).

12970 Never plant a crop till the new moon pours (M, 21, Pleasant Grove, 1961); Plant when the moon is tipped like a cup so water will run out (F, Du, SLC, 1963).

12971 Plant crops in a growing moon or they will die (F, 20, Swiss, SLC, 1965).

12972 If you plant your crops when the moon is getting larger--from crescent to full-- you will have good crops (M, Kearns, 1958). Cf. Brown 7974.

Light of the Moon, Full Moon

12973 If you plant by moonlight, your plants will grow better (F, 68, SLC, 1923).

12974 Plants will grow best if planted in the light of a new moon (F, 21, SLC, 1964).

12975 Plant all leafy vegetables in the light of the moon (F, Moab, 1953). Cf. Brown 7972f.

12976 If you plant seeds in the sunlight, they won't come up. They have to be planted in the light of the moon (F, Eng, SLC, 1960).

12977 Plant root vegetables in the light of the moon and leafy vegetables in the light of the day (M, 47, Hunter, 1930).

12978 When you plant dry seeds, plant them when the moon is starting to get full and that will guarantee results that when you boil them, after they have grown, they will be tender (F, Gr, SLC, 1957).

12979 The increase in size of the moon from new moon to full moon is believed to influence favorably the growth of plants. This is called sympathetic magic (M, Ephraim, 1895).

12980 A full moon makes crops grow better (M, SLC, 1964); You must plant a garden in the right sign, such as after a full moon (F, 73, Midway, 1972).

12981 Plant crops on a full moon night and a full harvest you will reap (M, 21, SLC, 1955).

12982 The best time to plant the crops in the springtime is to plant the seeds under the blessings of a full moon (M, 20, SLC, 1960).

12983 Farmers must plant crops during a full moon period or they will fail (F, SLC, 1959).

12984 Crops sown with a full moon will be ready a month earlier than crops sown with the waxing moon (F, 74, SLC, 1964).

12985 You are not supposed to plant a crop in the full of the moon (M, 49, Bountiful, 1964); If you plant seed in the full of the moon, you will have bad luck (F, SLC, 1929).

Waning Moon, Dark of the Moon, Etc.

12986 Plant all root vegetables in the ground during the old of moon and all other vegetables during new moon (M, Logan, 1970).

12987 Always plant root vegetables when the moon is waning (F, SLC). Brown 7987.

12988 If you plant your crops when the moon is getting smaller--from full to crescent-- you will have poor crops (M, Kearns, 1958).

12989 Plant anything in the dark of the moon for good results (F, 63, Monroe, 1964). Brown 7989.

12990    Plant your seeds by the moon--dark side for underground vegetables, light side for above-ground vegetables (F, 70, SLC, 1964); If crops grow below the ground, they should be planted in the dark of the moon; if they grow above the ground, they should be planted in the light of the moon (M, 49, Midvale).

12991    Plant tubers or root vegetables in the dark of the moon and leafy vegetables in the light of the moon (F, 67, SLC, 1970). Cf. Brown 7991.

12992    Seeds shouldn't be planted in the dark of the moon, or the crop will not turn out good (M, 49, saddle maker, SLC, 1961).

12993    Certain seeds must not be planted in the dark of the moon, or the crop will fail (F, 30, Amalga, 1940).

12994    All vegetables bearing underground will go to root or turn into root if planted in the dark of the moon (M, Draper, 1926).

Signs of the Zodiac, Holidays, Seasons, Etc.

12995    Don't do any planting on Ascension Thursday (M, 45, Bountiful, 1964). Cf. Brown 8015.

12996    Never plant a crop on the thirteenth of the month (M, 54, SLC, 1964).

12997    Plant on Saturday and the crops will fail (M, 84, Centerville).

12998    Always plant seeds on Sunday morning before breakfast (F, SLC, 1957).

Various Notions about Planting

12999    Plant your crops by the instructions found in the Almanac (F, 71, Centerville, 1963).

13000    It brings bad luck not to plant seed after the soil has been prepared for planting (M, 37, SLC, 1951).

13001    A crooked row holds more seeds (M, 80, Provo, 1950).

13002    Crops should be planted from north to south rather than from east to west (M, 63, Riverside, 1920).

13003    A farmer plants the seeds with his bare hands in order to give them life (M, SLC, 1937).

13004    If a corpse is taken across a field, that field will become barren, no matter how fruitful it may have been before (M, SLC, 1953).

CROPS, CULTIVATION

13005    Sunspots control the growth of crops (M, Marysvale, 1951).

13006    The Indians prayed and danced for rain so they would have a healthy crop (F, 37, SLC, 1964).

13007    On January 6th if a person will take pussy willows and holy water to the fields and then plant the pussy willows at the corners of the fields, and put holy water on them, they will have good crops (F, SLC, 1958).

13008    If the wooden figurine of a woman is placed in the ground near a crop, it will insure a fertile crop (F, SLC, 1959).

13009    If a farmer looks and sees a ring around the moon, he will have a good crop (M, 20, Magna, 1963).

13010    Spit when you see a rainbow so your crops will grow luxuriantly (F, Vernal, 1920).

13011    If a container of fresh earth is buried at the beginning of the season, you will get good crops (M, 19, SLC, 1963).

13012    If the wine ferments heavily in barrels on Christmas Eve, a good wine year will follow (F, 85, SLC, 1964).

13013    If the sun shines through the apple trees on Christmas Day, there will be an abundant crop the following year (F, Brigham City, 1960).

13014    A dry June is a sign of healthy crops (M, St. George, 1959). Cf. Brown 8037.

13015    Heavy snowstorms indicate an excellent spring crop (F, SLC, 1960). Cf. Brown 8035.

13016    A year of snow, a year of plenty (F, 50, SLC, 1964). Cf. Brown 8032ff.

13017    If you look at a new moon over your right shoulder, you'll have bad luck, and your crops for that month will grow very slowly and poorly (M, 70, SLC, 1964).

13018    Patches failing to grow in a cultivated field are inhibited by demons or evil spirits (M, Helper, 1959).

13019    Don't allow roosters to sit on manure, or the crops will fail (F, 60, Ger, SLC, 1965).

13020    The crops will not grow if it hails for three days straight (M, SLC, 1964).

13021    If a crow lands on the roof at dawn, the crop will be poor that year (M, 54, farmer, Manti, 1948).

13022    If you see crows flying in the rain, it means a famine is coming (F, 19, SLC, 1950).

13023    If a rooster crows at night, you can expect that your crops will be destroyed (F, 54, SLC, 1964).

13024    Bees sunning in swarms foretell a bad crop (M, 43, Orem, 1964).

13025    If you bring a hoe into the house or put it on the back porch, you will have bad crops that year (F, SLC, 1958).

13026    If you covet your neighbor's crop, your own crops will be destroyed (M, 23, SLC, 1961).

## VEGETABLES, CROPS, ETC.

### BEANS, PEAS

13027    In leap year beans grow the wrong way (M, SLC, 1964).

13028    You must always plant string beans with the rows pointing toward the north so they will grow tall (F, 47, SLC, 1926).

13029    Plant beans in the light of the moon to insure a bounteous crop (F, 67, SLC, 1963).

13030    Plant beans only at night when the moon is full, otherwise one will not have a good crop (M, SLC, 1955). Brown 8061.

13031    Beans must be planted in the old of the moon to prevent them running to vines (F, 85, SLC, 1964).

13032    Beans must be planted in the dark of the moon (M, Clinton, 1959). Cf. Brown 8063.

13033    Put a yarn string over beans to prevent frost from having an effect on them (Anon, SLC, 1959).

13034    Kidney beans will not grow unless they are planted on the 3rd day of May (F, SLC, 1950).

13035    Plant peas in the light of the moon to insure a bounteous crop (F, 67, SLC, 1963). Cf. Brown 8201.

### CARROTS, TURNIPS

13036    Planting such things as carrots below the ground in bright moonlight will bring a good crop (F, SLC, 1964).

13037    Always in the dark of the moon you planted things that grew under the ground such as potatoes and carrots (F, Moab, 1953); If you plant carrots in the dark of the moon, just as it starts up, you will have better luck with them than if the moon is waning (F, Moab, 1953).

13038    If you plant turnips in the dark of the moon, just as it starts up, you will have better luck with them than if the moon is waning (F, Moab, 1953).

13039    The time to sow turnips is on July 25, if one wants a good crop (M, 43, American Fork, 1929).

### POTATOES

#### General Beliefs and Practices

13040    When planting potatoes put some onion in the eye of the potato and it will always have water (M, 70, Copperton, 1964).

13041    If you plant potatoes on Friday, you will have a better crop (M, SLC).

13042    If you want a good crop, you should plant your potatoes on Good Friday (M, 21, Logan, 1972); To insure an abundant potato crop . . . (F, SLC, 1961). Brown 8229.

13043    It is unlucky to plant potatoes on Good Friday (M, Ger, SLC, 1963).

13044    According to the Irish, you should plant your potato crop on St. Patrick's Day (M, 18, SLC, 1957). Brown 8227.

13045    Plant potatoes with eyes up, or if planted with eyes down, they will use all strength pushing up through the cut potato, therefore, the harvest of potatoes will be small (F, SLC, 1961).

13046    If you cut potatoes and turn the eyes up, they will withstand the frost (F, SLC, 1961).

13047    Potatoes should be planted on a starry night to assure plenty of eyes (F, Ogden, 1917).

#### New Moon, Light of the Moon, Etc.

13048    In order for potatoes to grow successfully they must be planted by the new moon (F, SLC, 1963). Cf. Brown 8218.

13049    The planting of potatoes by moonlight insures good growth (F, Price, 1958).

13050    Plant potatoes by the light of the moon and you will have an abundant crop (M, 56, Provo, 1964).

13051    Plant your potatoes in the light of the moon so the eyes can see to grow (F, 47, SLC).

13052    Plant potatoes in the light of the moon and all you will get is the tops (F, 63, Monroe, 1964).

13053    If you plant potatoes in the light of the moon, they will rot in the ground (M, Layton, 1934).

13054    The time to plant potatoes is when the moon is shaped so that it will hold water, not when water can run out of it (F, Spanish Fork, 1895).

#### Full Moon

13055    Plant potatoes only under the light of a full moon (M, Ogden, 1961); . . . for a bounteous crop (M, 54, SLC, 1915). Brown 8219.

13056    Don't plant your potatoes until there is a full moon or your crop will fail (F, 70, Provo, 1900); . . . or they will rot (M, SLC, 1959).

13057    If you plant potatoes during a full moon, they won't grow (F, 65, SLC, 1964).

#### Waning Moon, Dark of the Moon

13058    Potatoes planted in the waste of the moon will go to tops (M, SLC, 1957).

13059    Plant potatoes in spring in the dark of the moon (F, 67, SLC, 1964). Cf. Brown 8221.

13060    Plant potatoes in the dark of the moon for a good crop (F, 18, SLC, 1964); If you plant potatoes in the dark of the moon, you will have bigger potatoes and less vines; if you plant them any other time during the month, you will have a lot of vine, but scrawny potatoes (F, Springville, 1967); . . . to prevent them running to vines (F, 63, Roosevelt, 1964). Brown 8223.

13061 Plant potatoes in the dark of the moon so they go underground (F, SLC); . . . so they'll put the tubes underneath the ground instead of on top. In this way, you get fewer vines and more potatoes (M, Lehi, 1957).

13062 Don't plant potatoes in the dark of the moon, or they'll grow down instead of up (F, 69, SLC, 1965).

13063 If you plant potatoes by the moon, if planted in the dark, they'll grow to vines (F, SLC, 1960); . . . they will all be tops (F, 88, SLC, 1964).

13064 Wait until the last dark of the moon in May before planting your potatoes, so that frost will not ruin the crop (F, Moroni, 1970).

CABBAGE, LETTUCE, SPINACH, PARSLEY

13065 Plant cabbage on St. Patrick's Day to have success (M, 24, SLC, 1950). Brown 8098.

13066 My mother used to plant her cabbage seed by the signs in the head so it would all head out and be a big head (F, Moab, 1953). Brown 8096.

13067 Cabbages must be planted in the full moon or when grown, they will run to seed and have no heart (M, Ger, SLC, 1963). Cf. Brown 8095.

13068 Lettuce is best planted on St. Valentine's Day, February 14 (M, Roy, 1929).

13069 Plant all above-ground crops such as spinach, etc., in the light of the moon so that the crop will be successful (F, SLC, 1964).

13070 Plant parsley during the light of the moon, so it will grow up instead of having lots of roots (F, SLC, 1958).

CUCUMBERS

13071 My mother used to plant her cucumbers by the signs in the arms, so that the cucumbers would be long and slim and not chubby (F, Moab, 1953). Brown 8167.

13072 Plant cucumbers on the first Sunday in June before sun up. Cucumbers will not grow unless planted at this particular time (F, 75, Smithfield, 1970). Cf. Brown 8172.

13073 Plant cucumbers after the sun goes down (M, SLC, 1950s).

13074 If you plant cucumbers with your mouth open, the bugs will not bother them while they are growing (M, Eng, SLC, 1965).

13075 The cucumber crop will all spoil if a menstruating woman walks through it (F, SLC, 1959).

ASPARAGUS, ONIONS, MUSHROOMS

13076 If you want your asparagus really to develop the following year, stop cutting it when the peas come on (F, SLC, 1957).

13077 It is unlucky not to leave always one stem of an asparagus in the bed to blossom (M, 34, Garland, 1940).

13078 Don't plant onions in the dark of the moon, or they'll grow down instead of up (F, SLC, 1965).

13079 Never plant onions and potatoes in the same row, because the onions get in potatoes' eyes and make them cry so they can't see to come up (F, 20, SLC, 1963).

13080 In dry years in Salome onions were planted in between the rows of potatoes. They had to scratch the onions to make the potatoes' eyes water enough to irrigate the rest of the garden (M, Provo, 1963).

13081 Mushrooms are poisonous unless gathered when the moon is full (M, Kaysville, 1942).

TOMATOES, PEPPERS

13082 If you plant tomatoes by moonlight, they will grow especially large and juicy (M, 53, Logan, 1926).

13083 Always in the light of the moon you plant things like tomatoes (F, Moab, 1953).

13084 One should always plant plants that grow on top of the ground during full moon in the moonlight, as for example tomatoes (F, Bingham, 1924).

13085 Never plant tomatoes before Decoration Day, or you will not get a good yield (M, Bountiful, 1950).

13086 When you plant your tomatoes, dig the dirt up and turn it over three times. Then the tomatoes will grow bigger and juicier (M, 58, Logan, 1935).

13087 If you want to raise a lot of strong pepper, make a person with a strong temper mad and get him to plant the seeds. But don't let the person know or suspect your design; catch him off guard (M, 54, Midvale, 1964). Brown 8184.

CORN

13088 If the dibble, the pointed implement used to make the holes in the ground, be thick, it will swell the ears of the corn (M, 46, Midway, 1935).

13089 Corn should be planted on a full stomach (M, Midway, 1929).

13090 In planting corn, always plant four kernels in the mound: one for the cutworm, one for the crow, one to rot, and one to grow (F, SLC, 1961); . . .

one for the worms, one for the birds, and two for the kettle (M, 44, Layton, 1970).

13091  In order for corn to grow successful it must be planted by the new moon (F, SLC, 1963).  Brown 8106ff.

13092  Plant corn only during the quarter moon (F, SLC, 1961).

13093  Plant corn in the light of the moon to insure a bounteous crop (F, 67, SLC, 1963).

13094  Only plant corn during a full moon--this will ensure a successful crop (F, 24, Orderville, 1948); . . . it will grow better (F, 65, SLC, 1962).  Cf. Brown 8116ff.

13095  Indians believed that they should never plant corn until the leaves on the trees were the size of a young rabbit's ear (F, SLC, 1957); Plant corn when leaves of white oak are the size of squirrel's ears (M, 80, SLC, 1960).  Cf. Brown 8137f.

13096  When April blows her horn (thunder), it's good for the corn (M, 19, Logan, 1950).  Cf. Brown 8128.

13097  Plant corn when you hear the first coo of the dove (M, SLC, 1960).  Cf. Brown 8135.

13098  If you plant corn in with fish, you get a better crop (M, 36, Murray, 1945); . . . make the corn crop grow sooner (F, 53, Bountiful, 1964).

13099  Corn four inches high on the fourth of July will mature (M, 44, Layton, 1970).

13100  An ear of corn with seven or fourteen rows is lucky and means a good harvest (M, 24, SLC, 1964).

13101  If locust blooms are heavy, expect a large corn crop (F, 46, SLC, 1931). Brown 8146.

13102  If it rains on the fourth of July, there will be no corn (M, 37, SLC, 1943).

13103  It is bad luck to harvest corn under a full moon (F, 20, SLC, 1955).

13104  It's good luck to find a red ear of corn (F, 40, Logan, 1938).  Brown 8160.

## SUGAR CANE

13105  The time to plant sugar cane is at noon. This will make it sweeter by drying up the juice and leaving the saccharine matter.  If planted in the morning, its joints will be too long; if in the middle of the day, they will be short (M, 46, Midway, 1930).

## FORAGE CROPS, HAY, GRASS, HERBS, ETC.

13106  Never let your husband put hay up on Sunday in the field, because the hay will mildew or burn and will be hard on the animals that have to eat it (F, 76, Payson, 1900).

13107  Don't cut hay if you have a north wind (M, Midvale, 1940).

13108  If it thunders on April Fool's Day, the farmer shall harvest a huge crop of hay (F, 78, Dan, SLC, 1965); . . . on All Fools Day . . . (M, 22, SLC, 1961).

13109  If you water the grass at night, it will keep free of weeds (M, 56, Provo, 1964).

13110  If you will water your lawn at night, the grass will grow greener (M, 53, Logan, 1929).

13111  Watering the lawn in sunshine harms the grass (F, 54, SLC, 1930s).

13112  If you water your lawn on Sunday, it will not grow (F, 40, Bountiful, 1926).

13113  Don't plant your own sage plant; let the giver do it (F, SLC, 1959).  Cf. Brown 8258.

## GRAIN

13114  Wheat will always grow if you sow by the light of the moon (M, SLC, 1964); You are supposed to plant barley, grain, oats, or any other kind of grains in the light of the moon (M, 27, W. Jordan, 1950).  Cf. Brown 8285.

13115  Planting grain during the full moon makes the harvest more successful (M, SLC, 1961).  Cf. Brown 8278f.

13116  Never plant wheat in the wane of the moon (M, SLC, 1958).

13117  The Danes named the last sheath of wheat "The Maren," and they danced around it during their harvest festivals (M, Dan, SLC, 1965).

13118  Before sowing barley the seed should be run through a man's shirt to insure fertility (M, 56, Midway, 1964).

13119  In the mountains east of Kaysville and Layton, the last snow to melt was seen as the shape of a horse from the valley. The farmers would not water their grain until the "snow horse" had melted through the middle (M, 52, Layton, 1916).

13120  A year without skating is bad for the barley (M, 27, Logan, 1963).  (Ice and frost are apparently meant.  --Eds.)

13121  Never plant your grain when the wind is blowing from the north, because it won't grow (M, 23, SLC, 1964).

13122  The earlier one plants his grain, the larger his crop will be (M, SLC, 1964).

13123  If bees swarm around a dead tree, then the price of grain will be high (M, 83, 1920).

13124  It is good luck to glean the last sheaf of grain on a field that has been harvested (M, Kaysville, 1958).

13125  You should sing while scattering oats, and the crop will be more abundant (F, Moab, 1953).

13126 Chinese farmers go out and say "bad rice" so the birds won't come and eat it (M, SLC, 1956).

## VINES

13127 Prune grape vines in February or else they will bleed (F, Moab, 1953).

13128 In Magna melons don't grow very well because the vines grow so fast that they wear the melons out by dragging them around the ground (M, 18, SLC, 1963).

13129 Plant all above-ground crops such as squash in the light of the moon so that the crop will be successful (M, SLC, 1964).

13130 Plant watermelon on the first day of April before the sunrise in the morning (M, Provo, 1972). Cf. Brown 8310, 8313.

13131 Plant squash after the 21st of June, or the bugs will eat it (F, Spanish Fork, 1934).

## HARVESTING

13132 The moon affects the harvest (M, SLC, 1959). Cf. Brown 8327.

13133 A green Christmas brings a heavy harvest (M, 40, W. Jordan, 1963).

13134 A wet March makes a bad harvest (M, 63, Riverside, 1920).

13135 A cold April gives bread and wine (M, 30, Ger, SLC, 1958).

13136 If May is wet and cool, it will fill the barn and barrel full (M, 30, Ger, SLC, 1958).

13137     When the swallow's nest is low,
     You can safely reap and sow.
     (F, SLC, 1961).

13138 If the pigeons move out of the barn, the crops will be bad that year (M, 23, SLC, 1958).

13139 During the last quarterly conference the leaders of the LDS Church had said that 1953 would be a bad year, and 1954 would be "really bad." Mrs. K said that her failure to grow a good garden this year, for the first time in her life, she had taken as confirmation of this warning (F, Moab, 1953).

13140 A broken plow blade means a poor harvest year (M, 48, SLC, 1963).

13141 Those crops which are cultivated or worked on during the Sabbath day will die and not produce a harvest (M, SLC).

13142 Seeds must be sown after midday for better yields at harvest (M, 53, Midvale).

13143 Always hoe to end of the row before stopping to insure all the crop being harvested (F, SLC, 1961).

13144 If a neighbor has a better harvest than you, he has enticed the fertilizers from your soil to his. Turn about is fair play (M, Mex, Cedar City, 1964).

13145 Never harvest only on a full moon (M, 23, SLC, 1964). Cf. Brown 8328.

13146 Fruits and vegetables should be gathered in the dark of the moon so they will not spoil (F, 40, Sandy, 1936).

13147 Farmers should never harvest every piece of fruit or vegetable, or all their grain, for if they do, they will not have a good crop the following year (F, 52, SLC, 1963).

13148 If you kill a toad, it will cause a famine (F, 45, SLC, 1930s).

13149 To dream of a harvest is a most favorable dream (F, SLC, 1964).

## PESTS

13150 If a scarecrow is placed in a cornfield or a garden, it will frighten the crows away (M, 79, Pleasant Grove, 1890). Cf. Brown 8335.

13151 To keep birds out of orchards use a scarecrow (F, Moab, 1953).

13152 Some people tie rags to fences to scare the birds from the orchards (F, Moab, 1953).

13153 To keep birds out of orchards, use a bright shiny can and put it on a stick up high. The winds will cause it to rattle and glitter (F, Moab, 1953); "We had birds in the cherries, and we had a wire and had a can of rocks on it, and when the wind blew, it would rock and scare the birds" (F, Moab, 1953).

13154 Go out in your corn patch, and say, "Bad corn, bad corn, bad corn," and the birds will stay away (M, SLC, 1959).

13155 To keep away the crows, pieces of a coffin are scattered in the center of the field of grain (M, SLC, 1959); Put a piece of the wood from a coffin in a field, and the sparrows will not vex it (M, Eng, lawyer, SLC, 1957).

13156 Manure was tied around a tree to kill the insects (M, SLC, 1946).

13157 Put fish heads in a gopher hole and the gopher will come up. Then shoot him with a shotgun (F, 21, Monticello, 1971).

## VARIOUS BELIEFS AND PRACTICES INVOLVING GARDEN AND FARM

13158 A person with a green thumb can grow anything (F, 57, SLC, 1964).

13159 Never thank anyone for seeds. It's bad luck (F, SLC, 1920); . . . the seeds will not grow (M, SLC, 1965); If anyone gives you a plant, don't say thank you, because it will die (F, 61, Mt. Pleasant, 1931). Brown 5359, 8044, 8352ff.

13160 When seeds are given you, it is bad luck to carry them home yourself. They must be sent home by another, or they will not come up (M, 30, St. George, 1959).

13161  If you ask for a start from a plant, it will not grow, but if you steal the start, the plant will grow (F, SLC, 1951).  Brown 8355.

13162  If you steal a slip, it will die (M, 24, SLC, 1950s).

13163  A well rig dragged across a field condemned the crop for the entire year, and it was allowed to rot in the field. The farmers would use nothing mechanical (M, 34, Granger, 1964).

13164  Women should not be allowed in the fields, because they don't know how to bring the seed up.  This is so especially during the spring before the seed has sprouted (M, 20, SLC, 1951).

13165  It is considered bad luck if one of the farmers breaks a handle on a coffee or tea cup during the planting season (M, 51, Randolph, 1917).

13166  Kill a toad and your garden won't grow. Toads eat insects (M, Vernal, 1945).

13167  You can cut down more brush on June 2 than ten men at any other season (M, Roy, 1935).

13168  Never sweep dirt outside after dark, because if you do, it means your crops will fail when you harvest them (F, 19, Monticello, 1960).

13169  When you use an axe, spit on your hands for good luck (M, 91, SLC).

13170  When two people hit the garden tools together while they are working, it's a sign that they will work together the next year (F, Ogden, 1961).  Cf. Brown 8357, 8359.

13171  If a rake falls with its teeth upwards, it is bad luck (M, 44, Hyrum, 1930). Cf. Brown 8358.

13172  Never pick a shovel up by the blade end because it's bad luck (M, 67, SLC).

13173  Unless a farmer cuts himself with his new tool, he will never be able to use it well (F, 42, Copperton, 1936).

13174  It is bad luck to close a gate which you find open (F, SLC, 1949).

## FLOWERS, SHRUBS

13175  Spring flowers will be more beautiful and grow better if you plant them on Valentine's Day (F, Ogden, 1961).

13176  If you thank a person who gives you flowers, they won't grow (M, SLC, 1957); Don't thank a person for a start of a shrub.  It's bad luck (F, Tooele, 1920). Cf. Brown 8365f.

13177  After you have planted a flower, do not look at it for two weeks or it will not grow (F, SLC, 1943).

13178  If you plant flowers when the moon is full, you will have more blooms (F, 69, SLC, 1964).

13179  If you find a four-leaf clover in your lawn, you should pick and save it until it turns brown and then plant it in a flower pot with a flower, or near some plant, and it will make the plant grow better (F, 58, SLC).

13180  It is believed that in order to make flowers bloom, you have to water them frequently with fresh, warm blood (M, 23, SLC, 1964).

13181  If you keep water constantly on a rock, roots will sprout (M, 40, SLC, 1933).

### Various Flowers and Shrubs

13182  It is bad luck if a geranium has more than three blooms on the same stem in one year, for the root will be damaged for life (M, SLC, 1949).

13183  If you steal a slip of English ivy, it will grow much better than if it is given to you (F, Provo, 1958).

13184  If you pick lilacs, they won't grow back next year (F, Springville).

13185  Sweet peas should always be planted on Good Friday for best results (F, Helper, 1930).

13186  You must steal the start for a wandering Jew plant, or it won't grow (M, 36, Sandy, 1945).

## TREES

13187  The planting of a tree shows faith in the future (F, 20, SLC, 1953).

13188  If you are setting out a tree, and name it after a large person, it will grow to be a large tree (F, 45, SLC, 1936).

13189  When you plant a tree, plant a tin can with it, for it is believed that the tree can use the iron from the can in its growth (F, Lehi, 1925).

13190  An evergreen that is planted without putting a penny in the hole first will die (M, SLC).

13191  Plant a pine tree, and you will pine (F, Weber Co, 1958).

13192  If you prune a tree in the light of the moon, it will not die (M, SLC, 1961).

13193  There will not be any chestnuts if it rains on the fourth of July (M, 37, SLC, 1942).

13194  When you plant an almond seed in the ground you must wrap it in cotton and the almonds that grow on the tree will be tender and tasty (F, SLC, 1957).

13195  If fruit trees are planted without a dead animal buried under their roots, they will not bear crops (F, 70, Centerville, 1920s).  Cf. Brown 8376.

13196  Never pick the last apple, pear, peach or any other fruit on a tree, or the next year no fruit will grow, or you will have a smaller crop (M, 76, Kamas, 1910).

13197    Put iron filings and shavings under apple trees to give the apples a good red color (M, SLC, 1953). Cf. Brown 8409f.

13198    If a fruit tree does not bear, drive a spike into it (F, 75, Huntington, 1931).

13199    Drive nails in trees that do not bear fruit (F, Lehi, 1930). Cf. Brown 8414f, 8434.

13200    The fruit on a tree will die if counted before picked (M, SLC, 1959).

13201    Frost will not kill the fruit if a candle is burning under the tree (M, SLC, 1930).

13202    If a man prunes a cherry tree, he will cut down on his crop of cherries (M, Perry, 1900).

13203    To burn or cut down a cherry tree brings bad luck (M, Ogden, 1961).

13204    It's bad luck to burn a peach tree (F, Murray, 1957).


FENCES, SHINGLES, ETC.

13205    Shingles must be put on at a certain time of the year, or they will curl up (F, Sandy, 1957). Cf. Brown 8466ff.

13206    If a fence is built at the wrong time of the year, the lower rail will sink into the ground (F, Sandy, 1957). Cf. Brown 8465.

13207    If you chop your own wood, it warms you twice as much (F, 78, Logan, 1947).

# Selected Bibliography

This bibliography is generally limited to titles in folk belief and superstition, but it rightfully includes entries from collateral fields--from folk medicine, from witchcraft and ghostlore, and from other kinds of folk legends strongly underlain by folk belief. Featured in this connection are the well-known western legend cycles of the vanishing hitchhiker and the Three Nephites; also the Latin American legends of La Llorona and El Mal Hijo. Coverage of the bibliography centers mainly in Utah and the Intermountain West, but the range has been widened to take in areas westward from the Great Plains and the Southwest all the way to the Pacific Coast. To provide a more ample matrix for these western American materials, however, standard collections from many parts of the country, and a few from Europe and elsewhere as well, have justifiably found a place. This broader coverage, of course, is calculated to underscore the strong ethnic flavor of the Utah Collection. Finally, several titles on special subject fields and individual motifs have been added from outside the geographical area represented by the bibliography. These detailed listings have been introduced to open up many categories and subcategories within the widely ramifying field of popular belief and superstition. These riches can be generously glimpsed throughout the Utah corpus, and their variants are to be found in pleasing array in state and regional collections throughout the land. For more extended references the reader should consult the bibliographies in the Frank C. Brown Collection for North Carolina (Vols. VI-VII) and in the three-volume edition of Newbell Niles Puckett's Popular Beliefs and Superstitions from Ohio (1981). Wayland D. Hand's Magical Medicine, published in 1980, places on the record a good bibliography of a special category of folk medical belief and custom almost limitless in scope and variety. (The only title cited consistently in the annotations, as indicated above, is the Frank C. Brown Collection of North Carolina Folklore. This work has been provided with a suitable short-title entry; other references are given such entries only if they are listed more than once. To have carried all articles and books cited in the body of the work would have lengthened and particularized the bibliography beyond the intention of the editors.)

ABBREVIATIONS

AFFword    Arizona Friends of Folklore Word. Flagstaff.

CFQ    California Folklore Quarterly. Berkeley and Los Angeles, 1942-1946. See Western Folklore.

FFC    Folklore Fellows Communications. Helsinki.

HFB    Hoosier Folklore Bulletin. Bloomington, Ind., 1942-1945.

JAF    Journal of American Folklore. Boston.

KFR    Kentucky Folklore Record. Bowling Green, Ky.

MAFS    Memoirs of the American Folklore Society. Boston and New York.

MF    Midwest Folklore. Bloomington, Ind.

NCF    North Carolina Folklore. Chapel Hill, N.C.

NMFR    New Mexico Folklore Record. Albuquerque, N.M.

NYFQ    New York Folklore Quarterly. Ithaca, N.Y.

PTFS    Publications of the Texas Folklore Society. Austin.

SFQ    Southern Folklore Quarterly. Gainesville, Fla.

TFSB    Tennessee Folklore Society Bulletin. Maryville, Tenn.

WF    Western Folklore. Berkeley and Los Angeles (succeeding the California Folklore Quarterly after Vol. 5).

Allen, John W. Legends and Lore of Southern Illinois. Carbondale, Ill., 1963.

Allison, Lelah. "Folk Beliefs Collected in Southeastern Illinois," JAF 63 (1950): 309-24.

Anderson, John Q. "Magical Transference of Disease in Texas Folk Medicine," WF 27 (1968): 191-99.

_____. Texas Folk Medicine: 1,333 Cures, Remedies, Preventives & Health Practices. Austin, 1970.

Arrendondo, Art. "La Llorona in Flagstaff," AFFword 2 (January 1973): 21-28.

Augar, Pearl Hamelin. "French Beliefs in Clinton County," NYFQ 4 (1948): 161-71.

Aurand, A. Monroe, Jr. Popular Home Remedies and Superstitions of the Pennsylvania Germans. Harrisburg, 1941.

_____. The Pow-Wow Book. A Treatise on the Art of "Healing by Prayer" and "Laying of Hands," etc., Practiced by the Pennsylvania Germans and Others, etc. Harrisburg, 1929.

Bacon, Jerry V. "Medicine and Ghosts," Southwest Folklore 2 (Summer 1978): 15-30.

_____. "Medicine, Magic, Spirits, and Cuisine," Southwest Folklore 2 (Winter 1978): 1-9.

Baker, Pearl, and Ruth Wilcox. "Folk Remedies in Early Green River," Utah Humanities Review 2 (1948): 191-92.

Bakker, C. Volksgeneeskunde in Waterland: een Vergelijkende Studie met de Geneeskunde der Grieken en Romeinen. Amsterdam, 1928.

Bancroft, Caroline. "Folklore of the Central City District, Colorado," CFQ 4 (1945): 315-42.

Barreras, Ramona. "Spanish-American Belief Tales," AFFword 2 (January 1973): 3-16.

Baughman, Ernest W. "Folk Sayings and Beliefs," NMFR 9 (1954-1955): 23-27.

Bayard, Samuel P. "Witchcraft Magic and Spirits on the Border of Pennsylvania and West Virginia," JAF 51 (1938): 47-59.

Baylor, Dorothy J. "Folklore from Socorro, New Mexico," HF 6 (1947): 138-50.

Beardsley, Richard K., and Rosalie Hankey. "The Vanishing Hitchhiker," CFQ 1 (1942): 303-35.

Beck, H. P. "Herpetological Lore from the Blue Ridge," MF 2 (1952): 141-50.

Beckwith, Martha Warren. "Signs and Superstitions Collected from American College Girls," JAF 36 (1923): 1-15.

Berdau, Emil. "Der Mond in Volksmedizin, Sitte and Gebräuchen der mexikanischen Grenzbewohnerschaft des sudlichen Texas," Globus 88 (1905): 381-84.

Bergen, Fanny D. Animal and Plant Lore Collected from the Oral Tradition of English Speaking Folk. MAFS 7. Boston and New York, 1899.

_____. Current Superstitions Collected from the Oral Tradition of English Speaking Folk. MAFS 4. Boston and New York, 1896.

Black, Pauline Monette. Nebraska Folk Cures. University of Nebraska Studies in Language, Literature, and Criticism, 15. Lincoln, 1935.

Black, William George. Folk-Medicine: A Chapter in the History of Culture. Publications of the Folk-Lore Society, 12. London, 1883.

Bogusch, E. R. "Superstitions of Bexar County," PTFS 5 (1926): 112-125.

Bourke, John G. "Popular Medicine, Customs, and Superstitions of the Rio Grande," JAF 7 (1894): 119-46.

Brand, John. Observations on the Popular Antiquities of Great Britain, Chiefly Illustrating the Origin of Our Vulgar Customs, Ceremonies and Superstitions. Edited by Sir Henry Ellis. 3 vols. London, 1901-2.

Brendle, Thomas R., and Claude W. Unger. Folk Medicine of the Pennsylvania Germans. The Non-Occult Cures. Proceedings of the Pennsylvania German Society, XLV. Norristown, Pa., 1935.

Brewster, Paul G. "Beliefs and Customs." In The Frank C. Brown Collection of North Carolina Folklore, I, 223-82. Durham, N.C., 1952.

Bridges, Stephen. "'The Hank,' A Winslow Legend," AFFword 4 (January 1975): 38-43.

Briggs, Katharine. An Encyclopedia of Fairies: Hobgoblins, Brownies, Bogies and Other Supernatural Creatures. New York, 1976.

Brown, Frank C. Frank C. Brown Collection of North Carolina Folklore. 7 vols. Durham, N.C., 1952-64. (Vols. VI-VII, Popular Beliefs and Superstitions from North Carolina, edited by Wayland D. Hand, 1961-64. Cited: Brown [entry no.].)

Browne, Ray B. Popular Beliefs and Practices from Alabama. University of California Publications: Folklore Studies, Vol. 9. Berkeley and Los Angeles, 1958.

Brooks, Juanita. "Frontier Birth Beliefs," WF 29 (1970): 53-55.

Brunvand, Jan Harold. "Folklore and Superstition in Idaho," Idaho Yesterdays 6 (1962): 20-24.

_____. "Folklore of the Great Basin," Northwest Folklore 3 (Summer 1968): 17-32.

_____. "Miscellany of Idaho Superstitions," SF 22 (1963): 202-3.

_____. "Modern Legends of Mormondom, or, Supernaturalism is Alive and Well in Salt Lake City." In American Folk Legend: A Symposium, edited by Wayland D. Hand, 185-202. Berkeley and Los Angeles, 1976.

Bryan, Naomi Ruth. "Children's Customs in San Mateo," WF 8 (1949): 261.

Burridge, Gaston. "Does the Forked Stick Locate Anything? An Inquiry into the Art of Dowsing," WF 14 (1955): 32-43.

Bushnell, John H. "Medical Folklore from California," WF 6 (1947): 273-75.

Busse, Norma. "Superstitions of the Theater," WF 8 (1949): 66-67.

Cannell, Margaret. Signs, Omens, and Portents in Nebraska Folklore. University of Nebraska Studies in Language, Literature, and Criticism, XIII. Lincoln, Nebraska, 1933.

Cannon, M. Hamlin. "Angels and Spirits in Mormon Doctrine," CFQ 4 (1945): 343-50.

Carlock, Barbara. "Tornado Tales of Northeastern Colorado," WF 21 (1962): 103-8.

Carranco, Lynn. "A Miscellany of Folk Beliefs from the Redwood Country," WF 26 (1967): 169-76.

Chavez, Tibo. New Mexican Folklore of the Rio Grande. Portales, N.M., 1972.

Cheney, Thomas E., Austin E. Fife, and Juanita Brooks, eds. Lore of Faith and Folly. Salt Lake City, 1971.

Clar, Mimi. "Russian Folk Beliefs Collected in Los Angeles," WF 17 (1958): 123-26.

Clark, Joseph D. "Madstones in North Carolina," NCF 24 (1976): 3-40.

Cordova, Gabriel. Magic Tales of Mexico. M.A. thesis, Texas Western College, University of Texas, 1951.

Cox, John Harrington. "The Witch Bridle," SFQ 7 (1943): 203-9.

Creighton, Helen. Blue Nose Ghosts. Toronto, 1957.

_____. Bluenose Magic. Popular Beliefs and Superstitions in Nova Scotia. Toronto, 1968.

_____. Folklore of Lunenburg County, Nova Scotia. National Museum of Canada, Bulletin, No. 117, Anthropological Series No. 29. Ottawa, 1950.

Crosby, John R. "Modern Witches of Pennsylvania," JAF 40 (1927): 304-9.

Cross, Tom Peete. "Witchcraft in North Carolina," Studies in Philology 16, No. 3 (1919): 217-87.

[Culin, Stewart]. "Concerning Negro Sorcery in the United States," JAF 3 (1890): 281-87.

Cunningham, Keith K. "The Vanishing Hitchhiker in Arizona--Almost," Southwest Folklore 3 (Winter 1979): 46-50.

Curtin, L. S. M. Healing Herbs of the Upper Rio Grande. Los Angeles, 1965.

_____. "Pioneer Medicine in New Mexico," Folk-Say. Norman, Okla., 1930. Pp. 186-96.

Dalyell, John Graham. The Darker Superstitions of Scotland. Glasgow, 1835.

Davenport, Gertrude C. "Folk-Cures from Kansas," JAF 11 (1898): 129-32.

Davidson, Levette J. "Superstitions Collected in Denver, Colorado," WF 8 (1954): 184-89.

Davis, Henry C. "Negro Folk-Lore in South Carolina," JAF 27 (1914): 241-54.

Day, Cyrus L. "Knots and Knot Lore," WF 9 (1950): 229-56.

Demetrio y Radaza, Father Francisco. Dictionary of Philippine Folk Beliefs and Customs. 4 vols. Cagayan de Oro City, P.I., 1970.

Dobie, J. Frank. "Weather Wisdom of the Texas-Mexican Border," PTFS 2 (1923): 87-99.

Dodson, Ruth. "Folk-Curing among the Mexicans," PTFS 10 (1932): 82-98.

Dorson, Richard M. "Aunt Jane Goudreau, Roup-Garou Storyteller," WF 6 (1947): 13-27.

_____. Bloodstoppers and Bearwalkers: Folk Traditions of the Upper Peninsula. Cambridge, Mass., 1952.

Dresslar, Fletcher Bascom. Superstition and Education. University of California Publications in Education, V. Berkeley, California, 1907.

Driver, Harold E. "A Method of Investigating Individual Differences in Folkloristic Beliefs and Practices," MF 1 (1951): 99-105.

Dundes, Alan. "Brown County Superstitions," MF 11 (1961): 25-56; also reprinted as "The Structure of Superstition," in Alan Dundes, Analytic Essays in Folklore, 88-94. The Hague, 1975.

Earthman, Glen. "Superstitions from Denver," WF 16 (1957), 132-33.

Edwards, G. D. "Items of Armenian Folk-Lore Collected in Boston," JAF 12 (1899): 97-107.

Elworthy, Frederick Thomas. The Evil Eye, An Account of This Ancient and Widespread Superstition. London, 1895.

Ericson, Eston Everett. "Nebraska Folklore and Popular Sayings," Folk-Lore 49 (1938): 148-53.

Espinosa, Aurelio M. "New-Mexican Spanish Folk-Lore," JAF 23 (1910): 395-418.

Fauset, Arthur Huff. Folklore from Nova Scotia, MAFS XXIV. New York, 1931.

Federal Writers' Project of the WPA. Idaho Lore. Caldwell, Idaho, 1939.

_____. "Proverbs, Prophecies, Signs and Sayings," Nebraska Folklore, Pamphlet No. 9, pp. 1-3, 4-7, 9. Lincoln, 1937.

_____. "Proverbs, Prophecies, Signs and Sayings," pt. II., Nebraska Folklore, Pamphlet No. 10, pp. 6-9. Lincoln, 1937.

Fife, Austin E. "Birthmarks and Psychic Imprinting of Babies in Utah Folk Medicine." In American Folk Medicine: A Symposium, edited by Wayland D. Hand, 273-83. Berkeley and Los Angeles, 1976. Cited: Fife, "Birthmarks."

_____. "The Cycle of Life among the Folk." In Lore of Faith & Folly, edited by Thomas E. Cheney, Austin E. Fife, and Juanita Brooks, 223-41. Salt Lake City, University of Utah Press, 1971.

_____. "Folk Belief and Mormon Cultural Autonomy," JAF 61 (1948): 19-30.

_____. "Folk Elements in the Formation of the Mormon Personality," Brigham Young University Studies 1 (1960): 1-17.

_____. "Folkways of a Mormon Missionary in Virginia," SFQ 16 (1952): 92-123.

_____. "Folkways of the Mormons from the Journals of John D. Lee," WF 21 (1962): 229-44.

_____. "The Legend of the Three Nephites among the Mormons," JAF 53 (1940): 1-49.

_____. "Pioneer Mormon Remedies," WF 16 (1957): 153-62.

_____. Saints of Sage and Saddle. Bloomington, Ind., 1956. Reprinted Salt Lake City, 1980. See esp. pp. 109-17 ("The Devil's Advocate"). (With Alta S. Fife.)

_____. "Virginia Folkways from a Mormon Journal," WF 9 (1950): 348-58.

Fogel, Edwin Miller. Beliefs and Superstitions of the Pennsylvania Germans. Americana Germanica, XVIII. Philadelphia, 1915.

Foster, George M. "Relationships Between Spanish and Spanish American Folk Medicine," JAF 66 (1953): 201-17.

Frazer, James George. The Golden Bough. A Study in Magic and Religion. 12 vols. 3rd ed. London, 1911-15.

Freud, Ralph. "George Spelvin Says the Tag: Folklore of the Theater," WF 13 (1954): 245-50.

Friend, Hilderic. Flowers and Flower Lore. New York, 1891.

Funk, William D. "Hiccup Cures," WF 9 (1950): 66-67.

Fyffe, Prudence. "Remedies," AFFword 4 (July 1974): 6-14.

Gardner, Emelyn Elizabeth. Folklore from the Schoharie Hills, New York. Ann Arbor, 1937.

Garriott, Edward B. Weather Folk-Lore and Local Weather Signs. U.S. Department of Agriculture, Bulletin, No. 33, Weather Bureau, No. 294. Washington, D.C., 1903.

Gaster, Theodore. The Holy and the Profane. New York, 1955.

Gelber, Mark, and Marjorie Kimmerle. Popular Beliefs and Superstitions from Colorado. Boulder, 1967. (Library deposit copy.)

Georges, Robert A. "The Greeks of Tarpon Springs: An American Folk Group," SFQ, 29 (1965): 129-41.

Gillis, Everett A. "Zodiac Wisdom," WF 16 (1957): 77-89.

Graalfs, Luise. "Bad-luck Superstitions on the Campus (U.C.)," WF 8 (1949): 264.

Granger, Byrd Howell. A Motif Index for Lost Mines and Treasures Applied to Redaction of Arizona Legends, and to Lost Mine and Treasure Legends, Exterior to Arizona. FFC 218. Helsinki and Tucson, 1977.

_____. "Naming in Customs, Beliefs, and Folk Tales," WF 20 (1961): 27-37.

_____. "Of the Teeth," JAF 74 (1961): 47-56.

Gregor, Walter. Notes on the Folk-Lore of the North-East of Scotland. Publications of the Folk-Lore Society, VII. London, 1881.

Grendon, Felix. "The Anglo-Saxon Charms," JAF 22 (1909): 105-237.

Grieve, Mrs. M. A Modern Herbal. 2 vols. New York, 1971. (Dover Publications reprint.)

Gross, Dan. "Folklore of the Theater," WF 20 (1961): 257-63.

Halpert, Herbert. "The Devil and The Fiddle," HFB 2 (1943): 39-43.

Halpert, Violetta Maloney. "Death Beliefs fro Indiana," MF 2 (1952), 205-19.

Hand, Wayland D. "American Analogues of the Couvade." In Studies in Folklore in Honor of Distinguished Service Professor Stith Thompson, edited by W. Edson Richmond, 213 29. Indiana University Folklore Studies, No. 9, Bloomington, Ind., 1957.

_____. American Folk Medicine: A Symposium. Publications of the UCLA Cente for the Study of Comparative Folklore and Mythology, No. 4. Berkeley and Los Angeles, 1976. (25 essays.)

_____. "American Witchcraft and Conjury: A Comparison," Mannus. Deutsche Zeitschrif für Vor- und Frühgeschichte 44 (1978): 36-43. (Festgabe fur Prof. H. R. Ernst Burgstaller.)

_____. "California Bell Legends: A Survey," CFQ 4 (1945): 18-28.

_____. "California Miners' Folklore: Below Ground," CFQ 1 (1942): 24-46.

_____. "California Miners' Folklore: Above Ground," CFQ 1 (1942): 127-53.

_____. "La Creencia y la supersticion folkloricas," Folklore Americas 25 (1965): 3-16.

_____. "Crossing Water: A Folkloristic Motif." In For Max Weinreich on His Seventieth Birthday: Studies in Jewish Languages, Literature and Society, 82-92. The Hague, 1964.

_____. "The Evil Eye in Its Folk Medical Aspects: A Survey of North America." In Actas del XLI Congreso Internacional de Americanistas, México, 2 al 7 septiembre, 1974. 3 vols. Vol. III, 183-89. Mexico City, 1976. Cited: Hand, "Evil Eye."

_____. "'The Fear of the Gods': Superstition and Popular Belief." In Our Living Traditions: An Introduction to American Folklore, edited by Tristram Potter Coffin, 215-27. New York and London, 1968.

_____. "Folk Belief and Superstition: A Crucial Field of Folklore Long Neglected." In Folklore Today: A Festschrift for Richard M. Dorson, edited by Linda Degh, Henry Glassie, and Felix J. Oinas, 209-19. Bloomington, Ind., 1976.

_____. "Folk Beliefs and Customs of the American Theater: A Survey," SFQ 38 (1974): 23-48.

_____. "The Folk Healer: Calling and Endowment," Journal of the History of Medicine and Allied Sciences 26 (1971): 263-75. Cited: Hand, "Folk Healer."

_____. "The Folklore, Customs, and Traditions of the Butte Miner," CFQ 5 (1946): 1-25, 153-78.

_____. "Folklore from Utah's Silver Mining Camps," JAF 54 (1941): 132-61. Cited: Hand, "Utah's Silver Mining."

_____. "Hangmen, the Gallows, and the Dead Man's Hand in American Folk Medicine." In Medieval Literature and Folklore Studies. Essays in Honor of Francis Lee Utley, edited by Jerome Mandell and Bruce A. Rosenberg, 323-29, 381-87. New Brunswick, N.J., 1970.

_____. "Jewish Popular Beliefs and Customs in Los Angeles." In Studies in Biblical and Jewish Folklore. MAFS 51 (1960): 309-26.

_____. Magical Medicine: The Folkloric Component of Medicine in the Folk Belief, Custom, and Ritual of the Peoples of Europe and America. Berkeley and Los Angeles, 1980. (23 original essays.) Cited: Hand, "Magical Medicine."

_____. "A Miscellany of Nebraska Folk Beliefs," WF 21 (1962): 257-78.

_____. "A North Carolina Himmelsbrief." In Middle Ages-Reformation-Volkskunde. Festschrift for John G. Kunstmann. Chapel Hill, N.C., 1959. Pp. 201-7.

_____. "Padepissers and Wekschissers: A Folk Medical Inquiry into the Cause of Styes." In Folklore Studies in Honour of Herbert Halpert: A Festschrift, edited by Kenneth S. Goldstein and Neil V. Rosenberg. St. John's, Newfoundland, 1980.

_____. "'Passing Through': Folk Medical Magic and Symbolism," Proceedings of the American Philosophical Society 112 (1968): 379-402. Cited: Hand, "Passing Through."

_____, ed. Popular Beliefs and Superstitions from North Carolina. Vols. VI-VII of the Frank C. Brown Collection of North Carolina Folklore. Durham, N.C., 1961-64. Cited: Brown (entry no.).

_____. "Popular Beliefs and Superstitions from Oregon," CFQ 4 (1945): 427-32.

_____. "Popular Beliefs and Superstitions from Pennsylvania," KFQ 3 (1958): 61-74; 4 (1959): 106-20.

_____. "'That the Child May Rise in the World': A Folk Belief and Custom of the Nursery," Transactions & Studies of the College of Physicians of Philadelphia, 42, No. 1 (July 1974): 77-80. (This number was a Festschrift for Samuel X. Radbill.) Cited: Hand, "That the Child May Rise."

_____. "The Three Nephites in Popular Tradition," SFQ 2 (1938): 123-29.

_____. "Will-o'-the-Wisps, Jack-o'-Lanterns and Their Congeners: A Consideration of the Fiery and Luminous Creatures of Lower Mythology," Fabula. Journal of Folktale Studies 18 (1977): 226-33.

Hankey, Rosalie. "California Ghosts," CFQ 1 (1942): 155-77.

Handwörterbuch des deutschen Aberglaubens. Edited by Eduard von Hoffmann-Krayer and Hanns Bächtold-Stäubli. 10 vols. Berlin and Leipzig, 1927-42. Cited: HDA.

Harris, Jesse W. "Some Southern Illinois Witch Lore," SFQ 10 (1946): 183-90.

Hastings, James, ed. Encyclopedia of Religion and Ethnics. 13 vols. Edinburgh, 1908-26. (Reprint ed., New York, 1956-60.)

Hatfield, Sadie. "Folklore of Texas Plants," PTFS 18 (1943): 157-62.

Hawes, Bess Lomax. "La Llorona in Juvenile Hall," WF 27 (1968): 153-70.

Hazlitt, W. Carew. Faith and Folklore: A Dictionary of National Beliefs, Superstitions and Popular Customs, Past and Current, with Their Classical and Foreign Analogues. 2 vols. London, 1905. (An alphabetical arrangement of Brand, above.)

Henderson, William. Notes of the Folk-Lore of the Northern Counties of England and the Borders. New ed. Publications of the Folk-Lore Society, II. London, 1879.

Hendricks, G. D. "Don't Look Back," PTFS 30 (1961): 69-75.

Herron, Miss, and Miss A. M. Bacon. "Conjuring and Conjure-Doctors in the Southern United States," JAF 9 (1896): 143-47.

Herzfeld, Elsa G. "Superstitions and Customs of the Tenement-House Mother," Charities 14 (1905): 983-86.

Hohman, John George. Long Lost Friend, or, Book of Pow-Wows. Edited by Monroe Aurand, Jr. Harrisburg, Pa., 1930.

Holland, William R. "Mexican-American Medical Beliefs: Science or Magic," Arizona Medicine 20, No. 5 (May 1963): 89-101.

Hovorka, O. v., and A. Kronfeld. Vergleichende Volksmedizin: Eine Darstellung volksmedizinischer Sitten und Gebräuche, Anschauungen und Heilfaktoren, des Aberglaubens und der Zaubermedizin. 2 vols. Stuttgart, 1908-9.

Hunter, Carolyn. "Ethno-Quackery: Wart Cures," AFFword 4 (January 1975): 3-7.

Hurley, Gerard T. "Buried Treasure Tales in America," WF 10 (1951): 197-216.

Hurt, Wesley R. "Spanish-American Superstitions," El Palacio 47 (1940): 193-201.

Hurston, Zora. "Hoodoo in America," JAF 44 (1931): 317-417.

Hyatt, Harry Middleton. Folk-Lore from Adams County, Illinois. Memoirs of the Alma Egan Hyatt Foundation. New York, 1935. 2d ed. 1965.

_____. Hoodoo, Conjuration, Witchcraft, Rootwork. 5 vols. Memoirs of the Alma Egan Hyatt Foundation. Quincy, Ill., 1970-78. Cited: Hyatt, Hoodoo.

Inwards, Richard. Weather Lore. 4th ed. London, 1950.

Jacobs, W. D. "Dangerous Money," NMFR 7 (1952-53): 20. (Two-dollar bills.)

Jahoda, Gustav. The Psychology of Superstition. London, 1969.

Janvier, Thomas A.  "Mexican Superstitions and Folk-Lore," Scribner's Magazine 5 (March 1889): 349-59.

Jeffrey, Lloyd N.  "Snake Yarns of the West and Southwest," WF 14 (1955): 246-58.

Johnson, Clifton.  What They Say in New England: A Book of Signs, Sayings, and Superstitions.  Boston, 1896.

Jones, Louis C.  "The Devil in York State," NYFQ 8 (1952): 5-19.

_____.  "The Evil Eye among European-Americans," WF 10 (1951): 11-25.

_____.  "The Ghosts of New York: An Analytical Study," JAF 57 (1944): 237-54.

Jones, Michael Owen.  "Folk Beliefs: Knowledge and Action," SFQ 31 (1967): 304-9.

Jones, Suzi.  Oregon Folklore.  Eugene, Ore., 1977.

Kanner, Leo.  "Superstitions Connected with Sneezing," Medical Life 38 (1931): 549-75.

Killion, Ronald G., and Charles T. Waller.  A Treasury of Georgia Folklore.  Atlanta, 1972.

Kimmerle, Marjorie M.  "A Weather Almanac for Colorado," The Colorado Quarterly 7 (1958): 68-79.

Kittredge, George Lyman.  Witchcraft in Old and New England.  Cambridge, Mass., 1929.

Knortz, Karl.  Amerikanischer Aberglaube der Gegenwart: Ein Beitrag zur Volkskunde.  Leipzig, 1913.

Koch, William E.  Folklore from Kansas: Customs, Beliefs, and Superstitions.  Lawrence, 1980.

_____.  "Hunting Beliefs and Customs from Kansas," WF 24 (1965): 165-74.

Lake, Mary Daggett.  "Superstitions about Cotton," PTFS 9 (1931): 145-52.

Lathrop, Amy.  "Pioneer Remedies from Western Kansas," WF 20 (1961): 1-22.

Lee, Hector.  The Three Nephites: The Substance and Significance of the Legend in Folklore.  University of New Mexico Publications in Language and Literature, No. 2.  Albuquerque, 1949.

Lick, David E., and Thomas R. Brendle.  Plant Names and Plant Lore among the Pennsylvania Germans.  Proceedings and Addresses of the Pennsylvania German Society, XXXIII, 1923.

Loomis, C. Grant.  "Some American Folklore of 1880," CFQ 4 (1945): 417.

_____.  "Chinese Lore from Nevada, 1867-1878," CFQ 5 (1946): 185-96.

_____.  "Indications of Miners' Medicine," WF 8 (1949): 117-22.

Lowrimore, Burton.  "California Superstitions," CFQ 4 (1945): 178.

McAtee, W. L.  "Odds and Ends of North American Folklore on Birds," MF 5 (1955): 169-83.

McKinney, Ida Mae.  "Superstitions of the Missouri Ozarks," TFSB 18 (1952): 104-9.

Mills, Randall V.  "Superstitions," WF 11 (1952): 43-45.

Mockler, W. E.  "Moon Lore from West Virginia," Folk-Lore 50 (1939): 310-14.

Montell, William Lynwood.  Ghosts along the Cumberland: Deathlore in the Kentucky Foothills.  Knoxville, 1975.

Morel, Robert, and Suzanna Walter.  Dictionnaire des Superstitions.  Verviers, 1972.

Moya, Benjamin S.  Superstitions and Beliefs among the Spanish-Speaking People of New Mexico.  M.A. thesis, University of New Mexico, Albuquerque, 1940.

Mullen, Patrick B.  "The Function of Magic Folk Belief among Texas Coastal Fisherman," JAF 82 (1969): 214-25.

Naff, Alixa.  "Belief in the Evil Eye among the Christian Syrian-Lebanese in America," JAF 78 (1965): 46-51.

Newell, Jane H.  "Superstitions of Irish Origin in Boston, Mass.," JAF 5 (1892): 242-43.

Newell, William Wells.  "The Ignis Fatuus, its Character and Legendary Origins," JAF 17 (1901): 39-60.

Noall, Claire.  "Medicine among the Early Mormons," WF 18 (1959): 157-64.

_____.  "Superstitions, Customs, and Prescriptions of Mormon Midwives," CFQ 3 (1944): 102-14.

Odell, Ruth.  "Mid-Western Saliva Lore," SFQ 14 (1950): 220-23.

Padilla, Floy.  "Witch Stories from Tapia Azul and Tres Fulgores," NMFR 6 (1951-52): 11-19.

Papanikolas, Helen Zeese.  The Peoples of Utah.  Salt Lake City, 1976.

_____.  Toil and Rage in a New Land: The Greek Immigrants of Utah.  Salt Lake City, 1974.

Papashvily, Helen.  "The World in a California Street: Stockton, 1911-1920," WF 10 (1951): 117-25.

Parler, Mary Celestia.  Folk Beliefs from Arkansas.  15 vols.  Fayetteville, Ark., 1962.  (Library deposit copy.)

Pearce, T. M.  "The Bad Son (El Mal Hijo) in Southwestern Spanish Folklore," WF 9 (1950): 295-301.

Penrod, James H.  "Folk Beliefs about Work, Trades, and Professions from New Mexico," WF 17 (1968): 180-82.

Phillips, Henry, Jr.  "First Contribution to the Folk-Lore of Philadelphia and Its Vicinity," American Philosophical Society.  Proceedings, Vol. XXV, No. 128, March 1888, 159-70.

Pickard, Madge E., and R. Carlyle Buley.  The Midwest Pioneer.  His Ills, Cures, and Doctors.  Crawfordsville, Ind., 1945.

Pound, Louise. "Nebraska Snake Lore," SFQ 10 (1946): 163-76.

Probert, Thomas. Lost Mines and Buried Treasures of the West. Berkeley and Los Angeles, 1977.

Puckett, Newbell Niles. Folk Beliefs of the Southern Negro. Chapel Hill, N.C., 1926.

_____. Popular Beliefs and Superstitions: A Compendium of American Folklore from the Ohio Collection of Newbell Niles Puckett. Edited by Wayland D. Hand, Anna Casetta, and Sondra B. Thiederman. 3 vols. Boston, 1981.

Radford, E., and M. A. Radford. Encyclopedia of Superstitions. London, n.d. [1947].

Randolph, Vance. Ozark Superstitions. New York, 1947.

Richardson, Clement. "Some Slave Superstitions," The Southern Workman 41 (1912): 246-48.

Robbins, Rossell Hope. The Encyclopedia of Witchcraft and Demonology. New York, 1959.

Roberts, Hilda. "Louisiana Superstitions," JAF 40 (1927): 144-208.

Rogers, E. G. "I Wish I May, I Wish I Might," TFSB 13, No. 1 (1947): 36-41.

_____. "Switching for Water," TFSB 21 (1955): 108-11.

Rogers, W. Stuart. "Irish Lore Collected in Schenectady," NYFQ 8 (1952): 20-30.

Roy, Carmen. Litterature Orale en Gaspésie. Ottawa, 1955.

Rumley, Barbara C. "Superstitions in San Francisco," WF 9 (1950): 159-60.

Rupp, William J. Bird Names and Bird Lore among the Pennsylvania Germans. Pennsylvania German Society. Proceedings and Addresses, Vol. 52. Norristown, Pa., 1946.

Russell, Louise. "Llorona Legends Collected from Junior High School Students in Greeley, Colorado," AFFword 4 (July 1974): 1-3.

Sackett, S. J., and William E. Koch, Kansas Folklore. Lincoln, 1961.

Scott, Florence Johnson. "Customs and Superstitions among Texas Mexicans on the Rio Grande Border," PTFS 2 (1923): 75-84.

Sébillot, Paul. Le Folk-Lore de France. 4 vols. Paris, 1904-7.

Seligmann, S. Der Böse Blick und Verwandtes. Ein Beitrag zur Geschichte des Aberglaubens aller Zeiten und Völker. 2 vols. Berlin, 1910.

Shenk, G. F. "The Cross of Salt," NMFR 1 (1947-48): 40-42.

Shoemaker, Henry W. "Neighbors: The Werwolf [sic] in Pennsylvania," NYFQ 7 (1951): 145-55.

_____. Scotch-Irish and English Proverbs and Sayings of the West Branch Valley of Central Pennsylvania. Reading, Pa., 1927.

Simmons, Frank. "The Wart Doctor," PTFS 14 (1938): 192-94.

Smith, Walter R. "Animals and Plants in Oklahoma Folk Cures," Folk-Say: A Regional Miscellany, edited by B. A. Botkin, 69-78. Norman, Okla., 1929.

_____. "You Can't Tell about the Weather," Folk-Say: A Regional Miscellany, edited by B. A. Botkin, 173-85. Norman, Okla., 1930.

Soland, Craig. "Ghost Stories from Cottage II," AFFword 3 (July 1973): 1-24.

_____. "More Ghost Stories from Cottage II: A Study in Institutional Collecting Technique," AFFword 3 (January 1974): 1-33.

Steiner, Roland. "The Practice of Conjuring in Georgia," JAF 14 (1901): 173-80.

Stephens, Claude E. "Witching for Water in Oregon," WF 11 (1952): 204-7.

Stout, Earl J. Folklore from Iowa. MAFS, XXIX. New York, 1936.

Strecker, John K. "Folk-Lore Relating to Texas Birds," PTFS 7 (1928): 25-37.

_____. "On the Origins of Reptile Myths," PTFS 5 (1926): 70-77.

_____. "Reptiles of the South and Southwest in Folk-Lore," PTFS 5 (1926): 56-69.

Swainson, Rev. Charles. The Folk Lore and Provincial Names of British Birds. Publications of the Folk-Lore Society, XVII. London, 1886.

Tally, Frances. "American Folk Customs of Courtship and Marriage: The Bedroom." In Forms Upon the Frontier, edited by Austin and Alta Fife, and Henry H. Glassie, 138-58. Utah State University Monograph Series, 16, No. 2. Logan, Utah, 1969.

Thiselton Dyer, T. F. British Popular Customs, Present and Past. London, 1876.

_____. The Ghost World. London, 1893.

_____. The Folk-Lore of Plants. New York, 1889.

Thomas, Daniel Lindsey, and Lucy Blayney Thomas. Kentucky Superstitions. Princeton, N.J., 1920.

Thompson, Lawrence S. "More Buzzard Lore," KFR 4 (1958): 155-62.

Turner, Tressa. "The Human Comedy in Folk Superstitions," PTFS 13 (1937): 146-75.

Vogt, Evon Z., and Ray Hyman. Water Witching, U.S.A. Chicago, 1959.

Walker, Warren S. "Water-Witching in Central Illinois," MF 6 (1956): 197-203.

Wallrich, T./Sgt. Bill. "Superstitions and Air Force," WF 19 (1960): 11-16.

Walton, Miranda Snow. "Wyoming Pioneer Superstitions," WF 9 (1950): 161-62.

_____. "Wyoming Weather Lore," WF 9 (1950): 162.

Ward, Donald J. "Weather Signs and Weather Magic: Some Ideas on Causality in Popular Belief," Pacific Coast Philology 3 (1968): 67-72.

Waugh, F. W. "Canadian Folk-Lore from Ontario," JAF 31 (1918): 4-82.

Webb, Wheaton P. "Witches in the Cooper Country," NYFQ 1 (1945): 5-20.

Weiner, Harvey. "Folklore in the Los Angeles Garment Industry," WF 23 (1964): 17-21.

Welsch, Roger L. A Treasury of Nebraska Pioneer Folklore. Lincoln, Neb., 1966.

Whitney, Annie Weston, and Caroline Canfield Bullock. Folk-Lore from Maryland. MAFS, XVIII. New York, 1925.

Whitten, Norman E., Jr. "Contemporary Patterns of Malign Occultism among Negroes in North Carolina," JAF 75 (1962): 311-325.

Williams, Phyllis H. South Italian Folkways in Europe and America. A Handbook for Social Workers, Visiting Nurses, School Teachers and Physicians. New Haven, Conn., 1938.

Wilson, Charles Morrow. "Folk Beliefs in the Ozark Hills," Folk-Say (1930): 157-72.

Wilson, Eddie W. "American Indian Concept of Saliva," MF 1 (1951): 229-32.

_____. "Some American Fishing Superstitions," MF 5 (1955): 217-20.

Wilson, Howard Barrett. "Notes of Syrian Folk-Lore Collected in Boston," JAF 16 (1903): 133-47.

Wilson, William A. "A Bibliography of Studies in Mormon Folklore," Utah Historical Quarterly 44 (1976): 389-94.

_____. "Mormon Legends of the Three Nephites Collected at Indiana University," Indiana Folklore 2 (1969): 3-35.

_____. "The Paradox of Mormon Folklore," Brigham Young University Studies 17 (1976): 40-58.

_____. "The Vanishing Hitchhiker among the Mormons," Indiana Folklore 8 (1975): 79-97.

Winslow, David J. "Occupational Superstitions of Negro Prostitutes in an Upstate New York City," NYFQ 24 (1968): 294-301.

Wintemberg, W. J. Folk-Lore of Waterloo County, Ontario. National Museum of Canada, Bulletin, No. 116. Anthropological Series No. 28. Ottawa, 1950.

Woodhull, Frost. "Ranch Remedios," PTFS 8 (1930): 9-73.

Woods, Barbara Allen. "The Devil in Dog Form," WF 13 (1954): 229-35.

Yoffie, Leah Rachel. "Popular Beliefs and Customs among the Yiddish-Speaking Jews of St. Louis, Mo.," JAF 38 (1925): 375-99.

Young, Kimball, and T. D. Cutsforth. "Hunting Superstitions in the Cow Creek Region of Southern Oregon," JAF 41 (1928), 283-85.

Zucker, Konrad. Psychologie des Aberglaubens. Heidelberg, 1948.

# Index

Abdomen: 252, 534
Abnormal, children: 225, 897, 937f.
Abominable Snowman: 10394
Abortion: 143ff.; --, preventing
Abracadabra: 2601, 3584
Abscess: 2905ff., 3077; --, hand: 2907; --,
    finger: 2907; --, foot: 2907
Absence: 4511
Absent, soul: 1417
Absent-minded: 2842
Absorb: 2735
Absorption: 783
Accident: 1089, 2806ff., 3816ff., 2285, 6301,
    6330, 6512, 7130, 7196, 7669, 7728, 7747,
    7777, 7790, 8867, 9007, 9228, 9785, 12746;
    --, auto: 11778; --, averting: 279, 6150;
    --, death by: 10663; --, fatal: 2810; -- in
    mine: 7086ff., 7088, 7108, 7114, 9648; --,
    preventing: 7649, 7652, 7860; --, seeing:
    345, 963; --, stopping at: 2820; -- in
    threes: 2806
Accident prone: 2823
Ace: 4813, 8584, 10438; --, black: 8583; -- of
    hearts: 8569; -- of spades: 8561, 8570,
    8585, 8607f., 9630ff., 10439; --, pair of:
    8609.
Aches, indicator of weather: 10803ff., 10844;
    -- of feet: 1716
Aches and pains: 2908ff.
Acid: 1929, 3644, 5913
Acidity: 1068
Acid stomach: 4048
Acne: 2917ff.
Acorn: 2222, 2276, 10509f., 12946; -- in
    window: 6482; as indicator of winter:
    10773f.
Acorn tea: 3945
Acquaintance: 8331
Actor: 7154ff., 7169, 7172ff., 7179, 7188,
    7194, 8277
Adam's apple: 1625
Adder: 12358; --, killing: 8507; --, skin of:
    6415, 12364
Addled: 1014
Address book: 4670
Admiring: 1167, 1197
Adoption: 50
Adult, child sleeping with: 919
Adulteress: 2349f.
Adultery: 5419
Adults, hair of: 651
Affair: 4556; --, love: 4501, 4796, 5097, 5085
Affection: 4862, 4990, 5520, 6544
Affectionate: 2352
Afflicted: 970
Afterbirth: 264, 852; -- of cow: 12752; --,
    disposing of: 302ff. See also Placenta
Afterlife: 1297, 9717, 9753, 9759, 10010
Afternoon, born in: 868
Afterpains: 306
Agate: 718, 3688
Age: 278, 2196, 4867
Agnus: 2882
Agreement: 7247

Ailment: 2733, 2742, 2761
Ailments, mental and emotional: 5167ff.
Air: 2501; --, bad: 7086; --, corrupted: 2581;
    --, dark: 6237; --, night: 2657, 3279,
    3323, 3773, 11501f.; --, stagnant: 2652;
    --, warm: 10052. See also Night air
Airplane: 48, 291, 7880f., 9348, 9611, 10398,
    11583; --, dreaming of: 7305. See also
    Plane
Airplane crash: 7883ff., 11550
Airplane sickness: 3790
Alarm clock: 12640
Albatross: 7035ff.; --, killing: 7041f., 12344
Albinism: 1020
Albino: 1020, 9008, 12584
Alcohol: 217, 953, 1450, 1920, 1927, 1929,
    2715, 4027, 4041
Alcohol, rubbing: 2918, 3842
Alcoholic (adj.): 217, 1000
Alcoholic (n.): 219, 1932
Alcoholism: 218, 1930
Alder bark tea: 2747
Alfalfa: 3752; -- leaves: 2749; -- tea: 2757,
    3350, 3904
All Fools Day: 13108
Alligator: 1218; --, teeth of: 720
All Souls Day: 9984
Almanac: 8956, 12999
Almond: 5197, 5336, 6008, 6039f., 9747; --,
    candied: 4741, 5561; --, Jordan: 5501; --
    seed: 13194
Alone: 1922, 8853
Alphabet: 4690, 7965
Alpine, Utah: 7068
Altar: 5438, 9105, 9208
Alum: 3146, 3303, 3753, 12821; -- syrup: 3987
Aluminum: 5834, 7400; --, cooking in: 3122,
    3468
Amber: 2661, 4994; -- beads: 3240, 3537, 3932,
    4028
Ambition: 862
Ambulance: 2598, 2821, 7870f., 9610
American League: 8705
Amethyst: 1926
Ammonia: 296, 3700
Amputation: 2826ff., 2831
Amulet: 7005ff., 8850, 10466, 10504ff.,
    10508ff., 10563, 10565ff., 10568ff.,
    10573ff.; --, badger's tooth: 8545; --, bat
    heart: 8693; --, toad heart: 7557
Anaphrodisiac: 4993f.
Ancestors: 20, 610, 5934
Anchor: 6974
Anemia: 3032
Angang: 4589, 4591, 4623, 5475f., 5478, 6960,
    7057, 7635, 7704ff., 7727, 7776, 7870,
    8938, 9006, 9011, 9066, 9785ff., 11827
Angel: 16, 1349, 1516, 6427, 8652, 9659, 9570,
    9918f., 10248, 10671, 10988, 11407, 11944;
    --, conversing with: 743, 747; --, dreaming
    of: 8347; --, kissed by: 689; -- of death:
    1233, 2664, 9878; -- Moroni: 4860, 4905f.,
    10004
Anger: 6544, 8638, 12900; --, Lord's: 11698

Angleworm: 11285
Angry: 1397, 1595, 1754, 1758, 2859
Animal: 7871, 9009, 9894f., 11908ff., 13106;
    --, albino: 12584; -- in body: 2792f.; --,
    burying alive: 2673; --, call of: 11705; --
    at Christmas: 11896ff.; -- curing disease:
    2786; --, dead: 9001, 11915, 13195; --,
    death of: 2640; --, eating: 1739; --,
    handling: 654; -- in house: 7936; --,
    howling of: 9380; -- as indicator of
    weather: 10708ff., 10849ff., 10875, 11025;
    --, injured: 2709; --, killing: 3364, 8994,
    8999, 9003, 9669; --, freshly killed: 3457;
    --, language of: 11914; --,
    legendary/mythical: 12575ff.; --, life span
    of: 791; --, looking at/seeing: 679, 973;
    --, making friends with: 2431; -- as
    mascot: 8686; --, mating of: 5291; --,
    mistreating: 9896; --, mysterious: 8864;
    --, protecting from lice: 12684; --,
    resemblance to: 359ff.; -- seeing spirits:
    10626; -- sensing earthquake: 11500; --,
    speaking: 11897; --, speaking of: 7033; --,
    taming: 12583; --, wild: 7134, 9810,
    11916f., 12165; -- as witch: 10040; --,
    wounding: 9004
Animal bite: 3367
Animal fur: 10731ff., 10784f.
Animal husbandry: 12583ff.
Anise: 8980
Ankle: 2607, 3921, 3923, 6899; --, left: 4574;
    --, ribbon on: 930, 1196; --, sprained:
    4040, 12742
Anniversary: 5371
Ant bed: 925.  See also Ant hill
Ant eggs: 4993
Ant hill: 4237, 12459; --, sleeping on: 3136.
    See also Ant bed
Antidote: 3001, 3591, 3712
Ants: 4356, 10696, 12455ff.; --, dreaming of:
    574, 6278, 12460; --, eating: 2488; --,
    first: 2488; -- as indicator of weather:
    10858, 10893, 10907, 10937, 10961, 11081f.,
    11279; --, killing: 6366, 7558; --,
    stepping on: 3835, 12457; --, sting of:
    3709f.  See also Red ant
Apartment: 6270
Aphrodisiac: 4961ff., 4966ff., 4978ff.
Apostate: 9957, 10202
Apostles: 3858, 11573
Apparition: 11923
Appendicitis: 2697, 2921ff.
Appendix: 2924, 2926
Appetite: 2130f., 4698
Apple: 1465, 1523, 2495, 2550, 3448, 4244ff.,
    4683ff., 6038, 6986, 9566, 10227; --
    blossom: 11202; --, bobbing for: 4685; --,
    burying: 4245; -- cider: See Vinegar and
    Apple vinegar; -- core: 2795; --, falling:
    8049; --, feeding to pig: 4246; --, green:
    109, 2922, 4047; -- juice: 3529; --, last:
    13196; --, peeling: 5101, 5771, 5773; --
    peeling: 4694ff., 5772; --, rotten:
    3525; -- seeds: 565, 2921, 3734, 4686f.; --
    skin: 10781; --, stealing: 326, 4047; --
    stem: 4690ff., 8512; -- tree: 2795, 13013,
    13197; -- vinegar: 3860
Application: 3212ff., 3327ff.
Apricot stones: 2796
Apricot tree: 2796
April: 1424, 4173, 10801, 10986, 11205, 11438,
    13096, 13130, 13135; --, born in: 9921,

11745, 11760; --, last night of: 4616; --
    rainwater: 2146, 3413; --, wedding in:
    5282ff.
April conference: 9956
April Fool's Day: 11901f., 13108; --, wedding
    on: 5697
Apron: 4587, 8076, 8130, 9225; --, blue: 5500;
    --, getting wet: 1924, 5165; --, losing:
    8362; --, wearing backwards: 6706; --,
    wearing wrong side out: 6688, 6905; --,
    white: 7057.
Apron strings: 7153
Arch, of foot: 1715f.
Arches National Monument: 10267
Architect: 7117
Archway: 5112
Argopelter: 12579
Argument: 5080, 8314, 8351, 8367, 8374, 8398,
    8407, 8426, 8466, 8469, 8475, 8515, 8519
Arising: 185, 491, 1761ff., 5632, 6648, 10188.
    See also Bed, getting out of
Aristocrat: 2355
Arizona mosquito plant: 3706
Arm: 2656, 4029; --, baby's: 373, 909; --,
    brass on: 3923; --, breaking: 3495, 3502,
    8324; --, cutting: 2293; --, folding: 1636;
    --, itching: 8325; --, left: 1637, 6650;
    --, mole on: 1404; --, right: 6648, 7611,
    8693; --, severed: 965, 2692, 2827, 2830;
    --, sign in: 13071; --, spot on: 468
Arms, position at burial: 9740; --, crossing:
    1665, 9934; --, folding: 5006; --, hairy:
    2264, 7445; --, interlocking: 4722; --,
    measuring: 9072
Arnica: 4036
Arrow: 6939, 7237
Arteries, hardening of: 1399
Art gallery: 842
Arthritis: 2928ff., 11008, 11216
Article, lost: 9916, 11618
Artist: 842, 844, 2331
Artistic: 2332ff.
Asafetida: 933, 2277, 3679, 3965; -- bag: 1121,
    2613, 2739, 2873, 3241, 3313, 3777, 3796,
    3947, 4004, 4435, 10293, 10133
Ascension Thursday, planting on: 12995
Ashes: 3541, 4858, 5756, 6102, 6373, 9357,
    11823, 12684; --, burying: 12551; --, cross
    of: 11190; -- as curing agent: 2683; --,
    eating: 2683; -- on forehead: 10239; --,
    hot: 3321; -- in shoe: 3756; --, sweeping:
    9356; --, taking out: 6175ff.
Ashes of the dead, disposal of: 9816
Ash tree: 851
Ash twig: 12716
Ash Wednesday: 11320, 12684
Ash wood: 2825, 7135
Asparagus: 1748, 13076f.
Aspen: 4229, 12924; -- bark: 2748.  See also
    Quakin' asp
Aspirin: 1925, 2729, 3203
Ass, hairs of: 1129, 4442
Assassination: 7573
Assault: 7139
Asthma: 2947ff., 3872
Asthma boil: 2949
Astrologer: 11728, 11730
Astrology: 11727ff.
Astronomer: 11775
Athlete: 8668, 8675, 8679f.
Athlete's foot: 3757
Athletic contest: 8666, 8684

Basque: 7136, 8623, 9976
Bastard: 824.  See Wedlock, out of
Bat (animal): 362, 1502f., 7937, 9441,
    12175ff.; -- in the belfry: 9941; --, bite
    of: 2897; -- in house: 6503; --, heart of:
    8693; -- as indicator of weather: 10934,
    11274; --, killing: 9442; -- pissing on
    head: 2972
Bat, baseball: 8716ff., 8723, 8747
Bath: 1589, 2634f., 3873, 3955, 4108, 8588,
    11382; --, baby's: 1037, 1090; -- during
    menstruation: 1971; --, milk: 1412; --,
    steam: 3235; --, sulphur: 3949; -- in
    winter: 3181
Bathe: 2718, 11860.  See also Shower
Bather's rash: 3873
Bathing: 1769ff., 3714, 8642, 11818; -- baby:
    1105; --, curative properties of: 2681,
    4181; -- of pregnant woman: 134, 188f.,
    317; --, time of: 1771
Bathing (swimming): 8855.  See also Swimming
Bath night: 8230
Bath powder: 4433
Bath tub: 150, 8575, 12416; --, direction of:
    1989, 6435; --, singing in: 8643
Batter, baseball: 8711, 8729ff.
Batter, spoiling of: 5783; --, stirring:
    5782ff., 5797f.
Batting average: 8723, 8735
Battle (n.): 7688; --, sea: 7012
Battlefield: 6393, 9122
Bawling out: 6692
Bay leaf: 4762f., 9569, 12926f.; -- under
    pillow: 4763
Bay rum: 1450
Beach: 3757, 9276
Beads: 1625, 3334, 3536f., 6898, 10571; --,
    amber: 3240, 3932, 4028, 4994; --, black:
    4992; --, glass: 4028; --, stringing: 9912
Beak: 10296
Beans: 2489, 3458, 13027; --, brown: 4259; --,
    burying: 3786, 4254ff.; --, rubbing on
    mole: 3786; --, planting: 4261, 13029ff.;
    --, red: 4257; --, rubbing on wart: 4263;
    --, white: 9543
Bear: 6797, 7828, 9996, 10710, 11720, 12159ff.,
    12576; -- cub: 9019; --, hibernation of:
    10742; -- hunting: 9019
Beard: 2263, 3871, 7123, 11844; -- of corpse:
    9882; --, girls growing: 1624; --, shaving:
    1622; --, white: 2708, 12035
Bear tracks: 10789, 12581f.
Beast: 10732, 10849, 11312ff.
Beating, child: 1197; -- tin pans: 301
Beau: 4503, 4508f., 4535, 4627, 4631; --,
    losing: 5099ff.
Beautiful: 158, 1448, 1495, 2144, 2557
Beauty: 1546, 1736, 2134ff.; -- of babies:
    797ff.; -- marks: 2137; -- sleep: 2003
Beaux: 5045
Beaver: 10709, 12166; -- dam: 10748
Bed: 69, 1026, 6435ff., 9313, 9660, 10241; --,
    axe under: 116, 244, 252, 267f., 306; --,
    baby: 1137; --, before: 1790; --, bird on:
    9456; --, blessing the: 5611; --, booties
    on: 1141; --, bottom of: 1875; --, broom
    on: 9330; --, butter under: 117; --,
    clothing on: 6756; --, coat on: 9218; --,
    cork in: 3316; --, direction of: 1414,
    2188, 9309f., 9676; -- of dying person:
    9173, 9815; --, eating in: 1098, 6096; --,
    eggs on/under: 1195, 6442; --, falling off:

1296, 1375, 1941; --, feather: 6444, 9148;
    --, foot over: 1996; --, getting out of:
    1758ff., 1970, 11784.  See also Arising;
    --, goblins under: 10389; --, going to:
    1791, 1795, 1799, 1801, 1866, 1876, 1883f.,
    1997, 2000, 2003, 2013, 2550, 2578, 3216,
    3508, 4127, 4745, 4759ff., 5079, 5191; --,
    hat on/under: 2562, 5680, 6774ff., 6778,
    6989, 7169f., 8131, 8840, 9220, 9675; --,
    wearing hat in: 6779; --, horseshoe under:
    4167; --, knife under: 253f., 2648, 2912;
    --, laughing in: 2515; --, making: 104,
    234, 1097, 2558, 5147, 7642, 8781, 9308;
    --, moon shining on: 11604; --, nails in
    front of: 245; --, penny under: 7417; --,
    potato under: 110, 3250; --, protection
    against storm: 11377; --, purse on: 6856;
    --, right side: 495, 4033; --, scissors
    under: 2912; --, shoe beside: 4744; --,
    shoes on/under: 2014, 2563, 3320, 6523,
    6809ff.; --, shoes pointing at: 2023; -- of
    sick person: 2642, 9137; --, singing in:
    8633, 8644; --, sitting on: 2835, 6304,
    6440; --, spider on: 8156; --, spirits
    under: 1995; --, stocking on: 1872, 5558;
    --, strange: 1821; --, sweeping under: 313,
    2645, 9138, 9328; --, three in: 2007; --,
    trousers on: 100; --, turning: 552; --,
    umbrella on: 2642, 6523, 8484, 9361; --,
    uranium under: 2945, 3926; --, water under:
    2985, 4752; --, weapon on: 6441
Bedbug: 12176; --, boiled: 3458; -- in
    ointment: 3410
Bedfellow: 2024
Bedpost: 4753, 4755
Bedroom: 4757, 6445, 9505; --, flowers in:
    2571, 6486, 9553; --, red: 4991
Bedroom eyes: 1545
Bed sores: 2985
Bedwetting: 1021ff.  See also Enuresis
Beef: 363; --, birthmark resembling: 389; --,
    burying: 3293; --, butchering: 12759f.; --
    juice: 2874; -- tea: 2770
Beefsteak: 3422, 4242; --, raw: 3086, 3527.
    See also Steak
Beehive: 11280
Beekeeper: 3723
Beer: 1510, 1908ff., 1914, 2415, 4891, 5929ff.,
    8622, 12064; --, egg in: 4971; --, souring
    of: 5931; --, washing hair in: 1433; -- and
    oysters: 3483
Beer bottle: 2270
Beer can: 8923
Bees: 5904, 7336, 10176, 12495ff., 13024,
    13123; --, burning: 3756; -- as indicator
    of death: 9521f.; -- as indicator of
    weather: 10759f., 10793, 11083, 11280; --,
    dreaming of: 7335; -- in house: 7918, 8151;
    --, killing: 7337; --, moving: 12702; --,
    moving on Good Friday: 12700; --, selling:
    12699; --, settling: 12703ff.; --,
    stealing: 12709; --, swarm of: 6414, 12495,
    12698; --, telling the: 2585, 9520, 12701,
    12707f.
Bee sting: 3689ff., 3888, 8510, 12499f., 12500,
    12502f.
Beeswax: 3553
Beet field: 2828
Beet juice: 4249
Beetle: 9523, 12461ff.; --, black: 9524; --,
    killing: 12463
"Beetle Eyes": 7797

Blizzard: 11416, 11428
Blond: 753
Blonde (adj.): 2384
Blonde (n.): 2380, 2399, 2406, 2846, 4871,
    5152f., 11805
Blood: 389, 1391ff., 2510, 3369, 3830, 6979,
    9681, 12764, 12790, 12935; -- ailments:
    1036f.; --, bad: 859, 2671, 3057, 3839; --
    bath: 8999; -- brothers: 2293; --, calf:
    3281; --, cat: 2788, 4212, 4216; --,
    changing direction of: 3045; -- changing
    when baptised: 9965; --, chicken: 3101; --,
    circulation of: 3034; --, coagulation of:
    12815; -- used in conjury: 10116; --,
    drinking: 2251, 3281; --, dreaming of:
    1812; --, drying up of: 1394f.; -- from
    finger of murderer: 7579; -- on flowers:
    13180; --, fresh: 3281; --, giving: 1268;
    --, good: 859; --, impurities of: 1036,
    3057, 3839; --, life's: 1367; --, low:
    3033; --, mammal: 11481; --, mole: 3885; --
    poisoning: 270, 1037, 2698, 3047ff.; -- of
    pregnant woman: 192; -- pressure: 3053ff.;
    --, purify: 3035, 3039f., 3042f., 3046,
    3058, 3370, 4045; --, shedding: 7576f.,
    10636; --, sheep: 3443; --, sight of: 980,
    12242; --, sign of death: 9057; --,
    signature in: 10219; --, snake: 378; --,
    spilling: 10663, 12010; --, spitting:
    12446; -- spot: 2545; --, stopping:
    2709; -- suckers: 1398, 3138; --, sucking:
    3976, 6556, 12178; stepping in: 2084; --
    thickener: 3044; -- thinner: 3044; --
    thinning: 3041; --, toad's: 4224; -- tonic:
    3036ff.; -- from wart: 4256, 4261, 4284;
    --, washing in: 8999
"Blood Wings": 7142
"Bloody Stake": 10085
Bloom: 9152
Bloomers: 11195
Blossom: 2746
Blouse: 2814, 6686
Blowing as cure for thrush: 1116; -- dandelion:
    566; -- on dice: 8614; -- into ear:
    3392f.; -- into paper bag: 3627; -- into
    sore throat: 4015; -- onto tonsils: 4141
Blowsnake: 12372, 12378
Blue: 394, 502f., 525f., 922, 1354, 2160, 2688,
    4592, 5387f., 6535, 6543, 6976, 8025,
    11195, 11333, 11879; -- apron: 5500; --
    clay: 3653; -- eyes: 5155, 8258; -- garter:
    5225; -- moon: 4837; -- pennant: 6984; --
    stones: 3001, 3591, 3712; --, touching:
    8010; --, wearing: 5390ff., 5424ff., 6727
Bluebird: 4636, 5952, 10680, 12251ff.
Blue ox: 11476
Bluestone: 4986
Blue vitriol: 12589
Bluish: 3758
Blushing: 8059
Boasting: 683, 7993, 8912, 9000
Boat: 6976, 7011, 7020, 7043, 7065; -- of
    eggshell: 10038; --, fishing: 7055f.; --,
    sinking of: 6980. See also Ship
Bobby pin: 4579, 4583, 8733. See also Hairpin
Bodily functions: 482ff.
Body: 2273, 2284, 2548, 2670; -- association
    with celestial bodies: 1413; --, baby's:
    331, 371, 381, 399; --, child's: 332, 372;
    --, composition of: 1415; --, dead: 349,
    1341, 3844, 4982, 10265, 10666; --, devil
    in: 2037; --, digging up: 9755; --, eyelash

on: 1576; --, good: 1418; --, pull of
    gravity on: 1414; -- hair: 1514; --,
    healthy: 902; --, herbs on: 2609; --,
    human: 10844ff.; --, humors of: 2671; --,
    infection in: 3669; --, parts of: 2742; --
    of pregnant woman: 332, 340, 358, 361, 383,
    459; --, rubbing: 2715, 2787; --, scabs on:
    3946; --, spirit in: 3665, 3681; --, spirit
    leaving: 1808, 2036f., 2043f., 2674f.; --,
    stepping over: 2005; --, soul leaving:
    1807; -- in trance: 1417; --, vapors of:
    2671; --, wrapping: 2248.  See also Corpse
    and Dead
Bog sprite: 10348
Boils (n.): 2410, 3057ff.
"Bole": 105
Bomb, atomic: 11734
Bone: 4243, 8718, 10580; --, aching: 10845f.,
    11007, 11009, 11216; --, bat: 6504; --,
    broken: 3490ff., 3498f., 3501.  See also
    Fracture; --, feeling in: 8272; --, fish:
    208, 4075ff., 7007, 8901, 10473; --, ham:
    3884; -- matter: 2698; --, rabbit: 10499;
    --, severed: 2827; --, turtle: 7008; --,
    strong: 723; --, weak: 724
Bonfire: 11193
Bonnet: 1139, 1364.  See also Cap
Bonny: 422, 427
Boogy man: 1219ff.  See also Buggerman
Book: 817, 1262, 1284, 1685, 1979, 7605, 12865
Book of Mormon: 2688, 9954, 10011
Boot: 453, 7075, 7133, 12636
Booties: 1141
Boots: 6800, 7075, 7098, 7132, 7655, 8874
Borax: 6367
Border state: 7892
Boric acid: 3753
Born, under zodiac: 2453, 2427
Borrowing: 5389ff., 5641, 6171, 6388, 6792,
    5897, 5900, 5918, 6930ff., 8416, 8451ff.,
    8471, 11776, 12032; -- salt: 2212, 8401ff.
Bosom: 2502, 4652
Boss: 1728, 2370, 5379, 5694, 5696ff.
Bossy: 2370
Botanicals: 2730ff.
Bottle: 1912, 3076, 3151, 3963
Bottling: 210.
Bottom, baby's: 1039, 1104
Bouncing: 251
Boundary: 2071
Bouquet, bridal: 5221f., 5226, 5462ff., 5466;
    --, wedding: 4947.  See also Flowers,
    bridal
Bourbon, medicinal use of: 2721
Bow (ribbon): 65, 4947
Bow, of vessel: 6982, 7003
Bow and arrow: 1318, 8921, 9761
Bowl (n.): 772, 2070, 6145
Bow-legs: 992ff.
Bowling: 8884ff., 11358; -- ball: 8884, 8887
Bow tie: 4823
Boxes: 1385
Boxing: 8879ff.; -- glove: 8879f.
Boy: 464, 467, 5138, 8181; --, birth of: 7431;
    --, bride holding: 524, 5557; --, crazy:
    4506; -- as first-footer: 8264
Boyfriend: 938, 4474, 4498f., 4523, 4546, 4557,
    4571f., 4574, 4579, 4586, 4588, 4595, 4598,
    4658, 4709, 4736, 4757, 4765, 4772, 5561,
    6637, 6865; --, losing: 5101, 5107ff.,
    5113; --, unfaithful: 5106, 5666
Boys, bad: 2; --, family of: 575

Bra: 1628, 6770
Bracelet: 6892; --, ankle: 4574; --, brass: 3922; --, copper: 3720, 3921; --, coral: 1162
Bragging: 2553, 7993, 10522f., 11527
Brahma bull: 8845
Brain: 1735ff.; --, addled: 1014; -- ailments: 3078ff.; --, baby's: 819; --, blood in: 3370; -- cells: 2840, 3080; --, cow's: 5864; --, damaged: 153; -- food: 1261, 1283, 1742f., 3081, 3083; --, infection of: 2693; --, shallow: 2852; -- waves: 7083
Brains: 598, 2297, 2851; --, calf: 2320; --, dead people's: 12892; --, rabbit: 722
Bramble bush, creeping under: 2988
Bran: 2771, 3795
Brandy: 4000
Brass: 3922ff., 12827; -- bracelet: 2942; -- ring: 3318; -- rod: 10458
Brave: 2470
Bravery: 6538, 7562
Bread: 918, 1211, 1630, 2772, 3121, 3142, 3488f., 4075, 5164, 5646, 5838ff., 6026, 6028, 7956, 8024, 8168ff., 9296ff., 10130, 11802, 13135; -- baked on Good Friday: 5852; -- baked on New Year's: 2590; --, baking: 5014f., 5788; --, blessing: 5791; --, breaking: 5845; --, burning: 4710, 5015, 5657, 6023, 8385, 9298, 11225; --, burying: 4371; --, buttering: 5846; --, Christmas: 6006; --, crosses on: 5791f.; -- crumbs: 6081; -- crust: 1462, 1474, 1513, 4078, 4119, 8645; --, cutting: 1210, 5847f., 6025, 7502, 8386; -- dough: 2792, 4709, 4448; --, dropping: 5842; --, Easter: 6002f.; -- failing to rise: 5789; --, finding: 5844; --, floating to discover drowned body: 9702f.; --, giving away: 9300; --, hiding: 7313; --, kneading: 5791; --, last piece of: 2258, 4711, 5025, 5175, 5195, 5839f.; --, moldy: 3489; -- in pocket: 10576; --, putting money in: 5475, 5994, 6006; --, second piece: 6024; -- soup: 265; --, stepping on: 5843; --, taking another piece: 8387; --, taking into new home: 6291ff.; --, throwing away: 5840, 6021f.; --, toasted: 4371; --, upside down: 5850f., 9299, 9680, 10190, 10269; --, white: 41
"Bread and butter": 685, 2113, 3718, 4711, 7771, 8026, 8520, 8527ff.
Bread and milk: 1198f., 3050, 3061, 3327, 3339, 3648, 3961, 4134
Breadboard: 4764
Breakage: 6146ff., 11554
Breakfast: 1791; --, before: 1542, 1752, 1779, 1796f., 1825ff., 1881, 1960, 3275, 4537, 4544, 4800, 5069, 5081, 6903, 7376, 8139, 12998; --, marrying before: 5328; --, singing before: 7222, 9120; --, sneezing before: 9107; --, telling dream before: 9102; --, walking before: 2637; --, whistling before: 8650
Breaking: 62, 65, 559f., 1334, 2070, 2426, 2513, 2536, 4769
Breast: 631f., 627, 6770; --, caking: 628; --, cancer of: 3138; --, development of: 1628; -- feeding: 115. See also Nursing. --, left: 4465; -- milk: 1115; --, veins on: 2349. See also Bust
Breastbone, chicken: 10750, 10788
Breast fever: 632
Breath: 5822; --, baby's: 1366; --, bad: 2967; --, cat sucking: 742, 1366, 1992; -- used in curing: 928, 1116; --, holding: 3611, 3621ff., 7840, 7847f., 8799, 9853ff., 12500, 12528. See also Wind
Breathe: 2581, 3612, 3770. See also Inhale
Breathing: 1077, 2151, 1343, 1735, 1776, 3261, 3613, 3628; -- illness: 2952
Breech birth: 287ff., 803, 839, 1089
Breeding, good: 2356

Breeze, warm: 10605
Brew (n.): 1480
Brick: 2176, 3232f.; --, last: 7122; -- laying: 7119
Bridal book: 5053, 5230, 5732
Bridal couple: 9209
Bridal party: 5480
Bridal Veil Falls: 11475
Bride: 560, 3016, 4564, 4918, 4944, 5047, 5052, 5174, 5188, 5214, 5216ff., 5227f., 5242, 5244, 5253, 5257f., 5261, 5293, 5330, 5333, 5341, 5350f., 5353ff., 5358f., 5361, 5367ff., 5388f., 5395ff., 5432, 5434f., 5442ff., 5454, 5458ff., 5471f., 5474f., 5477, 5482, 5489, 5493, 5514, 5517, 5535, 5539, 5545, 5556, 5559f., 5562f., 5569, 5572ff., 5576f., 5586, 5589f., 5615, 5618, 5620f., 5632, 5634ff., 5644ff., 5691, 5699, 5709, 5719, 5726, 5731, 5734, 9203, 9205, 10668; -- arising on wedding day: 5348; --, behavior of: 93, 685; --, death of: 9212, 9677; --, dreaming of: 9211; --, groom seeing: 5339, 5342, 5481; --, happy: 5247f., 5250, 5255, 5295; -- holding boy in lap: 470, 524; --, kissing: 5495ff.; -- looking in mirror: 5374ff., 5488; --, sad: 5255; --, sneezing: 5363; -- rehearsing wedding: 5343; -- stealing: 5346; -- stepping on husband's foot: 5486; -- stepping on pomegranate: 5553; --, wedding clothes of: 5380ff.
Bridegroom: 5223, 5346, 5354, 5474; -- seeing bride: 5481. See also Groom
Bridesmaid: 5047ff., 5055, 5219, 5222, 5344f., 5558, 5597
Bride-to-be: 4912, 4942, 4947, 5397
Bridge (card game): 8581ff.
Bridge: 4638, 5005, 7684, 7837, 7840, 7849, 7852, 7854f., 7858, 9769, 10197, 10391, 11712; --, crossing: 5112, 7838, 7846ff., 9693; --, passing under: 7827ff.; --, walking under: 7872
Brigham tea: 2749, 3035, 3905
Bright (smart): 793, 820, 1007f., 2299
Brilliant: 812, 822, 1920
Brimstone: 4387
Brine: 3416, 9926
Britches, hole in: 1602, 8112; --, money in: 7283
Broad bean flowers: 9968
Broccoli: 486
Bronchitis: 2593, 3084f.
Brook: 8534, 11860
Broom: 2175, 6183, 6192, 6202ff., 6287ff., 7503, 7567, 8196, 8198f., 10030, 12685; -- behind door: 8110f.; --, borrowing: 8471, --, breaking: 4769; --, burning: 6289; --, buying in May: 8470, 9331; -- over doorstep: 8197; --, gift of: 5469; --, hitting with: 2424, 7566, 9329; --, janitor's: 4768; --, jumping over: 5618, 6209; --, new: 6203ff., 6207f., 6288, 6291, 6294, 9332; --, old: 6205, 6288; -- on bed: 9330; -- on shoulder: 2180; --, stepping over: 105, 5039, 5617, 6209; -- stopping witch: 10047, 10069; -- straw: 4406, 5903, 10090, 12551; --, sweeping baby with: 759; --, sweeping feet: 514; --, tripping over: 6211
"Broomie:" 12016
Broomstick: 1718
Brother: 7585, 8355
Brother-in-law: 264
Brow: 2852
Brown: 361f., 374, 1410f., 4009, 5807; -- bag: 3789; -- bean: 4259; -- egg: 5896; -- paper: 3771, 3790, 3815; --, wearing: 5428f., 6736
Brownette: 5153
Brownies: 10396
Bruise (n.): 1695, 3086ff., 3112, 4111, 4456
Bruise (vb.): 331

Bruja: 4978
Brunette: 2373, 2406, 5137, 5152f., 8252
Brush (n.): 11099, 13167
Brushing: 279
Bubble gum: 8751
Bubbles: 5748, 6170, 6232, 7323f., 11138; -- in coffee: 6050, 6052, 8167; -- in tea: 4718, 6051, 8164; --, wishing on: 6051
Bucket: 2097, 6981
Buckeye: 2619, 3896, 10511
Buckshot: 3859, 3930
Buckskin: 3800
Buds: 10764
Buffalo: 8022; --, killing: 12118, 12121; -- tallow: 3155, 3837; --, white: 12118ff.
Bug: 3347, 5582, 6216, 10960, 12521, 13074, 13131; --, killing: 11080; -- in poultice: 2785
Buggerman: 1219. See also Boogy man
Buggy: 3358, 9607
Building (n.): 6259, 6271, 6551, 7117, 7121, 11766, 12078, 12335
Bull: 8846, 8850, 12757; --, dreaming of: 4627, 11995; --, mad: 11992ff.; --, sign of the: 2453
Bullet: 3821, 4141, 4461, 9022, 9199, 9967, 10325; --, eating: 1490; immunity to: 3544, -- in mouth: 2268; --, silver: 10289, 10326, 10676, 12766
Bullfighting: 8849
Bullfrogs: 3775. See also Frogs
Bull-headed: 2453
Bull rope: 8844
Bull snake: 12370
Bumblebee: 7338, 7918, 8152, 12497; --, killing: 12504
Bump (n.): 1526, 1679, 2141, 2372, 2340, 4111, 7610
Bump (vb.): 330
Bumping: 1422, 1639, 1991
Bunion: 3297; -- as indicator of weather: 10804, 10847, 11007, 11011
Bunkhouse: 7128
Bunyan, Paul: 11476
Burdock: 3906
Burglar: 7553f., 7561
Burial: 2016ff., 9755ff., 9803ff.; -- of children: 1389f.; -- clothing: 9802; -- at crossroads: 3396; --, live: 2673; -- of murdered victim: 7580; -- position: 9805ff., 10677; --, proper: 10640; --, raining at: 9915
Burn (n.): 355f., 3091ff., 6124
Burn (vb.): 2034
Burning: 8032; -- afterbirth: 303; -- of ears: 1535ff.; -- hair: 1500; -- as punishment: 2574; -- spiders: 2230; -- witch: 2366
Bursitis: 11010
Burying, chicken liver: 1120; -- child's fingernails: 851; -- dishrag: 2295; -- hair: 1488, 1501; -- placenta: 302ff.; -- tooth: 710; -- weather: 9858ff.
Bus: 7866ff., 8683; -- ticket: 1943, 2117, 11584
Business: 7216, 7222, 7229, 7233f., 7239; --, finding: 7227; --, starting: 7220; --, successful: 7214, 7219; -- transaction: 7224f., 7230
Busts: 1630. See also Breast
Butchering: 12591ff., 12758ff.
Butte: 11476

Butter: 117, 265, 1211, 3095, 3202, 3306f., 8024, 12716f., 12899, 12901f.; -- on cat's paws: 12624; --, churning: 5882ff., 10381; --, dislike of: 212; -- plaster: 3228; --, unsalted: 3095; -- on warts: 4415; --, washing hair with: 1481
Buttercup: 4438, 4665, 12717, 12719, 12901
Butterfly: 624, 4648, 7490, 7907, 8691, 9732, 12464ff.; --, black: 9526f., 12466; --, dead: 12467; -- in house: 4649, 8154; --, killing: 6643, 9525, 12472; -- as indicator of weather: 10908; --, white: 4650, 12464f.
Buttermilk: 2207, 9279; --, washing with: 1407, 1445, 2148f., 3520
Butterpflaster: 3219
Buttocks: 389
Button: 4601, 4882, 6768; -- in cake: 1245, 5058, 5235, 7474; --, counting: 5171, 6957; --, dropping: 6632; --, finding: 6631, 7628, 7966, 8358; -- as gift: 6630; --, holding: 7721, 7723, 9855; --, losing: 6634; --, pearl: 3419; --, sewing on: 1738, 5034, 6573; -- on string: 533; --, touching: 9781f.
Buzzard: 2226, 9499, 10482, 12341; -- as indicator of death: 9499; -- as indicator of weather: 10935, 11066

Cab: 7800, 7802
Cabbage: 1, 3055, 5757, 5989, 11834; -- juice: 4184; -- leaves: 3766; --, planting: 13065ff. See also Red cabbage
Cabin: 7699
Cactus: 1492, 3067; -- roots: 2773
Cage: 12490, 12605
Cain, descendants of: 1514, 10009
Cake: 5016, 6041; --, baking: 4713f., 5796ff., 5809, 5811, 8171; --, birthday: 1243ff., 4782, 5235, 7474; --, brown: 5807; --, falling: 5797, 5799, 5801ff., 5805, 9301; --, first: 5590, 5808; --, feeding to groom: 5556; --, fruit: 5584, 5598; --, last piece: 5026; --, penny in: 7519; -- under pillow: 4714; --, upside down: 5806; --, wedding: 5212ff.; --, white: 5807
Calamity: 6082, 7751, 9078
Calendar: 9641, 11779ff.
Calf: 12746, 12748ff., 12754ff.; --, blood of: 3281; --, weaning of: 12755f.
"Call": 825
Caller: 8152, --, first: 8244. See also Visitor
Calling on: 280. See also Visiting
Calluses: 3295
Calm: 11211
Calomel root: 4058
Calories: 5854, 5928
Calumet: 10968, 12590
Calving: 12748ff.
Camel: 12167
Cameo: 4571
Camomile tea: 3185, 3377, 3674
Camp: 12386
Camphor: 1050, 2614, 2737, 2774, 3212, 3224, 3315, 3432, 3574, 3663
Camphor ice: 3550
Camping: 12386
"Camp-robber": 9010
Campsite: 12157, 12165, 12382
Can (n.): 5754f., 13153, 13189
Canary: 12239ff., 12605ff.; --, dead: 7577, 12242; -- in house: 6497; --, killing:

Celery: 42, 5910; -- brain food: 1742; -- juice: 2956; -- nerve medicine: 2870
Celestial bodies: See heavenly bodies
Cell, prison: 7595
Cellar: 1221, 11154, 11380; -- door: 6331
Cello: 1889, 2537
Cells, brain: 2840
Cemetery: 2295, 4210, 4372, 9579, 9773f., 9812, 9819, 9835, 9838, 9840ff., 9852ff., 10657ff., 12334, 12891; --, burying dishrag in: 4314; --, passing: 139, 157, 9853
Centipede: 12522f.
Cents: 4392
Ceremony: 2081
Chafing: 1039
Chain: 6899; --, silk: 4025
Chair: 6423ff., 8472, 9067, 9257, 9749; --, breaking: 4731; --, bride's: 5559; --, changing: 8576; --, circumambulating: 6425, 8577f., 8592; --, falling over: 5205; --, knocking over: 7152; -- leg: 3494, 9690; --, rocking: 6429ff., 6434, 8221, 9388, 10653; -- rocking by itself: 9259; --, rocking empty: 2559, 6431f., 9258, 10224, 11174; --, shoes on: 7590; --, spoon under: 512; --, sweeping under: 7470; --, tipping over: 5030; --, turning: 8473f., 8591; --, twirling: 6428; --, whirling: 9255
Chairs, back to back: 8220, 9256
Chalk: 3491, 12524
Challenge: 7532
Chamberlain, Wilt: 8786
Chamber lye: 3153; --, as croup cure: 1070. See also Urine
Chameleon: 2620
Chamois jacket: 3332
Champagne: 1911, 1917, 3563, 6995ff.; -- glass: 6074
Change (vb.): 2217, 2295
Change, facial: 2347
Changeling: 1165f., 10393
Chant (n.): 4210, 4355, 8778; --, rain: 11181
Chant (vb.): 4406
Chapel: 8852
Chapping: 3152ff.
Character: 855, 7146, 2340f., 2343ff., 2359f., 2376, 2450f., 2465, 2475
Characteristics, inherited: 856
Charcoal: 1463; -- croup cure: 1071
Chariot: 11351
Charley horse: 472, 3319
Charm (n.): 4572, 5547, 7877, 10157, 10296, 10466ff., 10489, 10565, 12352; -- bracelet: 10570; --, good luck: 2606, 8868f.; -- passed male to female: 10092; --, verbal: 262, 10587ff.
Charm (vb.): 4331, 4393, 10092, 12354, 12388
Charmer, wart: 4402ff.
Chartreuse: 4819
Chased, dreams of being: 1871
Chastisements: 1215ff.
Chastity: 5411, 5433; --, losing: 5162. See also Virtue, losing
Cheater: 7217
Cheating: 11791
Cheek: 4483; --, birthmark on: 378; --, burning: 8283; --, color on: 461; --, dimple in: 2392, 7571; --, eyelash on: 1581; --, itching: 9053; --, left: 4549; --, rosy: 1521ff.
Cheek bones: 2452
Cheerful: 891, 2401

Cheese: 5216, 7483, 12635; --, feeding to "little people": 10381; --, green: 11591; -- improving memory: 2838; -- riddance of tapeworm: 4116; -- turning into rat: 12140; --, wearing on body: 2616
Cheese and milk: 3274
Cheesecloth: 3870, 4459
Cheese mold: 3956
Chef: 5739
Cherries: 396f., 2509
Cherries and milk: 2923, 3471, 4049, 5913, 9280ff.
Cherry: 13153; -- pie: 6047; -- pit: 3532; -- stone: 2796, 2921; -- tree: 13202f.; --, wishing on: 5905, 6032
Cherub: 4520
Chest, birthmark on: 362; --, crushed: 2707; --, diseases of: 2743; --, hair on: 1509ff., 2264, 7280; --, mole on: 464, 2503; --, pain in: 3592; --, pneumonia of: 3850; --, spreading poultice on: 2774; -- baby's: 1366
Chest ailment: 3156
Chest cold: 3213, 3221, 3225f.
Chestnut: 2487, 3072, 3898, 13193; -- leaves: 4437; -- around neck: 3804, 3335; -- relieving pain: 2915
"Chewing ice": 2239
Cheyenne warrior: 9199
Chick: 12669
Chicken: 4628ff., 11186, 12671f., 12676, 12687ff., 12831; --, birthmark from: 387; --, birthmark on: 12659; -- blood: 3101; -- bone: 2655; -- breast bone: 10750; -- coop: 4001, 12369, 12681. See also chicken house; --, crowing of: 8143, 9426ff.; --, dead or dying: 3781, 3836; --, disease of: 12683ff.; -- drippings: 3295; -- droppings: 4001; --, drowning of: 12658; -- entrails: 3855; -- feathers: 10751; --, feeding: 4287; -- gizzard: 1073, 2951, 3641, 4066; --, hatching: 12662; -- heart: 2142, 4758, 4967; -- house: 12685. See also Chicken coop; --, killing: 2926, 3656, 3855, 3976, 9427, 12184, 12691; -- laying eggs: 9988, 12682; --, live: 3220, 3855; -- liver: 122, 1120; -- pecking wart: 4225; --, setting: 12650ff.; -- without head: 5865; -- as indicator of weather: 10788, 10891, 11046ff., 11263; -- wing: 3319; -- yard: 4311. See also Hen, Rooster and Cock
Chicken backbone, divination by: 9430
Chicken hawk: 12687f.
Chief: 5171
Chilblains: 3157ff.
Child: 164, 6140, 7563, 8176, 8178, 8183, 8196, 9192, 9895; --, birthmarks on: 321; --, birth of: 12627; --, crawling: 8217; --, dead: 76, 608; --, dreaming of: 5160; --, dropping: 1091; --, first: 158, 5557, 5594; --, gifted: 810; --, good: 425; --, last: 2672; --, male: 6958; --, newborn: 269; --, sick: 2672; --, tenth: 11569; --, unborn: 199ff., 328, 343, 353, 482, 886, 946, 1335, 1338f. See also Baby, unborn; Fetus; --, out of wedlock: 7546. See also Children
Child-bed fever: 319
Childbirth: 245, 308; --, difficult: 236; --, easy: 254; --, pain of: 1967, 1975; --, preventing: 121, 125
Childhood, masturbation in: 1011
Childless: 35, 41, 44, 5560

11177; --, wearing backwards: 4759,
6696ff.; --, wearing in game: 8680f.; --,
wearing inside out: 6674ff., 6691ff.,
10127; --, wedding: 4476, 4995; --, white:
9224.  See also Clothing
Clothesline: 294, 6238, 10730, 11324; --,
dreaming of: 9224, 9337.  See also Washline
Clothespin: 1592, 3802
Clothing: 769, 4584ff., 4837, 5544, 6737ff.,
7965, 8850; --, baby's: 1142; -- buttoned
wrong: 6707ff.; -- chewed by mouse: 6582;
--, color of: 6722ff.; -- in conjury:
10117; -- of the dead: 76; --, mend while
wearing: 6573, 6575, 8076; --, new:
6641ff., 9801; --, praying over: 3459; --,
protective: 3542; --, sew while wearing:
2853; --, washing: 191; --, wearing
backwards: 6675; --, wearing inside out:
6690, 10152; --, wearing in basketball
game: 8788; --, worn in game: 8675
Clouds: 10685, 10882f., 11193, 11308, 11357,
11650; --, red: 10827f., 11248; -- as
indicator of weather: 10900, 10929, 10972,
10985, 11116, 11429
Clove: 4155
Clove syrup: 4153
Clover: 3600, 12861ff.; --, eight-leaf: 12873;
--, five-leaf: 12862, 12872; --, four-leaf:
4669ff., 12861ff., 13179; --, one-leaf:
7977; --, six-leaf: 12862, 12873f.
Clover Blossom tea: 3037
Club (weapon): 7582
Coach: 8681f., 8761, 8766
Coal: 8201, 11485, 11890; --, carrying:
8243ff., 11803; --, gift of: 8245, 8247;
--, hot: 1056; --, live: 278; --, sitting
on: 9909
Coal mine: 7077
Coal oil: 1072, 2829, 3208, 3324, 3328, 3528,
3710, 3770, 4016, 12818.  See also Kerosene
Coat: 4585, 4883, 6709f.; -- on bed: 9218; --,
sewing hair into: 4964; --, sewing pigeon
into: 10229; --, sticking pin in: 6600,
8546; --, thread on: 8132
Cobweb: 2999, 3139, 3572, 3813, 4356, 5044ff.,
11095, 12560ff., 12587, 12601; -- as
indicator of weather: 10964.  See also
Spider webs
Cock: 8661, 12666; --, crowing of: 7905, 11052.
See also Rooster
Cock crow: 10330
Cocklebur: 4655
Cockroach: 12524
Cocktails: 1455
Cocoa: 7323
Coconut milk: 3908
Coffee: 727, 1410, 1713, 1750, 1898, 5742,
5926, 6050, 7322, 7956, 7958; --, black:
112; --, bubbles in: 6052, 7317f., 7464,
8167; -- as indicator of weather: 10941,
11169
Coffee cup: 6049, 13165
Coffee grounds: 5927, 6053, 7915, 8166, 8984;
--, burning: 5927; --, telling fortune by:
10442f.; --, smoking: 3552
Coffee pot: 5013, 5742
Coffin: 1385, 9045, 9646f., 9739, 9753, 9866,
11508; --, child's: 1389; --, direction of:
6437; --, dreaming of: 9096, 9751; --,
pieces of: 13155; --, silver nails in:
10662.  See also Casket
"Coffin handle": 6381

Coffin nail: 3936, 6261
Coin: 7374ff., 7487, 11640f.; -- in bread:
5994, 6006; -- in cake: 1244; --, carrying:
2294, 7516, 10310, 10549ff.; -- in
divination: 530ff.; --, dropping: 7382; --
on eyelids of dead: 9736; --, finding:
7374ff.; --, flipping: 7384f.; --, giving
to child: 282; --, giving with gift: 6609,
6924; --, gold: 5994; --, head of: 7379,
7385; --, hole in: 7381; --, lucky: 7388,
8871; --, medicinal use of: 3825, 4401; --,
paying with: 5960; -- in return for sharp
gift: 8414; -- in shoe: 7461; --, rubbing:
7517; --, silver: 5454, 5589, 5760, 5762,
6128, 9736, 10562, 11832, 12766; -- in
statue: 8687; --, throwing in fountain:
7422ff.; --, throwing in pond: 7428; --,
throwing over shoulder: 7886; --, throwing
in waterfall: 7427; --, turning in pocket:
11664
Coincidence: 10544
Coitus: 592; -- during pregnancy: 806
Coke: 1925
Cold (illness): 1042ff., 1080, 2593, 3163,
3175ff., 3182, 3313, 3447; --, chest: 3766
Cold man: 11455
Cold sore: 3263ff.
Colic: 1051ff., 3272f.
Collar: 6972, 7871, 9610
"Collery marbles": 3174
Colony of ants: 12459.  See also Ants
Color: 2343, 2479, 2505, 8154; -- in dream:
1816
Color (complexion): 403
Color blind: 11993
Colors, school: 8671
Colt: 12796ff.
Comb (n.): 1480, 5119, 10569; --, black:
3436f.; --, breaking: 6846; --, dropping:
1435, 6841ff., 8135; -- as gift: 8380
Combat: 5489, 7141
Combing: 568
Comet: 2540, 10902, 11698ff.; -- as sign of
depression: 7521
Comfrey tea: 2757, 2947
Command, born to: 1313
Common sense: 6544
Commotion, dream of: 1850
Communication with dead: 2330
Companion: 2112, 5157, 9205
Company: 1388, 7915, 8090, 8093, 8099, 8103,
8109, 8123ff., 8131f., 8136, 8139ff., 8146,
8155, 8159, 8165f., 8168, 8170f., 8175,
8187, 8189ff., 8193f., 8199f, 8203, 8205,
8215, 8218, 8220f., 8228ff.; --, bad: 2386;
--, unwelcome: 8098
Compassion: 2250
Complexion: 2143ff.; -- of child: 751ff.
Compliment (n.): 1153, 1169, 7995, 10145
Concentrate: 203, 516, 2329f.
Conception: 90ff., 95f., 100, 412, 448ff., 903,
950, 953ff., 999; -- of animal: 12586; --,
preventing: 120.  See also Contraception
Concert: 846
Conference, L.D.S.: 13139
Confession: 7582, 9177, 9924
Confetti: 10306
Confinement: 234, 317
Congestion: 3213, 3766, 3770
Congratulate: 57
Conjury: 10092ff., 10110ff., 10117ff.
Conscience: 10020; --, guilty: 2348

Creek water: 4317
Creeping under bramble bush: 2988
Cremation: 9274
Creosote bush tea: 2932
Crew (n.): 7017
Crib: 922, 1165.  See also Cradle
Cricket: 9529, 10008, 12473ff.; --, black:
    12480; --, chirping of: 10720, 10805; -- on
    hearth: 7340; -- in house: 6550; -- as
    indicator of death: 9530; -- as indicator
    of weather: 10757, 10974, 11086, 11281f.,
    11450f.; --, killing: 7971, 10859, 11085,
    12476, 12478ff., 12727, 12731; --, Mormon:
    12479; --, seeing a: 4645; --, stepping on:
    12483
Crime: 7540, 10591, 10635
Criminal (n.): 7543, 7546; --, executed: 7596;
    --, freeing: 7593f.  See also Lawbreaker;
    Thief
Crimson: 3846, 6544
Cripple: 7387
Crippled: 2800ff.; -- child: 967f.
Criticize: 972
Crocheting: 9746
Crops: 12957, 12962, 12969ff., 12987, 12992,
    13005ff., 13039, 13041f., 13050, 13055f.,
    13060, 13064, 13075, 13093f., 13098, 13101,
    13122, 13125, 13129, 13138, 13141, 13143,
    13147, 13163, 13168, 13195; --, destroying:
    12766; --, good: 12336; --, planting:
    12963ff., 12996f., 12999; --, poisoning of:
    12960
Cross (adj.): 883, 1758, 1760, 1765, 2408
Cross (n.): 549, 1129, 5320, 5327, 7093, 7264,
    7699, 9913, 10234, 10307, 10325, 10231,
    10335ff., 10353, 10566, 11840, 12690,
    12924; -- of ashes: 11190; -- on ass's
    back: 4442; -- on bread: 5791f.; -- causing
    rain: 11184; --, in the form of: 5558,
    5920, 9302, 11297; -- on home plate: 8739;
    --, sign of: 1301, 3289, 5787, 5791, 5943,
    9914, 9935, 9945, 10232; -- of tar: 6268;
    -- of water: 3747
Cross (vb.): 1061
Crossbeam: 6106
Crosses, on hand: 556
Cross-eyes: 997, 1061ff., 1066, 1571ff.,
    3424ff., 3429, 7160, 7707f., 8541, 10139
Crossing: arms: 1665, 4494, 4497, 9934; --
    feet: 5111, 6577; -- felt: 8620; --
    fingers: 1279, 1574, 1687ff., 2103, 2114,
    5116, 6518, 7658, 7768, 7812, 7821f., 7825,
    7835, 7846, 7848, 7854, 7861, 8014, 8037,
    8077ff., 8669, 9855, 11789, 12028; -- in
    front of: 6239; -- hands: 4493ff., 5111,
    6089, 8328, 9934; -- knife and fork: 8425,
    9267; -- knives: 2815, 8426, 9265; -- legs:
    237, 293, 992, 1061, 1338, 1710ff., 4188,
    4728, 4743, 6091, 7825, 9934f.; -- one's
    self: 8085, 10196, 12321; -- path: 2531,
    7729f., 7732f., 7735ff.; -- railroad
    tracks: 2107; -- silverware: 6109; --
    slippers: 6825; -- thumbs: 2450
Crossroads: 4091, 4212, 4859, 10161, 10231; --,
    burial at: 3396, 4336.  See also
    Intersection
Crosswise: 539, 6580, 9644
Croup: 3323ff., 3327ff., 7249; --, cures for:
    1068ff.; -- string: 3331
Crow (n.): 10, 12312, 12317ff., 13021f., 13090,
    13150, 13155; --, cawing of: 9492; --
    crossing path: 7732; --, dead: 12603; --

flying: 10694, 12724; -- as indicator of
    death: 9490ff.; -- as indicator of weather:
    10857, 11067; --, seeing: 9145; --,
    talking: 12318; -- in yard: 2530
Crowd: 2129, 9097
Crowing, of rooster: 3427
Crown, of head: 1320f., 1421, 7609; --, double:
    653; -- of feathers: 9314
Crucifix: 10233, 10403
Crucifixion: 9934
Crumbs: 1462, 2325, 7503; --, cake: 5587
Crust: 1462, 1474, 1513, 1521, 1630, 4119; --,
    black: 1462
Crutches: 2108, 3495, 7890
Cry (vb.): See Weep
Crying: 9040; --, baby's: 618ff., 641, 736,
    853, 905f., 1191, 1351, 1778ff., 1787ff.;
    -- on birthday: 1230, 1239ff.; --, child's:
    878, 1149, 1313; --, dream of: 1964; --
    before eating: 1961f.; -- in movies: 1209;
    --, pregnant woman's: 882f.; -- on wedding
    day: 5370f., 5492f.
Crystal ball: 10432f., 10666
Cuckoo: 7332ff., 12266ff.; -- as indicator of
    weather: 10936, 11059f.
Cuckoo clock: 12269
Cucumber: 5758f.; --, planting: 13071ff.; --,
    raw: 3476; --, sliced: 3403, 5758; -- and
    ice cream: 3172; -- juice: 3136, 3515; --
    and milk: 3475; -- peel: 3576
Cud, loss of: 12732f.
Cue stick: 8892
Cuff links: 10572
Culinary practice: 5735ff.
Cup: 3614, 8460; -- on grave: 9826
Cupboard: 6291, 7508
Cupid: 4520
Cupping: 3076, 3151, 3963, 3989
Curb: 2078, 2098
Curd, in stomach: 1088
Cure (n.): 2679; --, miraculous: 2685ff.; --,
    religious: 2685ff.; --, spontaneous: 3555
Cure-all: 2721, 2726, 12860.  See also Panacea
Curfew: 10614
Curious: 2482
Currant tea: 3838
Curse (n.): 1176, 1195, 5482, 5946, 6100, 6400,
    6463, 6493, 6840, 7765, 8039, 9176, 9196,
    9834, 10013, 10591; --, breaking: 10114; --
    of Cain: 10009; -- causing cancer: 3131; --
    of death: 10643; --, evil: 989; -- of God:
    10024
Curse (vb.): 1190, 8037, 8911, 9906f., 10036,
    10058, 10170
Cursed: 733, 927, 8034ff., 8038
Curtain: 1331, 4375, 9377, 11871
Curtain rising: 7167
Custard pie: 4715
Customer: 7223; --, first: 7149, 7233, 7235
Cut (n.): 3336ff., 3978, 4458; --, bleeding:
    2998; --, open: 3658; --, treating: 12588
Cutlery: 4958
Cutting one's self: 6464
Cutworm: 13090
Czech wedding: 5500

Daddy longlegs: 10464, 12554f., 12745; --,
    killing: 11287; -- as indicator of rain:
    11098
Daffodil: 7351
Dairy: 12720
Dairy products and meat: 3479

Depression: 12340; --, monetary: 7499, 7521
Descendants: 1514
Desert: 2543, 12386
Desire (n.): 241, 396, 8031
Desire (vb.): 221
Desk: 6383; --, hat on: 9221
Dessert: 760
Destination: 6986, 7866
Destiny: 1293, 10430, 11727
Detergent: 6232
Develop: 1158
Development, of child: 200
Devil: 1350, 1671, 1709, 2047, 2554, 4724,
    5150, 5781, 5786, 6099, 6670, 8573, 8648,
    9691, 9976, 10058, 10163ff., 10250, 10342,
    11354, 12170, 12802; -- beating wife:
    11005f., 11345, 11406; --, blinding: 10243;
    -- bound by God: 9992; --, casting out:
    2689; -- coming for soul: 9575; --,
    dispelling: 301, 618, 2037; -- entering
    body: 1227; --, feeding: 6020, 9905, 10191;
    --, invoking: 10221ff.; --, physical
    appearance: 10194ff.; --, possession by:
    1188ff., 10202ff.; --, power of: 2688; --
    in pregnant woman: 160; -- quarreling:
    11006; --, spell of: 8539; -- in soul:
    2879; --, warding off: 5436, 6175, 6296,
    10230, 12827.  See also Satan
Devil pact: 10219
Devil's darning needle: 1604.  See also Darning
    needle; Dragonfly
Devil's wife: 11405
Dew: 3511, 4675, 11194; -- from cow pie: 3510;
    --, washing in: 2136
Diabetes: 3349f.
Diabetes, winter: 4444f.
Dial (of watch): 7255
Diamond (card): 8568
Diamond (jewel): 2218, 4923f., 5517, 6874,
    6877; -- as indicator of weather: 10837; --
    particles: 3420; -- ring: 563, 4922, 4936,
    5515ff.; -- shape: 6439, 9312
Diamond fold: 6246
Diaper: 72f.; --, changing: 73, 752; --,
    dreaming of: 8350; --, soiled: 4145; --,
    wet: 1082, 1408, 2920, 3103, 3519
Diaper rash: 1103.  See also Rash
Diarrhea: 1073, 3351ff.
Dibble: 13088
Dice: 8605, 8610ff.
Die (vb.): 2227f.  See Pass away
Diet (n.): 483, 1145, 2499, 5928.  See also
    Weight loss
Dieting: 1804
Digestion: 1805
Digits: 1083
Digitus medicus: 3994
Dignity: 6861
Dike:  9695
Dill: 2057
Dill pickles: 172.  See also Pickles
Dime: 7786, 8248, 8593, 10560, 12065; -- in
    cake: 1245, 5058, 5235, 7474; -- in
    divination: 532; --, finding: 7396f.; --,
    giving for gift: 5470; --, boiling with
    mushrooms: 5760; -- in plumb pudding: 5196;
    -- in shoe: 4904, 5452; -- in new home:
    6293; -- from tooth fairy: 702, 704; --
    burying warts: 4392; --, wearing: 2607
Dimple: 688f., 1400, 2363, 2392, 2400, 2412,
    4479, 4483, 7571, 10217

Dinner: 1782, 1790, 1796f., 1877, 2209, 5966,
    8092, 8139, 8144, 8192, 8194; --, formal:
    6086; --, going out to: 5949
Dinner table: 1791
Diphtheria: 1074, 3360ff.
Direction: 1806, 2013, 2111, 4619, 4771, 6352,
    7638, 8137; -- of bathtub: 6435; -- of bed:
    6435ff., --, change of: 3424; -- East to
    West: 5784; --, reversing: 5741, 5783; --,
    stirring in same: 5782, 5796ff.
Dirt: 4982, 5756, 5836, 5910, 6213, 7471; --,
    churchyard: 4981; --, dreaming of: 11479;
    --, eating: 176f., 1145f., 9596; --,
    graveyard: 3937; --, sweeping: 5037, 6179
Dirty: 72
Disability: 2801
Disagreement: 8519
Disappointment: 1563, 1637, 5399, 5895, 6122,
    6139, 6511, 6666, 6695, 6829, 6832, 6843,
    6845, 6942
Disaster: 1571, 2077, 5974, 6374, 6470, 6506,
    6511, 6528, 6999f., 7014, 7018, 7025, 7027,
    7669f., 7739, 7894, 10535, 11255, 11700,
    11723, 11971, 12146, 12215, 12274, 12478;
    --, dreaming of: 2522; -- in mine: 7114
Discretion: 6861
Disdainful: 2474
Disease: 2581, 2585, 4113, 9128ff.; -- of
    animal: 12595; --, bacterial: 2555; --,
    catching: 2599; -- of cattle: 12734; -- of
    chest: 3156; --, childhood: 1020ff.; --,
    circumscribing: 3797, 3799f.; --,
    communicable: 2602, 2555; --, contagious:
    2614, 2626, 2672; --, curing: 2605, 2671,
    2673, 2710, 2723, 2786, 2788; --, death
    from: 3417; --, falling of: 3797, 3799; --,
    feeding: 2632; --, mention of: 310; --,
    preventing: 931, 2591f., 2596f., 2603,
    2615, 2620, 7010, 9014, 12804; --,
    protecting from: 12114; --, respiratory:
    2593; --, spiritual: 2691; --, spreading
    of: 2589; --, supernatural: 2677; --,
    susceptible to: 917; --, transference of:
    3167, 3889, 4229; --, warding off: 933,
    2595, 2601, 2608, 2613, 2679
Disfigured: 347, 1066
Dishcloth: 6161, 9250; --, boiling: 4766; --,
    burying: 4296, 4302, 4304, 4315, 4317; --,
    dropping: 8190, 8469; --, rubbing on wart:
    4293; --, stealing: 4295, 4299
Dishes: 9763, 10249; --, breaking: 5333, 5350,
    5564, 6146ff., 6275, 8102, 9720; --,
    devil's: 10177; --, dropping: 8187; --,
    first set of: 5647; -- on grave: 9825; --,
    washing: 571, 5032, 5165, 6048, 6134,
    6167ff., 7642, 8179, 8182, 8188, 8194,
    11383
Dishonest: 2375, 2403
Dishonesty: 2376
Dishrag: 12733, 12752; --, burying: 2295, 4164,
    4297, 4305, 4307ff., 4310ff., 4316; --,
    dirty: 4294, 4300f.; --, dropping: 4765,
    6162ff., 7925, 8048, 8092, 8190ff.; --,
    stealing: 4164, 4295; --, throwing over
    shoulder: 6160
Dish towel: 3615, 4279; --, burying: 4306; --,
    dropping: 7626, 8092, 8189, 9375; --, using
    together: 6159
Dishwater: 5031, 5210, 8983
Disinfect: 3362
Disinfectant: 269, 2727, 3341
Dislike: 212, 231

water: 7917, 11460f., 11467; -- of
clothesline: 9224, 9337; -- of coffin:
9096, 9751; -- in color: 1884ff.; -- of
commotion: 1850; -- of cream: 7912; -- of
crowd: 9097; -- of crying: 1964; -- of
danger: 1859; -- of the dead: 3845, 7898,
7943, 8210, 9092f., 9095, 9101, 9154,
9156f., 9193, 9627, 9735, 10638, 11023; --
of death: 87f., 1839, 4517, 4804ff., 7301;
-- of dirt: 11479; -- of dirty water: 8349;
-- of disaster: 2522; -- of dog: 8491f., --
of dress: 5008; -- of drowning: 9698f.; --
of dying: 8346, 9086f., 9091; -- of eating:
1851, 8383; -- of eggplant: 11839; -- of
eggs: 1834, 1853, 5892, 7329, 7485, 7491,
8496f.; -- of failure: 1860; -- of falling:
1854, 9099; -- of fire: 1835, 1847, 7899,
8477f., 10020; -- of fish: 78, 11461; -- of
floating: 9698; -- of flood: 11204; -- of
flowers: 7353, 9547, 9549; -- of fly:
12492; -- of food: 9275; -- of fruit: 1849,
9295; -- of funeral: 4804; -- of future
husband: 4714; -- of future spouse: 4739,
4741, 4747f., 4751ff., 4756, 4758f., 4763,
4767, 4832, 4843ff., 5595ff., 5598ff.; --
of ghosts: 193; -- of gift: 9619; -- of
God: 9657; -- of gold: 7270, 7432; -- of
grapes: 1783; -- of grave: 9844; -- of
green: 1837; -- of hair: 1437; -- of
harvest: 13149; -- of hat: 6721; -- of
hawk: 6962, 11839; -- of hay: 12936; -- of
heaven: 9971; -- of hedge: 12913; -- of
hell: 9977; -- of home: 4513; -- of horse:
2533, 4626f., 7484, 8493, 12009; -- of
horseshoe: 7328; -- of house burning: 7492,
9351; -- of kissing: 1948, 3464; -- of
letter: 7939; -- of lice: 2523, 7341, 9531;
-- of the living: 9154, 9620; -- of lizard:
8508, 12432; -- of lover: 4750; -- of
marriage: 5007; -- of meat: 2813, 9290,
9682; -- of mice: 7330, 12143; -- of milk:
54; -- of mill: 9961; -- of money: 2519,
4514, 7302ff.; -- of monster: 346; -- of
mountain: 9597; -- of mud: 2528, 9594,
11480; -- of muddy water: 2812, 7931,
9594f., 11465, 11467; -- of nakedness:
9090; -- of Negro: 8031; -- of Nephite
descendants: 7068; -- of nest: 6911; -- of
nuts: 7469; -- of opposite sex: 4761; -- of
pain: 2811; -- of parrot: 7560; -- of
penny: 7403; -- of person: 7896; -- of pig:
9422; --, pleasant: 12926; -- of being
pregnant: 2272; -- of property: 7522; -- of
rain: 1846; -- of rat: 8486, 12137; -- of
rattlesnake: 12410; -- of riches: 1861; --
of rifle: 7929; --, sad: 53; -- of seeing
someone: 8351; -- of shoes: 4606; -- of
shrub: 7433; -- of silver: 1836, 7269; --
of smelling: 1848; -- of snake: 1982, 2524,
4643, 8498ff., 8505ff., 9517, 12409ff.; --
of snake bite: 12412; -- of spider: 7342,
8511; -- of split hoof: 10180; -- of
strange place: 7306; -- of strawberries:
9287; -- of sweetheart: 4578, 4743, 4762,
4840; -- of swimming: 8857, 9595; -- of
tears: 1858; -- of teeth: 1613f., 1616,
2517, 7443, 8322f., 9061ff.; -- of train:
9606; -- of trees: 7433; -- of true love:
4745, 4836, 4841; -- of valley: 2520; -- of
washing diapers: 8350; -- of water: 1226,
1838, 2508, 2527, 2799, 11462ff., 11466; --
of wedding: 64, 2521, 4518, 5729ff., 7897,

9201f.; -- of white: 9100; -- of white-
haired man: 2704, 9197; -- of white horse:
9418, 12023f.; -- of wind: 1852, 8348; --
of witch: 7927; -- of wolf: 7728
Dream (vb.): 1834ff., 4515, 5561, 6270, 8279
"Dream cake": 5602
Dreaming: 2025, 4935, 8344ff.
Dreams: telling: 1826ff., 1830ff., 9092, 9102;
-- three in succession: 1855ff., 4742
Dress (n.): 1924, 2492, 4594ff., 4597, 4601,
4823f., 4869, 5052, 6717, 6728, 6762,
6764f., 6767f., 7964, 8076, 8154; -- on
backwards: 2814; --, bridal: 5290, 5398,
5404, 5435; --, dreaming of: 5008; --,
cutting out: 6562, 6569, 6572; --, getting
wet: 5168; --, making: 6559f., 6570; --,
maternity: 77; --, mend while wearing:
8360; --, new: 4838, 6641ff., 6645, 6712f.;
--, sewing: 4770, 4964, 6619, 9369; --,
taking off: 6655; --, tearing: 4600; --,
trying on: 5190; --, wedding: 4651, 5051,
5227, 5374, 5396; --, white: 5008; -- on
wrong side out: 6687, 10075
Dressing, for burns: 3096
Dressing, order of: 6647ff.
Dressing, for wounds: 2831
Dressing room: singing in: 7194; --, whistling
in: 7190f., 7203f., 8689
Dressmaker: 7145
Dress rehearsal: 7182ff.
Drink (n.): 6033; --, cold: 3127; --, last:
5198, 11795; --, soft: 2122
Drink (vb.): 3612ff.
Drinking: 1938; -- alcohol: 1907f., 1927f.,
2169; -- beer: 1510; -- blood: 2251; --
carrot juice: 1411; --, cure for: 1934; --
coffee: 1410, 1750, 1898; -- hot drinks:
1899; -- hot water: 1752; -- lemon juice:
1804; -- during menstrual period: 1972; --
milk: 1399, 2178; -- mineral waters: 2718;
-- of pregnant woman: 1340; -- from river
Nile: 7887; -- sea water: 2206ff.; -- tea:
994; -- water: 1896f., 2168, 2179; -- water
and molasses: 1406; -- wine: 1236
Drinks, mixing: 2551
Driver: 7860
Driveway: 7805
Drop (vb.): 10, 1935, 2514, 6107f.
Droppings: chicken: 1722, 4001; --, cow: 3660;
--, sheep: 3451, 3779
Dropsy: 3370ff.
Drought: 10923f., 11182
Drowned body, finding: 9701ff.
Drowning: 1340, 7006, 7048, 9687ff.; -- of
baby: 229; -- of fetus: 299f.; --, dream
of: 88, 2216; --, preventing: 10584; --,
protection against: 1356, 9603; --, rescue
from: 8935; --, revived from: 2706
Drunk (intoxicated): 218, 999, 1919, 1924ff.
See also Intoxicated
Drunkard: 1930ff., 5168ff. See also Drunks
Drunks: 1930ff. See also Drunkard
Drugs (n.): 2714, 4438; --, yellow: 3717
Duck (n.): 12201ff., 12696; --, blind: 12202;
--, causing black plague: 2989; --, eating:
5990; --, migration: 10754; --, nesting of:
12206; -- as indicator of storm: 11264
Dugout: 8709
Dull: 1920
Dullard: 2853
Dumb (adj.): 2846ff., 2854
Dumb (speechless): 2690

Electric chair: 7595
Electricity: 3046, 11731
Elephant: 11045, 12124ff.; --, pink: 1932, 12124
Elevator: 11541
Eleven: 1003, 1792, 1798, 1962, 4689, 7786, 7802, 8606, 8663, 11570, 11589; -- o'clock: 8091, 8124, 11187, 11209
Eleventh: 1236, 6284, 11773
Elf: 245, 10352; -- souring milk: 5878. See also Elves
Elk's tooth: 10476
Elm: See Slippery elm
Elopement: 5233
Elves: 10349ff., 10360, 10363, 10390. See also Elf
Embarrassed: 1497
Embers, dead: 6177
Emerald: 2660, 3286, 4569, 6878; -- ring: 4925
Emergency: 5527
"Emo": 10659; --, grave of: 2194, 9833
Emotion: 212, 6544
Emotional: 1482; -- ailments: 995ff.; -- states: 2859ff.
Employment, change of: 6963
Enemy: 1493, 7586, 8276, 8322, 8336, 8401, 8424, 8426, 8439, 8452, 8478, 8486, 8497f., 8502ff., 8507f., 8511, 8525, 9347, 9381, 10037, 10123, 10604, 12765; -- of the church: 10013; --, protecting against: 8534; --, shaking stick at: 8274. See also Foe
Energetic: 2468
Energy: 2257, 2715
Engagement: 23, 915, 4494, 4907ff., 4918ff., 5212; --, breaking: 4932ff.; --, time of: 4929ff.; --, secret: 4493
Engineer: 7123
English ivy: 13183
Enterprise: 6962
Entertainment: 9872, 9876
Entrails, chicken: 3855
Enuresis: 1029.  See also Bed wetting
Envious: 2417
Epidemic: 2687, 3847; --, cholera: 3171
Epilepsy: 1078, 3395f.
Epiphany: 11840
Epitaphs: 2839
Epsom salts: 2723, 2908, 3090, 3662, 4037, 4110
Equator: 11245
Equinox: 12762
Eraser: 573, 584
Errand: 1256
Error: 1282, 8755
Eruption: 9129
Erysipelas: 3397
Esteem: 4550
Eternity: 5523
Ether: 1456
Eucalyptus leaves: 3247
Even ash: 12928f.
Evergreen: 790, 13190
Evil (adj.): 871, 879, 1643, 1655, 2384f., 6887, 8303, 8537, 10024, 10370, 11318
Evil (n.): 437, 970, 1709, 2075, 2577, 2711, 6313, 6795, 6810, 6993, 7994, 8574, 9922, 10124ff., 10467, 11526, 11609, 11699, 11822, 12185, 12239, 12327, 12477; --, avoiding: 5997; --, casting: 5440; --, possessed by: 1186; --, protect from: 1184; --, sign of: 7039; --, warding off: 5484, 5936, 6976, 9945, 10124

Evil eye: 926f., 943, 1167ff., 10037, 10138ff.; --, abating: 10159ff.; --, preventing: 10147ff.
Evil powers: 9691
Evil spells: 7020, 10036; --, breaking: 6158
Evil spirits: 278, 837, 1178ff., 1187, 1995, 2037, 2589, 3556, 4026, 5626, 9003, 9838, 10202, 10215, 10250ff., 10653, 10968, 12389, 13018; --, appeasing: 5540; --, casting out: 10121; -- causing epilepsy: 3395; -- causing mental illness: 2880; --, dispelling: 6995; --, driving out: 2674ff.; --, exorcizing: 29705; -- leaving body: 618; --, possessed by: 576, 945, 2689; --, protecting from: 1165, 1181ff., 1185, 5517; --, ridding: 5736; --, sucking out: 3989; --, warding off: 2647, 3230, 5436, 5485, 6035, 6255, 6336, 7756, 9723, 10157, 10272ff.  See also Spirit
Ewe: 11118
Exam: 1272ff., 6897
Ex-convict: 7542
Excrement: 1845, 10115
Execution: 7587
Exercise: 132, 1971
Expecting a child: 511.  See also Pregnant
Experience: 342, 350, 1482
Explosion, in mine: 7092, 7097, 7101
Expressive: 1544
Eye: 1540ff., 1552ff., 1788, 3417ff.; --, beady: 7543; --, bedroom: 1545; --, big: 2353; --, birds pecking out: 12222; --, black: 1551, 2377, 3422ff.; --, bloodshot: 3416; --, blue: 872, 1546ff., 1551, 2139, 2398, 5155, 8258; --, blue and green: 679; --, bright: 1552; --, brown: 681, 876, 1545, 1551, 2265, 2378, 5137, 8054; -- of cat: 10479; --, charm like: 10467; --, cinder in: 7607, 10990; --, circles under: 1131; --, close-set: 2357, 2435, 2442, 2454, 2471, 4473, 4553, 7549; --, closing: 7846ff., 7855, 9016, 11687; --, color of: 678, 5137; --, crossing: 3006; -- of dead: 9164f., 9179f., 9736f., 9743; --, extra: 10006; --, far-set: 2391; --, film over: 12590; -- of fish: 6886; --, foreign particle in: 3408f., 3411, 3419; --, glass: 10312; --, gray: 1551, 2441, 5137; --, green: 680, 805, 1549ff., 2417, 2434, 2441, 8054; --, hazel: 1544; --, hooded: 2328; --, hot iron held to: 7562; --, image of: 10131, 10155; --, inflamed: 3405; --, itching: 1557ff., 1950, 4466, 7279, 8282; --, left: 1560f., 1568ff., 1789, 1963, 2120, 5074, 7920; --, look in: 2342, 2374ff., 2403; --, looking bull in: 1194; --, looking lion in: 12131; --, meeting of: 4986; --, moon shining in: 11608; -- of peacock feather: 6747; -- of potato: 13040, 13045ff., 13051, 13079; --, powerful: 736; --, protruding: 2429; --, red: 12145; --, right: 1557ff., 1565ff., 1787, 1963, 2621, 4466, 7279, 7900, 7909; -- sewn by darning needle: 8064; --, sharp: 1552; --, shifty: 2376; --, shutting: 5576, 12105; --, slanted: 10047; -- of snake: 1095; --, sore: 3399, 3401ff., 3406f., 3410, 3413ff.; --, sty in: 1024, 4083ff., 4096ff.; --, twitching: 1564, 4466, 8106; --, watering of: 2418, 5767, 5769; --, weak: 3399, 3402; --, white of: 3758; --, wide-set: 2305; -- of wolf: 2621

dropping: 4701, 6097, 7924; --, evil eye
in: 10147; --, fighting over: 6144; --,
giving away: 5738, 6004, 7507, 8250; --,
hair in: 1150, 6100; --, holiday: 5988ff.;
--, hot: 2542; --, Italian: 2493; --, last
piece of: 5022ff., 10366; --, left over:
12961; --, natural: 1937; --, passing at
table: 6089, 9274; --, passion: 4971; --,
rich: 1866; --, salting: 5100, 5943; --,
scarcity of: 6014f., 6017ff., 6023ff.; --,
scraping off plate: 4700; --, seasoning:
8398; --, shortage of: 6027; --, souring
the: 5922; --, sticking of: 5743; --,
stirring of: 5741; --, taboo: 9277; --,
throwing away: 6019ff.; --, wasting: 2214,
7468; -- as indicator of weather: 11170,
11224
Food fallacies: 5913, 9277ff., 9289
Food poisoning: 3468ff.  See also Poisoning
Fool: 1002f., 2860, 8034, 8036, 8313; --,
kicking: 1596; --, kissing: 1947, 1950,
1953ff., 1957f.; --, in love with: 4473;
--, meeting a: 1594, 7717; --, shaking
hands with: 1662, 1664, 1666f., 8188
"Fool Hen": 1010
Foot: 1996; -- asleep: 1718, 3747, 8336; --,
baby's: 1049; --, fast on: 803; --, hopping
on one: 6355; --, itching: 2335, 4873; --,
left: 499, 1765, 1767, 4030, 4368, 6124,
6313f., 6653, 7000, 7624, 7639; --, nail
in: 3764; --, onion on: 3738; --, --,
paralyzed: 3835; --, right: 498f., 1731,
2069, 2247, 4143, 4368, 5490, 5620, 6315,
6346, 6649, 6669f., 6714, 6795, 7623; --,
sign of: 12593; --, slipper on one: 9112;
--, standing on one: 2809; --, stepping on:
5486, 5698f.; --, stubbing: 8094; --,
sweeping: 7567; --, trouble with: 3749; --
of wild animal: 11909; --, wrong: 1762f.
Football: 8757ff.; -- clothing: 8765ff.
Footprints: 2083, 3557
Footsteps: 2100, 4147
Forbidden: 1654
Forearm: 1396, 7802
Forefinger: 3633, 3762, 4104, 7843.  See also
Finger
Forehead: 5682; --, baby's: 1354; --, birthmark
on: 818; --, center of: 1429; --, high:
2297, 2308, 2318; --, kissing on: 4550; --,
streak on: 351; --, widow's peak on: 5181;
--, wrinkles on: 555, 4480
Foreign land: 5281
Foreseeing, gift of: 834
Foreskin: 942
Forest: 7891, 12878
Forgetfulness: 2832ff.
Forgetting: 1869, 4378, 4429, 8069f.
Forgiven: 8085
Fork: 1659, 4732, 5098, 5164; -- under chair:
512; --, dropping: 4733f., 4932, 5097,
6132f., 7959, 8175f., 8180ff., 8434f.; --,
placing on eye: 3423; -- on grave: 9826; --
in milk: 12738; -- as indicator of rain:
11172; --, two: 5714, 6135
Formaldehyde: 3362
Fortune: 5305, 12600
Fortune cookie: 10422
Fortune teller: 10407ff.
Fortune telling: 9629, 10407ff.
Forty: 10154, 10712, 10805; -- days: 307, 5636,
5932, 9870ff., 11870
Forty-nine: 9874f.

Forty-one: 1943
Forty-two: 11587
Forward: 1256, 3507, 6210, 7757
Foul line: 8701
Foundation: 7119; -- of house: 6256
Fountain: 3412, 10424; --, throwing coins into:
2662, 7422ff.
Fountain of Trevi: 7886
Fountain of Youth: 2280
Four: 81, 546, 1089, 1102, 1665, 2058, 4106,
4443, 4494f., 4529, 4672, 4686f., 4741,
4753, 4762, 4915, 5890, 9640, 11555f.,
12233, 12551, 13090; -- of card suit: 8584;
-- in a row: 4842; -- days: 3413; -- years:
6459; -- o'clock: 12235; -- of clubs: 8567;
-- of hearts: 8569; -- of spades: 8585
Four-leaf clover: 2900, 7352, 10029, 10516f.
Fourteen: 7758, 10805, 13100
Fourth: 1856, 2055
Fourth of July: 8705
Fowl: 4632, 12684
Fox: 7729, 9006f., 10790, 12153f.; -- fat:
3391; -- holes: 9347
Foxglove: 3601
Fracture: 3490ff.  See also Bone, broken
Fraternity: 1269
Frazier's Axle Grease: 3104
Freak: 352
Freckles: 463, 2862, 3504ff., 3510ff., 3513ff.,
7454; --, cause of: 755, 3503, 3509; --,
getting rid of: 1082
Freeze (n.): 11445
Freight car: 7876
French whore house: 9349.  See also Whore house
Freya: 6640
Friday: 1263, 1770, 6083, 6299, 6543, 7452,
7535, 7715, 8671, 10434, 10459, 11141f.,
11244, 11754ff.; --, baking on: 5807; --,
born on: 413, 418ff., 898, 9665; --, burial
on: 9803; --, doing business on: 7245f.;
--, courting on: 4870f.; --, cutting hair
on: 1498, 2970, 7495; --, cutting nails on:
1701ff., 1709, 4144, 4504; --, dreaming on:
1830; --, dying on: 9665; --, eating on:
1748, 5858; -- eating mustard on: 3280; --,
first: 10813, 11754; --, journey on: 9613;
--, laughing on: 1803; --, marrying on:
5322ff., 5326f.; --, moving on: 6281; --,
planting on: 13041; -- pilot day: 11754;
--, plowing on: 12956; --, quilting on:
6638; --, raining on: 10955; --, sailing
on: 7002, 7062; --, sewing on: 6571, 9369;
--, sneezing on: 1779, 2047f.; --, starting
job on: 6968f., 7120, 9028, 11755ff.; --,
traveling on: 7669f.; --, washing hair on:
3580; --, weather on: 10814f.; -- the
seventh: 8953; -- the thirteenth: 437f.,
2560, 2817, 2970, 3283, 5323, 6084, 6457,
6514, 6726, 7670, 9215, 9791, 11782ff.,
12454
Friend: 4571, 5117, 5380, 6864, 7682ff., 7897,
8223, 8331, 8334, 8344, 8348, 8368, 8374f.,
8382, 8411, 8421ff., 8428, 8435, 8441f.,
8457, 8461, 8475, 8487, 8491ff., 8495f.,
8512f., 8516, 8530, 9524, 9584, 9612, 9764;
--, death of: 9114, 9197; --, deceitful:
8499f., 8506; --, false: 2381; --, finding:
8377; -- hooking fingers with: 2115; --,
hungry: 8387; --, losing: 8275, 8277, 8284,
8323, 8359, 8361f., 8378, 8386, 8440, 8444,
8460 8476, 8501, 8530; --, making: 2431;
--, meeting: 7218, 8330; --, new: 8358,

9615, 9619; -- baby shower: 526; --, first: 5211; --, sharp: 3682, 6128, 6921ff., 8411ff., 9616; --, unwrapping: 4944, 6918; --, wedding: 65f., 560, 583, 4948, 5468
Gift of Blarney: 7997
Gift of gab: 7997
Gifted: 825
Gifts, magical: 839
Gin: 1915, 4969
Ginger: 2854
Ginger beer: 8246
Ginger tea: 3189, 3351, 3449, 3778, 4011
Ginseng: 2221, 2649, 9903; -- roots: 2732, 12880
Girl: 38, 465, 500, 505, 1945, 1986, 2231, 2381, 2399, 4554, 4605, 5138; --, birth of: 7431; -- as first footer: 8267; --, giggling: 12188; --, redheaded: 12034; --, seeing: 2065, 8833; --, single: 5214; -- sinking into the earth: 8621; --, unmarried: 4733, 4853, 5037, 5057. See also Girls
Girl friend: 4499, 4557, 4604, 4816, 5098, 5113, 5711
Girls: 2856; --, development of: 1630; --, sexual activity with: 2891; --, whistling: 1624, 8655, 8661f. See also Girl
Give away: 75, 77, 4397, 6936
"Given the eye": 1176
Giver: 67
Gizzard, chicken: 1073, 2951, 3641, 4066
Glass: 5073; --, blue: 11333; --, breaking: 564, 2285, 5127, 5499, 5565, 5638, 6074, 6157f., 6275, 9720f., 9868; --, drinking: 1900, 1914, 5744, 6064f., 9271f.; --, drinking from wrong side: 3614; -- as indicator of rain: 11167; --, reflection in: 2283; --, seeing moon through: 11646; --, throwing in fireplace: 5567; --, throwing over shoulder: 5566; --, water: 6063; --, wine: 7683
Glass beads: 4028
Glasses, eye: 2163, 2301, 3398, 3400, 7723, 11647; --, breaking: 6848f.
Glass eye: 10312
Glassware: 6156ff.
Gloves: 6652, 6829ff., 8382, 8977; --, conjuring with: 10118; --, dropping: 6829ff.; --, finding: 6835; --, gift of: 4588, 5091, 8381; --, hanging up: 7532; --, left: 5459; --, losing: 6834; -- in mine: 7077; --, right: 6651, 12739; --, throwing into fire: 2642
Glowworm: 12571
Glycerin: 4014
Gnome: 5878, 10399
Goal: 8895
Goat: 4405, 11339, 11828, 12112f., 12804; --, billy: 12860; --, black: 10461; --, diseases of: 12736; -- as form of devil: 10197; --, seeing: 1094; -- milk: 488; -- tallow: 3222
Go away: 4369. See also Decrease; Wear away
Goblet: 6156
Goblin: 10032, 10283, 10385ff., 12803; -- souring milk: 5878
God: 1397, 2573, 2576, 7071, 8659, 9762, 9907f., 9979, 10008, 10176, 10184, 10318, 10990, 11146, 11346f., 11349ff., 11371, 11706, 11881; --, cursing 9656, 9906; --, dreaming of: 9657; -- father of twin: 596; --, fingers of: 12306; --, grace of: 413,

429; --, institution of: 7378; --, messengers of: 12219; --, praying to: 2693; --, punishment by: 952, 2801, 2879; --, seeing: 650; -- of skiing: 8876; -- of war: 896; --, will of: 91. See also Lord
"God bless you": 920, 927, 2045, 2600
Goddess: 5295
Godly: 413
Gods: 9910, 11341, 12120
Going steady: 4882, 4903ff.
Goiter: 3535ff.
Gold: 257, 280, 529, 1067, 1312, 1612, 2220, 3024, 7070, 7083, 7268, 7351, 8249, 10463ff., 12233; --, breaking: 4911; -- coin: 5994; --, dreaming of: 7270, 7432; -- dust: 7554; -- earrings: 2595, 3402; --, finding: 6938; --, locating: 7083ff.; --, pot of: 10358, 10379f., 10464; -- mine: 7071; -- nugget: 11508; -- piece: 280, 5706, 6003, 7266, 10563; -- ring: 3740, 4100ff., 4382ff., 5503, 5520, 6867; -- at end of rainbow: 10465; -- thimble: 4102; --, vein of: 7069, 7112; -- watch: 3593
Golden: 6037
Goldenrod: 1590, 3902
Golden seal: 2731, 3132, 3145f.
Goldfish: 6505, 9519, 12240; -- bowl: 6505
Golf: 8808ff.; -- ball: 8811ff.; -- club: 8808, 8810, 8817; -- cup: 8815; -- match: 8809; -- tee: 8818f.
Good Friday: 5324, 6001, 11723, 11845f.; --, bread baked on: 5852; --, breaking pottery on: 6480; --, eggs laid on: 12677; --, entering mine on: 7089; --, doing business on: 7246; --, hammering on: 6361; --, planting on: 13042f., 13185; --, removing bees on: 12700; --, sweeping on: 6216; --, washing hair on: 3580; --, weaning on: 635
Good looking: 2142
Good-natured: 627, 2396f.
Goofang fish: 12580
Goofer dust: 4979
Goose: 12207; --, cackling of: 6910; --, eating on New Year's: 7462; --, walking on grave: 9050; -- dung: 2983; -- grease: 1123, 3224; -- pimples: 9050. See also Geese
Gooseberry thorn: 4384
Gopher: 10711, 13157; -- hole: 13157
Gossip (n.): 8279, 8300, 8431, 8487
Gossip (vb.): 2192, 8315, 8321, 8356, 8468
Gout: 3540
Gown: 9371; --, wedding: 5395ff.
Grabbing: 332, 340
Grace: 895
Grade (n.): 1272
Graduation: 7476
Grain: 12820, 13114f., 13119, 13124, 13147, 13155; --, feeding to birds: 6017; --, harvesting: 575; --, picking up: 6183; --, planting: 13121f.; --, price of: 13123; --, throwing at wedding: 5552
Grand Canyon: 11476
Granddaddy longlegs: 3498, 12556
Grandfather: 1119
Grandmother: 926, 1631, 9039
Grandmother's back, breaking: 2965
Grandparents: 614
Granny knot: 7126
Grant, President H. J.: 9986
Grape: 12957; --, dreaming of: 1783; -- juice: 5935; -- root: 3146; -- seeds: 2223, 2796, 2921. See also Malaga grape

Grapefruit: 3134, 3533

Grapevine: 1491

Grass: 1386, 1593, 6547, 8817, 11048, 11482, 12117, 12878, 13109ff.; --, cobwebs on: 10964; -- under gallows: 12877; -- in hat: 8750; -- on murderer's grave: 7585; -- in shoe: 2181; -- as indicator of weather: 11101, 11421; --, wild: 12715

Grass Creek: 10985

Grasshopper: 12506ff.; -- causing cancer: 3129; -- as indicator of weather: 10963

Grasshopper juice: 3011

Grave: 4215, 9297, 9301, 9353, 9363, 9381, 9399, 9556, 9571, 9724, 9760, 9776, 9812, 9820ff., 9841, 9843, 9861ff., 10330, 10592; --, child's: 1390; -- clothes: 9741; --, crawling over: 3077; --, digging: 6360; --, digging up: 9831; -- dirt: 1146; --, dreaming of: 1864, 9844; --, dropping article in: 10119; --, Emo's: 2194; --, goose walking on: 9050; --, lying on: 10205; --, murderer's: 7585; --, open: 5494; --, plowing: 9830; --, pointing at: 9973; --, rabbit running over: 9048, 9052; --, raining on: 9576; --, no rest in: 7596; --, snake crawling over: 9051; --, stepping on: 1342, 2173, 9846ff.; --, turning over in: 9187; --, walking over: 1864, 2588, 9046, 9049, 9058, 10601; --, yellow lilies on: 7597

Gravestone: 2839, 9823

Graveyard: 3788, 4209, 4215f., 8981, 9578f., 9593, 9777, 9837, 9839; --, ghosts in: 10658; --, passing: 10602

Graveyard dirt: 3937, 7553, 9060, 10123

Gravity: 1414

Gravy: 3473, 5818

Gray: 1476, 5262, 6540, 11993; --, wearing: 5428

Grease: 250, 632, 3223, 3239; --, animal: 2982; --, axle: 3366; -- on cat's feet: 12624; --, goose: 3324

Greasewood: 12953

Greasing, hips of pregnant woman: 239

Great Mother Dog: 11652

Greatness: 869

Great Salt Lake: 11472; --, curative properties of: 2719

Great Spirit: 9544, 12117

Great White Throne: 10271

Greece: 11840

Greedy: 2441, 2447

Greek: 1438, 1617, 7719, 9934, 11341, 11852; -- Church: 549, 5057; -- Orthodox Church: 5568, 9914, 9945; -- wedding: 5486, 5501, 5541, 5561, 5564

Green: 27, 1265, 1291, 2416f., 2595, 4822f., 5422, 6536, 6543, 7651, 7801, 8822f., 8827, 8830, 9354, 9579, 13133; -- apple: 4047; -- aspirin: 2729; -- chewing gum: 2552; --, dreaming of: 1837; -- fingers: 1684; -- fruit: 3173; --, gifts wrapped in: 4948; -- leaves: 6250; -- plant: 6269; -- stick: 4349f.; -- tomatoes: 5911; -- twig: 5750; --, wearing: 2182, 5421, 5425ff., 5432, 6728ff., 6769, 7171, 8829, 8875, 9216, 10373, 11841f., 12381

Green beans: 487, 4260

Green chili: 12155

Green room: 7166

Greens: 1880, 6035

Gremlin: 8808, 10398

Greyhound: 8826

Griddle: 5743; -- cakes: 3647

Grief: 6647, 8091

Grieving: 9075

Grimee: 10402

La grippe: 3736f.

Groom: 560, 4746, 4918, 5221, 5224, 5228, 5242, 5296, 5333, 5339, 5341, 5347, 5357ff., 5379, 5443, 5450, 5477, 5484, 5491, 5495f., 5499, 5535, 5539, 5556, 5563, 5569, 5573, 5590, 5612, 5618, 5635, 5669, 5679, 5691, 5699, 5706, 5726, 9205; -- carrying bride: 5622; --, congratulating: 5676; --, dancing with: 93; --, death of: 9212; -- kissing bride: 5340; -- looking in mirror: 5377; -- seeing bride: 3016, 5342; -- seeing wedding gown: 5400f., 5435; --, sneezing: 5363; --, touching: 5231. See also Bridegroom

Groom-to-be: 4912

Grouchy: 884, 1758, 1765f., 2006, 2409

Ground: 2267, 6622, 10696, 11067, 11190, 12883; --, burying medicine in: 3598; --, drawing circle on: 11189; --, digging into: 11477; --, hallowed: 9804; --, movement of: 7087; --, pleasant: 1720; --, shaking of: 7125; --, slapping: 8900; --, spitting on: 12043; --, strange: 7620, 7622; --, sweeping: 6207; --, urinating on: 4087; --, water from: 1905

Groundhog: 10713ff., 12169; -- day: 10712, 10811, 11886, 12169; -- seeing its shadow: 10686f.; -- as indicator of weather: 10851, 10905, 10958, 11043

Grounding wire: 2096

Grouse: 1010

Growing pains: 1083

Growth, of beard: 1622; -- of brain: 1739; -- of child: 302, 757ff., 779; -- of eyelashes: 1587; -- of fingernails: 1698; -- of hair: 1498; -- of nose: 1591; --, stunting: 761ff., 766ff., 2169ff.; -- of tooth: 707

Guesser: 5064

Guest: 5432, 5501, 5782, 5942, 6039, 6069, 6077, 8104, 8133, 8176, 8185, 8204, 8216, 8219; --, first: 6275; --, unwelcome: 8092

Guest room: 6190

Guilt: 8083

Guinea egg: 4798

Guinea pig: 9440, 12135

Gullible: 2413

Gum, chewing: 1633, 1749, 2118, 2552, 3596, 7239, 8721

Gums, baby's: 714, 717; --, bleeding the: 4124; --, child's: 722, 932

Gum wrappers: 2269

Gun: 6365, 8921, 9020ff., 12392; --, dead man's: 9026; --, placing on bed: 6441

Gunpowder: 2720, 3149, 4141, 4166, 4461, 8997, 12647; --, gargling with: 4014; -- preventing conception: 120

Gypsy: 1217, 2666, 2668, 3402, 7599, 9171, 10097, 10410; --, meeting: 7711


Habit: 204, 11596

Hack (n.): 5430

Hail: 11394, 13020

Hair: 22, 651ff., 1424ff., 1431ff., 1449ff., 1499ff., 1737, 2242, 2463ff., 4481, 4485, 5068, 5119, 7949, 7989, 9739, 10471; --, abundant: 658, 1308; --, animal: 11918; -- of ass: 4442; --, baby's: 227, 656, 788; --, black: 669, 1474f., 2334, 3436, 5183, 9067, 12171; --, bleaching: 9997; --, body: 1514, 2261; --, bride's: 560; --, brown: 5141; --, cat: 5130; --, chest: 1509ff., 2274, 2356, 5139f.; --, child's: 651, 914, 1117, 1389; --, chopped: 4118; --, coarse: 2850; --, color of: 678, 1469ff., 2343, 2399, 4837, 4962; --, combing: 40, 1435ff., 2832, 3436f., 4484, 5355, 5440, 6845, 8135, 10624; --, conjuring with: 10110ff., 10115; --, corpse: 9882; --, cowlick of: 1505ff.; --, curling: 2981; --, curly: 658ff., 1434, 1458ff.; --, cutting: 671ff., 746, 780, 796, 1362, 1458, 1485f., 1488f., 1491, 1493ff., 2970, 2975, 3253, 3438f., 3544, 3559f., 5161, 7495, 7586, 9069, 10926; --, dark: 8242; --, disposal of: 2896, 9070, 9907; --, dog: 3367, 3974, 5130; --, dry: 4446; --, dyeing: 3078; -- on earlobes: 4996; --, ends of: 1487; --, facial: 1623;

Herb tea: 2757
Herd (n.): 12762
Herd (vb.): 1199
Herdsmen: 7135
Hereditary: 320
Heritage: 7605
Hernia: 286, 1086
Herring: 4716, 5991, 8971
Hex: 10057, 10098; --, breaking: 10078; --
    sign: 10125, 10290.  See also Witch sign
Hiccoughs: 758, 1051, 3603ff., 3621ff., 4540,
    8340; --, cause of: 3603, 3608
"Hickey": 3638
Hickok, Bill: 8609
Hickory: 3541; -- nut: 2938, 10514, 12948; --
    stick: 10452
Hide-and-seek: 10664
High brow: 2308
High heels: 226f., 1062
High school: 8671, 8787
Highstrung: 887
Highway: 6551, 7652
Hike (n.): 1772
Hiking: 12162
Hill: 1888, 4274; --, burial on: 9807
Hip joint: 3541
Hippocratic oath: 3003
Hips: 239, 471
Hoarseness: 3636
Hobo: 7143, 10655
Hoe (n.): 9364f., 9367, 13025
Hoe (vb.): 13143
Hog: 366, 12170f., 12831ff.; --, breathing on:
    3261; --, growth of: 10738; --, ill: 12834;
    -- jowl: 5999; -- lard: 260; -- melt:
    10739, 10786; -- as indicator of weather:
    10738, 10787, 10850, 11261.  See also Hogs
Hogan: 9174
Hogs: 12828, 12837; --, slaughtering: 12838ff.
Hole: 11478, 12955; -- in britches: 1602; -- in
    door jamb: 1117; -- in shoes: 2411; --,
    stepping in/on: 2070, 3784, 6145; --,
    walking over: 2095
Holiday: 549, 8231, 12655
"Holler tail": 12734
Hollow: 4
Holly: 11873; -- berry: 12881; -- tree: 4484
Holy Bible: 3744.  See also Bible; Holy Book
Holy Book: 10565
Holy Days: 9944
Holy Saturday: 11852
Holy Thursday: 11852
Holy Trinity: 11546
Holy Water: 10233, 10403, 11331, 13007; --,
    curative properties of: 2685.  See also
    Water
Home: 4639; --, arriving: 7662; --, dreaming
    of: 4513; --, entering: 4527, 5554, 5932,
    8246; --, head of: 5701; --, leaving: 2807,
    5373, 7639, 7645, 7696; --, new: 5574,
    6264, 6274f., 6279, 6291ff., 6494, 8390;
    --, 5373, 5627
Home base: 8722
Home plate: 8736f., 8739
Home run: 8719
Homesick: 2861
Homicidal: 7572
Homosexual: 12680
Homosexuality: 2182ff.
Honest: 2403ff., 8631
Honey: 1134, 1883, 1929, 2011, 2144f., 2724,
    2757, 2933f., 3062, 3145f., 3191, 3202,

3205, 3277, 3302, 3305, 3308, 3324, 3418,
    3530, 3554, 3853, 4002, 4118, 4120, 4432,
    5573f., 12707; -- in shoe: 5446; -- in
    tonic: 2768; -- and milk: 3488
Honeybee: 7973, 12498
Honeycomb: 3806
Honeymoon: 4813, 5221, 5297, 5539, 5571,
    5639ff., 5677ff., 5704
Honor: 6974
Hoodoo: 10113
Hoof, split: 10180
Hoof-and-mouth disease: 12739
Hook, fishing: 8977, 8989f.
Hoop, passing sheep through: 12859
Hoopsnake: 12424ff., 12923
Hoot owl: 9146
Hope: 1689, 1837, 8904; --, color of: 1837
Hope chest: 5178, 5734
Hope Diamond: 6876
"Hopping John": 7315
Hop roots: 3038
Hops, in pillow: 2643, 3915
Hopseed: 12815
Hop tea: 2760, 3783, 3957, 4060
Horehound: 3352; -- syrup: 3299; -- tea: 3190,
    3957
Horn: 1424, 1494, 4906, 7813, 7849ff., 8683;
    --, car: 11725; --, cow: 12711, 12738; --,
    wild animal: 11909
Horned toad: 12446.  See also Toad; Horny toad
Hornet nest: 10761, 10794
Hornet sting: 3707
Horns, of Mormons: 11904
Horny: 2239
Horny toad: 3889, 12448.  See also Horned toad;
    Toad
Horoscope: 10414, 11729
Horrible: 348
Hors d'oeuvre: 4712
Horse: 656, 936, 1060, 1126, 1426, 2033,
    7781ff., 9418ff., 9769, 9956, 9987, 11965,
    11996ff., 12598, 12771ff., 13119; --
    attracting lightning: 11996; --, behavior
    of: 11389; --, black: 4626, 9420, 12002f.,
    12791; --, branding of: 12825; --, brown:
    12795; -- buried with dead: 9761f.; --,
    castrating: 12822ff.; --, counting: 9795;
    --, diseases of: 12804ff.; --, dreaming of:
    2533, 4626, 7484, 8493, 12009, 12023f.; --,
    finding: 7692; -- in funeral procession:
    9776; --, gray: 12000f.; --, killer: 12016,
    12794; -- killed by evil eye: 10143; --,
    killed by lightning: 12826; --, killing:
    12010; --, mean: 12793; --, mounting:
    12784f.; --, phantom: 10647; --, piebald:
    4440, 11999; --, race: 8824; -- as
    indicator of rain: 11037ff., 11259; --,
    red: 12960; -- rolling over: 12011; --,
    rubbing: 2656; --, sacrifice of: 9776; --
    with sixth sense: 12014; --, skewbald:
    11999; --, stray: 12800; --, stumbling:
    12012; -- with sway back: 4439, 4622ff.,
    4764, 5474, 7326f., 7484, 7726, 7781ff.,
    8938, 9418, 9775, 9956, 10668, 12018ff.,
    12035ff., 12051ff., 12064ff., 12792, 12805,
    12809, 12939; --, white and gray: 12004; --
    with four white feet: 12006f., 12775; -- as
    indicator of winter: 10737
Horse chestnut: 2618, 2914, 3590, 3897, 10513,
    10515, 12776, 12949
Horsehair: 2033, 3411, 4454, 10291, 12436; --
    blanket: 12383; -- halter: 10344; -- rope:

INDEX 453

Knothole: 12637
Knots: 1332, 1335, 4331ff.; -- in handkerchief:
    1175; --, three: 3333; -- of tree: 5
Knowledge: 2298, 2326
Knuckle bone: 10484
Knuckles: 2930, 4500
Koliva: 9747
Kraut: 5831.   See also Sauerkraut; Sourkraut

L.D.S. Church: 9658, 9661
Label: 2270, 2415
Labor (childbirth): 235, 237, 243, 246ff.,
    249ff., 256; -- pains: 232, 257
Lack: 430
Lactation: 625ff.
Ladder: 6510; --, walking under: 773, 1289,
    3497, 5061, 6507f., 6511ff., 6970, 8843.
    See also Step ladder
Lady: 330; --, weeping: 10643
Ladybird: 12520
Ladybug: 4646f., 12510ff.; --, finding: 1259;
    --, killing: 7339, 12520; -- on person:
    6644; -- preventing fire: 6417; -- as
    indicator of weather: 10975
Lady friend: 4515
Lake: 4803, 8939; --, measuring depth of: 8902
Lamb: 4405, 10818, 11118, 12153; --, black:
    12853f.; --, butchering: 9421; --, first:
    12855f.; --, hair of: 4000; --, tail of:
    12111
Lame: 2802
Lameness: 1089
Lamp: 6375, 6377f., 7889, 9343f.; -- on grave:
    9824; -- as indicator of rain: 11173; -- in
    window: 7065
Lamp black: 3431.   See also Soot
Lamp chimney: 11508
Lamp post: 2112, 5115
Land, fertility of: 12954; --, foreign: 7619;
    --, reclaimed: 7076; --, value of: 12953
Landslide: 7109
Lap (n.): 70, 198; -- of bride: 5557; --,
    holding frog in: 3167
Lapel: 6600
Lard: 3212, 3225f., 3229, 3770, 3950, 3972,
    4018, 12686, 12841, 12844, 12847; -- on
    aches and pains: 2909; --, hog: 260, 519;
    -- in poultice: 2774; --, rubbing with:
    271f.; -- in salve: 2779, 2783; --, killing
    worms with: 1134
Lark: See Meadowlark
Lark Mining Co.: 7087
Larvae, wasp: 3814
Laryngitis: 3738
Last: 61, 68, 437, 551, 1907, 1913, 1979, 2258,
    4712, 5022ff., 5086, 5146, 5175, 5195,
    5198, 5206, 5230, 5839f., 6389, 6933, 7122,
    7404, 8784; -- child: 121, 2672; -- night
    of April: 4616; -- piece: 6103f.; -- rites:
    9176; -- snow: 3415
Last Supper: 5967, 9262
Latin race: 8398
Latins: 2241
Laugh (n.): 2858
Laugh (vb.): 952, 1242. 1786, 1797f., 1800ff.,
    1960ff., 2515
Laughing: 3833, 6111, 8684, 9679, 9783; --,
    dream of: 640
Laughing gas: 1785
Laundering: 9335
Laundry: 6229ff., 6240ff.
Laurel: 1089; -- tree: 4653

Lavendar: 4592, 9879
Lawbreaker: 7544.   See also Criminal; Thief
Lawn: 11179, 13110ff.
Lawsuit: 7533
Lawyer: 5171, 5173, 6956f., 7534
Laxative: 2749, 2758, 2769, 3207
Lay (vb.): 69, 1359
Layette: 1136, 1156
Laying-on-of-hands: 4404, 4407, 4462
Lazy: 868, 2422ff.
Lead (n.): 3800, 6037
Leadership: 2308
Leading man: 7163
"Lead masher": 10401
Lead necklace: 3821
Leaf: 12916ff.; --, falling: 3259; --, peach:
    4059; --, plantain: 568, 3365, 3693; --,
    raspberry: 3453; --, tomato: 3693.   See
    also Leaves
Leaflet: 12886
Leap frog: 764
Leap year: 314, 410, 4915ff., 13027.   See also
    New Year's
Learn: 1740
Learning capacity: 2856
Leather: 6749, 8977
Leaves: 9563, 10623, 11104, 11422; --, basil:
    549; --, eucalyptus: 3247; --, green: 2831;
    --, horehound: 3352; --, horsetail: 3353;
    --, laurel, 1089; --, mint: 3675; --,
    mustard: 2755; -- as indicator of weather:
    10765, 11109.   See also Leaf
Lecheman: 3994
Leeches: 2671, 3052
Lee Mansion: 10646
Left (adj.): 453, 466, 481, 494f., 508, 2020f.,
    8737, 10496f., 12109, 12322, 12566, 12749,
    12830; -- ankle: 4574; -- arm: 1396, 1637,
    6650; -- boot: 7075, 7133; -- breast: 4465;
    -- cheek: 4549; -- chest: 3592; --
    direction: 535, 1208, 1915; -- ear: 1949,
    4469, 7921, 8286, 8295, 8298f. 8302, 8304,
    8309; -- elbow: 1640, 7700; -- eye: 1561,
    1563, 1568ff., 5074, 7920; -- finger: 821;
    -- foot: 1719, 1965, 1767, 4030, 4368,
    6124, 6313f., 6653, 7000, 7624, 7639, 8336;
    -- forearm: 7802; -- glove: 5459; -- hand:
    540, 1652ff., 1662, 1669ff., 1685, 1957,
    2191, 2488, 3169, 3740, 4623, 4922, 5128,
    5508, 5516, 6061, 7374, 7447, 7803, 7852,
    7876, 7952, 8115, 8118, 8333, 8562, 8916;
    -- leg: 1763, 2362; -- lens: 6849; --
    nostril: 1391; -- palm: 7763, 7814; --
    pocket: 2618, 7475; -- shoe: 3633, 6656,
    6660ff., 6667f., 6795, 6821, 8746; --
    shoulder: 523, 1620, 1626, 2123, 2818,
    4242, 4268f., 4300, 4362, 4695ff., 4706,
    4795, 4831, 4910, 5341, 5358, 5763, 5765,
    5772, 5944, 5979, 5984, 6160f., 6461, 6599,
    6824, 7185, 7552, 7759, 8062, 8087, 8391,
    8393, 8405, 9401, 9589, 10070, 10242f.,
    12003; -- side: 1401, 1425, 1766, 1999,
    2041, 2094, 4143, 6815, 9226, 12942; --
    stocking: 6657; -- thumb: 2333, 2450, 3922,
    5694; -- toe: 1725, 5004; --, turning to:
    4042, 4290; -- wrist: 3920.
Left-handed: 1656, 2299, 2315, 2319, 7715,
    8540, 8706f., 10063
Left to right: 5799f., 7737, 7749, 11509
Legacy: 7604
Legs: 966, 1990; --, birthmark on: 390, 397;
    --, black: 8587; --, breaking: 8723; --,

---

Meeting, one's double: 2292; -- fool: 1594; -- funeral party: 139, 157; -- priest: 1292; -- someone: 2189; -- on stairs: 6351; -- woman: 7057
Melon: 5775, 13128; -- rind: 3516. See also Watermelon
Member, of family: 547, 2522
Membrane: 1356
Memorial Day service: 9888f.
Memorial services: 5057
Memory, loss of: 2838ff.
Men: 1632, 7636, 11765; --, big-footed: 2848; --, colored: 1634; --, lean: 2863; --, shape-changing: 11908; --, short: 2483; --, white: 1634
Mending: 1738, 6573, 6575, 6577ff.
Menopause: See Life, change of
Menstrual cycle: 3782
Menstrual pains: 3782f. See also Cramps
Menstrual period: 1453, 12894; --, swimming during: 2800
Menstruating: 1440
Menstruation: 24, 1966ff., 4113, 5823f.; --, bathing during: 1971; --, dating during: 1971; --, exercising during: 1971; --, swimming during: 1971. See also Menstrual period; Monthly period
Mental ailments: 995ff.; -- disorder: 2881; -- gifts: 808ff.; -- illness: 1012, 2878, 2880, 2894; -- powers: 1740, 2296
Mentality, low: 2857
Mentally ill: 2899; -- retarded: 998
Merchant: 5171, 7233
Meringue icing: 5816
Merry: 413, 6647
Merthiolate: 4013
Message: 3954, 7906, 7908, 7974
Messenger, angelic: 7080; -- of death: 9453
Mess kit: 7140
Metal: 5744, 9581, 11366, 11374; -- around arm: 2941; -- around finger: 2941; -- around leg: 2941; --, precious: 7083; --, sliver: 3960; --, touching: 11927
Meteor: 11684f., 11697. See also Star, shooting
Meteoric fragment: 11329
Mexican: 7093; -- chihuahua: 2952
Mexico: 5170; --, epidemic in: 2687
Mice: 12129, 12243, 12616f.; -- causing canker: 3142; --, dreaming of: 7330, 12143; --, getting rid of: 6371; --, killing: 7105; -- leaving mine: 7108; -- in mine: 7105; --, roasted: 1030; -- on ship: 7031
Midday: 13142. See also Noon
Middle: 2288, 6637
Middle-aged: 996
Midnight: 449, 587, 1902, 1984, 2001ff., 2486, 2532, 2899, 3077, 3425, 3559, 4209, 4211, 4214, 4276, 4314, 4317, 4336, 4355f., 4367, 4484, 4559, 4607, 4724, 4794, 4857, 6191, 6214, 6465, 6681, 7002, 7062, 7087, 7747, 8239, 8242, 8247, 9370, 9403, 9405, 9416, 9424, 9455, 9832, 9837, 9840, 9843, 9945, 10032, 10166f., 10205, 10255f., 10322, 10329, 10341, 10390, 10602, 10615, 10643, 10654, 10658f., 11393, 11738, 11796f., 11799, 11801, 11822, 11830, 11858, 11869, 11897ff., 11914, 11989, 12327, 12435; --, born at: 835f.
Midshipmen: 7874
Midwife: 12, 250, 255, 935f.
Migraine: 3569

Migration, of animals: 10734
Mild: 2393
Milk: 54, 723, 902, 1088, 1366, 1399, 1776, 2178, 3040, 3276, 3305, 3474, 3502, 3534, 3857, 4064f., 4117, 5103, 5876, 9279, 12642, 12646, 12721, 12728, 12832f.; -- causing arthritis: 2929; --, bathing in: 1412; --, bloody: 12724ff.; -- and bread: 3327, 3339, 3648, 3961, 4134; --, breast: 1080; -- causing cancer: 3124; -- and cheese: 3274; -- and cherries: 2923, 3471, 4049, 5913, 9280ff.; -- and chili: 9283; -- and choke cherries: 3471, 4074, 9281; --, cow's: 3953, 4217; -- and cucumbers: 3475; --, donkey's: 3521; -- and dried fruit: 5915; -- in eye: 3408; -- feeding to "little people": 10381, 10383, 10396; -- feeding to snake: 1198f.; -- and fish: 316, 3472, 4051, 5917; -- and honey: 2011, 3488; --, hot: 7467; --, human: 3388, 4970, 4985; --, last drop: 5022; --, mare's: 4441. See also Mare's milk; --, mother's: 626, 629f.; --, new: 3049; -- and orange: 3472, 5914; -- and oysters: 3482; --, pasteurized: 5875; -- and pickles: 3484, 3874, 4050; -- in poultice: 2772; --, producing more: 12719f.; -- and rhubarb: 9282; -- and seafood: 5917; --, skim: 5877; --, soaking in: 5780; --, sour: 2720, 5878ff., 10381, 12723; --, spilling: 6031, 12722; --, spoiling: 5873; --, stirring with knife: 5872; -- in tea: 6056; -- and tomatoes: 3486, 5916; --, warm: 5921; --, washing in: 2150
Milk fever: 12740
Milking: 12722, 12729
Milkmaid: 10392, 12729
Milk snake: 12371
Milkweed: 3978, 4289ff., 12882; --, burying: 4291; -- lotion: 2994; -- tea: 3370
Mill Creek Canyon: 12935
Mill, dreaming of: 9961; -- refusing to grind: 7539
Millennium, signs of: 9985ff.
Million years: 11838
Mince pie: 6046
Mind, losing one's: 2901; --, state of: 201; --, vacant: 2858; --, weak: 2844
Mine (n.): 10462; --, accidents in: 7086ff.; --, coal: 7077; --, entering: 7089; --, gold: 7071; --, locating: 7066f.; --, mice in: 7105ff.; --, music in: 7102; --, rats in: 7105ff.; --, uranium: 2946; --, whistling in: 7099ff.; --, women in: 7111ff., 9602
Miner: 7066ff., 7073f., 7077, 7079, 7087, 7089, 7093ff.
Minerals: 2490, 2931; --, locating: 7081
Mine shaft: 7095
Mining: 7080
Minister's son: 10019
Mink: 4813; -- coat: 4916
Mint, in house: 6491; -- tea: 2761, 3675
Minute: 2214
Miracles: 9955ff., 10666
Mirror: 233, 674, 711, 745, 801, 864ff., 1008, 1017, 1035, 1065, 1107, 1158ff., 1319, 1373f., 1520, 2290, 2631, 2885, 3841, 4787, 4799, 5374ff., 6446ff., 8475, 9320ff., 10187f., 10332, 10631, 11375, 11631; --, bird on: 12215; --, breaking: 5204, 6453ff., 9319; --, cracking: 6451; --,

11228ff., 11232, 11241; --, seeing over
shoulder: 7360, 11619ff., 11624ff.; --,
seeing through trees: 11648f.; --, seeing
through glass/window: 11644ff.; --, shining
on face: 9591; --, shrink of: 12839; --,
sign of: 1294; --, staring at: 843; --,
sunspots on: 7231; --, throwing tooth at:
710; -- turning to blood: 9999f.; --,
waning: 456, 554, 11605, 12763, 12839f.,
12987f., 13037f., 13116; --, waste of:
12839, 13058; --, waxing: 456, 12846,
12984; -- as wife: 11706; --, wishing on:
11633ff., 11640ff.
Moondog: 11232
Moonlight: 2900, 3480, 4223, 4271, 4354, 4828,
4832, 7682, 10343, 10671, 13036, 13049,
13082, 13084; -- causing blindness: 3012;
--, planting by: 12973; -- shining on face:
2901; -- through window: 2855
Moon-lilies: 3019
Moon rays: 751
Moon-struck: 2898
Moose: 12576
Mop: 6981, 8199
Mopping: 6186
Moral: 2450
Mormon: 3106, 5457, 7990, 10006ff., 10059,
10202, 10991, 11904; -- church: 2701,
10269; -- conference: 10991; --
missionaries: 9691; -- pageant: 10992; --
pioneer: 2707; -- settlers: 10456; --
temple: 10014
Mormonism: 7080
Morning: 278, 400, 448, 1108, 1224, 1542, 1554,
1768, 1771, 1778, 1795, 1798, 2065, 2089,
2586; --, early: 3510, 4543; --, wedding
in: 5329
Morning sickness: 183ff., 232, 500f.; -- pills:
503
Moron: 1010
Morose: 2863
Moslems: 10571
Mosquito: 8067, 11090; -- bite: 3701, 12528.
See also Bites, mosquito
Moss: 11107, 12934f.
Moth: 2534, 7974; --, white: 9528; -- as
indicator of winter: 10758
Mother: 54, 105, 242, 308, 400, 482, 1209,
1695, 2074, 2627, 3745, 5138, 5549, 5630,
6766; -- of bride: 5647; -- causing
accident to: 2819; --, death of: 9110,
9112, 9251, 9539; --, expectant: 199ff.,
235, 328, 332, 359ff., 368, 403ff., 459,
484, 527ff., 540f., 819, 840ff., 1118; --,
lying to: 3027; --, new: 311; --, nursing:
115
Mother Goose: 11403
Mother-in-law: 3018, 5353, 5573f., 5577, 5615,
5702f., 5705
Mother nature: 11401
Mother's back: 2962
Mother's bone: 3493
Mother's spine: 4034
Mother's toe: 4132
Mother-to-be: 340
Motion sickness: 3789f.  See also Car sickness
Motorcycle: 7865
Mountain: 9099; --, dreaming of: 9597; --,
sacred: 10016; -- graperoot: 2491; -- lion:
9433, 12132f., 12338.  See also Lion; --
men: 11358; -- rush: 3042, 3200, 3454, 3642
Mountains: 3358

Mt. Fujiyama: 11839
Mourner: 9726
Mournful: 299
Mourning: 6725, 9215f., 9748, 9800, 9869ff.;
--, sign of: 5417
Mourning dove: 9474f.
Mouse: 975, 7483, 7832, 12141ff.; -- chewing
clothing: 6582; --, feeding to child: 1029;
--, fried: 1030; --, getting rid of: 6371;
-- in house: 8141; --, killing: 1134; --,
roasted: 3780; -- running over person:
9439; --, scared by: 371ff.
Moustache: 5009.  See also Mustache
Mouth: 1939, 1955, 2128, 2268, 2266, 2514; --,
black: 11981; --, canker in: 3141ff.; --,
child's: 1126; -- of dead: 9743; --,
deformity of: 947; --, devil entering:
10209; --, food in: 9104; --, hair in:
1954, 5009; --, large: 854, 1635; --, loud:
2425; --, open: 9814, 13074; --, pencil in:
3618; --, position of: 8934; --, roof of:
3815; --, sewn up by dragonfly: 686f.,
1228, 8065; --, sewn up by darning needle:
1604, 8042, 8065; --, sewn up by mosquito:
8067; --, small: 685; --, snakes and toads
in: 8041; --, sore: 3943, 3987; --, sores
in: 3791
Mouthwash: 3147
Movement: 11504
Movie: 7194; -- stars: 7162
Moving, into new home: 6269ff., 6279, 6287,
6291ff.; --, portents of: 6276ff.
Mowing: 12958
Muck: 4350
Mud: 3687, 3708f., 3861f.; --, black: 3698,
3978; --, Denver: 3654; --, dreaming of:
2528, 9594, 11480; -- for pain: 2916; --
packs: 4418
Mulberry bush: 11904
Mule: 7072, 8039; --, kicked by: 369; --,
white: 7092, 12017; -- shoe: 12092
Mullein: 3768, 4012; -- tea: 4012
Mummy powder: 2189
Mumps: 40, 1095, 3792
Murder: 7571ff., 7574, 7586, 8538, 10652
Murderer: 7585, 10007
Muscular disease: 3801
Muscles: 1641
Muscavado sugar: 1125
Mush: 10350; -- poultice: 3803
Mushrooms: 10390, 12587, 12885, 13081; --,
canning: 5828; --, ring of: 10367; --,
testing for poison: 5760ff., 5828
Music: 845ff., 3713, 9036, 9871, 12354; --,
ghostly: 10654; -- in mine: 7102
Musician: 845ff., 2336, 7206f.
Musk: 2031
Muskrat: 657
Mustache: 1513, 1953.  See also Moustache
Mustang: 12016
Mustard: 3198, 3280; -- as abortifacient: 150;
-- bag: 2610; --, dry: 3214; -- leaves:
2755; -- plaster: 3213, 3736, 3851; --
seed: 10023, 10067, 10518, 12945; -- in
shoes: 3890; -- water: 3214, 3450, 3751
Mutton bone: 518
Mutton tallow: 625, 3155
Mystery (adj.): 1012, 7547
Mystery (n.): 1979
Mystic: 830
Mythology: 10007

Pants: 8765, 8875; --, new: 6645; --, inside
boots: 7131; --, outside boots: 7137; --,
wrong side out: 6676
Paper: 45, 3589, 3816, 4073, 4802, 6917; --,
brown: 3225, 3771, 3789f., 3815; --,
burning: 3940; -- under pillow: 4749; --
turning into rat: 12140; --, throwing over
shoulder: 12128; --, white: 3789, 12128;
--, wrapping: 4950; --, writing: 3374
Paper sack: 3232, 6971
Paper towel: 3615
Papoose board: 1183
Paprika: 8398
Paralysis: 3835f., 12352; --, facial: 2477
Parasol: 7316.  See also Umbrella
Paregoric: 2767
Parents: 744, 859, 953, 1006, 1020, 1200ff.,
1227, 1369, 11861; --, minding: 10389
Parish: 9482
Park City: 7097
Parrot: 12243; --, dreaming of: 7560
Parsley: 123, 5909; --, planting: 13070; --
tea: 2010, 2990, 3726
Parting: 8211
Partner: 8521
Party: 102, 5042, 6151, 6253, 6765, 7663, 8027,
8237, 8625f.; --, birthday: 1252; --,
dreaming of: 1893
Pass away: 547, 9124.  See Death; Die
Passage: 7659
Passenger: 7869
Passing between: 2112
Passing through: 12859; -- maple tree: 789; --
through window: 771; -- underneath horse:
1060
Passion: 4974, 5156, 8543
Passionate: 4969
Passion flower: 4673
Passion pills: 4973
Pastry: 5785, 6027, 6048
Pasture: 3510, 12715, 12743, 12761
Patch, over eye: 2120; --, of pig skin: 367
Path: 374, 1260, 7937; --, animal crossing:
12333; --, bird crossing: 4640; --, cat
crossing: 2531, 6034, 7326, 9383f.; --,
crossing: 7730, 7732f., 7735ff., 11827; --,
fox crossing: 7729, 9006; --, mouse
crossing: 975; --, woman crossing: 9006
Pathway: 5619
Patient (adj.): 2463
Patient (n.): 2516, 2633, 2654, 4129, 4443,
7152, 9129
Patriarch: 8239, 11801
Patriarchal blessing: 2696
Paw, double: 12608; --, mole's: 4151; --,
rabbit's: 10495f.
Pay (vb.): 2212
Peace: 9993, 12119; --, live in: 1775; --, one
thousand years of: 9992
Peach: 210, 2147; -- branch divining rod:
10455ff.; --, last: 13196; -- leaf tea:
2762, 4059; -- leaves: 3067, 3146, 4193; --
tree: 13204
Peacock: 12301ff.; -- feathers: 7158, 7513,
7653; -- feathers in house: 5634, 6500f.;
--, wearing feathers: 6747f., 12302; -- as
indicator of rain: 11062
Peanut: 8834, 8847, 12950; -- hulls: 7568
Pear: 289; --, last: 13196; -- tree: 9567
Pearl: 4568, 5356, 5461, 5709, 6881ff., 8376,
9238; -- button: 3419; -- necklace: 4874;
-- ring: 4568, 4926

Peas: 485, 4656, 5764, 13076; --, black-eyed:
43; -- on New Year's: 5996, 7315; --,
planting: 13035; --, rubbing warts with:
4263; --, shelling: 5763; -- in shoes: 775;
--, throwing into well: 4264
Pea soup: 4054
Pebble: 2266, 2294, 4366, 4803, 8534, 10264;
--, swallowing: 176
Peddler: 2716
Pedestal: 9810
"Pedittle": 4897
Pee (n.): 1044
Pee (vb.): 1149, 4135
"Peebent flowers": 1022
Peepstone: 12801
Peepstone Lady: 10666
Peepstone Woman: 9701, 12800
"Pee-the-bed": 1023
Pelican: 7059
Pen: 6545, 8447; --, silver: 10080
Pencil: 1278, 6770, 9379; -- in mouth: 3618; --
determining sex: 537ff., 573; -- between
teeth: 5769
Pendant: 6895
Pendulation: 527ff., 531, 533ff., 536f., 539,
541
Penis bone, of raccoon: 10485
Penmanship: 2484.  See also Handwriting;
Writing
Pennant: 6984
Pennies, jar of: 5735
Penniless: 7522
Penny: 4391, 7236, 7389, 7407ff., 10552ff.,
13190; -- exchanging for baby's tooth: 702;
-- on belly button: 286; --, burying: 4399;
--, in cake: 1245, 5058, 5235, 7474, 7519;
--, carrying: 7405, 7515; --, dreaming of:
7403; --, dropping: 7419; --, finding:
7263, 7409ff., 7475, 8708; -- on forehead:
3827; -- in gift: 3336, 4958, 6924f.,
6928f., 8370, 8381; --, giving: 3785; -- in
horseshoe charm: 10507; --, hot: 4103; --,
Indian head: 7420; --, giving with knife:
6127, 7600; --, last: 7404; -- under lip:
3826; -- in navel: 3634; -- around neck:
3538; --, new: 4400, 5449, 7412; --, old:
7413; -- under pillow: 3583, 3876; --,
giving with pin: 6609; -- in purse: 6854,
7404; --, rubbing with: 3638; --, rubbing
wart with: 4394ff.; --, giving with sharp
object: 8412, 8415f., 8419; -- in return
for sharp object: 8414, 8438, 8447; -- over
ship's bow: 7003; -- in shoe: 2594, 3045,
4605, 5177, 5391, 5447ff., 5453, 5455; --,
sitting on: 3828; -- in slipper: 8370; --,
throwing into fountain: 2662, 7422; --,
throwing over shoulder: 7418, 7421; --,
wishing on: 7402
Penny loafer: 10556
People, dead: 5923, 9304; --, old: 11826; --,
white: 7562
Pep: 2133
Pep club: 8782
Pepper: 2457, 3098, 3385, 3914, 3998, 4976,
5980; --, black: 1109, 2211, 4065; --,
borrowing: 5981; --, burning: 10298; --,
cayenne: 1229; --, green: 13087; --, hot:
4186; --, passing: 5977f., 8395; --, red:
2366, 4129, 10299, 12672; --, warding off
snakes: 12382; --, spilling: 5979, 8174,
8396; --, swallowing: 6726.  See also Black
pepper; Red pepper, Cayenne pepper

Peppermint: 3302; -- leaves: 3858; -- tea:
    2009, 2756f., 3357, 3675, 4061
Pepper vinegar: 2958
Perceptary [sic] perception: 838
"Perdiddle": 4898, 4901f.
"Perdidle": 7817
Perfect: 228
Performance: 7170, 7182, 7184, 7186ff., 7197
Performers: 6476
Perfume: 118, 6711
Period, menstrual: 24, 114, 1615, 5873, 9116
Permanent, hair: 169, 206, 659, 1453
Persimmon tree: 3165
Persistence: 2421, 2467
Person, brutal: 2850; --, character of: 11913;
    --, dark: 8256; --, dead: 6529, 7025; --,
    evil: 9897; --, fair-complexioned: 8257ff.;
    --, first: 7232; --, light-headed: 8257;
    --, meeting: 7704; --, thick-witted: 2850;
    --, unmarried: 5202; --, white: 8031
Personal possessions: 10117ff.
Personality: 855, 892, 2294, 2346f., 2370,
    4565, 5152; --, abnormal: 897; --
    projection: 2281ff.
Pests: 6366ff., 13150ff.
Pet (n.): 7034; --, sick: 2640
Petals: 4672
Petrel: 6992, 9917; -- as indicator of storm:
    11272
Petticoat: 983, 6766; -- under head: 4747; --,
    inside out: 6703.  See also Slip
Petting: 4891
Phantom: 10395; -- limb: 2826ff.
Pharmacy: 7239
Pheasant: 12304; -- nest: 12958
Philadelphia: 7874
Phlegm: 4131
Phlegmatic: 543
Phone: 7989, 9625, 11367
Phosphorus: 1740
Photograph (n.): 2284f., 6470, 9322
Photograph (vb.): 2287, 4939, 11936
Phrenology: 10429ff.
Phthisic: 2734
Physician: 10429.  See also Doctor; Healer
Pianist: 850, 2336
Piano: 847, 850, 8627, 10654; --, covering at
    death: 9715; -- key: 11514
Pickax: 12405
Picket fence: 2102
Pickle juice: 4108
Pickles: 187, 1973, 5080, 7394, 9285f.; --,
    craving for: 4703; --, dill: 3792; --,
    eating before bed: 1878; --, making: 5830;
    -- and ice cream: 173, 3484, 9284; -- and
    milk: 174, 3484, 3874, 4050; -- and
    strawberries: 175.  See also Dill pickles
Picture: 380, 394, 2282, 2284, 2554, 2668,
    4940, 5648, 5654, 6470ff., 6500, 7157,
    7209, 7881, 8694, 9324, 9326, 10103, 10384;
    --, baby's: 516; -- under eaves: 10102; --,
    fading of: 2535, 9323; --, hanging: 863;
    --, looking at: 890; -- of pregnant woman:
    162; --, taking: 2286, 2288f.; --, upside
    down: 10104; --, turning to wall: 9712ff.
"Pididle": 7816
Pie: 5017, 5855f., 6042ff.; --, baking: 5813;
    --, cherry: 6047; --, custard: 4715; --,
    cutting: 5159; --, dropping: 4097; --,
    eating before bed: 1867; --, last piece:
    5146; --, wishing on: 6042
Piebald: 4440
Pie lady: 5856
Piercing ears: 1079
Pig: 4246, 12829f., 12834, 12848; -- crossing
    path: 5478; --, demon in form of: 10247;
    --, devil in form of: 10201; --, frightened
    by: 367; --, killing: 10229; --, sign of
    luck: 7216; --, slaughtering of: 519, 9422,
    12842; --, spirits in: 10628; -- as
    indicator of storm: 11262; -- at
    Thanksgiving: 6012; --, touching: 131

Pigeon: 2447, 12247ff., 13138; --, killing:
    12250; -- as indicator of death: 9478ff.;
    --, raising: 12604; --, white: 9478, 9480f.
Pigeon-toed: 2447
Pig fat: 2624
Pigmentation: 4407
Pig's melt: 10716
"Pig tail": 8845
Pig trough: 5580
Pile, straw: 6
Piles (disease): 3837
Pilgrimage: 10016
Pillow: 9314f.; --, almonds under: 4741, 5561;
    --, bay leaf under: 4763, 12926f.; --, book
    under: 1284; --, cake under: 4714, 5214;
    --, down-filled: 11377; --, egg under:
    4751; --, eucalyptus leaves under: 3247f.;
    --, flower under: 10940; --, four-leaf
    clover under: 12870; --, hops in: 2643,
    3915; --, key under: 1184; --, knife under:
    1873; --, looking glass under: 4750; --,
    onion under: 3248; --, paper under: 4749;
    --, penny under: 3583, 3876; --, salt
    shaker under: 3284; --, tooth under:
    702ff.; --, topaz under: 1874; --, walnut
    under: 3082; --, wedding cake under: 4748,
    5586, 5595, 5598ff.; --, wood under: 492
Pills: 502
Pilot: 7877, 7879, 7881
Pilot Mountain: 10985
Pimple: 2410, 3839ff.; -- on tongue: 8318
Pin: 1142, 3959, 4585, 4956, 5052, 5190, 5460,
    6590ff., 6767, 7511, 7629, 8025, 8546,
    8869; -- under bed: 5336; --, boiling:
    10240; --, borrowing/lending: 6607ff.; --,
    bride's: 5227; --, crossing: 4376; --,
    dropping: 8226, 8449f.; --, finding: 4771,
    6596ff.; -- as gift: 4937, 5095, 8446,
    8448; --, passing: 8443; --, picking up:
    6583ff., 6591, 8440ff.; --, pricking with:
    3869; --, safety: 6601ff., 8451, 10577; --,
    determination of sex: 541; --, sticking in
    candle: 4784; --, sticking in image: 10099;
    -- between teeth: 5769; --, throwing away:
    5405, 6599; -- in voodoo doll: 10105ff.;
    --, buying wart with: 4393; --, rubbing on
    wart: 4378; --, sticking wart with:
    4373ff., 4377
Pinching: 7179
Pine: 13191; -- bough: 275; -- gum: 1805; --
    knot: 4179; -- needle: 4351
Pine nut: 10744; -- as indicator of winter:
    10776f., 10796
Pine tree: 3097, 3166, 9570; --, planting:
    8513; -- as indicator of snow: 11420
Pink: 502f., 525f., 1932, 6539, 6543; --,
    wearing: 5393, 5427, 5430
Pink eye: 3430
Piñon nut: 10776
Piñon tree: 3652, 4459
Pinto horse: 12015
Pin-up (n.): 7012
Pinworms: 1096, 4453.  See also Worms
Pioneer: 9955, 10803
Pipe, ceremonial: 10968
Pipe, lighting: 6398
Pipe cleaner: 4139
"Pissabed": 1023
Pissing: 8874; -- in road: 4427
Pistol: 9021.  See also Gun
Pit, cherry: 3532
Pit, mine: 7079, 7110
Pit, race: 8832
Pitch (n.): 3652; -- of piñon tree: 4459
Pitcher: 8708ff.; --, breaking: 2536, 3749; --,
    left-handed: 8706f.
Pitcher's box: 8709
Pitchfork: 6359, 12722
Piute Indians: 6496
Placard: 6548
Place, dry: 305; --, hidden: 788
Place setting: 9273

Placenta, burial of: 302; --, disposal of: 121; --, feeding to husband: 121.  See also Afterbirth

Plague: 3843ff.  See also Black plague

Plane: 7878, 7882; --, jumping from: 7142.  See also Airplane

Plane crash: 9664

Planet: 879, 896, 2427, 11732; --, position of: 11727

Plans: 11522

Plant (n.): 111, 1022, 2608, 2746, 2764, 10145, 12861ff., 12879, 13159f.; -- in body: 2794ff.; --, female: 2035; --, gift of: 9541; --, green: 6269; --, medicinal: 2733; --, middle of: 3156; --, parts of: 2742f.; --, planting by moon: 12963ff.; --, swamp: 12697; --, talking to: 12952; -- as indicator of winter: 10795ff.

Plant (vb.): 790, 1491

Plantain leaf: 568, 2905, 3365, 3692

Plantain weed: 8050

Planting: 12958, 12968ff., 12973ff., 12995ff., 12999ff., 13089ff.; -- by moon phases: 12963ff., 12986ff.; -- season: 13165

Plaque: 4123

Plaster: 3327, 3736; --, butter: 3219, 3228; -- of cow dung: 3297; --, falling: 9243; --, mustard: 3213, 3851; --, onion: 3215.  See also Poultice

Plate: 1265, 8185f., 9763, 10967; --, breaking: 5563, 5588, 9744; --, dinner: 6102; --, empty: 6154; --, leaving food on: 6094

Play (vb.): 1008, 1022, 1025, 1218, 1253ff., 1385

Play, stage: 7169, 7171, 7177, 7183

Player: 8809

Player, Gary: 8820

Pleasant: 1561

Pleased: 1561

Pleasure: 1540

Pledge (n.): 1269

Pleebamarnock: 11489

Plenty: 5538, 5999, 8244

Plow blade: 13140

Plowing: 12956ff.; -- a grave: 9830

Plugging: 3262; -- as ritual cure: 4169f.

Plum: 2224; -- pudding: 5196; -- tree: 9568

Plumage: 12226

Pneumonia: 1097, 2694, 3180, 3849ff., 10643; --, three-day: 3848

Pocket: 7389, 7478, 8545, 10576; --, acorn in: 2276, 10510; --, buckeye in: 10511; --, empty: 7496; --, hair in: 5484; --, horse chestnut in: 2618; --, key in: 8033; --, left: 7475, 10561, 10569; --, lemon in: 4755; --, money in: 4834, 10564; --, nickel in: 10559; --, nutmeg in: 4423; --, rabbit foot in: 10497f.; --, salt in: 4079; --, sharp object in: 6745; --, inside out: 10648

Pocketbook: 10576.  See also Purse

Pocket knife: 5675; --, as gift: 8417, 8420; --, lending: 6935.  See also Knife

Point (vb.): 1978, 2013f., 2023

Pointing: 6973, 11607, 11716; -- at star: 4204

Poison: 1199, 3343, 3713, 3981, 3984, 5834, 11408, 11501, 12117, 12450; -- in body: 1101, 1968; --, drawing out: 3692, 3696, 3698, 3708, 3711, 3852, 3980, 5758f.; --, sucking out: 3137

Poisoning: 3857f., 12834f.  See also Food poisoning

Poison ivy: 3859ff., 12886f.

Poisonous: 3019, 3475ff., 3481ff., 3637, 11997, 12202, 12447f.

Poker: 8595ff.; -- chips: 8602, 8605

Poker and tongs: 8481

Poke salad: 4046

Pole: 8532; --, walking around: 2099, 2109.  See also Telephone pole

Policeman: 9958

Polio: 3864.  See also Poliomyelitis

Poliomyelitis: 3864

Polish (nationality): 12112, 12158

Polite: 888

Polka-dotted: 969

Pollard ash: 12142

Poltergeist: 10403

Polygamy: 261, 807, 4191, 10014

Polywog: 12436

Pomegranate: 33, 5467, 11804; --, stepping on: 5553f.; -- juice: 3355

Pond: 1299, 7428

Pookeys: 1222

Pool (game): 8891ff.

Poor (adj.): 1245, 1305, 5058, 5171f., 5174, 5176, 5235, 5451, 6006, 6495, 6956f., 7474, 7504, 7509, 7511ff., 7519; -- house: 7506

Pop (vb.): 1682

Popcorn: 5019, 5995, 8848

Pop eye: 7807

Poplar: 790; -- as indicator of winter: 10725

Popover: 5819

Popsicle stick: 6092

Pop-top: 4757

Popularity: 2469

Population: 548

Porch: 2224, 9510, 12253; --, back: 10274, 13025; --, burying dishrag under: 4308; --, burying frog under: 4222; --, front: 4420, 6225, 8143; --, sweeping: 6199

Porcupine: 12152; -- quills: 12645

Pores: 1416, 2151

Pork: 1344, 2544, 3479, 12839, 12846; -- causing boils: 3059; -- fat: 3996; --, fresh: 3971; -- poultice: 2777; --, raw: 3294; --, salt: 3340, 3971, 3997, 3999, 4237, 12843.  See also Salt pork; --, sliced: 2907

Porpoise: 7045ff., 7054; --, killing: 7047, 7049; -- as indicator of storm: 11278

Porridge: 5197, 11887

Port: 7004; --, leaving: 7002

Portrait: 9324

Position: 1421, 1517

Possession, by devil: 1188ff., 10202ff.; -- by evil: 1186; -- by evil spirit: 576, 945

Post: 2113, 8518ff.

Postage stamp: 6937

Postum: 7323

Pot: 5745; --, boiling over: 5749f.; --, sitting over: 149

Potato: 4430; --, baked: 3386, 3467; -- under bed: 110, 3250; --, begged: 3891; --, boiled: 3218; --, burying: 4274ff.; --, carrying: 7010; --, eyes of: 4280f., 5766; -- growing in ears: 2798; -- mashed as poultice: 3093; --, planting: 4271f., 13037, 13040ff., 13048ff., 13058ff., 13079f.; -- in pocket: 2966, 3891ff., 10520; -- in purse: 10521; --, raw: 2937, 3317, 3848, 4126, 4266; --, ring of: 3894; --, roasted: 4138; --, rotten: 4268; --, rubbing wart with: 4265ff.; --, scraped:

Quakin' asp: 12925.  See also Aspen
Quarantine: 3361
Quarrel (n.): 4956, 5077, 5656, 5659, 8275,
    8280, 8314, 8324, 8335, 8365, 8368, 8383,
    8392, 8402, 8405f., 8423, 8426, 8435, 8449,
    8459, 8462, 8467, 8473, 8477, 8480f., 8483,
    8485, 8515, 8517, 8519, 8523; --,
    preventing: 8011
Quarrel (vb.): 1255, 2805, 5359, 8319, 8328,
    8404, 8414f., 8418, 8450, 8458, 8463, 8496,
    8527
Quarter: 11644
Quartz: 7069
Queen (card): 9633; -- of hearts: 8571; -- of
    spades: 8572
Queens: 8021
Queer: 2182f.
Question: 2026, 8216
Queue: 7712
Quick: 2462
Quick-witted: 2317
Quicksilver: 4980, 9703
Quill, porcupine: 12152
Quilt: 61, 1822, 5042, 6638
Quilting: 62, 6639
Quinine: 146, 1050
Quinsy: 3871f.
Quiver (vb.): 389

Rabbi: 10179
Rabbit: 6412, 7788, 10791, 11836, 11848ff.,
    12145ff.; --, eating: 726, 986; --,
    frightened by: 982; --, hunting: 9014ff.;
    --, killing: 3364, 12148; -- running over
    grave: 9048, 9052; --, seeing: 983; --,
    touching: 984; --, white: 11772; --, wild:
    5866; -- as indicator of winter: 10749
Rabbit bone: 10499
Rabbit brains: 722
Rabbit brush: 3735
Rabbit ear: 13095
Rabbit foot: 29, 721, 2954, 9840, 10310, 10472,
    10487ff.; --, brushing baby with: 279; --,
    finding: 12151; -- around neck: 2623
Rabbit tail: 10502
Rabies: 3368, 12643.  See also Dog bite
Raccoon's penis bone: 10485
Race horse: 8824
Race track: 8822
Racing, car: 8827ff.
Radar: 12177
Radiation: 11734
Radio: 3880, 11363, 11736
Radish: 3733, 4975
Radium rocks: 2716
Rag: 545, 4026, 10116, 13152; --, burying:
    4318; --, turning into rat: 12140
Rage: 6673, 8385
Railroad track: 2105f., 4532, 4589, 6606,
    10655; --, crossing: 2107, 2822, 5005,
    5109ff., 5236, 7818ff.
Rails: 2105
Rain (n.): 754, 3509, 5121, 5250, 7645, 8860,
    9381, 9861, 10685, 10695, 10726, 10868,
    10981ff., 10997, 12885, 13022, 13102,
    13193; --, animal indicator of: 11046ff.;
    -- at burial: 9915; --, causing: 11181ff.;
    --, cosmic indicator of: 11110ff.; --,
    domestic indicators of: 11164ff.; --,
    dreaming of: 1846; --, explanation of:
    10988ff.; --, causing fire: 6418; --,
    fishing in: 8959, 8961f.; --, forty days

and nights of: 11144; -- on open grave:
    9576; --, indicators of: 11007ff.; -- as
    indicator: 11136ff.; --, insect indicator
    of: 11079ff.; -- as indicator of snow:
    11253, 11434; --, moon as indicator of:
    11121ff.; -- in morning: 7228; --, plant
    indicators of: 11099ff.; --, spider as
    indicator of: 11092; --, star as indicator
    of: 11132; -- while sun is shining: 4962,
    9574, 11006; -- on Valentine's Day: 12682;
    --, weather as indicator of: 11153ff.; --
    on wedding: 4700, 5251ff., 5259f.  See also
    Weather, wet
Rain (vb.): 1235, 1460, 5665, 9575, 9858,
    9862ff., 10206, 10815, 12918
Rain barrel: 2254, 12416
Rainbow: 16, 10380, 10465, 10872, 11207,
    11712ff., 13010; --, double: 10887; --,
    sign for fishing: 8965; -- as indicator of
    weather: 10831, 10836, 10864, 10868,
    10886f., 10930, 11145ff, 11242, 11435.
Raincoat: 6771
Rain dance: 11182, 13006
Raining: 300, 8964, 9475; -- at time of birth:
    893
Rain rhyme: 11192
Rainstorm: 1161, 1484, 3581, 11484
Rainwater: 3512, 4071, 4352f., 12567, 12604; --
    as cosmetic: 2146; -- as hair conditioner:
    1484; --, May: 10993
Rainy: 455, 894
Rainy day, baking on: 5804; --, moving on: 6279
Raisin: 1028, 3728, 4010; -- in ear: 3387; --
    bound to navel: 269
Rake (n.): 2175, 10981, 13171
Ranch: 7136
Rash (adj.): 2428
Rash (n.): 1098ff., 3873ff., 9129.  See also
    Diaper rash
Raspberry: 395, 12957; -- tea: 246, 3373, 3453
Rat: 1368, 12137ff.; --, burying: 4621; --,
    dreaming about: 8486, 12137; --, frightened
    by: 375; --, getting rid of: 6372; -- in
    hair: 1435; --, killing: 12137; -- leaving
    house: 6506; --, scared by: 976; -- on
    ship: 7030, 7032; --, white: 10480; -- as
    indicator of winter: 10747; --, witch's
    familiar: 10043
Rat tail: 3211
Rattle, snake: 3570, 3887, 3970
Rattler: 12382
Rattlesnake: 3975, 3977, 10641, 12373ff.,
    12380, 12383f., 12386, 12398, 12401f.,
    12428; --, age of: 12373; -- charming
    birds: 12374; --, dreaming of: 12410; --
    form of devil: 10195; --, feeding: 1199; --
    gall: 2987; -- as guardian: 7554; --,
    holding: 9904; --, killing: 12392; --
    rattlers: 3966, 3970, 10483, 12373; --,
    wearing rattles: 2622; -- skin: 12376; --,
    strike of: 12404ff.
Raven: 3026, 9494, 12312ff.; -- as indicator of
    death: 9493ff.; -- as indicator of rain:
    11070
Raw: 389, 2142, 2155, 2210, 2785
Razor: 6942; -- as gift: 8411
Razor blade: 4388f.
Read: 820, 1012, 1979
Reading: 4082, 5054
Recipe: 5789
Recital, piano: 8627
Recognize: 2189

Rise: 1300

Risk (n.): 317

Ritual: 9660; -- cure: 2926f., 2940, 2946, 2952, 3136, 3167, 3220, 3260, 3262, 3281f., 3293, 3319, 3364, 3396, 3457, 3656, 3718, 3786, 3855f., 3882, 3885, 3889, 3976, 4068, 4094, 4146, 4169, 4176, 4208ff.

River: 263, 1904, 9593, 9698, 9701, 11454, 11494, 11840, 12171, 12417; --, bathing in: 2635; --, crossing twice: 9768; --, drinking from: 11470; --, fishing in: 8932; --, throwing ashes into: 9816; --, throwing woman into: 10054; --, washing in: 3235

Roaches: 6367

Road, forks of: 12595; -- as indicator of storm: 11252; --, intersection of: 10086; --, middle of: 4366; --, peeing in: 4135; --, pissing in: 4427; --, urinating in: 3143, 4087

Road runner: 9510

Roadway, disposal in: 4263

Robber: 7559

Robbery: 7548

Robbing: 5227

Robin: 11925, 12275ff.; --, first: 12277, 12283; -- as indicator of death: 9482ff.; --, killing: 3499, 12286f.; --, origin of redbreast: 12275; --, seeing: 7438; --, singing of: 9482; -- as sign of spring: 10681ff.; --, stamping: 12283f.; -- as indicator of weather: 10856, 10973, 11061, 11417, 11449; -- at window: 9147

Rock (n.): 3831, 4365, 4962, 6759, 6917, 8249, 11494, 11809ff., 13181; --, black: 7070, 11487; --, burying bean under: 4255; --, burying dishrag under: 4313; --, grey: 11488; --, hot: 3234; --, origin of: 11476, 11486; -- in shoe: 10582; --, spitting on: 2913, 3951, 4363; --, rubbing wart with: 4312, 4361, 4364; --, white: 9835

Rock candy: 3204, 3733

Rocking (vb.): 60, 572, 1014, 1084, 2559

Rockwell, Porter: 3544, 7586

Rocky Mountain oysters: 2236

Rodent: 374

Rodeo: 8835ff.; -- arena: 8847; -- equipment: 8841

Roman: 11341; -- blood: 8757; -- Catholic: 9660

Romance: 5120; -- breaking up: 5072, 5115, 5118, 5120, 5124

Romantic: 843

Rome: 7886, 11856

Roof: 697, 6250, 12184, 12496, 13021; -- of car: 7892; --, leaking of: 6528; --, new: 6253; --, stork nesting on: 12309; --, tin: 6418; --, touching: 7846

Rooftop: 7

Room, cleaning: 2646; --, dark: 266; --, entering/leaving: 6307; --, sick person's: 2650ff.; --, sleeping in: 1994

Roosevelt, President: 9196

Roost, ruling the: 5700

Rooster: 7248, 12192ff., 12666, 12668, 13019; --, black: 10481; --, blood of: 10135; -- crowing: 7531, 7934, 8142ff., 8146ff., 8494, 8662, 9423ff., 9428, 12194ff., 13023; --, feeding bean to: 4264; -- fighting: 8145; -- laying eggs: 12673; --, looking at: 3427; -- predicting future: 2247, 2875, 4966, 7533, 10074, 10149, 10423, 10481; -- stones: 10481; -- as indicator of weather: 10878, 11265f.   See also Cock

Root: 10028, 13181f.; --, bamboo: 11498; --, cactus: 2773; --, calomel: 4058; --, cattail: 3049; --, dandelion: 3038; --, ginseng: 2732, 12880; --, grape: 3146; --, hops: 3038; --, rhubarb: 2734; --, rose: 3405; --, sego lily: 2740; --, take: 1491; --, violet: 12900; --, wild cherry: 3132; --, wild grape: 2752

Rope: 1323, 1330, 12384ff., 12422; -- breaking in a hanging: 7593; -- of suicide victim: 7598

Rosary: 1843

Rose: 4675ff., 4934, 5065, 5126; --, first: 12909; --, red: 3032, 4674, 12908, 12910f.; --, roots of: 3405; --, white: 12907

"Rose cold": 3179

Rose leaf: 12906

Rosemary: 5472, 5483

Rose shape: 9315

Rose water: 1447, 2146, 4763, 4827

Rosin: 8844; -- box: 7202

Rosy: 1521ff.

Rot (vb.): 3293, 4234, 4238, 4251, 4266, 4274, 4279, 4296f., 4303, 4308, 4326, 4341, 4344, 4350, 4356.   See also Decay

Rotten: 4321

Roulette: 8617ff.

Round steak: 4052

Row (n.): 2056, 4843ff., 13001, 13028, 13079f., 13143

Royal: 1727

Rub (vb.): 271, 358, 402, 913, 931f., 1049, 1089, 1120, 1126, 1408, 1447, 1469, 1542, 1593, 1911

Rubarb Indian Speufick: 1133

Rubber: 10286

Rubber band: 4029, 8786

Rubbers (overshoes): 3399

Ruby: 2219, 3002, 3933, 6887f.

Rug: 6224f., 10315; --, white: 6481

Ruin (n.): 7524

Rum: 1447, 2981

Run (vb.): 1045, 1628

Runner: 12773, 12824

Running: 8799

Runs (football): 8760

Russia: 9996

Russian: 8624

Rust: 2254

Rusty: 754

Rye noodles: 2486

Sabbath, born on: 425; --, cutting fingernails on: 1706; --, housework on: 6215; --, sewing on: 6567; --, working on: 6965, 13141.   See also Sunday

"Sabre salve": 4464.   See also Weapon salve

Sack: 3628, 4260, 6546; --, burying: 4364; --, paper: 3232, 3625, 12621

Sacrifice (n.): 12595

Sacrifice (vb.): 653

Sad: 413, 882, 1558

Saddle: 4114

Saddlebag: 13

Saddle soap: 8844

Saddle sore: 12817

Sadness: 53, 200, 2583, 4516, 5959, 6883ff.

Safeguard: 1688

Safety: 2047, 6994

Safety pin: 562, 2566

Saffron: 3042, 3200, 3454, 3642; -- tea: 1100f.

lambing: 12858; --, out of: 6486, 9042; --, rainy: 9002
Seat: 6086
Sea water: 2672
Seaweed: 1475; -- as indicator of rain: 11108
Second: 3448, 4641, 7187; -- child: 636; -- helpings: 6105; -- Coming: 9930, 9995, 9998; -- sight: 827, 830
Secrecy: 4304, 4315, 4326, 4364, 4371, 4375
Secret: 1891, 2473, 5790, 6047, 8030, 9910, 10176, 12233
Secretly: 121
Sedative: 3377, 3945, 4193
Seduction: 2583
See: 81, 831, 833, 1560, 1564, 1638, 1757, 1834, 1885, 2065ff., 2120, 2162, 2557, 2598, 2658, 4479.  See also Look
Seeds: 19, 124, 2921, 9652, 12998, 13001, 13159f., 13164; --, almond: 13194; --, apple: 565, 2921, 3734, 4686f.; --, cabbage: 13066; --, cherry: 6047; --, dandelion: 1254, 11590; --, grape: 2223, 2921; --, lemon: 2921; --, linen: 4187; -- making pregnant: 108; --, mustard: 10023, 12945; --, orange: 2921; --, passing through shirt: 13118; --, planting: 12976, 12978, 12990, 12992f., 13000, 13003, 13087; --, pomegranate: 33; --, sowing: 13142; --, strawberry: 2921; --, swallowing: 2794; -- of wart: 4422; --, watermelon: 108, 2921, 2991, 3732; -- as indicator of winter: 10767
Seeing: 200, 322, 334, 348, 350f., 4085; -- accident: 354, 963; -- animal: 973; -- birds: 1371; -- black widow: 381; -- cripple: 968; -- cross-eyed person: 997, 1063; -- in the dark: 1552; -- deformed object: 961; -- dog: 409; -- eclipse: 1064; -- fire: 358, 962; -- freak: 352; -- something frightening: 960, 1482; -- into future: 2328; -- man with one leg: 966; -- mouse: 372; -- nut: 398; -- person: 405; -- rabbit: 982f.; -- reptile: 380; -- self: 674, 1008, 1017, 1035, 1107; -- snake: 978; --, taboo of: 4146; -- white cat: 4620; -- white horse: 4622
Seer: 830
Seerstone: 10433
Sego lily roots: 2740
Seizure: 1078.    See also Convulsions; Fits
Selfish: 2443
Sell: 74
Semen: 4191
Senna: 2758; -- leaves: 3303; -- tea: 1102, 3276
Sensation: 405
Sense: 819
Sensitive: 2464
Separate (vb.): 2111
Separation: 5122, 6622, 8521
September: 10741, 11439, 12761; --, marrying in: 5302f.
Sermon: 9210
Serpent: 10462
Serve, tennis: 8807
Serving, the last: 5023
Sesame seeds: 4973, 10663
Settler: 10591
Seven: 605, 1231, 1478, 1751, 1792, 1798, 1962, 2088, 2105, 2117, 4101, 4274, 4332, 4563, 4689, 4844ff., 4983, 5048, 5072, 5186, 5234, 5344, 5848, 5972, 6146, 6321, 6421,

6452, 6456ff., 6675, 7523, 7746, 7756ff., 7772, 7800, 7802, 8257, 8606, 8615, 9978, 9986f., 10588, 10712, 11143, 11535, 11559ff., 11656, 11937, 12030, 12056, 12059, 12098, 12233, 12419, 12478, 12549, 13100; --, counting to: 7697, 12260; -- devils: 12170; -- months: 1327; --, multiples of: 11560; --, unlucky: 8831; -- years: 1240, 1415, 3555, 5201, 5204, 5209, 5526, 6239, 6428, 6454, 6460f., 6463, 6516, 6526, 6752, 6775, 10699
Seven o'clock: 8124, 11187, 11209
Seventeen: 11589
Seventeenth: 440
Seventh: 546, 11469, 11562; -- child: 599; -- daughter: 832; -- son: 600, 830ff., 928, 1295, 1315, 3074; -- year: 5667
Seven-year-itch: 3949f.
Sewer: 6618, 6629
Sewing: 1336, 2426, 2853, 4770, 5034, 5106, 5395, 6554ff., 6561ff., 8450, 9368ff., 9681, 10186; -- ears: 684; -- on Sunday: 5035; -- while wearing garment: 1738, 5105; -- machine: 1336, 11366; -- shut: 1538, 1543, 1588, 1606
"Sewing shut": 1604
Sex: 544, 1981f., 4881; -- of child: 459, 466, 474, 478, 482f., 493, 496, 504, 510, 527f., 538, 543, 547, 550ff.; -- drive: 4975, 4991, 12521; --, illicit: 35; --, opposite: 3077, 3604, 4729, 4761, 4854, 4961, 8234; -- organs: 1634; -- urge: 1984.   See also Intercourse, sexual
Sexual: 2233; -- change: 2231; -- experience: 5134; -- intercourse: 586, 591; -- relations: 113, 184, 458; -- relationship: 2961
Shadow: 46, 3469, 8918, 10126, 10200, 10220, 10333, 10710ff., 11122, 11740, 11960; --, bird's: 12231; --, crossing: 4961; --, dog's: 8937; --, ghost's: 10594; --, groundhog's: 10851, 10905, 10958, 11043, 12169; --, seeing: 9127; --, ship's: 6978; --, stepping on: 2085, 2281; --, witch's: 10048.   See also Image
Shagbark hickory: 3541
Shake: 209
Shampoo: 1432, 1444
Shamrock: 12861, 12875
Shape: 336, 366, 369, 372, 375, 382, 391f.; --, changing: 11908, 12181
Share: 1773
Shark: 7052f.; --, tooth of: 10477
Sharp object: 4953ff., 5093, 5095f., 9616
Shave (n.): 1988, 7149; -- beard: 1622f.; -- legs: 1507f.
Shaving: 1286, 8666, 8894; -- head: 652
Shears under bed: 254.   See also Scissors
Sheep: 10016, 12109ff., 12718, 12805, 12852ff.; --, blood of: 3443; --, counting: 2012; --, disease of: 12737; --, finding drowned body with: 9705; --, meeting: 7727; --, passing through hoop: 12859; -- as indicator of weather: 11042, 11413; --, white: 12110
Sheep droppings: 3451
Sheep dung: 3534
Sheep fertilizer: 2775
Sheepherder: 7136f., 10483, 10833
Sheep intestine: 3278
Sheep manure tea: 3967
Sheet: 6439, 9312; --, changing: 8781; --, cork between: 3316

Shutters: 9254
Sick: 180, 311, 636, 905, 918, 920ff., 1198,
2497, 2513, 2516, 2523, 2529, 2532f.,
2542f., 2545, 2550ff., 2556, 2565, 2578,
2586, 2595, 2607, 2615, 2627, 2629, 2632,
2634f., 2640f., 2642, 2646ff., 2655ff.,
2660, 2662ff., 2667f., 2671, 2694, 3484,
3486, 12585; --, curing: 2685; --, moving:
9136; --, visiting: 9131f.
Sickly baby: 904
Sickly child: 916
Sickness: 310, 926, 2517f., 2526, 2530f., 2534,
2536, 2540, 2558, 2564, 2567ff., 2573,
2580, 2587, 2610, 2625, 2644, 5645, 9516,
9553, 9573, 9640, 12234; -- by conjury:
10096, 10100; -- from evil eye: 10143,
10145f.; --, curing: 2651, 2741, 2750,
2759, 2767, 2790; --, in family: 2538; --,
preventing: 2590, 2616, 2619, 2624; --,
protecting from: 932; --, sign of: 2510,
2524, 2528; --, warding off: 3367
Sick person: 2630, 2639
Sick room: 301
Side: 1083; --, left: 4143, 9226; --, right:
3597, 4057, 7706; --, wrong: 3614
Sideache: 3951f.
Sidehill dodger: 12577
Sidehill wampus cat: 12575
Sides, changing: 8343
Sidewalk: 2071, 2074ff., 2086, 2566, 3745,
4524, 5189, 6238, 8339, 10177, 12174; --,
crack in: 2819; --, sweeping: 6198
Sideways: 527
Sight: 342, 348; --, impaired: 3400; --, loss
of: 3018
Sign: 517, 1788f.; --, astrological: 634,
12980; -- in window: 2602
Signature, in blood: 10219
Signature, doctrine of: 2742
Silence: 4714, 8027ff., 8268, 11739
Silent prayer: 3412
Silk: 4025, 6840, 6913, 7878; --, black: 1074,
3255, 3872, 4341; --, red: 4325, 4337,
8693; -- scarf: 4827; -- stocking: 3230; --
thread: 4323ff., 4331, 4339
Silly: 865
Silver: 281f., 283f., 717, 1182, 1310, 1836,
3270, 3423, 3821, 5332, 5470, 6037, 7267,
7351, 8381, 12233, 12766; -- bullet: 10289,
10326, 10676; -- coin: 5454, 5589, 5760,
6128, 9736, 10562, 11832; -- dollar: 285,
2944, 6265, 6343, 7399, 7400f., 7791,
10561, 11831; --, dreaming of: 7269; --,
giving with sharp object: 8414; --, hiding:
7313; -- knife: 4464, 6127; -- money: 7792;
-- nails: 10662; -- piece: 5178; -- ring:
4100; -- spoon: 12698; --, turning in
pocket: 7390, 11642; --, vein of: 7112; --
warding off witches: 10080; --, killing
witch with: 10083
Silverware: 6108, 8421ff., 11368; --, crossing:
6109; --, dropping: 7959
Similia similibus curantur: 3367, 3969
Sin: 948, 950, 5843, 8083, 8999, 9892, 9923ff.;
--, removal of: 10087
Sincere: 1208, 2373
Sin-eater: 9163
Sing: 234, 848, 852, 860, 1026, 1179, 1224,
1790ff., 2227, 8553, 8631
Singe: 1487
Singeing: 1452
Singer: 851ff., 2234, 2338, 7207, 8630

Singing: 1192, 4726, 9122, 11176, 12720, 13125;
-- in bath: 8643; -- before bed: 11022; --
in bed: 8633, 8644, 10214; -- before
breakfast: 5081, 7222, 8636ff., 9120; -- of
children: 9767; -- at dinner: 8640; -- in
dressing room: 7194; -- in house: 8632,
10260; -- in morning: 8634ff.; -- at the
table: 5011, 5167, 7506, 8639, 8641,
10210ff.; -- in the theater: 7195; -- on
the toilet: 5010
"The Singing Bones": 7583
Single: 5061, 5068
Sink (n.): 5836
Sinus: 3645; -- trouble: 3953f.
Sissy: 781, 874
Sister: 5579, 5581
Sisterhood: 1268
Sister-in-law: 976
Sitting: 512; -- in direction of bathtub: 8575,
8586; -- in one spot: 2887
Six: 448, 1488, 1819, 3260, 4689, 5237, 5727,
7115, 7941, 9113, 9640, 9755, 10687, 10707,
10710, 10712f., 10726, 10809, 10851, 11043,
11143, 11321f., 11451f., 11757, 11949,
12169, 12233f., 12415; --, counting to:
12097; -- hours: 3479; -- months: 278, 769,
1065, 1159, 1325, 1373; -- o'clock: 9663,
11315
Sixpence: 1611; -- in Christmas pudding: 6007;
-- in shoe: 5391, 5447
Sixteen: 4032
Sixteenth: 440
Sixth: 9198; -- sense: 12014
Sixty: 10712
Size: 757
Skaters (insect?): 1398
Skates: 8862f.
Skating: 8862f., 13120
"Skeen dhu": 10287
Ski contest: 8878
Skiing: 8864ff.
Ski lift: 11582
Ski race: 8870, 8872, 8875
Ski season: 11399
Skin, baby's: 1102; --, cancerous: 3134; --,
care of: 1406ff., 2143, 2148, 2152; --,
cat: 3852, 4068, 4176; --, itching: 2323,
8105; --, light colored: 756; --, snake:
2248; --, washing: 3520
Skin ailments: 3955ff.
Skin eruptions: 2756
Skipper of ship: 10405
Skirt: 4598f., 4655, 6762f., 6766, 7962; --,
checkered: 8890; --, hem turned up: 6641f.,
7311; --, long: 7499
Skull: 10429; -- bumps on: 10431; --, releasing
evil spirits from: 2880; --, swearing on:
9653
Skunk: 3178, 8697, 12174; -- fat: 1050; --
odor: 6552f., 6750; -- oil: 3227, 3329,
3853, 3990
Sky: 2540, 5262, 11711; --, blue: 11196; --,
clear: 10882; --, dark: 10832; --, falling:
12259; --, looking at: 10404; --, mackerel:
11249; --, pink: 10825, 10834f., 11428; --,
red: 10822ff., 10832f., 10860, 10928,
10945, 11114, 11247, 11307; --, sheep:
11115; --, yellow: 11112
Slaughterhouse: 3281
Sleep (n.): 881, 1191, 1991ff., 2016ff.,
2022ff., 2499; --, bring on/induce: 739ff.,

2875; --, curing during: 2685; --, talking
in: 2027
Sleep (vb.): 328, 873, 875, 919, 959, 1015,
1284, 1629, 1745, 1761, 1790, 1800,
1820ff., 1863, 1873, 1875, 1882, 1961,
2009ff., 3120
Sleeper: 1807
Sleeping: 1587, 4756, 9591; -- on ant hill:
3136; -- with chihuahua: 2952; -- on cotton
mattress: 5639; -- in dead person's room:
9084; -- with eyes open: 9696; -- in
moonlight: 751, 2855, 2901; -- outside:
3347; -- position: 9080ff.; -- on sage
pillow: 2868; -- with stocking: 2565; --
together: 783, 8110; -- on tooth: 706
Sleeping bag: 12384
Sleeping clothes: 6682
Sleepwalk: 2028
Sleepwalker: 2025, 9085
Sleeve: 2621, 6694
Slice (vb.): 16
Slicker: 9960
Slingshot: 8921
Slip (clothing): 2354, 3891, 4596, 5655, 6685;
--, inside out: 8133; --, showing: 4586;
--, wearing backwards: 6702, 6905; -- as
indicator of weather: 10843.  See also
Petticoat
Slip (plant): 13162
Slip knot: 7126
Slippers: 6825; --, drinking out of: 1917; --
as gift: 6793, 8370; --, right: 5447
Slippery elm: 3304, 3541; -- tea: 2754, 3957.
See also Elm
Sliver: 3958ff.
Slob: 8092, 8194
Slot: 7379; -- machine: 8593f.
Slow, mentally: 917
Slug (animal): 12573f.
Slug, metal: 2073
Smaller: 767
Smallpox: 3964ff., 4174
Smart (adj.): 808, 812f., 1384, 2318ff.
Smell (vb.): 137, 142, 171, 207, 212, 1366,
2091
Smile (n.): 743, 7230, 9724, 9936; -- causing
blindness: 3015
Smile (vb.): 1400
Smith, Joseph: 3544, 7990, 10007; -- the
killing of: 10024
Smoke (n.): 278, 2115, 2134, 3666, 8022, 8024,
11208; --, blowing into ear: 1076, 3587;
--, cigarette: 3393; --, dreaming of: 1848;
--, inhalation of: 2593, 2677; --, pipe:
3393; -- rings: 7252; --, smelling of:
8927; --, tobacco: 2727; -- as indicator of
weather: 10842, 10943, 10965, 11161f.,
11288f., 11325
Smoke (vb.): 2033f.
Smoking (n.): 196, 221ff., 766f., 1884, 2170,
2498, 6324, 7166, 7252; -- causing cancer:
3114; -- mullein: 4012; -- of newborn: 278;
-- of person: 278
Snail: 2229, 12572
Snake: 3540, 3570, 5867, 9516f., 11920,
12345ff., 12435, 12505, 12890; --, black:
11185, 11344; --, blind: 12351; --,
burying: 11276; -- crawling over grave:
9051; -- crossing path: 378; --, cutting in
half: 12393f., 12397; --, dead: 12408; --,
dreaming of: 1982, 2524, 4643, 8498ff.,
8505ff., 9517, 12409ff.; -- drinking milk:
12370; --, dying: 12397ff.; --, eating:
2278; --, eyes of: 1095; --, feeding:
1198f.; --, handling of: 12359; --, hanging
on fence: 11072; --, head of: 10153; --,
from horsehair: 12413ff.; --, killing:
8502, 9928f., 9978, 11071, 11073, 12387ff.;
--, killing to cause rain: 11185; --, legs
of: 12346; --, looking in eye of: 12352f.;
--, mate of: 12395f.; --, poisonous: 12362;
--, protecting from: 6496; --, scared by:

376; --, seeing: 408, 978, 4644; --,
shedding tail: 12365; --, snow: 8864; --
stealing cow's milk: 12371f.; --, stepping
on: 12360; --, sting of: 12407, 12425; --
sucking eggs: 12369; --, swallowing young:
12356; --, tail of: 12390, 12397f.; --,
touching: 379; --, warding off: 12379ff.;
--, whip: 12357.  See also Black snake;
Bull snake; Garter snake
Snake bite: 1108, 3968ff., 3977ff., 3981ff.,
8504ff., 9517, 12412
"Snake eyes": 8616
Snake fat: 3969
Snake feeder: 12505
Snake food: 12893
Snake grass: 12348
Snake oil: 3348, 3886
Snake rattles: 3887
Snakeroot: 12379
Snakeskin: 10153, 12363; --, rubbing in hand:
6149; -- preventing fire: 6415
Snake track: 12361f.
Snakeweed: 2781, 12348, 12890
Sneaky: 2435
Sneeze (n.): 2037, 10215
Sneeze (vb.): 1194, 1746, 1779, 1823, 1956,
2036, 2038ff., 2043ff., 2050ff., 2506f.,
2600, 2638, 2888, 4541ff., 8044, 9754,
10276
Sneezing: 1530, 7073, 7247, 7955, 8124ff.,
8341, 9103ff., 10216; -- before breakfast:
6903, 8125; -- of cat: 3177, 5338, 12615;
-- five times: 8128; -- four times: 9108;
-- during sermon: 9210; -- seven times:
9109; --, spirit leaving body: 10253; -- on
Sunday: 2866; -- three times: 5002, 7299,
7458, 7954, 8128; --, travel portent: 7634;
-- as indicator of weather: 10966; --
during wedding: 9210; -- on wedding day:
5363, 5367f.
Sniff: 2677.  See also Inhale
Snore: 2061
Snow (n.): 2501, 6369, 10692, 10761, 10772,
10811, 10985, 10996, 11338, 11397ff.,
11424ff., 13016, 13119; --, explanation of:
11401ff., 11407; --, first: 1936, 3154,
3414, 3545, 11395, 11436; --, heavy: 10742;
--, indicators of: 11411ff., 11418ff.; --,
last: 3415; --, March: 1441; -- applied to
neck: 3811; --, rubbing with: 3157; --,
running in: 3524; -- while sun is shining:
11405f., 11427; -- on wedding day: 5267,
5269
Snow (vb.): 9863
Snow blindness: 3431
Snowdrift: 11400
Snowfall: 11399
Snowflake: 11426
Snow snake: 8864
Snowstorm: 10683, 11243, 11417, 11435, 13015;
--, first: 11396, 11423; -- on wedding day:
5268
Snuff: 12587
Soap: 3547, 3661, 3705, 6172, 7489, 8466, 9376;
--, borrowing: 6171; --, laundry: 3069; --,
making: 6173f.; -- in poultice: 2782, 3962;
-- and water: 8273
Soapweed tea: 3912
Soccer: 8895; -- match: 8894
Society: 12936
Socks: 1172, 6826, 8743ff., 8765, 8771, 12481;
--, athletic: 8678; --, basketball: 8790;
--, brick in: 3233; --, two different
colors: 8672; --, dirty: 3230, 3242, 3998,
4030, 8768f., 8790; --, golf: 8821; --,
hanging: 1872; --, hole in: 8129; -- around
neck: 3799; --, old: 3242; --, onion in:
3719; --, putting on: 6648; --, red: 4031;
--, right: 8682; --, soiled: 4031; --,
washing: 8673f.; --, wool: 3230, 3330,
3997, 4031, 4134; --, wrong side out: 6675,
6695

Soda: 119, 2998, 3213, 3699, 6552; -- fountain: 7239; -- pop: 3864; -- water: 1105
Softball: 8698
Soil (n.): 4280, 6553, 10296, 12961, 13144; --, strange: 7623; --, swallowing: 2797
Solan goose: 6975
Solder: 10415
Soldier: 7688, 9347; --, dreaming of: 1885
Sole of shoe: 4421, 8063
Solitaire: 6875
Son, oldest: 9274; --, seventh: 3074, 11562
Song: 852, 1179, 9121f., 11736; -- bird: 5349; --, school: 8782
Song book: 8628
Sons: 569; -- of Perdition: 10012
Soot: 1170, 1647, 3000, 5337, 8206f., 10841, 12587; --, chimney: 145. See also Lamp black
Sorcerer: 10244
Soreness: 3089, 3091, 3098
Sores: 3956, 3985ff.; --, body: 2719; --, cancer: 3132; --, festering: 3647; --, mouth: 3791; --, running: 3943
Sore throat: 1109
Sorority: 1268f.
Sorrow: 1085, 1436, 1558, 2047, 5256, 5634, 5907, 5943, 6194, 6574, 6591, 8216, 11398
Soul: 89, 624, 1194, 1417, 6455, 6992, 9313, 9575, 9585, 9714, 9716, 9722, 9746, 9753, 9772, 9817, 9828, 9866, 9887, 9966ff., 9984, 10058, 10244, 10460, 10604, 12593; -- of the dead: 12307; --, devil coming for: 10206; --, devil in: 2879; -- going up in flames: 9717; --, injured: 2281; -- leaving body: 1807, 2025, 9172; --, new: 259; --, possession of: 1227, 2282, 2284; --, restless: 10405
Souls, seven: 9978
Sound (n.): 10264
Soup: 7956, 8145; --, boiling: 2213, 6963; --, bread: 265; --, making: 5822
Sour: 413, 1915, 1973, 8920; -- cream: 1621
Sourkraut: See Kraut; Sauerkraut
South: 1894, 4647, 7631, 8970, 9821, 9943, 10919, 10936, 10971, 11319, 11503, 13002f., 12208; --, direction of sleeping: 1414, 2017, 2019
Southeast: 11416
South Pacific: 7139
Soybeans: 2166, 3197, 6011
Spade (card suit): 9628ff.
Spade (tool): 9363. See also Shovel
Spaghetti: 4702
Spanish: 7136, 10308; -- wedding: 5726
Spanked: 1237
Spark (husband): 4734
Sparks: 4779, 6402, 7960f., 11731
Sparrow: 7630, 13155; -- as indicator of death: 9485ff.; --, killing: 12265; --, singing: 9485
Spasm: 1081
Speak: 1091, 2068, 4652, 4755, 4818
Speaking: 11529; -- of last shift in mine: 7094; -- about someone: 11523; --, taboo of: 8619; -- in unison: 5359, 8001ff., 8012ff., 8019ff., 8530; --, without: 4759, 6335, 12077. See also Talking, without
Spear: 11347
Spearmint tea: 2009, 2757, 3675, 3957, 4062
Specks on fingernails: 1694
Spectacles: 10425
Speculation: 7305

Speech: 744f., 7990ff.; -- of animals: 836; --, loss of: 2690
Spell (n.): 1760, 5358, 6520, 6569, 7753, 7766, 7769ff.; --, bad: 1197, 7711; --, breaking: 10130, 12003; --, casting: 10097, 10112; --, evil: 1195; --, magic: 10093, 12445; --, warding off: 10120ff.
Spelling, of name: 8886
Spend: 2389
Spendthrift: 2388f.
Spice: 4977, 9747; --, medicinal use of: 1058; -- around neck: 10294
Spice bag: 713
Spider: 4356, 7908, 7975f., 8155f., 12532ff., 12745; -- on bed: 8156; --, black: 7344, 9536, 12539, 12547f.; --, burning: 2230; -- on clothing: 6753; -- crossing path: 7346; --, dreaming of: 7342, 8511; -- in hair: 1504; -- in house: 7343; -- as indicator of gold: 10463; --, killing: 2567, 7348f., 7524, 9536, 11097, 12548f.; -- on neck: 3262, 4151; --, seeing: 7919; --, stepping on: 3498, 7156, 12546f.; -- as indicator of weather: 11093ff., 11286; -- on wedding dress: 4651; --, white: 7345, 7976, 9537, 12538, 12546. See also Black widow
Spider bite: 3711ff., 12558
Spider web: 2950, 3000, 6264, 7440, 8155, 12562ff.; -- in house: 7347; -- as indicator of rain: 11092. See also Cobwebs
Spike: 13198
Spilling: 513, 1918, 2267, 5919f.
Spin: 532, 542, 1323
Spinach: 779, 1467, 1512, 1641, 2177, 2255; --, planting: 13069
Spine, ailments of: 4033f.; --, breaking: 4034; --, curved: 4033; --, mother's: 4034; --, father's: 4034
Spinning: 1317, 7064; -- wheel: 1323, 5874, 6640
Spinster: 5069. See also Old maid
Spinsterhood: 4995ff.
Spirit, of murdered person: 7583; --, possession of: 2282
Spirits: 20, 1177, 3665, 3681, 5428, 5430, 5871, 6193, 6227, 6345, 6432, 6539, 7066, 7427, 9192, 9643, 9654, 9708, 9712, 9716, 9721, 9725, 9730, 9808, 9814, 9816, 9832, 9840, 9870, 9883, 9897, 9900, 9911, 9973, 10265, 10268, 10360, 10530, 10566, 10596f., 10607f., 10610, 10613, 10615, 10617, 10623, 10626, 10628, 10632f., 10655, 10657, 10661, 10663, 10666, 11983; --, ancestral: 610; --, bad: 2128; --, banishing: 6011; --, breaking: 6455; -- clothed in white: 10640; --, exorcizing: 2705; --, hearing: 831; -- leaving body: 1808, 2025, 2036, 2043f.; --, losing: 2284; --, messengers of: 12219; --, night: 6579; --, releasing: 2693; --, residence of: 10622; --, seeing: 831, 835; --, summoning: 10629, 10631; --, warding off: 10129. See also Evil spirit
Spiritual being: 10593
Spiritualist: 7067
Spiritual world: 10612
Spirit world: 747, 10618
Spit (n.): 1044, 3069, 3633, 3698, 3702; --, locating lost object: 6951ff.; -- of toad: 4198. See also Saliva
Spit (vb.): 272ff., 401, 510, 663, 1573, 1644, 1773, 2062ff., 3092, 3288, 3343, 3378, 3446, 3586, 3630, 3951f., 4090f., 4304,

4359, 4363, 4370, 4394, 4426, 5000, 6510,
6642, 6698, 6713, 6715, 6720, 6760, 6909,
6951ff., 7191, 11468, 11488ff., 11510,
11602, 11638, 11662, 11915, 11926, 12019,
12026ff., 12043, 12094, 12096, 12390
Spite (n.): 1535, 8294
"Spit fire": 2369
Spitting: 6863, 7699, 7759ff., 7765, 7875,
12810, 13010, 13169; -- on baseball bat:
8719; -- in baseball mitt: 8720; -- on
bull's head: 8846; -- on dice: 8613; -- in
fire: 9981; -- on fishing bait: 8979; -- on
fish hook: 8978, 8980; -- on fishing worm:
8978; -- in hand: 4522, 4622, 7244, 7327,
8670; -- on home plate: 8736; -- on marble:
8896; -- on money: 7251; -- on rock: 2913;
-- over shoulder: 12080; -- into wind: 9005
Spleen: 4035; --, pig's: 10716
Splinter: 7570
Split (in bowling): 8888
Split end: 1452
Split lip: 987
Spoil: 947
Sponge: 3535
Spontaneous generation: 12523
Spook (n.): 10670
Spool: 535
Spoon: 3270, 4737f., 5744, 9268, 12706; --
burying: 4326; -- under chair: 512; --,
dropping: 59, 6138ff., 7959, 8176, 8184;
--, extra: 58; -- on eye: 3423; --, picking
up: 6142; --, silver: 283f., 5761; -- on
table: 589; --, two: 5715, 6277
Sporting equipment: 8692
Sporting teams: 8686
Sports: 4809, 8663ff.
Sports car race: 8834
Sports coat: 6635
Sportsmanship: 8802
Spot (n.): 351, 398, 468
Spots, black: 9421, 12634; -- on fingernails:
1694, 2383; -- on nose: 1590; --, white:
4503, 6902, 7615, 8334, 8826, 10428, 12773
"Spotting dead": 8897
Spouse: 4624, 5301, 9329, 9757; --, dominant:
5694ff.; --, dreaming of: 4747f., 4752; --,
future: 4707, 4741, 4795, 4802, 4813; --,
loss of: 5682ff.
Sprain: 4036ff.
Spring (season): 2488, 2494, 3412, 4641, 6751,
6878, 7138, 7438, 8507, 9473, 9579,
10678ff., 10695, 10705, 10707, 10710,
10770, 10991, 11338, 11424, 11440, 11455,
12212, 12464, 12466, 12470f., 12895, 12946,
13059; --, hearing bird in: 12271; --,
seeing bird in: 12277, 12283, 12297; --,
first day of: 3511, 4104; --, flowers
gathered in: 4661; --, time of conception:
903
Spring (water): 4798, 10246, 10259, 12439; --,
drinking from: 1906; --, finding a: 10448
Spring fever: 4044ff.
Springtime: 1987, 12111, 12909
Spring tonic: 3044
Spunky: 2457
Spurs: 7133, 8842
Spy (vb.): 1891
Squash: 13131; --, planting: 13129
Squirrel: 10717f.; --, crossing path: 7731; --,
dead: 6496; --, ear of: 13095; --,
hibernation of: 10742; --, hunting: 9018;
--, tail of: 1164; -- as indicator of
winter: 10743ff.
Stabbing, death from: 9616
Stable (n.): 12601, 12804
Staff of life: 9300
Stage: 7157f., 7166f., 7176, 7178, 7180
Stain, fruit: 6229
Stairs: 498, 1300, 1628, 4792, 5186ff.,
6350ff., 10610; --, burying dishrag under:
4309; --, falling down: 815, 1002; --,
falling up: 97; --, meeting someone on:
9115; --, tripping up: 7300

Stake: 2071, 10341
Stammer: 1113f.
Stammering: 4082
Stamp (n.): 7979ff., 9623
Stamp (vb.): 687
Stamping: 7802f., 7817, 7830, 7876; -- cars:
4900; -- hand: 4622f.
Stand (vb.): 113
Standing: 300; -- baby: 993; -- on head: 1059
Star: 4843, 9582ff., 11651ff., 11735; --, born
under: 7430; -- as child: 11706; --,
counting: 10228; --, design of: 3798; --,
determining character: 855; --, evening:
11658; --, falling: 89, 4847ff., 7355ff.,
7478, 7884, 9584ff., 10604, 11309, 11329,
11676ff., 11687ff.; --, four in a row:
4842; -- foretelling future: 10413; -- as
indicator of death: 9582ff.; -- as
indicator of frost: 11447; --, looking at:
4840ff.; --, morning: 4844; --, pointing
at: 4204, 9919, 11682; --, position of:
1293, 11727; -- as indicator of rain:
11110, 11130, 11132; --, shooting: 2658,
4849, 7479, 7886, 11677, 11695f.; -- as
indicator of storm: 11230; -- as indicator
of weather: 10821, 10871, 10890; --,
wishing on: 11658, 11661ff., 11668ff.
Starboard: 6985. See also Right
Starches (n.): 1940
Stare (n.): 736
Stare (vb.): 681, 843, 2065, 2290, 3942, 4084,
4841
Staring: 2886; --, cause of blindness: 3014; --
at moon: 382
Starling: 12261
Star sign: 3130
Starvation: 6024
Starving: 6135
Statue: 51, 7378, 7652, 8687, 10643; -- of
elephant: 12126
Status quo: 10545
Steak: 3422, 5778, 5862, 5909; --, burying:
4239; --, external application of: 4241.
See also Beefsteak
Steal: 326, 877, 1166, 1324, 3891
Stealing: 7557, 7562, 13161f., 13183, 13186; --
bacon: 4231; -- dishrag: 4164, 4295f.,
4309; -- dishcloth: 4299; -- hair: 4964; --
handkerchief: 4319; -- lima bean: 4254; --
meat: 4240; -- potato: 4278; -- as ritual
cure: 3293
Steam: 11153
Steamboat: 9957, 12771
Steam hut: 2635
Steel: 3421, 10084, 10674, 12405; -- in baby's
cradle: 1165; -- protection from
thunderstorm: 11384
Steel bar: 5931
Steer (n.): 12757
Stem: 8050; --, onion: 714
Stenographer: 7146
Step (n.): 2107; --, first: 6649
Step ladder: 6515. See also Ladder
Stepmother: 1210f.
Stepping: over afterbirth: 304; -- on ant:
3835; -- over baby: 763; -- on black
square: 1288; -- on bread: 5843; -- over
broom: 5039, 6209ff.; -- over child: 761,
1383; -- on contractor's marking: 7118; --
on crack: 1200, 1287, 9110; -- on cracker:
3492; -- on dart: 3602; -- over dead body:
10265; -- over dog: 364; -- over feet:
6187; -- over fishing line: 8974; -- over
fishing pole: 8975f.; -- on foot: 5486,
5698f.; -- in footprints: 3557; -- on foul
line: 8701; -- on granddaddy-longlegs:
3498; -- over grave: 1342, 2173; -- over
gun: 9023; -- on heel: 5125; -- on hole:
3784; -- on iron: 778, 1302; -- on knife:
6124; -- over legs: 293, 5003; -- on line:
4034, 6066, 6238, 7397, 8804; -- on
manhole: 5113; -- on/over nails: 126, 7565;

-- over person: 762, 2005, 2079; -- on
pomegranate: 5554; -- on rails: 5109; -- on
rusty nail: 3866f.; -- on shadow: 2281; --
on spider: 3498, 7156; -- on/over stone:
3493, 3507; -- over threshold: 987
Steps, five: 2808; --, retracing: 6735, 8531;
--, stumbling at: 8094
Sterile: See Barren
Sterility: 34ff., 42ff., 91, 5559f.; --,
overcoming: 50ff.
Stew: 1511
Stick: 5129, 6330, 7135, 8274, 8932; --, green:
4349f.; --, forked: 7084, 10444, 10449ff.;
--, measuring with: 1069; --, notching:
4345, 4347; --, pointing at person: 10096;
-- tying women to: 251
Stick pin: 6893
Stillbirth: 290ff., 296ff., 301, 1390
Stimulate: 1261
Sting, insect: 3687
Stinging nettle: 3862f.
Stingy: 873, 2442f., 2445ff.
Stink beetle: 12529
Stink bug: 11091, 12530
Stitch: 61, 5398, 5734, 6639, 8075, 9371
Stitches, taking out: 6563, 6565; --, taking
out with nose: 6566, 6636; --, taking out
with teeth: 6567
Stock: 12739
Stocking: 4609; --, black: 4211; --, bride's:
5558; --, hole in: 6827, 7963; --, left:
6657; --, losing: 6906; --, putting
on/taking off: 6657ff.; --, silk: 3230; --,
ski: 8877; --, sleeping with: 2565, 3879;
-- around throat: 3085; --, wrong side out:
6684, 10076
Stocking cap: 2977
Stock market, crash of: 11730
Stolen: 4047
Stomach: 239, 478, 528, 533, 1747, 2546, 2656,
4699; -- turning black: 1750; --, book on:
817; -- covered with cat skin: 2927; --,
curd in: 1088; --, dishwater on: 5031,
8188; --, full: 13089; --, gas in: 1056;
--, gum in: 2552; --, madstone in: 12117;
--, pains: 305; --, plants growing in:
2797; --, rubbing: 99, 5749; --, rooster's:
10481; --, seeds growing in: 108; --,
sleeping on: 328, 1629; --, sour: 4072; --,
touching: 339; -- ulcers in: 4185; --,
uneasy feeling in: 9058; --, wetting: 571;
--, worms in: 2792, 4448, 4450
Stomachache: 1110, 3562, 4047ff., 4055ff. See
also Bellyache
Stomach flu: 3673
Stomach lining: 3123
Stomp: 2339
Stone: 776, 2659, 3931, 4231, 4363, 5619,
11490ff., 11495, 12959; --, blood on: 3830;
--, blue: 3001, 3591, 3712; --, burying
string under: 4334; --, cold: 4163; --,
finding: 6940; --, hot: 3462; --, jade:
1052; --, red: 8355; --, rooster: 2247,
2875, 4966, 10481; --, spitting on: 4359;
--, stepping on/over: 3493, 3507; --,
turning into: 10665; --, rubbing on wart:
4263, 4360; --, white: 10149. See also
Toad stone
Storage house: 6268
Storekeeper: 7235
Stories, ghost: 193

Stork: 7ff., 82f., 12308ff.; -- bringing
children: 590; -- in chimney: 7439; --,
killing: 12311; -- preventing fire: 6416
Storm: 5074, 5266, 7064, 7676, 8963, 9381,
9901, 10404, 10591, 10865, 11069, 11209ff.,
11291ff., 11361, 11380, 11388, 11426,
11996, 12703; --, animal indicators of:
11256ff.; --, calling up: 7014; --,
causing: 7027; --, eating during: 11370f.;
--, first: 9577; --, foretelling: 7050; --,
frightened by: 407; --, indicator of:
11215, 11227ff.; --, smoke: 11288ff.; --,
standing in: 1484
Stove: 5737, 5980, 6175, 6227, 11823; --, coal:
5751; -- as indicator of snow: 11410; --,
washing dishes on: 5032
Stranger: 5288, 7706, 8091, 8112ff., 8147,
8156, 8160, 8187, 8198, 8207, 8213, 8220,
8254; --, accepting food from: 5835; -- in
black: 9650; --, kissing: 1956, 2047f.; --,
meeting: 4746, 7716, 8134; --, shaking
hands with: 1662
Strangle: 1330ff., 1336
Strangulation: 4074ff.
Straw: 6, 6948, 9431, 12431; --, broom: 4406,
8198; --, drinking: 2122, 4660, 4855f.
Strawberries: 175, 666, 755, 1879, 12957; --,
craving: 392; --, dreaming of: 9287; --,
planting: 10924
Strawberry birthmark: 324, 336, 392
Strawberry ice cream: 667
Strawberry patch: 393
Strawberry seeds: 2921
Streak: 351
Stream: 79, 3412, 3523, 4360, 11488, 12116; --,
crossing: 4752, 7894; --, disposing hair
in: 1488; --, looking into: 4800; --,
running: 4346. See also Water
Street: 2094, 2110, 7742; --, crossing: 2602,
2808, 7780; --, defecating in: 4088; --,
urinating in: 4203
Street car: 7869
Strength: 578, 778ff., 783, 2245ff., 2250ff.,
2261ff., 9004; --, losing: 6028; --,
sapping: 783, 2629
Stretch: 329
Striding, over broom: 105. See also Stepping
over
Strife: 8430
Strike, in bowling: 8889; --, fish: 8989; --,
second: 8724; -- out: 8710ff.
Strike (vb.): 1215
String: 527, 529ff., 540f., 1334, 2624, 3164,
3819f., 4032, 4340, 4828, 6740; --,
breaking: 6167; --, buckskin: 3800; --,
burning: 2683, 10237; --, burying: 4321f.,
4326f., 4332ff., 4336; --, chewing: 2853;
--, cutting: 4943, 7480; --, determining
sex of child by: 534; -- around finger:
1680, 2833, 3508, 4104, 6908; -- around
infection: 3665; -- around injury: 3681;
--, knotting: 3166, 3333; --, loose: 6739;
--, measuring with: 8902; -- around neck:
3256; --, red: 10156; --, silk: 8693; --
around toe: 4143; --, throwing away: 7525;
-- around wart: 4320ff.; --, wearing: 125;
--, wool: 3799; -- turning into worm: 8982;
-- around wrist: 4104
String beans: 13028
Stroke (n.): 4079; --, golf: 8810
Strong: 2450ff.
Stronger: 544

Swallow (vb.): 108, 176, 1633, 1749, 2132, 3609ff.
Swallow's nest: 10925
Swamp: 10348, 11502
"Swamper": 6186
Swamp fog: 3445
Swamp needle: 1604
Swan: 9511, 12209f.; -- song: 12210
Swear: 1228, 4826, 8040ff., 10169
Swearing: 1229, 5612, 5948, 9656, 9928; --, cure from: 1229; -- on skull: 9653
Sweater: 4775, 8878; --, wearing backwards: 6704
Sweatshirt: 8679, 8741f.
Swede: 8622
Sweep: 5142, 5148, 5151
Sweeping: 5207f., 5616, 6175, 6178ff., 6190ff., 7471, 7510, 8098f., 8196, 8201, 8444, 9329, 9331, 9719, 11796; -- of baby: 759; -- under bed: 313, 9328; --, cause of blindness: 3018; -- under chair: 7470; -- after dark: 9327, 13168; -- in doorway: 5038; -- of face: 275; -- over/under feet: 514, 749, 5036f., 5206, 7567; -- friends away: 8470f.; -- on Good Friday: 6216; -- on New Year's: 6200f.; -- at night: 8200, 10030; -- under someone: 6186ff.; -- after sunset: 10189
Sweet: 1154, 2397, 7996
Sweet balsam: 3042, 3200, 3454, 3642. See also Balsam
Sweetheart: 1709, 3464, 4467, 4505, 4541f., 4553, 4577f., 4596, 4602, 4636, 4647f., 4663, 4776, 4784, 4794, 4840, 4938, 5093, 6864, 7977; --, dead: 10603; --, dreaming of: 4743, 4762; --, loss of: 5089f., 5103f., 5112, 5119, 5125
Sweet oil: 3382
Sweet peas: 13185
Sweet potato: 9546; -- plant: 2568
Sweets: 483, 6274, 9748; --, craving: 484; -- causing diabetes: 3349
Swell (vb.): 139, 157, 1423
Swelling: 3698, 3793, 3862, 4039, 4110ff.; -- of eye: 3422; --, prevent: 9741
"Sewing shut": 1604
Swift (bird): 12295. See also Chimney swift
Swim: 1461
Swimmer: 2132, 8858
Swimming: 1398, 2497, 3865, 3985, 8859f., 9691, 11787; --, dream about: 8857, 9595; --, during menstruation: 2800
Swimming cramps: 3322
Swing (vb.): 528, 536
Switch (n.): 1551
Swollen: 462
Sword: 10137
Sword fish: 10474
Syphilis: 4113f. See also Venereal disease
Syrup: 3084, 3132, 3202, 3306, 4437; --, horehound: 3299
"Syrup of rhubarb": 2758
System: 3477; --, bodily: 1752, 1938, 3137, 3207

Tabasco sauce: 3201
Table: 4497; --, baby on: 1359; --, booties on: 1141; --, dinner: 6091, 6156; --, feet on: 8337; --, hat on: 6787; --, key on: 6533; --, knocking on: 6421; --, laughing at: 1801; --, raincoat on: 6771; --, seating at: 2560, 6082ff.; --, setting of: 58f.,

6109, 6117f., 6133, 8185f.; --, shoes on: 1365, 6808, 7501, 7590, 8365f., 9230f.; --, singing at: 860, 1791, 4537, 4726, 5011, 5167, 7506, 8641; --, sitting at/on: 4725, 4727ff., 5028f., 5104, 5169, 5199ff., 5705, 5717, 6049, 6382, 6420, 6422; --, sneezing at: 1823, 9103; --, spilling something on: 513, 5656, 5944, 5982; --, sweeping under: 6189; --, thirteen at: 9260ff., 11576; --, umbrella on: 6522; --, walking around: 8579, 8598; --, whistling at: 8647
Tablecloth: 1174, 8580; --, shaking: 5033, 6081; --, shaking after dark: 6080, 10263
Tablespoon: 2144, 6907
Tablet: 2728
Taboo, against iron: 9199; -- against taking picture: 8694, 9762; -- against turning head: 9205; -- against washing hands: 9012; --, wife on hunting trip: 8996; --, woman on fishing trip: 8928
Taboo day: 6964
Tack: 2964
Tag alder tea: 3043
Tail, of cat: 4094, 4213, 4619; -- of child: 975; -- of cow: 12767; -- of horse: 4454, 5193; -- of rabbit: 10502; -- of rat: 3211; --, red: 4630; -- of squirrel: 1164
Tailor: 8018
Take: 334. See also Steal
Talent: 840
Talisman: 10504
Talk (vb.): 995
Talk about: 1541, 3161, 3603, 4467, 4572, 4603, 7657, 8212, 8281, 8283, 8286ff., 8292ff., 8296ff., 8302, 8307, 8315ff.; 8325, 8332, 8340f., 8342, 8352, 8357, 8369, 8389, 8439, 8685, 8998, 9031; --, dreams: 1817
Talkative: 748
Talking: 7834, 8213; -- to one's self: 7258, 10182; --, without: 4760. See also Speaking, without
Tall: 764, 776, 2178ff., 2203, 2302, 2346
Tallow: 1049, 3764; --, buffalo: 3155, 3837; --, goat: 3222; --, mutton: 3155, 4459
Tan: 3518
Tannic acid: 3096
Tansy tea: 1111, 2957, 3727, 3957
Tape measure: 1152, 6629
Tapeworm: 4115. See also Worms
Tapioca pudding: 2995
Tar: 6728, 8760; --, eating: 3150
Tarantula bite: 3713, 9538
Tattoo: 7006
Taurus, sign of: 2453, 11393
Taw: 10581
Tea: 148, 994, 1106, 2744ff., 2807, 3096, 3406, 3579, 3673, 3853, 4720, 5103, 6056, 7320, 7322, 7957; --, acorn: 3945; --, alder bark: 2747; --, alfalfa: 2757, 2931, 3350, 3904; --, beef: 2770; --, Brigham: 2749, 3035, 3905; --, bubbles on: 4718, 6051, 7319, 7465, 8164; --, camomile: 3185, 3377, 3674; --, catnip: 1036, 1054f., 1101, 2751, 2756, 3186, 3273, 3875, 3907, 3957, 4055; --, cayenne: 3187; --, chimney soot: 4069; --, clover blossom: 3037; --, comfrey: 2757, 2947; --, creosote: 2932; --, currant: 3838; --, dandelion: 2757, 3038, 3909; --, dollar-leaf: 2967; --, fenchel: 1046; --, fennel: 1055; --, ginger: 3189, 3351, 3449, 3778, 4011; --, gold ring: 257; --, green: 727, 7651; --, herb: 2757; --,

4749, 4770, 4780, 4783, 4789, 4812, 4815,
4841, 4892, 4905f., 4980, 5002, 5048, 5068,
5238, 5241, 5345, 5534, 5601, 5716, 5731,
5792, 5890, 5912, 6035, 6093, 6146ff.,
6341, 6354, 6377, 6390f., 6394ff., 6398,
6423, 6510, 6712, 6718, 6731, 6762, 6867f.,
6896, 6903, 6933, 7161f., 7190, 7202, 7299,
7424, 7458, 7479, 7490, 7531, 7575, 7597,
7698, 7701, 7745, 7754, 7759f., 7815, 7851,
7864, 7869f., 7883, 7954, 8018, 8037, 8128,
8142, 8209, 8216, 8494, 8560, 8577, 8579,
8592, 8598, 8797, 8807, 8812, 8889, 8938,
9044, 9073, 9087, 9139f., 9257, 9308, 9311,
9313, 9345ff., 9372, 9395, 9403, 9415,
9423, 9428, 9454, 9491, 9514, 9580, 9607,
9640, 9689, 9788, 9833, 9841, 9942, 10100,
10161, 10196, 10378, 10522, 10525, 10540,
10561, 10589, 10612, 10687, 10700, 10771,
10891, 10927, 10959, 10966, 11071, 11139,
11229, 11233, 11317, 11452, 11468, 11534f.,
11544ff., 11589, 11598, 11635, 11692,
11776, 11965, 12011, 12055, 12058, 12233f.,
12262, 12299, 12305, 12404, 12468, 12567,
12598, 12629, 12702, 13020, 13086, 13182;
-- accidents: 2806, 7088; --, of card suit:
8584; -- cents: 7406; --, cycles of:
11547ff.; -- days: 2680; -- deaths:
9634ff.; -- generations: 10024; -- of
hearts: 8569; -- knots: 3333; -- minutes:
3298; -- months: 732, 1361, 2695; --,
multiples of: 11545; -- nights: 2680, 4746;
--, series of: 6409; -- sneezes: 3177; --
of spades: 8585; -- times: 1060, 2988,
4009; -- years: 6298
Threefold: 11553
Three Nephites: 9922
Threshold: 6345ff., 10236; --, crossing: 778,
5621ff., 9209; --, hanging onions before:
3171; --, stepping over: 987; --, tripping
over; 2440, 5622; --, walking over: 6347.
See also Doorwalk
Thrice: 5596, 6932
Thrive: 901
Throat, itching: 3175; --, mole on: 1405, 7456;
--, poulticing: 2787; --, sore: 3995ff.,
4003ff., 4013ff., 4024ff. See also Throat
ailments; --, stocking around: 3085.
Throat ailments: 4130f. See also Throat, sore
Throwing away: 4258, 4298f., 4374, 4376, 4396,
4398, 4583, 4749, 6555, 8990
Throwing, over back: 2488
Thrush (illness): 1115
Thumb: 1675ff., 2459, 3762, 5695, 6895, 7294f.,
7614, 8020; --, biting: 8335; --, bumps on:
1679; --, crooked: 2388; --, fingers under:
11968; --, dipping in flour: 5785; --,
green: 13158; --, itching: 8120; --,
kissing: 4509; --, left: 1208, 2450, 3922,
5694; --, licking: 7814, 12057, 12283; --,
line around: 2199; --, right: 2333, 5694,
7814; --, short: 2456; --, specks on: 7488;
--, tying string around: 2833; --, sucking:
802, 1147f.
Thumbnail: 8334
Thumbs, twiddling: 9765
Thunder (n.): 1424, 10679, 10707, 10903,
11004f., 11110, 11193, 11330, 11334ff.,
11374, 12180, 12430, 12661, 12703, 12706,
13096, 13108; --, devil beating his wife:
11345; --, explanation of: 11349ff.; --
souring milk: 5879; -- as indicator of
weather: 11296, 11430ff., 11446

Thunder (vb.): 12451
Thunder and lightning: 12661
Thunderbolt: 9580
Thundering: 8964
Thunderstorm: 11360, 11376f., 11390, 12209,
12662; -- causing beer to sour: 5931; --,
eggs laid during: 12674f.; --, frightened
by: 407
Thursday: 6536, 6543, 8671, 11751ff.; --,
cutting fingernails on: 1709; --, cutting
hair on: 7495; --, marrying on: 5320,
5326f.; --, moving on: 6280; --, traveling
on: 7668; --, sex on: 1984; --, sneezing
on: 2047f.; --, snowing on: 11397; --, time
of birth: 413, 416f.; --, filing toenails
on: 7452; --, wearing green on: 2182, 6730;
--, wearing yellow on: 2183. See also
Ascension Thursday
Thyroid extract: 4434
Ticket: 4825, 7867, 8822; --, bus: 7942
Tickling: 4080
Tidal wave: 11208
Tide: 447, 12850; --, ebb: 9153, 9662; --,
falling: 9662; --, incoming: 447, 8943; --,
rock: 7087
Tie (n.): 4822ff., 6893, 8363; --, black: 4821;
--, red: 4589, 7312. See also Necktie
Tie (vb.): 2247
Ties, railroad: 2106
Tiki charm: 29
Timbers: 7104
Time, of day: 412; --, telling: 11590, 11741,
12903
Time out: 8774
Timid: 2458
Timidity: 2459
Tin, using on table: 6101
Tin cans: 5543f.
Tincture of cantharides: 1450
Tinfoil: 7400
Tin pans: 301
Tire, flat: 7657, 7864, 10532
Tit, baby's: 934
Tithing: 8929
Titty bag: 3731
Toad: 1118, 3137, 3539, 12442ff.; --, crossing
path: 7735, 12444; --, curing sickness:
2790; --, killing: 3976, 4224, 11074,
12449, 12726, 13148, 13166; --, raining:
10994; --, toasted: 3372; --, touching:
3505; -- causing warts: 4195ff.; --,
rubbing on wart: 4221, 4223. See also
Horned toad; Horny toad
Toad-frog: 3167
Toad's heart: 7557
Toad spit: 4198
Toadstone: 2790
Toadstool: 10367f., 12885; -- causing warts:
4206
Toast (bread): 660, 1521, 3407, 3673, 4119,
5854; --, burnt: 1462, 1513, 3729, 5853
Toast, wedding: 5565, 5569
Toasting: 6075f., 7663
Tobacco: 1108, 2727, 3338, 8979, 12820; --, bag
of: 4288; --, chewing: 2993, 4128, 4156,
12648, 12732; -- on neck: 3246; --
poultice: 2784; --, using on snake bite:
3978f.
Tobacco juice: 3338, 3378, 3586, 3707, 12391,
12506f.; --, from grasshopper: 3129
Toe: 1751, 2029, 4414; --, big: 1727f., 3818,
4076, 4143, 5696, 8338, 11019; --,

---

breaking: 4132; --, first: 7494; --, great:
2370; --, hammer: 1730; --, itching: 8338;
--, left: 5004; --, long: 5143; --,
position for burial: 9742; --, second:
1727f., 2370, 5696, 7494; --, severed:
3000; --, stubbing: 1678, 1723ff., 4508,
5004, 6427, 7548; --, stumping: 1724, 4509;
--, touching: 7871; --, uneven: 728; --,
webbed: 1729, 7616; --, yarn around: 3715
Toe ache: 11326
Toenails: 9077; --, cutting: 1731ff., 4133; --,
dog's: 10296; --, filing: 7452; --,
ingrown: 1734, 4133f.; --, plugging in
tree: 4146
Toe shoe ribbons: 7198
Toe shoes: 7196, 7199.  See also Ballet shoes
Together: 63, 2111, 2113.  See also Unison
Toilet: 4340, 9905; --, public: 4190; --,
singing on: 5010
Toilet water: 664
Token: 5501
Tomatoes: 130, 1744, 1966, 2548, 3100, 3485f.,
3760; --, causing cancer: 3123; --,
craving: 399; --, green: 3793, 5911; -- and
milk: 3486, 5916; --, planting: 13082ff.;
--, raw: 3050
Tomato juice: 1393, 6750
Tomato leaf: 3693
Tomb: 9739, 9834
Tombstone: 4214, 10660
Tommy Knockers: 1223, 7103
Tongue: 704, 708f., 1229, 1607, 1619, 2603,
8630; --, biting: 8060f., 8290, 8319; --,
blister on: 3027ff.; --, canker on: 3141;
--, eating: 744; --, hair on: 1954; --,
long as dog's: 8068; --, loosen: 7997; --,
lumps on: 3030, 4136; --, paper under:
3816; --, pimple on: 3031, 8318; --, sharp:
8431; --, snake: 12407; --, sores on: 3030,
4135f.; --, splitting: 12227, 12318
Tonic: 2130, 2763f., 2746, 2748, 2752, 2754,
3755, 3760, 4003; --, spring: 2760, 2765f.,
2768
Tonsillitis: 4137
Tonsils: 4020, 4139
Tool: 13173; --, garden: 13170; --,
disappearing: 10269; --, grave digging:
9822; --, bringing indoors: 6358ff., 9362
Tooth: 700ff., 708ff., 1374; --, badger's:
8545; --, black: 709; --, burning: 710; --,
burying: 710; --, cutting: 785; --, elk's:
10476; --, falling out: 1616; --, filling:
1615, 1977; --, first: 785, 1309; --, gold:
708, 1612; --, grinding: 1132; --, hen's:
4149; --, horse's: 1126; --, hound's:
10478; --, long: 409; --, loose: 695; --,
loss of: 164; -- around neck: 3573; --,
pulling: 135, 327, 698, 700, 1616f., 1976,
7443; --, rhinoceros: 3359; --, rotting:
4126; --, shark's: 10477; -- as indicator
of storm: 11220; -- for a tooth: 7536; --,
wild animal: 11909
Toothache: 55, 180, 4142ff., 4160ff., 11007
Toothpaste: 4122
Toothpicks: 5203
Top (toy): 6955
Topaz: 1874, 2955, 8375
"Topping out": 6250, 7121
Tortilla: 5170, 5786
Touch (vb.): 131, 339, 358, 361, 371, 379, 381,
383, 389, 392, 520, 984, 1078, 1093, 1118,
1175, 1195, 1589, 1618, 2575
Tournament, basketball: 8791; --, golf: 8820
Towel: 561, 1774, 8462ff., 9339; --, burying:
4303; --, hot: 2925
Tower of London: 12315
Toy: 284, 1389, 10165
Track: 8799ff.
Track meet: 8800f.
Tracks, railroad: 2105, 2107
Tracks, spitting in: 7761

Tragedy: 644, 957, 6348, 6453, 6528, 11479; --,
in threes: 7161
Trail: 7730, 7891
Train: 7648, 7866, 7872ff., 9605f.; --,
counting cars on: 5056; --, dreaming of:
9606
Train whistle: 10613, 10984
Traitor: 6877
Trampling: 2960
Trance: 1417, 10432
Trash: 749, 7510; --, burning on Sunday: 10185
Travel (n.): 133, 7608ff., 7638, 7647, 7651.
See also Journey; Trip
Travel (vb.): 5249, 7616ff., 7631, 7653, 7783
Traveler: 7733, 10348
Tray: 1264, 7945
Treachery: 1852, 8508, 12273, 12432
Treacle: 2768
Treadle: 1336
Treasure, hidden: 10459ff.
Tree: 2111, 4056, 9306, 9521, 10145, 10622,
11392, 11648f., 12914ff., 13199; --, apple:
2795, 13013, 13197; --, ash: 851; --,
aspen: 4229; --, birch: 9819; --, bleeding
of: 12935; --, burying dishrag under: 4315;
--, burying fish under: 4227; --, cedar:
9571; --, cherry: 13202f.; --, climbing:
12166; --, dead: 9564, 13123; -- as
indicator of death: 9563ff.; -- as divisive
object: 5115, 5118, 8520, 8522ff., 8531;
--, dreaming of: 7433; --, elder: 4350,
11390; --, fir: 2224; --, flowering of:
12730; --, fruit: 9565, 13195, 13198; --,
getting under: 12272; --, goofer: 4979; --,
holly: 4484; --, immortal: 10058; --,
laurel: 4653; --, leafless: 10726; --,
lightning-struck: 4157, 7570, 12921, 11391;
--, maple: 789; --, memorial: 9819; --,
nailing into: 4226; --, naming: 13188; --,
oak: 4009, 4169, 4336.  See also Tree,
white oak; --, orange: 5465; --, peach:
13204; --, pear: 9567; --, persimmon: 3165;
--, pine: 3097, 3166, 8513, 9570, 11420;
--, piñon: 3652, 4459; --, planting:
13187ff., 13194; --, plugging: 4146, 12767;
--, plum: 2224, 9568; --, poplar: 10725;
--, pruning: 13192; --, standing under:
11000; -- killed by snake: 12923; -- stung
by snake: 12426; --, snowball: 12638; --,
stump of: 4315, 4353; --, burying thread
under: 4337; --, transplanting: 9571; --,
white oak: 4352.  See also Tree, oak; --,
willow: 2569.
Tree bark: 3343
Tree branches: 10300
Tree shavings: 4157
Tree trunk: 12934
Tremor: 981
Triangle: 2196, 10154
Tribe: 7562
Trip (n.): 7045, 7607, 7613, 7618, 7622,
7625f., 7628, 7630, 7634, 7640ff., 7646,
7648, 7650, 7654, 7657, 7670, 7689ff.,
7703, 7728, 7777, 7783, 7785; --, leaving
on: 7664, 7668f., 7672f., 7675; --,
postponing: 7633.  See also Journey; Travel
Trip (vb.): 2087f., 2090, 2440, 4524, 4526,
6356, 9114.  See also Stumble
Triplets: 592, 8019
Troll: 10391ff.
Troll doll: 10575
Trouble: 4883, 5145; --, financial: 2876, 7501
Trousers: 100, 6653, 7460
Trousseau: 5332, 5378, 5422
Trout: 8904ff., 8946, 8955
Truck: 7661ff., 7860
True: 8043f., 8046
Trumpet: 4905, 10004
Trunk: 5372, 6477
Trunk, elephant: 12125, 12127
Trust (vb.): 2433ff.
Trustworthy: 2406
Truth: 8045, 9177

Tub: 4106
Tuber: 12991
Tuberculosis: 4171ff.
Tuesday: 6543, 7715, 11747ff.; --, time of birth: 413, 867; --, going to sea on: 7001; --, washing hair on: 3435; --, beginning job on: 11748ff.; --, marrying on: 1020, 2496, 5316ff., 5326f.; --, moving on: 6280; --, cutting nails on: 1702, 1709; --, sewing on: 6569f., 9368; --, sneezing on: 1956, 2047f., 2506; --, the thirteenth: 5311; --, traveling on: 7666f.
Tumblebugs: 2785
Tumbler: 5012
Tumbleweed: 3977
Tumor, cancerous: 3134
Tuna fisherman: 7060
Tune: 8277
Tunnel: 5112, 7828, 7854f.
Turkey: 12695; -- backbone: 9430; -- feathers: 10752
Turn (vb.): 1179
Turning, around: 2065, 2124, 2295, 3617, 4241, 4290, 4355, 4528f., 4796, 6035, 6148, 7190, 7698, 7751f., 7754, 7756, 7758, 7761, 8007; --, back: 7689ff., 7696ff.; --, three times: 4042
Turnip: 1125; --, planting: 13038f.
Turpentine: 125, 138, 143f., 2603, 2726, 3224, 3229, 3326, 3341, 3636, 3770, 3995, 3997, 4018, 4098, 4130, 4140, 4453; --, bringing on labor: 247
Turquoise: 6889
Turtle: 11838, 12429ff.; --, eating: 2470
Turtle bite: 12430f.
Turtle bone: 7008
Turtledove: 4637
TV: 6476, 11365
"The Twa Sisters": 7583
Twelve: 4677, 4689, 4866, 5781, 5992, 7757, 9561, 9666, 10689, 11065, 11260; -- apostles: 3858; -- days: 1442; -- Holy Days: 9335; -- Holy Nights: 6640; -- months: 864; -- o'clock: 10816, 11265, 11315, 11599
Twentieth: 7573
Twenty: 439, 1478, 2205, 10859, 11068, 11123; --, counting to: 3623, 7697; --, dying before: 9117; -- minutes: 2808, 8027, 8029
Twenty-five: 5066; --, counting to: 12284
Twenty-four: 5616, 5722, 7986
Twenty-ninth: 9592
Twenty-one: 1915, 4825, 7867, 7942, 11584
Twenty thousand: 48
Twenty-three: 11585
Twice: 2052, 2057, 4640, 4783, 5047, 5718, 6932, 7633f., 7681, 9107, 11541, 11543, 11550
Twig, green: 5750; --, laurel: 4653; --, notching: 4346; -- as indicator of weather: 10923
Twins: 38, 576ff., 1371, 2291, 8019, 12858; --, death of: 9126, 9170; --, identical: 232
Two: 588f., 1372, 1478, 1483, 1486, 2111, 2513, 2634, 3260, 4021, 4497, 4629, 4719, 4732, 4737f., 4880, 5098, 5144, 5179, 5712, 5714f., 5718, 5846, 5855, 5890, 6158f., 6184, 6300f., 6303, 6354, 6391, 6446, 6468, 7444, 7486, 7610, 7966, 8211, 8220, 8794, 8807, 8815, 8905, 9268, 9516, 9640, 10589, 11537ff., 11666, 11911, 11939, 12233f., 12323, 12327, 12353, 12494; -- of card

suit: 8584; -- in chair: 6424; -- of hearts: 8569; -- knives: 2815; -- months: 780; -- of spades: 8585; -- years: 757, 796
Two-dollar bill: 6987, 7165, 7364ff., 8699, 9559, 10564
Two o'clock: 9663, 10816
Two-timing: 4788
Typewriter: 4861, 10183
Typhoid fever: 4178ff.

Udder: 12740
Ugly: 347, 799ff.
Uintah Basin: 2716
Ukufutwa: 278
Ulcers: 4183ff.; --, stomach: 4063
Ullr medal: 8876
Umbilical cord: 255, 545, 1183, 1330ff., 1335ff.
Umbilicus: 138
Umbrella: 6521ff., 8484, 9766, 11203; -- on bed: 2642, 9361; --, black: 6525f., 9359; --, opening in car: 7794; -- as gift: 6915; --, close before entering house: 6524ff.; --, opening in house: 2539, 2561, 5060, 6276, 6525ff., 8483, 9358ff., 11175; --, opening in theater: 7159
Umpire: 8735
Unbaptised: 624, 1352
Unblessed: 624
Unchristened: 1352
Uncle, death of: 9110
Unconscious: 2701
Underclothes: 1416, 9223
Undergarments, Mormon: 4989, 5457
Underground person: 1165
Undergrowth: 1117
Underpass: 7839, 7841ff., 7850f., 7857, 7859
Undershirt: 6701
Underwear: 6685, 8748f., 10910; --, wearing to bed: 3231; --, changing: 2217, 9222; --, long: 10704; --, red flannel: 3916; --, around throat: 2787; --, dipping in water: 3849; --, wrong side out: 6692f.
Undressed: 56.  See also Naked; Nude
Undressing: 6647
Unfaithful: 949, 2351
Unfeminine: 1710
Unhappiness: 1202, 5399f.
Unhappy: 900, 1230, 1239, 2515
Unhealthy: 903, 919, 1936
Uniform, athletic: 8676; --, basketball: 8792; --, dirty: 8677
Unison: See Together
United States: 9996
United States Naval Academy: 7874
Unity: 5725
Unknown (n.): 343
Unknown (adj.): 936
Unpleasant: 1846
Unruly: 894
Unsafe: 2049
Unseen: 936
Unselfish: 2387
Unsociable: 2480
Unstable: 2366, 2864
Untangle: 2121
Untidy: 1172
Up and down: 537
Upset, emotional: 357
Upside down: 760, 1916, 4799, 5929, 6049, 6773, 7979, 7981ff., 7985; -- horseshoe: 6340; -- picture: 6475

Wedding band: 528, 4383, 4921, 5511f., 5525, 5673f., 9212
Wedding banquet: 5575
Wedding bells: 4806
Wedding breakfast: 5350
Wedding cake: 5560, 5583ff.; --, cutting: 5591f., 5691; -- under pillow: 5586, 5595, 5597; --, wishing on: 5607
Wedding ceremony: 5242ff., 5399, 5481ff., 9208, 9210
Wedding clothes: 4476, 4995, 5378ff., 7498, 9056, 9071
Wedding day: 585, 5348ff., 5378, 5389, 5461, 5475, 5477, 5571, 5706; --, changing: 5719; --, dancing on: 5700; --, rain on: 5252, 5254, 5256f., 5259f., 5262f.; --, snowing on: 5267f., 5707
Wedding dinner: 5572
Wedding dress: 3016, 4651, 5399. See also Wedding gown
Wedding ensemble: 5402
Wedding gifts: 5468ff. See also Wedding present
Wedding gown: 5395, 5409ff. See also Wedding dress
Wedding march: 524, 5055
Wedding night: 564, 2187, 5251, 5267, 5392, 5586, 5610ff., 5630, 5635, 5637f., 5731, 9203
Wedding party: 5478
Wedding present: 561. See also Wedding gifts
Wedding reception: 5394, 5557, 5561ff., 5582
Wedding ring: 527, 4100f., 5596, 5688, 5690, 9213, 9756f.; --, broken: 5671; --, dropping: 5687; --, losing: 5531f., 5672; --, removing: 5526ff., 5688f. See also Ring, wedding
Wedding shower: 8412
Wedding trip: 5641
Wedging: 12767
Wedlock, out of: 34, 824, 951, 1009, 7546
Wednesday: 5863, 6543, 11903; --, cleaning house on: 6222; --, marrying on: 5319, 5326f.; --, cutting nails on: 1701, 1709; --, raining on: 10998; --, sneezing on: 2047f., 7955; --, time of birth: 413ff., 1307; --, washing clothes on: 6235
Weeds: 8983, 10768, 10772, 10800, 13109
Week: 515, 2047, 2049
Weekend: 7672
Weep: See Cry
Weeping: 5369, 5630, 7640, 8557
Weeping willow: 9572f., 12933. See also Willow
Weight: 777, 1804
Weight loss: 4430ff. See also Diet
Weird: 2182
Welding: 47
Well (adj.): 914. See also Healthy
Well (n.): 1299, 4264, 10167, 10246, 10259, 11474; --, throwing coins into: 7422, 7425f.; --, digging: 10444, 10451, 11651; --, drying up of: 9955; --, looking into: 4797, 4799. See also Wishing well
Well-bred: 870
Well rig: 13163
Well water: 11866
Well witching: 10456. See also Water witching
Werewolf: 10318ff., 10325f.
West: 3523, 4646f., 5191, 5474, 6437, 8968, 8970, 9943, 10899, 10929, 10932, 10957, 11307, 11311, 11630, 13002; --, bed facing: 2016, 9310; --, bury facing: 9805; --, head toward: 9082
Wet (adj.): 229
Wet dreams: 2237
Wetting: 69f., 649, 2091, 4089; -- in road: 4087. See also Urinating
Whale, white: 7055
Whale oil: 3297
Wheat: 28, 4285f., 9652, 9747; --, boiled: 5057; --, bouquet of: 5578; --, burying: 4286; -- offered at memorial: 9763; --, planting: 13114, 13116; --, stolen: 7539

Wheat germ: 2232
Wheaties: 2234
Wheel: 7793
Whip (vb.): 656, 1551, 2228
Whipped: 1224
Whipping: 1225
Whippoorwill: 2227, 9512, 12297ff.; --, call of: 4641
Whip snake: 12357
Whirl: 1806
Whirlpool: 9646
Whiskers: 1621, 1623, 2262; --, cat's: 12616; --, red: 5154
Whiskey: 1057, 1908f., 1912f., 1916, 1921, 2208, 3203ff., 3853, 3981, 4160, 6954, 7226, 10358, 12420; -- as cure-all: 2721; -- on snake bite: 3978
Whistle (n.): 11794
Whistle (vb.): 9856, 12485
Whistling: 2184, 5001, 7833, 7857, 8645ff., 9604, 10222, 10983, 12637; -- backstage: 7192; -- before breakfast: 1796; --, a breeze: 11303; -- in the dark: 8649, 10305; -- in the dressing room: 7190f.; -- in the editorial room: 7147; -- of girls: 1624; -- in house: 8648, 10221; -- during intercourse: xxxvii; -- in kitchen: 5739; -- in locker room: 8688; -- in mine: 7099ff.; -- at night: 7561, 10630; -- aboard ship: 7013ff., 7058, 11255; -- to attract snakes: 12366; -- on Sunday: 10221; -- in theater: 7193, 7195
White: 5417, 6534, 6976, 7659, 8824, 9618, 10491, 10569, 11956, 11961, 11963, 12005ff., 12781; -- aspirin: 2729, -- bean: 9543; -- bird: 9508, 12221; -- butterfly: 4650, 12464; -- cake: 5584, 5807; -- cat: 4620, 7325; -- cloth: 4799, 9033; -- clothes: 9224, 9337; -- cricket: 4645; -- dog: 12771; -- dove: 1370, 1372; --, dreaming of: 9100; -- dress: 5008; --, egg: 5896; -- feather: 2791; -- flowers: 6370, 9151, 9554, 9559; --, wrapped in: 4949; -- hair: 1479, 2884; -- hare: 7789; -- hen: 12183; -- horse: 4439, 4622ff., 4764, 5474, 7326, 7726, 8938, 9775, 9956, 10668; --, protecting from lightning: 11385; -- moth: 9528; -- mule: 7092, 12017; -- paper: 3789, 12128; -- person: 8031; -- pheasant: 12304; -- pigeon: 9478, 9480f.; -- rat: 10480; -- rider: 9420; -- rocks: 9835; -- rooster stone: 2247, 2875, 7533, 10074; -- rug: 6481; -- skin: 1408; -- specks: 1694; -- spider: 7345, 7976, 9537; -- spots: 4503, 7615, 8334, 8826; -- string: 4104; -- thread: 4584, 7964; --, wearing: 5409ff., 5412ff., 5431, 6722f., 6726, 7057, 8802, 8875, 8926, 10362, 10640, 10642, 11385; -- whale: 7055
White Lady of Spring Canyon: 10667
White liver: 9123
White oak: 4352, 13095
Whittling: 9982
Whooping cough: 1121ff., 4435ff.
Whore: 7210ff., 9349; -- house: See French whore house
Wick: 250, 7961
Wicked (n.): 12222
Wickedness: 2386
Widow: 3632, 5180ff., 5275f., 5473, 5682f., 9875, 9879; --, marrying: 5185
Widower: 4594
Widow's cap: 5180
Widow's hat: 5180
Widow's peak: 2139, 2271, 2309, 5182
Wife: 105, 350, 543, 4962, 5146, 5155, 5164, 5176, 5528, 5604, 5659, 5697f.; --, ambitious: 5649; --, choosing: 5135f.; --, coveting someone's: 2556; --, cranky: 5261; --, future: 4820, 5074; --, getting a: 4711, 4735; --, giving away: 5711; -- on hunting trip: 8996; --, infidelity of: